HANDBOOK OF
CLINICAL
INTERVIEWING
WITH ADULTS

HANDBOOK OF CLINICAL INTERVIEWING WITH ADULTS

Edited by

MICHEL HERSEN
Pacific University

JAY C. THOMAS
Pacific University

SAGE Publications
Los Angeles • London • New Delhi • Singapore

For information:

Sage Publications, Inc.
2455 Teller Road
Thousand Oaks, California 91320
E-mail: order@sagepub.com

Sage Publications India Pvt. Ltd.
B 1/I 1 Mohan Cooperative Industrial Area
Mathura Road, New Delhi 110 044
India

Sage Publications Ltd.
1 Oliver's Yard
55 City Road
London EC1Y 1SP
United Kingdom

Sage Publications Asia-Pacific Pte. Ltd.
33 Pekin Street #02-01
Far East Square
Singapore 048763

Printed in the United States of America.

Library of Congress Cataloging-in-Publication Data

Handbook of clinical interviewing with adults /editors, Michel Hersen and Jay C. Thomas.
    p. cm.
Includes bibliographical references and index.
ISBN 978-1-4129-1717-9 (cloth: alk. paper)
    1. Interviewing in psychiatry—Handbooks, manuals, etc. 2. Mental illness—Diagnosis—Handbooks, manuals, etc. I. Hersen, Michel. II. Thomas, Jay C., 1951-[DNLM: 1. Interview, Psychological—methods. 2. Mental Disorders—diagnosis. WM 141 H236 2007]

RC480.7.H37 2007
616.89′075—dc22

200700588

This book is printed on acid-free paper.

07   08   09   10   11   10 9 8 7 6 5 4 3 2 1

Acquisitions Editor:	Cheri Dellelo
Editorial Assistant:	Anna Mesick
Project Editor:	Tracy Alpern
Copy Editor:	Carol Anne Peschke
Typesetter:	C&M Digitals (P) Ltd.
Proofreader:	Anne Rogers
Cover Designer:	Edgar Abarca
Marketing Associate:	Amberlyn Erzinger

CONTENTS

PREFACE

The *Handbook of Clinical Interviewing With Adults* and the companion *Handbook of Clinical Interviewing With Children* have been designed by the editors to be the most comprehensive work in the area published to date. Indeed, in our review of existing literature on interviewing we were not able to find any comparable work of this magnitude and scope. Therefore, we see these two volumes as a pragmatic resource for interviewers in general and as a specific resource to be used by course instructors for teaching clinical interviewing with adults and children.

The *Handbook of Clinical Interviewing With Adults* is organized into three parts (Part I, "General Issues"; Part II, "Specific Disorders"; and Part III, "Special Populations and Issues"). The three parts of this volume were specifically selected to deal with the general and theoretical, the pragmatic with respect to diagnostic entities, and the more unusual with respect to special populations. Part I includes nine chapters dealing with general issues. Part II, "Specific Disorders," includes 12 chapters with a generally consistent format across chapters to the extent possible, as dictated by the relevant data. This approach was designed to serve as a pedagogic tool and should facilitate the work of both teachers and students, given its pragmatic focus. None of the competing volumes on adults or children handles the material in this fashion. Finally, in Part III, "Special Populations and Issues," topics given short shrift in all prior books on the topic are presented in seven chapters.

Recognizing that instructors using this handbook may decide to assign selected chapters to their students according to course requirements and time limitations, we have not attempted to remove any minor duplication of material that may occur across chapters. To the contrary, for the specific disorders, problems, and special topics, we see each chapter as representing the most up-to-date thinking with respect to interviewing strategies.

Many people have contributed to this handbook. First, we thank our eminent contributors, who agreed to share their expertise with us. Second, we thank Carole Londerée for her invaluable editorial assistance and sense of timing. Third, we thank Cynthia Polance, Heidi Meeke, and Christopher Brown for their technical assistance. And finally, we thank the editorial staff at Sage Publications for all their efforts.

Michel Hersen
Jay C. Thomas
Portland, Oregon

PART I

GENERAL ISSUES

1

PHILOSOPHICAL UNDERPINNINGS OF CLINICAL INTERVIEWING

JOHAN ROSQVIST, THRÖSTUR BJÖRGVINSSON, AND JILL DAVIDSON

Alice: "Please, Sir, which way do I go?"
Cheshire Cat: "That depends a great deal on where you want to go."

This quote from Lewis Carroll's *Alice in Wonderland* (1951) illustrates why clinicians interview patients. Without asking questions, how can any practitioner expect to provide an answer about where, potentially, to go? Without more completely understanding patients, or who they are and how they became that way, it is all but impossible to form a unified theory (i.e., a working hypothesis) to explain the phenomenon or circumstances that bring patients to seek professional assistance. In fact, interviewing is the single best link to understanding and appreciating patients and the predicaments they bring to the consulting room. By exploring past and present aspects of patients' experiences, practitioners can begin to find clues for how to unlock, undo, or change problematic behaviors, thoughts, and feelings.

When done well, interviewing can produce an understanding that allows practitioners to begin to offer suitable clinical recommendations about where to go and how to get there. The assumption that "you can't get there from here" is quickly

debunked through understanding. Such understanding often is what patients lack most when they present for professional help, leaving many to meander through life and its challenges. After all, if they already understood how their presenting complaints or problems worked, it is unlikely that they would seek our assistance. They already would have modified their behavior.

Thus, information is knowledge, and knowledge is power. This immovable truth is the cornerstone of all clinical enterprises and not only cuts across all health care professions but also represents a common-sense foundation to human existence and evolution. Knowledge about critical factors in a person's life is the key ingredient necessary for practitioners to develop an effective clinical plan. This has long been appreciated and is well illustrated in the ancient Zen aphorism, "Acquire knowledge. It enables its possessor to distinguish right from wrong; it lights the way to heaven; it is our friend in the desert, our society in solitude, our companion when friendless; it guides us to happiness; it sustains us in misery; it is an ornament among friends, and an armor against enemies" (Geary, 2005, p. 45). Information is the universal ingredient needed to help ameliorate patients' suffering or to solve any problem. Information is what helps anyone be more genuine and real (i.e., more effectively functioning). In most helping settings, therefore, interviewing remains the gold standard.

However, it is abundantly clear that interviewing has its own unique problems, challenges, and perhaps even ethical and legal issues. For example, any clinical activity, whether interviewing or more directly intervening through some specific clinical method or technique, is grounded in human relationships. This may sound elementary and simplistic at first blush, but it is critical to recognize just how vulnerable patients can feel in disclosing and discussing issues that may be blocking them from happiness, fulfillment, or love. Patients can feel so anxious about telling anyone their deepest, darkest fears, concerns, or problems that they are unable to explain themselves adequately. Unfortunately, without a clear picture of the human condition it can be extremely difficult for practitioners to point the way. Thus, the human relationship between the helping professional and the patient is of paramount importance because it is centrally influential and informative in the interview process (Sommers-Flanagan & Sommers-Flanagan, 1999).

People grow and develop optimally through connection with others. In fact, people are evolutionarily programmed to want to belong and become part of a group. Chiefly, there is safety in numbers. Or, rather, safety comes through others, as living in groups increased primordial odds of survival (Rosqvist, 2005; Skinner, 1963). However, when one does not feel safe (a construct influenced by a multitude of subjective variables) around another person, whether physically, emotionally, or spiritually, one generally will not draw that person closer or confide in that person. In order to interact at the depth of a clinical interview, patients must feel a minimal level of trust and comfort with their interviewers, no matter what type of helping professional conducts the interview. It is assumed that clinicians are competent in obtaining fully informed consent from prospective patients so that the clinical endeavor may proceed. Interviewers need to focus on patient communication rather than listening to their own thoughts and feelings. Interviewers

need to be able to develop a positive working relationship in order to accurately obtain assessment and diagnostic information. Considering all these varied aspects separately and apart from each other facilitates the interviewing task. Indeed, when the entire package of a clinical interview is combined, the total picture quickly becomes more challenging, even for seasoned practitioners or interviewers. The complexity of an interview situation increases further when a dyad of some type (e.g., a couple, a family, or a group) is the focus rather than an individual.

Clinical interviewing encompasses many challenges. Practitioners need specialized training and sufficient practice in order to carry it out properly. They need to do so with adequate depth and detail and with compassion and caring, remembering that the person interviewed is a human being who deserves respect and has inherent dignity and worth. It is all too easy to approach an interview as a technician, using proper technique but losing sight of the human connection that facilitates a productive interaction. The working relationship is a critical foundation for any interview. For without such a connection, the level of cooperation and participation from patients could be limited.

FREE-FLOWING VERSUS MORE STRUCTURED INTERVIEWS

Since the publication of the *Diagnostic and Statistical Manual* (*DSM;* American Psychiatric Association, 1952), agreement over definitions of mental illness and related criteria for diagnosis has been imperfect if not outright unsatisfactory. Reliability and validity have been called into serious doubt because little uniformity of diagnostic questions historically existed (Segal, Coolidge, O'Riley, & Heinz, 2006). Fortunately, the last 30 years of the 20th century produced great interest and work in developing standardized structured and semistructured interviews for diagnosing mental illness to address growing dissatisfaction with the traditionally more free-flowing interview.

Although more free-form interviews can yield useful information and data, structured and semistructured interviews are meant to minimize sources of variance in interviewer style and patient characteristics. For example, depending on experience levels, theoretical orientation, and other dispositional factors, several different interviewers are likely to produce varied outcomes. Such differences may be at the heart of why such broad reliability challenges historically appeared, often to a degree that rendered diagnoses thoroughly unreliable. Such low reliability in diagnostic clarity is a critical problem: Practitioners change what they do in treating their patients 50% of the time when they are given an accurate diagnosis. Such modification in therapeutic interventions suggests that accuracy in diagnostic clarity determines the appropriateness of a treatment for a given presenting complaint. In short, without an accurate diagnosis, it is often not clear what treatment to apply, or a generic form of a treatment may be applied, resulting in suboptimal outcomes. Historically, this may have been acceptable. But with the advent of empirically supported treatments, our interventions have become increasingly specific. We now target very specific pathologic mechanisms as certain disorders are better understood. Along with higher specificity in interventions, the field of clinical psychology has also enjoyed increasingly optimized outcomes. Such improvement has also created a greater demand for higher diagnostic accuracy. Indeed, use of more structured interviewing approaches is now common, if not required, in research settings. Most clinical settings are following suit.

Role of Interviewing in Functional Analysis, Treatment Planning, and Interventions

Information gathered during initial interviews, and potentially from follow-up data gathering, is critical for establishing an accurate diagnosis. This, in turn, is absolutely central to treatment planning and delivery. The task practitioners face during interviewing is to understand the patient's problem sufficiently to determine an appropriate intervention to modify behaviors, thoughts, and feelings. From a functional analytic perspective, all behaviors (whether good, bad, or indifferent) are learned and are always purposeful (i.e., they serve a distinct function for the person engaged in them). Indeed, interviewers focus their lines of questioning so as to understand environmental events that control and maintain behavior. Skinner (1989) suggested that behavior is the

product of three kinds of selection: natural selection, operant conditioning, and social contingencies. If practitioners accept this notion of the root causes of behavior in their exploration of human problems, it behooves them to evaluate biological influences, personal voluntary influences, and cultural influences. Such focus on behavior as multidetermined usually is illustrated when interviewers take a bio-psycho-social and spiritual interviewing approach. That is, clinicians systematically inquire into the biological, mental, sociocultural, and spiritual aspects of their patients. Although these domains do not necessarily represent the full uniqueness of individuals, a careful and comprehensive evaluation of such factors offers a representative view of human functioning. Such comprehensiveness is needed to produce meaningful diagnoses, the starting point for treatment planning and interventions. By removing irrelevant details from the content of the presented problems, the practitioner can understand the origin of idiosyncratic phenomena (Sturmey, 1996). After all, if contextual variables are identified about how particular phenomena are controlled, they can be changed. A thorough comprehension of problems therefore is still the key to ameliorating suffering. Without information, change is not possible.

Recommendations for New Practitioners and Interviewers

Initial interviews (often called intake interviews) probably are among the most challenging for beginning clinicians. Therefore, there are some benefits to selecting structured and semistructured interview formats. Indeed, these formats provide less experienced practitioners greater guidance and direction in what types of questions to ask. Structured interviewing formats often provide algorithmically discrete diagnostic decision trees, which, as previously noted, will remove much practitioner variance in diagnostic conclusions. In this fashion, structured interviews include standardized content, formats, and question orders that follow the *DSM* framework. After establishing a basic understanding of how to navigate through a decision tree interview, beginning interviewers often feel more confidence and comfort in interviewing patients. The ambiguity of the interviewing process is diminished. Interestingly, patients also report a higher degree of "feeling heard" and "feeling connected" when practitioners use standardized interviews rather than free-form interview formats. This is because the algorithm guides the interviewer to ask relevant and on-target questions rather than exploring irrelevant or marginally related topics.

INSPIRATIONS AND MOTIVATIONS FOR DOING GOOD INTERVIEWING

Because the clinical interview is the foundation for all subsequent clinical interventions, establishing and developing good interviewing skills is a prerequisite for any helping professional. It could be argued that practitioners with poor interviewing skills, especially those who also make care decisions for patients, represent a definite hazard to the very patients they set out to help. Most people know how to talk to others, but clinical interviewing is quite different from a normal conversation. In fact, it is impossible to be a good diagnostician or treatment provider without being a good interviewer. Being able to conduct good interviews is a prerequisite to providing proper care. Additionally, having basic social skills and clinical sensitivity to obtain patient cooperation and confidence will enable novice clinicians to overcome their initial reluctance to interact with distressed people. Such comfort probably is best established through frequent opportunities for practice with a range of different clinical presentations.

It is also important to note that proper interviewing techniques and more standardized interviewing formats can reduce a practitioner's legal liability. In certain types of interviews (e.g., child custody evaluations, disability assessments, trauma, and litigation proceedings) it is not unusual for findings to be questioned and legally scrutinized, in which case reliability and validity may be of much greater interest to the clinician. A clear clinical strategy for eliciting diagnostic information can remove doubt about practitioner bias.

Interviewing is a primary form of information gathering for clinicians, but it is not the only one. Cognitive, personality, and performance assessments have an important role to fill. They provide detailed, standardized comparisons, answer questions, and fill in gaps that interviewing alone cannot. However, they are expensive and time consuming, and their use must be justified. More targeted measures, such as those developed for specific complaints such as the Beck Anxiety Inventory (Beck & Steer, 1990), provide quantitative corroboration of a client's state and allow easy tracking of progress. Thus, interviewing typically is the primary mode of information gathering. It provides the clinician with the data and frame of reference that may direct the use of these other assessment methods. Ultimately, the interview is where the collaboration between clinician and client begins. Successful interviewing lays the foundation for meaningful change.

COMMENTS

Interviewing is the foundation for all psychology practice and therefore is clearly the basis of psychological service. No systematic way of helping patients exists without some form of gathering information about human functioning and the problems that arise through living with challenges. Difficulties in life appear to be a universal experience and can be argued to be a truth, if not the greatest truth of living. Buddha's Four Noble Truths hold that life is suffering, because human nature is not perfect, and neither is the world in which humans live (Peck, 1998). In every life there will be some physical suffering, such as pain, illness, injury, fatigue, old age, and ultimately death. Psychological suffering may also manifest itself as sadness, fear, frustration, and disappointment. Once this potentially uncomfortable truth is acknowledged, the difficulties better appreciated and further understood, it is possible to transcend all kinds of ailments of the human body, psyche, and spirit. Acceptance and mindfulness of naturally and normally occurring challenges are important in raising awareness of this human condition, but it may be more critical to understand how problems in living arise, are maintained, and remit in order for change to occur. After all, change is what most of psychology has framed as the premise for human existence and evolution of humankind. Change is our driving force. Change comes through understanding. Clinicians can acquire true understanding only through inquisitive dialogues, regardless of their theoretical frameworks. Clinical interviewing remains the tried and true path to such powerful knowledge, with the ultimate objective of change to relieve suffering.

ORGANIZATION OF THE BOOK

As will become apparent to the student reading this book, contemporary interviewing in clinical and counseling psychology is a complex endeavor that takes considerable knowledge. The next 27 chapters include a wealth of material that one must master in order to become a skilled interviewer. This material is divided into three parts: Part I, "General Issues," and Part II, "Specific Disorders," and Part III, "Special Populations and Issues."

The student needs to master all of the material herein and integrate it carefully while using himself or herself as the vehicle for eliciting relevant information from clients in a humane way. This book will open the door to the interviewing process, and practice and experience will cement the technique.

REFERENCES

American Psychiatric Association. (1952). *Diagnostic and statistical manual of mental disorders.* Washington, DC: Author.

Beck, A. T., & Steer, R. A. (1990). *Beck Anxiety Inventory manual.* San Antonio, TX: Psychological Corporation.

Carroll, L. (author), Geronimi, C. (director), & Jackson, W. (director). (1951). *Alice in Wonderland* [Motion picture]. Los Angeles: Universal Studios.

Geary, J. (2005). *The world in a phrase: A brief history of the aphorism.* New York: Bloomsbury.

Peck, M. S. (1998). *The road less traveled: A new psychology of love, traditional values and spiritual growth* (2nd ed.). New York: Touchstone.

Rosqvist, J. (2005). *Exposure treatments for anxiety disorders: A practitioner's guide to concepts, methods, and evidence-based practice.* New York: Routledge.

Segal, D., Coolidge, F. L., O'Riley, A., & Heinz, B. A. (2006). Structured and semistructured interviews. In M. Hersen (Ed.), *Clinician's handbook of adult behavioral assessment* (pp. 121–144). New York: Academic Press.

Skinner, B. F. (1963). Selection by consequence. *Science, 7,* 477–481.

Skinner, B. F. (1989). *Recent issues in the analysis of behavior.* Columbus, OH: Merrill.

Sommers-Flanagan, R., & Sommers-Flanagan, J. (1999). *Clinical interviewing* (2nd ed.). New York: Wiley.

Sturmey, P. (1996). *Functional analysis in clinical psychology.* New York: Wiley.

2

UNSTRUCTURED INTERVIEWING

SANDRA JENKINS

Clinical interviewing has occupied a long and extensive history as the basic clinical skill necessary for successful psychotherapy. Interviewing is the first step in the overall therapy process (i.e., interview, assessment, treatment, termination, and follow-up). Unstructured interviews are used to cover a broad range of possible data points for integration. Essentially, the clinician using unstructured interview techniques presumes that the most pertinent issues will present themselves spontaneously if an expansive net is cast over the client's mental processes, unhindered and uninfluenced by the therapist's preconceptions, perspectives, or assumptions. Access, to the fullest extent, to the real inner life of the client is the main goal. Spontaneity of responding is the key difference between *unstructured* and *structured* interview formats.

An unstructured interview format permits clients' mental processes and functioning to be revealed through their choice of words, meanings, and interpersonal styles. Presented with broad questions and given the opportunity to verbalize in any manner, the client's thoughts, memories, and feelings will emerge in a flow or stream of information. Spontaneous responses are especially important in this process, and every effort is made to obtain them. Interpretations of clients' spontaneous responses are used as indicators of their innermost feelings, thoughts, and values. To facilitate the appropriate interpretations it is important for the therapist to assume a particular stance or attitude. It is critical that the therapist avoid assuming that he or she understands completely a client's meanings and to maintain a position of openness and curiosity. The therapist's main role is to listen attentively and interpret the client's statements as clues to his or her general level of functioning, lifestyle development, interpersonal attitudes, underlying conflicts, and unresolved traumas. Observation of the client's nonverbal and verbal behavior is extremely important (Sullivan, 1954).

All interview formats have precise elements that structure the interview and subsequent outcomes. The setting, time constraints, and skill levels of the participants affect the quality and the flow of information. However, unstructured interview techniques do require an environment, an atmosphere, and attitudes that promote information collection. Every element must support the overall goal of collecting information in a manner that encourages the client to communicate freely, without distractions or inhibitions. From the very beginning of the interview, first impressions shape the ensuing relationship.

Unstructured interviewing is not synonymous with unplanned or unintentional interviewing. All clinical interviewing is defined and structured by both the therapist and the client.

Interviewing is inherently structured by the social norms of agreed-upon roles and the ensuing mutual understandings between the participants. Therapist-client interactions are also structured by the particulars of the therapy situation, such as the setting, time constraints, skill levels of both therapist and client, and purpose of the interview. In most situations therapists are expected to lead the interaction, guided by their theoretical orientation and level of training and experience.

PURPOSE

Interviewing styles, questions, and interactions follow from the purpose of the interview. An attorney has a very different purpose than an employer, a medical doctor, or a psychologist. Essentially, the purpose of any interview is to gather the necessary information to carry out some larger professional goal, such as diagnosis and treatment. Systematic information gathering allows an organized analysis, which is systematically integrated into hypotheses for diagnosis and treatment.

THEORETICAL ORIENTATIONS

The primary elements of theoretical orientations, roles, expectations, settings, time limits, purpose and goals, and therapist skill levels determine the features of unstructured interviewing. Theoretical foundations provide the logical sequence of questions to ask and the plausible observations to be made to arrive at a working hypothesis about the problems to be resolved. Different orientations use some techniques that are the same or similar but place the focus of the inquiry on different aspects of the client's responses. The interview process follows naturally from these theoretical orientations toward the development of the treatment goals.

An extensive life history usually is a substantial part of the information that is gathered in most therapy approaches. Past life events and overall life development are considered crucial diagnostic aspects of current problems in functioning. History taking of symptoms usually is accompanied by perusal of the overall life development history, including social, educational, and economic development.

Psychodynamic therapies, including psychoanalysis, have long used unstructured interview methods. Beginning with Freud, therapists adopted an unstructured model of interviewing as a procedure designed to allow the client to freely report whatever seemed relevant. In psychodynamic interviews the focus usually is on past events that were painful and traumatizing, leading to symptom development, which form the basis for current problems with appropriate functioning. The psychodynamic therapist pays particular attention to the client's relationship history, beginning with parents, siblings, and extended family members. Observations of the transference, or the client's responses to the therapist, are part of the assessment of past significant relationships. The quality of relationships, from childhood to current adult relationships, is examined for evidence of enduring relationship distress and difficulties that are rooted in the client's early life history. As the interview proceeds the therapist listens carefully to the history of origins and onset of symptoms. It is presumed that the client's traumatic experiences were rendered bearable and managed through use of defense mechanisms that keep the traumatizing events out of conscious awareness. Eventually, connections are drawn between past traumatizing experiences and the client's patterns of malfunctioning. As the proper interpretations reveal these connections between past and present, the client reaches insight, or awareness of the unconscious motives determining dysfunctional behavior (Yalof & Abraham, 2005).

This unstructured, fluid process fit very well with humanistic approaches, such as Gestalt therapies, which are predicated on treatment goals involving awareness, understanding, and insight. However, there are some key differences from psychodynamic therapies. The Gestalt therapist is more focused on assessment of present interactions between therapist and client than on past life events and historical relationships. Through use of present-tense dialogue the therapist observes and analyzes the client's present patterns of experience and awareness. It is assumed that the present subjective experience not only is more available and accessible but also is the most efficient means of effecting change. As the dialogue proceeds the therapist observes the unfolding and cresting of inner processes along a continuum of sensation, excitement, action, contact, reflection, and withdrawal. As patterned thoughts, feelings, and behaviors emerge the therapist empathizes with the client's present experience, attempts to understand phenomenological elements, and offers feedback. The client is then asked to reflect on his or her current experience and reconsider patterns of experience by engaging in an experiment. The experiment eventually leads to increasing awareness, followed by insight, leading to alternative conceptions and experiences (Woldt & Toman, 2005).

In cognitive and behavioral therapies the interview focuses on gathering specific symptom information and the specific factors maintaining those symptomatic behaviors. Interviews are not as fluid or as flexible because the focus is aimed at discovering and examining specific events, thinking patterns, and frequent behaviors. The interview also focuses on determining discrete environmental factors that reinforce and maintain dysfunctional behaviors. The client's past and current experiences and functioning are assessed to identify factors such as particular life events, developmental events, learning history, and cognitive schemas. Diagnostic efforts center on identifying current cognitive and affective precursors and environmental antecedents to problem behaviors. The cognitive therapist pays particular attention to the client's expression of underlying assumptions that motivate behavioral responses in a variety of possible situations. The behavior therapist focuses on past and present reinforcers of dysfunctional behaviors. Particular emphasis is placed on gathering a complete description of the target behavior, such as frequency, intensity, and duration. As the interview progresses the therapist formulates hypotheses about the factors causing and maintaining the target behaviors. Cognitive behavioral therapies are action oriented. The client is responsible for promoting change by monitoring, tracking, recording, and altering cognitions and behaviors. Motivation to sustain this change effort is achieved through the establishment of a strong, cooperative working alliance between client and therapist. It is also advisable to maintain and reinforce the quality of the working alliance by regularly soliciting feedback from the client about the therapist's ability to empathize with his or her concerns and problems. Usually the interview ends with the assignment of homework consisting of

reading materials and behavior change practice instructions (Beck, 1995; Padesky & Greenberger, 1995; Truax, 2002).

THE INITIAL INTERVIEW

The First Contact

First impressions begin when the first contact is made. If you have the services of a receptionist, be certain that he or she is well trained in receiving the general public with a tone that is welcoming and an attitude that is appropriate for greeting and informing people who are probably distressed and inquisitive. Rehearse the way the receptionist will answer the phone and take down information. Next, instruct the receptionist as to how to handle people in crisis and inform potential clients about scheduling appointments. Be certain that people are being received in a manner that is friendly and nondiscriminating with regard to race, gender, ethnicity, and other personal characteristics.

If you do not have a receptionist, then the greeting on your telephone serves that purpose. Your greeting informs potential clients about your attitudes and frame of mind as a professional as well as your availability. Greeting messages should be brief and positive in tone but not inappropriately cheerful.

The Setting

The interview format will differ depending on the clinician's practice setting. Interviews that take place in clinics, hospitals, community agencies, and campus counseling centers can all be quite different from one another. Clinical settings serving the general public differ from private practice settings in many fundamental ways. In public settings the information gathered is likely to be shaped by externally regulated policies that require collection of substantial amounts of personal data in a timeline format. For instance, a client file must contain information that is used to determine the client's appropriateness for treatment in that particular clinic. Information is then passed on to others in a chain of information gathering until a decision is reached as to whether to admit the client into treatment. Throughout the chain, specific increments of information are recorded in the file until a clinician is assigned or the client is referred elsewhere. In accordance with state regulations for public clinics, policy usually requires a certain amount of information to be recorded within a specified period of time. An established format usually is used, with a series of questions to be asked at each step in the procedure.

In a private setting the clinician is free to select content that fits his or her theoretical leanings and the current legal and ethical codes of practice. For the most part, the intake process can be determined by the psychologist's own style of information gathering. The private practitioner is free to ask questions as they develop spontaneously within the procedure and determine the timeframe based on the client's willingness to divulge at various times during the process (Armstrong, 2000).

The setting shapes the all-important first impression that a prospective client develops. It is important that this impression be a positive one. These early impressions are part of the therapy relationship. In the same way that we create vital impressions of our early relationship with people the second we enter their home, the client enters the therapy relationship forming opinions about the therapist and the therapy relationship based on his or her reactions to the professional setting.

Before you receive a client it is always advisable to examine every inch of the office setting, including the waiting room, if there is one. Your office space should be easy to find, well lit and ventilated, and as private as possible, with no noises filtering in from the outside, and it should be clean and attractive. A common courtesy is to provide a box of tissues within easy reach of wherever the client is likely to sit.

Some accoutrements are important to avoid, such as art or pictures that are too suggestive or that depict content likely to elicit certain emotions. Avoid pictures of family, children, and spouses, so as not to advertise your happy private life. Natural color tones and textures, with some splashes of more vibrant colors, provide a soothing and inviting atmosphere. Avoid furnishings that are uncomfortable to sit on for long periods. An atmosphere of comfort and neutrality is likely to help clients relax and focus on their internal processes without distractions.

Personal Appearance

How you dress is very important. Clothes should be comfortable but not too casual (save the jeans for later in your relationship). Avoid any clothing that calls attention to your political stances. As with your office space, an attitude of neutrality is both freeing and soothing to the stranger who has entered your space for the first time. Avoid clothing that is flashy, trendy, exceedingly odd or peculiar, or expensive looking. Clients respond best to a professional person who conveys a sense of comfort, is easygoing, takes pride in his or her appearance, is able to assume the role of an authority figure, and is capable of adequate self-care. When in doubt, clothes that convey a neutral message, in keeping with the culturally determined expectations for a professional role, are the most prudent option (Weinberg, 1996).

THE INTERVIEW PROCESS

Two strangers enter a room and one person, designated as the interviewing professional, instructs the other and then begins to ask questions. The other person, designated as the interviewee, responds to the questions and begins to reveal deeply personal information, including personal problems experienced in their past and current life.

For anyone who has seriously attempted to study the context of the first interview, one thing stands out: It is an unusual situation. How does a stranger entice another stranger to reveal so much on their first meeting together? The answer lies in certain aspects of the situation itself. First, the strangers share a common understanding about their respective roles. Second, the stranger assuming the role of interviewer is presumed to possess a set of skills and a body of expertise. Third, the stranger in the role of interviewee can reasonably expect that the interaction will benefit him or her in someway. Fourth, the setting and roles provide a definition of professional purposes and outcomes. Finally, any professional interaction is presumed to be about something important (Sullivan, 1954).

The interview can be broken down into stages or phases. Put simply, there is a life span quality to the process, featuring beginning, middle, and end stages. Each phase should be seen as one distinct aspect of the process, with its own planning and preparation.

Preparation

Careful and thoughtful preparation is the key to achieving the goals of the interview. The steps in preparation include clarity about the goals in each phase. In the beginning phase, two goals are equally important: Make a good first impression and establish sufficient rapport to encourage the client's openness and willingness to reveal personal information. In the middle phase the goal is to facilitate the gathering of enough information to begin the appropriate treatment or to make the appropriate referral. In the end phase the goals are to summarize information and close the interview. This should include some method for checking with the client to make sure the information and your understanding of its meaning are accurate and correct. Next, bring the interview to a close on a note that is proper for the kind of information that has been conveyed.

Before the interview begins it is advisable to review any information already known to you about the client. Establishing rapport should be planned according to cultural norms and expectations for respectful and proper behavior. Cultural norms of introduction can vary depending on ethnicity, age, gender, and marital status. Are you familiar with the differing norms? Do you know the proper way to introduce yourself and the task at hand with people from different cultural backgrounds? Will you need an interpreter? If so, make certain the interpreter is properly trained. Never use family members, especially children, as interpreters.

How did the client sound to you over the phone? How would you rate his or her degree of distress (high, medium, low)? Did the client sound especially anxious, cautious, depressed, or angry? Did the client seem more positive than negative, or the other way around? Was the client anxious to get an appointment? Was there a tone of desperation in the caller's voice? Was he or she experiencing a crisis? Will you need to do a risk assessment for possible harm to self or others? How and why was the person referred to you? Who referred the client, and how well do you know that referral source? These questions and answers are all part of the formulation of a first impression of the client, and some groundwork is laid for what to expect when we meet.

How much time is available? Normally, 50 to 60 minutes is needed to properly conduct an initial interview, and some clinicians prefer to schedule a longer amount of time than that. In this era of managed care many clinicians feel the pinch of time constraints on their billable hours and restrict their sessions accordingly. Make certain that enough time is available to achieve the goals of making a positive impression and establishing rapport. A timeframe that is too limited will give the impression that the client is not respected or valued or that his or her problems are not taken seriously.

Therapist's Attitudes and Personal Qualities

The interpersonal attitude that the therapist assumes during the interview greatly affects the process. Certain personal qualities are known to promote the establishment of rapport and enhance the gathering of vital information. The process is aided by attitudes of respect, openness, and curiosity. Respect does not necessarily mean agreement with the client or with things the client has done. Nor does it mean that we necessarily believe the client is "a good person." Respect means that we are meeting a stranger with a willingness to open ourselves to his or her point of view and offer assistance and understanding for his or her troubles.

The inevitable influence of personal values and biases is always an important consideration. Research shows that all of us are susceptible to the influence of biased preconceptions and attitudes. Different groups, regions, and age cohorts were raised with differing biases about differing groups of people. Personal life events can also create biased attitudes (e.g., in a therapist who was molested as child or treated badly by a member of a minority group). Recent research in bias shows that most Americans no longer espouse or admit to racist attitudes. Yet it is also evident from research conducted on unconscious cognitions that most of us still harbor biased thoughts and feelings.

Allowing ourselves to become aware of any prejudices we have is ethical, responsible clinical practice. Next, it is necessary to determine, as honestly as possible, the impact of our biases on our clinical practice. In coping our biases and prejudices an ethical clinician strives toward identification, careful monitoring, and appropriate referrals, when necessary. An ethical and responsible therapist will avoid working with clients on whom they are likely to impose a biased frame of mind.

Attitudes of openness and curiosity may be the most important interviewer attributes. Good unstructured interviewers take pleasure in meeting and getting to know new people. It is an opportunity to exercise one's abundant curiosity. Who is this person? What has this person's life entailed? What is this person's world view? What interesting experiences has this person had? Who and what matters most? Comprehending the totality of this new person is a welcome challenge. A stance of openness and curiosity allows for the flow of information to take any direction and follow any path and promotes awareness of many possible characteristics of the client's unique personhood (McWilliams, 2004).

Anxiety and Safety

Both strangers enter the interview with a set of expectations, but neither can be certain that those expectations will be met. For that reason a certain amount of anxiety is always present when the first interview begins. Indeed, anxieties for both people begin before they actually meet one another. For both parties there is always the looming basic question, "Will we like each other?"

Therapists wonder about their competencies and abilities to perform well with a new client that they have never encountered before. Will I know what to offer and how to respond, or will I feel completely stymied, inadequate, and lost? Anxiety-provoking questions such as these tend to occur no matter how long the therapist has been practicing and how skilled the therapist is. Although certain anxieties are likely to be more prominent in the novice, there is always the possibility that a new client will evoke feelings of ineptitude and self-doubt in an experienced therapist (Morrison, 1995; Wiger & Huntley, 2002).

For clients there are even more intense anxieties having to do with trust. Is the therapist a kind, patient, understanding, and competent person? Will I feel respected by the therapist, and will I feel confident that the therapist has

something to offer as a clinician? Am I wasting my time and money? What will I do if, after we meet, I do not feel good about the encounter, and how will I extricate myself? Maybe more important, there is anxiety about the potential power of an authority figure on whom the client wants to depend in his or her time of need. Anyone in such a position will have some fears that his or her own state of needfulness will create vulnerabilities that may prove to be liabilities. Many clients fear that their needs and emotions will become overwhelming and too intense for them to exercise sufficient self-control. Will they be able to protect themselves should the therapist be inept, too callous, or too controlling?

It is important to keep in mind that whatever the purpose or goals of a professional meeting, two people who are strangers to each other will each experience some amount of anxiety. Because anxiety cannot and should not be eliminated, controlling the amount and the source of anxiety is indicated.

To control inevitable anxieties the clinician should be aware of certain things. Careful monitoring of one's own anxiety offers important clues into our own and the client's functioning. Were there some indications on the phone that this may prove to be an especially difficult client? Are my anxieties signs of professional or personal shortcomings, such as an unacknowledged lack of expertise or the presence of personal biases? Am I ready to take on another client at this time, or should I accept the fact that my case load is already excessive?

Careful preparation and adherence to expected cultural and professional norms are indicated for the first meeting. Anxieties can be minimized for both strangers when the therapist maintains the usual cultural expectations associated with a professional interaction. It is also advisable to pace the first session slowly. Any questions remaining after that session can always be addressed in a later session. Do not try to eliminate anxiety by doing too much information gathering into the initial session, a mistake many novices make.

THE BEGINNING PHASE

The therapy process begins with the initial interview, which is used to provide an introduction to the process and to assemble the necessary information that will guide the process. Most practicing clinicians would agree that the initial interview is structured to produce certain interaction effects that will affect the subsequent therapy work. By no means is the initial interview the only interview; interviewing as information gathering continues in some way or other throughout treatment, but the initial interview sets the crucial expectations for what is to come. In the initial interview roles are established, and the relationship is defined.

Receiving and Greeting the Client

The manner in which you greet your clients for the first time begins the all-important first impression of you as a therapist. Both strangers are socially obligated to make the best possible impression on the other. Generally, clients should be received in whatever manner is proper and respectful for their cultural group (Mishne, 2002; Tseng & Streltzer, 2004). If the client is within the same age range or younger, using his or her first name is acceptable, but if the client is much older, then it is advisable to use his or her last name. Some clinicians prefer to initially address all of their clients by their last names (e.g., "Hello, Mr. Smith.") and allow clients to make it clear that they feel more comfortable being addressed by their first name (e.g., "Call me Hal."). Typically, Hispanic and Asian clients should be addressed with some formality, using a title (i.e., Mr., Ms., or Mrs.), followed by their last name. If the interview is conducted with a couple or family unit it is usually appropriate to address the person who called to make the appointment first, followed by the other adults, then their children. For Hispanic and Asian families it is best to address the husband first and then his wife (e.g., "Hello Mr. and Mrs. Blank.").

Much research evidence shows that minorities, especially in public clinics, are reticent to reveal information to a strange White person. Research on racial matching continues to show mixed results. Yet evidence mounts that race of interviewer does play a role in the information gathered. That is, minorities tend to offer different information depending on the race of the interviewer (Hersen & Turner, 2003).

It is customary to shake hands at the first face-to-face contact. However, it is advisable to wait for clients to offer their hands first. Touch, no matter how slight, is probably the most powerful signal of intimacy, actual or expected, in any culture. Many clients have histories of abuse, both physical and psychological. Until a solid basis for trust has developed, it is always possible that any touch, no matter the intentions, can be misinterpreted, creating unnecessary anxiety and distress. Never touch a client until the relationship is well established, and then only in ways that are completely within the norms of a professional relationship.

If you have a waiting room you may have a short distance to walk to arrive at your office. The walk to the office area can be anxiety provoking for both therapist and client because it can impose an ambiguous relational mood. Resist the temptation to fill this relational void with any chatter about clients or their problems. Hallways are not private spaces, and it is not wise to give the impression that anything the client says is not completely confidential. If you must engage in conversation, now is a good time to ask whether the client was able to find the office and a parking space without too much difficulty. Save any more meaningful conversation for after you have entered your office and shut the door.

Setting the Frame and Structure

Once they have entered the office, therapists intentionally differ in what they do next. Some therapists tell the client where to sit. This releases the client from having to make a decision, which can be awkward in a stranger's domain. Furthermore, it prevents the added awkwardness of what to do if the client chooses the therapist's favorite chair. Another reason for telling the client where to sit has to do with the therapy method. Some therapy orientations require certain seating arrangements to achieve the suitable interpersonal connection, and some therapists prefer to exercise control over the therapy process, such as sitting in a position where only they can see the clock.

Some therapists prefer to tell clients, "Sit wherever you like," and offer a variety of available seating possibilities. This leads the clients to a decision, and the therapist can then observe how they make that decision. Do they move quickly and decisively? Or do they waver and wait for cues from the therapist? Do they assume their seat nervously, or do they behave as if they have been coming to your office for some time and already feel some ownership of the space? Will they sit some distance from the therapist, or will they seek a chair that closes the distance? Do they prefer the chair as close to the door as possible, or will they enter into the inner recesses of the room?

Once seated, the therapist should begin the work of the interview. If you have not done so already, a polite inquiry as to whether the journey to your office was easy enough should be made. A brief introduction is now in order. What do you plan to do in this session? A brief overview can provide a sense of structure and give the relationship a set of clear expectations (e.g., "In this meeting I would like to begin by going over my treatment procedures and make sure that you understand your rights and responsibilities. Then I want to spend the rest of our time getting to know you and have you tell me about yourself and the reasons why you have come here today.").

Next it is expected that the therapist will introduce the necessary terms and conditions for treatment (e.g., fees), privacy rights including Health Insurance Portability and Accountability Act (HIPAA) documents, limits of confidentiality, and consent to treatment forms. It is wise to have well-written documents that can be read and discussed easily and quickly.

If you are taking notes it will become obvious when you lift pen to paper, but if you want to record this or other sessions, now is the time to get the client's permission. Note taking, especially in this first interview, is always advisable, and clients have come to expect it. However, do not allow note taking to interfere with the natural flow of emotions and information. Your attention should not stay too fixed on writing but on the client's attempt to be heard and to bond with you.

About 5 minutes is a reasonable amount of time to spend on these preliminary procedures. The therapist should remember that clients can be given copies of documents to take home and read at their leisure, and any questions raised can be addressed in the next session.

Some amount of anticipation has been rising between the first contact and the first interview, perhaps over a few weeks or a few months. It is not advisable to prolong the opportunity to let clients talk about the problems they are experiencing. During this interim anxieties are inevitably building, and people under stress often are anxious to get to the point.

Next it is customary to ask the client why he or she has come to see you. Several openings are acceptable. "Why have you come to see me?" is the simplest. Other possible opening questions include "What did you want to see me about?" or "What brings you here today?" At this point clients will begin to tell you about their problems and present the level of distress that they are undergoing.

THE MIDDLE PHASE

The use of unstructured interviewing during the initial contact is intended to maximize the amount and depth of the information gathered and to establish rapport. Rapport creates a trusting bond between therapist and client and encourages the client to reveal information that he or she might otherwise prefer to keep hidden. Essentially, it is believed that the more the client reveals, the more effective and useful the therapy can be. During this phase the therapist should remain attentive to both verbal and nonverbal information, including interpersonal styles, speech patterns, and the degree of self-awareness as well as the content of the information revealed. The therapist's inquiry skill levels determines how well information is gathered and how well rapport is established.

Asking Questions

Asking the appropriate questions is the essence of unstructured interviewing. Different frames of inquiry facilitate different responses on the part of the client. Questions that encourage a range of possible responses are best. This method allows a richness of responses that can aid in understanding and interpretation of revelations at the deepest possible levels of meaning. Typically, the kinds of questions that expedite spontaneous and deeper levels of responding include *open, focusing,* and *clarifying questions.*

Open questions begin with words that encourage the client to conduct an extensive scan of their inner processes in order to provide an answer. Open questions usually begin with "What," "How," or "When," or a statement such as "Tell me about. . . ." For instance, the therapist asks, "What do you want to talk about?" or "How do you feel about your marriage?" or "Tell me about yourself." In response to any question clients must formulate an answer by first focusing on and scanning through their internally organized environment, calling on their own unique processing. Open questions act as a projective technique to expand the boundaries of responses. Properly executed, open questions may prompt clients to respond in ways that even they had not expected, especially if they have never thoroughly considered the subject matter before.

Focusing questions ask the client to focus on a specific topic or some topic detail. A focusing question usually is phrased in the form of an open question but works to narrow the client's scanning toward specific content (e.g., "What was your childhood like?" "Tell me about your education background," "Who else is involved?" "How do you plan to deal with that?"). Focusing can help to fill in the details or allow a particular topic to be explored in more depth.

Clarifying questions ask the client to report enough specifics about a topic to eliminate vagueness or ambiguities that might hinder understanding or lead the therapist to make inaccurate assumptions. A clarifying question or statement has the advantage of making the topic and its meaning clearer to both client and therapist. Some examples of clarifying questions include "What do you mean by . . . ?" "Describe the last time you . . . ," Are you saying . . . ?" or "Give me an example of. . . . " Clarifying the subject expands the therapist's knowledge of emotional and behavioral patterns and conveys the therapist's intention to work toward as much understanding of the client's experiences as possible.

Open, focusing, and clarifying questions and statements achieve the goal of complex information gathering by opening up the inner world of experiences, emotions, values, intentions, needs, desires, and hopes. Conversely, some questions and statements should not be used because they tend to have the opposite effect. It is best to avoid *closed, leading,* and *why questions.*

Closed questions can be answered with a simple "yes" or "no" answer, limiting the range of responding. Closed questions usually begin with words such as "Are," "Did," "Can," and "Is" (e.g., "Are you happy?" "Did you want to come today?" "Can you tell me about your depression?" "Is it okay to ask you about . . . ?").

Leading questions suggest a right or desirable answer. The client may respond by providing it rather than responding more authentically. Some examples of leading questions include "Are you prepared to work hard to get better?"

"Is it okay with you to take medications?" or "How well do you think this session went?"

Why questions often have the effect of imposing a demand to explain or justify one's choices and behaviors. Clients may feel they have been put on the spot and respond defensively. In any case, they may not honestly know the answer but feel pressured to provide some reply, whether it is genuine or not. Examples of why questions are "Why don't you talk about sex?" "Why didn't you deal with that problem?" or "Why did you allow that to happen?"

Keeping the Information Flowing

Keeping the information flowing is also the goal of good interviewing. No matter how skillfully executed, a steady stream of questions can have a detrimental effect on the interview. Constant inquiry can create an ambiance more akin to an interrogation than an interview. The absence of mutual connection hinders development of rapport and trust. The flow of questions should be interrupted and integrated with statements that allow the client to pause and shift the focus onto the therapist's capacity to understand and empathize. This can be accomplished by using *empathy, paraphrasing,* and *summarizing.*

Empathic statements and comments address the client's feelings, using feeling words that capture the emotional content of the client's verbal and nonverbal messages. Empathy conveys warmth, caring, and nurturance. It is also an indicator that the client will be taken seriously and his or her problems will be attended to respectfully. Clients tend to develop trust more quickly with the skillful use of empathy. They also tend to offer more personal information if the therapist has demonstrated his or her capacity for affective comprehension and compassion.

Paraphrasing comments convey that the client's messages and meanings have been heard and understood. The therapist essentially repeats what the client has said but uses different phrasing to avoid being redundant. These comments tend to help the client feel heard and inclined to continue talking. If the client says, "Why do I do these things? I wish I could stop," the therapist might respond with, "You feel worried and frustrated and want more control over your life."

Summarizing comments are useful tools in pulling a sequence of client comments together into a meaningful whole. Again, the client feels heard but has the added sense that his or her comments have been processed at a comprehensive level, and the larger meanings are clear. Summarizing is also useful in unifying a list of complaints or concerns. This conveys that therapist has been attentive to all of the pertinent data, not just focusing on one problem or a single aspect of a problem. Summarizing can help a client clarify and keep track of his or her feelings and problems, instead of drifting in a state of confusion. Finally, summarizing can signal that the interview is drawing to a close, and the client will be encouraged to wind down and refrain from bringing forward new material.

Rhythms and Cadences

Every interview has a verbal tempo. Usually the interview begins at a slow pace as the client begins to feel connected to his or her feelings and a bond is formed with the therapist. As problems and complaints are drawn out into the open, the tempo and signs of tension tend to increase. The client often experiences increasingly powerful emotions, with a corresponding increase or decrease in his or her rate of speech. Typically, the tempo ebbs and flows as the interview progresses through different content areas. As the content becomes more sensitive, the therapist should take care to match the client's pacing as much as possible while continuing to make inquiries. It is usually better for therapists to pace inquiries too slowly, rather than too quickly, through sensitive and emotionally loaded content areas, to avoid causing the client to feel pushed or hurried along.

It is not uncommon for the interview to be punctuated by long pauses or silences. During these moments the interviewer should respond with appropriate matching of the mood. Many times novices are distressed by silence, believing that they have an obligation to fill these anxiety-provoking verbal voids by introducing topics or continuing to ask questions. This tendency is almost always a mistake and reveals more about the therapist's level of discomfort than the client's.

Silences can be quite appropriate and informative. The experienced interviewer learns to distinguish between different characteristics of silence. Some silences occur as the client turns inward to focus on sorting through a complex thought. Other silences denote the building of strong emotions that the client is struggling to restrain or control. Clients fall silent when their thoughts or feelings are difficult to express in words or when there are simply no words to articulate a powerful and momentous experience. If the emotional content is weighty and the client becomes silent, it is best for the interviewer to do likewise and wait for the client to resume talking. Therapist silence at such times conveys a respect for the client's feelings and prevents interruption of a significant inner process that may take some time to complete.

Different ethnic groups respond best to a verbal rhythm and tone that is familiar in their cultural experience. For instance, American Indians typically prefer a slower cadence and longer pauses than do European Americans. The right pacing for an American Indian interviewee is about half the speed suitable for European American cultural groups. A rate of speech that would be comfortable for an American from the East Coast, for instance, could be felt as rude and overbearing. Asian and American Indian cultures emphasize harmony and mindfulness, so a slower, lower, and softer tone of voice is also advisable.

INTERVIEW CONTENT

Typically, clients are first asked why they have sought therapy. This is followed by the taking of an extensive life history and some assessment inquiries. The reasons for seeking therapy, or life problem experiences, should be explored using empathy and paraphrasing to form a trusting connection. Clarifying and focusing questions and summarizing are used to make sure the information is perceived accurately.

The Life History

The information from the client's life history forms the basis for later hypotheses about diagnosis and treatment. The interviewer seeks to gather enough information to formulate a picture of the client's past experiences, life patterns, life choices, symptom patterns, and overall life development. Apart from the *what,* or content, it also pertinent for the interviewer to pay attention to *how* clients report their history for clues to their interpersonal style and ability to tell a story that is cohesive and coherent. During this phase of the interview clients' verbal and nonverbal behaviors express their overall ability to relate and their willingness to reveal.

The interviewer probably will begin by using an open inquiry (e.g., "Tell me about your life to this point."). From there the interviewer notices how the client proceeds. Does the client begin in early childhood and proceed from there to the present? If so, what does the client choose to tell us about, to emphasize, and to omit? What past experiences seem most relevant and important to the client? What past people and events have shaped the client's life, and what events have contributed to the client's problems? What happy themes does the client mention, and what setbacks, failures, and disappointments does he or she describe?

As the history unfolds the interviewer should be attentive to forming an impression of the person and his or her personality. The interviewer's curiosity should be activated. Is the client sociable and outgoing? Or shy and reticent? Does the client tell the story with feelings, values, and attitudes prominently displayed? Or does the presentation sound flat, like a recitation from the phone book? Is eye contact appropriate? Or is the client barely able to look at you? What messages does the client send through body language and postures? Does the client appear comfortable and at ease? Or does his or her posture express tension, disdain, and defensiveness? Does the client welcome talking about himself or herself? Is the client proud, self-deprecating, self-critical, grandiose, or balanced and realistic in his or her self-appraisal? What is the client's overall disposition or attitude about life? Is the client self-assured, hopeful, calm, and generally satisfied? Or, is it apparent that the client feels sad, angry, depressed, or despairing? Does the client have an appropriate sense of humor? Or does the client seem humorless, morbid, or bitter? Or does the client assume an inappropriate cheerfulness and gaiety about seriously painful and hurtful events?

Does the client speak slowly and clearly, or does he or she speak so rapidly that it is difficult to follow and take notes? Does the client respond straightforwardly and readily answer your questions, or does he or she respond with deflections, diversions, circumspections, and tangents?

Unless clients have rehearsed, either on their own or through many visits to a therapist's office, the history inevitably will be choppy and disjointed. Few people are able to give a complete account of a lifetime without some out-of-sequence or missing material. Furthermore, it is also likely, and quite common, for clients to censor some important material until trust has been better established. The interviewer should not expect to receive the whole story in the first interview. In later interviews the pieces will begin to fit together as deeper revelations emerge.

Within 50 to 60 minutes, depending on the client's mood and skill levels, it may not be possible to elicit more than the presenting problem and a brief life history. In most cases, however, the therapist should attempt to get as much pertinent overview information, with some key details, as possible. If time is limited, important information can be touched on briefly and rounded out later, but it is best to gather as much as possible in the first interview to lay the groundwork for a treatment plan.

Key information includes the client's date of birth, education history, employment history, marital or adult relationship history, children, friendships, and family of origin information including a description of parents, siblings, extended family members, and significant life events. It is also desirable to gather some information on alcohol and drug use, medical problems, legal problems, and any previous psychotherapy.

Assessment

At some point in the latter part of the middle phase, the interviewer should reflect on what he or she has ascertained that will guide and inform a preliminary diagnosis or diagnostic impression. Much has been learned at this point by careful and attentive listening and direct observation, but some specifics may still be needed. Are there signs of disorder? If so, the interviewer will want to get a detailed picture of symptom patterns. Most clients expect to be examined, to some extent, about behaviors that appear abnormal and usually are prepared to give in-depth responses to direct, diagnostically oriented questions.

A useful technique is to envelop each symptom in narrowing circles of history, influence, and impact. If the client shows signs of depression or despair, the interviewer should ask for an integrated symptom history (e.g., "As far back as you can remember, when did your depressed moods begin?" "How often have you felt depressed in the last year?" "On a scale of 1 to 10, how would you rate the intensity of your depressed moods?" "What events triggered your depression?" "How has your depression affected your work, your marriage, your family, your social life, or your hobbies?" or "Have you ever felt suicidal, and if so, did you have thoughts of harming yourself, did you have a plan for hurting or killing yourself, or have you ever done anything to hurt yourself when you were depressed?").

Moreover, the interviewer should take notice of speech, thought, or behavior patterns that indicate any signs of severe disorder. If there are any signs of severe disturbance, such as loose associations, incoherence, chaotic confusion, paranoid ideations, or preservations, be prepared to conduct a mental status exam. Ask about specific symptoms, including unusual somatic complaints, loss of memory, hallucinations, or delusions.

THE END PHASE

Bringing the interview to a close or end point should be done with some forethought. Avoid abrupt or sudden shifts in content or connection. Abruptness can be interpreted as rudeness or a desire to be rid of the client. A good way to signal the approaching end of the interview is to begin to summarize what has been discussed and what has been learned. Then save time for the client to ask questions, if any, as a gesture of mutuality. Remember, the client has just spent nearly an hour submitting to the leadership and inquiries of the interviewer and might appreciate an opportunity to balance, somewhat, the relative power positions. Allotting time for the client to ask questions demonstrates an interest in and respect for the client's independent initiative and contributions. This phase is also the proper time to discuss follow-up issues, if any, and transitions into treatment.

When summarizing what has been discussed, keep the summaries brief and segmented. For example, "You want to deal with your depression, which you have felt for some time." Pause for a second and then proceed, "You have tried therapy before, but with limited success, and this time you want to be clear about how the therapy will help you, so we should discuss this in detail at the next session." Pause again, then, "I will give it some thought for next time. Is that it? Do I have it, do you think I get what you were saying?"

Once it is established that you and the client have had a meeting of the minds, if there are follow-up issues raise them at this point (e.g., "I would like you take some tests to get a better fix on the extent of your depression and go over the results with you next time," "I want to encourage you to get a full medical exam to rule out the possibility of any medical problems that might be contributing to your depressed moods," or "I want to discuss the possibility of a psychiatric referral to have you evaluated for possible medications that might help your depression.").

Next, some transition into therapy, if that is indicated, or a referral to a suitable therapist should be completed. A good way to segue is to ask what the client would like to accomplish in therapy and determine whether the client is suitable for the type of therapy you offer or is someone you would welcome working with. An open or focused question is useful for getting this information. Some examples of useful questions are, "If we worked together in therapy and the therapy was successful, how would you and I both know that our work was successful?" Or, "What would tell you that our therapy work has succeeded?"

When the client is invited to ask questions it is advisable to be prepared for what might be asked. Generally speaking, honest and frank responses are appropriate to establish trust. Most clients can sense when the therapist is hedging or fabricating. If you are not sure what to answer or how to answer, it is best to admit that is the case. If you feel pressured to make promises, be advised that one common mistake, especially for novices, is to overpromise. "I don't know, I will think about it" is always preferable to making up answers to questions when you actually don't have a good answer.

When time is up, a simple statement will suffice to bring things to an end. "I'll see you next time," or "Our time is up for today." Many therapist find it hard to bring their sessions to a close, especially if the client has experienced intense emotions; they think it is imperative to allow the client time to calm down before stating that the time is up. Some clients seize on this empathic courtesy to extend the therapy time. Instead of reaching a calmer point, other continue to emotionally escalate. Some clients need to know that they are expected to leave at the end of the appointed time, and a gentle but firm expression that "it's time to leave" can help them learn to focus and modulate their feelings to fit within the allotted time.

At the end of the first session it is a common courtesy to escort the client back to the waiting area, elevator, or door. Many people fell some amount of disorientation after an emotionally intense experience. Helping them back to the point of origin often is helpful. A final statement such as "It was good to meet you" serves as an appropriate parting.

CASE EXAMPLE

The first contact with Susan H. (not her real name) is by phone voice message. She states her purpose very clearly: "This is Susan H., calling on Tuesday morning. I was referred to you by Dr. M. for some therapy. I would like an appointment. I can be reached at (phone number). Please return my call. Thank you." Her voice is clear, her speech is precise and well organized, but there is also a hint of stiffness and sadness or depression. She sounds pleasant but cautious. When she is reached via a return phone call, she says, with some slowness, "I was hoping to get an appointment to see you. I have been feeling in a rut lately, and my doctor thought therapy might help." She asks what times I have available but then suggests a timeframe when she is most available. The appointment is made, and I tell her how to find my office, including where to park, what floor, and the location of the receptionist and waiting room. Her response is affirmative.

My first impressions are forming. She seems to be a thoughtful person with good planning abilities. She also seems depressed but with her emotions well controlled. She is probably Caucasian and well educated. What does she mean by "in a rut"? How depressed is she? Is "a rut" her polite euphemism for "depressed" or "desperate"? There is no mention of symptoms that sound serious or unfamiliar to me as a clinician. I do not remember the doctor who referred her, but I do remember giving a talk to a group of physicians a few months ago. What did her doctor tell her about me? What did I say in the talk that made the doctor remember me? My own anxiety levels are low. My general sense is that she will be an interesting and comfortable client with whom to work.

Our appointment is for 5:00 p.m. the next Tuesday. At 4:45 p.m. I go to the receptionist to tell her that I am expecting a new client at 5:00 p.m. and to buzz me when she arrives. The receptionist says, "She's already here, in the waiting room." She is early. Why? Is she anxious to see me? Entering the waiting room, I see a nice-looking Caucasian woman, probably in her 30s, reading a magazine. She looks preoccupied but comfortable. She is used to this type of environment. As I approach her and introduce myself, two things become readily apparent. One, she is impeccably dressed in a manner that suggests a business or professional career life. The clothes are well chosen for her height and build (both within normal range); color tones are natural hues, with some brighter colors in her accessories. Her shoes are flat and sensible. Her hair and makeup are casual but studious looking. As she rises to greet me, she is pleasant but smiles only slightly; she gathers her things and does not offer her hand. This is a no-nonsense interpersonal approach. She intends to be amiable but get down to business.

Entering my office, I instruct her to sit where she likes. She chooses a comfortable proximity that conveys an appropriate level of intimacy and deference for the first meeting. Her movements are decisive; however, she seats herself in a somewhat heavy way, suggesting that she feels tired or burdened but resigned to the weighty decision to see a therapist. There is now a hint of anxiety and vulnerability. She is anxious to see how this will go. I take this as a good sign. A certain resistance has begun, indicating her awareness that she feels vulnerable and insecure but able to mange these anxieties. She anticipates the possibilities of opening her vulnerable self to a stranger, which suggests that on some level she is willing to do so.

I ask whether she found the office easily, but I am aware that small talk will feel frivolous to her. I sense a need in myself to form a connection as soon as possible, perhaps to alleviate her intensifying anticipations. I make a quick but considered decision to wait for a while before introducing treatment documents and confidentiality issues. I move rather quickly to business. "So why did you want to see me for therapy?"

"Don't you want me to fill out forms?" I reply that that can wait a bit. "Thank God. I was in no mood to do all that right now." She then talks about feeling too down lately to function well. She has trouble sleeping and feels tense and low in energy. I ask, "So are you depressed?" She sinks into her seat and considers the question, then says, with much hesitation, "I guess so, I suppose I am." I now have the sense that she is very emotionally constricted, perhaps too much so. She prefers to put her emotions aside and think her way through her problems rather than letting her emotions guide her. Are her feelings threatening to her? I continue, "Tell me about what your life has felt like lately."

She begins a description of mood problems and burdens at work, and a sense of alienation becomes apparent. She works as an administrator in a law firm and is struggling to keep up with the workload and high performance expectations. She states that her marriage is supportive. She has three children: a son aged 8, and another son aged 11, and a daughter who is 13. Her voice is now stilted and monotone, her rate of speech is slowing, and she seems to be withdrawing into herself. It crosses my mind to wonder whether she is angry. Then she admits that she has had trouble getting out of bed in the morning, and some evenings she goes straight to bed after work, and her husband and children have become worried about her. She states, "Sometimes I worry that I just can't do it anymore, it all feels like I'm on the brink of collapsing." I make two mental notes. First, her tone suggests more marital dissatisfaction than she has admitted to, so I need to know more about her family life, especially the quality of her marital relationship. Second, I must get more detailed information about the extent of her depressed mood and possible suicidal ideations.

Moving into life history information, I ask her, "Tell me about your life, starting with your childhood." I am aware of being anxious to hear this information; I anticipate that her history will provide clues about the origins of her depressive symptoms and emotional style. I am also beginning to get the feeling that she has a history of social alienation and loneliness, and I wonder whether her life story will confirm these impressions.

She tells her life story in a well-organized, linear fashion. She offers a good amount of detail. As I take notes, I notice she paces herself at a speed that is expeditious but comfortable enough for me to write down her story. I wonder whether she has been in therapy before.

Susan did indeed grow up a lonely only child. She was studious, well behaved, and responsible and worked hard in school to excel. She was also passive and shy. She had some difficulty making friends. She kept to herself a lot and spent much of her time alone in her room reading. Her

mother was abusive and distant. Her father was warm and sympathetic but submissive to his wife and was absent a lot working. As she tells her story I offer some clarifying questions (e.g., "What did your mother say to you?"), some focusing questions (e.g., "When did you first notice that?"), and summarizing. I feel my own sympathy for her growing. Given her business-mindedness, however, I keep my empathic statements limited to an occasional comment such as, "That must have been hard."

As can happen in any interview, I make a few mistakes. When she talks about an argument between her parents, her mother had said her father was "hopeless." I ask, "Did she mean she thought he was inadequate as a husband or a provider?" She stops and then starts and then stops again, struggling to formulate an answer. Obviously, my question is badly phrased and causes her to feel confused and frustrated. I interrupt her and state that I know it was a badly formed question and rephrase it to ask, "What did you think your mother meant?" After a pause she answers that she thought her mother had never appreciated her father and was inclined to nag and criticize him. She then proceeds in an even rhythm and flow; she seems to feel increasingly at ease and safe.

She begins to talk about her parents' marital problems, which reached a crisis point when she was 13. Her father threatened to leave, and a divorce seemed imminent. I ask, "So what happened next?" She answers, "My Dad broke down and decided to stay. They are both still living and will obviously be with each other until one of them dies. I may have been disappointed actually, that they didn't divorce. It was very hard living with my mother; it was hard on both of us [implying her and her father]. I left home to go to college at 18, and I will never go back." I wonder again about her anger, and because her own daughter is now 13, I wonder again about the state of her marriage.

Moving forward, she describes life in college and the first time she fell in love. She was far too shy and socially unskilled to make any approach or to respond well when he approached her, so the young man never knew how she felt. She met her husband at a time when she was ready to leave home forever. She describes her husband as intelligent and compassionate and a very responsible father. He enjoys the children and spends a lot of time with them. They rarely fight.

Nor do they tend to socialize with friends or other couples. Vacations are also rare because of their heavy work schedules.

I ask a focusing question: "How would you rate your sex life?" She hesitates in her thoughtful, perhaps censoring manner before answering, "Its okay, it's all right, there are no complaints." This response raises further questions in my mind. I get the impression that her marriage is definitely not as satisfying as she would like. Is there is a "sedate" relationship pattern lacking some important qualities, with tensions building underneath the surface? How much time does she spend with her children? Are there difficulties for her relating to them? Does she ever enjoy herself in any aspect of her life? What about her job? What are the causes of her distress at work? Considering the time remaining and confident that we have made an optimal connection to one another, I decide to shift into a semistructured format to obtain more details about her depression symptoms.

I begin by asking for a specific history of her symptoms: "When, as far back as you can remember, were you aware of being depressed?" She replies, "When, I guess since childhood, although I wasn't always clear about that fact. Sometimes I'm okay. But, no, before you ask, I've never thought seriously about killing myself." I am relieved, and I believe her, but I do want to know about key times and events when depression might be triggered, how she behaves when she is depressed, what has she tried in the past to relieve her depression, and so forth. It is advisable to tell her that we will both carefully monitor the severity of her depressed moods, and if she becomes suicidal we will consider a number of options to prevent a suicide. I now tell her that I want her to take the Minnesota Multiphasic Personality Inventory 2 and will be referring her to see a psychiatrist for an evaluation for medications. She agrees readily to both proposals, another clear sign that our connection is working well.

Next, questions designed to fill in the data are asked. I inquire about her date of birth, medical history, substance use, and any abuse history. Nothing remarkable is reported. Some inquires can round out the life events picture (e.g., "Who are the most important people in your life?" "What events have made you the happiest?" "What was the worst thing that has ever happened to you?"). My assessment has led to hypotheses about her symptoms and personality.

She is a high-functioning person with no signs of severe disorder. She is intelligent, responsible, and diligent. She shows signs of emotional constriction and social alienation. Her sadness and anger, along with other feelings, are deeply buried and rigidly controlled. She can be self-effacing, hard working, time conscious, and preoccupied with her demeanor and performance in a way that hint at perfectionist tendencies. There is a clear thread of family social isolation. Does she lack social skills, or does she find others so lacking that she prefers her own fantasies to actual human company? Is she obsessive or compulsive? In the next sessions I will pay more attention to perfectionistic strivings, perhaps leading to self-punitive tendencies, her work history and current work environment, and her feelings about her children.

Beginning the end phase, I ask whether she has had any previous therapy. She states, "Yes, for a short while in college, but I didn't like it. She was always late and her office was never clean!" Finally, she sounds angry and resentful, but it doesn't last. "No, I didn't stay because she was a million miles away sometimes; I didn't feel like she wanted to be bothered with me. No, actually, it was probably my fault, I just didn't know how to talk about myself back then, it was too hard to say what I thought or felt, so I really wasn't getting much good out of it." I make a mental note to avoid being late and to make sure that my office is never too cluttered. As for giving her the desired amount of attention and empathy, I am convinced that that concern has been satisfied.

Next, presuming that we will work together, I tell her it is time to go over the HIPAA and consent to treatment documents. She sighs but puts on her glasses and gives the materials and my overview spiel her full attention. I give her forms to sign and material to take home with her. I now ask, "So, say we have worked together and the therapy has been successful and we both know it has been successful, how would you know it has been successful?"

After a long and thoughtful silence she states, "I wouldn't feel so bad all of the time. I guess I would like a normal life, I mean. . . ." For the first time she looks away, breaking eye contact, and her voice breaks a little; clearly she is experiencing powerful emotions that she is struggling to control. After she composes herself she continues, "I haven't had much of a life really, I mean, I think other people have gotten more out of their lives. I would know it was successful if I wasn't afraid to live a halfway happy life, a life that I wanted." I see the results of our successful connection in her candor and her willingness to let her painful feelings reluctantly come through. Although many more questions are raised, it is time to end the interview.

I say, "Well, it is time for us to stop. I will think about what you have just said. It was good to meet you. I will see you next week." Susan looks toward the clock, surprised that the time has gone by so quickly, which I take to be another good sign that we have made a good connection. She says, "Oh, so it is." Then she rises, gathers her things, declines to be escorted back to the elevator, pauses at the door, looks back, smiles, and says, in a sincere voice, "Thank you."

I am convinced that our first interview was successful. There are many more questions to be asked. I am curious about the rest of her life, beliefs, values, and feelings that we did not yet touch upon. I look forward to seeing her again, working with her, and learning more about her.

SUMMARY

The unstructured interview has many advantages. One main advantage is the richness of information that ensues when client and therapist have the greatest possible freedom within which to operate. When the client is free to offer any possible perspective and the clinician can seize the moment as it arises to pursue any topic of clinical interest, information flows freely and naturally. Another advantage is that unstructured processes enhance the potential for depth of bonding between client and therapist, often leading to greater openness and trust.

Freedom of expression combined with ingenuity allows a process to develop that is an additional source of information. The interview is an interpersonal situation in which both the therapist and the client are engaged in a dynamic. This dynamic is a source of information about the client's interpersonal life and his or her preparedness for a therapeutic alliance. In a process that has been well planned and executed, attention is paid to the client's style of interacting as clues to disorders, resistances, and defenses that will become part of the therapy work. The client's verbal and nonverbal behaviors are then used to formulate a diagnostic impression that leads to a treatment procedure.

Client behaviors and responses to questions offer an expansive view of their personal and interpersonal development, skills, mental organization, and motivation levels. Despite careful planning and interview structures, both social and psychological, it is never possible to predict how things will unfold as two strangers interact. Once a connection has been made and the client is actively engaged in telling his or her story, it is impossible to know where the interview will lead. Therefore, it is wise to keep an open mind and learn from the process itself.

The unstructured format has important advantages but also some disadvantages. For many years unstructured interviewing was the primary format for gathering information pertinent to therapy goals and purposes. With the ascent of behavioral orientations, interviews needed to focus on specific symptoms and outcomes. In behavioral approaches sometimes the structured interview is found to be more suitable. Today, the relative merits of unstructured and structured interviews continues to be debated.

Some studies suggest that structured interviews work better when the goal is to arrive at a *Diagnostic and Statistical Manual*–oriented diagnosis. Structured interviews also tend to improve interrater reliability in settings that are intended for determinations based on specified diagnostic criteria, such as hospital emergency rooms. Other studies show that structured interviews reduce rater bias when used to gather information cross-racially. Structured interviews also appear to be more useful and reliable in employment decision making (Dougherty, Turban, & Callender, 1994; Huffcutt & Roth, 1998; Mantwill, Kohnken, & Aschermann, 1995; Miller, 2003; Orpen, 1985; Van Iddekinge, Raymark, & Roth, 2005).

Much depends on the purpose of the interview. If the main objective of the interview is a broad goal, such as getting to know someone, then unstructured interviews still offer the best method for achieving that goal. Unstructured interviewing techniques are designed to promote the emergence of information that may be known or unknown to the client. Certain aspects may be too threatening and are suppressed from the client's conscious awareness. Sometimes the client may not have associated different aspects of the problem as parts of the same problem. As the client engages in the unstructured interview, a process of discovery is shared by both parties.

REFERENCES

Armstrong, P. S. (2000). *Opening gambits: The first session in psychotherapy.* Northvale, NJ: Jason Aronson.

Beck, J. S. (1995). *Cognitive therapy: Basics and beyond.* New York: Guilford.

Dougherty, T. W., Turban, D. B., & Callender, J. C. (1994). Confirming first impressions in the employment interview: A field study of interviewer behavior. *Journal of Applied Psychology, 79*(5), 659–665.

Hersen, M., & Turner, S. (Eds.). (2003). *Diagnostic interviewing* (3rd ed.). New York: Kluwer Academic/Plenum.

Huffcutt, A. L., & Roth, P. L. (1998). Racial group differences in employment interview evaluations. *Journal of Applied Psychology, 83*(2), 179–189.

Mantwill, M., Kohnken, G., & Aschermann, E. (1995). Effects of the cognitive interview on the recall of familiar and unfamiliar events. *Journal of Applied Psychology, 80*(1), 68–78.

McWilliams, N. (2004). *Psychoanalytic psychotherapy: A practitioner's guide.* New York: Guilford.

Miller, C. (2003). Interviewing strategies. In M. Hersen & S. M. Turner (Eds.), *Diagnostic interviewing* (3rd ed., pp. 47–66). New York: Kluwer.

Mishne, J. (2002). *Multiculturalism and the therapeutic process.* New York: Guilford.

Morrison, J. (1995). *The first interview: Revised for the DSM-IV.* New York: Guilford.

Orpen, C. (1985). Patterned behavior description interviews versus unstructured interviews: A comparative validity study. *Journal of Applied Psychology, 70*(4), 774–776.

Padesky, C., & Greenberger, D. (1995). *Clinician's guide to mind over mood.* New York: Guilford.

Sullivan, H. S. (1954). *The psychiatric interview.* New York: W. W. Norton.

Truax, P. (2002). Behavioral case conceptualization for adults. In M. Hersen (Ed.), *Clinical behavior therapy: Adults and children* (pp. 3–36). New York: Wiley.

Tseng, W., & Streltzer, J. (Eds.). (2004). *Cultural competence in clinical psychiatry.* Washington, DC: American Psychiatry Publishing.

Van Iddekinge, C. H., Raymark, P. H., & Roth, P. L. (2005). Assessing personality with a structured employment interview: Construct-related validity and susceptibility to response inflation. *Journal of Applied Psychology, 90*(3), 536–552.

Weinberg, G. (1996). *The heart of psychotherapy: A journey into the mind and office of the therapist at work.* New York: St. Martin's Griffin.

Wiger, D. E., & Huntley, D. K. (2002). *Essentials of interviewing.* New York: Wiley.

Woldt, A. L., & Toman, S. M. (Eds.). (2005). *Gestalt therapy: History, theory and practice.* Thousand Oaks, CA: Sage.

Yalof, J., & Abraham, P. P. (2005). Psychoanalytic interviewing. In R. J. Craig (Ed.), *Clinical and diagnostic interviewing* (2nd ed., pp. 57–90). New York: Jason Aronson.

3

STRUCTURED AND SEMISTRUCTURED INTERVIEWS

JULIE N. HOOK, ELISE HODGES, KRISCINDA WHITNEY, AND DANIEL L. SEGAL

Diagnostic interviewing is one of corner-stones of modern clinical psychology. The earliest forms of interviewing typically involved a free-flowing, unstandardized format in which professionals relied on their clinical acumen to generate appropriate questions. As the field progressed, standardization of clinical diagnosis was emphasized, a concept marked by the publication of the first *Diagnostic and Statistical Manual of Mental Disorders* (*DSM;* American Psychiatric Association, 1952). Since that time, the *DSM* has gone through many revisions, and with its growth and development structured and semistructured interviews have also evolved, mirroring the *DSM* criteria.

The inherent nature of an unstructured interview leaves the type of questions and manner in which questions are asked to the discretion of the professional, which can be influenced by the professional's theoretical orientation, training, mood, and interaction with the patient. With the advent of structured interviews, several limitations of the unstructured interview were addressed. The structured interview provides a standardized method for asking and answering questions and recording and interpreting responses. As a consequence, variability and inconsistency across

professionals are decreased (Rogers, 2001; Segal & Coolidge, 2003). Improvement of diagnostic consistency has helped make the structured interview a useful tool not only in clinical practice but also in clinical research and training of professionals (Rogers, 2001).

In the past few decades, there has been a proliferation of structured interviews, and a number of important differences between instruments have emerged. First, the structured interview can vary in the stringency of the user's ability to deviate from the interview protocol. The most strict is a *fully structured interview,* which requires that all questions be asked as written, allowing few or no deviations from the interview format. Alternatively, a *semistructured interview* is less strict, typically beginning with standard questions but allowing optional probes or follow-up questions from the interviewer. Second, structured interviews vary in the content and depth of coverage. For example, some instruments may include most clinical (Axis I) or personality (Axis II) disorders, whereas others focus on a specific subset of disorders, such as anxiety or mood disorders, but with greater depth. Structured interviews have also been developed to assess specific areas of clinical interest (e.g., malingering, the five-factor model of personality). Third, the ease of use for the interviewer, the level of training needed to administer the measure, and the psychometric properties also differ between the different structured interviews.

Although there are advantages of structured interviews, critics of these instruments point out that their use can damage rapport, particularly in the context of a therapeutic relationship (Rogers, 2001; Rubinson & Asnis, 1989). Furthermore, a structured interview is only as valid as the diagnostic criteria on which it is based. Many researchers have argued that the *DSM* criteria should not be the sole determinant of diagnoses or be used as a substitute for clinical expertise (First, Frances, & Pincus, 2004). A structured interview can also limit the depth and breadth of coverage of particular diagnostic or clinical issues (Rogers, 2001; Rubinson & Asnis, 1989). Although there are advantages and disadvantages of relying solely on a structured interview, the interviewer is not prohibited from following up with individualized or unstructured questions (i.e., before or after the structured interview is completed).

This chapter first provides the reader with information to evaluate structured interviews, particularly in regard to psychometric properties. Next, a review of commonly used instruments of Axis I and II disorders is provided, followed by a chapter summary.

PSYCHOMETRIC CHARACTERISTICS

Reliability and validity are essential aspects of psychological measurement. Therefore, a review of these terms as they apply to structured interviews is provided.

Reliability

Reliability is the degree of consistency of a measure, such that a perfectly reliable measure theoretically would give the same result every time it was used (barring significant changes in the measured construct; Segal & Coolidge, 2006a). The reliability of structured interviews can be assessed at different levels of analysis, ranging from item-specific reliability within an interview to the resultant diagnoses. The majority of reliability studies of structured and semistructured interviews focus on diagnostic consistency across

raters (called interrater reliability) or across different points in time (called test-retest reliability; Rogers, 2001). In addition, but less often, the internal consistency within a measure is also reported (called coefficient alpha; Clark & Watson, 1995). However, because of the polythetic nature of most structured interviews, coefficient alpha is not considered an appropriate statistic in demonstrating reliability (Rogers, 2001).

Test-retest reliability is a measure of consistency of performance across time, such that a client is given a structured interview at time one and then administered the same interview by a different rater at another time. Two different raters are needed to ensure independence of assessment. Duration of the test-retest interval depends on the stability of the trait being measured. For example, personality disorders, which are thought to be quite stable over long periods of time, may necessitate a much longer test-retest interval than would a measure of an acute stress disorder. Interrater reliability is a measure of consistency across raters, in which one interview is performed with two or more raters observing (or evaluating) the interview; this type of reliability is one of the most commonly used methods of assessing reliability for the structured interview.

Interrater reliability estimates for categorical diagnoses typically are reported in terms of kappa, although Yule's Y and intraclass coefficient (ICC) are also used (Rogers, 2001). The kappa coefficient is the most commonly reported measure of agreement between two raters (Cohen, 1960). Although kappa does correct for chance agreements (Bakeman & Gottman, 1989), it may be influenced by base rates, making it difficult to compare kappas across studies (Thompson & Walter, 1988). Although Yule's Y is recommended for use with low–base rate phenomena (Spitznagel & Helzer, 1985; Summerfeldt & Antony, 2002), it is less commonly reported in validation studies. ICCs are used as measures of reliability when there are more than two raters (Keller et al., 1981). With large samples, ICCs are considered to be similar to a weighted kappa (Fleiss & Cohen, 1973).

Validity

Validity is the precision of measurement, how accurately a construct is assessed, and what can be inferred from the test scores (Anastasi &

Urbina, 1997; Segal & Coolidge, 2006b). Criterion-related and construct validity are the two most commonly examined types of validity for structured interviews.

Criterion-related validity is the degree to which scores on one measure predict scores on another measure considered to be the criterion or gold standard. This can be assessed at the same time (concurrent validity) or at a specified time in the future (predictive validity; Cronbach, 1990). Most studies that have examined criterion-related validity of structured interviews compare the consistency of a diagnosis from the interview to the diagnosis provided by an expert clinician or diagnostician. However, some critics argue that clinical judgment should not be considered a gold standard because of the inherent fallibility in clinical decision making (Garb, 2005). Predictive validity is of particular concern for measures designed to forecast future outcomes. An example would be the use of professional aptitude tests in determining a person's success or failure at a career.

Construct validity is the degree to which an obtained score reflects the theoretical true score of the phenomena under investigation (Cronbach & Meehl, 1955). Construct validity typically is examined through convergent and discriminant validity studies or a multitrait, multimethod matrix (Campbell & Fiske, 1959). In general, convergent validity is demonstrated when the score from one measure of a disorder is more highly related to a score of another measure of the same disorder than to a score from a measure of a different disorder. For instance, scores obtained from a new structured interview for anxiety disorders would be expected to be highly similar to the obtained score from an existing measure of anxiety disorder. On the other hand, to demonstrate the discriminant validity of a measure, one would expect that the obtained score would be less related to the scores from a measure of a dissimilar trait or disorder. In this example, the obtained score from the new structured interview of anxiety disorders should not be highly related to the obtained scores on an intelligence measure.

SEMISTRUCTURED INTERVIEWS FOR AXIS I DISORDERS

This section provides an overview of the measures including their development, administration

information, and a review of the literature related to reliability and validity (when available). Four of the most widely used semistructured interviews are reviewed: the Diagnostic Interview Schedule (DIS) for *DSM-IV,* the Structured Clinical Interview for *DSM-IV* Axis I Disorders (SCID-I), the Schedule for Affective Disorders and Schizophrenia (SADS), and the Anxiety Disorders Interview Schedule (ADIS) for *DSM-IV.* Each of these instruments assesses a variety of disorders and is useful in providing differential diagnoses.

Diagnostic Interview Schedule (DIS)

The DIS is a fully structured interview developed for clinicians and nonclinicians to assess a range of *DSM*-based psychiatric diagnoses (Robins, Cottler, Bucholz, & Compton, 1995). Because the DIS is completely structured with very specific questions and follow-up probes, the need for clinical judgment during questioning is minimized, which reduces reliance on the examiner's clinical training. The most recent version, DIS-IV (Robins et al., 1995), is based on the *DSM-IV* major psychiatric disorders.

The DIS was developed in 1978 at the request of the National Institute of Mental Health (NIMH) in response to the development of the Epidemiological Catchment Area (ECA) research program. This project resulted in a need for a comprehensive assessment tool that could be used for large-scale, multicenter epidemiological studies by interviewers with limited or varied clinical experience. Because the *DSM-III* (American Psychiatric Association, 1980) was in use at that time, many *DSM-III* disorders were the basis for the DIS and the ECA study. Over the course of changes associated with the *DSM,* the DIS followed, and upon publication of the *DSM-IV* (American Psychiatric Association, 1994), the DIS-IV was developed.

The interview begins by having the respondent provide demographic information and includes sections that pertain to chronological dates that aid the respondent's recall of symptom onset and also includes questions related to risk factors (e.g., living circumstances). The DIS then includes a series of questions that pertain to psychiatric symptoms in a standardized order. These questions are further organized into 19 modules that evaluate 30 *DSM-IV* Axis I psychiatric disorders including mood disorders, anxiety disorders, substance use disorders, and psychotic disorders, as well as antisocial personality disorder, coded on Axis II (Rogers, 2001). In most cases, the DIS modules are independent, unless one module precludes administration of another. For each module, if a symptom is reported as present, closed-ended questions are asked related to severity, frequency, and time course, as are questions that may provide information related to the potential for organicity (Summerfeldt & Antony, 2002). Once the core and probe questions have been asked, responses are coded as follows: 1 for *did not occur,* 2 for *lack of clinical significance,* 3 for *medication, drugs, or alcohol,* 4 for *physical illness or injury,* and 5 for *possible psychiatric syndrome.* If the number of symptoms for a threshold of a diagnosis is met, the interview proceeds. Additional questions are asked about the episode or disorder, including the frequency of occurrence, the respondent's age at onset, and age during the last occurrence. These data are then used to generate a diagnosis, including current and lifetime diagnoses.

No clinical experience is needed to administer the DIS, but familiarity with the administration protocol is recommended before use of the measure (Rogers, 2001; Summerfeldt & Antony, 2002). With users who are new to the DIS, administration of the entire measure may take up to 150 minutes. The format of the DIS allows omission of specific modules if the diagnosis is not being studied or if a diagnosis falls below the clinical threshold.

The psychometric properties of the DIS in its original and revised versions range from poor to excellent. Unfortunately, there have been only limited investigations of the psychometric properties of the DIS-IV, but because of the similarities across versions of the DIS, it has been proposed that research on the psychometric properties of prior versions is applicable to the DIS-IV (Rogers, 2001; Summerfeldt & Antony, 2002).

Investigations into the reliability of the DIS have yielded mixed results. Robins and colleagues (Robins, Helzer, Croughan, & Ratcliff, 1981; Robins et al., 1982) examined the test-retest reliability of the DIS-II, which focused on *DSM-III* lifetime disorders; results from these studies suggest moderate kappas for most assessed disorders. For later versions of the DIS, results were similar, citing mostly moderate agreements between raters across populations and over time. More recent studies, using the DIS-III (Vandiver &

Sher, 1991) found median kappa coefficients of .46 for current diagnoses and .43 for lifetime diagnoses over a period of 9 months.

Most studies examining validity for the DIS focus on concurrent or convergent validity using a kappa rating for a particular diagnosis across instruments. Overall, the reported kappas in validation studies are similar to the reliability studies, ranging from moderate to high agreement (Gavin, Ross, & Skinner, 1989; Whisman et al., 1989). For example, Robins et al. (1982) reported a mean agreement of .55 between lay-administered DIS and medical chart diagnoses. Whisman et al. (1989) compared diagnoses resulting from the DIS and the interview version of the Hamilton Rating Scale for Depression (Hamilton, 1960) and reported a high median ICC of .89 (moderate to high agreement).

Structured Clinical Interview of *DSM-IV* Axis I (SCID-I)

The Structured Clinical Interview for *DSM-IV* Axis I Disorders (SCID-I; First, Gibbon, Spitzer, Williams, & Benjamin, 1997a) is a semistructured interview designed for interviewers with clinical experience. The SCID-I provides diagnoses for many *DSM-IV* Axis I diagnoses. It is reported to be the most widely used diagnostic instrument in the United States (Rogers, 2001; Summerfeldt & Antony, 2002). The SCID-I has undergone revisions to mirror the most current *DSM* criteria. At present, the SCID-I has two versions: the SCID-CV (Clinician Version; First, Spitzer, Gibbon, & Williams, 1997) and the SCID-RV (Research Version; First, Gibbon, Spitzer, & Williams, 1996). The research version covers more disorders, subtypes, and course specifiers than the SCID-CV and consequently takes longer to administer.

The SCID-CV is designed for clinical settings and focuses on the most common diagnoses in clinical practice. The organization of the SCID-CV is hierarchical, with very specific decision trees and discontinuation criteria for each module. Like the DIS, it is also arranged in a modular format and covers many *DSM* Axis I diagnoses. Specifically, it includes the most commonly seen diagnoses in a clinical setting: mood episodes, mood disorders, psychotic symptoms, psychotic disorders, substance abuse disorders, and anxiety and other disorders. The organization of the SCID-CV is flexible, which allows an interviewer to supplement existing questions and alter the selection and order of administration of modules.

The SCID-I begins with a demographic information section and provides a 12-item screen to help determine which sections to administer or omit. Each module begins with specific diagnostic questions and offers additional probes for follow-up questions. The related *DSM-IV* diagnostic criteria for each disorder are presented. Each criterion is rated on a three-point scale: 1 for *absent or false*, 2 for *subthreshold*, and 3 for *true or present*. A fourth rating, ?, is used if there is insufficient information. Ratings are determined on the basis of the probe and the follow-up questions. Administration times range between 45 and 90 minutes.

Although there is limited research on the reliability for the full *DSM-IV* SCID-I, a great deal of data have been accumulated for earlier versions of the instrument. However, reliability estimates for the current SCID-I are at or above those reported for the earlier versions (Levin, Evans, & Kleber, 1998; Ventura, Liberman, Green, Shaner, & Mintz, 1998; Zimmerman & Mattia, 1998). Studies examining interrater reliability generally have focused on current, as opposed to lifetime, diagnoses. Reliabilities reported have been good, ranging from greater than .75 (Riskland, Beck, Berchick, Brown, & Steer, 1987) to greater than .85 (Sato, Sakado, & Sato, 1993; Williams et al., 1992; Zimmerman & Mattia, 1998). However, in one of the largest studies (Williams et al., 1992) of test-retest reliability, moderate reliabilities were reported (mean kappa = .61) for assessment of current diagnoses in a clinical population, with higher reliabilities reported for panic disorder. For the nonclinical group included in this study the reliabilities were low, with a mean kappa reported of only .37.

Regarding validation studies, Maziade et al. (1992) examined the concurrent validity of SCID-I mood and schizophrenic disorders and reported a high level of agreement (kappa = .83). However, in studies that have examined convergent validity of newer interview measures using the SCID-I as the gold standard, the reported values were not optimal. For example, Ross, Swinson, Larkin, and Doumani (1994) compared the computerized version of the DIS with the SCID-I among a group of substance abusers. A median kappa of .56 was reported for the most common substance abuse disorders; however, they reported poorer values in terms of the agreement between mood and anxiety disorders (median kappa = .22).

Schedule for Affective Disorders and Schizophrenia (SADS)

The SADS (Spitzer & Endicott, 1978) is an extensive, semistructured diagnostic interview covering 23 diagnostic categories. The SADS focuses primarily on the assessment of mood and psychotic disorders. The SADS is divided into two parts: Part I for current episodes and Part II for past episodes. The SADS-II is also known as the SADS-Lifetime version, or SADS-L. In addition, there is also the Schedule of Affective Disorders and Schizophrenia–Lifetime Anxiety version (SADS-LA; Manuzza, Fyer, Klein, & Endicott, 1986). The SADS is designed for use by those with clinical experience and training.

In Part I, symptoms are rated twice, first for the worst period of the current episode and second for the full duration of the current episode. By using comparative ratings, clinicians assess the severity of the disorder (Endicott & Spitzer, 1978). The SADS Part I takes approximately 45 to 75 minutes to administer, whereas the SADS Part II takes approximately 15 to 60 minutes. The SADS scoring results in reliable ratings of the severity of symptoms and is useful when evaluations are focused on prior diagnoses or when issues of response biases may be of concern. The SADS covers 23 psychiatric disorders with subcategories for schizophrenia, schizoaffective disorder, and major depression. The SADS was developed before the final revisions of the *DSM-III* and does not offer complete coverage of *DSM-IV* disorders. However, there is a large overlap in the range of symptoms in the SADS Research Diagnostic Criteria (SADS-RDC; Spitzer, Endicott, & Robins, 1975, 1978) and *DSM-IV* disorders.

In comparison to other semistructured interviews, the SADS emphasizes the degree of symptom impairment. That is, most mood, psychotic, and behavioral symptoms are rated on six-point scales ranging from 1 for *not at all* to 6 for *extreme* (unremitting symptoms of high intensity). Within this scale, a score of 3 is required to be *clinically significant*, and a score of 0 can be used to designate *no information*. Most questions also include a description and provide representative examples for ease of administration. The majority of other symptoms are rated on a three-point scale (1 = *absent*, 2 = *suspected or likely*, and 3 = *definite*), with 0 indicating *no information*. The SADS-II (lifetime) is rated dichotomously (*yes* or *no*) because of the difficulties patients often experience when asked to provide a retrospective rating of symptom severity. Finally, a global assessment scale is included that provides a single rating of functioning ranging from 1 to 100, based on 10 levels of impairment, with lower scores reflecting more severe impairment. The structure of the SADS includes three levels of inquiries, with optional probes that clarify incomplete or unclear responses. Furthermore, the SADS provides questions that the interviewer may ask if a particular response is unclear.

Development of the SADS stemmed from the need for a standardized clinical and research method for *DSM* psychiatric diagnoses and was devised as a method to differentiate between mood and psychotic disorders for the NIMH collaborative study of the psychobiology of depression (Rogers, 2001; Summerfeldt & Antony, 2002). NIMH researchers conducted several studies examining the reliability of the SADS (Andreasen et al., 1981; Endicott & Spitzer, 1978; Keller et al., 1981). These investigations focused on three issues: symptoms, summary scales, and diagnoses across current and lifetime episodes. The NIMH studies were comprised of large participant samples and a variety of psychiatric diagnoses. Generally, results of these studies supported the reliability of the measure. For example, Andreasen et al. (1981) used a sample of 50 inpatients and 50 outpatients to assess current and lifetime diagnoses; ICCs were strong, with values of .81 and .87. In another study examining the test-retest reliability of lifetime anxiety disorder diagnoses using the SADS-LA, Manuzza et al. (1989) reported moderate to excellent reliability ratings. Their group included 104 patients from an anxiety research clinic, with reliabilities ranging from .60 to .90 for generalized anxiety disorder, social phobia, panic disorder, agoraphobia, and obsessive-compulsive disorder. These authors also reported that the major sources of disagreement between raters included variation in patient reports and criterion ambiguity. In a review of the SADS, Rogers (2001) reported median kappas of .85 for diagnoses and .70 for individual symptoms and concluded that this measure is highly reliable.

Validity of the SADS has been examined through a number of studies that focused on criterion-related, convergent, and construct validity. For example, in terms of construct validity, Hokanson, Rubert, Welker, Hollander, and Hedeen (1989) found chronically depressed first-year college students who met criteria for depression on the SADS also had low social contact and increased stress. In terms of concurrent validity, Hesselbrock, Stabenau, Hesselbrock, Mirkin, and Myer (1982) examined concordance in diagnoses between the SADS-L and the DIS; they reported moderate to excellent kappas ranging from .72 to 1.0 (median of .76). In contrast, studies that have examined substance abuse populations have reported mixed findings. In a study comparing diagnoses based on the Personality Assessment Inventory (Morey, 1991) and the SADS, Rogers, Ustad, and Salekin (1998) found moderate correlations ranging between .40 and .67. Rogers, Sewell, Ustad, Reinhardt, and Edwards (1995) used the multitrait, multimethod matrix and found excellent discriminant validity with the SADS for depressive, schizophrenia, and bipolar disorders and moderate to good convergent validity.

Anxiety Disorders Interview Schedule (ADIS)

The ADIS was developed by Di Nardo, O'Brien, Barlow, Waddell, and Blanchard (1982) to provide reliable diagnoses of anxiety disorders and to distinguish between anxiety disorders and other frequently encountered comorbid mood disorders. In addition, this measure is designed to establish more precise information about symptoms of anxiety. The ADIS is a semistructured interview organized by diagnosis including generalized anxiety disorder, posttraumatic stress disorder, acute stress disorder, panic disorder, agoraphobia, specific and social phobias, and obsessive-compulsive disorder. The ADIS also includes sections that cover mood disorders, hypochondriasis, somatization, substance abuse, and psychosis. Furthermore, there are two versions of the adult ADIS-IV: the standard version, which provides information about current diagnoses only (Brown, Di Nardo, & Barlow, 1994), and the lifetime version (ADIS-IV-L; Di Nardo, Brown, & Barlow, 1994), which provides diagnostic information about past and current problems.

The ADIS-IV begins with questions pertaining to demographic information, description of the presenting problem, and information about current stressors. This portion is followed by sections for evaluating the presence of Axis I disorders. Many of the ADIS items are dichotomously formatted, and it includes nine-point scales to determine the intensity of specific symptoms for both severity and frequency. After symptom endorsement, more detailed questions regarding the *DSM-IV* criteria are asked. Symptom denial results in omission of that particular section. For patients with an anxiety disorder, the ADIS-IV can take approximately 2 hours to complete and can be administered by clinicians or trained paraprofessionals. The ADIS-IV also includes a treatment section (Summerfeldt & Antony, 2002), which offers a template for treatment and assessment of treatment progress.

The reliability studies examining the ADIS generally involve current diagnoses and have supported the reliability of the instrument. Kappa coefficients generally range from moderate to high. For example, Brown, Di Nardo, Lehman, and Campbell (2001) studied the interrater reliability of the ADIS-based anxiety and mood disorders in a group of 362 outpatients. For most of the diagnostic categories, reliabilities ranged from good to excellent, with kappas between .60 and .86. However, there were lower kappas in regard to dysthymic disorder and in some cases kappas as low as .22. In another comprehensive study of this instrument, Di Nardo, Moras, Barlow, Rapee, and Brown (1993) examined the test-retest reliability of the ADIS-R with a large group of participants ($n = 267$) across varying time points (e.g., 0–44 days) for six diagnoses. The median kappa was .65, with poorer findings for mood disorders than for anxiety disorders. Di Nardo et al. (1993) proposed that the poorer reliability probably resulted from a low base rate of occurrence of mood disorders in the study sample. Better reliabilities were reported by Abel and Borkovec (1995) in their study examining 40 outpatients with respect to generalized anxiety disorder.

There are no validity studies examining the full ADIS-IV. However, studies that have used the ADIS to examine features of specific anxiety disorders are thought to provide support for its construct validity (Summerfeldt & Antony, 2002). Rapee, Brown, Antony, and Barlow (1992) found that those diagnosed with panic disorder using the ADIS-R were more likely to react strongly to panic induction. However, Paradis, Friedman, Lazar, Grubea, and Kesselman (1992) reported more disappointing findings regarding the ADIS. Specifically, these researchers examined the diagnosis of panic disorders using the ADIS-R and compared these results to intake diagnosis. This study reported that 25% of those diagnosed with panic disorder by the ADIS did not receive this diagnosis at the intake evaluation.

SEMISTRUCTURED INTERVIEWS FOR AXIS II PERSONALITY DISORDERS

There are several well-constructed and popular semistructured interviews for the assessment and differential diagnosis of the *DSM-IV* Axis II personality disorders. These instruments are particularly valuable because clinicians and researchers alike have struggled with their ability to accurately diagnose personality disorders and distinguish one personality disorder from another (Coolidge & Segal, 1998; Westen & Shedler, 2000; Widiger, 2005; Widiger & Samuel, 2005). Interviews described in this section include the Structured Clinical Interview for *DSM-IV* Axis II Personality Disorders, the Structured Interview for *DSM-IV* Personality, the International Personality Disorder Examination, the Personality Disorders Inventory–IV, and the Diagnostic Interview for *DSM-IV* Personality Disorders. Before describing these instruments, we describe several options for how the selected personality disorder interview may be used in clinical and research settings.

The full semistructured interview may be used as part of a comprehensive and standardized intake evaluation. Although this strategy offers a wealth of diagnostic data and is common in research settings, routine administration is uncommon in the clinical setting because of the time needed for full administration. A more palatable variation on this theme is that sections of an interview may be administered after a traditional unstructured interview to clarify and confirm the diagnostic impressions. Widiger and Samuel (2005) recommended the strategy in clinical practice to first administer an objective self-report inventory followed by a semistructured interview focusing on the specific personality disorders that received elevated scores from the self-report screening. This strategy is responsive to time constraints in clinical practice but also allows collection of standardized, systematic, and objective data from the semistructured interview.

A final point to highlight is that before administration of any Axis II interview, the respondent's present mental state or Axis I conditions should be fully evaluated. Given that the self-report of enduring personality characteristics can be seriously compromised in a respondent who is acutely distressed or disorganized, this practice should not be surprising. The aim of personality assessment is to rate the respondent's typical, habitual, and lifelong personal functioning rather than acute or temporary state.

Structured Clinical Interview for *DSM-IV* Axis II Personality Disorders

The Structured Clinical Interview for *DSM-IV* Axis II Personality Disorders (SCID-II; First, Gibbon, Spitzer, Williams, & Benjamin, 1997b) was designed to complement the Axis I version of the SCID (described earlier). The SCID-II has a similar semistructured format as the SCID-I, but it covers the 10 standard *DSM-IV* personality disorders and depressive personality disorder and passive-aggressive personality disorder (listed as disorders to be studied further in an appendix of the *DSM-IV*).

The basic structure and convention of the SCID-II closely resemble those of the SCID-I. An additional feature of the SCID-II is that it includes a 119-item self-report screening component called the Personality Questionnaire, which may be administered before the interview portion and takes about 20 minutes. The purpose of the Personality Questionnaire is to reduce overall administration time because only the items that are scored in the pathological direction are further evaluated during the structured interview portion.

During the structured interview component, the pathologically endorsed screening responses are pursued to ascertain whether the symptoms are experienced at clinically significant levels. The respondent is asked to elaborate about each suspected personality disorder criterion, and specified prompts are provided. Like the Axis I SCID, the *DSM-IV* diagnostic criteria are printed on the interview page for easy review. The ratings of each diagnostic criterion are coded as follows: ? indicates *inadequate information*, 1 indicates

absent or false, 2 indicates *subthreshold*, and 3 indicates *threshold or true*. Twelve personality disorders are covered on a one-by-one basis. Each disorder is assessed completely, and diagnoses are made before the clinician proceeds to the next disorder. This modular format permits researchers and clinicians to tailor the SCID-II to their specific needs and reduce administration time. Clinicians who administer the SCID-II are expected to use their clinical judgment to clarify responses, gently challenge inconsistencies, and ask for additional information as needed to rate accurately each criterion. Collection of diagnostic information from collateral sources is permitted. Complete administration of the SCID-II typically takes less than 1 hour.

Training requirements and interviewer qualifications for the SCID-II are similar to those of the SCID-I. There is no clinician version of the SCID-II. The psychometric properties of the SCID-II are strong, and the interested reader is referred to First and Gibbon (2004) for a comprehensive review. Given the extensive coverage of the personality disorders, modular approach, and strong operating characteristics, the SCID-II is likely to remain a popular and effective tool for personality disorder assessment.

Structured Interview for *DSM-IV* Personality

The Structured Interview for *DSM-IV* Personality (SIDP-IV; Pfohl, Blum, & Zimmerman, 1997) is a comprehensive semistructured diagnostic interview for *DSM-IV* personality disorders. It covers 14 *DSM-IV* Axis II diagnoses, including the 10 standard personality disorders, self-defeating personality disorder, depressive personality disorder, negativistic personality disorder, and mixed personality disorder. Interestingly, the SIDP-IV does not cover *DSM* personality categories on a disorder-by-disorder basis. Rather, the *DSM-IV* criteria are reflected in items that are grouped according to 10 topical sections that reflect a different dimension of personality functioning: interests and activities, work style, close relationships, social relationships, emotions, observational criteria, self-perception, perception of others, stress and anger, and social conformity (Pfohl et al., 1997). These categories are not scored. Rather, they reflect broad areas of personal functioning under which personality disorder items can logically be subsumed.

For the most part, each SIDP-IV question corresponds to a unique *DSM-IV* Axis II criterion. The specific *DSM-IV* criterion associated with each question is provided for interviewers to easily see. All questions are always administered, and there are no skip-out options. Most questions are conversational in tone and open ended to encourage respondents to talk about their usual behaviors and long-term functioning. In fact, respondents are specifically instructed to focus on their typical or habitual behavior when addressing each item and are prompted to "remember what you are like when you are your usual self." Based on patient responses, each criterion is rated on a scale with four anchor points. A rating of 0 indicates that the *criterion was not present,* 1 corresponds to a *subthreshold level* where there is some evidence of the trait but it is not sufficiently prominent, 2 refers to the *criterion being present for most of the past 5 years,* and 3 signifies a *strongly present and debilitating level.* The SIDP-IV requires that a trait be prominent for most of the past 5 years to be considered a part of the respondent's personality. This "5-year rule" helps ensure that the particular personality characteristic is stable and of sufficient duration, as required by the general diagnostic criteria for a personality disorder described in *DSM-IV.*

A strong point of the organizational format by personality dimensions (rather than by disorders) is that data for specific diagnoses are minimized until final ratings have been collated on the summary sheet. This feature can potentially reduce interviewer biases, such as the halo effect or changing thresholds, if it is obvious that a respondent needs to meet one additional criterion to meet the threshold for diagnosis. This topical organization also makes the intent of the interview less transparent compared with the disorder-by-disorder approach of some other semistructured interviews.

Significant clinical judgment is needed to properly administer the SIDP-IV because interviewers are expected to ask additional questions to clarify patient responses when necessary. Also, data are not limited to self-report. Significant others who know the respondent well should be consulted when available, and a standard informed consent is included for informant interviews. Collateral information is particularly prized when one is evaluating personality disordered people, who may lack insight into their own maladaptive personality traits and distort facts about their strengths and limitations. Informants can also provide diagnostic data that can help resolve the state-trait distinction about specific criterion behaviors.

If discrepancies between sources of information are noted, interviewers must consider all data and use their own judgment to determine the veracity of each source. Making this distinction can be one of the challenges faced by SIDP-IV administrators. Given the multiple sources of diagnostic data, final ratings are made after all sources of information are considered. Such ratings are then transcribed onto a summary sheet that lists each criterion organized by personality disorder, and formal diagnoses are assigned. As required by the *DSM*, diagnoses are made only if the minimum number of criteria (or threshold) has been met for that particular disorder.

Administration requires knowledge of manifest psychopathology and the typical presentation and course of Axis I and II disorders (Pfohl et al., 1997). The SIDP typically takes 60 to 90 minutes for the patient interview, 20 minutes for interview of significant informants, and 20 minutes to fill out the summary score sheet. Studies documenting the strong psychometric properties of the SIDP are plentiful, and they are summarized in the manual for the instrument (Pfohl et al., 1997).

International Personality Disorder Examination

The International Personality Disorder Examination (IPDE; Loranger, 1999) is an extensive, semistructured diagnostic interview to evaluate personality disorders for the *DSM-IV* and the *International Classification of Diseases,* 10th edition (*ICD-10;* World Health Organization, 2004) classification systems. The IPDE was developed within the Joint Program for the Diagnosis and Classification of Mental Disorders of the World Health Organization (WHO) and U.S. National Institutes of Health, aimed at producing a standardized assessment instrument to measure personality disorders on an international basis. As such, the IPDE is the only personality disorder interview based on worldwide field trials. The *IPDE Manual* contains the interview questions to assess either the 10 *DSM-IV* or the 10 *ICD-10* personality disorders. The two IPDE modules (*DSM-IV* and *ICD-10*) contain both a self-administered screening questionnaire and a semistructured interview booklet with scoring materials.

The Screening Questionnaire is a self-administered form that contains 77 *DSM-IV* or 59 *ICD-10* items written at a fourth-grade reading level. Items are answered either *True* or *False*, and the questionnaire typically is completed in about 15 minutes. The clinician can score the questionnaire quickly and identify respondents whose scores suggest the presence of a personality disorder. Subsequently, the IPDE clinical interview is administered.

The IPDE interview modules (for either the *DSM-IV* or *ICD-10* systems) contain questions, each reflecting a personality disorder criterion, that are grouped into six thematic headings: work, self, interpersonal relationships, affects, reality testing, and impulse control (Loranger, 1999). Because disorders are not covered on a one-by-one basis, the intent of the evaluation is less transparent, similar to the SIDP-IV. At the beginning of each section, open-ended inquiries are provided to enable a smooth transition from the previous section and to encourage respondents to elaborate about themselves in a less structured fashion. Specific questions are subsequently asked to evaluate each diagnostic criterion. For each question, the corresponding personality disorder and the specific diagnostic criterion are identified with precise scoring guidelines.

Respondents are encouraged to report their typical or usual functioning rather than their personality functioning during times of episodic psychiatric illness. The IPDE requires that a trait be prominent during the past 5 years to be considered a part of the respondent's personality. Information about age of onset of particular behaviors is explored to determine whether a late-onset diagnosis (after age 25 years) is appropriate. When a respondent acknowledges a particular trait, interviewers follow up by asking for examples and anecdotes to clarify the trait or behavior, gauge impact of the trait on the person's functioning, and fully substantiate the rating. Such probing entails significant clinical judgment and knowledge on the part of interviewers about each criterion. Items may also be rated based on observation of the respondent's behavior during the session, which also takes clinical expertise. To supplement self-report, interview of informants is encouraged. Clinical judgment is needed to ascertain which source is more reliable if inconsistencies arise.

Each criterion is rated on a scale with the following definitions: 0 indicates that the behavior or trait is *absent or within normal limits,* 1 refers to an *exaggerated or accentuated degree of the trait,* 2 signifies *criterion level or pathological,* and ? indicates that the *respondent refuses or is unable to answer.* Comprehensive item-by-item scoring guidelines are provided in the manual (Loranger, 1999). At the end of the interview, the clinician records the scores for each response on the appropriate IPDE answer sheet. Ratings are then summed by hand or computer. The output is quite extensive, including the presence or absence of each criterion, the number of criteria met for each personality disorder, a dimensional score (sum of individual scores for each criterion for each disorder), and a categorical diagnosis (definite, probable, or negative) for each personality disorder (Loranger, 1999). Such comprehensive output is especially valued by clinical researchers and is an attractive feature of the IPDE.

The IPDE is intended for use by experienced clinicians who received specific training with the IPDE. Average administration time is 90 minutes for the interview, which can be reduced through use of the screening questionnaire (omitting interview items associated with unlikely personality disorders). Because the IPDE has been selected by the WHO for international application, it has been translated into numerous languages to facilitate transcultural research. Ample evidence of reliability and validity of the IPDE has been documented (Loranger, 1999; Loranger et al., 1994). Because of the instrument's ties to the *DSM-IV* and *ICD-10* classification systems and adoption by the WHO, the IPDE is widely used for international and cross-cultural investigations of personality disorders and their features.

Personality Disorder Interview–IV

The Personality Disorder Interview–IV (PDI-IV; Widiger, Mangine, Corbitt, Ellis, & Thomas, 1995) is a semistructured interview for assessment of the 10 standard personality disorders in the *DSM-IV* and the two proposed personality disorders (passive-aggressive and depressive) presented in the *DSM-IV* appendix as criteria sets provided for further study. The PDI-IV is appropriate for respondents age 18 years and older, and administration time is about 90 to 120 minutes.

A unique feature of the PDI-IV is that it is available in two separate versions, each with its own interview booklet. *The PDI-IV Personality*

Disorders Interview Booklet arranges the diagnostic criteria and corresponding questions by personality disorder. *The Thematic Content Areas Interview Booklet* organizes the criteria and questions by thematic content. The nine topical areas are attitudes toward self, attitudes toward others, security of comfort with others, friendships and relationships, conflicts and disagreements, work and leisure, social norms, mood, and appearance and perception. The questions for each diagnostic criterion are the same in each interview form, but the organization is different. The modular approach easily lends itself to focused and rapid assessment of particular personality disorders of interest to the researcher or clinician. A screening questionnaire is not provided for the PDI-IV.

The PDI-IV administration book includes questions for each of the 94 individual personality disorder diagnostic criteria, cross-referencing the *DSM-IV*. Instructions to interviewers and prompts and suggestions for follow-up questions are included. During administration, each criterion is rated on the following three-point scale: 0 indicates *not present,* 1 indicates *present at a clinically significant level,* and 2 indicates *present to a more severe or substantial degree.* A particular strength of the PDI-IV is its comprehensive manual (Widiger et al., 1995), which extensively discusses the history and rationale for each diagnostic question and problems that often arise in the assessment of each criterion.

After the interview is completed, the clinician summarizes responses to individual PDI-IV criteria and plots the overall dimensional profile. According to the manual, this profile may help clinicians rank multiple diagnoses by order of importance and identify characteristics in the respondent that are relevant to psychopathology and treatment. Output provided is both a dimensional rating for each personality disorder and a categorical rating. Reliability and validity data, as summarized in the manual (Widiger et al., 1995), are solid, although few psychometric studies by independent researchers have been conducted.

Diagnostic Interview for *DSM-IV* Personality Disorders

The Diagnostic Interview for *DSM-IV* Personality Disorders (DIPD-IV; Zanarini, Frankenburg, Sickel, & Yong, 1996) is a semistructured interview designed to assess the presence or absence of the 10 standard *DSM-IV* personality disorders as well as depressive personality disorder and passive-aggressive personality disorder in the *DSM-IV* appendix. Before administration of the DIPD-IV, assessment of the Axis I disorders and the respondent's general functioning (e.g., in the areas of work, school, and social life) is advised (Zanarini et al., 1996).

Like the SCID-II, the DIPD-IV interview is conducted on a disorder-by-disorder basis. The interview contains 108 sets of questions, each designed to assess a specific *DSM-IV* personality disorder diagnostic criterion. The initial question for each criterion is dichotomously formatted and is followed by open-ended questions for further exploration. The interview covers the past 2 years of the respondent's life with regard to thoughts, feelings, and behaviors that have been typical. Although respondents are the sole source of information for most of the diagnostic criteria, if a particular behavior exhibited during the interview contradicts the response, this may be used instead. Probing on the part of the administrator is encouraged if responses appear incomplete or untrue.

Each diagnostic criterion is rated on the following scale: 0 indicates *absent or clinically insignificant,* 1 indicates *present but of uncertain clinical significance,* 2 indicates *present and clinically significant,* and NA indicates *not applicable.* After all 108 criteria are rated, final categorical diagnosis for each personality disorder is made based on the number of criteria met. The final output is recorded as 2, indicating *yes* or *met full criteria,* 1 indicating *subthreshold* (one less than the required number of criteria), or 0 indicating *no.*

Information about administration and scoring of the DIPD-IV is sparse compared with the other Axis II semistructured interviews. Experience and knowledge of personality disorders are recommended for use of the DIPD-IV, and administration time typically is 90 minutes. The DIPD-IV is selected as the primary diagnostic measure for personality disorders in the Collaborative Longitudinal Personality Disorders Study, which is a large, multisite, prospective naturalistic longitudinal study of personality disorders and comorbid mental health problems.

SUMMARY

The interview in its broadest terms is an interaction between a professional and a client. As noted, the interview can take many forms, ranging from an unstructured interaction leaving the questions up to the interviewer to a fully structured question-and-answer format leaving no room for an off-the-cuff exchange. Certainly, structured and semistructured interviews have their drawbacks. Their use can detract from the first encounter, making it feel more sterile or distant. As previously noted, the validity of a structured interview depends on the accuracy of the diagnostic criteria on which it is based. Furthermore, the structured interview may be considered fallible in that most are heavily reliant on self-report data.

Despite these criticisms, structured and semistructured interviews offer a number of significant advantages. Most notably, structured interviews minimize the variability between professionals with standardization of assessment. Greater reliability of diagnosis is a precursor for greater validity or meaningfulness of the diagnosis. Advanced degrees typically are not required for the administration of these interviews, allowing their wider use. In addition, the psychometric properties of these instruments, particularly measures reviewed in this chapter, are quite promising. If the past several decades are a predictor of the future of structured interviews, then the field probably will continue to see new structured interviews and updates on existing measures. With the upsurge in the use of structured interviews, it is important to keep in mind that the administration of a structured interview does not prevent the user from supplementing with unstructured questions, before or after the structured interview, perhaps blending the best of both worlds.

References

Abel, J. L., & Borkovec, T. D. (1995). Generalizability of the *DSM-III-R* generalized anxiety disorder to proposed *DSM-IV* criteria and cross-validation of proposed changes. *Journal of Anxiety Disorders, 9,* 303–315.

American Psychiatric Association. (1952). *Diagnostic and statistical manual of mental disorders.* Washington, DC: Author.

American Psychiatric Association. (1980). *Diagnostic and statistical manual of mental disorders* (3rd ed.). Washington, DC: Author.

American Psychiatric Association. (1994). *Diagnostic and statistical manual of mental disorders* (4th ed.). Washington, DC: Author.

Anastasi, A., & Urbina, S. (1997). *Psychological testing* (7th ed.). Upper Saddle River, NJ: Simon & Schuster.

Andreasen, N. C., Grove, W. M., Shapiro, R. W., Keller, M. B., Hirschfield, R. A., & Mcdonald-Scott, P. (1981). Reliability of lifetime diagnosis. *Archives of General Psychiatry, 35,* 400–405.

Bakeman, R., & Gottman, J. M. (1989). *Observing interaction.* Cambridge, UK: Cambridge University Press.

Brown, T. A., Di Nardo, P. A., & Barlow, D. H. (1994). *Anxiety Disorders Interview Schedule for* DSM-IV *(ADIS-IV).* San Antonio, TX: Psychological Corporation.

Brown, T. A., Di Nardo, P. A., Lehman, C. L., & Campbell, L. A. (2001). Reliability of *DSM-IV* anxiety and mood disorders: Implications for the classifications of emotional disorders. *Journal of Abnormal Psychology, 110,* 49–58.

Campbell, D. T., & Fiske, D. W. (1959). Convergent and discriminant validation by the multitrait-multimethod matrix. *Psychological Bulletin, 56,* 81–105.

Clark, L. A., & Watson, D. (1995). Constructing validity: Basic issues in objective scale development. *Psychological Assessment, 7,* 309–319.

Cohen, J. (1960). A coefficient of agreement for nominal scales. *Educational and Psychological Measurement, 20,* 37–46.

Coolidge, F. L., & Segal, D. L. (1998). Evolution of the personality disorder diagnosis in the *Diagnostic and Statistical Manual of Mental Disorders. Clinical Psychology Review, 18,* 585–599.

Cronbach, L. J. (1990). *Essentials of psychological testing* (5th ed.). New York: Harper & Row.

Cronbach, L. J., & Meehl, P. E. (1955). Construct validity in psychological tests. *Psychological Bulletin, 52,* 281–300.

Di Nardo, P. A., Brown, T. A., & Barlow, D. H. (1994). *Anxiety Disorders Interview Schedule for the* DSM-IV: *Lifetime version.* San Antonio, TX: Psychological Corporation.

Di Nardo, P. A., Moras, K., Barlow, D. H., Rapee, R. M., & Brown, T. A. (1993). Reliability of *DSM-III-R* anxiety disorder categories: Using the anxiety Disorders Interview Schedule–Revised (ADIS-R). *Archives of General Psychiatry, 50,* 251–256.

Di Nardo, P. A., O'Brien, G. T., Barlow, D. H., Waddell, M. T., & Blanchard, E. G. (1982). *Anxiety Disorders Interview Schedule (ADIS).* Albany: Center for Stress and Anxiety Disorders, State University of New York at Albany.

Endicott, J., & Spitzer, R. L. (1978). A diagnostic interview: The schedule for affective disorders and schizophrenia. *Archives of General Psychiatry, 35,* 837–844.

First, M. B., Frances, A., & Pincus, H. A. (2004). DSM-IV-TR *guidebook: The essential companion to the* Diagnostic and Statistical Manual of Mental Disorders (4th ed., Text rev.). Washington, DC: American Psychiatric Publishing.

First, M. B., & Gibbon, M. (2004). The Structured Clinical Interview for *DSM-IV* Axis I Disorders (SCID-I) and the Structured Clinical Interview for *DSM-IV* Axis II Disorders (SCID-II). In M. J. Hilsenroth & D. L. Segal (Eds.), *Comprehensive handbook of psychological assessment: Vol. 2. Personality assessment* (pp. 134–143). Hoboken, NJ: Wiley.

First, M. B., Gibbon, M., Spitzer, R. L., & Williams, J. B. W. (1996). *Structured Clinical Interview for* DSM-IV *Disorders Research Version: Patient edition (SCID-I/P, ver. 2.0).* New York: New York State Psychiatric Institute, Biometrics Research Department.

First, M. B., Gibbon, M., Spitzer, R. L., Williams, J. B. W., & Benjamin, L. S. (1997a). *The Structured Clinical Interview for the* DSM-IV *Disorders (SCID).* Washington, DC: American Psychiatric Association.

First, M. B., Gibbon, M., Spitzer, R. L., Williams, J. B. W., & Benjamin, L. S. (1997b). *Structured Clinical Interview for* DSM-IV *Axis II Personality Disorders (SCID-II).* Washington, DC: American Psychiatric Press.

First, M. B., Spitzer, R. L., Gibbon, M., & Williams, J. B. W. (1997). *Structured Clinical Interview for* DSM-IV *Axis I Disorders (SCID-I): Clinician version.* Washington, DC: American Psychiatric Press.

Fleiss, J. L., & Cohen, J. (1973). The equivalence of weighted kappa and the intraclass correlation coefficient as measures of reliability. *Educational and Psychological Measurement, 33,* 613–619.

Garb, H. (2005). Clinical judgment and decision making. *Annual Review in Clinical Psychology, 1,* 67–89.

Gavin, D. R., Ross, H. E., & Skinner, H. A. (1989). Diagnostic validity of the drug abuse screening test in the assessment of *DSM-III* drug disorders. *British Journal of Addictions, 84,* 301–307.

Hamilton, M. (1960). A rating scale for depression. *Journal of Neurology, Neurosurgery, and Psychiatry, 23,* 56–62.

Hesselbrock, V., Stabenau, J., Hesselbrock, M., Mirkin, P., & Myer, R. (1982). A comparison of two interview schedules: The Schedule for Affective Disorders and Schizophrenia—Lifetime and the National Institute of Mental Health Diagnostic Interview Schedule. *Archives of General Psychiatry, 39,* 674–677.

Hokanson, J. E., Rubert, M. P., Welker, R. A., Hollander, G. R., & Hedeen, C. (1989). Interpersonal concomitants and antecedents of depression among college students. *Journal of Abnormal Psychology, 98,* 209–217.

Keller, M. B., Lavori, P. W., McDonald-Scott, P., Sheftner, W. A., Andreason, N. C., Shapiro, R. W., et al. (1981). Reliability of lifetime diagnoses and symptoms in patients with a current psychiatric disorder. *Journal of Psychiatric Research, 16,* 229–240.

Levin, F. R., Evans, S. M., & Kleber, H. D. (1998). Prevalence of adult attention deficit hyperactivity disorder among cocaine abusers seeking treatment. *Drug and Alcohol Dependence, 52,* 15–25.

Loranger, A. W. (1999). *International Personality Disorder Examination (IPDE)* DSM-IV *and* ICD-10 *modules.* Odessa, FL: Psychological Assessment Resources.

Loranger, A. W., Sartorius, N., Andreoli, A., Berger, P., Buchheim, P., Channabasavanna, S. M., et al. (1994). The International Personality Disorder Examination: The World Health Organization/Alcohol, Drug Abuse, and Mental Health Administration international pilot study of personality disorders. *Archives of General Psychiatry, 51,* 215–224.

Manuzza, S., Fyer, A. J., Klein, D. F., & Endicott, J. (1986). Schedule for Affective Disorders and Schizophrenia–Lifetime Version Modified for the Study of Anxiety Disorders (SADS-LA): Rationale and conceptual development. *Journal of Psychiatric Research, 20,* 317–325.

Manuzza, S., Fyer, A. J., Martin, L. Y., Gallops, M. S., Endicott, J., Gorman, J., et al. (1989). Reliability of anxiety assessment: I. Diagnostic agreement. *Archives of General Psychiatry, 46,* 1093–1101.

Maziade, M. R. A. A., Fournier, J. P., Cliche, D., Merette, C., Caron, C., Garneau, Y., et al. (1992). Reliability of best-estimate diagnosis in genetic linkage studies of major psychoses. *American Journal of Psychiatry, 149,* 1674–1686.

Morey, L. C. (1991). *Personality Assessment Inventory: Professional manual.* Tampa, FL: Psychological Assessment Resources.

Paradis, C. M., Friedman, S., Lazar, R. M., Grubea, J., & Kesselman, M. (1992). Use of a structured interview to diagnose anxiety disorders in a minority population. *Hospital and Community Psychiatry, 43,* 61–64.

Pfohl, B., Blum, N., & Zimmerman, M. (1997). *Structured Interview for* DSM-IV *Personality.* Washington, DC: American Psychiatric Press.

Rapee, R. M., Brown, T. A., Antony, M. M., & Barlow, D. H. (1992). Response to hyperventilation and inhalation of 5.5% carbon dioxide–enriched air across the *DSM-III-R* anxiety disorders. *Journal of Abnormal Psychology, 101,* 538–552.

Riskland, J. H., Beck, A. T., Berchick, R. J., Brown, G., & Steer, R. A. (1987). Reliability of the *DSM-III* diagnoses for major depression and generalized anxiety disorder using the structured clinical interview for the *DSM-III. Archives of General Psychiatry, 44,* 817–820.

Robins, L. N., Cottler, L., Bucholz, K., & Compton, W. (1995). *Diagnostic Interview Schedule, version IV.* St. Louis, MO: Washington School of Medicine.

Robins, L. N., Helzer, J. E., Croughan, J., & Ratcliff, J. S. (1981). National Institute of Mental Health Diagnostic Interview Schedule. *Archives of General Psychiatry, 38,* 381–389.

Robins, L. N., Helzer, J. E., Ratcliff, K. S., & Seyfried, W. (1982). Validity of the Diagnostic Interview Schedule, version II: *DSM-III* diagnoses. *Psychological Medicine, 12,* 855–870.

Rogers, R. (2001). *Handbook of diagnostic and structured interviewing.* New York: Guilford.

Rogers, R., Sewell, K. W., Ustad, K. L., Reinhardt, V., & Edwards, W. (1995). The Referral Decision Scale in a jail sample of disordered offenders. *Law and Human Behavior, 19,* 481–492.

Rogers, R., Ustad, K. L., & Salekin, R. T. (1998). Forensic applications of the PAI: A study of convergent validity. *Assessment, 5,* 3–12.

Ross, H. E., Swinson, R., Larkin, E. J., & Doumani, S. (1994). Diagnosing comorbidity in substance abusers. *Journal of Nervous and Mental Disease, 182,* 556–563.

Rubinson, E. P., & Asnis, G. M. (1989). Use of structured interviews for diagnosis. In S. Wetzler (Eds.), *Measuring mental illness: Psychometric assessment for clinicians* (pp. 43–66). Washington, DC: American Psychiatric Press.

Sato, T., Sakado, K., & Sato, S. (1993). Is there any specific personality disorder or personality disorder cluster that worsens the short-term treatment outcome of major depression? *Acta Psychiatrica Scandinavica, 88,* 342–349.

Segal, D. L., & Coolidge, F. L. (2003). Structured interviewing and *DSM* classification. In M. Hersen & S. Turner (Eds.), *Adult psychopathology and diagnosis* (4th ed., pp. 72–103). New York: Wiley.

Segal, D. L., & Coolidge, F. L. (2006a). Reliability. In N. J. Salkind (Ed.), *Encyclopedia of human development* (Vol. 3, pp. 1073–1074). Thousand Oaks, CA: Sage.

Segal, D. L., & Coolidge, F. L. (2006b). Validity. In N. J. Salkind (Ed.), *Encyclopedia of human development* (Vol. 3, pp. 1297–1298). Thousand Oaks, CA: Sage.

Spitzer, R. L., & Endicott, J. (1978). *Schedule for Affective Disorders and Schizophrenia: Change version.* New York: New York Biometrics Research.

Spitzer, R. L., Endicott, J., & Robins, E. (1975). *Research diagnostic criteria.* New York: New York State Psychiatric Institute, Biometrics Research.

Spitzer, R. L., Endicott, J., & Robins, E. (1978). Research diagnostic criteria: Rationale and reliability. *Archives of General Psychiatry, 35,* 773–782.

Spitznagel, E. L., & Helzer, J. E. (1985). A proposed solution to the base rate problem in the kappa statistic. *Archives of General Psychiatry, 42,* 725–728.

Summerfeldt, L. J., & Antony, M. M. (2002). Structured and semistructured diagnostic interviews. In A. M. Antony (Ed.), *Handbook of assessment and treatment planning for psychological disorders* (pp. 3–37). New York: Guilford.

Thompson, W. D., & Walter, S. D. (1988). A reappraisal of the kappa coefficient. *Journal of Clinical Epidemiology, 41,* 949–958.

Vandiver, T., & Sher, K. J. (1991). Temporal stability of the diagnostic interview schedule. *Psychological Assessment, 3,* 277–281.

Ventura, J., Liberman, R. P., Green, M. F., Shaner, A., & Mintz, J. (1998). Training and quality assurance with Structured Clinical Interview for *DSM-IV* SCID-I/P). *Psychiatry Research, 79,* 163–173.

Westen, D., & Shedler, J. (2000). A prototype matching approach to diagnosing personality disorders: Toward *DSM-V. Journal of Personality Disorders, 14,* 109–126.

Whisman, M. A., Strosahl, K., Fruzetti, A. E., Schmaling, K. B., Jacobson, N. S., & Miller, D. M. (1989). A structured interview version of the Hamilton rating scale for depression: Reliability and validity. *Psychological Assessment, 1,* 238–241.

Widiger, T. A. (2005). Personality disorders. In R. J. Craig (Ed.), *Clinical and diagnostic interviewing* (2nd ed., pp. 251–277). Lanham, MD: Jason Aronson.

Widiger, T. A., Mangine, S., Corbitt, E. M., Ellis, C. G., & Thomas, G. V. (1995). *Personality Disorder Interview–IV. A semistructured interview for the assessment of personality disorders. Professional manual.* Odessa, FL: Psychological Assessment Resources.

Widiger, T. A., & Samuel, D. B. (2005). Evidence based assessment of personality disorders. *Psychological Assessment, 17,* 278–287.

Williams, J. B. W., Gibbon, M., First, M. B., Spitzer, R. L., Davies, M., Borus, J., et al. (1992). The Structured Clinical Interview for *DSM-III-R* (SCID): Multisite test-retest reliability. *Archives of General Psychiatry, 49,* 630–636.

World Health Organization. (2004). *International classification of diseases* (10th ed.). Geneva, Switzerland: Author.

Zanarini, M. C., Frankenburg, F. R., Sickel, A. E., & Yong, L. (1996). *The Diagnostic Interview for* DSM-IV *Personality Disorders (DIPD-IV).* Belmont, MA: McLean Hospital.

Zimmerman, M., & Mattia, J. I. (1998). Psychiatric diagnosis in clinical practice: Is comorbidity being missed? *Comprehensive Psychiatry, 40,* 182–191.

4

MOTIVATIONAL INTERVIEWING

JENNIFER R. ANTICK AND KIMBERLY R. GOODALE

Motivational interviewing (MI) is a combination of both traditional and innovative methods. MI is traditional in that it relies on therapeutic concepts such as unconditional positive regard (Rogers, 1951, 1989) and has been hypothesized to represent an expert use of cognitive dissonance theory (Draycott, & Dabbs, 1998), self-determination theory (Deci & Ryan, 1985, 2000; Markland, Ryan, Tobin, & Rollnick, 2005; Sheldon, 2003; Vansteenkiste & Sheldon, 2006), and self-efficacy theory (Bandura, 1977). Prominently cited and traditional clinical concepts reflected in MI include the importance of empathy in the development of a therapeutic relationship and the need to tailor assessment and treatment to each client.

MI is postmodern in style, however. The social skills of the therapist also play an important role in MI (Moyers, Miller, & Hendrickson, 2005). The interview usually takes the form of a flowing conversation intended to assist the client in the direction of making the changes he or she is ready to make. The relationship between the motivational interviewer and client is power neutral, and at times the therapist is wisest to take a one-down position. The therapist does not presume to know better than the client about the client's life and circumstances, nor does the therapist presume to know the correct path to making change. Instead, the client is considered the expert on his or her experience, reasons for change, how change takes place in his or her life,

and, particularly important for MI, reasons against change.

MI recognizes as a key construct the ambivalence inherent in any decision-making process. Eliciting and articulating that ambivalence is one of the main activities in MI. The reasons for and against change have equal value in that the decisional balance must be explored for a person to make a commitment to change. Many other types of clinical interviews are structured as information-gathering sessions in which open- and closed-ended questions are asked in a linear, sequential fashion in order to validate or rule out different diagnostic classifications. Because many theoretical orientations and their concomitant methods assume treatment to be a natural outgrowth of the diagnostic process, the interview leads to treatment targets (behavioral, affective, cognitive) and potential methods of intervention. All of this further assumes the interviewer to have information critical to the client and the client to be ready to make changes. In stark contrast, MI assumes the client to be the expert in his or her own change processes. It further assumes that clients are ambivalent about change and should be expected to move through stages of readiness to change and to be in need of facilitation rather than intervention per se.

This chapter reviews the intrinsic assumptions of Mi and the core tasks and skills involved and briefly considers the literature examining a variety of applications.

CENTRAL ASSUMPTIONS OF MI

Ambivalence is central to the change process (Center for Substance Abuse Treatment [CSAT], 1999; Miller & Rollnick, 1992, 2002). The motivational interviewer understands that ambivalence about making changes is normal and appropriate. It is neither pathology nor something to be avoided. Instead, ambivalence is to be explored and made plain, without judgment.

All changes have positive and negative consequences (CSAT, 1999; Miller & Rollnick, 1992, 2002). Helping clients identify their reasons for and against change will help them move closer to resolving their ambivalence and make said change. To be effective, the therapist cannot have a vested interest in whether a particular path is followed.

The arguments for and against change are on the mind of a person considering making change (Miller & Rollnick, 1992, 2002). If a therapist argues for a change, he or she leaves the client to argue (internally or externally) against the change. The skilled motivational interviewer creates an environment in which it is safe for the person to sort these concerns out and possibly argue for the change. This represents respect for the client's idiosyncratic needs in committing to change.

Confrontation does not expedite change. A motivational interviewer demonstrates, in all activities, recognition of the client's autonomy. Many interviewing methods use confrontation to some extent, even if it is mild from the interviewer's perspective. In avoiding confrontation, MI is a very practical approach. People make change with or without us. Acknowledging free will in the decision-making process can help facilitate an honest conversation about barriers the client perceives to be in the way.

Readiness to change is different from willingness to change or interest in change and different from readiness to seek help. The to-do list for any interview should be guided by the client's readiness to change or stage of change (Prochaska, DiClemente, & Norcross, 1992; Prochaska & Norcross, 2001; Prochaska et al., 1994). Prochaska et al. (1992) observed that both natural and therapist-facilitated change involved progressing through five stages, later called the stages of change. Although the exact number of stages has been debated, the construct appears to hold up under scrutiny, and clients find the concepts to have face validity.

Clients may be at different points of readiness for a large change or, more likely, for aspects of making the changes at the time of interview. Both the flexibility of the interviewer in adapting to the client's needs and the client's readiness can make all the difference in whether the client will make good use of the time and come back at a later date. Most important, many traditional interviewing methods assume the client is in the action stage, ready and raring to go. However, research suggests that only a fraction of clients arrive for their first interview truly ready for action. In fact, in some studies, as few as 20% of clients were categorized as being in the action or preparation stage. A full 40% of clients were categorized as in the contemplation stage, with an additional 40% not even considering making a change (precontemplation) (Biller, Arnstein, Caudill, Federman, & Guberman, 2000; Prochaska et al., 1992; Prochaska & Norcross, 2001). Retention rates in therapy suggest that these are unlikely to be isolated findings. Several authors have found that the client's stage on entry into treatment and the match between therapist language and client commitment language were important predictors of client retention and therapy outcome (Amrhein, Miller, Yahne, Palmer, & Fulcher, 2003; CSAT, 1999; Moyers & Rollnick, 2002; Prochaska & Norcross, 2001).

In order to best facilitate progress without pushing harder for change than the client, one must tailor the interview to the client's readiness. This may mean that the interview is preliminary, a preview for a future conversation that may lead to treatment. The unfortunate alternative is a mismatch that is unlikely to lead to a positive or fruitful therapeutic interaction. Worse yet, the client may feel certain that therapy does not help. The main problem may be that the therapist confuses readiness to seek help with readiness to change (Freyer et al., 2005). A successful motivational interviewer recognizes and acknowledges the current situation. Instead of trying to convince the client of the need for change, the therapist invites the client to determine the best course of action for himself or herself and thereby invites the client to discover his or her own reasons and need for change.

MI can be as brief as a single interview or modified to be the mainstay of treatment as motivational enhancement therapy (Miller, 2000). MI rightly assumes a single session, the modal number of sessions across therapies (McCambridge & Strang, 2004). No matter how talented, a therapist in search of a therapy goal is preoccupied by diagnostic and treatment planning processes. In choosing to work within a single-session framework, the therapist can be less focused on an agenda of paperwork and treatment plans and instead fully attentive to the immediate conversation and issues at hand for the client. Viewed in this way, MI looks and sounds less like a method and more like a form of communication. If more interactions follow, it is because the client determines that therapy is the best course of action at that time. For this reason, treatment planning is a creative process when one is using MI techniques.

The client is whole. Like other strengths-based methods, MI assumes the client to have many of the requisite skills and abilities to improve his or her own life (Lewis & Osborn, 2004; Viner, Christie, Taylor, & Hey, 2003). The client is not broken or needing to be fixed, taken apart, analyzed, educated, or told what to do. The client has strengths and resources that are not being used or not fully being used that can be brought to bear on his or her present situation. Clients may determine that they need to increase their skill levels or learn new ways of dealing with challenges, or they may find that they have the information they need and just need to apply it. People are assumed to have a natural inclination toward health and wellness, and therapists can facilitate the process in partnership with the client.

MI is transtheoretical, client centered, and directive all at the same time. Because MI is not based on a particular theory of pathology but instead a theory of facilitating change, it can be used in conjunction with many theoretical approaches but not all. It is a natural match with integrative approaches that emphasize what are now called the common factors in therapy (Hubble, Duncan, & Miller, 1999).

Core Tasks and Skills Involved in MI

As originally outlined by Miller and Rollnick (1992), four major principles underlie the approach to MI.

- Expressing empathy
- Developing discrepancy
- Rolling with resistance and avoiding argumentation
- Supporting self-efficacy

Expressing empathy is one of the most important elements of any therapy. It is not so much an emotional response or verbal expression of sympathy as a clinical activity. Demonstrating empathy is the therapist's skill of understanding the client's concerns, feelings, and situations in a way that communicates respect and acceptance. Roots of this activity are in the works of Carl Rogers. Rogers believed that healthy change can take place when clients are encouraged to discuss and explore their experiences without negative judgment, criticism, or blaming (Rogers, 1951, 1989). An empathetic therapist creates a supportive and open environment where clients feel safe in exploring their issues and discussing their personal reasons for change. MI also goes beyond Rogers's precepts in that it openly acknowledges the directive, if subtle, nature of the therapeutic interaction. Rogers was said to believe that he did not influence his clients' choices until his graduate students demonstrated otherwise.

The key to understanding clients and expressing empathy lies in reflective listening. Reflective listening entails focusing on each new client statement and making reflections and summaries of these statements to ensure accuracy and understanding. This type of active listening is nonjudgmental and conveys acceptance to the client. It does not mean that the therapist necessarily needs to agree with the client or approve of the client's situation. It is possible to understand and accept a person's situation without approving of it (Bundy, 2004). Empathy is expressed through the therapist's desire to understand and accept the client's perspective. In order to facilitate the conversation and demonstrate that you understand (as opposed to stating that you understand), you must listen very carefully and, without interrupting, restate in your own words what the client has communicated to you. Then, you must check back and make sure you are correct in your understanding before moving on. With clients who are feeling stuck or misunderstood (by anyone) this can be a true gift and can assist them in truly moving on.

Developing discrepancy is a valuable therapeutic technique to elicit change in clients. Change will not come about unless clients become aware of the gap between where they currently are and where they want to be. Most clients already come to therapy with some ideas about wanting to change but feel stuck or ambivalent. The key is to get the client to discuss how his or her current behaviors are getting in the way of an ultimate desired goal. In other words, the client needs to present his or her own reasons for wanting to change instead of the therapist imposing reasons for doing so. According to Miller and Rollnick (1992), "People are often more persuaded by what they hear themselves say than by what other people tell them" (p. 57).

One way to develop discrepancy is to have a dialogue regarding both sides of the client's ambivalence. Elicit from the client the pros and cons of the situation, including the positive and negative aspects of the client's behaviors from the client's point of view. This is the essential task of decisional balance, and it allows the client to explore and develop his or her own reasons for maintaining the current behavior and his or her own goals or need for change. The therapist's true task is to normalize and amplify the ambivalence, not argue for one position or another.

The therapist can help direct the dialogue through some simple strategies and questioning (CSAT, 1999). Some strategies include asking clients to discuss the good things and the bad things about their behavior. Explore with clients what their lives would be like if they didn't engage in the target behavior and what their lives would be like if they changed. Ask what clients imagine will happen if they continue down the same path or where they see their lives 5 years from now. Discuss in detail the clients' goals and things they want and elicit from them how their current behavior gets in the way of achieving those things. When clients offer something bad about their behavior, ask them to elaborate and talk more about it. Once clients have accepted their own arguments and reasons for change, they can begin to move toward that change.

Rolling with resistance and avoiding argumentation are companion activities that take significant determination on the part of the therapist. Many clients have had negative experiences with previous therapists or social contacts that have pushed a particular agenda. The successful motivational interviewer does not argue for any particular outcome but instead uses reflective listening to help the client explore his or her ambivalence about making change. Miller and Rollnick (1992, 2002) suggest that arguing for change leaves the client to argue against change and that this is a natural human response to being pushed in a particular direction. The metaphor often used to explain this interaction is the difference between wrestling and the martial art of aikido (Scales, Miller, & Burden, 2003; Sheldon, 2003). It is an apt metaphor, as any experienced therapist can recall verbally wrestling or playing devil's advocate or in some way opposing or proposing an alternative perspective with a client. When opposing or directly challenging a client's beliefs, attitudes, or ideas about his or her situation, we leave the client to defend his or her decisions and become opponents in an argument instead of facilitators of the desired process.

In aikido, the skilled martial artist uses the momentum of the opponent's assault (verbal in this case) to disarm his or her argument, essentially allowing it to unfold uncontested and fall flat. This approach is also reminiscent of mindfulness approaches in that the therapist notes the opportunity to engage in an adversarial exchange with the client and lets it pass without response or, better yet, with a reflective statement. Direct confrontation and arguing change to the client are inconsistent with the other principles of MI. The therapist cannot express empathy and understanding to a client when he or she is actively arguing for change instead of discussing the client's reasons for maintaining the behavior. Similarly, discrepancy cannot be amplified between where the client is currently and where he or she wants to be if the client feels the need to defend his or her position and dispute reasons for change.

Ultimately, becoming argumentative with the client, although with good intentions, leads to further resistance to change. According to Miller (2004), "resistance is only the patient giving voice to the other side of ambivalence, to the nonchange side of the internal argument" (p. 4). In order for the therapist to move the client toward change, the beliefs that underlie the behavior must be delicately and tactfully challenged. When done skillfully, this technique can shift the client's perspective from the nonchange side of the argument and lead to openness to new ways of acting. The client is led to take an objective look at both the reasons for maintaining the behavior and the positive aspects of change.

There are several approaches of rolling with resistance that can maintain the discrepancy between where the client is and where he or she wants to be. As a general principle of rolling with resistance, the therapist remembers that the client is the expert in his or her own dilemma and invites the client into the problem-solving process. Asking for clarification or elaboration with genuine interest is helpful in avoiding argumentation. Other techniques include restating the client's arguments for and against change in the same sentence and eliciting additional reasons for and against change to continue the conversation. Generally, the therapist should not impose his or her own views and opinions on the client. Rather, both the client and the therapist should generate and consider new information and perspectives. This approach actively engages the client in the problem-solving process and reduces the chance that he or she will take an oppositional stance.

Supporting self-efficacy is more than an emotional or verbal affirmation or a compliment. In MI, one supports the client's self-efficacy by noting or commenting on specific aspects of his or her perspective, experience, or skill set that might be helpful in resolving the client's concerns. In essence, you are affirming the person's ability to get through the difficult changes that are ahead of him or her. In order to accomplish this, however, the therapist must pay close attention to evidence of the client's previous successes, skills, and capacities to be successful in the future. If self-esteem and self-efficacy result from mastery and confidence in one's abilities to meet life's challenges, then the therapist has a significant opportunity to make useful observations in this regard. The next step is to communicate clearly to the client that he or she is capable and has expertise to draw on in the current situation by eliciting positive statements about the change process and past attempts at change.

Eliciting motivational self-statements (motivation for change) is a critical aspect of this discussion. Clients express reasons for change in the course of uninhibited change talk, and the skilled interviewer pays close attention to these and asks for information about the client's self-motivational statements in the context of reasons against change.

Scaling questions may also be helpful in this regard. Clients can be asked on a scale of 1 to 10 how strongly they are motivated to change, how important change is to them, or how confident they are that they can make a change. This type of questioning leads to change talk. For example, if the therapist asks how confident a client is on a scale of 1 to 10, regardless of the answer, he or she can make further inquiries into the reasons for that level of confidence. In addition, the therapist can discuss with the client what it would take to move up one point on the confidence scale. Assisting the client in breaking large goals into smaller, doable but meaningful chunks can also help a client see the tasks ahead as within his or her abilities.

MI uses another classic therapeutic method in its reliance on open-ended questions as the mainstay of conversation. It is intended to give clients the greatest possible opportunity to express themselves in their own words and to help them hear their own language about change, thereby amplifying the distance between current behavior and the client's goals. Ultimately, the motivational interviewer is listening for information about readiness to change, reasons for and against change, how the person has made change in the past, and motivational self-statements.

Having described the basic components of MI, it is important to note that the acquisition of these therapeutic skills entails detailed instruction and supervision. Miller and others have written extensively about the training process involved in teaching practitioners to perform the tasks involved in MI (Baer et al., 2004; Barsky & Coleman, 2001; Madson, Campbell, Barrett, Brondino, & Melchert, 2005; Miller, 1996; Miller & Mount, 2001; Miller, Yahne, Moyers, Martinez, & Pirritano, 2004; Moyers, Martin, Manuel, Hendrickson, & Miller, 2005; Moyers, Miller, et al., 2005; Shafer, Rhode, & Chong, 2004). Tools to assist in training are available and can improve the structure of MI supervision (Rosengren, Baer, Hartzler, Dunn, & Wells, 2005).

Other disciplines have followed suit with peer-reviewed articles regarding the training of first-year medical students, dental students, and nurses to use MI techniques in their interactions (Britt, Hudson, & Blampied, 2004; Brown & Oriel, 1998; Koerber, Crawford, & O'Connell, 2003; Lange & Tigges, 2005; Miller, 2001; Miller & Johnson, 2001; Poirier et al., 2004; Rollnick, 2001). It is often cited as a general approach to increase compliance with difficult medical regimens or reduce substance use in specific at-risk populations, such as pregnant women and people with cancer (Gibson & Gibson, 2000; Handmaker, Miller, & Manicke, 1999; Tappin et al., 2005; Velasquez et al., 2000; Wakefield, Oliver, Whitford, & Rosenfeld, 2004).

Medical applications are promising opportunities given how much behavior change is needed to implement most medical treatment plans (Berdoz, Conus, & Daeppen, 2005; Emmons & Rollnick, 2001; Resnicow et al., 2002). Care settings can include the traditional outpatient mental health setting, acute care, inpatient drug and alcohol treatment centers, primary care settings, inpatient psychiatric treatment settings, and public health settings (Baker et al., 2002; Bechdolf et al., 2005; Dunn, 2003; Dunn, Deroo, & Rivara, 2001; McCambridge & Strang, 2003; Petersen et al., 2004; Sindelar, Abrantes, Hart, Lewander, & Spirito, 2004; Stotts, Schmitz, Rhoades, & Grabowski, 2001; Swanson, Pantalon, & Cohen, 1999). Lay applications are also on the increase with attempts to train peer counselors (Gray, McCambridge, & Strang, 2005) and church leaders (Resnicow et al., 2001) to facilitate desired changes in health-promoting behavior.

The primary goal is to increase adherence at all points along the continuum: treatment initiation (Carroll, Libby, Sheehan, & Hyland, 2001), attendance and treatment adherence (Gance-Cleveland, 2005; Ossman, 2004; Possidente, Bucci, & McClain, 2005; Rusch & Corrigan, 2002), participation (Erickson, Gerstle, & Feldstein, 2005; Shinitzky & Kub, 2001), frequency of self-motivational statements, treatment retention (Secades-Villa, Fernande-Hermida, & Arnaez-Montaraz, 2004), and continuation of gains after conclusion of treatment (Miller, 2005). Although there is some loss of treatment gain over time, clients exposed to MI still show significantly better retention of therapy gains over non-MI groups of clients (Burke, Arkowitz, & Menchola, 2003; Calhoun & Admire, 2005; McCambridge & Strang, 2005; Miller, 2005; Rubak, Sandbaek, Lauritzen, & Christensen, 2005).

The training of nontherapists to use MI techniques has resulted in a different set of considerations (Resnicow et al., 2002). Although they are assumed to be transferable across health care disciplines, MI techniques build on basic therapeutic methods, few of which are emphasized or taught in detail in nursing, dental, or medical schools.

A second area of consideration involves the need for reliable measures of the relevant constructs and their consistent use in assessing the usefulness of MI techniques. Clinician perception, although important, is not a reliable indicator of proficiency (Moyers, Martin, et al., 2005;

Moyers, Miller, et al., 2005). Health care environments, similar to general mental health environments, benefit from structure to ensure that patients benefit from the use of MI methods. Measures can be helpful to use in supervision and training. Miller and Rollnick (2002) provide detailed transcribed interviews demonstrating MI, and video demonstrations may also be used to train the therapist interested in MI. Short outcome measures are recommended as a method of assessing the application of these skills in the context in which they are being applied (Carey, Purnine, Maisto, & Carey, 1999; Lane et al., 2005).

The list of MI applications continues to expand. A sample of current topics in peer-reviewed journals reveals a diverse collection of health care services integrating or focusing on MI. Researchers report success with patients at risk for diabetes (Carino, Coke, & Gulanick, 2004) and those already diagnosed with diabetes (Channon, Huws-Thomas, Rollnick, & Gregory, 2005; Channon, Smith, & Gregory, 2003; Doherty & Roberts, 2002; Draycott & Dabbs, 1998). HIV treatment providers report positive results from the use of MI to increase adherence to antiretroviral regimens (Adamian, Golin, Shain, & DeVellis, 2004; Cooperman & Arnsten, 2005; Dilorio et al., 2003), reduce HIV risk (Harding, Dockrell, Dockrell, & Corrigan, 2001; McVinney, 2004; Parsons, Rosof, Punzalan, & DiMaria, 2005), and increase HIV testing (Foley et al., 2005).

Traditional MI applications continue to include goals for reducing alcohol, tobacco, marijuana, and other drug use independent of or concurrent with other mental health treatments (Barrowclough et al., 2001; Brown et al., 2003; Graeber, Moyers, Griffith, Guarjardo, & Tonigan, 2003; Hohman, 1998; Knight et al., 2005; Martino, Carroll, Kostas, Perkins, & Rounsaville, 2002; Martino, Carroll, O'Malley, & Rounsaville, 2000; Miller, Yahne, & Tonigan, 2003; Mullins, Suarez, Ondersma, & Page, 2004; White & Pollex, 2005) and are joined by efforts to increase exercise adherence in preventive cardiology, chronic heart failure, and cardiac rehabilitation (Belg, 2003; Brodie & Inoue, 2005).

Family therapists and nurse practitioners alike are discussing the virtues of MI in increasing adherence with children, adolescents, and their families (Erickson, Gerstle, & Feldstein, 2005) for medical and psychological treatments as well as marital therapy (Cordova, Warren, & Gee, 2001).

Eating and weight disorder treatments also appear to be enhanced with the inclusion of MI principles and techniques (Smith, Heckemeyer, Kratt, & Mason, 1997; Tantillo, Bitter, & Adams, 2001; Thorpe, 2003; VanWormer & Boucher, 2004; Wilson & Schlam, 2004), as do contraceptive counseling efforts (Petersen et al., 2004). Within mental health, an increase in efforts to encourage smoking cessation for patients with psychotic disorders is under way, using MI, and compliance with the complex treatments designed for dually diagnosed adults can be addressed without the classic control issues (Steinberg, Ziedonis, Krejci, & Brandon, 2004; Van Horn & Bux, 2001).

Mandated and forensic clients also appear to respond to MI methods, reflecting increased participation in groups and improvements in targeted symptoms (Lincour, Kuettel, & Bombardier, 2002). Occupational medicine is finding a role for MI in clients scheduled for return to work (Miller & Moyers, 2002).

Additional targets include reducing smoking by parents with young children in the home (Emmons et al., 2001), helping patients with mixed anxiety and depression follow through with treatment recommendations (Westra, 2004), improving insight and treatment in schizophrenia (Chanut, Brown, & Dongier, 2005; Rusch & Corrigan, 2002), and increasing adherence to exercise regimens by patients with fibromyalgia (Jones, Burkhardt, & Bennett, 2004).

Summary

The basic skills necessary to perform the tasks of MI are a part of most clinical training. The real difference is in how much effort is expended in attending explicitly to reflective listening and facilitating change talk over confronting, educating, or challenging clients to try to make change. The wide array of current applications is both striking and impressive. It speaks directly to psychological and medical providers' need for interviewing methods that enhance the treatment process. It is likely that the applications will eventually narrow to the patient care settings and populations for whom it is found to be most effective. In the interim, the findings in support of MI suggest that broad appeal is warranted.

The initial interview often is laden with myriad tasks that make connecting personally with a client difficult. What MI lacks in obvious structure it more than makes up for with substance. In a motivational interview, one can effectively begin a therapeutic relationship, elicit confidence about making change, pace readiness for change, identify initial goals for treatment, identify past successful change, determine barriers to change, and glean client strengths and resources that are essential to planning treatment.

MI has limitations and takes special training and supervision. However, MI takes less time than many comparable strategies to produce behavior change. It is most helpful as a prelude, an introduction to treatment and, interestingly, most helpful for those who are determined by traditional methods to be resistant to change or those who have negative assumptions about their ability to make change. This combination of flexibility, directiveness, and client-centeredness may be the reason MI has been adopted worldwide as a method of enhancing treatment from the first point of contact.

References

Adamian, M. S., Golin, C. E., Shain, L. S., & DeVellis, B. (2004). Brief motivational interviewing to improve adherence to antiretroviral therapy: Development and qualitative pilot assessment of an intervention. *AIDS Patient Care & Standards, 18,* 229–238.

Amrhein, P. C., Miller, W. R., Yahne, C. E., Palmer, M., & Fulcher, L. (2003). Client commitment language during motivational interviewing predicts drug use outcomes. *Journal of Consulting & Clinical Psychology, 71,* 862–878.

Baer, J. S., Rosengren, D. B., Dunn, C. W., Wells, E. A., Ogle, R. L., & Hartzler, B. (2004, January 7). An evaluation of workshop training in motivational interviewing for addiction and mental health clinicians. *Drug & Alcohol Dependence, 73,* 99–106.

Baker, A., Lewin, T., Reichler, H., Clancy, R., Carr, V., Garrett, R., et al. (2002). Motivational interviewing among psychiatric in-patients with substance use disorders. *Acta Psychiatrica Scandinavica, 106,* 233–240.

Bandura, A. (1977). Self-efficacy: Toward a unifying theory of behavior change. *Psychological Review, 84,* 191–215.

Barrowclough, C., Haddock, G., Tarrier, N., Lewis, S. W., Moring, J., O'Brien, R., et al. (2001). Randomized controlled trial of motivational interviewing, cognitive behavior therapy, and family intervention for patients with comorbid schizophrenia and substance use disorders. *American Journal of Psychiatry, 158,* 1706–1713.

Barsky, A., & Coleman, H. (2001). Evaluating skill acquisition in motivational interviewing: The development of an instrument to measure practice skills. *Journal of Drug Education, 31,* 69–82.

Bechdolf, A., Pohlmann, B., Geyer, C., Ferber, C., Klosterkotter, J., & Gouzoulis-Mayfrank, E. (2005). Motivational interviewing for patients with comorbid schizophrenia and substance abuse disorders: A review. *Fortschritte der Neurologie-Psychiatrie, 73*, 728–735.

Belg, A. J. (2003). Maintenance of health behavior change in preventive cardiology. *Behavior Modification, 27*, 103–131.

Berdoz, D., Conus, M. K., & Daeppen, J. B. (2005). Helping patients with risky health behaviors: Some suggestions for motivational interviewing. *Revue Medicale Suisse, 1*, 2453–2456.

Biller, N., Arnstein, P., Caudill, M. A., Federman, C. W., & Guberman, C. (2000). Predicting completion of a cognitive-behavioral pain management program by initial measures of a chronic pain patient's readiness for change. *Clinical Journal of Pain, 16*, 352–359.

Britt, E., Hudson, S. M., & Blampied, N. M. (2004). Motivational interviewing in health settings: A review. *Patient Education & Counseling, 53*, 147–155.

Brodie, D. A., & Inoue, A. (2005). Motivational interviewing to promote physical activity for people with chronic heart failure. *Journal of Advanced Nursing, 50*, 518–527.

Brown, R. A., Ramsey, S. E., Strong, D. R., Myers, M. G., Kahler, C. W., Lejuez, C. W., et al. (2003). Effects of motivational interviewing on smoking cessation in adolescents with psychiatric disorders. *Tobacco Control, 12*(Suppl. 4), 3–10.

Brown, R. L., & Oriel, K. (1998). Teaching motivational interviewing to first-year students. *Academic Medicine, 73*, 589–590.

Bundy, C. (2004). Changing behaviour: Using motivational interviewing techniques. *Journal of the Royal Society of Medicine, 97*(Suppl. 44), 43–47.

Burke, B. L., Arkowitz, H., & Menchola, M. (2003). The efficacy of motivational interviewing: A meta-analysis of controlled clinical trials. *Journal of Consulting & Clinical Psychology, 71*, 843–861.

Calhoun, J., & Admire, K. S. (2005). Implementing a predictive modeling program, part II: Use of motivational interviewing in a predictive modeling program. *Lippincott's Case Management, 10*, 240–245.

Carey, K. B., Purnine, D. M., Maisto, S. A., & Carey, M., P. (1999). Assessing readiness to change substance abuse: A critical review of instruments. *Clinical Psychology Science and Practice, 6*, 245–266.

Carino, J. L., Coke, L., & Gulanick, M. (2004). Using motivational interviewing to reduce diabetes risk. *Progress in Cardiovascular Nursing, 19*, 149–154.

Carroll, K. M., Libby, B., Sheehan, J., & Hyland, N. (2001). Motivational interviewing to enhance treatment initiation in substance abusers: An effectiveness study. *American Journal on Addictions, 10*, 335–339.

Center for Substance Abuse Treatment. (1999). Enhancing motivation for change in substance abuse treatment. *Treatment Improvement Protocol (TIP) Series, 35*. DHHS Pub. No. (SMA) 99-3354. Washington, DC: U.S. Government Printing Office.

Channon, S., Huws-Thomas, M. V., Rollnick, S., & Gregory, J. W. (2005). The potential of motivational interviewing. *Diabetic Medicine, 22*, 353.

Channon, S., Smith, V. J., & Gregory, J. W. (2003). A pilot study of motivational interviewing in adolescents with diabetes. *Archives of Disease in Childhood, 88*, 680–683.

Chanut, F., Brown, T. G., & Dongier, M. (2005). Motivational interviewing and clinical psychiatry. *Canadian Journal of Psychiatry—Revue Canadienne de Psychiatrie, 50*, 548–554.

Cooperman, N. A., & Arnsten, J. H. (2005). Motivational interviewing for improving adherence to antiretroviral medications. *Current HIV/AIDS Reports, 2*, 159–164.

Cordova, J. V., Warren, L. Z., & Gee, C. B. (2001). Motivational interviewing as an intervention for at-risk couples. *Journal of Marital & Family Therapy, 27*, 315–326.

Deci, E. L., & Ryan, R. M. (1985). *Intrinsic motivation and self-determination in human behavior.* New York: Plenum.

Deci, E. L., & Ryan, R. M. (2000). The what and the why of goal pursuits: Human needs and the self-determination of behavior. *Psychological Inquiry, 11*, 227–268.

Dilorio, C., Resnicow, K., McDonnell, M., Soet, J., McCarty, F., & Yeager, K. (2003). Using motivational interviewing to promote adherence to antiretroviral medications: A pilot study. *Journal of the Association of Nurses in AIDS Care, 14*, 52–62.

Doherty, Y., & Roberts, S. (2002). Motivational interviewing in diabetes practice. *Diabetic Medicine, 19*(Suppl. 3), 1–6.

Draycott, S., & Dabbs, A. (1998). Cognitive dissonance. 2: A theoretical grounding of motivational interviewing. *British Journal of Clinical Psychology, 37*, 355–364.

Dunn, C. (2003). Brief motivational interviewing interventions targeting substance abuse in the acute care medical setting. *Seminars in Clinical Neuropsychiatry, 8*, 188–196.

Dunn, C., Deroo, L., & Rivara, F. P. (2001). The use of brief interventions adapted from motivational interviewing across behavioral domains: A systematic review. *Addiction, 96*, 1725–1742.

Emmons, K. M., & Rollnick, S. (2001). Motivational interviewing in health care settings: Opportunities and limitations. *American Journal of Preventive Medicine, 20*, 68–74.

Emmons, K. M., Hammond, S. K., Fava, J. L., Velicer, W. F., Evans, J. L., & Monroe, A. D. (2001). A randomized trial to reduce a passive smoke exposure in low-income households with young children. *Pediatrics, 108*, 18–24.

Erickson, S. J., Gerstle, M., & Feldstein, S. W. (2005). Brief interventions and motivational interviewing with children, adolescents, and their parents in pediatric health care settings: A review. *Archives of Pediatrics & Adolescent Medicine, 159*, 1173–1180.

Foley, K., Duran, B., Morris, P., Lucero, J., Jiang, Y., Baxter, B., et al. (2005). Using motivational interviewing to promote HIV testing at an American Indian substance abuse treatment facility. *Journal of Psychoactive Drugs, 37*, 321–329.

Freyer, J., Tonigan, J. S., Keller, S., Rumpf, H., John, U., & Hapke, U. (2005). Readiness for change and readiness for help-seeking: A composite assessment of client motivation. *Alcohol & Alcoholism, 40*, 540–544.

Gance-Cleveland, B. (2005). Motivational interviewing as a strategy to increase families' adherence to treatment regimens. *Journal for Specialists in Pediatric Nursing: JSPN, 10,* 151–155.

Gibson, A., & Gibson, T. (2000). Motivational interviewing. *Practising Midwife, 3,* 32–35.

Graeber, D. A., Moyers, T. B., Griffith, G., Guajardo, E., & Tonigan, S. (2003). A pilot study comparing motivational interviewing and an educational intervention in patients with schizophrenia and alcohol use disorders. *Community Mental Health Journal, 39,* 189–202.

Gray, E., McCambridge, J., & Strang, J. (2005). The effectiveness of motivational interviewing delivered by youth workers in reducing drinking, cigarette and cannabis smoking among young people: Quasi-experimental pilot study. *Alcohol & Alcoholism, 40,* 535–539.

Handmaker, N. S., Miller, W. R., & Manicke, M. (1999). Findings of a pilot study of motivational interviewing with pregnant drinkers. *Journal of Studies on Alcohol, 60,* 285–287.

Harding, R., Dockrell, M. J., Dockrell, J., & Corrigan, N. (2001). Motivational interviewing for HIV risk reduction among gay men in commercial and public sex settings. *AIDS Care, 13,* 493–501.

Hohman, M. M. (1998). Motivational interviewing: An intervention tool for child welfare case workers working with substance-abusing parents. *Child Welfare, 77,* 275–289.

Hubble, M. A., Duncan, B. L., & Miller, S. D. (1999). *The heart and soul of change: What works in therapy.* Washington, DC: American Psychological Association.

Jones, K. D., Burckhardt, C. S., & Bennett, J. A. (2004). Motivational interviewing may encourage exercise in persons with fibromyalgia by enhancing self efficacy. *Arthritis & Rheumatism, 51,* 864–867.

Knight, J. R., Sherritt, L., Van Hook, S., Gates, E. C., Levy, S., & Chang, G. (2005). Motivational interviewing for adolescent substance use: A pilot study. *Journal of Adolescent Health, 37,* 167–169.

Koerber, A., Crawford, J., & O'Connell, K. (2003). The effects of teaching dental students brief motivational interviewing for smoking-cessation counseling: A pilot study. *Journal of Dental Education, 67,* 439–447.

Lane, C., Huws-Thomas, M., Hood, K., Rollnick, S., Edwards, K., & Robling, M. (2005). Measuring adaptations of motivational interviewing: The development and validation of the behavior change counseling index (BECCI). *Patient Education & Counseling, 56,* 166–173.

Lange, N., & Tigges, B. B. (2005). Influence positive change with motivational interviewing. *Nurse Practitioner, 30,* 44–53.

Lewis, T. F., & Osborn, C. J. (2004). Solution-focused counseling and motivational interviewing: A consideration of confluence. *Journal of Counseling and Development, 82,* 38–48.

Lincour, P., Kuettel, T. J., & Bombardier, C. H. (2002). Motivational interviewing in a group setting with mandated clients: A pilot study. *Addictive Behaviors, 27,* 381–391.

Madson, M. B., Campbell, T. C., Barrett, D. E., Brondino, M. J., & Melchert, T. P. (2005). Development of the motivational interviewing supervision and training scale. *Psychology of Addictive Behaviors, 19,* 303–310.

Markland, D., Ryan, R. M., Tobin, V., & Rollnick, S. (2005). Motivational interviewing and self-determination theory. *Journal of Social and Clinical Psychology, 24,* 811–831.

Martino, S., Carroll, K., Kostas, D., Perkins, J., & Rounsaville, B. (2002). Dual diagnosis motivational interviewing: A modification of motivational interviewing for substance-abusing patients with psychotic disorders. *Journal of Substance Abuse Treatment, 23,* 297–308.

Martino, S., Carroll, K. M., O'Malley, S. S., & Rounsaville, B. J. (2000). Motivational interviewing with psychiatrically ill substance abusing patients. *American Journal on Addictions, 9,* 88–91.

McCambridge, J., & Strang, J. (2003). Development of a structured generic drug intervention model for public health purposes: A brief application of motivational interviewing with young people. *Drug & Alcohol Review, 22,* 391–399.

McCambridge, J., & Strang, J. (2004). The efficacy of single-session motivational interviewing in reducing drug consumption and perceptions of drug-related risk and harm among young people: Results from a multi-site cluster randomized trial. *Addiction, 99,* 39–52.

McCambridge, J., & Strang, J. (2005). Deterioration over time in effect of motivational interviewing in reducing drug consumption and related risk among young people. *Addiction, 100*(4), 470–478.

McVinney, D. (2004). Motivational interviewing and psychotherapy. *Focus: A Guide to AIDS Research, 19,* 4–6.

Miller, C. E., & Johnson, J. L. (2001). Motivational interviewing. *Canadian Nurse, 97,* 32–33.

Miller, J. H., & Moyers, T. (2002). Motivational interviewing in substance abuse: Applications for occupational medicine. *Occupational Medicine, 17,* 51–65.

Miller, W. R. (1996). Motivational interviewing: Research, practice, and puzzles. *Addictive Behaviors, 21*(6), 835–842.

Miller, W. R. (2000). Motivational enhancement therapy: Description of counseling approach. In J. J. Boren, L. S. Onken, & K. M. Carroll (Eds.), *Approaches to drug abuse counseling* (pp. 89–93). Bethesda, MD: National Institute on Drug Abuse.

Miller, W. R. (2001). Comments on Dunn et al.'s "The use of brief interventions adapted from motivational interviewing across behavioral domains: A systematic review." *Addiction, 96,* 1770–1772.

Miller, W. R. (2004, January–February). Motivational interviewing in service to health promotion. *Art of Health Promotion,* 1–9.

Miller, W. R. (2005). Motivational interviewing and the incredible shrinking treatment effect. *Addiction, 100,* 421.

Miller, W. R., & Mount, K. A. (2001). A small study of training in motivational interviewing: Does one workshop change clinician and client behavior? *Behavioural and Cognitive Psychotherapy, 29,* 457–471.

Miller, W. R., & Rollnick, S. (1992). *Motivational interviewing: Preparing people to change addictive behavior.* New York: Guilford.

Miller, W. R., & Rollnick, S. (2002). *Motivational interviewing: Preparing people to make change* (2nd ed.). New York: Guilford.

Miller, W. R., Yahne, C. E., Moyers, T. B., Martinez, J., & Pirritano, M. (2004). A randomized trial of methods to help clinicians learn motivational interviewing. *Journal of Consulting & Clinical Psychology, 72,* 1050–1062.

Miller, W. R., Yahne, C. E., & Tonigan, J. S. (2003). Motivational interviewing in drug abuse services: A randomized trial. *Journal of Consulting & Clinical Psychology, 71,* 754–763.

Moyers, T. B., Martin, T., Manuel, J. K., Hendrickson, S. M., & Miller, W. R. (2005). Assessing competence in the use of motivational interviewing. *Journal of Substance Abuse Treatment, 28,* 19–26.

Moyers, T. B., Miller, W. R., & Hendrickson, S. M. (2005). How does motivational interviewing work? Therapist interpersonal skill predicts client involvement within motivational interviewing sessions. *Journal of Consulting & Clinical Psychology, 73,* 590–598.

Moyers, T. B., & Rollnick, S. (2002). A motivational interviewing perspective on resistance in psychotherapy. *Journal of Clinical Psychology, 58,* 185–193.

Mullins, S. M., Suarez, M., Ondersma, S. J., & Page, M. C. (2004). The impact of motivational interviewing on substance abuse treatment retention: A randomized control trial of women involved with child welfare. *Journal of Substance Abuse Treatment, 27,* 51–58.

Ossman, S. S. (2004). Motivational interviewing: A process to encourage behavioral change. *Nephrology Nursing Journal: Journal of the American Nephrology Nurses' Association, 31,* 346–347.

Parsons, J. T., Rosof, E., Punzalan, J. C., & DiMaria, L. (2005). Integration of motivational interviewing and cognitive behavioral therapy to improve HIV medication adherence and reduce substance use among HIV-positive men and women: Results of a pilot project. *AIDS Patient Care & Standards, 19,* 31–39.

Petersen, R., Payne, P., Albright, J., Holland, H., Cabral, R., & Curtis, K. M. (2004). Applying motivational interviewing to contraceptive counseling: ESP for clinicians. *Contraception, 69,* 213–217.

Poirier, M. K., Clark, M. M., Cerhan, J. H., Pruthi, S., Geda, Y. E., & Dale, L. C. (2004). Teaching motivational interviewing to first-year medical students to improve counseling skills in health behavior change. *Mayo Clinic Proceedings, 79,* 327–331.

Possidente, C. J., Bucci, K. K., & McClain, W. J. (2005). Motivational interviewing: A tool to improve medication adherence? *American Journal of Health-System Pharmacy, 62,* 1311–1314.

Prochaska, J. O., DiClemente, C. C., & Norcross, J. C. (1992). In search of how people change. *American Psychologist, 47,* 1102–1114.

Prochaska, J. O., & Norcross, J. C. (2001). Stages of change. *Psychotherapy, 38,* 443–448.

Prochaska, J. O., Velicer, W. F., Rossi, J. S., Goldstein, M. G., Marcus, B. H., Rakowski, W., et al. (1994). Stages of change and decisional balance for twelve problem behaviors. *Health Psychology, 13,* 39–46.

Resnicow, K., Dilorio, C., Soet, J. E., Ernst, D., Borrelli, B., & Hecht, J. (2002). Motivational interviewing in health promotion: It sounds like something is changing. *Health Psychology, 2,* 444–451.

Resnicow, K., Jackson, A., Wang, T., De, A. K., McCarty, F., Dudley, W. N., et al. (2001). A motivational interviewing intervention to increase fruit and vegetable intake through Black churches: Results of the Eat for Life trial. *American Journal of Public Health, 91,* 1686–1693.

Rogers, C. (1951). *Client-centered therapy.* New York: Houghton Mifflin.

Rogers, C. (1989). *The Carl Rogers reader.* H. Kirschbaum & V. L. Henderson (Eds.). New York: Houghton Mifflin.

Rollnick, S. (2001). Comments on Dunn et al.'s "The use of brief interventions adapted from motivational interviewing across behavioral domains: A systematic review." Enthusiasm, quick fixes and premature controlled trials. *Addiction, 96,* 1769–1770.

Rosengren, D. B., Baer, J. S., Hartzler, B., Dunn, C. W., & Wells, E. A. (2005). The video assessment of simulated encounters (VASE): Development and validation of a group-administered method for evaluating clinician skills in motivational interviewing. *Drug & Alcohol Dependence, 79,* 321–330.

Rubak, S., Sandbaek, A., Lauritzen, T., & Christensen, B. (2005). Motivational interviewing: A systematic review and meta-analysis. *British Journal of General Practice, 55*(513), 305–312.

Rusch, N., & Corrigan, P. W. (2002). Motivational interviewing to improve insight and treatment adherence in schizophrenia. *Psychiatric Rehabilitation Journal, 26,* 23–32.

Scales, R., Miller, J., & Burden, R. (2003). Why wrestle when you can dance? Optimizing outcomes with motivational interviewing. *Journal of the American Pharmacists Association: JAPhA, 43*(5 Suppl. 1), S46–S47.

Secades-Villa, R., Fernande-Hermida, J. R., & Arnaez-Montaraz, C. (2004). Motivational interviewing and treatment retention among drug user patients: A pilot study. *Substance Use & Misuse, 39,* 1369–1378.

Shafer, M. S., Rhode, R., & Chong, J. (2004). Using distance education to promote the transfer of motivational interviewing skills among behavioral health professionals. *Journal of Substance Abuse Treatment, 26,* 141–148.

Sheldon, K. M. (2003). Reconciling humanistic ideals and scientific clinical practice. *Clinical Psychology: Science and Practice, 10,* 302–315.

Shinitzky, H. E., & Kub, J. (2001). The art of motivating behavior change: The use of motivational interviewing to promote health. *Public Health Nursing, 18,* 178–185.

Sindelar, H. A., Abrantes, A. M., Hart, C., Lewander, W., & Spirito, A. (2004). Motivational interviewing in pediatric practice. *Current Problems in Pediatric & Adolescent Health Care, 34,* 322–339.

Smith, D. E., Heckemeyer, C. M., Kratt, P. P., & Mason, D. A. (1997). Motivational interviewing to improve adherence to a behavioral weight-control program for older obese women with NIDDM. A pilot study. *Diabetes Care, 20,* 52–54.

Steinberg, M. L., Ziedonis, D. M., Krejci, J. A., & Brandon, T. H. (2004). Motivational interviewing with personalized feedback: A brief intervention for motivating smokers with schizophrenia to seek treatment for tobacco dependence. *Journal of Consulting & Clinical Psychology, 72,* 723–728.

Stotts, A. L., Schmitz, J. M., Rhoades, H. M., & Grabowski, J. (2001). Motivational interviewing with cocaine-dependent patients: A pilot study. *Journal of Consulting & Clinical Psychology, 69,* 858–862.

Swanson, A. J., Pantalon, M. V., & Cohen, K. R. (1999). Motivational interviewing and treatment adherence among psychiatric and dually diagnosed patients. *Journal of Nervous & Mental Disease, 187,* 630–635.

Tantillo, M., Bitter, C. N., & Adams, B. (2001). Enhancing readiness for eating disorder treatment: A relational/motivational group model for change. *Eating Disorders, 9,* 203–216.

Tappin, D. M., Lumsden, M. A., Gilmour, W. H., Crawford, F., McIntyre, D., Stone, D. H., et al. (2005). Randomised controlled trial of home based motivational interviewing by midwives to help pregnant smokers quit or cut down. *British Medical Journal, 331*(7513), 373–377.

Thorpe, M. (2003). Motivational interviewing and dietary behavior change. *Journal of the American Dietetic Association, 103,* 150–151.

Van Horn, D. H., & Bux, D. A. (2001). A pilot test of motivational interviewing groups for dually diagnosed inpatients. *Journal of Substance Abuse Treatment, 20,* 191–195.

Vansteenkiste, M., & Sheldon, K. M. (2006). There's nothing more practical than a good theory: Integrating motivational interviewing and self-determination theory. *British Journal of Clinical Psychology, 45,* 63–82.

VanWormer, J. J., & Boucher, J. L. (2004). Motivational interviewing and diet modification: A review of the evidence. *Diabetes Educator, 30,* 404–406.

Velasquez, M. M., Hecht, J., Quinn, V. P., Emmons, K. M., DiClemente, C. C., & Dolan-Mullen, P. (2000). Application of motivational interviewing to prenatal smoking cessation: Training and implementation issues. *Tobacco Control, 9*(Suppl. 3), 36–40.

Viner, R. M., Christie, D., Taylor, V., & Hey, S. (2003). Motivational/solution-focused intervention improves HbA1c in adolescents with Type I diabetes: A pilot study. *Diabetes Medicine, 20,* 739–742.

Wakefield, M., Oliver, I., Whitford, H., & Rosenfeld, E. (2004). Motivational interviewing as a smoking cessation intervention for patients with cancer: Randomized controlled trial. *Nursing Research, 53,* 396–405.

Westra, H. A. (2004). Managing resistance in cognitive behavioural therapy: The application of motivational interviewing in mixed anxiety and depression. *Cognitive Behaviour Therapy, 33,* 161–175.

White, L. G., & Pollex, S. S. (2005). Tobacco: Motivational interviewing to empower behavior change. *Texas Dental Journal, 122,* 528–532.

Wilson, G. T., & Schlam, T. R. (2004). The transtheoretical model and motivational interviewing in the treatment of eating and weight disorders. *Clinical Psychology Review, 24,* 361–378.

5

MENTAL STATUS EXAMINATION

MICHAEL DANIEL AND TRACY CAROTHERS

The mental status examination (MSE) is an interview screening evaluation of the most important areas of a patient's emotional and cognitive functioning (Daniel & Crider, 2003). The MSE gives the clinician a structured framework by which to conduct the evaluation (Robinson, 2001) and arrive at a more reliable diagnosis or at least develop a working hypothesis about diagnosis. The MSE consists of observations of the patient's verbal and nonverbal behavior and the patient's report of subjective experience. Many authors note that the MSE is to psychiatric diagnosis what the physical examination is to medical diagnosis (Robinson, 2001). The MSE can be helpful in distinguishing between organic and functional disorders (Carlat, 2005; Robinson, 2001; Strub & Black, 2000).

The purpose of the MSE is to provide a framework for the comprehensive evaluation of mental functioning that increases objectivity and reliability of the data and subsequent diagnosis. It is important to develop a standardized approach for conducting an MSE that includes assessment of the critical domains described in this chapter. A standardized approach increases reliability of the MSE and should include the behavioral referents on which interpretations are based (Daniel & Crider, 2003; Hales & Yudofsky, 2004). According to Strub and Black (2000), standardization of the MSE increases the accuracy of identifying organic disorders and

describing the patient's current level of functioning. Although some MSE questions can be embedded in the initial intake interview with the patient, it also is important to administer the MSE in a hierarchical manner, evaluating basic functional abilities before assessing more complex abilities such as language and verbal reasoning. Straying from this approach increases the likelihood of misdiagnosis (Strub & Black, 2000).

Although a standardized approach is important for reliability of the MSE, it must be balanced with the flexibility necessary to create a comfort level for the patient that will produce valid data. The patient is most likely to feel at ease, and the clinician most likely to obtain valid data, if the MSE flows smoothly and has a conversational quality, especially at the beginning of the interview. It is important to convey a genuine sense of concern and empathy to the patient (Shader, 2003). In addition to rapport, environmental influences should be considered such as privacy (Shader, 2003); a patient may very well respond differently if assessed while lying on a gurney in a busy emergency room than she would in an office with the door closed.

Finally, ambiguous findings often are clarified with information obtained during the MSE in the context of a thorough psychosocial and psychiatric history. Remember, the MSE is a snapshot of the patient's current experience, and its significance is fully evident only with the perspective of the patient's history. Because the MSE is a picture of the patient's functioning at that moment, reevaluation may be necessary if there is a change in the patient's condition (Shader, 2003). In addition, it is essential to consider medical problems and medications as possible etiologic factors. General knowledge of the overlapping etiology of medical disorders and psychiatric symptoms along with accurate information about the patient's current medical status will prevent misdiagnosis that could have serious consequences (Daniel & Crider, 2003).

There are various ways of organizing the domains assessed during an MSE (e.g., see Daniel & Crider, 2003). The domains assessed vary slightly according to the purpose of the MSE (e.g., administered for psychiatric evaluation vs. neurologic evaluation). We first will discuss domains that are common to psychiatric and neurologic MSEs followed by a discussion of the unique components included in a neurologic MSE.

APPEARANCE

Appearance is what the patient looks like. A patient's appearance should be documented with sufficient detail so that another person could read the description and have a vivid picture of what the patient looks like (Hales & Yudofsky, 2004; Robinson, 2001). If the patient is evaluated again in the future, the initial documentation will provide valuable information about any change in appearance that may reflect a change in the patient's psychiatric status (Daniel & Crider, 2003). MSE references state that patient characteristics such as gender; height; weight; hair color, style, and quality; facial hair; facial expressions; eye movements and level of eye contact; tattoos; scars; grooming; cleanliness; jewelry; skin texture; actual and stated age; signs of intoxication; and physical limitations or disabilities should all be noted (Carlat, 2005; Daniel & Crider, 2003; Hales & Yudofsky, 2004; Robinson, 2001; Shader, 2003).

Appearance can also provide the clinician with clues to psychiatric diagnosis or level of functioning (Carlat, 2005; Robinson, 2001). A patient who enters the office wearing wrinkled clothing with holes, has matted, unkempt hair, and appears unbathed may be depressed or psychotic, whereas the patient who enters the office with endless energy, talking rapidly and wearing outrageous attire may be experiencing a manic episode. Other psychological disorders such as anorexia nervosa and trichotillomania may be suggested by emaciation and patches of missing hair, respectively (Robinson, 2001). Appearance can also provide the clinician with information about the patient's level of self-esteem and self-care (or lack thereof) and about whether the patient is attempting to make some type of personal statement, as is well illustrated by Carlat's (2005) example: "She wore a T-shirt with the slogan, 'Every day I'm forced to add one more name to the list of people who piss me off'" (p. 124).

Occasionally, appearance can provide the clinician with information about the possibility of organic disease. For example, a patient who enters the office with half of his face shaved or has not dressed appropriately on one side of his or her body is exhibiting signs of unilateral neglect (Strub & Black, 2000).

BEHAVIOR

Behavior is how the patient acts, verbally and nonverbally. Assessment of the patient's behavior is done throughout the MSE. Behavioral observations are a critical part of the MSE because specific behaviors often are representative of specific neurological disorders and therefore can assist the clinician in determining whether the patient has a psychiatric or organic dysfunction. *Level of consciousness* often is categorized under either *appearance* or *behavior*. Level of consciousness can be conceptualized on a continuum, from a low level of consciousness to hypervigilance. A patient is considered to have a normal level of consciousness if he or she is alert, responds appropriately to the interview, and is normally aware of internal and external stimuli (Strub & Black, 2000). A patient with a low level of consciousness has decreased alertness and may appear lethargic. A hypervigilant patient will appear restless, easily startled, and much attuned to what is happening in the room and in the surrounding environment (Daniel & Crider, 2003). *Acute confusional state* is readily identified through behavioral observation. These patients often are inattentive, and their conversations are inconsistent and confabulatory. Their level of consciousness fluctuates (Strub & Black, 2000). It is important for clinicians to be aware of these types of behaviors because they often represent acute medical problems (Strub & Black, 2000); they also may reflect acute psychotic conditions.

Robinson (2001) defines *mannerisms* as exaggerated behaviors that are socially appropriate but unusual. They are unique to the individual, and it is likely that the individual is unaware that he or she is engaging in the behavior. Mannerisms do not necessarily mean the patient has psychiatric illness; however, the presence of mannerisms should be considered in relation to the patient's history and other information gained from the MSE (Daniel & Crider, 2003). *Compulsions* are behaviors or mental acts that a patient feels compelled to repeatedly perform. Compulsive behavior usually is a way to reduce or prevent distress related to obsessive thoughts. Compulsions occur in obsessive-compulsive disorder and Tourette syndrome.

In addition to providing the clinician with information about possible psychiatric and organic disorders, the patient's behavior can significantly affect the results of the rest of the MSE (Strub & Black, 2000). For example, when the patient is confused, uncooperative, or having difficulty sitting still, it will be difficult to obtain meaningful data for many aspects of the MSE.

Motor Activity

Motor activity is the type and quality of the patient's movements. Astute observation of motor activity can play an important role in the differential diagnosis of psychological and neurological disorders. Whether or not the patient is experiencing decreased or increased motor activity and the specific qualities of the motor activity are essential in the differential diagnosis of organic and psychiatric disorders.

The terms *psychomotor retardation* (decreased motor activity), *akinesia* (absence of movement), *hypokinesia* (decreased movement), and *bradykinesia* (slowed movement) often are used interchangeably. However, *psychomotor retardation* is a term used to refer to decreased motor activity caused by a psychological condition (Robinson, 2001), whereas *akinesia, hypokinesia,* and *bradykinesia* are used to describe decreased movement caused by organic dysfunction. Subcortical disorders result in abnormal motor activity, including Parkinson disease, Huntington disease, progressive supranuclear palsy, and AIDS-related brain

deterioration. Decreased motor activity in patients with Parkinson disease is evidenced by difficulty initiating movements, rigidity in movements, and a shuffling gait. Psychomotor retardation sometimes is present in patients with psychological disorders such as schizophrenia, depression, and narcolepsy (Robinson, 2001). *Catatonia* is a form of psychomotor retardation in which a patient is immobile and does not respond to stimuli that would typically illicit a response. Catatonia is typically seen in patients with schizophrenia. Whereas a patient with catatonia cannot be easily moved, a patient with *catalepsy* (or *waxy flexibility*) is immobile but can assume a posture for a prolonged period of time.

Other patients present with increased motor activity, or *psychomotor agitation.* Agitation, or increased motor activity, is manifest as fidgeting and hand-wringing (Robinson, 2001). Psychomotor agitation can occur in anxiety disorders, agitated depression, manic episodes, and patients using stimulant drugs. Agitated motor activity is not a common symptom of neurological disease, although can occur in the acute period after a traumatic brain injury. Agitated motor activity also could be the result of medication or other substance use. *Akathisia* is increased motor activity such as fidgeting, rocking, and pacing that is typically the result of antipsychotic medication (Robinson, 2001). *Tardive dyskinesia* exclusively affects psychiatric patients and results from long-term use of dopamine antagonist medication. Tardive dyskinesia most commonly affects the muscles of the face, especially the lips and mouth, and appears as a writhing or tic-like movement. *Tremors* are involuntary movements that typically occur in the distal parts of the body (i.e., hands and feet). A resting tremor is common in patients with Parkinson disease and is often characterized as a pill-rolling tremor. Resting tremor generally stops when the patient begins to move. In contrast, intention tremor generally occurs during movement and disappears when the patient is at rest. Intention tremors can occur in patients with cerebellum damage. It is important to note that older adults often have tremors as a result of nonspecific infirmities of age. *Choreiform* movements are a wide variety of involuntary movements that have a rapid, highly complex and jerky quality; they are typical of Huntington disease. Often people with choreiform movement disorders are skillful at "finishing" the involuntary movement to make it look intentional and functional and thereby disguise its involuntary nature.

Tics are involuntary, stereotyped, sudden movements (e.g., blinking, head jerking, teeth grinding) or vocalizations (e.g., throat clearing, humming, clicking) and can be complex (Daniel & Crider, 2003; Robinson, 2001). *Echopraxia* (mimicking another person's movements) is a complex motor tic, and *palilalia* (patient's repetition of his or her own words), *echolalia* (patient's repetition of others' words), and *coprolalia* (patient saying profanity or obscenities) are complex vocal tics. Patients who experience tics may not express them during the MSE because they typically occur in response to increased discomfort or distress (Robinson, 2001). Tics can occur in "normal" people, and if tics are present they should be considered with findings in other aspects of the MSE.

ORIENTATION

Orientation is awareness of personal identity, current location, time, and present circumstances. The majority of patients are oriented in all these spheres, although it is not unusual for a patient to be off on the date (Carlat, 2005; Daniel & Crider, 2003). Patients who fail in one of these areas often have some form of brain dysfunction (e.g., delirium or dementia). Disorientation is rare in patients with psychological disorders, except those with the most severe disturbance (Daniel & Crider, 2003).

In most cases the patient's orientation to person, location, and circumstances can be determined within the first few minutes. It is likely that the patient will tell you his or her name after you introduce yourself and indicate whether he or she is oriented to location and circumstances after you make a general inquiry such as "What led up to you being here?" Information regarding date can be obtained by asking the patient to write his or her name and the date on a piece of paper when doing visual memory testing. If the clinician is still unsure of the patient's orientation he or she should directly question the patient ("Where are you right now?" or "What is the date?"). Any dimensions to which the patient is not spontaneously oriented should be assessed with simple multiple choices: "Are you in a doctor's office, hospital, or clinic?" Or for more disoriented patients: "Are you in a church, hospital, or school?" The patient who responds correctly to multiple-choice items is better oriented than one who does not.

ATTITUDE

Attitude is how the patient feels and what he or she thinks about participating in the MSE. In addition to verbal statements, attitude is revealed through facial expressions, posture, and eye contact. A patient's attitude may change during the MSE (Carlat, 2005) depending on the topic at hand. It is important to take note of any shifts in attitude during the MSE (Hales & Yudofsky, 2004), the behaviors that typify the change, and the topic that accompanied it. Of course, attending to the patient's attitude, willingness to participate, and interpersonal behavior during the MSE is important in order to obtain valid results. Fortunately, many patients are cooperative throughout the MSE, and they are described as *cooperative, responsive,* and *open.*

However, some patients are *guarded or suspicious,* reluctant to answer questions for fear that the information they provide will be the basis for bias against them in the hospital, in the clinic, or by the doctor. Other patients may be *hostile* because they are angry about whatever circumstances led to their referral for an MSE; often they feel they have no problems and view their referral for an MSE as part of a malicious plot against them or the failure of others to understand their circumstances. *Passive* patients do not volunteer information; when they are asked questions, their answers are incomplete and unelaborated.

The patient's attitude may shed light on various disorders or the patient's current level of functioning. Patients with certain types of personality disorders and those seeking to gain something from the results of the MSE may be manipulative or evince feeling of entitlement. Those who have had contact with multiple mental health providers may be wary or distrustful. Patients in severe distress or pain may be preoccupied.

SPEECH AND LANGUAGE

Language is the use of symbols to communicate. *Speech,* one of four general modes of language, is what the patient says and the quality of how he or she talks. The patient's speech must be assessed before the patient's thought process or the content of thought because the primary way to obtain information about these areas, and other areas of cognitive functioning, is through speech (Carlat, 2005; Strub & Black, 2000). A patient's speech can also provide the clinician with information about current emotional state (Shader, 2003). If the patient has no obvious impairments in language, as evidenced by his or her ability to understand the examiner and respond appropriately during the examination, no further language evaluation is needed. However, if speech impairment is present, the clinician needs to determine whether the impairment is caused by psychological or organic dysfunction.

Only a brief overview of language functioning is possible here; refer to Strub and Black (2000) for a more detailed description of language. From a cognitive perspective, language generally is divided into four domains, as illustrated in Table 5.1. *Aphasia* is impairment of language caused by brain damage and is broadly classified into two general syndromes: nonfluent, mostly associated with frontal brain damage, and fluent, mostly associated with temporoparietal damage. *Nonfluent aphasia* is characterized by slow, labored, halting speech with difficulty saying words. Auditory-verbal comprehension is less affected, but often there are comprehension deficits for statements when the grammatical structure is important in conveying the meaning (e.g., distinguishing between "the child called for her mother," "the mother called for her child," and "the mother was called by her child"). *Fluent aphasia* is characterized by impaired auditory-verbal comprehension and speech that generally is normal in rhythm, intonation, and quantity but is a meaningless mix of nonsense words (*neologisms* or *jargon*) and real words. For the most part, nonfluent aphasics are aware of their language deficits, whereas fluent aphasics are not. Reading and writing deficits are associated with both types of aphasia. *Dysnomia*, or word retrieval deficit, is a common symptom of most aphasia syndromes. When cerebrovascular accident is the cause of aphasia, it often produces symptoms of both syndromes; aphasia also can result from head injury and dementia. For the most part, speech deficits are apparent in conversation. If it appears the patient is experiencing subtle word-finding problems unrelated to psychiatric disturbance, referral for neuropsychological or speech pathology evaluation is indicated. If the patient gives unreliable or incoherent answers to questions, comprehension may be at issue and can be tested at a basic level. Place three or four common items in front of the patient (e.g., a pen, cup, book, and key) and say "I want to make sure you can understand what I'm saying, so I'm going to ask you to do some things with these objects on the table. Point to the ____," completing the statement with each item in turn. If the patient is successful at this level, then give three or four instructions that include two or more objects (e.g., "Put the pen in the cup," "Put the key on top of the book," or "Put the cup between the pen and key."). You can also use prompts such as "Show me the one you use to unlock a door." Anything other than perfect performance indicates that the patient is not reliably processing language, and it is important to determine whether it represents a neurological or psychiatric problem. The patient who passes this simple comprehension screening but still appears to have comprehension deficits that appear unrelated to psychiatric disturbance should be referred for a more comprehensive evaluation. *Dysarthria* is distorted pronunciation caused by impaired neuromuscular control of oral and facial muscles and results from a number of developmental disorders and acquired brain injury. Organic disorders can be differentiated from psychiatric disorders if characteristics of speech deficits are noted and explored in more detail (e.g., age of onset, duration).

The quality of a patient's speech should always be noted because it can provide information about possible psychiatric diagnoses. For example, manics often interrupt or respond without pause with rapid, pressured speech that parallels racing thoughts. Significantly depressed patients have slow speech of low volume, little variation in intonation, increased response latencies, and little initiation; the speech of some schizophrenics has the same qualities but often has bizarre content.

Table 5.1	Broad Domains of Language	
	Receptive	*Expressive*
Auditory	Auditory-verbal comprehension	Speech
Visual	Reading	Writing

SOURCE: From Daniel, M. & Crider, C. "Mental status evaluation." In Michel Hersen & Samuel Turner (Eds.), *Diagnostic Interviewing*, Third Edition. Copyright © 2003, New York: Kluwer Academic/Plenum Publishers. Used with kind permission of Springer Science and Business Media.

MOOD AND AFFECT

Affect and mood are the key features of many emotional disorders. *Mood* is the internal emotional state of the patient and generally is considered more stable over time, changing over days and weeks. Assessment of mood is subjective because it is often based solely on patient report (Robinson, 2001; Shader, 2003). *Affect* is the patient's external expression of emotional state, is influenced by context, and may change from moment to moment. Assessment of affect is somewhat more objective because it is observable by others (Shader, 2003). Although mood and affect typically are in concordance, some people (typically those with psychiatric disorders) experience discordant mood and affect.

The term *euthymic* is used to describe normal mood. According to Robinson (2001), abnormal mood can be categorized into four types: dysphoric, euphoric, angry or irritable, and apprehensive. *Dysphoria* occurs when a patient feels sad or depressed. Dysphoric mood is the primary feature of depressive disorders; however, it can also be seen in bipolar disorders, anxiety disorders, and personality disorders. Dysphoric mood can also occur as a response to a major life event (e.g., the death of a loved one) or in reaction to current medical status (e.g., diagnosis of cancer). *Euphoria* is extreme elation and happiness. Patients experiencing euphoria do not come to the attention of clinicians as often as those with dysphoric mood; however, euphoria is common in some psychiatric disorders such as schizophrenia, when patients are experiencing a manic episode, or during a substance-induced state. *Angry* or *irritable* mood can occur in patients who are experiencing a manic episode, are depressed, or have anxiety disorders or personality disorders. For patients with organic disorders, angry or irritable mood can be seen in patients with dementia and prefrontal lobe dysfunction. Angry mood is expressed through belligerence, confrontation, and opposition. There are many reasons why a patient may appear anxious during the MSE; however, when anxiety is accompanied by worry, dread, and fear that interfere with daily functioning, this reflects *apprehensive* mood. Apprehension is common in anxiety disorders and can also occur in depression, paranoia, and certain medical conditions. An extreme form of apprehension is *panic attack*, in which the patient experiences sweating, rapid heartbeat, chest pain, and a feeling of impending death.

Because affect is determined through observation of the patient's behavior, the clinician needs to record verbal as well as nonverbal emotional expression. Behaviors such as crying, yelling, laughing, smiling, and grimacing, tone of voice, posture, and hand gestures all define affect (Daniel & Crider, 2003). As with mood, the primary characterization of affect is type. Authors differ in the various ways to describe affect (Carlat, 2005; Daniel & Crider, 2003; Robinson, 2001; Shader, 2003). Examples of adjectives used to describe affect are *anxious, worried, tense, sad, depressed, happy, bright, bitter, defensive, indifferent, distant, apathetic,* and *disgusted.*

Once type has been determined, other qualities of affect should be assessed. Carlat (2005) describes four qualities of affect: stability, appropriateness, range, and intensity. *Stability* is how modulated and steady affect is. It is normal to have variability in affect within an MSE; however, extreme and rapid changes in affect, or *lability,* are associated with psychological and neurological disorders. Patients suffering from mania, personality disorders such as borderline personality or histrionic personality, or dementia and those with right hemisphere cerebrovascular accident may present with labile affect (Carlat, 2005; Daniel & Crider, 2003; Robinson, 2001). *Appropriateness* is how well the patient's affect matches the topic he or she is discussing (Daniel & Crider, 2003). Affect is classified as *congruent,* meaning the patient's emotional expression is in accord with reported mood, or *incongruent,* meaning the patient's emotional expression is discordant with reported mood. For example, affect would be considered congruent for the patient who cries when talking about a traumatic experience, whereas affect would be considered incongruent if the same patient laughed while talking about the traumatic event. *Range* is the breadth of emotional expression. As with stability, it is normal for a patient to show variability in affect throughout the MSE. However, if the patient has a *restricted or constricted* affect—that is, shows little variability in the type of affect expressed—he or she may be suffering from a psychiatric disorder such as a mood disorder, schizophrenia, or obsessive-compulsive disorder (Carlat, 2005; Robinson, 2001) or may be manifesting the effects of brain injury. *Intensity* is the strength or magnitude of an emotional response. Affective intensity can be thought of as falling along a continuum from low to high (Robinson, 2001), with normal intensity, usually described as *animated,* in the middle. Someone with animated affect typically responds to situations in a fashion similar to the "average person" (Daniel & Crider, 2003). Patients on the low end of the continuum have little emotional expression and have *blunted* or *flat* affect. Flat affect is seen in patients with schizophrenia, obsessive-compulsive disorder, prefrontal lobe damage, and Parkinson disease. Patients on the high end of the intensity continuum have *exaggerated* affective responses. Patients with anxiety disorders, mania, and histrionic, narcissistic, and borderline personalities often experience exaggerated affect (Carlat, 2005; Daniel & Crider, 2003; Robinson, 2001).

Thought and Perception

Thought is the internal dialogue that occurs in the patient's mind. *Perception* is the patient's process of recognizing and understanding external events and circumstances (Robinson, 2001). It is essential that the patient's speech and language skills be assessed before thought and perception are evaluated because they can only be inferred from what the patient says. If a patient has logical thoughts, expresses them in an organized manner, and is realistic when interpreting events, he or she does not have a thought or perception disorder. Thought and perception disturbances are the hallmark of psychosis; however, they can be present in severe mania and depression (Daniel & Crider, 2003). Open-ended questions give more opportunity for subtle thought disorders to manifest (Shader, 2003).

Most references on MSE distinguish two aspects of thought: process and content. *Thought process* is how a patient forms and organizes thoughts (Robinson, 2001). Although sometimes it is not clear whether a patient's thought process is normal, certain types of thought processes are considered disordered. *Circumstantiality* is the mildest form of thought disorder and can often be seen in normal people (Carlat, 2005). When circumstantial, the patient provides very detailed, overelaborative responses that eventually get to the point and are generally relevant to the content of the discussion (Robinson, 2001).

Circumstantiality may reflect normal conversation style, obsessive thinking, anxiety, or below-average intelligence and is described clinically in patients who suffer from dementia and temporal lobe epilepsy (Carlat, 2005; Robinson, 2001). *Tangentiality* is thought that strays from the topic at hand and never returns; speech is understandable and thoughts usually are logical, but they are not relevant (Carlat, 2005; Robinson, 2001). *Flight of ideas* is rapid speech that changes quickly from one topic to another. The patient's ideas are somewhat logical, and the ideas usually are associated to one another. Flight of ideas is manifest in mania as pressured speech and can also appear in patients with psychotic disorders (Robinson, 2001). *Loose associations* (also called *thought derailment*) are thoughts that have no logical association, although sentences remain grammatically correct. Loose associations are seen in patients with schizophrenia (Robinson, 2001). *Word salad* is the most extreme form of thought process disturbance. There is no logical association between words, although prosody of speech and word articulation are intact (Robinson, 2001). *Neologisms* are made-up words and are common in fluent aphasia and psychotic speech; therefore, differential diagnosis of thought disorder and fluent aphasia should be considered when neologisms are present (Carlat, 2005; Daniel & Crider, 2003; Robinson, 2001).

Thought blocking is another type of thought disturbance. Thought blocking occurs when the patient loses his or her train of thought in mid-sentence. When patients return to talking, they have changed subjects and do not remember what they were talking about before the interruption. *Perseveration* is the repetition of a word, phrase, or idea resulting from failure to properly inhibit and cease a response when it no longer is appropriate. At extreme levels, the patient may repeat the same word or phrase in a mechanical and rote manner, relevant or not, regardless of redirecting prompts; this typically occurs in psychotic and severely brain-damaged patients. At a less severe level, the patient may perseverate on a topic or idea that continually intrudes despite change of topic; this may be associated with psychosis or obsessive-compulsive disorder (Daniel & Crider, 2003). *Clang associations* are the production of words or phrases based on rhyming sound (Daniel & Crider, 2003). *Echolalia* occurs when a patient repeats what he or she hears another person say. Echolalia can occur in aphasia, psychotic disorders, and dementia (Daniel & Crider, 2003; Robinson, 2001).

As noted earlier, many features of thought disorder can be seen in aphasia and other medical conditions as well as psychosis. In order to distinguish aphasia from thought disorder, a clinician could ask the patient to read a passage from a book, write a paragraph, or repeat a phase because thought disorders typically do not interfere with these mental processes (Robinson, 2001).

Thought content is what the patient thinks about, as reflected in what he or she talks about. Thought content is assessed as soon as the interview begins. What the patient chooses to talk about at the beginning of the interview may give the clinician an idea of what is important to the patient (Robinson, 2001). *Obsessions* "are persistent ideas, thoughts, impulses, or images that are experienced as intrusive and inappropriate and that cause marked anxiety or distress" (American Psychiatric Association, 2000, p. 457). Common obsessions include fear of contamination, a need for order, consistent repeated doubt about the completion of an important task, sexual imagery, and aggressive impulses. Obsessions often are accompanied by compulsions, which are actions performed by the patient as a way to reduce the anxiety he or she has about the obsession. Common compulsions include washing, checking, and ordering.

The best way to find out whether a patient is experiencing obsessions is to ask about them. Robinson (2001) suggests using the following questions to elicit whether the patient has obsessive thoughts: "Do you experience repetitive thoughts that you can't stop?" "Do they feel like your own thoughts?" "Are you forced to think something against your will?" or "Do you have intrusive thoughts about . . . (contamination, hurting someone, having to count something, etc.)?" (p. 200).

A *phobia* is a fear of an object or situation that is not threatening; however, when encountered by the patient it causes severe distress and anxiety (Daniel & Crider, 2003). Often, the patient is aware that his or her fear and anxiety is irrational (i.e., ego-dystonic), but the patient still goes to great lengths to avoid the situation or object. There are many different types of phobias; however, we will briefly discuss only three types. *Social phobia* is diagnosed when a patient avoids public places or social functions for fear of being humiliated or embarrassed. This fear is so great that it impairs social or occupational functioning. *Specific phobia* is an irrational fear of a specific object or situation (e.g., spiders, snakes, bridges, driving, flying). *Agoraphobia* is fear of open or public places, based on the fear that the person may not be able to escape the situation and may have a *panic attack* (Daniel & Crider, 2003). Agoraphobia often causes patients to restrict themselves to home.

One of the critical areas of the MSE is assessment of *suicidal* or *homicidal ideation* because this represents one of the major areas of risk for the patient, others the patient comes in contact with, and the clinician (i.e., liability) (Carlat, 2005; Daniel & Crider, 2003). Presence or absence of suicidal or homicidal ideation or intent should always be documented in the MSE report. It is often difficult for new clinicians to broach the topic of suicide with patients. However, suicidal ideation is common among patients suffering from depression. The patient may feel a sense of relief that the clinician asked about suicide and, as a result, feel more open to discussing it with the clinician (Carlat, 2005). The first step is to ask about suicidal thoughts (e.g., "Sometimes when people are depressed and feeling down they have thoughts of harming themselves. Do you ever feel this way?"). If the patient admits having these thoughts, it is important to determine whether the patient actually has a plan or whether the patient has merely passive thoughts (Carlat, 2005; Daniel & Crider, 2003). Ask whether the patient has a plan, what the plan is (noting the extent of detail and lethality of method), whether the patient has means to execute the plan (e.g., access to a weapon or lethal medication), and whether the patient has done anything to initiate the plan (e.g., written a letter to his or her family, written a will) (Daniel & Crider, 2003). Other risk factors to assess are age (i.e., older people are at higher risk for suicide), gender (i.e., males are more likely to commit suicide), past suicide attempts, presence of a mental illness (i.e., mood disorder, schizophrenia, personality disorder, or anxiety disorder), and alcohol or drug abuse (Daniel & Crider, 2003; Robinson, 2001).

Homicidal ideation or thoughts of assaulting someone do not need to be assessed in every patient; however, the clinician should ask about homicidal ideation when a patient talks about being angry or hostile toward someone in particular (Carlat, 2005). Homicidal ideation can be assessed with the same basic approach used for evaluating suicidal ideation. Patients with anti-social personalities, paranoid ideation, substance abuse, or a history of violence are most likely to plan violence (Carlat, 2005; Daniel & Crider, 2003). (See Robinson, 2001, for a thorough review of assessment of suicidal and homicidal patients.)

Perception is the patient's interpretation of external events and circumstances; delusions are impairments in this interpretation. *Delusions* are "false beliefs that are not corrected by an appeal to reason or by contradictory evidence" (Shader, 2003, p. 14). Delusions range from plausible (the police are following me) to bizarre (the doctor has placed an electronic chip in me so the police can track where I go). They also vary in their organization and stability over time. Patients can have many delusions that are either highly interrelated (i.e., they are systematized) or have little connectedness (i.e., they are nonsystem-atized) (Daniel & Crider, 2003; Robinson, 2001). It is essential that the clinician be aware of cul-tural factors that could influence a patient's thought content. Also, it is important to deter-mine whether the irrational belief is consistent or whether the patient changes his or her beliefs during the interview; if the latter happens, then the thought does not qualify as a delusion. Shader (2003) recommends that clinicians use the following questions when they suspect delu-sional thoughts but need to probe further: "Do you feel that anyone has it in for you or that you are being watched?" "Do you ever feel someone else is controlling your mind or your thoughts?" "Do you have experiences that you don't think you could easily explain to others?" or "Do you feel you have special powers or that you are des-tined for a special role or job?" (p. 15).

There are many different types of delusions. *Paranoid delusions,* especially *persecutory* ones, are the most common in psychiatric patients (Daniel & Crider, 2003; Robinson, 2001). Common themes are that the patient is being monitored, followed, or poisoned or that his or her personal possessions are being stolen (Robinson, 2001). Patients with this type of delusion often spend large amounts of time trying to confirm whatever they suspect is happening (Robinson, 2001). *Grandiose delusions* are irrational beliefs that the patient has exceptional skills, status, or posi-tion. These patients often claim that they have some special power or privilege and that they are

confidants of prominent people (Daniel & Crider, 2003). Delusions of grandeur are common in patients who have been diagnosed with schizo-phrenia or are experiencing a manic episode (Robinson, 2001). *Somatic delusions* relate to physical symptoms and medical problems. In less severe forms, these delusions are plausible symp-toms, and it is important to rule out medical dis-orders. Patients who have been diagnosed with depression or schizophrenia or are experiencing alcohol or cocaine withdrawal commonly have somatic delusions (Robinson, 2001). *Ideas of refer-ence* are delusions that some unrelated thing is sending special and specific messages to the patient. Most commonly this involves the media (i.e., television or newspaper). *Delusional jealousy* is an unfounded belief that one's partner is unfaithful. *Erotomanic* delusions occur when the patient believes that someone, usually a famous person, is in love with him or her. These patients often spend a great deal of time attempting to have direct contact with the famous person, some-times with tragic consequences (Daniel & Crider, 2003; Robinson, 2001).

Auditory hallucinations occur most often in psychiatric patients, especially those with schiz-ophrenia. They usually consist of hearing voices but can include sounds other than voices and may include a voice calling their name, using full sentences, and saying derogatory things about the patient (Daniel & Crider, 2003; Robinson, 2001). There are different types of auditory hal-lucinations: *command hallucinations* (hearing a voice that gives an instruction), *audible thoughts* (hearing their own thoughts as if they were spo-ken out loud for everyone to hear), *voices argu-ing or discussing* (hallucinatory voices arguing about the patient), and *running commentary* (comments about the patient regarding an ongoing activity) (Robinson, 2001).

Visual hallucinations occur among psychiatric patients; however, they more often represent neurological dysfunction. *Olfactory* and *gustatory hallucinations* are more likely to be related to neurological dysfunction, especially temporal lobe epilepsy and dysfunction of the limbic system or frontal lobes (Daniel & Crider, 2003; Robinson, 2001). *Tactile hallucinations* such as insects crawl-ing on the skin are also common with neurologi-cal dysfunction, especially alcohol or drug withdrawal (Daniel & Crider, 2003; Robinson, 2001). *Hypnagogic* and *hypnopompic hallucina-tions* occur when the patient is either falling asleep or waking from sleep. These hallucinations occur when the patient is experiencing sleep paralysis and dreaming while he or she is awake. Some normal people experience these types of hallucinations, and often they do not represent a psychiatric problem (Daniel & Crider, 2003; Robinson, 2001). Hypnagogic and hypnopompic hallucinations are associated with narcolepsy (Hales & Yudofsky, 2004; Robinson, 2001). Unformed and short-lived hallucinations such as flashes of light, ringing, buzzing, and faint odors or tastes are more likely to be related to neurologic dysfunction than to a psychiatric condition (Daniel & Crider, 2003; Robinson, 2001).

Depersonalizations are patients' feelings that they are not themselves. The patient may report feeling strange, as though outside his or her body and watching what is occurring. Depersonalization is a common experience among patients with psychiatric disorders, especially those who have experienced a traumatic event. *Derealization* is a patient's feeling that the environment has changed in some way and, as a result, feels strange or foreign. Derealization can be seen in patients with schizophrenia (Hales & Yudofsky, 2004; Robinson, 2001). Clinicians should be aware that although these perceptual disorders are common in some psychiatric disorders, some normal people also have these experiences (Robinson, 2001).

INSIGHT AND JUDGMENT

Insight is the patient's level of awareness regarding his or her disorder and the ability to think about the cause of the illness in a reasonable manner (Hales & Yudofsky, 2004; Robinson, 2001). Level of insight can provide some indication of the patient's potential to benefit from psychological treatment. Although insight usually is assessed throughout the MSE, what the patient says at the beginning of the MSE when allowed to talk about what brought him or her to the occasion of the MSE is especially informative. Carlat (2005) suggests asking the patient questions such as "What do you think needs to happen for your life to improve?" or "Why do you think you've been having these problems?" (p. 140). The patient's ability or inability to understand he or she has a problem usually is apparent with direct questioning. If the clinician prefers to use more objective measures, insight questionnaires can be used (see Robinson, 2001, for more information).

Judgment is the ability to make and execute good decisions. Making good decisions entails identifying and weighing essential information, making a rational decision, and acting on that decision in an appropriate manner (Daniel & Crider, 2003; Hales & Yudofsky, 2004; Robinson, 2001). Poor judgment may result from limited cognitive ability or inability to effectively apply rational decisions when confronted with everyday circumstances. Most patients who are seen for an MSE have impaired judgment to some degree. Often, clinicians assess judgment by asking patients how they would solve a common, everyday problem (e.g., "What would you do if you found a stamped envelope on the ground?"). However, this type of questioning often does not provide a reliable indication of the patient's judgment (Carlat, 2005; Daniel & Crider, 2003; Robinson, 2001). The clinician is more likely to get an accurate measure of a patient's ability to make good judgments by asking questions that actually pertain to the patient (e.g., "Are you planning to go back home?" after the patient has been physically abused yet again by a spouse). Also, it is important to consider the patient's past behavior as an indication of his or her judgment (Daniel & Crider, 2003).

Impaired insight and judgment are common among patients with psychiatric disorders. Impaired insight can be seen in patients with schizophrenia, patients experiencing a manic episode, and those with histrionic or borderline personality disorders. In addition to patients with psychiatric disorders, patients with neurological dysfunction such as right hemisphere cerebrovascular accident, traumatic brain injury, and dementia often have little insight regarding their illness (Daniel & Crider, 2003).

ATTENTION AND CONCENTRATION

Attention is "the patient's ability to attend to a specific stimulus without being distracted by extraneous internal or environmental stimuli" (Strub & Black, 2000, p. 40). *Concentration* requires that a patient attend to information over a longer period of time. *Working memory* involves manipulating and processing the contents of what is attended to. References on MSE typically use only the terms *attention* and *concentration;* however, ability to attend to information is critical for more complex cognitive abilities such as language comprehension, visuospatial processing, and memory. If attention is impaired, it is likely that other cognitive abilities also are impaired, and the results of the MSE may be somewhat skewed by attention problems (Robinson, 2001). Observing the patient and asking some simple questions is a first step in determining whether the patient is attending to what is going on during the MSE. Is the patient able to sit and focus on the conversation, or is he or she looking around the room and asking the clinician to repeat questions (Carlat, 2005; Robinson, 2001)?

More formal testing can also be used to assess the patient's level of attention and concentration. Probably the most common test of attention is the digit span test; however, it is not useful with patients who have language disorders because it will be confounded by their verbal deficits (Daniel & Crider, 2003; Robinson, 2001; Strub & Black, 2000). Patients are tested using both forward and backward span; the latter requires the patient to rehearse numbers while manipulating them, making it more sensitive to attention problems. Tell the patient, "I am going to say some numbers, and after I'm finished your job is to say the numbers back to me in the same order I said them." The numbers are presented at the rate of one per second. Most patients will be able to start with three digits. After the digits forward task is complete, say, "I am going to say some more numbers; this time, when I'm finished your job is to say them backward." Again, present the numbers at a rate of one per second. See Table 5.2 for average performance for different age groups.

Commonly used tests of concentration include asking the patient to spell a word backward and the serial seven subtraction test. Passing the former does not rule out a concentration problem, but failing it demonstrates one.

The latter test requires the patient to start at a specified number (usually 100) and subtract by sevens. Other versions of this test have been used (e.g., serial subtraction by threes or adding by a specific number). Although this test appears to be useful with patients, keep in mind that as many as 58% of normal people make some errors on these types of tasks (Robinson, 2001; Shader, 2003; Strub & Black, 2000).

Many psychological and neurological disorders are associated with impairment in attention and concentration. Depression, anxiety, somatoform disorder, and psychotic disorders all can influence a patient's performance on attention and concentration tests. Neurological dysfunctions such as right hemisphere cerebrovascular accident, cortical and subcortical dementias, and delirium cause deficits in attention and concentration (Daniel & Crider, 2003; Robinson, 2001). Patients with attention-deficit/hyperactivity disorder (ADHD) often perform these short attention and concentration tasks adequately. ADHD can be diagnosed with a thorough history and neuropsychological testing. When one is testing a patient's attention and concentration, it is also important to consider the influence of current medications (Robinson, 2001).

MEMORY

Memory is a complex cognitive ability that involves storing information in the brain and recalling or recognizing it later (Daniel & Crider, 2003; Strub & Black, 2000). Intact attention and concentration are necessary for effective memory. In order to create new memories the patient must first attend to a stimulus, encode information about the stimulus, retain and store the information, and later retrieve the information from memory (Robinson, 2001). For purposes of the MSE, we divide memory into *remote, recent, immediate,* and *delayed.* The first two are recall of events from many years and a few days to months ago, respectively; the latter two are the types of memory evaluated by MSE cognitive tests.

Evaluation of remote and recent memory is obtained when one is taking a history of recent events and psychosocial background. Key aspects of this information are verified (e.g., by family) to determine the reliability of memory is these areas. Immediate and delayed memory can be evaluated

Table 5.2	Average Digit Span Performance by Age		
Age	*20–64*	*65–69*	*70–89*
Digits forward	6–8	6–8	6–7
Digits backward	5–7	5–6	4–5

SOURCE: Adapted from the Wechsler Memory Scale III (Wechsler, 1997).

using the three-object recall (Carlat, 2005; Daniel & Crider, 2003; Robinson, 2001). The clinician tells the patient, "I am going to say three words, and I want you to remember them" (e.g., *screwdriver, compassion, brown*). The patient's comprehension of the words is verified by his or her accurate repetition of all three. Although many references on MSE only mention testing auditory-verbal memory, it is important to also test visual-graphic memory (Daniel & Crider, 2003). Have the patient copy three figures; we use those in Figure 5.1.

Tell the patient you will ask him or her to draw the figures again later from memory. Continue the MSE for 20 minutes, keeping the patient engaged with other activities to ensure that he or she is not rehearsing the words or figures. Then ask the patient to recall the words. For any words not spontaneously recalled, give a cue: "One of the words was a tool [feeling, color]." If the word is not recalled with the cue, give multiple-choice recognition: "Was the word *pliers, wrench,* or *screwdriver* [*frustration, compassion,* or *admiration; brown, black,* or *gray*]?" Then ask the patient to draw the three figures again. For any figures not spontaneously recalled, horizontally present the target figure with the foils in Figure 5.2 for multiple-choice recognition; be sure that the target figure appears in a different position (i.e., first, second, or third) for each trial.

Almost all normal people under the age of 70 will remember all three words immediately; people over 70 may spontaneously remember only two and should at least recognize the third in multiple-choice format. Almost everyone under age 60 will remember all three figures. Ability to recall and draw figures after a delay declines steadily after 60, and many normal people in their 70s and 80s will recall only one or two of the drawings; however, most people older than 60 will recognize the figures in multiple-choice format that they do not recall spontaneously. Poor memory performance can vary depending on whether psychological or organic dysfunction is involved. As a rule, patients with psychological disorders often do better on cued or recognition memory than on uncued recall; however, this pattern also is characteristic of subcortical disorders. In contrast, patients with neurological disorders such as traumatic brain injury, cerebrovascular accident, and cortical dementia do not do well on delayed or cued recall; patients with severe brain damage (e.g., advanced stages of cortical dementia) probably will be impaired in all aspects of memory. When patients with mood or anxiety disorders show deficits on memory tests, their difficulty probably is secondary to psychological disturbance and not a result of a true memory deficit. Impaired remote or recent memory with mostly intact immediate and delayed memory is almost always associated with psychological disturbance, including dissociative disorder and malingering. The possibility of malingering should always be considered when there is the

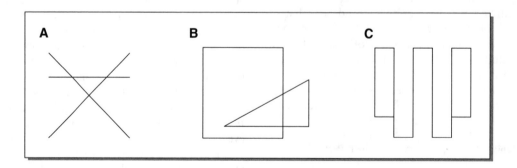

Figure 5.1   Figures for Memory Test

SOURCE: From Daniel, M. & Crider, C. "Mental status evaluation." In Michel Hersen & Samuel Turner (Eds.), *Diagnostic Interviewing*, Third Edition. Copyright © 2003, New York: Kluwer Academic/Plenum Publishers. Used with kind permission of Springer Science and Business Media.

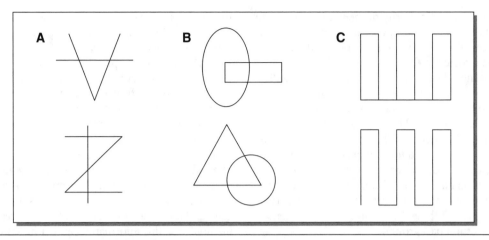

Figure 5.2   Multiple-Choice Figures for Figure Recognition

SOURCE: From Daniel, M. & Crider, C. "Mental status evaluation." In Michel Hersen & Samuel Turner (Eds.), *Diagnostic Interviewing*, Third Edition. Copyright © 2003, New York: Kluwer Academic/Plenum Publishers. Used with kind permission of Springer Science and Business Media.

opportunity for secondary gain. If memory dysfunction is apparent during the MSE or if the clinician is unsure about the patient's memory ability, referral should be made for neuropsychological evaluation.

INTELLECTUAL ABILITY

Intelligence is the patient's overall level of cognitive ability relative to others his or her age and can be only grossly estimated in an MSE. Typically, level of education is the best indicator of intelligence. However, if the patient has limited education but has been successful in a demanding career, it is likely that his or her occupational status is a better indicator of intellectual ability than educational attainment. For example, if the patient dropped out of school in the 11th grade but runs a successful computer consulting business, it is likely that his or her intellectual abilities are higher than his or her education would predict (Daniel & Crider, 2003). In the MSE the patient's use of vocabulary, ability to give concise but thorough answers, and ability to independently comprehend the implications of statements are indications of intellectual level. If an accurate measurement of intelligence or abstract thinking ability is needed, the patient should be referred for neuropsychological evaluation.

ABSTRACT THINKING

Abstraction is the capacity to recognize and comprehend relationships that are not immediately or concretely apparent. All MSE references recommend that abstraction be tested using two tests: similarities and proverb interpretation (Daniel & Crider, 2003; Hales & Yudofsky, 2004; Robinson, 2001; Strub & Black, 2000). The similarities test is administered by asking the patient how two objects or items are alike (e.g., "How are a couch and a chair alike?"). Items increase in difficulty as the test is administered. Patient responses are classified as correctly abstract, correct but concrete, or incorrect. Proverb interpretation entails asking the patient to explain an abstract general meaning of a concrete statement. Proverbs also are administered in ascending difficulty (e.g., "What does this saying mean?"). Responses are scored along the same continuum as similarities. For both similarities and proverb interpretation, patients of low education and low occupational status are expected to get only the simplest items correct. Patients with a high school education and average occupational attainment should get the majority of the items correct. If a patient with advanced education and high occupational success only answers two or three of the items correctly, the possibility of brain dysfunction should be considered (Strub & Black, 2000).

Both proverb interpretation and similarities require that, in addition to abstract ability, the patient has general knowledge of the terms used in the test questions. These test items can be culturally biased, and it is important to be aware of the cultural limitations of such tests (Robinson, 2001; Shader, 2003). Shader suggests use of the following "bias-free" proverbs, but interpretation even of these appears likely to be influenced by cultural background.

"What goes around comes around."

"Don't judge a book by its cover."

"People who live in glass houses shouldn't throw stones."

"The bigger they are, the harder they fall."

Neurological MSE

Although both psychiatric and neurological MSEs generally include the areas outlined in this chapter, there are important differences. The diagnostic focus of each is different (psychological vs. neurocognitive disorders). The MSE often attempts to distinguish between the two or identify the comorbidity of them. Given the neurological MSE's focus on neurological disorders, it includes assessment of motor and sensory processing as well as a more in-depth evaluation of higher-level cognitive functions in areas such as constructional ability, calculations, abstraction, reasoning, and problem solving. Evaluation of these areas of cognitive functioning is essential because although the patient may appear to be functioning adequately on other aspects of the MSE, he or she may not perform adequately on tasks that require the use of higher-level cognitive abilities. These abilities are more sensitive to the effects of brain damage, and deficits in these areas may be the first signs of brain dysfunction (Strub & Black, 2000).

Dysfunction of motor processing is seen in *apraxia,* impairment in selecting, planning, and performing well-learned movements (Strub & Black, 2000). *Agnosia* is dysfunction of perception

that impairs the patient's ability to recognize an object or information that is presented in a certain modality (i.e., visual, tactile, auditory). Apraxia and agnosia appear in a various forms, necessitating a variety of assessment techniques. *Constructional ability* involves visually perceiving an object, recognizing the parts of the object, and integrating those parts (Strub & Black, 2000). Tasks of constructional ability typically involve motor integration. Constructional abilities can be assessed using a variety of tests ranging from copying a figure to three-dimensional block construction. *Calculation ability* involves having general knowledge of mathematical concepts, manipulating this information, and, if in written form, perceiving the numbers and signs and spatially aligning written problems (Strub & Black, 2000). Assessment of a patient's ability to calculate often is broken down into different components in order to determine the exact nature of dysfunction. See Strub and Black (2000) for information about specific tests and scoring criteria in these areas. As noted earlier, it is important to assess language ability, attention, and memory before assessing higher cognitive functions because the latter rely on these basic abilities (Strub & Black, 2000).

Age and Cultural Considerations

It often is necessary to modify the MSE to accommodate children, older adults, and patients from various cultural backgrounds. Specific information about conducting an MSE with children is beyond the scope of this chapter; however, Robinson (2001) provides useful information on this topic.

Sometimes it is necessary to speak more slowly and loudly when assessing older adults. Although nearly yelling an MSE is tiring and can feel awkward, for patients with decreased hearing acuity it is the only way to obtain valid results. It is not uncommon for older adults to become nervous if they know they are being evaluated for psychological purposes (Robinson, 2001), and extra efforts may be needed to help set the patient at ease. Consideration of educational background is especially important with older adults because it is not uncommon for these patients to have achieved low levels of education. Assessing affect and congruence of affect and mood must include consideration of the patient's medical history. For example, there may be no psychological significance in the incongruence of a report of feeling happy and a flat affect in a patient with Parkinson disease because flat affect may be the result of motor impairment. Circumstantial speech is common among older adults (Robinson, 2001). Older adults have a great deal of life experience and stories they often like to share. Older adults have higher rates of depression and suicide. The majority of indicators of depression are similar to those of younger patients (e.g., decreased interest in activities, feelings of hopelessness); however, older adults tend to have more somatic complaints, and physical symptoms are not as reliable an indicator of depression (Robinson, 2001). There are many reasons older adults are at a high risk for suicide, and a thorough suicide assessment should be conducted with every older adults who is referred for an MSE. Aging affects performance on cognitive tests. Verbal abilities and general fund of knowledge remain intact as a person ages, whereas speed, visuospatial abilities, and construction abilities decline with age.

The MSE can result in inaccurate diagnosis if cultural factors are not considered. Consideration of cultural background is especially important when one is evaluating thought content, perception, speech, and abstract thinking. For example, it is common in some cultures to believe in seeing visions of or talking with loved ones who are dead. If present, this type of cultural background must be deftly considered during evaluation for a thought disorder in the patient who reports hearing voices or having visions of dead loved ones. Of course, it is important to consider a patient's nonnative English-speaking status if the MSE is conducted in English because this is a potential confound for all verbal parts of the MSE. Some of the questions and items described in this chapter for evaluation of abstract thinking have significant limitations for patients who have limited English fluency or are from different cultures. The items on these tests can be unfamiliar or have different significance that makes them unsuitable to assess abstract thinking in these patients.

SUMMARY

The MSE is a picture of the patient's current cognitive and emotional functioning. To be most meaningful, information obtained during the MSE must be considered in the context of psychosocial and historical information with reference to collateral sources of information whenever possible. Cultural and age factors should always be considered when one is making a diagnosis regarding mental illness. General knowledge of the overlapping etiology of psychiatric and medical processes is important to prevent misdiagnosis.

A psychiatric MSE typically includes evaluation of appearance, behavior, motor activity, orientation, attitude, speech and language, mood and affect, thought and perception, insight and judgment, attention and concentration, memory, intellectual ability, and abstract thinking. Simple cognitive tests typically are administered. A neurological MSE includes these areas of functioning with the additional evaluation of motor and sensory processing, constructional ability, and calculation ability.

REFERENCES

American Psychiatric Association. (2000). *Diagnostic and statistical manual of mental disorders* (4th ed.). Washington, DC: Author.

Carlat, D. J. (2005). Mental status examination. In D. J. Carlat (Ed.), *The psychiatric interview: A practical guide* (pp. 122–142). Philadelphia: Lippincott Williams & Wilkins.

Daniel, M., & Crider, C. (2003). Mental status evaluation. In M. Hersen & S. M. Turner (Eds.), *Diagnostic interviewing* (3rd ed., pp. 21–46). New York: Kluwer Academic/Plenum.

Robinson, D. J. (2001). *Brain calipers: Descriptive psychopathology and the psychiatric mental status examination* (2nd ed.). Port Huron, MI: Rapid Psychler Press.

Shader, R. I. (2003). The mental status examination. In R. I. Shader (Ed.), *Manual of psychiatric therapeutics* (pp. 9–16). Philadelphia: Lippincott Williams & Wilkins.

Strub, R. L., & Black, R. W. (2000). *The mental status examination in neurology* (4th ed.). Philadelphia: F. A. Davis.

Wechsler, D. (1997). *Wechsler Memory Scale* (3rd ed.). San Antonio, TX: The Psychological Corporation.

6

MULTICULTURAL ISSUES

DANIEL S. MCKITRICK, TIFFANY A. EDWARDS, AND ANN B. SOLA

The ability to accurately and effectively assess the complex context of culture is at the heart of competent multicultural practice (e.g., Hays, 2001; Pedersen, 1990; Sue, Ivey, & Pedersen, 1996; Sue & Sue, 2003). Giving adequate attention to sociocultural issues is a complex, potentially overwhelming task. The wealth of guidelines and other professional directives affecting multicultural practice is testimony to the intricacies of that field. Examples in the American Psychological Association (APA) alone range from those that are specifically focused on multicultural practice to general guidelines and directives that include mention of multicultural practice. Examples with a specific focus include "Guidelines for Providers of Psychological Services to Ethnic, Linguistic, and Culturally Diverse Populations" (APA, 1993) and "Guidelines on Multicultural Education, Training, Research, Practice, and Organizational Change for Psychologists" (APA, 2003). General examples that make references to multicultural practice include the "Ethical Principles of Psychologists and Code of Conduct" (APA, 2002), the *Standards for Educational and Psychological Testing* (American Educational Research Association, American Psychological Association, & National Council on Measurement in Education, 1999), and the *Policy Statement on Evidence-Based Practice in Psychology* (APA, 2005).

Another important source of direction for negotiating the complexities of multicultural practice also began within the APA (Division 17, counseling psychology): the multicultural competencies (Sue et al., 1982). Subsequently refined, within APA and the American Counseling Association (e.g., Arredondo et al., 1996; Sue, 2001; Sue, Arredondo, & McDavis, 1992; Sue et al., 1998), a recent version has been integrated with the APA multicultural guidelines (APA, 2003), endorsed by the various national ethnic minority associations, and called "characteristics of culturally competent helping" (Council of National Psychological Associations for the Advancement of Ethnic Minority Interests, 2003, pp. 5–7).

Within the field of multicultural practice, one of the most complicated areas is multicultural assessment (e.g., Dana, 2000; Malgady, 1996; Ridley, Li, & Hill, 1998). The guidelines and directives not only call attention to problems of inadequate multicultural assessment but also provide some direction for addressing them. Further identification of problems and suggestions for remedy come from the multicultural assessment literature.

This chapter is designed to help the reader map and manage the territory of multicultural assessment, particularly multicultural clinical interviewing. In pursuit of that goal, first we provide some key definitions. Next, we give a context for multicultural clinical interviewing.

This context includes a sense of the central role of multicultural interviewing in the multicultural assessment process and a developmental perspective of multicultural assessment. Then, we characterize the current developmental phase of multicultural assessment as including frames for systematically integrating and applying the overwhelming multitude of issues and suggestions related to multicultural competence in assessment. We overview an exemplary frame, the Multicultural Assessment Procedure (MAP) (Ridley, Li, et al., 1998), and highlight the role of the clinical interview within that model. Then we offer refinements to the MAP and its clinical interviewing process. Finally, we apply this information to a specific population, Latinos.

DEFINITIONS

Five definitions are central to this chapter: *culture, multiculturalism, multicultural assessment, multicultural clinical interviewing,* and *multiculturally competent assessment and clinical interviewing.* All of these definitions are based on those used in the MAP (Ridley, Hill, & Li, 1998; Ridley, Li, et al., 1998), with some modifications.

Culture

Ridley, Li, et al. (1998) borrow their definition of culture from Marsella and Kameoka (1989):

Culture is shared learned behavior that is transmitted from one generation to another for purposes of human adjustment, adaptation, and growth. Culture has both external and internal referents. External referents include artifacts, roles, and institutions. Internal referents include attitudes, values, beliefs, expectations, epistemologies, and consciousness. (p. 233)

In keeping with their overall thoughtful approach, Ridley, Li, et al. (1998) list five ways this definition is important to assessment:

• It implies that, because culture is so pervasive, it is important to collect and "process a broad range of data" (p. 834).

• There are more obvious (external) and less obvious (internal) types of data that need to be considered.

• Because individuals vary in the extent to which they share with their cultural groups their adherence to various aspects of the culture, there are going to be important within-group differences between individuals of any cultural group.

• Because culture does not make up the total of any individual's world experience, it follows that individuals within any culture have behaviors, views, and feelings that are not typical of others in their culture.

• Because culture is defined so generically, many groups may be considered as cultures, including the most often considered ethnic and racial groups and groups defined by gender, age, socioeconomic status, and others.

This appears to be what is commonly described in the literature as a broad definition of culture (Pedersen, 1997), in contrast to a narrow definition, which includes only race and ethnicity. A broad or narrow definition of culture affects what is communicated in broad or narrow definitions of multiculturalism.

Multiculturalism

Proponents of a narrow definition of multiculturalism (e.g., Carter, 1995; Helms & Richardson, 1997) want to make sure attention to ethnicity and race is not diluted. A strong argument can be made for the tenacity of racism and ethnic bias in mainstream U.S. culture, the importance of prioritizing its study and alleviation, and the tendency for people to avoid this difficult subject by focusing on other less difficult topics. Proponents of the broad definition of multiculturalism (e.g., Hays, 2001; Sue & Sue, 2003) agree with the need to make sure attention to race and ethnicity is not neglected or avoided through attention to other cultural issues. Yet they believe that there is value in considering other cultural factors that also potentially make people vulnerable to discrimination.

Ridley, Li, et al. (1998) take a potentially confusing dialectical stance on multiculturalism: They combine an extremely broad stance and a narrow stance. They take a very broad position in recommending "everyone should be assessed in light of sociocultural influences" (p. 851). From their perspective, the question "is never 'Is culture relevant to a particular client?' A better question is this: 'How is culture relevant to understanding this client?'" (p. 857).

At the same time, Ridley, Li, et al. (1998) incorporate special attention to nonmainstream clients, who often need modifications in standard assessment practices. Although they acknowledge this need for modification across the broad range of cultural factors (e.g., age, religion, gender), they narrow their scope to race and ethnicity.

We suggest clarifying their position on multiculturalism by examining their rationales for using a broad definition. They emphasize a science-based rationale of considering a broad range of sociocultural factors so as to promote thorough assessment of all clients' cultural contexts. However, at various points in their work, they also implicitly endorse another rationale, that the broad definition helps address the many opportunities for misunderstanding and bias across the various multicultural populations. This is a common rationale in the literature. For instance, Hays (2001) cites research suggesting that "prejudice is lower when one holds the 'knowledge structures' to categorize others as having multiple group memberships" (p. 6). We recommend making both of these rationales explicit.

So the result is that we define multiculturalism extremely broadly so as to enhance the accuracy and comprehensiveness of attention to all clients by taking into consideration relevant sociocultural factors. We adopt the comprehensive list of sociocultural factors provided in the APA multicultural guidelines (APA, 2003): "race, ethnicity, language, sexual orientation, gender, age, disability, class status, education, religious/ spiritual orientation, and other cultural dimensions" (p. 380). Yet because of the especially pervasive influences of racism and ethnic bias, we choose to focus especially on sociocultural factors affecting ethnic and racial minority clients. (See APA, 2003, for further definition of race and ethnicity.) Although this definition necessarily limits focus on clients from other minority groups and from mainstream clients, it is assumed that clients from these groups also would benefit from attention to sociocultural factors. Furthermore, it is assumed that all clients have multiple group characteristics (e.g., age, religion, gender) that vary in significance across situations and that all clients would benefit from attention to these characteristics. The importance of these characteristics will be discussed later in this chapter.

Multicultural Assessment

We attempt here to bring together the main defining points of multicultural assessment, which are embedded in the MAP (Ridley, Li, et al., 1998; Ridley, Hill, et al., 1998), into an explicit definition: Multicultural assessment is a logical and necessary extension of standard assessment in which a traditional underemphasis on sociocultural factors is remedied. This traditional lack of sensitivity to sociocultural factors has caused corresponding potential insensitivities and biases in the assessment process, especially for racial and ethnic minorities. Therefore, multicultural assessment refines standard assessment in order to give sociocultural factors adequate attention and to modify related causes of potential insensitivity and bias in the assessment process.

This definition embraces both the demands for social responsibility and the demands for scientific integrity from the various APA guidelines. These issues will be discussed in more detail in following sections.

Multicultural Clinical Interviewing

Multicultural clinical interviewing contains extensions and refinements of standard clinical interviewing that parallel refinements to standard assessment contained in multicultural assessment. More specifically, multicultural clinical interviewing, in addition to its standard functions of gathering medical, psychiatric, and social information, "serves as the fundamental medium for gathering cultural information" (Ridley, Li, et al., 1998, p. 872). This is consistent with the bio-psycho-social-cultural theoretical model adopted by Ridley, Li, et al. Also, multicultural clinical interviewing is an important adjunct to a variety of approaches used to gather covert cultural information, especially when these approaches are not normed on target minority clients, have language limitations, or have any number of other problems that lead to potentially inaccurate and biased assessment results. As with multicultural assessment, multicultural clinical interviewing also addresses assessment process issues that potentially lead to insensitivities and bias.

Multiculturally Competent Assessment and Clinical Interviewing

Multiculturally competent assessment and clinical interviewing should follow the various professional guidelines for competent practice intentionally, systematically, and effectively and should incorporate developments in the professional literature that pertain to these guidelines. The goal is to demonstrate "the ability and committed intention to consider cultural data in order to formulate accurate, comprehensive and impartial case conceptualizations" (Ridley, Hill, & Wiese, 2001, p. 32).

A Context for Multicultural Clinical Interviewing

In order to provide a context for multicultural clinical interviewing, first we describe the central role of multicultural clinical interviewing, within the more general practice of multicultural assessment. Then, we offer a developmental perspective of multicultural assessment. This perspective clarifies the need to consider the clinical interview within the frame of the MAP (Ridley, Li, et al., 1998).

The Central Role of Multicultural Clinical Interviewing

The purpose of clinical diagnostic assessment is to identify the client's presenting problem, contextualized in his or her multidimensional environments, while establishing therapeutic rapport. Initial information gathering usually is done largely through clinical interviews. These interviews provide a framework for understanding clients, which leads to preliminary diagnoses, case formulations, and general outlines for treatment goals. Morrison (1995) stated just this. He held that skilled interviewers maintain three common characteristics: They gain the most comprehensive and accurate data relevant to diagnosis and treatment, complete interviews efficiently, and lay the foundation for a good working relationship.

In standard assessment procedures, the clinical interview is crucial. Wiger and Huntley (2002) state, "A comprehensive mental health interview is the cornerstone of obtaining an accurate diagnosis and providing on target treatment" (p. 1).

Maruish (2002) goes further:

> The primacy of the clinical interview over the other means used to gather assessment information cannot be emphasized heavily enough. Information from other sources is important, but it often is indirect, second-hand information that either has been colored by others' perceptions of the patient, is inferred from other information, or lacks the degree of detail or specificity that the clinician would have pursued if the clinician were the one who gathered the information. (p. 17)

In addition to its central goal of gathering standard data and cultural data, multicultural clinical interviewing has other important functions in the multicultural assessment process. Ridley, Li, et al. (1998) recommend a cyclical assessment process in which one "can recycle through the MAP process at any point when new information is either acquired or required" (p. 868). Therefore, clinical interviewing is not limited to the initial stage of assessment. Also, Ridley et al. use a postassessment narrative, in addition to the usual clinical interviewing. The postassessment narrative is done through follow-up questioning that is done by means of a clinical interviewing process.

A Developmental Perspective

Although multicultural practice has been described as the fourth force in psychology since the early 1990s (Pedersen, 1991), various discriminatory, biased practices, mostly at the nonconscious level (Ridley, 1995), have hindered the development of accurate clinical judgment and ethical multicultural assessment practice and have elicited a large array of suggestions from the literature for remedy.

Culture, especially race, was once considered a nuisance variable in assessment. Often practitioners operated from the deficit hypothesis (Jones & Thorne, 1995). That is, cultural differences found in assessment scores were attributed to historical cultural deprivation, isolation, and impoverishment instead of barriers in language, problems in methodological development and normative samples, sociohistorical status and context, or assessor bias. This deficit hypothesis assumes an ethnocentric perspective that mainstream U.S. culture considers the appropriate and normative way of being.

Malgady (1996), Dana (1998, 2000, 2001), and others have argued that standard assessment instruments, procedures, and systems (e.g., *Diagnostic and Statistical Manual of Mental Disorders, Fourth Edition* [*DSM-IV-TR;* American Psychiatric Association, 2000]) have been used as if they were etic (universal), when in fact they reflect a Western European emic (group-specific) focus. Sociocultural differences among clients have been downplayed or ignored, resulting in myriad problems, such as misdiagnosing and over-pathologizing and underpathologizing clients (Dana, 2001).

Implications for Clinical Judgment. Ignoring relevant diagnostic information can lead to errors in judgment. Several common judgment errors can derail the diagnostic process. Confirmatory bias, type I and II errors, and ignoring the base rates are among the most damaging forms of diagnostic prejudice. Confirmatory bias occurs when a clinician misinterprets or disregards relevant information in favor of a presupposed hypothesis. When the clinician misreads new data as evidence for the original hypothesis, the initial belief is confirmed and strengthened (Rabin & Schragg, 1999). In fact, new information can have a polarizing effect, intensifying adherence to the original belief (Lord, Ross, & Lepper, 1979). Type I error occurs when a clinician falsely rejects the null hypothesis (a false positive), whereas a type II error occurs when a clinician falsely confirms the null hypothesis (a false negative). The null hypothesis traditionally has been used in clinical practice to assume the client operates in a normal range of functioning. When practitioners ignore the base rates of a given disorder in a given population, they increase the likelihood of occurrence of type I or type II errors. Base rates are "the probability or proportion of actual positives that exist in the total sample" (Wiggins, 1973, p. 244). They provide a guide from which one can predict a given disorder in a specific context. When base rates are low, prediction is difficult, whereas when base rates are high, prediction is more accurate (Kamphius & Finn, 2002). For more information about the use of base rates, see Kamphius and Finn.

Assessor bias is an overarching concept that includes the previously discussed forms of prejudice. Dana (1993) describes assessor bias as the homogenization of all clients through the use of scientific method without critical thought. More specifically, he refers to the use of standardized assessments normed and developed for primarily White populations that derive unfair interpretations. Although Dana discusses assessor bias in terms of psychometric assessment, it is applicable to the diagnostic interview. For example, psychometric instrumentation often is used in collaboration with the diagnostic interview to establish clinical decisions.

These errors negatively affect every client. However, they have a poignantly assiduous impact on ethnically diverse clients. Specifically, these errors reinforce stereotyping and discriminatory practices against clients of color (Lonner & Ibrahim, 2002). Bhugra and Bhui (1999) have referred to psychiatry and psychology as forms of social control of ethnic minority patients' cultural variations. They consider misdiagnosis or underdiagnosis based on ethnic differences to be forms of individual and institutional racism. It is an individual form in that it occurs on a small scale between a therapist and his or her client. However, it is an institutional form in that diagnoses are based on syndrome sets established by and for Western, White patients.

Confirmatory bias in clinical assessment can stem from clinicians who refuse to actively commit themselves to self-reflective awareness of their personal biases and bracket off interpersonal judgments based on cultural difference. Type I and II errors may carry different discriminatory weights for ethnic minorities. Malgady (1996) theorizes that type I errors hold less bias against racial minorities than type II errors. Because type I errors are allowed only a .05 probability and type II errors are granted a .20 probability, type II errors have tended to reinforce and advocate for minimizing group differences. Essentially, the null hypothesis assumes that a clinically inconsequential difference or no difference exists between the mainstream group and ethnic minority groups. Therefore, the null hypothesis acts as a form of color-blindness in diagnostic hypothesis testing; cultural variables such as different symptom expressions, cultural defenses, and acculturation are overlooked.

Often these errors also cause discriminatory long-term consequences for non-White help seekers. For example, Bhugra and Bhui (1999) state that ethnic minority patients are more likely to receive more drastic forms of treatment such as electroconvulsive therapy and larger dosages of neuroleptics, tranquilizers, and antidepressants than their White counterparts. Diagnostic labels also tend to be more severe. For example, African Americans are diagnosed with schizophrenia more often than Whites, whereas Whites are more often diagnosed with less severe affective disorders such as depression and anxiety disorders (McNeil & Kennedy, 1997). Such biases lead to long-term labeling at an individual level and reinforcement of stereotyping against racial minority groups at professional and societal levels.

Implications for Ethical Practice. Not only are these errors problematic for clients, they raise ethical concerns for practitioners. The APA's (2002) "Ethical Principles of Psychologists and Code of Conduct" delineate several codes specifically addressing cultural difference, assessment, and competence. Psychologists are mandated to operate within the boundaries of their professional competence and obtain relevant training and consultation before working with populations with which they have little or no experience (Standard 2.01). In addition, they are required to maintain competence over time working with specific populations (Standard 2.02). Psychologists are also prohibited from any form of unfair discrimination, including against racially different others (Standard 3.01). Psychologists may use only assessment tools with adequate reliability and validity or established strengths for the given populations with which they work. Finally, all assessment tools, including the clinical interview, should consider the client's language preference (Standard 9.02). Therapists who commit such errors on a regular basis practice outside the boundary of multicultural competence and may be vulnerable to suit or ethical complaints.

Suggestions for Remedy. The multicultural assessment literature has a growing abundance of suggestions for remedying these potential sources of clinical judgment error and unethical practice. The large range of suggestions reflects the complexities of the field and tends to overwhelm the practitioner (Ridley, Hill, et al., 1998). In developing the MAP, Ridley, Li, et al. (1998) sorted many suggested clinical practices from the literature into 16 categories: using emic criteria without slipping into extreme cultural relativism, making appropriate cultural use of standard assessment tools, using nonstandard approaches (e.g., postassessment

narratives, constructivist strategies, and idiographic approaches) with awareness of their limitations, using measures constructed for particular groups without neglecting within-group variance, using the *DSM-IV* in culturally appropriate ways, considering clients' psychocultural adjustment (e.g., regarding acculturation, biculturalism, world view, and cultural identity), matching client and therapist expectancies for assessment, making culturally based defenses explicit (e.g., "color blindness, color consciousness, cultural transference, cultural countertransference, pseudotransference, cultural ambivalence, overidentification, and identification with the oppressor" [Ridley, Li, et al., 1998, p. 843]), using behavioral analyses with attention to potential clinician bias, reaching agreement with clients as to conceptualization of their problems, demonstrating their credibility to clients (e.g., via showing expertise, being nondefensive, and self-disclosing), respecting and supporting clients' belief systems, being aware of one's own cultural background and related influences in potential bias, using a variety of means to broaden one's approach to assessment (e.g., using multiple information sources and methods of data collection), using adequately trained interpreters and translators who meet wide-ranging criteria, and considering input from extended family members.

This list was not intended to be exhaustive, and there have been many more suggestions for remedy since the list was compiled. Nonetheless, simply reading through the list demonstrates why a number of authors recognized the rich but patchwork nature of the literature and began to offer frames for systematizing an approach to multicultural practice (e.g., Berg-Cross & Takushi-Chinen, 1995; Grieger & Ponterotto, 1995; Jacobsen, 1988). Despite these efforts, it has been evident that there still was not a process that adequately addressed multicultural issues (e.g., Hall, 1997; Turner, Hersen, & Heiser, 2003). In order to remedy this shortcoming, Dana (2001) argues for "major modifications in diagnostic practices" (p. 102), and Ridley, Li, et al. (1998) advocate a "reconceptualization" (p. 849) of the assessment framework.

MAP: A FRAME FROM WHICH TO BUILD

Perhaps the most comprehensive, ambitious of the above frames is Ridley, Li, et al.'s (1998) MAP. Early reviewers captured some of its hallmark qualities: The MAP took on "the formidable task of integrating what is thought about and, in some instances, known about multicultural assessment and merged this material with a scientific methodology of hypothesis testing" (Spengler, 1998, p. 930), and the MAP "represents the integration of a myriad of powerful and thought-provoking elements that challenges us to reexamine and reconceptualize the salience of culture in the assessment process" (Constantine, 1998, p. 922).

Overview of MAP

Another hallmark feature of the MAP is the careful and thoughtful groundwork on which it is built. After reviewing, categorizing, and critiquing the literature on multicultural assessment, Ridley, Li, et al. (1998) identify the integrating thread of their critical analysis:

> Because theory guides practice, the lack of a conceptual framework hinders the development of clear assessment guidelines. Due to this absence of testable theoretical principles and practical guidelines, a scientific basis for multicultural assessment has not evolved. These problems are compounded by bias in the literature that treats the process as though it is primarily the assessment of ethnic minorities by White clinicians. (p. 851)

Ridley, Li, et al. (1998) then explain how the MAP addresses these issues "by systematizing current suggestions into a conceptual framework that is relevant to any multicultural clinician/client relationship and explicated in a concrete clinical procedure" (p. 851). From here, they proceed to describe the 10 "foundation principles" underlying their philosophy (theory) of assessment, "eight critical issues that are highly relevant" (p. 859), and four areas of "clinical judgment pitfalls and debiasing strategies to deal with these pitfalls" (p. 883).

On the above groundwork, Ridley, Li, et al. (1998) construct the MAP in four phases: Phase 1, collect salient and nonsalient cultural data with multiple methods; Phase 2, interpret the data, forming a working hypothesis; Phase 3, incorporate the cultural data with other clinical data, test the working hypothesis, and refine it as appropriate; and Phase 4, arrive at a "sound, accurate, and complete" (p. 883) assessment decision, based on

hypothesis testing. The overall procedure is characterized, first, by having guidelines and "microdecisions" delineated within each of the four phases. Second, the process is flexible, systematic and logical, so as to promote thorough analysis of complex issues. Third, the MAP requires the clinician to reflectively recycle through the assessment process on a routine basis.

Clinical Interviewing in the MAP

As described earlier, the clinical interview in the MAP may be used during a postassessment interview and at almost any point as the clinician cycles and recycles through the assessment process. However, the clinical interview is used primarily in Phase 1, as the main means of collecting data. Therefore, Phase 1 is considered closely here.

The emphasis of Phase 1 is on cultural data collection rather than on data collected in standard clinical interviewing. Ridley, Li, et al. (1998) identify many examples of cultural variables, including acculturation, history, economics, politics, language, religious practices, experiences with racism and prejudice, and cultural values affecting communication, orientation to time and space and property, modes of learning, and work attitudes.

Clinical data are broken into two categories, overt and covert data, each of which also is broken into the subcategories of cultural and idiosyncratic data. Cultural data are normative emic data, and idiosyncratic data are individual data. Overt data "(e.g., obvious mannerisms, expressions, and self-disclosures)" (Ridley, Li, et al., 1998, p. 872) are readily identified. Covert data "(e.g., unresolved and unexpressed conflicts, implicit cultural values and assumptions, repressed memories)" (p. 872) generally require probing.

The clinical interview in the MAP is the main tool for collecting overt data. Overt cultural data come from two main sources: information the client shares in the role of cultural expert, in order to answer questions the clinician has about the client's culture, and information the clinician elicits through other means that do not burden the client with responsibility to educate the clinician. The Person-In-Culture Interview (Berg-Cross & Takushi-Chinen, 1995) is recommended for the latter purpose. This interview schedule will be discussed in detail later, as applied to Latino clients.

After collecting overt data, the clinician faces the first of two microdecision points in Phase 1: "Do I have enough data to make a sound assessment decision?" The answer to this question very rarely is "Yes." The complexities of culture in combination with the myriad idiosyncratic data almost always necessitate moving beyond the salient information and considering covert data. This brings the clinician to the second microdecision: "How do I best collect nonsalient information?" Covert cultural data are best collected with a variety of methods, which may include clinical interviewing but also other methods, such as life histories, behavioral observations, input from family, and assessment of clients' psychocultural adjustment (e.g., acculturation, world view, and racial and ethnic identity).

REFINEMENT SUGGESTIONS FOR MAP CLINICAL INTERVIEWING

One of many laudable features of the MAP is its heuristic value. Ridley and his associates want the MAP to "generate scientifically thoughtful inquiry that will improve its conceptual organization" (Ridley, Li, et al., 1998, p. 851) and hope that colleagues' research and experience with MAP will inspire constructive "critiques to further refine the MAP's structure and to strengthen its methods" (Ridley, Hill, et al., 1998, p. 947). This notion of ongoing thoughtful updates is consistent with multiculturally competent practice, as reflected, for example, in the APA (2003) multicultural guidelines and Derald Wing Sue's (2003) integration of the multicultural guidelines with the multicultural competencies. In that spirit, some suggestions for refinement of the MAP are offered here. It is beyond the scope of this chapter to give more than a few examples:

Explicitly incorporate the APA multicultural guidelines (APA, 2003) into the MAP. The goals of the multicultural guidelines are to advocate for multicultural conscience in clinical practice and training, education, and research; to provide basic information and references on empirical research on the field of multicultural psychology; and to develop a paradigm to frame future research and practice. Three guidelines are specifically relevant to client assessment.

Guideline One states "Psychologists are encouraged to recognize that, as cultural beings, they may hold attitudes and beliefs that can detrimentally influence their perceptions of and interaction with individuals who are ethnically and racially different from themselves" (APA, 2003, p. 17). Takushi and Uomoto (2001) identify Harry Stack Sullivan as the first psychologist to describe the clinician as the assessment instrument in the clinical interview. As with error in any assessment tool, clinician bias may influence the true outcome. More specifically, bias may occur not only in the form of the explicit content present in the interaction but also in the form of perceived characteristics about the actors in the interaction (Kunda & Thagard, 1996). Therefore, Dana (1993) calls for clinicians to differentiate between genuine etics and imposed etics during assessment. Genuine etics are universal values espoused by all cultures. These may include community, family, celebration, and labor. However, although all cultures embody these characteristics, each culture conveys these universal facets in unique ways. An imposed etic in the United States is a Eurocentric or Americentric value that is erroneously assumed to be universal. Guideline One implies that practitioners need to recognize how imposed etics can result in unfairly differential treatment of ethnic minority clients (APA, 2003). Automatic stereotypes and prejudices that occur based on the cultural milieu to which a clinician adheres can lead to miscommunication (Fiske, 1998) and outgroup discrimination (Hewstone, Rubin, & Willis, 2002).

Guideline Two states, "Psychologists are encouraged to recognize the importance of multicultural sensitivity/responsiveness, knowledge, and understanding about ethnically and racially different individuals" (APA, 2003, p. 25). In doing so, psychologists must first accept that each person's phenomenological experience is derived in part from his or her cultural lens, as suggested by Guideline One. Then they must strive to understand the impact of stigma on minority individuals' psychological, behavioral, and emotional events (Crocker et al., 1998). Stigma related to being an ethnic minority in a prejudiced society has been associated with reduced willingness to seek or participate in treatment (U.S. Department of Health and Human Services, 2001). Additionally, variations in *DSM-IV* diagnostic symptoms (Cheng, Leong,

& Geist, 1993; Okazaki, 1997), cognitive orientations (Robinson-Zanartu, 1996), world view and social networks, and persistence in treatment (Anderson, 1995) have all been associated with ethnic difference. Guideline Two suggests that practitioners be mindful of cultural variation and actively gain broader cultural knowledge of emic criteria.

Guideline Five states, "Psychologists strive to apply culturally-appropriate skills in clinical or other applied psychological practices" (APA, 2003, p. 43). Guideline Five suggests more than merely appreciating ethnic diversity but implies a candid effort to modify treatment and assessment for culturally different clients. For example, alteration of standardized assessment aligns with Guideline Five. Lonner and Ibrahim (1996) propose methods for using standardized assessment with non-White clients. They posit that the use of construct-based tests, or theoretically derived tests, may impose Western etics on the test taker. Therefore, these tests should be used sparingly unless psychometric research validates the preferred measure for a target population.

Also, Lonner and Ibrahim (1996) suggest consideration of the ethical use of measures. They advise that tests be used to "identify potential for growth" in a multicultural context (p. 311) rather than highlight deficits. Dana (2001) suggests three means for reducing bias in diagnostic assessment: Modify the use of standardized *DSM-IV* diagnostic instruments, use standardized cultural orientation measures in combination with *DSM-IV* instruments, and use only measures with appropriately normed populations. Unfortunately, many of the measures most commonly used by psychologists are not appropriately normed on minority populations (Dana, 1993).

Lonner and Ibrahim (2002) suggest caution when interpreting response sets, which may be influenced by ethnicity. Response sets such as acquiescence, social desirability, evasiveness, inconsistency, and extremity can alter the results of an assessment protocol. Additionally, they discuss the mode of response and test content (verbal vs. nonverbal). For clients with limited English proficiency, cultural sensitivity to the mode of response and test content may dramatically change results. Recognizing the impact of cultural variation on monocultural instruments can improve the accuracy of diagnosis.

Appropriate standardized assessment and clinical interviewing of culturally different clients provide psychologists adequate information to conceptualize a client in context. Guideline Five mandates integration of a client's relevant acculturative history, language proficiencies, familial orientation, and culture-specific community resources (APA, 2003). Moreover, broad clinical assessment should smoothly guide useful interventions. For example, identification of a client's acculturative identity should lead the clinician to use culture-specific, culture-blended, or Western interventions.

Clarify how to do multicultural assessment ethically. Ridley, Hill, and Wiese (2001) have developed an impressively detailed model for ethical assessment practice. Replicating the care and thoroughness shown in the development of the MAP, they first identify competence as the overriding principle. Then they describe four pertinent ethical standards, three basic multicultural assessment activities, and five guidelines designed to help assessors to connect the ethical standards to basic multicultural activities, in other words, to operationalize the standards.

Give explicit ideas for appropriate use of the DSM-IV-TR. Roysircar (2005) gives a good overview of the shortcomings of the various *DSM-IV-TR* provisions for attending to culture, concluding that they fall short of providing "a comprehensive delineation of multicultural variability" (p. 22). Hays (2001) concurs and goes on to suggest several ideas for compensating, including the novel addition of an Axis VI, which incorporates her ADDRESSING acronym in order to list pertinent cultural data related to age, developmental disability, religion, ethnicity, socioeconomic status, sexual orientation, indigenous heritage, national identity, and gender. Kress, Eriksen, Rayle, and Ford (2005) offer more guidelines and also include several questions for the assessor to consider before making a diagnosis.

Expedite integration of cultural data with other data in the clinical interviewing process. One simple act can contribute much to accomplish the aim of Ridley, Li, et al. (1998) to make all assessment multicultural: Integrate the collection of cultural data with the collection of other data on the clinical interview form. Ponterotto, Gretchen, and Chauhan (2001) take a step in that direction by incorporating basic demographic data into their "Holistic Idiographic Framework for Practice." Roysircar (2005) does the same with a brief "Clinician Intake Form." Gallardo-Cooper (2001) adds a cultural data section to a standard clinical interview format and insinuates cultural sensitivity throughout the interview process in the "Culture-Centered Clinical Interview," discussed later in this chapter.

Put less focus on the individual client and more on the family. Although Ridley, Li, et al. (1998) and other scholars (e.g., Dana, 1993; Paniagua, 1994) emphasize the importance of involving the family in multicultural assessment, Ridley, Li, and Hill seem reluctant to include the family in the MAP assessment process. For instance, in the clinical interview, they suggest bringing in family "when clients are too impaired to provide sufficient information" (p. 871). Also, in their case example, they brought in the client's family only when the client "insisted" (p. 890).

Two final suggestions for refinement will be discussed in the context of an application of semistructured multicultural clinical interviewing to Latino clients.

APPLICATION EXAMPLE: THE LATINO CLIENT

Two main issues relevant to refinement of the MAP are pertinent to this application: how the MAP handles the tension between needing to consider clients from the emic perspective and needing to not stereotype clients by overemphasizing the emic perspective and the utility of the distinction in the MAP between overt and covert data. Two semistructured interview schedules, the Person-in-Culture Interview (PICI; Berg-Cross & Takushi-Chinen, 1995) and the Culture-Centered Clinical Interview (CCCI; Gallardo-Cooper, 2001), will be applied for use with Latino clients and will be considered in the context of these two main issues. First, however, a very brief description of some Latino emic variables is presented.

Latino Emic Variables

In a recent critical review of the literature on the clinical interview with Latinos, Sola (2006) identifies six cultural values that repeatedly are identified as being especially relevant to the interview process:

1. Latinos tend to construe the self as being collectivistic, as interdependent on others and not necessarily separate from other social units (e.g., Santiago-Rivera, Arredondo, & Gallardo-Cooper, 2002; Sue & Sue, 2003).

2. The most important social unit is the family (e.g., Falicov, 1998; Marin & Marin, 1991).

3. *Personalismo,* the collectivist belief that personal relationships are valued above all else, is fostered in the family (e.g., Chong, 2002; Levine & Padilla, 1980).

4. Interpersonal *respeto* (respect) is maintained in conversation through appropriate use of formal and informal Spanish pronouns and verb tenses (e.g., Garcia, 1996; Santiago-Rivera et al., 2002).

5. Traditional gender roles call for men's *machismo* (including honor, moral courage, and loyalty and responsibility to family, friends, and community) (e.g., Morales, 1996; Torres, Solberg, & Carlstrom, 2002) and women's *marianismo* (including devotion to family, self-sacrifice, spirituality, and nurturance) (e.g., Chong, 2002; Sue & Sue, 2003).

6. Religion and spirituality, most often Catholicism and sometimes in combination with indigenous beliefs, are central in the lives of most Latinos (e.g., Chong, 2002; Santiago-Rivera et al., 2002).

Numerous other emic variables may be significant factors in the clinical interview with Latino clients, such as language, *DSM-IV-TR* cultural syndromes and traditional emotional distress symptoms, history of oppression and racism, and experience of economic hardship (e.g., Barona & Santos de Barona, 2003).

PICI

Ridley, Li, et al. (1998) do not offer much specific direction about how to conduct the clinical interview. However, they do suggest using the PICI as an option. Use of a semistructured interview such as PICI is recommended in the multicultural literature (e.g., Turner, Hersen, & Heiser, 2003). This format provides the flexibility often needed for diverse clients while also offering more precision and consistency than afforded by unstructured interviews.

The PICI is a set of 25 open-ended questions that are designed to help gain cultural understanding of clients without stereotyping them

(Berg-Cross & Takushi-Chinen, 1995). The authors note that all of their experience with this interview format has been among urban, educated populations, and it may be inappropriate for some groups. The tension between emphasis and overemphasis on the emic perspective is addressed by assessing the individual's expression of a range of generic cultural issues, such as those identified in Ridley, Li, and Hill's 16 categories of current suggestions from the multicultural assessment literature. These cultural issues are accessed through questions generated from the theories of Western humanistic, psychodynamic, existential, and family system psychotherapies. The notion is that the clients are characterizing their own versions of their respective group cultures, through their responses to the universal cultural items.

Some may question whether it is appropriate to consider generic cultural issues within a frame of Western psychotherapy questions. However, PICI's generic approach to emic issues helps to avoid overemphasis on the emic perspective but may offer some difficulties for Latino clients. First, the style of questioning is direct and may be considered rude, insensitive, threatening, and disrespectful to the Latino client (Santiago-Rivera et al., 2002). Second, the format does not allow one to build rapport before discussing difficult topics. There is no opportunity to *placticar* (use personal small talk). Instead, the first question asks the client about "the problem." Moreover, it is unlikely that the clients, or family members who are present during the clinical interview, will be comfortable discussing how the problem affects them (Chong, 2002). This question requires family members to be disloyal to one another and violates the cultural value of familism.

Next, Latino clients may have a difficult time understanding how some of the questions in this format pertain to a clinical interview. Various studies have shown that Latino clients come away from therapy confused because the counselor asks questions that seem irrelevant and intrusive. Also, they may be offended and confused by the PICI question that has them describe an embarrassing experience. Instead of promoting trust and respect, this question may be considered a threat to their personal dignity (Santiago-Rivera et al., 2002). They may answer out of respect for the clinician's authoritative position, but it is likely that they will not return for another visit.

Several other questions on the PICI may be difficult for Latino clients because of gender issues. Some questions require the client to share painful experiences, information regarding a lack of resources, or information related to the safety of the family, and may be threatening to a Latino male client. Conveying to a stranger that he is not able to live up to his duty to protect, provide for, and defend his family could be a direct threat to his manhood (Torres et al., 2002). A Latina client who subscribes to the paradigm of *marianismo* is socialized to not ask for help or discuss personal problems outside the family (Gil & Vazquez, 1996). Discussing family problems related to insufficient resources and safety may be uncomfortable for a married Latina client because she may perceive it as an act of disloyalty toward her husband. Sharing with a stranger that she is unhappy or in pain may contradict her self-image of being the strongest and most self-sacrificing member of the family.

Finally, the PICI seems to assess more covert than overt data. This seems odd, given that Ridley, Li, et al. (1998) characterize the PICI as appropriate mainly for collecting overt data. But, as will be discussed later, a mixed emphasis on overt and covert data seems to be an artifact of extant semistructured multicultural clinical interview frames.

CCCI

Like that of the PICI, the format of the CCCI is well suited to Latino clients (Gallardo-Cooper, 2001). Also, as in the PICI, in the CCCI process clients use their own words to describe their individual experiences of generic cultural issues, including many of the 16 current suggestions from Ridley, Li, et al. (1998). However, several of the problems resulting from using the PICI with Latino clients are avoided through the incorporation into the CCCI of attention to key Latino emic variables. Sensitivity to all the common cultural values identified in Sola's (2006) literature review, and other Latino cultural values, is incorporated into the CCCI.

Much of the CCCI's cultural sensitivity is afforded by the nature of its semistructured format. The interviewer using the CCCI is not given direct questions to use in assessing cultural data, as is done in the PICI, but instead has topic areas to cover, such as sociopolitical issues, immigration history, and spiritual issues. This format allows the clinician to be sensitive to cultural cues and adjust the interview accordingly. For instance, the flexibility of the format permits the clinician to build rapport and trust and encourages client self-disclosure (Gallardo-Cooper, 2001; Santiago-Rivera et al., 2002). The relaxed form of communication encouraged by the format promotes *personalismo* and encourages the client to *platicar* (Santiago-Rivera et al., 2002). To *platicar* is to maintain a pleasant atmosphere while having a personal small talk.

The flexible CCCI format also allows the client to direct the clinician toward topics that are comfortable and not threatening. More difficult subjects should be discussed after there is sufficient rapport. A clinician should be aware that Latino clients may have legitimate concerns as to how information they give in a clinical interview could be used against them. They may not trust a clinician's guarantee of confidentiality because of past infringements. Some clients may have an inherent fear of institutions because of experiences in their native country. Others may be residing illegally or be living with family or friends who do not have residency or legal status. All of these circumstances and beliefs may dampen the clients' willingness to speak freely about their lifestyle until they know the clinician can be trusted (Sue & Sue, 2003).

In addition to the attention given to emic issues by means of the CCCI's flexibility, special attention is given to some emic issues by means of emphasis. For example, level of acculturation is addressed in several different ways throughout the CCCI. Specific acculturation scales also are recommended. Additionally, the CCCI includes an assessment of language skills. A thorough evaluation of a client's language skills is important because ample research suggests that misdiagnosis of bilingual clients is associated with the language spoken during the clinical interview (e.g., Grand, Marcos, Freedman, & Barroso, 1977; Guttfreund, 1990). Such misdiagnoses include both type I and type II errors (Del Castillo, 1970; Marcos, 1976).

So, with the CCCI, the balance between emphasis and overemphasis of emic focus is handled differently than in the PICI. Attention to emic issues specific to Latino clients makes the CCCI more user friendly, at the risk of overemphasizing the emic perspective. However, like the PICI, the CCCI is designed to counteract that risk by encouraging client individual expression. Also, the CCCI cultural dimensions are embedded in a traditional clinical interview format, with attention to diagnosis, medical history, educational and vocational functioning, and the like. This mediates the emic focus while facilitating the incorporation of cultural data into all other types of data for ready integration into conceptualization, diagnostic, and treatment processes.

As regards the MAP distinction between overt and covert data, the CCCI thoroughly mixes attention to the two.

Implications for Refinement of the MAP

Our recommendations regarding refinement of the MAP are as follows.

Follow the lead of both the PICI and the CCCI in dividing attention between individual and generic emic perspectives. Furthermore, as with the CCCI, include sufficient flexibility in the interview process to allow attention to specific emic issues pertinent to interviewed clients. However, be cautious about overemphasizing attention to specific emic issues (Sue, 2003). Stuart (2004) has developed an approach designed to help the assessor avoid overemphasis of emic data through 12 specific skills derived from the multicultural assessment literature. In their characteristically thoughtful and comprehensive style, Ridley and his associates (Ridley, Hill, Thompson, & Ormerod, 2001) have developed a comprehensive set of assessment practice guidelines, designed to promote systematic assessment and holistic integration of clients' multiple cultural identities. These guidelines form an idiographic perspective on assessment that helps assessors avoid making "generalizations about clients based on race, gender, age, sexual orientation, and socioeconomic status without fully exploring the nuances of these qualities in the lives of individual clients" (p. 193). Pedersen (1997) suggests expanding such consideration to the full array of broad cultural variables (e.g., adding religion and disability). Pedersen also describes a tool called the Interpersonal Cultural Grid that can be used to help assess which of a client's cultural identities are most salient in any given situation.

Expect to collect both overt and covert cultural data in the clinical interview. The distinction in the MAP between using the clinical interview largely to collect overt versus covert data is confusing and is further clouded by the use of clinical interviewing throughout the assessment in a cyclic manner. In addition to the CCCI and the PICI, several other semistructured multicultural assessment interview frames reviewed by Ponterotto et al. (2001) all seem to mix attention to overt and covert data. Therefore, this mix may be hard to avoid in the semistructured interview format.

SUMMARY

In the labyrinth of multicultural clinical practice, one of the more complex areas is multicultural clinical assessment. Clinical interviewing plays a central role in that assessment process. A growing professional literature and many practice guidelines and other professional directives offer abundant suggestions and mandates for navigating multicultural assessment activities so as to avoid common pitfalls and to arrive at accurate, effective, relevant assessment results. However, only recently has multicultural assessment reached the stage at which the potentially overwhelming number of suggestions for competent practice have been organized in order to construct detailed plans of action for the assessment process.

One particularly laudable such plan, the MAP, was developed by Ridley, Li, et al. (1998). In the MAP, Ridley and his associates have integrated myriad suggestions for competent multicultural assessment into a systematic and comprehensive process. Clinical interviewing has key functions throughout the process. Walking a fine line between traditional empiricism and postmodern constructivism, Ridley and associates have successfully fashioned an approach that applies the invaluable tools of the scientific method in a flexible and culturally sensitive assessment process. Ambitiously, they have made sound arguments for applying this process to clinical assessment for all clients. Finally, Ridley and associates have detailed their MAP so carefully and fully that theoreticians, researchers, and practitioners easily can critique the approach and offer ideas for refinement. Ridley and several associates have contributed several important improvements since the MAP was first developed, and they have extended an open invitation for continuing constructive feedback. Unable to resist the invitation, this chapter's authors have identified some possible refinements and look forward to reading about future developments as they surface in the literature.

REFERENCES

American Educational Research Association, American Psychological Association, & National Council on Measurement in Education. (1999). *Standards for educational and psychological testing.* Washington, DC: Authors.

American Psychological Association. (1993). Guidelines for providers of psychological services to ethnic, linguistic, and culturally diverse populations. *American Psychologist, 48,* 45–48.

American Psychiatric Association. (2000). *Diagnostic and statistical manual of mental disorders* (4th ed., Text rev.). Washington, DC: Author.

American Psychological Association. (2002). Ethical principles of psychologists and code of conduct. *American Psychologist, 57,* 1060–1073.

American Psychological Association. (2003). Guidelines on multicultural education, training, research, practice, and organizational change for psychologists. *American Psychologist, 58,* 377–402.

American Psychological Association. (2005). *Policy statement on evidence-based practice in psychology.* Washington, DC: Author.

Anderson, N. (1995). Behavioral and sociological perspectives on ethnicity and health: Introduction to the special issue. *Health Psychology, 14,* 589–591.

Arredondo, P., Toporek, R., Brown, S., Jones, J., Locke, D., Sanchez, J., et al. (1996). Operationalization of the multicultural counseling competencies. *Journal of Multicultural Counseling and Development, 24,* 42–78.

Barona, A., & Santos de Barona, M. (2003). Recommendations for the psychological treatment of Latino/Hispanic population. In Council of National Psychological Associations for the Advancement of Ethnic Minority Interests (Ed.), *Psychological treatment of ethnic minority populations* (pp. 19–23). Washington, DC: Association of Black Psychologists.

Berg-Cross, L., & Takushi-Chinen, R. (1995). Multicultural training model and the Person-In-Culture Interview. In J. Ponterotto, J. Casas, L. Suzuki, & C. Alexander (Eds.), *Handbook of multicultural counseling* (pp. 333–356). Thousand Oaks, CA: Sage.

Bhugra, D., & Bhui, K. (1999). Racism in psychiatry: Paradigm lost—paradigm regained. *International Review of Psychiatry, 11,* 236–243.

Carter, R. (1995). *The influence of race and racial identity in psychotherapy.* New York: Wiley.

Cheng, D., Leong, F., & Geist, R. (1993). Cultural differences in psychological distress between Asian and American college students. *Journal of Multicultural Counseling and Development, 21,* 182–200.

Chong, N. (2002). *The Latino patient: A cultural guide for health care providers.* Yarmouth, ME: Intercultural Press.

Constantine, M. (1998). Developing competence in multicultural assessment: Implications for counseling psychology training and practice. *Counseling Psychologist, 26,* 922–929.

Council of National Psychological Associations for the Advancement of Ethnic Minority Interests (Ed.). (2003). *Psychological treatment of ethnic minority populations.* Washington, DC: Association of Black Psychologists.

Crocker, J., Major, B., & Steele, C. (1998). Social stigma. In D. Gilbert & S. Fiske (Eds.), *The handbook of social psychology* (Vol. 2, 4th ed., pp. 504–553). New York: McGraw-Hill.

Dana, R. (1993). *Multicultural assessment: Perspectives for professional psychology.* Boston: Allyn & Bacon.

Dana, R. (1998). Personality assessment and the cultural self: Emic and etic contexts as learning resources. In L. Handler & M. Hilsenroth (Eds.), *Teaching and learning personality assessment* (pp. 325–346). Mahwah, NJ: Erlbaum.

Dana, R. (2000). Psychological assessment in the diagnosis and treatment of ethnic group members. In J. Aponte & J. Wohl (Eds.), *Psychological intervention and cultural diversity* (pp. 59–74). Boston: Allyn & Bacon.

Dana, R. (2001). Clinical diagnosis of multicultural populations in the United States. In L. Suzuki, J. Ponterotto, & P. Meller (Eds.), *Handbook of multicultural assessment: Clinical psychology and educational applications* (2nd ed., pp. 101–131). San Francisco: Jossey-Bass.

Del Castillo, J. (1970). The influence of language upon symptomatology in foreign-born patients. *American Journal of Psychiatry, 127,* 242–44.

Falicov, C. J. (1998). *Latino families in therapy: A guide to multicultural practice.* New York: Guilford.

Fiske, S. (1998). Stereotyping, prejudice, and discrimination. In D. Gilbert & S. Fiske (Eds.), *The handbook of social psychology* (4th ed., Vol. 2, pp. 357–411). New York: McGraw-Hill.

Gallardo-Cooper, M. (2001). *Culture-centered clinical interview.* Unpublished manuscript.

Garcia, W. (1996). *Respeto:* A Mexican base for interpersonal relationships. In W. B. Gudykunst, S. Ting-Tommey, & T. Nishida (Eds.), *Communication in personal relationships across cultures* (pp. 137–155). Thousand Oaks, CA: Sage.

Gil, A., & Vazquez, C. I. (1996). *The Maria paradox.* New York: Perigee.

Grand, S., Marcos, L. R., Freedman, N., & Barroso, F. (1977). Relation of psychopathology and bilingualism to kinesic aspects of interview behavior schizophrenia. *Journal of Abnormal Psychology, 86,* 492–500.

Grieger, I., & Ponterotto, J. (1995). A framework for assessment in multicultural counseling. In J. Ponterotto, J. Casas, L. Suzuki, & C. Alexander (Eds.), *Handbook of multicultural counseling* (pp. 357–374). Thousand Oaks, CA: Sage.

Guttfreund, D. G. (1990). Effects of language usage on the emotional experience of Spanish-English and English-Spanish bilinguals. *Journal of Consulting and Clinical Psychology, 58,* 604–607.

Hall, C. (1997). Cultural malpractice: The growing obsolescence of psychology with the changing U.S. population. *American Psychologist, 52,* 642–651.

Hays, P. (2001). *Addressing cultural complexities in practice: A framework for clinicians and counselors.* Washington, DC: American Psychological Association.

Helms, J., & Richardson, T. (1997). How "multiculturalism" obscures race and culture as differential aspects of counseling competency. In D. Pope-Davis & H. L Coleman (Eds.), *Multicultural counseling competencies: Assessment, education and training, & supervision* (pp. 60–79). Thousand Oaks, CA: Sage.

Hewstone, M., Rubin, M., & Willis, H. (2002). Intergroup bias. *Annual Review of Psychology, 53,* 575–604.

Jacobsen, F. (1988). Ethnocultural assessment. In L. Comas-Diaz & E. Griffith (Eds.), *Clinical guidelines in cross-cultural mental health* (pp. 135–147). London: John Wiley & Sons.

Jones, E., & Thorne, A. (1995). Rediscovery of the subject: Intercultural approaches to clinical assessment. In N. Rule-Goldberger & J. Bennet-Veroff (Eds.), *The culture and psychology reader* (pp. 720–740). New York: New York University Press.

Kamphius, J., & Finn, S. (2002). Incorporating base rate information in daily clinical decision-making. In J. Butcher (Ed.), *Clinical personality assessment: Practical approaches* (2nd ed., pp. 256–268). London: Oxford University Press.

Kress, V., Eriksen, K., Rayle, A., & Ford, S. (2005). The *DSM-IV-TR* and culture: Considerations for counselors. *Journal of Counseling and Development, 83,* 97–104.

Kunda, Z., & Thagard, P. (1996). Forming impressions from stereotypes, traits and behaviors: A parallel-constraint-satisfaction theory. *Psychological Review, 103,* 284–308.

Levine, E. S., & Padilla, A. M. (1980). *Crossing cultures in therapy: Pluralistic counseling for the Hispanic.* Belmont, CA: Wadsworth.

Lonner, W., & Ibrahim, F. (1996). Appraisal and assessment in cross-cultural counseling. In P. Pedersen, J. Draguns, W. Lonner, & J. Trimble (Eds.), *Counseling across cultures* (4th ed., pp. 293–322). Thousand Oaks, CA: Sage.

Lonner, W., & Ibrahim, F. (2002). Appraisal and assessment in cross-cultural counseling. In P. Pedersen, J. Draguns, W. Lonner, & J. Trimble (Eds.), *Counseling across cultures* (5th ed., pp. 355–379). Thousand Oaks, CA: Sage.

Lord, C., Ross, L., & Lepper, M. (1979). Biased assimilation and attitude polarization: The effects of prior theories on subsequently considered evidence. *Journal of Personality and Social Psychology, 37,* 2098–2109.

Malgady, R. (1996). The question of cultural bias in assessment and diagnosis of ethnic minority clients: Let's reject the null hypothesis. *Professional Psychology: Research and Practice, 27,* 73–77.

Marcos, L. R. (1976). Bilinguals in psychotherapy: Language as an emotional barrier. *American Journal of Psychotherapy, 30,* 552–560.

Marin, G., & Marin, B. V. (1991). *Research with Hispanic populations.* Newbury Park, CA: Sage.

Marsella, A., & Kameoka, V. (1989). Ethnocultural issues in the assessment of psychopathology. In S. Wetzler (Ed.), *Measuring mental illness: Psychometric assessment for clinicians* (pp. 231–256). Washington, DC: American Psychiatric Press.

Maruish, M. (2002). *Essentials of treatment planning.* New York: Wiley.

McNeil, J., & Kennedy, R. (1997). Mental health services to minority groups of color. In T. Watkins & J. Callicut (Eds.), *Mental health policy and practice today* (pp. 235–257). Thousand Oaks, CA: Sage.

Morales, E. (1996). Gender roles among Latino gay and bisexual men: Implications for family and couple relationships. In J. Laird & R. J. Green (Eds.), *Lesbians and gays in couples and families: A handbook for therapists* (pp. 272–297). San Francisco: Jossey-Bass.

Morrison, J. (1995). *The first interview.* New York: Guilford.

Okazaki, S. (1997). Sources of ethnic difference between Asian American and White American college students on measures of depression and social anxiety. *Journal of Abnormal Psychology, 106,* 52–60.

Paniagua, F. (1994). *Assessing and treating culturally diverse clients: A practical guide.* Thousand Oaks, CA: Sage.

Pedersen, P. (1990). Complexity and balance as criteria of effective multicultural counseling. *Journal of Counseling and Development, 5,* 550–554.

Pedersen, P. (1991). Multiculturalism as a fourth force in counseling. *Journal of Counseling and Development, 70,* 5–25.

Pedersen, P. (1997). *Culture-centered counseling interventions.* Thousand Oaks, CA: Sage.

Ponterotto, J., Gretchen, D., & Chauhan, R. (2001). Cultural identity and multicultural assessment: Quantitative and qualitative tools for the clinician. In L. Suzuki, J. Ponterotto, & P. Meller (Eds.), *Handbook of multicultural assessment: Clinical psychology and educational applications* (2nd ed., pp. 67–100). San Francisco: Jossey-Bass.

Rabin, M., & Schragg, J. (1999). First impressions matter: A model of confirmatory bias. *Quarterly Journal of Economics, 114,* 37–82.

Ridley, C. (1995). *Overcoming unintentional racism in counseling and therapy.* Thousand Oaks, CA: Sage.

Ridley, C., Hill, C., & Li, L. (1998). Multicultural assessment: Reexamination, reconceptualization, and practical application. *Counseling Psychologist, 26,* 827–910.

Ridley, C., Hill, C., Thompson, C., & Ormerod, A. (2001). Clinical practice guidelines in assessment: Toward an idiographic perspective. In D. Pope-Davis & H. Coleman (Eds.), *The intersection of race, class, and gender in multicultural counseling* (pp. 191–211). Thousand Oaks, CA: Sage.

Ridley, C., Hill, C., & Wiese, D. (2001). Ethics in multicultural assessment: A model of reasoned application. In L. Suzuki, J. Ponterotto, & P. Meller (Eds.), *Handbook of multicultural assessment: Clinical psychology and educational applications* (2nd ed., pp. 29–45). San Francisco: Jossey-Bass.

Ridley, C., Li, L., & Hill, C. (1998). Revisiting and redefining the multicultural assessment procedure. *Counseling Psychologist, 26,* 939–947.

Robinson-Zanartu, C. (1996). Serving Native American children and families: Considering cultural variables. *Language, Speech, and Hearing Services in Schools, 27,* 373–384.

Roysircar, G. (2005). Culturally sensitive assessment, diagnosis, and guidelines. In M. G. Constantine & D. W. Sue (Eds.), *Strategies for building multicultural competence in mental health and educational settings* (pp. 19-38). New York: Wiley.

Santiago-Rivera, A., Arredondo, P., & Gallardo-Cooper, M. (2002). *Counseling Latinos y* la familia: *A practical guide.* Thousand Oaks, CA: Sage.

Sola, A. (2006). *Conducting the clinical interview with Latinos.* Unpublished manuscript, Pacific University, Forest Grove, OR.

Spengler, P. (1998). Multicultural assessment and a scientist-practitioner model of psychological assessment. *Counseling Psychologist, 26,* 930–938.

Stuart, R. (2004). Twelve practical suggestions for achieving multicultural competence. *Professional Psychology: Research and Practice, 35,* 3–9.

Sue, D. (2001). Multidimensional facets of cultural competence. *Counseling Psychologist, 29,* 790–821.

Sue, D. (2003). Cultural competence in the treatment of ethnic minority populations. In Council of National Psychological Associations for the Advancement of Ethnic Minority Interests (Ed.), *Psychological treatment of ethnic minority populations* (pp. 3–7). Washington, DC: Association of Black Psychologists.

Sue, D., Arredondo, P., & McDavis, R. (1992). Multicultural counseling competencies and standards. A call to the profession. *Journal of Counseling and Development, 70,* 477–486.

Sue, D., Bernier, J., Durran, M., Feinberg, L., Pedersen, P., Smith, E., et al. (1982). Position paper: Cross-cultural counseling competencies. *Counseling Psychologist, 10,* 45–52.

Sue, D., Carter, R., Casas, J., Fouad, N., Ivey, A., Jensen, M., et al. (1998). *Multicultural counseling competencies: Individual and organizational development.* Thousand Oaks, CA: Sage.

Sue, D., Ivey, A., & Pedersen, P. (1996). *Multicultural counseling theory.* Pacific Grove, CA: Brooks/Cole.

Sue, D. W., & Sue. D. (2003). *Counseling the culturally diverse: Theory and practice* (4th ed.). New York: Wiley.

Takushi, R., & Uomoto, J. (2001). The clinical interview from a multicultural perspective. In L. Suzuki, J. Ponterotto, & P. Meller (Eds.), *Handbook of multicultural assessment: Clinical psychology and educational applications* (2nd ed., pp. 47–66). San Francisco: Jossey-Bass.

Torres, J. B., Solberg, V. S. H., & Carlstrom, A. H. (2002). The myth of sameness among Latino men and their machismo. *American Journal of Orthopsychiatry, 72*(2), 163–181.

Turner, S., Hersen, M., & Heiser, N. (2003). The interviewing process. In M. Hersen & S. Turner (Eds.), *Diagnostic interviewing* (3rd ed., pp. 3–20). New York: Kluwer Academic/Plenum.

U.S. Department of Health and Human Services. (2001). *Mental health: Culture, race and ethnicity.* A supplement to *Mental health: A report of the Surgeon General.* Rockville, MD: U.S. Department of Health and Human Services, Substance Abuse and Mental Health Services Administration, Center for Mental Health Services.

Wiger, D., & Huntley, D. (2002). *Essentials of interviewing.* New York: Wiley.

Wiggins, J. (1973). *Personality and prediction: Principles of personality assessment.* Reading, MA: Addison-Wesley.

7

SELECTING TREATMENT TARGETS AND REFERRAL

PAULA TRUAX AND SARA WRIGHT

One the primary goals of the interview and self-report assessments discussed in the preceding chapters is identification of a treatment focus. Typically, treatment focus is a combination of the overall reasons therapy was sought with the specific goals for change. This treatment target (e.g., depressed mood) then becomes the centerpiece of treatment planning, goals are related to the target (e.g., reduce depressed mood from the severe range to the minimal range), interventions are designed to produce positive change in the treatment target (e.g., increase pleasurable and mastery activities), and outcome assessment evaluates progress on the treatment target (e.g., Beck Depression Inventory–II [BDI-II]; Beck, Steer, & Brown, 1996). However, given the myriad issues that a client brings to treatment, it can often be difficult to identify the most appropriate treatment target. The current chapter first discusses reasons for focused treatment and then clarifies the issues involved in selecting a target and the steps for moving from a general target to specific goals and outcome assessments. The therapeutic use of goal development and outcome assessment is addressed, along with considerations for appropriate referral.

REASONS FOR FOCUSED TREATMENT

Treatment varies widely on the diffuse versus focused continuum depending on the therapist's theoretical orientation and the client's and therapist's preferences for therapy style. Although most clinicians and clients would agree that neither extreme is ideal, research suggests that more focused treatment may yield advantages over more diffuse treatments. In particular, more focused therapy tends to be more effective (Craske, Maidenberg, & Bystritsky, 1995) and generally preferred by clients (Hecker, Fink, & Fritzler, 1993). Although clear treatment foci tend to lead to better outcomes, some exceptions include clients who are in early stages of change, more resistant to therapy, or most interested in self-growth or existential issues (Beutler et al., 1991).

IDENTIFYING A TREATMENT TARGET

First and foremost, perhaps the most salient aspect of selecting a treatment target is an understanding of the concerns that led the client to seek treatment or the referral question posed by any referring source. Self-referred clients often begin the initial assessment with concerns about specific symptoms or situations that led to help seeking. Likewise, external referral sources also identify possible symptoms or situations causing clinically significant distress for the referred client. Often, it is the desire for relief of these very symptoms that prompted the client to seek services. Thus, in most cases, the selected treatment targets should be closely related to the concerns that initiated therapy. For example, the treatment target for a client who self-refers to therapy because of difficulty sleeping, low interest, lethargy, difficulty concentrating, and feeling entirely ineffectual probably would be depression. Similarly, for a client referred by an employer concerned about client substance abuse, the treatment target is likely to involve substance abuse. Although there are some exceptions to the rule that the presenting concern should guide the treatment target choice, the actual reasons that led to treatment seeking should generally be included in the treatment target list.

Second, often a number of concerns are presented at the initial assessment. Prioritization of these concerns is an important key to outcome, retention, and compliance. Hatcher (1999) found that therapist impressions of the client-therapist collaboration were associated with both client and therapist estimates of client improvement. In particular, issues such as the nature and severity of presenting concerns, client preference, stage of change, research on effective treatments, feasibility of treatment (e.g., managed care limitations), and demographic issues such as age, disability, and cultural issues will be addressed in this chapter.

One of the first issues to consider in prioritizing treatment targets is the nature and severity of the presenting concerns. Linehan (1993) suggests an algorithm for determining priority treatment targets based on the nature of a client's concerns. This decision-making process always prioritizes suicidal behavior first, followed by therapy-threatening behavior and then severe quality-of-life–threatening behaviors. As Linehan (1993) adeptly points out, "no psychotherapy is effective with a dead patient" (p. 124); thus, any client behavior that suggests imminent suicidality becomes the priority at any point in treatment. Suicidal behaviors include direct suicidal threats, recent suicide attempts, intentional self-harm with or without suicidal ideation (e.g., cutting or burning self with a cigarette), and significant

ideation and intent accompanied by a specific, lethal, available, proximal plan. Although suicidal ideation alone is cause for concern, Linehan indicates that it need not become the number one treatment priority unless it is new or unexpected, is very distressing, or interferes with therapy goal attainment. Significant therapy-threatening behaviors that endanger therapy continuation should be addressed next. Examples of therapy-threatening behaviors include being late or absent from scheduled therapy sessions, not completing homework, or being nonparticipative in session. Finally, severe quality-of-life behaviors such as significant substance abuse, domestic violence, homelessness, or any other behavior that would substantially threaten occupational, social, or familial stability would be targeted next. If these three priority issues are either absent or have been resolved, other therapeutic concerns become treatment targets.

Severity is perhaps the most important issue in determining priority of the remaining treatment targets because more severe concerns generally should be addressed first. However, severity is a multifaceted concept that may encompass subjective distress, chronicity, and impact on functioning. Subjective distress is the amount of emotional pain the client experiences as a result of the problem. Prioritization based on subjective distress might involve a rank ordering of the subjective units of distress scales (0 = *no distress*, 10 = *extreme distress*) for each of the presenting concerns. Chronicity, the duration of a potential treatment target, may be measured with an interview such as the Longitudinal Interval Follow-up Evaluation (Keller et al., 1987) Finally, impact on functioning for physical, social, occupational and academic, and familial areas may be assessed with a self-report instrument such as the SF-36 (Ware, Snow, Kosinski, & Gandek, 1993). Furthermore, a multitude of instruments are available to measure the combined severity (i.e., distress, chronicity, and impact) of specific concerns such as depression (BDI-II; Beck et al., 1996) or anxiety (State-Trait Anxiety Inventory; Spielberger, Gorsuch, Lushene, Vagg, & Jacobs, 1983). See resources such as the *Practitioner's Guide to Empirically Based Measures of Depression* (Nezu, Ronan, Meadows, & McClure, 2000), *Practitioner's Guide to Empirically Based Measures of Anxiety* (Antony, Orsillo, & Roemer, 2001), *Measures for Clinical Practice, Volumes 1 and 2* (Corcoran & Fischer, 2000a, 2000b) for many severity measures. Although at first glance, severity alone may appear sufficient for identifying a treatment target, multiple concerns may be of comparable severity, or the severity dimensions may not be congruent. For example, a client may present with debilitating, distressing panic attacks and depressed mood.

A second issue in treatment target prioritization is the research on effective treatments. Such research may point either to one target most likely to yield a positive outcome or to a particular ordering of targets. For example, research on comorbid depression and marital distress found that when marital therapy alone was compared with individual cognitive therapy for depression and combined marital and cognitive therapy, marital therapy had the most positive outcome for both depression and marital distress (Jacobson, Dobson, Fruzzetti, Schmaling, & Salusky, 1991). Similarly, for concomitant depression and panic, an initial focus on the panic appears to lead to a reduction in depression, and depression does not appear to impede panic treatment (Tsao, Mystkowski, Zucker, & Craske, 2002), whereas most evidence for depression treatment with comorbid panic suggests that panic does reduce short- and long-term outcomes for depression (Brown, Schulberg, Madonia, Shear, & Houck, 1996). Findings such as these may be helpful when they exist; however, such research often is absent or equivocal. In these cases, issues such as stage of change and client preference should play a greater role in prioritizing treatment targets.

Third, readiness for change may vary across presenting concerns. For example, a client may present with potential treatment targets of depression and substance abuse. The client might be highly motivated to reduce the depression but less motivated to reduce the substance use. This concept of readiness for change can be assessed with the Rhode Island Change Assessment Scale (Dozois, Westra, Collins, Fung, & Garry, 2004) and classified into one of four categories: precontemplative (i.e., does not recognize a problem exists), contemplative (recognizes problem; unsure whether costs of change outweigh the benefits), action (recognizes problem and is taking steps to change problem), and maintenance (recognizes problem and has initially resolved problem). Treatment outcome research on stage of change suggests that later stages of change predict better treatment outcome than earlier stages

of change (Brown, Melchior, Panter, Slaughter, & Huba, 2000; Clements-Thompson, Klesges, Haddock, Lando, & Talcott, 1998; Scott & Wolfe, 2003; Treasure, Katzman, Schmidt, Troop, Todd, & de Silva, 1999). Furthermore, stage of change may be increased through the development of a good therapeutic alliance. Thus, beginning with a treatment target the client is motivated to change (e.g., depression) might enhance the therapeutic alliance and increase the probability that the stage of change for the remaining targets (e.g., substance abuse) may change. Targeting a goal that the client is unmotivated or unwilling to change may be more likely to lead to therapy dropout. For example, Booth, Dale, and Ansari (1984) found that clients seeking treatment for substance abuse were more successful in reducing drinking when they chose their goals rather than when the goals were imposed by the therapists.

Fourth, a close cousin to stage of change is client preference. Preference may be an especially salient prioritization variable for maintaining the client in therapy. Several researchers have pointed to the importance of involving clients in treatment planning to improve retention, compliance, and treatment satisfaction (Noble & Douglas, 2004). Client preference may be measured through an interview probe such as, "In consideration of your depression, alcohol use, and job satisfaction, which concern would you most like us to focus on initially?" Although clients may not always choose the most severe concern or even the most relevant concern, meeting client preferences may facilitate the therapeutic alliance and eventually increase the client's stage of change for the more severe concerns. Sobell, Sobell, Bogardis, Leo, and Skinner (1992) found that 87% of problem drinkers preferred self-selection of therapeutic goals over therapist selection; furthermore, they felt more confident they would achieve self-selected goals.

Fifth, feasibility of any treatment target must also be considered. Examples of issues that affect the feasibility of the treatment plan include the availability of time and money and a client's intellectual ability to complete the treatment as planned. Furthermore, feasibility is affected by the availability of training or supervision for the designated therapist. One of the initial steps in prioritizing treatment targets is to assess client resources. That is, what are the client's insurance limitations and potential willingness to self-pay when these benefits are exhausted? What amount of time each week and over time is the client able or willing to devote to therapy? What is the client's ability to understand and implement an effective treatment for the treatment target? Although a treatment target such as distress caused by a chronic history of childhood sexual abuse is unlikely to be successful for a client with four sessions to devote to therapy, a target of improving sleep hygiene may lead to significant improvement within these constraints.

Finally, understanding the role of client variables in the client's presenting concern is also central to the development of a treatment target and plan. Consistent with the American Psychological Association (APA) guidelines for culturally competent therapy (Arredondo et al., 1996), Hays (2002) proposes a model known as the ADDRESSING framework for conceptualizing client variables for clients and therapists.

A = Age and generational differences

D = Disability (developmental)

D = Disability (acquired)

R = Religion and spiritual orientation

E = Ethnicity

S = Socioeconomic status

S = Sexual orientation

I = Indigenous heritage

N = National origin

G = Gender

Hays recommends applying the ADDRESSING framework to each client to facilitate culturally responsive diagnosis and treatment planning based on the role of cultural privilege on presenting concerns and treatment plan.

CASE ILLUSTRATION

The following case will be used to illustrate the identification of treatment targets and subsequent goal-setting.

Ms. B, a 22-year-old employed, single Asian engineering student, presented with a primary concern of 2 months of persistent depressed mood with an upset stomach, no interest in previous activities, decreased appetite, insomnia, very low energy, intense guilt, and difficulty

concentrating. She reported that she hardly slept, stayed in her dorm room, did not talk to friends, and had recently quit going to class. She acknowledged passive suicidal thoughts within the past week (i.e., "I hoped that the bad dream would leave me dead"). She denied having any history, plan, or intent, however. Instead, she said that she would "never do that" because of how it would affect her family (deterrent). She also noted a secondary concern related to a sexual assault that occurred 2 years ago. She said she had increased anxiety in public places, avoidance of being alone, and flashbacks about the incident. Although she admitted distress about these symptoms, she was ambivalent about treatment for these symptoms. Instead, she requested help with her depression. Her BDI-II was 31, placing her in the severe depression range (Beck et al., 1996), and on a measure of posttraumatic stress disorder symptoms called the Impact of Events Scale (Horowitz, Wilner, & Alvarez, 1979; Sundin & Horowitz, 2003) she scored a total of 38, with 18 for avoidance and 20 for intrusion. These scores are at least one standard deviation below the means for veterans seeking service for trauma (McFall, Smith, Roszell, Tarver, & Malas, 1990).

Axis I: 296.22 Major Depressive Disorder, Single Episode

309.81 Posttraumatic Stress Disorder

Axis II: V71.09 No diagnosis

Axis III: Noncontributory

Culturally, the application of the ADDRESSING model to Ms. B suggests the following:

A, E, N, G = 22-year-old, second-generation single female, only child of Thai parents.

D/D = No disabilities.

R = Conservative Baptist. Her father's grandparents converted from being Buddhists to Baptists.

S = Upper middle class; both parents are engineers with a high-tech firm.

S = Heterosexual.

I = Identifies as Asian American and grew up in a Caucasian neighborhood.

The following dialogue with Ms. B illustrates how the process of identifying treatment targets may proceed. This process occurs in the first and second sessions and involves four general steps in which the therapist summarizes the primary areas of concern or possible treatment targets, asks the client whether there are other targets, presents a rationale for narrowing the focus, and helps the client to prioritize targets based on nature, severity, research, readiness for change, preference, feasibility, and client variables.

Therapist: Based on what we have been talking about in the last couple of sessions, it sounds like there are a few areas in which you would like to see improvement such as feelings of depression, anxiety about the rape, and avoidance of places that remind you of the rape [summarizing]. How well does this represent the areas you are concerned about?

Ms. B: Yeah, I guess that about sums it up.

T: Is there anything I have left out [other targets]?

Ms. B: No, not really. My stomach is really bothering me, I can't go to class until my stomach feels better. I wouldn't be able to concentrate. My doctor said nothing is wrong with me. He said it was depression and that I should talk to someone. That's why I called you.

T: Our bodies are so responsive to our moods! It is not uncommon for people with depression and anxiety to notice changes in their digestive systems [acknowledging role of culture in symptoms; Lippincott & Mierzwa, 1995; Nguyen, 1982]. I think this would be important for us to monitor. I would like you to continue to follow up with your doctor, however, if your stomach continues to bother you over the coming weeks.

Ms. B: That sounds fine.

T: One thing that is really helpful to you making progress in therapy is to narrow our focus. You might have seen that you do best in school when you are focused on one class at a time rather that three at one time. Therapy is a bit like that. If we try to address the depression, anxiety, and avoidance all at once, we are less likely to make progress in any area [presenting rationale]. What would you say is the highest priority for you [prioritizing]?

Ms. B: I don't know! They all seem important and all kinda rolled up into one! But I really don't feel ready to think about the rape or face anything related to it. I guess I would just like to feel better, sleep better, and start going to class again. Maybe if I felt better, I could face the rape.

T: Yeah, sometimes it can be hard to separate one problem from another. The more anxious you are, the more you avoid; the more you avoid friends and familiar places the more you stay in your room and get depressed. I just want to clarify, when you said you want to "feel better" did you mean you would like to feel less sad?

Ms. B: Yeah, I'd like to stop crying all the time and sleep better.

T: Okay, so you would like to work on the depression and your sleep first, is that correct [preference]?

Ms. B: Yeah.

T: I think that is a good place to start. The research on treatment of depression symptoms like yours suggests that it is best to feel more stable than you are right now to begin treatment for rape-related trauma [Scott & Stradling, 1997]. Further, your insurance covers 20 sessions, and based on my experience and the research, there is a very good chance that we can make good progress on your depression in that time [feasibility]. The other issue I think you and I should talk about is your thoughts of wishing you would die. I know you said that you are not currently having thoughts of hurting yourself but that you have had thoughts that you would be better off dead within the past week. I think it is likely that you will start to feel more hopeful as we work on the depression, but I want to make sure that we have a plan for these feelings [nature].

Ms. B: I don't like feeling so sad that I am having these thoughts. But I can say with the utmost confidence that I would never do anything to take my own life. I just knew when I felt that hopeless it was time to get some help!

T: I am glad you had the courage to seek help. This is the first step to feeling better. Maybe you and I can just form an "anti-harm contract" that outlines what you will do if you were to get to feeling especially hopeless again. Would you be willing to do that?

Ms. B: No problem.

In this example, the therapist is able to use the client's presenting concerns and begin to form a treatment target. One of the most difficult things for clients to do is to determine what specifically they would like to work on. The therapist can help the client organize his or her concerns into goals.

TRANSFORMING TREATMENT TARGETS INTO GOALS

A treatment target is the general destination for therapy; a treatment goal is a more specific description of the therapeutic destination. Possible treatment targets for Ms. B might be depression, anxiety, or avoidance, whereas treatment goals might include any of the following:

- Reduce depressed mood from the severe range on the BDI-II to the minimal range.

- Reduce the intensity of anxiety while confronting avoided places from 10 (0 = *no anxiety* to 10 = *most intense anxiety every experienced*) to 3.

- Increase percentage of time that avoided places are entered when encountered from 10% of the time to 80%.

This process of moving from targets to specific goals is vital to effective, efficient therapy. Not only does goal setting tend to lead to shorter therapies with better outcomes (James, Thorn, & Williams, 1993), it also begins to shape the therapeutic content, defines an end point to treatment, and facilitates client-therapist collaboration and client expectations (cf. Lambert & Barley, 2001). The goal content provides the focus of treatment because it often develops directly from the presenting problems. This connection between the presenting problem and the treatment goals should be clear for both the client and therapist. Furthermore, goal setting often is the starting point of a more cohesive treatment framework.

Prochaska and Norcross (1999) state that a meaningful advantage to having a cohesive theoretical framework is that it "delimits the amount of relevant information, organizes that information, and integrates it all into a coherent body of knowledge that prioritizes our conceptualization and directs our treatment" (p. 5). When both the client and the therapist have a clear therapeutic destination, therapy is less likely to wander. Additionally, appropriate treatment goals are imperative to identifying the most relevant and effective treatment interventions. Furthermore, the goal-setting process is an important entrée to a strong therapeutic alliance; one of the three core elements of therapeutic alliance is the client's perception that his or her goals are aligned with those of the therapist (Tracey & Kokotovic, 1989). Finally, goal setting may increase client hope. Positive expectations such as these have also been often associated with improved therapeutic outcomes (cf. Drisko, 2004; Sotsky et al., 1991).

Aside from the direct effects of goal setting for the client, the development of clear, realistic goals helps to meet the demands of the current managed care environment. Managed care organizations almost unanimously require that treatment plans include specific symptom descriptions and treatment targets, regardless of the therapist's theoretical orientation (Antonuccio, Thomas, & Danton, 1997). Additionally, therapists who are able to present cohesive treatment plans are more likely to successfully petition for additional sessions (Castonguay, Schut, Constantino, & Halperin, 1999). Finally, managed care review boards may better understand treatment plans that include specific treatment goals and therefore be more likely to grant additional sessions (Hoyt, 1995).

Specific, Measurable, Attainable Goals

Goals with clear behavioral targets and well-defined end points are more likely to lead to the positive benefits of goal setting outlined earlier. For example, James et al. (1993) found that chronic headache patients who established specific timeframes for their goals had less headache pain and needed less pain medication than those with less specific timelines (e.g., "as long as you can"). Similarly, goal specificity has been associated with more successful outcomes in industrial organizational research for areas such as negotiation

(Zetik & Stuhlmacher, 2002) and work tasks (Winters & Latham, 1996). To this end, the SMART criteria developed by Locke and Latham (1990) often are used. That is, therapeutic goals are specific, measurable, anchored, and realistic and have a timeline.

- *Specific:* Goals should target specific variables with observable referents that are relevant to the client's presenting concerns (e.g., intensity of depressed mood, frequency of night awakenings). The specificity helps to determine the most accurate treatment intervention.

- *Measurable:* Goals should include an observable, objective scale of measurement that is meaningful to the client (e.g., on a scale of 0–10, daily frequency).

- *Anchored:* To assess whether sufficient progress was made, goals should include both the current level and the desired level at the end of treatment (e.g., intensity of depressed mood will be reduced from a daily average of 9 to a daily average of 5).

- *Realistic:* Goals should be realistic given the client's current and past functioning and available treatment time. It is important to distinguish between ideal and realistic because they are not always the same.

- *Timeline:* Goals should include a target date for the goals to be accomplished. On the target date, the goals should be reviewed with the client to determine whether the goals have been resolved or need to be renewed.

Collaboration

Effective identification of treatment targets entails collaboration between client and therapist. Without this key component, even the most apparently perfect goals are likely to be unsuccessful. In a review of the literature on goal collaboration and therapeutic outcome, Tryon and Winograd (2001) found that clients who reported that they had been collaboratively involved in goal setting generally had better outcomes. Collaborative goal setting begins with the therapist's enthusiasm, confidence, and a clear rationale. If therapists are unclear, unmotivated, or uninterested in setting treatment goals, clients are likely to adopt the same stance. Next, the therapist should engage the client in a discussion about what he or she would like to accomplish in therapy.

For Ms. B, the discussion about selecting treatment targets includes examining her goals using the SMART criteria.

Therapist: One thing that might really help us be clear about the direction we are heading would be to get more specific about our goals; let's make sure that each of these goals is specific, measurable, anchored, and realistic and includes timelines. I heard you say that your primary goal is feeling less depressed. You noted that, in particular, you would like to be sleeping better. Is that correct?

Ms. B: Yeah, I feel exhausted and depressed all day because I'm sleeping less than I used to.

T: Let's get that goal of sleeping better more specific. Is it simply the amount of sleep or the quality of sleep [specific]?

Ms. B: Just the amount of sleep, because once I am able to fall asleep, I sleep just fine.

T: Okay, so let's specify that this treatment goal is to increase the time spent sleeping. First, we need to know how much you are sleeping. How can we measure your current hours of sleep [anchored]?

Ms. B: Well, I could write down when I fall asleep and when I wake up.

T: Great! Tracking your sleep for the next week will give us helpful information about how much you are sleeping now. How much time would you like to be sleeping in a typical night [measurable]?

Ms. B: Well, I used to sleep 8 hours a night and was never tired during the day. I would be happy with getting back to the usual.

T: So the desired amount of night per night is 8 hours. Does this amount seem realistic to you [realistic]?

Ms. B: It seems a long way off right now, but I guess if I was sleeping better just a couple of months ago, I might be able to get back to that.

T: That's great! Let's think about how long it might take for us to accomplish this goal. Realistically, sleep improves gradually as your depressed mood lifts. Since we are committing to 20 sessions of therapy, we could review this goal in 10 weeks to assess our progress. How does that sound [timeline]?

Based on this discussion, Ms. B and her therapist developed the following goal:

- Increase average duration of sleep each night from 2 hours/night to 8 hours/night by the 20th week of therapy.

Challenges

As mentioned earlier, the centerpieces of successful goal setting are specificity and collaboration. Developing specific goals in collaboration with clients can be particularly challenging when clients present very general goals, such as "I want to feel better." This is especially true if the client is severely distressed and has difficulty focusing and creating specific goals. When clients are vague, the therapist's role is to help specify these goals by asking questions ("What is one sign that would indicate you are feeling better?") and offering suggestions ("I wonder if worrying less during each day would be a sign that you are less anxious and more confident."). Additionally, therapists can help clients by staying on track and approaching each goal individually. Therapists should keep in mind that the behaviors related to each goal should be within the client's control, related to presenting concern, and within the therapist's purview. For example, a goal of eating less than 20 fat grams per day is more likely to be successful than a goal of losing 10 pounds; food intake is more directly within client control than actual weight loss. Finally, it is important for therapists to avoid being trapped by vague goals because they sound ideal, such as "I want to achieve genuine acceptance of all aspects of self." Although this may be true for clients, the work for therapists is to apply the SMART criteria to transform the goal into one that can be achieved through treatment interventions.

Another challenge is goal setting with clients who are mandated or in the early stages of change. First, it is important for therapists to acknowledge mandated clients' level of motivation and ambivalence about therapy. Ideally, the process of setting goals itself would motivate clients. A structured opportunity for clients to visualize life changes may be inspirational. However, if the process does not appear to motivate clients, therapists may take a more active and directive role in developing treatment goals. Motivational interviewing has been found to be effective with both mandated clients and clients in the early stage of change (Miller & Rollnick, 2002). In fact, with these clients, the first goal may simply be increasing motivation to change through therapy (Hersen & Van Hasselt, 1998). With a mandated client, a likely starting point in goal setting is the referral reason (i.e., reduce substance use or reduce incidence of anger outbursts). If the client is not motivated to work on these goals or does not feel that these goals are achievable, the therapist and client may need to create smaller, more achievable goals or address a related goal that the client is more motivated to change (e.g., improve relationship with husband; improve sleep). As noted earlier, collaborative goal setting leads to better therapeutic outcomes than therapist-imposed goals (James et al., 1993). Finally, any successes or achievements by the client should be acknowledged and celebrated to encourage continued progress toward the treatment goals.

Goal Setting Across Theoretical Orientations

Although treatment goals are created collaboratively, regardless of theoretical orientation, therapist orientation largely influences specific treatment targets. Therapeutic orientations include hypotheses about causes of the presenting problem that dictate intervention and treatment direction. Because psychodynamic theory focuses on the role of early emotional experiences in creating psychological defenses, psychodynamic treatment goals may involve forming transference neuroses and working through resistance to create more appropriate defenses. Cognitive theory is based on the idea that unhelpful thinking and core beliefs are influencing present problems; therefore, the goal of treatment is to create more adaptive self-statements. Additionally, behavior therapists are interested in behavioral contingencies and may create treatment goals that focus on changing the consequences associated with the antecedent. Gestalt therapists' goals in therapy are to increase client awareness of current experience and to meet the present needs of the client. Despite clinicians' varying therapeutic orientations, the treatment goals should be specific to the client's presenting problem and the approach acceptable to the client (Hersen & Van Hasselt, 1998).

MEASURING PROGRESS

One of the primary reasons for specific goal setting is to clearly establish a treatment destination. The utility of this process is mediated by measurement of goal progress. Clearly, setting treatment goals is not worthwhile if no attempt is made to check progress. More important, however, monitoring progress is the best way for clinicians and clients to evaluate whether progress is being made. If progress is slow or nonexistent, the clinician may focus on changing interventions early in treatment. In an original study (Lambert, Whipple, Smart, et al., 2001) and a replication (Lambert, Whipple, Vermeersch, et al., 2001). Lambert and colleagues found that therapists who were given client progress feedback were more likely to have successful outcomes with the clients who were having a poor initial response to treatment. Outcome measure feedback to clients also predicted better outcome than for those with no feedback (Hawkins, Lambert, Vermeersch, Slade, & Tuttle, 2004). Also, monitoring progress through measures provides a clear signal of when therapy can be terminated successfully. Therefore, it is important to set an expectation when developing treatment goals that these goals will be monitored regularly throughout the therapy. The therapist can collaborate with the client concerning type and frequency of measurements.

Perhaps the most important reason for measuring goal attainment is that it provides an objective view of therapeutic change. This view may facilitate treatment planning, client moralization, therapeutic alliance, and termination. Although treatment planning usually occurs early in therapy, it should be considered dynamic based on therapeutic progress. Whipple, Lambert, Vermeersch, Smart, Nielsen, and Hawkins (2003) found that therapists who were given suggestions for intervention modification based on client measures of outcome, stage of change, therapeutic alliance, and social support had better outcomes than those who did not receive advice. Second, measurement of progress may facilitate

client moralization during crucial phases of therapy. Even for clients making good therapeutic progress overall, each week is variable. Weekly in-session review of client outcomes may help clients to see outcome trends that overshadow a difficult week. Furthermore, if adequate change is not occurring, this measurement may highlight why change is sluggish. For example, simultaneous monitoring of mood and activity may indicate that a client feels less depressed when engaging in pleasurable activities, whereas mood is lower when activity is stalled. Third, measurement may bolster the therapeutic alliance if the therapist regularly reviews and interprets findings with the client. Research on weekly measurement suggests that clients generally dislike outcome assessment when they receive no feedback; in contrast, they tend to feel more positively about therapy and measure completion when they receive regular feedback (Halperin & Snyder, 1979). Finally, outcome measurement helps clients and therapists determine an appropriate termination point. Without this measurement, termination may be determined more subjectively by variables such as client liking for therapist or therapy. This may be less of a concern for self-pay clients; however, for clients relying on third-party payment, prudent use of resources is vital.

The next dialogue occurs in a later session with Ms. B. The therapist is monitoring the progress on treatment goals.

Therapist: One of the goals in your treatment plan was to increase the amount of sleep from 5 hours to 8 hours a night. We have been talking about ways to achieve this goal, such as cutting down on midday naps. How many hours a night have you been sleeping in the past week?

Ms. B: Well, I'm pretty sure I have been getting more.

T: That sounds like good news. What leads you to believe that?

Ms. B: I just feel better. And I have been writing down when I go to sleep and when I wake up, like we talked about, but I haven't actually calculated the numbers.

T: I'm glad you are feeling better, and I am impressed you have been tracking and recording your sleep patterns. Let's take the time in session to calculate exactly how many hours you have been getting and compare the numbers to our goal of 8 hours. It's important to know how close we are to our goal!

In this brief exchange, the therapist is acknowledging Ms. B's improved mood and the success of monitoring her sleep. However, the therapist is going beyond the client's verbal impressions by asking for specific, concrete information about the amount of hours she is sleeping.

Types of Outcome Measurement

Successful measurement entails careful selection of outcome measures and involves a number of dimensions including data collection method, level of specificity, and level of standardization. As a rule, however, all measurement should be easy to complete, reliable, and sensitive to change. First, one should consider several different measurement types, ranging from self-monitoring to self-report to clinician observation. Self-monitoring is a helpful way for clients and therapists to increase their awareness of current symptoms. The sleep diary is a good example of a self-monitoring instrument that might be used with Ms. B for variables such as sleep efficiency and number of night awakenings (Morin, 1993). Although observation by clinicians or others (e.g., parents, teachers, caregivers) is a common assessment method for children or the cognitively impaired, it is not often used with non–cognitively impaired adults aside from in-session observation. Self-report is by far the most commonly used assessment method with adults. This usually involves retrospective reports of behavior or mood over a specified preceding period of time (e.g., 1 week, 1 month). Verbal self-reports may also be collected in-session through therapist questions such as "How many nights over the past week have you had no night awakenings?" Verbal self-report is most successful when the therapist has brief list of questions that are repeated each session. Although either questionnaire or verbal self-report provides the most direct assessment of cognitive and emotional experiences, they have many of the commonly documented difficulties of retrospective reports, such as inaccuracy caused by client efforts at social desirability, faulty memory, or client lack of awareness (cf. Schwarz, 1999). A combination of clinician

observation, self-monitoring, and self-report questionnaires is ideal.

Second, regarding specificity, measurement can vary from global symptom distress (e.g., the Global Distress Scale on the Brief Symptom Inventory; Derogatis & Melisaratos, 1983) to more problem-specific measures such as the BDI-II (Beck et al., 1996) or the Pittsburgh Sleep Quality Index (Buysse, Reynolds, Monk, Berman, & Kupfer, 1989; Carpenter & Andrykowski, 1998). Furthermore, more specific aspects of particular problems may also be measured. For example, the extent of depressogenic thinking might be measured with the Dysfunctional Attitudes Scale (Weissman, 1980) or unhelpful sleep beliefs with the Dysfunctional Beliefs and Attitudes About Sleep Scale (Morin, Stone, Trinkle, Mercer, & Remsberg, 1993). In most cases, the instruments should measure specific goals, and both broad and narrow measures should be used to comprehensively measure progress (Woody, Detweiler-Bedell, Teachman, & O'Hearn, 2003).

Third, therapists must weigh the advantages and disadvantages of both standardized and idiographic approaches. Ideally, standardized measures such as the BDI-II have been normed on clinical and nonclinical populations and have demonstrated internal and external reliability as well as validity. On the other hand, idiographic measurement is developed uniquely for each client (e.g., subjective units of distress, $0 = no$ *depression* and $10 = the most depressed ever been$). Standardized measurement allows comparison of the client's distress level with those of clinical and nonclinical populations. Additionally, the magnitude of therapeutic change can be evaluated for clinical significance. That is, it can be determined whether the client's change is large enough that it is unlikely to be caused by measurement error and whether the posttest score is more likely to be from the clinical or nonclinical populations (Jacobson & Truax, 1991). The main deterrents to using standardized measures to measure clinical progress are that available measures may be expensive, cumbersome, or inadequately specific. Alternatively, idiographic measurement solves most of the problems raised by standardized assessment while forgoing many of the advantages. Idiographic assessment may involve verbal or written questions about intensity (e.g., "Please rate your sleep quality from $0 = worst quality ever$ to $10 = entirely restful$"), frequency (e.g., "How many times did you wake up for more than 1 minute?"), duration (e.g., "How many minutes did you lay in bed before falling asleep?"), or qualitative data (e.g., "Please write the most worrisome thoughts you had while awake in bed.") and can be tailored directly to client concerns. Of course, the results of these assessments can be compared only with the client's own scores. Often, careful assessment involves some combination of standardized and idiographic assessment. Idiographic assessment alone typically is not advised, however, because no conclusions can be made about whether clinically significant recovery is reached.

Frequency of Outcome Assessment

Once the types of measures have been decided, the next step is determining how often and when to give the measures. There is no clear consensus on how often to give measures to clients, but research has shown the importance of giving measures multiple times over the therapy. General agreement among researchers is that clinicians should give measures at least before treatment, at mid-treatment, and after treatment. Woody et al. (2003) suggest a general guideline of giving measures early and often. Measures may be given more frequently at the beginning of treatment in order to establish a clear baseline and monitor early progress. If clients are given measures too rarely, clinicians are likely to miss important changes or patterns in symptoms or behavior. However, clinicians should be cautious about giving measures too often because research suggests that giving measurements at every session can lead to an artificial improvement in scores. Longwell and Truax (2005) investigated the effects of repeated measurement with the BDI-II by randomly assigning college students to one of the following 2-month assessment schedules: weekly, monthly, or bimonthly. Whereas the monthly and bimonthly assessment groups had stable scores, the weekly assessment group had significant decreases in BDI-II scores. No groups received treatment or had a change in additional bimonthly-only assessment with other depression assessment measures. Taken together, these findings suggest that the BDI-II loses validity with weekly assessment, whereas it appears to retain validity with monthly and bimonthly assessment. Although it is unknown, based on these findings, whether this validity decline is unique to the BDI-II or is more ubiquitous across self-report questionnaires, these findings suggest that monthly assessment may be ideal.

Challenges

Common challenges to successful outcome assessment include low client motivation to complete measures and lack of correspondence between measures or observations. Client motivation may be affected by a number of factors. Perhaps the most important factor is therapist attitude and collaboration. A common but significant mistake by beginning clinicians is to have clients complete measures on a regular basis but never talking about the results in session. By doing this, the clinician is sending the message to the client that these measures are not important. The client may then become sloppy, inaccurate, or resentful when completing the measures. Clinicians can talk about the previous week's measures in session or even quickly score the current measures while the client is waiting before starting the session. The clinician can then begin the session by checking in with the client on whether the measures are an accurate reflection of the client's perceptions. The check-in also provides information about how clients are feeling about progress and opens to door to discussion of compliance issues in treatment. A therapist who is enthusiastic about the clinical role of outcome assessment and clearly explains the rationale is more likely to enlist client cooperation. In particular, regularly reviewing the results and using them as a clinical tool (e.g., pointing out the relationship between changes in sleep behaviors and sleep quality) is more likely to lead to client compliance. A second drain on client motivation is unnecessarily long, cumbersome, or frequent assessment. It is vital that clinicians choose efficient, easy-to-complete measures for frequent assessment. Short forms of commonly used measures such as the Beck Depression Inventory–Short Form (Reynolds & Gould, 1981) may be particularly useful for weekly assessment. The following is an example of how the therapist may review the outcome assessment with Ms. B.

Therapist: I really appreciate how willing you have been to think about your goals for treatment. I can see that you would really like to start feeling better.

Ms. B: I am desperate to improve my life. I already feel a little bit better because

I am starting to do something about my problems by coming to therapy. I hope this continues.

T: I am optimistic that through good hard work by you and me, you will start to notice some improvement in your mood and sleep as well as your school performance.

Ms. B: Yeah, I really hope so.

T: Because change often happens a little at a time and may wax and wane over days or weeks, it can be very helpful for us to measure your progress with some brief questionnaires and review them each week.

Ms. B: I really don't like filling out questionnaires. It is so boring and I just have to face how bad things are.

T: It is common for people to feel this way, especially at the beginning of therapy. I am also invested in making sure that these measures don't take too long and that we review them regularly, so we can use the results to make decisions about treatment. Would you be willing to complete one brief measure a week? It would take 5 minutes or less.

Ms. B: Yeah, I would be willing to do that, especially if I could learn more about myself.

T: We could alternate questionnaires and have you complete this assessment of your mood, called the Beck Depression Inventory–Short Form, one week and this brief sleep measure [Pittsburgh Sleep Quality Index] the next week. Would you be willing to complete both this week so that we can have a baseline measurement?

Ms. B: Sure! That doesn't sound like a big deal.

A second challenge is a lack of agreement between questionnaires and client verbal report or therapist observation. Therapists should explore the reasons behind this discrepancy. The mismatch may result from the uniqueness of the client's experience while filling out the measures. For instance, the client may be extremely anxious while waiting for the therapy session to begin. Conversely, the client may be trying to project a socially desirable image or be extremely optimistic about meeting with the therapist. Either way, if the results are skewed by clients' presession thoughts or feelings, it is important that the

therapist encourage honest self-appraisal and emphasize the questionnaires' timeframes (e.g., "How has your mood been over the last week?"). If the measures' results are inaccurate for some other reason, such as poor vision or limited vocabulary, the therapist should problem solve with the client to increase the accuracy. Again, it is imperative that the therapist convey the importance of the measures to the client.

Reviewing Progress With Client

Once the clinician has verified with the client that the measures' results are a reasonably accurate reflection of the client's experience, the therapist should discuss the results in a meaningful way. Results should never be framed in a pass-fail context but rather as an opportunity to reflect on therapy. If the measures are showing progress toward treatment goals, the therapist should acknowledge the successes and congratulate the client. Also, the therapist may want to inquire about what the client thinks has led to or contributed to the progress. If the measures are showing no progress toward the goals, the therapist should also acknowledge this and ask the client what he or she believes is the reason for the lack of change. Clients may appreciate this consumer-oriented approach, in which their satisfaction (or dissatisfaction) can be openly discussed. The therapist may want to problem solve with the client about obstacles to success (e.g., if client is not doing homework) and propose changes in treatment interventions. Finally, it is important to remember that no progress or worsening of symptoms in the first few sessions may be a sign that either the treatment plan or the therapeutic alliance is amiss. Because dropout is particularly likely when clients are demoralized by continued distress despite treatment, it is important that the client and therapist reevaluate the treatment direction and make changes as necessary. The following is a dialogue with Ms. B that illustrates how to introduce and discuss the results of measures with clients.

Therapist: Welcome back! I have looked over your measures and want to discuss with you how well the measures match with your experience over the last week. The first one I would like to discuss is the one that measures changes in your mood and other signs of depression, such as changes in sleep and appetite. Compared to last time you filled this out, which was 2 weeks ago, your scores have not changed in any noticeable way. How well does this match with how you have been feeling in the last 2 weeks?

Ms. B: That sounds about right. I have been feeling the same for the last couple weeks; I am still sad and having difficulty focusing at school.

T: How would you feel about putting this lack of improved mood on our agenda today? I think it's really important that we figure out why this is happening and come up with some ways to improve your mood.

Ms. B: Yeah, I would really like to be able to function better at school. I just don't feel like I have the energy or focus to really concentrate and put effort into studying.

T: It sounds like this is a high-priority issue, so let's spend some time today working on ways to boost your mood and concentration.

REFERRALS

Because clinicians have an ethical responsibility to provide the best possible care for clients, a central part of identifying treatment targets and treatment planning is identifying the need for a referral as either an adjunct or an alternative to treatment with the assessing clinician. The reasons for a referral include a lack of therapist expertise for client presenting concern, a lack of progress after beginning therapy, or enhancement of ongoing treatment with the assessing therapist. Perhaps the most common reason for referral is inadequate expertise. The APA Code of Conduct (2002) clearly states, "Psychologists provide services, teach, and conduct research with populations and in areas only within the boundaries of their competence, based on their education, training, supervised experience, consultation, study, or professional experience" (p. 1063). Although competence and incompetence are not dichotomous, a general guideline for evaluating whether a therapist should continue with a case or make a referral is the use of a cost-benefit analysis. For therapists in remote locations with few viable referral sources, the costs of a referral may outweigh the benefits of treating cases closer

to the edge of competence. In urban areas with many specialists, referrals should be more common for client concerns not central to therapist competence (APA, 2002). When possible, referrals should be made immediately after assessment unless the problem emerges later in therapy. Referrals that occur after the therapy relationship has commenced often involve more emotional costs (i.e., ending of the initial therapeutic relationship) than those that occur earlier in the process.

Exceptions to the very early referral include lack of progress, new client concerns that are outside the therapist's competence, therapeutic relationship difficulties, or significantly increased severity (e.g., suicidal crisis). The APA Code of Ethics (2002) states, "Psychologists strive to benefit those with whom they work and take care to do no harm" (p. 1062). When the client fails to make expected progress (Lambert, Hansen, & Finch, 2001), it is incumbent on the therapist to consider the costs and potential benefits of changes to the treatment plan or a referral. Similarly, if a new problem arises during treatment that is outside the therapist's scope of expertise, a referral should be made at that point. Additionally, if a client and therapist have an unresolvable conflict, the therapist should initiate a referral. For example, the therapist may have difficulty helping a woman who wants to work on ensuring the success of an emotionally abusive relationship. In this case, the therapist needs to be aware of whether his or her own values are negatively affecting treatment and, if so, refer the client out. A client may also initiate the process by requesting a different therapist. For example, a client may express a preference for another modality of treatment, such as group therapy. Of course, if a client becomes imminently suicidal or homicidal at any point in the assessment or treatment phase, treatment intensity normally should be increased. This might include hospitalization or a referral to a resource that can provide more intensive services. Of course, the therapist should take care that clients are not abandoned in crisis. Rather, the therapist must carefully monitor the transfer or referral for a suicidal client and ensure that a successful transition was made.

Finally, referrals often are adjunctive to treatment with an assessing clinician. Examples of possible therapy augmenting referrals include medication, testing, or group, family, or couple therapy. Although the literature on the added benefit of medication with psychotherapy is mixed for some conditions such as mild to moderate depression or anxiety disorders, medication should always be considered as an adjunct to psychotherapy for psychosis, bipolar disorder, or severe or chronic depression (cf. Otto, Smits, & Reese, 2005) or for clients who request a medication referral. Although the reasons for referrals for testing vary widely, they may include neuropsychological testing for clients with head injuries or recent changes in cognitive functioning, learning disability assessment for clients with chronic difficulties functioning at work or school, or personality testing to facilitate treatment planning. Referrals for additional therapy modalities may be appropriate for clients who are having any of the following problems in addition to individual concerns: marital or relationship problems, child-rearing problems, a particular skill deficit that may benefit from a psychoeducational group (e.g., assertiveness, parenting skills), or interpersonal problems that might benefit from a process group.

When making a referral, the therapist should take certain steps to ensure that it is successful for the client. The first step is for clinicians to educate themselves on possible referral sources in their communities. Ideally, clinicians have a list that includes resources for a variety of problems. The second step is to talk with the client about the reasons for the referral and collaboratively decide about the best possible referral resources. If the client does not feel that the referral source will be helpful, the client is less likely to follow up (Hersen & Van Hasselt, 1998). Therefore, it is important to be specific and clear about what the referral source can provide and how to contact the professional. Additionally, the clinician should contact the referral source and inform him or her of the client's presenting problem, provided the client has provided authorization. The referral therapist then has the choice about whether to treat the client. If the referral therapist chooses not to treat the client, it is that therapist's obligation to refer the client to another treatment provider. If these steps are taken, the referral process should be successful for all parties involved.

Challenges may arise during the referral process. A common challenge is a client who appears hesitant to take the steps to continue treatment with the referral source. When this happens, it is important for the clinician to express confidence in the referral therapist and problem solve with the client. The initial therapist may help the client determine when to call the new therapist and even what to say. If the referral is for additional treatment, such as a psychiatric consultation, the therapist should follow up with the client to ensure that it happened and to assess client reactions to the referral. Another challenge may be the clinician's reluctance to end treatment with a client. In this case, consultation and supervision may be necessary. With awareness of these potential challenges, clinicians can address them and provide an efficient and successful referral.

Summary

Identification of treatment targets, goals, and outgoing outcome assessment are the foundation to successful intervention. The prioritization of treatment targets involves clarifying the nature and severity of client concerns, treatment outcome research, readiness for change, client preference, feasibility, and client variables such as culture. Key ingredients to effective negotiation of this treatment planning are the therapist's presentation of a clear rationale, collaboration with the client, and a good therapeutic alliance.

References

American Psychological Association. (2002). Ethical principles of psychologists and code of conduct. *American Psychologist, 57,* 1060–1073.

Antonuccio, D. O., Thomas, M., & Danton, W. G. (1997). A cost-effectiveness analysis of cognitive behavior therapy and fluoxetine (Prozac) in the treatment of depression. *Behavior Therapy, 28,* 187–210.

Antony, M. M., Orsillo, S. M., & Roemer, L. (2001). *Practitioner's guide to empirically based measures of anxiety.* New York: Kluwer Academic.

Arredondo, P., Toporek, R., Brown, S. P., Sanchez, J., Locke, D. C., Sanchez, J., et al. (1996). Operationalization of the multicultural counseling competencies. *Journal of Multicultural Counseling and Development, 24,* 42–78.

Beck, A., Steer, R., & Brown, G. (1996). *Manual for the BDI-II.* San Antonio, TX: The Psychological Corporation.

Beutler, L. E., Engle, D., Mohr, D., Daldrup, R. J., Bergan, J., Meredith, K., et al. (1991). Predictors of differential response to cognitive, experiential, and self-directed psychotherapeutic procedures. *Journal of Consulting and Clinical Psychology, 59,* 333–340.

Booth, P. G., Dale, B., & Ansari, J. (1984). Problem drinkers' goal choice and treatment outcome: A preliminary study. *Addictive Behaviors, 9,* 357–364.

Brown, C., Schulberg, H. C., Madonia, M. J., Shear, M. K., & Houck, P. R. (1996). Treatment outcomes for primary care patients with major depression and lifetime anxiety disorders. *American Journal of Psychiatry, 153,* 1293–1300.

Brown, V. B., Melchior, L. A., Panter, A. T., Slaughter, R., & Huba, G. J. (2000). Women's steps of change and entry into drug abuse treatment: A multidimensional stages of change model. *Journal of Substance Abuse Treatment, 18,* 231–240.

Buysse, D. J., Reynolds, C. F., Monk, T. H., Berman, S. R., & Kupfer, D. J. (1989). The Pittsburgh Sleep Quality Index: A new instrument for psychiatric practice and research. *Psychiatry Research, 28,* 193–213.

Carpenter, J., & Andrykowski, M. A. (1998). Psychometric evaluation of the Pittsburgh Sleep Quality Index. *Journal of Psychosomatic Research, 45*(1), 5–13.

Castonguay, L. G., Schut, A. J., Constantino, M. J., & Halperin, G. S. (1999). Assessing the role of treatment manuals: Have they become necessary but nonsufficient ingredients of change? *Clinical Psychology: Science and Practice, 6,* 449–455.

Clements-Thompson, M., Klesges, R. C., Haddock, K., Lando, H., & Talcott, W. (1998). Relationships between stages of change in cigarette smokers and healthy lifestyle behaviors in a population of young military personnel during forced smoking abstinence. *Journal of Consulting and Clinical Psychology, 66,* 1005–1011.

Corcoran, K., & Fischer, J. (2000a). *Measures for clinical practice: A sourcebook: Vol. 1. Couples, families, and children* (3rd ed.). New York: Free Press.

Corcoran, K., & Fischer, J. (2000b). *Measures for clinical practice: A sourcebook: Vol. 2. Adults* (3rd ed.). New York: Free Press.

Craske, M. G., Maidenberg, E., & Bystritsky, A. (1995). Brief cognitive-behavioral versus nondirective therapy for panic disorder. *Journal of Behavior Therapy and Experimental Psychiatry, 26,* 113–120.

Derogatis, L., & Melisaratos, N. (1983). The brief symptom inventory: An introductory report. *Psychological Medicine, 13*(3), 595–605.

Dozois, D. J., Westra, H. A., Collins, K. A., Fung, T. S., & Garry, J. K. (2004). Stages of change in anxiety: Psychometric properties of the University of Rhode Island Change Assessment (URICA) scale. *Behaviour Research and Therapy, 42*(6), 711–729.

Drisko, J. W. (2004). Common factors in psychotherapy outcome: Meta-analytic findings and their implications for practice and research. *Families in Society, 85,* 81–90.

Halperin, K. M., & Snyder, C. R. (1979). Effects of enhanced psychological test feedback on treatment outcome: Therapeutic implications of the Barnum effect. *Journal of Consulting and Clinical Psychology, 47,* 140–146.

Hatcher, R. L. (1999). Therapists' views of treatment alliance and collaboration in therapy. *Psychotherapy Research, 9,* 405–423.

Hawkins, E. J., Lambert, M. J., Vermeersch, D. A., Slade, K. L., & Tuttle, K. C. (2004). The therapeutic effects of providing patient progress information to therapists and patients. *Psychotherapy Research, 14,* 308–327.

Hays, P. A. (2002). *Addressing cultural complexities in practice.* Washington, DC: American Psychological Association.

Hecker, J. E., Fink, C. M., & Fritzler, B. K. (1993). Acceptability of panic disorder treatments: A survey of family practice physicians. *Journal of Anxiety Disorders, 7,* 373–384.

Hersen, M., & Van Hasselt, V. B. (1998). *Basic interviewing: A practical guide for counselors and clinicians.* Mahwah, NJ: Lawrence Erlbaum.

Horowitz, M. J., Wilner, N., & Alvarez, W. (1979). Impact of event scale: A measure of subjective stress. *Psychosomatic Medicine, 41,* 209–218.

Hoyt, M. F. (1995). *Brief therapy and managed care: Readings for contemporary practice.* San Francisco: Jossey-Bass.

Jacobson, N. S., Dobson, K., Fruzzetti, A. E., Schmaling, K. B., & Salusky, S. (1991). Marital therapy as a treatment for depression. *Journal of Consulting and Clinical Psychology, 59,* 547–557.

Jacobson, N. S., & Truax, P. (1991). Clinical significance: A statistical approach to defining meaningful change in psychotherapy research. *Journal of Consulting and Clinical Psychology, 59,* 12–19.

James, L. D., Thorn, B. E., & Williams, D. A. (1993). Goal specification in cognitive-behavioral therapy for chronic headache pain. *Behavior Therapy, 24,* 305–320.

Keller, M. B., Lavori, P. W., Friedman, B., Nielsen, E., Endicott, J., McDonald-Scott, P., et al. (1987). The Longitudinal Interval Follow-Up Evaluation: A comprehensive method for assessing outcome in prospective longitudinal studies. *Archives of General Psychiatry, 44,* 540–548.

Lambert, M. J., & Barley, D. E. (2001). Research summary on the therapeutic relationship and psychotherapy outcome. *Psychotherapy: Theory, Research, Practice, Training, 38,* 357–361.

Lambert, M. J., Hansen, N. B., & Finch, A. E. (2001). Patient-focused research: Using patient outcome data to enhance treatment effects. *Journal of Consulting and Clinical Psychology, 69,* 159–172.

Lambert, M. J., Whipple, J. L., Smart, D. W., Vermeersch, D. A., Nielsen, S. L., & Hawkins, E. J. (2001). The effects of providing therapists with feedback on patient progress during psychotherapy: Are outcomes enhanced? *Psychotherapy Research, 11,* 49–68.

Lambert, M. J., Whipple, J. L., Vermeersch, D. A., Smart, D. W., Hawkins, E. J., Nielsen, S. L. et al. (2001). Enhancing psychotherapy outcomes via providing feedback on client progress: A replication. *Clinical Psychology and Psychotherapy, 9,* 91–103.

Linehan, M. M. (1993). *Cognitive-behavioral treatment of borderline personality disorder.* New York: Guilford.

Lippincott, J. A., & Mierzwa, J. A. (1995). Propensity for seeking counseling services: A comparison of Asian and American undergraduates. *Journal of American College Health, 43,* 201–204.

Locke, E. A., & Latham, G. P. (1990). *A theory of goal setting and task performance.* Englewood Cliffs, NJ: Prentice Hall.

Longwell, B. T., & Truax, P. (2005). The differential effects of weekly, monthly, and bimonthly administrations of the Beck Depression Inventory-II: Psychometric properties and clinical implications. *Behavior Therapy, 36,* 265–276.

McFall, M. E., Smith, D. E., Roszell, D. K., Tarver, D. J., & Malas, K. L. (1990). Convergent validity of measures of PTSD in Vietnam combat veterans. *American Journal of Psychiatry, 147,* 645–648.

Miller, W., & Rollnick, S. (2002). *Motivational interviewing: Preparing people for change* (2nd ed.). New York: Guilford.

Morin, C. M. (1993). *Insomnia: Psychological assessment and management.* New York: Guilford.

Morin, C. M., Stone, J., Trinkle, D., Mercer, J., & Remsberg, S. (1993). Dysfunctional beliefs and attitudes about sleep among older adults with and without insomnia complaints. *Psychology and Aging, 8,* 463–476.

Nezu, A. M., Ronan, G. F., Meadows, E. A., & McClure, K. S. (2000). *Practitioner's guide to empirically based measures of depression.* New York: Kluwer Academic.

Nguyen, S. D. (1982). Psychiatric and psychosomatic problems among Southeast Asian refugees. *Psychiatric Journal of the University of Ottawa, 7,* 163–172.

Noble, L. M., & Douglas, B. C. (2004). What users and relatives want from mental health services. *Current Opinion in Psychiatry, 17,* 289–296.

Otto, M. W., Smits, J. A. J., & Reese, H. E. (2005). Combined psychotherapy and pharmacotherapy for mood and anxiety disorders in adults: Review and analysis. *Clinical Psychology: Science and Practice, 12,* 72–86.

Prochaska, J. O., & Norcross, J. C. (1999). *Systems of psychotherapy: A transtheoretical approach.* Pacific Grove, CA: Brooks/Cole.

Reynolds, W. M., & Gould, J. W. (1981). A psychometric investigation of the standard and short form Beck Depression Inventory. *Journal of Consulting and Clinical Psychology, 49,* 306–307.

Schwarz, N. (1999). Self-reports: How the questions shape the answers. *American Psychologist, 54,* 93–105.

Scott, M. J., & Stradling, S. G. (1997). Client compliance with exposure treatments for posttraumatic stress disorder. *Journal of Traumatic Stress, 10,* 523–526.

Scott, K. L., & Wolfe, D. A. (2003). Readiness to change as a predictor of outcome in batterer treatment. *Journal of Consulting and Clinical Psychology, 71,* 879–889.

Sobell, M. B., Sobell, L. C., Bogardis, J., Leo, G. I., & Skinner, W. (1992). Problem drinkers' perceptions of whether treatment goals should be self-selected or therapist-selected. *Behavior Therapy, 23,* 43–52.

Sotsky, S. M., Glass, D. R., Shea, M. T., Pilkonis, P. A., Collins, J. F., & Elkin, I. (1991). Patient predictors of response to psychotherapy and pharmacotherapy: Findings in the NIMH Treatment of Depression Collaborative Research Program. *American Journal of Psychiatry, 148,* 997–1008.

Spielberger, C. D., Gorsuch, R. L., Lushene, R., Vagg, P. R., & Jacobs, G. A. (1983). *Manual for the State-Trait Anxiety Inventory (Form Y).* Palo Alto, CA: Mind Garden.

Sundin, E. C., & Horowitz, M. J. (2003). Horowitz's Impact of Event Scale evaluation of 20 years of use. *Psychosomatic Medicine, 65,* 870–876.

Tracey, T. J., & Kokotovic, A. M. (1989). Factor structure of the Working Alliance Inventory. *Psychological Assessment, 1,* 207–210.

Treasure, J. L., Katzman, M., Schmidt, U., Troop, N., Todd, G., & de Silva, P. (1999). Engagement and outcome in the treatment of bulimia nervosa: First phase of a sequential design comparing motivation enhancement therapy and cognitive behavioural therapy. *Behaviour Research and Therapy, 37,* 405–418.

Tryon, G. S., & Winograd, G. (2001). Goal consensus and collaboration. *Psychotherapy: Theory, Research, Practice, Training, 38,* 385–389.

Tsao, J. C. I., Mystkowski, J. L., Zucker, B. G., & Craske, M. G. (2002). Effects of cognitive-behavioral therapy for panic disorder on comorbid conditions: Replication and extension. *Behavior Therapy, 33,* 493–509.

Ware, J. E., Jr., Snow, K. K., Kosinski, M., & Gandek, B. (1993). *SF-36 health survey. Manual and interpretation guide.* Boston: The Health Institute, New England Medical Center.

Weissman, A. (1980). *Assessing depressogenic attitudes: A validation study.* Paper presented at the 51st Annual Meeting of the Eastern Psychological Association, Hartford, CT.

Whipple, J. L., Lambert, M. J., Vermeersch, D. A., Smart, D. W., Nielsen, S. L., & Hawkins, E. J. (2003). Improving the effects of psychotherapy: The use of early identification of treatment and problem-solving strategies in routine practice. *Journal of Counseling Psychology, 50,* 59–68.

Winters, D., & Latham, G. P. (1996). The effect of learning versus outcome goals on a simple versus a complex task. *Group & Organization Management, 21,* 236–250.

Woody, S. R., Detweiler-Bedell, J., Teachman, B. A., & O'Hearn, T. (2003). *Treatment planning in psychotherapy: Taking the guesswork out of clinical care.* New York: Guilford.

Zetik, D. C., & Stuhlmacher, A. F. (2002). Goal setting and negotiation performance: A meta-analysis. *Group Processes & Intergroup Relations, 5,* 35–52.

8

SUICIDE RISK ASSESSMENT

ELIZABETH T. DEXTER-MAZZA AND KATHRYN E. KORSLUND

S uicide continues to be a major health concern for all ages in the United States (Murphy, 2000). Recent statistics show that it is the 11th leading cause of death in the United States (McIntosh, 2006). According to the American Association of Suicidology (AAS; McIntosh, 2002), 787,000 people attempt suicide each year, and for every 25 attempts there is one death. The National Vital Statistics Report (Murphy, 2000) indicated an overall decrease in suicide-related deaths dating back to 1979 and up to data from 1998. The rate decreased from 11.7 to 10.4 per 100,000 people, and more recently it decreased 1.9% between 1997 and 1998. Although overall rates of suicide decreased from 1994 to 2000, there was a slight increase in 2001 and 2002 (McIntosh, 2004). Furthermore, the distribution of rates varies across age, gender, and race; whereas some categories have decreased, others have increased.

One important issue in studying and reviewing research examining suicide and suicidal behaviors is the terminology used by different authors. Reynolds and Mazza (1994) note that the description of suicidal behaviors has varied over time and that there is a continuum of suicide behaviors, ranging from suicide ideation to suicide attempts to deaths due to suicide. They defined *suicide ideation* as thoughts about self-inflicted injuries or death, including plans, means, and outcomes of suicidal behaviors. Suicide

attempts included self-injurious behaviors with some level of intent to die. Finally, *suicide* was defined as any intentional self-inflicted injurious behavior that leads to death. Current literature also suggests the use of other terminology (Linehan, 1993; Rudd, Joiner, & Rajab, 2001). Linehan considered *suicidal threats* to include statements of intent without action, and *almost suicidal behaviors* to include actions of intent without actual completion, such as putting a gun in the mouth but not shooting. She also used the term *parasuicidal,* a term originally coined by Kreitman in 1977 (as cited in Linehan, 1993), to refer to "nonfatal, intentional self-injurious behavior that results in actual tissue damage, illness, or risk of death. [It also includes] any ingestion of drugs or other substances not prescribed or in excess of prescription with clear intent to cause bodily harm or death" (Linehan, 1993, p. 14). However, it does not include death due to suicide, suicidal threats, suicide ideation, or almost suicidal behaviors (Linehan, 1993). Because of the continued lack of specificity and support for this term internationally, Linehan has dropped the term *parasuicide* in her current work. The problem with this term is that it does not provide the behavioral specificity that this field is lacking. Similar confusion is present in the literature from the United Kingdom. Deliberate self-harm has become the accepted term in the United Kingdom to describe similar behaviors

(Hawton, Harriss, Simkin, Bale, & Bond, 2004). However, this term does not discriminate between suicide attempts and nonsuicidal self-injury. Furthermore, Rudd and colleagues used the presence of intent to die to distinguish between instrumental behaviors and suicidal behaviors. According to their definition, people engaging in instrumental behaviors have no intent to die. Rather, the function of the behavior can be considered to be help seeking, punishment of others, or attention seeking (Rudd et al., 2001). Upon comparison, instrumental and parasuicidal behaviors appear to have some similarities in definition, which may lead to confusion on the part of readers and researchers who are assessing clients and determining appropriate interventions. Rudd and colleagues further distinguish suicide attempts with injuries and suicide attempts without injuries using level of lethality. Furthermore, intent is an important variable to consider in determining suicide risk. It would be unseemly for us to provide our own terminology; this would only add to the confusion of the field because there is no agreed-upon nomenclature. However, we encourage others to be as behaviorally specific as possible, especially when distinguishing nonsuicidal self-injurious behaviors and suicidal behaviors (e.g., specifying intent, lethality, specific behavior).

DEMOGRAPHIC CHARACTERISTICS OF SUICIDE

Given different types of suicidal behavior, prevalence rates and characteristics of people who engage in such behavior vary depending on the type of the suicidal behavior considered. In this section, characteristics of people who engage in suicidal behavior are considered, with the primary focus on those who die by suicide.

Gender

In 2003, approximately 1.3% of deaths in the United States were caused by suicide (McIntosh, 2006). Of the 31,484 suicides in 2003, males made up the majority of this group, with 25,203 deaths, versus 6,281 for females. These data are consistent with those of previous years, suggesting that males are four to five times as likely to die by suicide as females; however, females report attempting suicide two to three times as often as males

(McIntosh, 2006; National Institute of Mental Health, 1999).

Methods

According to McIntosh (2006), among the common methods used to commit suicide, firearms (53.7%) are the most frequently used, followed by hanging or suffocation (21.1%). The third cause of death is by poisons (17.3%). Other less lethal means included jumping from high places, cutting and piercing, drowning, jumping or lying in front of moving objects, or purposefully burning or setting fire to self (7.9%).

As mentioned previously, males are more likely to die by suicide than females. This is because males tend to use more lethal means than females (McIntosh, 2000). Use of the most lethal means to commit suicide in 1998 (i.e., firearms and explosives) varied by gender, with 61.6% of males and only 38.4% of females using these methods. The second most common method by males (19.2%) and females (16.8%) was hanging, strangulation, or suffocation. For all other methods of suicide, rates of use were higher for females than males. Based on the 4:1 ratio of suicide between males and females, percentages based on methods were higher for females even though the actual number of suicides was greater for males in 1998.

Age Groups

The problem of suicide varies greatly by age group. As stated previously, suicide is the 11th leading cause of death in the United States for all races and both genders. However, it is the fourth leading cause of death for people who are 9–14 years old, third for people 15–24 years old, second for people 25–34 years old, fourth for people 35–44 years old, sixth for people 45–54 years old, and eighth for people 55–64 years old (Anderson, 2001). Although suicide did not rank in the top 10 causes of death for people over the age of 65 in 2003, the rate of suicide among older adults was 14.6 per 100,000 (McIntosh, 2006). From 1979 to 1998, the rate of suicide for the 5- to 14-year-old cohort doubled from 0.4 to 0.8 per 100,000 and decreased to 0.6 per 100,000 in 1999. It also increased from 17.9 to 21.0 for those 85 years and older and again decreased in 1999 to 19.2 per 100,000. Furthermore, the rates for all other age groups have decreased (McIntosh, 2000).

Race

Race is another important factor by which suicide varies. Although suicide rates are lower among African Americans than among Caucasians, rates increased significantly between 1950 and 1981; in the 15- to 24-year-old cohort alone it increased by 214% and 133% for African American males and females, respectively (Health, 1984, as cited in Baker, 1990). Rate of suicide peaked at 12.5 per 100,000 African Americans in 1993. Since then, the rate for both genders has steadily decreased and was at 6.2 in 1998 (Joe & Kaplan, 2001) and 5.1 in 2003 (McIntosh, 2006). Similar to the national statistics on overall rates, African American males are still six times more likely to commit suicide than African American females (Joe & Kaplan, 2001).

The Native American population also has experienced an increase in suicide rates in recent decades. According to the Centers for Disease Control and Prevention (CDC, 2000), Native American suicide rates were 1.5 times the national average from 1979 to 1992. Furthermore, during this time period, 64% of suicides among Native Americans were accounted for by males between the ages of 15 and 24 (CDC, 2000). Literature suggests a connection between suicide and the decrease of young Native Americans adhering to traditional family living (Berlin, 1987). Such incongruence between family members, the tribe, and the young adult may lead to an increasingly chaotic family and adult alcoholism, both risk factors for suicidal behavior (Berlin, 1987; Westefeld et al., 2000). Furthermore, levels of acculturation of young Native Americans may also serve as a risk factor for suicide among this population, which may account for varied suicide rates across tribes. For example, tribes such as the Navajo, which have stronger tribal support and live in more remote areas, have lower rates of suicide than tribes that experience higher levels of acculturation (Middlebrook, LeMaster, Beals, Novins, & Manson, 2001).

SPECIFIC RISK FACTORS FOR SUICIDE

A wide variety of factors must be considered when one is assessing the level of suicide risk in any person. Although there is a common acceptance and support of general risk factors for suicide, we are lacking in the understanding and dissemination of risk factors for specific populations, including psychiatric inpatients, prison or jail inmates, single versus multiple attempters, and people with specific disorders (e.g., bipolar disorder, major depressive disorder, schizophrenia). This section provides a detailed description of both general and specific risk and protective factors for suicide.

Assessing a person's level of potential for suicide risk encompasses two primary components: the clinical and empirical assessment of risk factors. Most often, the clinician makes the most accurate estimation of risk by completing a thorough assessment of objective risk factors before making any decisions based on clinical experiences (Motto, 1991). First, it is important to understand the demographics of the person being assessed and the suicide rates for each demographic group. Unfortunately, we have not yet developed a composite score of risk factors to predict suicide. Therefore, we must look at the number of current risk factors that are present and estimate the suicide risk for each individual. Risk factors can be organized by history of behaviors, current behaviors, recent problems, current mental status, and chronic problems (Table 8.1).

For the general populations risk factors for imminent suicide include major depression with severe anhedonia, agitation or global insomnia, recent loss (e.g., death, loss of employment), isolation from others, current alcohol or substance use, hopelessness, frequency, intensity, and duration of suicidal ideation, development of method, availability and access to means, presence of suicide preparatory behaviors (e.g., giving away belongings, writing a will or suicide note, tying up loose ends such as financial or business responsibilities) dissatisfaction with therapy, or recent publicity about a suicide (Linehan, 1993). It is imperative that all therapists and mental health practitioners have these risk factors memorized and easily accessible because you never know when you may find yourself in a crisis situation with a client. As mentioned previously, these are the general risk factors that must be taken into consideration in assessing all clients. However, specific risk factors for different populations also must be addressed.

Previous Suicide Attempts

The best predictor of future behavior is past behavior. We have heard this saying over and over

Table 8.1   Risk and Protective Factors for Suicide

Risk Factors	Protective Factors

History
    Ambivalent suicide attempt
    Suicide attempts (i.e., clear intent to die)
    Medically significant attempt or self-injury
    Family history of suicidal behavior
	Current
	    Hope for the future
	    Self-efficacy in problem area
	    Attachment to life
	    Responsibility to children, family, or others,
	        including pets, whom client would not
	        abandon

Current
    Plan or preparation (including specific method
        and time)
    Suicide ideation (frequency, duration, intensity)
    Suicide intent (including client belief that he or
        she is going to commit suicide or hurt self)
    Preferred method available or easily obtained
    Lethal means (of any sort) available or easily
        obtained
    Precautions against discovery (e.g., deception
        about timing, place)
 	
    Isolation
    Substance use (including alcohol and prescription
        meds in the past 3 hours)
    First 72 hours of incarceration
	Attachment to therapy and at least one therapist
	    Therapist attached (will stay in contact)
	    Embedded in protective social network or family
	    Fear of social disapproval for suicide
	    Fear of act of suicide, death, and dying or no
	        acceptable method available
	    Belief that suicide is immoral or that it will be
	        punished (high spirituality)
	    Commitment to live and history of taking
	        commitments seriously or reason to trust
	        this commitment
	    Client willing to follow crisis plan

Current mental status
    Major depression plus
        Severe turmoil, anxiety, panic attacks, mood
            cycling
        Severe global insomnia
        Severe anhedonia
        Inability to concentrate
        Psychosis (voices telling client to commit suicide)
        Severe hopelessness	

Recent
    Prompting events for previous suicide attempt
        or significant self-injury
    Sudden loss (other negative event)
    Abrupt clinical change (either negative or positive)
    Indifference or dissatisfaction with therapy	

Chronic or usual
    Physical pain
    Impulsiveness	

SOURCE: Adapted from University of Washington Behavioral Research and Therapy Clinics Imminent Risk and Severe Self-injury Risk and Treatment Actions Note (2004).

again when referring to clients. When it comes to suicide, we know that presence of one or more past suicide attempts increases the current risk of suicide. Clark, Gibbons, Fawcett, and Scheftner (1989) suggest that suicidal behavior may be explained by the trait hypothesis, or that suicidal behavior is caused by a "latent person-specific trait" (p. 42) in people with affective disorders. Their study identified a significant relationship between history of past attempts and future attempts. However, they did not find the recency of the previous attempt to be related to future attempts. Rudd et al. (2001) have also reported significant differences in the risk profile of those who are considered multiple attempters (one or more previous suicide attempts) and single attempters. Furthermore, the level of lethality of previous suicide attempts also is a determining factor in suicide risk (Modai, Kuperman, Goldberg, Goldish, & Mendel, 2004). Modai and colleagues determined that those with previous medically serious suicide attempts have a higher level of suicide risk than those who have made less serious attempts. Furthermore, they identified previous medically serious suicide attempts as the most powerful risk factor for determining the current estimate of suicide risk.

When evaluating past suicide attempts, it is important to distinguish between intent and lethality. Although someone may state that he or she intended to kill himself or herself, you must also evaluate the level of lethality determined by the means. For example, a client with direct intent to kill herself may take four sleeping pills with the belief that those four pills would be lethal, whereas someone else with no intent or ambivalent intent and the desire to sleep may take 50 sleeping pills. The level of lethality and medically serious outcomes would place the latter client at a higher level of estimated risk. Whereas some clients are acutely aware of the risk factors associated with taking excessive amounts of medications or mixing medications, many are not. Therefore, it is important to assess for both the type and amounts of medication the client has available.

Family History of Suicide

A family history of suicidal behaviors may increase a person's estimated level of risk to moderate. The increased risk may result from the modeling of suicidal behaviors in a family pedigree or may be more specifically caused by a genetic or biological trait passed through family pedigrees. In the early 1980s, studies found that 34–48% of people who engaged in suicidal behaviors had a family history of suicidal behaviors (Murphy & Wetzel, 1982; Roy, 1983). Roy (1992a) combined several studies examining the concordance rates of suicide in monozygotic and dizygotic twins. He found a 13.2% concordance rate for monozygotic twins and a 0.7% rate for dizygotic twins. In addition to the twin studies, Roy (1992a) also reviewed adoption studies that were carried out in Denmark. These studies examined the biological family histories of 57 adopted people who committed suicide out of a large sample of adopted people ($n = 5{,}483$). Two hundred sixty-nine biological relatives of the 57 who committed suicide were identified; 12 (4.5%) biological relatives also committed suicide, whereas none of the adoptive relatives committed suicide. Furthermore, in 1985 Egeland and Sussex reported their findings from a study of eight family pedigrees of the Amish in Lancaster, Pennsylvania. All eight of these family pedigrees were loaded with an array of affective disorders. However, in four of the families there were a total of 26 suicides, whereas there were none in the other four, showing that suicide may occur independent of affective disorders. Based on the studies summarized here, there may be a distinctive genetic factor that increases the risk for suicidal behaviors.

Presence of Mental Disorders

The mental health of adults in the United States has become a matter of concern, especially in the area of suicide. Studies over the past 30 years indicate that 90% of adults who commit suicide have a psychiatric disorder at the time of their death (Kaplan & Harrow, 1999). Furthermore, the diagnosis of a personality disorder presents a significant increase in suicide risk when it is comorbid with a primary major affective disorder or a psychotic disorder (Hansen, Wang, Stage, & Kragh-Sorensen, 2003; Moran et al., 2003).

Mood and Anxiety Disorders

According to the *Diagnostic and Statistical Manual of Mental Disorders, Fourth Edition, Text Revision (DSM-IV-TR;* American Psychiatric Association, 2000), 15% of those diagnosed with major depressive disorder (MDD) and 10–15% of those diagnosed with bipolar I disorder will die by suicide. However, other studies have challenged the rate for MDD as being inflated. Blair-West, Cantor, Mellsop, and Eyeson-Annon (1999) believe that the current population suicide rates would have to be much higher if the rate of 15% were true, given that MDD has a prevalence rate of 17%. They suggest the rate to be much lower, only 3.4%, for MDD. Additionally, it is unclear whether the prevalence rate of suicide for bipolar disorder is accurate. Some have reported the suicide rate for the bipolar disorders to be less than that of MDD (Angst, Stassen, Clayton, & Angst, 2002; Hoyer, Olesen, & Mortensen, 2004), whereas others have reported a mean rate of 19% in bipolar disorder (Goodwin & Jamison, 1990). Regardless, we know that the diagnosis of a mood disorder significantly increases the level of suicide risk.

Affective disorders and anxiety disorders have been studied extensively with regard to level of suicide risk. Chioqueta and Stiles (2003) report significant differences in the effects of these disorders on suicide risk. They measured suicide risk by level of suicide ideation and the presence of hopelessness rather than actual behavior. However, suicide ideation not only has been identified as a prerequisite for suicide attempts but also has several overlapping risk factors with suicide attempts (Sokero et al., 2003). Chioqueta and Stiles found dysthymia to be significantly related to increased levels of hopelessness, whereas MDD and bipolar disorder are associated with increased suicide ideation. Furthermore, there was an interaction effect between depression and anxiety. Suicide ideation is significantly elevated in those with a primary diagnosis of either MDD or dysthymia when higher levels of anxiety are also present. However, suicide ideation is not affected when an anxiety disorder is the primary diagnosis and depressive symptoms occur.

Schizophrenia

One disorder that seems to be resistant to treatment and has a high incidence rate for suicide is adult schizophrenia (Caldwell & Gottesman, 1992; Meltzer, 1998; Modestin, Zarro, & Waldvogel, 1992). In addition to having a high rate for suicide, this population also tends to use more lethal and violent means to complete suicide than nonschizophrenic suicides (Heila et al., 1997). Suicide is the leading cause of premature death among patients with schizophrenia (Caldwell & Gottesman, 1992; Modestin et al., 1992; Roy, 1992b). There is a reported lifetime prevalence rate of 10% for completed suicides and 18–55% for attempted suicides in this population (Gupta, Black, Arndt, Hubbard, & Andreasen, 1998; Meltzer, 1998). As compared to the general population, base rates for suicide among patients diagnosed with schizophrenia are extremely high. Studies consistently find rates between 350 and 600 per 100,000 schizophrenic people per year (Caldwell & Gottesman, 1992). Predicting suicide in patients with schizophrenia can be difficult because they give few or no immediate warnings and rarely communicate

their suicidal intent directly (Nyman & Jonsson, 1986). Studies have reported factors including age of onset, illness duration, hospitalization history (including aftercare), previous suicide attempts, depression, and psychosis (Gupta et al., 1998; Heila et al., 1997; Kaplan & Harrow, 1999; Modestin et al., 1992). People diagnosed with schizophrenia are at highest risk for suicide immediately after they are first diagnosed, and although the risk decreases over time, they continue to remain at risk for the rest of their lives. Remarkably, all studies agree that the period immediately after hospital discharge is a period of extremely high risk (Roy, 1992b). Meltzer (1998) and Roy (1992b) both state that there is an increased risk during the 6-month period after the first admission for schizophrenia. This may explain the high suicide risk in younger diagnosed people based on age of onset. Research has shown that only about 10% of people with schizophrenia who commit suicide are responding to command hallucinations (Heila et al. 1997). It is often believed that a person with schizophrenia uses suicide as an attempt to escape the hallucinations or the despair that is caused by the symptoms of the illness.

Hospitalization

For generations, people have been admitted to the hospital for psychiatric care when they are thought to be at imminent risk of completing suicide. However, current literature suggests that risk for suicide may increase around hospital admissions. Hoyer and colleagues (2004) report the day after discharge to have the highest risk of suicide for people with an affective disorder and the day of admission as the second. Dong, Ho, and Kan (2005) found five additional risk factors for suicide when assessing the suicides of 92 inpatient suicides in a case-controlled study over a 2-year period in Hong Kong. The strongest predictor of completed suicide was a history of deliberate self-harm behavior, followed by "admission due to suicidal behavior, depressive symptoms at time of suicide, away without leave during admission, and extra-pyramidal side effects/akathisia at time of suicide" (p. 97). Therefore, when estimating the level of risk for suicidal patients and determining whether hospitalization should be considered, it is important to address whether you believe your patient may benefit from hospitalization. Hospitalization does not guarantee safety from suicide.

Incarceration

Many people believe that suicidal people are safe once they are incarcerated. However, suicide is considered to be one of the leading causes of death in jails in the United States (Hayes, 1997, as cited in Goss, Peterson, Smith, Kalb, & Brodey, 2002). Several prevention programs and suicide risk screening programs have been implemented in the penal system both nationally and internationally. Several risk factors have been identified that are specific to those incarcerated in the literature. General factors include active substance abuse, previous psychiatric diagnosis, age over 40 years, homelessness, one prior incarceration, and incarceration for a violent offense (Blaauw, Kerkhof, & Hayes, 2005; Goss et al., 2002). More specifically, at the time of the suicide, inmates may also experience increased agitation or anxiety, inmate conflict, fear, or disciplinary action (Way, Miraglia, Sawyer, Beer, & Eddy, 2005). Additionally, there has been discrepancy in the literature as to whether there is a higher level of risk in the first 24 to 72 hours of incarceration as opposed to later time points (Hayes, 1989). Goss and colleagues recently reported that risk is elevated at all time points and that completing accurate assessments of all inmates upon intake is the most effective method of prevention; 25% of those who made suicide attempts had never received a mental health evaluation.

Protective Factors

So far we have discussed several potential risk factors for suicide, factors that may increase the likelihood of a person attempting or completing suicide. Fortunately, there are also several protective factors that can decrease the likelihood of suicide (see Table 8.1). As with all behavioral assessments, it is important to identify both problems (e.g., risk factors) and strengths (e.g., protective factors) with all clients in order to determine a more accurate estimated level of risk.

Overview of the Study of Suicide Assessment

Suicide risk assessment is distinct from suicide prediction. Despite the obvious appeal of predicting a deadly act before it occurs, accurate prediction of suicide for a given individual is nearly impossible. This is because human behavior is complex, and suicide is an uncommon behavior. Predictions based on low base rate behaviors produce high false-positive and false-negative rates on account of statistical problems inherent in the calculations. A seminal study conducted by Pokorny (1983) illustrates this phenomenon. In his study, 4,800 psychiatric patients were followed for 5 years. Using a variety of items and scales demonstrated to be good predictors of suicide in previously published studies, they predicted 1,241 patients to suicide. At the conclusion of the 5-year period, there were 67 completed suicides. Of the predicted 1,241 cases, 35 individuals were correctly predicted to commit suicide. This results in a predictive value (the proportion of true suicides out of all positive predictions) of 2.8% for the prediction tools used in the study. Other prediction models have produced similar results (e.g., Clark, Young, Scheftner, Fawcett, & Fogg, 1987; Goldstein, Black, Nasrallah, & Winokur, 1991; Motto, Heilbron, & Juster, 1985).

Given that most people who appear suicidal do not attempt suicide and that among those who do, few actually die, predicting that a given individual will *not* suicide results in a prediction that is correct most of the time. In this fashion we avoid the overprediction problem. However, an actuarial approach such as this is unacceptable to most clinicians because it fails to detect those who will suicide.

This has led many clinicians to become skeptical of all suicide evaluation instruments, protocols, checklists, or other empirical modes of assessment. Instead, risk assessment has been accomplished via clinical intuition, which tends to rely on subjective indicators of risk (e.g., "Do I feel worried about this patient's ability to keep himself or herself free of harm?"). However, such judgments generally fail to yield accurate risk profiles (Gale, Mesnikoff, Fine, & Talbot, 1980; Pokorny, 1962). This is because such approaches tend to emphasize ideographic factors rather than assessment of a standardized array of risk factors, often resulting in failure to assess a critical element.

In contrast to suicide prediction, suicide risk assessment focuses on *suicide potential* or the estimated *risk* of suicidal behavior rather than predicting the behavior itself. Suicide risk assessment is a comprehensive evaluation of empirically identified immediate and long-term suicide risk factors, as well as protective factors that mitigate risk, to determine current risk of suicidal behavior. Thus, suicide risk assessment identifies those who are in an elevated risk group.

Beyond risk assessment, this form of evaluation provides invaluable clinical information for managing suicidal crises and developing treatment plans. What is critical to keep in mind is that suicide risk is not a static variable; it is a vacillating state that will emerge and recede over time. Therefore, suicide risk assessment must be conducted on an ongoing basis. Methods of assessment include self-report inventories, structured and semistructured interviews, suicide assessment protocols, and behavioral analysis.

Assessment Strategies

Structured and Semistructured Interviews. The structured interview is a highly systematized format designed to ensure that the assessment is conducted in a standardized fashion. The interviewer is directed to conduct the evaluation according to a verbatim script; every question is asked in exactly the same way, ensuring uniformity of the information gathered. Such standardization establishes the reliability of the assessment from administration to administration, both across and within individuals.

Semistructured interviews are not as highly structured and permit interviewers to modify the phrasing of the questions. The dialogue format of the interview permits the interviewer to seek additional information to clarify or expand a response and to tailor the assessment to the individual by use of a screening format in which failure to meet criteria for a particular item allows the interviewer to skip to the next relevant question. Thus, semistructured interviews vary in format, content, and length from administration to administration.

At the completion of the interview, whether structured or semistructured, a determination of suicide risk is made. This is most often based on a summation of several behaviorally anchored rated items. The semistructured interview benefits psychometrically from the systematic approach of the structured interview, and its flexibility mitigates against problems of assessment burden, poor comprehension, impaired cognition, and low reading level inherent in other methods. For this reason, the semistructured format is a staple in suicide risk assessment.

Self-Report Inventories. Self-report inventories are easy to administer and in most cases are easy to score. More and more, traditional paper-and-pencil measures are available for administration by computer, thus streamlining the administration and scoring procedure. Suicide risk assessment inventories range from just a few items tapping a single-dimension construct to multiple-item, multidimensional scales. Most scales use true-false or Likert-type scales. Self-report inventories share the benefits of structured instruments in terms of standardized format. Challenges associated with the self-administered instruments include reading comprehension problems, vision impairment, and lack of opportunity for respondents to seek clarification on item meaning.

Sample Suicide Assessment Battery. The following section describes the format, administration, usage, and psychometric properties of five instruments used in the suicide treatment research studies at the University of Washington Behavioral Research and Therapy Clinics ("the Linehan research lab"). (For a comprehensive review of these and other instruments widely used in the field of suicide assessment and treatment, see Brown, 2004.) Two of the instruments use a self-report format, and two use a clinical evaluator in completing a checklist or conducting an interview.

Some instruments focus on detailed evaluation of a specific area of suicide assessment (e.g., suicide ideation), whereas others offer a more comprehensive assessment of multiple domains. All the instruments reviewed here are intended for a general adult psychiatric population. (For a review of instruments relevant to child and adolescent populations, see Goldston, 2000). It is difficult to make recommendations regarding the selection of specific assessment tools because decisions will be influenced largely by the context of the assessment (i.e., population, setting, accompanying assessments) and purpose of evaluation.

Reasons for Living. The Reasons for Living inventory (Linehan, Goodstein, Nielsen, & Chiles, 1983) consists of 48 items measuring the positive side of suicidal ambivalence. Items were developed from surveys administered to nonpatient samples of college students, adults, and senior citizens who were asked about their reasons for living. This instrument is unique in that it measures a protective factor believed to mitigate suicide vulnerability. The self-administered inventory items are rated on a six-point Likert scale reflecting six distinct domains: Survival and Coping Beliefs, Responsibility to Family, Child Concerns, Fear of Suicide, Fear of Social Disapproval, and Moral Objections. Scoring consists of summing all items and dividing by the number of items for each subscale and scale total.

The authors report strong internal consistency, with Cronbach alphas ranging from .72 to .92 for each subscale and .89 for the total scale. These estimates of reliability have been generally replicated by other investigators, who obtained a range of .79 to .91 for each scale, .70 for the total inventory, and a test-retest reliability coefficient of .83 (Osman, Jones, & Osman, 1991). The scale is intended for adults and has been found to differentiate suicide attempters from suicide ideators (Linehan et al., 1983), suicide attempters from nonattempters (Malone et al., 2000; Mann, Waternaux, Haas, & Malone, 1999; Osman et al., 1999), and people who have previously experienced suicide ideation from those who have not in both psychiatric and general populations (Connell & Meyer, 1991; Osman et al., 1993; Strosahl, Chiles, & Linehan, 1992). Short forms and modified versions have been developed for screening purposes and for adolescent, college, geriatric, non-English-speaking, and forensic populations.

Suicidal Behaviors Questionnaire–Revised. The Suicide Behaviors Questionnaire (Linehan, 1996) is a 34-item self-report assessment of multiple dimensions of suicidal behavior. Assessment domains include past, present, and future suicidal ideation, communication, and intent; suicide plans, acts, and availability of methods; and social deterrents, attitudes toward, and expectancies of suicidal behavior. The instrument has been used in a variety of suicide research studies and has solid psychometric properties with internal reliability coefficients ranging from .73 to .92 (Addis & Linehan, 1989). Abbreviated and clinician-administered versions have been developed but are less widely used.

Suicide Attempt Self-Injury Interview. The Suicide Attempt Self-Injury Interview (SASII; Linehan, Comtois, Brown, Heard, & Wagner, 2006) is a comprehensive interviewer-administered instrument that assesses multiple factors involved in nonfatal suicide attempts and intentional self-injury including variables related to method, lethality, impulsivity, and consequences of the act; suicide intent, ambivalence, and other motivations; antecedent events and states of mind (e.g., alcohol consumption, command voices); likelihood of rescue; and habitual self-injury behaviors. It is designed to avoid confounding behavior or topography with function or intent. It obtains detailed information on each episode of suicidal behavior separately. Previous versions of the SASII called the Parasuicide History Interview have been used in a variety of suicide research studies. The SASII has been found to have very good interrater reliability and sufficient validity (Linehan et al., 2006).

Lifetime Parasuicide Count. The Lifetime Parasuicide Count (Linehan & Comtois, 1996) is a clinician-administered measure developed as a brief yet detailed survey of past suicidal behaviors. Historical behavior is categorized into suicide attempts, ambivalent suicide attempts, and nonsuicidal self-injury. Information is obtained on the first instance, the most recent instance, and the most medically severe instance of behavior. The Lifetime Parasuicide Count was designed for use with adults but has also been used with an adolescent population. A past-year measure has been developed for use as a screening tool for research studies.

Clinical Assessment

In practice, assessment and intervention are two elements of the same task: treatment of the patient. Therefore, they will be linked by the theoretical philosophy underpinning the treatment approach. In this chapter, clinical risk assessment and intervention have been separated for the purpose of clarifying the essential elements of the assessment task. We present the clinical method of risk assessment here, using a model consistent with a biosocial theory of disorder and behavioral approach to intervention.

As noted earlier in this chapter, previous suicidal behavior is a risk factor for future suicidal behavior. Therefore, detailed assessment of past suicidal behavior is a critical component of evaluation. At the start of treatment, the therapist should take a comprehensive history of all previous suicidal behaviors, taking care to assess in detail the full spectrum of behavior from vague wishes to die to near-lethal suicide attempts.

Information about suicidal behavior may be spontaneously communicated to therapists, family, friends, or other people in the patient's environment. Alternatively, therapists may have to elicit information. Baseline assessment of current and past suicidal behavior should take place with all new clients, regardless of whether patients appear to be currently suicidal. That said, data show that mental health professionals do not routinely inquire about suicidal behavior, even when the client has made a recent suicide attempt (Coombs et al., 1992). Thorough assessment before the start of treatment establishes baseline suicidality. Moreover, data obtained from the assessment provide a framework for future evaluation should a suicide crisis emerge during treatment.

Formal Risk Assessment. At the start of treatment the therapist conducts a formal and detailed long-term and immediate suicide risk assessment. This information becomes the idiographic correlate to the risk factor data from the empirical literature. With some patients, suicidal ideation may be a common background theme to their lives and not indicate elevated risk, whereas for others the bare hint of morbid thoughts is cause for alarm. Understanding the context of past behaviors provides an invaluable framework from which to launch therapy and is a key element to risk assessment.

The formal suicide risk evaluation requires the clinician to assess and document risk for each domain. During the course of treatment, substantial changes in the client's life circumstances will periodically require the therapist to conduct the formal evaluation anew. Patients should be asked about suicidal behaviors per se and about times when they intentionally harmed or injured themselves with no thought of committing suicide. The prompting events (e.g., sudden loss) for historical behaviors should be identified as well as what means were used and how they were obtained. The environmental picture should be painted with as much detail as possible: Was the behavior impulsive or planned? Did the patient make preparations of any sort, such as taking precautions against intervention or seeking out preferred means? What was the patient's emotional tone at the time: sad, angry, scared? What were his or her expectations: death, discovery, relief? See Table 8.1 for a full review of risk and protective factors that should be assessed in detail. One additional point that is imperative in a suicide

risk assessment is in regard to multiple methods. We have already discussed the importance of assessing for method of suicide. However, it is important to not stop asking the question after you receive the first answer. Often patients have been thinking about multiple methods of suicide. Therefore, you must continue to ask, "Have you thought of any other ways of committing suicide?" until the client responds with a "no."

Behavioral Analysis. Because of its emphasis on detail, precision, clarity, and specificity, behavioral analysis is an excellent vehicle for suicide risk assessment. Moreover, it constitutes a synthesis of the empirical risk factor and clinical insight models of assessment. As a method of suicide risk assessment, behavioral analysis most often occurs in the context of treatment: individual psychotherapy sessions, medication management visits, and telephone crisis calls.

Across the course of treatment the provider must monitor all forms of suicidal behaviors, including suicidal ideation or wanting to be dead, planning or threatening suicide, and all instances of suicide attempts and nonsuicidal self-injurious acts. As treatment progresses, the clinician should periodically ask whether the client has made any plans for a suicide attempt or has the means to carry out a suicide attempt. With the chronically suicidal patient it is particularly important for the therapist to engage in open and matter-of-fact dialogue about suicide risk and self-injury on a routine basis (e.g., "Have you purchased any razor blades lately?" "Do you have any out-of-date prescriptions stockpiled at home?").

Increases from baseline levels of suicidality or marked changes since the last therapeutic contact should be individually assessed and analyzed as part of treatment. We have found that the use of daily self-monitoring forms ensures that the therapist is kept apprised of day-to-day shifts in suicidality. Although daily diaries are not essential for risk assessment, several points argue for their use: As suicidal behavior decreases, therapists are less likely to inquire about changes, and clients are less likely to spontaneously report increases; if other behaviors are recorded on the form, patterns contributing to increased suicidality can be observed and inform judgment; and a wealth of data suggest that self-monitoring a behavior is itself a treatment intervention (so called "reactive treatment effect"), so mere observation of suicidal targets may decrease risk over time.

Analysis starts with behaviorally defining the problem (specifying the behavior as, e.g., a suicide attempt, intentional nonsuicidal self-injury, or increased suicidal ideation), its context, topography (frequency, intensity, duration), function, and consequences. In contrast to the assessment conducted before treatment, this analysis is circumscribed to the current instance of suicidal behavior or risk, not suicidal crises more generally. The analysis is conducted in painstaking detail. Therapist and patient work collaboratively to understand the environmental events, cognitive and emotional experiences, and behavior of the client that led to the suicidal behavior or increased risk.

At other times there may be no overt shift in suicidality. Self-monitoring cards may reflect consistently high ratings of suicidality that are customary for the patient. In this instance the therapist must remain alert for subtle communications suggesting that more detailed assessment is necessary. Examples include statements by patients that they "can't stand it any longer," that "things are not working out," or that others they care for would be "better off" without them.

Whether detected as part of routine monitoring or in the course of treatment, once it is clear that suicide is on the patient's mind the therapist must evaluate immediate risk factors.

SUICIDE RISK ASSESSMENT TRANSCRIPT

The following therapy excerpt demonstrates several of the elements of suicide risk assessment that may show up in the context of treatment. The session is with Jessica, a 23-year-old Caucasian college student who has been episodically suicidal since she was 17 years old. She has a history of two suicide attempts, the first being an overdose of Tylenol PM with clear intent to die. She made the suicide attempt 2 weeks before her 17th birthday, just after a breakup with her boyfriend. She was found by her parents the morning after the overdose, was rushed to the emergency room by ambulance, and spent several days in intensive care. After discharge she was referred for individual and family therapy and was started on a selective serotonin reuptake inhibitor. She describes the second suicide attempt as more ambivalent. This attempt was in the context of a fraternity party on her college campus. She reports that she was drinking heavily and feeling sad and lonely.

She started taking pills her friend gave because her friend said that they would make her less sad. She said she went home after the party and felt even more sad and alone. She ran the bathtub full of warm water, got in, and started to cut her wrists (a behavior she had been engaging in off and on since age 13). She reported that she felt "disconnected" from her body and that the sensation associated with the cuts was not painful but comforting. She continued to sit in the tub and lightly but repeatedly cut herself until her roommate came home approximately an hour later. She was taken to the campus health center, where she was evaluated and admitted to the psychiatric service. After 3 days she was released and referred for dialectical behavior therapy.

At the time of this session Jessica met diagnostic criteria for an Axis I diagnosis of dysthymic disorder and an Axis II disorder of borderline personality disorder and has been in therapy for approximately 1 month. We join the session in progress.

Therapist: You seem really sad and angry today, and you keep saying that you don't know how much longer you can keep trying. You've said this a few times today. Tell me, have you been thinking about suicide?

Jessica: [No reply.]

T: Is that right?

J: Well . . . I really have a lot of problems right now and I don't know how to solve them. It seems like my life is falling down around my shoulders and I'm sort of like backed into a corner and either I get help and it works or I die. I don't know. I just. . . . I wouldn't be here any more. I wouldn't have to feel this way. And, my family wouldn't have to deal with me being like this all the time.

T: All things being equal, would you rather die or solve the problems?

J: I hate my life and my friends and my parents. I have huge fights with everyone. I am dying right in front of everybody and nobody can see me. I just can't deal with anything. I get so angry that I just want to die!

T: So, where does that leave you?

J: I don't know. I just really don't know. I can't stand things the way they are!

I just feel so overwhelmed and I can't stand it! I can't stand it and I just start crying and crying. Even I can't stand myself, I'm so pathetic!

T: Are you thinking about trying to kill yourself? So, what's your plan? If you were to kill yourself, how would you do it?

J: I'd drive my car into a ravine.

T: What do you think would happen to you? Do you expect you'd be dead if you did that?

J: Yes. I don't know. I'd probably screw that up, too.

T: Which ravine?

J: The one off the top of the old highway.

T: Did you drive to your appointment with me today?

J: Yes.

T: Well, I can't very well have you drive away from here then, can I?

J: What do you mean?

T: I can't very well have you drive off to kill yourself from your therapist's office, now can I? I think we'll have to figure out how to solve your problems instead.

J: I guess.

T: Do you think you'll change your mind after session?

J: Yes. No. I, um, I don't know.

T: I don't know either. I think you better give me your car keys and we'll call you a cab to get you home today.

J: [Shakes head no.]

T: Yes. Give me your keys.

J: I'll just find another way [reaching into her purse for the car keys].

T: Well, that's true, you can, but at least I have to block off as many roads to suicide as I can [accepting the keys]. But if you found another way, what would it be?

J: [No response.]

T: Do you want help not to kill yourself? Or have you decided to do this?

J: [No response.]

T: Jessica? Talk to me.

J: I'm thinking about this.

T: That's good.

J: Well, if you really think we can solve some of these problems. . . .

T: I do. But it will take a little time, and it will take effort on both our parts. So, first things first. I need you to agree to give us a little time to work on solving the problems.

J: How long?

T: I don't know. But there's no point in us working like hell trying if you're just going to decide to kill yourself in the end. So can we agree that you're giving up this idea of being dead?

J: Well, we'll see where we are [laughing and nodding yes].

T: I'm serious about this. Do you agree to not kill yourself or try to?

J: Yes.

T: You're going to genuinely throw yourself into it? I mean completely and genuinely from the bottom of your soul to the top of your head?

J: Yes.

T: I'm taking you at your word for that. So tell me, did you wake up in the morning feeling the way you do today?

J: Yes.

T: Did you feel this way yesterday morning?

J: Um, I don't know. I can't remember. I don't think so.

T: So we know yesterday morning you weren't feeling this way, but sometime between yesterday and this morning you began feeling badly.

J: Right.

T: So, when did you first start feeling like maybe you would be thinking about suicide more seriously?

J: Um, it actually started last night. I just kind of lost my control over the way I was feeling because I was at my folks' place for dinner with my sister and her boyfriend and friends of theirs, and I just felt so out of place. I was exhausted from work and school, and I just sort of started slipping.

T: What do you mean?

J: I started to feel real shaky on the inside. You know? Like I might just come apart or shut down or scream or something.

T: I know this is hard. This is what we need to do a lot of if we're going to figure out what your patterns are and what leads you to feel so overwhelmed. It seems like it comes out of the blue, but the truth is something in the environment or inside of you put this in motion, and if we can figure it out, we'll be a step closer to solving the puzzle and your pain.

The session continues with emphasis on identifying the specific prompting events that led to the immediate suicide crisis. Then, the stage is set for generating solutions to the client's immediate problems. As the session comes to a close, the therapist returns to the issue of suicide and asks several more questions to assess suicide risk status.

Therapist: So, how is your level of distress right now?

J: Better. I feel better. It feels, more . . . manageable.

T: Truly?

J: Yes.

T: Good. Now, what we need to be ready for is that you might have another wave of feeling really overwhelmed, sad, and angry, and what we need to do is get you ready to deal with that so that suicide doesn't look like a workable option to you.

J: Right.

T: So, tell me, right now, how high is your urge to kill yourself?

J: Zero.

T: Really?

J: Really.

T: I've got your car key and will hold onto it for the week. What other methods do you have that you could use to kill yourself?

J: Well, I guess I could jump off a bridge or run into traffic, but I just don't really

see myself doing those things. They're too . . . I don't know. I can't see myself doing those.

T: What *do* you see yourself doing? I mean, if you were to start thinking about suicide again?

J: I can't shoot myself because I don't have a gun. I don't even know how to fire a gun. I don't see the point of overdosing—that just got me very sick. Cutting simply makes a mess of my arms and gets my roommate involved in my life. I'm sort of out of options.

T: That's very good. So, we're still left with what you could see yourself doing if you were to start to think about suicide again.

J: I won't. I don't see that happening. If I started to feel like that again I'd probably just cut.

T: "Just cut!" As if that's going to somehow win favor with me?

J: Well, you know what I mean.

T: Yes, I do. And, I'm all for it—not trying to kill yourself, that is. We just have to drop the cutting as the solution.

J: I won't cut if I feel okay.

T: Yes, I know. What we need is an ironclad agreement that you won't cut or try to kill yourself whether you feel okay or not.

J: I know. It's just that it's hard to sit here and say to you that I won't do those things. I can't read the future, and I don't want to let you down saying one thing and doing another.

T: That's very good, because I don't want that either. We'll have to figure out a way for it to really be true by it being true.

J: Okay.

T: So now that we're agreed on that, what could disrupt this plan of ours? What do we need to be vigilant for in the coming week so that nothing disrupts your resolve?

J: Umm. . . . You've got my car keys, so that pretty much rules out the car. I don't have any razor blades at home.

T: Do you have them somewhere else? Like in your purse?

J: [laughing] No, but I could always get them!

T: Right, so how are we going to work to prevent that?

J: I don't know. Maybe I could put a note on my billfold reminding me not to buy any.

T: Do you think that would work?

J: Yes.

T: Even if you were really upset—sad and angry—you think that would stop you?

J: Yes. It would at least slow me down and make me think about what I was doing. Sometimes I just don't think. I get upset and I do things.

T: Good. So, note to remind you to slow down and think. What would the note say?

J: Just that. "Think!" No, better still, "Make It True!"

T: Perfect! Here's some sticky notes [hands notes to client]. Go ahead and make out one now for your billfold.

J: [Takes the notes and writes one out.]

T: So, let's review. You're saying that you're in for this: no suicide, no cutting, and no trying to suicide. Right?

J: Yes.

T: Let me hear it from you.

J: I'm not going to kill myself or try to.

T: And. . . .

J: And not cut myself.

T: Very good. Now, tell me something, why are you saying this?

J: Well . . . well. . . . You pretty much convinced me. I don't have a shot at my life without trying, and the only way to try is to do it, and to do it I have to make it true.

The therapist spends the remainder of the session teaching the client strategies to get through difficult moments and rehearsing these strategies in response to imaginal increases in suicidal urges. The client is also reminded that additional coaching is available should she forget her new strategies or have a recurrence of suicidal thinking and urges that she cannot treat sufficiently with her new skills.

ASSESSMENT OBSTACLES

The assessment of suicidal behaviors is fraught with multiple obstacles. The following section outlines several issues for the clinical assessor to be alert to and suggestions for navigating the problems.

Stance on Suicide

In this chapter we assume that the clinician is on the side of life. However, this is an arguable position. Studies of therapists' attitudes toward elective suicide show that many among our ranks support the patient's right to suicide (Werth & Cobia, 1995; Werth & Liddle, 1994). Personal, moral, and ethical philosophies, as well as religious values and life experiences, influence the clinician's views. The position one adopts in assessing and treating suicidal patients matters, and it is critical that the clinician be clear on his or her position with regard to suicide before the suicide crisis.

Planting the Seed of Suicide

One barrier to suicide risk assessment is the fear that asking questions about suicide may lead to increased suicide risk or even directly prompt suicidal behavior in previously nonsuicidal but "vulnerable" people (Pearson, Stanley, King, & Fisher, 2001). Such fear may inhibit the very assessment that is necessary for accurate assessment and intervention. In a study examining patterns of self-reported suicidality and distress during research assessments among 63 women meeting criteria for borderline personality disorder and current and chronic suicidality, Reynolds, Lindenboim, Comtois, Murray, and Linehan (2006) found no evidence to support this fear. In fact, they discovered that changes in suicidality after assessments (including specific and detailed assessment of past suicidal behavior and current ideation, intent, and plans) were small and infrequent. Moreover, they found that suicidality was just as likely to *decrease* after an interview. This resonates with what many clinical suicidologists have discovered: Questions about suicide often are met with relief and unburdening of thoughts and feelings carefully guarded from family and friends.

Knowing What to Say and How to Say It

Unless they treat suicidal people as a specialty, many treatment professionals feel uncomfortable asking about suicidal behavior directly. However, there may be no single more important area of assessment where direct and straightforward questioning is needed. Conducting an effective risk assessment requires that the assessor have full command of suicide-related language. Assessors must be ready to use terms such as *suicide, death, dead, decapitate, cut, sever, burn, disembowel, pierce, self-immolation, vein, blood,* and *vomit.* We recommend rehearsing such words out loud or with a colleague until you can deliver them without flinching.

Community Expectations and Legal Liability

Suicide or the threat of impending suicide by a patient can be one of the most stressful experiences for the treating clinician (Hellman, Morrison, & Abramowitz, 1986; Roswell, 1988). The likelihood that mental health professionals will encounter patient suicide is not insignificant. Studies have reported that between 15% and 62% of psychiatrists have had a patient die by suicide (Brown, 1987b; Chemtob, Bauer, Hamada, Pelowski, & Muraoka, 1989; Litman, 1965; Schnur & Levin, 1985). Among psychologists the estimate of patient suicide is between 14% and 28% (Bongar, Cleary, & Sullivan, 2002; Brown, 1987a; Chemtob et al., 1989), and among clinical social workers the figure is 33% (Jacobson, Ting, Sanders, & Harrington, 2004).

Fear of patient suicide is compounded by expectations of patients' families and the larger community that treatment professionals can and will predict suicidal behavior. Moreover, the legal system expects clinicians to foresee suicidal behavior, a position that has affected the standard of care for treatment and assessment of suicidal people. Therefore, concern over the legal ramifications of patient suicide may drive risk assessment procedures rather than a systematic approach derived from empirically based guidelines.

Difficulty of Treating Suicidal People

Suicide risk assessment may reveal the need for risk management or intervention. These activities require additional resources and thus present excess burdens, not the least of which is knowing what to do. Despite the frequency of suicide and related behaviors among people receiving mental health treatment, many therapists are ill equipped to treat the acutely suicidal person.[1]

Assessment of Suicide in a Psychotic Population

Among the severely mentally ill, several additional challenges in assessing suicide vulnerability are encountered. In addition to the multiple problems experienced by nonpsychotic suicidal patients, these patients may demonstrate loosening of associations and significantly impaired reality testing. They may experience command hallucinations or have delusional belief systems that contribute to self-harmful and suicidal behavior. People directed to engage in potentially lethal behavior by command hallucinations rarely identify the event as a suicide attempt. Therefore, additional care must be exercised in assessing suicide in this population because these people may be falsely classified as representing low suicide risk. Making the diagnostic task even more difficult, these people often suffer diminished cognitive capacity, flexibility, and conceptual organization to resist potentially harmful impulses, to evaluate alternative problem-solving strategies, or to reliably report suicidal distress.

Despite the significance of suicide among people diagnosed with schizophrenia, little research has focused on the development of an assessment tool to assist clinicians in making judgments about suicide risk in this population. Therefore, risk assessment has been accomplished via clinical intuition or application of risk assessment tools designed for nonpsychotic populations that fail to take into consideration the complexities noted earlier. Two instruments have been developed to address this shortcoming: the Interview for Suicide in Schizophrenia (Turner, Korslund, Barnett, & Josiassen, 1998) and the InterSePT Scale for Suicidal Thinking (Lindenmayer et al., 2001).

Suicide Prevention Contracts

Suicide prevention contracts or no-suicide contracts are widely used by mental health practitioners when working with suicidal clients;

however, these contracts are also infrequently studied and have almost no empirical data. According to *Black's Law Dictionary* (Black, 1957), in the simplest terms a contract implies the creation, modification, or destruction of a legal relationship. Therefore, the question must be asked when a client signs a no-suicide contract, "What relationship is being created, modified, or ended?" A no-suicide contract is not a legally binding contract and will not stand up on its own in a court of law. In a survey of Harvard Medical School Faculty, more than 70% of psychiatrists and psychologists reported that they regularly used a used a no-harm contract with patients, and more than 75% stated that the contracts were recommended at their place of employment. However, more than 60% reported receiving no training in the use of the contracts (Miller, Jacobs, & Gutheil, 1998).

For more than 30 years, mental health practitioners have been using these contracts as a method of suicide intervention and liability risk management despite the lack of empirical evidence to support them or the lack of training received in using them. It is important to note that a signature on a sheet of paper cannot ensure the safety of any person. These contracts can provide both the clinician and the client with a false sense of security. Many of us probably have heard stories from colleagues, mentors, or even clients about times when no-suicide contracts have worked. And more times then not, it is likely that there was a strong relationship between the clinician and client that can account for the commitment to safety made by the client regardless of the signature on the sheet of paper. Receiving a commitment to safety from a suicidal client can be of great benefit when used as a part of crisis planning and intervention strategies. By developing a crisis plan for what a client may do if he or she becomes suicidal or urges to suicide increase and determining what may get in the way of those actions, a therapist may strengthen the client's commitment to using the plan. This in turn will provide the therapist with additional information about the client's current level of risk.

Putting It All Together: Determining Level of Risk

Now that we have reviewed all the risk and protective factors for suicide, methods of assessment,

barriers to assessment, and the use of no-suicide contracts, another question arises: "How do we put it all together to determine whether my client will kill himself or herself?" Unfortunately, this question cannot be answered with certainty. Given the low base rate behavior of suicide and suicide attempts, as a field we are still unable to predict outcome. Therefore, each clinician must take into account each of the risk factors discussed in this chapter, balanced with the protective factors, and determine the estimated level of risk. Therefore, it is important to have a strong understanding of the weight each risk factor may add to a clinical profile of suicide risk. For example, the data show that Caucasian men between the ages of 25 and 44 are at a higher level of risk than African American women. However, those who have a history of multiple suicide attempts and access to means are at greater risk than those who don't. Therefore, there is no way for us to provide a straightforward algorithm of estimated level of suicide risk. Each individual's risk must be determined by assessment of all domains of risk through multiple methods and modes (e.g., self-report measures, clinical interview, other-report measures, behavioral observation), consultation with colleagues, and study of the literature for documented risk factors.

Summary

A detailed, straightforward, evidence-based assessment of suicide risk can still only estimate risk at best. We have no ability to predict who will and will not kill himself or herself. In order to do accurate on-the-spot assessments, it is important to memorize all the risk factors discussed in this chapter.

There is one major limitation to this chapter. Now that you have learned about assessing someone for risk of suicide, you need to decide what to do, especially if you decide to treat the person on an outpatient basis. Rarely in clinical practice are assessment and treatment separated. However, based on the parameters of this chapter, we did not address the treatment side of managing suicidal people. For further information on how to treat suicidal people on an outpatient basis, we suggest reading Linehan's 1993 text, *Cognitive-Behavioral Treatment of Borderline Personality Disorder*, or Rudd, Joiner, and Rajab's 2000 text, *Treating Suicidal Behavior*. Finally, it is important to note that simply reading about the methods of suicide risk assessment does not mean that one knows how to conduct the assessment. One must practice conducting thorough assessments through role-plays and clinical supervision from a trained mental health professional.

NOTE

1. A discussion of intervention strategies for the suicidal patient is beyond the scope of this chapter. We direct the interested reader to Linehan (1999).

REFERENCES

Addis, M., & Linehan, M. M. (1989). *Predicting suicidal behavior: Psychometric properties of the Suicidal Behaviors Questionnaire.* Poster presented at the annual meeting of the Association for the Advancement of Behavior Therapy, Washington, DC.

American Psychiatric Association. (2000). *Diagnostic and statistical manual of mental disorders* (4th ed., Text rev.). Washington, DC: Author.

Anderson, R. N. (2001). Deaths: Leading causes for 1999. *National Vital Statistics Report, 49,* 1–88.

Angst, F., Stassen, H. H., Clayton, P. J., & Angst, J. (2002). Mortality of patients with mood disorders: Follow-up over 34–38 years. *Journal of Affective Disorders, 68,* 167–181.

Baker, F. M. (1990). Black youth suicide: Literature review with a focus on prevention. *Journal of the National Medical Association, 82,* 495–507.

Berlin, I. N. (1987). Suicide among American Indian adolescents: An overview. *Suicide and Life-Threatening Behavior, 17,* 218–232.

Blaauw, E., Kerkhof, J. F. M., & Hayes, L. M. (2005). Demographic, criminal, and psychiatric factors related to inmate suicide. *Suicide and Life-Threatening Behavior, 35*(1), 63–75.

Black, H. C. (1957). *Black's law dictionary* (4th ed.). Eagan, MN: West.

Blair-West, G. W., Cantor, C. H., Mellsop, G. W., & Eyeson-Annon, M. L. (1999). Lifetime suicide risk in major depression: Sex and age determinants. *Journal of Affective Disorders, 55,* 171–178.

Bongar, B., Cleary, K., & Sullivan, G. (2002). The considerations of age and critical risk factors when working with the suicidal client. *Behavioral Emergencies Update, 3*(2).

Brown, G. K. (2004). *A review of suicide assessment measures for intervention research with adults and older adults.* Bethesda, MD: National Institute of Mental Health. Available at http://www.nimh.nih.gov/suicide research/adultsuicide.pdf

Brown, H. (1987a). The impact of suicide on therapists in training. *Comprehensive Psychiatry, 28,* 101–112.

Brown, H. (1987b). Patient suicide during residency training: Incidence, implications, and program response. *Journal of Psychiatric Education, 11,* 201–216.

Caldwell, C. B., & Gottesman, I. I. (1992). Schizophrenia: A high-risk factor for suicides. *Suicide and Life-Threatening Behavior, 22*(4), 479–493.

Centers for Disease Control and Prevention. (2000). *Suicide in the United States.* Retrieved February 19, 2001, from http://www.cdc.gov/ncipc/dvp/suifacts.htm

Chemtob, C. M., Bauer, G. B., Hamada, R. S., Pelowski, S. R., & Muraoka, M. Y. (1989). Patient suicide: Occupational hazard for psychologists and psychiatrists. *Professional Psychology: Research and Practice, 20,* 294–300.

Chioqueta, A. P., & Stiles, T. C. (2003). Suicide risk in outpatients with specific mood and anxiety disorders. *Crisis, 24,* 105–112.

Clark, D. C., Gibbons, R. D., Fawcett, J., & Scheftner, W. A. (1989). What is the mechanism by which suicide attempts predispose to later suicide attempts? A mathematical model. *Journal of Abnormal Psychology, 98,* 42–49.

Clark, D. C., Young, M. A., Scheftner, W. A., Fawcett, J., & Fogg, L. (1987). A field test of Motto's risk estimator of suicide. *American Journal of Psychiatry, 144,* 923–926.

Connell, D. K., & Meyer, R. G. (1991). The Reasons for Living inventory and a college population: Adolescent suicidal behaviors, beliefs, and coping skills. *Journal of Clinical Psychology, 47*(4), 485–489.

Coombs, D. W., Miller, H. L., Alarcon, R. D., Herlihy, C., Lee, J. M., & Morrison, D. P. (1992). Presuicide attempt communications between parasuicides and consulted caregivers. *Suicide and Life-Threatening Behavior, 22*(3), 289–302.

Dong, J. Y. S., Ho, T. P., & Kan, C. K. (2005). A case-control study of 92 cases of in-patient suicides. *Journal of Affective Disorders, 87,* 91–99.

Egeland, J. A., & Sussex, J. N. (1985). Suicide and family loading for affective disorders. *JAMA, 254,* 915–918.Gale, S. W., Mesnikoff, A., Fine, J., & Talbot, J. A. (1980). A study of suicide in state hospitals in New York City. *Psychiatric Quarterly, 52,* 201–213.

Goldstein, R. B., Black, D. W., Nasrallah, A., & Winokur, G. (1991). The prediction of suicide: Sensitivity, specificity, and predictive value of a multivariate model applied to suicide among 1906 patients with affective disorders. *Archives of General Psychiatry, 48,* 418–422.

Goldston, D. (2000). *Assessment of suicidal behaviors and risk among children and adolescents.* Technical report submitted to NIMH under contract no. 263-MD-909995. Retrieved from http://64.136.148.48/pdfs/0822childmental.pdf

Goodwin, F. K., & Jamison, K. R. (1990). *Manic depressive illness.* New York: Oxford University Press.

Goss, J. R., Peterson, K., Smith, L. W., Kalb, K., & Brodey, B. B. (2002). Characteristics of suicide attempts in a large urban jail system with an established suicide prevention program. *Psychiatric Services, 53*(5), 574–579.

Gupta, S., Black, D. W., Arndt, S., Hubbard, W. C., & Andreasen, N. C. (1998). Factors associated with suicide attempts among patients with schizophrenia. *Psychiatric Services, 49*(10), 1353–1355.

Hansen, P. E. B., Wang, A. G., Stage, K. B., & Kragh-Sorensen, P. (2003). Comorbid personality disorder predicts suicide after major depression: A 10-year follow-up. *Acta Psychiatrica Scandinavica, 107,* 436–440.

Hawton, K., Harriss, L., Simkin, S., Bale, E., & Bond, A. (2004). Self-cutting: Patient characteristics compared with self-poisoners. *Suicide and Life-Threatening Behavior, 34,* 199–208.

Hayes, L. M. (1989). National study of jail suicides: Seven years later. *Psychiatric Quarterly, 60,* 7–29.

Heila, H., Isometsa, E. T., Henriksson, M. M., Heikkinen, M. E., Marttunen, M. J., & Lonnqvist, J. K. (1997). Suicide and schizophrenia: A nationwide psychological autopsy study on age- and sex-specific clinical characteristics of 92 suicide victims with schizophrenia. *American Journal of Psychiatry, 154*(9), 1235–1242.

Hellman, I. D., Morrison, T. L., & Abramowitz, S. I. (1986). The stresses of psychotherapeutic work: A replication and extension. *Psychological Medicine, 42,* 197–205.

Hoyer, E. H., Olesen, A. V., & Mortensen, P. B. (2004). Suicide risk in patients hospitalized because of an affective disorder: A follow-up study, 1973–1993. *Journal of Affective Disorders, 78,* 209–217.

Jacobson, J. M., Ting, L., Sanders, S., & Harrington, D. (2004). Prevalence of and reactions to fatal and nonfatal client suicidal behavior: A national study of mental health social workers. *Omega, 49*(3) 237–248.

Joe, S., & Kaplan, M. S. (2001). Suicide among African American men. *Suicide and Life-Threatening Behavior, 31,* 106–121.

Kaplan, K. J., & Harrow, M. (1999). Psychosis and functioning as risk factors for later suicidal activity among schizophrenia and schizoaffective patients. *Suicide and Life-Threatening Behavior, 29*(1), 10–24.

Lindenmayer, J. P., Czobor, P., Alphs, R., Anand, R., Islam, Z., & Pestreich, L. (2001). The InterSept Scale for Suicidal Thinking (ISST): A new assessment instrument for suicidal patients with schizophrenia. *Schizophrenia Research, 49*(Suppl. 1–2), 5.

Linehan, M. M. (1993). *Cognitive-behavioral treatment of borderline personality disorder.* New York: Guilford.

Linehan, M. M. (1996). *Suicidal behaviors questionnaire.* Unpublished manuscript. Seattle: Department of Psychology, University of Washington.

Linehan, M. M. (1999). Standard protocol for assessing and treating suicidal behaviors for patients in treatment. In D. G. Jacobs (Ed.), *The Harvard Medical School guide to suicide assessment and intervention* (pp. 146–187). San Francisco: Jossey-Bass.

Linehan, M. M., & Comtois, K. (1996). *Lifetime parasuicide history.* Unpublished manuscript. Seattle: Department of Psychology, University of Washington.

Linehan, M. M., Comtois, K. A., Brown, M. Z., Heard, H. L., & Wagner, A. (2006). Suicide Attempt Self-Injury Interview (SASII): Development, reliability, and validity of a scale to assess suicide attempts and intentional self-injury. *Psychological Assessment, 18,* 303–312.

Linehan, M. M., Goodstein, J. L., Nielsen, S. L., & Chiles, J. A. (1983). Reasons for staying alive when you are thinking of killing yourself: The Reasons for Living Inventory. *Journal of Consulting and Clinical Psychology, 51,* 276–286.

Litman, R. (1965). When patients complete suicide. *American Journal of Psychotherapy, 4,* 570–576.

Malone, K. M., Oquendo, M. A., Haas, G. L., Ellis, S. P., Li, S., & Mann, J. J. (2000). Protective factors against suicidal acts in major depression: Reasons for living. *American Journal of Psychiatry, 157,* 1084–1088.

Mann, J. J., Waternaux, C., Haas, G. L., & Malone, K. M. (1999). Toward a clinical model of suicidal behavior in psychiatric patients. *American Journal of Psychiatry, 156,* 181–189.

McIntosh, J. (2000). *U.S.A. suicide: 1998 official final statistics.* Retrieved October 18, 2000, from http://www.suicidology.org/index.html

McIntosh, J. (2002). *U.S.A. suicide: 2000 official final data.* Retrieved October 18, 2002, from http://www.suicidology.org/associations/1045/files/2000 datapg.pdf

McIntosh, J. (2004). *U.S.A. suicide: 2004 official final data.* Retrieved February 1, 2006, from http://www.suicidology.org/associations/1045/files/2002 datapg.pdf

McIntosh, J. (2006). *U.S.A. suicide: 2004 official final data.* Retrieved February 21, 2006, from http://www.suicidology.org/associations/1045/files/2004 datapgv1.pdf

Meltzer, H. Y. (1998). Suicide in schizophrenia: Risk factors and clozapine treatment. *Journal of Clinical Psychiatry, 59*(3), 15–20.

Middlebrook, D. L., LeMaster, P. L., Beals, J., Novins, D. K., & Manson, S. M. (2001). Suicide prevention in American Indian and Alaska Native communities: A critical review of programs. *Suicide and Life-Threatening Behavior, 31,* 132–149.

Miller, M. C., Jacobs, D. G., & Gutheil, T. G. (1998). Talisman or taboo: The controversy of the suicide-prevention contract. *Harvard Review of Psychiatry, 6*(2), 78–87.

Modai, I., Kuperman, J., Goldberg, I., Goldish, M., & Mendel, S. (2004). Fuzzy logic detection of medically serious suicide attempt records in major psychiatric disorders. *Journal of Nervous and Mental Disease, 192*(10), 708–710.

Modestin, J., Zarro, I., & Waldvogel, D. (1992). A study of suicide in schizophrenic in-patients. *British Journal of Psychiatry, 160,* 398–401.

Moran, P., Walsh, E., Tyrer, P., Burns, T., Creed, F., & Fahy, T. (2003). Does co-morbid personality disorder increase the risk of suicidal behavior in psychosis? *Acta Psychiatrica Scandinavica, 107,* 441–448.

Motto, J. (1991). An integrated approach to estimating suicide risk. *Suicide and Life-Threatening Behavior, 21,* 74–89.

Motto, J., Heilbron, D., & Juster, R. (1985). Development of a clinical instrument to estimate suicide risk. *American Journal of Psychiatry, 142,* 680–686.

Murphy, G., & Wetzel, R. (1982). Family history of suicidal behaviors among suicide attempters. *Journal of Nervous and Mental Disease, 170,* 86–90.

Murphy, S. L. (2000). Deaths: Final data. *National Vital Statistics Reports, 48,* 1–15.

National Institute of Mental Health. (1999). *Suicide facts.* Retrieved July 6, 2001, from http://www.nimh.nih.gov/research/suifact.htm

Nyman, A. K., & Jonsson, H. (1986). Patterns of self-destructive behaviour in schizophrenia. *Acta Psychiatrica Scandinavica, 73,* 252–262.

Osman, A., Gifford, J., Jones, T., Lickiss, L., Osman, J., & Wenzel, R. (1993). Psychometric evaluation of the Reasons for Living inventory. *Psychological Assessment, 5*(2), 154–158.

Osman, A., Jones, T., & Osman, J. R. (1991). The Reasons for Living inventory: Psychometric properties. *Psychological Reports, 69,* 271–278.

Osman, A., Kopper, B. A., Linehan, M. M., Barrios, F. X., Gutierrez, P. M., & Bagge, C. L. (1999). Validation of the Adult Suicidal Ideation questionnaire and the Reasons for Living inventory in an adult psychiatric inpatient sample. *Psychological Assessment, 11,* 115–223.

Pearson, J. L., Stanley, B., King, C. A., & Fisher, C. B. (2001). Intervention research with persons at high risk for suicidality: Safety and ethical considerations. *Journal of Clinical Psychiatry, 62,* 17–26.

Pokorny, A. D. (1962). Characteristics of forty-four patients who subsequently committed suicide. *Archives of General Psychiatry, 2,* 314–323.

Pokorny, A. D. (1983). Prediction of suicide in psychiatric patients: Report of a prospective study. *Archives of General Psychiatry, 40,* 249–257.

Reynolds, S. K., Lindenboim, N. L., Comtois, K. A., Murray, A., & Linehan, M. M. (2006). Risky assessments: Participant suicidality and distress associated with research assessments in a treatment study of suicidal behavior. *Suicide and Life-Threatening Behavior, 36,* 19–34.

Reynolds, W. M., & Mazza, J. J. (1994). Suicide and suicidal behaviors in children and adolescents. In W. Reynolds & H. Johnston (Eds.), *Handbook of depression in children and adolescents* (pp. 525–579). New York: Plenum.

Roswell, V. A. (1988). Professional liability: Issues for behavior therapists in the 1980s and 1990s. *Behavior Therapist, 11,* 163–171.

Roy, A. (1983). A family history of suicide. *Archives of General Psychiatry, 40,* 971–974.

Roy, A. (1992a). Genetics, biology, and suicide in the family. In R. W. Maris, A. L. Berman, J. T. Maltsberger, & R. I. Yufit (Eds.), *Assessment and prediction of suicide* (pp. 574–588). New York: Guilford.

Roy, A. (1992b). Suicide in schizophrenia. *International Review of Psychiatry, 4,* 205–209.

Rudd, M. D., Joiner, T., & Rajab, M. H. (2001). *Treating suicidal behavior: An effective, time-limited approach.* New York: Guilford.

Schnur, D. B., & Levin, E. H. (1985). The impact of successfully completed suicides on psychiatric residents. *Journal of Psychiatric Education, 9,* 127–136.

Sokero, T. P., Melartin, T. K., Rytsala, H. K., Leskela, U. S., Lestela-Mielonen, P. S., & Isometsa, E. T. (2003). Suicidal ideation with attempts among psychiatric patients with major depressive disorder. *Journal of Clinical Psychiatry, 64,* 1094–1100.

Strosahl, K., Chiles, J. A., & Linehan, M. (1992). Prediction of suicide intent in hospitalized parasuicides: Reasons for living, hopelessness, and depression. *Comprehensive Psychiatry, 33,* 366–373.

Turner, R. M., Korslund, K. E., Barnett, B. E., & Josiassen, R. C. (1998). Assessment of suicide in schizophrenia: Development of the Interview for Suicide in Schizophrenia. *Cognitive and Behavioral Practice, 5*(2), 139–169.

Way, B., Miraglia, R., Sawyer, D., Beer, R., & Eddy, J. (2005). Factors related to suicide in New York State prisons. *International Journal of Law and Psychiatry, 28*(3), 207–221.

Werth, J. L., & Cobia, D. C. (1995). Empirically based criteria for rational suicide: A survey of psychotherapists. *Suicide and Life-Threatening Behavior, 25,* 231–240.

Werth, J. L., & Liddle, B. J. (1994). Psychotherapists' attitudes toward suicide. *Psychotherapy: Theory, Research, and Practice, 31,* 440–448.

Westefeld, J. S., Range, L. M., Rogers, J. R., Maples, M. R., Bronley, J. L., & Alcorn, J. (2000). Suicide: An overview. *Counseling Psychologist, 28,* 445–510.

9

WRITING UP THE INTAKE INTERVIEW

DANIEL L. SEGAL AND PHILINDA S. HUTCHINGS

The ability to craft a clear, comprehensive, and professional intake evaluation report is a top skill possessed by seasoned mental health professionals. However, this task often seems overwhelming to the beginning clinician, who is concurrently facing the challenges of learning other basic interviewing and psychotherapy skills. But imagine a clinician who conducts a whole course of treatment without formally documenting anything about why the client came for services, what problems he or she initially had, and what treatment recommendations and goals were established. How could this practitioner justify the type of treatment provided and gauge whether treatment was successful?

Indeed, standards of the field today dictate that psychological services be adequately documented (Wiger, 2005; also see American Psychological Association, 1993). Such documentation provides some degree of professional accountability and also serves the therapeutic function of helping the clinician think clearly about the case. No matter what clinical specialty or type of setting in which clinicians work, they probably will be responsible for writing at least some form of intake report. Historically, however, many psychology training programs have not provided much formal classroom training in professional report writing. Students often were left to their own devices to

learn how to write intake reports, and they often did so through informal means: studying old intake reports in their clients' charts or borrowing model reports from more experienced students or teachers. This chapter was written to address this gap and provide a more formal resource for clinicians to use. The purpose of this chapter is to assist clinicians in their report writing by offering practical and explicit guidelines to help them prepare well-written, thorough, and clinically useful intake reports. A sample intake evaluation report and an intake report checklist are provided in the appendixes to be used as training tools.

However, it should be stated at the outset that there is no single correct way to format and write an intake report. There are few absolutes when it comes to report writing. Perusal of reports from diverse mental health professionals will show that the documents vary widely. It is likely that different clinical supervisors will modify some aspect of report writing to satisfy their particular desires and the specific requirements of the setting (e.g., inpatient or outpatient). This should not be a source of great anxiety or concern. The general format and style of the intake report described here is a generic template that can be modified to suit different clinicians, their supervisors, and diverse patient populations. Additionally, the write-up of the intake report and the issues discussed here are not tied to any particular psychological theoretical orientation. Rather, most of the information is intended to apply to clinicians with diverse theoretical approaches.

This chapter describes the typical sections of an intake report and discusses strategies to successfully organize and prepare each part. Throughout, common errors and possible alternative or ameliorative strategies are highlighted. Examples culled from real reports are liberally provided to enhance understanding of the material. In all cases, identifying information has been altered to protect confidentiality of clients.

As is true with all clinical skills, improvement comes with practice and thoughtful consideration of the feedback from clinical supervisors and colleagues. A clinician's first few reports probably will not be as clear and comprehensive as later ones, but we hope that the guidelines in this chapter will enhance these initial attempts and provide a solid base from which to build and improve. We also want to highlight the point that intake report *writing* cannot be completely separated from intake *interviewing*. Therefore, many suggestions include tips about information that must be asked of clients or assessed during the intake session to demonstrate how that information might be presented in a report. For further information and guidance about interviewing strategies and the general process of clinical interviewing, several resources are available (Craig, 2005; Evans, Hearn, Uhlemann, & Ivey, 2004; Hersen & Van Hasselt, 1998; Morrison, 1995; Othmer & Othmer, 2002a, 2002b).

GOALS OF THE INTAKE SESSION AND PURPOSES OF THE INTAKE REPORT

The intake session (or initial consultation) usually is the first face-to-face formal contact between clinician and client. Although there is some variability across clinicians and settings, the typical intake session is scheduled for 1–2 hours. Length of the interview is affected by the complexities of clients' problems and their ability and willingness to work cooperatively with the clinician. In our experience, at least 90 minutes is necessary to allow completion of paperwork (e.g., a client data sheet, informed consent forms, baseline self-report rating scales) and a reasonably thorough evaluation. In some cases,

several meetings are necessary. In general, the goals of the initial meeting are to

- Establish rapport with the client and begin to form the therapeutic alliance

- Collect relevant data about the client and his or her problems and history to determine the initial treatment plan and treatment contract

We emphasize that the first goal (to establish rapport) is paramount. If clinicians were to pay more attention to one of these two aims, it is advisable to emphasize rapport. Additional details and data can be collected in later sessions, but not if the client prematurely terminates treatment because of the clinician's failure to promote a safe environment and therapeutic relationship. Indeed, a strong alliance between clinician and client is widely regarded as essential to the psychotherapeutic process (see Castonguay & Beutler, 2005).

When clients present for an evaluation, they are often in a great deal of emotional pain. They are often demoralized and hopeless because their efforts to address their problems have failed or have had only limited impact. They can benefit by simply having an opportunity to share their story with a compassionate and attentive listener. With each intake session, clinicians have an opportunity to begin the process of healing and growth and to nurture the development of a therapeutic relationship with the client. They accomplish these tasks by using their basic psychotherapeutic skills, such as reflecting feelings and content, clarifying and summarizing, providing emotional support, communicating empathy, and being compassionate, genuine, and caring. In contrast, clinicians who fire off question after question as if they are on a fact-finding mission are clearly missing the therapeutic potential of the intake session.

As clinicians are establishing rapport, they are also gathering data about the client's current and past problems, social history, medical history, and mental status. Clinicians also usually incorporate a process of differential diagnosis. (For extensive coverage of this diagnostic process, see Craig, 2005; First, Francis, & Pincus, 2002; Hersen & Turner, 2003; Othmer & Othmer, 2002a). Treatment recommendations and feedback usually are provided to the client at the end of the session. During this session, a great deal of important clinical information is amassed, although the unfolding of this complex information often is haphazard and confusing. The written intake report is the outcome of that initial evaluation and serves several important purposes.

- Writing the report helps clinicians to organize the wealth of critical information gleaned from the client during the intake session.

- Writing the report assists clinicians in thinking about initial case conceptualization, diagnosis, and treatment planning.

- The report provides a detailed description of the client's current psychological and social functioning. This record is valuable during ongoing treatment because it can be consulted whenever the clinician is confused about something or has forgotten some important information. Clinicians often find it helpful to review the report before their sessions to refresh their memory and make sure that important topics or themes are not neglected.

- Because the report is a snapshot of the client's functioning at one point in time, it can serve as a baseline against which therapeutic progress can be measured at later dates.

- The report serves as the official documentation or record of the initial intake session and remains in the client's confidential chart during and after treatment. It may offer clinicians some protection if they are sued or if a complaint is filed against them to a state licensing board or a professional organization (e.g., American Psychological Association). Although this official report can be requested by clinicians and other professionals who provide services for the client at a later point, a copy may not be sent out until the client gives permission to do so. This is accomplished by having the client sign a release of information form that describes the information to be released and to whom. Likewise, at intake, clinicians can request that their clients sign a release so that clinicians may receive documentation (e.g., intake reports, testing reports, medical summaries) and communicate with diverse professionals, paraprofessionals, and family members who are included in the treatment. Reports from other professionals usually are especially helpful in elucidating the client's difficulties, history, and changes in functioning.

GENERAL CONSIDERATIONS AND CONVENTIONS

In the written intake report, how should clinicians refer to the person they are writing about? There are no definitive rules, but the following guidelines provide assistance. It is always appropriate to refer to the person as "the client" or "the patient." For example, "The client reports that he has been drinking six beers each night for the past 2 weeks." Sometimes, the formal name of the client may be reported, and this is acceptable as long as the name remains consistent from one usage to the next. For example, a student referred to the client's full name at the beginning of a report (Mr. Robert Johnson) but then used derivations of the name in other sections (e.g., Robert Johnson, Robert, and Bob). If you are including the client's name in the body of the report, it is suggested to use the entire full name (Mr. Jeremy Jones) or the formal last name (Mr. Jones). It is best to avoid using first names or nicknames only. Use of the client's last name denotes respect and a professional relationship.

When should the intake report be written? In general, it is advisable to start organizing and writing the report as soon as possible after the completed interview. This way, the information is fresh and clear. In cases where students had the unfortunate experience of conducting several intakes before attempting the write-ups, the result was confusion about the facts of the cases on the part of the student and a disappointed or irritated supervisor. Clinics often have policies about when drafts of the intake report are to be completed. For example, practicum students may be required to submit a first draft version within 5 days of the intake session. A copy of the draft report typically is placed in the client's chart concurrent with submission to the supervisor, and this draft serves as a temporary document until the final report is completed. This is because crises can develop during clinical work with distressed clients, and incomplete information in the chart is better than no information at all.

Many supervisors provide extensive feedback or comments on early drafts, and it would not be uncommon to revise the report several times before it is finally accepted and signed by a supervisor. View the supervisor's feedback as an opportunity to improve, and try to remain positive and receptive to the advice. Remember, the clinician's name will forever be linked to the report, so it is important to produce an accurate and professional product. One should keep in mind that the client, other people, agencies, or the courts may gain access to the document. Clinic policies usually dictate when a final report is completed and placed in the client's chart (e.g., 2 weeks from initial contact). In training settings, the final document is signed and dated by both the student clinician and the supervisor.

Write-ups should include notification that the report is confidential. Just as the content of a psychotherapy or psychological testing session is confidential, so are written intake reports, psychological testing reports, and progress notes. It is important that confidentiality and its limitations be discussed with clients at the beginning of the intake session so that they understand that confidentiality is not absolute. Situations in which confidentiality must be broken include serious concerns about suicidal or homicidal behavior or suspected child or elder abuse. As noted earlier, clients can authorize release of the intake report and other clinical documents to anyone they choose as long as consent to release the information is provided in writing. In cases in which clients do not give their consent (i.e., the records are subpoenaed by a court order from a judge), the issue becomes more complex and should be discussed with a supervisor or seasoned colleague.

PROFESSIONAL WRITING

When writing the intake report, remember that information is being received primarily from one source: the client. This information should not be viewed as the absolute representation of the truth. Indeed, the information is not necessarily factual but rather is only the client's view of the situation. This is an important distinction to make. Because intake interviewers do not know much about the veracity of the client's statements, it is advisable to regularly preface statements in the report with qualifiers. The following are some options and examples: "The client reports [states, relates, says, describes, indicates, notes, elaborates] that he was married seven times, all to millionaires." Other conventions are to write that "According to the client . . . ," "As described by the client . . . ," or "The client

reportedly. . . . " Avoid using the terms *alleges* and *claims* because they may sound judgmental.

It is especially important to preface statements that are potentially controversial or untrue. As an example, it is best to write, "The client describes his father as a severe alcoholic" rather than "The client's father is a severe alcoholic." Similarly, write, "The client reports that she was sexually assaulted by her previous psychotherapist" rather than "The client was sexually assaulted by her previous psychotherapist." As a rule, preface more statements than not and certainly preface any statements that are potentially controversial, untrue, or slanderous.

When information about the client is received from other sources, such as family members, caretakers, teachers, physicians, attorneys, or other documents and reports, it is important to specify the source of the information, as in "The client's wife reports that he has difficulty remembering to take his medication" and "According to medical records received from the client's primary physician, the client has a history of high blood pressure and poorly controlled diabetes." It may also be important to indicate how the information was received and the estimated reliability of it, as in "The client's mother states she received a report from the school that the client is unable to sit still in class, but she does not recall when or from whom she received the report." Sometimes, different sources provide conflicting information, and this should be described as clearly as possible: "According to the client's wife, the client uses cocaine on a daily basis. The client reports much less regular use, about once a month."

Another writing issue concerns verb tense in the report, whether present tense or past tense is used (e.g., "The client characterizes [characterized] his relationship with his wife as close and supportive"). Although there are no definitive rules, and either tense is acceptable, it is important that the verb tense remain consistent within and between sections of the report. A report with inconsistent verb tenses will look sloppy and read poorly. An exception is the mental status examination section, which typically is written in the past tense (e.g., "Speech *was* [not is] tangential.").

Objective writing is another potential challenge for the beginning clinician. The trick here is to translate client statements into objective, behaviorally specific terms. In one report, a student wrote, "The client partied a lot during college." Obviously, this is what the client said, but from this description, is the exact nature of the client's experience clear? What exactly does "partied" mean, and how much is "a lot"? It is critically important that the write-up be objective and provide specific data, or it will start to look like one long quote from the client forever mired in the client's subjective experience. When asked to rewrite and clarify the communication from the client, the student was able to revise the sentence as follows: "The client reports a long history of alcohol and recreational drug use dating back to 2004, when he was an undergraduate student at University of Mississippi. He relates that he regularly drank beer to excess (approximately six to eight beers) about 4 to 5 days each week, and smoked marijuana on most weekends. He also describes having numerous fights in bars and several episodes in which he drove while intoxicated, with one arrest." This is much more objective, specific, and informative than the previous comment.

Consider the following example: "The client wants his wife to get off his back!" A possible objective rewrite of this statement would be, "The client notes that his wife regularly nags him about his lack of participation in household chores, and he elaborates that he wants her to stop but is unsure how to handle the situation." Try to replace the client's slang and colloquialisms with objective, clinical terms. For example, replace "crabby" with "irritable," "cracked-up" with "became psychotic," and "nervous" with "anxious."

It is also important to provide in the report as many specific details about the client's current functioning and history as possible. For example, instead of writing, "The client grew up in a small Southern town," state, "The client grew up in Ocean Springs, a small town in southern Mississippi." Instead of reporting, "The client completed graduate school," write, "The client graduated with PhD in philosophy from Tulane University." It is also advisable to provide specific dates in the report when possible. Instead of noting that "The client was hospitalized during her adolescence after making a suicide attempt" or that "The client was hospitalized 10 years ago," provide the specific dates of the event: "In October 1996, the client (age 16 at the time) reportedly was hospitalized for 11 days at Shady Oaks inpatient psychiatric unit following her suicide attempt, consisting of swallowing 50 tablets of Valium and cutting her left wrist." The

referent "10 years ago" will have a different meaning when someone reads the report at later time, but dates of important events remain constant regardless of when the report is read. Avoid using the term *issues* as well (e.g., "The client has anger issues [medical issues, family issues].")). Rather, state what the problem is specifically. As can be easily seen, more details and dates are better than less, and they make the report more descriptive and potentially useful in treatment.

A related problem in some reports is the excessive use of quotations. It is often easy to remember interesting and vivid quotes from the client, and it is tempting to include them in the report. However, a reliance on quotes often limits clarity, specificity, and objectivity. Consider the following example: "According to the client, his boss is 'a real pain in the rear.'" What does the client mean exactly by "pain in the rear"? What specifically does the boss do that the client finds irritating? It is important to document these specific events clearly. The statement can be rewritten as follows: "According to the client, he frequently becomes irritated at his boss at Burrito World. The client elaborates that his boss demands that work be done on time, frequently criticizes the client when he takes a nap at work, and threatens to fire the client when he comes to work under the influence of LSD. The client notes that his boss is 'a real pain in the rear.'" These statements shed more light on what is happening at work.

As another example, consider the following use of quotes from the client: "The client describes her brother as 'odd, weird, a real nerd.'" From this quote, is it really clear how the brother behaves specifically? Does he suffer from a serious mental disorder such as schizophrenia? Or does he just like to watch *Star Trek* reruns and play fantasy games? It would be best to replace the quote with a clear description of the brother's behavior. We advise clinicians to use quotes only *after* describing the facts objectively." Quotations can add flavor to the facts but do not describe them. Students who rely excessively on quotes should practice writing reports without any quotes. This strategy challenges them to think about what the client is communicating and to ask for clarification and elaboration. Once the student is more proficient at objective writing, quotes may be added, but only to spice up and personalize the report.

Jargon should also be avoided in intake reports and intake interview sessions. Examples of jargon include "The client demonstrated a *strong transference reaction* to the interviewer," "The client appears *fixated at the oral stage* of development," "The client suffers from a *Type-A personality*," and "The client seems to have lots of *boundary issues*." Clinicians may know what they mean by those terms, but others reading the report may not. It is good practice to write the report so that it can be understood by someone without significant formal training in psychology. As we described earlier, with the client's permission, reports may be released to others, and in many cases the recipients will not be mental health professionals (e.g., lawyers, primary care physicians, disability evaluators, and family members). Jargon typically is vague and abstract. It inhibits the flow of a well-written report. (*Note:* An exception to this rule is the clinical formulation section, which by definition incorporates the language of a particular psychological theory.)

Clients themselves sometimes use jargon or labels, especially those who are psychologically sophisticated. Even in these cases, jargon has no place in the report. Ask clients to describe the behaviors that the label implies. A client explained emphatically at the beginning of the intake session that she was a "coda," evidently meaning a "codependent." Upon gentle questioning, this client described vividly many specific behaviors that had led her to think of herself as a "coda." This specific information was documented in the report (e.g., "The client describes herself as unassertive, gullible, afraid to be alone, insecure, and dependent on others for self-esteem. She relates a long history of repetitive and destructive relationships with chemically dependent and abusive individuals whom she tries to help"). Some clients likewise use slang terms to describe themselves or others (e.g., "crazy," "nutty," "superhuman," "cool," "a worry wart," "has a bad attitude," "a loser"). Like jargon, such terms should be avoided in a professional report.

The intake report is focused on describing the client. Therefore, the clinician's self-disclosures or personal opinions are best left out of the report (e.g., "I felt sad for the client when he discussed his painful childhood." "The client should not be so bitter about her divorce because it probably was for the best anyway."). Rather than including personal reflections in the written report, the clinician should discuss his or her feelings with a supervisor or colleague, which can lead to a greater understanding of oneself and of one's client.

SECTIONS OF THE INTAKE REPORT

The sections commonly provided in comprehensive intake reports are presented in Table 9.1. In fact, our template for the formal write-up is divided into these discrete segments, making the final document organized and efficient. As each section is discussed, it may be helpful to consult the sample intake evaluation report presented in Appendix 9.A. A checklist for writing the intake report is also provided (Appendix 9.B).

Table 9.1   Sections of a Typical Intake Evaluation Report

- Title and identifying data
- Referral source
- Informants
- Presenting problem (or chief complaint)
- History of presenting problem (or history of chief complaint)
- Other relevant history (or psychosocial history)
- Medical history and current medications
- Mental status examination and client strengths
- Clinical formulation (or case conceptualization)
- *DSM-IV-TR* multiaxial diagnostic impressions
- Tentative treatment goals and strategies

Title and Identifying Data

Typically, the name and address of the clinician or service agency are listed at the top of the report. Recall that reports often are requested and released (with the client's permission) to outside agencies or professionals. Many professionals use letterhead stationery or electronic templates for this purpose. The title "Intake Evaluation" or "Diagnostic Interview" should be included below the address, as well as notification (printed or stamped, preferably on each page of the report) that the report is confidential. Next, identifying demographic information is presented. In our template, the following data are provided: full name of client, gender, date of birth, age, level of education, name of interviewer, date of examination, employment status, and marital status. Think of these as minimally required demographics. Additional demographic information one may list includes ethnicity, nationality, cultural factors, primary language, and current medications. Most of this demographic information can be found on the forms clients fill out before being interviewed. Make sure this information is complete before proceeding.

Referral Source

The referral source answers the question, "Who sent the client?" Important facts prompting the initial evaluation and specific referral questions should be noted. Common referral sources include family doctors or general practitioners, nurses, psychiatrists, crisis lines, local mental health or social service agencies (e.g., county mental health department, area agency on aging), probation officers, courts for mandated treatment, other psychotherapists who are unable to treat the client, clergy, employers, family members, friends, and teachers. Some clients are referred for follow-up psychotherapy after discharge from a psychiatric inpatient unit. Other clients are self-referred, which means that they have decided for themselves that a mental health evaluation is warranted and no other agency, individual, or professional has specifically recommended treatment. The following are examples of write-ups: "The client was referred for a psychological assessment and possible psychotherapy by Sue Levy, MD, the client's local family doctor." "The client was self-referred for evaluation of depression and substance abuse." "The client was referred by Debbie Royal, MSW, a social worker at a local acute-term care nursing home, The Manors, for evaluation of the nature and extent of psychiatric disability." "The client was referred by Daniel Heimlich from El Paso County Probation and Parole for psychological assessment and treatment planning after the client was found walking the streets naked, disoriented, and singing showtunes."

Informants

This section describes all sources of information used in the report. If the client and nobody else was interviewed, state that the client attended the session alone. In some cases, however, there may be multiple informants. For example, parents often are interviewed when they bring their children in for evaluation. Sometimes, people seeking treatment are severely impaired (e.g., those who are actively psychotic, disorganized, or cognitively impaired) and therefore are unable to provide a great deal of accurate information. In these situations, data gathering often is facilitated by the participation of family members, spouses, or significant others who know the client well. These people often can provide more thorough

and reliable information about the client's current and past functioning. Entire families may be interviewed during a family psychotherapy evaluation. Finally, some clients bring prior records from outside sources or professionals (e.g., medical records, reports from previously seen mental health professionals, disability documents, discharge reports from psychiatric facilities). State clearly whether any prior records are available and reviewed for the report.

Presenting Problem

The presenting problem refers to the client's present difficulties and is written in the report in terms of psychiatric symptoms and signs experienced by the client. A clear and descriptive presenting problem is a crucial aspect of the intake report. If the presenting problem is not clearly elicited in the interview and delineated in the write-up, the rest of the report will follow this faulty lead and remain off track. Unfortunately, the presenting problem (in terms of symptoms and signs) is not always readily apparent. Besides symptoms, clients often express their problems in terms of patterns of maladjusted behavior (e.g., repeatedly fired from jobs, repeatedly entering into relationships with abusive partners, repeatedly having conflict with authority figures), stressors (e.g., divorce, death or loss of a close family member or friend, bankruptcy, poverty, being a victim of a crime), or interpersonal conflicts.

More generally, clients typically present at intake as either symptom or stressor focused. Clients with a symptom-focused presentation often list a litany of disturbing psychological and physical symptoms that they find distressing and from which they want relief. It is often easy to describe the presenting problem for such clients. For example, a client brought in a typed, two-page list of symptoms for review. This action may also be diagnostically useful (e.g., it may indicate obsessive-compulsive personality disorder features). It is common for anxious and depressed clients to see their symptoms as things to get rid of, and these clients often can describe a diverse array of symptoms that are experienced as ego-dystonic. For example, a depressed client may report a dysphoric mood ("feeling blue" in her words) and having an excessive appetite, weight gain, and trouble concentrating. The clinician may then inquire directly about other symptoms of a major depressive episode (e.g., sleep disturbance, loss of interest in activities, low energy, psychomotor retardation or agitation, feelings of worthlessness, and thoughts of death or dying) to flesh out other aspects of the problem or disorder experienced by the individual. If additional symptoms are elicited or reported (at any time during the interview), regardless of whether they are part of the same syndrome or disorder (in this case major depression), they should be listed in the presenting problem. This last point is especially important because many clients present with signs and symptoms of diverse psychiatric disorders, rarely presenting with the prototypical picture of a single disorder.

Another point to emphasize is that clinicians should not leave it up to the client to accurately report all symptoms because clients are not experts in psychopathology and often do not recognize some symptoms. People with certain disorders (e.g., schizophrenia, personality disorders, substance-related disorders) often lack insight into their condition and therefore may be unaware that they suffer from a mental disorder (Othmer & Othmer, 2002a). Such people may clearly exhibit overt signs of the disorder (e.g., hallucinations and delusions in people with schizophrenia; flamboyant, dramatic, seductive, and superficial behavior in people with histrionic personality disorder; evidence of tolerance and withdrawal symptoms in people with alcohol dependence) but will not report them. It is the intake interviewer's job to identify and understand all psychiatric symptoms and signs experienced by the client, whether or not the client recognizes such symptoms and signs. Then, they should be listed in the presenting problem section in descriptive, objective terms. For clients with symptom-focused presentations, clinicians should evaluate thoroughly why clients are seeking help now and what have they done to try to address or resolve the problem up to the present time (an assessment of coping).

In contrast to symptom-focused clients, those with a stressor-focused presentation pose a different challenge. These people typically complain about current stressors with which they are struggling. For example, one client complained that her main problem was that she caught her boyfriend with another woman and subsequently ended the relationship. Another client reported that the main difficulty was that he recently relocated to a new city and started a demanding graduate program. It is critical to ask clients who present with stressors to explore and describe the specific ways in which the stressors are affecting them. In this way, current symptoms can be elicited. For example, the previously mentioned woman revealed that as a result of the breakup she increased her alcohol consumption to the point of daily drinking; was feeling increasingly depressed, angry, lonely, and suicidal; and also experienced increased appetite, irritability, and lethargy. In the second example, the displaced graduate student said that because of the recent changes in his life he was experiencing panic attacks, poor concentration, difficulty falling asleep, ruminative thoughts, upset stomach, and diarrhea. These presenting problems (in terms of psychiatric symptoms and signs) should be reported in the presenting problem section.

Note that the environmental stressors are not actually the presenting problem; rather, the presenting problem refers to symptoms and signs. Therefore, stressful experiences such as being fired from a job, being diagnosed with stomach cancer, and being rejected by one's partner are not part of the presenting problem, at least as it is conceptualized here. However, these stressors are exceptionally important to elicit and understand, and they have their rightful place in the next section of the report ("History of Presenting Problem").

In the presenting problem section, make sure to be comprehensive in listing symptoms and signs. Some clients may suffer from more than one disorder; they may suffer from diverse symptoms of several disorders, never fulfilling criteria for any specific one; they may suffer from problems that are not easily identifiable as being a part of any syndrome (e.g., excessive anger, loneliness); or they may have personality disorder or features of a personality disorder.

Regarding the personality disorders, each is defined by a list of criteria and diagnostic thresholds (e.g., the individual must meet five of the nine criteria to be diagnosed) just like the clinical disorders listed on Axis I. However, personality disorders are known to be especially difficult to diagnose and conceptualize (Coolidge & Segal, 1998; Segal & Coolidge, 2001; Segal, Coolidge, & Rosowsky, 2006; Westen & Shedler, 2000; Widiger, 2005). When personality disorder features are present, it is important to describe the personality disorder symptoms in the presenting problem section. With a narcissistic client, for example, the symptoms may be reported as "The client also presents with a longstanding pattern of viewing himself as superior to others, overvaluing his accomplishments, craving admiration, being insensitive to others' feelings and needs, reacting to criticism with rage and depression, and having a sense of entitlement." In most cases of personality disorder, symptoms of an Axis I clinical disorder (or multiple clinical disorders) probably will be present as well, and these symptoms should be understood as part of the presenting problem.

In any case, the major point is that *all symptoms and signs* should be recorded in the presenting problem section. Notably, all symptoms should be described as specifically as possible. Some dimensions of symptoms to note include frequency, duration, and intensity. For example, the symptom "sleep disturbance" is unclear. Does the client have trouble falling asleep or staying asleep, does the client have frequent nightmares, or does the client wake up after sleep but not feel rested? How many nights each week does it happen? Clear, behaviorally specific descriptions of symptoms make a report stand out. An excellent and clinically rich resource for diverse descriptions of disorders, clinical constructs, and symptoms is provided by Zuckerman (2005). Factors that influence the meaning of signs and symptoms should be also described, such as cultural context. For instance, it is not uncommon in some cultures to report hearing the voices of departed loved ones during times of stress or as part of normal experience, and this should not necessarily be interpreted as auditory hallucinations indicating psychosis in people raised in such cultures (Castillo, 1997). Finally, if the evaluation was occasioned by a hospitalization of the client, the reason for the hospitalization should be clearly described.

History of Presenting Problem

In the template we are presenting, this section includes three important components that help clarify and expand on the presenting problem already noted. These components are onset, precipitants (or stressors), and course. Each should be assessed and described fully in this section of the report.

Onset addresses the questions "When did the symptoms and signs listed in the presenting problem first become apparent?" or "When did the symptoms begin?" With a depressed client, for example, ask, "When did you first start having

some of the symptoms of depression we have been discussing?" It may also be helpful to ask clients when they were free of all symptoms: "Up until what age were you free of any problems?" Sometimes, clients cannot accurately pinpoint (or even approximate) when their symptoms began. This is especially likely in cases where the disorder had an insidious onset or when clients lack insight into the problem. In these cases, document that "The client was unable to identify the approximate onset of his symptoms."

Related to onset are *precipitants,* or *stressors,* that typically occur before the appearance or worsening of symptoms. Describe precipitants clearly in the report to help the reader understand the context in which symptoms or distress have developed in the client's life. Some clients can provide lengthy descriptions of numerous life stressors, and all relevant details should be put in this section. It may be helpful to ask what else was happening in the client's life at the time the symptoms began, even if the client sees no relationship between these events and the symptoms experienced. If the client cannot identify any stressors, precipitants, or life changes, state so in the report.

The third variable, *course,* characterizes how the client's symptoms have changed, if at all, since the onset. Have the symptoms gotten better over time? Worse? Better for 3 months, then worse for the past 6 months? Was there a previous episode of the problem years ago and a recurrence in the past year? Has there been no change in the symptoms since they started? Whatever the facts, state them in the report. The following is a brief example of a description of onset, precipitants, and course: "The client relates that his depressive symptoms began around April 2006. According to the client, he was fired from his job as a computer programmer in February 2006, his wife filed for divorce 2 weeks later, and in late March his pet golden retriever died from kidney disease. Since that time, his symptoms have gotten progressively worse up to the present evaluation (June 2006)." Most full write-ups will be much longer and more complex.

Other Relevant History

This section of the report includes information generated from the social history part of the interview. This section provides a thorough overview of the client's life besides the presenting problem. Whereas the presenting problem section is problem focused, this section is *person focused*. This distinction is important because clinicians treat people with mental health problems, not the problems themselves, in a vacuum.

Moreover, this description of background information relevant to the present difficulties is critical because it helps place the clients and their problems in a context of general functioning. Regarding early life, it is often helpful to indicate whether there were any complications at birth, where the client grew up, and how many siblings were in the family and describe the birth order, school performance, social development, and any significant events or problems (e.g., traumas, illnesses, disabilities, abuse) in early and middle childhood and adolescence.

The focus then turns to the adult years, where the client's functioning in many major areas is described. These domains include educational history, work history, dating or marital history, sexual history, interpersonal relationships with family and friends, legal and criminal history (especially any current litigation or criminal proceedings), medical problems, religious or spiritual background and values, current social life, leisure activities, important life events and transitions, and psychoactive substance use history (alcohol and other psychoactive substances, whether legal or illegal). Regarding psychoactive substance use, relevant information includes the specific substances used, quantity and frequency of use, route of administration, signs of tolerance or withdrawal, negative consequences associated with substance use, relationship between substance use and the client's problems, and any self-perceived benefits of substance use.

In addition, the client's history of episodes of mental illness and treatment (called the client's past psychiatric history) should be clearly listed, preferably in chronological order. Dates of all previous mental health contacts, previously established diagnoses, the reasons for treatment and treatments offered, the number of sessions, the names of treating clinicians and hospitals, responses to treatment, and the reason for terminating treatment should be included, when available. Additionally, previously prescribed psychotropic medications are part of the past psychiatric history. Such data about the client's past psychiatric treatment can greatly assist the clinician in reconstructing past diagnoses from other clinicians and identifying responses to certain types of intervention (e.g., cognitive

psychotherapy, medications) that may be replicated or avoided, depending on experiences of the client.

Similarly, always assess and comment on any family history of mental illness, substance use, and suicide (called family psychiatric history). Clearly describe whether any family members have been diagnosed, treated, or hospitalized for psychiatric problems. Also indicate whether mental illness seems to have been present but left untreated. The client's family psychiatric history is important because many disorders have a genetic component, and it can also speak to the environment in which the client was raised. Many clinicians also make a statement in the report about the presence or absence of a history of physical abuse, emotional abuse, sexual abuse, sexual assault, intimate partner violence, or any other type of abuse or trauma. If clients report not having these experiences, state so in the write-up.

Medical History and Current Medications

In this section the client's relevant medical history is recorded, including significant medical problems or disorders. Medications that the client is taking should also be listed, whether they are prescribed or over-the-counter. It may be important to report use of nutritional supplements, vitamins, or unusual amounts of food or drink as well, including drinking large amounts of coffee or caffeinated soft drinks or taking many different vitamins and food supplements daily. For prescribed medications, list the name, dosage, and prescribing doctor if possible. It is also helpful to state the type of medication or what the medication was prescribed for (e.g., antidepressant, antianxiety, antipsychotic, hypnotic, pain relief).

Mental Status Examination and Client Strengths

The mental status examination (MSE) often is considered to be the cornerstone of a psychiatric evaluation. This assessment focuses on the client's present functioning in the here and now, as observed by the clinician. This information often is critical in the diagnostic assessment when combined with other parts of the intake evaluation such as the presenting problem, history of the presenting problem, and psychiatric treatment history. Therefore, some form of MSE should be carried out on all clients at intake. However, the depth of the evaluation often is based on severity of the client's illness, with more disturbed people needing more comprehensive and formal testing of mental status. This section of the report is devoted to a description of the information generated from the MSE part of the interview. The report should include a statement about each MSE variable assessed during the interview. If the behavior or response was completely normal, then state this rather than omitting it.

Many MSE sections begin with a description of the client's demographics (age, gender, ethnicity), appearance, attire, grooming, hygiene, and eye contact. If some of this information has been presented in earlier sections of the report, usually it does not need to be repeated here. Provide enough information so that the reader can easily visualize the client's physical appearance at the interview. Definitely note anything unusual about the person (e.g., wore neck brace, malodorous, rashes on skin, fingernails bitten, six bows in hair stacked on top of each other). Also comment on the person's behavior during the interview (e.g., fell asleep several times, hands tightly clasped, frequently cried, paced around the room, sucked thumb) and the attitude of the client toward the interviewer (e.g., cooperative, suspicious, hostile, guarded, seductive, manipulative). If the client's attitude is labeled negatively, make sure to clearly describe the client behaviors that led to this inference. These vivid descriptions of appearance and behavior often provide diagnostic clues.

Next, describe the client's mood (e.g., euthymic, anxious, dysphoric, euphoric, irritable) and affect (e.g., broad, restricted, flat). Characterize the person's speech in terms of loudness, speed, and organization of thoughts (e.g., soft, loud; rapid, pressured, average rate; logical, coherent, goal directed, loose associations, circumstantial, tangential, word salad, or senseless speech). Include comments about the cognitive functions of orientation (to time, place, person, and situation), attention, concentration, fund of knowledge (appropriate to educational and sociocultural background), and recent and remote memory. Provide a gross estimate of intelligence level. Provide a description of the reliability or quality of information obtained from the client. Is the person a poor or excellent historian? Make sure to include assessments of the client's awareness (of having a problem) and insight (into the causes of the problem and the impact it is having on the client's life). Describe the client's judgment. To what extent is the client able to solve his or her problems in a realistic way and make reasonable plans for the future? The MSE variables of awareness, insight, and judgment usually are described on a continuum ranging from extremely poor or nonexistent to excellent. In addition, always ask directly and comment in the report about the extent to which there is suicidal or homicidal ideation, plan, or intent and about the presence or absence of delusions and hallucinations. Finally, it is common to include strengths in the MSE section. This can balance out the report and focus on positives that exist with all clients. A positive asset search during the interview often reveals important strengths of the client that may be helpful in implementing treatment. Some examples of client strengths include their motivation for treatment, good verbal skills, intelligence, perseverance, ability to maintain employment, ability to live independently, ability to maintain positive relationships with family or friends, and no cognitive impairment.

Clinical Formulation

This section describes the clinician's theoretical analysis of the current case, addressing the specific questions "What has caused the person's present difficulties (symptoms) to develop?" and "What maintains those symptoms?" It is important to understand that in some cases problems are *caused* by one set of reasons but are *maintained* by another set. For example, a client withheld sex from her husband after she learned of his infidelity (the cause). Over time she forgave him but continued to avoid physical intimacy because she had become obese and felt uncomfortable about her body (maintaining factors). Additionally, relevant issues related to the culture, ethnicity, gender, sexual orientation, and religious or spiritual beliefs of the client should be described. Based on the clinician's particular theoretical orientation (e.g., psychodynamic, cognitive-behavioral, humanistic, existential, family systems), educated hypotheses about the origins of the person's problems are offered. The conceptualization attempts to explain how the client came to have these particular problems at this time according to a particular theoretical orientation. Obviously, there is no definitive right or wrong way to conceptualize a case.

Different theories offer a different conceptualization. However, it is important to thoroughly learn the language and concepts of a particular model and to remain consistent within the formulation so that you do not throw a panoply of different models together without a rationale for doing so. Clinicians who are having trouble with case formulation (and most beginning clinicians do) should look to a supervisor or colleague for guidance and support.

DSM-IV-TR Multiaxial Diagnostic Impressions

This section supplies a full diagnosis based on criteria for mental disorders listed in the *Diagnostic and Statistical Manual of Mental Disorders* (*DSM-IV-TR*; American Psychiatric Association, 2000). The *DSM-IV-TR* includes a multiaxial system, which involves assessment of different domains of client functioning. There are five distinct axes in the DSM system, and the report should include information on *each one*.

- Axis I includes clinical disorders (e.g., bipolar disorder, generalized anxiety disorder, alcohol dependence, anorexia nervosa, schizophrenia, adjustment disorder) and other conditions that may be a focus of clinical attention (e.g., bereavement, phase of life problem, parent-child problem).

- Axis II includes the 10 standard personality disorders (paranoid, schizoid, schizotypal, antisocial, borderline, histrionic, narcissistic, avoidant, dependent, and obsessive-compulsive) and mental retardation. In the interview, always screen for lifelong maladjustment and lifelong recurrent coping deficits, which can alert the clinician that a personality disorder or features of a personality disorder may be present. However, it often takes several sessions to formally diagnose these complex disorders. Interestingly, Axis II may also be used to list prominent maladaptive personality disorder *features* that do not meet the diagnostic threshold. Habitual use of maladaptive defense mechanisms may also be listed on Axis II, although this technique appears uncommon in clinical practice.

Note: For both Axis I and Axis II, if the client meets the formal diagnostic threshold for a specific disorder, clinicians should write out the full name for each disorder (including subtypes, specifiers, and severity ratings, if applicable) and provide the official numeric diagnostic code for each disorder as listed in the *DSM-IV-TR*. It is imperative that diagnoses listed on Axis I or Axis II be fully supported by symptoms listed in the presenting problem section and the timeframe of the problem described in the history of the presenting problem section. Indeed, there should not be any surprises in this diagnostic section. In cases of diagnostic uncertainty, clinicians may record the word "(Provisional)," following the tentative diagnosis. If the client does not meet criteria for any Axis I or Axis II disorder, the *DSM-IV-TR* code V71.09 is available to indicate "No diagnosis."

- Axis III includes general medical conditions. All medical problems relevant to the person's current functioning or potential management of the case should be recorded. It is acceptable to use the client's self-report in cases where there are no medical charts to verify, but it will be necessary to request medical records and communicate with the client's physician (with the client's permission and a signed release of information) if the medical picture significantly influences or complicates the presentation of current problems, case formulation, or treatment.

- Axis IV is for reporting of environmental and psychosocial stressors. Note all stressors currently affecting the client. Whereas the *DSM-IV-TR* provides general categories of stressors (e.g., social problems, economic problems), it is advantageous to report the specific stressors experienced by the client (e.g., conflict with peers, severe financial pressures, victim of a violent crime). Usually, stressors within the past year are noted, except for certain diagnoses on Axis I, such as posttraumatic stress disorder, where the trauma is recorded on Axis IV regardless of when it occurred.

- On Axis V, record judgments concerning the client's overall level of functioning. Use the Global Assessment of Functioning (GAF) Scale in the *DSM-IV-TR*, which provides ratings on a standardized scale ranging from 0 to 100, with higher scores reflecting higher functioning. Consider the extent to which the person's symptoms have been interfering with school, work, family relationships, social life, and health, and make an overall GAF rating. Typically, the client's current GAF score is provided. Many clinicians supplement the current rating with GAF ratings for other times, such as the highest level in the past year or upon admission to a psychiatric facility.

An important point to emphasize here is that the diagnosis and case formulation together facilitate the development of a treatment plan.

Tentative Treatment Goals and Strategies

This final section often is the most important. Here, the clinician should clearly state any professional recommendations based on the full evaluation of the client. Possible recommendations include individual psychotherapy; couple psychotherapy; family psychotherapy; group psychotherapy; referral for personality, intelligence, or neuropsychological testing; referral for social work services; referral to medical professionals to rule out organic causes of psychiatric symptoms; referral to support or educational groups; consultation with psychiatrist for possible pharmacotherapy; hospitalization (for acutely suicidal, homicidal, or psychotic people); another evaluation in 3 or 6 months to see whether current functioning or impairment worsens; or no treatment indicated at present.

If some form of psychotherapy is recommended, the clinician should state the tentative goals of the treatment, the estimated prognosis, the expected length of treatment, and the plan to review treatment progress after a specified period of time (e.g., 6 weeks, 10 weeks). Regarding the goals of treatment, they are often are concordant with the presenting problem. For example, if the client presents with prominent symptoms of an eating disorder (e.g., low weight, refusal to eat food, and distorted body image), some goals of psychotherapy might reasonably be to increase weight, increase caloric intake, increase healthful eating behaviors, and reduce distortions in body image. As another example, with a depressed client who is unassertive and isolated, treatment goals may be to reduce depression, increase assertive communication, and improve interpersonal skills.

Most models of psychotherapy support the tenet that goal setting should be a collaborative process between the clinician and client. It is certainly important that clients be aware of at least some of the goals of treatment, and this treatment contract often is negotiated at the end of the initial interview. In many cases, there will be a specific document describing treatment goals, objectives, and strategies (called a treatment plan) that will be completed by the clinician and possibly the client during the early phases of psychological intervention (see Hersen & Porzelius, 2002; Jongsma & Peterson, 2003). Prognosis is the prediction of the probable course and outcome of the client's problems (or mental disorder). Prognosis alternatively can be viewed as the likelihood of recovery from a disorder or illness and as such can be conceptualized as being on a continuum (e.g., from poor to excellent). A number of variables factor into determination of prognosis, including levels of awareness of the problems and insight, the chronicity of the problems, and the client's motivation to get better. To the extent that clients have poor awareness and insight, a long history of being symptomatic without periods of relief, and limited motivation, their prognosis usually is poor.

Summary

Intake interviewing and report writing are important and highly valued skills for clinicians to practice, hone, and master. This chapter has reviewed the purposes of the intake interview and intake report and has provided suggestions to help produce well-written and thorough reports. A general template for the intake report was provided, each section of the report was discussed, and guidelines for organization and professional writing were provided. Remember that the format and sample report presented here are not definitive models. Rather, clinicians are encouraged to modify and adapt the information to meet their particular needs. Although the process of conducting an interview and writing the report may seem intimidating, especially for beginning clinicians, with practice and experience the process will become more natural and efficient. Regardless of individual differences in style, fostering a safe and positive therapeutic relationship, conducting a thorough evaluation of the client, and crafting a solid intake report are necessary components of successful psychological treatment.

ACKNOWLEDGMENTS

We thank Molly Maxfield, MA, for her helpful comments on an earlier version of this chapter. We dedicate this chapter to our students because their many drafts of reports, tough questions, innovations, and innocent blunders helped shape and refine our ideas.

REFERENCES

American Psychiatric Association. (2000). *Diagnostic and statistical manual of mental disorders* (4th ed., Text rev.). Washington, DC: Author.

American Psychological Association. (1993). Record keeping guidelines. *American Psychologist, 48,* 984–986.

Castillo, R. J. (1997). *Culture and mental illness: A client-centered approach.* Pacific Grove, CA: Brooks/Cole.

Castonguay, L. G., & Beutler, L. E. (Eds.). (2005). *Principles of therapeutic change that work.* New York: Oxford University Press.

Coolidge, F. L., & Segal, D. L. (1998). Evolution of the personality disorder diagnosis in the *Diagnostic and Statistical Manual of Mental Disorders. Clinical Psychology Review, 18,* 585–599.

Craig, R. J. (Ed.). (2005). *Clinical and diagnostic interviewing* (2nd ed.). Lanham, MD: Jason Aronson.

Evans, D. R., Hearn, M. T., Uhlemann, M. R., & Ivey, A. E. (2004). *Essential interviewing: A programmed approach to effective communication* (6th ed.). Belmont, CA: Thomson Wadsworth.

First, M. B., Francis, A., & Pincus, H. A. (2002). DSM-IV-TR *handbook of differential diagnosis.* Washington, DC: American Psychiatric Publishing.

Hersen, M., & Porzelius, L. K. (Eds.). (2002). *Diagnosis, conceptualization, and treatment planning for adults: A step-by-step guide.* Mahwah, NJ: Lawrence Erlbaum.

Hersen, M., & Turner, S. M. (Eds.). (2003). *Diagnostic interviewing* (3rd ed.). New York: Springer.

Hersen, M., & Van Hasselt, V. B. (Eds.). (1998). *Basic interviewing: A practical guide for counselors and clinicians.* Mahwah, NJ: Lawrence Erlbaum.

Jongsma, A. E., & Peterson, L. M. (2003). *The complete adult psychotherapy treatment planner.* Hoboken, NJ: Wiley.

Morrison, J. (1995). *The first interview: Revised for DSM-IV.* New York: Guilford.

Othmer, E., & Othmer, S. C. (2002a). *The clinical interview using* DSM-IV-TR: *Vol. 1. Fundamentals.* Washington, DC: American Psychiatric Publishing.

Othmer, E., & Othmer, S. C. (2002b). *The clinical interview using* DSM-IV-TR: *Vol. 2. The difficult patient.* Washington, DC: American Psychiatric Publishing.

Segal, D. L., & Coolidge, F. L. (2001). Diagnosis and classification. In M. Hersen & V. B. Van Hasselt (Eds.), *Advanced abnormal psychology* (2nd ed., pp. 5–22). New York: Kluwer Academic/Plenum.

Segal, D. L., Coolidge, F. L., & Rosowsky, E. (2006). *Personality disorders and older adults: Diagnosis, assessment, and treatment.* New York: Wiley.

Westen, D., & Shedler, J. (2000). A prototype matching approach to diagnosing personality disorders: Toward *DSM-V. Journal of Personality Disorders, 14,* 109–126.

Widiger, T. A. (2005). Personality disorders. In R. J. Craig (Ed.), *Clinical and diagnostic interviewing* (2nd ed., pp. 251–277). Lanham, MD: Jason Aronson.

Wiger, D. E. (2005). *The clinical documentation sourcebook: The complete paperwork resource for your mental health practice.* Hoboken, NJ: Wiley.

Zuckerman, E. L. (2005). *Clinician's thesaurus* (6th ed.). New York: Guilford.

APPENDIX 9.A   INTAKE EVALUATION

Aardvark Counseling Center
291 Anteater Road
Colorado Springs, CO 80933

INTAKE EVALUATION
CONFIDENTIAL

Name: Isabel Illustration   Examiner: Sandy Student, MA

Gender: Female   Date of Examination: 9/7/2006

DOB: 3/22/49   Employment Status: Unemployed

Age: 57   Marital Status: Married

Level of Education: High School

Referral Source:

Ms. Illustration is a 57-year-old, married, White woman referred to Aardvark Counseling Center by Dr. Ima Smart, her internist, for psychological assessment and psychotherapy. The client states that she was referred after she had an uncontrollable crying spell in her physician's office and revealed thoughts of suicide to the physician.

Informants:

The client attended the session alone. However, she brought records from a prior psychiatric hospitalization and several handwritten notes from her daughter to the session, and they were reviewed for this report.

Presenting Problem:

The client presents with the following symptoms: depressed mood, frequent crying, loss of pleasure in activities, trouble falling asleep, overeating and weight gain, lethargy, poor concentration, low self-esteem, helplessness, and infrequent thoughts of wishing she were dead. She also complains of increased social isolation and worry about the future. She sees herself as significantly depressed, although she states that she does not know why she is depressed. The client describes several physical problems including headaches, occasional dizziness, constipation, infrequent stomach pain, and aching joints.

History of Presenting Problem:

The client reports that she first experienced symptoms of depression around April 1997. She relates that at that time she and her husband moved from California to Colorado because of business opportunities for her husband. She states that she missed her children, who lived near her in California, and that she subsequently became increasingly isolated in Colorado. She notes that her depressive symptoms worsened over the next year, and in May 1998, she was voluntarily hospitalized for 5 days in the adult psychiatric unit at St. Luke's Hospital for severe depression and suicidal thoughts. She reportedly was prescribed the antidepressant medication Paxil (20 mg/day) but notes that she stopped it soon after discharge because of unpleasant side effects. She states that in June 1998 she received follow-up individual psychotherapy with local psychologist, Dr. Em Pathy. The client relates that her symptoms slowly remitted and that she ended psychotherapy in January 2000. The client characterizes the treatment as being cognitive-behavioral in nature. She reports that for the next several years she experienced few symptoms until about age 53 (2002). Since that time, the client reports chronic and debilitating depressive episodes lasting several months at a time. These episodes include all the symptoms noted previously. The current episode reportedly began around February 2006, after conflict with her husband greatly intensified. She relates that at that time the family's financial difficulties mounted and that she and her husband were forced to file for bankruptcy. She also relates that in March 2006, her son was diagnosed with a malignant brain tumor and has a poor prognosis. Her symptoms reportedly have progressively worsened since their onset. The client indicates that she has not sought treatment since her psychotherapy in 1998. The client denies ever experiencing symptoms of hypomania or mania.

Other Relevant History:

Ms. Illustration grew up in Sunnyside, California, a rural farm town. She is unaware of any complications during her birth or postnatal difficulties. She reportedly reached all developmental milestones without delay. She describes a difficult childhood working on the family farm, in extreme poverty. She characterizes her childhood and adolescence as extremely lonely and reports a longstanding difficulty expressing herself to others and a pattern of letting others take advantage of her. She states, "I have always been a doormat for stronger people to walk all over." She is the youngest in a sibship of two. She states that she has a distant relationship with her brother, who lives in New York. According to the client, her brother was the favorite of both parents and received special attention from them that she never received. She describes both of her parents as chronically pessimistic and elaborates that they both were harshly critical toward her, almost never supportive or encouraging.

Ms. Illustration reports that she met her future husband at age 17 and married at age 18 (1967), primarily to be able to leave her family home and start a new life for herself. The couple has two children who live close to each other in California. She states that she is close to her daughter (age 34) and her daughter's two children but is unable to see them often because of geographic separation. She states, "I miss them dearly." She reports a conflictual relationship with her son (age 31), whom she characterizes as demanding and inconsiderate. According to the client, her son was diagnosed with a cancerous brain tumor in March 2006 and has a poor prognosis for recovery. She states, "He's doomed, and I just will not be able to survive it either." The client's father reportedly died in 1991, and the client's mother has lived with the client's daughter in California since that time. The client states that her mother has not adjusted well to the death of her husband and has been chronically depressed.

The client reports that she graduated from high school and worked on and off during much of her adult life as a housekeeper. In 1992, she reportedly received training as a nurse's aide and worked for many years as a home health aide. She states that in February 2002 she lost her job when the home health agency went out of business and that she has not worked since then. The client notes that both of her parents have a history of depression, and her mother was briefly hospitalized in 1992 after a suicide attempt. She also suggests that her father had an undiagnosed alcohol problem. She states that she never got along with her father and did not like that he spent the family money on alcohol. She describes her mother as negative, critical, and demanding. She characterizes herself as a nonpracticing Catholic. She reports no history of criminal or legal problems with the exception of the pending bankruptcy.

Her husband reportedly works as manager of a local restaurant and bar. The client describes a stormy and conflictual relationship with her husband, with reported infidelity on his part. She states that initially the relationship was satisfactory but that for the past 4 years they have frequently argued about diverse topics such as finances, children, and leisure activities. The client reports that her husband frequently gambles away his earnings, stays out overnight on a regular basis, and maintains romantic relationships with several female bartenders at his restaurant. She states, "His cheating is so obvious it makes me sick." The fighting reportedly escalated in February 2006, when her husband reportedly lost their remaining savings in a gambling binge and paid for an abortion for one of his bartenders. The client also provides her perception that her husband generally does not care about her, but he seems to become more responsive when her depression worsens. She describes having few hobbies or interests and characterizes her local social support network as limited. She states that since February 2006 she has become increasingly withdrawn from her only local friend. She indicates that she does not feel comfortable telling her friend about her problems with her husband, and instead she avoids seeing her friend. She denies a history of drug or alcohol abuse. In addition to the history of recurrent depression in both parents, the client reports that her brother is a recovering alcoholic and that two paternal uncles committed suicide. She reports no other significant family history of mental illness. She also reports no history of physical abuse, sexual abuse, or intimate partner violence.

Medical History and Current Medications:

Significant medical problems that the client reports include headaches, occasional dizziness, constipation, infrequent stomach pain, and osteoarthritis. Current prescribed medications include Tylenol with codeine (dosage unknown, as needed for pain) and Celebrex (200 mg/day, a nonsteroidal anti-inflammatory agent), both prescribed by the client's primary physician, Dr. G. E. Smith. Over-the-counter medications include a daily multivitamin, frequent use of Mylanta and Pepcid (for acid indigestion and heartburn), and occasional aspirin. The client states she smoked one pack of cigarettes daily from the age of 18 to 35 and then successfully stopped (1984).

Mental Status Examination and Client Strengths:

Ms. Illustration presented as a short, overweight, White woman who appeared older than her stated age. She wore a pink jumpsuit that had several holes in it. She generally appeared well groomed, with the exception of dirty fingernails. She initially appeared visibly anxious and described feeling dizzy during the early part of the interview. She attended the interview alone. The client demonstrated poor eye contact and appeared to be shy. Despite some initial shyness, she was increasingly cooperative throughout the interview and appeared to be an organized and reliable historian. Her mood was dysphoric, and her affect was broad. Her speech was soft but logical, coherent, relevant, and goal directed. Her attention and concentration were generally adequate, although she seemed to lose her focus several times during the interview. Recent and remote memory were grossly intact. Her fund of knowledge was adequate, and she appeared to be of average intelligence. The client was aware that she is depressed, although her insight into the causes of her depression and the impact of the depression on her life was poor. Her judgment was fair. She was oriented to time, place, person, and the situation, with no evidence of a formal thought disturbance. She reported never experiencing delusions or hallucinations. She admitted to current infrequent, passive suicidal ideation but denied current suicidal plan or intent. She also denied any homicidal ideation, plan, or intent. Her strengths include a supportive relationship with her daughter, her stated desire for help, and previous positive response to psychotherapy.

Clinical Formulation:

Ms. Illustration has suffered bouts of clinically significant depression for many years. Her positive family history of depression, alcohol abuse, and suicidal behavior further indicates a biological basis. The current episode appears to be related to increased conflict with her husband, worsening financial pressures, and a serious illness in her son. According to the cognitive-behavioral model, the client seems to hold several depressogenic core beliefs, particularly the schema that she is worthless and helpless. She also seems to process information in depressogenic ways, prone to the cognitive distortions of catastrophizing, personalization, and arbitrary inference. Behaviorally, the client's rate of participation in pleasurable events has decreased, which probably exacerbates her depressive symptoms. The client also seems to have some difficulty with assertiveness and appropriate expression of feelings.

DSM-IV-TR **Multiaxial Diagnostic Impressions:**

Axis I: 296.33 Major depressive disorder, recurrent, severe without psychotic features (provisional)
Axis II: Deferred
Axis III: Headaches, occasional dizziness, constipation, infrequent stomach pain, osteoarthritis
Axis IV: Psychosocial stressors: unemployment, isolation, conflict with husband, bankruptcy, son diagnosed with serious illness
Axis V: Current GAF, 50; highest GAF past year, 63

Tentative Treatment Goals and Strategies:

It is recommended that the client be accepted for individual psychotherapy on a priority basis, with the goals of reducing depression, reducing social isolation, increasing the rate of pleasurable activities, and increasing assertive communication. Because she responded well in the past to a cognitive-behavioral approach, this method should be considered. Furthermore, a referral for a psychiatric evaluation for consideration of psychotropic medications is recommended. The client's level of suicidal thinking should be closely monitored and regularly reevaluated. Prognosis for this client's full recovery is guarded. Estimated length of treatment is 30–45 sessions, with a plan to review in 8 weeks.

Sandy Student, MA
Psychology Trainee

Thomas Therapist, PhD
Psychologist (Supervisor)

APPENDIX 9.B   INTAKE REPORT CHECKLIST

General Considerations and Conventions

1. ☐ Formal name of client used
2. ☐ Verb tense consistent within sections
3. ☐ Document proofread

Professional Writing

1. ☐ Statements regularly prefaced with qualifiers
2. ☐ Client statements translated objective, behaviorally specific terms
3. ☐ Slang and colloquialisms replaced with objective, clinical terms
4. ☐Specific details provided when possible
5. ☐ Specific dates provided when possible
6. ☐ Quotes infrequently used
7. ☐ Quotes used only after the facts have been described objectively
8. ☐ No jargon in report
9. ☐ No self-disclosures in report

Sections of the Report

A. Title and Identifying Data

1. ☐ Name and address of clinician or service agency provided
2. ☐ Labeled "Intake Evaluation"
3. ☐ Labeled "Confidential"
4. ☐ Complete identifying demographic information provided

B. Referral Source

1. ☐ Referral source clearly stated
2. ☐ Important facts prompting the assessment noted
3. ☐ Specific referral questions noted

C. Informants

1. ☐ All sources of information noted

D. Presenting Problem

1. ☐ Presenting problem stated in terms of psychiatric symptoms and signs
2. ☐ All psychiatric symptoms and signs listed, regardless of whether client is aware of them
3. ☐ Symptoms described as specifically as possible (frequency, duration, intensity)

E. History of Presenting Problem

1. ☐ Onset of presenting problems clearly stated
2. ☐ Precipitants or environmental stressors described
3. ☐ Course of presenting problems specified

F. Other Relevant History

1. ☐ Siblings and birth order reported
2. ☐ Early childhood, middle childhood, and adolescence described
3. Adult history described:
   ☐ Educational history
   ☐ Occupational history
   ☐ Dating and marital history
   ☐ Sexual history
   ☐ Interpersonal relationships with family and friends
   ☐ Current social life
   ☐ Legal and criminal history
   ☐ Religious or spiritual identification
   ☐ Leisure activities
   ☐ Substance use history

4. ☐ Client's past psychiatric history
5. ☐ Family psychiatric history
6. ☐ History of physical or sexual abuse, sexual assault, and intimate partner violence

G. *Medical History and Current Medications*
1. ☐ All significant medical problems or medical conditions noted
2. ☐ All medications taken by client listed, including prescribed and over-the-counter medications (dosage provided, if known)

H. *Mental Status Examination and Client Strengths*
1. ☐ Client demographics
2. ☐ Appearance, attire, grooming, hygiene
3. ☐ Eye contact
4. ☐ Behavior during interview
5. ☐ Attitude toward interviewer
6. ☐ Mood and affect
7. ☐ Speech and organization of thoughts
8. ☐ Orientation
9. ☐ Attention and concentration
10. ☐ Fund of knowledge
11. ☐ Recent and remote memory
12. ☐ Estimate of intelligence
13. ☐ Reliability of information
14. ☐ Awareness and insight
15. ☐ Judgment
16. ☐ Suicidal and homicidal ideation, plan, or intent
17. ☐ Delusions and hallucinations
18. ☐ Strengths

I. *Clinical Formulation*
1. ☐ Theoretical analysis of the current case provided
2. ☐ Hypotheses about origins and maintaining factors of presenting problems noted

J. DSM-IV-TR *Multiaxial Diagnostic Impressions*
1. ☐ Each of the five axes addressed
2. ☐ Full name for each Axis I and Axis II disorder provided (including subtypes and specifiers)
3. ☐ Official code numbers provided for each disorder on Axis I and Axis II
4. ☐ Diagnosis supported by symptoms in the presenting problem and history of presenting problem sections
5. ☐ On Axis III, general medical conditions noted
6. ☐ On Axis IV, psychosocial and environmental problems noted
7. ☐ On Axis V, current functioning noted using the Global Assessment of Functioning (GAF) scale

K. *Tentative Treatment Goals and Strategies*
1. ☐ Professional recommendations stated
2. ☐ Tentative goals of treatment listed
3. ☐ Prognosis provided
4. ☐ Estimated length of treatment stated
5. ☐ Plan to review progress in psychotherapy reported

PART II

SPECIFIC DISORDERS

10

MAJOR DEPRESSIVE DISORDER

KEITH S. DOBSON AND MARTIN C. SCHERRER

DESCRIPTION OF THE DISORDER

Both depression and the often comorbid condition of anxiety, as Dozois and Dobson (2004) recently observed, "are frequently referred to as the common colds of mental disorders" (p. 1). Though accurate in its reflection of the widespread nature of depression, such a view fails to reflect just how debilitating and costly this condition is to those who experience it and to society in general (Dozois & Dobson, 2004).

Accurate assessment of clinical depression is a critical step in the conceptualization and treatment planning process, and a central element of such assessment is clinical interviewing. After a brief review of the depressive disorders, we will examine interviewing strategies in general and in the context of major depressive disorder and then consider behavioral assessment and differential diagnosis. Finally, we will address the implications for assessment in terms of treatment planning, with particular emphasis on cognitive-behavioral models of case formulation as an avenue through which ideographic information is applied to a general and empirically supported intervention.

DSM-IV-TR Depressive Disorders

The *Diagnostic and Statistical Manual of Mental Disorders* (*DSM-IV-TR*; American Psychiatric Association [APA], 2000) includes under "Mood Disorders" the conditions with the defining feature of a disturbance in mood. Three categories are delineated: the depressive disorders, the bipolar disorders, and two disorders based on etiology, mood disorder due to a general medical condition and substance-induced mood disorder. The absence of past manic, mixed, or hypomanic episodes distinguishes the depressive from the bipolar disorders. The focus of the present discussion is on the depressive disorders, including major depressive disorder, dysthymic disorder, and depressive disorder not otherwise specified, each of which is briefly discussed in turn. Before addressing these disorders, we will outline the diagnostic criteria for a major depressive episode because these criteria are crucial in diagnosing the various depressive disorders.

Major Depressive Episode. A major depressive episode is defined as a period of at least 2 weeks involving a range of symptoms that represent a change from prior functioning and are present for most of the day, nearly every day. At least five of nine specific symptoms are required, with at least one of the symptoms involving either a predominantly depressed or irritable (i.e., in children or adolescents) mood or markedly diminished interest or pleasure in all or almost all activities. Additional symptoms include a significant change in appetite or weight; change in sleep patterns (insomnia or hypersomnia); psychomotor disturbance (agitation or retardation); fatigue or loss of energy; feelings of worthlessness or excessive guilt; diminished ability to think or concentrate, or indecisiveness; and recurrent thoughts of death, suicidal ideation, or a suicide attempt or specific plan. Such symptoms must cause clinically significant distress or impairment in functioning and do not meet criteria for a mixed episode, which involves symptoms of a manic episode in addition to a major depressive episode. Furthermore, the symptoms must not be caused by a substance or general medical condition and are not better accounted for by bereavement, which is defined as a period of grief occasioned by the death of a lost one, lasting less than 8 weeks.

Major Depressive Disorder. The defining feature of major depressive disorder (MDD) is the presence of one or more major depressive episodes in the absence of a manic, mixed, or hypomanic episode. The presence of a single major depressive episode results in the diagnosis of MDD, single episode, whereas two or more major depressive episodes separated by at least 2 consecutive months result in the diagnosis of MDD, recurrent. A number of specifiers are available to further elaborate the clinical status and features of the current episode.

Current severity is indicated as mild, moderate, or severe (with or without psychotic features, which may be mood-congruent or -incongruent). The *chronic* specifier is indicated if criteria for MDD have been met continuously for at least 2 years. The *catatonic features* specifier is indicated when the clinical picture is characterized by marked psychomotor disturbance (including symptoms such as motoric immobility, excessive and apparently pointless motor activity, and peculiar or stereotyped movements). A loss of pleasure or a lack of reactivity to usually pleasurable stimuli, in addition to symptoms such as early morning awakening and excessive or inappropriate guilt, indicates the *melancholic features* specifier. The *atypical features* specifier is indicated by mood reactivity and at least two additional features, such as significant weight gain or increased appetite, hypersomnia, and sensitivity to interpersonal rejection. The *postpartum onset* specifier is used when the onset is within 4 weeks postpartum. Finally, longitudinal course specifiers include *with and without full interepisode recovery,* determined by whether full remission is attained between major depressive episodes, and the *seasonal pattern* specifier indicates a seasonal

pattern to the onset and remission of major depressive episodes.

Dysthymic Disorder. Dysthymic disorder has as its central feature a chronically depressed mood for most of the day, more days than not, that lasts at least 2 years. In addition, at least two of the following symptoms are present: appetite disturbance, sleep disturbance, low energy or fatigue, low self-esteem, poor concentration or indecisiveness, and hopelessness. During the 2-year period, the person has never been without these symptoms for more than 2 months at a time and has never experienced MDD. However, the diagnosis may be made if a person experienced MDD with full remission before developing dysthymic disorder. Also, after the initial 2 years of dysthymic disorder, a person may experience superimposed episodes of MDD, resulting in both diagnoses (also called double depression). Specifiers for dysthymic disorder include *early onset* (before age 21 years) and *late onset* (21 years or older), and with *atypical features,* which follows the criteria as defined for MDD.

Depressive Disorder Not Otherwise Specified. The *DSM-IV-TR* (APA, 2000) includes the not otherwise specified (NOS) category for conditions with depressive features that do not meet criteria for other depressive disorders. Examples include premenstrual dysphoric disorder, minor depressive disorder, recurrent brief depressive disorder, and postpsychotic depressive disorder of schizophrenia (suggested research criteria for these conditions are provided in the *DSM-IV-TR's* Appendix B: "Criteria Sets and Axes Provided for Further Study"). Also falling in the depressive disorder NOS category are instances wherein MDD is superimposed on another disorder, such as delusional disorder, psychotic disorder NOS, or the active phase of schizophrenia, as long as the symptoms do not better meet the diagnosis of schizoaffective disorder. The NOS category is also used when it is unclear whether a depressive disorder is primary or due to a substance or general medical condition.

The Impact and Cost of MDD

The depressive disorders take a substantial toll on both the individuals who experience them and society at large. Depression has been rated by the World Health Organization as the number one cause of disability in the world (Muñoz, Le, Clarke, & Jaycox, 2002) and has been found to negatively affect physical health (e.g., increased rates of cardiac problems) and interpersonal relationships (e.g., troubled parent-child relationships, increased rates of divorce) (Dozois & Westra, 2004; Gotlib & Hammen, 2002). Depression is also associated with significant role impairment, comparable to that caused by seriously impairing chronic physical disorders (Kessler, 2002). For example, a recent large-scale epidemiological examination of MDD, the National Comorbidity Survey Replication (NCS-R), found that of respondents with MDD, 96.9% reported at least some, 87.4% at least moderate, 59.3% severe or very severe, and 19.1% very severe role impairment associated with their depression (Kessler et al., 2003). Given its early age of onset (i.e., median age of onset is in the mid-20s), depression can also negatively affect critical life course role transitions, including educational attainment, entry into the labor force, parenting, and marital timing and stability (Kessler, 2002).

The social cost of depression is high as well. Much of the role impairment caused by the disorder is seen as reduced work performance, with some estimates placing the annual cost of depression in terms of lost productivity in the United States at more than $33 billion (Kessler, 2002). For example, the NCS-R found that respondents with 12-month MDD reported an average of 35.2 days in the past year when they were unable to work or carry out normal activities, which is more than twice the less than 15 days recently reported for most chronic conditions (Kessler et al., 2003). Depression is not only one of the most common disorders faced by mental health professionals but also one of the most costly (Dozois & Westra, 2004).

The Epidemiology of MDD

Given recent estimates, such as that almost 20% of the U.S. population at one point in their lives will experience a clinically significant episode of depression, the disorder is among the most common psychiatric conditions (Gotlib & Hammen, 2002). In terms of point prevalence, community self-report surveys indicate that as many as 20% of adults and 50% of children and adolescents report experiencing depressive symptoms for recall periods between 1 week and

6 months (Kessler, 2002). Rates of *DSM* major depression, as identified by structured diagnostic interviews, are much lower, at less than 1% in children, up to 6% in adolescents, and 2–4% in adults (Kessler, 2002). This discrepancy in findings between symptom screening measures and diagnostic interviews is worth consideration because it underlines the importance of attending to subsyndromal symptoms, particularly given evidence that such symptoms may predict later onset of major depression (Kessler, 2002).

Large-scale epidemiological investigations of the prevalence of depression have varied in their findings. For example, findings from the most recent epidemiological survey carried out in the United States, the NCS-R, which was conducted in 2001–2002 and used *DSM-IV* criteria, estimated the prevalence of MDD to be 16.2% for lifetime and 6.6% for the 12 months before assessment (Kessler et al., 2003). These estimates are much higher than those from the Epidemiological Catchment Area study carried out approximately two decades earlier, which estimated prevalence rates for MDD using *DSM-III* criteria to be 3.0–5.9% for lifetime and 1.7–3.4% for 12 months (Weissman, Bruce, Leaf, Florio, & Holzer, 1991). A number of reasons for such discrepancy have been proposed, including methodological differences across surveys, less reluctance to admit depression in more recent cohorts, and a genuine increase in the prevalence of depression in recent cohorts (Kessler, 2002), particularly among young people (Gotlib & Hammen, 2002).

The Course of MDD

The typical onset of depression is in adolescence, and the disorder is increasingly being understood as often involving a chronic or recurring course (Gotlib & Hammen, 2002). Epidemiological data indicate that the risk of initial onset of depression is fairly low until the early teens, when it begins to rise in a linear fashion, and the slope of this increase has become increasingly steep in more recent age cohorts (Kessler, 2002; Kessler et al., 2003). The course of an untreated major depressive episode is variable but typically lasts 4 months or longer (APA, 2000). Although they may change in severity, the specific symptoms endorsed by people with major depressive disorders appear to remain stable over the course of the disorder (Minor, Champion, & Gotlib, 2005).

Even after recovery from an episode after treatment, many people continue to experience symptoms and psychosocial impairment, and residual symptoms are associated with a more severe relapsing and chronic course of the disorder (Judd et al., 1998, 2000). More than 80% of people with a history of major depression experience recurrent episodes (Kessler, 2002), and rates of recurrence increase and time between episodes decreases with each successive episode (Boland & Keller, 2002). A number of risk factors for recurrent depression have been identified, including a history of frequent or multiple episodes, double depression, and long duration of individual episodes (Boland & Keller, 2002).

Comorbidity and MDD

It has been noted that "the existence of 'pure' depressive states may be quite rare" (Clark, Beck, & Alford, 1999, p. 23) and that comorbidity among people with depression is the "norm" (Kessler, 2002). Particularly high rates of comorbidity are observed between depressive disorders and anxiety disorders, schizophrenia, substance abuse, and eating disorders, and depression often is comorbid with a range of medical conditions (Belzer & Schneier, 2004; Dozois & Dobson, 2002). For example, the NCS-R found that 72.1% of respondents with lifetime MDD also met criteria for at least one of the other *DSM-IV* disorders assessed, with the highest rate of comorbidity observed with anxiety disorders (59.2%), followed by impulse control disorders (30.0%; e.g., bulimia, conduct disorder, antisocial personality disorder) and substance use disorders (24.0%) (Kessler et al., 2003).

In the event of comorbidity, depression generally is secondary, occurring after the onset of the comorbid condition. This pattern occurs more often for some comorbid conditions, such as anxiety disorders, than for others, such as substance use disorders, and more often among men than women (Kessler, 2002; Kessler et al., 2003). Consideration of comorbid conditions in the assessment of depression is critical because comorbidity is generally associated with greater psychosocial impairment and poorer treatment response and outcome (Boland & Keller, 2002; Dozois & Dobson, 2002).

Interviewing Strategies

Structured Diagnostic Interviews

Structured diagnostic interviewing has been called a necessary tool in assessing psychological disorders, given the complexity of current diagnostic systems such as the *DSM-IV-TR* (Barbour & Davison, 2004). Structured diagnostic interviews exhibit a number of advantages over their unstructured or less structured counterparts. For example, they lessen the possible impact of interviewer bias, they are generally more comprehensive and ensure adequate coverage of symptoms, and they have been shown to improve diagnostic reliability (Groth-Marnat, 1999). Therefore, structured and semistructured diagnostic interviews have become the standard in research situations and are becoming the "hallmark of empirically driven clinical practice" as well (Summerfeldt & Antony, 2002, p. 3).

The selection of a particular interview is based on a number of potential considerations, including coverage and content. Coverage includes whether the interview covers the disorders of interest and such factors as time period of interest and course of the disorder. *Content* refers to such issues as whether the interview was developed for and validated with (or is generally applicable to) the population of interest; psychometric factors, involving consideration of reliability and validity in terms of the diagnoses and population of interest; and practical issues, such as length of the interview and training requirements (Summerfeldt & Antony, 2002). The Schedule for Affective Disorders and Schizophrenia (SADS) and the Structured Clinical Interview for *DSM-IV* Axis I Disorders (SCID) are commonly used examples of structured diagnostic interviews that exhibit excellent psychometric properties and have been identified as the best methods for diagnosing mood disorders (Dozois & Dobson, 2002). Each of these structured interviews will be addressed in turn.

Schedule for Affective Disorders and Schizophrenia. The SADS (Endicott & Spitzer, 1978) is one of the earliest attempts to address diagnostic error through structured interviewing. Developed before the *DSM-III*, which introduced the use of explicit diagnostic criteria, the SADS relies on the research diagnostic criteria (RDC) of Spitzer,

Endicott, and Robins (1978). Since its introduction, the SADS has undergone a number of expansions, and several versions are available, each developed for a specific purpose (Summerfeldt & Antony, 2002). Some versions differ in terms of the temporal focus of assessment; the regular version (SADS) differentiates symptoms experienced over the past year from past history of mental disorders, the lifetime version (SADS-L) considers all current and past symptoms, and the change version (SADS-C) assesses change in symptoms over time. Other versions have been developed for use with specific disorders; for example, the SADS-LB provides expanded coverage of bipolar disorder, the SADS-LA does so for anxiety disorders, and recent versions, such as the SADS-LA-IV, have begun to incorporate *DSM-IV* in addition to RDC criteria (Summerfeldt & Antony, 2002).

Of the available versions, the SADS and SADS-L are the most widely used. The SADS-L provides lifetime coverage, and the SADS provides more information about current episodes (Summerfeldt & Antony, 2002). Twenty-three major diagnostic categories, as defined by the RDC, are covered by the SADS, with the mood disorders category including major depressive, manic-depressive, and minor depressive disorders. Scores on eight dimensional summary scales are also provided, four of which assess aspects of depression, including depressive mood and ideation, endogenous features, depressive-associated features, and suicidal ideation and behavior.

Although the general format differs across versions, the SADS generally consists of three components. The first component is a brief overview of the client's background and demographics, such as education, peer relations, and hospitalizations, and an assessment of the course of any past illnesses. Part I of the diagnostic part of the SADS assesses individual symptoms of the disorders covered, both for the worst period of the current episode and for the current period, defined as the past week, which is meant to minimize the impact of daily symptom fluctuation. Most symptoms are rated on multipoint scales (i.e., three- or six-point scales) in terms of frequency and intensity, with a rating of 0 applied if the item is not applicable or there is no information available. Cut points on these scales identify clinically significant symptoms, and numeric ratings are also accompanied by descriptive severity anchors.

Whereas Part I focuses on individual symptoms, Part II is organized by specific syndrome, with questions for each section that assess screening criteria, individual symptoms, degree of impairment or severity, and associated features. Specific symptoms are rated in a dichotomous fashion ("yes" or "no"), and clinically significant ratings are used to determine RDC diagnosis. As a semistructured interview, the SADS provides a number of levels of inquiry for each symptom, including standard questions, optional probes, and nonstandardized questions to clarify responses. Also, the interviewer may choose to skip sections of the interview based on the interviewee's responses to screening questions. Additional sources of information, such as medical records and family members, may also be consulted to enhance diagnostic accuracy.

The SADS displays strong psychometric properties. Evidence from a number of studies indicates good to excellent reliabilities for the SADS at all levels of assessment, including diagnosis, summary scales, and specific symptoms (Summerfeldt & Antony, 2002). There is also considerable evidence for the validity of SADS diagnoses (e.g., concurrent, predictive validity); for example, SADS diagnosis and summary scale scores have been found to predict course, symptoms, and outcome for a range of disorders, including schizophrenia, bipolar disorder, and major depression (Summerfeldt & Antony, 2002). In terms of the assessment of depression in particular, the SADS has demonstrated high interrater reliability, and has been found to correlate with independent measures of depression (Dozois & Dobson, 2002).

The SADS is not without limitations (Summerfeldt & Antony, 2002). The SADS assesses fewer diagnoses than other diagnostic interviews. With an administration time of approximately 90–120 minutes, the SADS is also quite lengthy, and its use takes considerable training, both of which may limit its use in clinical settings (Dozois & Dobson, 2002). However, its strengths include its ability to make fine distinctions between subtypes of mood disorder and its strong psychometric properties and extensive research base (Dozois & Dobson, 2002; Summerfeldt & Antony, 2002). Although its utility in some clinical situations may be limited, the SADS is particularly suited to research situations requiring diagnostic precision (Dozois & Dobson, 2002).

Structured Clinical Interview for DSM-IV *Axis I Disorders.* The SCID-I (First, Spitzer, Gibbon, & Williams, 1995, 1996) probably is the most widely used semistructured diagnostic interview among North American researchers (Summerfeldt & Antony, 2002). Originally introduced to increase diagnostic reliability by operationalizing *DSM-III* diagnostic criteria, the SCID has undergone a number of revisions, with the most recent version reflecting *DSM-IV* criteria. A separate version of the SCID is available for diagnosing Axis II personality disorders (SCID-II), and there are two primary versions of the SCID available for assessment of Axis I disorders: a clinical version (SCID-CV) and a research version (SCID-I). The SCID-CV was designed to assess the disorders most commonly seen in clinical settings (e.g., mood, substance use, and anxiety disorders), whereas the SCID-I is much longer and allows assessment of more disorders and more in-depth examination of subtypes and course and severity specifiers.

The SCID allows the assessment of 51 *DSM-IV* Axis I disorders, organized in terms of nine diagnostic modules (mood episodes, psychotic symptoms, psychotic disorders differential, mood disorders differential, substance use disorders, anxiety disorders, somatoform disorders, eating disorders, and adjustment disorders), and the interview can be customized to include only the modules deemed relevant. Like the SADS, the SCID begins with an open-ended overview of demographic information and the patient's current presenting complaint and level of functioning, as well as history of psychopathology and treatment, which not only provides the interviewer with important information but also assists in building rapport and providing context for the subsequent interview (Summerfeldt & Antony, 2002). A series of 12 questions are then administered to determine which modules to administer before the interview proper begins.

Depending on the modules used, the SCID varies in length. Each diagnostic section includes both required probe questions and suggested follow-up questions. Based on the respondent's answers, the interviewer determines whether diagnostic criteria are absent, subthreshold, or present, with a fourth option available if information is insufficient to rate a given item. Both probe and follow-up questions, which may involve asking for specific examples, are used as necessary, and a skip-out option is also available if the interviewee does not meet a critical criterion required for a given disorder. Administration time generally varies between 45 and 90 minutes, although the average interview for depressed people generally takes less than 60 minutes (Dozois & Dobson, 2002).

The SCID for *DSM-IV* is new, and therefore there is little evidence supporting its psychometric properties (Nezu, Nezu, McClure, & Zwick, 2002). However, reliability data are available for earlier versions of the SCID, which indicate wide variability in interrater agreement (as assessed by the kappa coefficient) across disorders and within categories, including depression (Dozois & Dobson, 2002). Findings in general indicate acceptable reliabilities for disorders commonly seen in clinical settings, including major depressive disorder and anxiety disorders (Summerfeldt & Antony, 2002). As Summerfeldt and Antony observe, the variability in reported kappas may result at least in part from variation in the skill and training of the interviewer because the SCID relies largely on clinical judgment and diagnostic skill. The validity of the SCID depends largely on the validity of the *DSM-IV*, to which it is aligned. There is some evidence for correspondence between the SCID and other standardized measures and symptom ratings, but determining validity is difficult given the lack of a diagnostic gold standard (Dozois & Dobson, 2002). As Summerfeldt and Antony observe, further investigation of the validity of the SCID is warranted.

The SCID shares a number of the limitations of the SADS, including the need for training on the part of interviewers. Summerfeldt and Antony (2002) note a number of other limitations, including possible threats to reliability arising from its semistructured format, greater susceptibility to response styles and deliberate faking because of its high face validity, and the fact that information about subthreshold conditions is lost because of its decision tree format and use of skip-outs. However, these authors also point to the SCID's many advantages, including its breadth of coverage and its alignment with the *DSM*. Compared with the SADS, the SCID is more comprehensive, takes less time to administer, is more congruent with *DSM-IV* criteria, and offers a clinician version; therefore, it may be the preferred structured interview in diagnosing depression (Dozois & Dobson, 2002).

Clinician Rating of Symptoms: The Hamilton Rating Scale for Depression. The Hamilton Rating Scale for Depression (HRSD; Hamilton, 1960, 1967) is the most commonly used clinician rating instrument of depressive symptoms (Dozois & Dobson, 2002). Widely used in both clinical and research settings, the HRSD is commonly viewed as a gold standard among depression scales and was designed to assess severity of symptoms among people diagnosed with a depressive disorder and to assess change in symptoms over time (Nezu et al., 2002). The HRSD is not a structured interview, but it does rely on information gathered through an interview procedure. Specifically, the scale consists of 21 items and takes approximately 10 minutes to complete after a 30-minute, open-ended interview to gather the required information. Other sources may also be interviewed if the accuracy of the patient's report is in question (Hamilton, 1967). Of the 21 items of the original HRSD, 17 are scored in terms of severity during the past few days or week. Items focus largely on behavioral and somatic symptoms of depression, such as insomnia, psychomotor retardation, and appetite and weight change, although specific items differ across versions (Nezu, Ronan, Meadows, & McClure, 2000).

The fact that numerous versions of the HRSD are in use complicates examination of the scale's psychometric properties across investigations. However, the HRSD appears to be a reliable measure that is sensitive to treatment change, and several lines of evidence support its validity (Dozois & Dobson, 2002; Nezu et al., 2002; Nezu, Ronan, et al., 2000). Some of the identified limitations of the HRSD include an emphasis on somatic items relative to mood and cognitive symptoms, lack of evidence for discriminant validity, inconsistent item weightings, and a focus on symptoms over the past week rather than 2 weeks, as required by *DSM-IV* diagnostic criteria (Dozois & Dobson, 2002). Despite these limitations, the measure exhibits high clinical utility and research applicability (Nezu, Ronan, et al., 2000); given its utility in assessing treatment targets and outcome, along with its widespread use, Dozois and Dobson recommend routine use of the HRSD in clinical practice.

Clinical Interviewing

As noted earlier, structured interviews, such as the SADS and SCID, probably represent the optimal assessment strategy if the goal is diagnosis and are particularly well suited to research situations necessitating a high degree of diagnostic precision (Dozois & Dobson, 2002). The utility of such measures in clinical situations is limited, however, and clinicians are more likely to use less structured and formal interviews, often called clinical interviews, in order to assess client symptoms (Barbour & Davison, 2004). As Dozois and Dobson (2002, p. 272) observe, "much of the information necessary for the assessment of depression results from the clinical interview."

The format and specific content of the clinical interview depend on a number of factors, including the particular goal of the assessment and the theoretical orientation of the interviewer (Barbour & Davison, 2004; Groth-Marnat, 1999). For example, whereas a more client-centered clinician might work to enhance the process of self-change through a more nondirective interview style, a behavioral interview probably would work to obtain particular information about external consequences of behavior through more structured questioning (Groth-Marnat, 1999). Some general areas of assessment include the history of the problem, such as initial onset, antecedents and consequences, and treatment history; family background, including family constellation, cultural background, and emotional and medical history; and personal history, including pertinent information regarding infancy, childhood, adolescence, and early, middle, and late adulthood (Groth-Marnat, 1999). A combination of both open-ended and more directive questioning is generally used, depending on client characteristics and the type of information required. Several texts are available that provide in-depth information and recommendations for the initial clinical interview (e.g., Morrison, 1995; Othmer & Othmer, 1994).

Among the greatest advantages of less structured interviewing are its flexibility and ideographic focus, which allows in-depth exploration of particular issues through follow-up on specific responses (Groth-Marnat, 1999). Such interviews can be modified depending on the particular situation and also allow the development of rapport and client-self-exploration (Groth-Marnat, 1999). However, although flexibility is one of the greatest inherent strengths of the clinical interview, it is also associated with the potential weakness of interviewer bias (i.e., the halo effect, confirmatory bias, the primacy effect), which may negatively affect reliability and validity (Groth-Marnat, 1999). Therefore, both the advantages and the disadvantages of the various forms of interviewing must be weighed in relation to the goals and demands of the assessment situation when one is deciding which particular format (i.e., clinical or structured diagnostic) of interview to use.

The Clinical Interview and Depression. As previously noted, the clinical interview plays an important role in the assessment of depression, and Dozois and Dobson (2002) outline a number of basic considerations in interviewing depressed patients. It is crucial to ensure that interviewees are provided with information regarding what will be required of them throughout the assessment, and a clear rationale should also be provided. For example, Dozois and Dobson note that depressed people tend to be sensitive to being interrupted, so such specific issues should be addressed at the onset of the interview. Depressed people should be made to feel relaxed and should not be rushed through the interview, particularly given such symptoms of depression as psychomotor retardation. The experience of depression varies across individuals, so the interviewer may begin by asking the patient to describe the presenting complaints and particular experience with the disorder in his or her words. A tendency to exhibit negative biases on the part of depressed people may influence such reporting, however, so it is useful to check on the accuracy of the patient's report over the course of the interview.

It is important throughout the interview to attend to specific details of symptoms, and the primary areas requiring assessment reflect the major systems affected in major depression, including the affective, cognitive, behavioral, somatic, and social (Dozois & Dobson, 2002). For each symptom domain and for each specific symptom criterion, it is important to obtain a sense of severity, which can be accomplished through the use of quantitative measures and through qualitative descriptions provided by the patients. Individuals vary in the way they describe their symptoms, and the interviewer may have to translate the patient's idiosyncratic descriptions when assessing diagnostic criteria. It may also be useful to consult with significant others who may provide further information about more observable symptoms the person is reporting. As Dozois

and Dobson point out, a detailed review of symptoms "not only helps in making appropriate diagnoses and treatment recommendations, it also conveys messages that the interviewer is interested in the patient and knowledgeable about the symptoms and difficulties that he or she is experiencing" (p. 273).

Consideration of both frequency and number of past depressive episodes is important for several reasons, including accurate diagnosis, and because such information is related to speed of recovery and risk of relapse (Dozois & Dobson, 2002). However, unintentional memory biases have been found to negatively affect the reporting of such information as age of first episode and past number of episodes (Dozois & Dobson, 2002). Therefore, Dozois and Dobson recommend a number of techniques, including ensuring that the interviewee is aware of the time period being assessed (e.g., the past 2 weeks when assessing MDD) and providing contextual cues when discussing past episodes (e.g., special occasions).

Assessment of the interviewee's history includes attending to a wide range of variables (Dozois & Dobson, 2002). Past psychiatric and medical conditions of both the interviewee and his or her family should be considered, along with current comorbid disorders, which may have important implications for diagnosis and treatment. Treatment history, which might include psychiatric hospitalization, psychotherapy, medications, electroconvulsive therapy, and self-help groups and products, should also be assessed because such information might suggest resources for change. Other important areas to assess include behavioral indices of depression, factors that may be maintaining the depression, the patient's level of motivation for change, and areas of strength, such as strong social support, which may be exploited in treatment.

Suicide assessment is an important feature of the assessment of depressed patients. Assessing suicide risk is difficult because of its low base rate, so in addition to being open and frank about suicidality, the clinician should ask about a number of potential risk factors (Dozois & Dobson, 2002). Risk factors that have been identified in the literature include hopelessness, impulsivity, substance abuse, a mental or physical disorder, and social isolation, and these should be kept in mind in addition to immediate suicide indicators such as a specific plan, timeframe, and available means (Dozois & Dobson, 2002). Psychometric instruments such as the Beck Hopelessness Scale (Beck, Weissman, Lester, & Trexler, 1974) may also assist in assessing risk, in addition to drawing on clinical experience and intuition. Dozois and Dobson recommend that, ultimately, the clinician must often conduct a "mental factor analysis" of risk factors, self-report scores, and the results of direct questioning in assessing suicide risk (see Meichenbaum, 2005, and Stolberg, Clark, & Bongar, 2002, for more thorough discussions of assessment of suicide risk in depression).

Interviewing for Therapy. Data from the assessment in general, and through interviewing procedures in particular, provide crucial information for case conceptualization and treatment planning. Although there is a range of basic areas of assessment in clinical interviewing of people with depression, the particular theoretical paradigm in which the interviewer is operating influences both the kinds of questions that are asked and the way the information obtained is interpreted (Barbour & Davison, 2004). The treatment of depression has been informed by identification and advancement of empirically supported treatments, with a number of specific interventions, including cognitive-behavioral therapy (CBT), behavior therapy, and interpersonal therapy, having a sufficient database to warrant being considered empirically supported (Chambless et al., 1998; Chambless & Ollendick, 2001). Whereas an interview taking place in the context of behavior therapy, for example, probably would involve a functional analysis of the specific conditions under which a behavior does or does not occur (Barbour & Davison, 2004), an interviewer working in the interpersonal therapy framework would attempt to identify major interpersonal problem areas and place the client's experience of depression in its interpersonal context (Weissman, Markowitz, & Klerman, 2000).

Interviewing for cognitive therapy (CT) or CBT also involves attending to particular issues. Widespread use of CBT-based interventions in treating depression is supported by a large body of evidence attesting to its efficacy and effectiveness. Aaron Beck's CT represents the best-established of the available CBT interventions (Hollon, Haman, & Brown, 2002) because CT has been shown to be effective in more randomized control trials than any other psychosocial intervention, and CT has been shown to be at least as effective in treating depression and more effective

in preventing relapse than antidepressant medication (Persons, Davidson, & Tompkins, 2001). Some considerations in interviewing for CT will be examined briefly (cf. Beck, Rush, Shaw, & Emery, 1979).

As Beck et al. (1979) observe, therapy begins with the initial contact between the therapist and patient, and often this initial contact takes the form of the clinical interview. Some of the primary goals of the initial interview include the formation of the working relationship, which includes development of rapport; the gathering of important information, including the identification of target symptoms for intervention; and the use of specific cognitive techniques, which are aimed to produce at least some symptom relief. From the onset, the therapist works with the patient to establish a collaborative therapeutic relationship and to socialize the patient to therapy by using explicit and relevant examples to illustrate the cognitive model, including the link between negative thinking and unpleasant emotions. Providing a clear rationale for therapy and asking the patient for feedback is also important in the initial session, as is the identification of target symptoms. Behavioral or cognitive techniques are introduced, depending on presenting symptoms, with the goal of producing symptom relief, which further improves the therapeutic relationship and increases the patient's confidence in the efficacy of the therapy (see also Beck, 1995, for a further discussion of CT).

Beck et al. (1979) discuss several other considerations that are relevant in interviewing depressed patients. For example, it is important to recognize the validity of the negative ideas and beliefs held by the patient to himself or herself and to try to understand the basis of such beliefs rather than attempt to dispute them too early in the course of the interview or therapy in general. The level of structure and activity should also be adjusted as appropriate. For example, the therapist generally is more active early in therapy, including during the initial interview, and especially so with more severely depressed patients. The use of questioning is central to CT, not only as a means to gather information but also as a therapeutic tool in identifying, considering, and correcting negative cognitions and beliefs. Finally, eliciting feedback (e.g., about therapy, homework assignments, or the therapist) is particularly important with depressed patients, who may fear rejection or criticism from the therapist.

INTERVIEWING OBSTACLES AND SOLUTIONS

As indicated earlier, clinical interviewing with depressed patients can take various forms. There are areas that are typically assessed regardless of the theoretical orientation of the interviewer (e.g., presenting symptoms); however, the focus of the interview for therapy generally reflects the broader context of the particular treatment being implemented. Therefore, clinical interviewing plays a crucial role in case conceptualization and treatment planning.

Approaching the Assessment of Depression

Before examining the particular strategy of clinical interviewing and the depressive disorders, it is useful to consider the more general context of the assessment of depression. As Nezu et al. (2002) observe, a number of key issues guide the assessment process and selection of procedures, including the goals of the assessment, who is to be assessed, the value of a given assessment measure, and the source of the information provided. Each of these issues will be examined briefly, beginning with the goal of the assessment.

There are many different possible reasons or goals for the assessment of depression. These include screening, diagnosis and classification, description of symptoms, clinical hypothesis testing, treatment planning, prediction of behavior, and assessment of treatment outcome, and it is important to consider such particular goals when choosing assessment procedures and measures (Nezu et al., 2002). For example, measures used for screening purposes should display criterion-related validity and other characteristics such as sensitivity and specificity, whereas those used for diagnosis should be considered in terms of content validity and, if clinical judgment is involved, interrater reliability.

The question of who is being assessed is relevant to the appropriateness of the measure used (Nezu et al., 2002). Age, comorbid conditions, and ethnic and cultural background should all be taken into account because all these factors may influence the expression of depressive symptoms. When possible, measures developed specifically for use with certain populations with depression should be used, such as the Children's Depression Inventory (Kovacs, 1992), the Calgary Depression Scale for Schizophrenia (Addington, Addington, & Maticka-Tyndale,

1993), and the Vietnamese Depression Scale (Kinzie et al., 1982).

Nezu et al. (2002) stress consideration of the value of a given assessment tool, which is a function of both the likelihood that the chosen measure will provide information relevant to the goal of the assessment and the cost-benefit ratio of the use of a measure. The measure's psychometric properties, including the various facets of reliability and validity, should be examined, as should issues such as the time involved, practicality of administration, potential risks or ethical violations, and incremental validity. Ultimately, measures with strong psychometric properties and a positive benefit-to-cost ratio should be chosen.

The source of the information is another important consideration, where measures of depression can be categorized as either self-report or clinician rated (Nezu et al., 2002). Although self-report measures are brief, they are more susceptible to respondent bias, whereas clinician-rated measures may take longer but be more reliable. Therefore, a combination of both types of measures is generally recommended, in addition to a consideration of the four general issues raised by Nezu et al. (2002).

An abundance of measures of depression and depression-related constructs are available to researchers and clinicians. A recent volume by Nezu, Ronan, et al. (2000), for example, discusses more than 90 depression-related measurement tools. However, Nezu, Nezu, and Foster (2000, p. 17) point out that "although excellent assessment tools exist for many different clinical problems, the tools are only as good as the skill of the craftsperson who uses them," and much skill is needed in choosing which assessment measure to use for a given individual and purpose. Nezu, Nezu, et al. (2000) outline a 10-step set of heuristics to facilitate this decision-making process, which will be considered briefly here.

The first step involves determining the goal of the assessment, which may include screening, diagnosis, case formulation, treatment planning, and outcome evaluation. If the goal is to assess treatment outcome, for example, the selected measure should assess behaviors targeted by treatment, display good test-retest reliability in the absence of treatment, and be sufficiently sensitive to detect change. The second step is to adopt a system approach, which involves using multiple assessment measures and procedures to accomplish the various goals of the assessment (i.e., a multimethod, system-oriented approach). The third step is to individualize assessment and identify obstacles (e.g., limited motivation on the part of the person being assessed or limited experience of the assessor), and the fourth step involves adapting the assessment to overcome obstacles, where the assessor might ask himself or herself, "What assessment procedures should I incorporate to maximize the chances of obtaining valid, reliable, and comprehensive information about this client for my particular assessment goal?" (Nezu, Nezu, et al., 2000, p. 21).

The fifth step involves generating a variety of assessment strategies for each focal area, which includes self-report inventories, interviews, and behavioral observation, and the sixth step involves generating multiple ideas for each strategy. The seventh step involves conducting a cost-benefit analysis, where the likelihood and value of outcomes is evaluated for each assessment goal and range of measurement alternatives. At the eighth step, the measures with the highest utility (those with the highest benefit-cost ratio) are selected, and at the ninth step, the selected procedures are implemented, which may entail adapting a particular measure for a specific situational context. Finally, the tenth step involves monitoring the effects and determining whether the assessment procedure has generated useful, valid, and reliable information.

Although such an involved approach to the selection of assessment approach may appear quite time-consuming, Nezu, Nezu, et al. (2000) point out that such a guided approach ultimately saves time and increases efficacy of assessment in both research and clinical situations. As reflected by the model proposed by Nezu, Nezu, et al., the importance of using multiple strategies in the assessment of depression cannot be overstated. Indeed, accurate assessment of depression entails use of multiple strategies, including structured and unstructured interviews, clinician ratings, and self-report inventories, ideally obtained from multiple perspectives, including the patient, significant others, and the clinician (Dozois & Dobson, 2002). Each of these assessment strategies has advantages and disadvantages that must be considered.

Structured interviews, such as the SCID-I (First et al., 1995, 1996) and the SADS (Endicott & Spitzer, 1978), offer a number of advantages related to assessment in general and depression in particular, including greater reliability than unstructured interviews and, in the case of the SCID and the SADS, strong reliability and validity in assessing mood disorders (Dozois & Dobson, 2002; Groth-Marnat, 1999). However, such interviews are lengthy and generally require extensive training to administer with adequate reliability (Dozois & Dobson, 2002).

Self-report measures and clinician rating scales offer a convenient means to assess symptoms and are particularly useful in identifying targets for treatment and assessing change over the course of therapy (Dozois & Dobson, 2002). A large number of self-report measures are available that exhibit strong psychometric properties and provide valuable information, such as the Beck Depression Inventory (BDI-II; Beck, Steer, & Brown, 1996). However, self-report measures exhibit a number of general limitations, such as vulnerability to response bias and misinterpretation, and some are particularly relevant to the assessment of depression. For example, self-report measures are not appropriate for use with people with thought disorder or impaired reality testing or concentration (Dozois & Dobson, 2002). Such limitations necessitate the use of self-report measures in conjunction with other procedures rather than as the sole method.

Finally, clinician rating scales are a third commonly used assessment method, with the most common such measure being the HRSD (Hamilton, 1960, 1967). Clinician rating scales offer a number of distinct advantages, including providing a standardized format for clinicians to follow, allowing clinicians to follow up on inconsistent or incomplete responses, and providing information beyond that gained through self-report measures (Dozois & Dobson, 2002; Nezu, Ronan, et al., 2000). In terms of the latter advantage, self-report measures tend to provide more severe ratings of symptoms than clinician ratings, largely because of a lack of a normative database on the part of patients (Dozois & Dobson, 2002). Therefore, and as is the case with the assessment of depression in general, combining various procedures and measures is crucial for an accurate and complete assessment of depression.

The clinical interview is widely recognized as one of the most important tools for gathering information in both clinical and research situations (Barbour & Davison, 2004; Dozois & Dobson, 2004; Groth-Marnat, 1999). As evidenced by the preceding discussion, the assessment of depression should draw on multiple methods and sources, and a number of considerations must be taken into account in their selection (Nezu, Ronan, et al., 2000; Nezu et al., 2002). It is important for the clinician to recognize consistent patterns of response across different types of measures of sources of information but also to recognize the possible importance of intermeasure inconsistency. With this broader context in place, the role of clinical interviewing in the assessment of depression in particular will now be addressed.

CASE ILLUSTRATION

Simone Walsh was a 40-year-old Caucasian woman who was referred by her family physician to a local mental health center because of ongoing concerns about her performance at work and apparent signs of depression, including crying at work. The psychologist who saw Simone at the center, Dr. Guillermo Hernandez, began the assessment by asking Simone to briefly describe the troubles she had been having at work or in other settings. Simone described a series of depression-related symptoms, including sad mood, loss of interest in many areas, self-denigrating thoughts, sleep disturbance (waking up in the night or early morning and difficulty returning to sleep), feeling slowed down, fatigue, and problems with concentration and thinking. She said that the onset of these problems had been about 6 months earlier, around the time that her husband of 14 years had suddenly advised her that he was leaving the relationship for another. Dr. Hernandez recognized that these symptoms met the *DSM-IV* criteria for major depressive episode, nonmelancholic subtype, but that Simone had not mentioned suicidal thoughts or behavior. On inquiry, Simone denied that she had any current thoughts in this direction, primarily because of the devastating effect it would have on her 5-year-old daughter.

Dr. Hernandez then inquired about Simone's history of depression. She responded by indicating that she had one similar episode in the past, when she was 23 years old, after she had left home and moved to a new city after finishing college. She reported feeling isolated and "frozen" for a period of 2 or so months at that time, a problem that eventually resolved as she became more engaged with activities and social relationships in her new setting. Further inquiry revealed no

other apparent disorders. Simone did acknowledge the occasional use of alcohol to dull her senses (she also admitted to extensive marijuana use during college), and she indicated that she had been a shy child and socially anxious young adult, but these problems were not as great as in the past. Dr. Hernandez also questioned Simone about other legal or illegal drugs she might be taking that could simulate depression and about possible medical disorders, but she said that these considerations did not apply. Given this information, Dr. Hernandez revised his diagnostic impression to one of major depressive disorder, recurrent.

In order to further evaluate severity of Simone's adaptive functioning, Dr. Hernandez administered both the HRSD 17-item version and the BDI-II. The HRSD yielded a score of 25, which is in the moderate range of depression severity. The BDI-II score of 34 was seen as roughly comparable to the HRSD score and again placed Simone in the moderate range of severity for depressed patients. Of importance, item 9 on the BDI (suicidality) was rated 0, indicating a lack of active suicidal thinking, but item 2 (hopelessness) was 2, indicating a fairly strong endorsement of future pessimism. On inquiry, Simone admitted that she wondered whether her current problems would ever improve. The problems that she listed included isolation and loneliness, the lack of an intimate adult relationship, being overwhelmed as a mother at times (e.g., she said that she often managed to get what had to be done completed but that she "collapsed" once her daughter was in bed), poor work performance, and financial worries since her marital separation.

Dr. Hernandez, and the clinic in which he worked more generally, favored an evidence-based approach to the treatment of mental health problems. He had determined that cognitive-behavioral therapy was indicated for the problems Simone was presenting, and he shared a brief description of the model and his treatment recommendation with her. She generally agreed with the need for help, and she expressed some enthusiasm for the practical, problem-oriented strategy that Dr. Hernandez was offering. To begin this process, Dr. Hernandez elected to supplement the assessment information he already had with a behavioral assessment strategy. Specifically, he asked Simone to keep a daily diary of her activities, indicating for each hour the major task or event she was involved with (Beck et al., 1979; Beck, 1995). As part of this record keeping, he also asked Simone to indicate whether she had any sense of mastery (success, completion), or pleasure associated with these events. This strategy provided a realistic sense of Simone's range of activities and her functional status.

In summary, Dr. Hernandez's assessment strategy was simple and clinically focused. Although he used a diagnostic interview, it was unstructured and not as systematic as alternatives, such as the SCID. He used two severity measures, one interviewer based and one self-report, and because the results of these two measures were approximately equal, they helped to reinforce the model of the patient's depression as being of moderate severity. Finally, Dr. Hernandez used a self-report instrument to collect functional behavioral information, which could be used both for planning new activities in CBT ANS to index change in functional range and quality of activities over time. Dr. Hernandez was aware of other possible assessment targets, such as Simone's attitudes or attributional style, and the need to revisit the issues of hopelessness and suicidality over time. He was also mindful that although the patient had reported that she was (just) managing her parenting responsibilities and work performance, it might be necessary to obtain collateral and independent assessments in either or both of these areas if her depression did not respond to treatment or if her adaptive functioning seemed to be getting worse. With this information at hand, Dr. Hernandez concluded the assessment phase and initiated treatment.

MULTICULTURAL AND DIVERSITY ISSUES

Although depression may be viewed as a universal human condition, research interest in variation in the incidence, specific symptoms, meaning, and treatment of depression across ethnic or cultural groups has expanded significantly over the past decade (Gotlib & Hammen, 2002). Findings from such research, and increasing cultural diversity in both Canada and the United States, point to the need for clinicians to attend to individual differences when assessing depressive disorders.

For example, there are a number of recognized differences in the expression of particular symptoms of depression across cultures. Findings indicate that people from non-Western cultures (e.g., Filipino, Arab, Turkish, Japanese, Korean) are more likely to emphasize somatic symptoms of depression than depressed Westerners, with proposed reasons for this discrepancy including beliefs about the integration of mind and body, decreased emphasis on emotional expression, or stigma associated with mental illness among non-Western cultures (Gotlib & Hammen, 2002; Tsai & Chentsova-Dutton, 2002). Similar differences have also been found between particular ethnic groups. For example, whereas depressed African Americans have been found to report increased somatic symptoms, depressed European Americans have been found to be more likely to report such symptoms as suicidal ideation and guilt (Tsai & Chentsova-Dutton, 2002). Such differences in symptom expression clearly may complicate assessment and ultimately diagnosis of depressive disorders.

Use of structured diagnostic interviews among people from non-Western cultures or ethnic minorities is complicated by the fact that the diagnostic criteria underlying such interviews are derived from Western conceptions of psychopathology (e.g., the *DSM-IV-TR*; APA, 2000). As discussed earlier, significant variations in symptom expression across culture and ethnic groups may occur, as in the case of depressive disorders, and therefore it cannot be assumed that information obtained from assessment methods such as structured interviews will necessarily generalize across cultural and ethnic groups. There is evidence that structured diagnostic interviews may reduce the effects of cultural bias on psychiatric diagnosis (e.g., in the assessment of panic disorder); however, such interviews may also result in misdiagnosis of particular disorders for a number of reasons, not the least of which may be language barriers (Barbour & Davison, 2004). In conducting any form of psychological assessment, it is crucial to consider social and cultural factors that may affect symptoms and ultimately diagnosis, and clinicians must educate themselves if they are unfamiliar with the cultural or ethnic group to which the person they are assessing belongs (Barbour & Davison, 2004).

With publication of the *DSM-IV*, attempts were made to incorporate specific, culturally relevant information into the diagnostic nomenclature (APA, 1994). For example, a specific "Outline for Cultural Formulation," which includes consideration of such factors as the patient's cultural identity and cultural explanations of the patient's illness, and a "Glossary of Culture-Bound Syndromes" appear in an appendix of the manual. Other models designed to increase attention given to cultural and other individual differences in diagnosis have also been proposed. Hays's (2001) ADDRESSING framework provides a heuristic for clinicians of specific individual difference factors (e.g., ethnicity, indigenous heritage, national origin, gender) that should be considered in conducting assessment and therapy with diverse populations.

In addition to a general consideration of issues of culture and ethnicity, there are a number of specific factors that the clinician should consider when conducting interviews with people of diverse backgrounds. Hays (2001) describes a range of differences in nonverbal communication, such as use of physical gestures, extent of direct eye contact, and use of silence, across cultural groups that the interviewer should attend to. For example, although direct eye contact is generally valued in Western culture, many non-Western cultures instead view indirect eye contact as both the norm and as a sign of respect toward those in authority. Depression itself can also influence a person's movements and mannerisms, including hand movements, eye contact, and rate of speech (Dozois & Dobson, 2002; Rehm, 1987; Schelde, 1998a, 1998b). Therefore, it is important that clinicians not only attend to cultural variations in nonverbal communication over the course of the interview but also consider the impact of both culture and depression on observed behavior.

DIFFERENTIAL DIAGNOSIS AND BEHAVIORAL ASSESSMENT

Differential Diagnosis

The differential diagnosis of the depressive disorders is complicated by the fact that depressive symptoms are associated with a range of psychological and medical conditions and that depressive disorders often are comorbid with other disorders (Boland & Keller, 2002; Dozois & Dobson, 2002). However, the *DSM-IV-TR* (APA, 2000) provides explicit guidance in the differential diagnosis of major depressive episodes and the depressive disorders. Diagnostic criteria for a major depressive episode include that symptoms

are not caused by a general medical condition or substance and are not better accounted for by bereavement. MDD is distinguished from a mood disorder due to a general medical condition and a substance-induced mood disorder, as determined by whether the mood disturbance is found to result from a general medical condition or a substance, respectively. After the death of a loved one, bereavement would be diagnosed unless symptoms persist for more than 2 months or include symptoms such as marked functional impairment, suicidal ideation, or psychomotor retardation.

MDD must also be distinguished from a number of other diagnoses (APA, 2000). In older adults, it is important to determine whether cognitive symptoms are caused by MDD or dementia, which is accomplished through a thorough medical evaluation and evaluation of symptom onset, course, and treatment response; for example, dementia typically is associated with a premorbid history of cognitive decline, whereas an abrupt cognitive decline is generally seen with the onset of MDD. MDD can be distinguished from a manic or mixed episode by the absence of manic symptoms. Both MDD and attention-deficit/hyperactivity disorder (ADHD) can involve symptoms of distractibility and low frustration tolerance, and caution should be used in diagnosing both in the case of children with ADHD if the primary mood disturbance is irritability. In the event that a psychosocial stressor precedes the onset of MDD, adjustment disorder with depressed mood may be the appropriate diagnosis if full MDD criteria are not met.

Diagnostic criteria for major depression include exclusionary criteria that the MDD is not better accounted for by schizoaffective disorder and is not superimposed on schizophrenia, schizophreniform disorder, delusional disorder, or psychotic disorder not otherwise specified (APA, 2000). Schizoaffective disorder may be differentiated from major depression by its requiring a period of at least 2 weeks of delusions or hallucinations in the absence of prominent mood symptoms, and the *DSM-IV-TR* observes that although depressive symptoms may be present during psychotic disorders, they are often considered to be associated features of these disorders and do not warrant a separate diagnosis. However, if full criteria for MDD are met, the diagnosis of depressive disorder NOS may be made in addition to the diagnosis of schizophrenia, delusional disorder, or psychotic disorder NOS. MDD must also be distinguished from dysthymic disorder, which is accomplished on the basis of severity, chronicity, and persistence. Dysthymic disorder requires the presence of depressive symptoms over a period of 2 years, compared with 2 weeks for MDD, and is generally associated with chronic, less severe symptoms that persist for many years. MDD must also be distinguished from a mood disorder caused by a general medical condition, substance-induced mood disorder, or dementia, as described in reference to MDD.

Finally, diagnostic criteria for dysthymic disorder stipulate that the mood disturbance is not better accounted for by MDD; that there has never been a manic, mixed, or hypomanic episode and that criteria are not met for cyclothymic disorder; that the disturbance does not occur exclusively during the course of a chronic psychotic disorder; and that the symptoms are not caused by a substance or general medical condition. Although dysthymic disorder and MDD share many symptoms, they do differ in terms of onset, course, and severity. Furthermore, both disorders may be diagnosed if no MDD was present for the first 2 years of the dysthymic disorder or if there has been a full remission of the MDD before the onset of dysthymic disorder (i.e., double depression). Accurate differential diagnosis and thorough assessment, including structured diagnostic interviews, increase the reliability of diagnosis and identification of comorbid conditions and are critical for case formulation and treatment planning (Dozois & Dobson, 2002).

Behavioral Assessment

As noted earlier, MDD involves a range of systems that affect functioning in a number of areas, including the affective, cognitive, behavioral, somatic, and social domains, many of which are amenable to behavioral assessment procedures (Dozois & Dobson, 2002). A number of the diagnostic criteria for MDD, such as depressed affect and psychomotor agitation or retardation, are directly observable (APA, 2000), and major theoretical and therapeutic models of the disorder, such as Beck's cognitive model (e.g., Beck et al., 1979; Clark et al., 1999), focus on the relationship between emotion, cognition, and behavior. Although an exhaustive examination of behavioral assessment of depression is beyond the scope of the present discussion, the role of

behavioral assessment in the context of clinical interviewing will be discussed briefly (see Haynes & Heiby, 2004, and Haynes & O'Brien, 2000, for comprehensive examinations of behavioral assessment).

There are several behavioral indicators that the interviewer should attend to while interviewing depressed patients. Depression can affect a person's appearance, movements, and mannerisms (Dozois & Dobson, 2002). For example, research has found that depressed people exhibit less eye contact and hand movements and a lower rate of speech (Rehm, 1987). A number of these features, such as eye contact and speech rate, have also been found to improve as people recover. For example, Schelde (1998a, 1998b) has found depression to be characterized behaviorally by primarily a reduction in social interaction and secondarily by reduced self-occupation and body mobility. More specifically, behavioral markers of depression in this research included nonspecific gaze, withdrawal, and reduced mouth movements, and markers of recovery included social interest, social smile, and social initiative. Such findings have implications for interviewing depressed patients. For example, Schelde (1998b) observes that although depressed people may talk, their answers are brief and they tend not to display accompanying facial expressions and gestures. Such nonverbal communication can provide important information about the patient's current emotional state.

In addition to informal observation of behavioral symptoms and indicators of depression, the interview can also involve more formalized methods of behavioral assessment, such as a functional analysis of the patient's difficulties. "A functional analysis . . . aims to determine the conditions under which particular behaviors occur or do not occur, and whether they are followed by reinforcing or punishing events" (Barbour & Davidson, 2004, p. 185). Obtaining clear examples and definitions of any terms used by the depressed patient to describe his or her symptoms is crucial in order to operationally define the patient's difficulties, and the functional analysis can suggest hypotheses regarding causal factors of problem behaviors and indicate areas for intervention (Barbour & Davidson, 2004). For example, recent behavioral activation treatments for depression emphasize the use of functional analysis as a tool to examine the ideographic environmental contingencies that maintain depressed behavior, to assess the specific needs and goals of the patient, and to target behavior that is likely to improve quality of life (Hopko, Lejuez, Ruggiero, & Eifert, 2003). Thus, results from the functional analysis play an important role in informing the therapy to follow.

Behavioral assessment also constitutes an important element of many behavioral and cognitive-behavioral interventions for depression (e.g., Beck, 1995; Hopko et al., 2003). For example, in CBT, behavioral interventions often are undertaken before cognitive ones because change in behavior is generally easier and may itself lead to more positive thoughts about certain situations (Dobson & Khatri, 2002). Among the more prominent behavioral techniques used in CBT are self-monitoring and activity scheduling, both of which entail repeated behavioral assessment on the part of the patient (DeRubeis, Tang, & Beck, 2001).

Self-monitoring involves having the patient record his or her activities and associated moods in a detailed manner (e.g., every hour) for a specified period of time, such as 1 week. Self-monitoring serves a number of functions, including informing both the therapist and patient of how much time is being devoted to certain activities, and provides a baseline to which future ratings can be compared (DeRubeis et al., 2001). Activity scheduling involves developing a schedule of activities that the patient found pleasurable from the self-monitoring exercise, activities that the patient enjoyed in the past but has been avoiding during the depression, or new activities that may be rewarding (DeRubeis et al., 2001). As part of the exercise, the therapist can have the patient test certain hypotheses, for example, by having the patient record predicted levels of enjoyment or mastery and compare them to actual ratings after completing the activities (Beck, 1995). Ongoing assessment over the course of therapy plays a number of important roles in terms of monitoring change over time, including allowing the therapist to identify any problems or areas for modification in treatment, and encouraging patients by providing clear evidence of progress (Dozois & Dobson, 2002).

In addition to the assessment of behavior, CBT interventions for depression also focus on assessing cognition. Although the therapist does attend to cognition in the initial interview, much of the formal assessment of the patient's thoughts and beliefs takes place as therapy progresses, with a central tool being the use of the Dysfunctional Thoughts Record (DTR; Beck, 1995). The DTR is a worksheet that the patient uses to record and respond to distorted cognitions and is a central technique through which cognitive restructuring is accomplished in CBT. Similar to other behavioral assessment techniques in terms of its requirement that the patient record situations in specific detail and on a regular basis, the DTR asks patients to record situations and the associated automatic thoughts, emotions, adaptive responses, and the outcome (i.e., in response to the adaptive response) (Beck, 1995). Like other behavioral assessment techniques, the DTR is reviewed regularly during therapy sessions. Furthermore, a range of self-report measures are available for the assessment of cognitive content and processes in depression, which may be useful therapeutically (see Blankstein & Segal, 2001, for further discussion).

SELECTION OF TREATMENT TARGETS AND REFERRAL

As previously discussed, there are many different possible reasons for the assessment of depression (Nezu et al., 2002; Nezu, Nezu, et al., 2000). However, one of the most important goals is the development of a solid case conceptualization and treatment plan, which depends on information derived from the assessment such as appropriate diagnosis and an understanding of the presenting problems and their severity (Dobson & Dozois, 2002). Accurate diagnosis is important, for example, in determining what specific symptoms to target first in instances of depression comorbid with other disorders (Dobson & Dozois, 2002) and in selecting a particular intervention to use for a particular disorder, based on its level of empirical support (Chambless & Ollendick, 2001). Of course, implementation of an empirically supported treatment with a particular patient requires consideration of much more than diagnosis alone, and a thorough case conceptualization is crucial for treatment planning. A particularly relevant model of case conceptualization in the treatment of depression is that of Persons and colleagues (Persons & Davidson, 2001; Persons et al., 2001), which is based on Beck's cognitive theory of depression.

"A case formulation," as defined by Persons et al., "is an idiographic (individualized) theory that explains a particular patient's symptoms and problems, serves as the basis for an individualized treatment plan, and guides the therapy process" (2001, p. 25). Persons et al. argue that evidence-based clinical practice requires that the clinician translate the nomothetic to the ideographic by tailoring empirically supported treatment protocols (e.g., CBT for depression) to the treatment of an individual patient in an evidence-based manner. This evidence-based formulation-driven approach to treatment relies heavily on data collected during the initial assessment, which leads to the case formulation that is based on hypotheses regarding possible mechanisms causing or maintaining problem behaviors, and the case formulation is in turn used to develop the treatment plan. Assessment continues over the course of treatment and is used to modify the treatment as necessary. Clinical decision making is guided by the empirical literature, and the therapist is guided by the case formulation rather than a list of interventions. Furthermore, the formulation and the treatment plan are based on a nomothetic formulation and protocol, respectively, with strong empirical support. Thus, treatment remains nomothetic in terms of drawing on an empirically supported intervention (e.g., CBT for depression) but is also idiographic in the way the protocol is implemented for the particular patient.

A cognitive-behavioral case formulation and treatment plan consist of a number of specific elements (Persons & Davidson, 2001; Persons et al., 2001). The "Identifying Information" section consists of demographic and background information (e.g., age, ethnicity, living situation) and is followed by the "Problem List," which is a comprehensive list of any problems the patient is experiencing in the symptoms, interpersonal, occupational, medical, financial, housing, legal, and leisure domains. Problems are further viewed in terms of Beck's three-component system of cognitive, behavioral, and mood symptoms of depression, which in turn leads to intervention suggestions. Though not strictly a component of case formulation, a "Diagnosis" section is included because of the utility of diagnosis in case formulation and treatment planning. For example, a diagnosis of depression implies certain schema about the self, world, and future and also suggests empirically supported nomothetic interventions.

The next section, "Working Hypothesis," consists of a number of subsections that are derived directly from Beck's theory of depression and may be modified depending on the particular cognitive-behavioral theory used (Persons et al., 2001). It is here that the nomothetic is translated to the ideographic. Persons et al. describe subheadings including "Schema," "Precipitating and Activating Situations," "Origins," and "Summary of the Working Hypothesis," which is described as the heart of the formulation and involves a description of how the particular patient learned particular schema that are now being activated by external events, in turn resulting in the identified symptoms and problems.

"Strengths and Assets," the next section of the formulation, involves noting patient strengths and assets (e.g., social skills, support network) that may be drawn on in designing interventions. The final section, which is based on the formulation, is the "Treatment Plan." This section includes a number of subsections specific to a cognitive-behavioral approach, including "Goals (Measures)," which involves collaboratively setting goals that are described in concrete terms and are assessed in terms of progress made over the course of therapy; "Interventions," where the specific interventions are related to the deficits described in working hypothesis, address problems from the problem list, and facilitate accomplishment of goals; and "Obstacles," where the therapist attempts to predict any difficulties that may arise in therapy in order to prevent or overcome them as needed.

SUMMARY

Assessment procedures play a central role not only at the initial stage of the cognitive-behavioral case formulation, but also during implementation of the intervention derived from it. As evidenced from the preceding discussion, a cognitive-behavioral case formulation contains a great deal of information, which can be derived using a number of assessment strategies, including the initial clinical interview. As Persons et al. (2001) note, much of the required information can be assessed by simply asking the patient directly. Thus, a clinical interview conducted in the context of the cognitive-behavioral case formulation approach includes assessment of areas specific to this model, such as information relevant to the problem list and working hypothesis (i.e., schema, activating situations, origins) and more general areas (e.g., depressive symptoms, behavioral assessment).

As Persons and colleagues (Persons & Davidson, 2001; Persons et al., 2001) acknowledge, there is little empirical support for the utility of the use of case formulation to guide intervention. However, the approach does rest on a foundation of empirically supported approaches as a guide for specific interventions, and Persons and Davidson recommend that therapists adopt one of the nomothetic formulations used in empirically supported therapies for the disorder being treated as a guide for the working hypothesis. Furthermore, a number of models of case conceptualization are available within the nomothetic cognitive-behavioral approach. However, as Nezu, Nezu, Peacock, and Girdwood (2004) observe, these variations share a number of important similarities, including an emphasis on the importance of individualized assessment in order to better understand the individual patient and the problems he or she is experiencing and similarities in the design of individual treatment protocols. Thus, models of case conceptualization such as that proposed by Persons and colleagues highlight the central role of assessment, including clinical interviewing in its various forms (i.e., structured diagnostic interviews and clinical interviews), not only in identifying areas of difficulty that a patient is experiencing but also in informing individualized and empirically based interventions to address those difficulties.

REFERENCES

Addington, D., Addington, J., & Maticka-Tyndale, E. (1993). Rating depression in schizophrenia: A comparison of a self-report and an observer-report scale. *Journal of Nervous and Mental Disease, 181,* 561–565.

American Psychiatric Association. (1994). *Diagnostic and statistical manual of mental disorders* (4th ed.). Washington, DC: Author.

American Psychiatric Association. (2000). *Diagnostic and statistical manual of mental disorders* (4th ed., Text rev.). Washington, DC: Author.

Barbour, K. A., & Davison, G. C. (2004). Clinical interviewing. In M. Hersen (Series Ed.), S. N. Haynes & E. M. Heiby (Vol. Eds.), *Comprehensive handbook of psychological assessment: Vol. 3. Behavioral assessment* (pp. 181–193). Hoboken, NJ: Wiley.

Beck, A. T., Rush, A. J., Shaw, B. F., & Emery, G. (1979). *Cognitive therapy of depression.* New York: Guilford.

Beck, A. T., Steer, R. A., & Brown, G. K. (1996). *Manual for the BDI-II.* San Antonio, TX: Psychological Corporation.

Beck, A. T., Weissman, A., Lester, D., & Trexler, L. (1974). The measurement of pessimism: The Hopelessness Scale. *Journal of Consulting and Clinical Psychology, 42,* 861–865.

Beck. J. S. (1995). *Cognitive therapy: Basics and beyond.* New York: Guilford.

Belzer, K., & Schneier, F. R. (2004). Comorbidity of anxiety and depressive disorders: Issues in conceptualization, assessment, and treatment. *Journal of Psychiatric Practice, 10,* 296–306.

Blankstein, K. R., & Segal, Z. V. (2001). Cognitive assessment: Issues and methods. In K. S. Dobson (Ed.), *Handbook of cognitive-behavioral therapies* (2nd ed., pp. 40–85). New York: Guilford.

Boland, R. J., & Keller, M. B. (2002). Course and outcome of depression. In I. H. Gotlib & C. L. Hammen (Eds.), *Handbook of depression* (pp. 43–60). New York: Guilford.

Chambless, D. L., Baker, M. J., Baucom, D. H., Beutler, L., Calhoun, K. S., Crits-Christoph, P., et al. (1998). Update on empirically validated therapies, II. *Clinical Psychologist, 51,* 3–16.

Chambless, D. L., & Ollendick, T. H. (2001). Empirically supported psychological interventions: Controversies and evidence. *Annual Review of Psychology, 52,* 685–716.

Clark, D. A., Beck, A. T., & Alford, B. A. (1999). *Scientific foundations of cognitive theory and therapy of depression.* Toronto: Wiley.

DeRubeis, R. J., Tang, T. Z., & Beck, A. T. (2001). Cognitive therapy. In K. S. Dobson (Ed.), *Handbook of cognitive-behavioral therapies* (2nd ed., pp. 349–392). New York: Guilford.

Dobson, K. S., & Khatri, N. (2002). Major depressive disorder. In M. Hersen (Ed.), *Clinical behavior therapy: Adults and children* (pp. 37–51). New York: Wiley.

Dozois, D. J. A., & Dobson, K. S. (2002). Depression. In M. M. Antony & D. H. Barlow (Eds.), *Handbook of assessment and treatment planning for psychological disorders* (pp. 259–299). New York: Guilford.

Dozois, D. J. A., & Dobson, K. S. (2004). The prevention of anxiety and depression: Introduction. In D. J. A. Dozois & K. S. Dobson (Eds.), *The prevention of anxiety and depression: Theory, research, and practice* (pp. 1–6). Washington, DC: APA Press.

Dozois, D. J. A., & Westra, H. A. (2004). The nature of anxiety and depression: Implications for prevention. In D. J. A. Dozois & K. S. Dobson (Eds.), *The prevention of anxiety and depression: Theory, research, and practice* (pp. 9–41). Washington, DC: APA Press.

Endicott, J., & Spitzer, R. L. (1978). A diagnostic interview: The schedule for affective disorders and schizophrenia. *Archives of General Psychiatry, 35,* 837–844.

First, M. B., Spitzer, R. L., Gibbon, M., & Williams, J. B. W. (1995). *Structured clinical interview for* DSM-IV *Axis I disorders.* New York: Biometrics Research Department.

First, M. B., Spitzer, R. L., Gibbon, M., & Williams, J. B. W. (1996). *Structured clinical interview for* DSM-IV *Axis I disorders, clinician version (SCID-CV).* Washington, DC: American Psychiatric Press.

Gotlib, I. H., & Hammen, C. L. (2002). Introduction. In I. H. Gotlib & C. L. Hammen (Eds.), *Handbook of depression* (pp. 1–20). New York: Guilford.

Groth-Marnat, G. (1999). *Handbook of psychological assessment* (3rd ed.). Toronto: Wiley.

Hamilton, M. (1960). A rating scale for depression. *Journal of Neurology, Neurosurgery and Psychiatry, 23,* 56–62.

Hamilton, M. (1967). Development of a rating scale for primary depressive illness. *British Journal of Social and Clinical Psychology, 6,* 278–296.

Haynes, S. N., & Heiby, E. M. (Eds.). (2004). *Comprehensive handbook of psychological assessment: Vol. 3. Behavioral assessment.* Hoboken, NJ: Wiley.

Haynes, S. N., & O'Brien, W. H. (Eds.). (2000). *Principles and practice of behavioral assessment.* New York: Kluwer Academic.

Hays, P. A. (2001). *Addressing cultural complexities in practice: A framework for clinicians and counselors.* Washington, DC: APA Press.

Hollon, S. D., Haman, K. L., & Brown, L. L. (2002). Cognitive-behavioral treatment of depression. In I. H. Gotlib & C. L. Hammen (Eds.), *Handbook of depression* (pp. 383–403). New York: Guilford.

Hopko, D. R., Lejuez, C.W., Ruggiero, K. J., & Eifert, G. H. (2003). Contemporary behavioral activation treatments for depression: Procedures, principles and progress. *Clinical Psychology Review, 23,* 699–717.

Judd, L. L., Akiskal, H. S., Maser, J. D., Zeller, P. J., Endicott, J., Coryell, W., et al. (1998). Major depressive disorder: A prospective study of residual subthreshold depressive symptoms as predictor of rapid relapse. *Journal of Affective Disorders, 50,* 97–108.

Judd, L. L., Paulus, M. J., Schettler, P. J., Akiskal, H. S., Endicott, J., Leon, A. C., et al. (2000). Does incomplete recovery from first lifetime major depressive episode herald a chronic course of illness? *American Journal of Psychiatry, 157,* 1501–1504.

Kessler, R. C. (2002). Epidemiology of depression. In I. H. Gotlib & C. L. Hammen (Eds.), *Handbook of depression* (pp. 23–42). New York: Guilford.

Kessler, R. C., Berglund, P., Demler, O., Jin, R., Koretz, D., Merikangas, K. R., et al. (2003). The epidemiology of major depressive disorder: Results from the National Comorbidity Survey Replication (NCS-R). *Journal of the American Medical Association, 289,* 3095–3105.

Kinzie, J. D., Manson, S. M., Vino, T. D., Tolan, N. T., Anh, B., & Pho, T. (1982). Development and validation of a Vietnamese language rating scale. *American Journal of Psychiatry, 139,* 1276–1281.

Kovacs, M. (1992). *Children's Depression Inventory manual.* New York: Multi-Health Systems.

Meichenbaum, D. (2005). 35 years of working with suicidal patients: Lessons learned. *Canadian Psychology, 46,* 64–73.

Minor, K. L., Champion, J. E., & Gotlib, I. H. (2005). Stability of *DSM-IV* criterion symptoms for major depressive disorder. *Journal of Psychiatric Research, 39,* 415–420.

Morrison, J. (1995). *The first interview: Revised for* DSM-IV. New York: Guilford.

Muñoz, R. F., Le, H.-N., Clarke, G., & Jaycox, L. (2002). Preventing the onset of major depression.

In I. H. Gotlib & C. L. Hammen (Eds.), *Handbook of depression* (pp. 343–359). New York: Guilford.

Nezu, A. M., Nezu, C. M., McClure, K. S., & Zwick, M. L. (2002). Assessment of depression. In I. H. Gotlib & C. L. Hammen (Eds.), *Handbook of depression* (pp. 61–85). New York: Guilford.

Nezu, A. M., Nezu, C. M., Peacock, M. A., & Girdwood, C. P. (2004). Case formulation in cognitive-behavior therapy. In M. Hersen (Series Ed.), S. N. Haynes & E. M. Heiby (Vol. Eds.), *Comprehensive handbook of psychological assessment: Vol. 3. Behavioral assessment* (pp. 402–426). Hoboken, NJ: Wiley.

Nezu, A. M., Ronan, G. F., Meadows, E. A., & McClure, K. S. (2000). *Practitioner's guide to empirically based measures of depression.* New York: Kluwer.

Nezu, C. M., Nezu, A. M., & Foster, S. L. (2000). A 10-step guide to selecting assessment measures in clinical and research settings. In A. M. Nezu, G. F. Ronan, E. A. Meadows, & K. S. McClure (Eds.), *Practitioner's guide to empirically based measures of depression* (pp. 17–24). New York: Kluwer.

Othmer, E., & Othmer, S. C. (1994). *The clinical interview using DSM-IV: Vol. 1. Fundamentals.* Washington, DC: American Psychiatric Press.

Persons, J. B., & Davidson, J. (2001). Cognitive-behavioral case formulation. In K. S. Dobson (Ed.), *Handbook of cognitive-behavioral therapies* (2nd ed., pp. 86–110). New York: Guilford.

Persons, J. B., Davidson, J., & Tompkins, M. A. (2001). *Essential components of cognitive-behavior therapy for depression.* Washington, DC: APA Press.

Rehm, L. P. (1987). The measurement of behavioral aspects of depression. In A. J. Marsella, R. M. A. Hirschfeld, & M. M. Katz (Eds.). *The measurement of depression* (pp. 199–239). New York: Guilford.

Schelde, J. (1998a). Major depression: Behavioral markers of depression and recovery. *Journal of Nervous and Mental Disease, 186,* 133–140.

Schelde, J. (1998b). Major depression: Behavioral parameters of depression and recovery. *Journal of Nervous and Mental Disease, 186,* 141–149.

Spitzer, R. L., Endicott, J., & Robins, E. (1978). Research diagnostic criteria. *Archives of General Psychiatry, 35,* 773–782.

Stolberg, R. A., Clark, D. C., & Bongar, B. (2002). Epidemiology, assessment, and management of suicide in depressed patients. In I. H. Gotlib & C. L. Hammen (Eds.), *Handbook of depression* (pp. 581–601). New York: Guilford.

Summerfeldt, L. J., & Antony, M. M. (2002). Structured and semistructured diagnostic interviews. In M. M. Antony & D. H. Barlow (Eds.), *Handbook of assessment and treatment planning for psychological disorders* (pp. 3–37). New York: Guilford.

Tsai, J. L., & Chentsova-Dutton, Y. (2002). Understanding depression across cultures. In I. H. Gotlib & C. L. Hammen (Eds.), *Handbook of depression* (pp. 467–491). New York: Guilford.

Weissman, M. M., Bruce, M., Leaf, P., Florio, L., & Holzer, C. (1991). Affective disorders. In L. Robins & E. Regier (Eds.), *Psychiatric disorders in America* (pp. 53–80). New York: Free Press.

Weissman, M. M., Markowitz, J. C., & Klerman, G. L. (2000). *Comprehensive guide to interpersonal psychotherapy.* New York: Basic Books.

11

BIPOLAR DISORDER

SHERI L. JOHNSON, LORI EISNER, AND RANDY FINGERHUT

DESCRIPTION OF THE DISORDER

Bipolar disorder is a serious psychiatric disorder characterized by extreme difficulties in social and occupational functioning (Mitchell, Slade, & Andrews, 2004). The disorder is projected to become the sixth leading cause of medical disability worldwide by 2020 (Murray & Lopez, 1997). Fortunately, mood-stabilizing medications have been shown to reduce the risk of symptoms, hospitalizations, and even suicide (Angst, Angst, Gerber Werder, & Gamma, 2005; Baldessarini & Tondo, 2003; Goldberg, 2004). Recognition of this disorder is the first step toward providing effective care.

Despite the clear advantages of careful diagnosis, many mental health practitioners do not screen for this condition. For example, in one survey 79% of providers reported that they did not routinely screen for bipolar disorder (Brickman, LoPiccolo, & Johnson, 2002). Among people with bipolar disorder attending support groups, patients reported that it took them an average of more than 5 years to obtain the diagnosis of bipolar disorder (Lish, Dime Meenan, Whybrow, & Price, 1994). In a large community study, less than half of patients with bipolar disorder reported receiving treatment within the past year (Kessler, Rubinow, Holmes, Abelson, & Zhao, 1997). Sadly, treatment of depression without accurate diagnosis of a history of mania

can create substantial difficulties because antidepressant medications in the absence of mood-stabilizing medications have been found to trigger episodes of mania (Ghaemi, Lenox, & Baldessarini, 2001). Therefore, one vital public health goal is to increase recognition of this disorder by mental health practitioners.

The Diagnostic and Statistical Manual of Mental Disorders (*DSM-IV-TR;* APA, 2000) recognizes several forms of bipolar disorder, each defined on the basis of manic symptoms of varying duration and severity: bipolar I disorder, bipolar II disorder, cyclothymia, and bipolar disorder not otherwise specified (NOS). Bipolar I disorder is defined by one or more lifetime episodes of mania. According to *DSM-IV-TR,* a manic episode is defined by intense euphoric or irritable mood, accompanied by three associated symptoms (four if mood is irritable only). Associated symptoms can include decreased need for sleep, elevated self-esteem, distractibility, increased talkativeness, increased goal-directed activity, and excessive involvement in high-risk pleasurable activities (Table 11.1). To meet diagnostic criteria for mania, these symptoms must either create severe impairment for at least 1 week or be severe enough to necessitate hospitalization. The episode of mania can be accompanied by simultaneous symptoms of depression, in which case it is called a mixed episode. Despite the name *bipolar,* depression is not required for a diagnosis of bipolar I disorder. Nonetheless, episodes of major depression are common for people with this disorder (see Table 11.1 for diagnostic criteria of depression).

Bipolar I disorder is the most severe form of the disorder, but a variety of milder forms of disorder have been defined, including bipolar II disorder, cyclothymia, and bipolar disorder NOS. Bipolar II disorder is defined by at least one lifetime hypomanic episode, along with episodes of major depression. Although hypomanic episodes are defined by the same symptoms as those used to define manic episodes, a hypomanic episode need only last 4 days and results in distinct changes in functioning rather than severe impairment. Cyclothymia is defined by frequent fluctuations between manic and depressive symptoms that do not meet the severity or duration criteria for mania or hypomania. The person must experience frequent mood fluctuations for at least 2 years (1 year in a child or adolescent). Finally, bipolar disorder NOS is defined by manic symptoms that do not meet either the frequency, duration, or severity criteria.

Bipolar I disorder and bipolar II disorder are both episodic: Symptoms can be absent for years at a time. Therefore, diagnosis rests on careful coverage of lifetime episodes, because even a 70-year-old person who last experienced a manic episode during childhood still qualifies for the diagnosis of bipolar disorder. Although some people go for a decade without symptoms, persistent subsyndromal symptoms of depression are normative (Judd et al., 2002). Moreover, even on adequate levels of lithium, most people experience further episodes within a 5-year period (Keller, Lavori, Kane, & Gelenberg, 1992).

INTERVIEWING STRATEGIES

A collaborative approach to the interview process helps set the tone for later treatment sessions. It may be useful to spend time initially setting expectations for the clinical interview. The clinician can explain the purpose of the interview (i.e., to gather information about the client to use for planning treatment) and can distinguish assessment from therapy goals. In addition, use of active listening skills (e.g., open questions, validating feelings, and reflective listening) can build rapport, which in turn can maximize patient disclosure.

Table 11.1   *DSM-IV* Criteria

Manic Episode:

1. A period of 1 week or longer where mood is abnormally euphoric or irritable. (NOTE: The duration can be shorter than 1 week if mood changes result in hospitalization.)

2. Must have three or more symptoms (four if mood is irritable) during mood changes:
   - Elevated view of oneself
   - Feels rested despite decreased sleep
   - Pressured speech
   - Racing thoughts
   - Easily distracted
   - Increase in goal-directed behavior or agitation
   - Increased engagement in high-risk activities

Major Depressive Episode:

1. A period of 2 weeks or longer where individual is persistently depressed or anhedonic.

2. Must have five or more symptoms most of the day nearly every day during this period:
   - Depressed mood
   - Anhedonia
   - Significant increases/decreases in weight or appetite not due to dieting
   - Significant increases/decreases in sleep
   - Significant increases/decreases in motor activity
   - Fatigue
   - Lowered self-esteem
   - Concentration difficulties
   - Suicidal ideation

SOURCE: Adapted from American Psychiatric Association (2000).

Typically, a clinical interview should start with an assessment of the patient's presenting problems. A good interviewing strategy is to begin with an open-ended question (e.g. "What has brought you to see me?"). This allows the patient time to tell his or her story. The interviewer can then follow up with more specific questions to gather information about bipolar symptoms.

One of the difficult aspects of diagnosing bipolar disorder is that a clinician must be careful to capture manic and depressive symptoms. Although people with bipolar disorder are much more likely to seek treatment for depressive symptoms, epidemiological studies document that

about 20–33% of people with bipolar disorder experience unipolar mania (cf. Karkowski & Kendler, 1997; Kessler et al., 1997). Longitudinal evidence suggests that many people who initially report unipolar mania develop depressive episodes over a 15- to 20-year period (Solomon et al., 2003).

For each pole, areas to focus on include disruptions in mood, sleep, energy, behavior, cognition, and self-esteem. See Table 11.2 for a list of typical questions we use to begin to assess symptoms of depression and mania. It is advisable to start with less threatening questions with patients who are fearful or defensive. Generally speaking,

---

Table 11.2   Suggested Probes for Assessing Depression and Mania

---

Depression:

Have you ever had a period of 2 weeks or longer where you felt depressed most of the day, nearly every day?

Have you ever had a period of 2 weeks or longer where you the activities you usually enjoyed were less pleasurable?

During that time:
How was your sleep?
How was your energy?
How did you feel about yourself?
Did you feel lethargic or agitated?
Did you have suicidal thoughts?
How was your concentration?

Other signs of depression:
Did life feel more difficult for you?
Did you lose faith in yourself?
Were you less social than usual?

Mania:

Have you ever had a period of 1 week or longer of where you felt happier than circumstances dictated most of the day, nearly every day?

Have you ever had a period of 1 week or longer of where you felt extremely irritable most of the day, nearly every day?

During that time:
What was your energy like?
How many hours per night were you sleeping? Did you feel rested or tired?
Did you notice any changes in your behavior?
Did you have any new or unusual ideas or goals? What were they?
How was your confidence?
Were you more talkative than usual? Did others notice or comment on this?
What was your concentration like?

Other possible signs of mania:
Did you change your dress or appearance?
Did you find that you got more accomplished?
Did you find yourself more sexually desirable?
Did life seem more exciting to you?
Did people seem too slow?

---

many patients are more open to discussing their depressive symptoms than their manic symptoms because depressive symptoms often are less stigmatizing. Within depression or mania probes, clinicians may first cover more objective symptoms, such as sleep patterns, concentration, or appetite before asking about the patient's mood. Recent evidence supports the idea that probing for increases in activity may be particularly helpful for identifying manic episodes (Akiskal & Benazzi, 2005).

A number of standardized instruments have been designed to capture the diagnosis of bipolar disorder (e.g., the Structured Clinical Interview for *DSM-IV*; First, Spitzer, Williams, & Gibbon, 1997; and the Schedule for Affective Disorders and Schizophrenia; Endicott & Spitzer, 1978) and the severity of symptoms (e.g., the Bech-Rafaelsen Mania Scale [BRMS]; Bech, 2002; Bech, Bolwig, Kramp, & Rafaelsen, 1979; and the Modified Hamilton Rating Scale for Depression [HAM-D]; Miller, Bishop, Norman, & Maddever,, 1985). The diagnostic interviews provide not only suggested probes but also thresholds for when to consider a symptom clinically significant.

In conducting any assessment of the severity of bipolar symptoms, clinicians should be aware that rates of completed suicide are about 12–15 times higher in those with bipolar disorder than in the general population (Angst, Stassen, Clayton, & Angst, 2002). After cardiovascular events, suicide is the most likely cause of death for people with bipolar I disorder (Angst et al., 2002). Rates of

violence are also higher than in the general population (Corrigan & Watson, 2005). Therefore, it is important to assess for suicidal and homicidal risk. Asking specific questions about the presence and intensity of the patient's suicidal and homicidal thoughts, whether he or she has a specific plan and the means to carry it out, and the level of intent in carrying out a plan can help clarify the patient's risk of harm to self and others. Obtaining details on prior suicide attempts is also important.

The clinician should gather information about the patient's social and medical history. Given the highly heritable nature of bipolar disorder, family history of mood disorders should provide helpful information. Childhood events and traumas are also important to cover. An understanding of the patient's relationships within and outside of the family can help in treatment planning. The clinician should ask about the patient's medical history and substance use history because these are potential confounds in diagnosis of bipolar disorder.

Once the clinician has developed an understanding of the patient's symptoms, he or she should establish a timeline for their development. The clinician should inquire as to when the patient first noticed a change in his or her mood and when it reached a level that caused impairment. We find it helpful to use a lifechart (Denicoff et al., 1997) to capture the time course of episodes, antecedents, and consequences (Figure 11.1). Typically, we use one line of the lifechart to draw manic and depressive episodes,

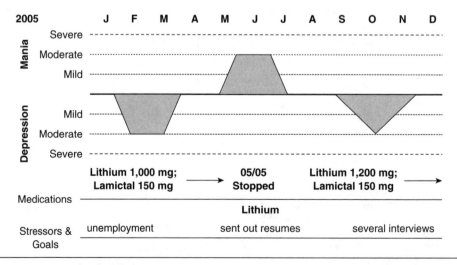

Figure 11.1   Example of a Lifechart

one for treatment, and one for life events. The interviewer can alternate his or her questioning to focus on events, mood changes, behavioral responses, and consequences to behavioral choices. Lifecharts can vary substantially in their level of detail. When interviewees have experienced more than six episodes, we often focus on understanding the pattern of symptoms over the past 2 years. When interviewees report few episodes, we draw the pattern for the entire life course. We often find it helpful to ask the patient to draw patterns as we watch or even to take the lifechart home and add to it during the week.

In drawing out the symptom line, we are interested in the severity of episodes but also the nature of prodromal periods, because a better understanding of the rapidity of onset can help in planning strategies to prevent psychosocial problems as symptoms begin. We also use this as an opportunity to describe mixed episodes (periods of simultaneous depression and mania), which have been shown to be a predictor of poor treatment outcome (Kruger, Young, & Braunig, 2005). We cover subsyndromal symptoms, which can indicate a need for more intensive treatment with medication or psychotherapy.

We then use a second line to record treatment history, including medications, dosages, and periods of nonadherence. This often provides robust data about which medications have been effective and provides a concrete image for patients of the costs of nonadherence, which is all too common in this disorder (Basco & Rush, 1995; Keck, McElroy, Strakowski, & Stanton, 1996; Svarstad, Shireman, & Sweeney, 2001).

We use a third line to note major life events and changes. Much evidence supports major life events as a predictor of depression within bipolar disorder (Johnson & Fingerhut, 2004), and so careful questioning can often help capture events that preceded a bipolar episode. The interviewer should note stressful life events such as job changes, health problems, interpersonal losses, or financial difficulties. Bipolar disorder often takes quite a toll on a person's relationships, finances, and career, so it is important for interviewers to understand changes in these domains that unfold consequent to episodes. Although it is time-consuming, understanding the costs associated with this illness can help motivate patients for treatment.

One should consider the clinical interview as an initial step in the assessment of bipolar disorder.

Ideally speaking, the clinician should monitor bipolar symptoms on an ongoing basis. This can be done in a diary format. The patient can monitor his or her sleep, mood, medication compliance, and use of alcohol and drugs on a daily basis.

INTERVIEWING OBSTACLES AND SOLUTIONS

Interviewing people with bipolar disorder can pose a number of challenges to the clinician. For example, symptoms of mania may interfere with the conversational flow of the interview. After discussing this issue, we turn to two particular issues that may lead patients to minimize their bipolar symptoms: poor insight and concerns about stigma.

Manic Symptoms and Conversational Flow

Patients who are experiencing current symptoms of mania may exhibit pressured speech. Beyond this, it is important to note that many clinical interviews place the interviewer in a dominant role, and a manic patient may deeply resent this type of exchange. Overly structured interviews, in which a patient has little room to decide when to elaborate on concerns, can be particularly frustrating for patients in this state. Therefore, it may be useful to give patients permission to ask questions, voice concerns, or choose the order of topics to be covered. That is, we recommend finding small ways to restore some of the balance of power in allowing acutely manic patients opportunities to influence the interview process. Beyond this, we often find it helpful to note that we hope to cover a vast number of questions and to highlight that they will get chances to share other stories at the end of the interview. If a patient is acutely manic, breaking the interview up into smaller time periods can be helpful; it is often easier for patients to stay focused for brief periods of time.

Lack of Insight Into Symptoms

Insight into manic symptoms has been found to drop dramatically as people become manic (Dell'Osso et al., 2002). This is not surprising when one considers how cognition seems to shift with episode status. Bipolar patients may exhibit state-dependent changes in their ability to recognize or recall their symptoms. For instance, patients in the midst of a manic episode may find it more difficult to remember details of their depressive history. Indeed, people who are experiencing acute mania often are poor at recognizing any signs of threat, much less their own dangerous warning signs. As an indicator of how profound such deficits can become, consider a study of facial affect recognition. Lembke and Ketter (2002) showed participants pictures of extremely intense emotional facial expressions and asked them to choose which emotion was being displayed. Although there is evidence that people with bipolar disorder are extremely sensitive to facial cues of negative affect during periods of remission (Harmer, Grayson, & Goodwin, 2002), people who were acutely manic were uniquely unable to recognize negative facial expressions. Imagine, then, how difficult it would be to evaluate complex interpersonal cues in a rich environment. Not surprisingly, during a manic episode, people can be oblivious to signs of distress or concern in others. They are also likely to be motivated to pursue their own personal goals, moving at lightning speed in a burst of confidence, such that people who provide negative feedback are ignored.

This presents quite a paradox for interviewers who would like to make a diagnosis of an acute manic episode. They can expect that many patients will not acknowledge concerns and do not want to hear negative feedback. Interviewers should keep feedback extremely behavioral and build consensus with a person step by step (e.g., first in regard to changes in concrete areas such as sleep, then in regard to activities, then in regard to romantic relationships) rather than attempting to quickly label a manic episode as such. That is, patients often can endorse concerns about not sleeping more readily than they can accept a full diagnosis of mania; we often work to facilitate good medical care for their difficulty sleeping.

As manic symptoms remit, insight often improves. Research also suggests that people develop better insight into illness as they age (Kleindienst, Engel, & Greil, 2005). Nonetheless, some patients have poor memories for the jumbled events of a manic episode, and others might not want to remember the events. We find that a calm, nonconfrontational stance can help promote enough rapport to facilitate discussion of these difficult experiences.

Given difficulties with insight and recall, family interviews can be helpful in piecing together details. Clinicians can maximize the reliability of their interviews by using multiple sources. If possible, clinicians should get patients' consent to interview loved ones who know the patient well and can report on his or her history. Clinicians are also advised to get permission to access the patients' past records of inpatient and outpatient medical and psychological treatment.

In one innovative study, researchers videotaped psychotic behavior at the time of hospital admission, and 6 weeks later they reviewed these tapes with patients (Davidoff, Forester, Ghaemi, & Bodkin, 1998). Although one can imagine that patients might have found these videos shocking, those who viewed the tapes sustained longer periods of time before rehospitalization than those who did not view such tapes. At times, family members may be able to provide a less shocking version of this sort of feedback to help patients understand the nature of symptoms that they may not fully remember.

Patient Concerns About Stigma

In keeping with a collaborative approach, clinicians may devote a portion of the interview to explaining the patient's diagnosis. Clinicians can use this time to understand the fears patients have about the disorder. Most patients find the process of diagnosis to be intensely stigmatizing. Self-blame can be reduced by honest discussion of the highly genetic basis of this disorder. Nonetheless, deep fears about the meaning of a bipolar diagnosis usually are not addressed just by the knowledge that this is a biologically driven disorder. Many clients have family members or friends with a history of bipolar disorder, and most have witnessed periods of untreated symptoms creating painful embarrassment and intense interpersonal rejections.

Our approach to stigma is to assume that people have views about what a diagnosis means and to ask about these views in detail before proceeding with diagnosis. Supportive psychoeducation can go a long way toward correcting some myths (e.g., bipolar disorder gets worse over time, people with bipolar disorder cannot work or must live in hospitals). In respect to some beliefs, we find it helpful to frame the purpose of diagnosis, which ultimately is to help in the process of treatment and regaining control. Written material can help challenge myths and fears. The National Institute of Mental Health

Web site provides free brochures with up-to-date information (http://www.nimh.nih.gov/healthinformation/bipolarmenu.cfm).

Some concerns about stigma are realistic: A recent survey suggests that most mental health consumers report stigma from family members, from employers, and even within their religious organizations (Wahl, 1999). Therefore, in exploring potential negative aspects of hearing a diagnosis, it is important for a clinician not to automatically dismiss fears and concerns. Rather, therapists can work with clients to minimize the negative consequences of the disorder for relationships, careers, and other important aspects of life.

Without overt discussion of these types of fears, the process of diagnosis can be overwhelming for many patients. For patients with severe mental illness, rates of suicide are particularly high in the first year after an initial diagnosis and hospitalization. Diagnosis, then, is a vulnerable time that requires delicate sensitivity to the best means of combating hopeless images of bipolar disorder.

Finally, we find it helpful to approach diagnosis as a process rather than a singular piece of feedback. Often, patients begin considering evidence that they have bipolar disorder only weeks into treatment, as they begin to develop more trust in the therapist. Over time, they gradually accept different facets of the disorder, perhaps beginning with an acknowledgment of certain symptoms and moving toward the understanding that symptoms could be of concern in the future. In one study, we found that acceptance of the need for treatment was multifaceted and included acknowledgment of previous and future symptoms, acceptance of the need for medications, difficulties letting go of positive aspects of mania such as energy and increased sociability, and willingness to tolerate the sometimes severe side effects of mood-stabilizing medications (Johnson & Fulford, under review).

CASE ILLUSTRATION

Although we certainly have met people who readily reviewed their symptoms and then easily accepted the diagnosis of bipolar disorder, this has been fairly rare in our experience. More commonly, a person who has not been previously diagnosed can find the interview difficult to complete: He or she may be vague about details, have trouble discussing concerns, or be unsure of the timing or severity of such concerns. In such cases, we often bring family members in for an interview. Often, it takes us several sessions to really help a patient integrate feedback from family members in a way that he or she finds useful and informative. Therefore, we have chosen a case illustration of a person who had difficulty recognizing signs of the disorder. To protect the identity of our client, we have changed several features of this story, at times incorporating details from more than one client to represent the general process of obtaining and sharing a diagnosis.

Stan was a 52-year-old married man who ran a small jewelry store. After hearing a community talk on bipolar disorder, Stan called to find out more about a treatment trial we were conducting, which included free psychotherapy. As part of that program, we screened Stan with the Structured Clinical Interview for *DSM-IV* (SCID) to determine whether he met diagnostic criteria for bipolar disorder.

In reviewing the events leading up to his interview, Stan reported that he and his wife separated in February, and shortly thereafter he was placed on a mood stabilizer. His wife accepted him back into the house on the condition that he continue to take medication for bipolar disorder. He stated that he had accepted his bipolar disorder and the need for treatment.

During the SCID, Stan endorsed a number of behaviors that were congruent with mania, but he denied that his behaviors were symptoms. For example, when asked about periods of irritability, he reported that he had suffered through two argumentative encounters with police in the past year. Although these seemed to be significant signs of irritability, Stan denied that anything was amiss with his condition during these incidents, stating that he had been unfairly treated by the police. Similarly, he described himself as 100% confident in his abilities but denied that he was experiencing any increase in self-esteem. His speech was pressured, but he stated that he was "always a talker." Although he endorsed sleeping only 4 hours per night, he stated that he had "always been a high-energy guy." Even though he described himself as diagnosed with bipolar disorder, Stan could not identify a single symptom that he saw as manic, nor could he identify a distinct time period of manic behavior. At the end of the SCID, the interviewer was unable to state whether he met criteria for a manic episode, and we decided it was worth gaining his wife's perspective.

At a joint session the next week, Stan's wife gave a detailed overview of her concerns. She noted that Stan had always had more energy, more confidence, and less need for sleep than most people. For some time, these had seemed like distinctive strengths. Over the years, these characteristic behaviors sometimes became more intense, but not in a way that could be clearly characterized as episodic until February. In February, Stan began to demonstrate pressured speech and argumentativeness to an extent that friends expressed concerns to Stan's wife. She noted that during that time his sleep had diminished to a few hours per night, his spending had increased, and his driving had become more reckless. By her report, he met criteria for a manic episode in February. According to his wife, Stan began to calm down when mood-stabilizing medication was started. During the marital session, Stan was extremely distressed; with each symptom his wife described, Stan either denied the behavior or justified his reactions.

In many ways, the initial assessment with Stan was typical: At one level, he was able to acknowledge concerns about bipolar disorder. But he found the process of discussing these symptoms overwhelmingly difficult, he was unable to provide a clear image of any specific symptom, and he could not define the time course of any symptoms. At the same time, he showed a number of strengths: He presented as an intelligent and successful man who was motivated to engage in treatment and curious to learn more about bipolar disorder.

The therapist cautiously agreed to see Stan for treatment but let Stan know that psychotherapy would involve helping him learn to recognize symptoms of mania. Without the ability to label these symptoms, she warned Stan, efforts to learn to control these symptoms were not likely to go far. She agreed to begin by meeting with him and seeing whether they could jointly build a better sense of what the symptoms were and how to label them.

At the next session, Stan emphasized that he had already accepted that he had bipolar disorder and that he was taking medication, so he did not expect that this would ever be a problem again. Even as Stan denied any concerns about

symptoms, he appeared to be experiencing some mild hypomanic symptoms: His speech was pressured, and his affect remained intense. Indeed, the therapist in the next office complained about the volume of Stan's voice. While providing reinforcement for his willingness to accept the diagnosis and the need for medications, the therapist began to discuss Stan's fears about what would happen if he were symptomatic. It seemed that Stan was concerned about how manic symptoms could threaten his marriage. Most important, though, he seemed to view symptoms in a black-and-white manner; he seemed to equate the idea of having one symptom with being "manic."

To combat Stan's fears about identifying symptoms, the therapist introduced the idea of manic "blips" as a common phenomenon in bipolar disorder. To reinforce the idea that manic symptoms could vary on a continuum, Stan and the therapist began to develop a personal checklist for him, which described different symptoms of mania and possible levels of severity. In using this scale, Stan was able to see that even though he had a couple mild symptoms, his symptoms were not at a full-blown level. This insight seemed to help him consider his symptoms more calmly. With these gains, Stan was in an excellent place to begin practicing mood management skills and monitoring their success.

DIFFERENTIAL DIAGNOSIS AND BEHAVIORAL ASSESSMENT

Diagnosing bipolar disorder is difficult because of its overlap with a number of other psychological disorders. In one major community study, 100% of people with bipolar I disorder met criteria for a comorbid psychiatric condition (Kessler et al., 1997). In this section we discuss disorders that resemble bipolar disorder and suggestions for differential diagnosis.

Major Depressive Disorder

Most people with bipolar disorder experience episodes of depression, and they often seek treatment for depression without reporting their history of mania. Moreover, it can be difficult to differentiate major depressive episodes with prominent irritability from mixed episodes (APA, 2000). Both types of episodes are marked by symptoms of irritability, sleep disturbance, and concentration difficulties. To qualify for a mixed episode, however, a person must meet criteria for both a manic episode and a major depressive episode nearly every day for at least 1 week.

Substance-Related Disorder and Mood Disorder Caused by a General Medical Condition

Diagnostic criteria for bipolar disorder specify that mood-related symptoms cannot be caused by the direct effects of a substance or a general medical condition. The most common substance involved in inducing manic episodes is antidepressant medication. Indeed, by one estimate, as many of 20% of people with bipolar spectrum disorder develop hypomanic or manic symptoms when treated with antidepressants alone (Ghaemi, Hsu, Soldani, & Goodwin, 2003). Current treatment guidelines suggest that antidepressant medications should be administered only in combination with a mood-stabilizing medication. Manic episodes that are triggered by antidepressant medication are diagnosed as substance-induced mood disorders.

Other substances that are particularly likely to trigger manic episodes include cocaine and stimulants. These substances directly increase the level of dopamine in the synaptic cleft and therefore may directly challenge the pathways involved in the genesis of manic episodes (Winters, Johnson, & Cuellar, under review).

Beyond these substances, intoxication or withdrawal from a broad range of substances often causes mood changes, impulsive or reckless behavior, and sleep disturbance. Medical conditions such as multiple sclerosis, stroke, and thyroid disease can also produce symptoms that mimic symptoms of mania or depression. It is therefore advisable to inquire as to whether the patient has had a recent physical exam.

Efforts to distinguish between a bipolar disorder and a substance-induced mood disorder are complicated by the fact that almost half of people with bipolar disorder abuse substances at some point during their lives (Brown, Suppes, Adinoff, & Thomas, 2001; Chengappa, Levine, Gershon, & Kupfer, 2000; Zarate & Tohen, 2001). It is therefore necessary to look at the temporal patterns between substance use and symptoms. It is sometimes necessary to defer a bipolar diagnosis until a sufficient period of detoxification has occurred.

Schizophrenia and Schizoaffective Disorder

Differentiating between bipolar disorder and psychotic disorders can be quite difficult in that mood disturbances often are linked with psychosis. Between one third and one half of patients with bipolar I disorder report psychotic symptoms (Judd et al., 2002; Lenzi, Rinaldi, Bianco, Balestri, & Marazziti, 1996), particularly during acute periods of mania (Black & Nasrallah, 1989). Psychotic symptoms tend to be present for less than 2 weeks per year (Judd et al., 2002).

If psychotic symptoms occur only during manic or depressive episodes, the patient would be diagnosed with bipolar disorder with psychotic features. When psychotic symptoms are more prominent, other diagnoses should be considered. Schizoaffective disorder is diagnosed when psychotic symptoms occur for 2 weeks or more outside the context of a mood episode. For schizophrenia, mood symptoms are brief relative to psychotic symptoms. Finally, a patient may be given dual diagnoses of schizophrenia and bipolar disorder if symptoms of both syndromes are present at a level that meets diagnostic criteria (APA, 2000).

Personality Disorders

Rates of comorbid personality disorders within bipolar disorder range from 33% to 50%, with particularly high rates when personality disorders are assessed during symptomatic periods (Ucok, Karaveli, Kundakci, & Yazici, 1998). Borderline personality disorder, histrionic personality disorder, and antisocial personality disorder, in particular, share symptoms with bipolar disorder. Patients with borderline personality disorder exhibit affective instability, impulsivity, and self-damaging behavior. Those with histrionic personality disorder can display seductive sexual behavior, rapidly shifting emotions, exaggerated expression of emotion, and self-dramatization. People with antisocial personality disorder have impulsive behavior, irritability, and antisocial behavior. Bipolar disorder can be distinguished from these personality disorders in that its symptoms are episodic and tied to mood changes. Therefore, it is important that clinicians examine the course of a patient's symptoms, specifically looking at mood patterns and their relationship to behavioral difficulties.

Generalized Anxiety Disorder

Restlessness, concentration difficulties, irritability, and sleep disturbance are characteristic of both generalized anxiety disorder (GAD) and bipolar disorder. However, the two disorders are easy to differentiate. In bipolar disorder, the aforementioned symptoms are related to episodic mood changes, whereas in GAD they are not. In addition, although people with GAD and bipolar disorder both have problems sleeping, bipolar patients feel rested despite their lack of sleep. According to the *DSM-IV* (APA, 2000), if a patient's GAD symptoms are confined to the course of a mood episode, he or she should be diagnosed with mood disorder and not GAD.

MULTICULTURAL AND DIVERSITY ISSUES

Intriguingly, rates of bipolar I disorder are about 1% across countries when studies are conducted using standardized interviews applied by similarly trained interviewers (Weissman, Bland, Joyce, & Newman, 1993). Some variability is apparent when studies have relied on different measures and training procedures for conducting diagnostic interviews, but such variability could reflect methodological differences (Noaghiul & Hibbeln, 2003). Nonetheless, rates of seafood consumption appear to explain some of the modest variability in rates of disorder across countries. That is, countries with higher rates of bipolar disorder tend to be those with low rates of seafood consumption (Noaghiul & Hilburn, 2003), consistent with the idea that omega-3 fatty acids are protective against mood disorders.

Little work has examined the course and outcome of bipolar disorder across different cultural groups. Similarly, little is known about how culture influences symptom expression. However, it is worth noting that in the United States, minority status has been tied to lower use of psychiatric treatment services (Wang et al., 2005). Therefore, culture may influence attitudes and expectations about treatment.

SELECTION OF TREATMENT TARGETS AND REFERRAL

The clinical interview should help set goals for treatment. This is best done within a collaborative framework. The patient should have input on what he or she would like to accomplish in therapy. The clinician helps the patient define goals that are specific, realistic, and measurable.

Medications are the bedrock of treatment for this disorder (Goldberg, 2004). The first medication that was found to be helpful in the treatment of manic symptoms was lithium, and to this day there is more evidence to support the efficacy of lithium than any other medication for bipolar disorder (see the APA Practice Guidelines, Hirschfeld et al., 2002). Beyond evidence from double-blind randomized trials that lithium reduces the severity of symptoms and the frequency of episodes (Prien, 1984), lithium is the first treatment shown to reduce suicidality (cf. Kessing, Sondergard, Kvist, & Andersen, 2005). Therefore, lithium is the first-line treatment.

Despite strong evidence for the efficacy of lithium, the side effects of lithium can be quite difficult to tolerate. About three quarters of people report side effects from lithium, which include excessive thirst, frequent urination, memory problems, tremor, weight gain, drowsiness, and diarrhea (Goodwin & Jamison, 1990). Antiseizure medications, such as valproate, have fewer side effects and have been shown to be effective mood-stabilizing agents in a series of trials.

Generally, mood-stabilizing medications have been found to be less effective in reducing depression symptoms than manic symptoms (Hlastala et al., 1997). To supplement mood-stabilizing medications, patients often are prescribed antipsychotic medications, antidepressants, and a range of other novel medication treatments (Rivas Vazquez, Johnson, Rey, Blais, & Rivas Vazquez, 2002). Antidepressants must be prescribed with caution, given the risks of inducing manic symptoms; current policy recommendations state that mood-stabilizing medications should be started before antidepressant medications are prescribed (Hirschfeld et al., 2002).

Although medications are the central treatment, there are several reasons that psychotherapy may be helpful as an adjunct to medication. Psychosocial interventions have been found to help improve adherence and decrease rates of hospitalization (Scott, 2004). Adherence is a particularly important goal in that in one major community survey, only 20% of people with bipolar disorder reported receiving outpatient treatment in the past year (Kessler et al., 1997). Even among those receiving outpatient treatment, as many as 75% have been found to experience disruptions in consistent medication maintenance within a 1-year period (Unutzer, Simon, Pabiniak, Bond, & Katon, 2000). Many patients have great fear about taking medications, and it is important to assess and discuss these fears.

Psychosocial treatment may also be helpful in restoring aspects of a person's life that are damaged by this disorder; relationships, occupations, and finances each suffer a fairly dramatic toll with each episode. One third of people remain unemployed a full year after hospitalization for mania (Harrow, Goldberg, Grossman, & Meltzer, 1990). Because family conflict, life stress, social isolation, and negative cognitive styles clearly predict the course of the disorder (Johnson & Meyer, 2004), interventions designed to help reduce these potential triggers of symptoms are important (Johnson & Leahy, 2004). Indeed, cognitive, interpersonal, family, and group therapies have been found to reduce symptoms, particularly depressive symptoms, in a series of trials (Colom et al., 2003; Frank et al., 2005; Lam et al., 2003; Miklowitz, George, Richards, Simoneau, & Suddath, 2003).

SUMMARY

Bipolar disorder can have serious consequences, making early detection and accurate diagnosis essential. A failure to screen for manic symptoms often leads to improper treatment, with severe implications for a patient's health and functioning.

We recommend a collaborative interviewing strategy beginning with the patient's presenting problem, followed by specific questions to capture both manic and depressive symptoms. It may be easier to begin with objective symptoms before moving into more difficult questions surrounding the patient's mood. Because high rates of suicide accompany this disorder, it is essential for clinicians to assess current and past suicidal ideation, plans, intent, and attempts. Instruments such as the SCID, HAM-D, and BRMS can be used to guide and provide structure to the clinical interview. Once manic and depressive symptoms have been identified, a lifechart is a useful tool to ascertain the time course of episodes, antecedents, and consequences. A comprehensive interview helps identify comorbid conditions and rule out other Axis I and Axis II disorders.

Interviewing a person with bipolar disorder may pose many challenges, and interviewers will need skill for dealing with potential problems such as pressured speech, poor insight, and concerns about stigma. Providing acutely manic patients with opportunities to influence the interview process, keeping feedback extremely behavioral, adopting a calm nonconfrontational stance, conducting family interviews, and understanding what a diagnosis means to the patient are strategies that can facilitate the diagnostic process. Concerns about stigma may particularly interfere with treatment seeking for some minorities. Sensitivity to the complexity of this disorder combined with an informed interviewing style can lay the groundwork for a collaborative treatment effort between clinician and patient. With accurate diagnosis, both medication and psychosocial treatments have much to offer for a person with bipolar disorder.

REFERENCES

Akiskal, H. S., & Benazzi, F. (2005). Optimizing the detection of bipolar II disorder in outpatient private practice: Toward a systematization of clinical diagnostic wisdom. *Journal of Clinical Psychiatry, 66,* 914–921.

American Psychiatric Association. (2000). *The diagnostic and statistical manual of mental disorders* (4th ed., Text rev.). Washington, DC: Author.

Angst, F., Stassen, H. H., Clayton, P. J., & Angst, J. (2002). Mortality of patients with mood disorders: Follow-up over 34–38 years. *Journal of Affective Disorders, 68,* 167–181.

Angst, J., Angst, F., Gerber Werder, R., & Gamma, A. (2005). Suicide in 406 mood-disorder patients with and without long-term medication: A 40 to 44 years' follow-up. *Archives of Suicide Research, 9,* 279–300.

Baldessarini, R. J., & Tondo, L. (2003). Suicide risk and treatments for patients with bipolar disorder. *Journal of the American Medical Association, 290,* 1517–1519.

Basco, M. R., & Rush, A. J. (1995). Compliance with pharmacotherapy in mood disorders. *Psychiatric Annals, 25,* 269–279.

Bech, P. (2002). The Bech-Rafaelsen Mania Scale in clinical trials of therapies for bipolar disorder: A 20-year review of its use as an outcome measure. *CNS Drugs, 16,* 47–63.

Bech, P., Bolwig, T. G., Kramp, P., & Rafaelsen, O. J. (1979). The Bech-Rafaelsen Mania Scale and the Hamilton Depression Scale: Evaluation of homogeneity and inter-observer reliability. *Acta Psychiatrica Scandinavica, 59,* 420–430.

Black, D. W., & Nasrallah, A. (1989). Hallucinations and delusions in 1,715 patients with unipolar and bipolar affective disorders. *Psychopathology, 22,* 28–34.

Brickman, A. L., LoPiccolo, C. J., & Johnson, S. L. (2002). Screening for bipolar disorder. *Psychiatric Services, 53,* 349.

Brown, E. S., Suppes, T., Adinoff, B., & Thomas, N. R. (2001). Drug abuse and bipolar disorder:

Comorbidity or misdiagnosis? *Journal of Affective Disorders, 65,* 105–115.

Chengappa, K. N. R., Levine, J., Gershon, S., & Kupfer, D. J. (2000). Lifetime prevalence of substance or alcohol abuse and dependence among subjects with bipolar I and II disorders in a voluntary registry. *Bipolar Disorders, 2,* 191–195.

Colom, F., Vieta, E., Martinez Aran, A., Reinares, M., Goikolea, J. M., Benabarre, A., et al. (2003). A randomized trial on the efficacy of group psychoeducation in the prophylaxis of recurrences in bipolar patients whose disease is in remission. *Archives of General Psychiatry, 60,* 402–407.

Corrigan, P. W., & Watson, A. C. (2005). Findings from the National Comorbidity Survey on the frequency of violent behavior in individuals with psychiatric disorders. *Psychiatry Research, 136,* 153–162.

Davidoff, S. A., Forester, B. P., Ghaemi, S. N., & Bodkin, J. A. (1998). Effect of video self-observation on development of insight on psychotic disorders. *Journal of Nervous and Mental Disease, 186,* 697–700.

Dell'Osso, L., Pini, S., Cassano, G. B., Mastrocinque, C., Seckinger, R. A., Saettoni, M., et al. (2002). Insight into illness in patients with mania, mixed mania, bipolar depression and major depression with psychotic features. *Bipolar Disorders, 4,* 315–322.

Denicoff, K. D., Smith Jackson, E. E., Disney, E. R., Suddath, R. L., Leverich, G. S., & Post, R. M. (1997). Preliminary evidence of the reliability and validity of the prospective life-chart methodology (LCM-p). *Journal of Psychiatric Research, 31,* 593–603.

Endicott, J., & Spitzer, R. (1978). A diagnostic interview: The Schedule for Affective Disorders and Schizophrenia. *Archives of General Psychiatry, 35,* 837–844.

First, M. B., Spitzer, R. L., Williams, J. B. W., & Gibbon, M. (1997). *Structured Clinical Interview for DSM-IV (SCID).* Washington, DC: American Psychiatric Association.

Frank, E., Kupfer, D. J., Thase, M. E., Mallinger, A. G., Swartz, H. A., Eagiolini, A. M., et al. (2005). Two-year outcomes for interpersonal and social rhythm therapy in individuals with bipolar I disorder. *Archives of General Psychiatry, 62,* 996–1004.

Ghaemi, S. N., Hsu, D. J., Soldani, F., & Goodwin, F. K. (2003). Antidepressants in bipolar disorder: The case for caution. *Bipolar Disorders, 5,* 421–433.

Ghaemi, S. N., Lenox, M. S., & Baldessarini, R. J. (2001). Effectiveness and safety of long-term antidepressant treatment in bipolar disorder. *Journal of Clinical Psychiatry, 62,* 565–569.

Goldberg, J. F. (2004). The changing landscape of psychopharmacology. In S. L. Johnson & R. L. Leahy (Eds.), *Psychological treatment of bipolar disorder* (pp. 109–138). New York: Guilford.

Goodwin, F. K., & Jamison, K. R. (1990). *Manic-depressive illness.* New York: Oxford University Press.

Harmer, C. J., Grayson, L., & Goodwin, G. M. (2002). Enhanced recognition of disgust in bipolar illness. *Biological Psychiatry, 51,* 298–304.

Harrow, M., Goldberg, J. F., Grossman, L. S., & Meltzer, H. Y. (1990). Outcome in manic disorders: A naturalistic follow-up study. *Archives of General Psychiatry, 47,* 665–671.

Hirschfeld, R. M. A., Bowden, C. L., Gitlin, M. J., Keck, P. E., Suppes, T., Thase, M. E., et al. (2002). Practice guideline for the treatment of patients with bipolar disorder (2nd ed.). In *American Psychiatric Association practice guidelines for the treatment of psychiatric disorders* (pp. 547–634). Washington, DC: American Psychiatric Association.

Hlastala, S. A., Frank, E., Mallinger, A. G., Thase, M. E., Ritenour, A. M., & Kupfer, D. J. (1997). Bipolar depression: An underestimated treatment challenge. *Depression and Anxiety, 5,* 73–83.

Johnson, S. L., & Fingerhut, R. (2004). Negative cognitions predict the course of bipolar depression, not mania. *Journal of Cognitive Psychotherapy, 18,* 149–162.

Johnson, S. L., & Fulford, D. (under review). *Development and validation of a measure of treatment attitudes in bipolar disorder.* Unpublished manuscript.

Johnson, S. L., & Leahy, R. L. (2004). *Psychological treatment of bipolar disorder.* New York: Guilford.

Johnson, S. L., & Meyer, B. (2004). Psychosocial predictors of symptoms. In S. L. Johnson & R. L. Leahy (Eds.), *Psychological treatment of bipolar disorder* (pp. 83–105). New York: Guilford.

Judd, L. L., Akiskal, H. S., Schetteler, P. J., Endicott, J., Maser, J., Solomon, D. A., et al. (2002). The long-term natural history of the weekly symptomatic status of bipolar I disorder. *Archives of General Psychiatry, 59,* 530–537.

Karkowski, L. M., & Kendler, K. S. (1997). An examination of the genetic relationship between bipolar and unipolar illness in an epidemiological sample. *Psychiatric Genetics, 7,* 159–163.

Keck, P. E., McElroy, S. L., Strakowski, S. M., & Stanton, S. P. (1996). Factors associated with pharmacologic noncompliance in patients with mania. *Journal of Clinical Psychiatry, 57,* 292–297.

Keller, M. B., Lavori, P. W., Kane, J. M., & Gelenberg, A. J. (1992). Subsyndromal symptoms in bipolar disorder: A comparison of standard and low serum levels of lithium. *Archives of General Psychiatry, 49,* 371–376.

Kessing, L. V., Sondergard, L., Kvist, K., & Andersen, P. K. (2005). Suicide risk in patients treated with lithium. *Archives of General Psychiatry, 62,* 860–866.

Kessler, R. C., Rubinow, D. R., Holmes, C., Abelson, J. M., & Zhao, S. (1997). The epidemiology of *DSM-III-R* bipolar I disorder in a general population survey. *Psychological Medicine, 27,* 1079–1089.

Kleindienst, N., Engel, R. R., & Greil, W. (2005). Which clinical factors predict response to prophylactic lithium? A systematic review for bipolar disorders. *Bipolar Disorders, 7,* 404–417.

Kruger, S., Young, L. T., & Braunig, P. (2005). Pharmacotherapy of bipolar mixed states. *Bipolar Disorders, 7,* 205–215.

Lam, D. H., Watkins, E. R., Hayward, P., Bright, J., Wright, K., & Kerr, N. (2003). A randomized controlled study of cognitive therapy for relapse prevention for bipolar affective disorder: Outcome of the first year. *Archives General Psychiatry, 60,* 145–152.

Lembke, A., & Ketter, T. A. (2002). Impaired recognition of facial emotion in mania. *American Journal of Psychiatry, 159,* 302–304.

Lenzi, A., Rinaldi, A., Bianco, I., Balestri, C., & Marazziti, D. (1996). Psychotic symptoms in mood disorders:

Evaluation of 159 inpatients. *European Psychiatry,* *11,* 396–399.

Lish, J. D., Dime Meenan, S., Whybrow, P. C., & Price, R. A. (1994). The National Depressive and Manic-Depressive Association (DMDA) survey of bipolar members. *Journal of Affective Disorders, 31,* 281–294.

Miklowitz, D. J., George, E. L., Richards, J. A., Simoneau, T. L., & Suddath, R. L. (2003). A randomized study of family-focused psychoeducation and pharmacotherapy in the outpatient management of bipolar disorder. *Archives of General Psychiatry,* *60,* 904–912.

Miller, I. W., Bishop, S. B., Norman, W. H., & Maddever, H. (1985). The Modified Hamilton Rating Scale for Depression: Reliability and validity. *Psychiatry Research, 14,* 131–142.

Mitchell, P. B., Slade, T., & Andrews, G. (2004). Twelve-month prevalence and disability of *DSM-IV* bipolar disorder in an Australian general population survey. *Psychological Medicine, 34,* 777–785.

Murray, C. J., & Lopez, A. D. (1997). Mortality by cause for eight regions of the world: Global burden of disease study. *Lancet, 349,* 1498–1504.

Noaghiul, S., & Hibbeln, J. R. (2003). Cross-national comparisons of seafood consumption and rates of bipolar disorders. *American Journal of Psychiatry, 160,* 2222–2227.

Prien, R. F. (1984). Drug therapy in the prevention of recurrences in unipolar and bipolar affective disorders: Report of the NIMH Collaborative Study Group comparing lithium carbonate, imipramine, and a lithium carbonate–imipramine combination. *Archives of General Psychiatry, 41,* 1096–1104.

Rivas Vazquez, R. A., Johnson, S. L., Rey, G. J., Blais, M. A., & Rivas Vazquez, A. (2002). Current treatments for bipolar disorder: A review and update for psychologists. *Professional Psychology: Research and Practice, 33,* 212–223.

Scott, J. (2004). Treatment outcome studies. In S. L. Johnson & R. L. Leahy (Eds.), *Psychological treatment of bipolar disorder* (pp. 226–241). New York: Guilford.

Solomon, D. A., Leon, A. C., Endicott, J., Coryell, W. H., Mueller, T. I., Posternak, M. A., et al. (2003). Unipolar mania over the course of a 20-year follow-up study. *American Journal of Psychiatry, 160,* 2049–2051.

Svarstad, B. L., Shireman, T. I., & Sweeney, J. K. (2001). Using drug claims data to assess the relationship of medication adherence with hospitalization and costs. *Psychiatric Services, 52,* 805–811.

Ucok, A., Karaveli, D., Kundakci, T., & Yazici, O. (1998). Comorbidity of personality disorders with bipolar mood disorders. *Comprehensive Psychiatry,* *39,* 72–74.

Unutzer, J., Simon, G., Pabiniak, C., Bond, K., & Katon, W. (2000). The use of administrative data to assess quality of care for bipolar disorder in a large staff model HMO. *General Hospital Psychiatry, 22,* 1–10.

Wahl, O. F. (1999). Mental health consumers' experience of stigma. *Schizophrenia Bulletin, 25,* 467–478.

Wang, P. S., Lane, M., Olfson, M., Pincus, H. A., Wells, K. B., & Kessler, R. C. (2005). Twelve-month use of mental health services in the United States: Results from the National Comorbidity Survey Replication. *Archives of General Psychiatry, 62,* 629–640.

Weissman, M. M., Bland, R., Joyce, P. R., & Newman, S. (1993). Sex differences in rates of depression: Cross-national perspectives. *Journal of Affective Disorders, 29,* 77–84.

Winters, R. W., Johnson, S. L., & Cuellar, A. K. (under review). *Regulatory deficits in unipolar depression and bipolar disorder.* Unpublished manuscript.

Zarate, C. A. J., & Tohen, M. F. (2001). Bipolar disorder and comorbid substance use disorders. In J. R. Hubbard & P. R. Martin (Eds.), *Substance abuse in the mentally and physically disabled* (pp. 59–75). New York: Marcel Dekker.

12

SCHIZOPHRENIA

DAVID ROE, ABRAHAM RUDNICK, AND KIM T. MUESER

DESCRIPTION OF THE DISORDER

Schizophrenia is a complex psychiatric illness characterized by many difficulties such as psychosis, apathy, social withdrawal, and disrupted functioning. It is considered to be the most severe and disabling of all adult psychiatric illnesses. The lifetime prevalence of schizophrenia in the general population is approximately 1% (Keith, Regier, & Rae, 1991). In general, the prevalence of schizophrenia is remarkably stable across a wide range of different demographic and environmental conditions, such as gender, race, religion, population density, and level of industrialization (Jablensky, 1989). However, schizophrenia is more common in some social circumstances, such as urban areas of industrialized countries (Peen & Dekker, 1997).

Because of its complexity, assessment of the disorder is necessarily broad based and involves various clinical interviews. In order to understand the wide scope of assessment, interviewing, and treatment, it is important to first review the diagnostic criteria and core psychopathology that define the illness and the common associated features, including comorbid disorders, that complicate the clinical picture.

Current classifications of schizophrenia are based primarily on the work of Kraepelin, who focused on the long-term deteriorating course of the illness (which he called dementia praecox),

and Bleuler, who emphasized the core symptoms of the disorder as difficulties in thinking straight (lose associations), incongruous or flattened affect, loss of goal-directed behavior or ambivalence caused by conflicting impulses, and retreat into an inner world (autism, as coined by Eugene Bleuler). The two major classification systems, the *Diagnostic and Statistical Manual of Mental Disorders* (*DSM*; American Psychiatric Association, 1980, 1994) and the *International Classification of Diseases* (World Health Organization, 1992) both specify that the diagnosis of schizophrenia is based on the presence of specific symptoms, the absence of other symptoms, and psychosocial difficulties that persist over a significant period of time. Symptoms and impairments must be present in the absence of general medical or so-called organic conditions (e.g., substance abuse and neurological disorders such as Huntington's disease) that could lead to a similar clinical presentation.

Core Symptoms and Impairments of Schizophrenia

For descriptive purposes, the core symptoms of schizophrenia are divided into three broad categories: positive, negative, and cognitive symptoms or impairments.

Positive symptoms are the *presence* of perceptual experiences, thoughts, and behaviors that are ordinarily absent in people without a psychiatric illness. The typical positive symptoms are hallucinations (primarily hearing, but also feeling, seeing, tasting, or smelling in the absence of environmental stimuli), delusions (false or patently absurd beliefs that are not shared by others in the person's environment), and disorganization of thought and behavior (disconnected thoughts and strange or apparently purposeless behavior). Some positive symptoms are considered highly specific, such as first-rank symptoms (e.g., delusions of thought insertion or auditory hallucinations with a running commentary), and perhaps even pathognomonic (particularly affect, i.e., emotional expression, that is inappropriate to the content of the person's thoughts at that time). For many people with schizophrenia, positive symptoms fluctuate in their intensity over time and are episodic, with approximately 20–40% experiencing persistent positive symptoms (Curson, Patel, Liddle, & Barnes, 1988).

Negative symptoms are the opposite of positive symptoms in that they are defined by the *absence* of behaviors, cognitions, and emotions ordinarily present in people without psychiatric disorders. Common examples of negative symptoms include constricted or flat affect (diminished or absent expressiveness of facial expression, other body language or voice tone), anhedonia (loss of pleasure), anergia (loss of energy or initiative or ability to follow through on plans), and alogia (diminished amount or content of speech). All of these negative symptoms are common in schizophrenia, and they tend to be stable over time (Mueser, Bellack, Douglas, & Wade, 1991). Furthermore, negative symptoms have a pervasive impact on the ability of people with schizophrenia to engage and function socially and to sustain independent living (Pogue-Geile, 1989).

Cognitive impairments in schizophrenia include deficits in attention, memory, and executive functions (e.g., planning ahead, abstract thinking, and cognitive flexibility), and although in many cases they are stable, there is some evidence that they can worsen over time in late adulthood (Kurtz, 2005), particularly for a subgroup who have poor outcomes from early on. These impairments interfere with the person's ability to focus for sustained periods of time, which is highly related to functional disability, resulting in significant disruption to independent community living and work. Among the various cognitive impairments involved, there is

evidence that social cognition is also impaired (Penn, Corrigan, & Racenstein, 1998) and that this impairment tends to be stable over time. This may result in poor social skills, leading to further problems in community integration.

Functional Disability and Handicap or Disadvantage

In addition to requiring presence of specific symptoms, modern diagnostic systems also require evidence of sustained functional disability (e.g., more than 6 months for *DSM-IV*) for the diagnosis of schizophrenia. Common difficulties in psychosocial functioning include problems fulfilling the roles of a worker, student, or homemaker, poor social relationships, and difficulties to care for oneself (e.g., disrupted grooming, hygiene, ability to cook, clean, do laundry, and attend to health care needs).

Although most people with schizophrenia indicate that competitive employment is a primary goal of theirs, a small minority (less than 15%) are actually working at any given time (Cook & Razzano, 2000; Drake et al., 1999). Problems in functioning contribute to difficulties in several other areas, resulting in handicap or disadvantage. The poor financial standing of many people with schizophrenia may cause them to reside in impoverished living conditions (e.g., in neighborhoods rife with substance abuse and crime) and to maintain poor dietary practices. Therefore, treatment for schizophrenia often entails substantial attention to the most common consequences of disrupted functioning in schizophrenia, such as unstable or unsafe housing, inadequate food and clothing (especially for homeless people), and neglected health problems.

Associated Features

Positive, negative, and cognitive symptoms and impairments and functional disability include the core characteristics of schizophrenia, there are additional associated problems. These include affective disorders such as postpsychotic depression (many times leading to suicide, which occurs in up to 10% of people with schizophrenia), anxiety disorders such as obsessive-compulsive and posttraumatic stress disorder, increased use of illicit drugs and alcohol, aggression (mainly if the person has previous aggression, nonadherence, and substance use), limited insight into illness, and poor treatment adherence.

INTERVIEWING STRATEGIES

Development of more reliable criteria for schizophrenia in the *DSM-III* (American Psychiatric Association, 1980) was an extremely important development because until then the reliability of the diagnosis was low (Matarazzo, 1983). The main advantage of structured interviews is that they provide a standardized approach for gathering information, which reduces the variability of the assessment. Among the most important contributions to increased reliability were the development and use of interviewing strategies. Another advantage is that it provides guidelines for determining whether a specific symptom exists. On the downside, in order to fully benefit from the advantages of structured interviews, a fair amount of training and persistence are needed.

A comprehensive assessment interview should commence with evaluation of basic characteristics of the disorder, followed by frequently associated features and common comorbid diagnoses. In the following section we focus on interviewing strategies for assessing these areas.

Specific Domains of Assessment

A wide range of assessment instruments, divided primarily into self-report and interview-based instruments, has been developed to evaluate the severity of psychiatric symptoms. The Structured Clinical Interview for *DSM-IV* (SCID; First, Spitzer, Gibbon, & Williams, 1996) is the most widely used diagnostic assessment instrument for research studies of people with psychiatric disabilities in the United States. Psychiatric rating scales, based on semistructured interviews, have also been developed to provide a useful, reliable measure of the wide range of psychiatric symptoms commonly present in people with a psychiatric disability. These scales typically contain between 1 and 50 specifically defined items, each rated on a severity scale of five to seven points. Some interview-based scales have been developed to measure the full range of psychiatric symptoms, such as the Brief Psychiatric Rating Scale (BPRS; Lukoff, Nuechterlein, & Ventura, 1986) and the Positive and Negative Syndrome Scale (Kay, Opler, & Fiszbein, 1987), whereas other interview-based scales have been designed to tap specific dimensions, such as the Scale for the Assessment of Negative Symptoms (Andreasen, 1984) and the Hamilton Depression Rating Scale (Hamilton, 1960). The same classification holds true for self-report scales.

Interview-based psychiatric rating scales typically include a combination of symptoms elicited through direct questioning and symptoms observed in the course of the interview, as well as symptoms elicited by a collateral history taking (from caregivers and clinical documentation). For example, on the BPRS, depression is rated by asking questions such as "What has your mood been lately?" and "Have you been feeling down?" Mannerisms and posturing, on the other hand, are rated based on the behavioral observations of the interviewer. Psychiatric symptom scores can be either added up to get an overall index of symptom severity based on a rating scale or summarized in subscale scores corresponding to symptom dimensions such as negative, positive, and comorbid (affective and other) symptoms.

Positive and Negative Symptoms and Cognitive Impairments

Mental health professionals may use a variety of methods to assess positive and negative symptoms and cognitive impairments, including personal observation, interviews with collaterals, tasks, and use of standardized scales—clinician rated as well as self-report—designed to measure one type of symptom or all symptoms. The most widely used instruments include the BPRS (Lukoff et al., 1986; Overall & Gorham, 1962), the Scale for the Assessment of Negative Symptoms (SANS; Andreasen, 1982), the Scale for the Assessment of Positive Symptoms (SAPS; Andreasen, 1984), and the Positive and Negative Syndrome Scale (PANSS; Kay et al., 1987), all of which are designed to be administered as semistructured clinical interviews. The BPRS was developed as a general measure of severe psychopathology in psychiatric disorders and includes items relevant to positive, negative, disorganization, and mood symptoms (Mueser, Curran, & McHugo, 1997). The SANS was developed to measure the negative symptoms of schizophrenia, and factor analyses indicate three correlated clusters of symptoms: apathy-anhedonia, blunted or flattened affect, and alogia-inattention (Sayers, Curran, & Mueser,

1996). The SAPS was developed to assess the positive symptoms of schizophrenia, including hallucinations, delusions, bizarre behavior, and disorganized thought. The PANSS incorporates all the 18 items of the original BPRS and includes additional items tapping negative symptoms, cognitive impairments, and comorbid symptoms. Cognitive impairments can be assessed by a wide variety of instruments, mainly addressing working memory, attention or vigilance, verbal learning and memory, visual learning and memory, speed of processing, reasoning and problem solving, and social cognition (Bilder, 2006).

Role Functioning

Role functioning is the extent to which a person is able to meet the expectations of socially defined roles, such as employee, student, parent, or spouse. People with schizophrenia often have difficulty securing and sustaining competitive employment and therefore supporting themselves. The effects of schizophrenia on work productivity have been documented extensively (Marwaha & Johnson, 2004). People typically have difficulty getting jobs, working the number of hours required by many jobs, and keeping jobs.

Schizophrenia can also affect school performance because of the early age of onset, often leading patients to prematurely terminate educational attainment (Kessler, Foster, Saunders, & Stang, 1995). Dropping out of school early is problematic for many patients for a variety of reasons, including feelings of failure and lower levels of education, which are also a disadvantage when they are trying to enter the workforce (Mueser, Salyers, & Mueser, 2001).

In terms of assessment, work-related problems can be evaluated by obtaining information such as the type of job a person has, the wages and benefits paid, the number of hours worked, and satisfaction with the job. Work history information may be similarly obtained, such as prior jobs the person has had, the longest duration of competitive employment, wages and hours worked at the last competitive job, and reasons for job termination. This information is readily obtained through a direct interview with the patient and others.

Some structured interviews of social functioning also contain questions about work performance, such as the Social Adjustment Scale-II (Schooler, Hogarty, & Weissman, 1979).

Observational measures of the quality of vocational functioning have also been developed, such as the Work Behavior Inventory (Lysaker, Bell, Bryson, & Zito, 1993). Observational measures such as these generally rely on another person who can complete the measure, such as the employer. Therefore, these measures are limited to vocational settings in which the patient has disclosed his or her disability to the employer or in which all the workers have a disability.

Independent Living and Self-Care Skills

Self-care skills involve the behaviors or activities of daily living (ADLs) necessary to maintain one's health, to present in a socially appropriate manner, and to meet one's basic living needs. Common self-care skills include personal hygiene and grooming, dental care, and self-managing illnesses such as diabetes. Independent living skills are known as instrumental ADLs (I-ADLs), or skills necessary for living on one's own, such as the ability to use public transportation, budget money and pay bills, do laundry, cook, and maintain one's apartment safely.

One of the best-validated instruments for assessing these skills is the Independent Living Skills Survey (Wallace, Liberman, Tauber, & Wallace, 2000). This measure includes both a client and a staff (or significant other) version and assesses a wide range of specific behaviors related to self-care and independent living. Many other instruments for measuring community functioning also tap some independent living skills, such as the Social and Adaptive Functions Evaluation (Harvey et al., 1997) and the Multnomah Community Ability Scale (Barker, Barron, & McFarlane, 1994).

Assessing Associated Features

Because schizophrenia usually affects many aspects of the person's life, it is essential to assess also the common associated features of the illness mentioned earlier, which include affective and anxiety disorders, substance abuse, lack of insight, and nonadherence.

Affective and Anxiety Disorders. People with schizophrenia disproportionately suffer from a lack of positive feelings (anhedonia) and high levels of negative affect, particularly depression, anxiety, and hostility (Blanchard & Panzarella,

1998; Glynn, 1998). Therefore, mood and level of anxiety are clearly important domains to assess in formulating a treatment plan, particularly given evidence that negative affect is associated with a poorer clinical course in people with schizophrenia (Blanchard & Panzarella, 1998).

Several instruments can be used to assess mood and anxiety, including the Beck Depression Inventory (BDI; Beck & Beck, 1972) and the Spielberger State-Trait Anxiety Scale (STAI; Spielberger, Gorsuch, & Lushene, 1970). The BDI and STAI, both of which are self-report tools, also have the advantage of being empirically validated and may be repeated frequently to monitor depression and anxiety throughout the course of treatment. A schizophrenia-specific instrument with good psychometric properties that was generated specifically for depression in schizophrenia is the Calgary Depression Scale for Schizophrenia (Addington, Addington, & Schissel, 1990). Posttraumatic stress disorder (PTSD) can be screened for by the PTSD Checklist (Blanchard, Jones-Alexander, Buckley, & Forneris, 1996), which is a self-report measure that requires respondents to rate the degree to which they experience each of the 17 PTSD symptoms identified in the *DSM-IV* in relation to a prespecified traumatic event.

Substance Abuse. Given the high prevalence of substance abuse in schizophrenia, a comprehensive assessment should explore active substance use, both past and present. One such instrument, the Dartmouth Assessment of Lifestyle Instrument (DALI; Rosenberg et al., 1998), is an interviewer-administered scale that may be completed in approximately 6 minutes and was designed as a brief screen for detecting substance use disorder in people with severe mental illness, including schizophrenia. Items on the DALI address patterns of substance use, loss of control, consequences of use, dependence in terms of physiological syndromes, and subjective distress.

Even if substance use is denied, some measure of caution should be maintained, particularly for young, single men with lower-than-average levels of education, given that these men have the highest rates of substance use comorbidity (Mueser et al., 2000). If substance use is suspected, random urine drug screens and interviews with close informants may be conducted to test for current or recent substance use. People who acknowledge a substance use history should be monitored closely because of the chronic, relapsing nature of substance use disorders.

Poor Treatment Adherence. Studies have demonstrated that up to 55% of people with schizophrenia have significant difficulty following treatment recommendations, including taking medications as prescribed (Fenton, Blyler, & Heinssen, 1997). Poor treatment adherence is associated with increased symptom levels and functional disability and higher rates of relapse and rehospitalization. A more thorough assessment of adherence to medication regimens should include evaluation of barriers to adherence, including unpleasant side effects, complexity of medication regimens, cognitive impairment, poor insight or awareness of illness and of the need for treatment, poor alliance with mental health care providers, insufficient supervision during administration, family beliefs about illness or medications, mental status or current symptoms (e.g., paranoia about medications), and perceived benefit of medications (Cramer & Rosenheck, 1999; Kemp, Hayward, Applewaite, Everitt, & David, 1996; Weiden et al., 1994). Standardized scales designed to evaluate treatment adherence and attitudes toward medications may help identify targets for intervention. One such measure is the Rating of Medication Influences (ROMI) scale (Weiden et al., 1994). Other instruments include the Drug Attitudes Inventory (Hogan, Awad, & Eastwood, 1983), a self-report measure of willingness to take medications, and the Neuroleptic Dysphoria Scale (Van Putten & May, 1978), designed for use with acutely psychotic people.

INTERVIEWING OBSTACLES AND SOLUTIONS

Psychiatric diagnosis uses generic clinical assessment skills, such as combining open-ended and close-ended questions, as well as specialized skills that are needed to overcome obstacles associated with the psychiatric impairments. In this section we discuss such common obstacles, and proposed solutions to them, focusing on people with schizophrenia.

Obstacle 1: Preinterview Baggage

Obstacle: Some of the obstacles may begin even before the interviewee has attended the interview or met the interviewers. These may be related to the interviewee's feelings, expectations, and concerns, perhaps based on past experience. For instance, even before coming to the interview the interviewee may feel threatened, expect to be harshly judged and criticized, and be concerned about the possible consequences of the interview. Such preinterview feelings may manifest themselves in a range of different ways. For example, an interviewee who is feeling threatened may be very guarded or may be aggressive as a response to his or her perceived threat. Similarly, an interviewee who expects to be judged harshly may be hesitant at best or, worse, reluctant and oppositional to reveal anything and may even be hostile and antagonistic toward the interviewer. Finally, an interviewee who is concerned with the consequences of the interview might be busy trying to guess how he or she might best respond to questions asked by the interviewer, which would seriously threaten the validity of the information elicited.

Solution: Because the effectiveness and quality of all interviews depend on rapport, a starting point for the interviewer meeting an interviewee with the aforementioned concerns would be to develop empathy and understanding of the potential origins of the interviewee's baggage. This may include recognizing that the interviewee may have been in several clinical settings and situations that he or she perceived as threatening (e.g., being interviewed at a teaching hospital in front a group of trainees who were all strangers), was indeed judged harshly (e.g., for discontinuing medication against medical advice or using substances), or suffered from negatively perceived consequences of previous interviews (e.g., forced interventions or involuntarily hospitalization). In addition, the interviewer may use his or her clinical skills to help the interviewee feel more comfortable by expressing concern and empathy and greeting the interviewee and his or her story in a nonjudgmental manner. It is often useful in such cases to focus on the interviewee's immediate emotions and needs and address the discomfort that he or she might be feeling ("I have a sense that you are not feeling very comfortable. I was wondering whether you might be willing to share how you are feeling right now."). In addition to addressing the interpersonal context, there are several practical ways in which the interviewer can help the interviewee feel more at ease. Examples include introducing himself or herself and describing what to expect in terms of the format of the interview (its nature, rationale, and length) and what will follow in a clear and detailed manner. The interviewee should then be invited to ask questions and express any concerns, which should be addressed before proceeding. Forming a collaborative atmosphere in which the interviewee actively participates in an interview rather than being a passive subject is important. In addition, respecting the interviewee's style and pacing oneself to better match the interviewee's pace gradually increases the interviewee's trust and participation. Finally, when the interviewee is uncomfortable, it is particularly useful to start the interview with a warmup phase that includes easy-to-answer, factual questions to help the interviewee become more at ease. As the interviewee feels more comfortable, follow-up questions can be particularly helpful to gather more information about particular areas of significance.

Obstacle 2: Lack of Insight Into Illness

Obstacle: Because the interview usually takes place in a clinical setting (outpatient clinic or hospital), a typical early question is "What brought you here?" or "How did you come to be in the hospital?" This question is meant to provide a neutral stimulus to encourage the interviewee to reveal the sequence of events that preceded current treatment and to help obtain an overview of the present episode. One potential obstacle is that the interviewee may lack insight into the behaviors, experiences, or beliefs that characterize the current episode and preceded current interventions or hospitalization. The interviewee may deny having a problem altogether ("I do not know, everything was just fine."), believe that a problem led to being treated but that the problem was not his or hers ("They [family] wanted me taken away because they needed the room in the house."), or believe that he or she has a problem but that it is not a mental problem ("I was feeling weak and they wanted to do some tests on me"). These cases, reflecting various degrees and styles of lack of insight, which is common among people with schizophrenia, present a potential obstacle for the interviewer seeking to obtain an overview of the current episode and psychiatric history.

Solution: Although it may be frustrating for the interviewer, it is not useful to be confrontational or repeat the question with the hope that the interviewee will eventually "gain insight." It is important instead to acknowledge the potential value in the information collected rather than get angry or anxious about failing to elicit the desired information. Information collected from an interviewee who seems to have limited insight into his or her condition may be of value for several reasons. First, discrepancies between the perceptions of interviewees and mental health providers may not always indicate lack of insight (Roe, Lereya, & Fennig, 2001). Second, even if the interviewee clearly lacks insight, it is clinically useful to explore and understand how different events are perceived and experienced by the interviewee (Roe & Kravetz, 2003). In addition, in some cases lack of insight may serve as a defense from the threat to self posed by the illness and its social and personal meaning (Roe & Davidson, 2005). Therefore, acknowledging the clinical value of the interviewee's report, even if it is not consistent with that of the interviewer, may help the interviewer convey genuine respect for the interviewee's views rather than become inpatient, angry, or confrontational regarding the interviewee's "lack of insight."

Obstacle 3: The Guarded and the Suggestible Interviewee

Obstacle: The validity of the information collected may be seriously compromised in the extreme cases of the particularly guarded or suggestible interviewee. At one extreme, the guarded interviewee may not reveal much information, particularly in relation to symptoms. Because clinical assessment in psychiatry depends to a great degree on self-report, interviews with guarded interviewees may create the false impression that the person experiences fewer symptoms than he or she actually does. At the other extreme is the suggestible interviewee, who is easily influenced by the interviewer's questions and comes to believe that he or she has experienced any symptom he or she is asked about and therefore might be assessed as being more symptomatic than he or she really is. Regardless of which of

the two extremes a person is at, the information collected through the interview may not accurately reflect the person's condition.

Solution: There are several possible solutions to these problems. First, the interviewer can be explicit about the value of eliciting the most valid information and its importance in helping to generate the most beneficial and tailored treatment plan. Second, the interviewer can gently test whether the interviewee understood the questions. Third, once he or she identifies such a tendency, the interviewer should be particularly careful with leading questions that imply to the interviewee what the "right" answer is (which would motivate the guarded interviewee to deny the symptom and the suggestible interviewee to become convinced he or she has it). Finally, it is important that the interviewer use his or her judgment and clinical skills and evaluate whether other sources (including observations within the interview) are consistent with the interviewee's self report.

Obstacle 4: Assessing Symptoms

Obstacle: Many obstacles to collecting reliable information during an interview are intensified when one is trying to elicit information about symptoms. As already discussed, interviewees often deny having symptoms altogether, are reluctant to discuss these experiences, or are highly suggestible and easily convinced that they have many of the symptoms asked about. All of these obstacles make it particularly difficult to achieve the primary goal of a diagnostic interview: to assess interviewees' symptoms in a reliable manner. The inherent difficulty is that because of the absence of laboratory test markers and indicators, psychiatric diagnosis depends heavily on self-report, which is subject to many distortions.

Solution: Ironically, the interview's inherent limitations are also its strength because the complex process and data it reveals can facilitate the generation of diagnostic hypotheses. For instance, by evaluating the content and logical flow of the interviewee's verbalization, the interviewer may be able to learn about the presence of symptoms such as hallucinations and thought disorganization (e.g., loose associations, circumstantiality, and thought blocking). Although delusions may be readily assessed at times because of the interviewee's preoccupation with the theme or idea, at other times more engagement in lengthier discussions is needed before the interviewee begins to reveal much about these delusional ideas. In addition, observations of the interviewee's behavior and affective expressivity during the interview can detect symptoms such as constricted or inappropriate affect. Finally, the interviewer may ask himself or herself whether he or she is losing track of the point the interviewee is trying to make, which can serve as a useful cue to consider different symptoms such as tangential speech or derailing.

Obstacle 5: Symptoms Getting in the Way

Obstacle: The core symptoms of the disorder can make interviewing a person with schizophrenia difficult. Examples include the interviewee actively hallucinating, being delusional, displaying disorganized thought or behavior, or presenting with severe negative symptoms, cognitive impairments, or comorbid symptoms such as anxiety. Common effects of these symptoms and impairments are distraction of the interviewee, which disrupts the flow of the interview, and poor collaboration on his or her part.

Solution: There are various ways to address such disruptions. One way is to break up the interview into smaller parts in order to accommodate the person's attention span. This can involve taking more frequent rest breaks or conducting the interview over a few days. This approach can also be used within the interview by breaking questions down into smaller ones so that the interviewee can more easily retain and process the questions. Finally, it is often useful to identify incentives for the person to participate as fully as possible in the interview, both explaining the benefits of the interview, providing token rewards (e.g., refreshment breaks), and linking participation in the assessment to helping the person achieve some other personally desired goal.

Obstacle 6: The Importance of Context

Obstacle: Another obstacle is a lack of sufficient information on personal or cultural context within which the diagnostic information could be meaningfully understood. This can occur in transcultural situations if the interviewer is not versed in the interviewee's language and culture. It can also occur if insufficient time is allocated to the interview. Finally, it can also occur if there is lack of trust on the part of the interviewee, be it because of paranoia, a traumatic history with the health care system, unsatisfactory communication skills on the part of the interviewer, or other factors.

Solution: To understand the personal context it is useful to explore how symptoms relate to various domains of a person's life. To gather such information it is important that the interviewer ask about a range of other contexts, including work, living, leisure, and social relationships, to try to identify the often complex mutual influences between these contexts and symptoms. Another imperative aspect of the context is its longitudinal course (e.g., time of onset of the first psychotic episode), which would affect the developmental abilities of the interviewee (e.g., educational level and interpersonal experiences). Also, the interviewer should be sensitive to paranoia or a traumatic history on the part of the interviewee that may disrupt the interview, and use appropriate communication skills to build trust (e.g., fully disclosing the possible risks and expected benefits of the interview; giving the interviewee as much control as possible over the interview by asking open-ended questions and inviting the person to tell his or her life story; and using empathic verbalizations). Last but not least is the cultural and spiritual context. Because the interviewer functions as a yardstick to some degree in evaluating the interviewee's beliefs, it is imperative that the clinician be familiar with the interviewee's general and health beliefs in relation to those of the culture to which he or she belongs. The next section discusses cultural considerations in greater depth.

CASE ILLUSTRATION WITH DIALOGUE

Arthur, a 24-year-old bachelor who lives with his widowed mother, is referred by his family doctor for a psychiatric consultation because of prolonged social withdrawal. The family doctor provides information that Arthur was diagnosed with a first and only psychotic episode when he was 17. He was treated then for a couple of months with an antipsychotic medication that resolved his psychosis, after which he discontinued the medication, and since then he has not received psychiatric care. Because Arthur wants to be seen in consultation without his mother, the mother sends a letter to the consultant suggesting that Arthur was always somewhat withdrawn but that since his psychotic episode he has completely isolated himself, confining his life to watching TV, eating, and sleeping, and that he does not share his thoughts with her. The following are parts of the consultation interview, focusing on some of the aforementioned obstacles and solutions.

Interviewer: Hello, Arthur. My name is Dr. Paul Brown, and I am a psychiatrist. You can call me by my first or last name, whatever you feel most comfortable with. Please have a seat. . . . Do you know why your family doctor referred you to me?

Arthur: First I want to know what my mother wrote in the letter she sent you [obstacle number 1].

I: That's fair enough because your mother did not indicate that you should not know what she wrote in the letter. As I understand from your family doctor, you wanted to see me alone, without your mother. Therefore, she thought it would be helpful for me to know how she sees how you have been doing, considering that you live with her and that she has known you since you were born. Does that make sense?

A: I guess. So what did she write in the letter?

I: Actually, not a lot. Mainly that in the last few years you have been keeping to yourself, staying at home and making do with TV, eating, and sleeping. That also seems to be the reason for your family doctor referring you to me. What do you think about that?

A: She's always on my case, and now she has managed to bring the Doc into the loop. I have just not decided what I want to do in my life, so I am waiting it out.

I: It is very important for me to hear your perspective on what has been going on in your life. That is my purpose for this meeting, so that I can give you my impression of what's been going on in your life and whether there is anything that could be helpful to you. Is that okay? And would you have another purpose for this meeting?

A: My purpose was to know what my mother wrote to you in the letter. I know that now, so we can go on talking. Who knows, maybe you can help me understand why I am stuck.

I: In order to try to do that, I would need to ask you questions. The meeting will probably take around an hour or so. If you need a break, let me know, and we will do that. Can we start?

A: Sure.

I: Let's start with some basic facts. How old are you. . . .

I: You have told me that your relationship with the TV has become that of a love-hate one, because sometimes it is your friend and sometimes it is not. You seemed a bit reluctant to go into more detail [obstacle number 3]. Would you be comfortable explaining it to me, so I can understand what's going on in your life better?

A: You'll laugh at me.

I: I promise you I take you very seriously.

A: Sure?

I: My job is to help people, whatever they are experiencing. The more I know what you are experiencing, the more I can help you.

A: Okay. Sometimes the TV sends me messages. . . .

I: I notice that during our talk once in a while you seem to lose your thread of thought, so that I had to repeat some of my questions [obstacle number 5]. Did you notice that?

A: I am not used to talking so much, so maybe I am tired.

I: Do you lose your thread of thought at home?

A: Maybe.

I: There are many reasons why that could happen, and one of the things I can help out with is to find out how much of that is happening, and if so why. For that, I would need you to answer a few questions and to follow a few instructions. This will only take a few minutes. Can we do that now?

A: Go ahead.

I: This is called the Folstein Mini–Mental Status Examination. It is not about passing or failing, but rather gives both of us information on things like your concentration and memory. The first question is, what is the date today?

MULTICULTURAL AND DIVERSITY ISSUES

Understanding different cultural beliefs, values, and social structures can have important implications for the diagnosis of schizophrenia and its assessment. Ethnic groups may differ in their willingness to report symptoms, as illustrated by one study that reported that African American interviewees were less likely to report symptoms than Hispanics or non-Hispanic Whites (Skilbeck, Acosta, Yamamoto, & Evans, 1984). In addition, many other studies have found that African Americans are more likely to be diagnosed with schizophrenia than other ethnic groups (Adams, Dworkin, & Rosenberg, 1984). Knowledge of cultural norms is critical in avoiding the possible misinterpretation of culturally bound beliefs and practices when arriving at a diagnosis. Several studies have shown that ethnic differences in diagnosis vary as a function of both the interviewee's and the interviewer's ethnicity (Loring & Powell, 1988). Of note, misdiagnosis of affective disorders such as schizophrenia is the most common problem with the diagnosis of ethnic minorities in the United States (Jones, Gray, & Parsons, 1981, 1983).

DIFFERENTIAL DIAGNOSIS AND BEHAVIORAL ASSESSMENT

Differential Diagnosis

The symptoms of schizophrenia overlap with those of many other psychiatric disorders, and therefore the presence of other syndromes should be assessed and ruled out before the diagnosis of schizophrenia can be made.

Schizoaffective and mood disorders are commonly confused with schizophrenia because they are mistakenly thought to simply assume the presence of both psychotic and affective symptoms (particularly in bipolar and psychotic depression types). But it is not the predominance of the psychotic versus the affective component that determines the diagnosis but rather the timing of the psychotic and affective symptoms. If psychotic symptoms always overlap with affective symptoms, the person is diagnosed with an affective disorder, whereas if psychotic symptoms are present in the absence of an affective syndrome, the person meets criteria for either schizoaffective disorder or schizophrenia. The distinction between schizophrenia and schizoaffective disorder is even more difficult because judgment must be made as to whether the affective symptoms have been present for a substantial part of the person's illness.

Although the differential diagnosis between schizophrenia and schizoaffective disorder is difficult, the clinical implications of this distinction may be less important than that between the affective disorders and either schizophrenia or schizoaffective disorder. Some research on family history and treatment response suggests that schizophrenia and schizoaffective disorder may be similar disorders and may respond to the similar interventions (Levinson & Mowry, 1991). Therefore, the information provided in this chapter on schizophrenia may also pertain to schizoaffective disorder, and the differential diagnosis between the two disorders may not be of major importance from a clinical perspective, particularly with recent research showing that some second-generation antipsychotic medications have not only antipsychotic properties but also mood-stabilizing properties (Citrome, Goldberg, & Stahl, 2005).

Recent research (Mueser, Goodman et al., 1998; Mueser et al., 2002) reveals high rates of exposure to trauma and PTSD comorbidity among people with severe mental illness such as schizophrenia. These findings and the overlap in symptom presentation make it a highly relevant disorder in schizophrenia assessment. Dissociative or reexperiencing symptoms such as trauma-related auditory phenomena and flashbacks may be mistakenly interpreted as schizophrenia (Sautter et al., 1999).

Substance use disorder, such as alcohol dependence or drug abuse, can be either a differential diagnosis to schizophrenia or a comorbid disorder. With respect to differential diagnosis, substance use disorders can interfere with a clinician's ability to diagnose schizophrenia and can lead to misdiagnosis if the substance use is covert (Kranzler et al., 1995). Psychoactive substances, such as alcohol, marijuana, cocaine, and amphetamines, can produce symptoms and dysfunction that mimic those found in schizophrenia, such as hallucinations, delusions, and social withdrawal (Schuckit, 1989). The most critical recommendations for diagnosing substance abuse in schizophrenia include the following: Maintain a high index of suspicion of substance abuse, especially if a interviewee has a past history of substance abuse; use multiple assessment techniques, including self-report instruments, interviews with interviewees, clinician reports, reports of significant others, and biological assays; and be alert to signs that may be subtle indicators of presence of a substance use disorder, such as unexplained symptom relapses, increased familial conflict, money management problems, and depression or suicidality. Once a substance use disorder has been diagnosed, integrated treatment that addresses both the schizophrenia and the substance use disorder is necessary to achieve a favorable clinical outcome (Mueser, Noordsy, Drake, & Fox, 2003).

Many general medical disorders, such as hyperthyroidism, and cognitive disorders, such as dementia of various types, can present with schizophrenia-like symptoms. Also, in many of these disorders the cognitive impairments are similar, such as in some cases of head injury. Therefore, distinguishing schizophrenia from these disorders may be difficult, particularly when past history is not conclusive (e.g., when a first psychotic episode started after head injury). Moreover, the impact of comorbidity (e.g., whether head injury that occurred after the onset of schizophrenia is contributing to symptom severity and cognitive impairment) may be very difficult to determine because the natural course of schizophrenia in itself is not a uniform one. Still, a thorough medical and psychiatric history is helpful in this respect, as are laboratory tests (e.g., blood tests for hormones and many other factors, brain imaging such as computed tomography and magnetic resonance imaging) to rule out or support general medical and cognitive disorders.

Behavioral Assessment

Schizophrenia is sometimes associated with disruptive behaviors, particularly when it is refractory to treatment (Brenner et al., 1990). Of most concern are behaviors that result in physical risk to the person with schizophrenia or to others, such as suicidality and aggression, respectively. These are more common in people with schizophrenia than in the general population, particularly in subgroups such as young men with schizophrenia (for depression) and nonadherent substance-abusing people with schizophrenia (for aggression). Although predicting risk and dangerous behavior is difficult, there are measures that attempt to do that, some with more success than others. Suicidality in general has been somewhat predicted by scales such as the Scale for Suicide Ideation (SSI; Beck, Kovacs, & Weissman, 1979). More recently, a schizophrenia-specific measure to assess suicidality has been developed, based on the SSI (Alphs et al., 2004). Both measures involve a structured interview. Aggression in general has been measured and predicted by many scales. In the context of severe mental illness, a scale developed to predict aggression in interviewees settings is the Broset Violence Checklist (Almvik & Woods, 1998; Almvik, Woods, & Rasmussen, 2000), which is based on clinician's observations. In the context of schizophrenia, scales such as the Violent Risk Appraisal Guide and the historical part of the risk assessment device HCR-20 have been used with moderate success to predict future violence in known offenders (Tengstrom, 2001).

SELECTION OF TREATMENT TARGETS AND REFERRAL

Considering the variability in symptoms, associated features, and comorbid diagnoses in schizophrenia, it is important that treatment for people with schizophrenia be individually tailored. A comprehensive assessment can help provide the information needed to identify specific disabilities that will serve as targets for change, which should be based on the interviewee's identified goals as much as possible (Anthony, Cohen, Farkas, & Gagne, 2002). This section describes treatment related to three broad areas that can be assessed using the interviewing strategies discussed earlier: symptoms, functioning, and quality of life. Although this division is somewhat arbitrary, because the three areas interact with one another, it provides a useful framework.

Symptom Target Interventions

Medication and Adherence Interventions. Antipsychotic medications are the most powerful single intervention to reduce symptoms and prevent relapses. They are most effective in their impact on positive symptoms and to a lesser degree on negative symptoms and cognitive impairments. Since the 1990s, various atypical or second-generation antipsychotics have been developed and have largely replaced the first-generation antipsychotics, which had more side effects, particularly more neurological side effects (admittedly, the second-generation antipsychotics demonstrate other disturbing side effects, such as hyperlipidemia and possibly diabetes mellitus). Of note, clozapine, which was discovered before the 1990s but has atypical properties, is widely agreed to be the treatment of choice for refractory schizophrenia (Gaebel, Weinmann, Sartorius, Rutz, & McIntyre, 2005). One of the most puzzling yet consistent findings is that despite evidence supporting the effectiveness of psychiatric medication (Thornley & Adams, 1998), only about half of people diagnosed with a severe mental illness and prescribed psychotropic medications use their medication as prescribed (Weiden & Olfson, 1995). A range of interventions have been developed to address this very challenge. Boczkowski, Zeichner, and DeSanto (1985) describe an example of the psychoeducational approach, in which individual medication regimens are carefully reviewed and written materials with information about the medications are provided. Similarly, behavioral tailoring interventions (e.g., Boczkowski et al., 1985; Cramer & Rosenheck, 1999) focus on helping interviewees develop specific cues that incorporate taking their medication with routine aspects of their daily activities. Finally, Kemp et al. (1996) describe compliance therapy, based on the principles of motivational interviewing (Miller & Rollnick, 2002), psychoeducation, and cognitive-behavioral techniques. This intervention provides information about the benefits and side effects of medications, highlights discrepancies between interviewees' actions, beliefs, and desires, emphasizes the value of staying well, and encourages self-efficacy with respect to taking medication.

Illness Management Interventions. There is growing recognition that the interviewee can take an active role in his or her own illness management (Mueser et al., 2002). Examples of treatment components that can enhance illness management include monitoring early signs of symptoms and relapse, developing plans in advance to deal with possible situations of worsening of symptoms, and developing coping skills to address stress.

Cognitive-Behavioral Therapy. Cognitive-behavioral therapy for psychosis conceptualizes delusions and hallucinations as distorted perceptions and beliefs that are resistant to disconfirmation but may be altered by reviewing objective evidence and encouraging consideration of alternative perspectives or adaptively coping with the psychotic symptoms. There are different variants of cognitive-behavioral therapy for psychosis, some restorative (i.e., attempting to reduce or eliminate the psychosis) and others compensatory (i.e., attempting to cope adaptively with the psychosis) (Rathod & Turkington, 2005). For example, it can aim to develop a collaborative relationship with the interviewee and to examine the conditions in which symptoms occur and then to consider alternative, more adaptive interpretations of reality. Therapists may begin to gently encourage interviewees to explore the evidence supporting psychotic beliefs, first targeting those that were identified as least firmly held. Although structured and systematic cognitive-behavioral therapy for psychosis is a new intervention, the data available to date support its effectiveness (Zimmermann, Favrod, Trieu, & Pomini, 2005).

Cognitive Remediation and Rehabilitation. Until recently, it was commonly argued that the cognitive impairments accompanying schizophrenia are irreversible and that not much can be done to improve on that. Lately, both psychopharmacological and psychosocial research suggests that some cognitive impairments can be reversed or compensated for. This is particularly important because cognitive impairments predict dysfunction, perhaps more than any other symptom or impairment in schizophrenia (Green, Kern, Braff, & Mintz, 2000). The second-generation antipsychotics may improve some cognitive functions in schizophrenia, although there are contradictory reports, and they do not seem to eliminate cognitive deficits (Rund & Borg, 1999). Cognitive training, also called cognitive remediation and cognitive rehabilitation, demonstrates an even more robust effect, restoring some cognitive functions, such as sustained attention, and compensating for others, such as disrupted short-term memory (Twamley, Jeste, & Bellack, 2003). However, the broader impact of cognitive rehabilitation on functioning remains less clear.

Functioning

Social and Independent Living Skills Training. Many people with schizophrenia report experiencing difficulty behaving appropriately or feeling comfortable in social situations, which often leads to social withdrawal and dysfunction. Over the past three decades, treatment for schizophrenia has encouraged active teaching methods such as didactic instruction, modeling, behavioral rehearsal, corrective feedback, role play, contingent social reinforcement, and homework. Several manualized skill training modules have been developed by various clinical academic centers, such as the Clinical Research Center for Schizophrenia and Psychiatric Rehabilitation at the University of California at Los Angeles. These modules have been empirically validated and used in several countries around the world (Liberman et al., 1998). Symptom self-management, recreation for leisure, medication self-management, community reentry, job seeking, workplace fundamentals, basic conversation skills, and friendship and dating skills are among the modules that are available, all of which use the same teaching techniques, including didactic instruction, role play, problem solving, homework, and in vivo behavioral rehearsal. These modules have been demonstrated to be effective in promoting significant learning of social and independent living skills in people with schizophrenia (Liberman et al., 1998) and, given their user-friendly nature, may be administered by a broad array of mental health professionals. Research on social skill training indicates that it is an effective and useful modality for improving adaptive social and role functioning (Bellack, 2004).

Family Interventions. The theoretical rationale for including family counseling derives from research suggesting that people living in families with high expressed emotion—that is, overt attitudes indicating criticism, dissatisfaction, hostility, and overinvolvement—were more vulnerable to relapse and rehospitalization (Budd & Hughes, 1997). Family intervention therefore was designed to teach more adaptive, less stressful family communication skills and problem solving through instruction and modeling of appropriate skills by a therapist. Over the past 20 years, several types of family intervention for schizophrenia have been developed. Common components that are offered in varying amounts include education about the illness, practical and emotional support, and skill development in communication, problem solving, and crisis management (Dixon, Adams, & Lucksted, 2000). Most successful family intervention programs are offered for a long period of time (more than 6 months) by mental health professionals involved in interviewees' treatment. Research has demonstrated that family interventions may help lower relapse rates (Pitschel-Walz, Leucht, Bäuml, Kissling, & Engel, 2001).

Integrated Dual-Diagnosis Treatment. Historically, treatment for people dually diagnosed with schizophrenia and a substance use disorder was either sequential or parallel (Drake & Mueser, 2000). Research has found that integrated psychiatry and addiction programs that engage such dually diagnosed patients in treatment for at least 1 year produce greater improvement in substance use outcomes (Drake, Mueser, Brunette, & McHugo, 2004). Several different programs based on the integrated approach have been developed. Their primary goal is to include an awareness of the implications of the substance use disorder into all aspects of the mental health treatment program. The most effective integrated treatment models are comprehensive in that they target not only the substance use but also the multitude of other behaviors and life circumstances, such as living environment and social networks, that may be maintaining it. Family involvement is based on the important role relatives can play in giving support and helping interviewees move forward on the road to recovery by developing motivation to address their dual disorders and use self-management strategies. For many interviewees, both disorders are persistent, and therefore their treatment usually entails a long-term approach (Mueser et al., 2003).

Vocational Rehabilitation. Given the potential benefits of work in terms of increasing activity, socialization, financial status, self-esteem, community tenure, and self-reported quality of life, stable employment should be included as a treatment goal if the interviewee expresses an interest in it. Past vocational approaches such as sheltered employment have been largely displaced by more independence-enhancing vocational approaches, such as supported employment. The Individual Placement and Support (IPS) model, which is perhaps the contemporary paradigm of supported employment, is based on the "place-train" approach to vocational rehabilitation. IPS is characterized by rapid attainment of competitive jobs in the community, the provision of support and training as needed after work has commenced, and attention to interviewee preferences in terms of the type of job sought and the nature of support provided (Becker & Drake, 1994). To ensure integration of vocational rehabilitation and clinical treatment, in the IPS model the employment specialist performs all vocational support functions (i.e., assessment, job search, and support) while working as an integral member of the interviewee's clinical treatment team. Controlled research on the IPS model has shown that it dramatically increases rates of employment compared to traditional train-place models or day treatment programs with adjunctive vocational rehabilitation (Bond, 2004; Drake et al., 1999).

Assertive Community Treatment and Case Management. People with schizophrenia who need assistance with several aspects of daily functioning such as work, housing, transportation, medication management, and money management may need aid from a variety of social service agencies. The growing appreciation of the complexity of coordinating the various services has led to the development of various case management models, including assertive community treatment (ACT; Stein & Santos, 1998). ACT is provided by a team of mental health professionals, including psychiatrists, nurses, social workers, occupational therapists, recreational therapists, case managers, and peer support workers, who work at the same facility. Because most mental health services are delivered directly by the ACT team members and not brokered to other providers, both coordination and continuity of care are greatly facilitated. Case loads are shared across clinicians so that one person is not solely responsible for coordinating the care of a particular group of clients, and ACT teams generally have low client to clinician or case manager ratios (e.g., 10:1 rather than the 30:1 of clinical case management). This allows more time to be spent assisting each client. ACT teams typically offer 24-hour (7 days a week) coverage and provide

most services in the community. Other case management models are less intensive, providing coordination of services with or without direct clinical care (Bond, Drake, Mueser, & Latimer, 2001; Mueser, Bond, Drake, & Resnick, 1998).

ACT addresses several of the problem domains that may be identified in a comprehensive assessment of functioning and often serves as a critical foundation for other treatment approaches intended to target those impairments and dysfunctions. For example, case managers are in an excellent position to monitor problems such as poor adherence with prescribed medications and substance use. Assistance with practical needs of daily living such as housing, transportation, and shopping undoubtedly helps clients maintain stable living arrangements and reduces stress, which is related to reduced time spent in hospitals and perhaps greater subjective quality of life (Mueser et al., 1998). Case managers also reduce stress by helping interviewees navigate the complexities of general medical services and social service agencies. Finally, assuming a positive working relationship, case managers may be able to convince reluctant interviewees to participate in useful treatment such as skill training, family work, or cognitive-behavioral therapy, and may be instrumental in encouraging competitive employment. Because of the higher intensity of services on ACT teams and their emphasis on outreach into the community, ACT services usually are reserved for a subgroup of people with schizophrenia who have difficulty managing their illness through the usual array of community mental health services and have histories of either frequent psychiatric hospitalizations or extremely impaired psychosocial functioning.

Quality of Life

Quality of life is narrowly defined as the person's subjective well-being in various domains of life. It is assessed in health care by many instruments, and there are now some measures of quality of life in the context of schizophrenia, such as the Quality of Life Interview (Lehman, Kernan, & Postrado, 1995) and the Wisconsin quality of life Index (Becker, Diamond, & Sainfort, 1993), which is unusual in that it has three versions: a self-report one, a clinician-rated one, and a family report one. Quality of life is indirectly affected by many factors, including the aforementioned interventions. It is also directly affected by some interventions. One such intervention is supportive psychotherapy, which may use person-centered, psychodynamic, and other techniques (Penn, Mueser, Tarrier, Gloege, & Serrano, 2004). Probably the most systematic approach to date to supportive psychotherapy is the psychodynamic approach (Winston, Rosenthal, & Pinsker, 2004). Importantly, it is different from exploratory psychotherapy, which is the more traditional type of psychodynamic psychotherapy, in that supportive psychotherapy generally attempts to avoid provoking anxiety in the client. Other interventions that affect quality of life directly are wellness enhancement, using more holistic approaches such as relaxation and facilitating and supporting spirituality. Finally, self-help positively affects quality of life, be it participation in a clubhouse, peer support, or other self-help initiatives.

SUMMARY

Schizophrenia is a severe, long-term, multifaceted and heterogeneous psychiatric disorder characterized by disruption in social functioning, in the ability to work, and in self-care skills and by the core symptoms of positive symptoms (hallucinations, delusions, disorganization), negative symptoms (alogia, apathy), and cognitive impairments (in attention, memory, and executive functions). Schizophrenia can be reliably diagnosed with structured clinical interviews, with particular attention paid to differential diagnosis and to commonly associated problems, such as substance use and posttraumatic stress disorder, which often complicate the clinical picture. Assessment for treatment and rehabilitation planning is a complex process that involves delving into a wide range of domains of impairment and functioning. Effective assessment is crucial to identifying the most important treatment and rehabilitation goals and to prioritize pursuit of those goals.

REFERENCES

Adams, G. L., Dworkin, R. J., & Rosenberg, S. D. (1984). Diagnosis and pharmacotherapy issues in the care of Hispanics in the public sector. *American Journal of Psychiatry, 141,* 970–974.

Addington, D., Addington, J., & Schissel, B. (1990). A depression rating scale for schizophrenics. *Schizophrenia Research, 3,* 247–251.

Almvik, R., & Woods, P. (1998). The Broset Violence Checklist (BVC) and the prediction of inpatient violence: Some preliminary results. *Psychiatric Care, 5,* 208–211.

Almvik, R., Woods, P., & Rasmussen, K. (2000). The Broset Violence Checklist: Sensitivity, specificity, and interrater reliability. *Journal of Interpersonal Violence, 15,* 284–296.

Alphs, L., Anand, R., Islam, M. Z., Meltzer, H. Y., Kane, J. M., Krishnan, R., et al. (2004). The International Suicide Prevention Trial (interSePT). *Schizophrenia Bulletin, 30,* 577–586.

American Psychiatric Association. (1980). *Diagnostic and statistical manual of mental disorders* (3rd ed.). Washington, DC: Author.

American Psychiatric Association. (1994). *Diagnostic and statistical manual of mental disorders* (4th ed.). Washington, DC: Author.

Andreasen, N. C. (1982). Negative symptoms in schizophrenia: Definition and reliability. *Archives of General Psychiatry, 39,* 784–788.

Andreasen, N. C. (1984). *The Scale for the Assessment of Positive Symptoms (SAPS).* Iowa City: University of Iowa.

Anthony, W., Cohen, M., Farkas, M., & Gagne, G. (2002). *Psychiatric rehabilitation* (2nd ed.). Boston: Center for Psychiatric Rehabilitation.

Barker, S., Barron, N., & McFarlane, B. (1994). *Multnomah Community Ability Scale: Users manual.* Portland: Western Mental Health Research Center, Oregon Health Sciences University.

Beck, A. T., & Beck, R. W. (1972). Screening depressed patients in family practice: A rapid technique. *Postgraduate Medicine, 52,* 81–85.

Beck, A. T., Kovacs, M., & Weissman, A. (1979). Assessment of suicidal intention: The Scale for Suicide Ideation. *Journal of Consultation and Clinical Psychology, 47,* 343–352.

Becker, D. R., & Drake, R. E. (1994). Individual placement and support: A community mental health center approach to vocational rehabilitation. *Community Mental Health Journal, 30,* 193–205.

Becker, M., Diamond, R., & Sainfort, F. (1993). A new patient focused index for measuring quality of life in persons with severe and persistent mental illness. *Quality of Life Research, 2,* 239–251.

Bellack, A. S. (2004). Skills training for people with severe mental illness. *Psychiatric Rehabilitation Journal, 27,* 375–391.

Bilder, R. M. (2006). Schizophrenia. In P. J. Snyder, P. D. Nussbaum, & D. L. Robins (Eds.), *Clinical neuropsychology: A pocket handbook for assessment* (2nd ed., pp. 398–414). Washington, DC: American Psychological Association.

Blanchard, E. P., Jones-Alexander, J., Buckley, T. C., & Forneris, C. A. (1996). Psychometric properties of the PTSD checklist. *Behavior Research and Therapy, 34,* 669–673.

Blanchard, J. J., & Panzarella, C. (1998). Affect and social functioning in schizophrenia. In K. T. Mueser & N. Tarrier (Eds.), *Handbook of social functioning in schizophrenia* (pp. 181–196). Boston: Allyn & Bacon.

Boczkowski, J. A., Zeichner, A., & DeSanto, N. (1985). Neuroleptic compliance among chronic schizophrenic outpatients: An intervention outcome report. *Journal of Consulting and Clinical Psychology, 53,* 666–671.

Bond, G. R. (2004). Supported employment: Evidence for an evidence-based practice. *Psychiatric Rehabilitation Journal, 27,* 345–359.

Bond, G. R., Drake, R. E., Mueser, K. T., & Latimer, E. (2001). Assertive community treatment for people with severe mental illness: Critical ingredients and impact on clients. *Disease Management and Health Outcomes, 9,* 141–159.

Brenner, H. D., Dencker, S. J., Goldstein, M. J., Hubbard, J. W., Keegan, D. L., Kruger, G., et al. (1990). Defining treatment refractoriness in schizophrenia. *Schizophrenia Bulletin, 16,* 551–560.

Budd, R. J., & Hughes, I. C. T. (1997). What do relatives of people with schizophrenia find helpful about family intervention? *Schizophrenia Bulletin, 23,* 341–347.

Citrome, L., Goldberg, J. F., & Stahl, S. M. (2005). Toward convergence in the medication treatment of bipolar disorder and schizophrenia. *Harvard Review of Psychiatry, 13,* 28–42.

Cook, J. A., & Razzano, L. (2000). Vocational rehabilitation for persons with schizophrenia: Recent research and implications for practice. *Schizophrenia Bulletin, 26,* 87–103.

Cramer, J. A., & Rosenheck, R. (1999). Enhancing medication compliance for people with serious mental illness. *Journal of Nervous and Mental Disease, 187,* 53–55.

Curson, D. A., Patel, M., Liddle, P. F., & Barnes, T. R. E. (1988). Psychiatric morbidity of a long-stay hospital population with chronic schizophrenia and implications for future community care. *British Medical Journal, 297,* 819–822.

Dixon, L., Adams, C., & Lucksted, A. (2000). Update on family psychoeducation for schizophrenia. *Schizophrenia Bulletin, 26,* 5–20.

Drake, R. E., McHugo, G. J., Bebout, R. R., Becker, D. R., Harris, M., Bond, G. R., et al. (1999). A randomized clinical trial of supported employment for inner-city patients with severe mental disorders. *Archives of General Psychiatry, 56,* 627–633.

Drake, R. E., & Mueser, K. T. (2000). Psychosocial approaches to dual diagnosis. *Schizophrenia Bulletin, 26,* 105–118.

Drake, R. E., Mueser, K. T., Brunette, M. F., & McHugo, G. J. (2004). A review of treatments for clients with severe mental illness and co-occurring substance use disorder. *Psychiatric Rehabilitation Journal, 27,* 360–374.

Fenton, W. S., Blyler, C. R., & Heinssen, R. K. (1997). Determinants of medication compliance in schizophrenia: Empirical and clinical findings. *Schizophrenia Bulletin, 23,* 637–651.

First, M. B., Spitzer, R. L., Gibbon, M., & Williams, J. B. W. (1996). *Structured Clinical Interview for DSM-IV Axis I Disorders: Patient edition* (SCID-I/P, Version 2.0). New York: Biometrics Research Department, New York State Psychiatric Institute.

Gaebel, W., Weinmann, S., Sartorius, N., Rutz, W., & McIntyre, J. S. (2005). Schizophrenia practice guidelines: International survey and comparison. *British Journal of Psychiatry, 87,* 248–255.

Glynn, S. M. (1998). Psychopathology and social functioning in schizophrenia. In K. T. Mueser & N. Tarrier (Eds.), *Handbook of social functioning in schizophrenia* (pp. 66–78). Boston: Allyn & Bacon.

Green, M. F., Kern, R. S., Braff, D. L., & Mintz, J. (2000). Neurocognitive deficits and functional outcome in schizophrenia: Are we measuring the "right stuff"? *Schizophrenia Bulletin, 26,* 119–136.

Hamilton, M. (1960). A rating scale for depression. *Journal of Neurology, Neurosurgery, and Psychiatry, 23,* 56–62.

Harvey, P. D., Davidson, M., Mueser, K. T., Parrella, M., White, L., & Powchik, P. (1997). Social-Adaptive Functioning Evaluation (SAFE): A rating scale for geriatric psychiatric patients. *Schizophrenia Bulletin, 23,* 131–145.

Hogan, T. P., Awad, A. G., & Eastwood, R. (1983). A self-report scale predictive of drug compliance in schizophrenics: Reliability and discriminative validity. *Psychological Medicine, 13,* 177–183.

Jablensky, A. (1989). Epidemiology and cross-cultural aspects of schizophrenia. *Psychiatric Annals, 19,* 516–524.

Jones, B. E., Gray, B. A., & Parsons, E. B. (1981). Manic-depressive illness among poor urban blacks. *American Journal of Psychiatry, 138,* 654–657.

Jones, B. E., Gray, B. A., & Parsons, E. B. (1983). Manic-depressive illness among poor urban Hispanics. *American Journal of Psychiatry, 140,* 1208–1210.

Kay, S. R., Opler, L. A., & Fiszbein, A. (1987). The Positive and Negative Syndrome Scale (PANSS) for schizophrenia. *Schizophrenia Bulletin, 13,* 261–276.

Keith, S. J., Regier, D. A., & Rae, D. S. (1991). Schizophrenic disorders. In L. N. Robins & D. A. Regier (Eds.), *Psychiatric disorders in America: The Epidemiologic Catchment Area Study* (pp. 33–52). New York: Free Press.

Kemp, R., Hayward, P., Applewaite, G., Everitt, B., & David, A. (1996). Compliance therapy in psychotic patients: Randomized controlled trial. *British Medical Journal, 312,* 345–349.

Kessler, R. C., Foster, C. L., Saunders, W. B., & Stang, P. E. (1995). Social consequences of psychiatric disorders, I: Educational attainment. *American Journal of Psychiatry, 152,* 1026–1032.

Kranzler, H. R., Kadden, R. M., Burleson, J. A., Babor, T. F., Apter, A., & Rounsaville, B. J. (1995). Validity of psychiatric diagnoses in patients with substance use disorders: Is the interview more important than the interviewer? *Comprehensive Psychiatry, 36,* 278–288.

Kurtz, M. M. (2005). Neurocognitive impairments across the lifespan in schizophrenia: An update. *Schizophrenia Research, 74,* 15–26.

Lehman, A., Kernan, E., & Postrado, L. (1995). *Toolkit for evaluating quality of life for persons with severe mental illness.* Baltimore, MD: The Evaluation Center at HSRI.

Levinson, D. F., & Mowry, B. J. (1991). Defining the schizophrenia spectrum: Issues for genetic linkage studies. *Schizophrenia Bulletin, 17,* 491–514.

Liberman, R. P., Wallace, C. J., Blackwell, G., Kopelowicz, A., Vaccaro, J. V., & Mintz, J. (1998). Skills training versus psychosocial occupational therapy for persons with persistent schizophrenia. *American Journal of Psychiatry, 155,* 1087–1091.

Loring, M., & Powell, B. (1988). Gender, race, and *DSM-III: A study of the objectivity of psychiatric diagnostic behavior. Journal of Health and Social Behavior, 29*, 1–22.

Lukoff, D., Nuechterlein, K. H., & Ventura, J. (1986). Manual for the Expanded Brief Psychiatric Rating Scale (BPRS). *Schizophrenia Bulletin, 12*, 594–602.

Lysaker, P. H., Bell, M. D., Bryson, G. J., & Zito, W. (1993). *Raters' guide for the Work Behavior Inventory.* West Haven, CT: Rehabilitation, Research, and Development Service, Department of Veterans Affairs.

Marwaha, S., & Johnson, S. (2004). Schizophrenia and employment: A review. *Social Psychiatry and Psychiatric Epidemiology, 39*, 337–349.

Matarazzo, J. D. (1983). The reliability of psychiatric and psychological diagnosis. *Clinical Psychology Review, 3*, 103–145.

Miller, W. R., & Rollnick, S. (Eds.). (2002). *Motivational interviewing: Preparing people for change* (2nd ed.). New York: Guilford.

Mueser, K. T., Bellack, A. S., Douglas, M. S., & Wade, J. H. (1991). Prediction of social skill acquisition in schizophrenic and major affective disorder patients from memory and symptomatology. *Psychiatry Research, 37*, 281–296.

Mueser, K. T., Bond, G. R., Drake, R. E., & Resnick, S. G. (1998). Models of community care for severe mental illness: A review of research on case management. *Schizophrenia Bulletin, 24*, 37–74.

Mueser, K. T., Corrigan, P. W., Hilton, D. W., Tanzman, B., Schaub, A., Gingerich, S., et al. (2002). Illness management and recovery: A review of the research. *Psychiatric Services, 53*, 272–284.

Mueser, K. T., Curran, P. J., & McHugo, G. J. (1997). Factor structure of the Brief Psychiatric Rating Scale in schizophrenia. *Psychological Assessment, 9*, 196–204.

Mueser, K. T., Goodman, L. B., Trumbetta, S. L., Rosenberg, S. D., Osher, F. C., Vidaver, R., et al. (1998). Trauma and posttraumatic stress disorder in severe mental illness. *Journal of Consulting and Clinical Psychology, 66*, 493–499.

Mueser, K. T., Noordsy, D. L., Drake, R. E., & Fox, L. (2003). *Integrated treatment for dual disorders: A guide to effective practice.* New York: Guilford.

Mueser, K. T., Salyers, M. P., & Mueser, P. R. (2001). A prospective analysis of work in schizophrenia. *Schizophrenia Bulletin, 27*, 281–296.

Mueser, K. T., Yarnold, P. R., Rosenberg, S. D., Swett, C., Miles, K. M., & Hill, D. (2000). Substance use disorder in hospitalized severely mentally ill psychiatric patients: Prevalence, correlates, and subgroups. *Schizophrenia Bulletin, 26*, 179–192.

Overall, G., & Gorham, D. (1962). The Brief Psychiatric Rating Scale. *Psychological Reports, 10*, 799–812.

Peen, J., & Dekker, J. (1997). Admission rates for schizophrenia in the Netherlands: An urban/rural comparison. *Acta Psychiatrica Scandinavica, 96*, 301–305.

Penn, D. L., Corrigan, P. W., & Racenstein, J. M. (1998). Cognitive factors and social adjustment in schizophrenia. In K. T. Mueser & N. Tarrier (Eds.), *Handbook of social functioning in schizophrenia* (pp. 213–223). Boston: Allyn & Bacon.

Penn, D. L., Mueser, K. T., Tarrier, N., Gloege, A., & Serrano, D. (2004). Supportive therapy for schizophrenia: A closer look at the evidence. *Schizophrenia Bulletin, 30*, 101–112.

Pitschel-Walz, G., Leucht, S., Bäuml, J., Kissling, W., & Engel, R. R. (2001). The effect of family interventions on relapse and rehospitalization in schizophrenia: A meta-analysis. *Schizophrenia Bulletin, 27*, 73–92.

Pogue-Geile, M. F. (1989). The prognostic significance of negative symptoms in schizophrenia. *British Journal of Psychiatry,* Suppl. 7, 123–127.

Rathod, S., & Turkington, D. (2005). Cognitive-behaviour therapy for schizophrenia: A review. *Current Opinion in Psychiatry, 18*, 159–163.

Roe, D., & Davidson, L. (2005). Self and narrative in schizophrenia: Time to author a new story. *Journal of Medical Humanities, 31*, 89–94.

Roe, D., & Kravetz, S. (2003). Different ways of being aware of and acknowledging a psychiatric disability. A multifunctional narrative approach to insight into mental disorder. *Journal of Nervous and Mental Disease, 191*, 417–424.

Roe, D., Lereya, J., & Fennig, S. (2001). Comparing patients and staff members' attitudes: Does patients' competence to disagree mean they are not competent? *Journal of Nervous and Mental Disease, 189*, 307–310.

Rosenberg, S. D., Drake, R. E., Wolford, G. L., Mueser, K. T., Oxman, T. E., Vidaver, R. M., et al. (1998). Dartmouth Assessment of Lifestyle Instrument (DALI): A substance use disorder screen for people with severe mental illness. *American Journal of Psychiatry, 155*, 232–238.

Rund, B. R., & Borg, N. E. (1999). Cognitive deficits and cognitive training in schizophrenic patients: A review. *Acta Psychiatrica Scandinavica, 100*, 85–95.

Sautter, F. J., Brailey, K., Uddo, M. M., Hamilton, M. E., Beard, M. G., & Borges, A. H. (1999). PTSD and comorbid psychotic disorder: Comparison with veterans diagnosed with PTSD or psychotic disorder. *Journal of Traumatic Stress, 12*, 73–88.

Sayers, S. L., Curran, P. J., & Mueser, K. T. (1996). Factor structure and construct validity of the Scale for the Assessment of Negative Symptoms. *Psychological Assessment, 8*, 269–280.

Schooler, N., Hogarty, G., & Weissman, M. (1979). Social Adjustment Scale II (SAS-II). In W. A. Hargreaves, C. C. Atkisson, & J. E. Sorenson (Eds.), *Resource materials for community mental health program evaluations* (pp. 290–303). DHEW Publication no. (ADM) 79-328. Rockville, MD: National Institute of Mental Health.

Schuckit, M. A. (1989). *Drug and alcohol abuse: A clinical guide to diagnosis and treatment* (3rd ed.). New York: Plenum.

Skilbeck, W. M., Acosta, F. X., Yamamoto, J., & Evans, L. A. (1984). Self-reported psychiatric symptoms among Black, Hispanic, and White outpatients. *Journal of Clinical Psychology, 40*, 1184–1189.

Spielberger, C. D., Gorsuch, R. C., & Lushene, R. E. (1970). *Manual for the State-Trait Anxiety Inventory.* Palo Alto, CA: Consulting Psychologists Press.

Stein, L. I., & Santos, A. B. (1998). *Assertive community treatment of persons with severe mental illness.* New York: Norton.

Tengstrom, A. (2001). Long-term predictive validity of historical factors in two risk assessment instruments in a group of violent offenders with schizophrenia. *Nordic Journal of Psychiatry, 55,* 243–249.

Thornley, B., & Adams, C. (1998). Content and quality of 2000 controlled trials in schizophrenia over 50 years. *BMJ, 317*(7167), 1181–1184.

Twamley, E. W., Jeste, D. V., & Bellack, A. S. (2003). A review of cognitive training in schizophrenia. *Schizophrenia Bulletin, 29,* 359–382.

Van Putten, T., & May, P. R. A. (1978). Subjective response as a predictor of outcome in pharmacotherapy. *Archives of General Psychiatry, 35,* 477–480.

Wallace, C. J., Liberman, R. P., Tauber, R., & Wallace, J. (2000). The Independent Living Skills Survey: A comprehensive measure of the community functioning of severely and persistently mentally ill individuals. *Schizophrenia Bulletin, 26,* 631–658.

Weiden, P. J., & Olfson, M. (1995). Cost of relapse in schizophrenia. *Schizophrenia Bulletin, 21,* 419–429.

Weiden, P., Rapkin, B., Mott, T., Zygmut, A., Horvitz-Lennon, M., & Frances, A. (1994). Rating of Medication Influences (ROMI) scale in schizophrenia. *Schizophrenia Bulletin, 20,* 297–307.

Winston, A., Rosenthal, R. N., & Pinsker, H. (2004). *Introduction to supportive psychotherapy.* Washington, DC: American Psychiatric Publishing.

World Health Organization. (1992). *International classification of diseases* (10th ed.). Washington, DC: Author.

Zimmermann, G., Favrod, J., Trieu, V. H., & Pomini, V. (2005). The effect of cognitive behavioral treatment on the positive symptoms of schizophrenia spectrum disorders: A meta-analysis. *Schizophrenia Research, 77,* 1–9.

13

PANIC AND AGORAPHOBIA

NORMAN B. SCHMIDT, JULIA D. BUCKNER, AND J. ANTHONY RICHEY

DESCRIPTION OF THE DISORDER

Panic disorder (PD) is an anxiety disorder that affects approximately 2% to 3% of the adult population at any point in time and is associated with poor physical health outcomes and high rates of health care use (Greenberg et al., 1999). According to the *Diagnostic and Statistical Manual of Mental Disorders, Fourth Edition* (*DSM-IV;* American Psychiatric Association [APA], 1994), the essential feature of PD is the presence of recurrent, unexpected panic attacks along with significant panic-related worry. Panic-related worry can take a number of different forms including persistent fears and concerns about having additional panic attacks (e.g., "Will I have another panic attack today?" "If I drive on the highway will I panic?"), worry about the possible implications or consequences of the panic attacks (e.g., "If I panic, I'll be incapacitated [die, faint, etc.].'"), or a significant behavioral change related to the attacks (e.g., phobic avoidance due to fears of panicking). Importantly, these panic attacks cannot arise solely from the direct physical effects of a substance (e.g., caffeine intoxication) or from a medical condition (e.g., hyperthyroidism). Finally, the panic attacks cannot be caused by some other mental disorder (e.g., social anxiety disorder, obsessive-compulsive disorder).

Because panic attacks are central to PD, a bit more clarification about their nature is needed.

Panic attacks involve an abrupt convergence (i.e., usually within a few minutes) of a number of autonomic and cognitive symptoms and typically result in intense fear or distress. According to the *DSM-IV* (APA, 1994), at least four symptoms must occur simultaneously for the panic attack to be considered a full-symptom panic attack. These symptoms include heart palpitations and chest pain, lightheadedness, nausea, flush or chill, shortness of breath, tingling sweating, feelings of unreality, and shaking. The subjective or cognitive symptoms include feelings of terror, fear of dying, and feeling out of control.

It is worth noting that significant heterogeneity exists in panic attacks, both across individuals and within an individual. In recent years, much attention has been devoted to elucidating the nature and phenomenology of panic attacks (Barlow, Brown, & Craske, 1994). In turn, such research not only has confirmed speculation that panic attacks are ubiquitous in clinical and nonclinical populations but has also resulted in increased recognition that panic attacks are not unidimensional with respect to clinical presentation. Rather, panic attacks are now viewed as heterogeneous in terms of their phenomenology, and interindividual heterogeneity regarding the experience of panic itself (i.e., across subjective, physiological, and behavioral domains) appears to be the rule clinically, not the exception.

In the past decade, several typologies have been developed to more fully account for the apparent heterogeneity in the phenomenon of panic (Klein & Klein, 1989; Ley, 1992; Whittal, Goetsch, & Eifert, 1996). The latest panic typology within the *DSM-IV* (APA, 1994) underscores the heterogeneity of panic symptoms by organizing panic in a polythetic fashion such that a panic attack may consist of physical (e.g., numbness, palpitations) or cognitive (e.g., fear of dying) symptom domains. The *DSM-IV* adopted a new panic attack typology that removed the diagnosis of panic attacks from the PD diagnostic section, where it had been in the *DSM-III-R*. The *DSM-IV* now allows recognition of three types of panic: unexpected, situationally bound, and situationally disposed. An unexpected (spontaneous, uncued) panic attack is defined as one that is not associated with a situational trigger (i.e., it occurs out of the blue). Because the *DSM-IV* requires that panic is recurrent, this would imply that at least two unexpected panic attacks are required for the diagnosis, but of course most people with PD experience much more. People with PD often have situationally predisposed panic attacks (i.e., those more likely to occur on, but not invariably associated with, exposure to a situational trigger). Situationally bound attacks (e.g., those that occur almost invariably and immediately on exposure to a situational trigger) can also occur in PD but are less common.

It is clear, then, that patients with PD typically present with a mixture of different types of panic attacks. It is also notable that although spontaneous or unexpected panic attacks often are characteristic of panic at the onset of PD, patients are more likely to establish links between panic and various situations over time, such that situationally disposed or bound panic becomes more common over the course of the disorder. The current empirical literature has not yet fully explored the importance of understanding the particular individual differences in panic, but some studies suggest that differences in panic may be consequential (Schmidt, Forsyth, Santiago, & Trakowski, 2002).

Finally, the frequency and severity of the panic attacks vary widely. For example, some people have moderately frequent attacks (e.g., once a week) that occur regularly for months at a time. Others report short bursts of more frequent attacks (e.g., daily for a week) separated by weeks or months without any attacks or with less frequent attacks (e.g., two each month) over many years. Limited-symptom attacks (i.e., attacks that are identical to "full" panic attacks except that the sudden fear or anxiety is accompanied by fewer than 4 of the 13 panic symptoms) are also very common in people with PD.

People with PD display characteristic concerns about the implications or consequences of the panic attacks. Some fear that the attacks indicate the presence of an undiagnosed, life-threatening illness (e.g., cardiac diseases, seizure disorder). Despite repeated medical testing and reassurance, they may remain frightened and unconvinced that they do not have a life-threatening illness. Others fear that the panic attacks are an indication that they are "going crazy" or losing control or are emotionally weak. We consider these specific concerns to be a key element in the assessment of patients because they will help direct cognitive behavioral treatment. Many people with recurrent panic attacks significantly change their behavior (e.g., quit a job, stop driving) in response to the attacks. Concerns about the next attack, or its implications, often are associated with development of avoidant behavior that may meet criteria for agoraphobia, in which case PD with agoraphobia is diagnosed.

Classification of PD and agoraphobia within the *DSM* has undergone significant changes over time and continues to be controversial (Cerny, Himadi, & Barlow, 1984). In particular, the *DSM* has substantially changed its description of the relationship between PD and agoraphobia. Marks (1970) originally suggested that agoraphobia was a phobic disorder arising from fears of public places that may or may not occur with panic attacks. Consistent with Marks's contentions, the *DSM-III* (APA, 1980) classified agoraphobia as a phobic disorder that could occur with or without panic attacks, whereas PD was considered to be a separate class of anxiety disorders called anxiety states or anxiety neuroses. Over time, however, as researchers increasingly recognized that agoraphobia often is a consequence of panic attacks, the *DSM* has reversed the relationship between these conditions such that in the *DSM-III-R* (APA, 1987) and *DSM-IV* (APA, 1994), agoraphobia is typically considered secondary to PD. Therefore, agoraphobic behaviors are now more commonly conceptualized as panic-related sequelae (Frances et al., 1993; Goldstein & Chambless, 1978; McNally, 1994).

This important change in nosology raises questions about the nature of agoraphobia. In the rare cases of agoraphobia without a history of panic attacks (Kearney et al., 1997; Lewinsohn, Zinbarg, Seeley, Lewinsohn, & Sack, 1997), agoraphobia is an autonomous diagnostic entity. These appear to be instances of people developing the classic fear and avoidance of crowds or open spaces without a history of panic (Hayward, Killen, & Taylor, 2003; Marks, 1987). The central criteria for this diagnosis include meeting diagnostic criteria for agoraphobia and failing to meet diagnostic criteria for PD.

In the majority of cases when an agoraphobia diagnosis is used, however, this diagnosis is not an independent diagnostic entity but it is simply a specifier attached to a PD diagnosis. Agoraphobia is used to indicate the severity of phobic avoidance behaviors exhibited by patients with PD. In these cases, the patient meets diagnostic criteria for PD along with the same criteria for agoraphobia specified in agoraphobia without history of PD. We suggest that this leads to the potential for confusion in the diagnostic system because *agoraphobia* is used as both a diagnostic entity (agoraphobia without history of PD) and a specifier (i.e., considered in cases of PD).

Many of the symptoms seen in panic attacks and PD are similar to those experienced in acute medical crisis (e.g., a heart attack), and many people seek immediate medical attention only to be told that their problems are psychological, not medical. Indeed, many people with PD have had repeated medical tests and have sought several "second opinions" because it is difficult to believe that one can experience such intense symptoms and not have a medical illness. On the other hand, certain medical conditions are associated with panic and may mimic panic symptoms.

The relationship between PD and nonpsychiatric medical illness is complex. It appears that nonpsychiatric medical conditions can contribute to the development of PD (Kahn, Drusin, & Klein, 1987; Raj, Corvea, & Dagon, 1993) or exacerbate PD symptoms (McCue & McCue, 1984). In addition, increasing evidence suggests that PD can contribute to the development of physical conditions or exacerbate existing physical conditions (Karajgi, Rifkin, Doddi, & Kolli, 1990; Kawachi et al., 1994). For example, longitudinal evaluation of PD indicates a higher risk

for a number of medical conditions (e.g., hypertension, migraine headaches, ulcer, thyroid disease) than in other anxiety conditions and the general population (Rogers et al., 1994). Therefore, careful screening for medical conditions is critical in evaluating for PD.

INTERVIEWING STRATEGIES

Interviewing strategies for PD should focus on the acquisition of pertinent information that will guide the clinician in making an accurate diagnosis. This information includes the presence and severity of the various symptom domains that constitute PD. This information is obviously useful, if not critical to developing the most efficacious treatment plan. In the context of treatment, clinicians are encouraged to develop interviewing strategies to evaluate treatment progress. In this section we focus the assessment on a number of symptom domains and also provide a guide for various interview and self-report measures that can assist in these assessments (see Antony, Orsillo, & Roemer, 2001).

Table 13.1 presents a list of interviewing and assessment strategies that are organized by symptom domain, with measures recommended to assess each domain. It is useful to dismantle PD across a number of domains that define the disorder as a means to describe the condition, document recovery from the disorder, and identify possible obstacles (e.g., depression) that can influence treatment response. In the case of PD, it is helpful to consider partial versus complete recovery. Partial recovery involves some symptomatic remission of the typical symptoms such as panic attacks or phobic avoidance. However, we define complete recovery more broadly and discuss this with every patient. In this conservative definition, complete recovery from PD involves four key dimensions: no more panic attacks, no more panic-related worry, no use of safety aids, and normal levels of anxiety sensitivity. The rationale for this conservative definition is that sometimes patients are infrequently panicking and may have limited avoidance behaviors. However, if they continue to show panic-related worry or anxiety sensitivity, they are at much greater risk for relapse. Similarly, the continued use of safety aids may mask the level of recovery. Therefore, we recommend that clinicians and patients show good awareness of these dimensions, starting with the initial assessment. It is helpful to keep these dimensions in mind in organizing the initial and ongoing assessment of patients.

Diagnosis

Obtaining an accurate diagnosis obviously is one of the central aims of the initial assessment. The use of structured interviews produces more reliable diagnostic inferences than diagnostic decisions made without the use of standardized instruments (Grove & Meehl, 1996). Unless the clinician is very familiar with *DSM-IV* criteria (APA, 1994), we recommend the use of

comprehensive structured clinical interviews such as the Structured Clinical Interview for *DSM-IV* (SCID-IV; First, Spitzer, Gibbon, & Williams, 1994) or the Anxiety Disorders Interview Schedule for *DSM-IV*: Lifetime (ADIS-IV; DiNardo, Brown, & Barlow, 1994). The SCID-IV and the ADIS-IV can be used at intake to rule out differential diagnoses and assess for comorbidity. Both interviews are excellent, although the ADIS provides more specific data about the condition apart from *DSM* criteria.

Assessment of PD should also include strategies to rule out medical conditions that mimic or exacerbate panic attacks (Barlow, 2002; Taylor,

Table 13.1   Domains to Include in Interviewing Strategies Aimed at Assessing Panic Disorder

Domain	*Assessment Tool*
Diagnosis	• SCID-IV or ADIS-IV • Medical evaluation
Panic attacks	• SCID-IV or ADIS-VI • PDSS
Anxious apprehension	• The Fear Questionnaire • PDSS • Scale 1 of the PAI
Safety aids	• Safety Aid Identification Form • Mobility Inventory
Anxiety sensitivity	• Anxiety Sensitivity • Body Sensations Questionnaire • Body Vigilance Scale
Comorbidity	• SCID-IV or ADIS-IV • Beck Depression Inventory–II • Social Interaction Anxiety Scale
Suicidality	• SCID-IV or ADIS-IV • Beck Scale for Suicide Ideation • Suicidal Ideation Scale
Core threat cognitions	• Agoraphobic Cognitions Scale • Scale 2 of the PAI
Self-efficacy in coping with panic	• Scale 3 of the PAI
General levels of anxiety	• Beck Anxiety Inventory • State-Trait Anxiety Inventory
Quality of life	• Global Assessment of Functioning • Sheehan Disability Scale • Quality of Life Inventory

NOTES: ADIS-IV = Anxiety Disorders Interview Schedule for *DSM-IV*: Lifetime; PAI = Panic Attack Inventory; PDSS = Panic Disorder Severity Scale; SCID-IV = Structured Clinical Interview for *DSM-IV*.

2000). Medical conditions that may resemble panic include endocrine disorders (e.g., hyperthyroidism, hypoglycemia), cardiovascular disorders (hypertension, congestive heart failure), respiratory disorders (e.g., asthma), neurological disorders (e.g., seizure disorders), and substance-induced panic as the result of substance withdrawal (e.g., alcohol, marijuana) or substance ingestion (e.g., caffeine, cocaine, amphetamines). We find that incorporating an interview or self-report instrument that asks about these conditions is very useful, but often referral to a physician is needed if the patient has not received a recent medical evaluation.

Treatment Targets

After diagnosis of PD has been established, it is recommended that the clinician gather information that will aid in the development of a treatment plan and provide baseline information that can be used to compare subsequent assessments in an effort to monitor treatment progress. Effective assessment of PD should include the assessment of six primary components: panic attacks, anxious apprehension or fear of panic, safety aids, anxiety sensitivity (fear associated with bodily sensations), comorbidity, and suicidality. Other domains that are useful to evaluate include core threat cognitions, self-efficacy in coping with panic, general levels of anxiety, and overall disability. Unless otherwise noted, these 10 areas should be assessed at intake and every 2 to 3 weeks throughout treatment to monitor treatment progress.

Panic Attacks. To understand the nature of panic attacks, it is important to assess the frequency, severity, and type (e.g., nocturnal, situationally bound) of panic experienced by the patient. At intake, panic attack characteristics can be assessed through clinical interview such as the SCID-IV and ADIS-IV. Additionally, panic attack severity can be assessed using a clinician-administered scale such as the PD Severity Scale (PDSS; Shear et al., 1997). The PDSS can be used to assess seven components of panic attacks during the past month. In fact, the PDSS provides a very useful and brief measure of functioning and symptom severity. In the ideal situation, panic attacks can be monitored using a prospective self-monitoring approach (e.g., the Texas Panic Attack Record Form) that reduces overreporting bias (Margraf, Taylor, Ehlers, Roth, & Agras, 1987). To accomplish this, forms are provided to the patient to complete each time he or she experiences a panic attack and turn in at the next therapy session.

Anxious Apprehension. Relative to panic per se, anxious apprehension—the level of worry a patient has about panicking—is more critical to creating impairment and disability. Many people experience panic, but few go on to experience PD. The distinction between these two groups has to do with whether someone develops anxious apprehension. The PDSS and the Fear Questionnaire (Marks & Mathews, 1979) and scale 1 of the Panic Attack Inventory (PAI; Telch, Brouillard, Telch, Agras, & Taylor, 1989) are examples of measures of anxious apprehension.

Safety Aids. Safety aids are actions the patient uses to provide temporary relief from anxiety and panic. There are true and false safety aids. True safety aids protect people from actual danger. However, false safety aids are behaviors used to cope with or prevent anxiety in situations in which there is no actual threat. Safety aids perpetuate anxiety because they prevent the patient from activating and challenging thinking errors that maintain anxious reactivity. There are five broad categories of safety aids: avoidance of bodily sensations, avoidance of situations, companions, medication and other substances, and idiosyncratic safety rituals.

Once the clinician has educated the patient about safety aids, the patient's particular safety aids can be identified either in session with the clinician's assistance or as homework. The PDSS also provides a measure of some important safety aids such as avoidance of situations and avoidance of sensations. Of course, the most common type of safety aid is phobic avoidance. Agoraphobic avoidance can be assessed with the Mobility Inventory (Chambless, Caputo, Jasin, Gracely, & Williams, 1985), a self-report measure consisting of 26 different situations that are typically the subject of agoraphobic avoidance. The patient rates degree of avoidance when alone and when accompanied, providing useful information on the safety aids of avoidance and use of companions.

Anxiety Sensitivity. Anxiety sensitivity refers to individual differences in the fear of arousal symptoms. Theoretical models suggest that fear of anxious arousal is a dispositional tendency that will lead to the development and maintenance of panic attacks (Maller & Reiss, 1992; Reiss & McNally, 1985). Moreover, treatment outcome research has shown that changes in anxiety sensitivity account for treatment response in cognitive-behavioral therapy (CBT; Smits, Powers, Cho, & Telch, 2004). It is therefore recommended to monitor anxiety sensitivity on a regular basis. The Anxiety Sensitivity Index (Peterson & Reiss, 1993) is the most widely used measure of anxiety sensitivity. Other measures to consider are the Body Sensations Questionnaire (Chambless, Caputo, Bright, & Gallagher, 1984), which asks patients to rate the extent to which they fear specific arousal-related bodily sensations. In addition, the Body Vigilance Scale (Schmidt, Lerew, & Trakowski, 1997) can be used to monitor conscious attention to internal cues.

Comorbidity. PD often co-occurs with other Axis I conditions, including other anxiety disorders and depression (Kessler, Chiu, Demler, & Walters, 2005). Because of this, and because panic attacks occur across a wide range of conditions, differential diagnosis can be challenging in PD. This is another reason we recommend the use of a comprehensive clinical interview such as the SCID-IV and the ADIS-IV. When comorbidity exists, it is often critical to ascertain the primary diagnosis. In many cases, PD appears to create secondary mood and anxiety problems. Treatment outcome data suggest that successful treatment of PD often leads to significant remission of co-occurring mood or anxiety disorder symptoms. However, there are many instances in which Axis I conditions are independent and may not be affected by the PD intervention. Also, there are instances in which these comorbid conditions may worsen during treatment.

Use of some substances is associated with panic symptoms. For example, panic attacks are associated with cannabis use (Zvolensky et al., 2006) and cigarette smoking (Zvolensky, Schmidt, & Stewart, 2003). In addition, PD is also highly comorbid with particular substance use disorders including alcohol use disorders (Kessler et al., 1997) and cannabis use disorders (Zvolensky et al., 2006). As noted earlier, in cases of patients presenting with panic and a history of substance use, it is important to determine whether the panic symptoms persist in the absence of substance use

and withdrawal to determine whether a diagnosis of PD is warranted. Furthermore, the assessment of substance use among people with PD is necessary to determine whether the patient engages in problematic substance use behaviors that could undermine treatment in at least two ways: Anxiolytic substances may interfere with activation of fear structure, and the patient may attribute successful completion of exposure exercises to the substance use rather than to newly acquired skills.

Suicidality. People with PD experience significantly greater levels of suicidal ideation and significantly more suicide attempts than people with other psychiatric conditions (Weissman, Klerman, Markowitz, & Ouellette, 1989). Furthermore, several anxiety-related variables are associated with suicidal ideation among people with PD after depression, including overall anxiety symptoms, level of anticipatory anxiety, avoidance of bodily sensations, vigilance toward bodily perturbations, and fear of cognitive incapacitation, is controlled for (Schmidt, Woolaway-Bickel, & Bates, 2001). It is therefore important to perform regular suicide assessments with patients with PD. It is recommended that the clinician interview the patient at intake and periodically throughout treatment on suicidal ideation and regularly administer self-report measures of suicidality, such as Beck Scale for Suicide Ideation (Beck, Kovacs, & Weissman, 1979) or the Suicidal Ideation Scale (Rudd, 1989).

Core Threat Cognitions. Core threat cognitions are unrealistic beliefs attached to the patient's alarm reaction. In the case of PD, core threat cognitions typically are concerned with one of three domains: physical threat, social threat (i.e., embarrassment), and loss of control. Evaluation of these domains is useful for the cognitive therapy component of the treatment and can be helpful in designing other types of interventions (e.g., interoceptive exposure). Intensity of various core threat cognitions can be assessed using self-report measures such as the Agoraphobic Cognitions Scale (Hoffart, Friis, & Martinsen, 1992) and scale 2 of the PAI (Telch et al., 1989).

Self-Efficacy in Coping With Panic. Increases in problem-focused coping appear to be related to outcome among patients with PD (Hino, Takeuchi, & Yamanouchi, 2002). Self-efficacy in coping with panic therefore can be used to provide a good gauge of the patient's perceived mastery of skills acquired over the course of treatment. Furthermore, poor panic-specific coping (compared with poor coping skills generally) is associated with increased panic responding (Schmidt, Eggleston, Trakowski, & Smith, 2005). This dimension can be assessed using scale 3 of the PAI (Telch et al., 1989). The PAI-3 can be used to specify persistent problem areas that warrant further treatment. Evaluating self-efficacy can also be particularly useful near termination to ensure that the patient feels confident in using newly acquired skills.

General Levels of Anxiety. It is sometimes useful to assess levels of overall subjective anxiety to provide an assessment of the general level of subjective distress. Two widely used measures are the Beck Anxiety Inventory (BAI; Beck, Epstein, Brown, & Steer, 1988) and the State-Trait Anxiety Inventory (STAI; Spielberger, Gorsuch, Lushene, Vagg, & Jacobs, 1983). One advantage of the BAI is that it takes less time to complete than the STAI. If the STAI is used, it is recommended that both the state and trait measures be administered at intake. However, in most cases only the state measure would be regularly readministered to monitor treatment progress.

Quality of Life. Given that PD is associated with marked impairment across several domains of functioning (Simon et al., 2002), it may be useful to assess the patient's level of overall functional impairment. This can be done with clinician ratings such as the Global Assessment of Functioning (APA, 1994) or self-report scales of functional impairment including the Sheehan Disability Scale (Sheehan, 1983).

INTERVIEWING OBSTACLES AND SOLUTIONS

When interviewing patients with PD, it is important to be aware of certain obstacles that could lead interviewers astray when it comes to diagnostic decision making, selection of treatment strategy, and selection of treatment targets. This section outlines difficulties commonly encountered in each of these three areas, their potential impact on diagnosis and treatment, and possible solutions.

Obstacles in Diagnostic Decision Making

We have established that diagnostic accuracy is a fundamental feature of the interviewing process. In fact, subsequent enterprises such as treatment, monitoring or measurement, and referral all hinge on the correct identification of the primary diagnostic entity. Therefore, the interviewer should be keenly aware of certain key features of PD that may influence the accuracy of the diagnosis.

When it comes to diagnostic errors, the interviewer must contend with one of two possibilities: false positives and false negatives. In the case of PD, false-positive errors may occur when various medical morbidities are mistaken for PD. White and Barlow (2002) outlined specific medical conditions that include panic-like symptoms such as endocrine disorders (e.g., hypothyroidism, hypoglycemia), cardiovascular disorders (e.g., mitral valve prolapse, cardiac arrhythmia, hypertension), respiratory disorders (e.g., asthma), and neurological disorders (e.g., multiple sclerosis). Each of these medical conditions creates symptoms that may mimic the physiological symptoms of panic attacks and therefore should be ruled out.

False-positive decisions carry with them their own set of risks, and another consideration is the possibility of false negatives. In PD, false negatives are more likely to occur when the chief presenting problem is not panic but rather a medical complaint. This is an issue of central importance, given that many panic patients first appear in a primary care setting. For example, Katon, Vitaliano, Anderson, Jones, and Russo (1987) found that 35% of patients in a primary care setting had diagnosable PD.

To minimize false-negative errors, interviewers should assess whether the physiological events are accompanied by subjective fear and whether the panic-like symptoms occur in the absence of real danger (i.e., they are not responses to a specific environmental stressor). If the patient reports excessive, unexpected fear, this would be consistent with a PD diagnosis instead of or perhaps in addition to the primary medical complaint.

Although a majority of people with PD report excessive fear in association with panic attacks, it is crucially important to note that a proportion of panic patients will not report fear in association with panic episodes. In the case of nonfearful PD (NFPD), patients typically experience a small number of somatic symptoms (particularly chest pain; Beck, Berisford, Taegtmeyer, & Bennett, 1990). However, there is a marked absence of affective and cognitive symptoms. Many of these cases present in various medical clinics. One way to distinguish NFPD from genuine cardiovascular conditions is by determining whether behavioral changes followed the onset of symptoms. The *DSM-IV* field trial found that among nonfearful panickers, significant behavioral changes developed after symptom onset. Therefore, it may be particularly informative to conduct a behavioral assessment in cases such as these.

Obstacles Influencing the Selection of Treatment Strategies

A variety of empirically validated treatments for PD are available. Pharmacological and psychological therapies are efficacious in reducing acute anxiety symptoms associated with PD. When making treatment recommendations, the interviewer should be generally aware of specific conditions that may be problematic for a particular treatment modality.

Interoceptive exposure is one of the front-line treatments for PD (Schmidt & Trakowski, 2004). In this approach, the feared sensations are provoked in a controlled setting, with the expectation that habituation will gradually extinguish the fear response. However, several diagnosis-specific and nonspecific obstacles could interfere with this particular treatment. For instance, a nonspecific obstacle to such an approach includes things such as age, whereby older or infirm patients may suffer adverse health consequences in response to prolonged exposure. Ethical considerations may limit panic provocation in younger patients. In instances such as these, the interviewer may want to focus on cognitive therapy, which in isolation has been shown to produce significant relief from panic symptoms (Clark, 1986). On the other hand, sometimes patients may have difficulty understanding the cognitive aspects of the condition. In these cases, and with children, it is helpful to adopt a more behavioral intervention strategy that focuses on exposure.

Pharmacological treatments for PD have received wide empirical support. Most psychopharmacological treatments for PD are safe and non–habit forming. However, one important consideration when one is making a recommendation for pharmacological treatment is whether the patient has a history of substance abuse or dependence. Benzodiazepines in particular carry a specific risk for tolerance, abuse, and dependence (Shader & Greenblatt, 1993). Therefore, the interviewer should carefully consider the risk associated with benzodiazepines when making treatment recommendations, particularly with patients who have a history of substance use problems.

Obstacles Influencing the Selection of Treatment Targets

Often the interviewer must identify specific areas on which subsequent treatment will focus. Generally speaking, once a diagnosis is established, this information provides a reasonable amount of guidance as to the specific symptoms to be treated. However, because PD symptoms are heterogeneous, the particular symptoms and response patterns vary greatly from patient to patient. Therefore, it is important for the interviewer to have a grasp not only of likely treatment targets but also of obstacles that could interfere with their detection or successful resolution.

In the treatment of PD, therapy typically focuses on two target areas: cognitive symptoms and behavioral symptoms. Cognitive symptoms include the patient's thoughts and beliefs about the catastrophic nature of panic episodes. Behavioral symptoms can include such things as agoraphobic avoidance of certain people or locations, safety behaviors meant to increase a feeling of subjective security, and interoceptive avoidance, which involves the avoidance of specific activities that could elicit panic-like sensations (e.g., exercise).

In terms of cognitive symptoms, a fairly extensive body of literature suggests that a majority of patients with PD experience catastrophic cognitions during panic attacks (Ottaviani & Beck, 1987; Salkovskis & Clark, 1990; Westling & Öst, 1993). On the other hand, there are patients with PD who do not report catastrophic ideation. When there is no clear recognition of catastrophic ideation, certain elements of treatment (e.g., cognitive therapy) may not be feasible. Another obstacle that may interfere with the identification of these symptoms is the significant variability in *types* of panic-related cognitions. For instance, factor analytic studies support existence of three major types of catastrophic cognitions that occur in the context of panic attacks: physical collapse, mental collapse, and social collapse (Chambless et al., 1984; Telch et al., 1989). Furthermore, the relative primacy of each area may vary widely from patient to patient (i.e., some people may endorse fears of fainting, whereas others may fear primarily public embarrassment due to overt symptoms of panic). Therefore, the interviewer should identify which of these areas is primary because research suggests that the manipulation of so-called hot cognitions will have a direct impact on the likelihood of successful treatment (Hicks et al., 2005; Keijsers, Hoogduin, & Schapp, 1994).

Behavioral symptoms of PD are also heterogeneous. Similar to the problems the interviewer may encounter in the realm of cognitive symptoms, the subtlety and variety of behavioral symptoms may complicate their identification. Therefore, it is important to be aware of the various types of behavioral symptoms, which will inform subsequent treatment recommendations. Principal among the behavioral symptoms of PD is interoceptive avoidance. Given that many patients with PD demonstrate sensitivity to and fear of bodily perturbations, it stands to reason that the person will take steps to avoid situations in which they are evoked. For instance, exercise, certain foods or drinks (especially caffeinated beverages), and even sexual relations may all be avoided in an attempt to elude physiological hyperarousal. The interviewer should take a careful inventory of situations and behaviors that evoke feared physiological sensations. Such a list should then be folded into treatment recommendations because exposure sessions should focus on the very situations in which the patient is likely to encounter aversive interoceptive experience.

Another subtle but problematic type of behavioral symptom is a safety behavior (i.e., safety aid). These are actions designed to bolster subjective feelings of safety or security in situations that normally cause the patient distress. For example, patients with PD may travel to certain places only if they have a "safe person" with them, or they may carry "safety" objects, such as a cane, water bottle, lucky charm, or pill bottles. The array of potential safety cues and behaviors is virtually limitless (Salkovskis, Clark, & Gelder, 1996). The

key point is that safety is falsely attributed to the presence of the person or trinket (rather than the innocuous nature of the situation), which therefore diminishes the effectiveness of exposure. Therefore, the interviewer should assess idiosyncratic habits that the patient may use to deal with situations that would typically result in a panic attack. Furthermore, these should also be outlined in treatment recommendations so that they may be eliminated before exposure work.

CASE ILLUSTRATION WITH DIALOGUE

The following case is adapted from a history of a patient who is fairly typical of those with severe PD with agoraphobia in terms of onset, symptoms, and course. In this particular case, the patient has a prior diagnosis of PD, but the key questions are very similar in cases after there is a clear acknowledgment of panic. Interviews often begin with the patients providing a concise history of their panic.

Therapist: So you have been diagnosed with panic disorder. Give me a brief history by telling me when it first began, how it has run its course, and the ups and downs, and then let me know how it is affecting you currently.

Patient: I am really embarrassed to tell you what panic disorder has done to my life because I feel like a neurotic mess. My first attack happened 10 years ago at the airport where I was picking up my husband. I hadn't had much sleep that week because both my daughter and son had been sick, and my husband was out of town. I was late for the plane, and I'm nervous being in airports and flying in general. I had taken a new route and had gotten lost. I was feeling generally disoriented I think from the lack of sleep and just nerves in general. I went to the gate, and it was the wrong gate, and that made me feel a little mixed up. It turns out that my husband had told me the wrong flight number. But I'm thinking, "Am I a little bit crazy here?" and then I started to run as fast as I could to the airline desk to find out what the right gate was.

When I started to run I got very, very lightheaded. I thought I was going to pass out right there in the airport, and

I didn't know if I could get myself out of this. There was a cop standing there, and I told him that I might pass out, and I gave him my name and phone number. Well, that got him very excited. He asked if he should call the medics, and I said I don't know, I might be okay. He went ahead and called the medics, so they came, and that actually made me more nervous.

T: So at this point, were you actually having a panic attack?

P: Not yet, but when the medics came, they put this thing on my finger to measure the oxygen in your blood, and it came out with a reading of *no oxygen*. The medics totally freaked out, and it was like they all had panic attacks at that point. And they were shouting, "Get the oxygen!" and I'm like, "Oh my God." So now it's getting worse, and at this point I would say it was a panic attack. It was horrible. They brought in a stretcher and oxygen. I mean, here I am in the middle of the airport with this whole hook-up, and they're scurrying around like I'm about to die. This didn't help my anxiety much. They put me in the ambulance, and then they started putting the pulse thing on themselves, and they couldn't get readings either. I kept saying, "But I'm breathing." So anyway, once I found out that the equipment was malfunctioning, everyone felt much better, and I felt much better.

T: Wow, so at the time you were having some scary thoughts like "I'm about to pass out" or "I'm not getting enough oxygen." Were there other scary thoughts you were having at the time? . . . [Note that in this case the patient has already reported at least one threatening thought. Often, patients will simply say they had a panic attack and that it was terrible but will not provide information about the specific nature of their ideation. When that is the case, asking something like "I understand you were panicking, but what was so frightening?" or "What sorts of scary thoughts were you having when you were panicking?" is helpful. This provides the interviewer with critical information about what we sometimes call core threats, or ideas that are

sufficient to provoke panic in anyone who believes them. Sometimes this process is confusing to patients, and it is also helpful to say, "You've said that you were panicking, but you didn't always have that term—*panic attack*. Think back to when you hadn't ever heard of a panic attack; what did you think was happening?" You might also say, "If I were to insert the thought 'I'm having a panic attack' into someone's head, how would that make them feel? It probably wouldn't make any sense unless they knew what a panic attack was. I'm trying to get at the meaning of a panic attack for you."]

T: That is an excellent account of how things got started. Now tell me about how panic developed over time.

P: Then about 2 weeks after that, I had another panic attack where I was in a department store and everything looked real bright, and I started feeling like "Oh my gosh, is something happening again?" and sort of lightheaded. Then I experienced something that I hadn't before, which I guess is called derealization, it seems like you're dreaming what's happening, things didn't seem real. To me, this was even more frightening than feeling like I was going to pass out because I thought now I'm losing my mind.

T: Did having panic attacks affect your behavior?

P: In addition to going to the emergency room about five times early on, my limitations increased over time. I was afraid to eat alone for fear that I might choke and die, and my kids would be alone in the house. I couldn't go out by myself unless it was right outside my condo, my own block. My husband and other family members have had to accompany me everywhere. I used to have daily attacks, but now I don't really. I tried a bunch of different medications, including Xanax and Prozac, but I couldn't stand how they made me feel in general, even though they made me feel less anxious.

T: Tell me more specifically about how your panic and fears of panic are affecting you right now.

P: I have basically stopped going out of the house most of the time. I use the excuse that I'm staying home with the kids, but that isn't really working anymore. My son is now a teenager, and he complains that I embarrass him by never going to school functions or his soccer games. I can't even go shopping with my daughter for school clothes. My husband has tried to be supportive, but dealing with a panic person can be a real chore. He had to drive me here today. I feel like a total mess. I alternate between feeling guilty, humiliated, and depressed and feeling really angry at this stupid disorder.

T: Most people that are as debilitated by panic as you are often will feel depressed; after all, your life has been really disrupted. Tell me more about your depression.

This is followed by an assessment of mood in this patient, including suicidal ideation and intent.

MULTICULTURAL AND DIVERSITY ISSUES

To date, most research on PD and other types of anxiety psychopathology has been conducted in the United States. However, psychological science must pursue information on issues pertaining to anxiety-related psychopathology across diverse populations. Such research activities benefit underserved populations and they permit the refinement of contemporary perspectives of anxiety and other types of psychopathology.

One central question is whether the condition we recognize as PD in North America is universally recognized or whether the *DSM-IV* (APA, 1994) notion of PD, which originates from medical doctrine that emphasizes biological commonality over cultural diversity, fails to adequately capture cross-cultural diversity. The empirical literature appears to suggest that *DSM* panic attacks and PD can be reliably diagnosed in other countries. For example, the Upjohn Cross-National Panic Study found that PD could be reliably diagnosed in Europe, Australia, and Central and South America, with symptom profiles being remarkably consistent across countries (Amering & Katschnig, 1990). However, as McNally (1994) points out, the Upjohn study did not establish the cross-*cultural* validity of PD because of the

substantial level of cultural similarity across the participating countries. To better establish cross-cultural validity, PD must be evaluated in less Westernized countries.

In fact, there have been several reports evaluating PD in African countries. In a study of Ugandan villages, Orley and Wing (1979) describe the existence of spontaneous panic attacks. Otakpor (1987) provides an account of several patients that appeared to have PD and were successfully treated with antidepressants. Also, *DSM-III* (Hollifield, Katon, Spain, & Pule, 1990) and *DSM-III-R* versions of PD have been diagnosed in Africa (Bertschy, 1992). There is also one report evaluating panic attacks in Iran (Nazemi et al., 2003). This report generally supports the idea of cross-cultural similarity of panic and PD among Iranian students. This literature obviously is fairly limited, but it is consistent with the idea that panic and PD are somewhat culturally universal.

On the other hand, there are also indications that PD is substantially affected by culture. For example, studies in India suggest different frequencies in certain panic attack symptoms and a much higher percentage of patients receiving an agoraphobia diagnosis (Neerakal & Srinivasan, 2003). Moreover, the sex ratio among those with agoraphobia is completely the opposite of that found in the United States. For example, Raguram and Bhide (1985) found that almost 85% of their agoraphobia patients were men. The explanation provided for these cross-cultural differences is that phobic avoidance would be difficult to detect in Indian women because many are forbidden to leave the home or can leave only when accompanied by a man.

There are also several instances of so-called culturally bound variants of panic and PD. In these cases, some of which are listed in the *DSM-IV* as culture-bound variants, the condition is similar to the Western diagnosis but differs in some substantive way. Kayak-angst (Amering & Katschnig, 1990) is a condition that resembles PD but is seen exclusively in male Eskimos. Kayak-angst involves feelings of terror, disorientation, and fear of drowning while kayaking far off shore. These attacks occur only at sea and dissipate once the person is back on shore. Koro describes a panic-like state surrounding fears that the penis is retracting into the body and occurs fairly exclusively in China and Chinese communities (Rubin, 1982). Sore-neck syndrome has been described as culture-bound variant of PD that occurs among Khmer refugees. Sore-neck syndrome involves fears that wind and blood pressure may cause blood vessels in the neck to burst, includes many symptoms of panic, and is highly comorbid with a PD diagnosis (Hinton, Um, & Ba, 2001).

One of the better-studied culture-bound syndromes that relates to PD is a condition called *ataques de nervios*, which translates to "attacks of nerves." As noted in the *DSM-IV-TR* (APA, 2000), *ataques de nervios* is an experience of distress characterized by a general sense of being out of control. The most common symptoms include uncontrollable shouting, attacks of crying, trembling, and heat in the chest rising into the head. Dissociative symptoms, suicidal gestures, and seizure or fainting episodes are observed in some episodes of *ataques de nervios* but not others. This syndrome is reported to occur typically after a distressing event such as an interpersonal conflict or the death of a loved one (Guarnaccia, DeLaCancela, & Carrillo, 1989). *Ataques de nervios* appear to have high prevalence rates in Hispanic countries (Guarnaccia, Canino, Rubio-Stipec, & Bravo, 1993) and high rates of comorbidity with a number of anxiety disorders including PD but also posttraumatic stress disorder and generalized anxiety disorder (Guarnaccia et al., 1993; Lewis-Fernández, Garrido-Castillo, et al., 2002). There have also been a number of studies demonstrating *ataques de nervios* among Hispanic samples in the United States (Salmán et al., 1998; Weingartner, Robison, Fogel, & Gruman, 2002).

With a similar presentation to panic attacks, several studies have evaluated the congruence between panic attacks and *ataques de nervios*. To date, this work has concluded that despite overlap, these are two distinct conditions that can both occur in the same person (Lewis-Fernández, Guarnaccia, et al., 2002; Liebowitz et al., 1994). Several symptoms have been reported to differentiate the two disorders; *ataques de nervios* are proposed to include fewer unprovoked episodes, more dissociative symptoms, and a slower crescendo than panic attacks (Lewis-Fernández, Garrido-Castillo, et al., 2002).

There is a wide range of perspectives on the impact of culture on the development of mental illness, including PD. A traditional psychiatric perspective indicates that biological forces determine the presence and the core aspects of the disorder, whereas cultural factors may affect the expression of the condition. For example, an underlying panic process may account for the emergence of panic in different cultures that will manifest itself as panic attacks, koro, or kayak-angst depending on cultural forces. On the other hand, Kleinman (1988) suggests that what is overlooked by this perspective is that the illness that emerges from a biological diathesis may be just as important as the underlying biological disease process. In other words, the interaction of culture with biological disposition may create important patterns in onset, course, treatment response, and so forth. For instance, among Cambodian refugees, orthostatic changes appear to be particularly provocative of panic attacks (Hinton, Pollack, Pich, Fama, & Barlow, 2005). Thus, cultural variables can be critical determinants of panic and PD.

DIFFERENTIAL DIAGNOSIS AND BEHAVIORAL ASSESSMENT

PD often can be mistaken for other psychiatric and nonpsychiatric disorders. We have already indicated the common problem of distinguishing PD from medical morbidities. In this section, we approach the issue of differential diagnosis between PD and other anxiety disorders, with a focus on behavioral assessment techniques.

Because patients with PD often suffer from social, physical, and occupational disability and suffer from mild to moderate levels of anxiety, it can sometimes be quite difficult to distinguish PD from other anxiety disorders (which generally share the same features). In particular, social anxiety disorder (SAD) and generalized anxiety disorder (GAD) should be ruled out because they can sometimes contain episodes of intense anxiety and panic attacks. Typically, this is accomplished by identifying the circumstances under which the patient becomes anxious and the content of the anxious apprehension. In the case of SAD, anxiety episodes typically occur exclusively in the context of social situations, whereas in PD, panic attacks also occur in nonsocial situations. However, some patients with PD have fears about social consequences that result from panic attacks. The basic issue to be considered is whether the patient has fears of panic per se. If this is the case, then PD is indicated. In the case of GAD, patients may also experience panic attacks along with excessive worry in any number of contexts. Once again, the critical issue is whether there is substantial worry about panic per se rather than worry about certain things that may or may not result in panic attacks.

In addition to evaluation of the central fear of panic, several laboratory and behavioral tests are available that can be used to distinguish PD from other anxiety disorders. These laboratory indices, sometimes called biological challenge tests, have a long history in PD. Biological psychiatrists began to use challenge tests, where the patient is exposed to a biological substance, to evaluate the purported neurobiology of PD. Challenge agents include norepinephrine, cholecystokinin, isoproterenol, caffeine, lactate, and high doses of carbon dioxide. Psychologists have also used challenges to understand cognitive parameters that affect fearful responding. A behavioral extension of the challenge task would include interoceptive assessment (Schmidt & Trakowski, 1994). This assessment involves the intentional generation of physical sensations through various exercises such as spinning or running in place. Both biological challenges and interoceptive exercises often create anxiety and even panic in patients with PD.

Although there are not clear data regarding how other anxiety patients respond to challenges or interoceptive exercises, it would be very unusual for a patient with PD to report no or little anxiety during these exercises (Schmidt & Trakowski, 1994). Therefore, challenge or interoceptive assessment can help to rule out PD when there is little or no fear. However, a positive fear response to these assessments does not rule out other anxiety conditions.

SELECTION OF TREATMENT TARGETS AND REFERRAL

The information collected during assessment interviews is vital to the determination of treatment targets and referral. Because we have already outlined symptom targets, this section of the chapter outlines the current research findings on treatment type, including combined (psychosocial plus pharmacological) treatment for PD.

Psychosocial Treatments

Several psychosocial treatments have been found to be efficacious in PD treatment, including in vivo exposure (Mathews, Gelder, & Johnston, 1981), cognitive therapy (Beck & Emery, 1985; Clark, 1986), and CBT (Barlow, Craske, Cerny, & Klosko, 1989; Telch et al., 1993). CBT is generally considered the treatment of choice for PD (Otto & Deveney, 2005). Historically, the practice of encouraging patients to repeatedly confront situations that produce intense fear and avoidance (i.e., in vivo exposure) has been the hallmark of behavioral treatments for agoraphobia and panic. The newer CBT protocols derived from this framework focus on correcting the patient's hypersensitivity to bodily sensations and the misinterpretation of these sensations as signaling immediate threat. The main components of treatment typically include education, training in cognitive reappraisal (i.e., cognitive restructuring), repeated exposure to bodily sensations connected to the fear response (i.e., interoceptive exposure), and repeated exposure to external situations that trigger a fear response (i.e., in vivo exposure).

When the newer CBT protocols are used, the question arises as to the selection of treatment targets and the sequencing of treatment. Exposure treatments can vary widely in their execution. For instance, exposure can be administered in a gradual, hierarchical fashion or in a more intensive manner, be therapist directed or patient directed, and involve in vivo or interoceptive exposure. The choice of treatment strategy should be guided by the information collected during intake and depends on the types of situations feared by the particular patient and individual differences in areas such as the patient's level of avoidance and anxiety sensitivity. Unfortunately, there is no clear empirical evidence to guide such choices.

There are some circumstances under which treatment may deviate from traditional CBT protocols for PD. For example, if the suicide assessment reveals that the patient is presenting with a high level of suicide-related dangerousness, treatment should begin with crisis management (see Rudd, Joiner, & Rajab, 2001). Additionally, it may be the case that a patient's comorbid conditions interfere with treatment delivery. Patients with comorbid mood disorders may demonstrate a decreased interest or motivation to engage in difficult exposure tasks without the assistance of psychopharmacological or psychosocial treatments targeting depressive symptoms. Similarly, patients with comorbid substance use disorders may benefit from brief motivational interviewing (see Miller & Rollnick, 2002) to increase motivation to change problematic substance use behaviors before engaging in treatment for PD.

Pharmacotherapy

In addition to psychosocial treatments, several classes of medication have been efficacious in ameliorating panic-related symptoms in a number of double-blind placebo-controlled trials. Antidepressants, particularly selective serotonin reuptake inhibitors, have become the medication of choice in PD treatment, reducing symptoms without causing the withdrawal and dependency that can occur with benzodiazepines. A recent meta-analysis concluded that selective serotonin reuptake inhibitors and tricyclic antidepressants are equally efficacious, although there may be a higher dropout rate among patients who use tricyclics (Bakker, van Balkom, & Spinhoven, 2002).

Combined Psychopharmacological and Psychosocial Treatments

Use of combined treatment approaches, in which the administration of medication is coupled with psychosocial intervention, is a common method for most mental disorders (see Sammons & Schmidt, 2001, for a review). For instance, Pincus et al. (1999) found that nearly 90% of patients of psychiatrists were receiving medication and that 55.4% of outpatients received both medication and psychotherapy. Use of combined treatment approaches is particularly evident in the treatment of PD. One possible explanation for the high rate of combined treatments in clinical practice is that mental health professionals may regard this approach as the most effective mode of intervention.

Common rationales for combining psychosocial and pharmacological treatments include treatment specificity, facilitation of psychosocial treatment with pharmacotherapy, and facilitation of pharmacotherapy with psychosocial treatment (see Telch & Lucas, 1994). The treatment specificity line of reasoning relies on the assumption that drug and psychological treatments affect different facets of a disorder. For example, medication could be used to affect neurobiological features of the disorder, whereas psychosocial interventions may address behavioral aspects. In comparison, the psychosocial facilitation argument suggests that the primary mode of treatment should be psychological, but the adjunctive use of medication may be indicated in some cases.

Unfortunately, despite the intuitive appeal of combined treatments for PD, there is little research to support the assumption that combined treatment approaches are superior to singular interventions (see Sammons & Schmidt, 2001). The few studies that have reported long-term efficacy indicate that the preliminary benefits of combined treatment are lost during follow-up and that in some cases combined treatment may yield poorer long-term outcome. For example, Barlow, Gorman, Shear, and Woods (2000) found that although combined imipramine plus CBT resulted in better outcome at posttreatment and postmaintenance, CBT alone predicted the best outcome at 6-month follow-up. The addition of imipramine to CBT appeared to reduce the long-term efficacy of CBT. Furthermore, CBT did not mitigate relapse after medication discontinuation.

SUMMARY

In summary, although the literature suggests that combined treatments may promote some short-term beneficial effects, combined treatments appear to lose their advantage in the long term and in some cases may have deleterious effects. On the other hand, it is worth considering the possibility that these medication trials typically must be discontinued at the end of treatment. The length of medication treatment may not be sufficient in these cases to produce the desired neurobiological changes. Therefore, long-term benefits of combined treatments may be underestimated. Furthermore, although it is somewhat surprising that combined treatments are not more efficacious for people with PD, a variety of factors may contribute to the lack of clear advantages, including the way in which the treatment approach is explained (or not explained) to the patient, a tendency to overrely on medication (or under rely on cognitive-behavioral skills), and misattribution of gains. Further work is needed to clarify these important issues.

Practical Recommendations for Treating PD

What do the data suggest for clinicians? For both unmedicated and medicated patients, tentative treatment algorithms can be derived based on the current research findings. When an unmedicated patient presents for treatment, it appears to be most conservative to start with a trial of CBT without pharmacological intervention because the data suggest that the singular effects of CBT will be highly effective for the majority of patients. Yet there are several instances in which CBT should be immediately combined with pharmacological intervention. For example, a PD patient with co-occurring severe depression may not be capable of undertaking a CBT trial and should be considered for a combination of CBT with antidepressant medication.

As for medicated patients, data do not indicate that the addition of CBT will yield positive benefits. However, there are some instances when the clinician may want to consider CBT for medicated patients. For example, CBT has been shown to be effective for medicated patients who do not respond to pharmacotherapy (Otto, Pollack, Penava, & Zucker, 1999). Similarly, CBT often is useful if medication discontinuation is a treatment goal because CBT can be helpful in discontinuing antidepressants and benzodiazepines (Schmidt, Woolaway-Bickel, Trakowski, Santiago, & Vasey, 2002; Whittal, Otto, & Hong, 2001).

REFERENCES

American Psychiatric Association. (1980). *Diagnostic and statistical manual of mental disorders* (3rd ed.). Washington, DC: Author.

American Psychiatric Association. (1987). *Diagnostic and statistical manual of mental disorders* (3rd ed., Rev.). Washington, DC: Author.

American Psychiatric Association. (1994). *Diagnostic and statistical manual of mental disorders* (4th ed.). Washington, DC: Author.

American Psychiatric Association. (2000). *Diagnostic and statistical manual of mental disorders* (4th ed., Text rev.). Washington, DC: Author.

Amering, M., & Katschnig, H. (1990). Panic attacks and panic disorder in cross-cultural perspective. *Psychiatric Annals, 20,* 511–516.

Antony, M. M., Orsillo, S. M., & Roemer, L. (2001). *Practitioner's guide to empirically based measures of anxiety.* New York: Kluwer Academic/Plenum.

Bakker, A., van Balkom, A. J. L. M., & Spinhoven, P. (2002). SSRIs vs. TCAs in the treatment of panic disorder: A meta-analysis. *Acta Psychiatrica Scandinavica, 106,* 163–167.

Barlow, D. H. (2002). *Anxiety and its disorders* (2nd ed.). New York: Guilford.

Barlow, D. H., Brown, T. A., & Craske, M. G. (1994). Definitions of panic attacks and panic disorder in

the *DSM-IV:* Implications for research. *Journal of Abnormal Psychology, 103,* 553–564.

Barlow, D. H., Craske, M. G., Cerny, J. A., & Klosko, J. S. (1989). Behavioral treament of panic disorder. *Behavior Therapy, 20,* 261–282.

Barlow, D. H., Gorman, J. M., Shear, M. K., & Woods, S. W. (2000). Cognitive-behavioral therapy, imipramine, or their combination for panic disorder: A randomized controlled trial. *Journal of the American Medical Association, 283,* 2529–2536.

Beck, A. T., & Emery, G. (1985). *Anxiety disorders and phobias: A cognitive perspective.* New York: Basic Books.

Beck, A. T., Epstein, N., Brown, G., & Steer, R. A. (1988). An inventory for measuring clinical anxiety: Psychometric properties. *Journal of Consulting and Clinical Psychology, 56,* 893–897.

Beck, A. T., Kovacs, M., & Weissman, A. (1979). Assessment of suicidal intention: The Scale for Suicide Ideation. *Journal of Consulting and Clinical Psychology, 47,* 343–352.

Beck, J. G., Berisford, M. A., Taegtmeyer, H., & Bennett, A. (1990). Panic symptoms in chest pain patients without coronary heart disease: A comparison with panic disorder. *Behavior Therapy, 21,* 241–252.

Bertschy, G. (1992). Panic disorder in Benin, West Africa. *American Journal of Psychiatry, 149,* 1410.

Cerny, J. A., Himadi, W. G., & Barlow, D. H. (1984). Issues in diagnosing anxiety disorders. *Journal of Behavioral Assessment, 6,* 301–329.

Chambless, D. L., Caputo, G. C., Bright, P., & Gallagher, K. (1984). Assessment of fear in agoraphobics: The Body Sensations Questionnaire and the Agoraphobic Cognitions Questionnaire. *Journal of Consulting and Clinical Psychology, 52,* 1090–1097.

Chambless, D. L., Caputo, G. C., Jasin, S. E., Gracely, E. J., & Williams, C. (1985). The Mobility Inventory for Agoraphobia. *Behaviour Research and Therapy, 23,* 35–44.

Clark, D. M. (1986). A cognitive approach to panic. *Behaviour Research and Therapy, 24,* 461–470.

DiNardo, P. A., Brown, T. A., & Barlow, D. H. (1994). *Anxiety Disorders Interview Schedule for DSM-IV: Lifetime Version (ADIS-IV-L).* Albany, NY: Graywind.

First, M. B., Spitzer, R. L., Gibbon, M., & Williams, J. B. (1994). *Structured Clinical Interview for Axis I DSM-IV Disorders: Patient edition* (SCID-I/P, Version 2.0). New York: Biometrics Research Department, New York State Psychiatric Institute.

Frances, A., Miele, G. M., Widiger, T. A., Pincus, H. A., Manning, D., & Davis, W. W. (1993). The classification of panic disorders: From Freud to *DSM-IV. Journal of Psychiatric Research, 27,* 3–10.

Goldstein, A. J., & Chambless, D. L. (1978). A reanalysis of agoraphobia. *Behavior Therapy, 9,* 47–59.

Greenberg, P. E., Sisitsky, T., Kessler, R. C., Finkelstein, S. N., Berndt, E. R., Davidson, J. R., et al. (1999). The economic burden of anxiety disorders in the 1990s. *Journal of Clinical Psychiatry, 64,* 1465–1475.

Grove, W. M., & Meehl, P. E. (1996). Comparative efficiency of informal (subjective, impressionistic) and formal (mechanical, algorithmic) prediction procedures: The clinical-statistical controversy. *Psychology, Public Policy, and Law, 2,* 293–323.

Guarnaccia, P. J., Canino, G., Rubio-Stipec, M., & Bravo, M. (1993). The prevalence of *ataques de nervios* in the Puerto Rico disaster study: The role of culture in psychiatric epidemiology. *Journal of Nervous and Mental Disease, 181,* 157–165.

Guarnaccia, P. J., DeLaCancela, V., & Carrillo, E. (1989). The multiple meanings of *ataques de nervios* in the Latino community. *Medical Anthropology, 11,* 47–62.

Hayward, C., Killen, J. D., & Taylor, C. B. (2003). The relationship between agoraphobia symptoms and panic disorder in a non-clinical sample of adolescents. *Psychological Medicine, 33,* 733–738.

Hicks, T. V., Leitenberg, H., Barlow, D. H., Gorman, J. M., Shear M. K., & Woods, S. W. (2005). Physical, mental, and social catastrophic cognitions as prognostic factors in cognitive-behavioral and pharmacological treatments for panic disorder. *Journal of Consulting and Clinical Psychology, 73,* 506–514.

Hino, T., Takeuchi, T., & Yamanouchi, N. (2002). A 1-year follow-up study of coping in patients with panic disorder. *Comprehensive Psychiatry, 43,* 279–284.

Hinton, D. E., Pollack, M. H., Pich, V., Fama, J. M., & Barlow, D. H. (2005). Orthostatically induced panic attacks among Cambodian refugees: Flashbacks, catastrophic cognitions and associated psychopathology. *Cognitive and Behavioral Practice, 12,* 301–311.

Hinton, D., Um, K., & Ba, P. (2001). A unique panic-disorder presentation among Khmer refugees: The sore-neck syndrome. *Culture, Medicine and Psychiatry, 25,* 297–316.

Hoffart, A., Friis, S., & Martinsen, E. W. (1992). Assessment of fear of fear among agoraphobic patients: The agoraphobic cognitions scale. *Journal of Psychopathology and Behavioral Assessment, 14,* 175–187.

Hollifield, M., Katon, W., Spain, D., & Pule, L. (1990). Anxiety and depression in a village in Lesotho, Africa: A comparison with the United States. *British Journal of Psychiatry, 156,* 343–350.

Kahn, J. P., Drusin, R. E., & Klein, D. F. (1987). Idiopathic cardiomyopathy and panic disorder: Clinical association in cardiac transplant candidates. *American Journal of Psychiatry, 144,* 1327–1330.

Karajgi, B., Rifkin, A., Doddi, S., & Kolli, R. (1990). The prevalence of anxiety disorders in patients with chronic obstructive pulmonary disease. *American Journal of Psychiatry, 147,* 200–201.

Katon, W., Vitaliano, P. P., Anderson, K., Jones, M., & Russo, J. (1987). Panic disorder: Residual symptoms after the acute attacks abate. *Comprehensive Psychiatry, 28,* 151–158.

Kawachi, I., Colditz, G. A., Ascherio, A., Rimm, E. B., Giovannucci, E., Stampfer, M. J., et al. (1994). Prospective study of phobic anxiety and risk of coronary heart disease in men. *Circulation, 89,* 1992–1997.

Kearney, C. A., Albano, A. M., Eisen, A. R., Allan, W. D., & Barlow, D. H. (1997). The phenomenology of panic disorder in youngsters: An empirical study of a clinical sample. *Journal of Anxiety Disorders, 11,* 49–62.

Keijsers, G. P. J., Hoogduin, C. A. L., & Schapp, C. P. D. R. (1994). Prognostic factors in the behavioral treatment

of panic disorder with and without agoraphobia. *Behavior Therapy, 25,* 689–708.

Kessler, R. C., Chiu, W. T., Demler, O., & Walters, E. E. (2005). Prevalence, severity, and comorbidity of 12-month *DSM-IV* disorders in the National Comorbidity Survey Replication. *Archives of General Psychiatry, 62,* 617–627.

Kessler, R. C., Crum, R. M., Warner, L. A., Nelson, C. B., Schulenberg, J., & Anthony, J. C. (1997). Lifetime co-occurrence of *DSM-III-R* alcohol abuse and dependence with other psychiatric disorders in the national comorbidity survey. *Archives of General Psychiatry, 54,* 313–321.

Klein, D. F., & Klein, H. M. (1989). The substantive effect of variations in panic measurement and agoraphobia definition. *Journal of Anxiety Disorders, 3,* 45–56.

Kleinman, A. (1988). *Rethinking psychiatry: From cultural category to personal experience.* New York: Free Press.

Lewinsohn, P. M., Zinbarg, R., Seeley, J. R., Lewinsohn, M., & Sack, W. H. (1997). Lifetime comorbidity among anxiety disorders and between anxiety disorders and other mental disorders in adolescents. *Journal of Anxiety Disorders, 11,* 377–394.

Lewis-Fernández, R., Garrido-Castillo, P., Carmen Bennasar, M., Parrilla, E. M., Laria, A. J., Ma, G., et al. (2002). Dissociation, childhood trauma, and *ataque de nervios* among Puerto Rican psychiatric outpatients. *American Journal of Psychiatry, 159,* 1603–1605.

Lewis-Fernández, R., Guarnaccia, P. J., Martínez, I. E., Salmán, E., Schmidt, A., & Liebowitz, M. (2002). Comparative phenomenology of *ataques de nervios,* panic attacks, and panic disorder. *Culture, Medicine and Psychiatry, 26,* 199–223.

Ley, R. (1992). The many faces of Pan: Psychological and physiological differences among three types of panic attacks. *Behaviour Research and Therapy, 30,* 347–357.

Liebowitz, M. R., Salmán, E., Jusino, C. M., Garfinkel, R., Street, L., Cardenas, D. L., et al. (1994). *Ataque de nervios* and panic disorder. *American Journal of Psychiatry, 151,* 871–875.

Maller, R. G., & Reiss, S. (1992). Anxiety sensitivity in 1984 and panic attacks in 1987. *Journal of Anxiety Disorders, 6,* 241–247.

Margraf, J., Taylor, C. B., Ehlers, A., Roth, W., & Agras, W. S. (1987). Panic attacks in the natural environment. *Journal of Nervous and Mental Disease, 175,* 558–565.

Marks, I. M. (1970). The classification of phobic disorders. *British Journal of Psychiatry, 116,* 377–386.

Marks, I. M. (1987). Behavioral aspects of panic disorder. *American Journal of Psychiatry, 144,* 1160–1165.

Marks, I. M., & Mathews, A. M. (1979). Brief standard self-rating for phobic patients. *Behaviour Research and Therapy, 17,* 263–267.

Mathews, A. M., Gelder, M. G., & Johnston, D. (1981). *Agoraphobia: Nature and treatment.* New York: Guilford.

McCue, E. C., & McCue, P. A. (1984). Organic and hyperventilatory causes of anxiety-type symptoms. *Behavioural Psychotherapy, 12,* 308–317.

McNally, R. J. (1994). *Panic disorder: A critical analysis.* New York: Guilford.

Miller, W. R., & Rollnick, S. (2002). *Motivational interviewing.* New York: Guilford.

Nazemi, H., Kleinknecht, R. A., Dinnel, D. L., Lonner, W. J., Nazemi, S., Shamlo, S., et al. (2003). A study of panic attacks in university students of Iran. *Journal of Psychopathology and Behavioral Assessment, 25*, 191–201.

Neerakal, I., & Srinivasan, K. (2003). A study of the phenomenology of panic attacks in patients from India. *Psychopathology, 36*, 92–97.

Orley, J., & Wing, J. K. (1979). Psychiatric disorders in two African villages. *Archives of General Psychiatry, 36*, 513–520.

Otakpor, A. N. (1987). A prospective study of panic disorder in a Nigerian psychiatric out-patient population. *Acta Psychiatrica Scandinavica, 76*, 541–544.

Ottaviani, R., & Beck, A. T. (1987). Cognitive aspects of panic disorders. *Journal of Anxiety Disorders, 1*, 15–28.

Otto, M. W., & Deveney, C. (2005). Cognitive-behavioral therapy and the treatment of panic disorder: Efficacy and strategies. *Journal of Clinical Psychiatry, 66*, 28–32.

Otto, M. W., Pollack, M. H., Penava, S. J., & Zucker, B. G. (1999). Group cognitive-behavior therapy for patients failing to respond to pharmacotherapy for panic disorder: A clinical case series. *Behaviour Research and Therapy, 37*, 763–770.

Peterson, R. A., & Reiss, S. (1993). *Anxiety Sensitivity Index Revised test manual.* Worthington, OH: IDS.

Pincus, H. A., Zarin, D. A., Tanielian, T. L., Johnson, J. L., West, J. C., Pettit, A. R., et al. (1999). Psychiatric patients and treatments in 1997: Findings from the American Psychiatric Practice Research Network. *Archives of General Psychiatry, 56*, 441–449.

Raguram, R., & Bhide, A. V. (1985). Patterns of phobic neurosis: A retrospective study. *British Journal of Psychiatry, 147*, 557–560.

Raj, B. A., Corvea, M. H., & Dagon, E. M. (1993). The clinical characteristics of panic disorder in the elderly: A retrospective study. *Journal of Clinical Psychiatry, 54*, 150–155.

Reiss, S., & McNally, R. J. (1985). The expectancy model of fear. In S. Reiss & R. R. Bootzin (Eds.), *Theoretical issues in behavior therapy* (pp. 107–121). New York: Academic Press.

Rogers, M. P., White, K., Warshaw, M. G., Yonkers, K. A., Rodriguez-Villa, F., Chang, G., et al. (1994). Prevalence of medical illness in patients with anxiety disorders. *International Journal of Psychiatry in Medicine, 24*, 83–96.

Rubin, R. T. (1982). Koro (*shook yang*): A culture-bound psychogenic syndrome. In C. T. H. Friedmann & R. A. Faguet (Eds.), *Extraordinary disorders of human behavior* (pp. 155–172). New York: Plenum.

Rudd, M. D. (1989). The prevalence of suicidal ideation among college students. *Suicide and Life-Threatening Behavior, 19*, 173–183.

Rudd, M. D., Joiner, T., & Rajab, M. H. (2001). *Treating suicidal behavior.* New York: Guilford.

Salkovskis, P. M., & Clark, D. M. (1990). Affective response to hyperventilation: A test of the cognitive model of panic. *Behavior Research and Therapy, 28*, 51–61.

Salkovskis, P. M., Clark, D. M, & Gelder, M. G. (1996). Cognition-behaviour links in the persistence of panic. *Behaviour Research and Therapy, 34*, 453–458.

Salmán, E., Liebowitz, M. R., Guarnaccia, P. J., Jusino, C. M., Garfinkel, R., Street, L., et al. (1998). Subtypes of *ataques de nervios:* The influence of coexisting psychiatric diagnosis. *Culture, Medicine and Psychiatry, 22*, 231–244.

Sammons, M. T., & Schmidt, N. B. (Eds.). (2001). *Combined treatments for mental disorders: A guide to psychological and pharmacological interventions.* Washington, DC: American Psychological Association.

Schmidt, N. B., Eggleston, A. M., Trakowski, J. H., & Smith, J. D. (2005). Does coping predict CO_2-induced panic in patients with panic disorder? *Behaviour Research and Therapy, 43*, 1311–1319.

Schmidt, N. B., Forsyth, J. P., Santiago, H. T., & Trakowski, J. H. (2002). Classification of panic attack subtypes in patients and normal controls in response to biological challenge: Implications for assessment and treatment. *Journal of Anxiety Disorders, 16*, 625–638.

Schmidt, N. B., Lerew, D. R., & Trakowski, J. H. (1997). Body vigilance in panic disorder: Evaluating attention to bodily perturbations. *Journal of Consulting and Clinical Psychology, 65*, 214–220.

Schmidt, N. B., & Trakowski, J. (2004). Interoceptive assessment and exposure in patients with panic disorder: A descriptive study. *Cognitive and Behavioral Practice, 11*, 81–91.

Schmidt, N. B., Woolaway-Bickel, K., & Bates, M. (2001). Evaluating panic-specific factors in the relationship between suicide and panic disorder. *Behaviour Research and Therapy, 36*, 635–649.

Schmidt, N. B., Woolaway-Bickel, K., Trakowski, J. H., Santiago, H. T., & Vasey, M. (2002). Antidepressant discontinuation in the context of cognitive behavioral treatment for panic disorder. *Behaviour Research and Therapy, 40*, 67–73.

Shader, R. I., & Greenblatt, D. J. (1993). Use of benzodiazepines in anxiety disorders: Reply. *New England Journal of Medicine, 329*, 1501.

Shear, M. K., Brown, T. A., Barlow, D. H., Money, R., Sholomskas, D. E., Woods, S. W., et al. (1997). Multicenter collaborative Panic Disorder Severity Scale. *American Journal of Psychiatry, 154*, 1571–1575.

Sheehan, D. V. (1983). *The anxiety disease.* New York: Scribner.

Simon, N. M., Otto, M. W., Korbly, N. B., Peters, P. M., Nicolaou, D. C., & Pollack, M. H. (2002). Quality of life in social anxiety disorder compared with panic disorder and the general population. *Psychiatric Services, 53*, 714–718.

Smits, J. A. J., Powers, M. B., Cho, Y. R., & Telch, M. J. (2004). Mechanism of change in cognitive behavioral treatment of panic disorder: Evidence for the fear of fear mediational hypothesis. *Journal of Consulting and Clinical Psychology, 72*, 646–652.

Spielberger, C. D., Gorsuch, R. L., Lushene, R., Vagg, P. R., & Jacobs, G. A. (1983). *Manual for the State-Trait Anxiety Inventory (Form Y).* Palo Alto, CA: Consulting Psychologists Press.

Taylor, S. (2000). *Understanding and treating panic disorder: Cognitive-behavioural approaches.* New York: Wiley.

Telch, M. J., Brouillard, M., Telch, C. F., Agras, W. S., & Taylor, C. B. (1989). Role of cognitive appraisal in panic-related avoidance. *Behaviour Research and Therapy, 27*, 373–383.

Telch, M. J., & Lucas, R. A. (1994). Combined pharmacological and psychological treatment of panic disorder: Current status and future directions. In B. E. Wolfe & J. Maser (Eds.), *Treatment of panic disorder: A consensus development conference* (pp. 177–179). Washington, DC: American Psychiatric Association.

Telch, M. J., Lucas, J. A., Schmidt, N. B., Hanna, H. H., Jaimez, T. L., & Lucas, R. A. (1993). Group cognitive-behavioral treatment of panic disorder. *Behaviour Research and Therapy, 31*, 279–287.

Weingartner, K., Robison, J., Fogel, D., & Gruman, C. (2002). Depression and substance use in a middle aged and older Puerto Rican population. *Journal of Cross-Cultural Gerontology, 17*, 173–193.

Weissman, M. M., Klerman, G. L., Markowitz, J. S., & Ouellette, R. (1989). Suicidal ideation and suicide attempts in panic disorder and attacks. *New England Journal of Medicine, 321*, 1209–1214.

Westling, B. E., & Öst, L.-G. (1993). Relationship between panic attack symptoms and cognitions in panic disorder patients. *Journal of Anxiety Disorders, 7*, 181–194.

White, K., & Barlow, D. H. (2002). Panic disorder and agoraphobia. In D. H. Barlew (Eds.), *Anxiety and its disorders: The nature and treatment of anxiety and panic* (2nd ed., pp. 328–379). New York: Guilford.

Whittal, M. L., Goetsch, V. L., & Eifert, G. H. (1996). Introduction of a dynamic, idiographic model for identifying panic. *Journal of Anxiety Disorders, 10*, 129–144.

Whittal, M. L., Otto, M. W., & Hong, J. J. (2001). Cognitive-behavior therapy for discontinuation of SSRI treatment of panic disorder: A case series. *Behaviour Research and Therapy, 39*, 939–945.

Zvolensky, M. J., Bernstein, A., Sachs-Ericsson, N., Schmidt, N. B., Buckner, J. D., & Bonn-Miller, M. O. (2006). Lifetime associations between cannabis use, abuse, and dependence and panic attacks in a representative sample. *Journal of Psychiatric Research, 40*, 477–486.

Zvolensky, M. J., Schmidt, N. B., & Stewart, S. H. (2003). Panic disorder and smoking. *Clinical Psychology, 10*, 29–51.

14

SPECIFIC PHOBIA

LAURA L. VERNON

DESCRIPTION OF THE DISORDER

Specific phobias, formerly called simple phobias in the *Diagnostic and Statistical Manual of Mental Disorders, Third Edition* (*DSM-III-R;* American Psychiatric Association [APA], 1987), are characterized by extreme fear and avoidance of a particular object or situation. This response is persistent and irrational and may be provoked merely by the anticipation of the situation. The phobic person experiences the fear nearly every time the phobic stimulus is encountered. To warrant a diagnosis, symptoms must cause significant impairment in functioning or be the source of significant distress. In adults, the person must also recognize that the fear is excessive or unreasonable. For example, blood-injection-injury (BII) phobic people fear and avoid medical and health care situations (e.g., doctors, hospitals, medical appointments). They report worrying about whether the phobia would prevent them from obtaining essential medical procedures or from taking their children for medical checkups (Öst, 1989; Öst, Hellström, & Kåver, 1992; Thyer, Himle, & Curtis, 1985).

Types

The *DSM-IV* identifies five types of specific phobias: animal type (e.g., spiders, snakes, dogs, mice), natural environment type (e.g., heights, storms, water), BII type, situational type (e.g.,

airplanes, elevators, enclosed places, driving), and other type (e.g., vomiting, choking, or contracting an illness). Animal and height phobias are the most common (Bourdon et al., 1988; Curtis, Magee, Eaton, Wittchen, & Kessler, 1998).

Specific phobias are currently split into different types based on arguments that the types are characterized by distinct ages of onset, gender prevalence rates, comorbidity patterns, physiological responses, and apprehension foci (see Antony & Swinson, 2000, and Barlow, 2002, for brief reviews). For example, there is evidence that fainting in response to phobic stimuli is specific to BII phobia (Öst, 1992) and that the onset of animal and BII phobias is generally earlier than situational and height phobias (Barlow, 2002). Claustrophobics are more fearful of bodily sensations than snake and spider phobics (Craske & Sipsas, 1992), and such fears appear to contribute to their fear and avoidance of enclosed spaces (Smitherman, Hammel, & McGlynn, 2003). Furthermore, there is emerging evidence that differences in interoceptive fears between the phobias may have treatment implications. Craske, Mohlman, Yi, Glover, and Valeri (1995) report that cognitive treatment targeting misinterpretation of bodily sensations was effective for claustrophobia but not snake and spider phobia. However, Antony, Brown, and Barlow (1997a) argue that assigning phobias to types is problematic for a number of reasons, including problems in research on the types and unclear guidelines for distinguishing them (e.g., whether dentist phobia is a form of BII phobia).

Epidemiology

In the United States, lifetime prevalence rates are approximately 11% for specific phobias (Eaton, Dryman, & Weissman, 1991; Kessler et al., 1994). However, internationally, lower rates typically are reported (Barlow, 2002), and exact rates are unclear because of variability in sampling, populations, and assessment techniques.

The median age of onset for specific phobia is approximately 15 (Magee, Eaton, Wittchen, McGonagle, & Kessler, 1996). However, the typical age of onset appears to vary by phobia type, with animal and BII phobias beginning in childhood and situational and height phobias beginning in adolescence or adulthood (Barlow, 2002). There is some evidence that subclinical fear typically begins years before the onset of clinical phobias (Antony et al., 1997a), suggesting the utility of early assessment and interventions.

Etiology

The two-factor theory proposed by Mowrer (1939, 1947) forms a foundation for many current theories regarding fear acquisition. The theory posits acquisition through classical conditioning, in which a previously neutral stimulus is paired with an aversive stimulus, perhaps during a traumatic experience. For instance, a person might develop a flying phobia after being on an airplane that had engine trouble and needed to make an emergency landing. The two-factor theory further posits symptom maintenance via operant conditioning. By avoiding or escaping from encounters with the feared stimulus, phobic people can reduce their anxiety, which is negatively reinforcing and increases the likelihood of future avoidance. Furthermore, theorists have added that avoidance prevents habituation and the disconfirmation of negative beliefs about the phobic stimulus.

Over the years there has been some support for the two-factor theory. In several samples conditioning experiences appear to have a role in the onset of the majority of claustrophobia and dental phobia cases and to a lesser extent in animal and blood phobias (Öst, 1987). However, one major criticism of the theory is that a large subset of people can't recall a direct conditioning experience preceding phobia onset (Rachman, 1990).

Naturalistic examinations of nonclinical populations also reveal that direct conditioning experiences fail to account for all subthreshold fears (Kleinknecht, 1982; Vernon & Berenbaum, 2004).

Rachman (1976, 1977) provides an expanded model of phobia acquisition to account for onset caused by vicarious acquisition and information transmission or instruction. In vicarious conditioning, a person might witness someone else's traumatic experience or witness someone behaving fearfully, as when parents model fear of dogs to their children. This has been observed in laboratory rhesus monkeys that learned to fear snakes after observing their parents behave fearfully with toy and live snakes (Mineka, Davidson, Cook, & Keir, 1984). In addition, in acquisition through information or instruction a person could develop a phobia after hearing about plane crashes on the news or being consistently warned by parents about the dangers of flying.

Although some studies provide support for these acquisition pathways (McNally & Steketee, 1985; Menzies & Clarke, 1993; Merckelbach, Arntz, & de Jong, 1991; Merckelbach & Muris, 1997), others do not report the expected group differences in frequency of acquisition experiences between phobic and nonphobic people (Di Nardo et al., 1988; Graham & Gaffan, 1997; Menzies & Clarke, 1995a; Poulton, Davies, Menzies, Langley, & Silva, 1998; Poulton, Menzies, Craske, Langley, & Silva, 1999). The three pathways do not appear to explain all phobias, nor does the model explain why some people do not develop phobias despite numerous acquisition experiences (see Antony & Barlow, 1997, for discussion).

In addition, Menzies and Clarke (1995b) have attempted to explain phobias that seem to occur in the absence of conditioning experiences, theorizing a fourth acquisition pathway. They propose that evolutionarily relevant stimuli (e.g., animals, heights, water) may not require a conditioning experience in order for a phobia to develop, whereas evolutionarily neutral situations (e.g., doctors, dentists, flying) may require such acquisition pathways. There is some support for this notion (Harris & Menzies, 1996; Menzies & Harris, 1997). For a full discussion, see the February 2002 special issue of *Behaviour Research and Therapy*.

Although acquisition and maintenance theories of phobia typically have been fear-based, Davey and colleagues (Davey, 1992; Davey, Forster, & Mayhew, 1993; Matchett & Davey,

1991) propose a disease avoidance model of animal phobia focusing on the potential contribution of disgust. Simply put, the model suggests that it was evolutionarily adaptive for humans to avoid, via disgust, animals deemed dirty, contaminated, or diseased. Support for the disease avoidance model suggests that disgust may play an important role in several types of specific phobia.

Disgust

Until recently fear has been the primary focus of phobia research, but disgust is emerging as an important area of study in its own right. Fear and disgust are both thought to be avoidance-motivated emotions, and in addition to the copious evidence of behavioral avoidance of frightening objects there is emerging evidence of avoidance of a range of disgusting objects (Rozin, Haidt, McCauley, Dunlop, & Ashmore, 1999; Woody & Tolin, 2002). Disgust and behavioral avoidance have often been indirectly examined in the specific phobias via phobics' interactions with contaminated items. For example, it has been found that spider phobics are less likely than nonphobics to eat, or report a willingness to eat, snacks over which a spider had walked (de Jong, Andrea, & Muris, 1997; Mulkens, de Jong, & Merckelbach, 1996). Disgust also appears to contribute more directly to spider avoidance (Woody, McLean, & Klassen, 2005), although not all studies have reported disgust-motivated avoidance behavior in animal phobic people (Klieger & Siejak, 1997; Vernon & Berenbaum, 2002), perhaps because of differences in contamination risk between the approach and avoidance tasks used. The relationship between disgust and avoidance has not yet been clarified.

In general, there is evidence documenting disgust responses to spiders and BII stimuli, particularly among phobic people. Disgust responses have been demonstrated via self-report during exposure to pictures of spiders (Tolin, Lohr, Sawchuk, & Lee, 1997) and during in vivo exposure to a spider (Vernon & Berenbaum, 2002; Woody & Tolin, 2002). Facial electromyelograms consistent with disgust have been found during guided imagery involving a spider (de Jong, Peters, & Vanderhallen, 2002), and facial expressions of disgust have been noted in response to a live spider (Vernon & Berenbaum, 2002). Although both spider phobic and nonphobic control groups report disgust in response to spiders, spider phobic people commonly report

significantly stronger disgust to spiders and to disgust stimuli than do nonphobic controls, regardless of the form of the stimulus and the assessment method used (de Jong & Muris, 2002; de Jong et al., 2002; Sawchuk, Lohr, Tolin, Lee, & Kleinknecht, 2000; Sawchuk, Lohr, Westendorf, Meunier, & Tolin, 2002; Tolin et al., 1997; Vernon & Berenbaum, 2002; Woody & Tolin, 2002). Similarly, disgust appears to play an important role in BII phobia (Sawchuk et al., 2000, 2002; Tolin et al., 1997; Tolin, Sawchuk, & Lee, 1999).

INTERVIEWING STRATEGIES

Selecting an Interview Format

Diagnostic interviews vary in the extent to which they are structured and standardized. At one extreme, structured interviews have precisely worded questions to be given in a certain order and include a decision tree for the interviewer to follow. Sections, or modules, typically begin with a broad screening question, which if answered affirmatively leads the interviewer to ask a series of specified follow-up questions. If the screening question or a certain number of follow-up questions are answered negatively, the interviewer is directed to go on to the next module. Structured interviews do not permit the interviewer to vary the phrasing or order of questions or add topics or questions. Their rigid structure is designed for interviewers with little clinical experience or for computer administration, both of which seem to be related to a loss of diagnostic accuracy (Antony, Downie, & Swinson, 1988; Komiti et al., 2001; Ross, Swinson, Larkin, & Doumani, 1994).

At the other end of the continuum are unstructured interviews, which are idiosyncratically conducted by expert clinicians. The interviewer generates all questions and follow-up questions. Although unstructured interviews address the disadvantages of structured interviews, including flexibility and time efficiency, they are not without drawbacks. When clinicians produce interview topics and questions without external aid or prompting, there is the possibility that important areas of inquiry will be skipped or forgotten. In fact, when diagnostic disagreements have been examined, a large number of them appear to be related to interviewer variability (see Blanchard & Brown, 1998, for a review).

Semistructured interviews offer a compromise between the strengths and weaknesses of the structured and unstructured interviews. For this reason, they are quite popular with researchers and practitioners alike. They are designed for use by trained clinicians and provide a standardized set of basic interviewing questions but allow changes in question order or the addition of follow-up questions. Semistructured interviews also leave final diagnostic decisions to the judgment of the interviewer. For this reason, they are not appropriate for administration by lay interviewers. However, when semistructured interviews are conducted by properly trained clinicians they can have reasonably strong interrater reliability. They typically take 1–4 hours to administer. Examples of semistructured interviews including specific phobia modules are the Structured Clinical Interview for the *DSM-IV* (SCID-IV; First, Spitzer, Gibbon, & Williams, 1996, 1997) and the Anxiety Disorders Interview Schedule for *DSM-IV* (ADIS-IV; Brown, Di Nardo, & Barlow, 1994; Di Nardo, Brown, & Barlow, 1994). The ADIS was designed specifically to target the anxiety disorders and therefore is quite comprehensive in its coverage not only of anxiety disorder diagnostic criteria but also of information regarding etiology and course. However, the ADIS is less comprehensive in its coverage of other Axis I disorders and does not address Axis II disorders, so supplementing it with additional assessments may be necessary. On the other hand, the SCID includes modules concerning a broad range of Axis I and II disorders but is less detailed regarding anxiety disorders. A thorough comparison of the ADIS and the SCID can be found in Antony and Swinson (2000).

Interviewers may want to consider whether a structured, semistructured, or unstructured interview format is most appropriate for their goals, schedule, and setting. This judgment should take into consideration the psychometric properties of the instrument, the population for which it was designed, how ratings are made (e.g., categorical symptom ratings are made on the SCID, dimensional ratings are made on the ADIS), the degree of necessary training and experience of the interviewer, and whether computerized versions are available.

Basic Areas of Assessment

Regardless of the type and format of interview used, a number of basic areas of assessment for specific phobias should be covered. These include current symptoms, level of distress and impairment, the influence of environmental factors, the presence of other symptoms and disorders, symptom history, and psychosocial, developmental, and treatment history.

First, clients should be encouraged to provide a detailed description of the presenting complaint in their own words. If the assessment is being conducted in a research setting in which specific phobias have been solicited, phobic fear and avoidance are more likely to be the presenting complaint. However, it is quite uncommon for clients to present for treatment of a single specific phobia. In most clinical settings clients may identify other problems initially. For instance, in the case study presented in this chapter a client who self-identified as suffering from posttraumatic stress disorder (PTSD) after a motor vehicle accident was determined to have driving phobia. Similarly, cases abound in which clients present with seeming specific phobia symptoms but eventually receive a different diagnosis, such as panic disorder with agoraphobia (PDA) or obsessive-compulsive disorder (OCD). Furthermore, multiple disorders may be present.

Specific phobias commonly occur in the presence of other Axis I disorders, particularly anxiety and mood disorders. It is important to determine whether phobic symptoms are better accounted for by another disorder. Furthermore, even in the case of an independently existing specific phobia, it is important to decide whether specific phobia is the principal diagnosis (associated with the most distress and impairment). Such determinations can be made after a careful assessment of the onset and course of symptoms, as well as levels of distress and impairment. It will also be useful to consider whether treatment for one disorder is likely to exacerbate the other. For example, it is not uncommon for stressful exposure treatments to exacerbate a preexisting substance use problem, suggesting that the substance use problem may need to be brought under control first or at a minimum monitored during anxiety treatment. Furthermore, the clinician should also address any substance use (e.g., caffeine, amphetamines) that may contribute to anxiety.

The client's initial description of the problem is likely to include aspects that may suggest several possible diagnoses. A systematic assessment of the client's signs and symptoms, including behavioral, cognitive, somatic, and emotional, will help to clear this up. Behaviorally, escape and avoidance symptoms are most common. A person with a height phobia may describe needing to leave a balcony because of anxiety, whereas a snake phobic may report running away from snakes. Furthermore, phobic people may avoid situations involving the potential for exposure. For example, dog phobics might change their jogging route to avoid a yard that contains a dog or turn down dinner at the home of a friend with a dog.

Along with such avoidance, phobic people often report cognitions that include unrealistically negative beliefs about the phobic object or one's response to it. Clients might describe irrationally negative thoughts about the phobic object's characteristics, such as the assumption that spiders or snakes will feel slimy or that birds will attack because they sense the client's fear. To assess such cognitions, the clinician may ask the client for predictions, querying, "If you were to encounter a dog unexpectedly, what do you think would happen?"

Examining the contribution of ongoing cognitive processes may also be useful. Processing biases for threat-relevant information have been widely found in the anxiety disorders (see Mathews & MacLeod, 1994, and Williams, Mathews, & MacLeod, 1996, for reviews) and are presumed to contribute to their maintenance. People with anxiety disorders, high trait anxiety, or induced anxious mood typically display attentional and interpretive biases for threat-relevant stimuli. Phobic fear and anxiety seem to direct attention toward potentially threatening stimuli and encourage threatening interpretations of ambiguous information (Becker & Rinck, 2004). For instance, when anxious people hear part of a phrase about "Little Susie's growth" they are more likely to make a threatening interpretation, assuming cancerous growth rather than normal developmental growth. A large number of experimental paradigms have been developed to test for such biases.

Because phobic people interpret phobic situations as highly threatening, it is not surprising that somatic symptoms typically are present. The evaluator should explore the presence of the physical sensations associated with fear, including elevated heart rate, trembling or shaking, tingling, dizziness, sweating, and chest pain. In fact, it is not uncommon for people with severe specific phobia to have situationally bound panic attacks in response to their phobic situation (Craske, 1991). Another subset of phobic people experiences situationally predisposed panic attacks, in which the attack does not occur upon every exposure to the situation but is more likely. Physiological monitoring, particularly during a behavioral assessment, can provide additional useful information in this area (Alpers, Wilhelm, & Roth, 2005; Cacioppo, Berntson, & Andersen, 1991; Hugdahl, 1988; Turpin, 1990). Given findings regarding the role of disgust in BII and animal phobias, physical responses such as nausea and vomiting should also be assessed, as should heart rate deceleration, which has been noted during disgust responses (Levenson, 1992). Assessors should also remain alert for a potential drop in heart rate, blood pressure, and muscle tone among BII phobic people because up to 70% report a history of fainting upon exposure to BII stimuli (Öst, 1992), suggesting the need for assessment of this area and, if present, appropriate measures before exposure treatment.

Information about cognitions and physical sensations provides indirect information regarding emotional responses, but the interviewer will also want to ask clients to describe and rate the intensity of various emotional responses. When the interview is combined with a behavioral assessment, the client's emotion ratings before, during, and after exposure to the phobic stimulus should be collected. Again, disgust should be explicitly assessed in cases of BII and animal phobia. Facial expressions, body posture, and vocal tone should be attended to. Disgust facial expressions typically include a raised upper lip and wrinkled nose, whereas raised eyebrows and a tense mouth indicate fear (Ekman, 1982; Ekman & Friesen, 1975).

When assessing for specific phobia signs and symptoms, it is important to determine whether they cause clinically significant impairment. In extreme cases the impairment is obvious, as when a spider phobic woman does not leave her house at night for fear of being unable to see and avoid spiders. In many cases, however, the impairment is questionable and the interviewer needs to probe the degree to which symptoms interfere with role responsibilities, job advancement, relationships, and daily activities. If the client is unable to provide examples of impairment or estimate the frequency or degree of interference, imaginary scenarios may be helpful. For example, the interviewer could ask whether the client could tolerate phobic exposure in order to get to a very important meeting on time (e.g., walking by a dog in an enclosed yard or taking an underpass with a spiderweb rather than walking the long way around). To warrant a diagnosis of specific phobia, clients must experience functional impairment or significant distress resulting from their fear or avoidance. This is the criterion that clients most often fail to meet. For instance, although a modest number of people fear and avoid spiders, they may feel that it is normal and justified and therefore are not distressed by it. Similarly, those living in areas where the phobic object is not common or those suffering from only mild aversion may not experience impairment.

Once the clinician has a good understanding of the client's symptoms, knowledge of the influence of environmental factors is also important. There are likely to be certain contexts that increase or decrease the level of distress caused by the phobic stimulus. A snake phobic might find a snake extremely distressing when loose in his yard, strongly distressing during a hike, and only moderately distressing in a glass aquarium at a zoo. A person with a fear of flying probably will find flying in a small commuter airplane on a stormy day much more upsetting than flying on a large jet airliner during good weather. The contextual factors that serve as safety signals and are reassuring can be as important as those that are distressing. For example, a young woman with insect phobia reported little insect fear when her mother, an entomologist, was present and could tell her which were poisonous. Such information about environmental factors can aid in planning treatment and constructing an exposure hierarchy so that clients are exposed to the majority of their fear-provoking triggers and gradually give up the use of safety signals.

In addition to a detailed description of the client's current symptom presentation, information should also be obtained about symptom history, incorporating acquisition, maintenance, and remission factors. Information should be collected regarding symptom onset, including situational factors such as etiology (e.g., vicarious learning), and personality factors such as emotional trait proneness (e.g., high trait anxiety or disgust sensitivity). Symptom course, including factors that may have contributed to exacerbation or remission, should also be investigated. For instance, naturalistic examinations have noted the role of increased factual knowledge and unexpected positive experiences with the stimulus in the remission of spider distress (Kleinknecht, 1982; Vernon & Berenbaum, 2004).

As in all psychological assessments, psychosocial, developmental, and treatment history and current situation should be addressed. What have the client's childhood, family, school, work, and dating experiences generally been? What are the client's current family situation, level of social support, and financial status? What are the client's skills, resources, deficits, and limitations? The clinician will also want to learn whether the client has previously sought psychological treatment and, if so, when, for what, and with whom, and what aspects of treatment were helpful or harmful. A release should also be obtained for previous psychological records and reports and any testing results, and permission should be sought to speak with former service providers.

The presence of Axis II disorders and medical, neurological, and cognitive conditions should also be assessed. The influence of Axis II disorders on symptom presentation and treatment should be considered. Ideally, the client will also be referred for a thorough medical examination because specific physical conditions may mimic or exacerbate anxiety, including endocrine, respiratory, and cardiovascular disorders. It may also be the case that the client has a condition that will limit or preclude certain treatment tasks. For example, a height phobic suffering from inner ear and balance problems or from a seizure disorder cannot safely complete in vivo exposure exercises involving precarious heights.

INTERVIEWING OBSTACLES AND SOLUTIONS

A number of interviewing obstacles are common in assessment of phobic anxiety and avoidance. For instance, in several situations and for different reasons, clients may not fully or adequately describe their symptoms. In some cases, clients may not appear to meet the diagnostic criterion requiring distress about their symptoms or recognition of the excessive or irrational nature of their fears. In most of these cases, a thorough, detailed, and careful follow-up is the solution.

It is not uncommon for clients to underestimate the scope of their difficulties. One particularly salient area in which underestimation occurs is in identification of avoidance behaviors. Naturally, clients are most likely to identify and report obvious avoidance, such as avoiding driving over bridges or looking out windows of tall buildings for a height phobia. They are often less aware of subtle avoidance, including being overly careful or needing excessive reassurance, such as needing someone to be nearby in order to climb a few steps on a ladder. Similarly, running away from spiders may be an obvious form of avoidance, whereas avoiding hiking or camping may be less noticeable because situations with the potential for exposure are avoided altogether. Furthermore, such activities may occur at a low base rate, making their avoidance less noticeable. It is often useful to have a list of situations and activities commonly avoided rather than relying on clients to list all their avoidance behaviors.

On the extreme end, avoidance can become a natural part of the routines of some clients. These people have adapted so well to their fears that avoidance may simply be habit, without the need for conscious thought or planning. In such cases it is not unusual for clients to deny having any fear and to be unaware of most of their avoidance behaviors. Because of their successful avoidance they may not have experienced fear recently. In such cases, a thought experiment with the client imagining contact and careful probing regarding cognitions can be useful.

In other cases, despite describing a full complement of phobic fear and avoidance symptoms, clients may not appear to qualify for a diagnosis because they initially deny distress regarding their symptoms and refute the idea that their reactions are excessive or unreasonable. In some sense it is not surprising that anxious clients would take this stance. Anxious people often overestimate the probability and valence of negative outcomes. For example, spider phobic people are more likely to make unrealistically negative attributions about spiders than nonphobic people (Riskind, Moore, & Bowley, 1995) and make higher probability estimates of being bitten and having the bite be harmful (Jones, Whitmont, & Menzies, 1996). Similarly, height phobics overestimate the likelihood of falling and being hurt in the fall (Menzies & Clarke, 1995b). Phobic people may also overrate the severity or uncontrollability of their own response to the phobic situation, such as a height phobic worrying about losing control and jumping off a high bridge (Antony et al., 1997a).

Given the perceptual and cognitive biases of anxious people, it is not surprising and is actually quite understandable that they see their responses as justifiable. Although there is some debate about the advisability of a diagnostic requirement of distress or insight regarding phobic symptoms (Jones & Menzies, 2000), sometimes careful questioning can reveal that the client does fit the criterion despite initial indications to the contrary. In some cases, clients do have distress or awareness about the excessiveness of their reactions but feel defensive, pressured, or misunderstood. In dealing with such clients it is important to validate the reality of their fear experience and make it clear that treatment will proceed at their pace. Clients who are not particularly psychologically minded may simply lack awareness of the impact of their symptoms. In such cases, prompting the client to be self-reflective with a series of questions may be useful ("Do you react more strongly to the stimulus than your friends and family?" "Do people who are close to you view your fear, disgust, and avoidance as excessive?" "If I waved a magic wand and took your reaction away, how might your life be changed?"). In the end, if clients are seeking treatment, learning about them may be more important than whether this criterion is ultimately met.

CASE ILLUSTRATION WITH DIALOGUE

To illustrate some key assessment issues described in this chapter, the following case is described. The client, Jenny, is a 32-year-old Caucasian woman who responded to a newspaper advertisement for a stress and anxiety clinic housed in a psychology department outpatient training clinic. Jenny is upper middle class, recently finished a graduate program, and works as a teacher. She has been married for several years. She and her husband moved to a small town one and a half years ago for Jenny to begin her teaching position. Jenny's husband is a consultant who works from home and travels fairly regularly. Jenny reports being happy with her work and relationships but is troubled by fear and avoidance of driving. Public transportation is not available in her town, and driving is a necessary part of daily life.

After a brief intake interview and explanation of clinic policies, Jenny was referred to the stress and anxiety clinic, and the SCID-IV interview was administered. The following excerpts have been adapted from an assessment interview that occurred over the course of multiple sessions.

Therapist:	What brings you in to the clinic today?	*Therapist:*	What prompted this change, Jenny?

Jenny: Well, something has to change. My husband is tired of driving me around, and he isn't always in town. He said I have to get back to driving.

T: So you have stopped driving?

J: Well, just cut back is more like it. I still drive when I need to, but I refuse to drive on the highway, and I try not to drive at night. It hasn't been that much of a problem until recently because I live really close to work. I just walk in to work, and if it is raining or something one of the girls gives me a lift home. But my husband has needed to travel a lot for work recently, and I didn't want to take him to the airport. His friend got sick and couldn't drive him at the last minute, and I refused. We got in a big fight. He started pointing out all the places I don't drive to and how there are friends and family I can't visit and how I couldn't pick up supplies last week and how much he has to do to try to take over.

T: I see, so you used to do more driving than you do now?

J: Yes, I used to be a really big driver, road trips and that kind of thing. Now I just don't enjoy driving any more; it makes me too anxious.

The client's initial description of her driving fear and avoidance symptoms could be part of a range of possible disorders. For instance, if her symptoms are caused by a fear of having panic attacks while driving and being unable to escape, she may have PDA. If her fear and avoidance are part of a stress reaction including reexperiencing, numbing, and hyperarousal after a traumatic automobile accident, then she may have PTSD. If her anxiety about driving is prompted by an obsessive concern that she has hit someone and a compulsive need to check that she has not done so, she may have OCD. If her fear and avoidance are circumscribed, then she may have a specific phobia, situational type. To make a distinction the interviewer needs more information about her symptoms and their onset.

Jenny: I got in a car crash about 8 months ago. I was driving. It was really scary. We were on the highway. My husband and I were in a big fight, and I told him he was clearly too angry to drive. Perfect, huh? How ironic. I told him I was calmer, so I should drive. So I was driving along and I went to change the radio station. When I looked up, we were about to hit this big truck that was right next to us. I swerved, and the next thing I knew we were upside down in the ditch.

T: Wow, how scary!

J: I know. I still remember the smell of the dirt. I was hanging upside down, and I could smell the dirt and grass, and the windshield was broken. I remember feeling kind of floaty, and then I wondered whether I was injured. I really couldn't tell, you know?

T: Uh huh. You were in shock?

J: Yes, I had to look down and check myself out to make sure I was all right. And I noticed I had broken my watch, and I was upset because my husband had given it to me. And then I remembered that he was in the car with me, and I had this moment of feeling like I swallowed my heart. But I looked over and he was okay. I mean, mostly okay. He had a cut on his head, and there was a little bit of blood, but he could look at me and talk to me and everything.

T: Good, good, so you were both basically okay?

J: Yeah, I guess you could say that. But boy, was I freaked out.

T: I bet.

J: I still feel horribly guilty about that, that my first thought was about myself. I mean, what kind of a person must I be to have completely forgotten that he was in the car? I haven't admitted that to him, that I was only concerned with myself first. I feel terrible. I could have killed my husband.

At this point, the client appears to be describing typical peritraumatic responses, including extreme fear and horror and possible dissociation (feeling "floaty" is a term that may indicate depersonalization), and a posttraumatic emotional response of shame and guilt. Because the client's experience qualifies as a trauma because of its life-threatening nature and her intense emotional response, the interviewer addressed PTSD symptoms.

Therapist: Scary stuff. Do you have thoughts or memories or nightmares about the car accident that you can't seem to shake?

Jenny: No, I don't think about it much anymore, and I never really had dreams about it. It did really bother me a lot right after it happened, though. We had to get a new car, and every time I saw that horrible car I would get upset.

T: How about now; do you get upset when things remind you of the accident now?

J: No, not really. I needed to talk about it a lot right afterwards, but now I think I have kind of worked it out of my system. My sister and I went over every detail of it, from beginning to end, so many times that now I can think about it more objectively.

T: How about when you are driving on the highway?

J: Yeah, I see what you mean. No, actually, I don't think my problem with the highway driving is because it makes me think about the accident.

T: So, you are okay thinking about the accident?

J: Well, yes and no. I mean, I can remember the accident and be calm about it. But at the same time the accident gave me this new viewpoint about cars. It's terrifying really, what cars can do. This sounds silly, but they are like these dangerous beasts to me.

T: Hmmm, say more.

J: Well, when I am driving, it makes me really tense because I never know what the car is going to do. I feel like it could just jump off of the road at any minute. I know it sounds crazy. It just feels so unpredictable, like the car might not do what I want it to. And that's too much for me. I get all panicky, and I just go right back home.

Although Jenny denied reexperiencing symptoms of PTSD in the preceding excerpt, at a later time the interviewer returned to the topic of reexperiencing and assessed for the presence of numbing and hyperarousal symptoms. After a thorough review of possible PTSD symptoms, it was determined that Jenny did not have PTSD. In the preceding excerpt, however, Jenny has raised the possibility of panic attacks. It is not yet clear whether her description of feeling "panicky" is simply a synonym to express her fear and anxiety or whether she is experiencing the physical and psychological symptoms of a panic attack. The interviewer chose to pursue this, asking questions about the panic.

Therapist: Jenny, can you describe for me how you feel when you get panicky?

J: Well, I start feeling kind of dizzy and faint, and my vision gets a little blurry, and I worry that it will make me crash. I feel like I can't get any air, a little like I am smothering, you know?

T: Uh huh. Anything else?

J: Well, my chest just feels really tight, and I can feel my heart racing. And my palms get sweaty. It starts to come on gradually, but then it gets worse and worse, and I feel like I'm going to pass out or lose my mind or something, and I have to either pull over or go right home.

With several more questions the interviewer establishes that the client is indeed regularly having full panic attacks that peak within 10 minutes. Next their origins are explored.

Therapist: When did the panic first start happening?

J: Oddly enough, it was when I was watching TV. My husband and I were just on the couch and suddenly I can't breathe, and I feel like I'm going to faint and like I'm going to jump out of my skin. It was so strange because we weren't even doing anything.

T: What was on TV?

J: Oh, good point. I never thought of that. The movie was pretty scary, actually, pretty tense. Maybe that was it. Do you think that could be why?

T: That definitely could have contributed, sure. What was going on in the movie?

J: No idea, I just remember that it was scary.

T: Sure, that could have pushed you over the edge. Sometimes there are other factors that can contribute to it, like whether things are tense in general or you have been drinking a lot of caffeine.

J: Oh yeah, I'm a caffeine fiend. I can drink a pot of coffee in the morning, if I have a lot of grading to do or something.

T: Well, that could definitely play a role too. How often do you drink coffee or caffeinated beverages?

J: Every day. I like my coffee in the morning, and then I drink cokes with lunch and dinner and snacks. So I probably have three or four cups of coffee and then another three or so cokes. Boy, that sounds like a lot when I say it now. I should probably cut back on that, shouldn't I? And I guess I do get stressed out pretty easily. I am kind of high strung.

The client went on to report that the panic attacks started a month after her accident and, with the exception of her first attack, are cued by driving. This suggests that her panic may occur as part of a driving phobia caused by the conditioning experience of her car accident. Later Jenny denied persistent worry about future attacks or their implications, but she reported some worry about whether the panic symptoms would lead to a car accident. Because she also alluded to anxiety before going on long trips, fear and avoidance about agoraphobic situations such as buses, trains, airplanes, and crowds were also explored. In the end, Jenny reported subthreshold anxiety and avoidance related to a number of agoraphobic situations. Because her avoidance of driving was her presenting complaint, and she reported marked fear in response to actual and anticipated driving situations, recognition that her fear was excessive, and significant life impairment, she was diagnosed with specific phobia, situational type,

and with PDA as a rule-out diagnosis. Jenny underwent exposure therapy, practicing driving in increasingly difficult situations and eventually driving on the highway at night. During the course of treatment Jenny developed frequent, apparently uncued nocturnal panic attacks. Treatment was supplemented with interoceptive exposure for her panic. After approximately 4 months of weekly treatment Jenny was able to successfully drive on the highway and was largely free of panic symptoms.

MULTICULTURAL AND DIVERSITY ISSUES

There is little evidence of multicultural influences in the specific phobias. There are some findings regarding gender, race, and ethnicity, but there are large gaps in the existing literature, with particularly little known about anxiety and phobias among Asian Americans and Native Americans. This section reviews evidence about specific phobias in diverse populations and related information from clinical and social psychology.

One particularly important diversity variable in the specific phobias is gender. Specific phobias are diagnosed more often among women than men, across a range of samples and phobia types (Curtis et al., 1998; Goisman et al., 1998; Himle, McPhee, Cameron, & Curtis, 1989). This gender difference has been attributed to bias in sampling and diagnostic criteria (Hartung & Widiger, 1998) and to differences in reporting, treatment seeking, and learning history (Antony & Barlow, 1997). In any event, women are likely to be disproportionately represented among those seeking assessment and treatment for phobias, and gender prevalence rates appear to vary as a function of age and type of phobia (Barlow, 2002).

Race is also likely to be an important variable in assessing for specific phobias. An early analysis of epidemiological data found that Black racial status was related to scores on a phobia scale (Warheit, Holzer, & Arey, 1975). Some more recent data suggests that African Americans, particularly women, are more likely to have phobias than are Caucasians (Robins & Regier, 1991; Zhang & Snowden, 1999).

Cultural, ethnic, and racial differences in symptom presentation should also be taken into account. For example, the interviewer should carefully assess physical complaints among minority populations because somatization is more common among African American, Hispanic, Native American, Alaska Native, and Asian populations (Hsu & Folstein, 1997; Robins & Regier, 1991; U.S. Department of Health and Human Services [USDHHS], 2001). A number of culture-bound syndromes seen in Hispanic Americans are particularly relevant in the assessment of anxiety and phobias, including *susto* (fright), *nervios* (nerves), and *ataque de nervios*. Although symptoms may include those that are typically associated with anxiety, such as trembling, the clinician should attend to a broader range of symptoms (e.g., crying, screaming, aggression, or dissociation for *ataque*) in identifying culture-bound syndromes (USDHHS, 2001).

Some knowledge of typical cultural differences in interpersonal interaction and reporting styles can also be helpful in an interview context. Cultural norms for body language and emotional expression vary. For instance, Asians and Asian Americans typically make less eye contact than other groups. They may also be less likely to identify and express emotions (Le, Berenbaum, & Raghavan, 2002). Interviewers should also be conscious of the influence of their own culture on their clinical judgment. An awareness of clinician-client cultural differences is particularly important in light of the typical discrepancy between the race and culture of the clinician and client (Holzer, Goldsmith, & Ciarlo, 1998), which may help account for the underdiagnosis of psychiatric disorders, particularly for African Americans and particularly for anxiety disorders (Kunen, Niederhauser, Smith, Morris, & Marx, 2005).

Underdiagnosis may also occur as a result of purposeful minimization of symptoms by the client. One reason for such misrepresentation is social desirability. For example, occasionally in our clinic male clients have had difficulty disclosing the extent of their phobic fear or disgust to an attractive female clinician. A lack of trust or rapport may also lead to initial distortion. In all such cases, behavioral assessment strategies can be particularly enlightening because the clinician has the opportunity to observe the extent of avoidance behavior and nonverbal behaviors such as posture and facial expression. Such information should be duly noted in final judgments about diagnosis and symptom severity.

The clinician should also attempt to determine the influence of cultural beliefs and meanings on symptom presentation. For example, among the Hmong, masks are a symbol of death. Recent Hmong immigrants may be expected to display strong fear reactions in response to masks worn at Halloween or Mardi Gras. Such culturally influenced reactions should not be considered psychopathological if they are normative for the culture, and the interviewer will need to investigate the customs and beliefs of the client's culture to make this determination. Birth country and level of acculturation should also be considered because these may function as risk or protective factors. For instance, people of Mexican origin living in the United States for longer periods of time appear to have higher phobia prevalence rates (Vega et al., 1998). The clinician should also consider whether cultural background may predispose certain populations to specific phobias. For example, because disgust responses have been linked to specific phobias and cultural differences in disgust have been reported (Haidt, Rozin, McCauley, & Imada, 1997; Rozin & Fallon, 1987), disgust sensitivity may be one important focus of clinical attention.

Because there is evidence that anxiety disorders are more likely for people with elevated stress, the interviewer should be sensitive to various experiential and environmental sources of stress, such as being the victim of a violent crime (see Kilpatrick & Acierno, 2003, for a review). Racial and ethnic minorities often are at higher risk for violent assault, particularly women (Greenfeld & Smith, 1999; Kilpatrick, Acierno, Resnick, Saunders, & Best, 1997), as are those in poverty (Reiss & Roth, 1993). Furthermore, some ethnic and racial minorities are overrepresented in high-risk groups such as those who are incarcerated, homeless, or refugees (USDHHS, 2001).

In other cases, environmental sources of stress may be fairly subtle, such as the effects of discrimination. A recent meta-analysis by Saucier, Miller, and Doucet (2005) suggests that racism has become more covert. Examinations of helping behavior found evidence that discrimination against Blacks is more likely when issues of race are not at the forefront and contextual factors provide an excuse (e.g., assistance would entail more risk, difficulty, or time) or, unfortunately, in cases of extreme emergency. Given that minority populations are more likely to experience violent crime, the availability of aid and assistance are important variables to consider. Not surprisingly, Black Americans report more stress in response to trauma than White Americans (Norris, 1992).

DIFFERENTIAL DIAGNOSIS
AND BEHAVIORAL ASSESSMENT

Accurate assessment is particularly important for differential diagnosis of specific phobias because the treatment of choice may vary between disorders. For the specific phobias, exposure-based treatments have received strong empirical support (Antony & Swinson, 2000; Hirai, Vernon, & Cochran, 2006). Although exposure-based techniques have been supported for a range of anxiety disorders, the focus of the exposure, the use of adjunctive treatment techniques, and the appropriateness of pharmacotherapy interventions vary from disorder to disorder. For example, if a fear of hospitals is a symptom of specific phobia, BII type, then treatment would involve graded exposure to hospitals. On the other hand, if a fear of hospitals is rooted in OCD obsessions about cleanliness and contamination, the exposure to hospitals would be only a small part of a treatment including exposure to a range of potentially contaminating stimuli and response prevention of compulsive washing after such exposure. Along the same lines, breathing retraining may be appropriate for a subset of clients with panic disorder (PD) but is unlikely to be needed by the majority of specific phobia clients (Antony & Swinson, 2000). Furthermore, combining cognitive and exposure-based therapeutic techniques appears quite useful for PD and social phobia, but there is little evidence of incremental efficacy from the addition of cognitive strategies for most specific phobias. Similarly, selective serotonin reuptake inhibitors and benzodiazepines have been shown effective for PD and social phobia, but there is no research demonstrating their efficacy for specific phobias, and there are some theoretical grounds for avoiding their use (Foa & Kozak, 1986).

Although differential diagnosis can have important implications for treatment planning, it can be particularly difficult in the anxiety disorders given their high symptom overlap. For instance, anxious apprehension may be symptomatic of many anxiety disorders, including specific phobia, social phobia, agoraphobia, and PD. However, in each case the target of the anxiety is different, such as anxiety regarding potential exposure to a feared situation, to negative evaluation, to inescapable situations, or to a situation eliciting a panic attack, respectively.

Comorbidity

There is evidence that specific phobias tend to be comorbid with one another and with other anxiety and mood disorders (Brown, Campbell, Lehman, Grisham, & Mancill, 2001; Curtis et al., 1998; Sanderson, Di Nardo, Rapee, & Barlow, 1990). It appears that when a specific phobia is the principal diagnosis, other comorbid disorders are less likely. However, specific phobias are rarely principal diagnoses and are much more common as an additional diagnosis, particularly accompanying other anxiety disorders (Sanderson et al., 1990). There is also some evidence that specific phobias may coexist less commonly with some disorders, such as bulimia nervosa and alcohol use disorders (Barlow, 2002).

Differential Diagnosis

The *DSM-IV* specifies that for a specific phobia diagnosis fear must not be better accounted for by another disorder. In the following sections recommendations are made for distinguishing specific phobia from PD and agoraphobia, social phobia, PTSD, and OCD.

PD and Agoraphobia. The presence of panic attacks can sometimes cause confusion about the appropriate diagnosis. It should be noted that panic attacks have been found to occur in conjunction with all of the anxiety disorders (see Craske, 1991, for a review of panic attacks and phobic fear). An excellent way to distinguish between specific phobia and PD is to assess what cues the panic attacks. In the context of a specific phobia, panic attacks usually are cued by situations or thoughts involving the phobic stimulus. In the driving phobia case study, Jenny initially reported having all of her panic attacks (except the first one) while driving. Clients with PD, on the other hand, typically report more frequent uncued panic.

Clients with specific phobia need not be able to link every panic attack to their phobic concerns, however. It may be the case that the client was not aware of the way in which "uncued" panic attacks were actually associated with the phobic stimulus. For example, Jenny's first panic attack occurred while she was watching a tense movie, and a scene (a car chase, perhaps) may have triggered thoughts or memories of her accident. It may also be true that not all panic attacks can be traced back to phobic triggers, yet a diagnosis of PD may still not be appropriate if the panic attacks developed after the specific phobia, increase in frequency or intensity when phobic symptoms peak, remit when phobia symptoms decline, or consist of only a couple symptoms (a minimum of four symptoms is required). Furthermore, people with PD typically report marked concern about their panic attacks, anxious anticipation of having another attack, and changes in their behavior to avoid future panic attacks. For those with panic attacks in the context of specific phobias, concerns about panic attacks are not central but instead are part of a larger complex of thoughts and behaviors related to the phobic stimulus.

A distinction between agoraphobia and specific phobia can also be difficult because the two may involve avoidance of similar situations. In such cases, the reasons behind the avoidance should be probed. Jenny's driving avoidance could signal agoraphobia if it was motivated by a fear that escape would be difficult (PDA if the need to escape was focused on a possible panic attack) instead of a fear of crashing. Similarly, avoidance of flying may point to PDA if the client does so out of fear of being trapped during a panic attack, especially if the client also avoids public transportation, elevators, and shopping malls.

Distinguishing situational phobias from PDA can be particularly difficult, and there has been some argument about whether claustrophobia may be a variant of PDA. The two seem to share comorbidity (Starcevic & Bogojevic, 1997), patterns of onset age and manner of acquisition (Öst, 1985, 1987), uncued panic (Craske, Zarate, Burton, & Barlow, 1993), fear and avoidance of interoceptive stimuli (Clark, 1986; McNally, 1990), and use of safety signals (Rachman, 1984; Sloan & Telch, 2002). Although Vickers and McNally (2005) report that fear of dying may distinguish PD from panic attacks. There is also some evidence challenging ideas of overlap between PDA and situational specific phobia, displaying differences between those with PDA and driving phobia (Antony et al., 1997a, 1997b).

It should also be noted that multiple diagnoses may be appropriate for some people. For example, had the client in the case study avoided driving both because of her fear of a crash (a symptom of specific phobia) and because of her fear of having a panic attack and being unable to escape (a symptom of PDA), consideration of both diagnoses would have been appropriate.

Social Phobia. Specific phobia and social phobia may also appear to share similar fear and avoidance symptoms. As with the distinction between specific phobia and PDA, information about the focus of the fear and the reasons for avoidance are paramount for determining the appropriate diagnosis. For example, Jenny described a fear of driving. Had her fear occurred only in the presence of other people and focused on looking foolish, incompetent, or unattractive, social phobia may have been a more apt diagnosis if she also had concerns about negative social evaluation in other situations. Similarly, avoidance of a range of other potential phobic situations, such as flying, eating in restaurants, or riding in elevators, may be motivated by social concerns or may be associated with a specific phobia. For instance, clients may avoid eating in restaurants for fear of choking and dying (symptom of specific phobia, other type) or for fear of embarrassing themselves (symptom of social phobia). Asking clients what they are afraid might happen in each situation or what the worst outcome would be can help tease apart these diagnoses.

Posttraumatic Stress Disorder. PTSD is another disorder that typically includes strong fear and avoidance responses. In our case illustration, Jenny developed fear and avoidance of driving after a serious automobile accident. Based on her description of the accident and her intense response, it would certainly meet diagnostic criteria for a trauma. However, PTSD is associated with a variety of reexperiencing symptoms, including intrusive and uncontrollable memories and images from the trauma, nightmares about the trauma, or, in extreme cases, flashbacks during which the person feels as though the trauma is actually happening all over again. Specific phobias do not include such reexperiencing symptoms, and Jenny did not report them. Nor did she report other symptoms of PTSD, such as numbing, including diminished positive affect or general hyperarousal symptoms such as trouble sleeping and an exaggerated startle response. Presence of reexperiencing, numbing, and hyperarousal symptoms is a useful way to distinguish between PTSD and specific phobia.

Obsessive-Compulsive Disorder. People with OCD may also occasionally appear to have specific phobias. Those with OCD may fear and avoid certain objects and situations because of obsessions. Antony and Swinson (2000) describe a woman who presented with an extreme fear and avoidance of snakes. Although she was initially thought to suffer from a snake phobia, in due course it was learned that her snake fear was part of a larger obsessive concern about contamination. The woman was diagnosed with OCD because her concern about snakes was only one fear among a broader set of obsessions. In our case illustration, Jenny might have been diagnosed with OCD if her avoidance of driving was caused by obsessions about having run someone over and the need to compulsively stop and check. Clients with OCD may be distinguished from those with specific phobia by the focus of their fear and by their need to perform compulsive rituals in response to their fear or anxiety.

Although issues pertaining to differential diagnosis have been reviewed for a number of anxiety disorders, it should be noted that situations of symptom overlap also arise with other disorders, particularly those in which fear is an important symptom, including hypochondriasis and anorexia nervosa. In most cases of differential diagnosis, it will also be useful to integrate interview findings with information obtained via questionnaires (a useful overview of those for specific phobia can be found in Antony, 2001), self-monitoring, and behavioral assessment.

Behavioral Assessment

Behavioral Approach Task. Avoidance is an integral part of the diagnostic criteria of specific phobia. Consequently, a behavioral approach task (BAT) with phobic stimuli has often been used as one index of phobia severity, along with reported fear during the BAT. The approach task, sometimes called a behavioral avoidance or assessment task, asks the client to enter a feared situation or approach a feared stimulus. The phobic stimulus may be approached down a walkway, or the client may perform several tasks that entail increasingly close contact with it (e.g., touching the outside of a mouse's cage, taking the cage lid off, touching the mouse using a pen, touching it with a bare finger).

Because of strong avoidance tendencies in specific phobia, clients may not have encountered the stimulus recently and may not clearly remember details of their reactions to it. A BAT allows exposure in a largely controlled way. The client can then give reports of thoughts, feelings, and physical sensations, and the clinician can observe subtle avoidance or other behaviors outside the client's awareness. The BAT also allows the clinician to gauge the accuracy of the client's self-report.

BATs have been used for initial assessment and to monitor treatment progress, outcome, and retention. In research on spider phobia, for instance, BATs with a live spider often are used as one index of symptom severity (Merckelbach, de Jong, Arntz, & Schouten, 1993; Mohlman & Zinbarg, 2000; Mystkowski, Mineka, Vernon, & Zinbarg, 2003).

BATs can include contrived, naturalistic, or imagined scenarios and settings. For example, in a contrived BAT, the client's approach to a caged animal can be measured in feet. In other cases, the number of tasks successfully performed with the stimulus may quantify approach behavior. Contrived BATs are especially popular in the assessment of specific phobias because they can be brief, portable, and easy to set up and can provide some objective measure of avoidance. Naturalistic BATs strive for greater external validity, asking the client to perform increasingly feared or avoided tasks in the natural environment. One example of naturalistic BATs are height avoidance tests, in which clients are asked to ascend to the highest level they can in a building with balconies, a multitiered parking garage, or a fire escape (Marshall, 1985; Williams, Turner, & Peer, 1985; Williams & Watson, 1985). There is also evidence that imaginal assessments including physiological monitoring can provide useful information about specific phobias (McGlynn & Vopat, 1994).

BATs can vary in terms of stimuli used, number of steps involved, instruction content, instruction timing, and positioning and behavior of the assessor. For instance, for an unbiased index of symptom severity clinicians will need to ensure that their demeanor, presence, or location is not perceived as overtly reassuring. The assessor can unwittingly become a safety signal, encouraging approach behaviors the client ordinarily would not be capable of performing and giving an underestimate of avoidance. When administered correctly, BATs can provide a wide variety of information, including approach distance, approach latency, subtle avoidance behaviors (e.g., turning one's face away, crossing arms defensively in front of one's body), facial expression, self-reported emotion and cognitions, and physiological response (e.g., heart rate, vagal tone, skin conductance, respiration, cortisol). If the BAT involves multiple steps, called a progressive BAT, such information may be taken at each step.

Ratings during a BAT often use subjective units of discomfort or distress (SUD) scales (Wolpe, 1973). They may use a 0–100 rating scale (0 = *no fear, disgust, discomfort, or avoidance,* 50 = *moderate,* 100 = *highest imaginable*). Other rating scales, such as 0–8 and 0–10, are also commonly used, as well as fear thermometers (Walk, 1956). Visual analog scales (McGlynn, Moore, Rose, & Lazarte, 1995) and dials allowing continuous input of fear levels (McGlynn, Rose, & Lazarte, 1994) have also been used.

Progressive BATS may involve a standard hierarchy of tasks specifically designed for the disorder or may be tailored to the specific fears and avoidance of the client. Although a standardized BAT can provide normative information allowing comparison across clients, those tailored to the client may be the most clinically informative. When selecting tasks for a BAT, the clinician may include multiple difficult and emotion-provoking tasks or steps representing a range of difficulty levels.

Biological Challenge. Another form of behavioral assessment is a biological challenge, such as carbon dioxide inhalation, which produces unpleasant physical sensations. In such cases, rather than be exposed to an external stimulus, the client is exposed to interoceptive stimuli. Although biological challenges typically are associated with PD, there is emerging evidence that natural environment and situational phobic people may also have strong reactions to the kinds of uncomfortable physical sensations produced by biological challenges (Antony et al., 1997b). For instance, reactions to biological challenges may be particularly illuminating with clients with claustrophobia symptoms. The same kinds of information gathered during a BAT can be collected during biological challenge tasks, and the same considerations apply.

SELECTION OF TREATMENT TARGETS AND REFERRAL

It is widely agreed that confronting one's phobic stimulus in some way is an essential ingredient in treatment for specific phobia. Researchers have found that exposure treatment is successful for phobias of spiders, snakes, rats, blood, dental procedures, flying, enclosed places, heights, and water (Antony & Swinson, 2000; Hirai et al., 2006). Current exposure-based treatments have their roots in systematic desensitization, imaginal flooding and implosion, and modeling. Exposure treatment manuals for specific phobias are widely available (e.g., Antony, Barlow, & Craske, 1997).

In exposure therapy for specific phobias, it is often the case that the behavioral tasks used for assessment can be adopted for in-session and between-session exposure practice. In most cases the client and clinician will develop a fear and avoidance hierarchy together. During assessment, the client will have generated examples of situations that are feared, avoided, or endured with difficulty. The clinician can review the list with the client and ask that he or she expand on it. When a representative list has been compiled, the client should rank the items from least to most feared and avoided. For example, an exposure hierarchy for blood phobia might include looking at photos of blood as an easy step, holding a sealed vial of blood as an intermediate step, and having blood drawn as a difficult step.

Once the list has been ordered the client should assign SUD ratings to each item. The list can then be modified and expanded based on the addition or subtraction of important components (e.g., safety signals, calming and controllable vs. frightening and unpredictable elements). It may be particularly important to break down tasks higher on the hierarchy into smaller parts if there is a big gap in the hierarchy between easy or moderate steps and a highly difficult step. For instance, a claustrophobic may find it easy to stand in a closet with the door ajar, assigning it a SUD score of 50. However, the same person may view the task as intolerable if the door is completely shut, rating it as 100. In this case, additional detail should be added to the hierarchy until more moderate ratings are achieved. After some discussion and brainstorming, the client and clinician might modify the "closed door" task to include being in a large empty closet with the door shut for 15 s with the light on, the client's hand on the doorknob, and the clinician immediately outside the door. Such modifications may change the client's rating to 75 and also emphasize that exposure will be gradual and under the client's control. The highest step on the hierarchy represents the ultimate goal of therapy and gives the clinician an objective measure of treatment success.

It has been suggested that in generating the hierarchy clinicians may initially want to avoid disclosing its purpose, lest the client withhold information (White & Barlow, 2002). Such a decision will require clinical judgment, weighing the degree of collaboration and rapport. If a client is sufficiently cooperative, open, trusting, and motivated, withholding information may be damaging to the working relationship and unnecessary. On the other hand, the hierarchy may overwhelm highly anxious and skeptical clients, and treatment information should be delayed until the client's confidence and motivation have increased.

Self-monitoring diaries before, during, and after treatment can serve a range of functions. They can be important for aiding in assessment and providing additional items or details for the fear and avoidance hierarchy. Additional self-monitoring forms should be completed during exposure practice and may also be used for other treatment exercises, such as cognitive restructuring. They may be carried around in a pocket or purse to record incidents of phobic fear or avoidance during and after treatment, as part of an ongoing assessment process.

Depending on the type and severity of the specific phobia and the existence of complicating disorders or conditions, the format and length of treatment may vary widely. Researchers have demonstrated the efficacy of 2.5- to 3-hour single-session exposure treatments for specific phobias (Arntz & Lavy, 1993; Hellström & Öst, 1996; Öst, 1989; Öst, Salkovskis, & Hellström, 1991). One-session group treatments have also been used successfully with up to eight clients (Götestam, 2002; Öst, 1996; Öst, Ferebee, & Furmark, 1997). In vivo observation and video observation of the exposure treatment of another client also appear to lead to symptom improvement, although

the most effective strategy was direct exposure experiences by the client (Götestam, 2002; Öst et al., 1997). A recent review suggests that motivated simple phobics may be the best candidates for self-administered treatments (Newman, Erickson, Przeworski, & Dzus, 2003).

Virtual reality (VR) treatment is another exciting form of exposure therapy (see Krijn, Emmelkamp, Olafsson, & Biemond, 2004, for a review). Although it does not appear especially effective for driving phobia (Wald, 2004), it has been used fairly successfully with spider phobia (Garcia-Palacios, Hoffman, Carlin, Furness, & Botella, 2002) and flying phobia (Mühlberger, Wiedemann, & Pauli, 2003; Mühlberger, Weik, Pauli, & Wiedemann, 2006; Rothbaum, Hodges, Anderson, Price, & Smith, 2002; Rothbaum, Hodges, Smith, Lee, & Price, 2000). Clients can venture into a computer-generated environment in which the therapist is able to control their exposure experience. For example, the possibility of rapid or unpredictable spider movement or a spider bite can be removed, and the spider's size, color, orientation, position, speed, and movements can be controlled. Flying phobics can undergo simulated takeoffs, landings, turbulence, and thunderstorms of carefully graduated severity. Perhaps the chief advantage of VR exposure is its cost-effectiveness. Time with a therapist and expensive elements such as taking a commercial airplane flight can be eliminated or reduced.

In cases in which exposure treatments are not available, the clinician should help the client find suitable resources. Sometimes clinicians do not have such referral information readily available, perhaps because the clinician is new to the area and operating independently or needs to refer a client to another location. In such circumstances national professional societies such as the Association for Behavioral and Cognitive Therapies, the Anxiety Disorders Association of America, and the APA can be invaluable. Some professional societies have online lists of professionals by specialty area and geographic location. Others have phone help and referral lines and e-mail groups for such questions. Regional and local professional organizations, such as the Midwestern Psychological Association and the Southeastern Psychological Association, and state and provincial professional societies (listed on the APA Web site) can also be quite useful.

As discussed earlier, the interview is a key aspect of assessment that is crucial for determining diagnoses, which in turn inform the selection of appropriate treatment strategies and referral. Furthermore, in the case of specific phobias, the information gathered in the assessment can be used immediately in generating an exposure hierarchy, which will guide treatment. Thus, in cases of referral, a clear and detailed report will be a useful aid to the treating clinician. Whether a single session, group format, or VR treatment is appropriate depends on the individual situation. A thorough assessment provides knowledge of the client, his or her signs and symptoms, and the broader context that will allow appropriate referrals and treatment planning. The interview serves as an important first step in the treatment process, not only for gathering information about the client and making a diagnosis but also for providing the client with a sample interaction with a mental health professional.

SUMMARY

This chapter described assessment strategies for specific phobia, briefly reviewing specific phobia types, epidemiology and etiology, and emerging evidence about the role of disgust. Interviewers are encouraged to use semistructured interviews when possible, and considerations for selecting structured, semistructured, and unstructured interview formats are reviewed, along with suggestions regarding basic assessment areas. Given the likelihood of interviewing obstacles, such as client minimization or misrepresentation of difficulties, clinicians should take steps to improve client awareness of symptoms through specific prompts regarding common types of obvious and subtle fear and avoidance behavior. The development and use of behavioral assessment strategies will also aid in the process. The role of gender and potential cultural, ethnic, and racial differences in symptom presentation, cultural beliefs, learning, and developmental history are explored. A case illustration of a driving phobia demonstrated interviewing techniques to assess symptom presentation, etiology, and course to clarify issues of differential diagnosis and comorbidity. Given the comorbidity of specific phobias with one another and with other anxiety and mood disorders, careful consideration of differential diagnosis is crucial for appropriate treatment selection.

REFERENCES

Alpers, G. W., Wilhelm, F. H., & Roth, W. T. (2005). Psychophysiological assessment during exposure in driving phobic patients. *Journal of Abnormal Psychology, 114*, 126–139.

American Psychiatric Association. (1987). *Diagnostic and statistical manual of mental disorders* (3rd ed., Rev.). Washington, DC: Author.

Antony, M. M. (2001). Measures for specific phobia. In M. M. Antony, S. M. Orsillo, & L. Roemer (Eds.), *Practitioner's guide to empirically based measures of anxiety.* New York: Kluwer Academic/Plenum.

Antony, M. M., & Barlow, D. H. (1997). Social and specific phobias. In A. Tasman, J. Kay, & J. A. Lieberman (Eds.), *Psychiatry.* Philadelphia: Saunders.

Antony, M. M., Barlow, D. H., & Craske, M. J. (1997). *Mastery of your specific phobia: Therapist guide.* San Antonio, TX: Therapy Works.

Antony, M. M., Brown, T. A., & Barlow, D. H. (1997a). Heterogeneity among specific phobia types in *DSM-IV. Behaviour Research and Therapy, 35*, 1089–1100.

Antony, M. M., Brown, T. A., & Barlow, D. H. (1997b). Response to hyperventilation and 5.5% CO_2 inhalation of subjects with types of specific phobia, panic disorder, or no mental disorder. *American Journal of Psychiatry, 154*, 1089–1095.

Antony, M. M., Downie, F., & Swinson, R. P. (1988). Diagnostic issues and epidemiology in obsessive compulsive disorder. In R. P. Swinson, M. M. Antony, S. Rachman, & M. A. Richter (Eds.), *Obsessive-compulsive disorder: Theory, research and treatment* (pp. 3–32). New York: Guilford.

Antony, M. M., & Swinson, R. P. (2000). *Phobic disorders and panic in adults: A guide to assessment and treatment.* Washington, DC: American Psychological Association.

Arntz, A., & Lavy, E. (1993). Does stimulus elaboration potentiate exposure in vivo treatment? Two forms of one session treatment of spider phobia. *Behavioural Psychotherapy, 21*, 1–12.

Barlow, D. H. (2002). *Anxiety and its disorders: The nature and treatment of anxiety and panic.* New York: Guilford.

Becker, E. S., & Rinck, M. (2004). Sensitivity and response bias in fear of spiders. *Cognition and Emotion, 18*, 961–976.

Blanchard, J. J., & Brown, S. B. (1998). Structured diagnostic interview schedules. In C. R. Reynolds (Ed.), *Comprehensive clinical psychology: Vol. 3. Assessment.* New York: Elsevier.

Bourdon, K. H., Boyd, J. H., Rae, D. S., Burns, B. J., Thompson, J. W., & Locke, B. Z. (1988). Gender differences in phobias: Results of the ECA community study. *Journal of Anxiety Disorders, 2*, 227–241.

Brown, T. A., Campbell, L. A., Lehman, C. L., Grisham, J. R., & Mancill, R. B. (2001). Current and lifetime comorbidity of the *DSM-IV* anxiety and mood disorders in a large clinical sample. *Journal of Abnormal Psychology, 110*, 49–58.

Brown, T. A., Di Nardo, P., & Barlow, D. H. (1994). *Anxiety Disorders Interview Schedule for the DSM-IV (lifetime version).* San Antonio, TX: Psychological Corporation.

Cacioppo, J. T., Berntson, G. G., & Andersen, B. L. (1991). Psychophysiological approaches to the evaluation of psychotherapeutic process and outcome, 1991: Contributions from social psychophysiology. *Psychological Assessment: A Journal of Consulting and Clinical Psychology, 3*, 321–336.

Clark, D. M. (1986). A cognitive approach to panic. *Behaviour Research and Therapy, 24*, 461–470.

Craske, M. G. (1991). Phobic fear and panic attacks: The same emotional states triggered by different cues? *Clinical Psychology Review, 11*, 599–620.

Craske, M. G., Mohlman, J., Yi, J., Glover, D., & Valeri, S. (1995). Treatment of claustrophobia and snake/spider phobias: Fear of arousal and fear of context. *Behaviour Research and Therapy, 33*, 197–203.

Craske, M. G., & Sipsas, A. (1992). Animal phobias versus claustrophobias: Exteroceptive versus interoceptive cues. *Behaviour Research and Therapy, 30*, 569–581.

Craske, M. G., Zarate, R., Burton, T., & Barlow, D. H. (1993). Specific fears and panic attacks: A survey of clinical and nonclinical samples. *Journal of Anxiety Disorders, 7*, 1–19.

Curtis, G. C., Magee, W. J., Eaton, W. W., Wittchen, H.-U., & Kessler, R. C. (1998). Specific fears and phobias: Epidemiology and classification. *British Journal of Psychiatry, 173*, 212–217.

Davey, G. C. L. (1992). Characteristics of individuals with fear of spiders. *Anxiety Research, 4*, 299–314.

Davey, G. C. L., Forster, L., & Mayhew, G. (1993). Familial resemblances in disgust sensitivity and animal phobias. *Behaviour Research and Therapy, 31*, 41–50.

Di Nardo, P. A., Brown, T. A., & Barlow, D. H. (1994). *Anxiety Disorders Interview Schedule for* DSM-IV. San Antonio, TX: Psychological Corporation.

Di Nardo, P. A., Guzy, L. T., Jenkins, J. A., Bak, R. M., Tomasi, S. F., & Copland, M. (1988). Etiology and maintenance of dog fears. *Behaviour Research and Therapy, 26*, 241–244.

Eaton, W. W., Dryman, A., & Weissman, M. M. (1991). Panic and phobia. In L. N. Robins & D. A. Regier (Eds.), *Psychiatric disorders in America: The Epidemiological Catchment Area study*. New York: Free Press.

Ekman, P. (Ed.). (1982). *Emotion in the human face* (2nd ed.). Cambridge: Cambridge University Press.

Ekman, P., & Friesen, W. V. (1975). *Unmasking the face: A guide to recognizing emotions from facial clues*. Englewood, NJ: Prentice Hall.

First, M. B., Spitzer, R. L., Gibbon, M., & Williams, J. B. W. (1996). *Structured Clinical Interview for* DSM-IV *Axis I Disorders: Patient edition (SCID-I/P, Version 2.0)*. New York: Biometrics Research Department, New York State Psychiatric Institute.

First, M. B., Spitzer, R. L., Gibbon, M., & Williams, J. B. W. (1997). *Structured Clinical Interview for* DSM-IV *Axis I Disorders (SCID-I): Clinical version*. Washington, DC: American Psychiatric Press.

Foa, E. B., & Kozak, M. J. (1986). Emotional processing of fear: Exposure to corrective information. *Psychological Bulletin, 99*, 20–35.

Garcia-Palacios, A., Hoffman, H., Carlin, A., Furness, T. III, & Botella, C. (2002). Virtual reality in the treatment of spider phobia: A controlled study. *Behaviour Research and Therapy, 40*, 983–993.

Goisman, R., Allsworth, J., Rogers, M., Warshaw, M. G., Goldenberg, I., Vasile, R. G., et al. (1998). Simple phobia as a comorbid anxiety disorder. *Depression and Anxiety, 7*, 105–112.

Götestam, K. G. (2002). One session group treatment of spider phobia by direct or modelled exposure. *Cognitive Behaviour Therapy, 31*, 18–24.

Graham, J., & Gaffan, E. A. (1997). Fear of water in children and adults: Etiology and familial effects. *Behaviour Research and Therapy, 35*, 91–108.

Greenfeld, L. A., & Smith, S. K. (1999). *BJS special report: American Indians and crime* (NCJ 173386). Washington, DC: U.S. Government Press.

Haidt, J., Rozin, P., McCauley, C., & Imada, S. (1997). Body, psyche, and culture: The relationship between disgust and morality. *Psychology and Developing Societies, 9*, 107–131.

Harris, L. M., & Menzies, R. G. (1996). Origins of specific fears: A comparison of associative and nonassociative accounts. *Anxiety, 2*, 248–250.

Hartung, C. M., & Widiger, T. A. (1998). Gender differences in the diagnosis of mental disorders: Conclusions and controversies in the *DSM-IV*. *Psychological Bulletin, 123*, 260–278.

Hellström, K., & Öst, L.-G. (1996). Prediction of outcome in the treatment of specific phobia: A cross validation study. *Behavioural Research and Therapy, 34*, 403–411.

Himle, J. A., McPhee, K., Cameron, O. G., & Curtis, G. C. (1989). Simple phobia: Evidence for heterogeneity. *Psychiatry Research, 28*, 25–30.

Hirai, M., Vernon, L. L., & Cochran, H. (2006). Exposure therapy for phobia. In D. Richard & D. Lauterbach (Eds.), *Comprehensive handbook of the exposure therapies*. New York: Academic Press.

Holzer, C. E., Goldsmith, H. F., & Ciarlo, J. A. (1998). Effects of rural-urban county type on the availability of health and mental health care providers. In R. W. Manderscheid & M. J. Henderson (Eds.), *Mental health, United States*. Rockville, MD: Center for Mental Health Services.

Hsu, L. K. G., & Folstein, M. F. (1997). Somatoform disorders in Caucasian and Chinese Americans. *Journal of Nervous and Mental Disease, 185*, 382–387.

Hugdahl, K. (1988). Psychophysiological aspects of phobic fears: An evaluative review. *Neuropsychobiology, 20*, 194–204.

Jones, M. K., & Menzies, R. G. (2000). Danger expectancies, self-efficacy and insight in spider phobia. *Behaviour Research and Therapy, 38*, 585–600.

Jones, M. K., Whitmont, S., & Menzies, R. G. (1996). Danger expectancies and insight in spider phobia. *Anxiety, 2*, 179–185.

Jong, P. de, Andrea, H., & Muris, P. (1997). Spider phobia in children: Disgust and fear before and after treatment. *Behaviour Research and Therapy, 35*, 559–562.

Jong, P. J. de, & Muris, P. (2002). Spider phobia: Interaction of disgust and perceived likelihood of involuntary physical contact. *Journal of Anxiety Disorders, 16*, 51–65.

Jong, P. J. de, Peters, M., & Vanderhallen, I. (2002). Disgust sensitivity in spider phobia: Facial EMG in response to spider and oral disgust imagery. *Journal of Anxiety Disorders, 16*, 477–493.

Kessler, R. C., McGonagle, K. A., Zhao, S., Nelson, C. B., Hughes, M., Eshleman, S., et al. (1994). Lifetime and 12-month prevalence of *DSM-III-R* psychiatric disorders in the United States: Results from the National Comorbidity Survey. *Archives of General Psychiatry, 51*, 8–19.

Kilpatrick, D. G., & Acierno, R. (2003). Mental health needs of crime victims: Epidemiology and outcomes. *Journal of Traumatic Stress, 16*, 119–132.

Kilpatrick, D. G., Acierno, R., Resnick, H. S., Saunders, B. E., & Best, C. L. (1997). A two year longitudinal analysis of the relationship between violent assault and alcohol and drug use in women. *Journal of Consulting and Clinical Psychology, 65*, 834–847.

Kleinknecht, R. A. (1982). The origins and remission of fear in a group of tarantula enthusiasts. *Behaviour Research and Therapy, 20*, 437–443.

Klieger, D. M., & Siejak, K. K. (1997). Disgust as the source of false positive effects in the measurement of ophidiophobia. *Journal of Psychology, 131*, 371–382.

Komiti, A. A., Jackson, H. J., Judd, F. K., Cockram, A. M., Kyrios, M., Yeatman, R., et al. (2001). A comparison of the Composite International Diagnostic Interview (CIDI-Auto) with clinical assessment in diagnosing mood and anxiety disorders. *Australian and New Zealand Journal of Psychiatry, 35*, 224–230.

Krijn, M., Emmelkamp, P. M. G., Olafsson, R. P., & Biemond, R. (2004). Virtual reality exposure therapy of anxiety disorders: A review. *Clinical Psychology Review, 24*, 259–281.

Kunen, S., Niederhauser, R., Smith, P. O., Morris, J. A., & Marx, B. D. (2005). Race disparities in psychiatric rates in emergency departments. *Journal of Consulting and Clinical Psychology, 73*, 116–126.

Le, H.-N., Berenbaum, H., & Raghavan, C. (2002). Culture and alexithymia: Mean levels, correlates and the role of parental socialization of emotions. *Emotion, 2*, 341–360.

Levenson, R. W. (1992). Autonomic nervous system differences among emotions. *Psychological Science, 3*, 23–27.

Magee, W. J., Eaton, W. W., Wittchen, H.-U., McGonagle, K. A., & Kessler, R. C. (1996). Agoraphobia, simple phobia, and social phobia in the National Comorbidity Survey. *Archives of General Psychiatry, 53*, 159–168.

Marshall, W. L. (1985). The effects of variable exposure in flooding therapy. *Behavior Therapy, 16*, 117–135.

Matchett, G., & Davey, G. C. L. (1991). A test of a disease-avoidance model of animal phobias. *Behaviour Research and Therapy, 29*, 91–94.

Mathews, A., & MacLeod, C. (1994). Cognitive approaches to emotion and emotional disorders. *Annual Review of Psychology, 45*, 25–50.

McGlynn, F. D., Moore, P. M., Rose, M. P., & Lazarte, A. (1995). Effects of relaxation training on fear and arousal during in vivo exposure to a caged snake among *DSM-III-R* simple (snake) phobics. *Journal of Behavior Therapy and Experimental Psychiatry, 26*, 1–8.

McGlynn, F. D., Rose, M. P., & Lazarte, A. (1994). Control and attention during exposure influence arousal and fear among insect phobics. *Behavior Modification, 18*, 371–388.

McGlynn, F. D., & Vopat, T. (1994). Simple phobia. In C. G. Last & M. Hersen (Eds.), *Adult behavior therapy casebook* (pp. 139–152). New York: Plenum.

McNally, R. J. (1990). Psychological approaches to panic disorder: A review. *Psychological Bulletin, 108*, 403–419.

McNally, R. J., & Steketee, G. S. (1985). The etiology and maintenance of sever animal phobias. *Behaviour Research and Therapy, 23*, 431–435.

Menzies, R. G., & Clarke, J. C. (1993). The etiology of fear of heights and its relationship to severity and individual response patterns. *Behaviour Research and Therapy, 31*, 355–365.

Menzies, R. G., & Clarke, J. C. (1995a). The etiology of acrophobia and its relationship to severity and individual response patterns. *Behaviour Research and Therapy, 33*, 795–803.

Menzies, R. G., & Clarke, J. C. (1995b). The etiology of phobias: A nonassociative account. *Clinical Psychology Review, 15*, 23–48.

Menzies, R. G., & Harris, L. M. (1997). Mode of onset in evolutionary-relevant and evolutionary-neutral phobias: Evidence from a clinical sample. *Depression and Anxiety, 5*, 134–136.

Merckelbach, H., Arntz, A., & de Jong, P. (1991). Conditioning experiences and spider phobics. *Behaviour Research and Therapy, 29*, 333–335.

Merckelbach, H., Jong, P. de, Arntz, A., & Schouten, E. (1993). The role of evaluative learning and disgust sensitivity in the etiology and treatment of spider phobia. *Advances in Behaviour Research and Therapy, 15*, 243–255.

Merckelbach, H., & Muris, P. (1997). The etiology of childhood spider phobia. *Behaviour Research and Therapy, 35*, 1031–1034.

Mineka, S., Davidson, M., Cook, M., & Keir, R. (1984). Observational conditioning of snake fear in rhesus monkeys. *Journal of Abnormal Psychology, 93*, 355–372.

Mohlman, J., & Zinbarg, R. E. (2000). What kind of attention is necessary for fear reduction? An empirical test of the emotional processing model. *Behavior Therapy, 31*, 113–133.

Mowrer, O. H. (1939). Stimulus response theory of anxiety. *Psychological Review, 46*, 553–565.

Mowrer, O. H. (1947). On the dual nature of learning: A reinterpretation of "conditioning" and "problem solving." *Harvard Educational Review, 17*, 102–148.

Mühlberger, A., Weik, A., Pauli, P., & Wiedemann, G. (2006). One-session virtual reality exposure treatment for fear of flying: 1-year follow-up and graduation flight accompaniment effects. *Psychotherapy Research, 16*, 26–40.

Mühlberger, A., Wiedemann, G., & Pauli, P. (2003). Efficacy of a one-session virtual reality exposure treatment for fear of flying. *Psychotherapy Research, 13*, 323–336.

Mulkens, S., Jong, P. de, & Merckelbach, H. (1996). Disgust and spider phobia. *Journal of Abnormal Psychology, 105*, 464–468.

Mystkowski, J., Mineka, S., Vernon, L. L., & Zinbarg, R. (2003). Changes in caffeine state enhance return of fear in spider phobia. *Journal of Consulting and Clinical Psychology, 71*, 243–250.

Newman, M. G., Erickson, T., Przeworski, A., & Dzus, E. (2003). Self-help and minimal-contact therapies for anxiety disorders: Is human contact necessary for therapeutic efficacy? *Journal of Clinical Psychology, 59,* 251–274.

Norris, F. H. (1992). Epidemiology of trauma: Frequency and impact of different potentially traumatic events on different demographic groups. *Journal of Consulting and Clinical Psychology, 60,* 409–418.

Öst, L.-G. (1985). Ways of acquiring phobias and outcome of behavioral treatments. *Behaviour Research and Therapy, 23,* 683–689.

Öst, L.-G. (1987). Age of onset in different phobias. *Journal of Abnormal Psychology, 96,* 223–229.

Öst, L.-G. (1989). One-session treatment for specific phobias. *Behaviour Research and Therapy, 27,* 1–7.

Öst, L.-G. (1992). Blood and injection phobia: Background and cognitive, physiological, and behavioral variables. *Journal of Abnormal Psychology, 101,* 68–74.

Öst, L.-G. (1996). One-session group treatment of spider phobia. *Behaviour Research and Therapy, 34,* 707–715.

Öst, L.-G., Ferebee, I., & Furmark, T. (1997). One-session group therapy of spider phobia: Direct versus indirect treatments. *Behaviour Research and Therapy, 35,* 721–732.

Öst, L.-G., Hellström, K., & Kåver, A. (1992). One versus five sessions of exposure in the treatment of injection phobia. *Behavior Therapy, 23,* 263–282.

Öst, L.-G., Salkovskis, P. M., & Hellström, K. (1991). One-session therapist-directed exposure vs. self-exposure in the treatment of spider phobia. *Behavior Therapy, 22,* 407–422.

Poulton, R., Davies, S., Menzies, R. G., Langley, J. D., & Silva, P. A. (1998). Evidence for a non-associative model of the acquisition of a fear of heights. *Behavior Research and Therapy, 36,* 537–544.

Poulton, R., Menzies, R. G., Craske, M. G., Langley, J. D., & Silva, P. A. (1999). Water trauma and swimming experiences up to age 9 and fear of water at age 18: A longitudinal study. *Behavior Research and Therapy, 37,* 39–48.

Rachman, S. J. (1976). The passing of the two-stage theory of fear and avoidance: Fresh possibilities. *Behavior Research and Therapy, 14,* 125–131.

Rachman, S. J. (1977). The conditioning theory of fear acquisition: A critical examination. *Behavior Research and Therapy, 15,* 375–387.

Rachman, S. J. (1984). Agoraphobia: A safety signal perspective. *Behavior Research and Therapy, 22,* 59–70.

Rachman, S. (1990). *Fear and courage* (2nd ed.). New York: Freeman.

Reiss, A. J., & Roth, J. A. (1993). *Understanding and preventing violence.* Washington, DC: National Academy Press.

Riskind, J. H., Moore, R., & Bowley, L. (1995). The looming of spiders: The fearful perceptual distortion of movement and menace. *Behavior Research and Therapy, 33,* 171–178.

Robins, L., & Regier, D. A. (1991). *Psychiatric disorders in America: The Epidemiologic Catchment Area study.* New York: The Free Press.

Ross, H. E., Swinson, R. P., Larkin, E. J., & Doumani, S. (1994). Diagnosing comorbidity in substance abusers: Computer assessment and clinical validation. *Journal of Nervous and Mental Disease, 182,* 556–563.

Rothbaum, B. O., Hodges, L., Anderson, P. L., Price, L., & Smith, S. (2002). Twelve-month follow-up of virtual reality and standard exposure therapies for the fear of flying. *Journal of Consulting and Clinical Psychology, 70,* 428–432.

Rothbaum, B. O., Hodges, L., Smith, S., Lee, J. H., & Price, L. (2000). A controlled study of virtual reality exposure therapy for the fear of flying. *Journal of Consulting and Clinical Psychology, 68,* 1020–1026.

Rozin, P., & Fallon, A. (1987). A perspective on disgust. *Psychological Review, 94,* 23–41.

Rozin, P., Haidt, J., McCauley, C., Dunlop, L., & Ashmore, M. (1999). Individual differences in disgust sensitivity: Comparisons and evaluations of paper-and-pencil versus behavioral measures. *Journal of Research in Personality, 33,* 330–351.

Sanderson, W. C., Di Nardo, P. A., Rapee, R. M., & Barlow, D. H. (1990). A description of patients diagnosed with *DSM-III-R* generalized anxiety disorder. *Journal of Nervous and Mental Disease, 178,* 588–591.

Saucier, D. A., Miller, C. T., & Doucet, N. (2005). Differences in helping Whites and Blacks: A meta-analysis. *Personality and Social Psychology Review, 9,* 2–16.

Sawchuk, C. N., Lohr, J. M., Tolin, D. F., Lee, T. C., & Kleinknecht, R. A. (2000). Disgust sensitivity and contamination fears in spider and blood-injection-injury phobias. *Behaviour Research and Therapy, 38,* 753–762.

Sawchuk, C. N., Lohr, J. M., Westendorf, D. H., Meunier, S. A., & Tolin, D. F. (2002). Emotional responding to fearful and disgusting stimuli in specific phobics. *Behaviour Research and Therapy, 40,* 1031–1046.

Sloan, T., & Telch, M. J. (2002). The effects of safety-seeking behavior and guided threat reappraisal on fear reduction during exposure: An experimental investigation. *Behaviour Research and Therapy, 40,* 235–251.

Smitherman, T. A., Hammel, J. C., & McGlynn, F. D. (2003, November). *Claustrophobia as a variant of panic disorder with agoraphobia?* Poster presented at the annual convention of the Association for Advancement of Behavior Therapy, Boston, MA.

Starcevic, V., & Bogojevic, G. (1997). Comorbidity of PDA and specific phobias: Relationship with subtypes of specific phobia. *Comprehensive Psychiatry, 38,* 315–320.

Thyer, B. A., Himle, J., & Curtis, G. C. (1985). Blood-injury-illness phobia: A review. *Journal of Clinical Psychology, 41,* 451–459.

Tolin, D. F., Lohr, J. M., Sawchuk, C. N., & Lee, T. C. (1997). Disgust and disgust sensitivity in blood-injection-injury and spider phobia. *Behaviour Research and Therapy, 35,* 949–953.

Tolin, D. E., Sawchuk, C. N., & Lee, T. C. (1999). The role of disgust in blood-injection-injury phobia. *Behavior Therapist, 22,* 96–99.

Turpin, G. (1990). Ambulatory clinical psychophysiology: Proceedings of a symposium held at the World Congress of Behaviour Therapy, Edinburgh, Scotland, September 1988. *Journal of Psychophysiology, 4,* 297–304.

U.S. Department of Health and Human Services. (2001). *Mental health: Culture, race, and ethnicity—A supplement to mental health. A report of the Surgeon General.* Rockeville, MD: Author.

Vega, W. A., Kolody, B., Aguilar-Gaxiola, S., Alderate, E., Catalano, R., & Carveo-Anduaga, J. (1998). Lifetime prevalence of *DSM-III-R* psychiatric disorders among urban and rural Mexican Americans in California. *Archives of General Psychiatry, 55,* 771–778.

Vernon, L. L., & Berenbaum, H. (2002). Disgust and fear in response to spiders. *Cognition and Emotion, 16,* 809–830.

Vernon, L. L., & Berenbaum, H. (2004). A naturalistic examination of positive expectations, time course, and disgust in the origins and reduction of spider and insect distress. *Journal of Anxiety Disorders, 18,* 707–718.

Vickers, K., & McNally, R. J. (2005). Respiratory symptoms and panic in the National Comorbidity Survey: A test of Klein's suffocation false alarm theory. *Behaviour Research and Therapy, 43,* 1011–1018.

Wald, J. (2004). Efficacy of virtual reality exposure therapy for driving phobia: A multiple baseline across-subjects design. *Behavior Therapy, 35,* 621–635.

Walk, R. D. (1956). Self-ratings of fear in a fear-invoking situation. *Journal of Abnormal and Social Psychology, 52,* 171–178.

Warheit, G. J., Holzer, C. E. III, & Arey, S. A. (1975). Race and mental illness: An epidemiologic update. *Journal of Health and Social Behavior, 16,* 243–256.

White, K. S., & Barlow, D. H. (2002). Panic disorder and agoraphobia. In D. H. Barlow (Ed.), *Anxiety and its disorders: The nature and treatment of anxiety and panic.* New York: Guilford.

Williams, J. M. G, Mathews, A., & MacLeod, C. (1996). The emotional Stroop task and psychopathology. *Psychological Bulletin, 120,* 3–24.

Williams, S. L., Turner, S. M., & Peer, D. F. (1985). Guided mastery and performance desensitization treatments for severe acrophobia. *Journal of Consulting and Clinical Psychology, 53,* 237–247.

Williams, S. L., & Watson, N. (1985). Perceived danger and perceived self-efficacy as cognitive determinants of acrophobic behaviour. *Behaviour Research & Therapy, 16,* 136–145.

Wolpe, J. (1973). *The practice of behavior therapy* (2nd ed.). New York: Pergamon.

Woody, S. R., McLean, C., & Klassen, T. (2005). Disgust as a motivator of avoidance of spiders. *Journal of Anxiety Disorders, 19,* 461–475.

Woody, S. R., & Tolin, D. F. (2002). The relationship between disgust sensitivity and avoidant behavior: Studies of clinical and nonclinical samples. *Journal of Anxiety Disorders, 16,* 543–559.

Zhang, A. Y., & Snowden, L. R. (1999). Ethnic characteristics of mental disorders in five U.S. communities. *Cultural Diversity and Ethnic Minority Psychology, 5,* 134–146.

15

SOCIAL PHOBIA

STEFAN M. SCHULZ, ALICIA E. MEURET, REBECCA LOH,
AND STEFAN G. HOFMANN

DESCRIPTION OF THE DISORDER

Social phobia (social anxiety disorder) is characterized by marked distress brought on during social or performance situations in which one may be subject to scrutiny by others. The disorder was first described in the literature in 1966 by Marks and Gelder. It often follows a chronic course (Amies, Gelder, & Shaw, 1983) and can negatively affect functioning in social, occupational, and other domains (Schneier et al., 1994; Stein & Kean, 2001).

Social phobia is a common anxiety disorder (Kessler, Chiu, Demler, Merikangas, & Walters, 2005). Epidemiological studies found a slightly higher prevalence rate in females than in males (3:2 female-to-male ratio; Kessler et al., 2005). The disorder is observed in all cultures, although the cultural mores of different societies can affect both presentation and prevalence of the disorder (Heinrichs, Rapee, et al., 2006). Public speaking is the most commonly feared social situation in U.S. studies (Pollard & Henderson, 1988). Other typical situations that may cause anxiety include eating or writing in public, initiating or maintaining conversations, meeting strangers, going to parties, and dating.

Diagnostic and Statistical Manual Diagnostic Criteria

According to the *Diagnostic and Statistical Manual of Mental Disorders* (*DSM-IV-TR;* American Psychiatric Association [APA], 2000), the defining feature is anxiety provoked by social or performance situations, and the *DSM-IV-TR* goes on to outline the typical presentation of social phobia and some exclusionary criteria for the diagnosis.

Researchers studying social phobia have noted heterogeneity across presentations of the disorder (Hofmann, Heinrichs, & Moscovitch, 2004). The *DSM-IV-TR* includes a *generalized subtype* specifier if the fears include "most social situations" (APA, 2000, p. 451). Unfortunately, there are no specific guidelines as to how many situations are considered "most," and people have interpreted the term in varying ways. For example, some assign a *generalized subtype* specifier if the person's fears affect a variety of social interaction situations (e.g., fear of initiating or maintaining a conversation), whereas the disorder is considered *nongeneralized,* or specific, if the fear is limited to performance situations (e.g., giving a speech, using public restrooms), even if multiple performance situations are problematic (Stemberger,

Turner, Beidel, & Calhoun, 1995; Turner, Beidel, & Townsley, 1992). Other authors distinguish between generalized, nongeneralized, and circumscribed subtypes, depending on the number of feared social situations (see Heimberg, Holt, Schneier, Spitzer, & Liebowitz, 1993, and Hofmann et al., 2004, for a review). Other systems that capture the heterogeneity of social phobia are based on the quality of the emotional expression in social situations (Hofmann et al., 2004) or cultural norms (Heinrichs, Rapee, et al., 2006; Hofmann & Barlow, 2002).

It remains uncertain whether these subtypes represent qualitatively or quantitatively different subgroups. Similarly, it remains unknown whether the diagnostic category social phobia and the highly comorbid Axis II category avoidant personality disorder (APD) represent distinct disease entities or whether they are simply extreme expressions of normal social anxiety. Another area of current research is the relationship between social phobia and shyness (Hofmann, 2000b). The diagnostic criteria of APD and social phobia overlap extensively, and studies have found that both feature high levels of social anxiety, high trait anxiety, greater overall psychopathology, depression, and poor overall psychosocial functioning (Turner et al., 1992). For our discussion, we subsume all subtypes under the term *social phobia* because there is no evidence that issues related to interviewing are subtype specific.

One final consideration in the clinical presentation of social phobia is its relationship to social skill deficits. Some early models of social phobia (e.g., Stravynski & Greenberg, 1989) implicated lack of social skills as the culprit underlying the anxiety. However, studies of social skills in people with social phobia have not demonstrated that difficulties in this arena consistently contribute to the origin or maintenance of the disorder (for review, see Stravynski & Amado, 2001). Nonetheless, it is recognized that some people with social phobia may indeed have deficiencies in social skills, and awareness of such difficulties is useful while one is interviewing patients with social phobia.

INTERVIEWING STRATEGIES

Structured Versus Unstructured Interviews

Clinical interviews can be either structured or unstructured. Some think that unstructured interviews offer greater flexibility, whereas others stress the importance of structured interviews in order to gather thorough and reliable information. Either approach is greatly enhanced through practice. An experienced clinician should be able to conduct a smooth interview while gathering enough information to formulate accurate diagnoses, regardless of the interviewing format he or she chooses.

A thorough understanding of the diagnostic criteria is essential for conducting a successful assessment interview. Although this is clearly important for unstructured interviewing, it is equally critical in structured interviews so that appropriate follow-up questions are asked. Many structured diagnostic instruments are available, including the Anxiety Disorders Interview Schedule for *DSM-IV* (ADIS-IV; DiNardo, Brown, & Barlow, 1994), the Structured Clinical Interview for *DSM-IV* (SCID-IV; First, Spitzer, Gibbon, & Williams, 1994), the Schedule for Affective Disorders and Schizophrenia (SADS; Endicott & Spitzer, 1978), and the Composite International Diagnostic Interview (Robins et al., 1988). Each instrument covers a range of psychological disorders and contains a specific section for diagnosis of social phobia. The interviews offer specific screening and follow-up questions while also allowing the clinician to ask additional questions necessary to clarify important points. Administration of the interviews typically requires training, and the instruments vary in their degree of structure. For example, the ADIS-IV leaves follow-up questions to the interviewer's discretion, whereas the SCID-IV offers sample follow-up questions to typical responses while also allowing the interviewer to generate other questions as necessary. The Composite International Diagnostic Interview is a fully structured instrument, and interviewers are trained to formulate standardized follow-up questions to reduce interrater variability.

Goals of the Interview

Potential goals of conducting an interview are establishing rapport, making the diagnosis, and gathering specific information about the client's clinical presentation that is relevant for treatment. Putting the client with social phobia at ease during the assessment is essential. Because many who suffer from social phobia may feel uncomfortable interacting with others, it is important to establish good rapport and to make the person feel comfortable during the interview. People with social phobia often find it helpful to learn that social phobia is a very common and very treatable condition. Patients also appreciate it if the therapist acknowledges the fact that an interview can be a very stressful social situation. The clinician might encourage the client to let him or her know how to make the interview process less stressful.

Assessment Measures

Assessment measures for social phobia include clinician-administered and patient-rated instruments. These measures may be used to supplement the information gathered during the assessment interview. We do not recommend using these assessment measures as the sole means for formulating a diagnosis. Proper diagnosis should be made only by trained clinicians. Ideally, we suggest that clinicians follow a structured diagnostic interview to ensure that important clinical information is gathered. Standardized measures will allow more objective validation of the clinical impression.

Clinician-administered scales include the Liebowitz Social Phobia Scale (Liebowitz, 1987) and the Brief Social Phobia Scale (Davidson et al., 1993). Both instruments measure fear and avoidance of common social situations that can be anxiety provoking. The Brief Social Phobia Scale also includes four items to assess somatic symptoms. Functional impairment may be assessed using the Sheehan Disability Scale (Sheehan, 1983) or the Liebowitz Self-Rated Disability Scale (Schneier et al., 1994).

Commonly used self-report measures of social phobia include the Social Phobia and Anxiety Inventory (Turner, Beidel, Dancu, & Stanley, 1989), the Social Interaction Anxiety Scale and the Social Phobia Scale (Mattick & Clark, 1998), and the Fear Questionnaire (Marks & Matthews, 1979). The Social Phobia and Anxiety Inventory measures both social phobia and agoraphobia and assesses specific thoughts, behaviors, and physiological symptoms. The Social Interaction Anxiety Scale focuses on anxiety caused by social interactions, and the Social Phobia Scale measures anxiety caused by performance situations (including such activities as eating and writing in front of others). The Fear Questionnaire allows the therapist to identify the client's primary phobia in order to assess the degree of distress and avoidance prompted by the situation.

Additionally, the Social Anxiety and Distress Scale (Watson & Friend, 1969), the Fear of Negative Evaluation Scale (Watson & Friend, 1969), the Social Interaction Self-Statement Test (Glass, Merluzzi, Biever, & Larsen, 1982), the Self-Statements During Public Speaking (Hofmann & DiBartolo, 2000), and the Cognitive-Somatic Anxiety Questionnaire (Schwartz, Davidson, & Goleman, 1978) were designed to measure specific aspects concomitant to social phobia.

General Issues

Before the start of the interview, it is recommended that the clinician provide the client with a few general guidelines and inform him or her of the nature and structure of the assessment. Assurances with regard to the confidentiality of the information can make the client feel more comfortable about disclosing sensitive information. It is helpful to remind the client about the purpose of the assessment and to tell him or her what kinds of questions can be expected. We advise that the clinician inform the client of the estimated duration of the interview. Anxiety about the overall process can be reduced through such explanations that familiarize the client with the interview format.

When interviewing, the clinician should be mindful about the use of open- and closed-ended questions. Open-ended questions (e.g., "How did this make you feel?") invite the client to describe experiences in his or her own words. Such narrative descriptions are a rich source of information and can help the interviewer determine topics worthy of further exploration. Closed-ended questions (e.g., "Did this make you feel upset?") make it possible to gather specific information quickly.

INTERVIEWING OBSTACLES AND SOLUTIONS

Because people with social phobia are especially concerned about the opinions of others, the clinician faces unique challenges when interviewing these clients. Given the nature of the disorder, the clinician may need to take extra care in putting the client at ease in order to make the assessment as productive as possible. For example, some people may have fears related to interacting with authority figures, whereas others may have anxiety related to feelings of being evaluated. An interview situation involves an evaluation by an authority figure. Awareness of the specific concerns of the client before the assessment interview can be very helpful. Where possible, we recommend having the client fill out self-report questionnaires to measure general or specific aspects of social anxiety before the interview. This can help guide the course of the assessment and alert the clinician to specific issues that may arise.

Fears of Interactions With Strangers

With all clients, establishment of rapport is important for conducting a successful interview. This is especially important when assessing people with social phobia, particularly if the anxiety is heightened during interactions with strangers. A warm, friendly attitude throughout the interview can help put the client at ease. Nonverbal behaviors (e.g., sympathetic smiles and understanding nods) can be reassuring. Severely anxious clients may avoid eye contact, and the clinician should not attempt to force clients to maintain eye contact. Skilled clinicians are able to infer the client's level of distress by monitoring his or her eye contact and nonverbal, paraverbal, and verbal behaviors.

The clinician may use open- and closed-ended questions strategically to make the assessment run more smoothly. People with social phobia who are afraid of the interview situation are likely to be more uncomfortable with open-ended questions than closed-ended questions, especially at the beginning of the interview. We recommend starting with closed-ended questions to acclimate the client to the question-and-answer format of the interview. It is important that the clinician adjust the type of questions to the client's comfort level during the interview without sacrificing the quality of the information gathered during the interview.

Fears of Interactions With Authority Figures

Some clients feel particularly apprehensive because the clinician represents an authority figure. It is always helpful to think of the assessment process as a collaborative effort in which two people work together toward a common goal. When the clinician adopts this attitude, it can be easier for the client to view him or her as less intimidating. Additionally, the client may feel threatened by items in the environment such as one-way mirrors, diplomas on the walls, or a large desk placed between interviewer and interviewee, and where possible, we recommend conducting the assessment in a warm environment rather than a cold office that displays the clinician's power and authority.

Fears of Evaluation

When the client has difficulty revealing personal information because of concerns about being evaluated, the clinician can be supportive in a number of ways. First, it may be helpful to remind the client about the confidentiality policy and the reasons for the assessment. Clients should be informed about who will and who will not have access to the information. We recommend that clinicians use empathy and express appreciation for how difficult the self-disclosure must be while stressing the importance of collecting information as completely and accurately as possible in order to make the assessment successful.

We recommend that clinicians adopt a nonjudgmental stance toward the interview and convey this attitude to the client both verbally and nonverbally. For example, the client may be reassured by reminders that many people have difficulties with social anxiety and that there is no reason to feel ashamed of it. It is helpful to make encouraging comments throughout the interview, but it is important that such comments be genuine and not contingent on the types of responses being given. We generally discourage clinicians from sharing their own social fears and concerns with their clients, although there may be exceptional circumstances in which it is appropriate. However, we believe that the potential harm that self-disclosure can cause to a therapeutic relationship does not outweigh the potential benefits.

When assessing people with social phobia, we recommend that clinicians allow extra time for the interview. People with social phobia can be sensitive to subtle verbal or nonverbal cues. Therefore, any sense of hurry on the part of the clinician may prompt the client to give abbreviated responses. This can result in inadequate information for making a diagnosis or may necessitate more time for the assessment in order to further explore important details. Because the interview often is a challenging social task in and of itself, frequent breaks could make the situation less challenging. Although this might add additional time to the interview, it can make the process less taxing for the client. At the same time, however, the clinician must avoid conducting an unnecessarily long interview because this can be tiring for both interviewer and interviewee. We recommend briefly discussing the length, number of breaks, and other issues related to the interview format at the beginning of the interview.

Social Skill Deficits

In some patients with social phobia, social anxiety may arise from a genuine lack of appropriate social skills. These patients may feel uncertain about how to behave during social interactions and are painfully self-conscious about their social skill deficits. During the assessment interview, these clients may appear nervous and awkward, and we recommend an accepting, nonjudgmental attitude from the clinician to help put the client at ease. Again, we advise that clinicians be explicit in letting clients know what will happen throughout the interview and what is expected of the interviewee because he or she may feel particularly anxious about behaving appropriately during the interview.

Problems With Assertiveness

Some clients with social phobia may have particular difficulties with assertiveness. This can be problematic during the assessment if it prevents the client from speaking up to clarify points of confusion or to inform the clinician of issues that have been overlooked. Throughout the assessment, it is important for the interviewer to offer the socially anxious client many opportunities to speak up. It can be helpful to reiterate information the client has just conveyed, and ask questions such as "Does that sound accurate to you?" We recommend that the clinician ask whether the interviewee has anything else to add before ending each topic of discussion and moving on to the next. If the client has nothing to say at that point, the clinician can offer assurances that the topic can be revisited if any other relevant information comes to mind later. However, the clinician should give the client enough time to answer these questions. People with social phobia often take long pauses during conversations for a variety of reasons. For example, the client might monitor his or her answers or prepare his or her nonverbal response. Such a safety behavior would be discouraged during treatment but should be accepted during the assessment interview because the clinician could otherwise miss important information.

CASE ILLUSTRATION WITH DIALOGUE

Here we provide a case illustration and an excerpt from the diagnostic interview of a patient with extreme fears in social situations.

John is a 48-year-old divorced man who presented to our clinic with concerns about what he described as "shyness that made it difficult for me to interact and get along with others." He reported that he had always been shy and anxious in social situations and that in the past 7 years, his shyness and social phobia had become disabling. He reported significant anxiety in multiple situations, including attending parties, participating in meetings and classes, talking in front of a group, speaking with unfamiliar people, talking to people in authority, dating, being assertive, and initiating and maintaining conversations. During his initial interview he noted that in these situations he is afraid that he will say something stupid or humiliating and that others will think poorly of him. He described multiple ways in which his social phobia interfered with his life. For example, he reported having to rely on his sister to interact for him in most social situations. He reported that his social phobia impeded his career advancement in that he had declined job offers and promotions because of his aversion to making presentations in front of and interacting with colleagues. The following is a part of his initial interview.

Interviewer:	John, do you remember the first time you felt your anxiety in social situations was incapacitating?
John:	Oh yes, I clearly remember the situation. I must have been about 8 years old or so. I was forced to participate in a Christmas play at school. It was just terrible.
I:	Can you tell me a bit more about what happened?
J:	Well, it's hard to talk about it even now. I get all anxious and stressed out just thinking about that day.
I:	I understand this must be distressing. Why don't you tell me what happened?

J: Hmmm. . . . I had a tiny role—just a couple of lines. I remember that I was obsessively practicing my lines for weeks and weeks, and I couldn't sleep in the nights leading up to the play. I had this ridiculous feeling I still have today: "How is it that everybody is excited about things like a play, or parties, and I just hate them so much?"

I: Did you try to get out of it?

J: Absolutely! On the day of the play, I felt sick to my stomach. Surely, it was all anxiety. I get the same feelings today.

I: I see. What other symptoms did you have?

J: I felt like my mind was wiped clean, and I couldn't remember a single word of what I had to say. Obliviously, my parents pushed me to go. The next thing I remember was walking on stage. God, I remember how the light felt so bright, and I felt like everybody in the audience stared at me and could see in my stupid face how terrified I was.

I: What happened next?

J: Hmmm. . . . I felt that my legs were wobbly and I couldn't move. My heart was beating like crazy, and I could feel the sweat running down my face. While I was waiting to say my line, my vision started to become blurry, you know, as if I would pass out any minute. Not only that—I was truly convinced that I would throw up or start crying. God, it was just pathetic. . . . When it was my turn, I heard myself saying the first lines, and then I remember nothing. I really felt as if I blanked. The next thing I remember was that I was walking off stage.

I: What happened then?

J: Well, I remember that I felt overwhelmed by relief, and at the same time I felt like the biggest idiot and failure.

I: I understand that you must have felt really awful in this moment. Did the event affect your performance at school?

J: I think it made everything worse. I totally started to withdraw from everything.

I: What do you mean by that?

J: Well, for example, in class I never raised my hand, and I was terrified that the teachers would call on me. I was sure all my classmates thought I was weird. It's funny—even today I am convinced most people think that. I guess that is why I never really had many friends. I just can't trust anyone. . . .

I: Does this issue of not trusting others affect other areas of your life?

J: Sure it does. It happens at work just like it did in school. The worst thing is talking to my colleagues, since I always feel that I say stupid things, and they only talk to me because they pity me.

I: Can you give me an example?

J: Well, last week there was a little gathering at the office. I dread these occasions and usually try to get out of them if I can. Everybody was standing around chatting, and one of my colleagues walked over to me and asked me if I had a nice weekend. I just nodded stupidly and turned all red. Before I could even get out a word, she was already talking to someone else.

I: And what happened afterwards?

J: Usually, I end up dwelling on these things, sometimes for weeks. I'd call myself names and beat myself up for acting stupidly. I sometimes create these fictional scenarios where I actually say and do what I should have. . . .

I: Do you think that this affects your performance at work?

J: Well, that's why I am here. I am sure sooner or later I will get laid off because of it.

I: What do you mean by "because of it"?

J: I can't do the work I would like to do because I am terrified to interact with others. I am sure that my bosses only assign me writing tasks because I am incapable of talking with customers. The problem is, I can't even concentrate on the writing task because I am constantly dwelling on what other people may think or say about me.

I: Mm-hmm. . . . I understand. Are there other situations that make you feel that same way?

J: Well, basically any situation where I have to interact with people. Even little things like ordering coffee are ridiculously hard for me. . . . I stumble over words and just feel awkward. It happens all the time that people have to ask me twice what I want because I simply can't speak up. That's why it's better for me to just not get into those situations.

I: And are there any other situations that you avoid or that would cause you great fear or anxiety to get into?

J: Any kind of social gathering: parties, private invitations, sometimes even family events. Can you imagine, I even started to avoid answering the phone.

I: Do you believe that your fear and anxiety in social situations are excessive or unreasonable?

J: Well, I know it is excessive; that's the whole problem. Everyone else is so much calmer and more competent than I am. I guess deep inside I know that I should not be so anxious about what other people think about me, but I just can't help it.

John was diagnosed with generalized social phobia and was offered individual cognitive-behavioral therapy (CBT). The information gathered during the ADIS-IV-L (DiNardo et al., 1994) suggested that he met criteria for a generalized subtype of social phobia. For example, he reported *experiencing exaggerated and persistent fear in multiple social situations,* such as work gatherings and private invitations (Criterion A). He further reported that he holds a strong *belief that people judge him* as being an awkward, incompetent person (Criterion A) and stated that his fears in these situations trigger *strong physical symptoms* such as heart racing and shakiness (Criterion B). The clinician's impression was that John has *insight* into the excessiveness of his fear of social judgment (Criterion C) and that he tries to *avoid social interactions or situations* or endures them with *great distress* when confronted unexpectedly or forced (Criterion D). John's description of his problem suggested that his *life is greatly impaired* in that he feels isolated, he has difficulty trusting others, and his work and social life have suffered (Criterion E). The specifier of *generalized* social phobia was given because of his *fear and avoidance of most types of social interaction* (as opposed to fear and avoidance limited to a specific domain such as public speaking).

MULTICULTURAL AND DIVERSITY ISSUES

Researchers have encountered social phobia in all countries in which the disorder has been studied, and it is recognized to affect people from a variety of social, cultural, and socioeconomic backgrounds. During an initial assessment, awareness of the background and life experiences of the client is essential for making a proper diagnosis and ensuring a smooth interview.

One specific example of the influence of culture on the expression of social phobia is *taijin kyofusho* (TKS), an emotional disorder that is believed to be particularly prevalent in the Japanese and Korean culture (Takahashi, 1989). A person with TKS is concerned about doing something or presenting an appearance that will offend or embarrass others. In contrast, social phobia in the Western culture is defined as the fear of embarrassing oneself. Awareness of different cultural phenomena in social phobia helps the clinician be sensitive to atypical presentations of the disorder.

Cultural norms and societal expectations can affect the presentation of social anxiety and shyness across a number of cultures (Heinrichs, Rapee, et al., 2006). For example, deferent and retiring behavior can be perceived as a weakness in Western cultures, whereas the same behavior suggests competence in China (Xinyin, Rubin, & Boshu, 1995). Thus, behaviorally inhibited people from these two cultures may have very different perceptions of their social competence. When forming clinical impressions, it is helpful to consider the presenting symptoms in the cultural context of the client.

Differing degrees of formality between assessor and client may be dictated by cultural expectations. Whereas Western attitudes may allow more collegial interactions in the assessment setting, people from some cultures (e.g., Korean, Japanese) may feel more comfortable adhering to rules of formality. Some people may be put at ease by being on a first-name basis with the interviewer, whereas such informality may cause distress in people raised in a culture with more firmly established rules of social hierarchy. It is recommended to err on the side of formality unless the client indicates otherwise.

The client's self-disclosure is essential in the assessment interview, yet this can be difficult for many people. In some cultures, self-disclosure may be considered entirely inappropriate between two people who do not know each other well. Additionally, clients from diverse backgrounds may struggle with discussing what they consider family secrets. Establishment and maintenance of good rapport are of particular importance in interviewing these clients, and extra time may be needed for the assessment so that the client does not feel rushed while trying to reveal sensitive personal information. The clinician can help put the client at ease by acknowledging the difficulties of self-disclosure and assuring the client that such feelings are normal. We advise the clinician to emphasize that the interviewing situation differs from everyday social interactions because the purpose of the interview is to gain information about the client that will be useful in treatment. We advise reminding the client that the information he or she shares will be kept confidential, which can also help assuage some fears.

Differential Diagnosis and Behavioral Assessment

Differential Diagnoses

Social phobia has many faces, and comorbidity with other disorders is the rule rather than the exception. A report of panic attacks in the context of social anxiety is a prevalent diagnostic issue. In this case a thorough exploration of the pathogenesis of the disorder provides the most valuable information. In *social phobia,* the fear of possible scrutiny by others typically develops long before the onset of panic attacks. They are usually limited to a typical set of social situations involving evaluation by others (e.g., public speaking). For those with social phobia who experience panic attacks, major concerns are related to appearing out of control in front of others and being able to escape the situation if necessary. At the same time, people with social phobia typically avoid a range of social situations in which panic attacks never occurred.

In *panic disorder with agoraphobia,* panic attacks may also occur in social situations, but usually they are not limited to evaluative social situations. Major concerns usually are related to fainting or dying of a heart attack. Sometimes, an initial onset of unexpected panic attacks in a social situation can lead to subsequent avoidance of similar situations thought to trigger the panic attacks. This might complicate a clear diagnosis because the onset of social fear may coincide with the development of panic attacks. However, if panic attacks are not limited to specific social situations only but occur unpredictably in a variety of other situations (e.g., alone on a bridge), panic disorder with agoraphobia is the more appropriate diagnosis. If somebody meets criteria for social phobia but also experiences unexpected panic attacks in nonsocial situations, both diagnoses can be given.

Distinguishing *agoraphobia without history of panic disorder* from social phobia can be complex because both disorders may involve the fear of possible humiliation. In social phobia, this would be the main characteristic defining all feared situations, whereas agoraphobia without history of panic disorder typically involves a set of situations, some of which may or may not involve scrutiny by others.

A close examination of the reasons for social avoidance is the key to distinguishing *separation anxiety disorder* from social phobia. People with separation anxiety disorder do not fear social situations themselves. Problems arise from being separated from a needed caretaker. Consequently, social avoidance may be reinforced by feelings of embarrassment and shame when a person wants to go home early, and he or she may need a parent when it's not developmentally appropriate.

Similar to social phobia, fears of being humiliated, scrutinized, or embarrassed in a social situation may also be essential concerns in *generalized anxiety disorder.* However, the fear and worries usually permeate a much broader range of issues. If clinically significant fear of embarrassment or humiliation is present in addition to other anxieties, both disorders may be diagnosed.

Specific phobias usually are elicited by a cluster of situations featuring distinct key stimuli, such as certain objects, situations, or a specific combination of them. In specific phobia, anxiety usually emerges regardless of whether evaluation is part of the situation, but this is the key element in social phobia.

Pervasive developmental disorders comprise a set of behavioral difficulties often associated with *autism*. Typical characteristics include poor social interaction and communication, social avoidance, and anxiety in new and unpredictable social situations. Milder expressions of the disorder may appear similar to social phobia. However, the ability to form meaningful relationships in social phobia is more constrained by the person's anxiety, not a lack of ability or interest in social interactions.

A lack of significant social relationships is also characteristic of *schizoid personality disorder*. This could be misinterpreted as avoidance behavior. However, the driving force is not anxiety but a lack of interest. Although some people with social phobia may lack social skills and practice to perform comfortably in social situations, they have the capacity and usually a strong interest in building social relationships with other people.

Depressed mood is characteristic for people with social phobia and often is a major motivation for seeking treatment. However, if depression is a reaction to the ongoing difficulties and limitations that accompany social phobia, it is usually possible to identify specific memories or thoughts that reinforce negative mood, such as difficult or embarrassing situations or missed opportunities. Furthermore, social avoidance can be a common characteristic in those with depression. However, people with social phobia avoid out of fear of being scrutinized and humiliated, whereas anhedonia or anergia is the reason in depression. Thus, a person with *major depression* or *dysthymic disorder* would demonstrate avoidant social behavior only during periods of low mood, whereas someone with social phobia shows more chronic patterns of social avoidance.

Other mental disorders or a *general medical condition* such as Parkinson disease, obesity, anorexia nervosa, facial disfigurement, body dysmorphic disorder, or stuttering might promote social anxiety and avoidance behavior. Caution is advised if there are signs of *substance abuse* or *substance dependence* because people with social phobia often try to alleviate anxiety and increase sociability by abusing alcohol or other substances. Primary substance abuse, on the other hand, can induce anxiety (e.g., sympathomimetics, caffeine, or heroin) and often leads to social withdrawal. If social avoidance is clinically significant but full criteria for social phobia are not met, a diagnosis of *anxiety disorder not otherwise specified* may be considered.

Finally, *performance anxiety, stage fright,* and *shyness* are common phenomena, especially in new and unfamiliar situations or when there is a risk of being scrutinized. The cutoff for clinical significance is not easy to define and may vary individually over time. A diagnosis of social phobia should be made only if the symptoms cause significant emotional distress (e.g., fear and avoidance) or functional impairment (e.g., questioning the ability to accomplish social, educational, or professional goals). Shyness when encountering new people, objects, or events (also called behavioral inhibition) and self-consciousness are discussed as precursors of social phobia during childhood. Therefore, exploring the pathogenesis may provide valuable information to corroborate the diagnosis for an adult.

Behavioral Assessment

Behavioral assessment can provide unique supplemental information to subjective reports, questionnaire data, and measures of psychophysiological reactivity. Its primary focus is on overt motoric behavior, such as entering feared social situations, degree of eye contact with an audience or individual cohort, or frequency and duration of pauses in a conversation. This section provides an overview of general principles and examples to help the practitioner create an optimal assessment strategy for people with social phobia.

One major concern in the assessment of behavior is the need to increase the reliability of the measurement. In this pursuit, a precise definition of the behavior under observation is crucial. Straightforward criteria such as "duration of a speech" and "frequency of eye contact" allow objective quantification (Hofmann, Gerlach, Wender, & Roth, 1997).

For recurring behavior, time-based logging (i.e., counting how often certain behaviors occur during a defined time interval) or event-based logging (i.e., recording the time for every occurrence of a behavior) is possible. Although the first strategy helps with observing frequent behavior, information about the timing in relation to co-occurring behavior is lost. Event-based logging helps to uncover possible causal relationships between different behaviors. However, tracking more than three items at a time might overburden a single observer. Minimizing the number of predefined measurement categories by differentiating them in accord with diagnostically relevant criteria improves efficiency and helps reduce the observational workload. In this context, it should be pointed out that a lack or reduction of behavior typically present in healthy people may provide even more clinically informative indicators than the presence of diagnostically distinctive characteristics. Examples include immobility (e.g., going blank when giving a speech), camouflage (e.g., blending into the background in a social gathering), or submission (e.g., avoiding confrontation, mitigation; Marks, 1987). Furthermore, generic categories such as verbal (content) versus nonverbal (paralinguistic [tone of voice, inflection, spacing of words, emphasis, and pauses] vs. proxemic-kinesic [body movement, gestures, and facial expressions]) behavior and approach versus avoidance reactions provide useful landmarks for creating concise measurement categories.

In addition to such a microanalysis of socially anxious behavior, a macro perspective on global indicators of social phobia (e.g., quality of social skills) can be implemented in a similar way (for a review, see Heinrichs, Gerlach, & Hofmann, 2006). For example, it usually yields highly reliable results to have two independent raters assess the overall impression they get about a certain person. However, one should note that this kind of assessment is susceptible to interpretation biases by the rater. A review by Scholing and Emmelkamp (1990) may supplement details about sophisticated coding systems for the analysis of different levels of behavioral specificity. Unfortunately, high reliability sometimes conflicts with the goal of increasing the validity of an assessment because naturalistic behavior in real-life settings tends to be highly unpredictable.

Self-monitoring is an option combining very high ecological validity with a reasonable level of reliability. Diaries and logbooks for recording particular behaviors are useful for homework assignments of behavior observations. Less reliable but often useful because of the instant availability of information are retrospective ratings (e.g., satisfaction with a social interaction) or estimations of the frequency of a certain behavior (e.g., cognitive restructuring, exercises completed). However, memory and self-enhancing bias are an important concern (Becker & Heimberg, 1988). To improve the validity of self-reports, for example, Mattick, Peters, and Clark

(1989) interviewed patients at each treatment session about their activities, independent from data collected in a diary. Compliance can be increased by involving the patient in the decision on what, and how, to record. People with social phobia tend to avoid social situations and interpersonal interactions, which would provide the most information about their issues. Therefore, one should be alert to subtle avoidance strategies when behavior with critical therapeutic value does not occur during the scheduled observation.

Standardized behavioral measures provide a strategy to overcome this problem. The most commonly feared situation in patients with social phobia, and in the general population, is public speaking. Therefore, the most widely used behavioral test in research and treatment is to give an impromptu speech in front of a small audience (two or three people). This test shows good reliability (Beidel, Turner, Jacob, & Cooley, 1989). Also, conversations with a same- or opposite-sex partner are commonly used (McNeil, Ries, & Turk, 1995). Situations such as performing under evaluation (e.g., solving simple mathematic problems on a blackboard while two observers watch) and situations necessitating self-confident appearance (arguing against another person with the opposite opinion) are valuable variations (Hofmann, 2000a). The main advantage of standardized tests is their comparability across individuals or groups.

One consequence of standardized evaluation criteria across all applications of the test is that a behavioral goal may be too easy to accomplish for some people and therefore might be of no diagnostic value. A common way to overcome this problem is to gradually increase the difficulty within a given task (single task, multiple step). To increase the sensitivity of a behavioral test, it should be made as easy as possible to avoid while quantitatively assessing this behavior. An example of such a behavioral avoidance test would be to arrange for a signal to quickly end the situation (e.g., holding up a stop sign).

Role plays are the typical format of behavioral tests. They usually consist of a series of enactments and simulations of social situations in the therapist's office or a research laboratory. The main advantage of this setting is a high level of control over situational and procedural details. However, the assessed person is aware that the situation is artificial and may not give a typical response to, for example, a confederate's sudden anger. Therefore, in highly structured role plays, confederates typically respond only minimally to keep the focus on the patient. The test usually lasts for a predetermined period of time (2–5 minutes) and targets one particular issue.

Standardized role play assessments are commonly used in research settings because of their high comparability and provide information for comparing an individual to representative data. One example is the Simulated Social Interaction Test (Curran, 1982; Curran et al., 1980). This test has been shown to have substantial discriminative validity, high test-retest reliability, good interrater reliability, good generalizability, and sensitivity to treatment change (Mersch, Breukers, & Emmelkamp, 1992). However, it is designed only for use with male subjects. Furthermore, Mersch et al. (1992) question the convergent validity of the test because of low correlations with other supposed measures of the same construct. Other standardized role play tests developed for research include the Taped Situation Test (Rehm & Marston, 1968), the Dating Behavior Assessment Test (Glass, Gottman, & Shmurak, 1976), and the Heterosocial Assessment Test (Perri & Richards, 1979).

Extended role plays are more realistic and individualized, but this increases the amount of idiosyncratic and unplanned interactions. The Social Interaction Test (Trower, Bryant, & Argyle, 1978) is an example that still offers a high level of standardization. It consists of three 4-minute interactions with a female and a male confederate. They are unaware of the conversation topic, but briefings, instructions, situational setting, and verbal and nonverbal behavior of the confederates are standardized. Usually, an independent judge and the confederates evaluate videotapes of the interactions (ratings of behavioral components and general impression ratings on 13 bipolar adjective scales) and write behavioral descriptions for the two general impressions considered most faulty. Gershenson and Morrison (1988) report details about psychometric characteristics, suggesting adequate reliability across different raters (e.g., lay vs. professional raters) and conversation topics, given appropriate training of the raters. Trower (1980) and Beidel, Turner, and Dancu (1985) provide support for convergent validity with clinical judgments of social skill deficits.

Individualized role play assessments allow a test to be optimized for specific individuals.

Barlow and Hersen (1984) provide detailed guidelines on how to construct such a test.

Altogether, behavioral tests have been shown to provide unique, reliable, and valid information for diagnosis and therapy of social phobia when applied appropriately. Self-monitoring and retrospective behavior ratings of the patient are especially useful for gathering information about behavior in real-life situations. Standardized tests and their individualized adaptations are necessary to examine situations that tend to be avoided. In their most common form, as role plays, behavioral tests can conveniently integrate diagnostic and therapeutic goals because they are a core element of most contemporary cognitive-behavioral programs for the treatment of social phobia (Heimberg & Becker, 2002).

SELECTION OF TREATMENT TARGETS AND REFERRAL

For the clinician, the assessment interview serves the purpose of gathering information necessary to make a diagnosis and identifying factors that may be of clinical relevance during treatment. For the client, the assessment often is merely a necessary first step in pursuing treatment, so he or she may be eager to discuss treatment options at the end of the assessment. This stage of the interview should include both selection of treatment targets and a dialogue about the different options available to the client. It is important to listen carefully to the client's needs and preferences and to work collaboratively to arrive at a treatment approach that is acceptable to client and that the clinician thinks will adequately address the identified problems.

For the many clients who present with comorbid disorders, the first step is to identify the primary problem that will form the main focus of treatment. In beginning this discussion, we recommend that the clinician provide an overview of the findings from the diagnostic interview and asks the client what he or she would like to address first in treatment. The patient usually can identify the problem he or she finds most distressing or impairing. Often, this problem will make a good primary treatment target because the patient is already motivated to address it. However, clinical judgment is advised in considering the feasibility of the patient's decision. Sometimes, for example, a comorbid disorder may interfere with the client's ability to successfully address his or her desired treatment target (e.g., treatment of social phobia may be hampered if the client clearly struggles with fatigue and amotivation caused by a major depressive episode).

The second step in selecting treatment targets is a discussion of the patient's goals (i.e., the major changes the patient would like to achieve during treatment). The patient may identify both specific goals, such as being able to give a presentation for a class, and more general goals, such as feeling more comfortable while interacting with strangers. The process of identifying treatment goals can help clarify for the client his or her reasons for pursuing treatment and can also be informative as the discussion turns to selection of a specific treatment approach.

Overview and Comparison of Treatment Options

Selective serotonin reuptake inhibitors (SSRIs) often are considered the first-line pharmacological treatment, although practitioners have also used benzodiazepines, beta blockers, monoamine oxidase inhibitors (MAOIs), and atypical antidepressants to treat social phobia, with varying degrees of success (for a thorough review, see Blanco, Schneier, & Liebowitz, 2001). CBT is the most widely supported psychological treatment approach for social phobia. It has demonstrated superior efficacy over nonspecific treatments such as support groups (Heimberg et al., 1990; Heimberg et al., 1994). More recent studies suggest that CBT is mediated through changes in maladaptive cognitions that are specific to the feared social situations (Hofmann, 2004). CBT often involves the combination of several cognitive and behavioral interventions, including psychoeducation, cognitive restructuring, exposure therapy, and possibly social skill training and relaxation training. This form of therapy can be administered individually or in a group setting.

Several meta-analyses have been conducted comparing the efficacy of pharmacological and psychological treatments for social phobia. These analyses suggest that treatments incorporating various aspects of CBT are largely efficacious in producing lasting improvements in social phobia symptoms (Taylor, 1996). One meta-analysis comparing CBT with pharmacotherapy found the two to be roughly equivalent on the whole but with much heterogeneity in the effectiveness of pharmacological treatments (Gould, Buckminster, Pollack, Otto, & Yap, 1997). Specifically, SSRI treatments were found to be significantly more efficacious than other treatments (both pharmacological and psychological), and treatment with beta blockers was not helpful. Use of MAOIs and benzodiazepines was equivalent to treatment with CBT. Studies that combined CBT components with non-SSRI medications fared slightly worse than treatment with either modality alone.

Research suggests that pharmacotherapy and CBT are equivalent in patient tolerability, with dropout rates averaging 10% for CBT and 14% for pharmacotherapy (Gould et al., 1997). However, the reasons for premature termination of treatment vary across these two modalities. Unpleasant side effects are a common cause for dropout with pharmacological treatments, and some people feel uncomfortable with the idea of relying on a medication to address psychological problems. Sometimes, a desire to remain medication-free can be the impetus for the patient to seek CBT, and a lack of time or motivation can lead to early termination.

Factors to Consider in Treatment Selection

Selection of any particular treatment approach for social phobia depends on a number of factors, such as the patient's expectations and commitment to treatment, the acceptability of different approaches to the patient, and his or her specific history and symptom profile. Many different options are available, including combinations of multiple approaches, so clinician and client should be able to decide on a treatment that is acceptable to the patient and that will properly address his or her specific needs.

With regard to treatment acceptability, the clinician should be mindful of any biases the patient has toward the different approaches. Some patients may reject the idea of pharmacotherapy, for example, out of fear of becoming dependent on medications. Others may feel too intimidated by the prospect of seeing a psychotherapist regularly to discuss difficult problems and may see medication as an easy alternative. In considering the client's preferences, it is important to dispel any misconceptions in order to help him or her make a fully informed decision. Sometimes the client can be persuaded to try a potentially helpful approach after receiving accurate information about what can be expected from the treatment. On the other hand, it can be detrimental for the clinician to push one particular treatment option if the patient is highly resistant to it.

CBT often is the treatment of choice for social phobia because it has demonstrated efficacy even long after termination (Heimberg, Salzman, Holt, & Blendell, 1993), whereas pharmacotherapy typically is effective only for the duration of use, and relapse rates are high after discontinuation (Gelernter et al., 1991). However, client motivation is a key component to the success of CBT. A good candidate for this therapeutic approach should feel committed to seeing a therapist regularly and should have the time and motivation to engage fully in homework assignments in order to benefit from treatment. If the patient is not sufficiently motivated to invest the time and effort necessary to make CBT work, pharmacotherapy is the more viable option.

CBT should be tailored to the patient's needs, such that individual treatment components are included to address specific areas of difficulty. Almost all CBT approaches for social phobia include some elements of psychoeducation, cognitive restructuring, and exposure therapy. Relaxation training is recommended when the patient has marked difficulties with physiological reactions to anxiety, and social skill training can be helpful when deficits in social skills are a major contributing factor to the patient's anxiety.

Group CBT for social phobia carries several advantages, such as numerous opportunities for spontaneous social interaction between group members, a supply of willing people to act as cohorts during in-session exposures, and a collaborative and supportive therapeutic environment. However, we do not recommend this approach for patients with severe social phobia, who may feel uncomfortable participating in a group. Additionally, patients with more atypical presentations of the disorder (e.g., those whose primary concerns are eating or writing in public) may be inappropriate for group treatment. Such patients may not be able to identify with the problems of others in the group, and excessive heterogeneity within a group can be an unnecessary burden on the therapist.

When selecting a treatment approach, we recommend that the clinician be attentive to client expectations. It is important that the client feel optimistic about the treatment he or she wishes to pursue, which can increase motivation and commitment. On the other hand, the clinician should manage the patient's expectations so he or she is realistic about what changes the treatment can bring. An open discussion about what can be reasonably expected from treatment can be very helpful in this regard.

One final, important consideration in selection of a treatment approach is the patient's previous treatment history. Here, it is necessary to ask what treatment the patient has had in the past and how beneficial it was. Disappointment over previous attempts can make a patient wary about pursuing the same type of treatment, but a discussion about factors that may have led to nonresponse can help determine whether another attempt under different circumstances may be more successful.

SUMMARY

Social phobia (social anxiety disorder) is the most common anxiety disorder and the third most common mental disorder in the population. The interpersonal nature of the interview presents a number of unique problems for this population. In this chapter, we outlined specific strategies for dealing with these issues. Advantages and disadvantages of structured and unstructured interviews, open-ended and closed-ended questions, and issues closely linked to social phobia, such as the fears of interacting with strangers and authority figures, social skill deficits, and problems with assertiveness, were discussed and illustrated with case examples. The chapter emphasized the importance of the client's cultural background, diversity issues, and differential diagnoses. We concluded with a brief review of behavioral assessment techniques and the selection of treatment targets and referrals.

REFERENCES

American Psychiatric Association. (2000). *Diagnostic and statistical manual of mental disorders* (4th ed., Text rev.). Washington, DC: Author.

Amies, P. L., Gelder, M. G., & Shaw, P. M. (1983). Social phobia: A comparative clinical study. *British Journal of Psychiatry, 142,* 174–179.

Barlow, D. H., & Hersen, M. (1984). *Single case experimental designs: Strategies for studying behavior change.* New York: Pergamon.

Becker, R. E., & Heimberg, R. G. (1988). Assessment of social skills. In A. S. Bellack & M. Hersen (Eds.),

Behavioral assessment: A practical handbook (pp. 365–372). New York: Pergamon.

Beidel, D. C., Turner, S. M., & Dancu, C. V. (1985). Physiological, cognitive and behavioral aspects of social anxiety. *Behaviour Research and Therapy, 23*, 109–117.

Beidel, D. C., Turner, S. M., Jacob, R. G., & Cooley, M. R. (1989). Assessment of social phobia: Reliability of an impromptu speech task. *Journal of Anxiety Disorders, 3*, 149–158.

Blanco, C., Schneier, F. R., & Liebowitz, M. R. (2001). Psychopharmacology. In S. G. Hofmann & P. M. DiBartolo (Eds.), *From social anxiety to social phobia: Multiple perspectives* (pp. 335–353). Boston: Allyn & Bacon.

Curran, J. P. (1982). A procedure for the assessment of social skills: The Simulated Social Skills Interaction Test. In J. P. Curran & P. M. Monti (Eds.), *Social skills training: A practical handbook for assessment and treatment* (pp. 348–373). New York: Guilford.

Curran, J. P., Monti, P. M., Corriveau, D. P., Hay, L. R., Hagerman, S., Zwick, W. R., et al. (1980). The generalizability of a procedure for assessing social skills and social anxiety in a psychiatric population. *Behavioral Assessment, 2*, 389–401.

Davidson, J. R. T., Potts, N. L. S., Richichi, E., Ford, S. M., Krishnan, R. R., Smith, R. D., et al. (1993). The Brief Social Phobia Scale. *Journal of Clinical Psychiatry, 52*, 48–51.

DiNardo, P. A., Brown, T. A., & Barlow, D. H. (1994). *Anxiety Disorders Interview Schedule for DSM-IV: Lifetime version (ADIS-IV-L)*. Albany, NY: Graywind.

Endicott, J., & Spitzer, R. L. (1978). A diagnostic interview: The Schedule for Affective Disorders and Schizophrenia. *Archives of General Psychiatry, 35*, 811–828.

First, M. B., Spitzer, R. L., Gibbon, M., & Williams, J. B. W. (1994). *Structured Clinical Interview for Axis I DSM-IV Disorders: Patient edition*. New York: Biometrics Research.

Gelernter, C. S., Uhde, T. W., Cimbolic, P., Arnkoff, D. B., Vittone, B. J., Tancer, M. E., et al. (1991). Cognitive-behavioral and pharmacological treatments of social phobia. *Archives of General Psychiatry, 48*, 938–945.

Gershenson, B., & Morrison, R. L. (1988). Social Interaction Test. In M. Hersen & A. S. Bellack (Eds.), *Dictionary of behavioral assessment techniques* (pp. 427–429). New York: Pergamon.

Glass, C. R., Gottman, J. M., & Shmurak, S. H. (1976). Response-acquisition and cognitive self-statement modification approaches to dating-skills training. *Journal of Counseling Psychology, 23*, 520–526.

Glass, C. R., Merluzzi, T. V., Biever, J. L., & Larsen, K. H. (1982). Cognitive assessment of social anxiety: Development and validation of a self-statement questionnaire. *Cognitive Therapy and Research, 6*, 37–55.

Gould, R. A., Buckminster, S., Pollack, M. H., Otto, M. W., & Yap, L. (1997). Cognitive-behavioral and pharmacological treatment for social phobia: A meta-analysis. *Clinical Psychology: Science and Practice, 4*, 291–306.

Heimberg, R. G., & Becker, R. E. (2002). *Cognitive-behavioral group therapy for social phobia: Basic mechanisms and clinical strategies*. New York: Guilford.

Heimberg, R. G., Dodge, C. S., Hope, D. A., Kennedy, C. R., Zollo, L., & Becker, R. E. (1990). Cognitive behavioral group treatment for social phobia: Comparison with a credible placebo control. *Cognitive Therapy and Research, 14*, 1–23.

Heimberg, R. G., Holt, C. S., Schneier, F. R., Spitzer, R. L., & Liebowitz, M. R. (1993). The issue of subtypes in the diagnosis of social phobia. *Journal of Anxiety Disorders, 7*, 249–269.

Heimberg, R. G., Juster, H. R., Brown, E. J., Holle, C., Makris, G. S., Leung, A. W., et al. (1994, November). *Cognitive-behavioral versus pharmacological treatment of social phobia: Posttreatment and follow-up effects*. Paper presented at the annual meeting of the Association for Advancement of Behavior Therapy, San Diego, CA.

Heimberg, R. G., Salzman, D., Holt, C., & Blendell, K. (1993). Cognitive-behavioral group treatment for social phobia: Effectiveness at five-year follow-up. *Cognitive Therapy and Research, 17*, 325–339.

Heinrichs, N., Gerlach, A. L., & Hofmann, S. G. (2006). Social skills deficit. In M. Hersen (Ed.), *Clinician's handbook of adult behavioral assessment* (pp. 235–252). Oxford, UK: Elsevier Academic Press.

Heinrichs, N., Rapee, R. M., Alden, L. A., Bogels, S., Hofmann, S. G., Oh, K. J., et al. (2006). Cultural differences in perceived social norms and social anxiety. *Behaviour Research and Therapy, 44*(8), 1187–1197.

Hofmann, S. G. (2000a). Self-focused attention before and after treatment of social phobia. *Behaviour Research and Therapy, 38*, 717–725.

Hofmann, S. G. (2000b). Treatment of social phobia: Potential mediators and moderators. *Clinical Psychology: Science and Practice, 7*, 3–16.

Hofmann, S. G. (2004). Cognitive mediation of treatment change in social phobia. *Journal of Consulting and Clinical Psychology, 72*, 392–399.

Hofmann, S. G., & Barlow, D. H. (2002). Social phobia (social anxiety disorder). In D. H. Barlow (Ed.), *Anxiety and its disorders: The nature and treatment of anxiety and panic* (2nd ed., pp. 454–476). New York: Guilford.

Hofmann, S. G., & DiBartolo, P. M. (2000). An instrument to assess self-statements during public speaking: Scale development and preliminary psychometric properties. *Behavior Therapy, 31*, 499–515.

Hofmann, S. G., Gerlach, A., Wender, A., & Roth, W. T. (1997). Speech disturbances and gaze behavior during public speaking in subtypes of social phobia. *Journal of Anxiety Disorders, 11*, 573–585.

Hofmann, S. G., Heinrichs, N., & Moscovitch, D. A. (2004). The nature and expression of social phobia: Toward a new classification. *Clinical Psychology Review, 24*, 769–797.

Kessler, R. C., Chiu, W. T., Demler, O., Merikangas, K. R., & Walters, E. E. (2005). Prevalence, severity, and comorbidity of 12-month *DSM-IV* disorders in the

National Comorbidity Survey Replication. *Archives of General Psychiatry, 62,* 617–627.

Liebowitz, M. R. (1987). Social phobia. *Modern Problems in Pharmacopsychiatry, 22,* 141–173.

Marks, I. M. (1987). *Fears, phobias, and rituals: Panic, anxiety, and their disorders.* New York: Oxford University Press.

Marks, I. M., & Gelder, M. G. (1966). Different ages of onset in varieties of phobias. *American Journal of Psychiatry, 123,* 218–221.

Marks, I. M., & Matthews, A. M. (1979). Brief standard rating for phobic patients. *Behaviour Research and Therapy, 17,* 263–267.

Mattick, R. P., & Clark, J. C. (1998). Development and validation of measures of social phobia scrutiny fear and social interaction anxiety. *Behaviour Research and Therapy, 36,* 455–470.

Mattick, R. P., Peters, L., & Clark, J. C. (1989). Exposure and cognitive restructuring for social phobia: A controlled study. *Behavior Therapy, 20,* 3–23.

McNeil, D. W., Ries, B. J., & Turk, C. L. (1995). Behavioral assessment: Self-report, physiology, and overt behavior. In R. G. Heimberg, M. R. Liebowitz, D. A. Hope, & F. R. Schneier (Eds.), *Social phobia: Diagnosis, assessment, and treatment* (pp. 202–231). New York: Guilford.

Mersch, P. P. A., Breukers, P., & Emmelkamp, P. M. G. (1992). The Simulated Social Interaction Test: A psychometric evaluation with Dutch social phobic patients. *Behavioral Assessment, 14,* 133–151.

Perri, M. G., & Richards, C. S. (1979). Assessment of heterosocial skills in male college students: Empirical development of a behavioral role-playing test. *Behavior Modification, 3,* 337–354.

Pollard, C. A., & Henderson, J. G. (1988). Four types of social phobia in a community sample. *Journal of Nervous and Mental Disease, 176,* 440–445.

Rehm, L. P., & Marston, A. R. (1968). Reduction of social anxiety through modification of self-reinforcement: An investigation therapy technique. *Journal of Consulting and Clinical Psychology, 32,* 565–574.

Robins, L. N., Wing, J., Wittchen, H. U., Helzer, J. E., Babor, T. F., Burke, J., et al. (1988). The Composite International Diagnostic Interview. An epidemiologic instrument suitable for use in conjunction with different diagnostic systems and in different cultures. *Archives of General Psychiatry, 45,* 1069–1077.

Schneier, F. R., Heckelman, L. R., Garfinkle, R., Campeas, R., Fallon, B. A., Gitow, A., et al. (1994). Functional impairment in social phobia. *Journal of Clinical Psychiatry, 55,* 322–331.

Scholing, A., & Emmelkamp, P. M. G. (1990). Social phobia: Nature and treatment. In H. Leitenberg (Ed.), *Handbook of social and evaluation anxiety* (pp. 269–324). New York: Plenum.

Schwartz, G. E., Davidson, R. J., & Goleman, D. J. (1978). Patterning of cognitive and somatic processes in the self-regulation of anxiety: Effects of meditation versus exercise. *Psychosomatic Medicine, 40,* 321–328.

Sheehan, D. V. (1983). *The anxiety disease.* New York: Bantam.

Stein, M. B., & Kean, Y. M. (2001). Disability and quality of life in social phobia: Epidemiologic findings. *American Journal of Psychiatry, 157,* 1606–1613.

Stemberger, R. T., Turner, S. M., Beidel, D. C., & Calhoun, K. S. (1995). Social phobia: An analysis of possible developmental factors. *Journal of Abnormal Psychology, 104,* 526–531.

Stravynski, A., & Amado, D. (2001). Social phobia as a deficit in social skills. In S. G. Hofmann & P. M. DiBartolo (Eds.), *From social anxiety to social phobia: Multiple perspectives* (pp. 107–129). Boston: Allyn & Bacon.

Stravynski, A., & Greenberg, D. (1989). Behavioral psychotherapy for social phobia and dysfunction. *International Review of Psychiatry, 1,* 207–218.

Takahashi, T. (1989). Social phobia syndrome in Japan. *Comprehensive Psychiatry, 30,* 45–52.

Taylor, S. (1996). Meta-analysis of cognitive-behavioral treatments for social phobia. *Journal of Behavior Therapy and Experimental Psychiatry, 27,* 1–9.

Trower, P. (1980). Situational analysis of the components and processes of behavior of socially skilled and unskilled patients *Journal of Consulting and Clinical Psychology, 48,* 327–339.

Trower, P., Bryant, B., & Argyle, M. (1978). *Social skills and mental health.* Pittsburgh: University of Pittsburgh Press.

Turner, S. M., Beidel, D. C., Dancu, C. V., & Stanley, M. A. (1989). An empirically derived inventory to measure social fears and anxiety: The Social Phobia and Anxiety Inventory. *Psychological Assessment, 1,* 35–40.

Turner, S. M., Beidel, D. C., & Townsley, R. (1992). Social phobia: A comparison of specific and generalized subtypes and avoidant personality disorder. *Journal of Abnormal Psychology, 101,* 326–331.

Watson, J., & Friend, R. (1969). Measurement of social-evaluative anxiety. *Journal of Counseling and Clinical Psychology, 33,* 448–457.

Xinyin, C., Rubin, K. H., & Boshu, L. (1995). Social and school adjustment of shy and aggressive children in China. *Development and Psychopathology, 7,* 337–349.

16

POSTTRAUMATIC STRESS DISORDER

Johan Rosqvist, Thröstur Björgvinsson,
Darcy C. Norling, and Berglind Gudmundsdottir

DESCRIPTION OF THE DISORDER

Although posttraumatic stress disorder (PTSD; American Psychiatric Association, 2000) was not formally recognized as a disorder per se until 1980, it is today considered one of the most serious and disabling anxiety disorders (Rosqvist, 2005). PTSD, or trauma and various stress reactions, is certainly not a new concept; in fact, the notion that people may experience psychological difficulties after exposure to traumatic situations has an extremely long history (Breslau, Peterson, Kessler, & Schultz, 1999; Finkelhor, Hotaling, Lewis, & Smith, 1990; Norris, 1992; Resnick, Kilpatrick, Dansky, Saunders, & Best, 1993).

Early literature is littered with references to problematic psychological sequelae that may follow threatening or harmful events. Andrews et al. (2003) point out that even in Homer's *Iliad*, nearly three thousand years ago, suggestions were made about "psychological problems following a traumatic experience" (p. 465). Later writers and philosophers (e.g., Shakespeare) are also known to have alluded to a particular set of symptoms that today we call PTSD or acute stress disorder (ASD; American Psychiatric Association, 2000). Although both PTSD and ASD are driven by trauma, the central difference between the two trauma-related anxiety disorders is that ASD occurs soon after trauma,

whereas PTSD occurs after a delay of at least a month (Rassin, 2005). Nonetheless, recent history, such as the American Civil War and World War I, also produced such early but not formally organized descriptions of these phenomena as *shell shock* and *battle or combat fatigue*. Fortunately, for many people with symptoms of PTSD, such problems subside with time, but some need formal intervention to achieve true relief. Although exposure to threatening or harmful life events is common, not everyone who is exposed to a potentially traumatic experience develops problems; indeed, PTSD lifetime prevalence rates are about 5% to 10%. Yet, importantly, high social costs are associated with the course and impact of PTSD ($3 billion per year from absenteeism and reduced productivity and disability) (McLean & Woody, 2001).

Indeed, anyone who has experienced a serious car accident, been the unfortunate victim of an assault, seen combat or war, or has found himself or herself in the midst of a natural disaster probably already understands that threatening experiences can be difficult to cope with in the moment. Nonetheless, most people somehow manage it. However, people may know substantially less about how to integrate such events and experiences into their own existing world view of presumed safety. Although most people probably do not have unrealistic views of just how safe our world is, most probably do not leave their homes each day with the expectation of encountering death and mayhem. Instead, most people appreciate the world as a place of relative safety where they are unlikely to be harmed, but they also probably acknowledge that chance exists (i.e., bad luck, though a statistical anomaly, does happen). Most probably also appreciate that there are things people can do to increase their odds of more favorable or positive daily experiences (e.g., do not drink and drive). Thus, on most days people assume that it will be just another uneventful day.

Although it is characterized by various symptoms, PTSD is perhaps best known for its effect on memory and the effect of troubling memories of past traumatic events on one's ability to live a productive and effective life in the present. This particular aspect of the disorder consists of intrusive thoughts and memories of the event and sometimes outright flashbacks to the event or dissociation from reality, to such an extent that the person feels as if the trauma is happening again, in the present. Continued perceptions of danger and harm often lead to extremely high arousal and flight responses in which the person experiencing flashbacks or disturbing memories may have a panic attack, flee, or display other signs of extreme fear, such as freezing and dissociating. Such people often go out of their way to prevent either the experience or the associated symptoms from recurring, so they often avoid both actively (e.g., avoiding physical locations, people, situations) and passively (e.g., through autonomic responses, such as feeling numb or being dissociative). Additionally, when people are aroused to this extreme level, it is often difficult to be attentive, display normal affect regulation, make basic decisions, and effectively engage in normal, everyday restorative behaviors (e.g., sleep). Over time, especially without formal treatment, PTSD worsens, making it increasingly difficult to function normally. Gross disability in all aspects of life is not unusual in patients with chronic, untreated PTSD.

The first formal criterion (Criterion A) for a diagnosis of PTSD is the experience of a traumatic event. This criterion is controversial in that authorities on the topic cannot seem to agree on a definition of *traumatizing*. It is important to note that *perception* of threat is actually a better predictor of PTSD than actual physical injury (Taylor, 2004), which leaves open the question of

cause and effect in the development of PTSD. After all, if all car accident victims automatically developed PTSD, as is not the case, then mental health clinics around the world could not possibly meet treatment demands of the sheer masses of people who presented with PTSD. Something else, beyond a threatening or harmful event, contributes to the development of PTSD. Especially in cases of litigation over injury and suffering, this can lead to accusations of malingering or the faking of symptoms or at least the suggestion that the problem is all in the victim's mind, which is undeniably true in that all psychological phenomena are psychologically derived.

The remaining three criteria are less controversial and more at the root of what practitioners actually set out to treat patients for (i.e., they cannot change that certain events have happened, but they can influence the most common problem sequelae). Criterion B is the "reliving cluster" of symptoms, which commonly consists of such things as negative, intrusive memories, intrusive images and other perceptions (e.g., smells, sounds), negative dreams and nightmares about the event, and actual flashbacks. The central tenet of this reexperiencing criterion is its invasive nature. It is not sufficient to simply ruminate or think a lot about the event; the intrusions must have an involuntary, uncontrollable quality to them whereby the sufferer cannot push these recollections away or turn them off. Researchers suggest that images are more common in PTSD than thoughts per se or lexical cognitions (Ehlers, & Steil, 1995; Ehlers et al., 2002). Others (de Silva & Marks, 1998) report that intrusive thoughts do not necessarily have to be about the event per se but can instead be questions about the event or questions based on the event and typically fall into three domains: threat and danger (e.g., "Am I safe?"), negative thoughts about the self (e.g., "Am I a bad person?"), and thoughts about the meaning of the event (e.g., "Why did this happen to me?"). Criterion C's central feature is in its focus on avoidance, whether voluntary or involuntary, of stimuli associated with the traumatic event. Classically, this criterion is marked by physical avoidance of locations, circumstances and activities, thoughts and feelings, and people that somehow would remind the person of traumatic events (e.g., avoiding driving or being a passenger in a car by someone who developed PTSD after a car wreck). This criterion also includes involuntary avoidance, such as numbing of general responsiveness to one's surroundings and internal world, so that sufferers "feel nothing," as much as that is humanly possible. Broadly, this often leads people to progressively restrict their lives to avoid recurrence of painful memories, which could be triggered by something as simple as a conversation with another person. Some may also begin to avoid things that trigger such memories (e.g., tall men with long hair, or who wear particular cologne, because of similarities to a perpetrator's characteristics or behavior). Criterion D is thought of as an arousal cluster of problems, with difficulty sleeping (often caused by nightmares), irritability or anger (often a side effect of hypervigilance), concentration difficulties, extensive vigilance, and exaggerated startle reflexes being most typical of the problem. This criterion is focused mostly on an overall and substantially increased arousal that is linked closely to hypervigilance.

The complete diagnosis of PTSD also includes criteria about duration (the disturbance must have lasted at least 1 month), and the aforementioned clusters must cause significant clinical impairment and personal distress to a degree that interferes with personal, social, occupational, and other important areas of life functioning. In fact, most people with PTSD do not function well in most life venues, and their impairment often is at the level of true disability.

INTERVIEWING STRATEGIES

Assessment of traumatic experience and its psychological consequences can be a difficult and complex process that involves consideration of multiple components as an integrated part of the interview. Although the scope of the interview may vary depending on the goals of the clinician (Keane & Barlow, 2002), getting detailed information may be particularly helpful in elucidating the client's unique experience and provide important information for treatment planning. During the interview, it is important for the clinician to be aware of his or her own emotional responses as the client describes his or her experience. It is critical for the clinician not to display discomfort or avoid asking questions about difficult traumatic experience because doing so may reinforce the client's avoidance behavior or even may confirm that such traumatic experience is unacceptable to

discuss (Orsillo, Batten, & Hammond, 2001). Therefore, the interviewer needs to become familiar with terms and phrases used in the interview and practice talking about sensitive topics (Rheingold & Acierno, 2003).

Right from the beginning of the interview it is imperative to exhibit empathetic listening skills and create a nonjudgmental atmosphere. Each interview should begin with an overview of what will take place. This will help create a supportive environment and may reduce the client's anxiety or discomfort. During the overview it is particularly important to acknowledge that talking about a traumatic experience and its consequences can be distressing, and therefore it is understandable that the client might want to avoid talking about the experience (Flack, Litz, & Keane, 1998). Furthermore, it is critical to explain why talking about the event and its consequences is an important step in determining the right treatment. Finally, it is important to be aware of that many trauma survivors suffer from chronic pain caused by injuries sustained during the event (Blanchard & Hickling, 2003). This may make it difficult for the client to endure sitting through an interview. Therefore, it may be helpful to allow the client to take breaks or make other arrangements that will make the assessment less physically strenuous.

Indeed, providing a brief overview of the interview process and acknowledging potential feelings patients may experience may facilitate a more thorough and complete interview. Such preambles and disclosures can ensure that patients are aware that information collected during the interview and assessment is central to proper diagnosis, assessment, treatment planning, and treatment. As stated previously, the understandable and common desire to avoid discussing traumatic experiences in detail may indeed produce incomplete responses, so an overview statement can be helpful. The following is a sample of an opening comment to someone who is being evaluated for PTSD and its treatment:

> Today I will be asking you many questions about events and circumstances that may be quite uncomfortable for you to talk about at length or in detail. Although it is possible that these questions may feel intrusive and unpleasant, I need to ask them to get as complete a picture, or understanding, as is possible about what has been going on for you lately and about the kinds

of things that have happened to you in the recent and distant past. I ask these questions because it is important for me to recognize all the areas that go into figuring out a meaningful plan to help you deal with the problems that bring you here today. I appreciate that some of these questions may make you feel anxious, or they may be difficult to talk about, but perhaps we can examine some ways of coping while we talk about these challenging topics so that you can manage such distressing feelings during and after this interview. I want to be absolutely sure that you know that ultimately the depth and details of the topics are up to you, and you should also know that we can go at whatever pace feels most tolerable to you. Please do not hesitate to tell me if you want to take a break, get something to drink, or use the restroom; again, while I ask these questions, I am ultimately interested in making sure you are as comfortable as you can be while I get to understand your experiences and concerns. Do you have any questions for me, or is there anything you would like to say before I begin to ask you some questions?

Overviews such as this help patients understand what will happen during the interview, and they can defuse much anticipatory anxiety and stress. Additionally, normalizing avoidance and anxiety responses is important and sets a supportive tone in which patients may feel safer to discuss challenging topics. After providing an overview of the interview, the clinician can move on to gathering information about the trauma event and its consequences. It will be particularly important to assess each of the four major areas: Trauma characteristics (Criterion A), history of other potentially traumatic experiences, 17 symptoms of PTSD, and other potential comorbid diagnoses (Resnick, Kilpatrick, & Lipovsky, 1991; Resick & Calhoun, 2001). Often it is helpful to start the assessment by asking the client to describe what led him or her to seek help. Starting out with an open-ended question not only provides important information about the client's main concern but also may give the interviewer an idea of the client's willingness to talk about the event and its consequences. Furthermore, this will allow the clinician to move logically into more detailed questions about characteristics of the event and individual responses to the trauma. This is necessary both to determine whether the event meets Criterion

A for PTSD and to identify possible factors that may predict the severity of posttraumatic symptoms (Resnick et al., 1991).

Numerous studies have documented that people often have a complex trauma history that may include diverse traumatic events such as serous accidents, physical assault, and rape. Therefore, it is essential to identify the trauma associated with the reported posttraumatic symptoms. Furthermore, a person with a complex trauma history may report a very different symptoms than a person with less extensive history (Resnick et al., 1991). Research has shown that the method selected to assess for prior trauma history may have great impact on the accuracy of what is reported (Keane, Weathers, & Foa, 2000). In particular, research has shown that survivors of different, potentially traumatic events often fail to disclose their experience when not asked directly. For example, it is certainly possible that trauma survivors choose not to disclose, but after rape it may certainly be possible for a woman to deny the event out of feelings of shame or self-blame, and she may not use the term *rape* to describe forcible sex perpetrated by a husband (Kilpatrick, 1983). Therefore, using behaviorally specific questions that leave little room for interpretation rather than unspecified subjective words or constructs provides more accurate assessment of prior potential trauma history. For example, one way to identify a history of rape using a behaviorally descriptive prompt might be asking, "Has a man or a boy ever made you have sex by using force or threatening to harm you or someone close to you? Just so there is no mistake, by sex we mean putting a penis in your vagina" (Resnick, Falsetti, Kilpatrick, & Freedy, 1996). During assessment of past trauma history it may be helpful for the interviewer to start with questions about noninterpersonal events and then gradually move into more sensitive events such as interpersonal crimes (Resick & Calhoun, 2001). In addition to asking whether a particular event has happened, it is necessary to follow up by asking about emotional responses to the event (i.e., whether the event meets Criterion A). This will allow the interviewer to determine whether further information is needed about the event and its impact on the client.

After a traumatic event that meets Criterion A is identified, an assessment of PTSD symptoms is in order. This should include evaluating each of the three symptom clusters of PTSD reviewed earlier. For each of the 17 symptoms it is necessary to determine whether the symptom is present after a specific traumatic event and to find out the frequency and intensity of each symptom. Finally, an assessment of how long the symptoms have been present is needed to determine whether the criterion for PTSD is met. During the evaluation of posttraumatic symptoms and throughout the assessment it is beneficial to pay attention to the client's report of situations he or she is avoiding and those that trigger upsetting memories of the event. Getting behavioral descriptions of how the client copes with these memories can be particularly helpful in understanding how the traumatic event is interfering with his or her life and what needs to be targeted in treatment. Additionally, an inquiry about several environmental factors should be made because they may influence the development or maintenance of PTSD. For example, social support has been identified as a strong predictor of PTSD across different populations (Brewin, Andrews, & Valentine, 2000). Also, it is important to examine other life stressors before and after the trauma and ask about family history of psychopathology and occupational adjustments that may have been made in response to the trauma (Resnick et al., 1991).

Several structured interviews have been developed to aid in the interview process. These measures have been shown to provide more reliable and valid assessment of PTSD. Furthermore, their use may improve treatment planning (Litz & Weathers, 1994), and therefore their use is highly recommended. Because space is limited, only a few of these assessment tools are reviewed in this chapter. The tools reviewed here are well established and have good psychometric properties. Broader overviews of measures can be found in Orsillo (2001) and Keane and Barlow (2002).

One of the most widely used and perhaps the most comprehensive diagnostic tools for PTSD is the Clinician-Administered PTSD Scale (CAPS; Blake et al., 1990). The CAPS is a structured interview that assesses all the 17 symptoms of PTSD and common associated features. An important aspect of the CAPS is that it assesses frequency and severity of each symptom using behaviorally anchored questions and scales. Additionally, the CAPS contains standardized questions assessing subjective distress, impairment in social functioning, and impairment in occupational or other important area of functioning caused by the PTSD symptoms. Psychometric data show that the CAPS is a sound measure of PTSD with excellent psychometric properties. The CAPS has strong support because of its good reliability and validity (Weathers, Keane, & Davidson, 2001) and has been shown to be sensitive to the detection of PTSD across different clinical populations (Blanchard et al., 1996; Mueser et al., 2001).

Another widely used and well-established structured interview to assess PTSD is the Structured Clinical Interview for *DSM-IV* (SCID-I; First, Spitzer, Gibbon, Williams, & Benjamin, 1996). In addition to PTSD, the SCID-I assesses the other Axis I and II psychiatric disorders. The PTSD module of the SCID assesses PTSD symptoms related to the most distressing event reported by the client. The SCID provides a count of numbers and results in a diagnosis. The PTSD module of the SCID appears to be both clinically sensitive and reliable. In particular, the SCID has shown excellent interrater reliability on assessment of symptoms across a variety of disorders (Skre, Onsted, Torgersen, & Kringlen, 1991; Ventura, Liberman, Green, Shaner, & Mintz, 1998).

Another commonly used structured interview is the Anxiety Disorders Interview Schedule (ADIS-IV; DiNardo, Brown, & Barlow, 1994). The ADIS-IV focuses primarily on assessing the anxiety and mood disorders. The PTSD section of the ADIS-IV uses closed-ended questions to assess the 17 symptoms of PTSD. After assessment of the symptoms, a series of questions to evaluate severity of the symptoms are asked. Finally, the interviewer assigns a global rating that indicates his or her judgment of the distress and impairment associated with the disorder. The ADIS-IV is recognized as providing reliable and valid diagnoses (Blanchard, Kolb, Gerardi, Rayan, & Pallmayer, 1986; Brown, DiNardo, Lehman, & Campbell, 2001; DiNardo, Moras, Barlow, Rapee, & Brown, 1993).

In addition to structured interviews, numerous self-report questionnaires have been developed to assess posttraumatic symptoms. Although most of these measures do not provide a diagnosis of PTSD, they can be helpful screening tools to identify clients who might benefit from further assessment (Brewin, 2005). A handful of measures have identified a cutoff score to aid in identifying clients who may suffer from PTSD. Two of these measures are the Impact of Event

Scale (IES; Horowitz, Wilner, & Alvarez, 1979) and the PTSD Symptom Scale–Self-Report (PSS-SR; Foa, Riggs, Dancu, & Rothbaum, 1993). The IES contains 22 items that are distributed across two subscales, which assess intrusion and avoidance. Test-retest reliability is good, and the scale appears to possess sound psychometric properties (Weiss & Marmar, 1997). The PSS-SR contains 17 items, reflecting the *Diagnostic and Statistical Manual of Mental Disorders, Fourth Edition (DSM-IV)* symptoms of PTSD, which are rated on a three-point Likert scale and summed to yield a total score. This measure has good test-retest reliability over a 1-month interval and high internal consistency (Foa et al., 1993). A score of 39 on the IES and a 15 on the PSS-SR for crime victims (Wohlfarth, van den Brink, Winkel, & ter Smitten, 2003) and a score of 27 on the IES and 15 on the PSS-SR for motor vehicle accident survivors (Coffey, Gudmundsdottir, Beck, Palyo, & Miller, 2006) have been identified as good cutoffs to use when determining who might benefit from further assessment of PTSD.

Interviewing Obstacles and Solutions

Challenges are likely to arise during the assessment of PTSD. These problems may vary slightly based on the type of traumatic event a person has experienced. For example, if a client's presenting trauma is rape by a man, this client may have great reservation about discussing the trauma with a male therapist. In addition, if a client was knocked unconscious during the traumatic event, the client's memory of the event may be impaired. In addition to problems that are specific to the traumatic event, some difficulties are common to all types of traumatic events. For example, most people who have experienced or witnessed a traumatic incident will have trouble discussing the event simply because the event in question is distressing. Despite the potential problems that may arise in PTSD assessment, most can be handled or even eliminated when dealt with appropriately.

By definition, people who are diagnosed with PTSD have experienced or witnessed a traumatic event. Discussing the traumatic event may result in distress for both the client and the therapist. As noted earlier, creating an environment in which the client feels safe and comfortable, the therapist should follow certain steps. Establishing rapport is crucial to the assessment phase and should be a principal focus of the first session. In addition, the therapist should adequately inform the client beforehand about what the assessment will entail and be prepared to pace the interview based on the client's emotional state. Despite many therapists' fear that asking clients about traumatic events will elicit extreme distress, researchers have found that discussing the event can actually decrease psychological symptoms and increase indices of physical health (Bricre, 2004; Brown & Heimberg, 2001; Petrie, Booth, Pennebaker, Davison, & Thomas, 1995). Therefore, questioning clients about traumatizing events should not be viewed as necessarily or inordinately upsetting and is actually more likely to be helpful.

Therapists may experience personal distress when assessing and treating trauma victims. Vicarious traumatization describes the transformation therapists may go through because of empathic engagement with clients' disturbing information (Pearlman & Saakvitne, 1995). With repeated exposure to vivid details of traumatic events, therapists may experience vicarious traumatization that continues to intensify if not suitably addressed (Brady, Guy, Poelstra, & Brokaw, 1999). In order to address this important concern, therapists are encouraged to seek supervision, support, and training in trauma assessment and treatment (Cunningham, 2004). In addition, researchers have found that therapists who are aware of their own personal history, maintain a regular self-care routine, and are spiritual report less distress as a result of working with trauma victims (Cunningham, 2004).

Traumatized clients are also likely to avoid answering questions or discussing topics related to the traumatic event, making it difficult to gather sufficient, important information relating to the trauma. Avoidance may present as emotional or cognitive suppression, denial, dissociation, distraction techniques, or memory impairment (Briere, 2004). For example, client who has experienced a motor vehicle accident may deny having bad dreams at night, may not remember important aspects of the accident, may dissociate when asked about the trauma or when retelling the story, may suppress emotions regarding the accident, and may avoid thinking about the accident by sleeping all day. These may all be symptoms of avoidance; however, particularly in accidents or more profound physical injury scenarios, it is crucial to sufficiently rule out undiagnosed head injury, which could well masquerade as some psychological symptoms (e.g., forgetfulness, dissociativeness).

Such denial or avoidance often results in the posttraumatic symptoms being less obvious during the assessment, which may result in difficulty in diagnosis. Unfortunately, underreporting and avoidance are difficult to identify through psychological tests. At present, therapists are limited to reliance on validity scales that measure defensiveness or a desire to look good (Briere, 2004). These scales are likely to identify extreme cases of underreporting; however, they are less likely to detect subtle attempts at underreporting or avoidance. The therapist therefore should not automatically rule out the possibility that a client has experienced or witnessed a traumatic event. This is not to suggest that therapists should assume that a client who denies a trauma history is simply "repressing" the event and instead is meant to remind therapists to consider this as a potential hypothesis.

In addition to the intentional denial or underreporting of a specific traumatic event, it is also plausible that the client can truthfully not remember the event in question. The client may have been unconscious during the event and, as a result, have little or no memory of the details of the event. For example, the client may have hit his or her head during a car accident and been knocked unconscious, or perhaps the client was drugged and then raped. Little research has been done on how this may affect the development of PTSD; however, beginning research suggests that PTSD and other psychiatric problems are as common in those who were briefly unconscious as in those who were conscious (Mayou, Black, & Bryant, 2000). In these situations, clinicians should do as much as they can to ensure that their inquiries and interventions do not persuade or elicit false reports (Briere, 2004). Gathering information from other sources may also prove beneficial in such situations.

In contrast to underreporting, forgetting, or denying traumatic events or symptoms, some clients may unintentionally misrepresent trauma histories or trauma-related symptoms (Briere, 2004). This may occur in the context of a severe personality disorder or psychosis; for instance, severe child abuse has been linked to borderline personality disorder and with some psychotic presentations (Briere, 2004). Such information therefore should not be discounted immediately

and instead, like all other information gained during an assessment, critically evaluated for the credibility of the report.

Although it is not as common, overreporting may also occur as part of a factitious disorder, in which the client may feel driven to report nonexistent traumatic events as a result of the psychological disorder (Briere, 2004). In addition, there may be a financial motivation for some trauma histories and trauma symptoms. This is especially true for forensic evaluations. A proficient forensic evaluation should always consider the possibility of malingering (Simon, 1995). Similar to underreporting, overreporting or the misrepresentation of a trauma history or trauma symptoms is difficult to assess. Overreporting may also be detected through the use of validity scale scores; however, researchers have found that people who genuinely experience distress and have been exposed to child sexual abuse, combat, or other traumas often score more deviantly on such validity scales, thereby reducing the utility of such scales with trauma victims (Briere, 2004; Elhai, Ruggiero, Frueh, Beckham, & Gold, 2002; Flitter, Elhai, & Gold, 2003).

Case Illustrations

The two case examples in this section show the diversity of symptoms and problems reported by people who have experienced traumatic events. Although both cases share similar features of PTSD, their presentations are different. Both the nature of the traumatic event and other related factors will play a role in how these cases are conceptualized and what treatment is selected.

Case 1

Anna is a 35-year-old married female homemaker who presented with complaints of anxiety, depression, and low motivation. According to Anna, these symptoms had been bothering her on and off since she was a sexually abused as a child. Anna reported that a 15-year-old neighborhood boy and family friend would come to her house, open his pants, and force her to touch his penis and bring him to climax. She denied vaginal or anal penetration. The abuse happened repeatedly over 1 year when she was around 9 years of age. Anna reported having been constantly fearful of the perpetrator and what might happen if her father found out about the abuse. The abuse ended after a disclosure to a female teenage friend who confronted the perpetrator. According to Anna, her symptoms escalated significantly a year before she sought therapy. She reported that two events led to the increased symptoms: One of her daughters turned the same age that she was when the abuse occurred, and she saw the perpetrator again when visiting her hometown. Anna stated that she had been hiding from her "big secret" for years, and it was not until she became overly concerned about her daughter's safety that she realized how much it was interfering with her life. Anna reported frequent intrusive thoughts about the abuse. These memories were distressing to her and were daily triggers for physical symptoms, such as accelerated heart rate, sweaty palms, and queasiness. Anna stated that she tried to stay busy to distract herself from these memories, but when that did not work she would go to sleep to get away from the memories. Also, Anna reported that she tried to avoid men who reminded her of the perpetrator. Anna stated that she often felt distant from people and felt unable to feel loving toward her family. Furthermore, she reported increased irritability and anger without being able to identify the source of the emotions. Anna commented that she often had difficulty concentrating and felt as if she had to be on guard constantly. She denied having difficulty sleeping at night but usually woke up feeling unrested. Anna described frequent panic attacks that were generally triggered by trauma reminders (e.g., seeing a man who looked like the perpetrator, hearing about an assault on the news, the smell of sweat, sexual relations with her husband), but sometimes they appeared to come out of the blue. As a result of these panic attacks she reported sometimes avoiding situations in which she had experienced panic in the past (e.g., a local shopping center, being intimate with her husband). Anna also reported feeling significantly depressed mood and loss of interest in most activities that she used to enjoy. Along with the depressed mood she reported loss of appetite, energy, and motivation. Anna denied suicidal ideations but reported feelings of worthlessness. As a result of her low motivation, Anna was having a hard time getting things done at home. Anna reported good support from her husband and their four daughters. In particular, her husband tried to help her around the house and drove the children to different activities. However, she stated that over the past year her symptoms had increasingly started to interfere with intimacy with her husband. Anna denied experiencing other past traumas. Anna stated that over the years she had on two different occasions sought treatment for anxiety and depression but never disclosed the abuse. Although Anna found therapy to be helpful, she stated that she knew that she needed to address her "big secret" to feel better. Anna's score on the IES was 47.

Case 2

Loren is a 36-year-old woman who lives with her second husband and a teenage son from her first marriage. Loren presented with significant symptoms of fear and avoidance after a motor vehicle accident that happened 2 years before she sought treatment. Loren was on her way home from work on a rainy afternoon when the accident happened. She was stopped at an intersection when she looked in her rear-view mirror and noticed a car approaching fast. Seconds later she felt the impact as the car rear-ended her. As a result of the impact, Loren's car was thrown into a spin, hit a barrier wall, and came to a stop. Loren was trapped in the car for some time before a rescue team was able to get her out using the "jaws of life." She reported believing that she was going to die. Loren was taken to a hospital, where she was examined and allowed to go home. As a result of her accident, Loren suffered two herniated disks and a tear in her lower back. Because of her injuries Loren has not been able to return to work as a full-time counselor. At the time of the interview, Loren reported severe physical pain due to her injuries and was taking medications to help manage her pain. In addition to the car accident, Loren reported two other traumatic experiences. Specifically, she reported being repeatedly physically abused by her first husband.

Loren reported significant posttraumatic problems associated with her motor vehicle accident. She reported daily intrusive thoughts about the accident and emotional and physical distress when exposed to accident-related cues. Loren reported daily struggles with these feelings, and at times she felt overwhelmed by her emotions. Her physical reactions included sweating, shaking, and shortness of breath, which often continued to upset her for a few hours. Loren reported having had frequent unpleasant dreams in which she was involved in different car accidents. The dreams usually woke her up, and it took her at least an hour to calm down and fall back to sleep. Loren stated that she actively avoids thinking and talking about the accident. Furthermore, she reported avoiding driving as much as possible. Specifically, she completely avoided driving on major highways, in heavy traffic (e.g., around noon or between 4 and 6 p.m.), and in bad weather. Loren commented that she was feeling distant and cut off from other people and emotionally numb most of the time. Loren reported a clear sense of foreshortened future and a "bad feeling" that she might die before her time. She reported feeling especially irritable most of the time and indicated that every little thing (e.g., her husband forgetting to bring milk home) would set her off. Despite significant effort she was usually not able to suppress her anger. Loren also reported difficulty concentrating. For example, she stated that before the accident she used to read a lot but afterward found it very hard to keep track of a story line in a book. Finally, Loren reported significant hypervigilance and strong startle reactions. Specifically, she stated that she was overly concerned about safety both while in the car and in her home. For example, while driving she constantly felt the need to look in the rear-view mirror, and at home she often checked to make sure her door was locked. Loren stated that she was bothered by her symptoms and felt that they were not manageable. She reported that her symptoms were significantly affecting her relationships with her family and friends.

Loren reported a period of depressed mood and loss of interest in her normal activities since the accident. Also, she reported significant loss of appetite, feeling fatigued yet unable to sleep, and was feeling guilty about her inability to handle her symptoms. Loren reported having thought about suicide (i.e., thoughts about taking all her prescribed pain medications at once) a few times since her accident. At the time of the interview, she stated that she was not having any thoughts of hurting herself. She stated that her depression was not as bad as before, and she was feeling more emotionally numb. Loren stated that her husband and son tried to be helpful, but most of the time she just wanted to be left alone. She stated that before the accident she used to be very active socially, work out, and entertain at her home. However, because of her fear of leaving the house and her physical limitations, she no longer participated in these activities and felt very isolated. Loren's score on the IES was 52.

DIFFERENTIAL DIAGNOSIS AND BEHAVIORAL ASSESSMENT

As noted earlier, trauma is part of modern life. Fortunately, most people exposed to trauma do not develop PTSD. Several factors increase the risk of PTSD after a traumatic event, including preexisting depression or anxiety disorder, family history of anxiety, female sex, and early separation from parents, to name a few (Breslau, Davis, & Andreski, 1991). It is therefore important to obtain a detailed history of the person presenting with the trauma in order to gauge previous coping strategies and to incorporate these findings into a comprehensive treatment plan.

Difficulties often arise when one is attempting to distinguish PTSD from other possible or additional diagnoses. PTSD is often present in the context of other symptoms and disorders. It has been demonstrated that people diagnosed with PTSD often also suffer from coexisting disorders, such as depression, anxiety disorders, alcohol and drug abuse, eating disorders, and borderline or antisocial personality disorder (Breslau & Davis, 1992; Briere, 2004; Green, Lindy, Grace, & Gleser, 1989). This high rate of overlap results partially from an actual comorbidity of various disorders with PTSD and partially from the fact that many of the criteria for depression and anxiety overlap with the criteria for PTSD, making it difficult to accurately diagnose (Briere, 2004). It is therefore imperative to evaluate for a wide range of psychological disorders when assessing the traumatized client. When one is assessing for PTSD, one or more comprehensive or general measures of psychological disturbance should be administered with measures that specifically assess for trauma symptoms. Additionally, data should be followed up with one or more clinical interviews (Briere, 2004).

For a diagnosis of posttraumatic disorder, according to *DSM-IV-TR* (APA, 2000), the client must experience the traumatic event as threatening to the life or physical integrity of himself or herself or others. Also, the response to the event involves intense fear, helplessness, or horror. Three symptom clusters define the disorder:

reexperiencing (e.g., nightmares, flashbacks, intrusive and distressing memories of the trauma), pervasive avoidance (e.g., not talking about the trauma, avoiding situations, circumstances, or people that remind the person of the trauma, and emotional numbing), and increased arousal and hypervigilance (e.g., disturbed sleep, exaggerated startle response, anger or irritability, and concentration problems).

After a traumatic event, a person initially receives a diagnosis of acute stress disorder if the symptoms occur within 4 weeks of the traumatic event and symptoms resolve after 4 weeks, according to *DSM-IV-TR*. However, the person is diagnosed with PTSD if the symptoms persist longer than 1 month. It is also important to differentiate between adjustment disorder and PTSD. The stressor must be of an extreme nature (i.e., threaten the life or physical integrity of the client or another) in order to meet PTSD criteria, but in adjustment disorder it can be of any severity (e.g., divorce). To differentiate PTSD from obsessive-compulsive disorder, intrusive thoughts that are experienced in PTSD must have a clear link to the traumatic event. These thoughts are different from recurrent intrusive thoughts in obsessive-compulsive disorder that are experienced as inappropriate and are not related to the events that triggered the trauma. It is also important to clarify that flashbacks that are experienced as part of PTSD are different from illusions, hallucinations, and other disturbances that are usually part of psychotic disorders.

PTSD often follows a chronic course and is often comorbid with other psychiatric disorders such as depression, other anxiety disorders, and substance abuse (Kessler, Sonnega, Bromet, Hughes, & Nelson, 1995). For example, of those who were screened in the Kessler et al. study, the major comorbid disorder was depression, with just under half (48%) of both males ($n = 139$) and females ($n = 320$) presenting with both PTSD and depression. It is very important to be aware that many people with PTSD who seek help initially present with comorbid depression as primary complaint, which often leads to failure to diagnose the primary PTSD. If left untreated, chronic PTSD can cycle into abuse of alcohol, drugs, and medication. Therefore, it is very important to assess for substance abuse in patients with PTSD (Kessler, 2000).

Often patients with PTSD also present with pain and various somatic symptoms. Therefore, careful consideration of the person's physical pain and other somatic complaints and their impact must be evaluated. In particular, it is important to assess how physical limitations or pain affect functioning. For example, a person with significant back injuries may avoid leaving the house not because of fear of trauma-related triggers or situations but rather because he or she is afraid of reinjury. Also, the person may report that he or she sleeps lot during the day but also report taking significant medication for chronic pain. Sedation and increased napping during the day may be common side effects of the medication; however, it also is possible that the person is using pain medication to help himself or herself avoid trauma-related thoughts. In such instances it is critical to evaluate possible overuse of medication and, if necessary, provide a referral to a doctor that specializes in pain management.

In addition to establishing the proper diagnosis of PTSD, it is essential to conduct a thorough behavioral assessment of the three symptoms clusters and the impact of these symptoms on the person's quality of life. In fact, in one study people with PTSD were found to experience greater impairment than people with major depression or obsessive-compulsive disorder across several domains of their life (Malik, Connor, Sutherland, Smith, Davidson, & Davidson, 1999). It is clear that the life of a person with PTSD is greatly affected by his or her symptoms, and he or she will avoid almost any reminders of the trauma. This avoidance can severely limit the person's mobility and functionality. Furthermore, the person may keep reliving the experience and have recurrent, intrusive thoughts about the trauma and struggle with sleep disturbances, hypervigilance, and irritability.

Assessing the erroneous and negative cognitions that the person may have about the traumatic event and their importance in maintaining the PTSD symptoms is essential. Foa and Jaycox (1999) propose that there are two themes of erroneous cognitions associated with the development and maintenance of PTSD: that the world is extremely dangerous (e.g., there is no place safe and people are not trustworthy) and that the person who experienced the trauma is extremely incompetent (e. g., he or she should have been able to prevent the trauma, and because it happened it is a sign of weakness). Once assessed and clarified, these erroneous negative cognitions can be challenged in a safe, nurturing therapeutic environment through various cognitive-behavioral interventions (Foa, Ehlers, Clark, Tolin, & Orsillo, 1999; Resick, Nishith, Weaver, Astin, & Feuer, 2002).

SELECTION OF TREATMENT TARGETS AND REFERRAL

Thorough behavioral assessment of the three symptom clusters defines the targets of treatment and other related factors that impede the person's ability to function. The behavioral assessment and diagnoses guide the treatment. If the person is struggling with alcohol or substance abuse, then it must be addressed before the trauma can be treated. However, some researchers state that it is important to address both substance or alcohol abuse and PTSD symptoms simultaneously (see Coffey et al., 2002). Regardless of whether a period of abstinence is required before the client engages in trauma treatment, it is imperative to evaluate and identify triggers for alcohol or drug cravings and establish a plan to prevent relapse.

Similarly, it has been shown that the client's level of depression greatly influences treatment outcomes, and therefore it is imperative to address severe depression before proceeding with the actual treatment of trauma. For example, if a person is not able to actively participate in treatment or get out of bed, is suicidal, and has other depressive symptoms, the first step in treatment may be to alleviate some of the depressive symptoms. This could be achieved by behavioral activation, followed by exposure-based cognitive-behavioral therapy. This applies to comorbid issues of panic attacks as well. Falsetti and Resnick (2000) designed multiple channel exposure therapy, which specifically treats comorbid PTSD and panic attacks.

Cloitre, Koenen, Cohen, and Han (2002) demonstrated that patients who struggled with affective dysregulation and received skill training in affective and interpersonal regulation followed by exposure treatment demonstrated significant improvements. Thus, enhancing emotional regulation (reduce affect dysregulation) can enhance the benefits of cognitive-behavioral therapy that uses exposure therapy.

Whether the person suffered from single-episode trauma (e.g., one rape) or repeated trauma (e.g., repeated sexual abuse) makes a tremendous difference in the selection of treatment targets

and referral. Nevertheless, a single traumatic event can lead to chronic PTSD. People who develop chronic PTSD often have more sophisticated avoidance mechanisms and more subtle ways to manage traumatic triggers. For example, they have much more practice in reorganizing their lives around their avoidance. A person who was traumatized by an automobile accident might take very elaborate and complex route to get to work and excuse the extra effort, stating, "It is not a big deal; it only takes 15 extra minutes," "I'm used to it by now," or "I don't ever drive on a busy road." After sexual assault the person may state, "I never go out after dark; it's not a big deal," "My friends know that I will not go out after 6 p.m., so they know not to ask." It is important to distinguish between safe choices and choices tied to a trauma-related trigger or avoidance. These factors influence the course of treatment and selection of treatment targets.

PTSD treatment outcomes have focused almost entirely on cognitive-behavioral therapies, and the data suggest that these interventions are efficacious (see Nemeroff et al., 2006). There are generally three subtypes of cognitive-behavioral interventions: exposure therapies, anxiety management, and cognitive therapies. Of those, exposure therapy is the most empirically supported therapy for PTSD (Nemeroff et al., 2006). One meta-analysis found that when clinician-rated measures were used, exposure therapy was more efficacious than any other type of treatment of PTSD (Van Etten & Taylor, 1998).

SUMMARY

In recent years the way PTSD is conceptualized has changed to reflect the generally accepted fact that traumatic experiences are more common than rare and, realistically, trauma and its potential negative human responses are not thought of as unusual anymore. Indeed, trauma and PTSD are now thought to be within the range of usual human experience, not outside. This de facto reality makes good clinical interviewing essential; given the nature of trauma and its potential deleterious sequelae, there is no better way to obtain needed information. Although an effective interview may seem tightly choreographed, the interviewer has to create an environment that imparts empathy, validation, and understanding while simultaneously eliciting data about the trauma and its effects. This can represent a challenge for the most seasoned interviewer, making practice and multiple interviewing experiences of paramount importance.

Novice interviewers faced with trauma, ASD, and PTSD may want to familiarize themselves with trauma-sensitive interview methods and role play multiple scenarios before encountering real survivors and victims. Good interview skills will elicit sufficient clinical information to inform accurate and complete diagnosis, case conceptualization, treatment planning, and, ultimately, intervention.

REFERENCES

American Psychiatric Association. (2000). *Diagnostic and statistical manual of mental disorders* (4th ed., Text rev.). Washington, DC: Author.

Andrews, G., Creamer, M., Crino, R., Hunt, C., Lampe, L., & Page, A. (2003). *The treatment of anxiety disorders: Clinician guides and patient manuals* (2nd ed.). New York: Cambridge University Press.

Blake, D., Weathers, F., Nagy, L., Kalouped, D., Klauminzer, G., Charney, D., et al. (1990). *Clinician-administered PTSD scale (CAPS)*. Boston: National Center for Post-Traumatic Stress Disorder, Behavioral Science Division.

Blanchard, E. B., & Hickling, E. J. (2003). *After the crash* (2nd ed.). Washington, DC: American Psychological Association.

Blanchard, E. B., Hickling, E. J., Taylor, A. E., Loos, W. R., Fornere, C. A., & Jaccard, J. (1996). Who develops PTSD from motor vehicle accidents? *Behaviour Research and Therapy, 34,* 1–10.

Blanchard, E. B., Kolb, L. C., Gerardi, R. T., Rayan, R., & Pallmayer, T. P. (1986). Cardiac response to relevant stimuli as an adjunctive tool for diagnosing post-traumatic stress disorder in combat veterans. *Behavior Therapy, 17,* 592–606.

Brady, J. L., Guy, J. D., Poelstra, P. L., & Brokaw, B. F. (1999). Vicarious traumatization, spirituality, and the treatment of sexual abuse survivors: A national survey of women psychotherapists. *Professional Psychology: Research and Practice, 30,* 386–393.

Breslau, N., & Davis, G. C. (1992). Posttraumatic stress disorder in an urban population of young adults: Risk factors for chronicity. *American Journal of Psychiatry, 149,* 671–675.

Breslau, N., Davis, G. C., & Andreski, P. (1991). Traumatic events and posttraumatic stress disorder in an urban population of young adults. *Archives of General Psychiatry, 48,* 216–222.

Breslau, N., Peterson, E. L., Kessler, R. C., & Schultz, L. R. (1999). Short screening scale for *DSM-IV* posttraumatic stress disorder. *American Journal of Psychiatry, 156,* 908–911.

Brewin, C. R. (2005). Systematic review of screening instruments for adults at risk of PTSD. *Journal of Traumatic Stress, 18,* 53–63.

Brewin, C. R., Andrews, B., & Valentine, J. D. (2000). Meta-analysis of risk factors for posttraumatic stress disorder in trauma-exposed adults. *Journal of Consulting and Clinical Psychology, 68,* 748–766.

Briere, J. (2004). *Psychological assessment of adult posttraumatic states: Phenomenology, diagnosis, and measurement.* Washington, DC: American Psychological Association.

Brown, E. J., & Heimberg, R. G. (2001). Effects of writing about rape: Evaluating Pennebaker's paradigm with a severe trauma. *Journal of Traumatic Stress, 14,* 781–790.

Brown, T., DiNardo, P., Lehman, C., & Campbell, L. (2001). Reliability of *DSM-IV* anxiety and mood disorders: Implications for the classification of emotional disorders. *Journal of Abnormal Psychology, 110,* 49–58.

Cloitre, M., Koenen, K. C., Cohen, L. R., & Han, H. (2002). Skills training in affective and interpersonal regulation followed by exposure: A phase-based treatment for PTSD related to childhood abuse. *Journal of Consulting and Clinical Psychology, 70,* 1067–1074.

Coffey, S. F., Gudmundsdottir, B., Beck, G. J., Palyo, S. A., & Miller, L. (2006). Screening for PTSD in motor vehicle accident survivors using the PSS-SR and IES. *Journal of Traumatic Stress, 19*(1), 119–121.

Coffey, S. F., Saladin, M. E., Drobes, D. J., Brady, K. L., Dansky, B. S., & Kilpatrick, D. G. (2002). Trauma and substance cue reactivity in individuals with comorbid posttraumatic stress disorder and cocaine or alcohol dependence. *Drug and Alcohol Dependence, 65,* 115–127.

Cunningham, M. (2004). Avoiding vicarious traumatization: Support, spirituality, and self-care. In N. B. Webb (Ed.), *Mass trauma and violence: Helping families and children cope* (pp. 327–346). New York: Guilford.

De Silva, P., & Marks, M. (1998). Intrusive thinking in posttraumatic stress disorder. In W. Yule (Ed.), *Post-traumatic stress disorder: Concepts and therapy* (pp. 161–175). New York: Wiley.

DiNardo, P., Brown, T., & Barlow, D. (1994). *Anxiety Disorders Interview Schedule for DSM-IV*. Albany, NY: Greywind.

DiNardo, P., Moras, K., Barlow, D., Rapee, R., & Brown, T. (1993). Reliability of *DSM-III-R* anxiety disorder category. *Archives of General Psychiatry, 50,* 251–256.

Ehlers, A., Hackman, A., Steil, R., Clohessy, S., Wenninger, K., & Winter, H. (2002). The nature of intrusive memories after trauma: The warning signal hypothesis. *Behaviour Research and Therapy, 40,* 995–1002.

Ehlers, A., & Steil, R. (1995). Maintenance of intrusive memories in posttraumatic stress disorder: A cognitive approach. *Behavioural and Cognitive Psychotherapy, 23,* 217–249.

Elhai, J. D., Ruggiero, K. J., Frueh, B. C., Beckham, & Gold, P. B. (2002). The Infrequency–Posttraumatic Stress Disorder Scale (FPTSD) for the MMPI-2: Development and validation with veterans presenting with combat-related PTSD. *Journal of Personality Assessment, 79,* 531–549.

Falsetti, S. A., & Resnick, H. S. (2000). Cognitive behavioral treatment of PTSD with comorbid panic attacks. *Journal of Contemporary Psychotherapy, 30*(2), 163–179.

Finkelhor, D., Hotaling, G., Lewis, I. A., & Smith, C. (1990). Sexual abuse in a national survey of adult men and women: Prevalence, characteristics, and risk factors. *Child Abuse and Neglect, 14,* 19–28.

First, M. B., Spitzer, R. L., Gibbon, M., Williams, J. B. W., & Benjamin, L. (1996). *Structured Clinical Interview for DSM-IV Axis I Disorders (SCID-I version 2.0).* New York: Biometrics Research Department, New York State Psychiatric Institute.

Flack, W. F., Litz, B. T., & Keane, T. M. (1998). Cognitive-behavioral treatment of warzone-related posttraumatic stress disorder: A flexible, hierarchical approach. In V. M. Follete, J. I. Ruzek, & F. R. Abueg (Eds.), *Cognitive-behavioral therapies for trauma* (pp. 77–99). New York: Guilford.

Flitter, J. M. K., Elhai, J. D., & Gold, S. N. (2003). MMPI-2 F scale elevations in adult victims of child sexual abuse. *Journal of Traumatic Stress, 16,* 269–274.

Foa, E. B., Ehlers, A., Clark, D., Tolin, D. F., & Orsillo, S. M. (1999). Posttraumatic Cognitions Inventory (PTCI): Development and validation. *Psychological Assessment, 11,* 303–314.

Foa, E. B., & Jaycox, L. H. (1999). Cognitive-behavioral theory and treatment of post-traumatic stress disorder. In D. S. Spiegel (Ed.), *Efficacy and cost-effectiveness of psychotherapy.* Washington, DC: American Psychiatric Press.

Foa, E. B., Riggs, D. S., Dancu, C. V., & Rothbaum, B. O. (1993). Reliability and validity of a brief instrument for assessing post-traumatic stress disorder. *Journal of Traumatic Stress, 6,* 459–473.

Green, B. L., Lindy, J. D., Grace, M. C., & Gleser, G. C. (1989). Multiple diagnosis in post-traumatic stress disorder: The role of war stressors. *Journal of Nervous and Mental Disease, 177,* 329–335.

Horowitz, M. J., Wilner, N., & Alvarez, W. (1979). Impact of event scale: A measure of subjective stress. *Psychosomatic Medicine, 41,* 209–218.

Keane, T. M., & Barlow, D. H. (2002). Posttraumatic stress disorder. In D. H. Barlow (Ed.), *Anxiety and its disorders* (2nd ed., pp. 418–453). New York: Guilford.

Keane, T. M., Weathers, F. W., & Foa, E. B. (2000). Diagnosis and assessment. In E. B. Foa, T. M. Keane, & M. J. Friedman (Eds.), *Effective treatments for PTSD* (pp. 18–36). New York: Guilford.

Kessler, R. C. (2000). Posttraumatic stress disorder: The burden to the individual and to society. *Journal of Clinical Psychiatry, 61*(Suppl. 5), 4–12.

Kessler, R. C., Sonnega, A., Bromet, E., Hughes, M., & Nelson, C. B. (1995). Posttraumatic stress disorder in the National Comorbidity Study. *Archives of General Psychiatry, 52,* 1048–1060.

Kilpatrick, D. G. (1983). Rape victims: Detection, assessment and treatment. *Clinical Psychologist, 36,* 92–95.

Litz, B. T., & Weathers, F. W. (1994). The diagnosis and assessment of post-traumatic stress disorder in adults. In M. B. Williams & J. F. Sommer (Eds.), *The handbook of posttraumatic therapy* (pp. 20–37). Westport, CT: Greenwood.

Malik, M. L., Connor, K. M., Sutherland, S. M., Smith, R., Davidson, R. M., & Davidson, J. R. (1999). Quality of life and posttraumatic stress disorder: A pilot study assessing changes in SF-36 scores before and after treatment in a placebo-controlled trial of fluoxetine. *Journal of Traumatic Stress, 12,* 387–393.

Mayou, R. A., Black, J., & Bryant, B. (2000). Unconsciousness, amnesia, and psychiatric symptoms following road traffic accident injury. *British Journal of Psychiatry, 177,* 540–545.

McLean, P. D., & Woody, S. R. (2001). *Anxiety disorders in adults: An evidence-based approach to psychological treatment.* New York: Oxford.

Mueser, K. T., Rosenberg, S. D., Fox, L., Salyers, M. P., Ford, J. D., & Carty, P. (2001). Psychometric evaluation of trauma and posttraumatic stress disorder assessments in persons with severe mental illness. *Psychological Assessment, 13,* 110–117.

Nemeroff, C. B., Bremner, D. J., Foa, E. B., Mayberg, H. S., North, C. S., & Stein, M. B. (2006). Posttraumatic stress disorder: A state-of-the-science review. *Journal of Psychiatric Research, 40,* 1–21.

Norris, F. H. (1992). Epidemiology of trauma: Frequency and impact of different potentially traumatic events on different demographic groups. *Journal of Consulting and Clinical Psychology, 60,* 409–418.

Orsillo, S. M. (2001). Measure for acute stress disorder and posttraumatic stress disorder. In M. M. Antony, S. M. Orsillo, & L. Roemer (Eds.), *Practitioner's guide to empirically based measures of anxiety* (pp. 255–307). New York: Kluwer Academic/Plenum.

Orsillo, S. M., Batten, S. V., & Hammond, C. (2001). Acute stress disorder and posttraumatic stress disorder: A brief overview and guide to assessment. In M. M. Antony, S. M. Orsillo, & L. Roemer (Eds.), *Practitioner's guide to empirically based measures of anxiety* (pp. 245–254). New York: Kluwer Academic/Plenum.

Pearlman, L. A., & Saakvitne, K. W. (1995). *Trauma and the therapist: Countertransference and vicarious traumatization in psychotherapy with incest survivors.* New York: Norton.

Petrie, K. J., Booth, R. J., Pennebaker, J. W., Davison, K. P., & Thomas, M. G. (1995). Disclosure of trauma and immune response to a hepatitis B vaccination program. *Journal of Consulting and Clinical Psychology, 63,* 787–792.

Rassin, E. (2005). *Thought suppression.* New York: Elsevier.

Resick, P. A., & Calhoun, K. S. (2001). Posttraumatic stress disorder. In D. H. Barlow (Ed.), *Clinical handbook of psychological disorders* (3rd ed., pp. 60–113). New York: Guilford.

Resick, P. A., Nishith, P., Weaver, T. L., Astin, M. C., & Feuer, C. A. (2002). A comparison of cognitive-processing therapy with prolonged exposure and a waiting condition for the treatment of chronic posttraumatic stress disorder in female rape victims. *Journal of Consulting and Clinical Psychology, 70,* 867–879.

Resnick, H. S., Falsetti, S. A., Kilpatrick, D. G., & Freedy, J. R. (1996). Assessment of rape and other civilian trauma-related post traumatic stress disorder: Emphasis on assessment of potentially traumatic events. In T. W. Miller (Ed.), *Stressful life events* (2nd ed., pp. 235–271). Madison, CT: International Universities Press.

Resnick, H. S., Kilpatrick, D. G., Dansky, B. S., Saunders, B. E., & Best, C. L. (1993). Prevalence of civilian trauma and posttraumatic stress disorder in a representative national sample of women. *Journal of Consulting and Clinical Psychology, 61,* 984–991.

Resnick, H. S., Kilpatrick, D. G., & Lipovsky, J. A. (1991). Assessment of rape-related post-traumatic stress disorder: Stressor and symptom dimensions. *Psychological Assessment: A Journal of Consulting and Clinical Psychology, 3*(4), 561–572.

Rheingold, A. A., & Acierno, R. (2003). Post-traumatic stress disorder (noncombat). In M. Hersen & S. M. Turner (Eds.), *Diagnostic interviewing* (3rd ed., pp. 345–361). New York: Kluwer Academic/Plenum.

Rosqvist, J. (2005). *Exposure treatments for anxiety disorders: A practitioner's guide to concepts, methods, and evidence-based practice.* New York: Routledge.

Simon, R. I. (Ed.). (1995). *Posttraumatic stress disorder in litigation: Guidelines for forensic assessment.* Washington, DC: American Psychiatric Press.

Skre, I., Onsted, S., Torgersen, S., & Kringlen, E. (1991). High interrater reliability for the Structured Clinical Interview for *DSM-IV* Axis I (SCID-I). *Acta Psychiatrica Scandinavica, 84,* 167–173.

Taylor, S. (Ed.). (2004). *Advances in the treatment of posttraumatic stress disorder: Cognitive-behavioral perspectives.* New York: Springer.

Van Etten, M. L., & Taylor, S. (1998). Comparative efficacy of treatments for posttraumatic stress disorder: A meta-analysis. *Clinical Psychology and Psychotherapy, 5,* 144–154.

Ventura, J., Liberman, R. P., Green, M. F., Shaner, A., & Mintz, J. (1998). Training and quality assurance with the Structured Clinical Interview for *DSM-IV* (SCID-I). *Psychiatry Research, 79,* 163–173.

Weathers, F., Keane, T. W., & Davidson, J. R. T. (2001). Clinician-administered PTSD scale: A review of the first ten years of research. *Depression and Anxiety, 13,* 132–156.

Weiss, D. S., & Marmar, C. R. (1997). The Impact of Event Scale—Revised. In J. Wilson & T. M. Keane (Eds.), *Assessing psychological trauma and PTSD* (pp. 399–411). New York: Guilford.

Wohlfarth, T. D., van den Brink, W., Winkel, F. W., & ter Smitten, M. (2003). Screening for posttraumatic stress disorder: An evaluation of two self-report scales among crime victims. *Psychological Assessment, 15,* 101–109.

17

GENERALIZED ANXIETY DISORDER

JONATHAN D. HUPPERT AND MICHAEL R. WALTHER

DESCRIPTION OF THE DISORDER

Generalized anxiety disorder (GAD) is a common disorder associated with significant distress and functional impairment. Using hierarchical exclusion rules for current panic and depression, Judd et al. (1998) report a lifetime prevalence of GAD of 3.6%. Similar results have been found when using *Diagnostic and Statistical Manual of Mental Disorders* (*DSM-III-R;* American Psychiatric Association [APA], 1987) criteria; the National Comorbidity Survey suggested a 12-month prevalence of 3.1% and a lifetime prevalence of 5.1% (Wittchen, Zhao, Kessler, & Eaton, 1994). More recently, data from the National Comorbidity Survey Replication (Kessler, Berglund, Demler, Jin, & Walters, 2005) found lifetime prevalence of 4.2% (using a 12-month minimum duration requirement) to 12.7% (using a 1-month minimum duration requirement), all using *DSM-IV* (APA, 1994) criteria. Females are more likely to receive a diagnosis of GAD than males (Grant et al., 2005; Kessler et al., 2005). The age of onset has ranged from childhood (Brown, Barlow, & Liebowitz, 1994) to early adulthood (early 30s, Grant et al., 2005; early 20s, Kessler et al., 2005).

Fortunately, advances in pharmacotherapy and psychotherapy have resulted in a greater likelihood of effective treatment (Mitte, 2005). However, before patients with GAD can be treated, they must be identified through a careful evaluation.

The goal of this chapter is to provide a thorough description of how to assess for GAD. First, we describe the diagnostic issues related to GAD, including diagnostic criteria and descriptive psychopathology. Then we discuss interviewing strategies related to GAD, including interview measures and self-report measures, and discuss possible obstacles a clinician may face when interviewing a patient with GAD. Then we discuss cultural and diversity issues related to GAD. Next, we discuss the differential diagnosis of GAD. Finally, we address the common treatment targets in GAD.

Diagnosis of GAD

GAD is a new diagnosis, changed from a "wastebasket" diagnosis pertaining to anyone suffering from anxiety who did not fit into another anxiety disorder listed in *DSM-III* to a discrete entity in *DSM-III-R* and *DSM-IV*.

According to *DSM-IV,* the diagnosis of GAD includes two major aspects: uncontrollable, unrealistic worry about more than one topic and accompanying physiological symptoms including muscle tension, difficulty sleeping, fatigue, restlessness or feeling keyed up or on edge, irritability, and difficulty concentrating. For a diagnosis of GAD, these symptoms must be persistent for a 6-month period and interfere with functioning or be distressing to the client. According to the *DSM-IV,* if these symptoms are better accounted for by another disorder, the diagnosis of GAD should not be made. In addition, the diagnosis of GAD cannot be made when it occurs solely during an episode of a mood disorder (i.e., major depression or dysthymia). The basic assumption behind this decision is that most people who are depressed are also anxious (see Barlow, 2002, for more details).

GAD has been shown to be a chronic disorder (Bruce et al., 2005), and as mentioned previously it typically presents in childhood (Brown et al., 1994) or early adulthood (Grant et al., 2005; Kessler et al., 2005). In view of these and other data, some argue that, in contrast to other anxiety disorders, a subtype of GAD (chronic, pervasive symptoms since childhood) may be better understood as an underlying personality trait that serves as a risk factor for anxiety disorders (Sanderson & Wetzler, 1991). However, recent research by Brown, Campbell, Lehman, Grisham, and Mancill (2001) suggests that some anxiety disorders such as social phobia may be likely to precede GAD. Other recent research suggests that the age of onset is commonly not in childhood (Kessler et al., 2005). Clinical experience suggests that a major stressor often exacerbates symptoms (e.g., the birth of a child or another role transition). Research (Wells, 1994b) and our clinical experience with GAD have led us to believe that people with GAD often report perfectionism, feel a greater need to control their environment, feel greater personal responsibility for negative events that occur or are predicted to occur in their environment, and have difficulty tolerating ambiguity (see Heimberg, Turk, & Mennin, 2004).

Phenomenology

Worry. Worry is the major cognitive component of GAD. Worries in GAD are thoughts and fears about future harm or negative outcomes and often are not completely formulated or thought through to the final concerns. Patients with GAD often describe worry episodes in which they think about one problem for a few moments and then move on to another worry. For example, one may think, "My husband is late. What if something happened to him on his way home? What if it was a car accident? How will I manage with the kids? What will happen to us financially? Is our insurance sufficient?" An important aspect of this worry is that the patient usually does not try to attempt to answer the questions he or she poses; instead, concerns stay threatening and ambiguous.

People who suffer from GAD tend to worry most of the day, nearly every day (Brown, O'Leary, & Barlow, 1993). However, it should be noted that worry in itself is not pathological. It is an attempt to predict future danger or to gain control over events that appear uncontrollable (and usually negative or dangerous; Rapee, 1991). However, it is clear that worry in GAD is dysfunctional in that it is, by definition, excessive or unrealistic and feels uncontrollable. As a result, patients tend to overpredict the likelihood of negative events and exaggerate consequences if the events were to occur (Brown et al., 1993; Butler & Mathews, 1983). Abel and Borkovec (1995) found that 100% of patients with GAD described their worry as uncontrollable, compared with none of the nonanxious controls. Additionally, anxious people tend to selectively attend to threatening, personally relevant stimuli (Mathews, 1990). Often there is an implied belief that worry will make the world more controllable and predictable. Consistent with this, worriers report five major functions of worry: superstitious avoidance of catastrophes, actual avoidance of catastrophes, avoidance of deeper emotional topics, coping preparation, and motivating devices (Borkovec, 1994).

Research supports the idea that pathological worry may have a functional role for patients with GAD. Worry has been shown to inhibit autonomic arousal in patients with GAD when they are shown aversive imagery (Borkovec & Hu, 1990). Counterintuitively, relaxation has been shown to increase the amount of worry in some patients with GAD (Borkovec, Shadick, & Hopkins, 1991). It is possible that for these patients, relaxation signals a lack of control, which triggers an increase in anxiety, or that patients sit quietly with their thoughts, resulting in greater exposure to their worries. Worrying may cause the avoidance of aversive imagery that is associated with an even greater emotional state (Borkovec et al., 1991). Therefore, worry may be maintained by both the avoidance of certain affective states and the reduction of anxious states through the decrease in arousal that occurs when someone worries. Research has recently supported the role of worry in avoidance of emotions (Mennin, Turk, Heimberg, & Carmin, 2003; Roemer & Orsillo, 2002).

Patients with GAD may also exhibit emotional dysregulation (Mennin, Heimberg, Turk, & Fresco, 2005). Mennin et al. found that students with GAD reported heightened intensity of emotions, poorer understanding of emotions, greater negative reactivity to emotional experience, and less ability to self-soothe after negative emotions than controls. Additionally, people with GAD have been found to endorse higher levels of emotional awareness than controls (Novick-Kline, Turk, Mennin, Hoyt, & Gallagher, 2005).

Although worry is an important component of GAD, Ruscio (2002) demonstrated that many people report excessive worry but do not meet criteria for GAD. Approximately one third of people in a college sample endorsed high levels of worry but did not meet criteria for GAD, and approximately 6% met criteria for GAD. Non-GAD worriers had less frequent, less excessive worry, more control over their worry, fewer physiological symptoms, and less distress and impairment. Therefore, the other criteria for GAD, including the physiological symptoms, are important to assess in evaluating a patient for GAD.

Somatic Symptoms. Patients with GAD experience unpleasant somatic sensations. Although they usually increase during a worry episode, both the worry and the somatic sensations can be described as persistent and pervasive. The most common somatic symptom reported by patients with GAD is muscle tension. Often associated with worry and tension, patients may experience other symptoms including irritability, restlessness, feeling keyed up or on edge, difficulty sleeping, fatigue, and difficulty concentrating. Because these symptoms may be the focus of concern for a patient with GAD, it is essential to evaluate them carefully, and they may be targets of treatment in their own right.

INTERVIEWING STRATEGIES

Initial Interview Stance

People with GAD may present as quite controlled, anxious, or irritable in the first session. Given their preoccupation with worry, they may come across as guarded or circumstantial in their speech. It can be tense or tiring to interview patients with GAD because their anxiety can be quite contagious, and trying to engage with them in a relaxed fashion can be tiring in its own right. Some people with GAD may be worried about whether seeking treatment is worthwhile or whether they are in the right place for treatment. They may be worried about answering questions fully or correctly. In addition, they may question the interviewer regarding their credentials or experience in order to seek reassurance that they are receiving high-quality care. Open-ended questions may be more difficult for them. However, most people with GAD are able to focus on the interview and describe their difficulties and concerns. If one does feel that the interviewee is quite distant, it is useful to ask what is going through his or her mind. If it becomes clear that the person is stuck on a worry, then acknowledging this as part of the problem can be useful. Another problem that can occur immediately in an interview with patients with GAD is that when asked what is bothering them or what brought them in for an evaluation, they may immediately begin describing a detailed problem and look for immediate advice or solutions. For such patients, it can be helpful to describe the desire for immediate relief and solutions as a core problem of some people who are anxious. Then, the assessor can state that the goal of the evaluation is to develop a complete picture of what is going on for the patient before addressing any individual issue. This may be disappointing for the patient, but suggesting that getting to know the whole patient and how he or she deals with problems is essential for helping him or her in the long term may be useful. In addition, the use of structured or semistructured interviews may help keep both the interviewer and the patient focused.

Tools for Assessment

The main structured or semistructured interviews used to assess GAD include the Hamilton Rating Scale for Anxiety (HAM-A; Hamilton, 1959) and general interviews for anxiety disorders such as the Anxiety Disorders Interview Schedule (ADIS-IV; Brown, Di Nardo, Lehman, & Campbell, 2001), the Structured Interview for *DSM-IV* (SCID; First, Spitzer, Gibbon, & Williams, 1995), or the Mini-International Neuropsychiatric Interview (Sheehan et al., 1998). The HAM-A, which measures general anxiety symptoms, is considered the gold standard interview for evaluating GAD symptoms. It is used in most clinical trials as the main outcome measure. Although there has been much controversy about the reliability of the HAM-A, Shear and colleagues (2001) recently developed a coding system that greatly improves the inter-rater reliability of this measure. Borkovec and colleagues (e.g., Borkovec, Newman, Pincus, & Lytle, 2002) use the HAM-A integrated with the ADIS in order to more fully evaluate GAD.

The HAM-A asks many questions about physiological symptoms of anxiety, even though many of these symptoms are excluded from the diagnosis of GAD in *DSM-IV*. Anxious apprehension and muscle tension are assessed along with cardiovascular, gastrointestinal, and other symptoms. Many patients with GAD are in frequent states of stress and tension and therefore experience many of these symptoms. However, one of the cardinal features of GAD according to *DSM-IV* is worry about a number of different areas, and the HAM-A does not inquire about this.

The ADIS is quite thorough in its evaluation of worry. The ADIS is designed to ask first whether a person experiences worry about a number of different areas that feels uncontrollable or exaggerated for the situation. This is an important aspect to evaluate because worry about financial ruin is quite realistic for a person who is significantly in debt, is unemployed, and has no support system. One line of questions that can help distinguish a stress reaction from GAD is to determine how the patient views his or her worrying compared with other people going through a similar situation. If the answer is that he or she is much more preoccupied with it than others would be and that this preoccupation seems to interfere with active planning and coping, then further inquiry into the symptoms of GAD is warranted. Another aspect of worry that the ADIS suggests evaluating is the different content area of worry. If someone is only concerned about his or her marriage and nothing else, then there are not multiple areas of concern, and alternative diagnoses should be considered. A systematic evaluation of different content areas of potential concern can be quite helpful. Some different areas of concern include family, friends, health, finances, one's job, and minor matters. Roemer, Molina, and Borkovec (1997) found that worriers are significantly more likely than other groups to worry about minor matters such as getting daily chores done. In addition to identifying content area, it is useful to know how excessive and how controllable the worry is. In addition, it is very useful to determine the percentage of the day that the patient engages in worry. A number of informal questions seem to help identify patients

with GAD, including "Are you a worrier?" "Have you always been a worrier?" "If someone else were to be experiencing the same life situation as you, would they be as worried as you are?" "Are you worried about worrying?"

Several self-report measures may also help supplement or expedite the interview process. The GAD-Q-IV is a self-report measure of GAD symptoms (Newman et al., 2002). The Penn State Worry Questionnaire (PSWQ; Meyer, Miller, Metzger, & Borkovec, 1990) measures uncontrollable worry, and the Intolerance of Uncertainty Scale (Buhr & Dugas, 2002; Freeston, Rhéaume, Letarte, & Dugas, 1994) measures one's perceived ability to cope with uncertainty. The Worry Domains Inventory assesses the areas of concern for the patient (Tallis, Eysenck, & Mathews, 1992). The metaworry inventory (Wells, 2005) also measures the concept of worry about worry. In addition, given recent theoretical accounts of emotional avoidance and interpersonal issues in GAD (Borkovec, Alcaine, & Behar, 2004; Newman, Castonguay, Borkovec, & Molnar, 2004; Roemer & Orsillo, 2002), one may want to examine emotional avoidance and interpersonal relationships. Specific methods have been developed to assess these issues (Roemer, Salters, Raffa, & Orsillo, 2005; Newman et al., 2004).

Given the high comorbidity of GAD and depression, it is useful to include a measure of depression as well. In fact, the Beck Depression Inventory (Beck, Rush, Shaw, & Emery, 1979) is the most common measure used within an assessment battery for GAD (Huppert & Sanderson, 2002). In addition, the Spielberger State-Trait Inventory (Spielberger, Gorsuch, Lushene, Vagg, & Jacobs, 1983) is another commonly used self-report measure in the assessment of GAD (Fisher & Durham, 1999). Finally, the Depression, Anxiety, and Stress Scales (DASS; Lovibond & Lovibond, 1995) evaluate the three constructs that the scale is named for, and patients with GAD tend to be elevated in both the depression and stress scales (see Brown, Chorpita, Korotitsch, & Barlow, 1997).

INTERVIEWING OBSTACLES AND SOLUTIONS

Different disorders tend to have different issues that become obstacles in the interview. In addition to difficult presentations and styles of interaction, patients with GAD may have difficulty providing some of the core details that would help the evaluation and may be a key part of the case formulation and treatment plan. For example, patients may have difficulty determining whether their worry is excessive. If they believe that they are engaging in worry in order to prevent catastrophe, they may believe that their worry is beneficial. One way to attempt to deal with this is to ask patients whether they are worried more than their significant others or whether friends and relatives have commented on the things they worry about. Many patients with GAD state that they are considered "worry warts" and have been worriers since childhood.

Another common problem when interviewing patients with GAD is that they may not be as aware of the content of their worries as they are of the physiological symptoms associated with their worrying. When asked about worry, they may say that they don't know, but they are just always anxious. One way of helping a patient think about worry is to explain that most of the time, there are triggers for feeling anxious, and then provide examples (e.g., worrying about finances, work, family, one's health).

Even if one is able to identify the global content of worries, many patients are unable to articulate the ultimate consequences of the worries. For example, if they say that they are very worried about their significant others, they may not be able to articulate what worries them. The patient may say something such as "I am afraid something bad will happen to them" but not expand on this at all. Usually, worries are fleeting ideas related to a theme that do not spiral down in a coherent fashion. The worry may be "My wife is late, what if she got in a car accident, or what if she got mugged? What if she is sick and didn't make it to the car?" This list of what-ifs is followed not by answers to the what-ifs but by other related questions.

Case Illustration With Dialogue

The following is an example of an assessment of an adult patient seeking treatment. In order to protect the identity of individual patients, this is a composite of a number of patients. Jack is a 45-year-old executive at a midsize company who called seeking treatment because he has been feeling stressed and tense a lot and feels that it is affecting his ability to work and his home life.

Jack was sent a self-report packet before his initial visit, which included the DASS-21 and the PSWQ. His scores on these measures were 75 on the PSWQ and 26 on the stress scale and 16 on the depression scale of the DASS, both in the clinical range for GAD.

Therapist:	So what brings you in for treatment?
J:	I don't know. I am not sure I should be here.
T:	Whose idea was it for you to come in?
J:	Mine.
T:	What were you thinking when you called and scheduled an appointment?
J:	I am too stressed out. But on the way here I began to think that being here is just going to stress me out more. I should be at work or at home, doing something about my problems, not here talking about them.
T:	It sounds like you are quite stressed out.
J:	Uh huh.
T:	Have you tried just doing things and ignoring your worries before?
J:	Yes.
T:	And how did it go?
J:	[irritably] All right, I get your point.
T:	Well, what kinds of things get you stressed out?
J:	What doesn't? I get stressed about work, about my family, about any time I have free. Free time is a luxury I don't have.
T:	So you feel like you need to keep busy all the time?
J:	There is just so much to do. At least when I am busy, I feel like I am making some progress. When I sit down, even for 5 minutes, I feel like I am wasting time, and I should be doing something. Thoughts just start racing in my mind.
T:	So it is hard to find time to just relax. That is common with people who have a lot of anxiety: The time that they want to feel relaxed ends up just being more stressful, with lots of worries.
J:	Exactly.

T: People feel stress differently. Some people feel it more in their bodies, like in muscle tension or in stomach aches or other gastrointestinal problems, and some feel it more in their heads, through headaches and dizziness. Still others feel it more in their heads, with racing thoughts, lots of what-ifs, and other worries. Or it could be a combination. How does your stress manifest itself?

J: Well, I get lots of worries about getting things done, and whether the quality is good enough at work. I feel a lot of muscle tension. These lead to me having a short fuse a lot. Even when I try to sleep, I have these worries keeping me awake, and my muscles are in knots.

T: So it sounds like you have a lot of worries, and muscle tension, sleep trouble, and irritability along with them?

J: Definitely, but what can you do to help me relax and get rid of these worries?

T: Well, the first thing to do to help anyone is to get a full, accurate picture of what is going on. That is my goal for today.

J: You mean you won't give me any way to stop this today?

T: Unfortunately, that is not the way things work. If I knew a quick fix, I would give it to you. However, once I have a good picture of what is going on, we can come up with a program that you agree to that may start helping you soon.

J: Well, all right, I guess. What else do you need to know?

T: Let's go through some questions a bit more systematically now, to make sure I cover all my bases. You said that you worry about work and home?

J: All the time. I can't even sit for 5 minutes without worries about work and my family creeping in quickly. I need to keep busy to try to feel better.

T: So what do you do to try to keep busy?

J: I need to keep my mind occupied. If I am home, I need to be reading the paper, watching something engaging on TV, listening to music, talking to someone, anything to distract me from my worries. I can't sit and play with my kids for more than 10 minutes without my mind going back to work, or thinking

about how I am going to pay for their colleges. They are only 5 and 8, but do you know how much college will cost? How am I supposed to pay for it?

T: So you worry about long-term finances, too.

J: You should, too.

T: So it sounds like you think that your worry may be useful at times? Well, let's talk more about that in a few more minutes. Do you worry about minor matters?

J: Yes. For sure. Like even how am I going to get the kids to their sports games on Saturday? Or how will I get all the forms I need to get done for work by Tuesday? Or will I get to the cleaners to pick up my stuff before they close?

T: Okay. How about your or your family's health?

J: Everyone is fine. I don't think about people getting sick, if that is what you mean. Though I do have thoughts about what would happen if my wife died. How would I manage? That kind of thing. But those thoughts come a lot less than work and kids. I guess I also worry that something could happen to my kids. I know it isn't likely, but you hear every once in a while about kids getting killed in car accidents, etc. Those thoughts pop into my mind from time to time.

T: And do you worry about your relationship with your wife or kids?

J: With my wife, I probably should more than I do. I know I snap at her too much, especially when she tells me not to worry about something, or tries to distract me while I am trying to figure something out.

T: So it sounds like your worry and anxiety interfere with your relationship with your wife in ways that you would like to change?

J: Definitely.

T: But not that you worry about your relationship like you worry about work, your kids, and minor matters.

J: Right. My kids I worry about more that way. I worry if I am a good enough father, whether something will happen to them, whether they will turn out okay. Being a parent is a lot of responsibility.

T: And you can never be sure how they will turn out in the end.

J: Right. But you need to try as hard as possible to prevent harm.

T: And worrying does that?

J: Yes.

T: Okay, so you have a lot of areas of worry. Do you feel that these worries are uncontrollable or excessive? By uncontrollable, I mean that it is difficult to turn your attention from them or stop them. By excessive, I mean, do you think that other people in your life situation (e.g., being married, full-time job in your line of work) would be as anxious and worried as you?

J: I can't stop if I want to, and I would like to be less stressed, more like other people are.

T: What percentage of the day do you think you are worrying?

J: 80.

The therapist then asks about physiological symptoms of GAD, including irritability, sleep loss, muscle tension, concentration, fatigue, restlessness, or feeling keyed up or on edge. Jack acknowledges all of these and does not meet criteria for other disorders. The end of the initial interview should describe findings about GAD and its treatment, orient the patient to the treatment model, and motivate the patient toward treatment.

Therapist: It is my impression that you have generalized anxiety disorder, or GAD. GAD is also known as the worry disorder. Many people with GAD describe having been a worrier since childhood.

Jack: Yes, that is definitely me.

T: Right. The cardinal signs of GAD are the uncontrollable, excessive worry and associated irritability, muscle tension, feeling keyed up, and difficulty with sleep. The good news is that the data are quite strong regarding the treatment of GAD. Most people describe significant reductions in worry and other symptoms with cognitive-behavioral therapies. These therapies tend to focus on the function of worry, which some researchers argue is to avoid negative feelings and outcomes. In addition, substantial amounts of research have demonstrated that people with GAD tend to notice and focus more on negative things and to interpret even things that are unclear in a more negative fashion. The goal of treatment will be to help you change these thought patterns and the physiological symptoms associated with them. But in order to do so, you may have to be more willing to give up some of the control you are trying to keep.

J: I don't know if I can do that.

T: Well, if you thought you could easily, you wouldn't be here. It is a good sign you didn't say "I will never do that." The first part of treatment is helping you learn why and how to do so. Any questions about anything I have gone over today?

MULTICULTURAL AND DIVERSITY ISSUES

A review of the literature on cultural and diversity issues in GAD returns few findings. Results from the National Comorbidity Survey Replication (Kessler et al., 2005) include the following statistically significant sociodemographic predictors of receiving a diagnosis of GAD (minimum 1-month duration): being younger than 60 years of age, having more than a high school education, having occupational statuses of unemployed or disabled, and being previously married, non-Hispanic White, and female. Using the same data, Ruscio et al. (2005) report a lower prevalence of GAD among males, non-Hispanic Blacks and Hispanics, and those who are unemployed. Data from Grant et al. (2005), who examined another U.S. sample, also found a lower risk of being diagnosed with GAD among Asians, Hispanics, and African Americans.

Data from nonclinical populations suggest some differences between ethnic groups in self-reported levels of worry. Results from a confirmatory factor analysis by Carter et al. (2005) show that African Americans scored significantly lower on the PSWQ than the White American group. In addition, an exploratory factor analysis of the PSWQ revealed two factors (general worry, worry absence) among White Americans and three factors (general worry, worry absence, and worry dismissal) among African Americans. The differences in subscale structure were minor according to the authors. In contrast, Novy, Stanley, Averill, and Daza (2001) found that English and Spanish versions of the PSWQ and other anxiety measures were equally reliable and valid, supporting the use of Spanish instruments in evaluating Hispanic patients.

Another study examining ethnic differences in worry in a college student population found no difference between ethnic groups (African American, Asian American, and Caucasians) in the degree to which they reported pathological worry (Scott, Eng, & Heimberg, 2002). However, there were some differences between ethnic groups relating to reported worry across several content areas. For example, African Americans reported less worry about work competence, future aims, relationship stability, and self-confidence than Asian Americans and Caucasians. However, African Americans reported the greatest amount of worry related to financial concerns.

Prevalence of GAD may vary across cultures. For example, in Mexico GAD prevalence (using a 12-month minimum duration) was reported to be 0.4% (Medina-Mora et al., 2005). Additionally, Lieb, Becker, and Altamura (2005) suggest a 2% prevalence rate of GAD in Europe (using a 12-month minimum duration). However, not all research has yielded similar findings. For example, Vega et al. (1998) report prevalence of GAD in Hispanics to be at least as high as in other ethnicities. Future researchers should target cultural and diversity issues related to GAD and other disorders. Overall, clinicians should take into account the possibility of differences in self-reported symptoms between ethnic groups.

DIFFERENTIAL DIAGNOSIS

Differentiating GAD from other anxiety disorders can be very complicated. First, worry is a common feature of anxiety disorders (e.g., worry about having a panic attack, worry about social situations, worry about germs). Additionally, there is a high level of comorbidity among the anxiety disorders, with GAD in particular, which requires one to consider diagnosing multiple disorders and making differential diagnoses (cf. Brown, Campbell, et al., 2001). The content and breadth of patient's concern are primary distinctions between GAD and other anxiety disorders.

Patients with GAD experience uncontrollable worry about several different areas in their life. In fact, they often worry about their worrying (known as metaworry; Wells, 1994b). On the other hand, patients with other anxiety disorders often are concerned about topics specific to their respective disorder.

Panic Disorder

Patients with panic disorder are worried about having a panic attack, or the consequences of experiencing certain bodily sensations. Generally, their focus is on internal states. What makes the differential diagnosis between panic disorder and GAD particularly difficult is that the worry experienced by patients with GAD can lead to a panic attack or panic-like symptoms. However, patients with GAD are concerned primarily about a future event, usually an external event or an illness, and not about having an immediate panic attack per se. Another distinction is the course of onset of worry versus panic. Focusing on the physical symptoms of their anxiety is a feature of some patients with GAD, and this can lead one to think that the preoccupation with bodily sensations is a sign of panic disorder. However, panic attacks occur suddenly, and their peak typically lasts for several minutes, whereas the onset and course of GAD-related anxiety usually are longer and more stable. However, distinguishing features of GAD and panic disorder may be fewer and slightly different in older treatment-seeking adults (Mohlman, de Jesus, Gorenstein, Kleber, Gorman, & Papp, 2004). They suggest that such features include patients with GAD generally endorsing more symptoms on the Beck Depression Inventory and symptoms of anger and hostility, and patients with panic disorder having elevated scores on measures of sympathetic nervous system arousal and more agoraphobic avoidance.

Social Phobia

Social concerns are a common area of worry for patients with GAD. As a result, patients with GAD often are diagnosed with comorbid social phobia (Sanderson, Di Nardo, Rapee, & Barlow, 1990). However, one major guideline for differentiating the two disorders can be made. GAD concerns are more global and focused on a number of different areas, which may include social situations. In contrast, patients with social phobia are specifically concerned with being evaluated, embarrassed, or humiliated in front of others.

Obsessive-Compulsive Disorder

Although the distinction between obsessive-compulsive disorder (OCD) and GAD seems obvious because of the behavioral rituals that are unique to OCD (Brown et al., 1994; Brown, Di Nardo, et al., 2001), some cases can be quite difficult to differentiate. Cases are especially complicated with patients with OCD who do not have compulsions or have only mental rituals. Assessing the focus of concern can help differentiate between obsessions and worries. Obsessions usually are short lived and focused on exaggerated or unrealistic expectations (e.g., "If I don't seal this envelope correctly, my wife will be injured on the way home from work"). Additionally, obsessions often follow an "if-then" form (e.g., "If I do or don't do or think something, then something bad will happen") or include vivid imagery (Wells, 1994a). Worry, on the other hand, usually is focused on future negative events that are not caused by the patient. Data from nonanxious subjects suggest that worry lasts longer, is more distracting, and usually consists of predominantly verbal thoughts as opposed to images (Wells & Morrison, 1994). Also, the thought content of a worry may be specified in a "what if" fashion but without a consequence being stated ("What if I get ill?"). Another common feature of patients with GAD and OCD is the fact that both may engage in reassurance-seeking behaviors that can be somewhat ritualistic and superstitious. Patients with GAD may report feeling compelled to act to neutralize a worry (Wells & Morrison, 1994; e.g., to call a family member at work to decrease worry about something happening to them) or to engage in other checking behaviors to see whether something bad has happened (Schut, Castonguay, & Borkovec, 2001). However, these behaviors are not as consistent, methodical, or ritualized as compulsive behaviors in patients with OCD.

Mood Disorders

The final distinction to be made is between GAD and mood disorders, especially major depression and dysthymia. More often than not,

anxiety symptoms occur in the context of depression, and therefore GAD is diagnosed as a separate disorder only when the symptoms have occurred independently of depression at some point. Regardless of *DSM* exclusionary criteria, the nature of cognitions associated with each disorder can be distinguished: Ruminations (common in depressive disorders) tend to be negative thought patterns about past events, whereas worries (associated with GAD) tend to be negative thought patterns about future events. This is consistent with theoretical conceptualizations of anxiety and depression that posit that depression is a reaction to uncontrollable, inescapable negative events leading to feelings of hopelessness, helplessness, and deactivation, whereas anxiety is a reaction to uncontrollable negative events that the person attempts or plans to escape from (for a more detailed explanation, see Barlow, Chorpita, and Turovsky, 1996). Brown, Campbell, et al. (2001) present data suggesting that without the rule-out criteria, 90% of patients diagnosed with dysthymia and 67% of patients diagnosed with major depression would be diagnosed concurrently with GAD, but with the rule-out criteria only 5% were diagnosed with GAD.

SELECTION OF TREATMENT TARGETS AND REFERRAL

There are a number of different theories of GAD, which suggest somewhat different treatment targets (see Heimberg, Turk, & Mennin, 2004). General treatment strategies include progressive muscle relaxation and cognitive restructuring (Leahy, 2004; see also Rygh & Sanderson, 2004, for a recent manual). Even the targets of cognitive restructuring differ according to different models of GAD. The most common issues are overestimations of the probability and cost of negative events (Butler & Mathews, 1983; Foa & Kozak, 1986), overestimation of threat as increasing over time (loomingness; Riskind & Williams, 2005), metaworry (Wells, 2005), and attention to threatening material and interpreting ambiguous information as threatening (attentional and interpretive biases; MacLeod & Rutherford, 2004). In addition to addressing cognitive distortions or biases, different psychological approaches address a number of other targets, including muscle tension (Borkovec, Grayson, & Cooper, 1978), sleep disturbance (Bélanger, Morin, Langlois, &

Ladouceur, 2004; Leahy, 2004), intolerance of uncertainty and problem solving (Dugas, Buhr, & Ladouceur, 2004), behavioral and emotional avoidance (emotional and behavioral; Borkovec et al., 2004), general affect regulation difficulties (Huppert & Alley, 2004; Mennin et al., 2003), mindfulness and acceptance of distress (Roemer, Orsillo, & Barlow, 2002), and interpersonal interactions (Crits-Christoph, Gibbons, & Crits-Christoph, 2004; Newman et al., 2004). Each of these targets is described briefly in this section.

Muscle Tension

Many cognitive-behavioral treatments for GAD include progressive muscle relaxation (PMR; Jacobson, 1938) to address physiological tension that characterizes GAD. However, other theories suggest that reduction of the core cognitive complaints will reduce muscle tension and that use of PMR can be an avoidance strategy. Thus, PMR is incompatible with treatments that focus on acceptance of distress rather than attempting to reduce it. However, some data suggest that PMR can be an effective technique for the treatment of GAD (Borkovec et al., 1987).

Sleep Disturbance

As noted in the diagnostic criteria, patients with GAD often have trouble falling or staying asleep, often because of their worries. At times PMR can be helpful in improving sleep. In addition, sleep hygiene can be important because some patients with GAD are so focused on trying to avoid negative outcomes that they do not follow normal sleep patterns. Therefore, sleep hygiene techniques can be useful for these patients (Leahy, 2004). Finally, some treatments for GAD improve sleep without directly addressing sleep habits (Bélanger et al., 2004).

Overestimation of Probability and Cost

Two of the major cognitive distortions that are emphasized in the anxiety disorders are overestimations of the probability of harmful events and the cost of mildly negative events (Beck & Emery, 1985; Foa & Kozak, 1986). For patients with GAD, probability of harm to oneself or one's family often is overestimated. The harm can be physical (e.g., illness, accidents), financial

(including fears of losing one's whole savings or getting fired), or emotional (people getting very angry, hurting people's feelings). Fears of future bad outcomes such as one's children not growing up to be happy may also be included here. For many of these overestimations, it is helpful to spiral down and attempt to learn more what the feared consequences are if these overestimated things were to occur. This often leads to catastrophic thoughts such as "If it was a car accident, then he is dead and I will never be able to cope." There are a number of distortions here that are probably increasing the patient's anxiety. There are two overestimations of harm: the likelihood of the car accident and the likelihood of death by a car accident. There are also two catastrophic thoughts: any car accident means death, and one cannot cope if one has a loss. Therefore, evaluating these thoughts can be an important aspect of understanding the thought processes in GAD, which must be targeted in treatment.

Loomingness

Recent findings suggest that there is a specific cognitive style related to anxiety in which people are more likely to perceive the risk of threats as increasing over time (Riskind & Williams, 2005). When asked whether bad things are more likely to happen as an event unfolds or time passes, people with anxiety, including patients with GAD, are more likely than depressed or nonanxious people to say "yes." Thus, another target of treatment may be addressing the belief of looming danger.

Metaworry

Another aspect of GAD that has been a focus of some work is the idea that patients with GAD worry about worrying, or metaworry (Wells, 2005). Metaworry may be an important target for treatment because it is not captured by the aforementioned appraisals of probability, cost, or loomingness. Beliefs about the uncontrollability and negative effects of worry may need to be addressed in treatment.

Attentional and Interpretive Biases

People with GAD not only have overestimations of probability and cost but also a number of other cognitive biases. The predominant information-processing problems they have are paying excessive attention to threat stimuli or having difficulty disengaging from threat stimuli (see MacLeod & Rutherford, 2004), developing threat interpretations in the face of ambiguity, and selectively remembering threat information. All of these biased processes can be viewed as targets for treatment. Many CBT treatments attempt to create situations in which patients strategically override these biases and rehearse alternative, adaptive strategies (Leahy, 2004). Furthermore, new procedures are in development to directly address these biases (see Mathews & MacLeod, 2005).

Intolerance of Uncertainty

One theory of GAD suggests that there are two main types of worry: worry about immediate issues and future, unrealistic worry. Both of these areas can be difficult for patients with GAD and therefore may be targets of treatment. The theory suggests that both types of worry are driven by the intolerance of uncertainty. People with GAD have been shown to be less able to tolerate uncertain outcomes than others (Dugas et al., 2004). This intolerance leads to worry about the many things in life that are ambiguous. The theory suggests separate methods of addressing more current worries and future, unrealistic worries. Future worries are addressed through practice in tolerating uncertain futures through imagery. More immediate issues are addressed through problem solving.

Problem-Solving Skills

Research by Dugas and colleagues (2004) and Davey (1994) suggests that people with GAD do not have trouble generating responses or solutions to problems but that they have trouble selecting solutions, particularly because they lack confidence in any solution. Thus, there is a problem-solving deficit in terms of selecting and executing solutions. This deficit may be a target of treatment, to be addressed through problem-solving skills.

Cognitive-Behavioral Avoidance

Models of GAD often suggest that patients with GAD attempt to avoid their feared outcomes through checking (Schut et al., 2001) or other behavioral avoidance strategies (Borkovec & Sharpless, 2004). In addition, significant research

is accumulating showing that patients with GAD engage in cognitive avoidance, often attempting to avoid thinking about negative outcomes (Borkovec et al., 2004). These types of avoidance are important targets of treatment for GAD in most theories.

Emotional Avoidance

In addition to cognitive and behavioral avoidance, the past decade has seen a reemphasis on emotions per se and emotional avoidance. For example, Roemer and Orsillo (2002) suggest that mindfulness and acceptance-based strategies are important ways of reducing emotional avoidance.

Affective Dysregulation

Related to the idea of emotional avoidance, data suggest that patients with GAD have significant problems with multiple stages of affect regulation, including identifying, labeling, tolerating, modulating, and self-soothing (Mennin et al., 2005). Therefore, identifying difficulties in affect regulation may be another important target of treatment. Huppert and Alley (2004) suggest that imaginal exposure to multiple emotions may be a way of developing affect regulation strategies.

Interpersonal Difficulties

As discussed earlier, relating to patients with GAD can be quite difficult because of their interpersonal style. This issue has been identified not just as a consequence of other GAD symptoms but also as an important target in itself (Crits-Christoph et al., 2004; Newman et al., 2004). Some data have revealed that patients who receive cognitive-behavioral therapy for GAD and continue to exhibit interpersonal difficulties do not respond to treatment (see Newman et al., 2004) and therefore that this target is essential for treatment. Others have shown that interpersonal difficulties addressed through a psychodynamic treatment that focuses on interpersonal relationships can be effective in reducing symptoms of GAD (Crits-Christoph, Connolly, Azarian, Crits-Christoph, & Shappell, 1996; Crits-Christoph, Gibbons, Narducci, Schamberger, & Gallop, 2005). Interestingly, in their treatment supportive and expressive components can be divided, and analyses suggest that expressive components are most related to treatment outcome

(Crits-Christoph et al., 1996). Both of these treatments suggest that directly addressing interpersonal difficulties is an important target in the treatment of GAD.

SUMMARY

GAD is a common, debilitating disorder that often goes untreated. A successful evaluation includes assessing many dimensions of worry and its antecedents and consequences and the physiological symptoms that are also associated with worry. Although GAD may overlap with a number of disorders, such as depression and the other anxiety disorders, it can clearly be differentiated, and doing so is an important part of treatment planning. In addition, there are many relevant treatment targets for GAD that should be identified and addressed.

REFERENCES

Abel, J. L., & Borkovec, T. D. (1995). Generalizability of *DSM-III-R* generalized anxiety disorders to proposed *DSM-IV* criteria and cross validation of proposed changes. *Journal of Anxiety Disorders, 9,* 303–315.

American Psychiatric Association. (1987). *Diagnostic and statistical manual of mental disorders* (3rd ed., Rev.). Washington, DC: Author.

American Psychiatric Association. (1994). *Diagnostic and statistical manual of mental disorders* (4th ed.). Washington, DC: Author.

Barlow, D. H. (2002). *Anxiety and its disorders* (2nd ed.). New York: Guilford.

Barlow, D. H., Chorpita, B. F., & Turovsky, J. (1996). Fear, panic, anxiety, and disorders of emotion. In D. A. Hope (Ed.), *Nebraska Symposium on Motivation: Perspectives on anxiety, panic, and fear* (pp. 251–328). Lincoln: University of Nebraska Press.

Beck, A. T., & Emery, G. (1985). *Anxiety disorders and phobias: A cognitive perspective.* New York: Basic Books.

Beck, A. T., Rush, A. J., Shaw, B. F., & Emery, G. (1979). *Cognitive therapy of depression.* New York: Guilford.

Bélanger, L., Morin, C. M., Langlois, F., & Ladouceur, R. (2004). Insomnia and generalized anxiety disorder: Effects of cognitive behavior therapy for GAD on insomnia symptoms. *Journal of Anxiety Disorders, 18,* 561–571.

Borkovec, T. D. (1994). The nature, functions, and origins of worry. In G. C. L. Davey & F. Tallis (Eds.), *Worrying: Perspectives on theory, assessment and treatment* (pp. 5–33). New York: Wiley.

Borkovec, T. D., Alcaine, O., & Behar, E. (2004). Avoidance theory of worry and generalized anxiety disorder. In R. G. Heimberg, C. L. Turk, & D. S. Mennin (Eds.),

Generalized anxiety disorder: Advances in research and practice (pp. 77–108). New York: Guilford.

Borkovec, T. D., Grayson, J. B., & Cooper, K. M. (1978). Treatment of general tension: Subjective and physiological effects of progressive relaxation. *Journal of Consulting and Clinical Psychology, 46,* 518–528.

Borkovec, T. D., & Hu, S. (1990). The effect of worry on cardiovascular response to phobic imagery. *Behaviour Research and Therapy, 28,* 69–73.

Borkovec, T. D., Mathews, A. M., Chambers, A., Ebrahimi, S., Lytle, R., & Nelson, R. (1987). The effects of relaxation training with cognitive therapy or nondirective therapy and the role of relaxation-induced anxiety in the treatment of generalized anxiety. *Journal of Consulting and Clinical Psychology, 25,* 883–888.

Borkovec, T. D., Newman, M. G., Pincus, A., & Lytle, R. (2002). A component analysis of cognitive behavioral therapy for generalized anxiety disorder and the role of interpersonal problems. *Journal of Consulting and Clinical Psychology, 70,* 288–298.

Borkovec, T. D., Shadick, R. N., & Hopkins, M. (1991). The nature of normal and pathological worry. In R. M. Rapee & D. H. Barlow (Eds.), *Chronic anxiety, generalized anxiety disorder, and mixed anxiety depression* (pp. 29–51). New York: Guilford.

Borkovec, T. D., & Sharpless, B. (2004). Generalized anxiety disorder: Bringing cognitive behavioral therapy into the valued present. In S. Hayes, V. Follette, & M. Linehan (Eds.), *New directions in behavior therapy* (pp. 209–242). New York: Guilford.

Brown, T. A., Barlow, D. H., & Liebowitz, M. R. (1994). The empirical basis of generalized anxiety disorder. *American Journal of Psychiatry, 151,* 1272–1280.

Brown, T. A., Campbell, L. A., Lehman, C. L., Grisham, J. R., & Mancill, R. B. (2001). Current and lifetime comorbidity of the *DSM-IV* anxiety and mood disorders in a large clinical sample. *Journal of Abnormal Psychology, 110,* 585–599.

Brown, T. A., Chorpita, B. F., Korotitsch, W., & Barlow, D. H. (1997). Psychometric properties of the Depression Anxiety Stress Scales (DASS) in clinical samples. *Behaviour Research and Therapy, 35,* 79–89.

Brown, T. A., Di Nardo, P. A., Lehman, C. L., & Campbell, L. A. (2001). Reliability of *DSM-IV* anxiety and mood disorders: Implications for the classification of emotional disorders. *Journal of Abnormal Psychology, 110,* 49–58.

Brown, T. A., O'Leary, T. A., & Barlow, D. H. (1993). Generalized anxiety disorder. In D. H. Barlow (Ed.), *Clinical handbook of psychological disorders* (2nd ed., pp. 137–188). New York: Guilford.

Bruce, S. E., Yonkers, K. A., Otto, M. W., Eisen, J. L., Weisberg, R. B., & Pagano, M., et al. (2005). Influence of psychiatric comorbidity on recovery and recurrence in generalized anxiety disorder, social phobia, and panic disorder: A 12-year prospective study. *American Journal of Psychiatry, 162,* 1179–1187.

Buhr, K., & Dugas, M. J. (2002). The Intolerance of Uncertainty Scale: Psychometric properties of the English version. *Behaviour Research and Therapy, 40,* 931–946.

Butler, G., & Mathews, A. (1983). Cognitive processes in anxiety. *Advances in Behaviour Research & Therapy, 5,* 51–62.

Carter, M. M., Sbrocco, T., Miller, O., Suchday, S., Lewis, E. L., & Freedman, R. E. K. (2005). Factor structure, reliability, and validity of the Penn State Worry Questionnaire: Differences between African-American and White-American college students. *Journal of Anxiety Disorders, 19*(8), 827–843.

Crits-Christoph, P., Connolly, M. B., Azarian, K., Crits-Christoph, K., & Shappell, S. (1996). An open trial of brief supportive-expressive psychotherapy in the treatment of generalized anxiety disorder. *Psychotherapy: Theory, Research, Practice, Training, 33,* 418–430.

Crits-Christoph, P., Gibbons, M. B. C., & Crits-Christoph, K. (2004). Supportive-expressive psychodynamic therapy. In R. G. Heimberg, C. L. Turk, & D. S. Mennin (Eds.), *Generalized anxiety disorder: Advances in research and practice* (pp. 293–319). New York: Guilford.

Crits-Christoph, P., Gibbons, M. B. C., Narducci, J., Schamberger, M., & Gallop, R. (2005). Interpersonal problems and the outcome of interpersonally oriented psychodynamic treatment of GAD. *Psychotherapy: Theory, Research, Practice, Training, 42,* 211–224.

Davey, G. C. L. (1994). Pathological worrying as exacerbated problem-solving. In G. C. L. Davey & F. Tallis (Eds.), *Worrying: Perspectives on theory, assessment and treatment.* New York: Wiley.

Dugas, M. J., Buhr, K., & Ladouceur, R. (2004). The role of intolerance of uncertainty in etiology and maintenance. In R. G. Heimberg, C. L. Turk, & D. S. Mennin (Eds.), *Generalized anxiety disorder: Advances in research and practice* (pp. 143–163). New York: Guilford.

First, M. B., Spitzer, R. L., Gibbon, M., & Williams, J. B. W. (1995). *Structured Clinical Interview for Axis I DSM-IV Disorders: Patient edition (SCID-P), (Version 2.0).* New York: Biometrics Research, New York State Psychiatric Institute.

Fisher, P. L., & Durham, R. C. (1999). Recovery rates in generalized anxiety disorder following psychological therapy: An analysis of clinically significant change in the STAI-T across outcome studies since 1990. *Psychological Medicine, 29,* 1425–1434.

Foa, E. B., & Kozak, M. J. (1986). Emotional processing of fear: Exposure to corrective information. *Psychological Bulletin, 99,* 20–35.

Freeston, M. H., Rhéaume, J., Letarte, H., & Dugas, M. J. (1994). Why do people worry? *Personality and Individual Differences, 17,* 791–802.

Grant, B. F., Hasin, D. S., Stinson, F. S., Dawson, D. A., Ruan, W. J., Goldstein, R. B., et al. (2005). Prevalence, correlates, co-morbidity, and comparative disability of *DSM-IV* generalized anxiety disorder in the USA: Results from the National Epidemiologic Survey on Alcohol and Related Conditions. *Psychological Medicine, 35,* 1747–1759.

Hamilton, M. A. (1959). The assessment of anxiety states by rating. *British Journal of Medical Psychology, 32,* 50–55.

Heimberg, R. G., Turk, C. L., & Mennin, D. S. (2004). *Generalized anxiety disorder: Advances in research and practice.* New York: Guilford.

Huppert, J. D., & Alley, A. C. (2004). The clinical application of emotion research in generalized

anxiety disorder: Some proposed procedures. *Cognitive and Behavioral Practice, 11,* 387–392.

Huppert, J. D., & Sanderson, W. C. (2002). Psychotherapy for generalized anxiety disorder. In D. J. Stein (Ed.), *Textbook of anxiety disorders* (pp. 141–155). Washington, DC: American Psychiatric Publishing.

Jacobson, E. (1938). *Progressive relaxation.* Chicago: University of Chicago Press.

Judd, L. L., Kessler, R. C., Paulus, M. P., Zeller, P. V., Wittchen, H. U., & Kunovac, J. L. (1998). Comorbidity as a fundamental feature of generalized anxiety disorders: Results from the National Comorbidity Study (NCS). *Acta Psychiatrica Scandinavica, 393,* 6–11.

Kessler, R. C., Berglund, P., Demler, O., Jin, R., & Walters, E. E. (2005). Lifetime prevalence and age-of-onset distributions of *DSM-IV* disorders in the National Comorbidity Survey Replication. *Archives of General Psychiatry, 62,* 593–602.

Leahy, R. L. (2004). Cognitive-behavioral therapy. In R. G. Heimberg, C. L. Turk, & D. S. Mennin (Eds.), *Generalized anxiety disorder: Advances in research and practice* (pp. 265–292). New York: Guilford.

Lieb, R., Becker, E., & Altamura, C. (2005). The epidemiology of generalized anxiety disorder in Europe. *European Neuropsychopharmacology, 15,* 445–452.

Lovibond, P. F., & Lovibond, S. H. (1995). The structure of negative emotional states: Comparison of the Depression Anxiety Stress Scales (DASS) with the Beck Depression and Anxiety Inventories. *Behaviour Research and Therapy, 33*(3), 335–343.

MacLeod, C., & Rutherford, E. (2004). Information-processing approaches: Assessing the selective functioning of attention, interpretation, and retrieval. In R. G. Heimberg, C. L. Turk, & D. S. Mennin (Eds.), *Generalized anxiety disorder: Advances in research and practice* (pp. 109–142). New York: Guilford.

Mathews, A. (1990). Why worry? The cognitive function of anxiety. *Behaviour Research and Therapy, 28,* 455–468.

Mathews, A., & MacLeod, C. (2005). Cognitive vulnerability to emotional disorders. *Annual Review of Clinical Psychology, 1,* 167–195.

Medina-Mora, M. E., Borges, G., Lara, C., Benjet, C., Blanco, J., & Fleiz, C., et al. (2005). Prevalence, service use, and demographic correlates of 12-month *DSM-IV* psychiatric disorders in Mexico: Results from the Mexican National Comorbidity Survey. *Psychological Medicine, 35,* 1773–1783.

Mennin, D. S., Heimberg, R. G., Turk, C. L., & Fresco, D. M. (2005). Preliminary evidence for an emotion dysregulation model of generalized anxiety disorder. *Behaviour Research and Therapy, 43,* 1281–1310.

Mennin, D. S., Turk, C. L., Heimberg, R. G., & Carmin, C. N. (2003). Focusing on the regulation of emotion: A new direction for conceptualizing and treating generalized anxiety disorder. In M. A. Reinecke & D. A. Clark (Eds.), *Cognitive therapy across the lifespan: Evidence and practice* (pp. 60–89). Cambridge: Cambridge University Press.

Meyer, T. J., Miller, M. L., Metzger, R. L., & Borkovec, T. D. (1990). Development and validation of the Penn State Worry Questionnaire. *Behaviour Research and Therapy, 28,* 487–495.

Mitte, K. (2005). Meta-analysis of cognitive-behavioral treatments for generalized anxiety disorder:

A comparison with pharmacotherapy. *Psychological Bulletin, 131,* 785–795.

Mohlman, J., de Jesus, M., Gorenstein, E. E., Kleber, M., Gorman, J. M., & Papp, L. A. (2004). Distinguishing generalized anxiety disorder, panic disorder, and mixed anxiety states in older treatment-seeking adults. *Journal of Anxiety Disorders, 18,* 275–290.

Newman, M. G., Castonguay, L. G., Borkovec, T. D., & Molnar, C. (2004). Integrative psychotherapy. In R. G. Heimberg, C. L. Turk, & D. S. Mennin (Eds.), *Generalized anxiety disorder: Advances in research and practice* (pp. 320–350). New York: Guilford.

Newman, M. G., Zuellig, A. R., Kachin, K. E., Constantino, M. J., Przeworski, A., Erickson, T., et al. (2002). Preliminary reliability and validity of the Generalized Anxiety Disorder Questionnaire—IV: A revised self-report diagnostic measure of generalized anxiety disorder. *Behavior Therapy, 33,* 215–233.

Novick-Kline, P., Turk, C. L., Mennin, D. S., Hoyt, E. A., & Gallagher, C. L. (2005). Level of emotional awareness as a differentiating variable between individuals with and without generalized anxiety disorder. *Journal of Anxiety Disorders, 19,* 557–572.

Novy, D. M., Stanley, M. A., Averill, P., & Daza, P. (2001). Psychometric comparability of English- and Spanish-language measures of anxiety and related affective symptoms. *Psychological Assessment, 13,* 347–355.

Rapee, R. M. (1991). Psychological factors involved in generalized anxiety. In R. M. Rapee & D. H. Barlow (Eds.), *Chronic anxiety, generalized anxiety disorder, and mixed anxiety depression* (pp. 76–94). New York: Guilford.

Riskind, J. H., & Williams, N. L. (2005). The looming cognitive style and generalized anxiety disorder: Distinctive danger schemas and cognitive phenomenology. *Cognitive Therapy and Research, 29,* 7–27.

Roemer, L., Molina, S., & Borkovec, T. D. (1997). An investigation of worry content among generally anxious individuals. *Journal of Nervous and Mental Disease, 185,* 314–319.

Roemer, L., & Orsillo, S. M. (2002). Expanding our conceptualization of and treatment for generalized anxiety disorder: Integrating mindfulness/acceptance-based approaches with existing cognitive-behavioral models. *Clinical Psychology, 9,* 54–68.

Roemer, L., Orsillo, S. M., & Barlow, D. H. (2002). Generalized anxiety disorder. In D. H. Barlow (Ed.), *Anxiety and its disorders: The nature and treatment of anxiety and panic* (2nd ed., pp. 477–515). New York: Guilford.

Roemer, L., Salters, K., Raffa, S., & Orsillo, S. M. (2005). Fear and avoidance of internal experiences in GAD: Preliminary tests of a conceptual model. *Cognitive Therapy and Research, 29,* 71–88.

Ruscio, A. M. (2002). Delimiting the boundaries of generalized anxiety disorder: Differentiating high worriers with and without GAD. *Journal of Anxiety Disorders, 16,* 377–400.

Ruscio, A. M., Lane, M., Roy-Byrne, P., Stang, P. E., Stein, D. J., Wittchen, H.-U., et al. (2005). Should excessive worry be required for a diagnosis of generalized anxiety disorder? Results from the US National Comorbidity Survey Replication. *Psychological Medicine, 35,* 1761–1772.

Rygh, J. L., & Sanderson, W. C. (2004). *Treating generalized anxiety disorder: Evidence-based strategies, tools, and techniques.* New York: Guilford.

Sanderson, W. C., Di Nardo, P. A., Rapee, R. M., & Barlow, D. H. (1990). Syndrome comorbidity in patients diagnosed with a *DSM-III-R* anxiety disorder. *Journal of Abnormal Psychology, 99,* 308–312.

Sanderson, W. C., & Wetzler, S. (1991). Chronic anxiety and generalized anxiety disorder: Issues in comorbidity. In R. M. Rapee & D. H. Barlow (Eds.), *Chronic anxiety, generalized anxiety disorder, and mixed anxiety depression* (pp. 119–135). New York: Guilford.

Schut, A. J., Castonguay, L. G., & Borkovec, T. D. (2001). Compulsive checking behaviors in generalized anxiety disorder. *Journal of Clinical Psychology, 57,* 705–715.

Scott, E. L., Eng, W., & Heimberg, R. G. (2002). Ethnic differences in worry in a nonclinical population. *Depression and Anxiety, 15,* 79–82.

Shear, M. K., Vander Bilt, J., Rucci, P., Endicott, J., Lydiard, B., Otto, M. W., et al. (2001). Reliability and validity of a structured guide for the Hamilton Anxiety Rating Scale (SIGH-A). *Depression and Anxiety, 13,* 166–178.

Sheehan, D. V., Lecrubier, Y., Sheehan, K. H., Amorim, P., Janavs, J., & Weiller, E., et al. (1998). The Mini-International Neuropsychiatric Interview (M.I.N.I): The development and validation of a structured diagnostic psychiatric interview for *DSM-IV* and *ICD-10. Journal of Clinical Psychiatry, 59*(Suppl. 20), 22–33.

Spielberger, C. D., Gorsuch, R. L., Lushene, P. R., Vagg, P. R., & Jacobs, A. G. (1983). *Manual for the State-Trait Anxiety Inventory.* Palo Alto: Consulting Psychologists Press, Inc.

Tallis, F., Eysenck, M. W., & Mathews, A. (1992). A questionnaire for the measurement of nonpathological worry. *Personality and Individual Differences, 13,* 161–168.

Vega, W. A., Kolody, B., Aguilar-Gaxiola, S., Alderete, E., Catalano, R., & Caraveo-Anduaga, J. (1998). Lifetime prevalence of *DSM-III-R* psychiatric disorders among urban and rural Mexican Americans in California. *Archives of General Psychiatry, 55,* 771–778.

Wells, A. (1994a). Attention and the control of worry. In G. C. L. Davey & F. Tallis (Eds.), *Worrying: Perspectives on theory, assessment and treatment* (pp. 91–114). New York: Wiley.

Wells, A. (1994b). A multi-dimensional measure of worry: Development and preliminary validation of the Anxious Thoughts Inventory. *Anxiety, Stress & Coping: An International Journal, 6,* 289–299.

Wells, A. (2005). The metacognitive model of GAD: Assessment of meta-worry and relationship with *DSM-IV* generalized anxiety disorder. *Cognitive Therapy and Research, 29,* 107–121.

Wells, A., & Morrison, A. P. (1994). Qualitative dimensions of normal worry and normal obsessions: A comparative study. *Behaviour Research and Therapy, 32,* 867–870.

Wittchen, H.-U., Zhao, S., Kessler, R. C., & Eaton, W. W. (1994). *DSM-III-R* generalized anxiety disorder in the National Comorbidity Survey. *Archives of General Psychiatry, 51,* 355–364.

18

EATING DISORDERS

TIFFANY M. STEWART AND DONALD A. WILLIAMSON

DESCRIPTION OF THE DISORDERS

Eating disorders may be conceptualized as having multiple symptom domains that are significant for the assessment, diagnosis, conceptualization, referral, and treatment process. These key domains include body size, restrictive eating, binge eating, compensatory behavior (e.g., purging), body image disturbance, and general psychopathology. It is important to assess eating disorders in a multidimensional fashion, capturing all the aforementioned domains and physical problems, medical conditions, and comorbid psychiatric disorders. (For an "at a glance" reference for comprehensive assessment of eating disorders, see Stewart & Williamson, 2006.)

This chapter provides an overview of one modality of assessment for eating disorders: interviewing techniques. This chapter focuses on anorexia nervosa (AN), bulimia nervosa (BN), binge eating disorder (BED), and eating disorder not otherwise specified (ED-NOS). Interview techniques may be used for the purpose of diagnosis, progress monitoring, or treatment outcome assessment. A brief summary of semi-structured interviews for the assessment of eating disorders and a description of an unstructured clinical interview are provided. Obstacles that arise in the interview process are discussed, with suggestions to guide a successful interview. A sample case illustration and interview dialogue

are also presented. Finally, information on differential diagnosis, behavioral assessment, multicultural and diversity issues, and treatment targets and referrals is summarized. The chapter begins with a brief description of the eating disorders.

Anorexia Nervosa

AN has been recognized as a psychiatric disorder for more than a century (Gull, 1874). Lifetime prevalence of AN is an estimated 0.5–3.7% of females (American Psychiatric Association [APA] Work Group on Eating Disorders, 2000), and it occurs 10 times more often in females than in males (Williamson, Zucker, Martin, & Smeets, 2001). A recent study showed 0.1–5.7% prevalence in females in Western countries specifically (Makino, Tsuboi, & Dennerstein, 2004). AN is the eating disorder most likely to result in severe medical consequences or death. The central diagnostic feature of AN is extreme weight loss. This weight loss often is achieved through restrictive eating or purgative behaviors (e.g., self-induced vomiting, excessive exercise). AN often is accompanied or maintained by an extreme fear of weight gain and body image disturbance, including body image distortion (overestimation of body size) or dissatisfaction with body size and shape. For a review of the diagnostic criteria for AN, see the *Diagnostic and Statistical Manual of Mental Disorders* (*DSM-IV*; APA, 1994).

People with AN often are in denial about the seriousness of their condition and minimize symptoms and consequences of restrictive eating, excessive exercise, and weight loss. AN is also associated with perfectionism and obsessive-compulsive symptoms. People diagnosed with AN often become withdrawn and do not participate in normal activities because they do not have the sufficient physical energy, because of depression or anxiety, or because they are engaging in the behaviors that maintain AN (e.g., excessive exercise or secretive restrictive eating). Medical consequences associated with AN are most commonly caused by chronic starvation. These symptoms include loss of or irregular menses, bradycardia, hypotension, cold intolerance, dry and brittle hair and nails, dehydration, and severe constipation (Pomeroy, 2004). Associated psychological disturbances include depression and anxiety and various personality disorders, with the most common being obsessive-compulsive personality disorder (Sansone, Levitt, & Sansone, 2005). Avoidant and borderline (most common in binge-purge subtype) personality disorders are also common.

Bulimia Nervosa

The syndrome of BN was first described by Russell (1979). For a review of the diagnostic criteria for BN, see the *DSM-IV* (APA, 1994). BN is characterized by repeated episodes of binge eating in which one feels a lack of control over the eating during the episodes (APA, 1994). These binge episodes are defined as objectively large. In the criteria for BN, an attempt is made to define an "objective" binge as eating a large amount of food in a short period of time. This definition has been interpreted many ways, but the general consensus is that the amount eaten is not an important distinction (Thaw, Williamson, & Martin, 2001). Another symptom of BN is the frequent use of purgative behaviors, including self-induced vomiting, laxative or diuretic abuse, restrictive eating, or excessive exercise to rid the body of calories or prevent weight gain. BN is also accompanied by concerns about body size and shape. Lifetime prevalence for BN is 1.1% to 4.2% for females (APA Work Group on Eating Disorders, 2000). Males with BN make up approximately 10% of all cases (Williamson et al., 2001). A recent study showed 0.3% to 7.3%

prevalence in females and 0% to 2.1% prevalence in males in Western countries (Makino et al., 2004).

People with BN often have a fear of gaining weight and fears of fatness that motivate extreme behaviors to maintain weight status (e.g., vomiting after eating a meal). Socially, people with BN become so involved with maintaining eating disorder behaviors that they have difficulty in interpersonal relationships or maintaining required school or social activities (e.g., attending classes and work obligations). These behaviors typically produce shame, which motivates concealment of the behaviors from peers and family members. Common medical consequences associated with BN may include dental erosion from vomiting, abrasions on fingers or hands from vomiting, and peripheral edema (Pomeroy, 2004). Associated psychological disturbances include depression, anxiety, and various personality disorders, with the most common being borderline personality disorder. Other associated personality disorders include histrionic and dependent personality disorders (Sansone, Levitt, & Sansone, 2005).

Eating Disorder Not Otherwise Specified

The ED-NOS category is characterized by various eating disorders that do not meet full diagnostic criteria for eating disorders as defined by the APA (1994). Fifty percent of people who present for eating disorder treatment fall into this category (Thaw et al., 2001). For a review of the description of ED-NOS, see the *DSM-IV* (APA, 1994). Examples of eating disorders that may fall into this category include BN type syndrome characterized by binges on objectively small amounts of food and purging, and AN without a loss of menses.

Binge Eating Disorder

BED is characterized by binge eating without the presence of compensatory behaviors such as self-induced vomiting or laxative use. For a review of the proposed diagnostic criteria for BED, see the *DSM-IV* (APA, 1994). Prevalence rates for BED are estimated anywhere from 2% in community samples to more than 25% in obese populations (treatment seeking; Yanovski, 1999). However, with the use of strict diagnostic criteria from the *DSM-IV,* full syndrome BED, on average, is found in less than 3% of treatment-seeking obese adults and roughly 1% or less of the adult community population (Williamson & Martin, 1999). Currently, the *DSM-IV* criteria for BED allow binges to be episodic or nonepisodic (Williamson & Martin, 1999). Thus, binge eating in this context may be defined as binge eating in discrete time periods, a constant overeating pattern throughout the day, or a "grazing" pattern of binge eating. This vague definition has led to difficulty in the diagnosis and classification of BED. People with BED typically express shame about their binge eating, concern about their weight (if they are overweight), and a loss of control over the episodes or continual overeating patterns. Socially, people with BED often binge in private and become more socially withdrawn at times to hide their behavior. The primary medical consequences of BED result from complications of overweight and obesity. Associated psychological disturbances include depression and anxiety. Recent review indicates that there is complex heterogeneity in Axis II disorders among people with BED (Sansone et al., 2005). Therefore, it is difficult to ascertain prevalence trends toward certain Axis II disorders in this eating disorder subgroup.

Interviewing Strategies

Semistructured Interview Strategies

The nature of semistructured interviews typically includes a general guide by which an interviewer follows a certain set of questions to interview a client. Most semistructured interviews require clinically trained interviewers (e.g., psychologists) to conduct the interview properly, and some interviews may require special intensive training specific to the measure itself (e.g., the Eating Disorder Examination [EDE]; Cooper & Fairburn, 1987).

Eating Disorders

The purpose of semistructured interviewing strategies for eating disorders is to assess the nature and severity of eating disorder symptoms. This section briefly summarizes the use of semistructured measurement tools in the assessment of eating disorder pathology. Two primary semistructured interviews for eating disorders are the EDE (Cooper & Fairburn, 1987; Fairburn & Cooper, 1993) and the Interview for the Diagnosis of Eating Disorders (IDED-IV; Kutlesic, Williamson, Gleaves, Barbin, & Murphy-Eberenz, 1998). One additional measure with comparable psychometric properties is the Structured Interview for Anorexic and Bulimic Syndromes for *DSM-IV* and *ICD-10* (SIAB-EX; Fichter & Quadflieg, 2000). The SIAB-EX generates diagnoses consistent with both *ICD-10* and *DSM-IV*. Finally, a measure that is used primarily for the assessment of the longitudinal course of psychopathology is the Longitudinal Interval Follow-Up Evaluation (LIFE; Keller et al., 1987).

Eating Disorder Examination. The EDE is a semistructured interview designed to assess the primary psychopathology of eating disorders. The EDE is in its 12th edition and is designed to assess the key features of eating disorders in two ways: the frequency of key behavioral features of eating disorders (e.g., purging) and dimensions of disturbance generated through specific subscales. The EDE includes four subscales: dietary restraint, eating concern, shape concern, and weight concern. Items are rated on a seven-point Likert scale, with the higher scores representing a higher level of severity or frequency. The EDE is conducted by the interviewer, and the interviewer rates the severity of the symptoms as reported by the participant in response to the questions. Because of its investigator-based format and its strong psychometric properties including validity and reliability, it has come to be viewed as the gold standard in the assessment of eating disorders (Grilo, 1998). Although it is a highly recommended measure, the EDE requires special training and is time consuming to administer, which may make it less attractive to use in certain protocols where time is a concern.

Interview for the Diagnosis of Eating Disorders. The IDED-IV is a semistructured interview designed specifically for differential diagnosis of eating disorders using the *DSM-IV* diagnostic criteria for eating disorders (APA, 1994). The IDED-IV questions are related directly to *DSM-IV* diagnostic criteria, and the questions enable the interviewer to establish the presence or absence of the specific diagnostic criteria related to AN, BN, BED, and other various subthreshold presentations of ED-NOS (e.g., night eating syndrome). The IDED-IV has good reliability and validity (Kutlesic et al.,

1998) and is a very user-friendly and reasonably efficient measure to use in clinical or research settings.

Longitudinal Interval Follow-Up Evaluation. The LIFE is a semistructured interview measure that is specifically designed for longitudinal study of mental disorders. A modified version for eating disorders has served as a primary measure of longitudinal studies of eating disorders (Grilo, 2005). The LIFE measure has been found to have adequate psychometric properties (Warshaw, Dyck, Allsworth, Stout, & Keller, 2001).

General Psychopathology

Axis I psychiatric disorders and personality disorders are common associated conditions with eating disorders (Grilo et al., 2003a, 2003b). These associated problems are important targets in assessment and are significant targets for case formulation and treatment. For Axis I disorders, the Structured Clinical Interview for *DSM* Axis I Disorders (SCID-I; Spitzer, Williams, Gibbon, & First, 1992; First, Spitzer, Gibbon, & Williams, 1996) is recommended. For Axis II disorders, there are five reasonably psychometrically sound semistructured interview measures: the Structured Clinical Interview for *DSM* Axis II Disorders (SCID-II; First et al., 1995), the Structured Interview for the *DSM-IV* Personality Disorders (Stangl, Phofl, Zimmerman, Bowers, & Corenthal, 1985), the Diagnostic Interview for Personality Disorders (Zanarini, Frankenburg, Chauncey, & Gunderson, 1987), the Personality Assessment Schedule (Tyrer, Strauss, & Cicchetti, 1983), and the Personality Disorder Examination (Loranger, 1988).

Unstructured Clinical Interview

An unstructured clinical interview is an alternative to the semistructured clinical interview approach. This approach to assessment and diagnosis is more informal and is not guided by specific questions that have been found to valid or reliable. Generally, this format is used when a more efficient collection of information is needed or an update on information is needed from an initial, more thorough assessment. A brief summary of recommended material for inclusion in a general clinical interview for eating disorders is presented in Table 18.1.

INTERVIEWING OBSTACLES AND SOLUTIONS

Obstacles in the Interview Process

Overvalued Ideas. In addition to the key domains of eating disorders, there are many underlying themes and cognitive beliefs that often aid in the maintenance of these disorders. Although the eating disorders AN, BN, ED-NOS, and BED have many differences, they often hold one key feature in common: overvalued ideas (Stewart, 2003). These overvalued ideas are strongly held beliefs that are extremely difficult, if not impossible, for the person to overcome without help. Furthermore, when others try to confront the person with regard to these beliefs, they are met with great resistance. This resistance may come in many forms, including omission of information, denial, minimization, normalization, or simply a lack of recognition that the nature of their behavior is not healthy. Western society values thinness. Therefore, dieting behaviors and exercise behaviors are viewed as "health" behaviors as well as a way to obtain thinness. These behaviors often are supported by society, especially with the current presence of the obesity epidemic. Therefore, it becomes difficult to determine when a health behavior becomes detrimental or beneficial to health. For example, an anorexic person presenting in an interview for an eating disorder may view herself or himself to be in line with the values of society (i.e., engaging in diet and exercise behavior) and may have even been supported for engaging in these behaviors (to a point) by friends and family. In contrast, a person presenting for help with bingeing and purging behaviors would not necessarily view these as "health" behaviors (although the goal of thinness is a valued "healthy" goal) and probably would be viewed by family and peers as "abnormal." Based on the values of society, certain thoughts and behaviors often are "normalized" by the patient and people around them until they become very extreme and threatening to health status, whereas other behaviors are not "normalized." Such patterns in belief systems and thoughts related to behaviors may determine how aware a person is of his or her problems and how willing the person is to cooperate with assessment, especially if the person believes that assessment or treatment may in some way force him or her to give up the overvalued beliefs surrounding his or her efforts to obtain thinness and other eating disorder behaviors.

Table 18.1   Basic Components of an Unstructured Clinical Interview for Eating Disorders

History and current experiences:
    Childhood (0–12 years)
    Adolescence (12–20 years)
    Young adulthood (20–35 years)
    Middle adulthood (35–49 years)
    Late adulthood (50 and older)
	• Patient medical history, including treatment
	• Family medical history
	• Patient psychological history, including treatment
	• Medication history
	• Weight history: weight changes
	• Developmental history: mental and physical
	• Key life events
	• Social history
	• Family environment
	• Education and work history
	• Overall life functioning

Current psychological symptoms	• Eating disorder symptoms • Body image disturbance • General psychopathology • Personality disorder symptoms • Self-perception: physical and mental • Self-esteem
Current behavioral symptoms	• Restrictive eating • Binge eating • Compensatory behaviors • Excessive exercise • Behaviors associated with general psychopathology (e.g., social isolation associated with depression) • Behaviors associated with personality disorders (e.g., cutting)
Current physical complications and/or medical consequences	• See Table 18.2 or Pomeroy (2004)

Partial Reporting. Partial reporting is common in patients referred to treatment by a family member, friend, or spouse. However, it can be observed in someone presenting for treatment who is self-referred. In the first case, patients who are not self-referred often are resistant to the interview process and may attempt to deceive the interviewer or omit pertinent information related to binge eating or weight control behaviors. Because these thoughts and behaviors often are secretive, they fear that exposure could lead to someone forcing them to change, leading them to be "fat" or "out of control." In the second case, even though some clients/patients present for treatment on their own and really desire an understanding of their problems and treatment, they are often embarrassed or ashamed to share details and may minimize behaviors or severity in order to appear socially desirable during the assessment process. Both of these cases serve as significant barriers to initial information collection.

The Inexperienced Interviewer

• *Don't walk in unprepared.* Very few interviews are designed for the inexperienced clinician. Furthermore, some of the well-established interviews require more intensive training even for experienced clinicians (e.g., the EDE). People with eating disorders are extremely difficult to assess and treat and have a highly specialized group of symptoms and behaviors. It is unwise to approach assessment, particularly an interview modality, with little or no experience with eating disorder populations.

• *Don't alienate.* People who present for assessment for eating disorders vary in family history, age level, and ethnic and cultural background. Furthermore, they often have unique life experiences. Even within diagnostic categories, no two cases ever look the same. Ideally, the patient should feel like part of the assessment team, working toward a common goal. Placing too much focus on the disorder itself and not on the person engaged in the interview can alienate the person and disengage him or her from the assessment process.

- *Don't be insensitive.* Professional distance from clients/patients is important. Interviewers with a history of eating disorders should not divulge this information to the client/patient. However, it is important that people being assessed and engaged in an interview feel as though they arc identified with and that their struggle is valid. Therefore, it is also not recommended to talk down to the interviewee. Taking either one of these approaches may eventually sabotage the overall rapport and effectiveness of therapeutic relationship for the purposes of assessment and treatment.

- *Don't push it.* Assessment for an eating disorder often involves fear, anxiety, and feelings of loss of control. The line between gathering details of symptoms and pushing the client to divulge personal information is a fine one. Assessment often is a gradual process, and trying to be too efficient or trying to obtain information aggressively will not promote the goal of an adequate assessment.

- *Don't plant ideas.* The power of implication can be significant during the interview. Don't suggest reasons why a person might have the eating disorder, particularly ones that have not been shown in the literature to have a causal relationship (e.g., sexual trauma). This type of suggestion could be damaging to people who have experienced this type of trauma but are not ready to divulge such things in the interview, and it could be damaging to people who have not experienced this type of trauma because it could give them ideas for processing when they are most vulnerable that are unrelated to their actual life experiences.

Recommendations and Solutions

Neutralization of Ideas. As a rule, the interview is not the time to challenge overvalued ideas; however, it is important to recognize the potential relevance of overvalued ideas. Working through overvalued ideas related to eating disorders is a long-term process and is best accomplished when genuine rapport and a commitment to the treatment process have been established. It's often the case that challenging some of these notions, even

minimally, without fully understanding them can threaten the credibility of the interviewer, compromise the interview, and make motivating the person to enter treatment difficult.

Gathering the Whole Story. In most cases, it is difficult to learn the full scope of the symptoms and severity in one interview. The initial interview can serve as a good basis from which to move forward in the assessment and treatment of eating disorders, however. In this process, it is important to act as a scientist, formulating hypotheses in order to ask additional questions needed to fill in any missing information. If an interviewee appears to be uncomfortable divulging certain types of information, it is important to note that because this information can be revisited when greater rapport is established. In most cases, it is necessary to corroborate reports with family members or friends. Furthermore, it is possible that certain behaviors that occur only in secret (e.g., bingeing and purging), which the client/patient is very ashamed of, may be observed only in a hospital setting.

The Experienced Interviewer

- *Do get proper training.* Interviewers should get the proper training in the use of semistructured interviews for eating disorders and should practice. Having colleagues simulate certain disorders in order to practice rating severity and to compare reliability with others' ratings will help beginning therapists become more precise information gatherers and symptom raters, which helps build confidence. This process eventually benefits both the interviewer and the client/patient, making the entire process more accurate and effective.

- *Do humanize the situation.* Reducing the stigma of eating disorders through education, including prevalence data, sociocultural influences, and maintenance factors can help the client/patient become more comfortable disclosing information as he or she feels understood and not "crazy." It is also important to take into account cultural considerations and developmental level. The more the interview process is tailored to the interviewee's greatest level of understanding and unique needs, the more willing he or she will be to cooperate with the process.

- *Do express empathy.* Maintaining authority and rapport is a delicate balance in any therapeutic relationship, but with regard to eating disorder assessment and treatment, this relationship is particularly difficult. This is the case because so often the client/patient believes that it is the interviewer's sole purpose to take control away from clients/patients and possibly make them do things against their wishes (e.g., eat larger amounts of food without purging or gain weight). Therefore, the interviewer should be as empathetic as possible, which enables rapport and validates the person's struggle. Furthermore, the clinician can use generic examples to illustrate points to express empathy or humanize details without making reference to eating disorder experiences he or she has had personally.

• *Do accept that comprehensive assessment is a process.* It is important to accept that not all of the necessary and relevant information can be obtained in one interview session. Assessment is a process, and significant amounts of information are learned over time. The interview often is one of the first steps in the process. In this step it is important to establish rapport, gather symptom information, make a diagnosis if possible, and formulate hypotheses about case formulation and maintenance factors in order to do further assessment and treatment planning.

• *Do allow each interview to be an individual information-gathering process.* The interview is designed for the purpose of gathering information. This preliminary process is not designed to guide or lead the client/patient to specific conclusions about his or her situation. The interview is the first step in this information-gathering process and is also designed to establish rapport with the patient. Because the entire assessment process may involve several meetings over time and other forms of assessment (e.g., behavioral assessment), typically a feedback session is conducted in which a case formulation may be hypothesized and discussed with the client/patient. However, it is important that the interview process remain one of discovery and not be influenced by preliminary hypotheses or biases on the part of the interviewer.

Case Illustration With Dialogue

The following dialogue is an excerpt from a semistructured diagnostic interview for eating disorders. The interviewer's questions are drawn from the IDED-IV, developed by Kutlesic et al.

(1998). This interview is designed to cover the bases of the core diagnostic features of eating disorders; however, additional questions often are needed to identify further relevant details for different interviewees. The following paragraphs describe the case example. The dialogue represents excerpts from a longer interview process.

The patient, Abby, was a 20-year-old single Caucasian woman who presented at a hospital treatment program for eating disorders, accompanied by her parents. She entered treatment at 5 feet, 6 inches tall and 98 pounds, with a body mass index (BMI) of 16. She had not had a menstrual period in 4 months and was experiencing fatigue and dehydration. Abby was somewhat resistant to entering treatment but was open to finding relief for some of her symptoms (e.g., the need to binge and purge). She did not feel that certain habits were "useful," and they were causing her to have physical complications, such as extensive dental problems (e.g., many root canals in a short period of time), fatigue (not as productive in her sports activities), stomach pain, and "bloating."

Abby was an athlete at an early age and excelled in a number of activities, including basketball. She was a good student in school and was the youngest sibling in her family, with two older sisters and one older brother, all of whom excelled at sports. Abby's family members were of normal weight, and Abby was worried that she would look like her sisters as she began to get older, which included a somewhat bulky, masculine body shape. She also had concerns about not living up to the achievement in sports that her sisters had accomplished. Even though she was a college student, she still lived at home with her parents. She did not socialize with college friends and maintain a normal college life (e.g., attending social activities). Abby maintained a fairly rigid schedule of exercise, schoolwork, and sports that resulted in emotional withdrawal from her parents. She often avoided family meals even though she had no social plans. She would engage in chores, such as mowing the grass (additional exercise), or say she would eat later, which usually resulted in night bingeing and purging via self-induced vomiting and exercise rituals including running and sit-ups.

Interviewer:	What are your current concerns regarding your eating and your body weight?
Abby:	I feel that my current body weight is okay, but I do not want to go over

100 pounds. I also really would like to gain control over my overeating because I am worried it will lead me to gain weight.

I: On a typical day, what do you eat?

A: I typically do not eat all day if I can. Sometimes I will drink some Diet Coke if I get hungry. At night, if I get really hungry, which I sometimes do, I will eat some salad, maybe some rice and meat with my family at dinner, and I will feel very full and fat.

I: When dieting, what do you eat?

A: I really do not "diet." I try to not eat as much as possible, as often as possible. People, in general, eat too much. They say it all of the time on the news. Everyone is fat, and everyone is getting bigger and bigger. It is a good thing to eat healthy [endorsement of "health" behavior].

I: When did you first begin to lose weight by restricting your eating?

A: About a year ago. I weighed myself in the locker room one day and realized I had reached 130 pounds. That is just too much. That is what "heavy" people weigh, and it was weighing me down on the basketball court. Also, my sisters weigh that much and they look big. They are a size 6. You just look better if you are thinner [possible endorsement of overvalued idea].

I: Are there any factors or situations that seem to *increase* your periods of restrictive eating?

A: When I am stressed out over a test at school or when I have a game coming up or something like that. I feel like I have to be "on," in other words, perform and look good doing it. Also, if I weigh in the morning and it's close to 100, then I need to bring it down. I have to be under 100 pounds to look good and play good [endorsement of overvalued idea].

I: Are there any factors or situations that seem to *decrease* your periods of restrictive eating?

A: Not really, because I've been doing this so long that now, when I try to

relax, it's all I can think about, and I'm constantly thinking about ways I can do a better job at getting my body into shape to do better at sports and look better [obsessional thinking]. It's a full-time job. You can't rest or it will sneak up on you [endorsement of a preoccupation with thinness]. You see all the time on TV, one minute a model is thin and the next she has gained like 20 pounds; that's totally out of control! That is why our country is so overweight [rationalization of the pursuit of extreme thinness due to idea that obesity is a problem].

I: Do you feel that your weight is normal right now?

A: Yes. I feel that I'm not one of those "sick" people that want to be 60 pounds or something, but I think 100 pounds is reasonable [denial and minimization of the seriousness of her BMI of 16]. It's what everyone wants to be. I think it is a healthy weight for me.

I: How often do you weigh yourself?

A: Usually at least twice a day, morning and night, but if I eat something, like at night, I'll weigh after I eat [reflects preoccupation with body size and weight].

I: What emotional reaction would you have if you gained 2 pounds?

A: I would do more exercise, probably try to bring it down again. If I could do that, I wouldn't react that much.

I: What emotional reaction would you have if you gained 5 pounds?

A: I would freak out and probably be really down. I probably wouldn't leave the house until I could lose it. I would run and mow the grass and stuff. I might add some sit-ups.

I: What emotional reaction would you have if you gained 10 pounds?

A: Honestly, that would never happen because I keep things too much under control. I can't even imagine. It's too hard to think about. I would be so down, but I would be panicked about how to get it off. When I think about it, my palms sweat [endorsement of severe fears of becoming fat or gaining small amounts of weight].

I: Do you wish to be thinner than you are now?

A: Hmmm, I could tone up a bit. I don't want to just be fit, I want to *look* fit.

I: Do you think or worry a lot about your weight and body size?

A: It's all I think about. I wake up in the middle of the night and think, "Hey, I can do a few sit-ups, I've got the energy." Sometimes, I never go back to sleep.

I: Do you ever feel fat?

A: Yes. My clothes touch me too much. Like when I eat, I feel my clothes, and I like them to feel loose, like I have room.

I: Tell me more about that.

A: If I eat too much, I don't do this too much, I feel bloated, and [voice lowers, expressing feelings of shame] I have to get rid of it. Sometimes, I throw up.

I: What is too much?

A: If I eat dinner with my family sometimes, they make me eat what they eat, like rice, salad, and meat. It's a lot and it makes my stomach hurt. I can't take it.

I: Do you ever binge [rapidly consume a large amount of food in a discrete period of time, e.g., 2 hours]?

A: Sometimes if I get really hungry and haven't eaten all day I will get up late at night when everyone is sleeping and eat some things [endorsement of hiding binge eating].

I: What kind of foods?

A: Like cereal, ice cream, things like that.

I: How much food do you eat during a binge?

A: Sometimes, half a box of cereal and maybe a pint of ice cream and some cookies if we have some.

I: How long does the eating last?

A: Not too long, maybe 30 minutes or so. That is about all I can take, and then I just feel sick, and disgusting, like I'm a bad person or something. I'm so ashamed [endorsement of shame surrounding binge eating].

I: Do you feel you can stop eating once a binge has begun?

A: No. Usually I'm kind of into it until I start feeling stomach pain, then, I wake up and realize, "Oh my gosh, if I don't stop, I'll get fat." I feel so out of control [endorsement of feeling out of control related to binge eating].

I: When binge eating, do you feel your eating is more rapid than normal?

A: Yes. I'm such a pig. I feel so full, like I could pop.

I: Do you ever feel as though you have overeaten when you eat small portions of certain fattening foods?

A: Yes. I feel full if I eat anything, especially if I've gone all day without eating. My stomach is shrunk, which is what I like. I have thrown up two cookies before because I could feel them in my stomach taking up space. Also, it just bothers me to know they are there.

I: Explain that.

A: I feel worse when I eat bad food than when I eat pure food. When I eat bad food, no matter how much, I don't want it in my body.

I: Define "bad food."

A: High carb, high sugar, high fat. Anything that can make me fat [defining "forbidden foods"].

I: Define "pure food."

A: Anything that is low in calories that cannot make me fat. Lettuce is a good example. No one can deny that lettuce is a health food [attempting to normalize thoughts and behavior].

Abby presented with low body weight, restrictive eating behavior, binge eating, and purgative behavior, including self-induced vomiting and excessive exercise. In addition, she would offer to do extra chores for her parents (e.g., mow the grass several times per week), and her parents would concede, not catching on to her intentions (i.e., to burn extra calories). Throughout the interview, Abby alluded to a strong fear of fatness and a drive for thinness, rationalizing that weight gain—or in her mind "obesity"—was "unhealthy." She also reported desiring a very low weight (100 pounds) for her height under the same caveat. Abby expressed shame related to her binge eating and reported engaging in behaviors to hide it. However, she endorsed her "healthy" behaviors and openly reported her exercise habits and her justification for why it was "healthy" behavior. She admitted to being preoccupied with her body size and weight and endorsed avoidance of forbidden foods. Abby also began to admit that on some level the thoughts and behaviors related to her eating disorder had become difficult to maintain even though she valued them, which was taken as a sign of some level of motivation for change. In sum, Abby was diagnosed with anorexia nervosa, binge-purge subtype, and was referred for treatment, beginning with an inpatient level of care to stabilize weight, reduce bingeing and purging behaviors, work toward healthy eating and exercise patterns, and reduce overvalued ideation related to eating, and body size and shape.

MULTICULTURAL AND DIVERSITY ISSUES

Over the years, research has challenged the notion that eating disorders and body image disturbances are limited to Caucasian populations, with more evidence that eating disorders and body image disturbance are present in men and women and in people of diverse ethnicities (e.g., African American, Latin American, and Asian populations: Yanovski, 2000). However, the presentations of such symptoms and concerns are complex and not fully understood. When assessing people for eating disorders, clinicians and researchers must take into account the intricate interactions between psychological, social, and ethnic factors that play a role in eating disorders. Throughout the literature, several important variables have emerged, including gender, ethnicity, and culture.

Men

Historically, research has focused on eating disorders and body image concerns in women. It is now clear that body dissatisfaction is common among men (Adams, Turner, & Bucks, 2005). The results of a recent study show that body dissatisfaction plays a key role in the relationship between homosexuality and eating disorder symptoms (Hospers & Jansen, 2005). However, body image concerns and eating disorders are not limited to homosexual men. Other issues related to body image concerns in men are steroid abuse (Blouin & Goldfield, 1995) and a "reverse anorexia nervosa" (Pope, Katz, & Hudson, 1993), later renamed "muscle dysmorphia" (Pope, Gruber, Choi, Olivardia, & Phillips, 1997). Muscle dysmorphia is characterized by the belief that the person looks small even though in reality he or she is of normal size or very muscular (Pope et al., 2005). This belief, not unlike other body image concerns, may lead men to engage in eating disorder behaviors to achieve their desired body size and shape, such as excessive exercise, unhealthy eating habits, and substance use.

African American and Hispanic Women

Overweight and obesity often are a risk factor for eating disorders. Given this fact, African American and Hispanic girls may be at risk for eating disorders because of their greater propensity for being overweight. African American women have been shown to be less likely to diet than their Caucasian counterparts (Akan & Grilo, 1995). African American women and adolescents have been shown to have less body size dissatisfaction and choose a larger "ideal body size" than Caucasian women in studies of body image (Stewart, Williamson, Allen, & Han, 2005; Williamson, White, Newton, Alfonso, & Stewart, 2005). However, in a recent study of psychiatrically hospitalized female adolescents, African American adolescents endorsed some eating disorder symptoms at similar rates as Caucasian girls (White & Grilo, 2005). Recent studies show that Latina adolescents (ages 11–20) have prevalence rates of eating disorders consistent with U.S. trends (Granillo, Jones-Rodriguez, & Carvajal, 2005). Body dissatisfaction, substance use, low self-esteem, and negative affectivity were some of the main risk factors for the development of eating disorders in this population. In a recent study examining predictors of body image dissatisfaction and disturbed eating attitudes and behaviors in African American and Hispanic girls, approximately 13% of the Hispanic girls and 10% of the African American girls met criteria for a diagnosis of a probable eating disorder. In this study, fear of negative evaluation was a key differentiating factor between the groups with eating disorder symptoms and groups without eating disorder symptoms (Vander & Thomas, 2004).

Asian Women

The study of body image disturbance and eating disorders in Asian populations has increased significantly in the past 20 years. Over this time period, research has generated conflicting results and many methodological problems associated with studying this population. The current *DSM* diagnostic criteria may not be appropriate for capturing eating disorder symptom patterns in Asian populations because they often present with different symptom profiles than their Western counterparts (Cummins, Simmons, & Zane, 2005). For example, it has been observed that some groups who receive treatment for eating disorders in Asian countries (e.g., Hong Kong, India) may be less likely to present with symptoms of body image disturbance than patients in Westernized countries. This makes it difficult to draw conclusions from studies directly comparing prevalence rates of eating disorders in Western countries and Asian countries. Furthermore, Asian countries are not homogenous. Research has yielded different results based on the population and country in which investigations have taken place.

Acculturation

Finally, there is a continuing debate on whether acculturation lends itself to higher or lower rates of eating disorders. A recent study concluded that the prevalence of eating disorders in non-Western countries is lower than that in Western countries but appears to be increasing (Makino et al., 2004). However, the results of many studies examining whether higher levels of acculturation led to higher levels of eating disorders in members of the minority group (e.g., Asians) acculturating to the dominant group (Westerners) are mixed. For a review, see Cummins et al. (2005).

Differential Diagnosis and Behavioral Assessment

In order to differentially diagnose AN, BN, BED, or ED-NOS, the interviewer must ask specific questions to determine the presence or absence of particular symptoms and the nature of those symptoms. The key domains that are used in differential diagnosis include body size, restrictive eating, binge eating, compensatory behavior (e.g., purging), body image disturbance, and general psychopathology. Furthermore, it is often beneficial to take into account physical complications and medical conditions (e.g., dehydration, constipation). Table 18.2 summarizes the primary symptoms required for differential diagnosis of AN, BN, ED-NOS, and BED.

Behavioral Assessment

It is useful to supplement interview methods with behavioral assessment methods and self-report methods to corroborate information obtained through interviews, particularly with regard to body image (Stewart & Williamson, 2004a). Furthermore, clients/patients with eating disorders often have special problems that are unique to concerns about eating and body size and shape, including body checking, food craving, and muscle dysmorphia (Stewart & Williamson, 2006). Two methods of behavioral assessment are described here.

Self-Monitoring. Self-monitoring of food intake is a method of gaining insight about the eating patterns or eating experiences of people diagnosed with eating disorders. Self-monitoring of food intake may include types and amounts of food eaten, temporal eating patterns, frequency and topography of binge episodes and purgative behavior, and mood before and after the meal (Williamson, 1990). There is controversy over the reliability and validity of self-reported binge-purge episodes and food intake (Anderson & Maloney, 2001). In addition, because of the shame they experience, some people with eating disorders deliberately minimize or deny eating pathology on self-report forms (Crowther & Sherwood, 1997). Despite these concerns, self-monitoring can be a useful clinical tool in addition to other measurement tools for the assessment of eating disorder symptoms.

Test or Therapeutic Meals. Test meals may be used as part of the assessment or treatment process for eating disorders. A test meal allows the clinician or researcher to observe the direct act of food consumption. This is particularly useful in the event that the client/patient omits key details about his or her eating habits during self-monitoring. This method of assessment may be used for observing eating behavior (e.g., rate of eating, anxiety while

Table 18.2   Guidelines for Differential Diagnosis of Eating Disorders

Eating Disorder Diagnosis	Presenting Symptoms for Diagnosis	Common Associated Symptoms	Common Physical Complications	Symptoms Contraindicated for Diagnosis
Anorexia nervosa, restricting type	• 15% below normal body weight • Severe restrictive eating • Fear of weight gain • Loss of menses • Body image disturbance	• Depression • Anxiety • Denial or minimization of the seriousness of weight status or weight loss	• Inanition • Bradycardia • Hypotension • Hair loss • Low body temperature • Dry skin • Lanugo • Brittle hair or nails • Loss of or irregular menses • Cold intolerance • Headache • Fatigue	• Normal weight or overweight • Binge eating • Purgative behavior
Anorexia nervosa, binge-purge type	• 15% below normal body weight • Severe restrictive eating • Fear of weight gain • Loss of menses • Presence of bingeing and purging • Body image disturbance	• Depression • Anxiety • Denial or minimization of the seriousness of weight status or weight loss	• All physical complications associated with restricting type possible • Physical complications with bulimia nervosa, binge-purge type possible	• Normal weight or overweight
Bulimia nervosa, binge-purge type	• Normal to 10% below or above normal weight • Frequent binge eating • Frequent purging, such as self-induced vomiting or misuse of laxatives, diuretics, or enemas • Body image disturbance	• Denial or minimization of binge-purge behaviors • Anxiety • Depression • Social isolation	• Erosion of dental enamel • Peripheral edema • Salivary gland enlargement • Abrasions on fingers or back of hand from self-induced vomiting • Fatigue • Headaches • Constipation • Abdominal bloating • Irregular menses	• Emaciation • Absence of bingeing and purging
Bulimia nervosa, nonpurging type	• Normal to 10% below or above normal weight • Frequent binge eating • Fasting or excessive exercise as compensatory behavior • Body image disturbance	• Shame regarding binge eating • Concern about weight • Anxiety • Depression	• Peripheral edema • Fatigue • Dry skin • Dehydration • Headaches • Constipation • Abdominal bloating • Irregular menses	• Use of vomiting, diuretics, or enemas as a method of purging
Binge eating disorder	• Frequent binge eating • Normal weight, overweight, or obese	• Shame regarding binge eating • Concern about weight • Anxiety • Depression • Social isolation	• Complications of obesity	• Compensatory behavior • Low to emaciated weight

eating, food mixing). Caloric intake may be calculated as well. Furthermore, with the use of a hierarchy of feared foods, this activity is useful as exposure with response prevention for the consumption of feared or "forbidden" foods and the act of consuming food in general (Stewart & Williamson, 2004c).

SELECTION OF TREATMENT TARGETS AND REFERRAL

The following are treatment targets as suggested by Stewart and Williamson (2004c). These targets are listed in the order in which they would logically be addressed in the treatment process.

1. The client/patient and family members must be educated with regard to eating disorders, body image, and the client's/patient's case conceptualization and process of treatment. This objective serves the function of putting to rest misconceptions and misinformation about eating disorders and treatment and provides accurate information to facilitate treatment and the client/patient and family roles in that process.

2. Medical complications that have developed as a result of starvation, binge eating, or purging must be corrected. In conjunction with this focus, the establishment of a healthy weight is key to reducing medical risk. The objective is that as the body weight stabilizes to a healthy level, clients/patients will become more cognizant of and responsive to other treatment modalities.

3. Establishment and stabilization of healthy eating patterns are essential for maintaining healthy weight, including a healthy schedule of eating, nutritionally sound eating (recommended content and quantity of food), and adherence to recommended meal plans.

4. Physical activity habits must be modified to promote healthy weight gain or loss, followed by healthy weight maintenance. A prescribed exercise plan to facilitate the client's/patient's recovery, eliminating compulsive exercise or sedentary behavior, is recommended. For example, anorexic clients/patients who need to gain weight may need no exercise for a length of time, whereas overweight clients/patients may need exercise in order to reach treatment goals.

5. Resolution of the psychological problems that contributed to the development and maintenance of the eating disorder is important in achieving remission or recovery. These psychological goals include enhanced awareness and processing of biased information and obsessive and rigid behaviors related to eating and weight.

6. Modification of body image disturbance is a core target to be addressed in treatment but often cannot be addressed until more critical elements are stabilized (e.g., refeeding). This involves many components that aim to promote the evolution of distorted and dissatisfied thoughts related to the body into a more neutral and accepting stance (Stewart, 2004).

7. Functioning in the social and family relationships must be enhanced, marked by greater overall comfort in relationships and enhanced cooperative and effective communication.

8. Strategies must be developed for relapse prevention, marked by sustained awareness of and adherence to health behaviors and establishment of and adherence to specific plans for the management of high-risk situations that may lead to recurrence of eating disorder perceptions, thoughts, beliefs, and behaviors.

SOURCE: Adapted from Stewart & Williamson (2004a).

With these targets in mind, different levels of care are needed for different levels of severity of eating disorders. Typically, people with greater medical risk (e.g., extremely low body weight) or severe behavioral patterns (e.g., severe purging) will need inpatient care. However, some people are well suited for care at lower levels (e.g., partial hospitalization or outpatient levels) and move toward a remission of symptoms with success. A summary of requirements for the different levels of treatment is provided in Table 18.3. For further information on multidisciplinary treatment of eating disorders and levels of care, see Stewart and Williamson (2004b).

SUMMARY

The assessment of eating disorders is complex. Psychological, behavioral, medical, and social factors coalesce to form the syndromes described by the *DSM-IV* diagnostic criteria. Eating disorders

Table 18.3   Eating Disorder Treatment Referral: Levels of Care

Level of Care	Criteria
Inpatient	**Criteria for Admission to Inpatient Level of Care** • The patient is medically unstable. • The patient weighs less than 85% of his or her ideal body weight. • The patient is suicidal or homicidal. **Criteria for Step Down to Lower Level of Care** • The patient is medically stable but may have binge-purge cycles and is participating in less restrictive eating. • The patient is 85–92% of his or her ideal body weight. • The patient is not homicidal or suicidal.
Partial hospitalization	**Criteria for Admission to Partial Hospitalization Level of Care** • The patient is medically stable but may have binge-purge cycles or restrictive eating. • Patient is not suicidal or homicidal. • Patient is motivated for treatment. • Patient has body weight that is between 85% and 92% of his or her ideal body weight. **Criteria for Step Down to Lower Level of Care** • The patient has had a significant decrease in binge eating and purging behaviors. • The patient is not suicidal or homicidal. • The patient is willing to participate in treatment and motivated. • The patient achieves a stable body weight greater than 92% of his or her ideal body weight.
Intensive outpatient	**Criteria for Admission to Intensive Outpatient Level of Care** • The patient is medically stable. • The patient is not suicidal or homicidal. • The patient exhibits a significant decrease in restrictive eating or binge-purge behaviors. • The patient exhibits improved nutrition. • The patient actively participated in the treatment process and discharge planning. • The patient continues to need structure. • The patient exhibits self-motivation to achieve recovery from eating disorder symptoms. **Criteria for Step Down to Lower Level of Care** • The patient is medically stable. • The patient is not suicidal or homicidal. • The patient's levels of bingeing and purging are not severe. • The patient's nutritional status is not severe. • The patient is willing to participate in the treatment planning and discharge planning process but continues to need structure in care. • The patient's body weight is greater than 92% of his or her ideal body weight.
Aftercare or traditional outpatient	• Individual outpatient treatment with a therapist or psychiatrist. • Weekly support group. • Family therapy. • Family support group.

are multifaceted disorders. In this regard, interview questions must span psychological, behavioral, medical, and social factors to help the interviewer gain a clear idea of the person's needs. Furthermore, although eating disorders share common patterns, eating disorders from individual to individual are rarely the same, particularly with regard to historical factors and variables that maintain the eating disorder symptoms. It is particularly important in the interview to cover these bases when gathering the details of each person's story. A key feature of some interviewees is a reluctance to come forward with information that they feel ashamed of, so an empathetic, understanding, and guiding approach is necessary in the interview process in order to reach a clinically relevant outcome. Finally, the interview process is key to the identification of all treatment targets, prioritization of those targets, and referral to appropriate treatment based on the urgency of the patient's needs and the assessment of treatment progress over time. The interview often acts as the core of the assessment, with behavioral assessment, self-report measures, and self-monitoring tools supplementing the information collected in the interview. Though often time consuming, the interview can be a remarkable tool for rapport building, diagnosis, case conceptualization, development of treatment targets and planning, and the measurement of treatment outcome.

REFERENCES

Adams, G., Turner, H., & Bucks, R. (2005). The experience of body dissatisfaction in men. *Body Image,* 2(3), 271–284.

Akan, G. E., & Grilo, C. M. (1995). Sociocultural influences on eating attitudes and behaviors, body image, and psychological functioning: A comparison of African-American, Asian-American, and Caucasian college women. *International Journal of Eating Disorders,* 18, 181–187.

American Psychiatric Association. (1994). *Diagnostic and statistical manual of mental disorders* (4th ed.). Washington, DC: Author.

American Psychiatric Association Work Group on Eating Disorders. (2000). Practice guideline for the treatment of patients with eating disorders (revision). *American Journal of Psychiatry,* 157(1), 1–39.

Anderson, D. A., & Maloney, K. C. (2001). The efficacy of cognitive-behavioral therapy on the core symptoms of bulimia nervosa. *Clinical Psychology Review,* 21, 971–988.

Blouin, A. G., & Goldfield, G. S. (1995). Body image and steroid use in male bodybuilders. *International Journal of Eating Disorders,* 18, 159–165.

Cooper, Z., & Fairburn, C. G. (1987). The Eating Disorder Examination: A semistructured interview for the assessment of specific psychopathology of eating disorders. *International Journal of Eating Disorders,* 6, 1–8.

Crowther, J. H., & Sherwood, N. E. (1997). Assessment. In D. M. Garner & P. E. Garfinkel (Eds.), *Handbook of treatment for eating disorders* (2nd ed., pp. 34–49). New York: Guilford.

Cummins, L. H., Simmons, A. M., & Zane, N. W. S. (2005). Eating disorders in Asian populations: A critique of current approaches to the study of culture, ethnicity, and eating disorders. *American Journal of Orthopsychiatry,* 75(4), 553–574.

Fairburn, C. G., & Cooper, Z. (1993). The eating disorder examination. In C. G. Fairburn & G. T. Wilson (Eds.), *Binge eating: Nature, assessment, and treatment* (pp. 361–404). New York: Guilford.

Fichter, M. M., & Quadflieg, N. (2000). Comparing self- and expert rating: A self-report screening version (SIAB-S) of the Structured Interview for Anorexic and Bulimic Syndromes for *DSM-IV* and *ICD-10* (SIAB-EX). *European Archives of Psychiatry and Clinical Neuroscience,* 250, 175–185.

First, M. B., Spitzer, R. L., Gibbon, M., & Williams, J. B. W. (1996). *Structured Clinical Interview for* DSM-IV *Axis I Disorders: Patient version (SCID-I, Version 2.0).* New York: New York State Psychiatric Institute.

First, M. B., Spitzer, R. L., Gibbon, M., Williams, J. B. W., Davies, M., Borus, J., et al. (1995). The Structured Clinical Interview for *DSM-III-R* Personality Disorders (SCID-II). Part II: Multisite test-retest reliability study. *Journal of Personality Disorders,* 9, 92–104.

Granillo, T., Jones-Rodriguez, G., & Carvajal, S. C. (2005). Prevalence of eating disorders in Latina adolescents: Associations with substance use and other correlates. *Journal of Adolescent Health,* 36(3), 214–220.

Grilo, C. M. (1998). The assessment and treatment of binge eating disorder. *Journal of Practical Psychiatry and Behavioral Health,* 4, 191–201.

Grilo, C. M. (2005). The use of structured instruments in the assessments of patients with eating disorders. In J. Mitchell & C. Peterson (Eds.), *The assessment of patients with eating disorders* (pp. 79–97). New York: Guilford.

Grilo, C. M., Sanislow, C. A., Shea, M. T., Skodol, A. E., Stout, R. L., Pagano, M. E., et al. (2003a). The natural course of bulimia nervosa and eating disorder not otherwise specified is not influenced by personality disorders. *International Journal of Eating Disorders,* 34, 319–330.

Grilo, C. M., Sanislow, C. A., Skodol, A. E., Gunderson, J. G., Stout, R. L., Shea, M. T., et al. (2003b). Do eating disorders co-occur with personality disorders?: Comparison groups matter. *International Journal of Eating Disorders,* 33, 155–164.

Gull, N. W. (1874). Anorexia nervosa (apepsia hysterica, anorexia hysterica). *Transactions of Clinical Endocrinological Metabolism,* 49, 806–809.

Hospers, H. J., & Jansen, A. (2005). Why homosexuality is a risk factor for eating disorders in males. *Journal of Social and Clinical Psychology,* 24(8), 1188–1201.

Keller, M. B., Lavori, P. W., Friedman, B., Nielson, E., Endicott, J., McDonald-Scott, P., et al. (1987). The Longitudinal Interval Follow-up Evaluation: A comprehensive method for assessing outcome in prospective longitudinal studies. *Archives of General Psychiatry, 44,* 540–548.

Kutlesic, V., Williamson, D. A., Gleaves, D. H., Barbin, J. M., & Murphy-Eberenz, K. P. (1998). The interview for the diagnosis of eating disorders–IV: Application to *DSM-IV* diagnostic criteria. *Psychological Assessment, 10,* 41–48.

Loranger, A. W. (1988). *Personality disorder examination.* Yonkers, NY: DV Communications.

Makino, M., Tsuboi, K., & Dennerstein, L. (2004). Prevalence of eating disorders: A comparison of Western and non-Western countries. *Medscape General Medicine, 6*(3), 49.

Pomeroy, C. (2004). Assessment of medical status and physical factors. In J. K. Thompson (Ed.), *Handbook of eating disorders and obesity* (pp. 81–111). New York: Wiley.

Pope, H. G., Jr., Gruber, A. J., Choi, P. Y., Olivardia, R., & Phillips, K. A. (1997). Muscle dysmorphia disorder. *Psychosomatics, 38,* 548–557.

Pope, H. G., Katz, D. L, & Hudson, J. I. (1993). Anorexia nervosa and "reverse anorexia" among 108 bodybuilders. *Comprehensive Psychiatry, 34,* 406–409.

Pope, C. G., Pope, H. G., Menard, W., Fay, C., Olivardia, R., & Phillips, K. (2005). Clinical features of muscle dysmorphia among males with body dysmorphic disorder. *Body Image, 2,* 395–400.

Russell, G. F. M. (1979). Bulimia nervosa: An ominous variant of anorexia nervosa. *Psychological Medicine, 9,* 429–448.

Sansone, R. A., Levitt, J. L., & Sansone, L. A. (2005). The prevalence of personality disorders among those with eating disorders. *Eating Disorders, 13,* 7–21.

Spitzer, R. L., Williams, J. B. W., Gibbon, M., & First, M. B. (1992). The Structured Clinical Interview for *DSM-III-R* (SCID): History, rationale, and description. *Archives of General Psychiatry, 49,* 624–629.

Stangl, D., Phofl, B., Zimmerman, M., Bowers, W., & Corenthal, C. (1985). A structured interview for the *DSM-III* personality disorders. *Archives of General Psychiatry, 42,* 591–596.

Stewart, T. M. (2003, November). *Light on body image: Acceptance through mindfulness.* An oral presentation presented at the Advancement of Behavior Therapy, Boston, MA.

Stewart, T. M. (2004). Light on body image treatment: Acceptance through mindfulness. *Behavior Modification, 28*(6), 783–811.

Stewart, T. M., & Williamson, D. A. (2004a). Assessment of body image disturbances. In J. K. Thompson (Ed.), *Handbook of eating disorders and obesity* (pp. 495–514). New York: Wiley.

Stewart, T. M., & Williamson, D. A. (2004b). Multidisciplinary treatment of eating disorders I: Structure and costs of treatment. *Behavior Modification, 28*(6), 812–830.

Stewart, T. M., & Williamson, D. A. (2004c). Multidisciplinary treatment of eating disorders II: Primary goals and content of treatment, a mindful approach. *Behavior Modification, 28*(6), 831–853.

Stewart, T. S., & Williamson, D. A. (2006). Eating disorders. In M. Hersen (Ed.), *Clinician's handbook of adult behavioral assessment* (pp. 253–278). Philadelphia: Brunner-Routledge.

Stewart, T. M., Williamson, D. A., Allen, H. R., & Han, H. (2005, October). *The Body Morph Assessment Version 2.0 (BMA 2.0): Psychometrics and interesting findings.* Poster presented at the North American Society for the Study of Obesity, Vancouver, BC.

Thaw, J. M., Williamson, D. A., & Martin, C. K. (2001). Impact of altering *DSM-IV* criteria for anorexia and bulimia nervosa on the base rates of eating disorder diagnoses. *Eating and Weight Disorders, 6*(3), 121–129.

Tyrer, P., Strauss, J., & Cicchetti, D. (1983). Temporal reliability of personality in psychiatric patients. *Psychological Medicine,13,* 393–398.

Vander Wal, J. S., & Thomas, N. (2004). Predictors of body image dissatisfaction and disturbed eating attitudes and behaviors in African American and Hispanic girls. *Eating Behaviors, 5*(4), 291–301.

Warshaw, M. G., Dyck, I., Allsworth, J., Stout, R. L., & Keller, M. B. (2001). Maintaining reliability in a long-term psychiatric study: An ongoing inter-rater reliability monitoring program using the longitudinal interval follow-up evaluation. *Journal of Psychiatric Research, 35,* 297–305.

White, M. A., & Grilo, C. M. (2005). Ethnic differences in the prediction of eating and body image disturbances among female adolescent psychiatric inpatients. *International Journal of Eating Disorders, 38,* 78–84.

Williamson, D. A. (1990). *Assessment of eating disorders: Obesity, anorexia, and bulimia nervosa.* Elmsford, NY: Pergamon.

Williamson, D. A., & Martin, C. K. (1999). Binge eating disorder: A review of the literature after publication of *DSM-IV. Eating and Weight Disorders, 4,* 103–114.

Williamson, D. A., White, M. A., Newton, R., Alfonso, A., & Stewart, T. M. (2005). Association of body size estimation and age in African-American females. *Eating and Weight Disorders, 10,* 216–221.

Williamson, D. A., Zucker, N. L., Martin, C. K., & Smeets, M. A. M. (2001). Etiology and management of eating disorders. In H. E. Adams & P. B. Sutker (Eds.), *Comprehensive handbook of psychopathology* (3rd ed., pp. 641–670). New York: Plenum.

Yanovski, S. Z. (1999). Diagnosis and prevalence of eating disorders in obesity. In B. Guy-Grand Ailhaud (Ed.), *Progress in obesity research* (pp. 229–236). London: Libby.

Yanovski, S. Z. (2000). Eating disorder, race, and mythology. *Archives of Family Medicine, 9,* 88.

Zanarini, M. C., Frankenburg, F. R., Chauncey, D. L., & Gunderson, J. G. (1987). The Diagnostic Interview for Personality Disorders: Interrater and test-retest reliability. *Comprehensive Psychiatry, 28,* 467–480.

19

Borderline Personality Disorder

Kathryn E. Korslund, Angela Murray, and Susan L. Bland

Description of the Disorder

Borderline personality disorder (BPD) is characterized by severe dysregulation across cognitive, behavioral, emotional, and interpersonal and intrapersonal spectrums. Emotional responses are intense and highly reactive. Episodes of depression, anxiety, and irritability are common, as are difficulties with anger and anger expression (both inhibited and explosive). Relationships may be intense and tumultuous; sensitivity to criticism and fear of rejection may result in concentrated efforts to avoid relationship rupture and preserve connections to significant people. In times of acute stress, cognitive processes may be affected, resulting in brief episodes of paranoia, delusional thinking, and a spectrum of dissociative experiences (e.g., depersonalization, derealization, amnesia). Additionally, identity disturbance, in the form of chronic feelings of emptiness and shifting values, preferences, and life goals, is common.

Suicidal behavior is common among people with BPD. In fact, BPD is one of only two *Diagnostic and Statistical Manual of Mental Disorders* (*DSM*) disorders for which suicidal behavior is a criterion (American Psychiatric Association [APA], 2000). It is estimated that approximately 80% of people with BPD will engage in some form of nonfatal suicidal behavior (i.e., intentional self-injurious act with or

without intent to die) (Clarkin, Widiger, Frances, Hurt, & Gilmore, 1983; Cowdry, Pickar, & Davies, 1985; Frances, Fyer, & Clarkin, 1986; Grove & Tellegen, 1991; Gunderson, 1984; Stone, 1993), and approximately 10% will die by suicide (Black, Blum, Pfohl, & Hale, 2004; Paris & Zweig-Frank, 2001). Suicide rates double among people with a history of previous suicidal behavior and triple for those meeting all nine *DSM-IV* BPD criteria (Stone, 1993; Stone, Hurt, & Stone, 1987).

The prevalence of BPD in the general population is approximately 1% to 2% (Samuels et al., 2002; Torgersen, Kringlen, & Cramer, 2001). Although it is disproportionately diagnosed in women (APA, 2000), the true prevalence by gender is unknown. Prevalence estimates for psychiatric samples range from 9% to 20% (Zimmerman, Rothschild, & Chelminski, 2005; Fossati et al., 2000), making BPD one of the most common personality disorders encountered in clinical settings.

Central to the definition of BPD are the qualities of pervasiveness and the longstanding nature of the disorder. However, recent research from two large-scale longitudinal studies is challenging this view of BPD. Data suggest that most patients exhibit substantial improvement over time, with many demonstrating complete remission from BPD diagnostic criteria (Paris & Zweig-Frank, 2001; Zanarini, Vujanovic, et al., 2003). However, people with BPD often have marked decrements in multiple areas of psychosocial functioning, resulting in a diminished quality of life for many. Such life dissatisfaction, combined with suicidal and other life-threatening behaviors, often results in extensive use of treatment resources.

INTERVIEWING STRATEGIES

Scope of Diagnostic Assessment

A range of assessment procedures are available for diagnosing BPD. The first task is to decide the scope of the assessment and determine which diagnostic tools are best suited to the task. The most comprehensive level of assessment is to assess for the presence of all Axis I and Axis II disorders. Given the evidence that most people meeting criteria for one personality disorder meet criteria for additional personality disorders (Zimmerman et al., 2005) and the impact of such co-occurrence and of Axis I disorders on treatment response (Akiskal, 2004; Paris, 2005b; Skodol et al., 2002; Smith, Muir, & Blackwood, 2004; Tyrer, 2004; Zimmerman & Mattia, 1999), this level of assessment may be warranted. However, consideration must be given to time and monetary constraints. When both are limited, a self-report questionnaire might be the only practical choice. However, it is critical to note that such an approach is not free of limitations and would limit the scope of the diagnostic assessment.

The diagnostic battery adopted by the University of Washington Behavioral Research and Therapy Clinics ("the Linehan research lab") uses standard tools from the clinical and research field for diagnosing Axis I and Axis II disorders. The battery consists of a combination of the Structured Clinical Interview for *DSM-IV* Axis I Disorders Patient Edition (SCID-I/P; First, Spitzer, Gibbon, & Williams, 1995) to assess for all Axis I disorders, the International Personality Disorder Examination (IPDE; Loranger, 1995) to assess for all Axis II personality disorders, and the BPD section of the Structured Clinical Interview for *DSM-IV* Axis II Personality Disorders (SCID-II; First, Spitzer, Gibbon, Williams, & Benjamin, 1996) to confirm the BPD diagnosis.

All three instruments possess sound psychometric properties, are easy to administer, and are routinely used in research. The IPDE is the most widely established measure of personality disorders currently available, being compatible with both the *DSM-IV* and the *International Classification of Diseases* (*ICD-10;* World Health Organization, 1992) classification symptoms, and is used by the World Health Organization. The IPDE is of particular value in a research setting because of its conservative guidelines that require a minimum of a 5-year history of current symptoms. This decreases the number of false-positive BPD diagnoses. The IPDE has the additional benefit of being scored categorically as well as dimensionally. We confirm the diagnosis with the SCID-II because most research clinicians use the SCID-II. The combination of the two measures constitutes a robust battery for BPD diagnosis that allows meaningful comparisons across various research studies locally and internationally.

The time estimated for collecting the aforementioned diagnostic information is as follows: 30 minutes for the SCID-I social history interview (precursor to the diagnostic interview), 90 minutes for the SCID-I, 45 minutes for the IPDE BPD section, 15 minutes for the SCID-II BPD section, and 2 hours to complete the remainder of the IPDE. Individual administration times may vary depending on complexity of symptoms and whether additional information (e.g., review of medical records, interviewing treating clinicians or significant family members) is required to make definitive diagnoses.

Outside the research context, the typical provider may feel overwhelmed at the prospect of dedicating the necessary financial and time resources to this type of comprehensive assessment. In a study comparing structured diagnostic measures with standard clinical assessment, Egan, Nathan, and Lumley (2003) advise clinicians to maximize efficiency by investing resources in comprehensive diagnostic assessment "rather than spending time forcing possibly misleading selections between diagnoses in patients who present a very complex diagnostic picture" (p. 449). They go on to state, "Without accurate diagnosis and consequent treatment planning for all disorders . . . treatment may be less effective" (p. 450). Thus, the frequent overlap of Axis I and Axis II diagnoses among those with BPD and the clinical complexity thereby introduced indicates that even beyond the research context, one could save time and money by getting a more complete clinical picture at the beginning.

Selection of Diagnostic Instruments

Beyond the unstructured clinical interview, there are three approaches to assessment and diagnosis of personality disorders: structured or semistructured interviews, self-report questionnaires, and clinician report inventories or checklists. In this section we discuss semistructured and self-report questionnaires because they are the most frequently used in clinical practice. (For a comprehensive review of the most commonly used instruments for assessment of personality symptoms, see Widiger, 2002.)

Semistructured Interviews

Five semistructured interviews are in use for personality disorder diagnosis based on the *DSM-IV* criteria: the IPDE (Loranger, 1995), the SCID-II (First, Gibbon, Spitzer, Williams, & Benjamin, 1997), the Structured Interview for *DSM-IV* Personality Disorders (Pfohl, Blum, & Zimmerman, 1997), the Personality Disorder Interview–IV (Widiger et al., 1995), and the Diagnostic Interview for Personality Disorders (DIPD-IV; Zanarini, Frankenburg, Sickel, & Yong, 1996).

To date, no empirical advantage has been identified for using one interview over another (Farmer & Chapman, 2002; Skodol et al., 2002; Zanarini, 2003). This is not to say that there are not pros and cons to the various approaches depending on the setting and context. For example, if time constraints are an issue, then there is much benefit to using the SICD-II, which takes the least amount of time to administer at 36 minutes (Beck, Freeman, Davis, & Associates, 1990), compared with the IPDE, which takes the most amount of time to administer (Widiger, 2002) at 2 hours and 20 minutes (Loranger et al., 1994). Additionally, both the SCID-II and IPDE have self-report questionnaires available that can be used as screening instruments in order to eliminate portions of the general personality disorder interview, thereby significantly decreasing assessment time (Widiger, 2002).

Self-Report Questionnaires

The following self-report questionnaires are the most commonly used self-report measures for the assessment of the *DSM-IV* personality disorders (Widiger, 2002): the Millon Clinical Multiaxial Inventory–III Axis II (Millon, Millon, & Davis, 1994), the Personality Diagnostic Questionnaire–4 + (Hyler, 1994), the Wisconsin Personality Disorders Inventory–IV (Klein & Benjamin, 1996), and the SCID-II PQ (First et al., 1997), for use with the SCID-II as a screening device. Additionally, according to a fairly new study, the Assessment of *DSM-IV* Personality Disorders Questionnaire (Schotte & De Doncker, 1996) appears to be a promising addition to this list (Schotte et al., 2004).

Although other measures, such as the Minnesota Multiphasic Personality Inventory (Butcher, Dahlstrom, Graham, Tellegen, & Kaemmer, 1989; Hathaway & McKinley, 1943), the Coolidge Axis II Inventory (Coolidge & Merwin, 1992), and the Personality Assessment Inventory (PAI; Morey, 1996) may provide valuable clinical information about personality traits and style, they are not included in the list provided here because they are not specifically tied to the *DSM-IV* personality disorder scales (Widiger, 2002).

Self-report measures for personality disorders have many advantages over interviewer-administered measures, such as shorter administration time, no interviewer bias, and less resource use in terms of staff training and time. Their primary disadvantage is that they are not recommended for diagnostic purposes because of their low diagnostic concordance with semistructured interviews and their tendency to overdiagnose co-occurring personality disorders (Beck et al., 1990; Farmer & Chapman, 2002; Hunt & Andrews, 1992; Modestin, Erni, & Oberson, 1998; Perry, 1992; Widiger, 2002). One possible exception to this is the Assessment of *DSM-IV* Personality Disorders Questionnaire (Schotte & De Doncker, 1996), which in a recent study showed good differential validity (ability to differentiate between symptomatic and nonsymptomatic clients), had decent convergent validity with the SCID-II, and did not over diagnose co-occurring personality disorders (Schotte et al., 2004).

Because of the problems noted earlier, self-report questionnaires are recommended primarily as tools to collect trait-specific information to supplement *DSM-IV* diagnoses (Beck et al., 1990; Skodol et al., 2002; Smith, Klein, & Benjamin, 2003) or as screening tools to be given before a semistructured interview. The McLean

Screening Instrument for Borderline Personality Disorder (MSI-BPD; Zanarini, Vujanovic, et al., 2003) is one such device. Adapted from the BPD module of the DIPD-IV for use as a screening device, the MSI-BPD is a BPD-specific instrument designed to inform additional assessment and not as a standalone diagnostic measure (Zanarini, Vujanovic, et al., 2003).

Successful screening reduces patient burden and maximizes assessment efficiency. Screening information directs the assessor to thoroughly evaluate only the personality disorders for which minimal endorsement has been made, the net effect of which is a reduction in assessor time and a corresponding reduction in assessment costs.

Dimensional Versus Categorical Approach to Diagnosis

The instruments described earlier are based on the *DSM-IV* diagnostic criteria. Recently, though, there has been controversy over the validity of the *DSM-IV* diagnosis of personality disorders. Peter Tyrer (2004) comments, "No one doing research on personality disorders is satisfied with the current diagnostic systems" (p. 371). In fact, the literature is full of articles questioning the *DSM-IV* criteria for Axis II disorders (Farmer & Chapman, 2002; Gabbard, 1997; Tyrer, 2004; Verheul, 2005; Widiger, Simonsen, Krueger, Livesley, & Verheul, 2005).

The most often cited deficiencies include extensive overlap between categories (Skodol et al., 1999), lack of distinction between discrete personality disorder categories and the lack of empirical support for the arbitrary cutoff points (Egan et al., 2003; Skodol et al., 2002; Widiger et al., 2005), the absence of a theoretical basis for each personality disorder (Farmer & Chapman, 2002), the heterogeneity within categories (Skodol et al., 1999), the lack of clinical utility (Skodol et al., 2002; Widiger et al., 2005), the lack of clear distinction between normal and abnormal personality (Farmer & Chapman, 2002; Skodol et al., 2002; Tyrer, 2004), and the inability to cover the breadth of personality psychopathology seen in clinical practice (Skodol et al., 2002; Widiger et al., 2005).

Because of these deficiencies, many researchers and clinicians are calling for a change in the way personality disorders are diagnosed. Rather than using the categorical model of classification, many are calling for dimensional models of classification either to replace the categorical approach or to supplement the current *DSM-IV* model (Beck et al., 1990; Clarkin, Hull, Canoter & Sanderson, 1993; Egan et al., 2003; Modestin et al., 1998; Skodol et al., 2002; Smith, Muir, & Blackwood, 2004; Tyrer, 2004; Widiger et al., 2005).

In light of this heterogeneity, both within and between categories, it can be beneficial to gather additional trait-specific information from clients diagnosed with BPD. Any two people given the *DSM-IV* BPD diagnosis are required to share only one criterion of the nine (Skodol et al., 1999) thus making generic treatment planning problematic. Distinguishing between underlying traits of the disorder can facilitate development of trait-specific treatments that target each client's most problematic areas. Several instruments have been developed specifically for measuring BPD traits and trait versus state aspects of BPD. These are described here to further aid clinicians in determining what to include in their assessment battery.

Instruments for BPD

A number of instruments have been developed specifically for BPD assessment. Two interviews, the PAI (Morey, 1996) and the Revised Diagnostic Interview for Borderlines (DIB-R; Zanarini, Gunderson, Frankenburg, & Chauncey, 1989) give the treatment provider more dimensional or trait-specific information related to BPD. Skodol et al. (2002) describe four subscales within the PAI—affective instability, identity problems, negative relationships, and self-harm—and note that the DIB-R differentiates between five components of the disorder: social maladaptation, impulsivity, affectivity, psychosis, and interpersonal relationships.

Another trait-specific questionnaire that has recently been developed is the Borderline Symptom List (Bohus et al., 2001). It is a 95-item self-rating scale developed from the *DSM-IV* criteria for BPD, the DIB-R, BPD experts, and feedback from patients with BPD. It was evaluated on 308 psychiatric patients in Germany who were diagnosed with BPD. Factor analysis of the results showed seven factors: self-image, affect regulation, auto-aggression, dysthymia, social isolation, intrusions, and hostility (Bohus et al., 2001).

The Questionnaire of Thoughts & Feelings (Renneberg, Schmidt-Rathjens, Hippin, Backenstrass, & Fydrich, 2005) is a new instrument that was constructed "to measure not only behavioral aspects of BPD but to focus on underlying cognitive assumptions and motivational aspects leading to behaviors typical for BPD." It is a 34-item questionnaire that takes 5–10 minutes to complete and is meant to measure the degree and content of cognition, which can then be used for treatment planning and evaluation. It is recommended primarily for the assessment of treatment outcome of cognitive-behavioral interventions for BPD (Renneberg et al., 2005).

The Zanarini Rating Scale for Borderline Personality Disorder (Zanarini, 2003), adapted from the BPD module of the DIPD-IV, is the first clinician-administered scale for the assessment of change in *DSM-IV* borderline behaviors. There are nine questions, each based on one of the nine BPD criteria of the *DSM-IV*. Each question is answered with respect to the preceding week and ranked according to a five-point severity rating scale. Ratings range from 0 to 4, with lower scores reflecting no or mild symptoms and higher scores reflecting more severe symptoms. Total scores range from 0 to 36. The scale was developed as an outcome measure intended to help the researcher or clinician better understand the changes in psychopathology that occur in treatment (Zanarini, 2003).

Another outcome measure with a 1-week timeframe is the Borderline Evaluation of Severity Over Time (Blum, Bartells, St. John, & Pfohl, 2002). This 15-item self-report measure, based on *DSM-IV* criteria, assesses three domains: negative thoughts and feelings, positive behaviors, and negative behaviors. Each item is rated on a five-point scale, with 1 = *none or slight* and 5 = *extreme*. The composite score yielded is between 12 and 72 (Blum, Pfohl, St. John, Monahan, & Black, 2002).

The PAI and the DIB-R are both measures in widespread use that are listed frequently in PsycINFO (PAI 250 times, DIB-R and DIB 107 times). The Borderline Symptom List, Borderline Evaluation of Severity Over Time, Zanarini Rating Scale for Borderline Personality Disorder, and Questionnaire of Thoughts & Feelings (and the MSI-BPD, described earlier) are relative newcomers that probably will be seen more frequently in future literature as time goes on. Which instruments to choose depends largely on the context (research or clinical), scope (single diagnosis or multiaxial assessment), frequency of administration, and available resources of the clinician.

The Diagnostic Interview

The context of the assessment probably will dictate who conducts the diagnostic interview. In many private practice settings a single provider conducts both the diagnostic assessment and treatment. On the other hand, group practices, hospital environments, and community mental health agencies are likely to have specialized personnel conducting assessment or treatment functions. Because of the requirements for blinded assessment methods, clinical research centers require that treatment and assessment functions be separated.

There are pros and cons to separated and integrated models of assessment. In integrated models, the assessment process lays the foundation for the therapeutic relationship and helps motivate clients to change. When assessment is separated from treatment, the diagnostic assessment is purely about the interview process and about collecting information to establish diagnoses. Much like a stenographer who keeps the court record or a journalist who collects facts, the assessor records the details of the clients' lives.

The relationship between the assessor and the client is important. Valid diagnosis depends on the accuracy of the information the client provides. Establishing rapport and creating an environment where the client feels safe to freely and honestly talk about the specifics of his or her life without fear of criticism or judgment is essential. Although the concept of the therapeutic alliance has received little empirical investigation in the context of psychiatric interviewing, it is no less important in assessment than in psychotherapy (Carlat, 2005).

There are many books about effective interviewing and what skills one needs to be an effective interviewer. They generally begin with setting the tone or establishing rapport and go on to discuss the different strategies used to motivate clients to change. Although the latter is important for those who conduct both assessment and treatment, it is establishing rapport that is singularly critical for assessment. Many consider Carl Roger's core conditions, a set of skills and an attitude on the part of the clinician (Cormier & Nurius, 2003; Sommers-Flanagan &

Sommers-Flanagan, 1999), essential to creating rapport during the interview.

For those conducting diagnostic assessments for BPD, creating an early therapeutic alliance is especially important. That said, it is also somewhat daunting because the disorder's hallmarks of intense emotionality, chaotic relationships, and recurrent suicidal behaviors make an assessment interview particularly difficult because the emotional reactions that can lead to these behaviors often are elicited in the context of interviewing.

However, it has been our experience that although clients often exhibit intense mood lability during the assessment interview, they rarely show pronounced increases in urges to self-harm or suicide. One possible explanation for this is that these behaviors, which often occur in the context of therapy, simply do not show up in assessment because of the distinctive, short-term, nontreatment quality of the assessment relationship. However, because emotional reactions can be more severe with BPD, Roger's core conditions are especially important points to consider when assessing clients with BPD.

These core conditions require that the interviewer show empathy, be genuine, and have positive regard for the client. In their book *Clinical Interviewing*, Sommers-Flanagan and Sommers-Flanagan (1999) state that "empathy elicits information. . . . When clients feel understood, they also tend to feel more open and willing to talk about their concerns in greater detail" (p. 135), which is exactly what is needed in assessments of clients with BPD.

With this in mind, be genuine, noncritical, nonjudgmental, accepting, and affirming. Use self-disclosure sporadically, but not inappropriately, and use humor to lighten things up. Stay professional but not detached, and show warmth. Show interest in the client's life and the people in the client's life. Show concern for the hardships in the client's life, but don't show pity or become overly emotional about the events that plague them.

Acknowledge the difficulty of the questions asked and the length of time needed to spend at the office or clinic. If a client does not understand a question, say that you did not explain it very well and then rephrase the question. Stop the interview if clients are too upset to continue. Offer to take a walk with them or talk to them about trivial things such as movies, books, or TV shows until they are able to continue. Treat them with compassion and sensitivity and help them to move through the difficult assessment process as easily and with as much dignity as possible. In return, you will have the privilege of setting down the details of their lives.

INTERVIEWING OBSTACLES AND SOLUTIONS

It has been our experience in working with clients with BPD that various obstacles in the assessment process tend to occur, some more often than others. Those of note are described in this section, with solutions that we have found to be helpful.

Assessment Versus Therapy

The clinical assessment process is difficult, and assessors need to be aware that many of the questions they pose are extremely painful for the client and can elicit intense emotional reactions. Moreover, when this occurs, clients may expect the assessor to act like a therapist and help them solve their emotional problems. In the context of the integrated model, seamless shifting between the two roles is possible. In the separated model, the challenge is to offer solace, compassion, and distraction rather than therapy. For this method to be successful, it is important to explain to the client, before the assessment begins, that treatment is a separate and distinct component from the assessment. For some clients this is a relief. For others, the prospect of telling the assessor the intricate details of their lives and then moving on to build a relationship with a provider constitutes a fresh wave of emotional pain. The intense emotionality of clients with BPD can make these transitions particularly painful.

Self-Harm During Interview

Although it is not common for clients with BPD to engage in self-harming behavior such as banging their head against the wall or scratching themselves with pins or paperclips during an assessment, it does occur. The practical approach is to tell them to stop the behavior immediately. Most patients will stop because you have acknowledged that their behavior is unacceptable. If they are unable to stop the behavior, then the interview must stop. Have patients take a break, go for a walk, have a cigarette break, or get something to eat until they are able to continue with the interview without harming themselves. Directed intervention may be uncomfortable for some assessors working from less directive models of assessment or treatment. However, clear instruction that the behavior must stop is essential with this population.

Another strategy is to have clients tell the assessor exactly when they are having the urge to harm themselves. When this happens, stop the interview and have clients stand up and move around the office for a few minutes. If they continue to have strong urges, or for those who use their hands for harming themselves, have them place their hands under their legs or give them something to hold, such as a stress ball, to keep their hands occupied.

Suicidal Patients During an Interview

Interviewing patients when they are feeling suicidal can be very stressful. The first step when you think someone is at risk for engaging in suicidal behaviors is to assess his or her level of risk. Once you have a clear picture of method, availability, lethality, and timeframe, your next step is to work to decrease the client's level of suicidal intent or bring additional caregivers in to increase postassessment monitoring and enhance safety. If possible, offer to take a walk with the client. The change of environment alone can help relax the client, as can the shift that takes place in the relationship between the assessor and client when they leave the office environment behind. Instead of a structured question and answer session, a conversation can now take place on a more intimate and less formal, though still professional, basis.

The goal is to continue to assess the client by asking questions that might pertain to the breadth, quality, and availability of the client's support system, any changes that have recently taken place in the client's life, his or her repertoires of positive self-soothing and distracting strategies, and his or her ability to use these strategies successfully in the past. Making reference to the positive things in the client's life and validating the client's feelings also help to reduce his or her overall level of distress.

If the client's suicidal intent decreases over the course of the walk, then the assessor can help the client make a detailed behavioral plan for the remainder of the day before leaving the clinic. If suicidality has not decreased and the assessment of lethality of the client's plan is high, friends or family members should be contacted to stay with the client, or the client should be taken to a nearby emergency room. It may be reassuring to know that in conducting research with clients with BPD who are acutely and chronically suicidal, we have found that detailed assessments rarely increase suicidality levels and, when they do, not significantly (Reynolds, Lindenboim, Comtois, Murray, & Linehan, 2006).

Mute Patients

It is challenging when clients come in and refuse to speak. In these instances information can be gathered in several different ways. It might be helpful to notice things about the clients, such as how they are dressed and what they are reading, and talk with the client about those things as a warm-up before interviewing him or her about intense interpersonal problems. As the interview begins, the assessor emphasizes that clients are experts about themselves and explains that by answering specific questions they will ultimately ensure that they get the best possible treatment because they know their problems, strengths, and situation better than anyone else. If the client is still unwilling to speak, then the last step would be to obtain copies of his or her records or interview family members for the assessment information.

Chronic Lateness or No-Shows

One of the most common and frustrating aspects of working with clients with personality disorders is the frequency with which they miss, reschedule, or arrive late for appointments. In clients with BPD, whose lives are in chronic chaos, this may be even more common. In order to reduce this problem, a reminder call the day before and the morning of the appointment may be necessary. This is standard protocol in our research clinic and has greatly reduced the problem.

Another strategy to draw clients to assessment appointments is to make the assessment environment an inviting place. Having coffee or tea available for when the patient arrives shows that you care about his or her well-being. Providing accurate directions and good parking or bus routes makes getting to appointments easier for the client. Beginning the assessment on time reduces apprehension and conveys to the client the message that he or she is important. Having snacks and hand lotion available during the assessment, taking frequent breaks, and conducting the assessment in a nicely furnished office will also help bring clients back to the clinic knowing that they will be treated with respect and will be in pleasant surroundings.

CASE ILLUSTRATION WITH DIALOGUE

The following is a transcript from a screening interview for BPD using the IPDE (Loranger, 1995). This transcript was chosen to illustrate assessment strategies in diagnosing BPD using the IPDE. Questions are asked based on the nine criteria for a *DSM-IV* diagnosis of BPD.

Patient Description

Bobby is a 29-year-old married woman who lives with her husband and two cats. Bobby earned her college degree 4 years ago. Her major in college was liberal arts. She has been working for the past 9 months in finance. Her work history has been irregular, with her current position being the longest job she held since graduating from college. She has been married for the past 2 years, during which time she and her husband have separated twice. She currently has a restraining order against a former boyfriend for harassment and stalking. Before getting married she was in a clean and sober house for 6 months. She was recently released from the hospital where she had been admitted after a suicide attempt by overdose on prescribed medications. Bobby ingested a nearly lethal amount of medication and spent 3 days in intensive care, followed by 2 days on a medical floor and then 7 days in a psychiatric unit. Bobby stated she that had planned the suicide attempt but then called 911 when she started to vomit.

Before the following transcript segment, the assessor spent several minutes casually chatting with the client and orienting her to the agenda for the assessment. The italicized sections of the transcript list symptoms of BPD from the IPDE. The questions that are in bold text are questions that appear in the interview and are to be asked

by the assessor. Supplement questions are at the discretion of the interviewer.

Identity Disturbance (There are five questions in this section; a positive score on two of the questions meets identity disturbance criteria.)

Assessor: **Let me ask some questions about the kind of person you are.**

Client: I don't know. I am nice, I guess, I am sad a lot, I really don't know.

A: **How would you describe your personality?**

C: Nice, I don't really know, I'm not sure who I am, I want to be whoever my husband and family want me to be. My mother thinks I am a good person, but my dad thinks I am crazy because I can't make up my mind about things. My husband just wants me to get help and get better.

A: **Have you always been like that?** Nice, a good person, not sure who you are and want to be whoever your family thinks you should be?

C: No.

[If the client responds that this is a longstanding pattern, this portion of the interview stops. If not, the assessor continues with questions to determine what precipitated the change. This is a critical element of making the diagnosis because situational variables such as trauma, cross-country moves, or significant illness may prompt such change and influence coding of this criterion.]

A: **When did you change?**

C: Oh, probably in high school things got all messed up.

A: **What were you like before?**

C: When I was in junior high and the beginning of high school I felt like I could do anything. I wanted to be a veterinarian. I love animals. I didn't think about who I was; I felt confident, I guess.

Identity Disturbance 1

A: **Do you think that one of your problems is that you're not sure what kind of person you are?**

C: I don't know who I am or what I should be doing.

A: How does that affect your life?

C: I am miserable. One day I listen to what my mother has to say about who I am supposed to be, and the next day I listen to what my husband has to say, and then I listen to the talk shows, and I get even more confused.

A: **Do you behave as though you don't know what to expect of yourself?**

C: I think so. I'm not sure what you mean.

A: Do you act like yourself when you are around people?

C: Sometimes.

A: **Are you so different with different people or in different situations that you don't behave like the same person?**

C: Yes, many times I do this.

A: Can you give me some examples?

C: Well, when I am at work, I act very professional and appear very competent because they act all professional and stuff; no one does anything wrong. When I am with my friends from my drinking and drugging days I act crazy because that is what they do. When I am with my husband I act nice and a lot of times helpless. He likes to take care of me; he would just die if he saw how I act at work and with my crazy friends because he doesn't see me that way. I am like a chameleon. I get nervous in new situations, so I watch how other people act, and I act like they do.

A: Have you always been like this?

C: Since I was in high school. People were mean to the kids who did not fit in. I haven't felt like I fit in since then, so I just act like those around me.

Identity Disturbance 2

A: **What would you like to accomplish during your life?**

C: To be happy, have a happy marriage.

A: What about a career?

C: Right now I want to be in finance.

A: **Do your ideas about this change often?**

C: Yes

A: Tell me about it.

C: I used to work in a restaurant, and I wanted to own a restaurant, and I wanted to be a veterinarian when I was in high school. I also started school to be a cosmetologist but quit. I watch a lot of TV, and I thought I should become a nurse or doctor or something like that, because a lot of shows looked fun. A couple of months ago I thought I should be a writer because I have a lot of ideas.

Identity Disturbance 3

A: **Do you have trouble deciding what's important in life?**

C: Yes, I don't know what is important.

A: How does that affect you or the way you live your life?

C: It causes me to make a lot of poor decisions and holds me back.

A: **Do you have trouble deciding what is morally right and wrong?**

C: Yes, I know stealing is wrong, but I do it anyway, and I know speeding is wrong, but I still speed, and I also am against drugs, but when I am with my friends and they offer me some pot I can't help myself. It really disgusts me. I always go against my principles.

Identity Disturbance 4

A: Do you have a lot of trouble deciding what type of friends you should have?

C: Yes, I never know who I should become friends with. If someone is nice to me I think that they should be my friend, and then I find out later that they steal. I don't know if I should stay friends with them. I get really confused about who I should have as a friend.

A: **Do the kind of people you have as friends keep changing?**

C: Yes. I have had people who are rockers, studious people, intellects, drug and alcohol addicts. I am always changing who I have as friends. I don't have any real long-term friends. I really would like to have the same friends. It makes it hard for me to have relationships because I am always changing.

Identity Disturbance 5

A: **Have you ever been uncertain whether you prefer a sexual relationship with a man or a woman?**

C: I don't know what I want sexually. I am attracted to men, but I also feel attracted to women. This has been bothering me a lot. I never wondered, but when I started college I felt very attracted to one of the other female students. We never did anything, but I have experimented with some women. I have a lot of shame talking about this because I was raised a Christian, and it is morally wrong, and I am married. I can't even talk to my husband about this.

Unstable, Intense Interpersonal Relationships

A: **Do you get into intense and stormy relationships with other people with lots of ups and downs? I mean, do your feelings about them run hot and cold or change from one extreme to the other?**

C: Oh yeah!

A: **In those relationships do you often find yourself alternating between admiring and despising the same person?**

C: That is so true of me. I love my husband so much. He is the best thing that has ever happened to me, but sometimes, like the other night when he told me that I should get a haircut, I just hated him. I even went upstairs to leave him because I just could not stand the thought of being near him for one more minute. This has happened with every boyfriend that I have had. I do this with my parents also. I think that they are the most caring and generous people that I have met, but sometimes I will go for weeks without talking to them because I think they are so awful.

Chronic Feelings of Emptiness

A: **Do you often feel empty inside?**

C: Yes.

A: **Does that upset you or cause any problems for you?**

C: It causes me to be depressed; I will cut a lot of times when I am empty just to fill up that void. I used to drink a lot when I felt empty. When I was in college I used to have sex with people I didn't know very well.

Frantic Efforts to Avoid Abandonment

A: **Do you ever find yourself frantically trying to stop someone close to you from leaving you?**

C: I do this all the time with my husband. Just the other day he had to go back to work, and I felt abandoned and begged him to stay home. Whenever we have a fight I beg him not to leave, and I even have run after him when he has driven away. I used to do this with my friends in high school. I would call them all the time because I was afraid they would leave me and I would be all alone. I have lost friendships over this because they think I am too needy.

Affective Instability

A: **Do you often change from your usual mood to feeling very irritable, very depressed, or very nervous?**

C: Yes, all the time. I have always been very moody. Just coming in here I was really nervous about this until I got to the parking garage, and the guy took forever to give me change. I became furious with him, and then I came in here and saw a homeless guy out in front of the building. I felt really depressed and sorry for him. I feel fine now, but when I get that intensity of my moods I feel out of control.

Intense Anger

A: **Do you sometimes get angrier than you should or feel very angry without a good reason?**

C: At the time it happens it feels like a good reason. When I was in the parking garage, I was so mad that when I got out of the car I slammed my car door and started kicking my car. I throw things sometimes when I get mad. I try not to throw things that are sentimental, but if I am in a rage then I can't help myself. Sometimes in stores I have embarrassed myself because the cashiers are stupid and slow, and I yell at them sometimes to hurry up. I've had the managers of several stores tell me to leave.

Paranoid Ideation or Dissociative Symptoms (five parts to this section)

A: **Sometimes when people are very upset or under a lot of stress, they have very unusual experiences. At times like this, have you ever experienced any of these? (1) Felt like you were in a dream and either you or the world around you wasn't real? (2) Felt like you were a detached spectator watching the world go on without being part of it? (3) Felt like you were outside of your own body, or some part of your body didn't belong to you? (4) Thought people could read your mind or already knew what**

your were thinking before your told them?
(5) Thought your mind, body, or behavior was under the control or influence of some force or person? Thought people had it in for you or were out to harm you?

C: Some of those things have happened to me. When I get really upset I get this surreal feeling, and I just sit there and watch things happen, and I don't even feel that I am there; it's like I am watching a movie. Sometimes this can last a couple of hours, and I don't even realize that time has gone by. I feel paralyzed when that happens, and my husband has had to shake me to get me out of it.

Recurrent Suicidal Behavior, Threats, and Gestures

A: Have you ever threatened to commit suicide, actually made a suicide attempt or gesture, or deliberately cut yourself, smashed your fist through a window, burned yourself, or hurt yourself in some other way?

C: Two weeks ago I overdosed on my medication because I wanted to kill myself. When I was a teenager I used to cut my arms when I got upset. I also tried to kill myself a couple of years ago by driving my car into a tree.

Impulsivity (There are a multitude of questions requiring two positive scores in the past 5 years in order to meet criteria.)

A: Have you ever had a problem with gambling or spending too much money?

C: I don't know. I am in credit card debt for $10,000, but isn't that what most people have?

A: Have your ever had a problem with drugs or alcohol?

C: I used to have a problem with alcohol and cocaine, but I have been clean and sober for the past two and one half years.

A: Have you ever gone on eating binges, so that it was a problem for you or others were concerned about you?

C: For about 6 months after I got married I used to secretly binge when my husband went to bed. I would eat large amounts of sweets several times a week. I gained 30 pounds during that time.

A: Have you ever shoplifted?

C: Not since I was in high school. My friends and I would go to the makeup counters and steal makeup all the time.

A: Do you get into sexual relationships quickly or without thinking of the consequences?

C: When I was in college I did. It was really bad. . . . I even ended up pregnant.

A: Have you ever taken unnecessary chances and risked harm or injury to yourself or others?

C: I don't think so.

A: Have you ever driven a car while intoxicated with alcohol or drugs?

C: I used to all the time, but not since I have been clean and sober.

A: Have you ever been stopped for the police for speeding or reckless driving?

C: I have gotten three speeding tickets in the last year.

This assessment vignette is typical of many of the subjects who participate in our research studies but may not be typical for those seeking BPD assessment in private practice or community-based organizations. Note that this case illustration reflected a person who met nine out of nine *DSM-IV* BPD criteria but that a positive diagnosis requires only five out of the nine to be met.

MULTICULTURAL AND DIVERSITY ISSUES

Minimal research has been done in the area of multiculturalism and personality disorders. Therefore, cross-culture community prevalence rates of personality disorders are mostly unknown (Akhtar, 1995; Paris, 1996, 1998). BPD has been reported most often in North America, Europe, and the United Kingdom, with infrequent reports of BPD in developing countries (Pinto, Dhavale, Nair, Patil, & Dewan, 2000). Cross-cultural research aside, attention to racial, ethnic, and cultural diversity as it pertains to personality disorders is rare even within a single cultural, geographic, or sociopolitical entity. Despite the increased focus on such issues in the past few years in the United States, very few studies have examined the prevalence of personality disorders across different groups, and where a study has been undertaken, findings are largely inconsistent (Chavira et al., 2003).

In a 1990 U.S. Epidemiologic Catchment Area study, demographic characteristics of those meeting criteria for BPD included being female, widowed, single, young, non-White, an urban resident, and of lower socioeconomic status (Swartz, Blazer, George, & Winfield, 1990). Another study that looked at the demographic profile of BPD in 23 studies found that patients meeting criteria for the disorder were similarly mostly young and female, but in contrast to the 1990 study it found that most people with BPD were White (Akhtar, Byrne, & Doghramji, 1986). Countering both these findings, one study of 1,583 psychiatric inpatients found no significant difference in the prevalence of BPD between Whites, Blacks, and Hispanics (Castaneda & Franco, 1985). Interestingly, the same study showed higher rates of BPD in women among Whites and Blacks but showed equal rates of BPD between Hispanic men and women. Another study of 554 patients taken from the recent Collaborative Longitudinal Personality Disorders Study showed higher rates of BPD in Hispanics than in Caucasian and African American participants and no significant gender by ethnicity interactions (Chavira et al., 2003).

In discussing the possible reasons for a higher rate of BPD in Hispanics, Chavira et al. (2003) note more frequent endorsements of intense anger, affective instability, and unstable relationships by Hispanics than by Caucasians. They speculate that the acculturation process for some ethnic minorities, which can include feelings of anxiety, emptiness, alienation, abandonment, loss of control, identity confusion (Hovey & Magana, 2002; Williams & Berry, 1991, as cited in Chavira et al., 2003), disruption of the family system, and intergenerational conflicts (Negy & Snyder, 2000, as cited in Chavira et al., 2003) might be one explanation for the higher rate of BPD found in the Hispanic group. Another explanation is that characteristics deemed acceptable in one culture, such as novelty seeking, quick temper, and extravagance, may be seen as pathological from a Western psychiatric standpoint and diagnosed as such by Western clinicians (Chavira et al., 2003). Both explanations point to the importance of taking cultural factors into consideration when looking at the prevalence of BPD across ethnic groups.

Culture is clearly important in a discussion of personality and its disorders. Because disorder is defined as a departure from the norm, it is critical to assess what defines the norm, and there is no better vehicle for that than culture. Even the concept of *personality* has a culturally defined base, and the one to which the label *disorder* is

attached is an extension of the Western cultural ideal of individualism. How well this fits the various people of the world or the cultural subsets represented in modern, Western, industrial societies is in question. We must look at how different cultures shape specific behavior and personality norms, how pathology is defined and expressed differently between cultures, and how the prevalence of personality disorders might change as the culture of an individual or population changes (Miller, 1996; Paris, 1996, 1998). For example, antisocial personality disorder was rarely seen in women when their behavior was strongly controlled by societal norms. As these norms shifted and women became free to express themselves, the prevalence of antisocial personality disorder among women increased (Bjorklund, 2006). In a similar fashion, in more traditional cultures or societies where compliance, indirect expression of emotions, and conformity are rewarded in order to keep the family or group intact, the symptoms of BPD such as impulsive action and excessive emotionality, traits associated with an individualistic, Western culture, tend to be discouraged (Paris, 1996, 1998).

Although traditional societies may play a role in discouraging and extinguishing expression of BPD behaviors, the disorder may be expressed in other ways. For example, in traditional societies people tend to show less psychological distress and disordered behavior (Murphy, 1982, as cited in Paris, 1996) and more physical or somatic distress (Leff, 1988, as cited in Paris, 1996). In her article on BPD in a social context, Miller (1996) discusses the different cultural expressions of distress, comparing BPD to certain "ethnic disorders" such as spirit possession, *nervios, susto,* and *latah,* and notes how all of these disorders tend to develop from problematic social histories, which leave people with a sense of social failure, inadequacy, marginality, and powerlessness.

As traditional societies modernize or as people from these societies immigrate to developed countries, roles and ties that were clear and guaranteed become unclear or perhaps nonexistent. The accompanying decrease in structure and clarity of individual, family, and community roles that traditional societies provide may lead some people in these communities to experience higher levels of discord and discomfiture consistent with criteria defining borderline personality disorder. Moreover, personality characteristics, such as dependency, that were adaptive in one culture become maladaptive in another and those that were previously seen as deviant, such as self-focus and individualism, become expected (Paris, 1996, 1998).

Thus, it is possible that the prevalence of BPD may increase with modernization and immigration because of the decrease in protective factors that traditional societies provide. It is also possible that BPD prevalence may increase in these circumstances because the change in culture allows a higher degree of acceptance of emotionally expressive and impulsive behaviors. Both are likely to play a role in the emergence of BPD within a culture and are important when one is considering how culture can affect the prevalence of BPD in different cultures. Moreover, because the definition of *disorder* and the diagnostic instruments reviewed in this chapter were developed from the Western cultural vantage point, care must be taken in the assessment process. That said, a standard for cultural competence in the assessment of something so culturally informed, shaped, and determined as personality, let alone its disorders, has not been identified. In the absence of such, the prospective assessor is encouraged to be as informed as possible about cultural norms and deviations for the various groups (e.g., racial, ethnic, religious) they encounter so that culturally normative behavior is not pathologized or disordered behavior normalized.

DIFFERENTIAL DIAGNOSIS AND BEHAVIORAL ASSESSMENT

BPD co-occurs with several Axis I disorders, most notably mood, substance use, anxiety, and eating disorders. It is important to note that the diagnostic criteria defining BPD are not an exclusive set; co-occurrence may reflect the overlap in diagnostic criteria of BPD with other disorders. Conversely, the observed co-occurrence may reflect the complexity and pervasiveness of BPD, the impact of multiple disorders, or common etiological factors. Prevalence estimates of co-occurrence of BPD with Axis I disorders vary widely. Such variation may be attributable to a variety of factors: the assessment approach (chart review, self-report screening, clinical interview, standardized interviews) and diagnostic criteria

(*DSM-III, DSM-III-R,* or *DSM-IV*); (2) experience, training, and reliability of diagnosticians; sample composition (e.g., community, clinical, inpatient, outpatient); and time focus (current or lifetime diagnosis).

Using structured interview methods and rigorous diagnostic specificity, co-occurrence of Axis I disorders in BPD samples have been estimated to range from 39% to 96% for mood disorders, 13% to 86% for substance use disorders, 7% to 99% for anxiety disorders, and 15% to 53% for eating disorders (Skodal et al., 1999; Trull, Sher, Minks-Brown, Durbin, & Burr, 2000; Zanarini et al., 1998a; Zanarini, Frankenburg, Hennen, Reich, & Silk, 2004; Zimmerman & Mattia, 1999). Among people with BPD selected for current suicidality (i.e., either a recent suicide attempt or a recent intentional self-injury with or without intent to die), 72% met criteria for current diagnosis of major depressive disorder, 78% met criteria for current diagnosis for any anxiety disorder, 40% met criteria for current substance use disorder, and 24% met criteria for current diagnosis of an eating disorder (Linehan et al., 2006).

BPD also co-occurs with other Axis II personality disorders (McGlashan et al., 2000; Zanarini et al., 1998b; Zimmerman et al., 2005). Each of the Axis II personality disorder groups (the so-called odd, anxious, and dramatic cluster disorders) has been observed in patients with BPD. In a general clinical sample of adults McGlashan et al. (2000) found that BPD significantly co-occurred with antisocial and dependent personality disorders. Zanarini et al. (1998b) examined comorbidity in a sample of 504 inpatients diagnoses with personality disorders and found that those with BPD had significantly higher rates of paranoid, avoidant, and dependent personality disorders than those without BPD and that although rates of avoidant and dependent personality disorders were similar across genders, men who met criteria for BPD were significantly more likely than women to meet criteria for paranoid, antisocial, narcissistic, and passive-aggressive personality disorders. In a sample of 101 women with BPD and recent suicidal and self-injurious behaviors, Linehan et al. (2006) found that 3% met criteria for a cluster A personality disorder, 10.9% met criteria for an additional cluster B personality disorder, and 25.7% met criteria for a cluster C personality disorder.

Borderline Personality Disorder Versus Bipolar Disorder

Since the advent of the *DSM-IV,* a tremendous amount of controversy has surrounded the Axis II personality disorders, not the least of which is the validity of the BPD diagnosis. The main argument is whether clients meeting BPD criteria should be considered part of the "bipolar spectrum" instead. Discussions of differential diagnosis have centered on distinguishing BPD from bipolar disorder (BD). Determining the presence or absence of BD has been one of the most difficult differential diagnosis issues in our research. The difficulty concerns the overlapping features of the two disorders, specifically affective instability and impulsivity (Benazzi, 2006; Paris, 2005a; Skodol et al., 1999) and, on a behavioral level, high novelty seeking, harm avoidance, low self-directedness, and low cooperativeness on a trait level (Akiskal, 2004).

According to Hutto (2001) the *DSM-IV* distinguishes between BD and personality disorders based on episodes. BD has discrete episodes in which features that are similar to those of BPD are present, but when the episode ends, patients are not symptomatic. Patients with BPD, on the other hand, continue to experience features that are present in BD regardless of episodes.

Many patients with BPD experience intense mood swings that usually last a few hours and sometimes can last for a couple of days (APA, 2000). By contrast, a manic episode is defined by a distinct period of abnormally elevated, expansive, or irritable mood that lasts 4 or more days (APA, 2000).

Another difference is in the impulsivity criterion. A patient in a manic episode can exhibit impulsive behavior. This impulsive behavior is out of the ordinary for the person and can cause painful consequences (i.e., buying sprees, sexual indiscretions, reckless driving). Borderline patients also may engage in impulsive behavior. This is a pattern of behavior over a long period of time that can include excessive spending, sexual activity, drug and alcohol problems, binge eating, shoplifting, and reckless endangerment. In contrast to BD, these are problems that occur on an ongoing basis, not just discrete episodes.

Magill (2004) found that obtaining an illness history is key to determining whether a patient has one or both disorders. Most people with a BPD diagnosis experience intense mood lability. This is short lived and usually is in response to external stimuli. People with BD also have this experience, but the duration of mood lability is experienced over several days or more and is not short lived. In screening people for possible inclusion in our BPD treatment studies, we have discovered that many of those referred to us with preexisting diagnoses of rapid cycling BD or cyclothymia do not meet criteria for those disorders. Detailed and careful assessment indicates that their symptoms are better accounted for by BPD, the essential feature being that the subjects may never have had a hypomanic episode, and their mood swings are mislabeled as a mood disorder instead of the mood lability of BPD.

According the *DSM-IV-TR,* BPD often co-occurs with mood disorders. The *DSM-IV* specification of episodes of distinct periods is paramount in determining the presence or absence of a bipolar diagnosis. A detailed interview with the client and significant others and a review of records may be necessary to distinguish the scope and specifics of behavioral episodes. If full criteria are met for both disorders, then a diagnosis of both disorders may be given. This is also true for BPD and other personality disorders that have overlapping features.

Other Axis II Disorders

Histrionic personality disorder (HPD) and BPD share similar features of rapid shifting of emotions and attention seeking. BPD differs in that its features are more self-destructive and intense (APA, 2000). The shifting emotions associated with HPD are associated with shallow expressions of emotions and are not internally intense. This is not to say that a person with BPD doesn't also have HPD or traits of HPD. It is our experience that most of our research subjects do not meet this particular criterion of rapid shifting of emotions because their emotions, although they may appear overly dramatic and superficial to the external observer, are not experienced as such by the subject.

Many people with BPD experience quasi-psychotic features. In our research these features rarely meet criteria for an independent psychotic disorder. They are better explained by either psychotic depression or the dissociative and paranoid symptom of BPD. People with BPD and paranoid personality disorder (PPD) have overlapping symptoms of thinking people are out to harm them. The BPD paranoid symptoms are transient and in response to external stimuli (Loranger, 1995). This is different from PPD because PPD symptoms are not necessarily in response to external stimuli. People with the paranoid symptoms of BPD are more likely to trust others after gaining familiarity with them, whereas people with PPD remain reticent.

Behavioral Assessment

The best way to assess BPD is to use semistructured clinical interviews like those mentioned earlier in this chapter. Using a semistructured clinical interview can help in discerning differences in diagnosis and co-occurrence of diagnosis. Self-report assessments are helpful but may give an inaccurate presentation of the person. With patients who are poor historians or who lack insight into their own behavior, a review of past records and clinical interviews with previous clinicians and family members might be needed for a diagnosis. Direct behavioral observation can also help in determining the presence or absence of BPD symptoms. Furthermore, information obtained in the context of therapy can help solidify provisional diagnosis.

Selection of Treatment Targets and Referral

Psychotherapy is the recommended treatment for BPD, with symptom-targeted pharmacotherapy serving in an adjunctive role (APA Work Group on Borderline Personality Disorder, 2001). Two psychotherapy approaches have been demonstrated as more effective than treatment as usual (i.e., existing community standards of care) in randomized controlled studies: dialectical behavior therapy (DBT; Linehan, 1993a, 1993b) and mentalization-based treatment (Bateman & Fonagy, 1999, 2001). Of the two, DBT has the most empirical support (Linehan et al., 1999, 2002, 2006; Linehan, Armstrong, Suarez, Allmon, & Heard, 1991; Linehan & Heard, 1993, Linehan, Heard, & Armstrong, 1993; Linehan, Tutek, Heard, & Armstrong, 1994; Verheul et al., 2003).

DBT is based on a conceptualization of BPD as a disorder of pervasive emotion dysregulation. Maladaptive behaviors are conceptualized as reducing (or, in the case of suicide, terminating) painful emotional states or are themselves a consequence of dysregulated emotion. Selection of treatment targets is based on a behavioral management and capability deficit model of BPD (Linehan, 1993a). There are two parts to the model: People with BPD are theorized to lack critical problem-solving, interpersonal, and self-regulation skills (including emotion-based skills such as distress tolerance and general self-management skills), and effective behaviors in the person's repertoire are inhibited by intense emotions, faulty beliefs and assumptions, or environmental contingencies that punish (or ignore) effective behavior and reward "borderline" behavior. Thus, principal treatment strategies include skill training, behavioral rehearsal, exposure techniques, cognitive modification, and contingency management procedures. Balancing this focus on change is the acceptance of the patient, the therapeutic relationship, and the world as it is.

People with BPD often are referred to treatment because of out-of-control behavior that poses immediate and serious risk of substantial harm or death. Treatment targets in the first stage of DBT are reducing life-threatening and suicide crisis behavior, reducing treatment-interfering behaviors that could lead to premature therapy termination, decreasing factors contributing to a diminished quality of life (e.g., Axis I disorders, homelessness) and increasing behavioral skills to manage behavior and emotions and build a life worth living. Once behavioral stability is achieved, treatment turns to increasing non-traumatic experiencing of emotions, resolving trauma-related issues of childhood, resolving the sense of incompleteness, and enhancing self-respect and freedom.

Standard DBT consists of weekly individual therapy, group skill training, a consultation team for the therapist, and telephone consultation to the patient as needed. Skill training focuses on the acquisition and strengthening of behavioral skills. Individual psychotherapy addresses motivational factors related to behavioral targets and strengthening and generalization of skills. The consultation team functions as therapy for the therapists; motivational factors and capability deficits of the treatment provider are addressed in a group therapy format by the other members of the consultation team. Telephone consultation is the purview of the individual therapist and is used to manage suicide crises and coach application of new skills to the real-world environment.

SUMMARY

People with BPD are common in clinical settings. Accurate assessment and diagnosis are critical for treatment. In this chapter we have reviewed several of the most commonly used instruments for personality disorder assessment in general and BPD in particular. The very qualities of the disorder often make assessment and diagnosis challenging. Strategies to maximize diagnostic efficiency and accuracy have been reviewed. Finally, empirically based treatment recommendations have been outlined.

ACKNOWLEDGMENTS

Writing of this manuscript was partially supported by grants 5 R01 MH034486-22 from the National Institute of Mental Health and 5 R01 DA014997-03 from the National Institute on Drug Abuse, Bethesda, Maryland. The authors thank the clinical assessors of the Behavioral Research and Therapy Clinics for their knowledge and expertise and all the subjects who have participated in our past and current studies.

REFERENCES

Akhtar, S. (1995). *Quest for answers: A primer of understanding and treating severe personality disorders.* Northvale, NJ: Jason Aronson.

Akhtar, S., Byrne, J. P., & Doghramji, K. (1986). The demographic profile of borderline personality disorder. *Journal of Clinical Psychiatry, 47*(4), 196–198.

Akiskal, H. S. (2004). Demystifying borderline personality: Critique of the concept and unorthodox reflections on its natural kinship with the bipolar spectrum. *Acta Psychiatrica Scandinavica, 110,* 401–411.

American Psychiatric Association. (2000). *Diagnostic and statistical manual of mental disorders* (4th ed., Text rev.). Washington, DC: Author.

American Psychiatric Association Work Group on Borderline Personality Disorder. (2001). Practice guideline for the treatment of patients with borderline personality disorder. *American Journal of Psychiatry, 158*(10), 1–52.

Bateman, A., & Fonagy, P. (1999). Effectiveness of partial hospitalization in the treatment of borderline personality disorder: A randomized controlled trial. *American Journal of Psychiatry, 156,* 1563–1569.

Bateman, A., & Fonagy, P. (2001). Treatment of borderline personality disorder with psychoanalytically oriented partial hospitalization: An 18-month follow-up. *American Journal of Psychiatry, 158*(1), 36–42.

Beck, T. A., Freeman, A., Davis, D. D., & Associates. (1990). *Cognitive therapy of personality disorders* (2nd ed.). New York: Guilford.

Benazzi, F. (2006). Borderline personality–bipolar spectrum relationship. *Progress in Neuro-Psychopharmacology and Biological Psychiatry, 30*(1), 68–74.

Bjorklund, P. (2006). No man's land: Gender bias and social constructivism in the diagnosis of borderline personality disorder. *Issues in Mental Health Nursing, 27,* 3–23.

Black, D. W., Blum, N., Pfohl, B., & Hale, N. (2004). Suicide in borderline personality disorder: Prevalence, risk factors, prediction and prevention. *Journal of Personality Disorders, 18*(3), 226–239.

Blum, N., Bartells, N., St. John, D., & Pfohl, B. (2002). *STEPPS manual.* Iowa City: University of Iowa.

Blum, N., Pfohl, B., St. John, J., Monahan, P., & Black, D. W. (2002). STEPPS: A cognitive-behavioral systems-based group treatment for outpatients with borderline personality disorder—A preliminary report. *Comprehensive Psychiatry, 43*(4), 301–310.

Bohus, M., Limberger, M. F., Frank, U., Sender, I., Grat Wohl, T., & Stieglitz, R. D. (2001). Development of the Borderline Symptom List (BSL). *Psychotherapy and Psychosomatic Medical Psychology, 51*(5), 201–211.

Butcher, J. N., Dahlstrom, W. G., Graham, J. R., Tellegen, A., & Kaemmer, B. (1989). *Minnesota Multiphasic Personality Inventory (MMPI-II): Manual for administration and scoring.* Minneapolis: University of Minnesota Press.

Carlat, D. J. (2005). *The psychiatric interview: A practical guide* (2nd ed.). Pennsylvania: Lippincott, Williams & Wilkins.

Castaneda, R., & Franco, H. (1985). Sex and ethnic distribution of borderline personality disorder in an inpatient sample. *American Journal of Psychiatry, 142*(10), 1202–1203.

Chavira, D. A., Grilo, C. M., Shea, M. T., Yen, S., Gunderson, J. G., Morey, L. C., et al. (2003). Ethnicity and four personality disorders. *Comprehensive Psychiatry, 44*(6), 483–491.

Clarkin, J. F., Hull, J. W., Canoter, J., & Sanderson, C. (1993). Borderline personality disorder and personality traits: A comparison of Structured Clinical Interview for *Diagnostic and Statistical Manual of Mental Disorders* Axis II Personality Disorders (SCID-II), borderline personality disorder and NEO-PI. *Psychological Assessment, 5*(4), 472–476.

Clarkin, J. F., Widiger, T. A., Frances, A., Hurt, S. W., & Gilmore, M. (1983). Prototypic typology and the borderline personality disorder. *Journal of Abnormal Psychology, 92*(3), 263–275.

Coolidge, F. L., & Merwin, M. M. (1992). Reliability and validity of the Coolidge Axis II Inventory: A new inventory for the assessment of personality disorders. *Journal of Personality Assessment, 59*(2), 223–238.

Cormier, S., & Nurius, P. (2003). *Interviewing and change strategies for helpers: Fundamental skills and cognitive behavioral interventions* (5th ed.). Pacific Grove, CA: Thomson/Brooks/Cole.

Cowdry, R. W., Pickar, D., & Davies, R. (1985). Symptoms and EEG findings in the borderline syndrome. *International Journal of Psychosomatic Medicine, 15*(3), 201–211.

Egan, S., Nathan, P., & Lumley, M. (2003). Diagnostic concordance of *ICD-10* personality and comorbid disorders: A comparison of standard clinical assessment and structured interviews in a clinical setting. *Australian and New Zealand Journal of Psychiatry, 37*(4), 484–494.

Farmer, R. F., & Chapman, A. L. (2002). Evaluation of *Diagnostic and Statistical Manual of Mental Disorders–IV* personality disorder criteria as assessed by the Structured Clinical Interview for *Diagnostic and Statistical Manual of Mental Disorders–IV* Personality Disorders. *Comprehensive Psychiatry, 43*(4), 285–300.

First, M. B., Gibbon, M., Spitzer, R. L., Williams, J. B. W., & Benjamin, L. S. (1997). *Structured Clinical Interview for* Diagnostic and Statistical Manual of Mental Disorders *Axis II Personality Disorders (SCID-II) personality questionnaire.* Washington, DC: American Psychiatric Press.

First, M. B., Spitzer, R. L., Gibbon, M., & Williams, J. B. W. (1995). *Structured Clinical Interview for* Diagnostic and Statistical Manual of Mental Disorders *Axis I Disorders: Patient edition (SCID-I/P, Version 2.0).* New York: Biometrics Research Department.

First, M. B., Spitzer, R. L., Gibbon, M., Williams, J. B. W., & Benjamin, L. (1996). *User's guide for the Structured Clinical Interview for* Diagnostic and Statistical Manual of Mental Disorders *Axis II Personality Disorders (SCID-II).* New York: Biometrics Research Department.

Fossati, A., Maffei, C., Bagnato, M., Battaglia, M., Donati, D., Donini, M., et al. (2000). Patterns of covariation of *Diagnostic and Statistical Manual of Mental Disorders–IV* personality disorders in a mixed psychiatric sample. *Comprehensive Psychiatry, 41,* 206–215.

Frances, A. J., Fyer, M. R., & Clarkin, J. F. (1986). Personality and suicide. *Annals of the New York Academy of Sciences, 487,* 281–293.

Gabbard, G. O. (1997). Finding the "person" in personality disorders. *American Journal of Psychiatry, 154*(7), 891–893.

Grove, W. M., & Tellegen, A. (1991). Problems in the classification of personality disorders. *Journal of Personality Disorders, 5*(1), 31–41.

Gunderson, J. G. (1984). *Borderline personality disorder.* Washington, DC: American Psychiatric Press.

Hathaway, S. R., & McKinley, J. C. (1943). *The Minnesota Multiphasic Personality Inventory* (rev. ed.). Minneapolis: University of Minnesota Press.

Hovey, J. D., & Magana, C. G. (2002). Psychosocial predictors or anxiety among immigrant Mexican migrant farmworkers: Implications for prevention and treatment. *Culturally Diversity & Ethnic Minority Psychology, 8*(3), 274–289.

Hunt, C., & Andrews, G. (1992). Measuring personality disorder: The use of self-report questionnaires. *Journal of Personality Disorders, 6*(2), 125–133.

Hutto, B. (2001). Potential overdiagnosis of bipolar disorder. *Psychiatric Services, 52*(5), 687.

Hyler, S. E. (1994). *The Personality Diagnostic Questionnaire 4+.* New York: New York State Psychiatric Institute.

Klein, M. H., & Benjamin, L. S. (1996). *The Wisconsin Personality Disorders Inventory–IV.* Madison: University of Wisconsin, unpublished test. Available from Dr. M. H. Klein, Department of Psychiatry, Wisconsin Psychiatric Institute and Clinic, 6001 Research Park Blvd., Madison, WI 53719-1179

Linehan, M. M. (1993a). *Cognitive-behavioral treatment of borderline personality disorder.* New York: Guilford.

Linehan, M. M. (1993b). *Skills training manual for treating borderline personality disorder.* New York: Guilford.

Linehan, M. M., Armstrong, H. E., Suarez, A., Allmon, D., & Heard, H. (1991). Cognitive-behavioral treatment of chronically parasuicidal borderline patients. *Archives of General Psychiatry, 48,* 1060–1064.

Linehan, M. M., Comtois, K. A., Murray, A. M., Brown, M. Z., Gallop, R. J., Heard, H. L., et al. (2006). Two-year randomized trial + follow-up of dialectical behavior therapy vs. therapy by experts for suicidal behaviors and borderline personality disorder. *Archives of General Psychiatry, 63,* 757–766.

Linehan, M. M., Dimeff, L. A., Reynolds, S. K., Comtois, K., Shaw-Welch, S., Heagerty, P., et al. (2002). Dialectical behavior therapy versus comprehensive validation plus 12 step for the treatment of opioid dependent women meeting criteria for borderline personality disorder. *Drug and Alcohol Dependence, 67,* 13–26.

Linehan, M. M., & Heard, H. L. (1993). Impact of treatment accessibility on clinical course of parasuicidal patients: In reply to R. E. Hoffman [Letter to the editor]. *Archives of General Psychiatry, 50,* 157–158.

Linehan, M. M., Heard, H. L., & Armstrong, H. E. (1993). Naturalistic follow-up of a behavioral treatment for chronically parasuicidal borderline patients. *Archives of General Psychiatry, 50*(12), 971–974.

Linehan, M. M., Schmidt, H., Dimeff, L. A., Craft, J. C., Kanter, J., & Comtois, K. A. (1999). Dialectical behavior therapy for patients with borderline personality disorder and drug-dependence. *American Journal of Addiction, 8*(4), 279–292.

Linehan, M. M., Tutek, D. A., Heard, H. L., & Armstrong, H. E. (1994). Interpersonal outcome of cognitive behavioral treatment for chronically suicidal borderline patients. *American Journal of Psychiatry, 151*(12), 1771–1776.

Loranger, A. W. (1995). *International Personality Disorder Examination (IPDE) manual.* White Plains, NY: Cornell Medical Center.

Loranger, A. W., Sartorius, N., Andreoli, A., Berger, P., Buchheim, P., Channabasavanna, S. M., et al. (1994). The International Personality Disorder Examination. The World Health Organization/Alcohol, Drug Abuse, and Mental Health Administration international pilot study of personality disorders. *Archives of General Psychiatry, 51,* 215–224.

Magill, C. (2004). The boundary between borderline personality disorders and bipolar disorder: Current concepts and challenges. *Canadian Journal of Psychiatry, 49,* 551–556.

McGlashan, T. H., Grilo, C. M., Skodol, A. E., Gunderson, J. G., Shea, M. T., Morey, L. C., et al. (2000). The collaborative longitudinal personality disorders study: Baseline Axis I/II and II/II diagnostic co-occurrence. *Acta Psychiatrica Scandinavica, 102,* 256–264.

Miller, S. (1996). Borderline personality disorder in cultural context: Commentary on Paris. *Psychiatry, 59*(2), 193–191.

Millon, T., Millon, C., & Davis, R. D. (1994). *Millon Clinical Multiaxial Inventory: III.* Minneapolis: National Computer Systems.

Modestin, J., Erni, T., & Oberson, B. (1998). A comparison of self-report and interview diagnoses of *Diagnostic and Statistical Manual of Mental Disorders III-R* personality disorders. *European Journal of Personality, 12,* 445–455.

Morey, L. C. (1996). *An interpretive guide to the Personality Assessment Inventory.* Odessa, FL: Psychological Assessment Resources.

Paris, J. (1996). *Social factors in the personality disorders.* New York: Cambridge University Press.

Paris, J. (1998). Personality disorders in sociocultural perspective. *Journal of Personality Disorders, 12*(4), 289–302.

Paris, J. (2005a). Borderline or bipolar? Distinguishing borderline personality disorder from bipolar spectrum disorders. *Harvard Review Psychiatry, 12,* 140–145.

Paris, J. (2005b). The diagnosis of borderline personality disorder: Problematic but better than the alternative. *Annals of Clinical Psychiatry, 17*(1), 41–46.

Paris, J., & Zweig-Frank, H. (2001). A 27-year follow-up of patients with borderline personality disorder. *Comprehensive Psychiatry, 42,* 482–487.

Perry, C. J. (1992). Problems and considerations in the valid assessment of personality disorders. *American Journal of Psychiatry, 149*(12), 1645–1653.

Pfohl, B., Blum, N., & Zimmerman, M. (1997). *Structured Interview for* Diagnostic and Statistical Manual of Mental Disorders–IV *Personality.* Washington, DC: American Psychiatric Press.

Pinto, C., Dhavale, H. S., Nair, S., Patil, B., & Dewan, M. (2000). Borderline personality disorder exists in India. *Journal of Nervous and Mental Disease, 188*(6), 386–388.

Renneberg, B., Schmidt-Rathjens, C., Hippin, R., Backenstrass, M., & Fydrich, T. (2005). Cognitive characteristics of patients with borderline personality disorder: Development and validation of a self-report inventory. *Journal of Behavior Therapy and Experimental Psychiatry, 36*(3), 173–182.

Reynolds, S. K., Lindenboim, N. L., Comtois, K. A., Murray, A., & Linehan, M. M. (2006). Risky assessments: Participant suicidality and distress associated with research assessments in a treatment study of suicidal behavior. *Suicide and Life Threatening Behavior, 36*(1), 19–34.

Samuels, J., Eaton, W. W., Bienvenu, J., Clayton, P., Brown, H., Costa, P. T., et al. (2002). Prevalence and correlates of personality disorders in a community sample. *British Journal of Psychiatry, 180,* 536–542.

Schotte, C., & De Doncker, D. (1996). *Assessment of* Diagnostic and Statistical Manual of Mental Disorders IV *Personality Disorders (ADP-IV) Questionnaire: Manual and norms.* Antwerp, Belgium: University Hospital Antwerp.

Schotte, C. K. W., De Doncker, D., Dmitruk, D., Van Mulders, I., D'Haenen, H., & Cosyns, P. (2004). Assessment of *Diagnostic and Statistical Manual of Mental Disorders IV* Personality Disorders (ADP-IV) Questionnaire: Differential validity and concordance with the semi-structured interview. *Journal of Personality Disorders, 18*(4), 405–419.

Skodol, A. E., Gunderson, J. G., Pfohl, B., Widiger, T. A., Lively, J. W., & Siever, L. J. (2002). The borderline diagnosis I: Psychopathology, comorbidity, and personality structure. *Biological Psychiatry, 51*(12), 936–950.

Skodol, A. E., Stout, R. L., McGlashan, T. H., Grilo, C. M., Gunderson, J. G., Shea, M. T., et al. (1999). Co-occurrence of mood and personality disorders: A report from the Collaborative Longitudinal Personality Disorders Study (CLPS). *Depression and Anxiety, 10,* 175–182.

Smith, D. J., Muir, W., & Blackwood, D. H. R. (2004). Is borderline personality disorder part of the bipolar spectrum? *Harvard Review of Psychiatry, 12*(3), 133–139.

Smith, T. L., Klein, M. H., & Benjamin, L. S. (2003). Wisconsin Personality Disorders Inventory–IV with the Structured Clinical Interview for *Diagnostic and Statistical Manual of Mental Disorders* Axis II Personality Disorders (SCID-II). *Journal of Personality Disorders, 17*(3) 173–183.

Sommers-Flanagan, R., & Sommers-Flanagan, J. (1999). *Clinical interviewing* (2nd ed.). New York: Wiley.

Stone, M. H. (1993). Long-term outcome in personality disorders. *British Journal of Psychiatry, 162,* 299–313.

Stone, M. H., Hurt, S. W., & Stone, D. K. (1987). The PI 500: Long-term follow-up of borderline inpatients meeting *Diagnostic and Statistical Manual of Mental Disorders–III* criteria: Global outcome. *Journal of Personality Disorders, 1,* 291–298.

Swartz, M., Blazer, D., George, L., & Winfield, I. (1990). Estimating the prevalence of borderline personality disorder in the community. *Journal of Personality Disorders, 4*(3), 257–272.

Torgersen, S., Kringlen, E., & Cramer, V. (2001). The prevalence of personality disorders in a community setting. *Archives of General Psychiatry, 58,* 590–596.

Trull, T. J., Sher, K. J., Minks-Brown, C., Durbin, J., & Burr, R. (2000). Borderline personality disorder and substance use disorders: A review and integration. *Clinical Psychology Review, 20*(2), 235–253.

Tyrer, P. (2004). New approaches to the diagnosis of psychopathy and personality disorder. *Journal of the Royal Society of Medicine, 97,* 371–374.

Verheul, R. (2005). Clinical utility of dimensional models for personality pathology. *Journal of Personality Disorders, 19*(3), 283–303.

Verheul, R., van den Bosch, L. M. C., Koeter, M. W. J., de Ridder, M. A. J., Stijnen, T., & van den Brink, W.

(2003). Dialectical behavior therapy for women with borderline personality disorder: 12-month, randomized clinical trial in the Netherlands. *British Journal of Psychiatry, 182,* 135–140.

Widiger, T. A. (2002). Personality disorders. In M. M. Antony & D. H. Barlow (Eds.), *Handbook of assessment and treatment planning for psychological disorders* (pp. 453–480). New York: Guilford.

Widiger, T. A., Mangine, S. L., Corbitt, E. M., Ellis, C. G., & Thomas, G. V. (1995). *Personality Disorder Interview–IV: A semistructured interview for the assessment of personality disorders. Professional manual.* Odessa, FL: Psychological Assessment Resources.

Widiger, T. A., Simonsen, E., Krueger, R., Livesley, J., & Verheul, R. (2005). Personality disorder research agenda for the *Diagnostic and Statistical Manual of Mental Disorders–V. Journal of Personality Disorders, 19*(3), 315–339.

World Health Organization. (1992). *International classification of diseases* (10th ed.). Washington, DC: Author.

Zanarini, M. C. (2003). Zanarini Rating Scale for Borderline Personality Disorder (ZAN-BPD): A continuous measure of *Diagnostic and Statistical Manual of Mental Disorders* borderline psychopathology. *Journal of Personality Disorders, 17*(3), 233–240.

Zanarini, M. C., Frankenburg, F. R., Dubo, E. D., Sickel, A. E., Trikha, A., Levin, A., et al. (1998a). Axis I comorbidity of borderline personality disorder. *American Journal of Psychiatry, 155,* 1733–1739.

Zanarini, M. C., Frankenburg, F. R., Dubo, E. D., Sickel, A. E., Trikha, A., Levin, A., et al. (1998b). Axis II comorbidity of borderline personality disorder. *Comprehensive Psychiatry, 39,* 296–302.

Zanarini, M. C., Frankenburg, F. R., Hennen, J., Reich, D. B., & Silk, K. R. (2004). Axis I comorbidity in patients with borderline personality disorder: 6-year follow-up and prediction of time to remission. *American Journal of Psychiatry, 161,* 2108–2114.

Zanarini, M. C., Frankenburg, F. R., Sickel, A. E., & Yong, L. (1996). *The Diagnostic Interview for Diagnostic and Statistical Manual of Mental Disorders–IV Personality Disorders (DIPD-IV).* Belmont, MA: McLean Hospital.

Zanarini, M. C., Gunderson, J. G., Frankenburg, F. R., & Chauncey, D. L. (1989). The Revised Diagnostic Interview for Borderlines: Discriminating borderline personality disorder from other Axis II disorders. *Journal of Personality Disorders, 3,* 10–18.

Zanarini, M. C., Vujanovic, A. A., Parachini, E. A., Boulanger, J. L., Frankenburg, F. R., & Hennen, J. (2003). A screening measure for borderline personality disorder: The McLean Screening Instrument for Borderline Personality Disorder (MSI-BPD). *Journal of Personality Disorders, 17*(6), 568–573.

Zimmerman, M., & Mattia, J. I. (1999). Axis I diagnostic comorbidity and borderline personality disorder. *Comprehensive Psychiatry, 40,* 245–252.

Zimmerman, M., Rothschild, L., & Chelminski, I. (2005). The prevalence of *Diagnostic and Statistical Manual of Mental Disorders–IV* personality disorders in psychiatric outpatients. *American Journal of Psychiatry, 162,* 1911–1918.

20

ALCOHOL AND OTHER DRUG DISORDERS

JON MORGENSTERN AND THOMAS IRWIN

DESCRIPTION OF THE DISORDERS

For the purposes of this chapter we will define alcohol and other drug use disorders consistent with the approach of the *Diagnostic Statistical Manual of Mental Disorders, Fourth Edition* (*DSM-IV*; American Psychiatric Association, 1994). *DSM-IV* groups substances into 11 pharmacological classes including alcohol, amphetamines, cannabis, cocaine, nicotine, and opiates. This chapter will not address nicotine because treatment of nicotine dependence differs substantially from that of other substance use disorders. In addition, *DSM-IV* divides substance use disorders into two major classifications—abuse and dependence—and provides a set of operational criteria to determine categorically whether these disorders are present or absent. *Abuse* is broadly defined as a maladaptive pattern of use leading to recurrent negative consequences such as legal problems. Dependence, a more severe disorder, is defined by presence of a cluster of symptoms indicating psychological and in many cases physiological dependence. *DSM-IV* also defines more minor disorder classifications such as substance intoxication, but these will not be discussed in this chapter.

Although *DSM-IV* provides an accepted and simplifying clinical heuristic for classification purposes, it is important for clinicians treating alcohol and other drug use disorders to understand a broader set of conceptual, empirical, and clinical knowledge that underlies the *DSM-IV* and other classification schemes. First, alcohol and other drug use problems are best understood as existing along a continuum of three interrelated dimensions: patterns of consumption, negative consequences, and dependence or addiction. In order to adequately characterize substance use issues for any client, clinicians should assess each of these domains within a continuous framework. Second, although the broad concepts of patterns of consumption, negative consequences, abuse, and dependence apply across different substance classes, their manifestations can be specific to each drug class. For example, dependence may manifest itself in different sets of symptom clusters in alcohol and in cannabis. Therefore, clinicians need general and substance class–specific knowledge to adequately assess and treat substance use problems.

Contemporary schemes for understanding substance use problems are strongly influenced by Edwards and Gross's (1976) work on the dependence syndrome and by an emerging public health framework (Saitz, 2005). The essential postulates of the dependence syndrome include clustering of cognitive, behavioral, and physiological elements that are related to a common process; distribution of these elements along a continuum of severity; and independence of dependence from negative consequences of use. These postulates set the stage for defining dependence and negative consequences as separate but related dimensions. Dependence is characterized by salience, impaired control, and manifestations of physiological dependence. Salience is defined by cognitive and behavioral preoccupation with the substance use to the exclusion of other valued activities. Impaired control is manifested by an inability to stop or control use despite knowledge of recurrent negative consequences. Physiological dependence is defined by the presence of tolerance, withdrawal, and use of substances to avoid withdrawal. Although *DSM-IV* provides an operational demarcation of presence or absence of dependence based on a threshold of three symptoms, studies have shown that dependence exists along a continuum of severity (Meyer, 2001), and measures are available that provide reliable and valid dimensional ratings (Cooney, Kadden, & Steinberg, 2005).

Negative consequences are problems that occur as a result of substance use. Negative consequences typically are grouped based on life domains such as social, health related, legal, and psychological. A wide variety of clinically informative measures provide dimensional ratings of negative consequences (Miller, Tonigan, & Longabaugh, 1995). People who are dependent invariably experience negative consequences. As substance dependence grows more severe, the experience of negative consequences increases across life domains. However, people can experience negative consequences without being dependent. *DSM-IV* defines abuse as the recurrent experience of negative consequences in the absence of dependence.

Patterns of consumption consist of the frequency, quantity, type, and route of administration of a substance. Patterns of consumption do not in themselves define substance use disorders. Therefore, knowing someone is a daily drinker doesn't indicate that he or she has a drinking problem. However, each feature of a pattern of use can have important assessment implications. For example, the oral ingestion of amphetamines

has much less addictive potential than smoking or injection (Hanson, 2002). Contemporary public health frameworks have attempted to place people into a unified classification framework based on consumption, consequences, and dependence (Institute of Medicine, 1990). Such classification helps to guide public policy and may be useful in communicating effectively with patients. For example, Richard Saitz (2005) defines a continuum of unhealthy alcohol use. People are classified as risky drinkers if they consume excessive amounts of alcohol that put them at future risk of disease, even if they currently not experiencing drinking problems. People are classified as problem drinkers if they drink excessively and experience occasional, mild problems, even if they do not meet *DSM-IV* criteria for alcohol abuse or dependence.

In summary, *DSM-IV* divides the major categories of substance use disorders into abuse and dependence. Although *DSM-IV* provides a useful heuristic, it is critical for clinicians to understand substance use problems along three interrelated dimensions of consumption, negative consequences, and dependence and to know how to assess the unique manifestations of these constructs across different substance classes. Readers interested in a more comprehensive explication of these issues can find it in recent books devoted to the topic of addiction (Donovan & Marlatt, 2005; Frances, Miller, & Mack, 2005).

INTERVIEWING STRATEGIES

There are many functions that interviewing serves when working with those who have substance use disorders. Strategies used for interviewing purposes depend heavily on the amount of time available to conduct the interview and its function, such as a brief assessment, structured intake interview, or an initial session that leads to ongoing treatment. For didactic purposes we will focus on the latter context, although the principles described here can apply to any context. The conduct of a good interview with any client requires knowledge, skill, and experience. This is especially true for clients with substance use disorders. The particular challenges in interviewing clients with substance use disorders stem from the client's ambivalence about change, the difficulty in accurately assessing this complex disorder, and, at times, the interviewer's beliefs or reactions to clients that can interfere with establishing rapport. The past 20 years have witnessed a sea change in approaches to interviewing substance-abusing clients and a revolution in the knowledge about the disorder. This sea change is represented in two conceptual and clinician approaches: motivational interviewing (Miller & Rollnick, 2002) and behavioral assessment. Each approach outlines a clear set of principles and techniques that can function on their own. However, most experts agree that the approaches complement each other. In this section, we describe motivational interviewing and its contribution to addressing obstacles typically encountered in developing a working relationship with substance use–disordered clients. We will also outline the principles of behavioral assessment, but we provide a description of behavioral assessment techniques in a later section.

Establishing Rapport and Facilitating Change

Motivational interviewing is a brief intervention strategy designed to mobilize a client's internal resources for change by increasing intrinsic motivation. Motivational interviewing is not just a set of techniques, but a style of being with people that shares many of the qualities of Rogerian therapy, such as therapist communication of empathy and genuineness. Perhaps the most innovative aspect of motivational interviewing is the assumption that even a brief encounter with a professional can facilitate change if that encounter is appropriately structured. This approach argues that any encounter with a patient should never be relegated solely to information collection but rather should be viewed in the context of a dynamic change process. Similarly, approaches that take a confrontational or even neutral information-gathering stance are likely to elicit client resistance and lead to inaccurate or incomplete information.

Clearly, the first challenge in interviewing any client is establishing rapport. Motivational interviewing posits that in order to establish rapport, therapists must understand client behavior within the conceptual frameworks of stages of change (Prochaska, DiClemente, & Norcross, 1992) and cognitive conflict theory (Orford, 1985). Both theories view client's attitudes toward change as dynamic, fluctuating based on interpersonal context, and multilayered. Stages of change theory

views clients' attitudes about changing any behavior as arrayed along a continuum of five distinct stages: precontemplation, in which the client does not believe he or she has a problem; contemplation, in which the client is concerned about the issue but not considering change just yet; preparation, in which the client acknowledges having a problem and is ready for change; taking action to change; and maintenance, in which the client has made changes and is working to maintain these changes. Identifying what stage of change a client is in is critical to the interviewing process and the establishment of good rapport. Cognitive conflict theory posits that ambivalence is the central feature of the struggle to overcome addictive problems, that ambivalence is present even when not apparent, and that ambivalence must be identified and engaged rather than overridden. A key aspect of motivational interviewing is identifying the occurrence of ambivalence via various manifestations of patient resistance and responding in a manner that engages rather than confronts the patient.

Motivational interviewing identifies four specific interviewing strategies as critical to establishing initial rapport: expressing empathy, developing discrepancy, rolling with resistance, and supporting self-efficacy. Expressing empathy involves the use of classic nondirective interviewing strategies, especially open-ended questions and reflective listening. If a client with a substance use problem feels that he or she is being listened to and understood in a nonjudgmental fashion, it dramatically increases the chances he or she will discuss sensitive topics that the therapist might not have had access to using a more neutral or confrontational stance. In addition, motivational interviewing has identified 12 typical types of therapist communications that can interfere with the self-disclosure process and are labeled roadblocks to communication. Use of nondirective counseling techniques, especially reflective listening and avoidance of communication roadblocks, provide a basis for the establishment of initial rapport, although motivational interviewing recommends several more advanced strategies.

Content Domains

Although motivational interviewing provides the strategies for facilitating rapport and mobilizing the change process, a complementary component of any interview is the collection of information needed for appropriate assessment and treatment planning. The literature on behavioral assessment of substance use disorders provides a comprehensive framework on what information should be collected and specific assessment techniques needed to ensure accurate reporting. Behavioral assessment entails a concrete and highly structured approach to gathering information. The behavioral assessment approach is clearly different from the one used in motivational interviewing. Experienced interviewers typically develop a feel for how to blend these approaches. Beginning interviewers are advised to start with motivational strategies and transition to more of a directive and structured approach after rapport has been established.

In this section, we describe the primary domains of behavioral assessment. This will provide readers with a context for understanding the case illustration. Then we will elaborate on each domain. A reasonably complete behavioral assessment should cover four content domains: descriptive features of the problem, learning factors that maintain the problem, the patient's views on change, and other information including environmental and social factors needed to determine the recommended setting, intensity, and foci of treatment, if treatment is warranted. Assessment of the descriptive features of the problem includes patterns of consumption, negative consequences, substance dependence and the assessment of co-occurring mental health, cognitive, and medical problems.

Empirical evidence provides strong support for the role of learning factors including classical and operant conditioning and cognitive mediation as key elements that maintain addictive behaviors (Rotgers, 2003). These factors are assessed via a functional analysis of substance use behaviors. A functional analysis begins with identification of the antecedents of substance use. These are either situational cues, such as the presence of the substances or surroundings associated with substance use such as a bar or club, or internal cues, such as negative mood states. These cues, or conditioned stimuli, trigger a highly automatized set of physiological, cognitive, and behavioral processes that often occur outside awareness. Cues trigger strong positive cognitive expectancies about the rewarding aspects of substance use, often accompanied by strong cravings to indulge. If they remain unchecked, these appetitive

processes lead to substance use. However, cues also set off higher-order cognitive control processes. These involve future judgments of the positive and negative consequences of use, coping actions that can be taken to restrain behavior, and the person's beliefs about whether he or she is capable of exercising self-control. A well-conducted functional analysis will yield a portrait of the factors that maintain addictive behaviors, including the set of situational factors that trigger use, positive and negative expectancies about use, the positive and negative consequences of use, coping behaviors available to the patient to exercise control, and situational self-efficacy judgments indicative of how well the patient feels he or she can control his or her behavior in tempting situations. These constructs will be elaborated on and illustrated in later sections.

A third content domain is the client's views about change. Although it may seem self-evident to the therapist that the client is engaged in self-destructive behavior, it is important to remember that any client change entails decision making and selection of alternative choices. Therefore, understanding the client's perspective on these issues is critical. Clients' views of change can be characterized by four domains: readiness to change; decisional balance; self-efficacy, or the belief that positive change can occur; and goal setting. Readiness to change has already been discussed. Decisional balance consists of cognitive appraisals about the likely positive or negative impacts of change, specifically the likely benefits of continuing to use substances and its costs as opposed to the likely benefits of reducing or stopping the use of substances and its costs. Novice therapists often fail to appreciate that substance abusers experience strong positive rewards from using despite the consequences and may see stopping use, at least initially, as a less attractive alternative. In addition to self-efficacy judgments about individual situations that trigger use (e.g., attending a party where liquor is served), clients also have generalized beliefs about their ability to change. These beliefs are intimately connected with judgments about self-worth, shame, and hopelessness and the desire to prevail over self-destructive behavior. Finally, clients have views about their goals for change. These include choices about moderating or reducing use versus quitting, choices about whether to attempt to change on one's own, and if one is seeking help, choices about whether to attend self-help groups or formal treatment.

A fourth and final content domain is environmental and other factors that influence the selection of setting, intensity, and foci of treatment. Clients with chronic and severe substance use disorders experience an array of medical and social problems that complicate treatment decisions. For example, if a client lives in a shelter surrounded by drug abusers, the appropriate recommendation for treatment will look quite different from that of the same client who lives with a supportive family. The American Society of Addiction Medicine Patient Placement Criteria (Mee-Lee & Shulman, 2003) provides an assessment framework for considering these issues and will be discussed in a later section.

INTERVIEWING OBSTACLES AND SOLUTIONS

Clients with substance use disorders often present special challenges. These problems entail minimization or even denial of factual aspects of the problem, a displacement of responsibility onto others, and a seeming indifference to even dire consequences of substance abuse. In the face of such behavior, it is not uncommon for professionals to conclude that most substance abusers are inherently dishonest and untrustworthy, that standard interview strategies are useless, and that more confrontational or coercive methods of information gathering are needed. An important first step in taking a more productive stance is to understand the factors that underlie surface manifestations of resistance and denial.

Cognitive conflict theory (Orford, 1985) views ambivalence about change as the core feature of addictive problems. Although people may present as either blithely uninterested in their problems or, conversely, unequivocally motivated to change the problem, a deep sense of ambivalence is invariably present. Equally important is the notion that at times of high conflict ambivalence usually is represented by "hot cognitions," which are not organized in coherent or rational systems. Thus, clients can present as indifferent or denying the problem in an interview and yet later experience intense panic and fear. Such defensive cognitive distortions are well described in the psychodynamic literature under the label of primitive defense mechanisms such as splitting (Kernberg,

1983). However, cognitive conflict theory posits these as temporary manifestations of a struggle with addiction rather than stable, enduring cognitive styles rooted in character pathology. Once it is viewed from this perspective, recognizing and addressing ambivalence is critical to effectively dealing with denial.

In addition, social stigma about substance abuse plays a profound role in the interview process. Self-disclosure of many private behaviors is problematic because they are viewed as socially undesirable. However, substance abuse typically is more stigmatizing because it is often viewed by society as morally reprehensible. By the time they seek help most clients have been told by others that their behavior is shameful and corrupt. Thus, clients enter the interview situation with at least the implicit expectation, often a reflection of their own internal perceptions, that therapists will judge them harshly as well. Failure to manage these expectations interferes with the process of self-disclosure.

Another more subtle but potentially powerful obstacle concerns a client's belief or self-efficacy about the ability to change. Almost without exception clients have experienced repeated failures to change their behavior on their own, and many have failed to resolve their problems even after treatment. Client resistance may reflect profound doubt about the ability to change and unwillingness to wholeheartedly engage in a process that will once again lead to deep disappointment. In addition, clients often have negative views of treatment and see placement in treatment as a stigmatizing and potentially punitive experience.

In addition to these psychological factors, other aspects of the setting and cognitive functioning of clients can present obstacles. Many clients with substance use disorders are referred for assessment by others, including family members, employers, and the criminal justice system. The extent to which information from the interview will be shared with others obviously is a complicating factor. Finally, clients with substance use disorders can experience cognitive problems as the result of either acute intoxication or the chronic effects of substances. These problems impair a client's ability to remember events. Cognitive impairment often goes undetected and is confused with resistance.

The natural tendency of most caring professionals when interacting with a client in denial, especially one facing imminent risks, is to confront, direct, advise, and warn clients. Unfortunately, these actions exacerbate the underlying causes of resistance, leading to surface compliance on the part of clients or outright argument and conflict. Instead, motivational interviewing recommends that therapists adopt a quite different stance, one that is client centered and attempts to engage rather than override ambivalence. This approach begins with use of nondirective counseling skills and attention to establishing good rapport. In addition, therapists help clients to develop discrepancies between their current behaviors and wished-for goals. For example, a therapist might use a value clarification task to initiate a discussion of goals or dreams a client has that have been thwarted by substance use. Developing discrepancies help clients become aware of their ambivalence and to turn "hot cognitions" into more organized constructs that are accessible to reasoning.

Another useful strategy to engage ambivalence is rolling with resistance. Clients can be expected to express resistance in overt or subtle ways during the interview. If the therapist takes on resistance directly by confronting it, the effect is often that the therapist ends up advocating the argument for change, while the patient argues against change. Instead, therapists are counseled to note resistance but deal with it in a way that facilitates the client's recognition of both sides of the issue. For example, rather than beginning by asking the client about the negative effects of substance use, the therapist might start by asking what the client enjoys about substance use. A final advanced interviewing strategy is supporting self-efficacy, or the client's belief in the possibility of change. Here again the focus is on a client-centered rather than prescriptive or didactic approach. Overall, motivational interviewing strategies are designed to manage the obstacles that underlie denial and resistance. Although motivational interviewing strategies facilitate greater client openness, it is important to recognize that for some clients coming to grips with the full extent of substance abuse can be a long and painful process. In these cases having additional sources of information about the client's behavior from family members, employers, and biological assessment of substance use can be extremely useful. (Interested readers can learn more about motivational interviewing in Miller & Rollnick, 2002, and Moyers & Waldorf, 2003.)

CASE ILLUSTRATION WITH DIALOGUE

A.R. is a client who has been seen in outpatient therapy for several months. He is a man in his mid-50s who has been drinking since his early college days. He has a successful life on almost any domain that could be measured. He is a husband to the woman he fell in love with in college. They have two sons who are young adults and have begun to be quite successful in their own careers. A.R. has been a successful lawyer for a large law firm in an urban area, in spite of, as he says, having a personality that might be suited to a more passive profession.

He acknowledges that he has very high levels of anxiety related to his profession and is uncomfortable when he is in litigation. He describes himself as passive and nonconfrontational and has used alcohol to help him cope with stress and anxiety associated with his career. To his credit, he used his own resources and professional help through psychotherapy to battle what was probably a very high level of social anxiety and kept it from interfering with his professional goals as a lawyer.

He sees that the culture and society around him and his profession have changed dramatically in the three decades since he first started working. Twenty-five years ago it was common to see professionals drink heavily even at lunch and go back to work afterward obviously impaired. Although he participated in this to some extent, he was always very cautious about his drinking and how it might affect his career. Mostly, drinking has been a way to relax after hard days and continues to serve this function even to this day. He states that weekends, particularly Sundays, are very stressful for him, and he rarely is able to enjoy his time because he is constantly thinking about the week ahead and the challenges he will have to face.

By his self-report, he states that he usually drinks two to three drinks on weekday evenings after getting home from work but that there are frequent occasions when he has more. He indicates that rarely will he have more than five or six in any given weekday evening. Weekends are different, though, and his drinking starts earlier in the day and lasts longer. One of his favorite things to do is to cook for the family on Sundays, and he enjoys drinking during the early afternoon and into the time when he starts his meal preparation. By the end of the meal, he has found himself going to sleep long before others are ready to retire because of his alcohol intake. This and other situations like it make him feel that he isn't connected to his family and friends as much as he would like.

He feels that drinking has caused some tension in his relationship with his wife, but his wife has been very supportive and patient with him over the years. The negative consequences of his drinking have not been extensive but have included some incidents when he has been embarrassed after getting too intoxicated at a dinner out with his wife and friends when he was slurring his words. His wife has been upset by this and similar incidents, and A.R. feels that he wants them to end.

Overall, A.R.'s profile fits that of a problem drinker with mild alcohol dependence. He is drinking more than 20 standard drinks per week. On weeks when he drinks heavily, he can consume more than 50 standard drinks. He experiences current negative consequences. Although these negatively affect his life, they are not severe. In addition, he experiences loss of control over drinking and salience in the sense that he has given up other valued activities in order to drink. However, he does not manifest *DSM-IV* symptoms of withdrawal or drinking to avoid withdrawal and therefore does not meet criteria for more severe dependence associated with physiological dependence.

A.R. has attempted to moderate his drinking for many, many years. He has tried disulfiram, naltrexone, and acamprosate as methods to reduce his cravings and alcohol intake. These have not been effective for him, he says. He has participated in many years of psychotherapy, mostly to cope with anxiety directly but also to help him discuss his drinking and try to keep it from getting out of control. Over the years, A.R. has had times when his drinking was successfully controlled, and he often wonders whether he can return to those drinking patterns. He was able to not drink during the week and limit weekend drinking to two or three drinks an evening.

One of the criteria A.R. used for choosing a professional was to find someone who would be willing to work with him on his drinking from a behavioral or cognitive-behavioral perspective. Early discussions about the philosophy of how people change were important to him, including a desire not to have to rely on religiosity or spirituality as a treatment component, which was something that had turned him off from Alcoholics Anonymous (AA). He also found the label *alcoholic* uncomfortable, but he did recognize that he was not always able to control his drinking. Powerlessness, the concept in AA that an alcoholic is completely unable to control his drinking, was something that puzzled him. He believed this to be inconsistent with his setting and trying to achieve goals related to drinking. He felt it might be possible to cope with alcohol problems in a similar way as he had with his problems with anxiety, via self-mastery. A.R.'s views and experience about change are similar to those of many problem drinkers. He is unsure whether he can successfully moderate his drinking. He has attended AA meetings, been treated with medications, and received psychotherapy. None of these approaches has worked especially well.

Probably because of his experiences in therapy, a positive therapeutic working alliance appeared to be achieved quickly. He seemed comfortable disclosing negative consequences related to drinking. Throughout the early sessions, motivational interviewing techniques were used, such as open-ended questions and reflective listening, to explore factors related to his drinking. Drinking had long been an important part of A.R.'s life, and he was not easily able to envision himself as a nondrinker (or ex-drinker). Throughout these sessions he was always highly ambivalent about change, and he recognized this ambivalence. He found it helpful to understand that ambivalence is a normal experience for people in his situation.

One of the difficulties A.R. faced as he weighed the positive and negative consequences of drinking is that he never experienced consequences so grave that he was in immediate danger. Instead, A.R. believed that the most powerful negative consequences were that drinking limited his ability to participate in activities that were meaningful to him and to fully enjoy time with his family. The positive side of drinking for him was that it was a fast and effective means of managing the anxiety he experienced from work, and it was helpful in getting him to relax after a long day of work. His father drank to excess and stopped only when a doctor told him that if he didn't stop drinking he would die. His father once commented to A.R. that quitting drinking is easy if you know that you will suffer grave physical effects quickly. This comment made an impression with A.R. because he knew that his situation wasn't as dire.

At the same time, however, he was very much aware that his drinking conflicted with things he valued dearly, such as his role as a father and husband. These realizations achieved via the use of motivational interviewing strategies helped A.R. become aware of this ambivalence while solidifying the therapeutic alliance.

Over the course of several sessions, it became apparent that his motivation for change fluctuated and to some degree depended on the successes and failures he had experienced in the prior week. In the first few sessions he was not interested in setting goals; rather, he wanted to discuss his options. Rather than pushing for change, the therapist reflected A.R.'s desire to make his own decisions. Eventually, A.R. asked for advice about setting drinking goals, and he and the therapist discussed what would be considered safe levels of drinking. Additionally, they compared what he might experience by trying to abstain altogether with the challenges of moderated drinking. From early in these discussions it was apparent that he wanted to choose moderation as an option to at least try and to perhaps shift to abstinence if these attempts were not successful. After about a month, A.R. decided that he wanted to try to moderate his drinking by not having any nights where he drank heavily, which was defined as more than three drinks. Also, he did not want to drink during the week, but only Friday through Sunday. A.R.'s selection of a goal was the end point in a process of struggling with his ambivalence, becoming aware of the positive and negative consequences of his drinking, and weighing various change options. His setting a clear goal for drinking was an important accomplishment that helped frame subsequent sessions.

It was always a pleasure to work with A.R., in large part because of his consistent attendance and his ability to discuss his successes and failures frankly without a great deal of defensiveness. It was not like him to hide what he saw as his failures or hide his shame or guilt when he had not been able to stop drinking during the week. At times, his emotions were quite evident in session, particularly when he felt that he had let his wife or children down during these episodes. Despite his nondefensive nature, A.R. did have some barriers that interfered with his ability to change. A.R. felt that having to quit drinking altogether was a sign of weakness. The idea of not drinking in a social setting was challenging not because he didn't have think he could accomplish this but because he didn't want to be perceived as a person who "couldn't drink," which he felt was a sign of weakness or inferiority. Additionally, he probably underestimated the quantity of drinking he was doing. He did not measure or count, and after getting started with a few beers or a few glasses of wine, he lost track of how much he had actually consumed. When asked to review his drinking experiences, he would often fail to include these heavy drinking episodes. Although this might be chalked up to "denial," a more clinically useful way to conceptualize this phenomenon is to attribute it to cognitive distortion that serves to protect a more functional view of oneself when reality is too threatening to consider closely.

Other barriers that A.R. experienced included a view of self-help programs that were somewhat unrealistic. Although he understood that social support was an important component, in previous attempts to attend AA meetings he had found it difficult to relate to others with similar circumstances. During the course of treatment, it was clear that he wanted to set his own agenda and that directive efforts to guide him would be met with resistance. He wanted collaboration rather than someone dictating what he should do and when.

Through a functional analysis with A.R., it became apparent that several key times posed a particular problem for his plan. First, weekdays were difficult because he commuted out of the city where he lived via commuter rail. Before getting on the train, he usually passed several beer vendors and often picked up a beer or two for the trip home on weekend nights. He believed that this trigger was the biggest barrier for him on weekdays and that if he could cope with the urge at this stage he would have a good chance of making it through the rest of the evening. However, weekday evenings were also difficult when he got home from work. He often got home from work before his wife did and would start dinner for the two of them. This usually included a glass of wine, which he would continue to consume throughout the evening. Uncorking a wine bottle had become strongly associated with his official end of the business day and a time when he could start to unwind from his job. Also, being alone, he did not have the support and or pressure from his wife to not have the wine.

Weekends were a little more difficult because these were days when A.R. wanted to limit his drinking instead of not drinking altogether. Information from the functional analysis suggested that drinking earlier, say with lunch, was not easy to manage for A.R. For him, it was easy to disregard his goal after one or two drinks, and if this occurred too early he would often think to himself, "I'm not going to be able to meet my goal for the day, so I might as well drink as much as I want." One or two beers during lunch would turn into many before the afternoon was over. Sundays were particularly difficult for him. He often cooked Sunday dinner for the family, and this process almost always included drinking wine throughout the meal preparation time, which could last much of the afternoon. He came to enjoy this activity very much because it gave him an opportunity to spend time with his family.

Probably the most powerful trigger A.R. faced each week was coping with the anxiety he experienced as Sunday morning turned into Sunday afternoon and A.R. started to contemplate the week ahead. His anxiety rose in a very predictable way, and by late Sunday afternoon A.R. would be ruminating about the challenges he didn't want to have to deal with at the office. Drinking wine afforded him the ability to not think about the difficulties until Monday morning. Further behavioral analyses indicated that it was likely that his drinking severely exacerbated the anxiety he experienced on Monday mornings, once the anxiolytic effects of the alcohol had worn off. Two examples from a functional analysis worksheet completed during treatment appear in Table 20.1.

During his treatment A.R. fluctuated in his motivation for change, which was reflected in his ambivalence in his goal choice. Once he had set goals for not drinking during the week and drinking in moderation on weekends, complete success occurred only occasionally. Most weeks he was not totally successful and would describe situations that had come up for which he made exceptions to his drinking goal. These exceptions would be explored in session to evaluate whether the goals he had set were appropriate and whether they should be reevaluated. This would usually end up with him reaffirming his goals and stating that he was comfortable with them as they were. After several months of therapy, he came in one day and described an event that had a very large impact on how he felt about his drinking, related to an acquaintance he had known for many years.

A.R.:   I'd like to start with something this week that had a big impact on me. And it has really changed the way I am thinking about my own life and what I should do. I've had a friend, not a great friend, but someone who has lived in my neighborhood for many years and who has kids about the same age as mine. He is a doctor who has been working for a hospital in the area. I'm not really sure what he does, but he's been at it for a long time and has done real well for himself and his family. He worked very long hours and didn't really

Table 20.1   Examples from A.R.'s Functional Analysis Worksheet

Trigger: Getting off work			
Thoughts and Feelings	*Response*	*Positive Consequences*	*Negative Consequences*
Wanting to relax after working, feeling tired and tense	Having a beer for the train ride home	Was able to forget about the day	Kept drinking and wasn't able to enjoy the evening with his wife
Trigger: Sunday afternoon			
Thoughts and Feelings	*Response*	*Positive Consequences*	*Negative Consequences*
Feeling anxiety about work on Monday	Drinking wine during the day while cooking	Was able to avoid thinking about the day	Feeling even more anxious on Monday morning Not enjoying the evening with his wife and kids

have a lot of time for his family. Anyway, I heard over the weekend that he overdosed on some kind of painkiller, which just surprised me. No one knew that he had a problem with it, but apparently he has been using drugs from the place he works for a long time.

Therapist: It sounds like that was difficult to hear.

A.R.:   The thing that got me was that you would never know that this was going on. He never seemed like the type to get involved with that kind of thing, and I never saw that he was affected in any way. I don't think other people saw it either.

T: So how did this change your thinking about your situation?

A.R.:   The thing that made me take notice is that it reminds me of myself and that I've had the ability to go through my life without my drinking being too noticed by others. I get by okay. The realization is that like him, I haven't been very good at balancing my life the way I'd like to. I work too much, and while I have a good relationship with my kids, I feel like I missed a big part of their growing up. The real issue is that I feel like the drinking takes me away from the most important things in life, much like the drugs probably did for him. It's like he had this whole separate life that existed without anyone else. It just seems sad to me. I don't want to end up sick or, even worse, wishing that I would have stopped drinking a long time ago.

T: So does this change how you want to proceed with things?

A.R.:   I think so. It certainly changes the way I've been thinking about my drinking and makes me think this is maybe more serious than I have wanted to believe. I've been wondering if it might be better to not drink altogether. I'm not sure how to go about doing that, but I'm starting to think in that direction.

Although this event did not have an immediate effect on his goals and behaviors, it certainly changed the way he thought about his drinking, and soon after this event he had another occurrence of drinking heavily and causing an awkward situation for his wife. One morning session after a holiday weekend, A.R. came to the office,

and the only way to describe his look was defeated. He went on to discuss the event.

Therapist: How was your holiday?

A.R.:   I've not had a good week. My wife and I had friends over for the holiday, and things just kind of slipped away from me. I had a great time putting things together for the meal and preparing for company. I did start drinking pretty early in the day, which was a big mistake I guess. I thought I was doing well. The meal went well, and everyone seemed to be enjoying themselves, including me. I'm not sure what happened really. I got really tired during the meal and afterwards was talking to the guests. I kind of had the impression at some point that our guests were slowly heading out to go home, so I went upstairs to take a nap. I kept sleeping through the rest of the afternoon and evening, and it was only the next day that I knew something was wrong. My wife was very upset with me and told me that she was disappointed that I just abandoned the party. Apparently people were not leaving, as I had thought, and my wife was in the position of having to tell people that I wasn't feeling well.

T: How are you feeling about that at this point?

A.R.:   Well, I feel bad that I let her down. That's what feels the worst right now. I'm not really sure what to do. I don't think I can do this anymore. I feel like I get it right a lot of the times but that sometimes it just kind of gets away from me.

T: So experiences like this make you wonder if it's worth it?

A.R.:   Very much. I just am tired of disappointing her and myself. I don't really know how to proceed here, though. I would like to walk away from drinking, but I don't really know how to. How do you just stop and not drink anymore?

T: It's hard to imagine what your life would look like if alcohol weren't a part of it.

A.R.:   I've been talking to my sister—the one that is in AA—about this stuff. She hasn't had a drink in many years and has really enjoyed it. She likes AA a lot but doesn't really go to meetings anymore. I don't think that it's right for me, but I am thinking that I might need to stop.

These events illustrate the expected unfolding process of change. A.R. has embarked on a plan to reduce drinking, is struggling to achieve his goals, and in the process obtains a deeper realization of the true cost of his drinking in terms of what he is giving up and the disappointment his drinking is causing to his wife. The therapist's role is help A.R. experience his disappointments and the consequences of his goal choice and use them to increase his motivation and efforts toward change. After these events, A.R. decided to try to go to some AA meetings in his area. Most often, he found it difficult to relate to others, and the concept of being powerless over alcohol was difficult to incorporate into his concept of change. Several ensuing discussions involved his ambivalence about abstinence and attendance at AA meetings. A.R. continued to struggle with whether to stop drinking altogether and eventually decided to continue to try to moderate.

A behavioral intervention strategy continued to be tailored for his goal choice, and a treatment plan was put together based on the functional analysis. The treatment plan for A.R. included a focus on several general tasks that would help him cope with the desire to drink. The first was to develop a plan to reduce the anxiety and tension related to his job. In analyzing some tools he had used in the past, A.R. reported that he had meditated and indicated that it had been helpful at one point, but he had gotten out of the habit. A daily meditation plan was developed, and he thought it would be a good idea to try to meditate three times a day, each for about 10 to 15 minutes.

The second task was to develop a support network. This proved to be somewhat difficult for A.R. It did not seem to be his nature to reach out to others in difficult times, which may have been one reason that self-help meetings were difficult. However, he did have a friend that he considered close enough to talk to, who also tended to drink a lot and who was also interested in limiting his alcohol intake. He thought that this might be a good place to start and was able to have several lunch meetings with this friend in order to discuss these issues.

The third task was to make attempts to use his time away from work in ways that were more rewarding. During a discussion of things that would serve this purpose, he mentioned that he had thought for many years that volunteering would be a very good thing to do. He had several ideas, which included the possibility of mentoring people who were interested in pursuing a career in law through a local college. A second idea was to involve himself in a local nonprofit that served the needs of underprivileged boys and girls. These discussions of volunteering were very exciting to A.R., and volunteering seemed to serve several functions. It provided a way to feel more connected to the community and also to help him feel that his time could be used in valuable ways because he often felt that the time he spent drinking was time being wasted. A fourth task was related to his overall health, which he recognized as being compromised by his drinking, at least in part because he didn't exercise as often as he thought he should.

Specific temporal tasks were also included in his treatment plan, which again were based on information from his functional analysis. The two primary scenarios that posed the most difficulty for him were related to when he got off work during the work week and weekend days, particularly Sundays, when he would be at home with nothing planned. For weekdays when he was getting off work and going home, he decided that going to the gym on his way home would be a way to feel more relaxed without having to drink. This also was helpful for him in another way. He felt it was easy to not pick up the beer at the train station if he knew that he was going for a workout. For the trip home, he would try to avoid the beer vendor areas as much as possible when walking through the train station.

The plan for times when he was at home in the evenings during the week and on weekends was to try to avoid going to the refrigerator and opening a bottle of wine or picking up a beer when he was by himself. The tools to help with this included making a phone call to his friend when he felt tempted to drink and trying not to spend as much time at home during downtimes. Of all the coping strategies available to him, A.R. particularly relied on cognitive strategies and decision-making tools as a way to cope with thoughts about drinking. For example, when necessary, he would attempt to think through what picking up a beer could lead to, challenging thoughts that it would be relaxing without also thinking about the potential negative consequences if he continued to drink.

A.R. was not always successful with these strategies, but was able to reduce his drinking through these techniques. A.R. remained committed to a moderation goal that included not having heavy drinking days and not drinking during weekday evenings, although at times he considered abstinence. He was able to develop a more positive lifestyle that included working out more frequently, and he continued to pursue activities that involved volunteering. Reaching out to others continued to be difficult for him. The friend that he had connected with ultimately was not that helpful in providing support for him. Although A.R. made many positive changes during treatment, he continued to be frustrated by his ambivalence about his drinking goals and the combination of his successes and failures in accomplishing the goals he set.

DIFFERENTIAL DIAGNOSIS AND BEHAVIORAL ASSESSMENT

Having introduced the basic concepts of motivational interviewing and behavioral assessment and illustrated their application in a case example, we now turn a more detailed explication of the types of information needed to assess substance use disorders and how this information is used to create an initial treatment plan. Assessment interviews must answer four broad questions. First, what is the nature of the substance use disorder, if present? Second, does the client have other problems, including other psychiatric disorders? If so, what is the relationship between these other problems and substance abuse, and how do these factors affect treatment? Third, what does the functional analysis indicate about the types of situations that trigger episodes of use, and what coping skill deficits and coping strengths does the client possess that can become potential targets of treatment? Fourth, what is the client's view of his or her problem and openness for change?

Substance Use

Substance use is a complex behavior, and accurate assessment entails use of several well-developed techniques. These techniques have been incorporated into existing measures. Familiarity with these measures, whether or not they are used as part of the interview process, will greatly improve interviewers' skills. To illustrate this point, let's consider how a client might respond to the question, "How much do you drink?" Clients might respond, "Well, not much," "I have a couple of drinks on the weekend," and so on. Such responses do not yield much information. The Timeline Followback Interview (Sobell & Sobell, 2000) is an excellent measure designed to assess patterns of substance use that incorporates several well-validated techniques needed to yield accurate assessment. These techniques include defining the content of alcohol in drinks based on a standard drink concept. A 12-ounce bottle of beer, a 5-ounce glass of wine, and a 1.5-ounce glass of hard liquor all contain one standard drink, or 9 grams of ethanol. In addition, the Timeline Followback Interview uses a calendar format as a memory aid and asks clients to review on a daily basis for a period of several weeks their patterns of substance use. Although such detailed techniques may seem like overkill to the novice interviewer, they typically yield invaluable data that help clarify not only the quantity and frequency of substance use but also a consumption pattern that may be linked to specific risk situations, such as heavy drinking on weekends. Use of this calendar method was invaluable in characterizing A.R.'s pattern of drinking.

It is helpful to classify negative consequences of substance use into life domains and characterize them on a continuum from mild to severe. Life domains include physical health, psychological problems, spouse or partner, family, friends, work, and legal. Gaining a clear understanding of the current (within the last several months) and past negative consequences is among the most useful ways to characterize the severity of substance use problems. Those with mild problems typically are functioning reasonably well in most domains but may have one domain that is especially problematic (e.g., a person who has several recent drunk driving arrests but whose other life domains appear intact). By contrast, people with multiple severe current and past consequences such as loss of several jobs, ruptured family relationships, and serious chronic medical and psychological problems that are the result of substance use clearly present a severe picture of the disorder. The Drinker Inventory of Consequences (Miller et al., 1995) is a well-validated measure of negative consequences of alcohol use that illustrates the concepts of different life domains and a continuum of severity.

Clinical diagnosis and severity of dependence complement assessment of patterns of consumption and negative consequences. Most assessment interviews require generation of a *DSM-IV* classification of abuse or dependence. Several semistructured diagnostic interviews exist that can provide useful didactic guides. Among the best for didactic purposes is the Substance Use Modules of the Structured Clinical Interview for *DSM-IV* (First, Spitzer, Gibbon, & Williams, 1996), which is a measure designed for use by clinicians. Assessment of the severity of dependence goes beyond assignment of a diagnosis to consider the extent of loss of control, salience, and neuroadaptation. For example, A.R. met criteria for alcohol dependence but experienced mild to moderate loss of control and salience, as evidenced by his ability to function well and set appropriate limits on his drinking in most situations. Assessment of physiological dependence, specifically withdrawal or use to avoid withdrawal, is important in assessing severity, especially with substances such as alcohol or opiates, where there are direct implications for selection of detoxification protocols.

Other Problems

Substance use disorders often co-occur with other Axis I and Axis II mental health disorders. At a minimum, it is important to determine whether a client meets criteria for other Axis I disorders and how the presence of these symptoms will affect treatment planning. Differential diagnosis of other mental health disorders among clients with active substance use disorders is complex, in part because chronic use of substances or acute intoxication can induce psychiatric symptoms or exacerbate symptoms in those who are vulnerable. For example, amphetamine use can cause hallucinations in someone without a history of psychosis or trigger these symptoms temporarily in someone vulnerable to psychosis. In neither case would separate treatment for psychosis be needed beyond perhaps a very brief stabilization period. As a general rule, it is important to determine whether an Axis I disorder is primary, defined as occurring before the substance use disorder or when the client was not using substances. If so, then it is likely that additional primary treatment for a mental health disorder will be needed. Axis II disorders also co-occur at high rates among clients with substance use

disorders (Verheul, Ball, & van der Brink, 1998). Although the reliability and validity of these diagnoses in the context of substance use disorders is uncertain, enduring character traits manifest in a wide array of contexts, such as impulsivity, affective instability, and sociopathy, have important implications for treatment planning.

It is also important to assess other areas of life functioning to determine whether they present problems that might interfere with initial treatment goals or might be positive supports. In clients who have a chronic history of substance use disorder, many areas of functioning are likely to be negatively affected. Several multidimensional assessment measures exist that provide comprehensive but brief coverage of relevant life domains. The Addiction Severity Index (ASI; McLellan & Kushner, 1992) is among the most widely used of these measures. The ASI uses semistructured interview strategies to obtain information about seven possible problem areas: alcohol use, drug use, psychiatric status, medical problems, family and social relationships, employment, and legal status. Interviewers who expect to be assessing clients with chronic substance use problems are strongly recommended to learn more about the ASI. Finally, interviewers should consider assessing cognitive impairment when clients present with clear memory or attentional problems because such problems can affect the ability to benefit from treatment.

Functional Analysis

Gaining a clear understanding of the nature of the substance use disorder, other psychiatric problems, and functioning in other life domains provides a framework for moving forward to analyze the antecedents that give rise to episodes of uncontrolled use. For clients with mild to moderate dependence, there are likely to be a few specific situations that trigger use. For example, antecedents for A.R. included leaving work and being home on Sunday. By contrast, clients with moderate to severe dependence are likely to experience loss of control in most situations. Similarly, knowing a client has a primary Axis I disorder can be helpful in forming hypotheses about the functional relationship between use and reduction of negative affect. In the case of A.R., drinking reduced intense experiences of anxiety. At times interviewers may assess a client who has recently relapsed after a period of extended abstinence. Assessment of relapse requires specialized knowledge and is beyond the scope of this chapter; a recent chapter by Dennis Donovan (2005) contains a comprehensive overview of the topic.

Although there is no set technique for conducting a functional analysis, interviewers may find it useful to introduce a functional analysis worksheet similar to that presented in Table 20.1. The worksheet provides an opportunity to educate the client about behavior analysis and specifically that substance use episodes involve triggering events, thoughts and feelings, actions, and the positive and negative consequences of those actions. For clinical and heuristic purposes antecedents can be categorized into proximal or immediate triggers and distal or broader problems that underlie vulnerability to use. Proximal antecedents typically are situations that become strongly associated with substance use, such as being in a bar, being in the company of others who use drugs, or particular times of the week. Distal antecedents are a broader set of general coping skill deficits. In A.R.'s case, high levels of anxiety related to work and his inability to manage that anxiety was a distal antecedent that exerted a broad influence over his excessive drinking.

In addition to identifying proximal and distal antecedents, interviewers should note coping capacities and deficits described throughout the interview because they will be important in determining treatment targets. Coping capacities can be usefully organized into proximal ones, related to handling immediate triggers to use such as strong urges, and distal or general coping skills, such as social, assertiveness, and communication skills, affect tolerance, and affect regulation. Also, it is useful to consider broad coping style. Does the client engage in approach coping such as active problem solving when confronting problems, or is coping characterized by avoidance, passivity, and escape? In addition to assessing internal coping capacities, it is important to assess environmental resources. The environment plays a critical role in maintenance and change of addictive problems (Moos, 2006).

Three characteristics of the environment are important to consider: restraint or structure, support, and provision of alternative rewards. Environments can provide strong restraint factors via social structure. For example, if the client is working full time, that activity presents an important restraint factor. Environment can also be supportive or interfering in efforts to change. For example, if a client's social network consists mainly of other heavy drinkers, then the social environment is likely to exert pressure to continue drinking. Finally, to what extent do the client's life circumstances provide alternative rewards via work, family, leisure, or community activities? Clients such as A.R., whose environment provides restraint in the form of social structures such as a job and family; a supportive social environment, and a meaningful investment in family, job, and community, are much more likely to change their behavior than clients who have fewer or none of these environmental features.

Client's Views on Change

The client's views on change include an assessment of readiness to change, decisional balance, situational and general self-efficacy, and selection of goals. These have been reviewed extensively in prior sections. A more complete explication of these concepts can be found in Miller and Rollnick (2002) and DiClemente (2003).

SELECTION OF TREATMENT TARGETS AND REFERRAL

Even a cursory familiarity with substance abuse treatment indicates the wide array of treatment options that vary from brief interventions of less than 10 minutes to 18- to 24-month residential treatment programs. The purpose of this section is to provide an introductory framework for treatment planning and refer interested readers to more specialized texts for additional information. One of the most comprehensive approaches to treatment selection is the American Society of Addiction Medicine Patient Placement Criteria (Mee-Lee & Shulman, 2003). The perspective presented here is consistent with that framework. Treatment for substance use disorder can be conceived as involving three phases, each with different targets: detoxification and stabilization, primary phase treatment, and continuing care. In addition, decisions about how to structure each phase, especially with regard to setting (inpatient vs. outpatient) and intensity are related to questions about the need for ancillary services, the existence of a supportive environment, and the involvement of other health care or system-level services such as criminal justice, child welfare, or social welfare.

A first question for assessment is whether clients need detoxification or a period of initial stabilization. Clients who use substances with classic withdrawal potential such as alcohol, sedatives, and opiates should undergo careful assessment of the need for detoxification. However, even other substances such as cocaine, which do not require specific medical care for withdrawal, have strong withdrawal potential that may necessitate high levels of structure and monitoring. Readers interested in detoxification issues are referred to Graham, Schultz, Mayo-Smith, Ries, and Wilford (2003) for a detailed discussion of each substance class. Even clients who are not experiencing withdrawal may need an initial period of stabilization before beginning treatment because of the exacerbation of acute psychiatric symptoms, intense mood fluctuations caused by high levels of recent use, inability to abstain from substance use without some external structure, temporary cognitive impairment or disorientation secondary to high levels of use, or medical problems that complicate or prevent a primary focus on reducing substance use. Detoxification and stabilization typically are conducted in inpatient settings. However, detoxification from alcohol, sedatives, and even opiates can be accomplished on an outpatient basis in cases uncomplicated by medical or psychiatric problems and with a client who is highly motivated and has a supportive social environment.

The target of primary treatment is reduction of substance use to an appropriately safe level, either abstinence or nonproblem use. A critical assessment question in planning primary treatment is whether the client has ancillary problems that necessitate concurrent treatment and whether the client's environment is sufficiently supportive and structured to allow outpatient care. An important and historically controversial issue has been whether primary treatment should always take place in residential or 28-day inpatient settings or can be accomplished in outpatient settings. The consensus, at least currently, is that primary treatment is recommended to occur in residential settings if clients have significant medical or psychiatric problems or live in social environments (e.g., homeless shelters, drug-saturated neighborhoods) that would not support recovery efforts (Finney & Moos, 2003). Clients who have psychiatric disorders need treatment that is integrated with primary addiction treatment. Similarly, if clients have basic needs, such as housing, transportation, or child care, these ancillary services should be provided as part of any treatment package.

Summary

Whatever the particular setting and package of services that make up primary treatment, the achievement of a sustained period of abstinence or nonproblem use requires a focus on a set of factors. These factors, or intermediate targets, include enhancing motivation, reducing cravings, increasing substance-specific and general coping skills, strengthening affect regulation, developing a social environment supportive of recovery, and developing alternative rewards and goals that are inconsistent with prior patterns of substance use. A variety of effective psychosocial interventions exist that, in general, target these factors (cf. Rotgers, Morgenstern, & Walters, 2003). For example, each of these factors was addressed in the cognitive-behavioral treatment of A.R. In addition, a variety of medications are available that, when delivered in the context of effective psychosocial interventions, can enhance outcomes. Interested readers are referred to Frances, Miller, and Mack (2005) for further discussion of the appropriate use of medication and counseling approaches.

Continuing care is the final phase of treatment. It is widely acknowledged that most clients should continue with some form of ongoing treatment even after achieving a stable period of abstinence or nonproblem use. This recognition is rooted in the emerging understanding that for many, substance dependence is a chronic illness that may recur repeatedly (McLellan, Lewis, O'Brien, & Kleber, 2000). The goals of continuing care are to help clients maintain behavior change, deal with slips or lapses without letting these events turn into full-blown relapses or a return to initial levels of problem use. In addition, continuing care can provide a forum for clients to begin to address broader rehabilitation goals such as job training and education.

References

American Psychiatric Association. (1994). *Diagnostic and statistical manual of mental disorders* (4th ed.). Washington, DC: Author.

Cooney, N. L., Kadden, R. M., & Steinberg, H. R. (2005). Assessment of alcohol problems. In D. M. Donovan & A. G. Marlatt (Eds.), *Assessment of addictive behaviors.* New York: Guilford.

DiClemente, C. C. (2003). *Addiction and change: How addictions develop and addicted people recover.* New York: Guilford.

Donovan, D. M. (2005). Assessment of addictive behaviors for relapse prevention. In D. M. Donovan & A. G. Marlatt (Eds.), *Assessment of addictive behaviors.* New York: Guilford.

Donovan, D. M., & Marlatt, G. A. (Eds.). (2005). *Assessment of addictive behaviors* (2nd ed.). New York: Guilford.

Edwards, G., & Gross, M. M. (1976). Alcohol dependence: Provisional description of a clinical syndrome. *British Medical Journal, 1,* 1058–1061.

Finney, J. W., & Moos, R. H. (2003). Effects of setting, duration, and amount on treatment outcomes. In A. W. Graham, T. K. Schultz, M. F. Mayo-Smith, & B. B. Wilford (Eds.), *Principles of addiction medicine* (3rd ed.). Chevy Chase, MD: American Society of Addiction Medicine.

First, M. B., Spitzer, R. L., Gibbon, M., & Williams, J. B. W. (1996). *The Structured Clinical Interview for DSM-IV Axis I Disorders: Patient edition (SCID-I/P, Version 2.0).* New York: Biometrics Research Department, New York State Psychiatric Institute.

Frances, R. J., Miller, S. I., & Mack, A. H. (Eds.). (2005). *Clinical textbook of addictive disorders* (3rd ed.). New York: Guilford.

Graham, A. W., Schultz, T. K., Mayo-Smith, M. F., Ries, R. K., & Wilford, B. B. (Eds.). (2003). *Principles of addiction medicine* (3rd ed.). Chevy Chase, MD: American Society of Addiction Medicine.

Hanson, G. R. (Printed April 1998, Reprinted January 2002). *Letter from the director. NIDA research report: Methamphetamine abuse and addiction.* Publication No. 02-4210. Bethesda, MD: National Institutes of Health.

Institute of Medicine. (1990). *Broadening the base of treatment for alcohol problems.* Washington, DC: National Academy Press.

Kernberg, O. F. (1983). The borderline patient. *Psychiatry* (Audio Digest), *11*(16).

McLellan, A. T., & Kushner, H. E. A. (1992). The fifth edition of the Addiction Severity Index. *Journal of Substance Abuse Treatment, 9*(3), 199–213.

McLellan, A. T., Lewis, D. C., O'Brien, C. P., & Kleber, H. D. (2000). Drug dependence, a chronic mental illness: Implications for treatment, insurance, and outcomes evaluation. *JAMA, 284*(13), 1689–1695.

Mee-Lee, D., & Shulman, G. D. (2003). The ASAM placement criteria and matching patients to treatment. In A. W. Graham, T. K. Schultz, M. F. Mayo-Smith, R. K. Ries, & B. B. Wilford (Eds.), *Principles of addiction medicine* (3rd ed.). Chevy Chase, MD: American Society of Addiction Medicine.

Meyer, R. E. (2001). Finding paradigms for the future of alcoholism research: An interdisciplinary perspective. *Alcoholism: Clinical and Experimental Research, 25*(9), 1393–1406.

Miller, W. R., & Rollnick, S. (Eds.). (2002). *Motivational interviewing: Preparing people for change* (2nd ed.). New York: Guilford.

Miller, W. R., Tonigan, J. S., & Longabaugh, R. (1995). *The Drinker Inventory of Consequences (DrINC): An instrument for assessing adverse consequences of alcohol abuse.* Project Match Monograph Series Vol. 4, NIH Publication No. 95-3911. Rockville, MD: National Institute on Alcohol and Alcoholism.

Moos, R. H. (2006). Social contexts and substance use. In W. R. Miller & K. M. Carroll (Eds.), *Rethinking substance abuse: What the science shows, and what we should do about it.* New York: Guilford.

Moyers, T. B., & Waldorf, V. A. (2003). Motivational interviewing: Destination, direction, and means. In F. Rotgers, J. Morgenstern, & S. T. Walters (Eds.), *Treating substance abuse: Theory and technique* (2nd ed.). New York: Guilford.

Orford, J. (1985). *Excessive appetites: A psychological view of addiction.* Chichester, UK: Wiley.

Prochaska, J. O., DiClemente, C. C., & Norcross, J. C. (1992). In search of how people change: Applications to addictive behaviors. *American Psychologist, 47*(9), 1102–1114.

Rotgers, F. (2003). Cognitive-behavioral theories of substance abuse. In F. Rotgers, J. Morgenstern, & S. T. Walters (Eds.), *Treating substance abuse: Theory and technique* (2nd ed.). New York: Guilford.

Rotgers, F., Morgenstern, J., & Walters, S. T. (Eds.). (2003). *Treating substance abuse: Theory and technique* (2nd ed.). New York: Guilford.

Saitz, R. (2005). Unhealthy alcohol use. *New England Journal of Medicine, 352*(6), 596–607.

Sobell, L. C., & Sobell, M. B. (2000). Alcohol Timeline Followback (TLFB). In American Psychiatric Association (Ed.), *Handbook of psychiatric measures* (pp. 477–479). Washington, DC: American Psychiatric Association.

Verheul, R., Ball, S. A., & van der Brink, W. (1998). Substance abuse and personality disorders. In H. R. Kranzler & B. J. Rounsaville (Eds.), *Dual diagnosis and treatment: Substance abuse and comorbid medical and psychiatric disorders.* New York: Marcel Dekker.

21

Sexual Dysfunction and Deviation

Tamara Penix and Dahamsara R. Suraweera

That the sexual dysfunctions and deviations are grouped together may seem appropriate at a cursory glance and inappropriate with a slightly more detailed look. Both categories have to do with sexuality, a decidedly unique set of behaviors that garner a great deal of attention. Furthermore, they are nonnormative forms of sexuality. However, a sharp divergence in the presentation of these problems quickly emerges. The former disorder entails a person being unable to move through the human sexual response cycle at will, thereby producing psychological distress or interfering with normal social functioning for the individual or dyad. For the latter, it is the sexual stimulus itself that is nonnormative, often resulting in distress or social dysfunction in the individual or in the inappropriate object of his or her sexuality. These categories are nearly opposites: One set of problems involves being unable to function sexually when that function is desired in some fashion, and the other involves functioning sexually when some aspect of the sexuality is deemed inappropriate.

Interviewing for these two kinds of problems entails appreciably different strategies. As a result, they will be handled separately in this chapter. One unifying theme is their most common obstacle: the difficulty of discussing sexuality forthrightly and accurately. Despite the ubiquity of

sexual commentary, full disclosure about one's sexuality, even in clinical settings, challenges the cultural prohibitions against it. Direct observation of human sexual problems is not done. There is consequently a problem of access to information requisite to solving sexual problems. All of the following recommendations refer to the goal of fully accessing relevant and accurate information about sexual behavior.

No structured clinical interviews specific to sexual dysfunctions or sexual deviance disorders were found for clinical use. The chapter aims to aid in structuring a sexual dysfunction or deviance interview.

Description of Sexual Dysfunction Problems

There are 11 categories of sexual dysfunction in the *Diagnostic and Statistical Manual of Mental Disorders Text Revision* (*DSM-IV-TR*; American Psychiatric Association [APA], 2000), very similar to those of the International Classification of Diseases (*ICD-10*; World Health Organization, 1992), 8 of them shared by women and men. They are further divided into four major categories, two additional context attentive categories, and the not otherwise specified (NOS) category. The four primary areas of diagnosis are the sexual desire disorders, sexual arousal disorders, orgasmic disorders, and sexual pain disorders. Also taken into account are sexual dysfunction caused by a general medical condition and substance-induced sexual dysfunction. Specifiers for each diagnostic category include whether the problem is lifelong or acquired, generalized or situational, and caused by psychological factors or combined factors (both psychological and physiological). The sexual desire disorders affecting both genders include hypoactive sexual desire disorder and sexual aversion disorder. The sexual arousal disorders include female sexual arousal disorder and male erectile disorder. Orgasmic problems include male and female orgasmic disorder and premature ejaculation in males. The final subcategory is the sexual pain disorders, which include dyspareunia in men and women and vaginismus in women.

Prevalence of the sexual dysfunctions in the population is unknown. It is essential to note that little is known about normative sexual practices and regular fluctuations in sexual desires and practices, thus rendering the diagnosis of a sexual dysfunction very subjective and dependent on clinician perceptions of marked distress or interpersonal difficulty. The most comprehensive study of the sexual dysfunctions to date (Laumann, Paik, & Rosen, 1999) found sexual desire disorders in the 30% range for women and 15% for men, 20% for female sexual arousal disorder and 10% for males, 25% for female orgasmic problems in the past year and 10% for males, 27% for premature ejaculation, 15% for female dyspareunia, and 3% for male dyspareunia. Vaginismus separate from a primary diagnosis of dyspareunia is rare according to a recent literature review by Reissing, Binik, Khalife, Cohen, and Amsel (2004).

The following are the essential features of each sexual dysfunction, taken from the *DSM-IV-TR* (APA, 2000). The second criterion for each problem is the presence of marked distress or interpersonal difficulty. The sexual dysfunction may not be better accounted for by another Axis I disorder (except another sexual dysfunction) and is not caused exclusively by the direct physiological effects of a substance (e.g., a drug of abuse, a medication) or a general medical condition (criterion C; APA, 2000).

Hypoactive Sexual Desire Disorder. Persistent or recurrently deficient (or absent) sexual fantasies and desire for sexual activity. The judgment of

deficiency is made by the clinician, taking into account factors that affect sexual functioning, such as age and the context of the person's life.

Sexual Aversion Disorder. Persistent or recurrent extreme aversion to, and avoidance of, all (or almost all) genital sexual contact with a sexual partner.

Female Sexual Arousal Disorder. Persistent or recurrent inability to attain, or to maintain until completion of the sexual activity, an adequate lubrication-swelling response of sexual excitement.

Male Erectile Disorder. Persistent or recurrent inability to attain, or to maintain until completion of the sexual activity, an adequate erection.

Female Orgasmic Disorder. Persistent or recurrent delay in, or absence of, orgasm after a normal sexual excitement phase. Women exhibit wide variability in the type or intensity of stimulation that triggers orgasm. The diagnosis of female orgasmic disorder should be based on the clinician's judgment that the woman's orgasmic capacity is less than would be reasonable for her age, her sexual experience, and the adequacy of sexual stimulation she receives.

Male Orgasmic Disorder. Persistent or recurrent delay in, or absence of, orgasm after a normal sexual excitement phase during sexual activity that the clinician, taking into account the person's age, judged to be adequate in focus, intensity, and duration.

Premature Ejaculation. Persistent or recurrent ejaculation with minimal sexual stimulation before, on, or shortly after penetration and before the person wishes it. The clinician must take into account factors that affect duration of the excitement phase such as age, novelty of the sexual partner or situation, and recent frequency of sexual activity.

Dyspareunia. Persistent or recurrent genital pain associated with sexual intercourse in either a male or female.

Vaginismus. Persistent or recurrent involuntary spasm of the musculature of the outer third of the vagina that interferes with sexual intercourse.

Sexual Dysfunction (specify) Due to a General Medical Condition (specify). Clinically significant sexual dysfunction that results in marked distress or interpersonal difficulty predominates in the clinical picture (Criterion A). There is evidence from the history, physical examination, or laboratory findings that the sexual dysfunction is fully explained by the direct physiological effects of a general medical condition (Criterion B). The disturbance is not better accounted for by another mental disorder (Criterion C).

Substance-Induced Sexual Dysfunction. Clinically significant sexual dysfunction that results in marked distress or interpersonal difficulty predominates in the clinical picture (Criterion A). There is evidence from the history, physical examination, or laboratory findings that the sexual dysfunction is fully explained by substance use because the symptoms in Criterion A developed during, or within a month of, substance intoxication or medication use is etiologically related to the disturbance (Criterion B). The disturbance is not better accounted for by a sexual dysfunction that is not substance induced. Evidence that the symptoms are better accounted for by a sexual dysfunction that is not substance induced might include the following: The symptoms precede the onset of the substance use or dependence (or medication use), the symptoms persist for a substantial period of time (e.g., about a month) after the cessation of intoxication or are substantially greater than what would be expected given the type or amount of the substance used or the duration of use, or other evidence of an independent non-substance-induced sexual dysfunction (e.g., a history of recurrent non-substance-related episodes).

For the sexual dysfunctions due to general medical conditions or substance use, it is specified whether the problem includes impaired desire, impaired arousal, impaired orgasm, or sexual pain. For the latter category, the diagnostician also specifies whether the onset is during intoxication.

INTERVIEWING STRATEGIES

The key to successful interviewing for the sexual dysfunctions is to build strong rapport rapidly. It is essential that clients acclimate to the interview situation, developing comfort, trust, confidence, and expectations that the dialogue is worthwhile and will lead to favorable outcomes. No data have been gathered thus far on the necessary and sufficient conditions for establishing rapport around sexual issues. The following recommendations are based on more general successful interviewing strategies and prevalent clinical practices.

A professional atmosphere and demeanor on the part of the clinician should be established. The environment should convey cleanliness and a sense of formality while remaining inviting. The interviewer should be on time and address the client formally. Clinic policies, informed consent, the limits of confidentiality, and release of information policies should be reviewed at the start of the interview and all questions answered before the clinician advances to the next step. It is important for the clinician to convey experience and comfort discussing sexual matters. Clients will take their cues in this regard from the interviewer. It may be useful to note the number of sexual dysfunction cases seen, years assessing and treating these problems, or any specialized training in the assessment and treatment of sexual dysfunctions.

Sexual issues should be discussed as openly as other topics, with full, soft eye contact and an unwavering demeanor. The interviewer should set a serious tone, one that may be loosened if the client demonstrates receptivity to humor by using it first. Humor may be used to increase the client's comfort; however, the humor should address the interviewing situation or the problem itself, not the client. Next, the interviewer may offer reassurances that sexual dysfunctions are common and that most are treatable. Interviewers should be aware of prevalence rates, in order to be able to produce them readily if asked, and the variety of available treatments. It is important to acknowledge how difficult it is to talk about a sexual problem and the relationship difficulties that may result (LoPiccolo, 2004). The client should be asked about any concerns about assessment or treatment in order to give the clinician the opportunity to alleviate any unrealistic fears or misconceptions about these endeavors.

One founded fear many clients have is discussing their sexual behavior in detail with a stranger. It is essential to lay the foundation for full disclosure of relevant information by elucidating the access problem. Behavioral assessments are not routinely conducted for problems of sexual dysfunction for privacy reasons. Clients must understand that the only way the clinician can access the problem is through the client's accurate description of its features and that greater accuracy leads to better assessment and treatment of the problem. It is critical that the clinician convey unflappability, genuine interest in the client, and concern for his or her welfare and sexual functioning. Finally, any cultural factors that may affect rapport should be acknowledged and addressed. Cultural dimensions on which the clinician and client may not be matched include age, gender, socioeconomic status, ethnicity, disability status, sexual orientation, spiritual beliefs, language, marital status, and ideological differences. It is important in the rapport-building phase to ascertain whether differences on any of these dimensions are important or of concern to the client. If a client identifies one or more category of concern, the interviewer may explore the origin of the concern and whether the difference could affect the assessment. Differences that the client perceives as affecting the interview and that cannot be resolved to his or her satisfaction are grounds for referral to another provider. See Hays (2003) for additional information on culturally sensitive assessment and intervention practices.

Once adequate rapport has been established, the interview takes on an investigative quality. The broad goals of the interview are to learn the parameters of the problem, to delineate its causal and maintaining factors, to understand the function of the symptom for the individual and the dyad, to identify potential targets for treatment, and to understand the palatability of and expectations for treatment as efficiently as possible. Toward these ends we have culled from the literature 20 general categories of questions that may be useful in gathering information, arranged from those that assess the most common features of these disorders to those that are rarer. A number of experts in the field of sexual dysfunction recommend this type of multidimensional approach to interviewing and assessment (Beck, 1995; Heiman, 2002; Kaplan, 1979; LoPiccolo & Friedman, 1988; Rosen & Leiblum, 1995; Trudel et al., 2001).

Demographic Information. It is important to know the client's age, ethnicity, marital status and presence of a regular sexual partner, sexual orientation, religious affiliation, income, level of education, and age and number of children because these variables may affect sexual functioning directly or indirectly. If the problem occurs in the presence of a regular sexual partner,

the client should be encouraged to include the partner in the interview. Ideally partners are interviewed separately and then jointly.

Problem Description. A detailed description of the problem is critical. This description should include the level and frequency of desire, arousal, orgasm, and genital pain, the degree of sexual satisfaction, subjective distress regarding the problem, and whether it is global or situational and lifelong or acquired (Heiman, 2002). In the case of a desire problem, it is important to note whether desire emerges once sexual activity is initiated (Letourneau & O'Donohue, 1993). If the problem is situational, follow-up questions must distinguish the features of contexts in which the problem arises from those in which it does not occur. Heiman encourages the interviewer to be aware of the affect and nonverbal behaviors surrounding the initial description. The features of actual sexual behavior must be voiced. These include the frequency, course, and sexual activities, evaluation of self and other, and satisfaction. Additional variables are participation in sexual activity when it is undesired, sexual activity outside the primary relationship, solo sexual activities, and use of the sex industry, ranging from using pornography to visiting strip clubs and prostitutes. Clients should address the presence of lubrication, swelling, or erection to sexual thoughts, to self-stimulation, and to stimulation by others. Finally, if the dysfunction occurred in the presence of another person, what was the reaction?

Medical History and Medications, Including Sexual Health. The first bit of essential medical information is the date of the last checkup and whether the sexual problem was addressed. Many sexual dysfunctions are partly or entirely physiological (Basson et al., 2001). The medical history should take into account all developmental abnormalities and insult, injury, and disease. Of particular interest are the client's medications because there are many with undesirable sexual side effects, including commonly used antidepressants and antihypertensives. Supplements and herbal remedies should be noted also because they may produce unpredictable side effects and are governmentally unregulated. Any sexual health problems should be identified, including any history of sexually transmitted disease and any problems necessitating a medical procedure involving the sexual organs.

Mental Health History and Current Psychological Functioning and Well-Being. The client's history of psychological functioning may be important. Clients should be asked whether they have ever been diagnosed with a major mental illness or received psychological or psychiatric treatment. The client's view of his or her current psychological functioning and sense of well-being warrant consideration. A number of psychological disorders and more transient emotional states may interfere with sexuality (Beck, 1995).

Substance Use. Like prescribed medications, illicit drugs and alcohol may interfere with sexual functioning and merit examination (APA, 2000).

Sexual History. A complete sexual history should be taken. This narrative should include the diagnostic elements of desire, arousal, orgasm, pain, and satisfaction for each type of sexual experience and partner. The features of partners and intimate relationships that included sex may be important as well. The clinician should distinguish the features of instances in which the sexual response cycle progressed uninterrupted from those that were cut short by dysfunction. Questions may focus on who was involved, which sexual thoughts or behaviors occurred, contextual factors that added to or detracted from the experience, and how the event ended. Common themes across sexual experiences and distinctions in those that were different may be noticed. Clients should be asked about their perception of their sexual skill. Use of contraceptives, pregnancy concerns, postpartum states, menopause, and surgeries such as hysterectomy are relevant. Experiences of sexual abuse and any related physical or psychological effects should be discussed at this time. LoPiccolo and Heiman (1978) suggest asking about the treatment of sexuality and affection in the family of origin, both overt and covert. They also propose exploring the affect associated with sex and the degree of enjoyment of other sensual experiences. Rates of lifetime sexual activity and the range of activities should be tracked (Hall, Andersen, Aarestad, & Barongan, 2000). Accounts should include extramarital sex, past or present.

Contextual Factors Including Stressors, the Environment, and Time. Queries must cover all elements that set the stage for sexuality. These include whether the environment supports sexual activity. The client may rate her or his stress with respect to how much of it there is and whether there is a perception of personal control over it. Does the client make time for sexual encounters? Is that time realistic or adequate to fulfill his or her sexual desires? What is the client's typical sexual environment like? Does the client have a space appropriate for uninterrupted sexual activity? Is it inviting? Do the client and his or her sexual partner maintain their attractiveness? Have the attractive features of a sexual partner changed in some discernible way? Is any novelty introduced into sexual relationships by the client or a partner? Does the client or partner have children who may be a concern during sexual activity? Is the couple trying to conceive a child? Is a woman in the dyad pregnant? Are the client and partner taking care of their physical and emotional needs?

Dyadic Adjustment. If the sexual dysfunction occurs in the context of an intimate relationship, the quality of that relationship should be explored. Questions should address relationship satisfaction, conflict and tension and its duration, roles in the couple, and power in the relationship. Unresolved conflicts have a way of affecting sexual intimacy. Relationship problems make participation in sex therapy less likely (Hawton & Catalan, 1986). Is there romantic love or compassion for the partner? This is the place to ask about sexual communication. Is communication about sex direct? Are the partners able to express their sexual preferences and desires? Who initiates sex, how, and how often? Desire discrepancy is an issue that must be addressed (Letourneau & O'Donohue, 1993). How often does each partner desire sexual contact, and how often does it materialize? The sexual drives of men and women peak at different ages (Letourneau & O'Donohue, 1993), potentially affecting a couple's sexual synchrony.

Sexual Attitudes and Beliefs and Perceived Sexual Norms. This category attempts to draw out the client's strongly held sexual ideas. Questions that may be useful here include the following. "From your perspective, who is permitted to have sex (e.g., ages, genders, orientations)?" "Who should not be having sex?" "What kinds of sexual activities are allowable?" "Which activities are unwise or not permissible?" "How do you think most people view sexual relationships?" "Are there any differences between how you approach sex and how other people do? If so, do those discrepancies concern you at all?"

Sexual Interests and Preferences. The focus of this category is the client's ideal interests and preferences and those of a partner if the sexual dysfunction involves the couple. What types of sexual partners and activities are of interest? Of these possible partners and activities, which ones are more and less preferred? Does the client think about sex at all? Are there common sexual activities or those preferred by a sexual partner that are aversive to the client? Does the client masturbate and, if so, how often, and is it a preferred sexual activity? Is there conflict in the sexual or gender orientation? Are there paraphilic interests? Letourneau and O'Donohue (1993, p. 94) describe the possibility of a "narrow sexual comfort zone" for people trying to balance an unnerving dependent attachment with a fear of real love and commitment. This is an issue that warrants exploration when a sexual dysfunction occurs within a dyad.

Sex-Related Cognitions. This is a more difficult category to describe because it can be highly individualistic. The major question that needs to be addressed is, "What kinds of associated thoughts arise when you think about sex during or outside a sexual encounter?" Important cognitions suggested by Lavie-Ajayi (2005) have to do with the meaning of the sex or orgasm, its importance, and the imperative to reach orgasm addressed by Potts (2000). Are there specific thoughts about whom or what the sex is for (Heiman, 2002)? Do thoughts about missing out or losing control arise? Is the dysfunction viewed as a sexual difficulty or a relational difficulty? Is there a perceived social stigma associated with not having orgasms? Body image concerns may emerge as well as judgments about a partner's body. Is there an acceptance of sexual differences from person to person?

Ravart, Trudel, Marchand, Turgeon, and Aubin (1996) suggest a number of different types of cognitions that may negatively affect sexual functioning. These include negative and causal attributions about events, negative self-talk, negative automatic thoughts, irrational beliefs about sex and relationships, sexual misconceptions, self-defeating attitudes, unrealistic expectations (especially hypersexual standards inducing performance anxiety; Letourneau & O'Donohue, 1993), aversive imagery, and antisexual thinking styles, which include focusing on the negative or unpleasant features of the partner, relationship, or sexuality in general. Letourneau and O'Donohue draw attention to the significance of incompatible sexual scripts, rendering it useful to discover how each partner views an ideal sexual encounter for comparison. Challenging cognitions may be accessed by asking about the incidence of nagging or worry thoughts and negative self-talk, strong ideas about the self or others including expectations, and beliefs about sex and relationships. The presence and content of aversive imagery or thoughts related to sex may also be examined.

Sex-Related Emotion. Several emotional states are implicated in sexual difficulties. These include anxiety, depression, anger, guilt, worthlessness, shame, and love. Clients may be asked whether any noticeable feelings arise in the contemplation of or participation in sexual activity and how they manage them if they do. Common anxieties include fears of losing control, pregnancy, becoming too close emotionally, and adequacy of performance (Letourneau & O'Donohue, 1993). An additional issue is whether there is subjective distress under sexual demand conditions.

Views of Cause and Solution. The client's view of what has caused the sexual dysfunction and the helpfulness of potential solutions are useful. Many clients present to their primary care physician for treatment of sexual concerns and often are surprised to be referred to a mental health professional. It is necessary to ascertain whether the client views the problem as entirely physiological in nature and whether he or she is amenable to psychological intervention. According to LoPiccolo (2004), men tend to seek a physical cause and a medical solution to sexual dysfunction.

Cultural Considerations. Sexual dysfunctions appear cross-culturally, with somewhat different prevalence rates in the few cross-cultural epidemiological studies that have been conducted (Hwang, 1999; Kadri, Mchichi Alami, & Mchakra Tahiri, 2002; Laumann, Paik, & Rosen, 1999). Cultural attributes that may influence these problems include culture-specific views of sexuality and sexual practices, prohibitions against sexual thoughts or activities, prescriptions for preferred sexual practices, views regarding men's and women's roles and how they should interact, and perspectives on sexual pleasure and procreation. It is up to the interviewer to assess cultural norms and how they may or may not affect the client's sexual functioning.

Concerns About Sex Therapy. Many clients who are assessed for sexual dysfunction harbor concerns about the potential recommendation of sex therapy (LoPiccolo, 2004). Asking about these fears permits the interviewer to dispel myths about common sexual therapies, particularly the concern that the therapist will engage in sexual activities with the client. Is the client motivated for and willing to comply with treatment, including completing homework?

Expectations for Change or Outcome. Expectations that the sexual dysfunction will be alleviated have been linked to better outcomes (Hawton & Catalan, 1986). Therefore, it is important to ask what the client expects from the interview and any interventions that may follow. This is a good opportunity for the interviewer to detect hopelessness in the client and to instill hope for change based on the latest research findings. LoPiccolo (2004) stresses the importance of a man seeing the benefit of therapy to himself and not simply to his partner in the case of premature ejaculation.

Accuracy of Sexual Knowledge. Sexual myths abound, and clients are as susceptible to them as anyone else. Based on the problem description, it is possible to determine the accuracy of the client's sexual knowledge in relevant areas. Questions such as the following may be helpful. "Do you think your experience is a common one?" "What do you think leads to your desired outcome?" "What has interfered with your desired outcome?" "How does the sexual response cycle generally progress? Is it always the same?" "Are there any beliefs about what should be stimulating or the kinds of fantasies one should have?" A woman who has never experienced an orgasm may not be aware that most women are not able to achieve orgasm from vaginal stimulation alone (Masters & Johnson, 1970). She may believe that there is something wrong with her body or mind, when in fact she may need greater skillfulness and breadth of stimulation to orgasm.

Body Self-Knowledge. These queries have to do with the client's understanding of his or her sexual functioning. Is he or she aware of natural sexual rhythms, such as being organically more interested in sexual activity during the few days of the month a female partner may be able to conceive a child? Does the client know how his or her body works? Does he or she know the type of stimulation or sexual activity that is interesting and linked with preferred sexual outcomes? Is there awareness of how to intensify or cool the sexual activity in order to increase one's or one's partner's sexual satisfaction?

Quality of Attention and Awareness. Is the client easily distracted from the sexual thought or experience occurring in the moment? Is it possible for the client to disconnect from disengaging thoughts and reconnect with sexual experience in the moment? Is the client willing to practice calming the mind and focusing solely on sex when time is set aside for it?

Prominent Sexual Memories. Asking the client about pervasive sexual memories, both positive and negative, can be revealing. Clients may idealize past sexual experiences or partners, they may have intrusive memories about bad sexual experiences, or they may experience guilt when reminded of a former sexual partner in a new sexual encounter. It may be useful to discuss the client's most vivid sexual memories relative to his or her current sexual functioning.

INTERVIEWING OBSTACLES AND SOLUTIONS

A number of obstacles arise during interviews in cases of sexual dysfunction. Perhaps the most important of these is discussing sexual beliefs and practices, particularly those that are unconventional. Several ideas for paving the way for sexual candor were offered earlier. The most important qualities of the interviewer bear repeating: professionalism, caring, and the unflappability that comes with experience and good training. Exhortations in praise of the value of honesty to positive outcome are also indispensable. A related obstacle is lack of access to the sexual partner or partners. The client may not want to have the partner involved. If the partnership is long term, it may be useful to appeal to outcome once again. A more accurate assessment presumably will lead to more appropriate intervention and a better resolution. Another impediment that may arise in these interview situations is the judgment or values of the clinician bleeding into the interview. Clinicians are members of cultural groups and the larger society, just as clients are. They have their own beliefs about sexuality and sexual values. It is crucial that these beliefs not be allowed to emerge and affect clients. For many clients the difficulty in accessing treatment for a sexual dysfunction is the fear of being evaluated. Clinicians must maintain the neutral stance in order to be effective. A useful exercise in this regard is exploring one's sexual attitudes, beliefs, and norms using the aforementioned questions. Holding those values with awareness and recognizing the effect of significant departures from those norms are good preparation for noticing when value differences arise in interviewing situations and taking care not to impose one's values on the client.

Interviewers need to keep in mind that the lack of objective behavioral criteria for many of the sexual dysfunctions is problematic and may lead to misdiagnosis, overdiagnosis, and possible stigmatization if one does not conduct a thorough and cautious interview. Nearly all of the sexual dysfunctions depend on the clinician's judgment relative to the client's self-reported private behavior. In some cases the clinician is asked to judge whether a person's "orgasmic capacity is less than would be reasonable for her age, sexual experience, and the adequacy of sexual stimulation she receives" (APA, 2000, p. 549). Other than age, which may not be an adequate marker of sexual drive depending on health status, these are highly subjective phenomena that a clinician may find it difficult to assess adequately. A proposed solution to this dilemma is to use the client and several of his or her closest friends and family members who are demographically similar as a reference group for sexual experience and the judgment of adequacy of sexual stimulation.

A related issue is what appears to be a tremendous amount of variability in individual sexual desire, fantasy, arousal, orgasm, and the associated satisfaction. Sexual desire easily fluctuates from several times a year to several times a day between individuals, and may even change significantly within the same person across a life span. It is paramount that the interviewer keep in mind this diversity when working with a particular client rather than comparing him or her with some perceived standard. What really seems to matter is the disparity between the client's sexual ideal and his or her reality and how the two may be brought a bit closer

together through as accurate information and behavior alteration as is available.

Last but not least, it should be acknowledged that little attention has been paid to sexual dysfunction in women (Bancroft, Loftus, & Long, 2003; Basson et al., 2001), so many of them may never have an opportunity to be assessed or treated. A reasonable solution may be to bring information about female sexual dysfunction and its treatment into the public eye, a task for which interviewers may be well suited.

Case Illustration

Marie is a married White female homemaker with two children, ages 3 and 6, who has presented for an assessment of sexual dysfunction on the recommendation of her psychologist. She received mental health treatment for approximately 1 year secondary to the reemergence of latent symptoms of posttraumatic stress disorder cued by the release of her rapist after a 10-year prison term. Marie expresses some hesitation discussing her sexual functioning with a stranger but states that she is willing to do it in order to make some positive changes in her marriage. She explains that she and her husband attempt to have intercourse approximately twice per month but only sometimes complete the act because it is too painful for Marie.

The clinician first focuses on building rapport with Marie, using the guidelines described earlier. The interviewer's aim is to help Marie feel comfortable disclosing all of the relevant information about her problem. Relevant demographic information is gathered. Marie and her husband do not have any strong cultural affiliations. Marie's husband is 2 years older than she is and works as a postal supervisor. He is unwilling to participate in the assessment because he views the problem as Marie's. The family is financially stable, and Marie is dependent on her husband economically. Marie describes the problem as excruciating vaginal pain (rated 8.5 on a scale with 10 as the most severe pain she has ever felt) that arises when she and her husband attempt sexual intercourse about twice monthly. She states that she braces herself against the pain so that her husband can experience an orgasm. The pain lasts as long as there is genital contact. No vaginal spasms were felt. She reports that she has never experienced an orgasm with her husband. She reports desire for sexual contact with her husband about once per week, which she never pursues. That desire usually is related to positive feelings about their relationship and is never accompanied by physiological arousal. Marie's husband initiates all of their sexual activities.

Marie reports she has experienced sexual intercourse without pain and with orgasm in the past, including after her rape and recovery. She currently experiences sexual arousal and orgasm with self-stimulation that requires approximately 1 hour of very soft and slow stimulation of her clitoris and no vaginal stimulation. She feels embarrassed about masturbating and judges that she is cheating her husband by having orgasms without him.

Marie's general medical history is unremarkable. She does not take any medications and is fit and in excellent health. She had chlamydia when she was 17 years old and two pregnancies as an adult. Marie was recently seen by a gynecologist for sexual pain. She has scar tissue inside her vagina, the result of a violent rape. Marie experienced mild vaginal pain during the examination. Her doctor confirmed the presence of areas of the vagina that were highly sensitive and others that were highly desensitized.

Marie was sexually active with boys in high school. She reports she did not particularly enjoy sexual intercourse, although it was not painful. She began experimenting sexually with a girlfriend. She had her first experiences of desire, arousal, and orgasm through this experience. After a 1-year relationship, she was cut vaginally during a violent rape at a party. She became a recluse, moving away from the area and changing her name out of fear after she testified against the perpetrator. She ceased all sexual activity until she met and married her husband several years later. She reports loving and trusting him immensely and finding her relationship extremely satisfying; however, they never had a satisfactory sexual relationship for him or for her. She states that sex with her husband has always been painful. They have never engaged in the extended foreplay or exclusive clitoral stimulation that makes orgasm possible for her. She thinks he would not be interested in that kind of sexual encounter, based on his resistance to such activities in the past, and she is afraid to initiate touching because it will lead to intercourse. She has found her husband supportive of her despite his frustration with their sexual relationship. She reports that he subdues his sexual desires most of the time because he knows sex is painful for her.

Marie cheated on her husband early in their marriage because of her strong desire for and arousal to another man. She was able to have an orgasm with him during extended lovemaking sessions, and intercourse was not painful. She reports that she has been afraid to discuss other ways of having sex with her husband because he was so generous as to take her back after the affair, and she would not like to remind him of it. Marie reports equal sexual interest in men and women but states she is pleased to be in her current relationship. She is satisfied with all other aspects of her life and their relationship. Marie is not under significant stress. She and her husband like their home and bedroom environment, and they have time together alone for sex after the children go to bed. Marie has accurate sexual knowledge. However, she views herself as deficient for being unable to climax without extensive gentle stimulation and views her husband's quick move to intercourse as "the right way." She is somewhat ashamed of her same-sex partnership in the past and thinks she may have contributed to her sexual problems by participating in that kind of sexual experimentation. She sees the psychological and physiological effects of the rape as causal as well as her affair, which she views as making the subject of her sexuality taboo. She also entertains the idea that she is "just not a sexual person." She is afraid if she does not fix the problem she may pursue another affair, or her husband will leave her. She presents no ideas about potential solutions, however, she emphatically states that her husband will not participate in sex therapy. She states that she has a strong faith in psychological interventions, is hopeful for change, and is willing to participate fully in the recommended interventions. She reports an acute awareness of sexual desire, arousal, and pain. Her attention does not waver. She knows how to pleasure herself sexually. Prominent sexual memories include the negative flashbacks to the rape, which occur rarely, and positive recalls of sex with her girlfriend and male lover.

Marie was diagnosed with dyspareunia. Primary targets of treatment were altering sex-related cognitions, bringing the husband into treatment to participate in talk therapy around sexual communication, and sexual skill lessons, including sensate focus and directed masturbation exercises.

MULTICULTURAL AND DIVERSITY ISSUES

Culturally competent assessment practice is mandated by the 2002 APA Ethical Code. The *DSM* admonishes its users to take into account cultural backgrounds that may influence sexual desire, expectations, and attitudes about sexual performance (APA, 2000). The sexual dysfunction literature is replete with warnings that many cultures view male and female sexuality differently, typically diminishing the importance of female desire, arousal, and orgasm and sanctifying those experiences for the male. These perspectives are presumed to affect sexual functioning. Religious prohibitions against sexuality outside approved relationships that typically involve joint child rearing are also noted as affecting sexual functioning. However, no studies were found linking particular cultural views of sexuality or practices and sexual dysfunction.

Appendix I of the *DSM-TR* (APA, 2000) provides useful recommendations for making a cultural formulation to complement other diagnostic considerations. The goal is to ascertain features of the client's culture that are relevant to the problem and its treatment. A narrative summary that addresses the following points is recommended.

- *Cultural identity of the individual.* Important cultural reference groups should be identified and acknowledged along with the level of acculturation into the major culture and language abilities, use, and preference.

- *Cultural explanations of the problem.* The meaning and perceived severity of the problem in the client's primary culture should be noted.

- *Cultural factors related to psychosocial environment and levels of functioning.* This includes both protective factors and stressors.

- *Cultural elements of the relationship between the client and the clinician.* Differences in culture should be acknowledged along with potential pitfalls such as establishing rapport, developing an egalitarian trusting relationship, and understanding the cultural meaning and significance of particular thoughts, feelings, and behaviors.

- *Overall cultural assessment for diagnosis and care.* The predicted influence of cultural variables on diagnosis, treatment planning, and intervention may be offered.

Culture matching, though often desired by clients, is often impossible. There is no contraindication to culturally diverse interview dyads in which the clinician is culturally sensitive and competent. Language differences may be overcome with the use of a professional translator. Children and family members of the client are not appropriate translators.

DIFFERENTIAL DIAGNOSIS

Comorbidity of the sexual dysfunctions and of sexual dysfunctions with other psychiatric disorders is high (Basson et al., 2001). A diagnostic study of 900 clients by Segraves and Segraves (1991) found that of 113 men with a sexual desire disorder, 47% had a secondary diagnosis of erectile dysfunction. For the 475 women with a sexual desire disorder, 41% also endorsed either an arousal or orgasm dysfunction, and 18% acknowledged both. The diagnostic task is to identify the problem as one involving sexual fantasy or desire, aversion to genital contact, lack of physiological arousal, delay or absence of orgasm, genital pain with or without vaginal spasms, or some combination, in which case multiple diagnoses are given. It is also imperative to determine whether the sexual problem is secondary to a medical condition such as multiple sclerosis, diabetes, abdominal surgery, bladder or bowel problems, or the effects of substances including antidepressants, over-the-counter medications, and recreational alcohol and drug use (Heiman, 2002).

SELECTION OF TREATMENT TARGETS AND REFERRAL

All of the data gathered through the methods described earlier are useful only if they inform a comprehensive treatment plan with jointly identified targets. Those targets should be the distal and proximal causal and maintaining factors for the thoughts, feelings, and behaviors of interest. These will be somewhat unique to each client and problem and are based on an analysis of the function of a particular symptom, its antecedents, and maintaining consequences. Common targets include altering the environment (e.g., making dates for sex), improving sexual and emotional communication, increasing sexual skill, attending relationship therapy, altering cognitions, treating mood disorders, altering contraception practices, and many others. Assessments of sexual dysfunction should routinely include coordination with the client's primary physician, given that the origins of many sexual dysfunctions are partly or entirely physiological. Referral to a psychiatrist may be warranted in the case of a primary or secondary co-occurring psychiatric disorder.

DESCRIPTION OF SEXUAL DEVIANCE PROBLEMS

Paraphilia is the formal term used to indicate a problem of sexual deviance. The implication of the word is that it has to do with aberrant love; however, it really has to do with sex, a different matter altogether. The *DSM-IV-TR* section on sexual deviance delineates a broad general category of recurrent, intense sexually arousing sexual fantasies, urges, and behaviors lasting at least 6 months that involve nonhuman objects, the suffering or humiliation of oneself or one's sexual partner, or nonconsenting people (Criterion A; APA, 2000). These thoughts, feelings, and behaviors range from those that garner attention only when they cause evident distress or a loss of social functioning in the afflicted person to those that may be unwanted or harmful to the object of the sexual behavior. The presumed nonnormative object of sexual desire is necessary for sexual arousal in some cases and in others may be featured in the sexual behavior. This often occurs during times of stress. There is little research on the paraphilias other than pedophilia, so the following information is necessarily limited. These issues are rarely diagnosed in general medical settings (APA, 2000). One must keep in mind that many people, if not most (true prevalence is unknown), eschew traditional avenues of treatment for the paraphilias. These behaviors often are unaccompanied by distress, and speaking about one's actual sexual behavior with a stranger remains taboo.

Nine major or more common paraphilias receive special categorization in the *DSM-TR*. A diagnosis of frotteurism, exhibitionism, pedophilia, or voyeurism is made if the person has acted on the sexual thoughts or they have caused significant distress or interpersonal difficulty. The diagnosis of sexual sadism is made only if the person has acted on sadistic sexual urges with a *nonconsenting* person or the urges have caused significant distress or interpersonal difficulty. For fetishism, transvestic fetishism, sexual masochism, and paraphilia NOS, the diagnosis is given if the sexual thoughts or behaviors cause clinically significant distress or impairment in social, occupational, or other important areas of functioning. The form of the behavior determines the exact diagnosis as follows:

Exhibitionism is exposing the genitals to an unsuspecting person.

Fetishism is using nonliving objects to achieve sexual gratification.

Frotteurism is touching and rubbing against a nonconsenting person.

Pedophilia is sexual activity with a prepubescent child or children (generally age 13 or younger). The person must be at least 16 years old and 5 years older than the child or children involved. Pedophilic subtypes have been proposed consisting of people who are attracted to males exclusively, females, both genders, and those limited to incestuous interests. They are further identified as exclusive or nonexclusive in their sexual interests.

Sexual masochism is receiving sexual pleasure from humiliation or suffering.

Sexual sadism is receiving sexual pleasure from inflicting humiliation or suffering.

Transvestic fetishism is receiving sexual pleasure from cross-dressing. One specifies whether gender dysphoria is a feature of this paraphilia.

Voyeurism is observing an unsuspecting person who is naked, in the process of disrobing, or engaging in sexual activity.

Paraphilia NOS is a nonspecific diagnosis for sexual behavior that may be considered aberrant but does not fall into one of the other more common categories. Telephone scatologia, receiving sexual pleasure from making obscene telephone calls to unsuspecting strangers, is one example.

The *DSM-TR* does not devote a specific category of disorder to those who sexually assault adults. These behaviors sometimes are diagnosed with paraphilia NOS or sexual sadism depending on the details and overall pattern of behavior.

Significant distress is not a necessary condition for the paraphilia diagnosis. For some paraphiliacs, it is the reaction of others and the ensuing social difficulties that are of concern rather than the behaviors in themselves. For some, significant distress, particularly depression, guilt, or shame, is associated with paraphilic thoughts and behavior. Many paraphiliacs are unable to connect with other people sexually because of their focus on the object of arousal. They are cut out of that part of human experience. It is often the sexual inflexibility of the paraphiliac that is remarkable. Whereas it is common for people to be interested in novel sexual experiences, paraphiliacs pursue novelty within a restricted range, around the non-normative object.

INTERVIEWING STRATEGIES

This section concentrates on assessment, diagnosis, and treatment planning for problems of sexual self-control. It is worth noting that clinical interviewing is also an integral part of risk assessment in forensic settings; however, a much more highly structured, semi-actuarial or fully actuarial approach is recommended to inform estimations of risk (Hanson, Morton, & Harris, 2003).

First we offer a selection of general strategies for successful interviewing with people with sexual deviance problems. Fifteen troves of pertinent information are then offered. It is possible that clinical interviewing that accesses accurate and relevant information efficiently is more difficult for issues of sexual deviance than for many other behavioral and psychological disorders. The difficulties discussed earlier in the chapter in discussing one's sexual ideas and practices are magnified by two additional sources of difficulty. First, it is not normative sexual interests that are the focus of these interviews. Clients are well aware that it is their abnormal sexual practices that are of interest. Thus, they are being asked to speak about private behaviors that are often abhorred or ridiculed by others. Moreover, many of the behaviors of interest are unlawful, and interviewers tend to be mandatory reporters of sexual crimes. People with sexually deviant behaviors who are also sexual offenders therefore present with additional motivation to maintain their silence. Once again, building rapport and establishing reasons for the interview that are useful to the client are paramount.

Several useful strategies may aid in building rapport quickly. The first is taking a down-to-earth, egalitarian stance with the client while conferring respect for the person, if not for the behaviors of interest. Interviewers should covey professionalism but not act superior to the client. People with sexual problems are accustomed to being devalued. An offer of respect and a sense of humanity can be unexpected and welcomed, opening the door for a positive interview. A related point is the importance of transmitting experience and comfort with sexually explicit discussions (Hunter & Mathews, 1997; Thornton & Mann, 1997). Many clients expect people to be uncomfortable with their sexual behavior and to judge it, and sometimes the client for it. It is important for the interviewer to overcome these preconceived ideas.

Rapport is also improved by predicting how the interview may be useful to the client. In forensic settings, it may be difficult for the client to ascertain any possible benefit to speaking candidly with an interviewer. In all cases it is useful to spark the client's motivation to respond with candor, emphasizing personally valued outcomes (Ward, McCormack, Hudson, & Polaschek, 1997). In interviews in which the benefit to the client is not an immediately obvious one, such as learning to manage a fetish, appealing to the client's need for disclosure and for relief may be effective. Clients with sexual deviance tend to feel burdened by their sexuality. Unburdening through self-disclosure often is an appealing proposition (Ward et al., 1997). Of course, this is successfully accomplished hand in hand with fully informed consent. Making clients aware that they may choose what to report and explaining the limits of confidentiality may encourage a sense that the client is in control of the boundaries of information. Wincze (2000) suggests that in order to introduce the least amount of error into the results, the assessor should begin with an assumption that the client will try to conceal important information.

Interviewers should be aware of the purpose of the interview, whether diagnostic, treatment oriented, or forensic in nature, and tell the client up front. In all cases involving sexually deviant behavior it is important to access collateral information, preferably before the interview with the client, in order to be able to address the minimization and denial of aspects of the behavior during the encounter (Ward et al., 1997).

Collateral information may include contacts with family members, arrest reports, victim statements, prior evaluations, and medical records to start (Krueger & Kaplan, 1997). The interview environment should be private and free of distractions. This may be difficult in a forensic setting but should be pursued nonetheless for better outcomes.

The following classes of information are ordered from those that would be expected to be the most useful to those that may be less relevant given the specific characteristics of the problem. They have been suggested by a number of researchers and clinicians in the field, including Abel (1989), Adshead (1997), and Ward et al. (1997), and by the available treatments for sexual deviance. Factors commonly correlated with sexual deviance and presumed to be causal include social skill deficits, deviant sexual arousal, distorted thinking, poor cognitive and emotional coping strategies, substance abuse, personality disorders, deviant sexual fantasy, a history of sexual victimization, young adulthood, sexual interest in children, a general criminal history, stranger, male or related victims if sexually abusive, sexual diversity, being single, and a history of dropping out of treatment (Hall, Andersen, et al., 2000; Hanson et al., 2003). Rapport is skillfully built with some subtlety by discussing nonsexual and noncriminal matters first and then moving into discussing criminal and sexual histories.

- *Demographics.* Sexual interests are affected by factors reflected in demographic information. Most relevant are age, gender, marital status, sexual orientation (including solely pedophilic interests), ethnicity, and income. Number of children and custody status may be useful as well.

- *Medical history, medications, and sexual health.* The first bit of essential medical information is the date of the last checkup and whether the sexual problem was addressed. The medical history should take into account all developmental abnormalities and insult, injury, and disease. Any history of head trauma should be addressed (McCormick, 2005). Also of interest are the client's medications because there are many with sexual side effects. One of our clients, an adolescent female with symptoms of a major depressive episode, was prescribed sertraline, which initiated manic symptoms including exhibitionism in the client. The behavior abated when the medication

was discontinued. The frustration of impotence has been cited by clients as a reason for rape with an object, although no formal studies of this phenomenon were found. Any sexual health problems must be identified, including any history of sexually transmitted disease, sexual injuries including hypoxia, and any problems necessitating a medical procedure involving the sexual organs.

- *Mental health history.* Of interest are prior diagnoses of Axis I or II mental disorders. Co-occurring disorders include the affective disorders and personality disorders, particularly antisocial personality disorder (Ertz, 1997; Hanson et al., 2003; Serin & Mailloux, 2003) and statistically uncommon but important psychopathy (Cale & Lillienfeld, 2004), in people with criminal sexual misconduct. Questions should also address any cognitive abnormalities, affective difficulties, especially emotional numbing (Ertz, 1997), current or past suicidality (Strosahl, 2004), dangerousness, and impulse control (Hucker, 2004).

- *Developmental history.* Early exposure to nonnormative behaviors is of interest, whether they are criminal or sexual in nature (Ward, McCormack, Hudson, & Polaschek, 1997). This includes exposure to pornography and violence. School conduct may also be explored.

- *Sexual history.* Interviewing around sexual history benefits from a developmental slant. One is interested in the client's earliest sexual experiences and objects of sexual desire, fantasy, and arousal and the significant experiences that follow through the life span. Initial and subsequent masturbation practices should be discussed, including frequency and associated fantasy. Both deviant and nondeviant sexual desires, fantasies, and experiences should be discussed, as should any history of being sexually abused (Barbaree & Seto, 1997). Experiences of sexual dysfunction are also relevant. If the client's sexual activities have involved another person, determine whether the sex was impersonal (Thornton & Mann, 1997) or more meaningful to the client.

- *Sexual urges, fantasies, and arousal.* The last category explored the client's actual sexual behavior. This one is concerned with a full exploration of the client's recent sexual desires, fantasies, and sources of physiological arousal. Once again the focus is on both deviant and nondeviant material. Queries should address descriptors of the objects of sexuality; characteristics of willing or unwilling partners, including gender, age, physical characteristics, and stranger status; and the importance of novelty to the mental or physical experience. Of special interest are preferred sexual scenarios. It is imperative to find out whether the client experiences any arousal to nondeviant interests and, if so, how it compares with arousal to his or her deviant interests.

• *Problem behavior.* In this section the deviant behavior is explored in greater depth, as recommended by Krueger and Kaplan (1997). Antecedents to the behavior and its consequences are discussed, along with its perceived impact on the client and others. The client's understanding of the problem is cued, as is whether he or she views it as problematic (Hunter & Mathews, 1997). Clients are asked how performing the behavior makes them feel during the fantasy stage, during the behavior, and afterward. The frequency of the behavior is addressed here, along with an estimate of its situational severity, if that varies. If the sexually deviant behavior is also a sexual offense, additional questions must be addressed. Ward and his colleagues (1997) and Serin and Mailloux (2003) offer suggestions for accessing relevant details about the behavior. It is important to know whether physical or psychological force was involved. How many instances of the offending behavior have there been? Was physical or psychological force used (Johnson, 1997)? Who are the victims, and what are their characteristics? Where does the offending typically occur? Does it include planning and grooming the victim to go along with the sexual misbehavior? What does the behavior achieve for the client? What is its function? Is the behavior impulsive or planned? Does the client take full responsibility for the behavior or deny, minimize, or blame the victim? If there is denial, is it of awareness, facts, impact, or responsibility (Palmer, 1997)? What is the client's relationship to his or her victim? Finally, what is the relative importance of or preference for nonconsenting sexual partners (Hanson & Harris, 1997)?

• *Sexual attitudes and beliefs.* This category attempts to draw out the client's strongly held sexual ideas. Questions that may be useful here include the following: "From your perspective, who is permitted to have sex (e.g., ages, genders, orientations)?" "Who should not be having sex?" "What kinds of sexual activities are allowable?" "Which activities are unwise or not permissible?" "How do you think most people view sexual relationships?" "Are there any differences between how you approach sex and how other people do? If so, do those discrepancies concern you at all?" It is important to access sexual offense supportive attitudes and beliefs in alleged or known offenders. Examples include viewing children as sexual beings and characterizing people who do not want to be exposed to exhibitionism as frigid. Cognitive distortions may be readily identified in this interview segment because they are often the byproducts of strongly held beliefs and are mental permission to offend. These include rationalization, minimization, justification, and all-or-none thinking. See Sbraga and O'Donohue (2004) for a more comprehensive discussion of sexuality-related cognitive distortions and their treatment.

• *Sexual knowledge accuracy.* The lack of accurate sexual knowledge has been implicated in the maintenance of deviant sexual behavior (Barbaree & Seto, 1997; Hunter & Mathews, 1997). For example, some exhibitionists view their behavior as an aphrodisiac for their victims. They imagine the victim accepting them once they have exposed themselves. They do not understand that being flashed by a stranger is unexpected and often frightening for victims. It is consequently important to assess the accuracy of the client's basic sexual knowledge and information about the paraphilia in question.

• *Criminogenic needs.* One of the best predictors of additional sexual offending behavior is a history of general criminal behavior (Hanson & Bussiere, 1998). This type of behavior has been conceptualized recently as serving the function of meeting a set of perceived needs for the offender (Andrews & Bonta, 1994). Chief among these needs are employment, relationships, emotional fulfillment, escape or avoidance, and belonging in a community (Serin & Mailloux, 2003). Indicators of criminogenic need consist of items such as criminal history, incarcerations, substance abuse, criminal attitudes, criminal associations, and a "predator/prey life view," as described by Ertz (1997, p. 14–4). It is important for the interviewer to discover not only the incidence of the aforementioned needs but also their function for the client.

- *Skill deficits.* A number of social skill deficits have been associated with paraphilic behavior (Langstrom & Grann, 2000; Nezu, Nezu, Dudek, Peacock, & Stoll, 2005; Ward, Hudson, Marshall, & Siegart, 1995). These consist of difficulties in conducting normative social relationships and include intimacy, problem solving, communication, assertiveness, and emotion regulation problems. Questions that may reveal some of these deficits include the following: "Is it hard for you to get close to other people?" "Do you find yourself in conflict with others more than you would like?" "Does it seem like other people take advantage of you?" "Is it difficult for you to handle some feelings like anger, anxiety, or depression?"

- *Treatment history and expectations.* Knowing the client's treatment history may provide pertinent information about the client's sexual functioning, how his or her problems were conceptualized, whether the treatment was at all successful and why or why not, how the client viewed that treatment and treatment in general, and ideas about new treatment recommendations. Some clients have unrealistic expectations for treatment (e.g., never having another fantasy about the deviant behavior), and this is the opportunity to preview realistic outcomes for the client and plant some seeds of hope for change if warranted.

- *Cultural concerns.* Cultural attributes theorized to influence these problems include culture-specific views of sexuality and sexual practices, prohibitions against sexual thoughts or activities, prescriptions for socially sanctioned sexual practices, views about men's and women's roles and how they should interact, and perspectives on sexual pleasure and procreation. It is up to the interviewer to assess cultural norms and how they may or may not affect the client's sexual functioning. A useful question in this regard is, "Are there any family or group beliefs that seem to affect your sexual behavior or the way you see sex or relationships between men and women?"

- *Strengths and lifestyle balance.* In preparing to make treatment recommendations, it is essential to understand the client's strengths and the healthful, positive aspects of life (whether present or ideal) that motivate her or him. Strengths may be found in many different aspects of the client's life, including cognitive or emotional abilities, physical health, good social supports, financial or career stability, commitment to children, and many others. Keeping in mind that for many people with detected sexual deviance problems sex has taken on a variety of functions edging out more prosocial activities and connections, it is important to identify vehicles for restoring balance in the lifestyle. In the most current nomenclature in the field of sexual offending, the goal is to create "good lives" (Ward & Stewart, 2003). This embraces the development of a healthy sex life, as a key aspect of a fulfilling and balanced existence.

INTERVIEWING OBSTACLES AND SOLUTIONS

The significance of building strong rapport quickly has been discussed several times in this chapter. There is nothing more important in interviewing about sexual behavior than overcoming the client's natural inclination to avoid the guilt, shame, and embarrassment that often accompany it. The accuracy this supports is presumed to have substantial weight in making a correct diagnosis that informs a useful and individually relevant treatment plan. That being said, the second most important obstacle is the lack of strong empirical research on the sexual deviance disorders. Most paraphilia treatment articles are either case studies or studies that included a small number of self-selected participants, leaving clinicians without a solid treatment foundation. It is difficult to inspire much confidence in a course of treatment that is essentially experimental. The only solutions to this problem are ethically explaining the experimental nature of the treatments, working from a solid theoretical foundation, ideally while collecting data on the interventions, and expanding the paraphilia research base.

Another interviewing obstacle is some clinicians' unwillingness or inability to maintain a respectful stance toward the client, separating the client as a person of worth from the behavior, which the interviewer may find distasteful or even horrifying. In this regard we recommend that clinicians practice these types of interviews repeatedly under intensive supervision during their graduate training, eliciting feedback about disrespectful nonverbal or verbal behaviors.

A helpful way of approaching these cases for some is to view the client as a product of his or her environment. Had the early environment been different, the client's behavior may have been different. Thus, it is the behavior that is deficient, not the client. If the deviant behavior is unlawful and involved victims, a related issue is maintaining that neutral stance and rapport while not colluding with the offender against the victim. It can be challenging to disagree with the client and do it agreeably. This may be achieved by withholding outright judgments of the behavior without offering any reinforcement for the client's behavior or his or her justifications for it.

The last major obstacle is managing discomfort. This regularly arises in two forms in these types of interviews: discomfort created by the clinician and that created by the client. Interviewers often feel uncomfortable when they challenge offenders' accounts of the problem behavior with collateral information and when they provide clients with feedback they do not want to hear (e.g., diagnosis of a paraphilia). Useful methods for being effective with these sensations include practicing often and exposing oneself to the unease repeatedly, being well prepared for sessions, having great familiarity with the details in the collateral information, not taking the offender's affect personally, and considering the greater good of getting the story straight—for the client and, perhaps, the community. The second category of discomfort is that produced by clients intentionally trying to test or titillate the clinician. This appears common, particularly if the clinician appears in any way inexperienced. Once again, it is the poise that comes with practice and experience that saves the day. A final, related issue is achieving privacy for confidentiality in the forensic setting while maintaining safety with clients with sexually abusive or violent pasts. Safety should always come first. Interviewers should work with security personnel in forensic settings to establish precedents for safe and private interviewing environments.

Case Illustration

Ray is a 20-year-old single White man who was referred by his probation officer for an assessment of his sexual behavior to determine his need for treatment. Ray is on probation for possession of marijuana and breaking into a vacant home to host a party there. He lives with his mother and 16-year-old sister, both of whom have reported missing undergarments. These items have been discovered in Ray's bedroom. Ray's mother has expressed concern to his probation officer that Ray may be a potential sexual offender, given his history of criminal offenses and the missing underwear. Ray is healthy and reports no history of disease or serious injury. He was prescribed alprazolam in jail to alleviate symptoms of anxiety, which he takes on an as-needed basis approximately six times per week. He also takes methylphenidate in the morning to alleviate hyperactivity. At age 5 Ray was diagnosed with attention-deficit/hyperactivity disorder, combined type. He reports that if he does not take medication he sleeps approximately 3 hours per night and cannot sit still for longer than a couple of minutes during the day. He finds it difficult to concentrate, even with the medication. He was not diagnosed with conduct disorder as a child and does not meet criteria for antisocial personality disorder. Ray drinks alcohol socially, which he describes as "about four drinks on a weekend night." He used marijuana three or four times per week before his recent arrest. He denies any subsequent use and use of any other substances. He said he was intoxicated on cannabis when he committed breaking and entering.

Ray's sexual history began with an instance of abuse. He was touched on the genitals by an adult male neighbor when he was 7. The man was arrested but never incarcerated and continued to live near the boy and to threaten him verbally throughout his childhood. His consensual sexual activities began when he was 16 with girls his age and older. He reports his enjoyment of traditional foreplay activities and sexual intercourse. He stated he has had approximately seven sexual partners, practiced safe sex with all of them, and is currently not having sex with anyone. He stated that some of his sexual relationships have been meaningful to him and that he has been in love with two of these girls but that sometimes the relationship was purely sexual. He emphasized that he was respectful of his partners and clear about his intentions. He has never had a homosexual or pedophilic encounter or any sexual dysfunction. He reports that he masturbates about once daily. He states that his interest in women's underwear began "by accident," when he was folding the family's clothes and admired them. He said he rubbed them in his hands, which made him feel aroused and have thoughts about having sex with one of his ex-girlfriends. He decided to keep them in order to be able to bring up the arousal at will for masturbation purposes. His curiosity extended gradually over several months to additional underwear. He stated he found the arousal strengthened when he introduced a new pair to his practice. In response to the interviewer's question about wearing the garments, he stated he did not put them on but preferred to hold them in his hand while masturbating. He stated with disgust that he has never had any sexual fantasies about his mother or sister. He acknowledged regular fantasies about sexual intercourse with an ex-partner. He stated that his arousal is greater with a "real person" but that he is unable to arrange regular sexual activities while living with his mother. He reported a fantasy of spanking a partner and being spanked if his partner was interested in trying it. He stated that he would not want to inflict pain but would like to feel a different kind of sensation during sex. He has never tried this with a partner. He estimates he has taken about 15 pairs of underwear over the past 3 months, about one a week. He said he feels excited when he takes the clothing and embarrassed when his mother confronts him about it. He said he is afraid there is something wrong with him sexually. He feels angry that he would be viewed as a potential abuser because he would never harm anyone sexually. He views his behavior as unusual but not harmful to him or to anyone else. He thinks his mother and sister are overreacting, because they have many pairs of underwear. Ray is unemployed because of his recent incarceration, but he is a skilled mechanic with a promised job when he is no longer on probation. He reports a close, caring relationship with his mother and several friends who know him well. He admits that he handles anxiety poorly and that his marijuana use was to "calm my nerves." He noted his friends do not have criminal histories and that he is opposed to harming anyone. He reported his crime as impulsive and "stupid." This was his first offense.

Ray appears socially skilled in every domain. He has never been treated for a sexual issue. He states he would like to understand his sexual behavior and to know his options for dealing with it. He would like to put his family at ease. He has no cultural concerns around sex. Ray's strengths are his adequate cognitive ability, his social support network, his social skill, his trade and the financial support of his mother, his physical health, and his sensitivity to others. Ray has many diverse interests that fill his time, including working on cars, fixing and selling antiques, expanding his music collection, and spending time with friends.

Ray was diagnosed with attention-deficit/ hyperactivity disorder, combined, generalized anxiety disorder, substance abuse in remission, and fetishism. Treatment plans include cognitive-behavioral treatment for improved impulse control and anxiety management, contingency management relative to criminal behavior, and management of his fetish behavior privately.

MULTICULTURAL AND DIVERSITY ISSUES

The sexual deviance literature is sparse with the exception of studies of sexual assault. There is an even greater need for information addressing multicultural issues in sexual deviance. Dominant theories of sexual deviance are embedded in a Western cultural context (Hall, Teten, & Sue, 2003) and primarily in the sexual behaviors of young males. It is these perspectives on normality and abnormality that are brought to bear on sexuality. An awareness that perceptions of appropriate behavior are culturally prescribed is essential because cultural group norms are important determinants of behavior. Dana (1995) identifies four issues that need to be addressed in a culturally competent assessment: cultural history and beliefs, acculturation status and cultural identity, health and illness beliefs, and appropriate language skills.

Behavior evolves through the cultural history and norms of groups of people, and each person belongs to a variety of different cultural groups by birth and often by choice. These groups may be ethnic, religious, gender, age, ideological, racial, or ability based. Although it is clear that cultural norms are influential, it is unclear precisely how they influence sexual behavior. Familiarity with cultural norms, which may entail an understanding of the history that shaped them, is necessary for full comprehension in an assessment. Although knowledge of general history and immigration may be useful in this regard, asking the client is the only way of understanding the specific elements of culture that may be relevant to the problem of interest.

For example, more than 500 American Indian tribal groups and more than 30 groups make up the "Hispanic" designator. Thus, knowing something about American Indians and Hispanics is *not* knowing something about an individual with membership in one of those groups.

Sexual behavior may be guided by the attitudes and beliefs of groups. Misogynistic and patriarchal beliefs have been implicated in sexually deviant behavior (Malamuth, Linz, Heavey, Barnes, & Acker, 1995). It also appears that collectivity versus individualism in groups differentially affects behavior, including sexual behavior (Hall, Sue, et al., 2000). Interpersonal concerns and social reputation are seen as a driving force in collectivist cultures, whereas intrapersonal interests may drive behavior in a more individualistic society. Depending on the sexual values of the culture, a greater concern for others in the group over the individual may be either protective or harmful (Hall & Barongan, 1997). The disapproval of others may be a powerful deterrent to sexually deviant behavior, or it may impede reporting of sexually deviant behaviors in order to maintain order in the group. Asian females my not report sexual assault, for example, because it is seen as less important than the need to maintain group cohesiveness (Dussich, 2001). Ethnic identity, the extent to which one subscribes to membership in a particular ethnic group, is also associated with adherence to particular cultural beliefs. The degree of acculturation to majority group norms is important to understand in determining whether beliefs about sexuality may be more like those of the majority group or may be more unique to a minority group. The stronger the ethnic identity and less assimilation into broader society, the greater the variability in socially acceptable beliefs from the majority. As Dana (1995) suggests, the view and production of sexually deviant behavior as healthy or unhealthy may be seen through different lenses, and as a result, culturally based interpretations of sexual behavior may clash. For example, some cultures view married women as the property of their husbands and view sexual behavior as an obligation of the woman to that relationship. If the wife did not consent to a sexual request by her husband and he had sexual intercourse with her anyway, some cultures would view this as rape, a sexually deviant behavior, whereas others would not see this as problematic. The same behavior may be viewed differently by different cultures. Conversely, there may be culturally distinct expressions of and moderators of psychopathology as well (Mahaffey, 2004). Carrasco and Garza-Louis (1997) provide the example of machismo and macho nonegalitarianism in some Hispanic cultures. Although there is often a value of different but respected roles for men and women in Hispanic cultures, machismo is the abuse of the power differential that accompanies those differences. The beliefs and behaviors of machismo are associated with sexually abusive behavior (Garza-Louis & Peralta, 1993).

Attention to language is essential in culturally competent interviewing. Ideally the client is able to listen and respond in his or her primary language in order to ensure that meaning and accuracy are not lost in translation. That being said, a clinical interview should not be conducted by a clinician who does not share the client's primary language without an interpreter. Family members and friends of the client (especially children) are not appropriate translators. Awareness of nonverbal communication is also important in the interview (Ertz, 1997).

It must be acknowledged that there is no evidence that ethnicity itself creates a risk for sexually coercive behavior, and there are similar rates of sexual abuse cross-culturally (Hall et al., 2003).

Finally, normative sexual differences across ages, genders, sexual orientations, and other cultural divides are not well understood, rendering issues of nonnormative sexuality across these domains even less well comprehended. The probability of paraphilic behavior is greater in young heterosexual males. The reasons for these differences are unknown.

DIFFERENTIAL DIAGNOSIS AND BEHAVIORAL ASSESSMENT

There are many healthy varieties in sexual fantasy and expression that should not be confused with paraphilic behavior. Sexual thoughts, feelings, behaviors, and objects are diagnosed only when they produce "clinically significant distress or impairment (e.g., are obligatory, result in sexual dysfunction, require participation of nonconsenting individuals, lead to legal complications, interfere with social relationships" (APA, 2000).

Unexpected sexual behaviors may also accompany disorders including schizophrenia, bipolar disorder, substance intoxication, mental retardation, dementia, and a personality change caused by a general medical condition (APA, 2000). According to the *DSM,* these secondary sexual deviance problems are distinct from a primary diagnosis in that the symptoms are present only during the course of the other mental disorder, the behaviors do not represent the client's preferred sexual activities, performance of the behaviors is isolated, and the behaviors have a later onset.

Each sexual deviance problem is uniquely focused and distinguished from others on that basis. However, the paraphilias are highly comorbid (Kafka & Prentky, 1994), and it is common for more than one paraphilia to be diagnosed for a single person. Clinicians may be curious about how to distinguish between fetishism, transvestic fetishism, and sexual masochism. In fetishism sexual arousal is associated with the object, and in transvestic fetishism it is wearing the clothing that is arousing. One form of sexual masochism is being forced to wear other-sex clothing. The arousal in this case is associated with that humiliation, not with the wearing or the clothing itself.

Behavioral observation is not conducted in assessment of the paraphilias for privacy reasons. A solid interview that rests on a functional analysis of the client's behavior including its antecedents, behavioral presentation and accompaniments, and consequences is very useful in creating a viable and individualized treatment plan (Sbraga, 2004; Serin & Mailloux, 2003).

SELECTION OF TREATMENT TARGETS AND REFERRAL

All data gathered through the methods described in this chapter are useful only if they inform a comprehensive treatment plan with jointly identified targets. Those targets should be the distal and proximal causal and maintaining factors for the thoughts, feelings, and behaviors of interest. These will be somewhat unique to each client and problem and are based on an analysis of the function of a particular symptom, its antecedents, and its maintaining consequences. Common targets include managing the environment through the acquisition of new coping skills, such as not going places that cue the behavior. Improving cognitive and emotional skills may be useful, such as altering cognitive distortions, accepting aberrant

sexual thoughts, acting in a value-based way, and learning to regulate intense emotion. Sexual arousal to deviant objects may be altered and managed through techniques such as masturbatory and verbal satiation, aversion therapy, and covert sensitization. However, no technique has been reliable in changing arousal from deviant objects to nondeviant objects. Consequently, if a client has an entirely paraphilic arousal, the problem may be exceptionally difficult to treat because of the prospect of having no satisfying sexual outlet. Assessments of sexually deviant behavior should routinely include coordination with the client's primary physician. Referral to a psychiatrist may be warranted in the case of a primary or secondary co-occurring psychiatric disorder or a severe sexual self-control disorder. Chemical and surgical castration significantly reduce sexual drive in males and reportedly produce a great deal of relief for many (Bradford, 1997). However, they are not a panacea. Reducing sexual urges and fantasies may not be sufficient to eliminate sexual behavior with alternative roots such as hostility toward women or belonging to a group such as a sadomasochism club. For these treatment needs, cognitive and behavioral interventions may be more conducive to creating meaningful change.

SUMMARY

The void of objective assessment tools for the sexual dysfunctions and deviations renders effective clinical interviewing crucial to positive intervention in these cases. Whereas clinical interviewing may be a useful supplement to the assessment enterprise in other clinical matters, it is paramount here. Unfortunately, interviewing around human sexuality is also hampered by sparse empirical investigation. Therefore, this chapter offers the most logical approach stemming from the available data, one that will need revision as this literature evolves.

For both sets of disorders the goal of professionally accessing relevant and accurate information about a person's most private behavior is, ironically, impeded by a lack of intimacy. It is the clinician's ability to convey and maintain professionalism while confidently, skillfully, and carefully engaging the client in a frank discussion of his or her most personal behavior that preserves the dignity of the client while permitting access to information essential to the change process. Complementing this fundamental task, the apparently broad variability in normative and healthy human sexual functioning should be emphasized throughout the interview and in any reports or recommendations it informs. Clinical interviewers who are accepting of their clients (if not their behavior), discreet, anchored by normative sexual knowledge, well informed about relevant and irrelevant content areas, and skilled in communication will be most effective in assessing and treating human sexual problems.

REFERENCES

Abel, G. G. (1989). Paraphilias. In H. I. Kaplan & B. J. Sadock (Eds.), Comprehensive textbook of psychiatry (5th ed., pp. 1069–1085). Baltimore, MD: Williams & Wilkins.

Adshead, G. (1997). Transvestic fetishism. In D. R. Laws & W. T. O'Donohue (Eds.), Sexual deviance: Theory, assessment, and treatment (pp. 280–296). New York: Guilford.

American Psychiatric Association. (2000). Diagnostic and statistical manual of mental disorders (4th ed., Text rev.). Washington, DC: Author.

Andrews, D. A., & Bonta, J. (1994). The psychology of criminal conduct. Cincinnati, OH: Anderson.

Bancroft, J., Loftus, M. A., & Long, J. S. (2003). Distress about sex: A national survey of women in heterosexual relationships. Archives of Sexual Behavior, 32, 193–208.

Barbaree, H. E., & Seto, M. C. (1997). Pedophilia assessment and treatment. In D. R. Laws & W. T. O'Donohue (Eds.), Sexual deviance: Theory, assessment, and treatment (pp. 175–193). New York: Guilford.

Basson, R., Berman, J., Burnett, A., Derogatis, L., Ferguson, D., Fourcroy, J., et al. (2001). Report of the International Consensus Development Conference on Female Sexual Dysfunction: Definitions and classifications. Journal of Sex and Marital Therapy, 27, 83–94.

Beck, J. G. (1995). Hypoactive sexual desire disorder: An overview. Journal of Consulting and Clinical Psychology, 63, 919–927.

Bradford, J. (1997). Medical intervention and sexual deviance. In D. R. Laws & W. T. O'Donohue (Eds.), Sexual deviance: Theory, assessment, and treatment (pp. 449–464). New York: Guilford.

Cale, E. M., & Lillienfeld, S. O. (2004). What every forensic psychologist should know about psychopathic personality. In W. O'Donohue & E. Levensky (Eds.), Handbook of forensic psychology (pp. 395–428). San Diego, CA: Elsevier.

Carrasco, N., & Garza-Louis, D. (1997). Hispanic sex offenders: Cultural characteristics and implications for treatment. In B. K. Schwartz & H. R. Cellini (Eds.), The sex offender: New insights, treatment innovations and legal developments (Vol. 2, 13-1–13–8). Kingston, NJ: Civic Research Institute.

Dana, R. H. (1995). Culturally competent MMPI assessment of Hispanic populations. Hispanic Journal of Behavioral Sciences, 17, 305–319.

Dussich, J. P. (2001). Decision not to report sexual assault: A comparative study among women living in Japan who are Japanese, Korean, Chinese, and English-speaking. International Journal of Offender Therapy and Comparative Criminology, 45, 278–301.

Ertz, D. J. (1997). The American Indian sexual offender. In B. K. Schwartz & H. R. Cellini (Eds.), The sex offender: New insights, treatment innovations and legal developments (Vol. 2, pp. 14-1–14-10). Kingston, NJ: Civic Research Institute.

Garza-Louis, D., & Peralta, F. (1993). The macho syndrome: Myths and realities of the Hispanic sex offender. Paper presented at the 1993 Annual Conference on Sex Offender Treatment, Huntsville, TX.

Hall, G. C. N., Andersen, B. L., Aarestad, S. L., & Barongan, C. (2000). Sexual dysfunction and deviation. In M. Hersen & A. S. Bellack (Eds.), Psychopathology in adulthood (pp. 390–418). Boston: Allyn & Bacon.

Hall, G. C. N., & Barongan, C. (1997). Prevention of sexual coercion: Sociocultural risk and protective factors. American Psychologist, 52, 5–14.

Hall, G. C. N., Sue, S., Narang, D. S., & Lilly, R. S. (2000). Culture-specific models of men's sexual coercion: Intra and interpersonal determinants. Cultural Diversity and Ethnic Minority Psychology, 6, 252–267.

Hall, G. C. N., Teten, A., & Sue, S. (2003). The cultural context of sexual aggression: Asian American and European American perpetrators. Annals of the New York Academy of Sciences, 989, 131–143.

Hanson, R. K., & Bussiere, M. T. (1998). Predicting relapse: A meta-analysis of sexual offender recidivism studies. Journal of Consulting and Clinical Psychology, 66, 348–362.

Hanson, R. K., & Harris, A. J. R. (1997). Voyeurism assessment and treatment. In D. R. Laws & W. T. O'Donohue (Eds.), Sexual deviance: Theory, assessment, and treatment (pp. 311–331). New York: Guilford.

Hanson, R. K., Morton, K. E., & Harris, A. J. R. (2003). Sexual offender recidivism risk: What we know and what we need to know. Annals of the New York Academy of Sciences, 989, 154–166.

Hawton, K., & Catalan, J. (1986). Prognostic factors in sex therapy. Behaviour Research and Therapy, 24, 377–385.

Hays, P. (2003). Addressing cultural complexities in therapy. Washington, DC: American Psychiatric Association.

Heiman, J. R. (2002). Psychologic treatments for female sexual dysfunction: Are they effective and do we need them? Archives of Sexual Behavior, 31, 445–450.

Hucker, S. J. (2004). Disorders of impulse control. In W. O'Donohue & E. Levensky (Eds.), Handbook of forensic psychology (pp. 471–487). San Diego, CA: Elsevier.

Hunter, J. A., & Mathews, R. (1997). Sexual deviance in females. In D. R. Laws & W. T. O'Donohue (Eds.), Sexual deviance: Theory, assessment, and treatment (pp. 464–480). New York: Guilford.

Hwang, M. Y. (1999). Sexual dysfunction. Silence about sexual problems can hurt relationships. Journal of the American Medical Association, 281, 584.

Johnson, S. (1997). Psychological force in sexual abuse: Implications for recovery. In B. K. Schwartz & H. R. Cellini (Eds.), *The sex offender: New insights, treatment innovations and legal developments* (Vol. 2, pp. 17-1–17-10). Kingston, NJ: Civic Research Institute.

Kadri, N., Mchichi Alami, K. H., & Mchakra Tahiri, S. (2002). Sexual dysfunction in women: Population based epidemiological study. *Archives of Women's Mental Health, 5,* 59–63.

Kafka, M. P., & Prentky, R. A. (1994). Preliminary observations of *DSM-III-R* Axis I comorbidity in men with paraphilias and paraphilia-related disorders. *Journal of Clinical Psychiatry, 55,* 481–487.

Kaplan, H. S. (1979). *The evaluation of sexual disorders.* New York: Bruner/Mazel.

Krueger, R. B., & Kaplan, M. S. (1997). Frotteurism assessment and treatment. In D. R. Laws & W. T. O'Donohue (Eds.), *Sexual deviance: Theory, assessment, and treatment* (pp. 131–151). New York: Guilford.

Langstrom, N., & Grann, M. (2000). Risk for criminal recidivism among young sex offenders. *Journal of Interpersonal Violence, 15,* 855–871.

Laumann, E. O., Paik, A., & Rosen, R. C. (1999). Sexual dysfunction in the United States: Prevalence and predictors. *Journal of the American Medical Association, 281,* 537–544.

Lavie-Ajayi, M. (2005). Because all real women do: The construction and deconstruction of female orgasmic disorder. *Sexualities, Evolution and Gender, 7,* 57–72.

Letourneau, E., & O'Donohue, W. (1993). Sexual desire disorders. In W. O'Donohue & J. H. Geer (Eds.), *Handbook of sexual dysfunctions: Assessment and treatment.* Boston: Allyn & Bacon.

LoPiccolo, J. (2004). Sexual disorders affecting men. In L. J. Haas (Ed.), *Handbook of primary care psychology* (pp. 485–494). New York: Oxford University Press.

LoPiccolo, J., & Friedman, J. (1988). Broad-spectrum treatment of low sexual desire: Integration of cognitive, behavioral, and systemic therapy. In S. R. Leiblum & R. C. Rosen (Eds.), *Sexual desire disorders.* New York: Guilford.

LoPiccolo, J., & Heiman, J. (1978). Sexual assessment and history interview. In J. LoPiccolo & L. LoPiccolo (Eds.), *Handbook of sex therapy* (pp. 103–112). New York: Plenum.

Mahaffey, M. B. (2004). Issues of ethnicity in forensic psychology: A model for Hispanics in the United States. In W. O'Donohue & E. Levensky (Eds.), *Handbook of forensic psychology* (pp. 808–851). San Diego, CA: Elsevier.

Malamuth, N. M., Linz, D., Heavey, C. L., Barnes, G., & Acker, M. (1995). Using the confluence model of sexual coercion to predict men's conflict with women: A 10-year follow-up study. *Journal of Personality and Social Psychology, 69,* 353–369.

Masters, W., & Johnson, V. (1970). *Human sexual inadequacy.* Boston: Little, Brown.

McCormick, N. B. (2005). Sexual difficulties after traumatic brain injury and ways to deal with it. *Archives of Sexual Behavior, 34,* 586–588.

Nezu, C. M., Nezu, A. M., Dudek, J. A., Peacock, M. A., & Stoll, J. G. (2005). Social problem-solving correlates of sexual deviancy and aggression. *Journal of Sexual Aggression, 11,* 27–36.

Palmer, R. (1997). Assessment and treatment of incest families. In B. K. Schwartz & H. R. Cellini (Eds.), *The sex offender: New insights, treatment innovations and legal developments* (Vol. 2, pp. 18-1–18-12). Kingston, NJ: Civic Research Institute.

Potts, A. (2000). Coming, coming, gone: A feminist deconstruction of heterosexual orgasm. *Sexualities, 3,* 55–76.

Ravart, M., Trudel, G., Marchand, A., Turgeon, L., & Aubin, S. (1996). The efficacy of a cognitive behavioural treatment model for hypoactive sexual desire disorder: An outcome study. *Canadian Journal of Human Sexuality, 5,* 279–293.

Reissing, E. D., Binik, Y. M., Khalife, S., Cohen, D., & Amsel, R. (2004). Vaginal spasm, pain and behavior: An empirical investigation of the diagnosis of vaginismus. *Archives of Sexual Behavior, 33,* 5–17.

Rosen, R. C., & Leiblum, S. R. (1995). Hypoactive sexual desire. *Psychiatric Clinics of North America, 18,* 107–121.

Sbraga, T. P. (2004). Sexual deviance and forensic psychology: A primer. In W. O'Donohue & E. Levensky (Eds.), *Handbook of forensic psychology* (pp. 429–470). San Diego, CA: Elsevier.

Sbraga, T. P., & O'Donohue, W. (2004). *The sex addiction workbook.* Oakland, CA: New Harbinger Press.

Segraves, K. B., & Segraves, R. T. (1991). Hypoactive sexual desire disorder: Prevalence and comorbidity in 906 subjects. *Journal of Sex and Marital Therapy, 17,* 55–58.

Serin, R. C., & Mailloux, D. L. (2003). Assessment of sex offenders: Lessons learned from the assessment of non-sex offenders. Sexual offender recidivism risk: What we know and what we need to know. *Annals of the New York Academy of Sciences, 989,* 185–197.

Strosahl, K. (2004). Forensic and ethical issues in the assessment and treatment of the suicidal patient. In W. O'Donohue & E. Levensky (Eds.), *Handbook of forensic psychology* (pp. 129–155). San Diego, CA: Elsevier.

Thornton, D., & Mann, R. (1997). Sexual masochism assessment and treatment. In D. R. Laws & W. T. O'Donohue (Eds.), *Sexual deviance: Theory, assessment, and treatment* (pp. 240–252). New York: Guilford.

Trudel, G., Marchand, A., Ravart, M., Aubin, S., Turgeon, L., & Fortier, P. (2001). The effect of a cognitive behavioral group treatment program on hypoactive sexual desire in women. *Sexual and Relationship Therapy, 16,* 145–164.

Ward, T., Hudson, S. M., Marshall, W. L., & Siegart, R. J. (1995). Attachment style and intimacy deficits in sexual offenders: A theoretical framework. *Sexual Abuse: A Journal of Research and Treatment, 7,* 315–335.

Ward, T., McCormack, J., Hudson, S. M., & Polaschek, D. (1997). Rape assessment and treatment. In D. R. Laws & W. T. O'Donohue (Eds.), *Sexual deviance: Theory, assessment, and treatment* (pp. 356–393). New York: Guilford.

Ward, T., & Stewart, C. A. (2003). Good lives and the rehabilitation of sexual offenders. In T. Ward, D. R.

Laws, & S. M. Hudson (Eds.), *Sexual deviance: Issues and controversies* (pp. 21–44). Thousand Oaks, CA: Sage.

Wincze, J. P. (2000). Assessment and treatment of atypical behavior. In S. R. Leiblum & R. C. Rosen (Eds.), *Principles and practice of sex therapy* (3rd ed., pp. 449–470). New York: Guilford.

World Health Organization. (1992). *ICD-10: International statistical classification of diseases and related health problems.* Geneva: Author.

PART III

SPECIAL POPULATIONS AND ISSUES

22

COUPLES

SARAH DUMAN, JED GRODIN, YOLANDA M. CÉSPEDES,
EMILY FINE, POORNI OTILINGAM, AND GAYLA MARGOLIN

This chapter highlights the ways in which interviews with couples are fundamentally different from interviews with individuals. We address two common types of couple interviewing: those conducted as part of therapeutic interventions when problems in the relationship are the presenting complaint (e.g., marital, family, or sex therapy) and those conducted when the partner's involvement and support can facilitate an ongoing individual treatment for a physical or mental health concern (e.g., partner input to make a major health care decision or to increase treatment compliance). Any type of couple interview, even a one-time consultation, raises questions about whose interests will be served. Who is the patient: one partner, both partners, or the relationship between the two partners? Answers to this question are inextricably linked to the goals of the couple session, which must be negotiated with both partners present. In any couple interview, the interviewer needs to demonstrate respect for the couple relationship as an important entity; at the same time, the interviewer needs to show sensitivity to each member of the couple and to be mindful of the individual partner's distinct opinions, goals, and reactions.

This chapter is written to convey the wide-ranging opportunities and unique challenges of conducting an interview with partners in an intimate relationship. We first offer a quick overview of distinguishing process features of couple interviews and of the content dimensions that are unique to relationship problems. We then present different modes of couple interviewing and how they map onto different phases of work with couples. We illustrate components of couple interviewing in one case involving issues of fidelity and trust. We also address special considerations regarding ethical, multicultural, and health issues in couple interviews. Our discussion of couple interviews refers to all intimate couples, regardless of marital status and sexual orientation. We use *spouse* and *partner* interchangeably. Whether or not two people are living together obviously affects the relevance of specific content areas, such as managing a shared household. Still, a couple approach to sessions is likely to be applicable for any two people who define themselves as a couple.

UNIQUE PROCESS FEATURES OF COUPLE INTERVIEWS

Three-Way Communication

The presence of both members of a couple in an interview creates a unique context for any communication. In individual interviews, the dialogue between one interviewer and one client contains both verbal and nonverbal channels of communication. Any one statement can convey different and potentially confusing messages across these channels of communication. In contrast to the two-way discussion that occurs in individual interviews, the three-way conversation of a conjoint couple interview opens up multiple levels of communication. In couple interviews, the interviewer is simultaneously involved in a conversation with each spouse, and the meanings attached to any one message are multiplied. Both partners hear the therapist's comments, yet they may not attach the same interpretations or meanings to the statements. For example, an interviewer's statement directed to a husband that he needs to take more responsibility for being compliant with medication may be intended also an indirect message to his wife that she needs to back away from dispensing her husband's medication. However, without a direct statement to the wife, she may not know whether she should take more or less responsibility for getting her husband to be compliant with medication. Directly assessing the husband's preference for whether he wants his wife to be more or less involved with his medication regimen is another important consideration.

Therapist as an Outsider

In the presence of both spouses, the interviewer is in the unusual situation of being the expert but also being an outsider. Spouses bring to the couple interview an indeterminate number of ongoing conversations with each other. Some of these conversations reflect topics that are receiving attention at home, whereas others reflect issues that date back to the beginning of their relationship but still are triggered with little provocation. Even a therapist who works with a couple over many sessions will have access to only a small portion of the important communications between spouses. Thus, the interviewer remains a newcomer to the long, complex, and intimate details of the spouses' lives. As a result, the interviewer may not notice or understand some of the private communications between spouses that transpire right in front of him or her. Interestingly, however, it is often the interviewer's attempts to make sense of couples' communications with one another that provide the most fertile territory for couple interviews.

Communication as the Essence

An in-depth understanding of communication serves important functions for both assessment and intervention in the couple interview. The ongoing process of clarifying the complexities of communication between the two partners and between each partner and therapist is a consistent, repeating, and vital part of the couple interview, regardless of whether the couple is just starting therapy or is many sessions into the therapeutic process. With both spouses present for a couple interview, it is essential that each partner understand not only the therapist's statements but also the partner's communications. This process of inspecting the multiple layers of meaning in communication and understanding the implications of one partner's statement for the other is the essence of the couple interview. The distinct advantage of conducting couple interviews with both spouses present is the opportunity to put communications under the therapeutic microscope—to help the speaker articulate his or her clear and heartfelt message and to help the listener accurately receive the content and affective level of the message.

Couple Interview as a Sample of Behavior

The couple interviewer is in a unique situation of having direct access to couple communications. Rather than rely on a client's report about a problem that occurred outside the therapy room, the couple interviewer directly observes the content and process of partners' communications with each other. In an individual interview, information is limited to one partner's description of his or her perceptions of the couple's communication style. At best, this might be a limited description; at worst, this could be a highly one-sided view that leads to misguided therapeutic interventions.

In couple interviews, the interviewer can directly observe communication processes; a sample of the couple relationship is brought into the interview session much as a patient is brought into an examining room. From an assessment perspective, time spent in the company of both spouses provides a window into the nature of their communication processes. Rather than rely on one partner's report of what is wrong with the relationship, the therapist uses her or his own eyes and ears to discern constructive and destructive patterns in the relationship. Even in interviews when one partner is assisting in the other's individual treatment, the couple interviewer can directly observe the manner in which assistance is offered and received. From an intervention perspective, communication exhibited in the interview represents the essence of what relationship therapy typically is designed to improve: how the partners get along with each other and how they handle conflict and demonstrate support and understanding.

Blurred Boundaries Between Assessment and Intervention

Conjoint couple interviews are replete with opportunities for each partner to hear new information or to learn something new about the partner, thereby blurring the boundaries between assessment and intervention. Even through straightforward, information-eliciting questions, one spouse might reveal information unknown to the other. Through a more active interviewing style, the couple interviewer can probe the couple to talk about a particular issue, to explain exactly why something is upsetting, to identify emotional reactions, and to link those emotions with specific events that just transpired in the session. Sometimes the couple interviewer purposely creates an environment in which spouses consider an issue from a new perspective or present their ideas in a new manner.

Thus, the couple interview presents limitless opportunities for transforming an ordinary statement into a communication that alters the way one or both partners view the relationship. Receiving previously unknown information from one's partner can propel someone to think and behave differently in the relationship. Interviewer strategies that elicit new information and new forms of expression are used to disrupt frequently repeated, nonproductive conversations.

Couple interviews also offer important opportunities for changing relationship processes and for eliciting partner support that are not available in individual interviews. With only a few exceptions (e.g., when one partner is at risk for physical or emotional harm), we maintain that relationship problems should be treated with both partners present. When clients in individual therapy identify relationship problems with their significant other as a major concern, our recommendation is to invite the partner into the ongoing therapy or to refer the couple to a therapist specifically trained in couple therapy. Doherty (2002) asserts that couple therapy is the recommended mode of intervention not only to maximize relationship benefits but also to minimize relationship harm. In addition, data clearly support including a partner in the therapy session to assist in the treatment of the other's individual problem (Baucom, Shoham, Mueser, Daiuto, & Stickle, 1998). Partners typically are willing to participate in one another's treatment if specifically asked and if shown how their participation can be beneficial.

DESCRIPTION OF RELATIONSHIP DISORDERS AND PROBLEMS

Relationship problems do not map neatly onto our current diagnostic schemes and are described only briefly in the *Diagnostic and Statistical Manual of Mental Disorders, Fourth Edition* (*DSM-IV;* American Psychiatric Association, 1994). An inadequate diagnostic scheme means that we lack a common language for recognizing, defining, and describing the characteristics or severity of relationship problems. Despite language in the *DSM-IV* about clinically significant impairment, we lack set criteria for a diagnosis of relationship disorders based on specific patterns of behavior, number of problems, length and seriousness of problems, or change from previous functioning. The raison d'être for relationship therapy arises from the consumer's perspective, when one or both partners decide that the relationship would benefit from outside intervention.

Couples who seek relationship therapy show remarkable variability across several important dimensions: scope of the problem, length of time problems existed, seriousness of the problems, and attributions about why problems exist. Each of these dimensions contributes to the presenting profile of the couple and must be explored in the first several meetings with a couple. These dimensions also contribute to therapeutic goals that are set and to strategies in working toward those goals.

First, with respect to scope, couples' reasons for seeking therapy can range from a few, highly specific complaints (e.g., "We disagree whenever money comes up but, when we are not talking about money, we really get along quite well.") to widespread discontent with the relationship (e.g.,

"We seem to disagree over everything these days."). Second, problems may be recent developments or longstanding issues, perhaps originating early in the relationship. Some couples seek therapy in the midst of an ongoing crisis, such as after the discovery of an affair or a particularly violent argument when they are convinced that the relationship is unlikely to survive without some help. Other couples report longstanding and pervasive problems, although a specific event still may have prompted the request for therapy. Still other couples, albeit a small number, seek relationship therapy as a preventive measure as they experience early stages of problems.

Third, couples vary in how seriously they view their relationship problems. One index of seriousness is how long they would tolerate being in the relationship in its current state or how many steps they have taken toward separation or divorce. Another index of seriousness is whether one or both partners have withdrawn from the relationship and have given up trying to make it better. Fourth, some partners attribute the cause of their problems to their own shortcomings or mistakes, whereas others attribute the problems to the partner or to more global, external circumstances, such as life stresses. The distinction between self and partner attributions often is linked to a partner's willingness to make personal changes.

An important consideration for couple interviewers is that the two partners are likely to differ in their perspectives on scope, length, seriousness, and cause of relationship problems. Each partner's perspective on these dimensions stems from her or his personal experience of distress, expectations for intimate relationships, and evaluation of what life would be like without the partner. Misunderstandings between partners about the seriousness of the problems, in addition to the problems themselves, are evident in statements such as "Why can't you understand how unhappy I am?" The couple interviewer needs to ensure that each partner has ample opportunity to express her or his opinions on these topics and to prevent one partner from becoming the spokesperson for the couple. Identifying and validating each partner's viewpoint on these issues are essential to being able to work effectively with the couple.

Partners' different perspectives on how they view their relationship problems also can intersect with different viewpoints on the usefulness of therapy. Therefore, interest in seeking therapy and in making therapy effective can be another point of disagreement between partners. A partner's lack of interest in therapy may reflect attitudes that the problems are not serious, are temporary, or are caused by circumstances that he or she cannot change. These attitudes are reflected in statements such as "The problems aren't really a big deal," "The problems will go away on their own as soon as I get another job," "We can solve the problems on our own," or "The problems would go away if my partner just changed his attitude or behavior." Alternatively, reluctance to enter therapy also may reflect the conclusion that the problems are so serious that the relationship is not worth saving. Each partner's thoughts and decisions about entering therapy must be expressed and understood by the interviewer and other partner.

MULTIDIMENSIONAL AND CONTEXTUAL UNDERSTANDING OF RELATIONSHIP DISTRESS

Figure 22.1 presents an overview of a multidimensional and contextual model for understanding relationship problems. The center of the model presents different content areas reflecting the scope of the problem. Process difficulties in communication and problem solving can affect each of these content areas. The outer circle of the diagram represents contextual and developmental dimensions that play a role in the development and course of the specific problems. Conducting a productive couple interview depends largely on knowing what contributes to positive and negative relationship functioning, particularly in light of the multitude of factors implicated in relationship dysfunctions. Because couples themselves are likely to spontaneously mention only a few of these factors, the interviewer needs to be active and thorough in collecting information.

Content of Problem Areas

Figure 22.1 offers a framework for considering four different dimensions of relationship problems. The two boxes on the left represent very different dimensions of a relationship. Closeness and intimacy reflect the private, personal, and affectionate dimensions of couple relationships—the

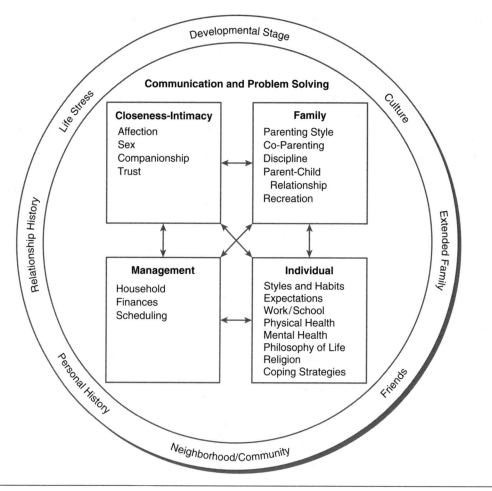

Figure 22.1   Multidimensional Contextual Model

aspects of relationships that typically bring partners together. Management represents the practical side of coordinating two lives and sharing a household. The boxes on the right represent how relationship problems intersect with individual problems and with family and parenting roles. Divergent individual styles, values, and preferences, although not dysfunctional for either individual, may clash and be a source of couple conflict. Likewise, parenting and the co-parenting relationship are important domains of how the couple functions.

Arrows between the four boxes represent the bidirectional and reciprocal influences between the dimensions. Problems in the intimacy realm may increase the likelihood of conflict over practical issues, and problems in the practical arena of relationships can erode intimacy.

Increasing attention is being paid to recursive influences between individual and relationship problems (Snyder & Whisman, 2003, p. 1). Couple problems often overlap with the psychological and physical problems of an individual partner (Baucom et al., 1998). Disentangling the specific ways in which relationship problems can contribute to individual problems (e.g., marital distress leads to depression) or individual problems can lead to relationship problems is an important focus in couple interviews.

Communication and Problem Solving

Communication deficits typically are the reason why disagreements about the topics in Figure 22.1 develop into problems. Disagreements about these topics are common and are not necessarily destructive to a relationship, particularly if the couple can resolve or set aside the disagreements. Disagreements become problematic when the couple experiences repeating and escalating patterns of negativity that cause significant pain to one or both spouses and lead to deterioration and divisiveness in the relationship. Yet another sign that conflict has become problematic is when it interferes with the partners' enjoying each other's company and feeling emotionally close. Problematic communication processes and areas of disagreement build on each other. Poor communication typically results in an increasingly wide range of conflict areas. When couples lack skill or motivation to collaborate toward mutually acceptable outcomes, even trivial disagreements can escalate into serious problems.

Three identifiable negative patterns often are found in distressed couples (Christensen & Pasch, 1993). In couples with a pattern of mutual escalation, both partners' negative and attacking behaviors lead to high levels of conflict escalation. In couples with a demand-withdraw pattern, one partner's accusations and demands contribute to the other's withdrawal, which further fuels the critical, demanding behavior. In mutually avoidant couples, the spouses choose to avoid their conflicts generally because they fear that open discussion will result in the high levels of conflict. Couples often show a combination of these patterns and, over time, can cycle from one pattern to another. Because couples themselves often do not recognize these patterns, the interviewer needs to reconstruct the pattern by collecting detailed information about how one relationship event is the stimulus for another event and how these events progress over time. These patterns are best understood when the interviewer works from the assumption that they are sustained by mutually reciprocal behaviors and cannot be attributed to the actions of one spouse alone.

Communication problems often stem from the different ways in which partners express and receive information, and specifically from their different ways of expressing emotion. Partners' beliefs that they should be compatible with one another often lead to a reluctance to articulate what they actually want in the relationship. Wile (1981) describes how this lack of entitlement often is misunderstood as demandingness on the part of one person. Partners may be unskilled in listening to one another. In efforts to defend their own positions, they may overlook points of commonality. Partners also vary widely in the extent to which they are comfortable with expressing disagreement and strong emotion (Margolin, 1987). In the early stages of a relationship, a reserved, somewhat withdrawn person may take pleasure in and find attractive the partner's spontaneity and intensity, only later to discover that this style is overwhelming during a conflict. Rather than either style being at fault, it is the difference in styles that can lead to incompatible, polarized positions where one complains about the other's demonstrative, argumentative style, and the other complains about the partner's aloof and withdrawn manner. The couple interview provides opportunity to directly observe and ultimately to transform these patterns.

Developmental and Contextual Variables

The outer ring of the Figure 22.1 lists a variety of developmental and contextual variables that, at different times, either can be strengths and resources for the couple or additional sources of stress. It is always important to consider the couple's problems in the context of the developmental stage of their relationship. The cognitive, emotional, and stylistic differences that partners bring to the relationship may not be evident until the couple faces a transition in their developmental stage. For example, when spouses face the time demands and role stresses that accompany the transition to parenthood, their different expectations and coping styles may exacerbate the challenges of this life change (Cowan & Cowan, 1990). In general, facing unfamiliar transitions or life stresses may bring to light differences in spouses' expectations that previously were not evident. Onset of health problems or disadvantageous financial circumstances may necessitate establishing a new balance between individual responsibilities, marital roles, and parenting roles and may create a need for support from the other spouse that previously was not necessary or even desirable (Whisman & Uebelacker, 2003).

For most couples, relationships with extended family and friends provide a combination of strengths and stresses. Partners may have different expectations about their level of involvement and that of the partner with the extended family. Relationships with extended family generally undergo adjustment over time because of deliberate decisions such as a move across the country or typical developmental factors such as the assistance needed by aging parents. Involvement with friends and community generally is an important source of support to couples, but sometimes, again possibly because of relocation, those supports are lacking or are readily available to only one partner.

Finally, partners bring their own life histories and histories of other relationships to their current relationship. Spouses develop personalized assumptions and expectations based on their histories. Spouses are exposed to styles of interaction in their family of origin, which they may adopt or reject. Either way, those learning histories and experiences in previous intimate relationships are likely to shape behavior in the present relationship. Tracing spouses' different pathways to their current interaction styles can be useful in building understanding and compassion and in reducing frustration and blame.

Summary

The multidimensional model presented in Figure 22.1 serves as a guide to information relevant to couple interviews. The interviewer collects information pertinent to these topics and helps the partners understand and clarify their thoughts and communications about salient topics in their relationship and about the connections between these topics. Improvement in the couple's interactions can result in resolution of the topics or greater understanding and acceptance of their differences on the topics. In the sections that follow, we provide further detail about the interviewing methods in the beginning and later phases of couple interviews. We also present information about interviewing with an appreciation for multiculturalism and for individual issues, such as physical and mental health problems.

INTAKE INTERVIEWS

Beyond orienting the couple to the interview situation, the priorities for intake interviews are to create a collaborative relationship and conducive environment for working with both partners, assess the couple's problems, assess relationship strengths and build positive expectations about therapy, observe the couple's communication style, and assign questionnaires for a standardized assessment. The initial welcome and orientation

to the session vary according to the referral question, but in all cases the interviewer needs to provide a general description of the purpose of this meeting and possible future meetings. During the informed consent process, the interviewer also needs to communicate applicable policies about confidentiality and about her or his obligations to report child or elder abuse or any intent to physically harm another person.

The initial session assesses problems and strengths in the relationship, with a primary focus on current functioning and an additional emphasis on relationship history (Jacobson & Margolin, 1979; Baucom, Epstein, & LaTaillade, 2002). Assessment of these areas may require more than one session. This process can begin with a simple statement, directed simultaneously to both partners, such as "I'd like to hear about what brought you here." In response to this question, it is likely that one or more topics will emerge as particularly problematic. The interviewer learns a lot about separate topics and connections between topics as the partners move from one issue to another in fluid and dynamic descriptions of their lives together. Beyond a description of the problem areas, the following additional information should be addressed:

- Events surrounding the decision to seek therapy at this time, including each partner's reactions to this decision

- Thoughts about where the relationship is headed

- The nature of the couple's daily interactions, including how this varies across days of the week

- The ways that the couple or partners individually have attempted to solve their problems

Create a Collaborative Working Relationship

The interviewer's efforts to create a conducive therapeutic environment involve establishing contact with each partner, perhaps even before the couple arrives. If the person not making the initial contact is reluctant to come to the session, the interviewer may want to have direct telephone contact with that partner. In the initial few moments of the session, the interviewer sets the stage for a collaborative relationship by balancing his or her communication with both partners. Simple but important steps include greeting each person by name; arranging the chairs so that both partners have equal access to the interviewer and also can face each other, and establishing eye contact with each partner when asking questions or making statements. The interviewer sets the tone that both partners are active participants in the session but ensures that each person has time to speak about a topic, without interruption or dispute from the partner. In this manner, the interviewer has the opportunity to hear and reflect on the unique experience of each partner and to communicate the value of the individual perspectives of each partner.

Assess Problem Areas

In the discussion of problem areas, it is important to focus on specific, detailed descriptions of the undesirable behaviors and the desired changes. The interviewer helps the couple translate and operationalize general complaints into specific behaviors. The interviewer also obtains a functional analysis of the problem behaviors to identify what variables control their occurrence or nonoccurrence and maintain them (Jacobson & Christensen, 1996). The functional analysis focuses on what conditions are antecedents and consequences to the problem behaviors. The goal is to identify variables that might be changed that, in turn, will influence the problems. With some problem behaviors, the interviewer might observe the antecedents and consequences in the session; however, generally the behaviors of interest occur outside the session. Thus, the interviewer typically needs to rely on the couple to provide information for a functional analysis.

The couple interviewer seeks to elucidate connections and patterns in the partners' interactions. Partners often have not thought about or have mistaken assumptions about the events that trigger the problematic behaviors. Awareness of one's own role in the sequence of problem behaviors may be lacking. For example, in the frequently occurring demand-withdraw pattern, the partner complaining about the other's withdrawal may fail to recognize the impact of his or her demanding behavior. The interviewer can help identify these patterns by prompting each partner to describe her or his thoughts and feelings when specific behaviors occur. Examining the cognitive, affective, and behavioral components

of one partner's reactions and how they connect to cognitive, affective, and behavioral reactions in the other partner reveal the relationship sequences. To obtain accurate descriptions about these interlocking reactions, the couple interviewer can assign between-session homework in which each partner individually records daily problem behaviors, his or her reactions to the behaviors, and the circumstances surrounding those events. Rather than discuss this information during the week, it is best for the couple to reserve their discussion until the next session. When each partner completes such a task, it often provides new and insightful information to the couple and to the interviewer about what variables influence the problem behaviors.

Assess Relationship Strengths

Assessment of strengths in the relationship serves the important function for both the couple and interviewer of providing balance for negative events that brought the couple to the session. The therapeutic conceptualization of the case rests on whether the couple is able to describe their strengths in an open and detailed manner, without sliding back into complaints and fault-finding. One strategy to help partners express what is positive in the relationship is to ask them what the relationship is like when the presenting problems abate. A dramatic way of eliciting this information is through what solution-focused couple therapists (e.g., Holt, 2002) describe as the "miracle question": "What would be different if your problems were miraculously solved overnight?"

Another strategy that elicits positive information in some couples is asking them to describe how they first got together as a couple. The initial phases of a relationship are positive for most couples, so the process of recalling those events often brings forth positive and caring descriptions. The interviewer can build on these affectionate moments by asking what attracted the partners to each other. However, couple interviewers need to be aware that some relationships do not have happy beginnings, and this discussion can bring forth reasons that the partners got together that are unrelated to positive qualities of the partner (e.g., being rejected in a previously failed relationship). This information is relevant to the assessment of the current relationship but will not advance the interviewer's goals of fostering a positive tone in the session and encouraging the partners to have positive expectations. Alternatively, partners' fond recollections and affirming statements about one another can foster a positive orientation to future work together (Gurman, 2002; Jacobson & Margolin, 1979).

Observe Couple Communication Processes

Whatever the topic of discussion, the couple interview provides information about how the couple communicates. Perhaps one member tends to be the spokesperson while the other person is quiet. Perhaps one partner subtly agrees or disagrees (head nodding, rolling eyes) with what the other says. By observing verbal and nonverbal communication processes, the interviewer can discern a great deal about each partner's frustration with the relationship and whether this frustration has eroded their respect for one another. The interviewer also might note that the couple communicates in an angry, blaming manner around some topics but appears supportive and respectful around other topics. These shifts in communication style are important in assessing the targets and strategies for intervention. The couple interviewer not only learns about the communication process but also can actively comment on and probe for different types of communication. For example, if a partner responds without seeming to hear what the other partner has said, the interviewer might interrupt and ask for a restatement, clarification, or paraphrase of the prior message.

Assigning Questionnaires for a Standardized Assessment

An efficient way to collect information about the wide-ranging topics described in Figure 22.1 is to collect information from standardized questionnaires about couple satisfaction (Snyder, 1979; Spanier, 1976), specific problems (Weiss & Birchler, 1975), attitudes about the marriage (Baucom & Epstein, 1990), and patterns of closeness and distance (Christensen & Heavey, 1993). These questionnaires serve several important functions. First, overall scores can be compared with population norms to get a general sense of the intensity of partners' dissatisfaction. Second, the partners' scores and answers to specific questions can be compared with one another to see whether partners are similar in their level of dissatisfaction in the sources of discontent. By assessing wide-ranging content areas, these questionnaires provide a quick overview about problem areas and strengths. They also provide information about sensitive problem areas a partner is reluctant to mention spontaneously in the interview.

The interviewer asks partners to fill out one or more of these questionnaires between sessions and bring them back to the next session. Once again, it is best if the partners complete the questionnaires without sharing the information with one another. When the couple comes back the next week, the interviewer should collect the forms and look them over before starting the second session. These questionnaires can be used to guide further assessment of problem areas in the subsequent session. To reinforce the importance of between-session assignments, the interviewer should begin the subsequent session by inviting the partners to share their thoughts in response to the homework assignments or to the previous session more generally.

INTERVIEWING DURING THE INTERVENTION PHASES OF THERAPY

A detailed description of interviewing during the intervention phases of therapy goes well beyond what we can discuss in this chapter. Excellent descriptions of the intervention phases of couple therapy are found elsewhere (e.g., Jacobson & Christensen, 1996; Jacobson & Margolin, 1979). Three intervention strategies for couple interviews deserve brief note here.

- *Getting the partners to join in empathic understanding of the problem.* In the presentation of couple problems, the partners often are at odds with one another; indeed, one partner often describes the other as the source of the problem. As Jacobson and Christensen (1996) describe, sometimes the objective of couple work is not necessarily to solve a problem but to promote the realization that the two partners can join together and support one another in their distress over a problem. Partners come to a more empathic understanding of one another through strategies that help partners to disclose soft emotions such as fear and insecurity that often underlie the hard emotions of anger and resentment and view their problems as part of a natural and understandable process of polarization caused by different personal styles rather than the intentional efforts to upset one another. Wile (1993, 2002) offers vivid examples of how the interviewer can help the couple feel emotionally connected through expression of heartfelt concerns. According to Wile, partners' efforts to stifle their concerns and avoid conflict are responsible for alienation in the relationship. Alternatively, the interviewer can highlight the validity of the partners' concerns and their feelings about those concerns. These efforts reduce partners' blame of themselves and one another and help them to generate a more understanding and collaborative stance toward their problems.

- *Communication training.* Structured communication training is used to foster understanding between partners by building skills in the expression and reception of the communication exchange (Jacobson & Margolin, 1979; Markman, Stanley, & Blumberg, 1994). The interviewer actively directs the flow of communication and slows down the communication exchange by delineating speaker and listener roles. Toward the goal of ensuring that messages are accurately sent and received, the interviewer inserts steps to check whether the listener heard the speaker's intended message. The listener or the interviewer paraphrases the speaker's message to clarify the speaker's message, and the speaker has the opportunity to revise or elaborate on his or her statement. Once both partners know that the initial message has been accurately stated and received, the speaker-listener roles can be reversed. The interviewer takes a directive role in teaching these communication skills by demonstrating and shaping specific speaker skills of brevity and clarity and specific listener skills of paraphrasing and reflection. Through these procedures, the interviewer works to extract the essential and fundamental sources of each partner's distress in an atmosphere of mutual respect. These procedures are likely to promote increased clarification and understanding of the problem, which will point to appropriate intervention strategies.

- *Problem solving.* Problem-solving training is the intervention strategy for examining and responding to situations that couples want to change but are in disagreement about how to change (Oliver & Margolin, 2003). When spouses are entrenched in different and inflexible

positions, problem-solving training can be used to identify solutions that partners have not yet considered. The interviewer guides the couple through several steps toward developing a mutually acceptable solution. First, the interviewer helps the couple define the problem in a way that is noninflammatory and that acknowledges how the problem affects both partners. Second, the interviewer guides the partners as they brainstorm and write down a broad menu of possible solutions. All discussion or evaluation of the merit of the ideas is postponed until the entire list is generated. Third, the partners separately rate the worthiness of every idea. The ideas rated as possibly or definitely worthy by one or both partners then are discussed. Fourth, the partners and interviewer together construct a trial plan that incorporates one or more of the ideas deemed acceptable by both partners; that plan is reevaluated and revised on a weekly basis. Through this process, partners move beyond their irreconcilable positions in favor of options they both recognize as possible solutions.

BYSTANDER AND INDIVIDUAL INTERVIEWS TO SUPPLEMENT COUPLE INTERVIEWS

Sometimes it is advisable to supplement the interview procedures previously described that involve both partners with two alternative types of interviews: the bystander interview and individual interviews. In the bystander interview, attention is directed primarily to one of the partners for a period of time—ranging from a few minutes to most of a session—while the partner observes. This type of interview is particularly useful when the interviewer wants to delve into a topic in depth with one partner without interference or debate from the other partner. The bystander interview can be an important learning experience for both partners and a source of insight for the interviewer. The right type of questions and comments might elicit new insights and new ways of looking at an issue for the person being interviewed. Accordingly, the partner being interviewed might formulate and articulate, perhaps for the first time, her or his previously unstated feelings on a topic. Similarly, the bystander partner has an opportunity to receive new information without any pressure to rebut what is being said or defend a previous position. Nonverbal reactions of the bystander partner often provide important information to the interviewer. Toward the end of this interview, it is important to include the bystander partner through inquiries about whether he or she learned anything new and, if so, what were her or his reactions.

Couple interviewers vary widely in the importance they place on individual interviews. Some couple interviewers believe that there always should be individual interviews as a way to establish rapport and validate the individual partners. That is, each partner has a separate and private opportunity to tell his or her story (Jacobson & Christensen, 1996). Other couple interviewers reserve the individual interviews for situations in which one or both partners appear reluctant or frightened to talk about a particularly sensitive topic, or the interviewer deems it necessary to have a private conversation with a partner about a potentially dangerous situation (e.g., domestic violence). In conducting individual interviews, it is important that each member of the dyad has an individual interview and knows the purpose of the interview.

CONFIDENTIALITY

At the beginning of any couple interview, it is important that the partners know the limits of confidentiality (Margolin, 1982). As in all therapy, clients need to know under what circumstances their private information might be shared with someone outside the therapy session. For couple interviews, partners need unambiguous information about the limits of confidentiality on information each might share with the interviewer. It is obvious that policies about confidentiality are needed when the interviewer holds individual interviews with each partner. However, policies about confidentiality are equally important even in conjoint interviewing. It is not unusual for one partner to find an opportunity to provide personal information to the interviewer; for example, in a telephone call, a written communication, or when the other partner steps out of the room.

Competing arguments can be made about the merit of not keeping any confidences between partners (e.g., confidences potentially breed alliances between the interviewer and one partner) or maintaining the confidentiality of information obtained from each partner (e.g.,

confidences promote open discussion about sensitive topics and elicit more honest answers about topics such as affairs). The most important guiding principle is that the partners know in advance what the policy is regarding confidential information. Then they can decide what they want to share under what circumstances with full knowledge of how the information might be used.

CASE ILLUSTRATION

Stacy, aged 26, requested therapy with her husband, Jim, aged 24. The couple had been together 8 years and had a 2-year-old child. Jim was an engineer and Stacy a nurse. After following consent procedures in the initial session, the interviewer first asked the couple what had brought them in for therapy. Jim immediately allowed Stacy to respond by saying, "I'll let her tell you. She's more upset about it." Stacy responded by explaining that Jim had recently been behaving suspiciously, and she suspected that he was having an affair after overhearing Jim in a phone conversation with an unfamiliar woman. She reported that other people confirmed her suspicions about Jim having an affair, yet she was not sure whether she should believe this information. She appeared both angry and saddened as she provided a lengthy description of her dissatisfaction with Jim's behavior. She even indicated that she was so disturbed by the possibility of infidelity that she would leave the relationship if she learned that Jim had lied to her about this situation. Jim remained quiet and essentially motionless during Stacy's several-minutes-long description.

The therapist then turned to Jim to allow him to respond and to articulate why he thought the couple might benefit from therapy. Jim did not directly deny Stacy's accusations. He acknowledged that Stacy did not trust him and that he wanted to increase her trust, although he did not indicate enthusiasm about coming to therapy. Throughout the first several minutes, the therapist made sure to attend to both partners, to answer each of their questions, and to reflect on their unique experience of entering therapy and dealing with this confusing and very troubling situation.

After several minutes trying to clarify each person's position on the presenting problem, the therapist transitioned into an assessment of current functioning in other domains. Stacy and Jim both reported that they divided responsibilities around the house and that both were devoted to and responsible for their toddler son. During assessment of these areas, both members of the couple spoke equally and respectfully, which was a style quite different from that displayed when they discussed the presenting problem. The therapist also asked for a description of how they generally handled disagreements. The partners agreed that, in most cases, Stacy was the one who got upset and Jim often deferred to her in order to keep the situation "calm." Toward the end of the session, the interviewer began to ask about the couple's relationship history, specifically about how they first met, as an opportunity for the partners to recall one another's positive attributes. The partners readily responded, speaking fondly of how they had met. Stacy was complimentary about how Jim had been a comfort to her during a time when her family of origin was having difficulties.

The initial interview with this couple yielded valuable information about the presenting problem, current functioning, and relationship history and provided the opportunity to observe the couple's communication style. Stacy's dissatisfaction around issues of trust was the primary motivator for the couple to enter therapy. This problem had serious ramifications for the future of the relationship. Despite her distress, her goals were not clearly formulated. Jim neither denied nor confessed to an affair, and his objectives for therapy also were unclear. The couple described a communication pattern that also was exhibited in the session: Stacy typically was the one who became angry and upset, instigated many of the arguments in the relationship, and, in general, exhibited high emotional intensity. Jim exhibited deference to Stacy, particularly around the issues of faithfulness and trust, and appeared to withdraw during conflict. A strength of the relationship was the warmth and affection the partners exhibited toward each other when discussing how they first met.

In the second session, the interviewer collected and quickly scanned several questionnaires the couple had completed. Interestingly, the questionnaires indicated that Jim experienced lower overall satisfaction with the relationship than did Stacy. Clearly the questionnaires had provided Jim a format for expressing his dissatisfaction, which he had not done in the previous session. This new information was very important to the

way the interviewer conceptualized the couple's issues and was a significant focus for the therapist's line of questioning in the second interview.

As the interviewer attempted to engage Jim in further assessment of his thoughts and feelings about the presenting problems of trust, he was somewhat reticent, and Stacy was quick to interrupt. To create an environment in which Jim would have time to formulate his thoughts and speak more freely, the interviewer switched to a bystander interview format. To set the stage for this interview focus, the interviewer pointed out how difficulties in a relationship are painful for both people, even if one person appears to be more outwardly upset. She also indicated that relationship problems are best understood by exploring how the actions of both partners sustain the relationship difficulties.

With encouragement and with questions that helped Jim put words to his experience, he described his frustration about the way Stacy had been treating him. He directly addressed Stacy's accusations and reported that he had not cheated on her but only had maintained a platonic friendship with another woman. He further reported that he had "not left the house or done anything without her permission" lately because she had become so suspicious and because her temper was so unpleasant. To avoid arguments, he chose not to respond to Stacy's accusations, even if they were untrue. When Stacy tried to interrupt, the therapist briefly acknowledged her statement but gently reiterated that she wanted to hear from Jim for a few minutes and that soon Stacy would have plenty of opportunity to speak. With that assurance, Stacy was able to concentrate on the conversation between the therapist and Jim.

The bystander interview, which lasted only 10 minutes, validated Jim's perspective in the eyes of both members of the dyad. After this interview, when the therapist asked Stacy for her thoughts, Stacy was able to say she had not realized how her suspicion and anger had affected Jim. She had been unaware of the extent to which Jim was distancing himself from the relationship and from her. The interviewer was encouraged by the extent to which Stacy acknowledged her role in the relationship problems and by her statement that she did not want to act that way any longer. Jim appeared relieved to hear these statements, a point he further confirmed in later intervention sessions. This interview had a powerful effect in bringing out new information that redefined the problem as a process involving both partners. The interview interrupted the one-sided accusations, provided Jim's assurance that he was not cheating on Stacy, and showed how Stacy's persistent attempts to engage Jim brought about the opposite effect: Jim's emotional withdrawal.

Based on clarification of the couple's problems in the first two sessions, the interviewer revisited the question of goals in the third session. She asked each partner what goals they wanted to accomplish in therapy and how they would know whether the goals were met. Jim's major goal was to regain Stacy's trust. Jim reported he would feel trusted when Stacy allowed him to go out with friends or to run errands on his own, without accompanying him. Stacy agreed that this was a worthy goal. She reported that she also wanted to increase her trust in Jim and not constantly wonder what Jim was doing when he was away from home. Discussion of these goals illuminated a pattern often found in couples with issues around trust: One partner's frequent tirades about trust results in the other partner's resentment, withdrawal, and even secretive behavior, which in turn fuels the first partner's suspicions (Margolin, 1981).

A therapeutic intervention that interrupts a spiraling pattern of suspicion and mistrust is to build in frequent, regularly scheduled discussions of trust (Margolin, 1985). This intervention first is introduced and practiced in the interview. Each partner rates, on a 1–10 scale, the answer to two questions: "How much how much do you trust your partner?" and "How much do you feel trusted?" Ratings are compared and discussed, with partners sharing why they rated one another high or low in trustworthiness. These procedures are repeated every week. Typically there are several outcomes to these "trust check-ins." Both partners share the responsibility for initiating discussions of mistrust. In the discussion, each spouse has an easy way of registering distrust by using the simple scale. In addition, however, the partner needs to provide a rationale for his or her mistrust. Overall, the partners become more aware of the cues they emit that they are or are not trustworthy. Having discussions on a frequent basis means that partners are not always angry and upset when they talk about trust issues. Suspicions are brought up early, before resentment builds. In addition, a check-in that occurs in the absence of suspicion provides confirmation of relationship trust, at least for the previous week. Over time, there can be growing evidence of ongoing relationship trust.

The interviewer introduced the trust check-in with Jim and Stacy. In the initial trust interview, the therapist first asked Jim about his trust levels, to make the point that they were both involved in building or eroding trust. Jim reported that he felt that Stacy trusted him at a level of 5 because Stacy had not been giving him as many indications of distrust as she had before. He said he trusted Stacy at a 9, with the clarification that "nothing is perfect." Stacy felt trusted at a 10 and was not disturbed by hearing that she was trusted only at a 9. Her trust for Jim was up to a 4 because she was more aware of his activities during the day. She noted that she still felt compelled to check his phone records. These interviews continued over the next few sessions. By the last interview, Jim's trust ratings remained high, and Stacy's rating of Jim rose to a 9. She attributed the high rating to Jim being less secretive and her being more informed of his activities through their daily talks.

As the couple dealt with issues of trust, they brought up additional treatment goals: Stacy wanted to get to know Jim better and to clarify whether she wanted to stay in the relationship. Jim wanted to stop avoiding conflict with Stacy and to articulate his viewpoints better. The next five sessions focused on communication training, with the interviewer guiding the partners to better articulate their ideas and listen carefully to one another. At several points in the intervention, the therapist used bystander interviews, particularly when Stacy became verbally aggressive or when Jim withdrew. The interview techniques in this case—validating each partner's perspective and changing the couple's communication pattern around issues of trust— renewed this couple's commitment to work together on their problems. After 10 sessions, they told the interviewer that the relationship was going better, and they were ready to solve additional problems on their own.

Multiculturalism and Couple Interviews

As noted in Figure 22.1, topics that are salient to couples often are contextually based, and problems may arise if the partners come from different cultural contexts, if they have different levels of identification with the same cultural context, or if they have different experiences as they go through the stress of migration and accommodate to a new situation (Falicov, 2003; McGoldrick, Giordano, & Pearce, 1996). Cultural differences commonly influence crucial domains of relationship functioning, including gender roles, family cohesion, emotional expression, relations with extended family, and religion (Crohn, 1998).

There is reason to consider the hypothesis that culture plays a role in the conflict of all couples. As McGoldrick et al. (1996, p. 6) state, "All marriages are to a degree cultural intermarriages. No two families share exactly the same cultural roots." Although a young couple may attempt to create their own customs and rituals as they develop their relationship, cultural influences from their families of origin are likely to impact their relationship perspectives and behaviors in subtle yet significant ways. Obtaining information about each partner's family of origin and larger cultural community is likely to identify positive and negative influences on the couple's current functioning.

Discussion of culture in the couple interview serves several important purposes. Such discussions often are informative to the couple and the interviewer in revealing ways in which the partners are unfamiliar with one another's culture or with the cultural impact on personal beliefs. Identifying cultural influences in the couple's current interaction patterns can result in new, nonblaming attributions, can normalize their experience of distress, and can reduce polarization (Falicov, 2003). Discussion of cultural influences also may bring to light previously unrecognized commonalities when partners believe that their cultural backgrounds are highly dissimilar (Hardy & Laszloffy, 2002).

The following case study highlights two important cultural issues. First, although both partners migrated to the United States, they experienced differences in mastering a new language, establishing a support network, and finding employment and had dissimilar reactions to leaving behind family and friends. In such cases, it is important to assess how long each partner has been in the United States, what motivated the migration, and who was left behind (Falicov, 2003). Second, although the couple shares a Latino background, they still held highly divergent ideas about gender roles. Coming from a similar culture does not mean that the two partners subscribe equally to the traditional cultural values; these differences can be particularly challenging as the couple is finding their way in a new culture.

Anita, age 32, and Roberto, age 35, were each of Argentinean background and had met in Argentina 6 years earlier. They married after 2 years of dating and began to discuss the possibility of moving to the United States soon after they wed. Roberto previously had spent time in the United States and was eager to return. Although Anita had not been to the United States before, she was happy to make the move with Roberto. At the time they entered therapy, Anita and Roberto had been married for 4 years and living in the United States for 2 years.

In their first session, Anita and Roberto indicated that they were entering therapy to improve their relationship after a separation that they had taken earlier that year. Before the separation, they were not communicating well and "simply not getting along." Anita returned to Argentina for 5 months while Roberto remained in the United States. Both described their time apart as immensely distressing, and Anita decided to return to the United States. Since their reunion, they experienced two primary problems: an inability to communicate effectively and a lack of understanding of the other person.

Through couple interviews, it became clear that "lack of understanding" was related to their different acculturation to American society. These differences had created conflict in their relationship, and their inability to communicate well had thwarted their efforts to resolve this conflict. Roberto had an excellent grasp of the English language, was pursuing an advanced degree at a prestigious university, and had made several close friends locally. Anita, on the other hand, did not feel comfortable communicating in English and, consequently, felt unprepared to take classes or to obtain a job. She also had not made any friends. Contrasting her current situation with her life in Argentina, Anita described how she previously had been working as a teacher and had a strong social network, whereas now she was "lost." Managing their household was a primary source of conflict. Roberto expected Anita to shoulder the majority of the responsibilities around the home and was pressuring her to take on additional responsibilities. Anita did not want the extra responsibilities, which Roberto could not understand.

The interviewer focused on the partners' different migration experiences with the goal of having the two partners listen to and understand each other's current experiences. Roberto had not previously heard Anita's comparison of her experiences in the United States and her home country or her desire to spend more time pursuing her career as opposed to investing more time in responsibilities around the home. As she saw it, taking more responsibilities around the home would prevent her from investing time in other areas of her life. However, Roberto did not realize that Anita wanted to pursue career opportunities, and consequently he suggested that she fill her time by engaging in household tasks. The interviewer worked to elicit information about Anita's struggle to adjust in the United States, which helped Roberto develop a better understanding of Anita's experience and of her needs and wishes. Moreover, by hearing Roberto discuss his own adjustment to a new culture, Anita was better able to understand the challenges of his experience and to learn about strategies that Roberto used to adjust to life in the United States. Discussion of each partner's experiences accommodating to a new culture increased the partners' empathy for one another and helped them understand the inevitability of certain stresses on their marriage. With new ways of thinking about the problems, the couple could take a collaborative stance toward solving some of their problems.

In addition to getting both partners to engage in empathic understanding of the problem, the interviewer also used communication training in the session. This couple displayed a demand-withdraw pattern when communicating, with Roberto often pushing for more emotional expression from Anita and Anita becoming quiet and nonresponsive. In addition to shaping speaker and listener skills, the therapist also videotaped the couple discussing a sensitive topic and allowed the couple to view their own interaction. Careful observation and discussion of the couple's communication patterns by the interviewer and couple slowed down the dialogue so that intended messages could be clearly understood.

SPECIAL POPULATIONS AND ISSUES IN COUPLE INTERVIEWS

Physical Disease and Couple Interviewing

Although couples might not connect health status with relationship problems, there is much evidence that relationship functioning affects physical health and vice versa (Burman & Margolin, 1992; Kiecolt-Glaser & Newton, 2001). Health conditions in one person can affect that person's mood and energy, which spills over into how that person functions as a companion and intimate partner. One person's ill health also can elicit both positive and negative reactions in the partner. Recent evidence also points to ways in which couple relationships can directly affect cardiovascular, endocrine, and immune functioning and affect illness processes indirectly through alterations in mood and health habits. Moreover, when one partner is ill, support in the couple relationship can influence treatment adherence and disease progression (Orth-Gomer et al., 2000). To learn about physical illnesses but not spend too much time obtaining this information, the couple interviewer can use a brief checklist as part of intake forms, on which each partner indicates current or recent health concerns. Chronic conditions, particularly those that restrict activities and predict deteriorating health and functioning, are important to include.

The couple interview is an opportunity for partners to learn more from one another about their separate and joint experiences in coping with illness. Partners may have a difficult time communicating about illness because of their concern that they will upset one another. The interviewer will want to learn about the onset of the condition and each person's subsequent adjustment. Was the illness present when the couple began their relationship? How has the illness affected roles in the relationship context? (For example, has one partner lost some of her or his independence while the other has assumed caregiving responsibilities? Has there been a shift in one partner's earning capacity, and if so, how does this affect the other partner and the couple? Is one person becoming increasingly housebound, and if so, what does this mean for the other partner?)

Consequences for the couple may include both positive and negative changes. For diseases with fluctuating symptoms, such as conditions involving chronic pain, it is important to assess how an intensification or deintensification of the symptoms affects the couple (Cano, Johansen, Leonard, & Hanawalt, 2005; Smith, 2003). How do the shifts in chronic pain affect the couple? What type of communication do they have around the shifting symptoms? The couple interview is a time in which partners can be encouraged to express their fears and frustrations and provide concrete and specific information to one another about what the partner could do that would be helpful in responding to illness. Baucom, Porter, Kirby, Gremore, and Keefe (2005) review psychosocial issues experienced by young women with breast cancer and highlight the importance of conjoint interviews with patients and their partners. Couple interviews can improve partners' abilities to communicate effectively, with specific attention to ways of providing emotional and practical support to one another.

Mental Health Problems and Couple Interviewing

Recent attention to connections between relationship adjustment and individual adult mental health problems comes from the fundamental assumption that individual disorders can be conceptualized and treated in the context of couple and family relations (Baucom et al., 1998). In general, stress transmission models suggest that an emotionally distressed person can place a burden on his or her partner and on the relationship. How the second partner responds to the burden can affect his or her own well-being and, similarly, can influence levels of support and conflict in the relationship. Alternatively, distress in the relationship can lead to individual adjustment problems in one or both partners.

Much evidence exists on the co-occurrence between marital conflict and certain disorders, such as depression and substance abuse (Whisman, 2001). Stress generation explanations of depression, for example, suggest that dysphoric people behave in ways that contribute to interpersonal conflict, which then maintains or exacerbates the depressive symptoms (Davila, 2001). Nondepressed partners also play a part in maintaining depressive responses and further perpetuating negative cycles of conflict and depression through their alternating patterns of supportive and attacking responses. Such variable reinforcement can generate continued patterns of depressive behaviors. Substance abuse and marital dissatisfaction similarly have bidirectional influences. Substance abusers often exhibit hostility or withdrawal in intimate relationships. However, these behaviors also are common in the non-substance-abusing partner. In the opposite direction, stress in the relationship commonly leads to sustained or exacerbated substance use (Fals-Stewart, Birchler, & O'Farrell, 2003). In some couples, substance abuse maintains equilibrium in the relationship such that cessation of the alcohol or drug use promotes new and different problems.

Beyond assessing for presence of mental health disorders in both partners, the couple interviewer can evaluate several possible connections between individual functioning and the relationship: Is one partner concerned about the other's emotional disorder? If so, what has the concerned partner done to be of assistance (or harm), and has that made the problem better or worse? In what ways does one partner's emotional disorder affect the other partner, the relationship, and other family roles such as parenting? Do changes, either positive or negative, in the mood or behavior of one partner affect the other partner or the relationship? Do changes in the relationship affect the severity of the emotional disturbance? How do patterns of the emotional disturbance fit with the couple's history? There is much variability across couples in the degree to which individual problems relate to couple problems and in the degree to which recovery from the individual or couple problems has a positive impact on the other. The challenge for the couple interviewer when exploring issues of individual disorders is to sustain the involvement of both partners and to engage both partners in generating hypotheses about links between individual and couple functioning.

Summary

The couple interview is a powerful tool for collecting wide-ranging information related to the mental and physical health of individuals and the functioning of couple and family units. Couple interviewers face some unique challenges: tracking information from multiple sources and on multiple levels, directing the flow of communication to maintain a productive level of involvement of each partner, and monitoring the nature of the interviewer-interviewee relationship with each partner. The interviewer has much to gain when both partners are part of the interview process. The couple interviewer learns far more on a content level through two different perspectives and through partners' reactions to one another's perspectives and also learns more on a process level by directly observing how the partners interact. Beyond advantages to the interviewer, the couple interview also provides benefits to the couple that are unattainable in individual interviews. A skillfully conducted couple interview is an opportunity for the couple to experience new ways of communicating and to acquire new understandings of themselves, one another, and the relationship.

Acknowledgments

This chapter developed out of a yearlong seminar and practicum class on couple and family therapy taught by Gayla Margolin. We thank the couples seen in this practicum for increasing our knowledge about couple interviewing. The case examples are disguised case descriptions of two of these couples. We also thank Benjamin Rottman for graphic design assistance.

References

American Psychiatric Association. (1994). *Diagnostic and statistical manual of mental disorders* (4th ed.). Washington, DC: Author.

Baucom, D. H., & Epstein, N. (1990). *Cognitive behavioral marital therapy*. New York: Brunner/Mazel.

Baucom, D. H., Epstein, E., & LaTaillade, J. J. (2002). Cognitive-behavioral couple therapy. In A. S. Gurman & N. S. Jacobsen (Eds.), *Clinical handbook of couple therapy* (3rd ed., pp. 26–58). New York: Guilford.

Baucom, D. H., Porter, L. S., Kirby, J. S., Gremore, T. M., & Keefe, F. J. (2005). Psychosocial issues confronting young women with breast cancer. *Breast Disease, 22*, 1–11.

Baucom, D. H., Shoham, V., Mueser, K. T., Daiuto, A. D., & Stickle, T. R. (1998). Empirically supported couple and family interventions for marital distress and adult mental health problems. *Journal of Consulting and Clinical Psychology, 66*, 53–88.

Burman, B., & Margolin, G. (1992). Analysis of the association between marital relationship and health problems: An interaction perspective. *Psychological Bulletin, 112*, 39–63.

Cano, A., Johansen, A. B., Leonard, M. T., & Hanawalt, J. D. (2005). What are the marital problems of chronic pain patients? *Current Pain and Headache Reports, 9*, 96–100.

Christensen, A., & Heavey, C. L. (1993). Gender differences in marital conflict: The demand-withdraw interaction pattern. In S. Oskamp & M. Costanzo (Eds.), *Gender issues in contemporary society* (pp. 113–141). Newbury Park, CA: Sage.

Christensen, A., & Pasch, L. (1993). The sequence of marital conflict: An analysis of seven phases of marital conflict in distressed and non-distressed couples. *Clinical Psychology Review, 13*, 3–14.

Crohn, J. (1998). Intercultural couples. In M. McGoldrick (Ed.), *Re-visioning family therapy: Race, culture, and gender in clinical practice* (pp. 295–308). New York: Guilford.

Cowan, P. A., & Cowan, C. P. (1990). Becoming a family: Research and intervention. In I. Sigel & G. Brody (Eds.), *Methods of family research* (Vol. 1, pp. 53–85). Hillsdale, NJ: Lawrence Erlbaum.

Davila, J. (2001). Paths to unhappiness: The overlapping courses of depression and romantic dysfunction. In S. R. H. Beach (Ed.), *Marital and family processes in depression: A scientific foundation for clinical practice* (pp. 71–87). Washington, DC: American Psychological Association.

Doherty, W. (2002). How therapists harm marriages and what we can do about it. *Journal of Couple and Relationship Therapy, 1*, 1–17.

Falicov, C. J. (2003). Culture in family therapy: New variations on a fundamental theme. In T. L. Sexton, G. R. Weeks, & M. S. Robbins (Eds.), *Handbook of family therapy: The science and practice of working with families and couples* (pp. 37–55). New York: Brunner-Routledge.

Fals-Stewart, W., Birchler, G. R., & O'Farrell, T. J. (2003). Alcohol and other substance abuse. In D. K. Snyder & M. A. Whisman (Eds.), *Treating difficult couples: Helping clients with coexisting mental and relationship disorders* (pp. 159–180). New York: Guilford.

Gurman, A. S. (2002). Brief integrative marital therapy: A depth-behavioral approach. In A. S. Gurman & N. S. Jacobson (Eds.), *Clinical handbook of couple therapy* (3rd ed., pp. 180–220). New York: Guilford.

Hardy, K. V., & Laszloffy, T. A. (2002). Couple therapy using a multicultural perspective. In A. S. Gurman & N. S. Jacobson (Eds.), *Clinical handbook of couple therapy* (3rd ed., pp. 569–593). New York: Guilford.

Holt, M. F. (2002). Solution-focused couple therapy. In A. S Gurman & N. S. Jacobson (Eds.), *Clinical handbook of couple therapy* (3rd ed., pp. 335–372). New York: Guilford.

Jacobson, N. S., & Christensen, A. (1996). *Integrative couple therapy: Promoting acceptance and change*. New York: W. W. Norton.

Jacobson, N. S., & Margolin, G. (1979). *Marital therapy: Strategies based on social learning and behavior exchange principles*. New York: Brunner/Mazel.

Kiecolt-Glaser, J. K., & Newton, T. L. (2001). Marriage and health: His and hers. *Psychological Bulletin, 127*, 472–503.

Margolin, G. (1981). A behavioral systems approach to the treatment of marital jealousy. *Clinical Psychology Review, 1,* 469–487.

Margolin, G. (1982). Ethical and legal considerations in marital and family therapy. *American Psychologist, 37,* 788–801.

Margolin, G. (1985). Building marital trust and treating sexual problems. In A. S. Gurman (Ed.), *Casebook of family therapy* (pp. 271–302). New York: Guilford.

Margolin, G. (1987). Marital therapy: A cognitive-behavioral-affective approach. In N. S. Jacobson (Ed.), *Psychotherapists in clinical practice* (pp. 232–285). New York: Guilford.

Markman, H. J., Stanley, S. M., & Blumberg, S. L. (1994). *Fighting for your marriage: Positive steps for preventing divorce and preserving a lasting love.* San Francisco: Jossey-Bass.

McGoldrick, M., Giordano, J., & Pearce, J. K. (1996). *Ethnicity and family therapy* (2nd ed.). New York: Guilford.

Oliver, P. H., & Margolin, G. (2003). Communication/problem-solving training. In W. O'Donohue, E. Fisher, & S. C. Hayes (Eds.), *Cognitive behavior therapy: Applying empirically supported techniques in your practice* (pp. 96–102). New York: Wiley.

Orth-Gomer, K., Wamala, S., Horsten, M., Schenck-Gustafsson, K., Schneiderman, N., & Mittleman, M. A. (2000). Marital stress worsens prognosis in women with coronary heart disease. *Journal of the American Medical Association, 284,* 3008–3014.

Smith, A. A. (2003). Intimacy and family relationships of women with chronic pain. *Pain Management Nursing, 4,* 134–142.

Snyder, D. K. (1979). Multidimensional assessment of marital satisfaction. *Journal of Marriage and the Family, 41,* 813–823.

Snyder, D. K., & Whisman, M. A. (2003). *Treating difficult couples: Helping clients with coexisting mental and relationship disorders.* New York: Guilford.

Spanier, G. B. (1976). Measuring dyadic adjustment. New scales for assessing the quality of marriage and similar dyads. *Journal of Marriage & the Family, 38,* 15–28.

Weiss, R. L., & Birchler, G. R. (1975). *Areas of change.* Unpublished manuscript, University of Oregon.

Whisman, M. A. (2001). The association between marital dissatisfaction and depression. In S. R. H. Beach (Ed.), *Marital and family processes in depression: A scientific foundation for clinical practice* (pp. 3–24). Washington, DC: American Psychological Association.

Whisman, M. A., & Uebelacker, L. A. (2003). Comorbidity of relationship distress and mental and physical health problems. In D. K. Snyder & M. A. Whisman (Eds.), *Treating difficult couples: Helping clients with coexisting mental and relationship disorders* (pp. 3–26). New York: Guilford.

Wile, D. B. (1981). *Couples therapy: A nontraditional approach.* New York: Wiley.

Wile, D. B. (1993). *After the fight: Using your disagreements to build a stronger relationship.* New York: Guilford.

Wile, D. B. (2002). Collaborative couple therapy. In A. S. Gurman & N. S. Jacobson (Eds.), *Clinical handbook of couple therapy* (3rd ed., pp. 281–307). New York: Guilford.

23

Intellectual Disability

Melissa L. González and Johnny L. Matson

This chapter focuses on the assessment of people with intellectual disability (ID) or mental retardation. Because there have been many recent advances in clinical practices and research in the area of ID, the chapter begins with a brief historical summary of the progress made in the services and treatments available for this population. The chapter then describes the core features of ID, dual diagnosis, differential diagnosis, and current assessment issues. Finally, the focus shifts to best practices in behavioral assessment for people with ID.

Throughout history there have been people deemed less or more capable than others. Over time, the view of the less capable person has changed with the needs and expectations of society (Scheerenberger, 1983). Over the years we have come to a better understanding of the etiological factors and illnesses associated with this population. The past 50 years have been marked by great progress in education and other services available for people with ID. Great strides have been made in treatment available for people with ID. Work by many researchers has provided a basis for behavior modification, which is an effective method for treatment of various deficits in social, adaptive, and communication skills for people with ID (Matson & Sevin, 1994). Another treatment approach, such as applied behavior analysis, which is more narrowly focused on operant behavior, has also become popular and well-researched method

of teaching new skills (Sturmey, 1998). Advances in treatment strategies for this population have been accompanied by many advances in clinical assessment (Matson & Sevin, 1994). The primary focus of this chapter is current assessment issues and practices for people with ID.

Issues such as the definition of ID, the role of the professional in the life of the person with ID, and the best way to study aspects of behavior in these people continue to be debated. Moreover, the term *mental retardation* for this population has been disputed. In 2001, the American Association on Mental Retardation decided to drop the term *mental retardation,* but no replacement term has been agreed upon. Many European countries and international journals, such as the *Journal of Intellectual Disability Research,* are currently using the term *intellectual disability* in place of *mental retardation* (Hodapp & Dykens, 2003). We will use the term *intellectual disability* in this chapter.

Description of the Problem

ID is characterized by three criteria: subaverage intellectual functioning, significant limitations in adaptive skills, and onset before age 18 (American Psychological Association [APA], 2000). Intellectual functioning is defined by the intelligence quotient (IQ). IQ is obtained with the use of one or more standardized, individually administered intelligence tests (e.g., Stanford-Binet, Wechsler Intelligence Scales; APA, 2000). To qualify as having subaverage intellectual functioning, a person must have an IQ of 70 or below, which is two standard deviations below the mean. Although IQ is a defining factor of intellectual functioning, there is widespread dissatisfaction with the reliance on measures of intelligence because of their covariation with socioeconomic factors (Flanagan, Genshaft, & Harrison, 1997). Blatt and Kaplan (1966) elucidated the problems and pitfalls of relying too heavily on IQ, thus highlighting the necessary consideration of adaptive behavior.

The second criterion, limitations in adaptive functioning, refers to the inability of a person to cope with life demands typical of someone of his age, background, and community surroundings (APA, 2000). This criterion requires significant skill impairment in two or more of the following areas: communication, self-care, home living, social and interpersonal skills, use of community resources, self-direction, functional academic skills, work, leisure, health, and safety (APA, 2000). Scales such as the Vineland Adaptive Behavior Scales (VABS) and the Vineland Adaptive Behavior Scales, 2nd edition (VABS-II) have been designed to assess levels of adaptive functioning (Sparrow, Balla, & Cicchetti, 1984; Sparrow, Cicchetti, & Balla, 2005). Although impairments in intellectual functioning are fairly stable past age 6, adaptive functioning skills are likely to improve with training. The VABS have been normalized on the general population, making it possible to derive overall and subscale adaptive behavior scores (Greenspan, 1999).

Onset before age 18 is the final criterion for a diagnosis of ID. Age of onset is associated with cause and level of intellectual impairment (APA, 2000). That is, more severe ID tends to be recognized earlier than milder levels of ID. In addition, ID associated with syndromes such as fragile X syndrome usually is diagnosed at birth, whereas ID with an unknown cause tends to be diagnosed later (Greenspan, 1999).

There are currently four degrees of ID that reflect the level of intellectual impairment: mild ID (IQ 50–70), moderate ID (IQ 35–55), severe ID (IQ 20–40), and profound ID (IQ below 25). The first level, mild ID, accounts for approximately 85% of all people with ID (APA, 2000; Greenspan, 1999). These people typically develop social and communication skills, have minimal sensorimotor impairment, and often are not easily distinguished from nondisabled people. People with mild ID usually achieve social and vocational skills but may need supervision, guidance, and assistance during stressful situations.

Moderate ID, the second level of impairment, accounts for approximately 10% of all people with ID. These people usually acquire communication skills during childhood. With moderate supervision, they profit from vocational training and attend to their own personal care. Generally, people with moderate ID adapt well to life in the community with supervision (APA, 2000).

The third level of impairment, severe ID, constitutes for 3%–4% of all people with ID. These people typically do not have communicative speech during early childhood but may learn to talk and gain some simple self-care skills and some preacademic skills during school age. People with severe ID usually need supervision in most settings (APA, 2000).

The final and most severe degree of intellectual impairment is profound ID. This level of impairment accounts for about 1% of all people with ID. ID in these people most often stems from an identified neurological condition. These people usually have impairment in sensorimotor functioning, communication, and self-care skills. However, these skill areas may improve with training (APA, 2000).

Etiology of ID

Predisposing factors to ID range widely and include biological, psychosocial, or a combination of factors. Heredity has been identified as one major predisposing cause. Errors of metabolism, as in Tay-Sachs disease, single-gene abnormalities, and chromosomal aberrations are associated with ID. Alterations in early embryonic development caused by chromosomal changes and prenatal toxins in syndromes such as Down syndrome and fetal alcohol syndrome, respectively, can also result in ID. Environmental factors before, during, and after birth affect the child's intellect. For example, fetal malnutrition, prematurity, hypoxia, viral infections, and trauma are common etiological factors. Moreover, nutritional deprivation, lack of social and linguistic stimulation, infections, traumas, and poisoning after birth may also account for impairments (APA, 2000; Leonard &

Wen, 2002). Although many etiological factors have been identified, approximately 30%–40% of cases of ID have no identified cause (APA, 2000).

Prevalence of ID

Prevalence rates of ID are approximately 1% (Larson et al., 2001; Leonard & Wen, 2002). However, rates have varied between studies because of differences in major definitions, classification systems, data collection, and sampling techniques (Roeleveld, Zielhuis, & Gabreels, 1997). Leonard and Wen's (2002) review of the literature asserts that prevalence of ID varies with gender, maternal race, socioeconomic status, and educational status. Richardson, Katz, and Koller (1986) found that males have a higher prevalence of ID than females. The gender difference has often been attributed to X-linked conditions, such as fragile X and unidentified X-linked conditions (Leonard & Wen, 2002). In addition, environmental factors influenced by social class have an impact on the prevalence of ID. Researchers have consistently found that the prevalence of mild ID has been strongly associated with low economic status and poor educational background of the mother (Decoufle & Boyle, 1995; Drews, Yeargin-Allsopp, Decoufle, & Murphy, 1995). Low birth weight is a common indicated risk factor that possibly results from maternal smoking and maternal urinary tract infections (Leonard & Wen, 2002).

DUAL DIAGNOSIS

People with ID are estimated to be three to four times more likely to have a psychiatric disorder than those in the general population (APA, 2000; Borthwick-Duffy, 1994). Dual diagnosis, the coexistence of ID and mental illness, is a new concept that has developed largely in the past 20 years. Historically, most professionals thought that people with ID were incapable of developing psychiatric disorders (Borthwick-Duffy, 1994). Abnormal behaviors were most often attributed to the person's ID rather than the presence of a mental illness (Schroeder, Mulick, & Schroeder, 1979). More recently, people with ID were viewed as susceptible to developing mental illness. However, this view held that a mental disorder of a person with ID is qualitatively different from the mental disorder of a person with no

intellectual impairment (Szymanski & Grossman, 1984). Current views of dual diagnosis are that people with ID are likely to have mental disorders similar to those in the general population. Moreover, it is generally recognized that these disabled people are more vulnerable to mental illness than their counterparts in the general population (Borthwick-Duffy, 1994).

Etiology of Dual Diagnosis

Organic, behavioral, developmental, and sociocultural models have been proposed as etiological theories for dual diagnosis (Matson & Sevin, 1994). Organic models of dual diagnosis focus on physiological, biochemical, and genetic factors that may predispose people to mental illness. For example, the high occurrence of people with Down syndrome developing Alzheimer's dementia suggests an underlying genetic cause of this disorder (Sovner & Pary, 1993).

Behavioral models emphasize the interactions between the individual and the environment. These models focus on the principles of classical conditioning, social learning theory, and operant psychology (Matson & Sevin, 1994). Pavlovian classical conditioning models have been discussed in the development of anxiety in the general population and in people with ID (Ollendick & Ollendick, 1982). Social learning theory suggests that fears and phobias may be the result of a person observing another's reaction to an event or object (Matson & Sevin, 1994). Operant models, on the other hand, are based on the principles of inadequate reinforcement of prosocial behaviors, inappropriate punishment, reinforcements of deviant response sets, and altered stimulus-response functions, such as decreased learning abilities (Matson & Sevin, 1994).

Developmental models suggest that development and sequences of cognitive development are fixed and universal. People with ID develop at slower rates than the general population. Thus, the behavior they exhibit indicates their delayed stage of development. For example, Sternlicht (1979) found that patterns of fears of institutionalized people with ID were typical of their developmental stage.

Another model, the sociocultural theory of dual diagnosis, highlights the social experience of the people and how they may affect psychopathology. For example, Reiss and Benson

(1984) pointed out the numerous negative experiences of people with ID, such as restrictive placements and social rejection, that may affect their mental health. Moreover, Rojahn and Tasse (1996) asserted that one possible explanation for the increased rates of psychopathology in people with intellectual deficits is their lack of coping skills. Not being able to cope with stressful situations may lead to a higher vulnerability to psychopathology and behavior problems. Subsequently, LaMalfa, Campigli, Bertelli, Mangiapane, and Cabras (1997) proposed a bio-psycho-social model of dual diagnosis. These authors suggested that each person has his or her own trajectory of development that is determined by both environmental and biological variables. Unlike more traditional models, this theory emphasizes individual differences in the development of psychopathology. Although there are several promising models for dual diagnosis, investigators should continue to study possible etiological factors of psychopathology (Matson & Sevin, 1994).

Prevalence of Dual Diagnosis

Similar to what was found in the prevalence studies of ID, prevalence rates of dual diagnosis in the disabled population are confounded with issues concerning definitions, diagnosis, sampling, and data collection (Borthwick-Duffy, 1994). Identifying dual diagnosis requires reliable and valid assessments of both ID and mental illness. Furthermore, sampling techniques complicate the task of estimating prevalence. Many investigations dealing with prevalence of dual diagnosis are based on samples of institutionalized people or service system databases. These samples tend to be skewed toward people with greater disability who are in need of services and therefore are unrepresentative of the intellectually disabled population. These issues result in inflated estimates of dual diagnosis (Borthwick-Duffy, 1994).

Borthwick-Duffy and Eyman (1990) asked, "Who are the dually diagnosed?" After reviewing demographics, adaptive and maladaptive behavior, and diagnostic information for clients receiving state services, the authors conclude that people who are referred for psychiatric evaluation and consequently dually diagnosed are likely to have higher cognitive capabilities. That is, people with the cognitive capacity to cause disruptions

in daily life and who lack social skills are more likely to be referred because of their challenging behaviors (e.g., aggression, unacceptable social behavior, and resistance). Furthermore, people residing in an institution are more likely to have access to qualified professionals to assess for psychopathology, thus increasing the likelihood of dual diagnosis. Finally, diagnostic overshadowing often plays a role in the prevalence rate of dual diagnosis across levels of ID. That is, people with profound intellectual deficits are less likely to be identified as mentally ill because of the severity of their intellectual deficits and the tendency to attribute abnormal behavior to low IQ rather than a psychiatric disorder.

Findings regarding the relationship of dual diagnosis with age, gender, residential setting, and intellectual level have been largely inconsistent. Many researchers assert that the prevalence of mental illness is highest among people with mild intellectual deficits. People with mild intellectual deficits are more likely to be aware of their limitations than people with more severe deficits. That said, Kerker, Owens, Zigler, and Horwitz (2004) hypothesize that people with mild intellectual deficits may be at a higher risk of reacting to stressful life events with an affective disorder. However, these authors also point out that the differences in prevalence estimates may result from the difficulties in diagnosing mental illness in people with severe intellectual deficits.

Certain mental illnesses are more prevalent in people with ID than in the general population. Kerker et al. (2004) report that adults with ID are more often diagnosed with anxiety and psychotic disorders than people without ID. Furthermore, Borthwick-Duffy and Eyman (1990) identified eight behaviors associated with dual diagnosis: depression, aggression, self-injury, resistive behaviors, temper tantrums, running or wandering away, adjustment changes in social relationships, and socially inappropriate behavior.

Differential Diagnosis

Although most professionals now recognize that people with ID are capable and likely to suffer from a mental illness, diagnosing the psychiatric disorder in these people is not easy. Deficits in communication and adaptive skills often make self-report of symptoms impossible, which is often the basis of diagnostic interviews and the criteria (e.g., flight of ideas, more talkative than usual, inflated self-esteem, feelings of worthlessness or inappropriate guilt) listed in the *Diagnostic and Statistical Manual of Mental Disorders, 4th Edition,* Text Revision (*DSM-IV-TR;* APA, 2000). Often these skill deficits are a roadblock in determining whether the abnormal behavior is caused by a psychiatric disorder, a brain injury associated with the intellectual deficits, or environmental factors (Reid, 1983).

Graham and Rutter (1968) found that although parents and teachers are able to describe their child's abnormal behavior, they are less proficient at interpreting the source of the behavior problem. In addition, Costello (1982) asserts that presence of mental illness in people with ID often results in an exaggerated interpretation of intellectual deficits. For example, Reiss, Levitan, and Szyszko (1982) conducted an experiment presenting a single case to many psychologists. The case description was identical except that it varied slightly in the description of the patient: Psychologists in Condition 1 were given background information indicating that the person was intellectually disabled, psychologists in Condition 2 were told the person was of normal intelligence, and psychologists in Condition 3 were told the person was an alcoholic. Findings from this study and replication studies indicated that the presence of ID decreased the importance or salience of abnormal behavior. This phenomenon, commonly called diagnostic overshadowing, is based on the tenet that intellectual deficit is such a salient feature of ID that any co-occurring abnormal behavior is attributed to such deficits. As time passes and more professionals have recognized that psychiatric disorders can and do manifest in the ID population, the current authors observe that the pendulum has shifted. There appears to be in many cases an overdiagnosis of psychiatric disorders in this population. One major reason for this phenomenon of "diagnostic undershadowing" may be the growing presence of psychotropic medications available and the influence of pharmaceutical companies on prescription and diagnostic practices.

Other factors contributing to problems with differential diagnoses in this population are that most professionals have had little exposure to people with ID and lack the expertise needed to treat this population (Matson & Sevin, 1994). Specific suggestions for conducting a thorough

behavioral assessment for people with ID, including behavioral observation techniques and the available assessment tools, will be outlined later in this chapter.

Clinical assessment of a person must capture his or her behavioral capabilities and limitations. Although diagnostic classification may be necessary for the person to receive the needed services, the main focus of the assessment should identify strengths and weaknesses and the behaviors that will be the targets of treatment (Beck, 1983). With this aim in mind, there are several techniques for assessment.

INTERVIEWING STRATEGIES

The clinical interview has been a popular method of clinical assessment for years because of its flexibility and convenience. Interviews typically are used to obtain a developmental history, assess current functioning, and identify treatment targets. One of its many advantages is that it lends itself to rapport building, which is an important factor in clinical assessment and treatment plan implementation (Merrell, 1994). Furthermore, it allows flexibility in obtaining information that might otherwise be overlooked. For example, the clinician can evaluate the client's characteristics such as social skills, verbal ability, and willingness to cooperate during an interview (Merrell, 1994). Moreover, interviewing is useful for obtaining the client's perspective on his or her own experiences (Wyngaarden, 1981). For people with limited capabilities, interviews are not as challenging as paper-and-pencil measures (Beck, 1983).

Often, interviews and structured questionnaires that were developed for the general population are used with people with borderline to mild ID. However, Finlay and Lyons (2001) caution clinicians that they should not assume these assessment tools are valid for this population; validity must be demonstrated. Although the clinical interview maintains an important aspect of clinical assessment with this population, it is relied on less heavily because of several problems relating to the cognitive and communication deficits associated with this population. These issues are discussed in more detail in the next section. Most often, the clinical interview is supplemented with third-party report, information gathered from standardized checklists, rating scales, and direct observations.

INTERVIEWING OBSTACLES AND SOLUTIONS

Despite the convenience of interviews, there are some drawbacks in applying them to this population. People with ID are a heterogeneous group; abilities vary widely from one person to the next. It is imperative that interviewers keep the client's cognitive, expressive, and receptive abilities in mind when conducting an interview and adjust the interview accordingly (Prosser & Bromley, 1998). People with more severe forms of ID are likely to have greater deficits in communication skills, thus making interviews with these people difficult, if not impossible. Beyond difficulties with communication during interviews, clinicians should also be aware that information gathered from interviews with people with ID must be used with caution (Sigelman, Budd, Spanhel, & Schroenrock, 1981b; Sigelman et al., 1980).

Sigelman, Schoenrock, et al. (1981) set out to examine the reliability and validity of information gathered through interviews with people with ID. Until this endeavor, little research had been done on response biases in the developmentally disabled population. Four separate studies were conducted to address the following questions: whether people with ID can respond to questions appropriately, how reliable their responses are over time, how valid the responses are (e.g., agreement with information from caregiver or records and freedom from systematic biases), and what types of questions optimize responsiveness and the reliability and validity of responses. Participants in the four studies included children and adults with varying levels of ID (i.e., ranging from mild to profound) and those living in an institutional and community settings.

Responsiveness

Overall, Sigelman, Schoenrock, et al. (1981) found that responsiveness is positively correlated to cognitive ability, with correlations ranging from $r = .41$ to .62; responsiveness to questions decreases as cognitive ability decreases. Only three people with profound ID passed the initial screening for the interview (i.e., emitting a word, sound, or gesture for three simple questions).

These three participants responded to very few questions during the interview, which led the researchers to conclude that verbal interviews were not feasible for people with profound ID. Though not surprising, this finding strongly supports supplementing interviews with information gathered from external sources (i.e., third-party report), especially for people with more severe cognitive deficits.

Responsiveness to interview questions was generally stable over time. That is, these researchers found that a person's level of responsiveness one week accurately predicted his or her level of responsiveness the next week. Furthermore, responsiveness clearly was a function of the type of questions asked. The relative difficulty of questions was stable across the participant samples. Understandably, questions that could be answered nonverbally (by pointing to a picture or indicating "yes" or "no") obtained the highest percentage of appropriate responses. Either-or questions elicited the next highest percentage of appropriate responses. Finally, multiple-choice questions and open-ended questions were found to have the lowest percentage of appropriate responses, and therefore were interpreted to be the most difficult for participants. Although these findings give us valuable information about the responsiveness of people with ID, the next section discusses the reliability of the responses provided.

Reliability

Overall, reliability of a response from one week to the next was considered to be marginally adequate. However, reliability did vary depending on the content and format of the question. For example, children living in an institution answered most consistently to questions about activities (93.5%) and least consistently to questions about rules and decision making (ranging from 56.1% to 77.3%; Sigelman, Schoenrock, et al., 1981). Open-ended questions yielded very little information. Many of the participants either did not respond or responded very little to these questions. Overall, yes-no questions had high reliability across the samples (89.8%) However, "yes" responses accounted for the majority. The authors caution that the reliability of these responses may be inflated by acquiescent responding, which is the tendency to answer a question affirmatively regardless of content (Cronbach, 1946).

Validity

Validity of responses was examined in two ways: comparing the participant's responses to alternative questions on the same topic and comparing the participant's responses to those of caregivers. Overall, acquiescence to questions was prevalent: 40%–50% of the participants contradicted themselves by answering "yes" to oppositely phrased questions such as "Are you happy?" and "Are you sad?" (Sigelman, Budd, et al., 1981b). These researchers also examined acquiescent responding by asking questions that should elicit a "no" response (e.g., "Are you Chinese?"). Participants often answered affirmatively to these questions as well. The tendency to acquiesce varied between questions, ranging from 28.0% to 73.1%. The lowest acquiescence rate was observed for questions demanding immediate and concrete information (e.g., "Right now, is it raining outside?"). These authors suggest that acquiescence is more likely to occur when the question is not understood or the answer is unknown or not accessible. Overall, results of this study indicate that acquiescent responding is more common among people with ID than in the general population. Furthermore, there were moderate negative correlations between acquiescent responding and IQ; participants with greater cognitive deficits were more likely to respond acquiescently (Sigelman, Budd, et al., 1981b). This finding was later replicated by Shaw and Budd (1982). Sigelman, Schoenrock, and colleagues (1981) argue against the use of yes-no questions with these people because of the prevalence of acquiescent responding in this population. These researchers suggest that yes-no questions should not be used without checks or should be avoided completely.

It was also noted that participants often answered questions in a manner that was inconsistent with their caregivers. Participant-caregiver agreement ranged from 59.3% to 64.5% across samples. Comparisons of the participant samples suggest that child-parent agreement is not sufficiently greater than resident-attendant agreement. Overall, participants and caregivers agree about two thirds of the time. Furthermore, it was noted that many of the participants could not accurately answer basic questions, such as giving their full name, spelling their name, stating their birthday, or describing the place where they lived.

These authors conclude that although the participants' responses often were reliable over time, they were not likely to be substantiated by information gathered from a caregiver (Sigelman, Schoenrock, et al., 1981).

Maximizing Responsiveness, Reliability, and Validity

Question Format. Sigelman, Schoenrock, and colleagues (1981) discuss the strengths and limitations of five types of questions: yes-no, either-or, picture choice, multiple choice, and open-ended questions. Although yes-no questions increase the likelihood of a response, they are also associated with acquiescent responding. Multiple-choice questions are also subject to response biases, where the participant has a tendency to choose the last option in the series. The major disadvantage of open-ended questions is that they often yield low responsiveness. However, open-ended questions requesting a single answer, rather than a list of responses, may be useful in obtaining meaningful information in interviews with this population (Sigelman, Schoenrock, et al., 1981). Sigelman, Budd, Winer, Schoenrock, and Martin (1982) examined the question format in terms of participant responsiveness, agreement with informants, and freedom from systematic response bias. These researchers concluded that verbal and pictorial multiple-choice questions proved to be a useful alternative to open-ended questions. Sigelman, Budd, Spanhel, and Schoenrock (1981a) evaluated either-or questions in comparison to yes-no questions in an adult institutionalized sample. They found that although either-or questions may be slightly more difficult to answer, the either-or format yields more valid responses than yes-no questions. Although either-or questions may introduce their own bias toward selecting the later of the two choices, it is not as pronounced as the acquiescence of yes-no questions. Wadsworth and Harper (1991) and Heal and Sigelman (1995) suggest that augmenting either-or choices with picture representations is beneficial for increasing responsiveness, reliability, and reducing response bias. Clinicians should be cautious with the use of closed questions (e.g., yes-no or multiple-choice questions) because there is a greater risk of acquiescence and other response biases with these formats. If clinicians choose to use these response formats, they should validate answers with either external reports or cross-questioning techniques (e.g., using reverse questioning such as "Are you happy?" and "Are you sad?").

Words and Terminology. Finlay and Lyons (2001) and Prosser and Bromley (1998) urge clinicians to use simple sentences during interviews. These authors suggest that clinicians avoid negatively worded questions and keep question structure and vocabulary simple. Because questions relating to time often pose problems for this population, Finlay and Lyons and Prosser and Bromley suggest that clinicians use significant events (e.g., birthdays, special holidays, trips) as time markers during interviews. Furthermore, Finlay and Lyons recommend asking about certain events separately rather than series of events. Questions should refer to specific, concrete events rather than elicit general statements. This practice increases the clarity of questions and is likely to elicit a more accurate response.

Setting the Stage. To further minimize these problematic issues, Prosser and Bromley (1998) make several recommendations for interviewing people with ID. First, these authors suggest that conducting the interview in a familiar setting, such as the home, day program, or work area, may help the person feel more relaxed and therefore more confident about providing information during the interview. Furthermore, these authors suggest opening the interview by explaining what the purpose of the interview is, what questions will be asked, who and what the information is for, why the information is important, how long the interview will take, and what the limits of confidentiality are. Prosser and Bromley suggest beginning the interview with easy questions that the person is able to answer accurately. Allowing the interviewee to meet success in answering questions in the beginning of the interview is likely to increase his or her confidence in answering questions and thereby increase the likelihood that he or she will answer more difficult questions later in the interview. This suggestion parallels research on behavioral momentum (Mace et al., 1988) showing that early success in compliance to demands probably will increase compliance when more difficult demands are presented. Finlay and Lyons (2001)

emphasize the importance of assuring the interviewee that the information will not be shared with his or her caregiver (if this is the case), especially when discussing sensitive topics. It is also recommended that clinicians remind the interviewee that it is acceptable to answer questions with "I don't know." Offering this option is important in guarding against acquiescence, which occurs typically when the question is not understood or the person does not know how to respond (Shaw & Budd, 1982). The clinician should also check the meaning of answers by eliciting examples. If the interviewee gives irrelevant examples in response to a question, this indicates that the interviewee does not understand what is being asked and that the clinician should adjust his or her questioning (Finlay & Lyons, 2001).

Depending on the cognitive and verbal capabilities of the person with ID, often a parent or a caregiver will be interviewed in place of the person in question (Beck, 1983), and as discussed previously, it is often desirable to interview caregivers to supplement or substantiate information gathered from the person with ID. The following section covers the use of third-party interviews as a supplement to interviews of people with ID.

Interviewing Caregivers

With the limitations of interviewing people with ID, it is not surprising that much of the research conducted with this population turns to caregiver informants. A variety of rating scales and structured interviews have been devised for use with third-party informants. One of the main advantages of conducting interviews with third-party informants is the ability to gather a substantial amount of information in a short period of time. Interviews typically cover a broad range of behaviors, including information about challenging behaviors or problems, adaptive behaviors such as social skills, communication skills, and daily living skills (Rush, Bowman, Eidman, Toole, & Mortenson, 2004).

Although the caregiver interview bears much weight in the behavioral assessments for this population, it too has been criticized. Hasan and Mooney (1979) indicate that misdiagnosis may be more common in this population because of the underreporting of symptoms by caregivers.

Because the validity of information gathered through interviews with the client or caregivers may be questionable at times, behavioral observations, standardized checklists, and rating scales are vital components of a thorough behavioral assessment with this population.

BEHAVIORAL ASSESSMENT

As with any behavioral assessment, a thorough clinical history should be taken and treatment targets should be formulated. To this end, it is important to take a variety of factors into account. People with ID have co-occurring deficits in adaptive and social skills and often exhibit behavioral excesses. Furthermore, people with ID are often prescribed various medications. Therefore, it is important that the clinician assess the various factors that interact and contribute to the client's behavioral presentation. Examining these factors systematically during assessment often provides the necessary information for an accurate diagnosis and effective treatment planning (Matson, Mayville, & Laud, 2003). In order to gather information about these factors, rating scales and behavioral observations typically are used. The remainder of this chapter focuses on behavioral assessment including the use of rating scales, behavioral observations, and functional assessment. In addition, several assessment tools developed specifically for use with people with ID are discussed.

Rating Scales

Rating scales are the most widely used assessment methods for this population. They are used to obtain information such as the frequency, duration, and severity of behaviors. Some advantages of rating scales are that they are efficient and easy to use and typically have better psychometric properties than interviews (Rush et al., 2004). Although rating scales often are used and typically are preferred over interviews for this population, there are some disadvantages, including the reliance on caregivers' subjective recollections of behavior. Another common criticism of indirect assessment is that informants may not be motivated, trained, or competent enough to respond accurately (Lalli, Browder, Mace, & Brown, 1993; Sturmey, 1996). Despite these problems, rating scales have been shown to

be useful in developing diagnoses and individualizing treatment plans (Matson, Mayville, & Laud, 2003). Several rating scales are available to assess varying aspects of behavior in people with ID, including psychopathology, adaptive behavior, social skills, challenging behavior, feeding problems, and medication side effects.

Psychopathology. Although currently there is a dearth of appropriate diagnostic criteria specifically for people with ID, several researchers have developed assessment scales to assess psychopathology in this population (Rush et al., 2004). Scales such as the Assessment of Dual Diagnosis (ADD; Matson, 1997), the Diagnostic Assessment for the Severely Handicapped–Revised (DASH-II; Matson, 1995a), the Psychiatric Assessment Schedule for Adults with Developmental Disabilities Checklist (PAS-ADD; Moss, Prosser, Costello, Simpson, & Patel, 1996), the Mini Psychiatric Assessment Schedule for Adults with Developmental Disabilities (Mini PAS-ADD; Prosser, Moss, Costello, Simpson, & Patel, 1997), and the Reiss Screen for Maladaptive Behavior (Reiss, 1988) are used to aid in the screening or diagnosis of psychopathology in the ID population.

The ADD was developed to screen for psychopathology in people with mild or moderate ID (Matson, 1997). This informant-based assessment tool comprises 79 items. An informant who has known the person for a minimum of 6 months rates the frequency, severity, and duration of the behavior for each item. There are 13 subscales, including Mania, Depression, Anxiety, Post-Traumatic Stress Disorder, Substance Abuse, Somatoform Disorders, Dementia, Conduct Disorder, Pervasive Developmental Disorders, Eating Disorders, and Sexual Disorders. Research by Matson and Bamburg (1998) examined the reliability and internal consistency of the scale on a sample of 101 adults with ID living in residential facilities and group homes. Tests of internal consistency, interrater reliability, and test-retest reliability yielded high to very high correlations.

Similar to the ADD, the DASH-II is an informant-based screening tool designed to evaluate psychopathology of people with severe and profound ID (Matson, 1995a). It is based on observable behaviors that can be reported by an informant who is familiar with the person with ID. This rating scale consists of 84 items across 13 subscales representing major psychiatric disorders: Anxiety, Depression, Mania, Pervasive Developmental Disorder or Autism, Schizophrenia, Stereotypies, Self-Injury, Elimination, Eating, Sleep, Sexual, Organic, and Impulse. The DASH-II has good psychometric properties. From a sample of 658 people with severe and profound ID, tests of interrater reliability, test-retest reliability, and internal consistency yielded high correlations (Matson, 1995a). Many of the subscales of the DASH-II have been validated in previous research with a severe and profound ID population (e.g., Pervasive Developmental Disorder or Autism, Depression, and Mania subscales; Matson & Smiroldo, 1997; Matson, Smiroldo, & Hastings, 1998; Matson, Rush, et al., 1999).

The PAS-ADD Checklist is a screening instrument that is completed by nonprofessionals who are familiar with the person with ID, with the aim to identify mental health problems and make informed referral decisions for adults with ID (Moss et al., 1996). The PAS-ADD Checklist comprises 29 items concerning psychiatric symptoms corresponding to *ICD-10* psychiatric diagnoses. Items are rated on four-point scale based on symptoms observed during the past 4 weeks. Item scores yield a total score and the following three subscale scores: affective or neurotic disorder, possible organic disorder, and psychotic disorder. It is recommended that those who score above one or more of the three thresholds be referred for further assessment by a mental health professional (Moss et al., 1998). Moss et al. (1998) examined the factor structure and internal consistency of the PAS-ADD Checklist in a sample of 201 people receiving health services in the United Kingdom. A factor analysis yielded an eight-factor solution that accounted for 65.3% of the variance, which included depression, restlessness, phobic anxiety, psychosis, hypomania, autistic spectrum, depression (suicidal thoughts and loss of self-esteem), and nonspecific. Internal consistency of the subscales was generally acceptable, with Cronbach's alpha coefficients ranging from moderate to high correlations. Interrater reliability was calculated for 66 people residing in a community or hospital setting; coefficients ranged from moderate to high correlations. In terms of validity, Moss et al. (1998) report that of the 59 participants in the validity study, the PAS-ADD yielded above-threshold scores for 26% of those with no current condition, 56% of those with a mild problem, and 92% of those with a severe disorder, as indicated by a consulting psychiatrist.

Unlike the PAS-ADD Checklist, the Mini PAS-ADD requires some training in its administration and provides more detailed information. The Mini PAS-ADD is an assessment schedule designed to identify psychiatric disorders based on *ICD-10* diagnoses in people with ID (Prosser et al., 1997). The Mini PAS-ADD comprises 86 items and yields the following subscales: Depression, Anxiety and Phobias, Mania, Obsessive-Compulsive Disorder, Psychosis, Unspecified Disorder (Including Dementia), and Pervasive Developmental Disorder. All items are rated on a four-point scale of severity. Prosser et al. (1998) examined the reliability and validity of the Mini PAS-ADD in a sample of 68 people with ID. Internal consistencies of the seven subscales ranged from high to very high correlations on Cronbach's alpha, whereas interrater reliability ranged from low to moderate correlations. Overall agreement for case identification was 75%. Furthermore, there was an overall correct classification rate of 91% when the Mini PAS-ADD was completed by psychiatrists. The overall correct classification rate was 81% when the Mini PAS-ADD was completed by members of the community support team.

The Reiss Screen for Maladaptive Behavior is an informant-based instrument for the screening of mental health problems in adolescents and adults with ID (Reiss, 1988). The scale consists of 38 items that informants rate on a scale from 0 to 2, with 0 = *no problem*, 1 = *the behavior is a problem*, and 2 = *the behavior is a major problem*. A factor analysis indicated eight subscales: Aggressive Behavior, Psychosis, Paranoia, Depression (Behavior Signs), Depression (Physical Signs), Dependent Personality Disorder, Avoidant Disorder, and Autism (Havercamp & Reiss, 1997). Sturmey, Burcham, and Perkins (1995) examined the psychometric properties of this scale in a sample of 60 people residing in a state school. They found good interrater reliability, modest to good test-retest reliability, and good internal consistency.

Adaptive Behavior. Assessing a person's adaptive behavior is an important part of an overall behavioral assessment. Adaptive behavior skills, including daily living, social, and communication skills, affect a person's ability to function effectively in society. An accurate assessment of a person's strengths and weaknesses in the domain of adaptive behavior allows the clinician to individualize the treatment plan. The VABS and the VABS-II (Sparrow et al., 1984; Sparrow et al., 2005) are a well-known informant-based measures of adaptive behavior. Four major domains of adaptive behavior are assessed: communication, daily living skills, socialization, and motor skills. These domains yield an adaptive composite score and age equivalent that can be used to evaluate a person's performance in comparison to his or her peer group, with a fifth domain targeting maladaptive behavior. Each item of the VABS is rated as 0 = *never*, 1 = *sometimes*, or 2 = *always*. The VABS have good psychometric properties with high to very high test-retest reliability coefficients and interrater reliability coefficients ranging from moderate to high.

Social Skills. Similar to adaptive behavior, social skills enable a person to interact appropriately with others and adjust to the world around him or her. Wing and Gould (1979) found that the severity of ID is related to deficits in social skills, such that those with more severe forms of ID have the greatest social skill deficits. There is also a negative correlation between social skills and the presence of maladaptive behavior (Duncan, Matson, Bamburg, Cherry, & Buckley, 1999; Matson, Smiroldo, & Bamburg, 1998). It is important to assess the client's social skills and deficits because they may aid in tailoring the intervention to the client's needs (Bielecki & Swender, 2004). The Matson Evaluation of Social Skills for Individuals with Severe Retardation (MESSIER; Matson, 1995b) and the Social Performance Survey Schedule (SPSS; Matson, Helsel, Bellack, & Senatore, 1983) are two rating scales available for assessing the social skills of people with ID.

The SPSS is a 57-item informant-based questionnaire developed to assess the strengths and deficits of social skills in people with mild or moderate ID (Matson et al., 1983). There are four subscales: appropriate social skills, communication skills, inappropriate assertion, and sociopathic behavior. The MESSIER, on the other hand, is an 85-item informant-based questionnaire designed to assess the social skills of severely and profoundly retarded people (Matson, 1995b). The items are grouped into six clinically derived subscales: Positive Verbal, Positive Nonverbal, General Positive, Negative Verbal, Negative Nonverbal, and General Negative. Informants are asked to rate each item

on frequency on a four-point Likert scale: *never* (0), *rarely* (1), *sometimes* (2), and *often* (3). The MESSIER and the SPSS have been found to have high internal consistency, high test-retest reliability, and a high interrater reliability (Matson, 1995; Matson, Carlisle, Bamburg, 1998; Matson et al., 1983; Matson, LeBlanc, Weinheimer, & Cherry, 1999).

Challenging Behavior. People with severe and profound ID living in institutions exhibit high prevalence rates of challenging behavior (Borthwick-Duffy, 1994). Challenging behaviors such as aggression and self-injury can be serious and common barriers to life in the community (Rojahn, Aman, Matson, & Mayville, 2003). Several rating scales have been developed to identify challenging behaviors in the ID population. These measures include the Aberrant Behavior Checklist (ABC; Aman & Singh, 1986) and the Behavior Problem Inventory (BPI; Rojahn, Matson, Lott, Esbensen, & Smalls, 2001). These empirically developed scales for challenging behavior often are used for assessing the effects of interventions (Rojahn et al., 2003).

The ABC is an informant-based rating scale developed to assess a wide range of behavior problems including self-injury, stereotypy, and aggressive or destructive behavior. There are five subscales comprising 58 items: Irritability, Agitation, Crying; Lethargy, Social Withdrawal; Stereotypic Behavior; Hyperactivity, Non-Compliance; and Inappropriate Speech. Various studies have shown the ABC to be a reliable and valid behavior rating scale (Aman, Singh, Stewart, & Field, 1985; Aman, Singh, & Turbott, 1987; Paclawskyj, Matson, Bamburg, & Baglio, 1997).

The BPI, on the other hand, addresses three challenging behaviors—self-injury, stereotypy, and aggressive or destructive behavior—in more detail. It has three subscales that were validated by factor analysis: Self-Injurious Behavior, Stereotyped Behavior, and Aggressive/Destructive Behavior. Each item is scored for frequency and severity. Several studies have provided evidence for the reliability and validity of this instrument (Rojahn et al., 2001, 2003).

Feeding Problems. Severe feeding problems are another challenging group of behaviors often displayed by people with developmental disabilities. These problems can cause serious health problems and greatly limit the person's ability for success in the community. Because the presence of feeding problems may pose serious health risks and interfere with the person's ability to transition to community settings, periodic screenings for feeding problems are warranted for this population. The Screening Tool for Feeding Problems is a 23-item informant-based measure designed to screen for a wide array of feeding problems (Matson & Kuhn, 2001). This measure consists of five subscales: Aspiration Risk, Selectivity, Feeding Skills, Refusal Related Behavior Problems, and Nutrition Related Behavior Problems. This measure has good psychometric properties. Tests of cross-rater reliability and test-retest reliability have yielded moderate correlation coefficients (Matson & Kuhn, 2001). In addition, the Rumination and Pica subscales have demonstrated criterion validity through correlation with *DSM-IV* diagnoses for rumination and pica (Kuhn & Matson, 2002).

Medication Side Effects. People with ID often have comorbid psychopathology and therefore are prescribed various psychotropic medications. It is not uncommon for these people to take these medications for extended periods of time. This approach can be problematic because side effects of medications often are associated with long-term and combined use. Given these facts, a screen for medication side effects is an essential part of a thorough assessment (Matson et al., 2003). The Matson Evaluation of Drug Side Effects (MEDS; Matson, Mayville, et al., 1998) is a broad assessment of medication side effects. The MEDS includes nine domains of medication side effects: cardiovascular and hematologic; gastrointestinal; endocrine and genitourinary; eye, ear, nose, and throat; skin, allergies, and temperature; central nervous system (CNS)-general; CNS-dystonia; CNS-parkinsonism and dyskinesia; and CNS-akathisia. Studies examining the psychometric properties support the reliability and validity of this rating scale (Matson, Mayville, Bamburg, & Eckholdt, 2001; Matson, Mayville, et al., 1998).

Because people with ID often are given antipsychotic medications, a regular screening for tardive dyskinesia is also necessary. The Dyskinesia Identification System: Condensed User Scale (Sprague & Kalachnik, 1991), a measure of extrapyramidal side effects (i.e., associated with abnormalities in movement) typically is used to assess for tardive dyskinesia in this population.

Research supports the reliability and validity of the instrument (Sprague & Kalachnik, 1991).

Seizures are also known to co-occur with ID at a high rate (Wilfong, 2002). Antiepileptic medications (i.e., anticonvulsants) are the most common and most effective method of treatment (Mycek, Harvey, & Champe, 1997). However, many antiepileptic medications typically used in this population (e.g., phenytoin, carbamazepine, valproic acid) are associated with significant side effects, including volatile behavior, impaired cognition, reduced motor skills, and sedation (Cole, 2002; Ruteccki & Gidal, 2002). The Scale for the Evaluation and Identification of Seizures, Epilepsy, and Anticonvulsant Side-Effects, Form B (Matson, 2000) was developed to monitor side effects that typically are associated with antiepileptic medications. This scale was developed for detecting changes in symptoms over time. It includes 14 domains of side effects: hematologic disturbance, electrolyte disturbance, hepatic disturbance, weight disturbance, respiratory disturbance, gastric disturbance, dermatological disturbance, hair change, gait disturbance, tremor, sedation, affect disturbance, cognitive disturbance, and drug-related dizziness. Preliminary studies examining reliability indicate moderately high interrater and adequate test-retest reliability (Matson, Laud, González, Malone, & Swender, 2005).

Behavioral Observations

Behavioral observations are an essential part of a behavioral assessment. Direct observation is widely recognized as an empirically supported assessment method (Merrell, 1994). Unlike clinical interview or rating scales, observational methods involve the clinician directly observing the targeted behavior. Therefore, these methods have an advantage over other methods in that they do not rely on a verbal report of symptoms by the client or the caregiver's recollection of behavior. Therefore, the information gathered through observations is more objective and reliable (Merrell, 1994; Rush et al., 2004). Furthermore, data gathered during behavioral observations are useful in developing interventions for the behavior. Some limitations to the use of behavioral observations are that they are often time and labor intensive. Also, the presence of the observer may alter the client's behavior, and so the observation may prove to be an inaccurate assessment. Finally, behavioral observations are not an optimal assessment method for low-frequency behaviors or highly variable behaviors; the behavior must occur during the observation for it to yield useful information (Beck, 1983).

The first step in using this technology is to operationally define the behaviors of interest. This is done so that the observer can record the occurrence of behavior systematically (Merrell, 1994). Several observational methods are available; the observational method chosen depends largely on the aspect of the behavior the clinician wants to assess (frequency, severity or intensity, duration), the setting in which it occurs, and the resources available to conduct the observation (e.g., time available to observe, number of observations, number of observers; Barrett, Ackles, & Hersen, 1986; Kazdin, 2001). Several techniques for direct observation are described briefly in the following paragraphs; the reader is referred to Mayville and Mayville (2004) for a more detailed description of these observation techniques.

Event recording involves a frequency count of behaviors as they occur (Cooper, Heron, & Heward, 1987). This approach is appropriate for behaviors that have a discrete beginning and end (e.g., head banging) and occur at low to moderate rates. Furthermore, event recording is recommended when there are consistent opportunities and lengths of time to respond. This recording technique may not be an optimal a choice if the duration of the behavior is inconsistent (Barrett et al., 1986; Mayville & Mayville, 2004).

Duration recording involves recording the duration of each episode of behavior from beginning to end. This method typically is used to observe behavior that is continuous and occurs at a high frequency or for extended periods of time (e.g., time of engagement with activities, skin picking; Mayville & Mayville, 2004).

Interval recording involves noting the occurrence of behavior within a prespecified interval of time. There are three types of interval recordings: partial interval, whole interval, and momentary time sampling. In partial interval recording the observer notes the occurrence of the behavior if it occurs at any point during the specified interval. In whole interval recording, on the other hand, the observer notes the occurrence of the behavior only if it occurs throughout the interval. Partial interval recording is most often used when the goal is to decrease the target behavior, whereas whole interval recording is used when the goal is to increase the target behavior (Mayville & Mayville, 2004). With momentary time sampling, the behavior must occur at the moment an interval ends for the observer to note the occurrence of the behavior. Momentary time sampling is most often used for behaviors that persist for long periods of time or occur at a high rate (e.g., stereotypic behavior at a high frequency; Bates & Hanson, 1983).

Latency recording involves recording the length of time between the presentation of a stimulus and the occurrence of the target behavior. This type of recording often is used to measure compliance with request (Mayville & Mayville, 2004).

Functional Assessment

Much of the research in the past 20 years has demonstrated that the function of behavior is the key to devising an effective behavioral intervention (Carr, 1977; Cooper & Harding, 1993). Carr asserts that aberrant behavior (e.g., self-injury) is complex and under the control of a number of motivational variables. Furthermore, he suggests that identifying the variables maintaining the behavior will lead to an effective treatment strategy. Carr, Robinson, and Palumbo (1990) assert that treatments based on behavior function can produce long-term effects, whereas protocol-based and crisis management strategies are only a temporary solution to the behavior problem. Therefore, a functional assessment of the aberrant behavior is considered best practice for developing effective treatments.

Three main approaches are suggested for functional assessment: indirect assessments, descriptive assessments, and experimental functional analysis. Although some experts clearly favor one approach over another (e.g., functional analysis; Baer, Wolf, & Risley, 1968; Iwata et al., 1994), all three of these approaches have the same goal: generating hypotheses of the functional variables maintaining a behavior. It is important to note that the extent to which an assessment approach approximates a functional relationship varies, along with other dimensions such as the time and resources needed to complete the assessment. A brief overview of these approaches to functional assessment will discuss the advantages and disadvantages of each approach.

Indirect Assessment. Indirect assessment involves asking a third party, usually a caregiver, to answer questions about the target behavior (e.g., likelihood of occurrence in certain situations, frequency of the behavior, severity). These assessments are removed from the time and place the actual target behavior occurs (Gresham, Watson, & Skinner, 2001). Indirect assessment techniques vary from informal interviews with caregivers to standardized assessment measures with known psychometric properties. Some of the advantages of indirect assessment include assessment efficiency, low cost and labor intensity, and usefulness for large groups. However, the clinician does not see the behavior first hand but relies on reports from caregivers (Paclawskyj, Matson, Rush, Smalls, & Vollmer, 2001). Many experts criticize this method because it relies on retrospective accounts and verbal representations of the target behavior in place of more formal evaluations (e.g., observation; Mace, Lalli, & Lalli, 1991).

A variety of indirect measures are available for use in functional assessment (e.g., the Motivation Assessment Scale [MAS], Durand & Crimmins, 1988; the Functional Analysis Interview Form, O'Neill, Horner, Albin, Storey, & Sprague, 1990; and the Functional Analysis Checklist, Van Houten & Rolider, 1991). Although Sturmey (1994) points out that many of these measures lack psychometric robustness, a more recent indirect assessment instrument, the Questions About Behavioral Function (QABF), is reported to have good psychometric properties (Matson & Vollmer, 1995). This assessment is given in an interview format with a respondent who is familiar with the person being assessed and the problem behavior targeted. Each question is scored on a Likert-type scale anchored with frequency descriptors of *Never, Rarely, Some,* and *Often.* The assessment yields a summary of endorsements for five categories reflecting hypotheses of behavioral function: attention, escape, physical, tangible, and nonsocial. The QABF has been reported to be a reliable and effective instrument to evaluate behavior function. Paclawskyj, Matson, Rush, Smalls, and Vollmer (2000) report good test-retest and interrater reliability, with item and total coefficients ranging from high to very high. Furthermore, Paclawskyj et al. report high internal consistency with coefficients for the individual subscales.

The convergent validity of the QABF with functional analysis and another commonly used indirect assessment, the MAS (Durand &

Crimmons, 1988) was examined by Paclawskyj et al. (2000). The QABF was found to have moderate agreement (69.2%) with the analog functional analysis, whereas there was lower agreement (53.8%) between the MAS and the analog functional analysis. Furthermore, the QABF has been demonstrated to be an effective assessment measure to aid in treatment development. Matson, Bamburg, Cherry, and Paclawskyj (1999) evaluated the validity and clinical utility of the QABF. Using a sample of 398 people with ID and aberrant behavior, these authors found that a clear behavioral function could be identified for the majority of the sample (84%). Moreover, people with treatments based on hypotheses generated from the QABF showed significantly greater reduction in the frequency of the targeted behavior than those whose interventions were based on standard treatment protocols.

Descriptive Assessment. Descriptive assessments involve the clinician observing the target behavior in its natural setting. This approach allows the clinician to note events surrounding the target behavior that may be a part of the maintaining contingencies. One major advantage to descriptive assessments is that they have high ecological validity; behavior is observed in the natural environment. However, limitations include the fact that the data are correlational in nature and therefore may be difficult to interpret. For example, if a person's screaming occurs in the presence of a tangible item, screaming may be associated with the presence of the tangible item but functionally related to some other environmental variable, such as the staff member who walks near the person's room when he or she has the tangible item. It is necessary to determine what is functionally related to the target behavior. Furthermore, the assessment may be quite time consuming and require extensive training (Sturmey, 1996). Various methods of descriptive assessment have been proposed; these range from use of scatter plots (Touchette, MacDonald, & Langer, 1985), to antecedent-behavior-consequence recording (Bijou, Peterson, & Ault, 1968) to more structured assessments, such as the Structured Descriptive Assessment (SDA), suggested by Anderson and Long (2002).

Scatter plot analysis typically consists of recording patterns of behavior across time. The relative rate of the behavior across time can be used to identify problems with stimulus control.

Scatter plots may help identify patterns of responding that suggest environmental variables that set the stage for the occurrence of the target behavior (Touchette et al., 1985). For example, a scatter plot may be used to assess the occurrence of the target behavior across staff members, times of day, and settings (Mayville & Mayville, 2004).

Antecedent-behavior-consequence recording involves recording events that occur immediately before, during, and after the target behavior (Bijou et al., 1968). This method of gathering data may identify relevant antecedents and consequences that are associated with the occurrence of the target behavior (Mayville & Mayville, 2004). Although these events identified through antecedent-behavior-consequence recording are only correlated with the occurrence of the target behavior, this information often lends itself to generating effective behavioral interventions.

With the SDA, participants are exposed repeatedly to four or five conditions similar to those in the experimental functional analysis procedures of Iwata, Dorsey, Slifer, Bauman, and Richman (1982/1994) in the natural environment. The advantage of the SDA is that it is as easy to implement as most descriptive assessments but as rigorous as the analog in terms of data and interpretation. These procedures were designed to increase the likelihood that specific environmental events would occur often enough to allow an adequate sampling of the co-occurrence with challenging behavior (Freeman, Anderson, & Scotti, 2000).

Experimental Functional Analysis. In contrast to the previously mentioned methods, experimental functional analysis requires the experimental manipulation of the target behavior in a controlled setting. Therefore, this approach calls for the direct observation and measurement of the problem behavior under test and control conditions in which some environmental variable is manipulated (Hanley, Iwata, & McCord, 2003). Iwata et al. (1982/1994) propose a model for assessing aberrant behavior in the presence of controlled contingencies involving positive, negative, and automatic reinforcement. This method involves the presence of establishing operations, discriminating stimuli, and consequences contingent on the target behavior. Another model, proposed by Carr and Durand (1985), systematically evaluates the target behavior under three conditions under which antecedent variables are

manipulated. The main advantage of these models is that they allow the clinician to examine the occurrence or nonoccurrence of the target behavior under controlled environmental contingencies and thereby demonstrate control over the target behavior. Moreover, the efficacy of treatments based on experimental functional analysis has been demonstrated (Kahng, Abt, & Schonbachler, 2001).

Many studies have demonstrated the effectiveness of this approach for generating useful hypotheses of behavioral function that lead to effective interventions. However, there are some criticisms to this approach to functional assessment. First, Sturmey (1994) asserts that the use of this approach may be impractical in some settings where the extensive expertise (i.e., specific clinical skills and knowledge) and resources (i.e., time for numerous trials and space for controlled setting) are not available. Second, it is necessary for the behavior to occur during the analog conditions to examine behavior function. Therefore, it may be difficult to examine the target behavior if it occurs at a low frequency. Similarly, it may be unethical to elicit the target behavior if it is serious or potentially life threatening (Sturmey, 1995). Third, Mace et al. (1991) suggest the possibility that shaping may occur. For instance, providing attention contingent on the occurrence of head banging repetitively over time may actually strengthen the reinforcing effects of the head banging and may maintain the behavior in the future. Finally, the clinician must infer that the variables maintaining the target behavior in the analog conditions are parallel to those in the natural environment (Mace et al., 1991).

Because identifying the function of an aberrant behavior is key to identifying an effective treatment, it is important to accurately assess behavioral function. The choice of approach to use in the functional assessment depends largely on the resources available and the frequency and severity of the target behavior.

RECOMMENDED PRACTICES

With the recent advances in assessment tools and increase in research on this population, it is recommended that a multimethod approach be taken to the behavioral assessment of people with ID (Rush et al., 2004). Assessments should include interviews with caregivers and the clients, when possible, and the use of behavioral observations and rating scales (Aman, 1991; Reiss, 1993). When appropriate, a functional assessment should also be conducted. Furthermore, the use of multiple informants may be helpful in gaining a comprehensive clinical assessment. These assessment tools used in conjunction with interviews will better equip the clinician to make informed clinical decisions for the treatment and diagnosis of the person with ID.

SELECTION OF TREATMENT TARGETS

With use of the previously mentioned assessment tools, the goals of treatment should be identified. When one is selecting treatment goals, the following criteria should be considered: the level of impairment or extent to which the client's functioning is impeded by a particular problem or behavior; behaviors that are dangerous to the client or others; behaviors that are of concern to the client or to significant others; behaviors that decrease risk for injury, illness, or physical or psychological dysfunctions; and behaviors that can lead to other appropriate behaviors (e.g., prosocial speech, taking medication as prescribed; Kazdin, 2001). After identifying the target of treatment, the clinician must also consider the situation, setting, and context variables that are present and may influence the effectiveness of the treatment (Kazdin, 2001).

SUMMARY

Much progress has been made in assessment for the ID population. Although traditional clinical interviews may be problematic with this population, a variety of other assessment tools have been developed and proven useful. Clinicians must take into account a variety of factors, including symptoms of psychopathology, adaptive skills and behavioral deficits, and the potential for medication side effects, when assessing a person with ID. Rating scales with good psychometric properties, behavioral observations, and functional assessments, when indicated, should be used in conjunction with information gathered in interviews. These tools should be used together during assessment to develop an accurate diagnosis and an effective treatment plan.

REFERENCES

Aman, M. G. (1991). Review and evaluation of instruments for assessing emotional and behavioural disorders. *Australia and New Zealand Journal of Developmental Disabilities, 17,* 127–145.

Aman, M. G., & Singh, N. N. (1986). *Aberrant Behavior Checklist: Manual.* East Aurora, NY: Slosson Educational Publications.

Aman, M. G., Singh, N. N., Stewart, A. W., & Field, C. J. (1985). Psychometric characteristics of the Aberrant Behavior Checklist. *American Journal on Mental Deficiency, 89,* 492–502.

Aman, M. G., Singh, N. N., & Turbott, S. H. (1987). Reliability of the Aberrant Behavior Checklist and the effects of variations in instructions. *American Journal on Mental Deficiency, 92,* 237–240.

American Psychological Association. (2000). *Diagnostic and Statistical Manual of Mental Disorders* (4th ed., Text rev.). Washington, DC: Author.

Anderson, C. M., & Long, E. S. (2002). Use of a structured descriptive assessment methodology to identify variables affecting problem behavior. *Journal of Applied Behavior Analysis, 35,* 137–154.

Baer, D. M., Wolf, M. M., & Risley, T. R. (1968). Some current dimensions of applied behavior analysis. *Journal of Applied Behavior Analysis, 1,* 91–97.

Barrett, R. P., Ackles, P. K., & Hersen, M. (1986). Strategies for evaluating treatment effectiveness. In R. P. Barrett (Eds.), *Severe behavior disorders in the mentally retarded* (pp. 323–357). New York: Plenum.

Bates, P. E., & Hanson, H. (1983). Behavioral assessment. In J. L. Matson & S. E. Breuning (Eds.), *Assessing the mentally retarded* (pp. 27–63). New York: Grune & Stratton.

Beck, S. (1983). Overview of methods. In J. L. Matson & S. E. Breuning (Eds.), *Assessing the mentally retarded* (pp. 3–36). New York: Grune & Stratton.

Bielecki, J., & Swender, S. L. (2004). The assessment of social functioning in individuals with mental retardation. *Behavior Modification, 28,* 694–708.

Bijou, S. W., Peterson, R. F., & Ault, M. H. (1968). A method to integrate descriptive and experimental field studies at the level of data and empirical concepts. *Journal of Applied Behavior Analysis, 1,* 175–191.

Blatt, B., & Kaplan, R. (1966). *Christmas in purgatory: A photographic essay on mental retardation.* Boston: Allyn & Bacon.

Borthwick-Duffy, S. A. (1994). Epidemiology and prevalence of psychopathology in people with mental retardation. *Journal of Consulting and Clinical Psychology, 62*(1), 17–27.

Borthwick-Duffy, S. A., & Eyman, R. K. (1990). Who are the dually diagnosed? *American Journal on Mental Retardation, 94*(6), 586–595.

Carr, E. G. (1977). The motivation of self-injurious behavior: A review of some hypotheses. *Psychological Bulletin, 84,* 800–816.

Carr, E. G., & Durand, V. M. (1985). Reducing behavioral problems through functional communication training. *Journal of Applied Behavior Analysis, 18,* 111–126.

Carr, E. G., Robinson, S., & Palumbo, L. W. (1990). The wrong issue: Aversive versus nonaversive treatment. The right issue: Functional versus nonfunctional treatment. In A. Repp & N. N. Singh (Eds.), *Perspectives on the use of nonaversive and aversive interventions for persons with developmental disabilities* (pp. 361–379). Sycamore, IL: Sycamore.

Cole, A. J. (2002). Evaluation and treatment of epilepsy in multiply handicapped individuals. *Epilepsy and Behavior, 3,* S2–S6.

Cooper, L. J., & Harding, J. (1993). Extending functional analysis procedures to outpatient and classroom settings for children with mild disabilities. In J. Reichle & D. P. Wacker (Eds.), *Communicative alternatives to challenging behavior* (pp. 41–62). Baltimore, MD: Brookes.

Cooper, J. O., Heron, T. E., & Heward, W. L. (1987). *Applied behavior analysis.* Columbus, OH.: Merrill.

Costello, A. (1982). Assessment and diagnosis of psychopathology. In J. L. Matson & R. Barrett (Eds.), *Psychopathology in the mentally retarded* (pp. 37–52). New York: Grune & Stratton.

Cronbach, L. J. (1946). Response sets and test validity. *Educational and Psychological Measurement, 6,* 475–494.

Decoufle, P., & Boyle, C. A. (1995). The relationship between maternal education and mental retardation in 10-year old children. *Annals of Epidemiology, 5,* 347–353.

Drews, C. D., Yeargin-Allsopp, M., Decoufle, P., & Murphy, C. C. (1995). Variation in the influence of selected sociodemographic risk factors for mental retardation. *American Journal of Public Health, 85,* 329–334.

Duncan, D., Matson, J. L., Bamburg, J. W., Cherry, K. E., & Buckley, T. (1999). The relationship of self-injurious behavior and aggression to social skills in persons with severe and profound learning disabilities. *Research in Developmental Disabilities, 20,* 441–448.

Durand, V. M., & Crimmins, D. B. (1988). Identifying the variables maintaining self-injurious behavior. *Journal of Autism and Developmental Disorders, 18,* 99–117.

Finlay, W. M. L., & Lyons, E. (2001). Methodological issues in interviewing and using self-report questionnaires with people with mental retardation. *Psychological Assessment, 13*(3), 319–335.

Flanagan, D. P., Genshaft, J. L., & Harrison, P. L. (1997). *Contemporary intellectual assessment: Theories, tests and issues.* New York: Guilford.

Freeman, K. A., Anderson, C. M., & Scotti J. R. (2000). A structured descriptive methodology: Increasing agreement between descriptive and experimental analyses. *Education & Training in Mental Retardation & Developmental Disabilities, 35,* 55–66.

Graham, P., & Rutter, M. (1968). The reliability and validity of the psychiatric assessment of the child II: Interview with the parent. *British Journal of Psychiatry, 114,* 581–592.

Greenspan, S. (1999). What is meant by mental retardation? *International Review of Psychiatry, 11,* 6–18.

Gresham, F. M., Watson, T. S., & Skinner, C. H. (2001). Functional behavioral assessment: Principles, procedures and future directions. *School Psychology Review, 30*(2), 156–172.

Hanley, G. P., Iwata, B. A., & McCord, B. E. (2003). Functional analysis of problem behavior: A review. *Journal of Applied Behavior Analysis, 36,* 147–185.

Hasan, M. K., & Mooney, R. P. (1979). Three cases of manic-depressive illness in mentally retarded adults. *American Journal of Psychiatry, 136,* 1069–1071.

Havercamp, S. M., & Reiss, S. (1997). Psychopathology in children and adolescents with developmental disorders. *Research in Developmental Disabilities, 18,* 369–382.

Heal, L. W., & Sigelman, C. K. (1995). Response biases in interviews of individuals with limited mental ability. *Journal of Intellectual Disability Research, 39,* 331–340.

Hodapp, R. M., & Dykens, E. M. (2003). Mental retardation (intellectual disability). In E. J. Mash & R. A. Barkley (Eds.), *Child psychopathology* (2nd ed., pp. 486–519). New York: Guilford.

Iwata, B. A., Dorsey, M. F., Slifer, K. J., Bauman, K. E., & Richman, G. S. (1982/1994). Towards a functional analysis of self-injury. *Journal of Applied Behavior Analysis, 27,* 197–209.

Iwata, B. A., Pace, G. M, Dorsey, M. F., Zarcone, J. R., Vollmer, T. R., Smith, R. G., et al. (1994). The functions of self-injurious behavior: An experimental-epidemiological analysis. *Journal of Applied Behavior Analysis, 27,* 215–240.

Kahng, S., Abt, K. A., & Schonbachler, H. E. (2001). Assessment and treatment of low-rate high-intensity problem behavior. *Journal of Applied Behavior Analysis, 34,* 225–228.

Kazdin, A. E. (2001). How to identify, define, and assess behavior. In *Behavior modification in applied settings* (2nd ed., pp. 67–97). Belmont, CA: Wadsworth.

Kerker, B. D., Owens, P. L., Zigler, E., & Horwitz, S. M. (2004). Mental health disorders among individuals with mental retardation: Challenging to accurate estimates. *Public Health Reports, 119,* 409–417.

Kuhn, D. E., & Matson, J. L. (2002). A validity study of the Screening Tool of Feeding Problems (STEP). *Journal of Intellectual and Developmental Disability, 27,* 161–167.

Lalli, J. S., Browder, D. M., Mace, F. C., & Brown, D. K. (1993). Teacher descriptive analysis data to implement interventions to decrease student problem behaviors. *Journal of Applied Behavior Analysis, 26,* 227–238.

LaMalfa, G., Campigli, M., Bertelli, B., Mangiapane, A., & Cabras, P. L. (1997). The psychopathological model of mental retardation: Theoretical and therapeutic considerations. *Research in Developmental Disabilities, 18,* 407–413.

Larson, S. A., Lakin, C., Anderson, L., Kwak, N., Lee, J. H., & Anderson, D. (2001). Prevalence of mental retardation and developmental disabilities: Estimates from the 1994/1995 national health interview survey disability supplements. *American Journal on Mental Retardation, 106,* 231–252.

Leonard, H., & Wen, X. (2002). The epidemiology of mental retardation: Challenges and opportunities in the new millennium. *Mental Retardation and Developmental Disabilities, 8,* 117–134.

Mace, F. C., Hock, M. L., Lalli, J. S., West, B. J., Belfiore, P., Pinter, E., et al. (1988). Behavioral momentum in the treatment of noncompliance. *Journal of Applied Behavior Analysis, 21,* 123–141.

Mace, F. C., Lalli, J. S., & Lalli, E. P. (1991). Functional analysis and treatment of aberrant behavior. *Research in Developmental Disabilities, 12,* 155–180.

Matson, J. L. (1995a). *The Diagnostic Assessment of the Severely Handicapped–Revised (DASH-II).* Baton Rouge, LA: Disability Consultants, LLC.

Matson, J. L. (1995b). *The Matson Evaluation of Social Skills for Individuals with Severe Retardation (MESSIER).* Baton Rouge, LA: Disability Consultants, LLC.

Matson, J. L. (1997). *The Assessment of Dual Diagnosis (ADD).* Baton Rouge, LA: Disability Consultants, LLC.

Matson, J. L. (2000). *Scale for the Evaluation and Identification of Seizures, Epilepsy, and Anticonvulsant Side Effects, B form.* Baton Rouge, LA: Disability Consultants, LLC.

Matson, J. L., & Bamburg, J. W. (1998). Reliability of the Assessment of Dual Diagnosis (ADD). *Research in Developmental Disabilities, 19,* 89–95.

Matson, J. L., Bamburg, J. W., Cherry, K. E., & Paclawskyj, T. R. (1999). A validity study on the Questions About Behavioral Function (QABF) scale: Predicting treatment success for self-injury, aggression and stereotypies. *Research in Developmental Disabilities, 20,* 163–176.

Matson, J. L., Carlisle, C. B., & Bamburg, J. W. (1998). The convergent validity of the Matson Evaluation of Social Skills in Persons with Severe Retardation (MESSIER). *Research in Developmental Disabilities, 19,* 493–500.

Matson, J. L., Helsel, W. J., Bellack, A. S., & Senatore, V. (1983). Development of a rating scale to assess social skill deficits in mentally retarded adults. *Applied Research in Mental Retardation, 4,* 399–408.

Matson, J. L., & Kuhn, D. E. (2001). *Screening Tool of Feeding Problems (STEP).* Baton Rouge, LA: Disability Consultants, LLC.

Matson, J. L., Laud, R. B., González, M. L., Malone, C. J., & Swender, S. L. (2005). The reliability of the Scale for the Evaluation and Identification of Seizures, Epilepsy and Anticonvulsant Side Effects–B (SEIZES-B). *Research in Developmental Disabilities, 26,* 593–599.

Matson, J. L., LeBlanc, L. A., Weinheimer, B., & Cherry, K. E. (1999). Reliability of the Matson Evaluation of Social Skills for Individuals with Severe Retardation (MESSIER). *Behavior Modification, 23,* 647–661.

Matson, J. L., Mayville, E. A., Bamburg, J. W., & Eckholdt, C. S. (2001). An analysis of side-effect profiles of anti-seizure medications in persons with intellectual disability using the Matson Evaluation of Drug Side Effects (MEDS). *Journal of Intellectual & Developmental Disabilities, 26,* 283–295.

Matson, J. L., Mayville, E. A., Bielecki, J., Barnes, H., Bamburg, J. W., & Baglio, C. S. (1998). Reliability of the Matson Evaluation of Drug Side Effects Scale (MEDS). *Research in Developmental Disabilities, 19,* 501–506.

Matson, J. L., Mayville, S. B., & Laud, R. B. (2003). A system of assessment for adaptive behavior, social skills, behavioral function, medication side-effects and psychiatric disorders. *Research in Developmental Disabilities, 24,* 75–81.

Matson, J. L., Rush, K. S., Smiroldo, B. B., Hamilton, M., Anderson, S. J., Baglio, C. S., et al. (1999). Characteristics of depression as assessed by the

Diagnostic Assessment for the Severely Handicapped II (DASH-II). *Research in Developmental Disabilities, 20,* 305–313.

Matson, J. L., & Sevin, J. A. (1994). Theories of dual diagnosis in mental retardation. *Journal of Consulting and Counseling Psychology, 62*(1), 6–16.

Matson, J. L., & Smiroldo, B. B. (1997). Validity of the mania subscale of the DASH-II. *Research in Developmental Disabilities, 18,* 221–226.

Matson, J. L., Smiroldo, B. B., & Bamburg, J. W. (1998). The relationship of social skills to psychopathology for individuals with severe and profound mental retardation. *Journal of Intellectual Disabilities Research, 23,* 137–145.

Matson, J. L., Smiroldo, B. B., & Hastings, T. (1998). Validity of the Autism/PDD subscale of the DASH-II. *Journal of Autism and Developmental Disabilities, 28,* 77–81.

Matson, J. L., & Vollmer, T. (1995). *Questions About Behavioral Function (QABF).* Baton Rouge, LA: Disability Consultants, LLC.

Mayville, E. A., & Mayville, S. B. (2004). Data collection and observation systems. In J. L. Matson, R. B. Laud, & M. L. Matson (Eds.), *Behavior modification for persons with developmental disabilities: Treatments and supports* (Vol. 1, pp. 130–159). New York: National Association for the Dually Diagnosed.

Merrell, K. W. (1994). *Assessment of behavioral, social & emotional problems: Direct and objective methods for use with children and adolescents.* New York: Longman.

Moss, S. C., Prosser, H., Costello, H., Simpson, N., & Patel, P. (1996). *PAS-ADD checklist.* Manchester: Hester Adrian Research Centre, University of Manchester.

Moss, S., Prosser, H., Costello, H., Simpson, N., Patel, P., Rowe, S., et al. (1998). Reliability and validity of the PAS-ADD checklist for detecting psychiatric disorders in adults with intellectual disability. *Journal of Intellectual Disability Research, 42,* 173–83.

Mycek, M. J., Harvey, R. A., & Champe, P. C. (1997). *Lippincott's illustrated reviews: Pharmacology* (2nd ed.). Philadelphia: Raven.

Ollendick, T. H., & Ollendick, D. G. (1982). Anxiety disorders. In J. L. Matson & R. P. Barrett (Eds.), *Psychopathology in the mentally retarded* (pp. 77–120). New York: Grune & Stratton.

O'Neill, R. E., Horner, R. H., Albin, R. W., Storey, K., & Sprague, J. R. (1990). *Functional analysis of problem behavior. A practical assessment guide.* Sycamore, IL: Sycamore.

Paclawskyj, T. R., Matson, J. L., Bamburg, J. W., & Baglio, C. S. (1997). A comparison of the Diagnostic Assessment for the Severely Handicapped–II (DASH-II) and the Aberrant Behavior Checklist (ABC). *Research in Developmental Disabilities, 18,* 289–298.

Paclawskyj, T. R., Matson, J. L., Rush, K. S., Smalls, Y., & Vollmer, T. R. (2000). Questions About Behavioral Function (QABF): A behavioral checklist for functional assessment of aberrant behavior. *Research in Developmental Disabilities, 21,* 223–229.

Paclawskyj, T. R., Matson, J. L., Rush, K. S., Smalls, Y., & Vollmer, T. R. (2001). Assessment of the convergent validity of the Questions About Behavioral Function scale with analogue functional analysis and the Motivation Assessment Scale. *Journal of Intellectual Disability Research, 45*(6), 484–494.

Prosser, H., & Bromley, J. (1998). Interviewing people with intellectual disabilities. In E. Emerson, C. Hatton, J. Bromley, & A. Caine (Eds.), *Clinical psychology and people with intellectual disabilities* (pp. 99–113). New York: Wiley.

Prosser, H., Moss, S., Costello, H., Simpson, N., & Patel, P. (1997). *The Mini PAS-ADD: An assessment schedule for the detection of mental health needs in adults with learning disability (mental retardation).* Manchester: Hester Adrian Research Centre, University of Manchester.

Prosser, H., Moss, S., Costello, H., Simpson, N., Patel, P. & Rowe, S. (1998). Reliability and validity of the Mini PAS-ADD for assessing psychiatric disorders in adults with intellectual disability. *Journal of Intellectual Disability Research, 42,* 264–272.

Reid, A. H. (1983). Psychiatric disorders in mentally handicapped children: A clinical and follow-up study. *Journal of Mental Deficiency Research, 24,* 287–298.

Reiss, S. (1988). Dual diagnosis in the United States. *Australia and New Zealand Journal of Developmental Disabilities, 14,* 43–48.

Reiss, S. (1993). Assessment of psychopathology in persons with mental retardation. In J. L. Matson & R. P. Barrett (Eds.), *Psychopathology in the mentally retarded* (2nd ed., pp. 17–39). Boston: Allyn & Bacon.

Reiss, S. A., & Benson, B. A. (1984). Awareness of negative social conditions among mentally retarded, emotionally disturbed outpatients. *American Journal of Psychiatry, 141,* 88–90.

Reiss, S., Levitan, G. W., & Szyszko, J. (1982). Emotional disturbance and mental retardation: Diagnostic overshadowing. *American Journal of Mental Deficiency, 6,* 567–574.

Richardson, S. A., Katz, M., & Koller, H. (1986). Sex differences in number of children administratively classified as mildly mentally retarded: An epidemiological review. *American Journal of Mental Deficiency, 91,* 250–256.

Roeleveld, N., Zielhuis, G. A., & Gabreels, F. (1997). The prevalence of mental retardation: A critical review of recent literature. *Developmental Medical Child Neurology, 39,* 125–132.

Rojahn, J., Aman, M. G., Matson, J. L., & Mayville, E. (2003). The Aberrant Behavior Checklist and the Behavior Problems Inventory: Convergent and divergent validity. *Research in Developmental Disabilities, 24,* 391–404.

Rojahn, J., Matson, J. L., Lott, D., Esbensen, A. J., & Smalls, Y. (2001). The Behavior Problem Inventory: An instrument for the assessment of self-injury, stereotyped behavior and aggression/destruction in individuals with developmental disabilities. *Journal of Autism and Developmental Disorders, 31,* 577–588.

Rojahn, J., & Tasse, M. J. (1996). Psychopathology in mental retardation. In J. W. Jacobson & J. A. Mulick (Eds.), *Manual of diagnosis and professional practice in mental retardation* (pp. 147–156). Washington, DC: American Psychological Association.

Rush, K. S., Bowman, L. G., Eidman, S. L., Toole, L. M., & Mortenson, B. P. (2004). Assessing psychopathology in individuals with developmental disabilities [special issue]. *Behavior Modification, 28,* 622–637.

Rutecccki, P. A., & Gidal, B. E. (2002). Antiepileptic drug treatment in the developmentally disabled: Treatment considerations with the newer antiepileptic drugs. *Epilepsy and Behavior, 3,* S24–S31.

Scheerenberger, R. C. (1983). *A history of mental retardation.* Baltimore: Brooks.

Schroeder, S. R., Mulick, J. A., & Schroeder, C. S. (1979). Management of severe behavior problems of the retarded. In N. R. Ellis (Ed.), *Handbook of mental deficiency, psychological theory and research* (pp. 341–366). Hillsdale, NJ: Erlbaum.

Shaw, J. A., & Budd, E. C. (1982). Determinants of acquiescence and naysaying of mentally retarded persons. *American Journal of Mental Deficiency, 87,* 108–110.

Sigelman, C. K., Budd, E. C., Spanhel, C. L., & Schoenrock, C. J. (1981a). Asking questions of retarded persons: A comparison of yes-no and either-or formats. *Applied Research in Mental Retardation, 2,* 347–357.

Sigelman, C. K., Budd, E. C., Spanhel, C. L., & Schoenrock, C. J. (1981b). When in doubt, say yes: Acquiescence in interviews with mentally retarded persons. *Mental Retardation, 2,* 53–58.

Sigelman, C. K., Budd, E. C., Winer, J. L., Schoenrock, C. J., & Martin, P. W. (1982). Evaluating alternative techniques of questioning mentally retarded persons. *American Journal of Mental Deficiency, 86,* 511–518.

Sigelman, C. K., Schoenrock, C. J., Spanhel, C. L., Thomas, S. G., Winer, J. L., Budd, E. C., et al. (1980). Surveying mentally retarded persons: Responsiveness and response validity in three samples. *American Journal Mental Deficiency, 84,* 479–486.

Sigelman, C. K., Schoenrock, C. J., Winer, J. L., Spanhel, C. L., Hromas, S. G., Martin, P. W., et al. (1981). Issues in interviewing mentally retarded persons: An empirical study. In R. H. Bruininks, C. E. Meyers, B. B. Sigford, & K. C. Lakin (Eds.), *Deinstitutionalization and community adjustment of mentally retarded people* (pp. 107–113). Washington, DC: American Association on Mental Deficiency.

Sovner, R., & Pary, R. J. (1993). Affective disorders in developmentally disabled persons. In J. L. Matson (Ed.), *Psychopathology in the mentally retarded* (2nd ed., pp. 87–138). Boston: Allyn & Bacon.

Sparrow, S., Balla, D., & Cicchetti, D. (1984). *Vineland Adaptive Behavior Scales: Interview edition survey form manual.* Circle Press, MN: American Guidance Service.

Sparrow, S., Cicchetti, D., & Balla, D. (2005). *Vineland Adaptive Behavior Scales, 2nd edition (VABS-II): Interview edition survey form.* Circle Press, MN: American Guidance Service.

Sprague, R. L., & Kalachnik, J. E. (1991). Reliability, validity and a total score cutoff for the Dyskinesia Identification System: Condensed User Scale (DISCUS) with mentally ill and mentally retarded populations. *Psychopharmacology Bulletin, 27,* 51–58.

Sternlicht, M. (1979). Fears of institutionalized mentally retarded adults. *Journal of Psychology: Interdisciplinary & Applied, 101,* 67–71.

Sturmey, P. (1994). Assessing the functions of aberrant behaviors: A review of psychometric instruments. *Journal of Autism and Developmental Disabilities, 24*(3), 293–304.

Sturmey, P. (1995). Analogue baseline: A critical review of the methodology. *Research in Developmental Disabilities, 16,* 269–284.

Sturmey, P. (1996). *Functional analysis in clinical psychology.* New York: Wiley.

Sturmey, P. (1998). Classification and diagnosis of psychiatric disorders in persons with developmental disabilities. *Journal of Developmental and Physical Disabilities, 10,* 317–330.

Sturmey, P., Burcham, K. J., & Perkins, T. S. (1995). The Reiss Screen for Maladaptive Behaviour: Its reliability and internal consistencies. *Journal of Intellectual Disability Research, 39,* 191–195.

Szymanski, L. S., & Grossman, H. (1984). Dual implications of "dual diagnosis." *Mental Retardation, 22,* 155–156.

Touchette, P. E., MacDonald, R. F., & Langer, S. N. (1985). A scatter plot for identifying stimulus control of problem behavior. *Journal of Applied Behavior Analysis, 18,* 343–351.

Van Houten, R., & Rolider, A. (1991). Applied behavior analysis. In J. L. Matson & J. A. Mulick (Eds.), *Handbook of mental retardation* (2nd ed., pp. 569–585). New York: Pergamon.

Wadsworth, J. S., & Harper, D. C. (1991). Increasing the reliability of self-report by adults with moderate mental retardation. *Journal of the Association for Persons with Severe Handicaps, 16,* 228–232.

Wilfong, A. A. (2002). Treatment considerations: Role of vagus nerve stimulator. *Epilepsy and Behavior, 3,* S41–S44.

Wing, L., & Gould, J. (1979). Severe impairments of social interaction and associated abnormalities in children: Epidemiology and classification. *Journal of Autism and Developmental Disorders, 9,* 11–29.

Wyngaarden, M. (1981). Interviewing mentally retarded persons: Issues and strategies. In R. H. Bruininks, C. E. Meyers, B. B. Sigford, & K. C. Lakin (Eds.), *Deinstitutionalization and community adjustment of mentally retarded people* (pp. 107–113). Washington, DC: American Association on Mental Deficiency.

24

NEUROLOGICALLY IMPAIRED CLIENTS

CHARLES J. GOLDEN AND ZARABETH L. GOLDEN

It is not unusual for clinicians involved in the evaluation of a client with possible neuropsychological or neuropsychiatry problems to rely more on test results than on the interview. There are several reasons for this tendency: a belief that clients referred from physicians or other professionals often have an adequate background identified, a reliance on standard scores rather than clinical knowledge and observation, a focus on using technicians to conduct most face-to-face contact, a lack of knowledge on how the interview may be a source of more than just answers to questions, and a failure to recognize the importance of specific observations or historical details. In reality, there are situations in which standardized tests and scores are essentially worthless, and one must rely on clinical interviewing to identify the correct diagnosis and course of treatment.

The general goals of an interview with neurologically impaired clients are much the same as those of an interview with any adult client, with differences in the degree and scope of the neurological history and data, which must be more comprehensive than in the standard psychological interview. However, even the gathering of this information is affected by the presence of any neurological symptoms and the manner in which those symptoms may affect the course and accuracy of an interview. Interviewers must be sensitive to presence of specific behaviors during an interview because the distinction between neurological disorders may hinge on very specific observations rather than more general findings seen in the standard interview. Such observations may help distinguish between a psychiatric or neurological disorder or between an attentional problem and a seizure disorder. Missing such important information can lead the clinician to the wrong diagnosis and treatment and result in delays in getting the client the best help. Finally, whenever possible, the quality of information gathered must be compared with information from interviews or records from collateral sources to ensure the accuracy of the finding.

The purpose of this chapter is to focus on what can be gathered from asking questions of the neurologically impaired client that differ from information we would gather from a nonneurological patient. Second, the impact of patient-specific symptoms such as aphasia on the interview process must be examined. Third, the importance of behavioral observations that may inform the diagnostic process will be examined. Then, the role of collateral interviews and specialized records will be discussed. Finally, specific issues related to the forensic interviews of these clients will be considered.

Specific Content Related to the Neurologically Impaired Client

The additional information needed when interviewing a neurologically impaired client pertains to the development of symptoms, including the sequence of events that led to the neurological disorder, course of the symptoms, and their current status. This information not only yields insight into the origin of the symptoms but also offers information on clients' understanding of their own problems. This information can also be used to detect stories that are neuropsychologically inconsistent and therefore may be misleading or even reflect malingering (although such inconsistencies may also reflect many other processes). The complexity of this information varies with the neurological disorders involved and the number of events or disorders involved.

Development of Symptoms

The development of symptoms in a neurological case can be very dramatic (e.g., in a severe head trauma after an accident) or more subtle and slow (e.g., in multiple sclerosis or many of the dementias). It is important to focus on when symptoms actually began. It is important to ask clients when their behavior began to change. Many people who are referred for neuropsychological evaluations for current problems have a history of past problems, such as learning disorders, alcohol or drug abuse, depression, and vocational problems. In head injuries seen by the current writers, more than 50% of the patients had difficulties that preceded head trauma. It is essential to separate preexisting symptoms from those that are new. This information is useful in understanding the neuropsychology of the disorder and focusing treatment on the symptoms that are most recent and more likely to respond to treatment.

When a client has had multiple problems, it can be effective to develop a clear timeline of potential neurological events and the development of the symptoms. Such timelines can identify whether symptoms are more likely to have psychological or neurological causes. For example, one patient came in after a mild head trauma (one with little or no loss of consciousness)

complaining of depression, memory problems, inability to work, problems with concentration, and inability to perform complex tasks. He had been diagnosed with postconcussion syndrome by his physician, who made the referral when the symptoms did not remit. The physician requested a neuropsychological evaluation to document disability caused by the head injury. However, a careful history revealed that the client had lost his job several days before the accident.

Closer inquiry revealed that the client's wife had left him 18 months earlier, which precipitated a slow decline in function. During this time the client slowly became less functional, receiving multiple warnings at work until he was finally fired. The accident occurred 3 days later and probably was caused by the client's inattention while driving. He was not taken to a hospital after the accident because he seemed to be fine. By the next day, he went to an emergency room complaining of neck stiffness. The physician was also concerned about his flat and depressed affect and his problem with reporting details of the accident. Despite a normal computed tomography scan and normal electro encephalogram (EEG), he was diagnosed with postconcussion syndrome. He was given medication for his pain and referred to a neurologist. By the time he saw the neurologist the patient's symptoms had become worse, possibly because of the medication and possibly because the client accepted the explanation that all his problems were caused by a head trauma.

When he was seen for the neuropsychological examination 3 months later, he was fully convinced that all his problems were caused by a head trauma. The neck pain had resolved itself, but he stated that his memory problems and his problems with concentration and completing complex (executive type) tasks had gotten worse. The client's mood had actually improved; he seemed almost elated at the idea that the head injury was the cause of his problems. He admitted that his wife had left him but insisted that none of the events was related to his current symptoms and blamed his firing on office politics. Testing confirmed extremely poor memory functioning, well beyond what would be expected with a mild head injury, and difficulty with complex tasks. During the interview, he was able to repeat every aspect of his prior treatment, even correcting the examiner once when he misquoted a date in the file. Thus, although the testing and initial history and referral clearly indicated problems arising from a head injury, the careful evaluation of how the symptoms developed pointed to an alternative explanation.

On the other hand, a client with a similar accident and recent history revealed a very different picture. The client suffered a mild head injury after an automobile accident accompanied by mild neck pain the next day. He was treated with medication and diagnosed with a mild whiplash syndrome. He stayed at home the next week with his family, resting. He then returned to work, where he was in a high-pressure job. He made several serious errors that came to the attention of his superiors. He was reassigned to a lower-level job after several days because he seemed unable to focus and to remember the details important for his job. He became increasingly depressed and frustrated and finally asked to take a medical leave of absence. He was diagnosed with major depression and placed on fluoxetine, but he did not respond. He was referred for testing to evaluate his personality decline and to recommend additional treatment.

The history revealed a high-functioning person who, although he was in a stressful and demanding job, performed at a very high level until the time of the accident. During the week he was at home (and wanting to get back to work), he had been irritable but had been able to deal with routine tasks. He had slept more than usual, but this had been attributed to his pain medication. Upon his return to work, the problems began to appear, and he became increasingly frustrated, depressed, and angry at himself for his problems and at others for pointing them out. He continued to decline as problems mounted first at work and then at home.

Despite the reported mildness of the head injury, his history suggested that he indeed had a neurological problem. His test results were actually better than those of the patient in the first example. However, based on the combination of history and tests results, the report suggested that the depression was a secondary rather than a primary problem and that the client indeed had a real neurological injury. On the basis of the report, a magnetic resonance imaging (MRI) scan was ordered, and there was residual evidence of bleeding in the deep frontal and temporal lobes. An MRI revealed slow metabolism in the frontal areas but hyperexcitability in the temporal area. Follow-up with a 24-hour EEG in the hospital indicated seizure spikes in the deep temporal lobe, resulting in complex partial seizures, which caused problems with his attention and emotional responses.

These two cases do not represent all the possibilities one might see but emphasize the need to take a careful history when physicians or others have already reached a conclusion. The variability of medical treatment for neurological disorders can lead to obvious but incorrect conclusions. It is not uncommon for the initial phases of degenerative disorders to be seen as psychological problems or for some psychiatric disorders to be misinterpreted as neurological disorders. These errors are compounded by the fact that doctors rarely take detailed histories because of the time and economic pressure to see as many patients as possible. In addition, in many cases, collateral sources of information are essential but rarely seen by physicians when an adult appears functional.

It should be mentioned that some neurological disorders do not have any clear cause of events that lead to their development. The most difficult to deal with are disorders that occur in utero or shortly after birth. Such disorders may be caused by genetic defects; maternal drinking, drugs, nutrition, disease, or injury; intrauterine problems; or labor difficulties. In many of these cases, the actual cause may never be identified, especially in adults. Such histories must remain somewhat speculative by necessity.

Course of the Symptoms

In assessing the development of symptoms, we must study the course the symptoms take over time once they are established. In the past, it has been stated that once symptoms have been established (e.g., after a head injury), they can only become better, not worse. This is a fallacy that can confuse the assessment of the course of the disorder. First, symptoms often get worse in disorders that may change over time. This includes the full range of degenerative disorders, which are most common in older adults but also strike younger people. Some degenerative diseases do not follow a linear course; they follow a pattern of exacerbation and remission that may be related to the disease process and to physical and psychological stress. The relationship to stressors may mislead the evaluator to think that stress is the major problem.

In addition, even time-limited disorders such as head injuries and strokes may have ongoing sequelae that change the course of the symptoms. As in the previous examples, many disorders can lead to seizures, which can interfere with cognitive, behavioral, and emotional processes. Seizures can be obvious (e.g., grand mal seizures), but they can often be more subtle. Some complex partial seizures may cause emotional changes that interfere with functioning. This can lead to depression, anxiety, panic attacks, or, in more severe cases, lead a person to physically attack another person. Some seizures result in only momentary losses of consciousness without motor symptoms, which can be easily missed. Again, good information on the course of the symptoms (how often they happen, when, under what circumstances, and under what physical and psychological stressors) is necessary.

People who have major strokes may have additional but smaller strokes that cause a stepwise decline in cognitive functioning without additional motor or sensory symptoms. Absence of such symptoms makes it more difficult for family or physicians to see the presence of the new strokes, but a careful history that reveals a stepwise decline in cognitive functioning can identify this pattern. This pattern is also useful in differentiating early cases of Alzheimer's disease (where the decline is more gradual) and multi-infarct dementia (where the decline is stepwise). People with bleeding in the brain secondary to trauma or leaking in the vessels of the brain may develop hematomas, which are essentially bags of blood that can enlarge and place pressure on brain matter. This pressure in turn may result in increasing cognitive, emotional, or sensory-motor symptoms even several weeks or months after the initial event. Similar problems can arise from hygromas, which are the consequence of leakage of cerebrospinal fluid. In all these cases a patient's symptoms will become increasingly worse.

Other potential causes of decline are secondary effects of treatment and secondary emotional reactions. Secondary effects of treatment can arise from several sources. A common one is fatigue: After a neurological insult people may have to work very hard in order to function at a normal or nearly normal level. Such people often use other areas of the brain to take over for the injured area, a process that is often inefficient and requires high levels of attention and focus. When such people are subjected to physical stress (e.g., a session of physical therapy) or psychological stress, they show declining cognitive function as they fatigue. Such decline may be misinterpreted as malingering or lack of effort, but this decline is similar to the physical decline we see in people who perform continued rigorous physical activity.

Another treatment effect can arise from medications. People with neurological problems often are on many medications that can affect brain function. Unfortunately, research on most of these medications focuses on the neurological side effects in people with normally functioning brains. The effects on people whose brain is not functioning in a normal manner are much less well understood and can be very unpredictable. Therefore, an analysis of what medications the client has been on and when must be projected against the course of the symptoms. A good interview can reveal patterns that point to a specific medication as the cause of the decline.

Emotional reactions can affect the client in a similar manner. As clients realize that they are unable to function, they may become frustrated, anxious, upset, depressed, or angry. These feelings can affect motivation but not as a result of choice by the client. They can also disrupt cognitive processes much in the same way as we see in fatigue. The increased behavioral and cognitive dysfunction lead to more emotional problems, which in return lead to more cognitive processes. If this cycle is not broken, the client can become totally incapacitated. Therefore, it is important to identify such a pattern as early as possible in the interview so that it can be treated promptly.

Current Status

It is important to establish the current status of each symptom. Clients may choose to discuss the problems they have had rather than what they have at the time they are seen. As a consequence, the interview must clearly distinguish what *was* true from what *is* true. Because many examinations are related to disability claims or insurance settlements or payments, clients may feel the need to emphasize their problems without being fully open about subsequent recovery. The interview must then focus on this issue so that the examiner understands the nature of the current complaints. Furthermore, the examiner must understand why the client is being seen at the exact time the interview is taking place. Although some evaluations may be routine reexaminations, most have a particular purpose, which can include a disability or insurance examination, the demands of a civil or criminal court case, loss of a job or spouse, failure at school or work, or a recent significant change in the client's status from a physical, psychological, or behavioral perspective. Knowledge of this reason is important so that the client's motivation may be better understood.

IMPACT OF PATIENT SYMPTOMS ON THE INTERVIEW

Understanding the impact of the patient's symptoms on the interview is vital in evaluating the accuracy and the meaning of the information given by the client. Neurologically impaired clients may have obvious difficulties in multiple areas, including speech difficulties, impaired speech comprehension, memory deficits (both short and long term), fatigue, limited insight and awareness, attention deficits, personality dysfunction, justification and exaggeration, and sensorimotor impairments.

Expressive Speech

An obvious and major problem in any interview is the ability of the client to respond to the interviewer's questions. Expressive speech problems can be seen as complete (i.e., no oral communication is possible) or partial (e.g., the client may have word finding problems, hesitate in pronouncing words, and produce nonsense words). Each of these presents a specific challenge to the interviewer.

Complete Loss of Speech. In these cases, the client is unable to produce any meaningful sounds and thus fully unable to communicate. However, when this severe language disorder is unaccompanied by a receptive speech disorder, alternative methods of communication can be established. These interviews often are slower and may possess less detail, but they allow at least a basic conversation with the client.

One obvious alternative is to allow the client to write or type his or her answers if writing skills have not been impaired. If a stroke has resulted

in an inability to speak and a paralysis of the dominant arm, the likelihood of communication by writing is less likely. In some cases, although there is no paralysis, writing is impaired in the same manner as the client's speech. Writing is most likely to be preserved when the injury is not to the area of the cortex that controls speech in the frontal lobe (also known as Broca's area) but to the system that communicates the intentions of the brain to the peripheral speech mechanism or to the mouth or vocal cords themselves. Thus, although there can be no guarantee that writing will work, it is generally the first alternative tried.

More serious problems arise when writing cannot be used as an effective method of communication. In these cases, alternative communication devices may be necessary. In people who maintain the ability to effectively control at least one hand and the ability to understand or read, a multiple-choice evaluation may be used in which the client points to the proper answer. In these cases, the client may be able to complete standardized questionnaires for specific purposes (which can also be administered on a computer with a touchscreen interface).

In other cases, the client may be able to make only a simple yes-no choice. These can be made in a wide variety of ways. The client may move one hand to indicate *yes* or the other to indicate *no.* He or she might move a single finger once for *yes* and twice for *no.* In a locked-in syndrome, a client may be cognitively intact but only able to blink, so he or she can blink once for *yes* and twice for *no* or look to the right for *yes* and left for *no.* All of these methods have also been adapted as computer interface methods, which can allow more flexibility. In one case seen by the senior author, eye movements were used to allow the client to move from letter to letter on a computer screen, which allowed the client to spell words letter by letter. In other systems, the client might move between symbols that represented specific responses such as "Yes," "No," "Maybe," "I am hungry," "I do not understand," and so on.

Word Finding. Word finding problems are not as serious as the complete loss of speech but require patience and additional time on the part of the interviewer. Word finding problems may be marked by several possibilities. The first is the obvious, in which the client is clearly seeking a word but cannot come up with it. Such people will search for a word until they find one or give up, but the word that is found may not be the right word. If the word that is used makes no sense in the context of the sentence, the fact that the wrong word is chosen is obvious. However, in some cases the client may pick a word in the same class (e.g., instead of "I was hit by a car," the client might say "I was hit by a plane."). Careful interviewing requires that any statements be verified with the client or others. An alternative response from clients is to use a made-up word (called jargon) that does not make sense. In some cases these words may appear to be the fusion of one or more real words or may simply be pure nonsense words with no meaning whatsoever.

Dysfluency. In some cases, the client has obvious problems marked by speech dysfluency. *Dysfluency* means that the rhythm, sound, and pattern of speech are disrupted. In such cases, it is obvious even to a casual listener that there is a speech problem of some kind. In fluent speech, if one were to listen to the speech without consideration for the content, everything would sound fine. Word finding difficulties may appear in either fluent or dysfluent speech.

The major characteristics of dysfluency are slowness of speech and unintelligibility. Dealing with both requires patience and additional time. When dysfluency is present, asking open-ended questions that call for long answers usually is not effective. Questions that can be answered more briefly generally are more effective. This may entail breaking down more general questions into a series of more limited questions. If more detailed answers can be eliminated, the length of the interview can be controlled more effectively.

Dysfluent speech may not be unintelligible, but the presence of unintelligibility must be dealt with carefully. The interviewer may ask the client to repeat the answer, but this will not necessarily produce a more understandable response. In addition, frequent requests to repeat also add to the patient's frustration with his or her symptoms and can cause anger and withdrawal from the interview. The better course is to use one of the alternative communication approaches as discussed earlier.

Diversity. Another related issue in our multicultural society is the issue of diversity. In general, the examiner must be aware of and practiced in the normal method of speaking with any person who is interviewed. The speech of someone whose method of speech before the neurological insult differs in such areas as rhythm, word choice, and pronunciation becomes much more difficult to understand with the aforementioned speech problems if you are not familiar with his or her normal speech. A person who is more acquainted with a given ethnic or cultural group's style of speech will generally do much better at understanding the speech when expressive speech problems are present.

Special problems may arise when a client is interviewed in a language other than his or her native language. Second languages are more easily disrupted after a neurological disorder even when both languages are well developed before the neurological impairment. In such cases, clients generally should be interviewed in their first language rather than one they learned later in life. The later the second language was learned, the more likely this problem is to arise.

Receptive Speech and Comprehension

Receptive speech and comprehension problems are an obvious and serious barrier to interviewing. If the client has a mild form, the interviewer may need to repeat many questions to ensure that the client comprehends. Errors of comprehension may lead to easy misinterpretation of questions, which will result in wrong answers. This is especially serious when one is asking yes-no questions, for which the wrong answer may easily be missed. It is much more effective (although more time consuming) to insist on longer answers in which the client must repeat the essence of the question, which allows the examiner to be certain that the question has been understood clearly.

Unfortunately, in many cases examiners choose to simplify questions so that it seems easier for the client to understand and answer them with short statements. However, the client can easily misunderstand these simpler questions as well. This can have especially serious consequences when the examiner is seeking information in a forensic or medical situation.

In a forensic setting, errors in comprehension (in the absence of fluency problems) may lead adversarially oriented examiners to conclude that the client is faking, malingering, or deliberately avoiding specific issues. For example, one client with a serious head trauma and bleeding in the left temporoparietal area of the brain (the area probably responsible for these deficits) was repeatedly labeled as a malingerer by the forensic psychologists hired by the prosecutor (who was charging him with a motor vehicle crime secondary to alcohol). They cited his "refusal" to directly answer the questions they asked, his inconsistencies when asked the same question in a different manner, and his "malingering" of confusion despite clear-cut neurological and neuropsychological evidence of the nature, location, and impact of his injuries.

Clients may misunderstand questions and fail to report relevant history in response to a medical question. This may cause the doctor to be unaware of specific allergies, history, or related medical care. This in turn may lead to poor and even dangerous care, which is later justified by the statement that the client did not report the problems to the physician or interviewer. Although the latter statement is true, it is the responsibility of the examiner to ensure that the neurologically impaired client does understand the questions. This can be done by asking the clients to reword and repeat several questions to ensure that they are comprehending the questions or by the use of more formal tests of receptive speech skills, although these are rarely used in most interview settings.

Memory

Another serious problem is memory disorders. These may take many forms. After a head injury or other neurological event, the client may lose memory for a period of time before the event (called anterograde amnesia), or he or she may lose memory for a period of time after the event (retrograde amnesia). Loss of memory may occur even though the client remains conscious during the period and is even able to respond and converse with others. Clients may have what appears to be a convenient loss of memory (e.g., inability to remember whether they had taken drugs before an accident), but these losses may be real. In some cases the length of amnesia lessens over time as the client recovers, although such lessening may be apparent only as the client fills in missing events with what he or she thinks should have happened or what others tell the client must have happened.

The filling in of events with false memories is difficult to confirm in some cases, but in other cases the emerging "memory" is clearly at odds with the facts of the case. For example, the examiner saw a young jogger found lying unconscious on the side of a rural road. Her head was bashed in on the left side. During neurosurgery, an impression of the wound strongly indicated a shape consistent with a side-view mirror. It was suggested that while jogging she was sideswiped by a mirror from a truck traveling on the narrow road in darkness. However, the jogger's family argued that she must have been attacked by someone. The client was in a coma for 6 weeks.

As she emerged from the coma and began to communicate, she was unable to remember the event or any events preceding the accident for 72 hours or following the event until she woke up from the coma. Her family kept pushing her to remember the event and shared with her their theories. Finally, after 8 months, she suddenly "remembered" the event, stating she had been attacked with a wooden baseball bat from behind by a man with a beard who tore her clothes off and attacked her before she lost consciousness. The story had several significant holes in it: There was no evidence that she was hit with a bat (no wood slivers or the shape of a bat), no evidence that her clothes had been ripped off, and no evidence that she had been sexually assaulted in any way. However, the story became increasingly complex, and the woman insisted it was true despite all physical evidence to the contrary. This complete belief in such false memories is not uncharacteristic of traumatized people who are unable to separate the false and real memories. Such false memories may also be comforting to the client because they provide explanations for missing periods of time, offer explanations for what might otherwise be seen as random events, and often are reinforced by family members, who are also looking for explanations.

Other memory disorders may be present as well. In some cases, new memories after an insult or the development of dementia may not be properly "saved." In extreme cases, no new memories may be formed at all. People with these rare disorders are unable to recognize the passage of time since their injury. For example, client J.P. had a bilateral stroke involving both hippocampi (located deep in the temporal lobes of the brain). As time passed, he always thought it was the day before his stroke. As his young child grew up, he failed to recognize him because he always looked for the "baby" and denied he had a grown child. He slowly became unable to recognize his wife as she aged (although he did notice a resemblance to his wife). He kept insisting he needed to go back to work and expressed great confusion when he was shown that his business was no longer located where he "knew" it was.

In less extreme cases, memories are partially formed but incomplete. In such cases, people fill in details in ways that they think are logical and fit their preconceptions and personality. This process occurs in most people because memories are rarely perfect. (This accounts for some of the variability in eyewitness recognition as well.) However, the memories after neurological injury are more impaired, so the reconstruction is more difficult and inaccurate. This again leads to inaccurate reports from the client, inconsistencies, and "recall" that is patently inconsistent with more objective accounts.

Another form of memory problems arises not from the absence of the memory but from an inability to access the memory when asked a specific question. Such people may be unable to answer a question initially when asked but may spontaneously recall the information at a later date or when asked the question again. This clearly leads to inconsistencies in self-reports, which interfere substantially with interviewing.

Fatigue

Fatigue does not cause neurological damage per se but often intensifies the symptoms of most of the problems described in other sections of this chapter. The client may show few obvious problems in speech or memory functions when well rested and not under physical or psychological stress. However, when the client is tired or stressed, his or her neurological function may decline. This is probably related to the way in which the brain reorganizes itself after a permanent brain injury. Brain circuits and cell clusters that are not routinely involved in a given cognitive behavior are recruited after an injury to produce an alternative system of brain cells to produce what appears to be the same behavior. The more effectively such an alternative system works, the more the original symptoms disappear.

However, although the new system seems to produce the same behavior, it usually has flaws: It may be less efficient, be less well organized, be unable to reproduce the exact behavior, or require more effort and focus than the original symptom. As a consequence, the new system is more subject to disruption than the older, generally more efficient and overlearned approach to the specific behavior. Thus, fatigue and stress lead to degradation of the new behavior and a reappearance of the symptoms that had been "cured." Interviews that take place under these conditions may fail to elicit accurate or useful information.

Insight and Awareness

In the evaluation of the neurologically impaired patient, the words *insight* and *awareness* often are used interchangeably when in fact they represent very different entities. After a brain injury, clients may have neither insight nor awareness. Awareness is the client's knowledge that a problem exists. In brain injury, the level of awareness may vary widely. In general, more concrete and obvious symptoms (e.g., the inability to walk or raise an arm or to speak) are more easily recognized or reported by the client.

However, this may not be true even for some very obvious injuries. In cases of unilateral neglect, clients may fail to recognize that one side of their body (most often the left side) is dysfunctional. Such clients, when shown their own paralyzed left hand, may observe that the hand does not work but will deny that the hand belongs to them. One client, an experienced bus driver, failed to recognize that he could no longer see in his left visual field. He began running into other vehicles, which he claimed "jumped out" at him. A farmer client in the Midwest reported that trees repositioned themselves in front of his tractors. Others simply walk into the left side of doors because they fail to account for the need to get the left side of their bodies through the door. They may be unable to dress because they cannot work with their left arm or leg.

Others recognize that they have legs or arms but do not acknowledge that they do not work. One hunter seen for treatment had hit a large male deer with his truck. The deer was thrown into the air and came down antlers first into the windshield. The hunter's frontal lobes were pierced through by the sharp antlers, essentially causing a frontal lobotomy. Although he was bilaterally paralyzed from the waist down, he was never aware that he was paralyzed. He repeatedly attempted to stand up from his bed or wheelchair, falling and injuring himself, all without recognition that his fall was the result of his own action. (He eventually needed to be constantly restrained for his own safety.)

More often, this lack of awareness is more common for cognitive and personality changes that are more subtle. Clients often are unaware that they have defects in judgment, that they are more irritable, that they are depressed, and that they are unable to do certain complex tasks. They often rely on overlearned responses rather than thinking through a specific intellectual challenge. When overlearned responses are adequate, they can function; when they are inadequate, they fail but do not recognize why.

The lack of awareness leads to serious problems in interviewing because the client will fail to report many of his or her problems. Indeed, the farmer with the dented tractor insisted that he was perfectly normal, as did the accident-prone bus driver. The man with the lower body paralysis was puzzled as to why he kept falling, blaming it on slippery floors or being pushed when asked to speculate. When the symptoms are obvious, it is not difficult for the observer to see the problems. However, when the symptoms are more subtle, it is easy to miss or ignore the client's problems. This again becomes serious in forensic settings, where the adversarial nature of the relationship may "reward" the interviewer when he or she misses symptoms that are inconsistent with the goals of the person who has hired the interviewer.

Related to the issue of awareness is insight. Insight is not just awareness of the symptoms but an understanding of where they come from and, more important, how they affect one's ability to function. This is extremely important in the neurologically impaired client because it is easy to teach the client the name and definition of his or her problem but much more difficult for the client to understand the implications of those deficits. One client readily acknowledged that he was irritable and made poor judgments, but he could not understand why his wife wanted to leave him because he had not "done anything" to her. Insight is essential during the interview if clients are to report how symptoms and problems affect their lives in any but the most general (and often inaccurate) terms. Lack of insight leads to inaccurate reports when an interviewer relies on just the client for a history and initial assessment.

Personality and Emotional Reactions

Personality dysfunction after a neurological insult arises from two sources: direct changes to the brain, which lead to alterations in mood or personality, and the client's reactions to the injuries, disorders, or their consequences, which can lead to depression, anxiety, or posttraumatic stress disorder. The latter category can be broken down further into reactions to physical changes such as paralysis or loss of vision (which themselves may or may not be related to the neurological injury) and reactions to perceived cognitive changes. In the case of all these symptoms, an analysis is complicated by the fact that symptoms may be related to the medical treatment of the disorder rather than the disorder itself, most often the secondary effects of medication. For example, medication for pain disorders may cause slowness, memory problems, difficulty in concentration, irritability, depression, and loss of judgment. Heavy sedation after a disorder often results in retrograde amnesia.

Reactions to neurological and physical deficits are associated with the degree of insight and awareness. In general, those with more awareness show more exaggerated reactions to their deficits than those with less awareness. This leads to the finding that a client with the least real problems (but with the most awareness) has worse personality and emotional reactions than the more severely injured client whose awareness is limited. In the case of the more mildly impaired client, the interviewer may see substantial exaggeration of symptoms caused by emotional reactions, whereas the more severely injured client may underreport and minimize problems. In addition, when the symptoms of the more mildly impaired client are challenged by professionals, the client may resort to further behavioral exaggeration to justify the seriousness of his or her symptoms. These factors must be considered and analyzed in the course of the interview so that the reliability of statements can be analyzed.

Overidealization of the Past

In giving a history, it is not unusual for a client to attribute all of his or her problems to the neurological condition. In such histories, the client (and even the family) presents himself or herself as without flaws before the disorder. It is very important to probe carefully to assess the degree to which a change has actually occurred. A client with a premorbid anger problem may blame his or her anger on a head trauma. Older clients with preexisting memory problems may blame all memory and cognitive problems on a small stroke or minor trauma. Only a full and careful history can get accurate information that allows an understanding of the actual cognitive and emotional effects of an injury, which in turn allows accurate diagnosis and understanding.

BEHAVIORAL OBSERVATIONS

Because the interview of the neurologically impaired client can be unreliable or even impossible using normal interviewing techniques, other methods of collecting information become especially important in many of these cases. One obvious alternative is observation of the client's behavior with regard to presentation of motor symptoms and specific cognitive and emotional problems. Usefulness of behavioral observations in these cases depends on both the accuracy of the observations and the knowledge of the examiner as to what behaviors have neurological significance. These behaviors are most often the consequence of the very behaviors that interfere with the traditional interview.

Motor Symptoms

Most easily observed are gross motor deficits. In more severe cases, clients can be paralyzed on one side of the body or in some cases on both sides. Unilateral motor impairment can be seen in the ability to use the hand or arm on one side of the body, or in some cases by the lack of movement of such limbs. Asking the client to do simple gross movements ("raise your hand") can reveal such problems easily, as can noting how the patient got into the interview room. Lesser problems can be noted by observing weaknesses, which can be reflected in abnormally slow movements or limps. Asking the client to squeeze your hand with each hand or to counter simple resistance (e.g., pushing your hand to the side) can reveal weakness in the arm.

More unusual movements are choreoid and athetoid movements, in which the client shows unusual and ungainly gross motor movements. The interviewer may also observe tics, sudden movements, or spasms in muscles that are not under voluntary control. Tics may include excessive or unusual blinking, shoulder shrugs, facial grimaces, hand jerks, or even involuntary vocal utterances, which may be sounds without meaning but also may be real words, including words considered offensive. Tremors are rhythmic movements most often seen in the hands, which can occur when the client is doing nothing (resting tremor) or when the client is attempting a specific motor task. All such behaviors should be observed and carefully described in terms of the actual motor behavior, its frequency, and any antecedent behaviors.

Seizures

One special class of motor disorders may arise from seizure disorders, although seizures are not limited to motor disorders. Most professionals are familiar with grand mal disorders, in which there is shaking of the entire body and a loss of consciousness. However, some motor seizures may be limited to one part of the body or may progress from one part of the body to another. These disorders may not be associated with a loss of consciousness and therefore may look voluntary. Other seizure disorders may result in repetition of an automatic behavior such as grabbing at something in the air, lip smacking, or repeatedly raising a hand. These automatic behaviors (automatons) can be quite simple or complex, but they are usually marked by mindless repetition. The client may appear to be conscious but usually is unresponsive and unaware of his or her own behavior.

Nonmotor seizures may be characterized by specific sensory experiences (e.g., smelling unpleasant smells that are not present, hearing sounds, or seeing visions) that may appear to be psychiatric in nature. Other seizures may involve involuntary experience of sensations such as fear, anger, anxiety, depression, or terror. Such people may act on such sensations by misinterpreting stimuli in their environment (e.g., when feeling sudden terror in the presence of another person, they will interpret that person as hostile or threatening and attack that person in order to "defend" themselves). These disorders are hard to diagnose without a thorough neurological workup, but the presence and pattern of these behaviors can be observed for further analysis and workup.

A final class of seizures may result in brief losses of consciousness without any associated motor behaviors. Such people may simply pause for tenths of a second up to several minutes. This behavior may occur occasionally or many times. One client seen by the authors was documented as having more than 100 seizures per minute, each lasting less than 1 second. Such problems can severely inhibit cognitive and motor skills, causing the person to be described as inattentive, unmotivated, or distracted. However, these seizures differ from simple inattentive or distracted behavior in the person's inability to respond to external stimuli during the seizure.

Language Disorders

Language disorders often are easy to observe when they interfere with expressive speech. In such cases, speech does not sound "normal"; the interviewer may be unable to precisely diagnose the disorder, but most professionals can make observations and describe the problems in the speech. Common disorders can include substituting real or made-up words in speech, an inability to come up with a specific word, a tendency to talk around a word or concept (circumstantial speech), slowness of speech when switching between syllables, an inability to repeat simple sentences or words, slurring, stuttering, loss of the rhythm of speech, speaking in a monotone, and inability to control the loudness of speech. People may cease to use basic connecting words such as *the, a,* or *an* or may speak in telegraphic speech marked by only a verb and noun (e.g., "Dog bark" rather than "The dog is barking"). Specific patterns of disorders may reveal specific types of lesions in the brain, often associated with disorders that create focal injuries such as a stroke, tumor, or even gunshot wound.

Receptive language disorders include mistaking a word for one that sounds alike (*double* for *bubble* or *fork* for *torque*), with the errors ranging from words that are very similar to words that are dissimilar. Sentences that are complex may be misunderstood until they are simplified, and abstract concepts may be misunderstood. Rapid speech may be misunderstood, whereas slower speaking of the same material may be intact. In some cases, the mistakes may be similar to those seen in a client with low intelligence or a lack of education or one who is not a native speaker of the language. However, the symptoms are found to occur when these factors do not seem likely, based on the client's background and past language history. These symptoms can be difficult to identify as neurological when these factors may apply and the history is not clear enough to identify whether there has been a change in language comprehension. In such cases, it remains important to describe the deficits as clearly as possible, even if their origin is unclear.

Attention Lapses

Attentional lapses are common after neurological injuries. During an interview these are characterized by the need to repeat questions, the need to reorient the client to the interview, and the client's inability to sit still and remain focused for longer periods of time. This must be distinguished from slowness in processing or responding (in which case the answer comes without repetition of the question if the interviewer is patient enough) or problems in comprehension in which the answer comes but seems to reflect a misunderstanding of the question. One way to test for these problems is to make questions simpler and to speak more slowly so the client can properly process the questions. As noted earlier, attentional problems may arise from seizures. In some cases these seizures may not be easily seen on routine EEGs and may be identified only from more sophisticated electroencephalographic analysis or extended electroencephalographic testing combined with constant behavioral observation.

Memory Problems

Some memory problems are very obvious when the client is unable to recall even basic historical information. Even in obvious cases, however, the interviewer should try to determine whether the problem is one of access to the memories or storage of memories. Access problems occur in people who are unable to answer direct questions but may reveal the information when speaking of another topic or when asked to recognize rather than recall the information.

Storage of memories is reflected in poor performance, whether in recognition or recall, and an inability to produce information under any conditions. When administering short-term mental status memory exams (e.g., remembering three words over 5 minutes) the interviewer should try a multiple-choice format if the client is unable to remember the words when asked to recall them. It is also important to push clients to guess when administering memory quizzes.

Other memory loss is less obvious in that clients sometimes report historical information as if they remember it when they do not. In such cases, the clients may be filling in or fabricating memories unknowingly. Even if they were given a reliable lie detector test, they would be judged as telling the truth when the information they are giving is actually false. There is also a need to distinguish memory problems from selective memory recall due to one's personal focus during the event. For example, drivers who go through a red light because they assumed it was green and did not actually look may remember (inaccurately) that the light was green when they went through the intersection.

THE ROLE OF COLLATERAL INTERVIEWS AND RECORDS

Because of the many problems involved with direct interviews of neurologically impaired subjects, the interviewer can easily underestimate or overestimate the client's problems even in the absence of overt or intentional malingering or motivational distortion. In such cases, there is a need to rely on collateral records and interviews. In doing this, however, one must not assume that such records are necessarily right or accurate; they may be subject to the exact same errors as a direct interview. In such records, one must distinguish between actual facts (the results of a medical test or direct observation), the client's statements, and the interviewer's opinions or interpretations. The weight that any individual record can be given depends on the source, the qualifications and training of the person presenting the information, and the circumstances under which the information was gathered.

Of foremost importance in records related to a neurologically impaired client is that symptoms are much more likely to be missed than erroneously observed (e.g., in patients with seizures who do not have severe motor symptoms or whose seizures happen rarely, symptoms may easily be missed in a routine, time-limited interview). Such symptoms may be misinterpreted as psychiatric symptoms or even as malingering. It should also be noted that seizures may not begin immediately after a neurological insult, showing up months or even years later. In other cases, subtle language deficits may be missed, as may milder cognitive problems. On the other hand, paralysis or global aphasia is quite unlikely to be missed.

Objective information generally is valued over opinion. Determining what has been observed rather than surmised is essential, as is recognizing what is significant to a neurological diagnosis and what is irrelevant. It is also important not to overestimate the value of neuroradiological or electrodiagnostic devices. EEGs miss up to 50% of all confirmed seizure disorders. Computed tomography scans and MRI can easily miss head traumas and other disorders. In addition, all these techniques must be interpreted by a skilled physician. The level and sophistication of a person's training may cause variations in the accuracy of an interpretation (just as it does in any diagnostic area).

In addition to records, one can conduct interviews with significant others and witnesses of the client's behavior. A weakness in such interviews is that the people with the most salient information about a client's behavior often are those who are closest to the clients personally. Although this is not surprising, it creates biases. A spouse, child, or parent may be in denial about the severity of problems the client is showing, making up excuses or even ignoring obvious behavior as irrelevant. It is again important to separate the opinions and conclusions of the interviewee from actual observations. There is also a clear tendency in close relatives or friends to overidealize the person before a neurological disorder (it is considered unseemly to speak badly of those who are sick or injured), so that they may make the person sound too perfect before the illness or injury. It is important to probe carefully for preexisting problems (made easier by giving the interviewee examples of common problems that "everyone has" so that reporting them does not appear disloyal). It is also important to note how consistent such reports are and whether they make sense.

FORENSIC INTERVIEWS

A special case of interviewing the neurologically impaired client is that of the forensic interview, whether done by the police, a lawyer, a psychologist, a physician, or another professional. Such interviews obviously are sensitive because they may involve large amounts of money in a civil case or someone's freedom (and even life) in a criminal case. Because neurologically impaired clients are difficult to interview accurately even under neutral or positive conditions, it is no surprise that interviews that are adversarial may not yield accurate and relevant information.

Suggestibility

As a result of problems with intelligence, memory, higher cognitive functions, and language comprehension, many of these clients can be intentionally and unintentionally led into appearing to make statements that may incriminate them or make them seem inconsistent or dishonest. In many police interviews, it is not unusual to mislead and confuse detainees using both nonexistent evidence and physical stress (interviewing over several hours), fatigue, deception ("We can help you if you admit you did XX; otherwise you will go to jail." or "We will let you go after you confirm you did this."), phony friendships, deceptions about basic rights, and misleading promises. Interviewers argue that these techniques are simply ways of getting at the truth, but they can also be used to coerce false confessions, especially in what is already a challenged population. It is essential that adversarial interviews be recorded so that a determination can be made about whether the interviewee fully understood his or her rights or the consequences of admitting to specific behaviors. Neurologically impaired people also are susceptible to suggestions as to what happened in memory gaps they cannot fill in themselves.

Confusion

Neurologically impaired clients can be easily confused into agreeing to statements that may falsely implicate them. Physical stress and fatigue can lead to a decrement in cognitive function that makes these people extremely vulnerable. A clever interviewer can manipulate such patients into a corner, leading them to make admissions that are deleterious (but not necessarily true) or lead them to make contradictory statements that compromise the perceived validity of all their statements. An ideal examination should be neutral and oriented toward discovering what actually occurred, but this happens rarely in an adversarial system.

Exaggeration

Neurologically impaired clients may fail to recognize their deficits and may conclude that they can run their own civil or criminal case on their own. The lack of judgment may convince them that they will do better if they exaggerate their symptoms. This leads to malingering behavior that is unnecessary to prove their case. Patients can easily be drawn into such exaggerations by a good examiner. This is often used to "prove" that the client is really not injured, although that conclusion has no basis in fact. An impaired client is just as likely or more likely than a nonimpaired client to choose to exaggerate as a "clever" way of controlling his or her case. For example, one client who had lost most of his anterior frontal lobe exaggerated his symptoms because he believed he would win more money, despite the fact that his real injuries were well documented and clearly supported the claim that he could no longer work or care for himself. After a deposition he even confided to the opposing attorney that there was nothing wrong with him but that he had fooled everyone (including the MRI, apparently). In another case, a client with a well-documented brain injury lied in a deposition about a minor decade-old criminal conviction because he thought that admitting to it would ruin his civil case against the person who injured him. When the judge learned the client had lied, the judge dismissed his suit outright. Such behavior can easily sabotage a court case even when the client is in the right. It is important to remember that although intellectually impaired clients may indeed malinger, that does not mean that they are not seriously impaired.

Emotional Reactions

Neurologically impaired clients often have poor control over emotional reactions. Therefore, they can be led (intentionally or unintentionally) to getting angry and essentially sabotaging themselves. Patient T.J.H. had a clear but focal brain injury. When testing with a supportive examiner, he produced normal test results except in the skills related to his specific injury. However, when tested by the defense psychologist, he became offended at her adversarial approach to the exam and refused to cooperate with any of her tests. She interpreted this as malingering and indicated that all of his claims were malingering. (It should be noted that this particular case was not malingering, as malingering is an attempt to deceive— pretending to cooperate while faking results— whereas refusing to cooperate is not an attempt to deceive but simply not to cooperate. This error is common in evaluations with this type of emotionally overreactive client.)

These clients can easily be made emotional by challenging them, questioning their truthfulness, or acting in a cold fashion while interviewing. Pushing the client to remember missing details can also lead to emotional dyscontrol. Thus, an interviewer can effectively sabotage an interview and therefore can truthfully report that the client was uncooperative.

Denial

Denial in clients is common after head injuries and other disorders. Such clients often deny symptoms that they have because of their lack of insight and awareness of their problems or the impact of their problems. Such people can be easily goaded into disagreeing with their own experts and casting doubt on their accuracy and reliability, even when such behavior runs counter to their own best interest and contradicts more objective evidence. These denials can be used by the opposite side to argue that the client clearly is the best judge of his or her condition. However, this claim is grossly misleading because the neurologically impaired client has a very poor ability to understand the impact of his or her own injury.

SUMMARY

It is evident that many of the symptoms associated with neurological dysfunction can limit the speed, accuracy, completeness, and validity of a clinical interview. The clinician must be aware of the factors that threaten the validity of the examination and weigh what information is of value and what is probably contaminated. The ideal interview is one in which the interviewer uses observation and probes to isolate the likely symptoms associated with the brain disorder while gathering information that is then validated by external records or interviews with those who know the client. Without this balance, conclusions that are based on interviews may be misleading or wrong.

On the positive side, observations made by a skilled examiner may allow identification of many of the symptoms caused by the brain disorder, which can lead to reasonable and often accurate diagnosis of the extent, impact, and cause of a neurological disorder, although the accuracy of such conclusions varies with the kind of disorder present and the neuropsychological knowledge of the examiner. In the hands of a skilled clinician, the interview-exam can often be as accurate as a comprehensive neuropsychological evaluation, although it is more subjective.

25

Older Adults

Lesley P. Koven, Andrea Shreve-Neiger, and Barry A. Edelstein

In 2002, one of out every 14 people on Earth (440 million) was 65 years of age or older, which was approximately 7% of the total population. The size of the older adult population is expected to double by 2020 (9% of the population) and more than triple by 2050 (17% of the population; U.S. Census Bureau, 2004). The world's older adult population grew by 795,000 per month in the year 2000. In 2002 the noninstitutionalized older adult population of the United States was 59.6 million (26.6 million men and 33 million women). The ratio of men to women decreases with age. For example, in 2002 there were 92 men per 100 women in the age range of 55–64; among those aged 65–74, there were 83 men per 100 women; for those aged 75–84, there were 67 men to 100 women, and among adults 85 years of age and older, there were 46 men per 100 women (Smith, 2003).

Older adults were predominantly White in the year 2003. Approximately 82.4% of the older adult (65+) U.S. population was White, 8.2% was African American, 2.8% was Asian or Pacific Islander, and less than 1% was American Indian and Native Alaskan Native. Older adults of Hispanic origin (who may be of any race) represented 5.7% of the population (Administration on Aging, 2004). The older adult population of the United States is less diverse than the younger population. Non-Hispanic Whites had the oldest age distribution in 2002, and American Indians and Alaska Natives, Asians and Pacific Islanders, and Hispanics had the youngest age distribution. Sixty-nine percent of the total population comprised non-Hispanic Whites, with larger proportions among the older adults. For example, for people 65–74 years of age, 80% are non-Hispanic Whites. Among people 85 years and older, 87% are non-Hispanic Whites (U.S. Census Bureau, 2004).

Cultural and Ethnic Issues

As younger adults age, the older adult population undoubtedly will become more diverse, calling for greater cultural competence among clinicians in the assessment interview. There are many reasons for clinicians to become culturally competent (Dana, 2000) and to have knowledge of the prevalence, incidence, and risk factors for mental disorders among older adult ethnic groups (Edelstein, Martin, & Koven, 2003). Psychiatric disorders can present and be experienced differently by different cultural groups. For example, the Hopi Indians of Arizona experience a disorder similar to major depression without the dysphoria (Mouton & Esparaza, 2000). The kinship systems of older adult ethnic groups often define group life and govern the individuals' relationships and status within the culture (Morales, 1999). Older adults tend to rely more on members of their kinship systems and their cultural traditions than younger adults. They may also be more devoted to folk beliefs, religious affiliations, and cultural traditions than their younger counterparts. In general, cultural and ethnic minority older adults tend to be more devoted to their unique cultures and family ties than younger ethnic minority adults (Morales, 1999). When these people encounter problems, the older adults are more likely than younger minority adults to seek assistance from family or community members and less likely to seek help outside the minority community. This is particularly true with psychological problems (Morales, 1999).

Culturally relevant information pertaining to salient environmental factors and psychopathology must be obtained in a fashion that is sensitive to the unique characteristics and history of each client (see Jones & Thorne, 1987). Understanding of the client's ethnic identity can be very helpful in establishing a working alliance and obtaining culturally relevant information. The interview might address spiritual beliefs (or their absence), health practices unique to the client's culture, perspectives on physical and mental health, and client and family expectations regarding mental health care (see Evans & Cunningham, 1996). Avoidance of idioms and colloquialisms in the interview can preclude misunderstandings and misinterpretations. If language difference is a barrier and no trained interpreter is available, one can access a language personal interpreter service through AT&T 24 hours a day at 800-528-5888. There is a sign-up fee, monthly charge, and charge per minute per call.

Several excellent resources regarding multicultural issues and older adults can be found. For example, Goldstein and Griswold (1998) address cultural variations in mental health and specific concerns and clinical manifestations of older adults. Haley, Han, and Henderson (1998) discuss special issues for older minority patients and provide examples of how cultural factors can influence the perception, conceptualization, and diagnosis of mental disorders. Hinrichsen (2006) provides a very thoughtful discussion of multicultural issues for practitioners working with older adults and offers recommendations for the practitioner and teacher. Finally, because the interview is the most commonly used assessment method, one should be aware of relevant cultural and ethnic factors when selecting assessment instruments (Rubio-Stipec, Hicks, & Tsuang, 2000).

BIASES AND MYTHS

Such phrases as "over the hill" and "don't be an old fuddy-duddy" begin to capture an element of what has become known as ageism (Butler, 1969). Butler likens ageism to racism and sexism. Although ageism can be directed at any age group, it is typically directed at older adults. People may be ageist not only with respect to others but also with respect to themselves because most younger adults will become older adults themselves. Butler (1980) describes three components of ageism: prejudicial attitudes toward older adults, old age, and the aging process; discriminatory practices against older adults; and institutional practices and policies that limit opportunities and deny older adults respect and freedom. It is important for clinicians to examine their own attitudes toward and practices with older adults and challenge those that reflect the misconceptions, errors, and stereotyping of ageism.

The myths of aging are ubiquitous, and clinicians are not immune to their effects. Among the many myths of aging (Palmore, 1999) are beliefs that older adults are sick and disabled, have many accidents in their homes, often live in nursing homes, no longer desire sexual activities, and are tired most of the time. In fact, the majority of older adults are healthy and have no limitations on their activities of daily living. Moreover, only 5% of older adults reside in long-term care facilities. Older adults also have fewer injuries in the home and a lower rate of acute illness than younger adults (Palmore, 1999). Healthy older adults have satisfying sexual relations into their 80s. In a survey of more than 10,000 older adults, Brecher (1984) found that 65% of women and 79% of men reported being sexually active. In a sample of 80- to 100-year-olds, Bretschneider and McCoy (1988) found that 62% of men and 30% of women reported currently having sexual intercourse.

COGNITIVE CHANGES IN NORMAL AGING

The cognitive operations involved in information processing, attention, and short-term memory have been the topic of extensive research in the psychology of aging. The study of these processes can be difficult because the majority of participants in a study may have risk factors associated with cognitive decline (e.g., hypertension). Similarly, educational attainment, health, and nutrition in infancy and childhood and exposure to illnesses make it difficult to study age-related changes in cognitive abilities because cohort effects can confound the results (Rubert, Loewenstein, & Eisdorfer, 2004). Despite these difficulties, there are several well-established findings with regard to changes in cognitive abilities associated with aging. Cognitive deficits associated with normal aging can have a significant impact on the interview process. It is important for clinicians to be aware of these cognitive changes so that the validity of the clinical assessment may be maximized.

A consistent finding in the cognitive aging literature is that reaction time increases with age. Salthouse (1996) proposed a general slowing hypothesis that states that increases in reaction time reflect a general decline of information processing speed in the aging nervous system. There is also some research to support an age-complexity hypothesis of reaction time, which suggests that because of the slowing of general processes in the nervous system, age differences increase with increasing complexity of the task (Whitbourne, 2000). It is therefore important for clinicians to speak slowly and present information at a slower pace when working with older adults, particularly when describing new or complex concepts and tasks. Similarly, older clients may need additional time to complete self-report questionnaires and may be slower to respond to interview questions. Therefore, clinicians may want to allow additional time when scheduling assessments with older adults.

Deficits in attention are thought to contribute in part to the slowing of reaction time with age, in addition to having an impact on age-related differences in working memory, reading comprehension, and everyday activities (Rogers & Fisk, 2001). Research on selective attention (attending to relevant information while inhibiting irrelevant information) suggests that older adults do show deficits in this area; however, such deficits are minimal in simple feature searches or when participants are given sufficient practice (Rogers & Fisk, 2001). Research also suggests that older adults show deficits in the ability to inhibit attention to irrelevant stimuli (Hasher & Zacks, 1988). Therefore, it is important for clinicians to eliminate any tangential or extraneous information from instructions and to conduct the assessment in a quiet environment without any stimuli that may distract the older client's attention.

Age-related changes are noticeable in older adults' working memory, the ability to hold information in storage while simultaneously processing new information. Declines in working memory may be related to reduced processing speed (Salthouse, 1993), or they may be related to older adults' difficulty in suppressing irrelevant information once it is called into their working memory (Radvansky, Zacks, & Hasher, 1996). Older adults may also have difficulty retrieving information from long-term memory, particularly if it has not been accessed for long periods of time (Whitbourne, 2000). Over time, memory for past events becomes less vivid and loses detail (Squire, 1989). Finally, research suggests that older adults have difficulties with some types of prospective memory, or memory for future intentions. There are few age differences across adulthood in the ability to perform tasks involving event-based prospective memory (being cued by one event with another). However, older adults show some deficits in their ability to perform time-based prospective memory tasks (e.g., remembering to take medications at certain times of the day; Park, Hertzog, Kidder, Morrell, & Mayhorn, 1997). Given these age-related declines in memory, clinicians may want to provide older adults with verbal or written reminders of instructions to assist with recall. Furthermore, it may be necessary to solicit information about clients from other sources (e.g., past medical records or reports from family members) if deficits in older adults' remote memory interfere with the delivery of accurate information.

CONSIDERATION OF SENSORY CHANGES WITH AGING

It is well established that vision and hearing decline with age. As a result, there is a change in the amount and quality of visual and auditory input that reaches the brain for subsequent processing. When interviewing older adults, it is necessary to consider these sensory changes to maximize the accuracy, reliability, and validity of the assessment.

Vision

Whereas the majority of older adults have fair to adequate vision (Pfeifer, 1980), some of the most severe age-associated decrements occur in the visual system. The level of acuity in 85-year-olds is approximately 80% less than that of people in their 40s, suggesting a loss of 2% per year (West et al., 1997). Indeed, when older adults were asked about their vision, visual acuity was listed as a primary complaint and was associated with unmet needs in daily activities and physical and emotional disabilities (Kline et al., 1992). Visual acuity may be maximized by raising the level of environmental illumination (Whitbourne, 2000). However, clinicians must be aware that older adults are also susceptible to glare, so sudden increases in light or exposure to scattered light can impair rather than improve visual acuity (Whitbourne, 2000). Materials printed on glossy surfaces are particularly vulnerable to glare (Storandt, 1994). During assessment, clinicians should try to balance the older adult's susceptibility to increased glare with the need for sufficient illumination.

Presbyopia is another normal age-related change in vision that creates difficulty focusing on near objects. With increased age, the lens becomes thicker and less elastic and is unable to change shape to focus on close objects (Winograd, 1984). Older adults may have to wear trifocals to achieve good focus of near, far, and middle-distance objects. In order to adequately focus on test materials, older adults may need to shift between components of their glasses to focus on materials presented at different distances, which may slow performance (Storandt, 1994). Clinicians should also be aware that presbyopia often leads to increasing difficulty reading small print. Whenever possible, stimuli should be made larger for older adults. One should consider having written or self-report instruments produced in larger print for use with older clients. Specifically, a 14-point font for written text has been found to maximize visual clarity for older adults with presbyopia (Vanderplas & Vanderplas, 1981). The ability to discriminate colors also diminishes with age, particularly in conditions involving inadequate illumination (Fozard & Gordon-Salant, 2001). Clinicians working with older adults should use materials with good contrast (e.g., black and white) to facilitate visual acuity.

The consequences of visual impairment for older adults are numerous. Visual deficits have been found to be related to intelligence; specifically, visual acuity was found to account for 41.3% of the variance in older adults' intellectual functioning (Lindenberger & Baltes, 1994). Visual impairment has also been found to be related to functional status decline (Stuck et al., 1999; Werner-Wahl, Schilling, Oswald, & Heyl, 1999), anxiety (DeBeurs, Beekman, Deeg, Dyck, & Tillburg, 2000), emotional well-being (Penninx et al., 1998, Werner-Wahl et al., 1999), and everyday activity levels (Marsiske, Klumb, & Baltes, 1997). As a result of visual deficits, older adults may also experience a change in social behavior, including withdrawal from activities requiring visual acuity and difficulty recognizing friends and acquaintances (Edelstein, Drozdick, & Kogan, 1998). It is important for clinicians to take age-related visual deficits into consideration when conceptualizing older adults' problems or changes in all of these areas.

Hearing

Hearing problems are the most common type of impairment reported by people aged 65 years and older (National Center for Health Statistics, 1995). A common communication problem described by older adults is difficulty understanding speech, particularly in environments with extensive ambient noise (Fozard & Gordon-Salant, 2001). Clinicians should be aware of clues that may signal hearing impairment, such as a history of ear infections, loud speech, requests for the interviewer to repeat statements, inability to distinguish the sound of one individual in a group of speakers, and the tendency to keenly watch the speaker's mouth (Vernon, 1989). However, clinicians may also want to directly ask older clients about any difficulties they have with hearing before beginning an interview.

The most common form of hearing loss in older adults is presbycusis, degenerative changes occurring in the cochlea or auditory nerve leading from the cochlea to the brain (Whitbourne, 2000). Presbycusis is most commonly associated with difficulty hearing high-pitched sounds. Female speakers with high-pitched voices should be sensitive to the fact that difficulty hearing high frequencies may impair communication with older adults, and attempts may be made to lower the pitch of their voices (Storandt, 1994). Older adults also commonly experience masking, or difficulty hearing normal speech when there is substantial background noise (Storandt, 1994). Therefore, a quiet environment is essential for interviewing older adults to limit interference. Additionally, when interviewing older adults, clinicians should ensure that clients have a clear view of their face to facilitate lip reading. Speech should be slowed without overarticulation, which can distort speech and facial gestures.

It is impossible to distinguish presbycusis, age-related hearing loss, from hearing loss by hereditary factors, noise exposure, disease processes, ototoxicity, or other exogenous events that occurred through the life span (Willott, 1991). However, multiple changes in the auditory system have been found with aging that make older adults particularly vulnerable to hearing loss. Such changes include a loss of inner and outer hair cells and supporting cells in the cochlea, a decrease of volume of strial tissue on the lateral cochlear wall, and a loss of neurons in the auditory nerve (Fozard & Gordon-Salant, 2001). Furthermore, older adults often have excessive ear wax in the ear canal and a calcification of the tympanic ring and ossicles of the middle ear, which lead to a loss in hearing sensitivity (Kline & Scialfa, 1996).

With the many improvements in hearing aids, much age-associated hearing loss can be corrected without an outwardly detectable device (Whitbourne, 2000). However, personality factors and gender play a role in hearing aid satisfaction and benefit. Older adults who are more extroverted have been found to derive greater benefit from their hearing aids (Cox, Alexander, & Gray, 1999). Additionally, older adults with an external locus of control find the increase in environmental sounds with their hearing aids to be more unpleasant than those with an internal locus of control, who feel that they have control over the rewards and penalties they receive (Fozard & Gordon-Salant, 2001). Women report greater satisfaction with hearing aids than men, who typically report a greater aversion to amplified environmental sounds (Fozard & Gordon-Salant, 2001). Thus, although clinicians should encourage older adults to bring their hearing aids to sessions and wear them during interviews, many older adults have difficulty with the use of amplification and may find wearing hearing aids to be more problematic than coping with diminished hearing acuity.

Communication problems with older adults may be exacerbated as people with hearing loss pretend to understand what is being said during the interview. More critically, reduced hearing acuity commonly has psychological effects. Decreased hearing sensitivity may limit one's enjoyment of social activities and the stimulation that other people and television provide. Withdrawal from other people (Vernon, 1989), depression (Vernon, 1989), denial (Vernon, Griffen, & Yoken, 1981), anxiety (DeBeurs et al., 2000), decreasing functional status (Stein & Bienenfeld, 1992), decreased intelligence and cognitive functioning (Marsiske et al., 1997; Wingfield, Tun, & McCoy, 2005), and rapid deterioration of cognitive functioning in older adults with dementia of the Alzheimer's type (Uhlmann, Larson, & Koepsell, 1986) may also occur in those with gradual hearing loss. Family members and friends may also withdraw from the hearing-impaired person because they are frustrated by efforts to communicate. Furthermore, older adults with hearing impairments may be misdiagnosed because they appear inattentive or withdrawn (Ferrini & Ferrini, 1993).

The aforementioned physiological changes can lead to significant changes in older adults' social behavior, mental health, intellectual abilities, and daily functioning. Clinicians must carefully assess for the presence and severity of sensory impairments when working with older adults. Attempts to minimize the extent to which vision and auditory impairments interfere with the clinical interview and assessment process will facilitate an accurate and reliable assessment. Clinicians must also consider sensory impairments when formulating a conceptualization of the client's presenting problems because erroneous conclusions may be made if these variables are neglected.

MEDICAL AND BIOLOGICAL CONSIDERATIONS

The majority of older adults have at least one chronic disease (Knight, Santos, Teri, & Lawton, 1995). Several diseases of older adults (e.g., chronic obstructive pulmonary disease [COPD], diabetes mellitus, cancer, hypothyroidism, coronary artery disease) can present with symptoms of psychiatric disorders, as a comorbid disorder, as a manifestation of the physical disease, or as a consequence of the physical disease. For example, Parkinson disease often presents with depression (Frazer, Leicht, & Baker, 1996). Starkstein, Preziosi, Bolduc, and Robinson (1990) report a 41% rate of depression among outpatients with Parkinson disease, with 50% of the depressed patients meeting criteria for major depression. COPD often is accompanied by depression, with approximately one quarter to one half of patients with COPD experiencing symptoms of depression (Murrell, Himmelfarb, & Wright, 1983). Van Manen et al. (2002) found the risk for depression among people with severe COPD to be 2.5 times that of controls. These people are also at risk for anxiety associated with the hypoxia and dyspnea that accompany the disease (Frazer et al., 1996). Finally, people with insulin-dependent and non-insulin-dependent diabetes are at risk for developing major depression, with a lifetime risk of approximately 32% (Frazer et al., 1996; Lustman, Griffith, Clouse, & Cryer, 1986). In their meta-analysis Anderson, Freedland, Clouse, and Lustman (2001) found that the presence of diabetes doubles the odds of developing comorbid depression.

Some medical disorders can first present as depression (e.g., pancreatic cancer, Parkinson disease). Similarly, urinary tract infection, which can cause confusion and agitation, can precede detection of the infection and can be misdiagnosed or inappropriately treated as an environmentally caused behavior problem.

To further complicate one's assessment efforts with older adults, most older adults are taking multiple medications. Older adults purchase 30% of all prescription drugs and 40% of all over-the-counter drugs (Williams, 2002) but make up only 13% of the U.S. population (U.S. Food and Drug Administration, 2003). Many commonly prescribed medications and several over-the-counter medications can produce psychological symptoms. For example, some of the inhalants used to treat COPD have the side effect of anxiety. Hallucinations, illusions, insomnia, and psychotic symptoms are possible side effects of various antiparkinsonian agents (Salzman, 2005). Benzodiazepines, used to treat sleep disorders in older adults, can lead to impaired cognitive functioning, confusion, and ataxia. Moreover, many

medications can interact with each other, producing adverse effects on cognition and behavior. Older adults differ from younger adults with regard to the absorption, distribution, metabolism, and excretion (pharmacokinetics) of drugs. For example, drugs often clear, through hepatic metabolism or renal function, more slowly in older than younger adults. Moreover, older adults can be more sensitive to medications than younger adults because of age-related changes in the body (e.g., change in organ function, loss of muscle tissue) that can cause the drug to be more concentrated in the blood. Finally, older adults may be more susceptible to the adverse effects of drugs than younger adults.

Age-related changes in older adult physiology also can affect the circadian rhythms that control a wide range of biological and psychological processes (e.g., body temperature regulation, hormone secretion, sleep-wake cycles, cognition). Each of these processes shows peaks and troughs throughout the 24-hour cycle. For example, various cognitive processes follow this rhythm, with peak performance associated with peak periods of physiological arousal (Bodenhausen, 1990). These peak periods vary with age, suggesting that cognitive assessment of older adults should take into consideration the person's peak and off-peak performance periods (Edelstein et al., 2003).

Sleep should be evaluated routinely when one is interviewing older adults. Inadequate sleep can lead to impaired cognitive performance, reduced energy, impaired concentration, and altered mood. Several age-related changes occur with different aspects of sleep. Age-related physiological changes contribute to alterations in sleep architecture (stages). Older adults tend to spend less time in deep sleep than younger adults, with older adults (particularly men) spending a smaller proportion of sleep time in stages 3 and 4 (delta sleep) than younger adults. Older adults are more likely than younger adults to experience advanced sleep phase syndrome (too early to bed, too early to rise), sleep apnea, restless legs syndrome, and periodic limb movement disorder (National Sleep Foundation, 2005). It is important to keep in mind that older adults need the same amount of sleep as younger adults. Although disrupted sleep is more common among older than younger adults because of age-related physiological changes, sleep problems among older adults often are tied to illnesses and medications also

(Barczi, 2005). For example, pain associated with arthritis can lead to problems initiating and maintaining sleep and to early morning awakening. The sleep deprivation can, in turn, increase the intensity of pain. Other disorders that disrupt, delay, or shorten sleep include gastroesophageal reflux disease, congestive heart failure, chronic obstructive pulmonary disease, end-stage renal disease, and diabetes (National Sleep Foundation, 2005).

AGE-RELATED CONSIDERATIONS IN THE ASSESSMENT OF MENTAL DISORDERS

Depression

Mood disorders in late life often are difficult to detect. There is significant heterogeneity in the presentation of mood disorders in older adults, in addition to comorbid medical conditions and a tendency for older adults to underreport the presence or severity of depressive symptoms (King & Markus, 2000). Nevertheless, the epidemiological data on depression in older adults suggest that it is less prevalent than in younger adults. Among community-living older adults, the prevalence of major depression is between 1% and 3% (Blazer, 1999). In contrast, in acute care or chronic care settings, prevalence rates range from 12% to 20% (Blazer, 1999). When clinically significant symptoms of depression that do not meet the full diagnostic criteria for major depression are considered, the picture is quite different. It is estimated that approximately 8–15% of community-living older adults experience symptoms of depression that interfere with their daily functioning (Blazer, 1999; Marin, 1990).

Presentation of depression among older adults often is very different than among younger adults. As a result, clinicians should be aware that the diagnostic criteria set forth in the fourth edition of the *Diagnostic and Statistical Manual of Mental Disorders* (*DSM-IV,* American Psychiatric Association [APA], 1994) may not adequately reflect the ways in which depressive disorders are experienced by older adults. The most common differences between older and younger adults in the presentation of depression include lower prevalence of dysphoria, fewer ideational symptoms (e.g., guilt, suicidal ideation), and higher rates of selected somatic complaints (e.g., constipation, aches, weight loss) among older adults

(Fiske, Kasl-Godley, & Gatz, 1998). Gatz and Hurwicz (1990) hypothesize that depressed older adults may be more likely to experience a lack of positive feelings rather than active negative feelings. Loss of interest, lack of energy, sleep disturbance, suicidal thoughts, and feeling blue have all been found to best distinguish depressed from nondepressed older adults (Koenig, Cohen, Blazer, Krishnan, & Sibert, 1993; Norris, Snow-Turek, & Blankenship, 1995). Finally, lethality of depression in old age distinguishes it from depression in younger adults. White men, particularly those with medical illnesses or living alone, show an increasing risk of suicide from age 60 to 85 (Conwell, 1994).

Anxiety

Anxiety disorders are the most prevalent group of disorders among older adults. At the same time, however, anxiety disorders remain less common among older adults than in any other age group (Gatz, Kasl-Godley, & Karel, 1996). Estimates range from 10% to 20% of older adults experiencing significant symptoms of anxiety (Banazek, 1997; Beekman et al., 1998). The most common anxiety disorders among older adults tend to be the phobias (agoraphobia, social phobia, specific phobia), with rates of 4.8%. Much lower prevalence rates have been reported for obsessive-compulsive disorder (0.8%) and panic disorder (0.1%). Generalized anxiety disorder appears to occur more often (4.6%), although the actual rate probably is higher given that these data were based on the *DSM-III-R* (APA, 1987) classification system, wherein generalized anxiety disorder was not diagnosed if any other disorder was present.

Although the frequency of anxiety symptoms appears to diminish in late life, the symptoms and characteristics of the anxiety disorders themselves appear to be consistent across age ranges (Stanley & Beck, 2000). However, there is some evidence that the prevalence and content of older adults' fears and worries are different from those of younger adults. For example, Liddell et al. (1991) note a significant decrease in fears with advancing age, and the nature of fears and worries also changes with age (Kogan & Edelstein, 2004). For example, Person and Borkovec found that older adults worried more about health, whereas younger adults worried more about family and finances (as cited in Scogin, Floyd, & Forde,

2000). Thus, the content of worry and fears may reflect developmentally appropriate themes across the life span (Stanley & Beck, 2000).

Personality Disorders

Prevalence rates for personality disorders (PDs) tend to be far more inconsistent and controversial than estimates for depressive and anxiety disorders. Such inconsistencies probably are attributable to the difficulties clinicians and researchers have in accurately diagnosing PDs in older adults but also are related to varying methods, sampling techniques, diagnostic measures, and diagnostic criteria (Segal, Coolidge, & Rosowsky, 2000). To illustrate, Cohen (1990) summarized surveys conducted in the 1980s that showed prevalence rates for PDs among older adults to range from 2.8% to 11%. In contrast, Segal et al. (1998) found rates of PDs to be as high as 63% among a group of senior center members who were administered the Personality Diagnostic Questionnaire Revised that used *DSM-III-R* criteria.

Definitive data are also lacking about the nature of PD symptoms across the life span. There continues to be a lack of consensus in the geropsychological literature as to whether PDs improve with advancing age (Segal et al., 2000). The *DSM-IV* suggests that some PDs (antisocial and borderline) tend to remit with age, whereas other PDs (obsessive-compulsive and schizotypal) tend to remain more stable. Indeed, the maturation hypothesis holds that "immature" personality types such as histrionic, narcissistic, antisocial, and borderline improve with age, whereas the "mature" personality types such as obsessive, schizoid, and paranoid worsen with age (Kernberg, 1984; Tryer, 1988). The improvement of personality disorders with age, such as borderline, may be related to normal decreases in activity level and increases in affective control found with age, leading to lower levels of affective instability and impulsiveness (Zweig & Hillman, 1999).

CONDUCT OF THE INTERVIEW

Informed Consent and Capacity to Consent

Obtaining informed consent from an older adult or legal guardian is a critical first step in the interview process (American Psychological Association, 1998; Halter, 1999). Although the majority of older adults, especially those between the ages of 65 and 79, are cognitively intact, the prevalence and incidence of dementia increase with age (Fitzpatrick et al., 2004). The effects of this disease can have a very gradual and subtle but significant impact on decision-making capacity. In neurodegenerative disorders (e.g., Alzheimer's disease) specific capacities (e.g., to consent to research, manage financial affairs, execute a will, drive, manage medications, live independently, or consent to medical treatment) inevitably will be lost over time (Marson & Hebert, 2005); however, the sequence and progression of these losses are largely unpredictable and may vary from person to person. Decision-making capacity varies greatly according to the degree and stage of cognitive impairment (Pucci, Belardinelli, Borsetti, Rodriguez, & Signorino, 2001).

When it is determined that an older adult does not possess decision-making capacity to offer informed consent to interview, the practitioner must obtain consent from the patient's surrogate decision maker and complete at least part of the interview with that person, who is often the primary caregiver. Surrogate decision makers play a critical role in offering consent for interview, at times participating in interview, and in facilitating access to health care services for many older adults. However, there are a few potential threats to validity and reliability that should be considered.

If the interview is to be conducted with both the client and his or her surrogate decision maker, it is important to remember that as with self-report by clients, self-report by surrogate decision makers may also be prone to psychometric threats. Although assessment of functional status via self-report by an older adult client typically is valid and reliable, Covinsky et al. (2000) found that this is not always so with other areas of functioning. For example, surrogates were more likely than the client to report increased functional dependence retrospectively, before a hospitalization, when in fact the client had been largely functionally independent according to medical records. Similarly, Neumann, Araki, and Gutterman (2000) found that caregivers with more caregiver duties and higher subjective distress provided more negative assessments of the care recipient's health and well-being than did the care recipient. Therefore, if a surrogate is to be used for informed consent and an information resource, one should consider the validity and reliability of the interview in light of the research indicating that surrogates may overreport or exaggerate functional dependency and minimize overall well-being for the cognitively impaired client.

Strategies for Addressing Interviewing Challenges

Older adults may offer interviewing challenges that are more common in older than younger adults. The greater likelihood of medical problems, cognitive decline, cognitive impairment, sensorineural changes, and generational (cohort) differences can all contribute to the challenges encountered by the clinical interviewer. This section addresses some of the more common challenges that arise during clinical interviews with older adults and identifies some possible solutions to the challenges.

Concealment and Resistance. Clinical presentations and endorsement of symptoms vary according to age and cohort (Edelstein et al., 2003; Yesavage, 1992). Prevalence of a socially desirable response bias in older adults, or the attempt to present oneself in a positive (and thus mentally healthy) light when self-reporting, has been well documented (Breemhaar, Visser, & Kleijnen, 1990; Cappeliez, 1989; O'Rourke et al., 1996). In addition to the perceived social stigma associated with presenting with a psychiatric problem, it is likely that some older adults feel they have much at stake when presenting for a clinical interview. They may believe (not always irrationally) that their honest disclosure of cognitive or psychological problems will result in further testing or scrutiny and may eventually result in the loss of freedoms or independence (e.g., driving, living independently). The older adult may actually conceal the "real problem" out of fear of stigmatization, perception of threats to independence, and perhaps a social desirability bias.

Clinicians may find it helpful to use empathy, tolerance, and nonjudgmental listening when a patient presents with multiple somatic problems that are believed to be symptoms of underlying psychopathology (Platt & Gordon, 2004; Steinmetz & Tabenkin, 2001). Platt and Gordon (2004) also recommend paying especially close attention to nonverbal communication (e.g., affect, motor behavior) when interviewing, which may

be less resistant to concealment than verbal forms of communication.

Techniques recommended for addressing concealment in clinical interview include the "plus minus approach," in which the interviewer balances the difficult questions with those that are less threatening. Thus, if a client reacts emotionally or becomes motorically agitated when a specific question is asked (e.g., "Have you recently wished you were dead or would fall asleep and not awaken?"), the interviewer may follow up with a more benign question (e.g., "How many grandchildren do you have?").

Another technique for dealing with a concealing client involves telling him or her that the interviewer is having a difficult time understanding what really happened or is happening. In doing this, the interviewer takes responsibility for the difficult interchange (e.g., it is his or her problem or inability to understand), leaving the client less defensive and perhaps more open to helping the interviewer understand. The interviewer can then follow up by asking open-ended questions, to which the client cannot answer with simple yes-no responses but rather must elaborate on events and feelings.

Thus far, strategies for addressing challenges when interviewing an older adult have related to a client who is purposefully concealing information and is thus resistant to interview. Nonvolitional clinical challenges also may occur during the older adult interview, one of which is fatigue.

Fatigue. As mentioned previously, older adults are at greater risk than their younger counterparts for experiencing sensory deficits (Whitbourne, 2000) and chronic pain (Helme & Gibson, 2001), which can make an interview especially taxing. In addition, the optimal time for performing cognitively demanding tasks tends to be in the morning for older adults because of age-related changes in circadian rhythms (Yoon, May, & Hasher, 1997), as previously noted. Attention is also better during these periods, when older adults are better able to inhibit distracting stimuli.

One strategy for preventing fatigue in the older adult client is to schedule interviews during the client's best time of day, or when he or she believes that his or her cognitive functioning is at its best. If this is not feasible, the interviewer should at least record the time of day in which the interview takes place so that potential influences on performance due to nonpeak assessment may be integrated into interpretation and case conceptualization. If the clinician is aware before assessment that an older adult client does indeed have sensory impairment or chronic pain, the clinical interviewer can be especially vigilant to monitor the client's energy level and apparent changes in concentration or attention as the interview proceeds. Changes in affect such as facial grimaces and somnolence should be noted because they may indicate increased fatigue, frustration, or pain (Cohen-Mansfield, 1999; Strauss, MacDonald, Hunter, Moll, & Hultsch, 2002).

If the client becomes too fatigued to continue, the clinical interview may be shortened so that only the most relevant information (e.g., mental status, presenting problem, brief medical history, past psychiatric treatment) is obtained. The interview also may simply be broken into two separate sessions so that a comprehensive evaluation occurs across two or more sessions.

Disinhibition. Another common challenge encountered when interviewing older adults, especially those with a fronto-temporal type dementia or executive dysfunction, is dealing with disinhibition. Disinhibition as a psychological construct has various components, including inability to suppress distractors (including internal stimuli), inability to control motoric or verbal responses, or inability to sustain attention (Nigg, 2000). Clinically, disinhibition occurs when a client is no longer able to monitor and control his or her behavior in a manner consistent with social norms. Disinhibition may become evident through verbal behavior (e.g., angry and emotional statements, verbal refusal to participate) or physical behavior (e.g., touching the interviewer inappropriately, becoming physically agitated or aggressive).

When a client evidences aggressive behavior, it is often in response to not having a need met, such as difficulties with orientation or frustration with the interview questions, impaired communication, or experience of pain (Talerico, Evans, & Strumpf, 2002). Thus, the interviewer may benefit from doing a brief functional assessment in an attempt to understand the function of the aggressive behavior and address that need by altering his or her own behavior (e.g., focusing on a different part of the interview that is less threatening or uncomfortable for the client, assessing current pain level). In other cases, however, the older adult is simply unable to monitor his or her behavior and must be redirected frequently.

For example, if a client touches the interviewer inappropriately (e.g., attempts to hug or touch the interviewer in a sexual way), one might tell the client that his or her behavior is inappropriate or that it is making the interviewer uncomfortable. Then, the interviewer might shake the client's hand in an attempt to model socially appropriate behavior and prevent further inappropriate behavior by modeling a socially appropriate response that is also incompatible with inappropriate touching. The interview may continue from there or may need to be discontinued depending on the client's ability to be redirected.

If a client is evidencing verbally inappropriate or irrelevant behavior due to disinhibition, the interviewer may listen to the client, acknowledge his or her desire to speak, and calmly but assertively redirect the client by following up with specific, direct, and pertinent interview questions. Using short, succinct questions that do not require sustained attention for a long period of time should also facilitate the interview. On occasion, the clinical interviewer will encounter an older adult whose disinhibited behavior precludes him or her from completing the interview, or the situation becomes a safety risk for the clinician. In these cases, behavioral observations should be carefully recorded and collateral information obtained from a surrogate or caregiver at another time.

PSYCHOMETRICS OF OLDER ADULT INTERVIEW ASSESSMENT

The evidence supporting the reliability and validity of older adult self-report is mixed. The reliability (across informants and time) can vary according to age (Achenbach, Krukowski, Dumenci, & Ivanova, 2005; Fuentes & Cox, 2000; Rodgers, Herzog, & Andrews, 1988). Reasons for this variability are many but may include older adult physical and mental health status changes, changes in physical functioning, and chronic cognitive impairment (Sager et al., 1992).

In their meta-analysis of cross-informant correlations with parallel self-report instruments, Achenbach et al. (2005) found fairly high correlations for substance abuse problems but less robust correlations for externalizing and internalizing problems. The authors conclude that because the correlations vary according to domain and content area, it is important to gather collateral information, especially for problems other than substance abuse, because it could increase the incremental validity of the assessment.

Reliability and validity of older adult self-report also appear to vary according to response format, question format, and content area sampled (Schwarz, 1999). For example, several studies indicate that using self-report for assessment of functional mobility appears to be a largely valid and reliable assessment mode because it correlates highly with true, observed functional mobility (Covinsky et al., 2000; DeBon, Pace, Kozin, & Kaplan, 1995). Similarly, in their literature review, Angel and Frisco (2001) conclude that older adult self-assessments of global health and specific functional capacities are generally valid and reliable.

In contrast, several studies have demonstrated that assessment of memory impairment through self-report is variable in terms of validity and reliability, especially in the case of the cognitively impaired client (Feher, Larrabee, Sudilovsky, & Crook, 1994; Kelly-Hayes, Jette, Wolf, D'Adostino, & O'Dell, 1992; Sunderland, Watts, Baddeley, & Harris, 1986). Validity of older adult self-reports of fatigue (Ekman & Ehrenberg, 2002) and life satisfaction (Rodgers et al., 1988) also varies in terms of internal consistency and poor agreement with observed behavior by others.

Thus, it appears that although the interview is a ubiquitous self-report method for obtaining clinically relevant information, it may prove vulnerable to various psychometric threats when used with older adults. The clinician will serve the client well and ensure a more valid assessment by being aware of these potential threats and supplementing the interview with collateral data (e.g., from records, informants) or using additional assessment measures to support conclusions drawn from interviews.

INTERVIEW FORMAT

Interviews vary in structure from free-flowing conversations with the goal of obtaining relevant information to highly structured diagnostic interviews that carefully guide the interviewer through a series of branching questions and probes. Although structured interviews offer diagnostic precision and strong reliability, they lack the flexibility and forgiving nature of unstructured interviews. The unstructured interview permits rephrasing of questions that appear unclear to the interviewee and the exploration of related topic areas that may be relevant to the presenting problems (Edelstein, Staats, Kalish, & Northrop, 1996). Moreover, the unstructured interview permits one to prompt and encourage responses and maintain the attention of interviewees who have difficulty concentrating.

Diagnostic interviews vary in structure, ranging from the semistructured Structured Clinical Interview for *DSM-IV-TR* Axis I Disorders (First, Spitzer, Gibbon, & Williams, 1996) to the more structured Diagnostic Interview Schedule IV (Robins et al., 1999). Although such interviews have been found reliable when used with older adults (Segal, Hersen, Van Hasselt, Kabacoff, & Roth, 1993), they often take a large amount of time to administer and can tax the physical and mental stamina of some older adults. More narrowly focused diagnostic interviews take less time to administer and consequently are less likely to be burdensome. For example, the Anxiety Disorders Interview Schedule–IV (Brown, DiNardo, & Barlow, 1994) has psychometric support for use with older adults (Diefenbach, Stanley, & Beck, 2001) and takes much less time to administer than the more comprehensive diagnostic interviews. Even if one chooses not to use a diagnostic interview, they can be rich sources of well-formulated questions that may be used in a more unstructured fashion.

SUMMARY

Older adults can offer unique and formidable challenges to the clinical interviewer for a variety of reasons that are discussed briefly in this chapter. The interview assessment of older adults can offer many of the elements and much of the intrigue of a good mystery novel. Each older adult presents with an array of problems that often have multiple determinants and potential solutions. The competent analysis of presenting problems entails an appreciation of the many age-related changes that can directly and indirectly affect the interview process and outcome. Supplementary reading in human development, older adult psychopathology, and the pharmacodynamics and pharmacokinetics of medications commonly used by older adults is strongly encouraged.

REFERENCES

Achenbach, T., Krukowski, R., Dumenci, L., & Ivanova, M. (2005). Assessment of adult psychopathology: Meta-analyses and implications of cross-informant correlations. *Psychological Bulletin, 131*(3), 361–382.

Administration on Aging. (2004). *A profile of older Americans: 2004.* Washington, DC: U.S. Department of Health and Human Services. Retrieved January 4, 2006, from http://www.aoa.gov/prof/Statistics/profile/2004/2004profile.pdf

American Psychiatric Association. (1987). *Diagnostic and statistical manual of mental disorders* (3rd ed., Rev.). Washington, DC: Author.

American Psychiatric Association. (1994). *Diagnostic and statistical manual of mental disorders* (4th ed.). Washington, DC: Author.

American Psychological Association. (1998). What practitioners should know about working with older adults. *Professional Psychology: Research and Practice, 29*(5), 413–427.

Anderson, R. J., Freedland, K. E., Clouse, R. E., & Lustman, P. J. (2001). The prevalence of comorbid depression in adults with diabetes: A meta-analysis. *Diabetes Care, 24,* 1069–1078.

Angel, R. J., & Frisco, M. L. (2001). Self assessments of health and functional capacity among older adults. *Journal of Mental Health and Aging, 7,* 119–138.

Banazek, D. A. (1997). Anxiety disorders in elderly patients. *Journal of the American Board of Family Practice, 10,* 280–289.

Barczi, S. R. (2005, December). Sleep disorders in the geriatric population: Implications for health—Medical illness, medications, and sleep in older adults. *Clinical Geriatrics* (Suppl.), 10–12.

Beekman, A. T. F., Bremmer, M. A., Deeg, D. J. H., Van Balkom, A. J. L., Smit, J. H., DeBeurs, E., et al. (1998). Anxiety disorders in later life: A report from the Longitudinal Aging Study, Amsterdam. *International Journal of Geriatric Psychiatry, 13,* 717–726.

Blazer, D. G. (1999). Depression. In W. R. Hazzard, J. P. Blass, W. H. Ettinger Jr., D. B. Halter, & J. G. Ouslander (Eds.), *Principles of geriatric medicine and gerontology* (4th ed., pp. 1331–1339). New York: McGraw-Hill.

Bodenhausen, G. V. (1990). Stereotypes and judgmental heuristics: Evidence of circadian variations in discrimination. *Psychological Science, 1,* 319–322, 1069–1078.

Brecher, E. (1984). *Love, sex, and aging.* Boston: Little, Brown/Consumer Reports.

Breemhaar, B., Visser, A., & Kleijnen, J. (1990). Perceptions and behaviour among elderly hospital patients: Description and explanation of age differences in satisfaction, knowledge, emotions and behaviour. *Social Sciences & Medicine, 31*(12), 1377–1385.

Bretschneider, J. D., & McCoy, N. L. (1988) Sexual interest and behaviour in healthy 80–102 year olds. *Archives of Sexual Behaviour, 17,* 109–129.

Brown, T., DiNardo, P., & Barlow, D. (1994). *Anxiety Disorders Interview Schedule adult version (ADIS-IV): Client interview schedule.* New York: Oxford University Press.

Butler, R. (1969). Ageism: Another form of bigotry. *The Gerontologist, 9,* 243.

Butler, R. (1980). Ageism: A foreword. *Journal of Social Issues, 36,* 8–11.

Cappeliez, P. (1989). Social desirability response set and self-report depression inventories in the elderly. *Clinical Gerontologist, 9*(2), 45–52.

Cohen, G. D. (1990). Psychopathology and mental health in the mature and elderly adult. In J. E. Birren & K. W. Schaie (Eds.), *Handbook of the psychology of aging* (3rd ed., pp. 359–371). San Diego, CA: Academic Press.

Cohen-Mansfield, J. (1999). Longitudinal predictors of non-aggressive agitated behaviors in the elderly. *International Journal of Geriatric Psychiatry, 14*(10), 831–844.

Conwell, Y. (1994). Suicide in elderly persons. In L. S. Schneider, C. F. Reynolds III, B. D. Lebowitz, & A. J. Friedhoff (Eds.), *Diagnosis and treatment of depression in late life* (pp. 397–418). Washington, DC: American Psychiatric Press.

Covinsky, K., Palmer, R., Counsell, S., Pine, Z., Walter, L., & Chren, M. (2000). Functional status before hospitalization in acutely ill older adults: Validity and clinical importance of retrospective reports. *Journal of the American Geriatrics Society, 48*(2), 164–169.

Cox, R. M., Alexander, G. C., & Gray, G. (1999). Personality and the subjective assessment of hearing aids. *Journal of the American Academy of Audiology, 10,* 1–13.

Dana, R. H. (Ed.). (2000). *Handbook of cross-cultural and multicultural personality assessment.* Mahwah, NJ: Lawrence Erlbaum.

DeBeurs, E., Beekman, A. T. F., Deeg, D. J. H., Dyck, R. V., & Tillburg, W. V. (2000). Predictors of change in anxiety symptoms of older persons: Results from the Longitudinal Aging Study Amsterdam. *Psychological Medicine, 30,* 515–527.

DeBon, M., Pace, P., Kozin, F., & Kaplan, R. (1995). Validation of self-reported dysfunction in older adults. *Journal of Clinical Geropsychology, 1*(4), 283–292.

Diefenbach, G. J., Stanley, M. A., & Beck, J. G. (2001). Worry topics reported by older adults with and without generalized anxiety disorder. *Aging and Mental Health, 5,* 269–274.

Edelstein, B. A., Drozdick, L. W., & Kogan, J. N. (1998). Assessment of older adults. In A. S. Bellack & M. Hersen (Eds.), *Behavioral assessment: A practical handbook* (4th ed., pp. 179–209). Boston: Allyn & Bacon.

Edelstein, B., Martin, R., & Koven, L. (2003). Psychological assessment in geriatric settings. In J. Graham & J. Naglieri (Eds.), *Handbook of psychology: Assessment of psychology* (Vol. 10, pp. 389–414). Hoboken, NJ: Wiley.

Edelstein, B., Staats, N., Kalish, K., & Northrop, L. (1996). Assessment of older adults. In M. Hersen & V. Van Hasselt (Eds.), *Psychological treatment of older adults: An introductory textbook* (pp. 35–68). New York: Plenum.

Ekman, I., & Ehrenberg, A. (2002). Fatigued elderly patients with chronic heart failure: Do patient reports and nurse recordings correspond? *International Journal of Nursing Terminologies and Classifications, 13*(4), 127–137.

Evans, C. A., & Cunningham, B. A. (1996). Caring for the ethnic elder. *Geriatric Nursing, 17,* 105–109.

Feher, E., Larrabee, G., Sudilovsky, A., & Crook, T. (1994). Memory self-report in Alzheimer's disease and in age-associated memory impairment. *Journal of Geriatric Psychiatry and Neurology, 7*(1), 58–65.

Ferrini, A. F., & Ferrini, R. L. (1993). *Health in the later years* (2nd ed.). Dubuque, IA: William C. Brown.

First, M. B., Spitzer, R. L., Gibbon, M., & Williams, J. B. W. (1996). Structured Clinical Interview for *DSM-IV* Axis I Disorders: Non-patient edition (SCID-NP, v. 2.0). New York: New York State Psychiatric Institute.

Fiske, A., Kasl-Godley, J. E., & Gatz, M. (1998). Mood disorders in late life. In B. Edelstein (Ed.), *Comprehensive clinical psychology: Vol. 7. Clinical geropsychology* (pp. 193–229). Oxford: Elsevier Science.

Fitzpatrick, A., Kuller, L., Ives, D., Lopez, O., Jagust, W., Breitner, J., et al. (2004). Incidence and prevalence of dementia in the Cardiovascular Health Study. *Journal of the American Geriatrics Society, 52*(2), 195–204.

Fozard, J. L., & Gordon-Salant, S. (2001). Changes in vision and hearing with aging. In J. Birren & K. W. Schaie (Eds.), *Handbook of the psychology of aging* (5th ed., pp. 241–266). San Diego, CA: Academic Press.

Frazer, D. W., Leicht, M. L., & Baker, M. D. (1996). Psychological manifestations of physical disease in the elderly. In L. L. Carstensen, B. A. Edelstein, & L. Dornbrand (Eds.), *The practical handbook of clinical gerontology.* Thousand Oaks, CA: Sage.

Fuentes, K., & Cox, B. (2000). Assessment of anxiety in older adults: A community-based survey and comparison with younger adults. *Behaviour Research and Therapy, 38*(3), 297–309.

Gatz, M., & Hurwicz, M. (1990). Are old people more depressed? Cross-sectional data on Center for Epidemiological Studies depression scale factors. *Psychology and Aging, 5,* 284–290.

Gatz, M., Kasl-Godley, J. E., & Karel, M. J. (1996). Aging and mental disorders. In J. Birren & K. W. Schaie (Eds.), *Handbook of the psychology of aging* (4th ed., pp. 365–382). San Diego, CA: Academic Press.

Goldstein, M. Z., & Griswold, K. (1998). Practical geriatrics: Cultural sensitivity and aging. *Psychiatric Services, 49,* 769–771.

Haley, W. E., Han, B., & Henderson, J. N. (1998). Aging and ethnicity: Issues for clinical practice. *Journal of Clinical Psychology in Medical Settings, 5,* 393–409.

Halter, J. (1999). The challenge of communicating health information to elderly patients: A view from geriatric medicine. In D. Park & R. Morrell (Eds.), *Processing of medical information in aging patients: Cognitive and human factors perspectives.* Mahwah, NJ: Lawrence Erlbaum.

Hasher, L., & Zacks, R. T. (1988). Working memory, comprehension, and aging: A review and a new view. In G. K. Bower (Ed.), *The psychology of learning and motivation* (Vol. 22, pp. 193–225). San Diego: Academic Press.

Helme, R., & Gibson, S. (2001). The epidemiology of pain in elderly people. *Clinical Geriatric Medicine, 17*(3), 417–431.

Hinrichsen, G. (2006). Why multicultural issues matter for practitioners working with older adults. *Professional Psychology: Research and Practice, 37,* 29–35.

Jones, E. E., & Thorne, A. (1987). Rediscovery of the subject: Intercultural approaches to clinical assessment. *Journal of Consulting and Clinical Psychology, 55,* 488–495.

Kelly-Hayes, M., Jette, A., Wolf, P., D'Adostino, R., & O'Dell, P. (1992). Functional limitations and disability among elders in the Framingham study. *American Journal of Public Health, 82*(6), 841–845.

Kernberg, O. (1984). *Severe personality disorders: Psychotherapeutic strategies.* New Haven, CT: Yale University Press.

King, D. A., & Markus, H. E. (2000). Mood disorders in older adults. In S. K. Whitbourne (Ed.), *Psychopathology in later adulthood* (pp. 141–172). New York: Wiley.

Kline, D.W., Kline, T. J. B., Fozard, J. L., Kosnik, W., Schieber, F., & Sekuler, R. (1992). Vision, aging, and driving: The problems of older drivers. *Journal of Gerontology: Psychological Sciences, 47,* P27–P34.

Kline, D. W., & Scialfa, C. T. (1996). Visual and auditory aging. In J. Birren & K. W. Schaie (Eds.), *Handbook of the psychology of aging* (4th ed., pp. 181–203). San Diego, CA: Academic Press.

Knight, B. G., Santos, J., Teri, L., & Lawton, M. P. (1995). The development of training in clinical geropsychology. In B. G. Knight, L. Teri, P. Wholford, & J. Santos (Eds.), *Mental health services for older adults: Implications for training and practice in geropsychology* (pp. 1–8). Washington, DC: American Psychological Association.

Koenig, H. G., Cohen, H. J., Blazer, D. G., Krishnan, K. R. R., & Sibert, T. E. (1993). Profile of depressive symptoms in younger and older medical inpatients with major depression. *Journal of the American Geriatrics Society, 41,* 1116–1176.

Kogan, J., & Edelstein, B. (2004). Modification and psychometric examination of a self-report measure of fear in older adults. *Journal of Anxiety Disorders, 18,* 397–409.

Liddell, A., Locker, D., & Burman, D. (1991). Self-reported fears (FSS-II) of subjects aged 50 years and older. *Behaviour Research and Therapy, 29,* 205–112.

Lindenberger, U., & Baltes, P. B. (1994). Sensory functioning and intelligence in old age: A strong connection. *Psychology and Aging, 9,* 339–355.

Lustman, P. J., Griffith, L. S., Clouse, R. E., & Cryer, P. E. (1986). Psychiatric illness in diabetes mellitus: Relationship to symptoms and glucose control. *Journal of Nervous and Mental Disease, 174,* 736–742.

Marin, R. S. (1990). Geriatric populations. In M. E. Thase, B. A. Edelstein, & M. Hersen (Eds.), *Handbook of outpatient treatment of adults: Nonpsychotic mental disorders* (pp. 513–539). New York: Plenum.

Marsiske, M., Klumb, P., & Baltes, M. M. (1997). Everyday activity patterns and sensory functioning in old age. *Psychology and Aging, 12,* 444–457.

Marson, D., & Hebert, K. (2005). Assessing civil competencies in older adults with dementia: Consent capacity, financial capacity, and testamentary capacity. In G. Larrabee (Ed.), *Forensic neuropsychology: A scientific approach*. Oxford: Oxford University Press.

Morales, P. (1999). The impact of cultural differences in psychotherapy with older clients: Sensitive issues and strategies. In M. Duffy (Ed.), *Handbook of counseling and psychotherapy with older adults* (pp. 132–153). New York: Wiley.

Mouton, C. P., & Esparza, Y. B. (2000). Ethnicity and geriatric assessment. In J. J. Gallo, T. Fulmer, G. J. Paveza, & W. Reichel (Eds.), *Handbook of geriatric assessment* (pp. 13–28). Gaithersburg, MD: Aspen.

Murrell, S. A., Himmelfarb, S., & Wright, K. (1983). Prevalence of depression and its correlates in older adults. *American Journal of Epidemiology, 117,* 173–185.

National Center for Health Statistics. (1995). *Vital and health statistics: Trends in the health of older Americans: United States, 1994.* Series 3: Analytic and Epidemiological Studies, No. 30. Publication No. 95-1414. Washington, DC: U.S. Department of Health and Human Services.

National Sleep Foundation. (2005). *Sleep and aging.* Washington, DC: Author. Available at http://www.sleepfoundation.org/sleeplibrary/index.php?id=64

Neumann, P., Araki, S., & Gutterman, E. (2000). The use of proxy respondents in studies of older adults: Lessons, challenges, and opportunities. *Journal of the American Geriatrics Society, 48*(12), 1646–1654.

Nigg, J. (2000). On inhibition/disinhibition in developmental psychopathology: Views from cognitive and personality psychology and a working inhibition taxonomy. *Psychological Bulletin, 126*(2), 220–246.

Norris, M. P., Snow-Turek, A. L., & Blankenship, L. (1995). Somatic depressive symptoms in the elderly: Contribution or confound? *Journal of Clinical Geropsychology, 1,* 5–17.

O'Rourke, N., Haverkamp, B., Rae, S., Tuokko, H., Hayden, S., & Beattie, B. (1996). Response biases as a confound to expressed burden among spousal caregivers of suspected dementia patients. *Psychology and Aging, 11*(2), 377–380.

Palmore, E. B. (1999). *Ageism: Negative and positive* (2nd ed.). New York: Springer.

Park, D. C., Hertzog, C., Kidder, D. P., Morrell, R. W., & Mayhorn, C. B. (1997). Effect of age on event-based and time-based prospective memory. *Psychology and Aging, 12,* 314–327.

Penninx, B. W. J. H., Guralnik, J., Simonsick, E., Kasper, J. D., Ferrucci, L., & Fried, L. P. (1998). Emotional vitality among disabled older women: The Women's Health and Aging Study. *Journal of the American Geriatrics Society, 46,* 807–815.

Pfeifer, E. (1980). The psychosocial evaluation of the elderly interviewee. In E. W. Busse & D. G. Glazer (Eds.), *Handbook of geriatric psychiatry* (pp. 275–284). New York: Van Nostrand.

Platt, F., & Gordon, G. (2004). *Field guide to the difficult patient interview* (2nd ed.). Philadelphia: Lippincott Williams & Wilkins.

Pucci, E., Belardinelli, N., Borsetti, G., Rodriguez, D., & Signorino, M. (2001). Information and competency for consent to pharmacologic clinical trials in Alzheimer disease: An empirical analysis in patients and family caregivers. *Alzheimer Disease & Associated Disorders, 15*(3), 146–154.

Radvansky, G. A., Zacks, R. T., & Hasher, L. (1996). Fact retrieval in younger and older adults: The role of mental models. *Psychology and Aging, 11,* 258–271.

Robins, L. N., Cotler, L. B., Bucholz, K. K., Compton, W. M., North, C., & Rourke, K. (1999). The Diagnostic Interview Schedule for *DSM-IV* (DIS-IV). St. Louis, MO: Washington University School of Medicine.

Rodgers, W. L., Herzog, A. R., & Andrews, F. M. (1988). Interviewing older adults: Validity of self-reports of satisfaction. *Psychology and Aging, 3,* 264–272.

Rogers, W. A., & Fisk A. D. (2001). Understanding the role of attention in cognitive aging research. In J. E. Birren & K. W. Schaie (Eds.), *Handbook of the psychology of aging* (5th ed., pp. 267–287). San Diego: Academic Press.

Rubert, M. P., Loewenstein, D. A., & Eisdorfer, C. (2004). Normal aging: Changes in cognitive abilities. In J. Sadavoy, L. F. Jarvik, G. T. Grossberg, & B. S. Meyers (Eds.), *Comprehensive textbook of geriatric psychiatry* (3rd ed., pp. 131–146). New York: W. W. Norton.

Rubio-Stipec, M., Hicks, M., & Tsuang, M. T. (2000). Cultural factors influencing the selection, use, and interpretation of psychiatric measures. In M. B. First (Ed.), *Handbook of psychiatric measures* (pp. 33–41). Washington, DC: American Psychiatric Association.

Sager, M., Dunham, N., Schwantes, A., Mecum, L., Haverson, K., & Harlowe, D. (1992). Measurement of activities of daily living in hospitalized elderly: A comparison of self-report and performance-based methods. *Journal of the American Geriatrics Society, 40*(5), 457–462.

Salthouse, T. A. (1993). Speed and knowledge as determinants of adult age differences in verbal tasks. *Journal of Gerontology: Psychological Sciences, 48,* P29–P36.

Salthouse, T. A. (1996). The processing-speed theory of adult age differences in cognition. *Psychological Review, 103,* 403–428.

Salzman, C. (Ed.). (2005). *Clinical geriatric psychopharmacology* (4th ed.). New York: Lippincott Williams & Wilkins.

Schwarz, N. (1999). Self-reports of behavior and opinions: Cognitive and communicative processes. In N. Schwarz, D. Park, B. Knauper, & S. Sudman (Eds.), *Cognition, aging, and self-reports* (pp. 17–44). Philadelphia: Psychology Press.

Scogin, F., Floyd, M., & Forde, J. (2000). Anxiety in older adults. In S. K. Whitbourne (Ed.), *Psychopathology in later adulthood* (pp. 141–172). New York: Wiley.

Segal, D. L., Coolidge, F. L., & Rosowsky, E. R. (2000). Personality disorders. In S. K. Whitbourne (Ed.), *Psychopathology in later adulthood* (pp. 141–172). New York: Wiley.

Segal, D. L., Hersen, M., Kabacoff, R. I., Falk, S. B., Van Hasselt, V. S., & Dorfman, K. (1998). Personality disorders and depression in community-dwelling older adults. *Journal of Mental Health and Aging, 4,* 171–182.

Segal, D. L., Hersen, M., Van Hasselt, V. B., Kabacoff, R. I., & Roth, L. (1993). Reliability of diagnosis in older psychiatric patients using the Structured Clinical Interview for *DSM-III-R. Journal of Psychopathology and Behavioral Assessment, 15,* 347–356.

Smith, D. (2003). The older population in the United States: March 2002. *Current Population Reports,* 2–5. Washington, DC: U.S. Census Bureau. Retrieved January 4, 2006, from http://www.census.gov/prod/2003pubs/p20-546.pdf

Squire, L. R. (1989). On the course of forgetting in very long term memory. *Journal of Experimental Psychology: Learning, Memory, and Cognition, 15,* 241–245.

Stanley, M. A., & Beck, J. G. (2000). Anxiety disorders. *Clinical Psychology Review, 20,* 731–754.

Starkstein, S. E., Preziosi, T. J., Bolduc, P. L., & Robinson, R. G. (1990). Depression in Parkinson's disease. *Journal of Nervous and Mental Disorders, 178,* 27–31.

Stein, L. M., & Bienenfeld, D. (1992). Hearing impairment and its impact on elderly patients with cognitive, behavioral, or psychiatric disorders: A literature review. *Journal of Geriatric Psychiatry, 25,* 145–156.

Steinmetz, D., & Tabenkin, H. (2001). The "difficult patient" as perceived by family physicians. *Family Practice, 18*(5), 495–450.

Storandt, M. (1994). General principles of assessment of older adults. In M. Storandt & G. R. VandenBos (Eds.), *Neuropsychological assessment of dementia and depression in older adults: A clinician's guide* (pp. 7–31). Washington, DC: American Psychological Association.

Strauss, E., MacDonald, S., Hunter, M., Moll, A., & Hultsch, D. (2002). Intraindividual variability in cognitive performance in three groups of older adults: Cross-domain links to physical status and self-perceived affect and beliefs. *Journal of the International Neuropsychological Society, 8*(7), 893–906.

Stuck, A. E., Walthert, J. M., Nikolaus, T., Bula, C. J., Hohmann, C., & Beck, J. C. (1999). Risk factors for functional status decline in community-living elderly people: A systematic literature review. *Social Science & Medicine, 48,* 445–469.

Sunderland, A., Watts, K., Baddeley, A., & Harris, J. (1986). Subjective memory assessment and test performance in elderly adults. *Journal of Gerontology, 41*(3), 376–384.

Talerico, K., Evans, L., & Strumpf, N. (2002). Mental health correlates of aggression in nursing home residents with dementia. *Gerontologist, 42*(2), 169–177.

Tryer, P. (Ed.). (1988). *Personality disorder: Diagnosis, management, and course.* London: Wright.

Uhlmann, R. F., Larson, E. B., & Koepsell, T. D. (1986). Hearing impairment and cognitive decline in senile dementia of the Alzheimer's type. *Journal of the American Geriatrics Society, 34,* 207–210.

U.S. Census Bureau. (2004). *Global population profile: 2002. International population reports.* Washington, DC: U.S. Agency for International Development.

U.S. Food and Drug Administration. (2003). *Medications and older people.* Rockville, MD: Author. Retrieved January 4, 2006, from http://www.fda.gov/fdac/features/1997/697_old.html

Vanderplas, J. H., & Vanderplas, J. M. (1981). Effects of legibility on verbal test performance of older adults. *Perceptual and Motor Skills, 53,* 183–186.

van Manen, J. G., Bindels, P. J. E., Dekker, F. W., Jzermans, C. J. L., van der Zee, J. S., & Schadé, E. (2002). Risk of depression in patients with chronic obstructive pulmonary disease and its determinants. *Thorax, 57,* 412–416.

Vernon, M. (1989). Assessment of persons with hearing disabilities. In T. Hunt & C. J. Lindley (Eds.), *Testing older adults: A reference guide for geropsychological assessments* (pp. 150–162). Austin, TX: PRO-ED.

Vernon, M., Griffen, D. H., & Yoken, C. (1981). Hearing loss. *Journal of Family Practice, 12,* 1053–1058.

Werner-Wahl, H., Schilling, O., Oswald, F., & Heyl, V. (1999). Psychosocial consequences of age-related visual impairment: Comparison with mobility-impaired older adults and long-term outcome. *Journal of Gerontology: Psychological Sciences, 54B,* P304–P316.

West, S. K., Munoz, B., Rubin, G. S., Schein, O. D., Bandeen-Roche, K., Zeger, S., et al. (1997). Function and visual impairment in a population-based study of older adults. *Investigative Ophthalmology & Visual Science, 38,* 72–82.

Whitbourne, S. K. (2000). The normal aging process. In S. K. Whitbourne (Ed.), *Psychopathology in later adulthood* (pp 141–172). New York: Wiley.

Williams, C. M. (2002). Using medications appropriately in older adults. *American Family Physician, 66,* 1917–1924.

Willott, J. F. (1991). *Aging and the auditory system.* San Diego, CA: Singular.

Wingfield, A., Tun, P., & McCoy, S. (2005). Hearing loss in older adults: What it is and how it interacts with cognitive performance. *Current Directions in Psychological Science, 14,* 144–148.

Winograd, I. R. (1984). Sensory changes with age: Impact on psychological well-being. *Psychiatric Medicine, 2*(1), 1–24.

Yesavage, J. (1992). Depression in the elderly: How to recognize masked symptoms and choose appropriate therapy. *Postgraduate Medicine, 91*(1), 255–261.

Yoon, C., May, C., & Hasher, L. (1997). Age differences in consumers' processing strategies: An investigation of moderating influences. *Journal of Consumer Research, 24,* 329–342.

Zweig, R. A., & Hillman, J. (1999). Personality disorders in adults: A review. In *Personality disorders in older adults: Emerging issues in diagnosis and treatment* (pp. 31–54). Mahwah, NJ: Lawrence Erlbaum.

26

SLEEP DISORDERS

SHAWN R. CURRIE AND JESSICA M. MCLACHLAN

PREVALENCE AND CORRELATES OF INSOMNIA

Trouble sleeping is a common mental health concern. In the general population, insomnia affects about 15.3% of adults (Lichstein, Durrence, Reidel, Taylor, & Bush, 2004). However, largely because of the inconsistent use of diagnostic criteria for defining insomnia, prevalence rates have varied between 9% and 20% depending on the survey (Ancoli-Israel & Roth, 1999; Ohayon, 2002; Partinen & Hublin, 2000). Using the *Diagnostic and Statistical Manual of Mental Disorders* (*DSM-IV*) criteria for primary insomnia, Ohayon (2002) estimates a prevalence of 6% in the general population. An additional 25–30% of adults complain of occasional or transient insomnia (Ancoli-Israel, & Roth, 1999; Ohayon, 2002). Clearly, insomnia affects a significant proportion of both Western and non-Western societies. Twenty-seven percent of the 26,000 patients from 15 countries that participated in the World Health Organization (WHO) International Collaborative Study on Psychological Problems in General Health Care (Üstün et al., 1996) reported persistent sleep difficulties. Prevalence rates of both chronic and transient insomnia tend to increase with age, reaching as high as 50% in some studies (Lichstein et al., 2004; Ohayon, 2002). Furthermore, in the U.S. population, insomnia is more prevalent in women than in men (18% vs. 12%, respectively; Lichstein et al., 2004).

APNEA AND OTHER SLEEP DISORDERS

After insomnia the most common sleep disorder is sleep apnea, which is characterized by the cessation of airflow through the mouth and nose at night. About 2% of women and 4% of men have sleep apnea (Partinen & Hublin, 2000). Unfortunately, because people with apnea generally breathe normally during the day, this very serious disorder often is undetected by medical personnel. Restless legs syndrome and periodic limb movement occur in the general population with about the same frequency as sleep apnea. Functional impairment associated with restless legs and periodic limb movements often is minimal, and so only the most severely affected people tend to seek medical treatment (Montplaisir, Nicolas, Godbout, & Walters, 2000). Dozens of other sleep disorders are described in the International Classification of Sleep Disorders-Revised (ICSD; American Sleep Disorders Association, 1997). The other noninsomnia sleep disorders typically are rare or occur primarily in children (Partinen & Hublin, 2000). All necessitate medical interventions that are beyond the scope of practice for most mental health clinicians. Therefore, the bulk of this chapter focuses on interviewing for the insomnia spectrum disorders.

INTERVIEWING STRATEGIES

Diagnostic Classification Schemes

Although the most widely used diagnostic system for insomnia is the *DSM-IV* (American Psychiatric Association, 1994), this scheme is not preferred by sleep specialists because of the purely descriptive nature of the criteria. The *DSM-IV* takes an atheoretical approach to the origin of mental disorders, so the cause of insomnia is not discussed in the diagnostic description. Primary insomnia in the *DSM-IV* is defined as at least 1 month of persistent difficulty initiating or maintaining sleep, or nonrestorative sleep that also interferes with the person's ability to function during the day or cause clinically significant distress. The ISCD (American Sleep Disorders Association, 1997) definition of psychophysiological insomnia is comparable to the *DSM* system in terms of the symptom severity but also specifies that the condition is maintained by learned cognitive and emotional arousal over the sleep experience. In this conceptual framework, insomnia is described as a condition of somatized tension and conditioned arousal leading to distress and decreased daytime functioning. Although there is often a precipitating event, many learned behaviors manifest in clients over time and are believed to play a dominant role in sustaining the insomnia. A primary goal of the clinical interview is to identify these learned behaviors so they may be targeted for change during treatment.

Unfortunately, neither classification scheme provides quantitative criteria for distinguishing normal from abnormal sleep. In order to differentiate between normal and abnormal sleep, researchers have adopted the following quantitative criteria to identify insomniacs: The person must have either a sleep onset latency (SOL) or a time awake after sleep onset (WASO) greater than 30 minutes for a minimum of three nights per week. Validity of these criteria was recently established by sensitivity-specificity analysis (Lichstein, Durrence, Taylor, Bush, & Riedel, 2003).

Sleep behavior can also be quantified in terms of how often the client wakes up (number of awakenings), the client's total sleep time (TST, in minutes or hours), the client's sleep efficiency (SEF, the ratio of hours slept to time in bed, up to a maximum of 100%), and the client's satisfaction with his or her sleep, generally called sleep quality (usually assessed with a numerical rating scale such as 0–10, with 0 = *extremely poor* and 10 = *extremely good*). Normative thresholds have also been defined for TST (less than 6.5 hours) and SEF (less than 85%) for distinguishing normal from abnormal sleep (Lacks & Morin, 1992; Morin et al., 1999; Smith, Nowakowski, Soeffing, Orff, & Perlis, 2003).

An important criterion for the clinical diagnosis of insomnia is evidence of compromised daytime functioning. Many people complain of poor sleep but report no distress or consequences to their daytime functioning (Fichten et al., 1995). Assessing consequences of sleep dysfunction in terms of work performance, vigor, mood, cognitive functioning, reliance on sleep medication, and overall quality of life is an equally important area of clinical interviewing. Roth (2004) recently reviewed the evidence that TST and measures of sleep continuity are correlated with alertness, memory, psychomotor performance, risk of car accidents, and pain threshold. Insomnia is also associated with increased depression (Breslau, Roth, & Rosenthal, 1996; Chang, Ford, & Mead, 1997; Ford & Kamerow, 1989), absenteeism (Zammitt, Weiner, & Damato, 1999), accidents (Balter & Uhlenhuth, 1992), and increased health care use (Simon & VonKorff, 1997).

Structured and Semistructured Interviews

Symptoms of insomnia are routinely assessed in mental health settings because disturbed sleep is a symptom of numerous psychiatric disorders in the *DSM-IV*. Therefore, questions about sleep quality often are asked in the context of a structured or semistructured interview for depression, anxiety, and a range of mental disorders. Such brief, global, retrospective assessments of sleep are not necessarily inaccurate, but they lack the depth of information necessary for properly diagnosing a sleep disorder. To plan specific interventions for sleep, a full-length interview is needed. The goals of the initial clinical interview can be broad or narrow, depending on the nature of the presenting complaint and the needs of the client. In general, the interview documents the severity and natural history of insomnia, screens for other sleep disorders, explores the contribution of psychological factors in the onset and maintenance of insomnia, and identifies what additional assessment procedures are needed. At a minimum, the clinical interview should collect sufficient information to make a preliminary diagnosis, screen for noninsomnia disorders, and rule out other causes of the person's sleep complaint. In most settings, a semistructured interview is the appropriate format for gathering information and building rapport with the client. Ideally, the clinician should strive to complete a comprehensive evaluation of the history of the client's sleep problem, including impact on daytime functioning, current sleeping habits, health behaviors (diet, exercise, and substance use), medical history and medication use, history of psychopathology, and past treatment for sleep problems, including attempts at self-management.

A structured interview for sleep disorders is also available to aid in diagnostic decision making. Schramm et al. (1993) developed the Structured Interview for Sleep Disorders for *DSM-III-R* (SIS-D) for use in psychiatric settings. The SIS-D consists of a structured inquiry about specific symptoms of sleep disorders as defined by the *DSM* classification scheme. Although it was originally developed using the *DSM-III-R* criteria (American Psychiatric Association, 1987), through several research studies, my colleagues and I have adapted the interview to include *DSM-IV* criteria (Currie, Clark, Rimac, & Malhotra, 2003; Currie, Wilson, Pontefract, & deLaplante, 2000). Also worth noting is the Sleep-EVAL system (Ohayon, 1996), a computerized interview for assessing sleep disorders in epidemiological research. Like our adaptation of the SIS-D, the Sleep-EVAL system uses a combination of *DSM-IV* and ICSD criteria in the determination of insomnia disorder. Structured interviews typically are reserved for research applications.

Functional Analysis

The functional analysis is considered the hallmark of behavioral assessment (Ollendick, Alvarez, & Greene, 2004). In the context of sleep assessment, a functional analysis would encompass a detailed evaluation of the precipitants, antecedents, possible secondary gains (e.g., sick role), and perpetuating factors functionally related to the sleep complaint. In clinical terms, a functional analysis is what distinguishes the assessment of insomnia as a disorder rather than a symptom of another condition. It should also identify the key maintenance factors in the client's insomnia, which will become the focal point of change during treatment.

A central tenet of the cognitive-behavioral model of insomnia is that insomnia is maintained by maladaptive sleep activities (Espie, 1991; Morin, 1993). These activities can be cognitive (covert) or behavioral (overt) (Morin, 1993). Overt maladaptive behaviors include using the bedroom for activities other than sleep or sex (e.g., watching TV, reading), engaging in stimulating activities before bedtime (e.g., problem solving with spouse, drinking coffee, exercise, working on the computer), and remaining in bed for long periods when not able to sleep. Incompatible cognitive activities could include using the presleep period for rehashing the day's events, focusing excessively on insomnia and its consequences, and trying to force the sleep process. The conditioning model of insomnia proposes that when sleep-incompatible behaviors are repeated over time, a mental association is formed between the bedroom and a state of arousal. Similarly, the bedroom environment and the usual temporal cues to sleep (i.e., the bedtime hour) lose their sleep-inducing properties. Additional cognitive responses (e.g., performance anxiety or apprehension while trying to fall asleep) may be formed as a consequence of repeated sleep-incompatible activities.

Inadequate coping attempts may further reinforce the persistence of insomnia. In many cases, the coping strategies insomniacs develop maintain rather than ameliorate the sleep disorder. For example, napping in response to a poor night's sleep, although immediately gratifying, can lead to additional sleep fragmentation at night. In response to daytime fatigue, insomniacs may consume excess caffeine and curtail daytime activities. Lack of regular exercise can further perpetuate poor sleep. Insomniacs often resort to sedative medications, both prescription and over-the-counter, in an attempt to improve their sleep. Pharmacological sleep aids have limited empirical evidence of long-term efficacy and are thought to maintain insomnia if taken for extended periods (Smith, Smith, Nowakowski, & Perlis, 2003).

A functional analysis should include a detailed inquiry of the client's attempts at self-management and the perceived benefits. Clients often are reluctant to abandon coping responses, even ones that seem to be incompatible with good sleep hygiene. Harvey (2002) introduced the concept of a sleep safety behavior, which is a maladaptive response to the anxiety caused by chronic insomnia. For example, the fearful thought that a poor night of sleep will impair performance at work may lead to the client calling in sick and trying to recover lost sleep by napping during the day.

Charles Morin (1993) provides a template for a detailed functional analysis. Key questions in the assessment include the following:

- What is your bedtime routine like?

- What do you do when you can't fall asleep or return to sleep?

- How is your sleep different when you go away from home?

- How does your sleep differ between weekdays and weekends?

- What things exacerbate your sleep problems?

- What are the things that improve your sleep?

- What impact does insomnia have on your life (mood, alertness, performance)?

- How do you cope with the impairment caused by your sleep problem? How effective are these strategies?

- How has your insomnia changed over time (getting better, getting worse, staying the same)?

- What prompted you to seek insomnia treatment at this time?

The functional analysis should be integrated with other sleep assessment procedures. These can include sleep questionnaires, self-monitoring, and collateral interviews. For example, the Dysfunctional Beliefs and Attitudes About Sleep Scale (Morin, 1993) can serve as a useful augment to the functional analysis. This scale assesses negative thoughts and unrealistic expectations about sleep, insomnia, and the consequences of sleep loss. A popular instrument in research (Espie, Inglis, Tessier, & Harvey, 2001) is equally effective as a clinical tool for identifying specific dysfunctional thoughts that may be maintaining sleep-incompatible behaviors. The client's highest score on the five subscales (misconceptions about the causes of insomnia, need for control over insomnia, magnifying consequences, unrealistic sleep expectations, and faulty beliefs about sleep-promoting practices) can be used to initiate discussion about the consequences of holding such negative thoughts. On a final note, the functional analysis does not end

with the assessment phase. Clinicians should continually assess the functional relationship between sleep behaviors and sleep quality throughout treatment.

A spouse or roommate can provide invaluable information on a client's sleep pattern that can assist in diagnosis and treatment planning. The observations of a bed partner can be especially helpful in ruling out noninsomnia causes of the client's poor sleep. A directed inquiry can help determine whether the sleep complaint is caused by sleep apnea, restless legs syndrome, periodic limb movements, or a parasomnia. Specific questions to ask collaterals include the following:

- Does the client snore loudly, gasp, choke, or stop breathing at night (symptoms of sleep apnea)?

- Does the client complain of creeping, crawling, or uncomfortable feelings in his or her limbs that is relieved by moving them (restless legs syndrome)?

- Do the client's legs or arms jerk repeatedly during sleep? Are you kicked in bed throughout the night (periodic limb movement)?

- Does the patient sleepwalk? Does he or she wake up during the night in a terrified state and have no memory of the event in the morning (night terrors)?

Collaterals can also corroborate the severity of primary insomnia symptoms. Insomniacs are known to overestimate sleep onset and underestimate sleep duration (Carskadon et al., 1976). In extreme cases (e.g., clients who report an SOL greater than 2 hours; SEF less than 60%), it is helpful to obtain a bed partner's estimate of time to fall asleep, sleep duration, and awakenings to assess whether sleep state misperception may be a factor. Finally, the collateral's assessment of lifestyle factors (caffeine use, alcohol consumption, exercise) and the impact of insomnia on the client (e.g., daytime fatigue) may assist in the overall evaluation and treatment planning.

Clinicians should also consider the bed partner's role in maintaining the client's insomnia or practice of maladaptive sleep behaviors. For example, a bed partner's insistence on watching television in bed may contribute to the insomniac's conditioned arousal in the sleep environment. Similarly, a bed partner's own irregular sleep pattern may be having a detrimental effect on the client's insomnia. On the positive side, bed partners can be sources of support for the client during cognitive-behavioral treatment. The implementation of stimulus control can be conjoint activity if some of the negative sleep behaviors are indirectly the result of the bed partner.

INTERVIEWING OBSTACLES AND SOLUTIONS

Overreporting of Sleep Dysfunction and Consequences

Objective-Subjective Discrepancy. Severity of sleep dysfunction reported by the insomniac often disagrees with other measures of sleep. In a landmark study, Carskadon et al. (1976) found that insomniacs overestimated time to fall asleep and underestimated sleep duration by approximately 30 minutes each. Similar studies conducted over the past 25 years have produced the same basic results (Edinger & Fins, 1995; Rosa & Bonnet, 2000). Good sleepers also overestimate SOL and underestimate TST although to a lesser degree. Summarizing across eight studies of good sleepers, Lacks (1987) found an average discrepancy between sleep diary and polysomnography (PSG) estimates for SOL of about 15 minutes in normal sleepers.

Several explanations have been advanced to explain the lack of agreement between self-reported and objectively measured sleep (see Currie, 2006). One possibility is that insomniacs exaggerate the severity of their sleep dysfunction. On personality tests, insomniacs score highly on measures of neuroticism and hypochondria (Morin, 1993; Rosa & Bonnet, 2000). These people may be predisposed to overreport symptoms of distress, including sleep problems (Smith, Smith, et al., 2003). This view is generally acknowledged, but most experts do not agree that insomnia is due solely to psychopathology and therefore does not represent a real health problem. Insomnia is similar to other psychophysiological disorders in that factors other than biology mediate the presentation and course of the condition.

The extent of exaggeration can vary from a matter of minutes to more than an hour (Currie, 2006; Rosa & Bonnet, 2000). The extreme end of the continuum is represented by the condition known as sleep state misperception (SSM). This is a subtype of insomnia in which clients are thought to confuse sleep and waking states to such an extreme degree that they often claim to get little or no sleep at all (Trinder, 1988). However, objective recordings reveal these people to have essentially normal sleep (SSM is also called subjective insomnia without any objective finding), yet their psychological profiles and self-reported daytime impairment are the same as those of insomniacs (Sateia, Doghramji, Hauri, & Morin, 2000). Although SSM is considered a distinct sleep disorder in the ICSD, many researchers argue that SSM represents the extreme of the subjective-objective discrepancy evident in all insomniacs (Edinger & Fins, 1995; Morin, 2000; Sateia et al., 2000; Trinder, 1988).

Cases of SSM or extreme exaggeration of insomnia severity present as interesting assessment challenges. Clinicians may be initially suspicious of claims of less than 4 hours of sleep per night, reported SEF values of 60% or less, or claims of going days with no sleep at all. Accompanying these extreme nocturnal symptoms may be excess claims of daytime impairment and health-related concerns. Clients may report exaggerated concerns that their insomnia will be fatal or may lead to other medical problems. Interestingly, research comparing insomniacs and normal sleepers has revealed few differences in daytime fatigue levels, cognitive functioning, or psychomotor performance between groups (Sateia et al., 2000). Such people tend to respond poorly to behavior-oriented treatment, often believing that only medication or compensatory sleep (i.e., napping) can ameliorate their symptoms.

Solutions. Interviewing clinicians should be aware that most insomniacs overreport symptoms to a certain degree. It is important to prioritize the subjective perception of inadequate sleep over any objective assessment results. Although self-report and PSG tend to produce different absolute sleep estimates, both generally indicate a sleep problem. Furthermore, diary and PSG measures tend to correlate highly with one another (Currie, 2006; Lacks, 1988). Clinicians need be concerned when the severity of self-reported insomnia seems extreme or highly improbable (e.g., claims of sleeping only 2–4 hours per night). Concern may also be raised when a client reports during the initial interview no variation in his or her nightly sleep pattern (e.g., reports sleep quality as being extremely poor every night of the week). Some suggested solutions for managing these clients include the following:

- *Objective sleep assessment.* Clients can be referred for an overnight PSG or, if available, arrange for several nights of actigraph recordings (Sadeh, Hauri, Kripke, & Lavie, 1995). The objective feedback may help correct clients' misperception about their sleep duration. They may obtain some relief knowing they are getting more sleep than originally estimated.

- *Self-monitor with a sleep diary.* Prospective self-monitoring is always a good assessment tool, but with these clients it can be invaluable to help document that some variation in sleep pattern occurs during a typical week. A limitation of retrospective reports is that clients make broad judgments about their sleep quantity and quality. They may selectively report on their most recent night of sleep or the worst-case scenario when making judgments rather than make a true personal average (Gehrman, Matt, Turingan, Dinh, & Ancoli-Israel, 2002).

- *Education on the nature of sleep and insomnia.* Emphasizing that sleep needs are highly individual may help to normalize clients' perceptions of their insomnia. Clients can be told that many people appear to function adequately on little total sleep time.

- *Construct an inventory of real and projected consequences.* Many insomniacs predict dire daytime consequences arising from their insomnia that in many cases never materialize (largely because they avoid the feared situation). Constructing an inventory of feared and actual consequences may help to correct the client's beliefs about the disabling nature of his or her insomnia.

- *Set realistic goals for improvement.* It would be unrealistic to expect a client with a self-reported SOL of 2 hours to fall asleep within 15 minutes with any kind of intervention. Accordingly, promising a client such a dramatic improvement is likely to result in disappointment when the treatment goal is not met and may reinforce the client's belief in the catastrophic nature of his or her sleep loss. Clients with extreme insomnia symptoms may be more receptive to treatment goals that are framed as a percentage improvement (e.g., a 25% reduction in SOL) rather than change in absolute time units.

Externalization of Causes of Sleep Dysfunction

Clients being interviewed in preparation for cognitive-behavioral treatment for insomnia should identify at least some behavioral or psychological factors contributing to their sleep problems. Although it is common for insomniacs to make attributions of cause to factors out of their control (e.g., medical conditions, weather, bed partner snoring), clients presenting with extreme attributional bias can pose a serious obstacle to psychological treatment. Like those with "catastrophic insomnia," these clients may resist the suggestion that changes in their own behavior are necessary to improve sleep.

Solutions. Foremost, one cannot assume that a client's externalization of the source of his or her sleep problem is completely in error. During the initial assessment, it is vital to establish that there is no underlying or external primary cause for the client's poor sleep. Clinicians should conduct a thorough medical and psychiatric history to rule out a primary disorder being the source of the client's insomnia. Similarly, it is important to rule out other sleep disorders, many of which can have symptoms similar to those of insomnia (e.g., insomnia and sleep apnea are both associated with daytime fatigue). Even after medical explanations for insomnia have been eliminated, clients may continue to blame their poor sleep on out-of-control factors. Suggested management strategies include the following:

- *Emphasize maintenance over etiological factors in insomnia.* The role of sleep habits, psychological state, and beliefs in maintaining poor sleep should be explained to the client. Some insomniacs may resist the idea of psychological factors being the cause of their sleep problem but are receptive to the notion that psychological and behavioral factors can maintain insomnia. We have found diabetes to be a good medical analogy to use with sleep clients. Although diabetes is caused by a biochemical imbalance, we also know that lifestyle and health behaviors can maintain and worsen diabetes even with insulin treatment. The successful management of diabetes requires behavior change and continued self-monitoring.

- *Self-monitoring of sleep hygiene adherence.* The sleep diary from Dr. Charles Morin's lab (described in Bouchard, Bastien, & Morin, 2003; provided in Currie, 2006) includes items for assessing good sleep habits. For example, clients are asked to report on the number of times they leave the bed when unable to sleep. Having the client monitor his or her sleep habits and practice of stimulus control may help to raise the client's awareness of the role of behavioral factors in insomnia.

- *Behavioral experiments.* A client can be encouraged to make a behavioral change to test the veracity of beliefs about the cause and behavioral treatment of sleep dysfunction. For example, many clients are reluctant to implement sleep restriction. The procedure involves having the insomniac reduce his or her time in bed to the total sleep time recorded during a baseline period. The aim of sleep restriction is to consolidate sleep into a shorter time period in bed (Morin, 1993). To many insomniacs the procedure seems counterintuitive given their preconceived belief about the need for more rather than less sleep. However, after trying it most clients are surprised to see how well it improves their sleep. The new information acquired through the behavioral experiment provides the impetus for changing a sleep-related belief.

Psychiatric Comorbidity

Comorbidity is a universal challenge that mental health clinicians face. Mental disorders rarely occur in isolation (Kaplan & Sadock, 2002), and sleep disorders are no exception (Ohayon, 2002). Specific issues in assessing primary and secondary insomnia are discussed later in this chapter. Comorbidity can be an obstacle during the clinical interview if clinicians find themselves unable to direct a focused discussion on sleep because the client seems overwhelmed with other mental health concerns. Clinicians may also encounter clients seeking an alternative treatment for their primary psychiatric illness. Clients who are refractory to conventional treatment may "doctor-shop" for a new therapist in a desperate attempt to relieve their symptoms. Such clients tend to have long but unsuccessful treatment histories including multiple therapists, hospitalizations, and numerous medication trials.

Solutions. There are no straightforward solutions for managing clients with moderate to severe psychopathology. Each case must be assessed individually and the decision to treat or not treat insomnia clearly explained to the client. Generally, the treatment of insomnia should not take precedence over another mental disorder, particularly one that is untreated or undertreated. In assigning treatment priority it is important to consider the client's preference, the stability of the comorbid condition, and his or her ability to fully engage in behavioral treatment for insomnia. On the other hand, medical or psychiatric comorbidity does not preclude focused treatment of insomnia. Nonpharmacological treatment for insomnia can be initiated concurrently if the other disorder is stable and the client is motivated to address the sleep disorder. Recent research suggests that targeting insomnia in treatment can alleviate depressive symptoms in the absence of any specific interventions for depression (Morawetz, 2003). Similarly, there is ample evidence of cognitive-behavioral therapy's efficacy in the treatment of secondary insomnia (Currie et al., 2000; Currie, Clark, Hodgins, & el-Guebaly, 2004; Lichstein, McCrae, & Wilson, 2003). If sleep-focused treatment is to be initiated, the goals of therapy and the role of the therapist should be conveyed unambiguously. Most important, treatment should be coordinated with the client's other care providers to avoid duplication of services. Furthermore, treatment providers should agree on the role of drug therapy as a complement to behavioral treatment.

Different Stages of Readiness to Change

The preceding obstacles centered on potential problems with the client. For the last obstacle, we discuss potential problems with the clinician's style of interviewing. Nonpharmacological treatment of insomnia is an action-oriented approach. Success in treatment requires the client to make clearly prescribed changes to his or her sleep habits to achieve a more satisfying sleep pattern. These can include avoiding napping, getting out of bed when not sleeping, restricting time in bed, and avoiding caffeine (Morin, 1993). These techniques are well researched and proven to be effective in treating insomnia (Morin, Hauri, et al., 1999). However, these methods also depend on the client's willingness to change and his or her ongoing adherence to behavior change. The stage of change model (Prochaska, DiClemente, & Norcross, 1992) has dominated the field of health psychology and behavioral medicine in the past 20 years. Although originally conceived for addictive behaviors, the principals of stage of change and the related motivational interviewing model (Miller & Rollnick, 2002) have been extended to other health behaviors (Resnicow, Dilorio, Borreli, Hecht, & Soet, 2002), including sleep treatment (Aloia, Arnedt, Riggs, Hecht, & Borrelli, 2004). Failure of the clinician to assess and match interventions to the client's stage of readiness to change can create frustration for both parties. Clinicians may assume the client is resistant, playing the sick role, or being difficult. Clients may experience the clinician as authoritative, demanding, insensitive to their difficulties in initiating change, and even confrontational. Some suggested solutions are as follows:

• *Plan interventions based on the client's personal goals for sleeping better and stage of readiness.* A central tenet of the motivational interviewing approach is that clients should develop their own reasons for change (Miller & Rollnick, 2002). In the case of insomnia, clients ideally should set their own goals for sleeping better. Motivation to change can be assessed by asking the client how improved sleep would enhance his or her quality of life. Nevertheless, the clinician cannot assume the client is ready to embrace the level of behavior modification needed to achieve better sleep in the cognitive-behavioral approach. Clients may want to sleep better but are poorly motivated to change their current habits to achieve this goal. Some useful questions to assess motivation are as follows:

- What are the advantages of changing some of your sleep habits? What are the advantages of things staying the same?

- What do you see happening in the next year if you make no changes to your sleep habits?

- How prepared do you feel to make changes to your current bedtime routine? What are some obstacles to changing your sleep schedule?

- What aspects of your sleep habits are you not interested in changing? Why?

• *Focus on small changes first.* For clients who are especially resistant to making large changes to their sleep habits, a gradual approach

to applying interventions is recommended. Clients can be presented with a menu of change options (e.g., sleep restriction, stimulus control, relaxation) and asked to pick one they feel ready to apply. Stimulus control, considered the core intervention in the behavioral treatment of insomnia, can be implemented gradually. For example, a client could start by adhering to a regular rising time every morning. The remaining instructions can be phased in over time. The downside with this approach is that clients may experience little improvement in their sleep by implementing only small changes and could get discouraged from taking further steps.

• *Emphasize personal choice.* The decision to change lies with the client. Some clients may opt to make no changes or pursue medication as an alternative to behavior therapy. Clinician should avoid arguing or using scare tactics (e.g., "Your sleep is only going to get worse if you don't start treatment.") to get clients to change. An overly directive approach is likely to be met with resistance in clients who are not convinced their sleep habits are maintaining their insomnia. In such cases, the clinician should focus on increasing the client's awareness of the relationship between sleep behaviors and sleep quality.

Case Illustration With Dialogue

The following case demonstrates a typical initial interview as part of the first phase of cognitive-behavioral therapy for insomnia. The case is also an illustration of the complex nature of insomnia when a history of another mental health problem is evident. In such cases, one cannot independently assess insomnia; the history and presentation of the other disorder must be considered.

Peter is a 38-year-old self-employed real estate agent. He lives with his wife of 12 years and their two daughters, aged 6 and 10. Peter was referred to a psychologist by his family doctor. The referral letter indicated no history of serious physical health problems but a recent history of alcohol dependence in early remission. In his 20s, Peter regularly binge drank (five or six drinks per occasion) about three times per week. Around age 28, he started to drink every evening to wind down. By age 35, Peter was drinking four or five drinks every night to help him sleep and more on the weekends when out with friends. Gradually, his sleep schedule became increasingly erratic. During a slump in the housing market, Peter's real estate business did poorly, and he became very depressed for about 3 months. This resolved, but he continues to experience periods of mild depression.

About 2 years ago, Peter's wife started to complain about his sleeping late and the decrease in income from his real estate job. After coming home from work one day, she was shocked to discover Peter still in bed at 4:30 p.m. with an apparent hangover. She insisted they see their family doctor together. Blood work revealed his liver enzymes to be significantly elevated, indicating significant alcohol consumption. At that point, Peter disclosed the full extent of his drinking and agreed to attend a residential alcohol program. Peter's last drink was about 5 months ago, but he reports strong urges to resume drinking. Despite the improvement in his drinking, Peter continued to experience insomnia and asked his family doctor to prescribe him something stronger for sleep (he takes 50 milligrams of trazodone both as a sedative and for depression). At that point, his family doctor referred him to the psychologist for assessment and treatment of insomnia.

Interviewer:	Good morning. What's your understanding about why your family doctor referred you to me?
Peter:	To be honest, I wasn't thrilled about seeing a shrink. However, my doctor wanted me to look at some ways of sleeping better without using drugs. He didn't want to prescribe me any sleeping pills because I'm an alcoholic.
I:	How are you making out with the alcohol problem?
P:	Pretty good; not a drop in 5 months. But I get urges every night to drink. That's why I asked for the sleeping pills. I figure pills are better for me than starting to drink again.
I:	It is not uncommon for alcoholics to continue to have sleep problems even after they quit drinking. It seems to take the brain a long time to recover from alcohol. We also know that sleeping pills are not a good long-term solution. In the end, they seem to help maintain the sleep problem rather than improve it.
P:	So what can I do?
I:	Before we get into treatment options, I would like to spend some time assessing your sleep. Is that okay?
P:	Sure.
I:	Let's go back to before your drinking got out of hand. How was your sleep as a teenager?
P:	I've always been a light sleeper, and I like to stay up late. In high school, my mother usually had to drag me out of bed in the morning.
I:	How did that affect your school performance?
P:	I was always tired and had trouble paying attention in class. I was an average student, however.
I:	What about in your 20s? How was your sleep then?
P:	I became a real night owl. I couldn't get to sleep before 1:00 or 2:00 a.m. and never could get up earlier than 10:00 a.m. It is one of the reasons I became a real estate agent. I figured it was more evening work and you could set your own hours.
I:	How did that work out?
P:	Pretty good at first. However, to be a good agent, you need to be available any time of the day. It was hard to make those morning appointments, I tell you. Whenever I had an early appointment, I would end up taking a nap later in the day to get ready for the evening appointments.
I:	How did that affect your home life?
P:	My wife understood at first. She has an 8 to 4 type job, so we hardly saw each other for most of the week. She didn't know about my sleeping in late and the naps. She found out when we had children. During her maternity leave, we were both home during the day, and she started to complain about my odd hours and that I wasn't helping out with the baby. When she went back to work, she had to take our daughter to day care at 7:30 in the morning because I was always too tired in the morning to take her.
I:	How did the drinking fit into this?

P: I used to drink with friends on the weekends and after getting home from work during the week. I found it helped me get to sleep. Without alcohol, I couldn't get to sleep until after 2:00 a.m. This went on for several years. Eventually I needed four or five drinks before bed.

I: How did it affect your sleep?

P: It would help me fall asleep, but I can't say I slept well. I'd usually wake up several times during the night. I also woke up with a hangover and was tired until late in the day.

I: What do you do when you wake at night?

P: I usually lie in bed trying to get back to sleep.

I: Do you ever get out of bed?

P: Usually not. Sometimes I won't fall back asleep at all, and I'll lie in bed until 10:00 or 11:00 a.m. until I finally get up. I still do that now. If I've had a bad night of sleep, I'll try to take a nap in the afternoon.

I: Tell me about a typical day for you right now.

P: I usually get up around 11:00 a.m. My wife and kids have left the house by that point. I will read the newspaper, check my work messages, and return any calls from clients. I always pray there will be no requests to show houses or meet with clients in the early afternoon. Around 1:00 p.m. I'll go to the office and do some paperwork. I come back home around 3:30 and take a 45-minute nap before my wife and kids get home. I'll usually have appointments to show houses starting at around 5:00 p.m. As a real estate agent, I do most of my client work in the evening. I'll meet with clients until about 8:00 p.m. Between clients I'll go to the coffee shop to eat and drink. After my last client, I'll go back to the office to drop off any paperwork. I usually get home around 9:30, except on Wednesday, when I go to my AA meeting. When I get home my wife and kids are already getting ready for bed. I will stay up watching TV until about 1:00 or 2:00 a.m.

I: Where do you watch TV?

P: Usually in the family room. Sometimes I'll watch TV in the bedroom after my wife falls asleep; it doesn't seem to bother her. Sometimes I'll fall asleep in the family room watching TV.

I: What's going through your head in the hours leading up to bedtime?

P: I'm usually thinking about work. I am very afraid of another downturn in the market. The last time that happened my sales evaporated on me and we had to rely on my wife's income for the family. I really don't have any other job skills. If I have a morning appointment with a client, I'll worry about not sleeping well. I watch TV to numb my brain before going to sleep. Now that I'm not drinking, I need something to turn off my thoughts.

I: How well does the medication work?

P: The trazodone used to make me a little sleepy but not anymore. I think it helps more with my depression than sleep.

I: How long does it take you to fall asleep on most nights?

P: Usually about three quarters of an hour, but some nights it seems like 2 hours.

I: How many nights a week does that happen?

P: About once or twice. Some nights I fall asleep right away, but that doesn't happen often.

I: What is different about the good and bad nights?

P: When I fall asleep right away it is usually after a very busy day when I've been going nonstop from the morning to evening.

I: How many hours of sleep do you get on a good night and a bad night?

P: A typical night I get about 5 to 6 hours. I usually wake up three or four times per night. On a good night a little longer, maybe 7 hours, and I wake up less often.

I: Do you snore? Do you wake up with a headache in morning?

P: My wife has said I snore sometimes.
I don't get morning headaches
anymore now that I've quit drinking.

At the end of this first interview, the clinician asked to speak to the client's wife, who was in the waiting room. The interviewer uses the opportunity to inquire about any symptoms of sleep apnea (loud snoring, periods of interrupted breathing) and restless legs syndrome or periodic limb movement. Apart from occasional snoring, the client presented with no symptoms of other sleep disorders. The client's wife also corroborated his sleep pattern and severity of insomnia.

Interviewer: You are not drinking now. How about
smoking?

Peter: I've cut down to half-pack a day.
I want to quit smoking too, but I'm
not ready yet.

I: How many cups of coffee do you have
a day?

P: I knew you were going to ask that.
I drink about four or five cups a day,
which I know is bad for sleep.

I: How many in the evening?

P: Most are in the evening. Like I said
before, between showing houses I go
to the coffee shop. I also take lots of
clients to the coffee shop to discuss a
house or sale. I know I should cut
back on coffee.

I: How about exercise?

P: I'm bad there too. I have a gym
membership, but I only go about
every other week.

I: What impact has your insomnia had
on your daily life?

P: It has certainly affected my work.
I avoid seeing clients in the morning
because I'm so tired. I usually defer
these clients to one of my colleagues,
which means lost business to me. A
successful real estate agent needs to be
available any time of the day. Even
without the morning clients, I feel
tired and irritable most of the day.
After my afternoon nap, I feel much
better. But then I'm drinking coffee all
evening, and I get so wired that I can't
fall asleep until 2:00 a.m.

I: What else?

P: I feel guilty that I'm not up in the
morning to help my wife get the kids
ready for school. I also don't get to say
goodbye to them, and most days
I don't see the kids until late at night,
when they are getting ready for bed.
My wife thinks I sleep in because I'm
lazy and I'm avoiding helping her in
the morning. I also worry that she
thinks I'm drinking again. She hasn't
said anything, but I can tell she is
suspicious with my staying up late. Of
course, the truth of the matter is that
I am very tempted to start drinking
again. I worry that if my sleep doesn't
improve, I'm going to give in one
night and take a few drinks to help me
sleep. Those feelings of temptation
just make my guilt even worse.

I: How does that guilt affect your day?

P: It doesn't help my mood, of course. It
adds additional stress on my day. I try
to make it up to my family by getting
dinner started before I have to leave
the house around 5:00 p.m.

I: What have you done on your own to
improve your sleep?

P: Other than drinking [laughing]? I've
experimented with taking the
trazodone. I've tried taking it late at
night, early in the evening, taking two
pills instead of one. I've even tried not
taking it.

I: What happens on nights you don't
take it?

P: Nothing. I sleep exactly the same.

I: What does that tell you about the pill?

P: It is not helping me sleep better. That's
why I wanted something stronger.

I: What else have you done to improve
your sleep?

P: I've tried going to bed earlier so
I would wake up earlier.

I: What happens?

P: If I go to bed at 10 or 11 p.m., I just
lie there for 2 hours. Sometimes I read
before I go to bed.

I: What do you read?

P: The newspaper, usually the real estate listings. I'm taking a correspondence course on accounting in preparation for doing a MBA, so I read some of my course material at night.

I: What about relaxing activities in the evening?

P: I watch TV, although I'm usually just killing time before I go to bed.

I: How would life be improved if you slept better?

P: I think I would have more enthusiasm for my work. I would be more productive if I could put in a full day instead of wasting the morning sleeping. It would be nice to get up in the morning with my wife and kids and have a regular work day. If I slept better I would be less tempted to drink.

I: What are the benefits of things staying the same?

P: I like the flexibility I have in my schedule. I've never been a morning person, so sleeping in late is nice. It also gets me out of helping my wife in the morning with the kids. My family doesn't ask much of me during the week because of my schedule. I know that is terrible to say, but it is the truth.

I: I'm going to give you some questionnaires to fill out and a sleep log to complete for 2 weeks. These will give me a better picture of your nightly sleep pattern now. Is that acceptable to you?

P: Yes.

The clinician gives Peter the Pittsburgh Sleep Quality Index (PSQI), the Beck Depression Inventory (BDI), the Beck Anxiety Inventory (BAI), and 2 weeks of sleep diaries to complete. The client returns in 2 weeks with the questionnaires and sleep logs completed. The clinician provides Peter with feedback on his questionnaire scores: PSQI = 15, BDI = 16 (mildly depressed), and BAI = 20 (moderately anxious).

Interviewer: Thank you for completing the sleep diary. How was it?

Peter: It was no problem. I found it helpful, actually. It made me realize how mixed up my sleep actually is. I can also see that I'm getting more good nights of sleep than I thought.

I: I could also see how irregular your sleep pattern is on the diary. Your time to bed can vary as much as 5 hours, some nights 10:00 p.m. and some nights 3:00 a.m. The same goes for your rising time. Interestingly, I noticed your sleep is most regular on the weekend. You're up by 7:00 a.m. on Saturday and Sunday, in bed by 11:00, and you don't nap at all on those days. You also sleep longer at night and wake up less often.

P: I get up early to take my son and daughter to hockey and dance class. Because I sleep in during the week, I agreed to organize the kids' weekend activities so my wife can sleep in, although she usually gets up with me anyway. I also agreed to not work on the weekend so I can spend time with the family. It is usually a full day of activities, so I'm exhausted by 10:00 p.m. and usually fall asleep without a problem.

I: Are you tired during the day on Saturday and Sunday?

P: Not usually.

I: It is interesting that when you don't have the opportunity to nap you don't feel the need to have one, and you actually sleep better at night.

P: I also find weekends more relaxing because I'm less stressed about work.

I: From the 2 weeks of sleep diaries I calculated some averages for you. For example, you take on average of 45 minutes to fall asleep, although this can range from 10 minutes on weekends to 2 hours during the week. You sleep an average of 6.5 hours per night and spend about 45 minutes awake throughout the night. However, you spend an average of 9 hours lying in bed. This makes your sleep efficiency, which is the percentage of time spent in bed actually sleeping, about 70%. Any amount below 85% is considered a problem. For your information, the cutoff we use in defining insomnia from time to fall asleep is 30 minutes. So there is no question that you have insomnia. Although you have some other problems in your life (which would explain the mild depression and anxiety you have), they don't appear to be severe enough to be the primary cause of your sleep problem. However, insomnia is not a simple disorder; it is affected by many factors, including a person's psychological state, lifestyle, physical health, and sleep environment.

P: What about my drinking? Did that mess up my sleep?

I: The two problems are definitely related. Research indicates that people with insomnia are more likely to develop a drinking problem, although the majority don't. In your case, you started drinking at night to wind down and fall asleep. Alcohol is effective in helping you fall asleep. But that is the only benefit. It disrupts your sleep more than it improves it. You wake up more often through the night, get a lighter sleep, and wake up earlier than you should. Then you feel tired during the day and might be tempted to take a nap. However, by doing this you are robbing yourself of nighttime sleep. When your bedtime rolls around, you are not ready to sleep, and you have another drink, starting the cycle again.

P: But I've quit drinking. Why do I still have insomnia?

I: As I said before, it seems to take the brain a long time to recover from years of heavy drinking. However, let's not forget that you had problems sleeping before you started drinking heavily. In fact, the sleep problem and your lifestyle seemed to contribute to your alcoholism. It stands to reason that the sleep problem would still be there even after you quit drinking. It also seems that the daily routine you had while drinking has continued into abstinence. Your sleep pattern continues to be very irregular: You sleep quite late into the morning and nap almost every afternoon. Furthermore, I see from your sleep diary you are actually drinking about seven cups of coffee a day.

P: I know. It is more than I originally thought. I need to cut down.

I: Research shows that people with insomnia take longer to eliminate caffeine from their system. This means that any coffee you drink from the afternoon on is going to disrupt your sleep at night.

P: So what can I do?

I: You are an ideal candidate for a nondrug approach to improving your sleep called cognitive-behavioral therapy. Research shows that it is more effective than pills in the long-term treatment of insomnia. In your case, I see a behavioral approach being the best fit for your sleep because your insomnia seems to be maintained by the highly chaotic sleep schedule you have developed over the years. Furthermore, you seem to sleep fine on the weekend. This says to me that you can sleep normally when your schedule is more regular. One possible treatment goal would be to make your weekdays more like your weekend schedule. What would be a reasonable weekday schedule for you?

P: I want to get up when my wife and kids get up. I could go to the office and work in the morning instead of leaving it until the afternoon. I could also see some clients in the morning instead of all in the evening. I would still have to see some clients in the evening, but I want to have dinner with my family like normal people. In the afternoon when there are not many clients to see, I could go to the gym.

I: Would seeing fewer clients in the evening seriously affect your business?

P: To be honest, no. There are lots of people who prefer to meet in the morning. I've always avoided morning appointments because I like to sleep in.

I: It sounds like changing your sleep schedule would still give you the flexibility you enjoy in your line of work. It would also get you up in the morning with your wife and kids.

The interviewer proceeds to negotiate some goals regarding the client's sleep schedule in preparation for implementing cognitive-behavioral therapy for insomnia.

DIFFERENTIAL DIAGNOSIS AND BEHAVIORAL ASSESSMENT

Primary Versus Secondary Insomnia

Insomnia is often comorbid with another medical or psychiatric disorder (Balter & Uhlenhuth, 1992; Lichstein, McCrae, et al., 2003; McCall & Reynolds, 2000). In fact, epidemiological studies have shown that the comorbidity of insomnia and psychiatric disorders occurs in 40–65% of cases (Lichstein, McCrae, et al., 2003; Ohayon, 2002), with certain patient groups being particularly vulnerable to sleep disturbances. For example, up to 70% of treatment-seeking patients with chronic pain report significant insomnia (Pilowsky, Crettenden, & Townley, 1985). High rates of insomnia are also associated with major depression, anxiety disorders (McCall & Reynolds, 2000), and alcohol dependence (Brower, 2001; Currie et al., 2003). However, because insomnia is a criterion for diagnosing several psychological disorders, it is possible that the degree of comorbidity is overestimated. Nonetheless, the lack of specificity in measurement is not sufficient to account for the rates of co-occurrence. Historically, disturbed sleep in these populations has been considered a consequence or symptom of the primary disorder. However, recently it has been found that insomnia often persists even after the primary disorder resolves (Currie et al., 2003; Lichstein, McCrae, et al., 2003). Therefore, if the marker of a primary disorder is that its successful treatment automatically leads to remission of the secondary disorder, there is little evidence that insomnia is necessarily a secondary disorder (Harvey, 2001). Furthermore, there is compelling epidemiological evidence that insomnia is a risk factor for the later development of major depression, anxiety disorders, and alcohol abuse (Ford & Kamerow, 1989; Weissman, Greenwald, Nino-Murcia & Dement, 1997; Wong, Brower, Fitzgerald, & Zucker, 2004).

The diagnosis of primary or psychophysiological insomnia can often be made by exclusion of other causes. In many cases, however, insomnia coexists as a distinct but functionally related condition to another psychiatric disorder, making differential diagnosis more difficult. Disentangling the source of overlapping symptoms can be assisted by ascertaining the onset of insomnia in relation to the onset of psychiatric illness, whether symptoms of insomnia persist during periods of full or partial remission of the psychiatric disorder, how the client distinguishes between disorders, and the relative severity of the psychiatric and insomnia disorders. The use of standarized instruments such as the BDI (Beck, Ward, Mendelson, Mock, & Erbaugh, 1961), the BAI (Beck, Epstein, Brown, & Steer, 1988), and a brief diagnostic interview can assist in diagnosis and in quantification of the severity of comorbid psychiatric symptoms.

Screening for Other Sleep Disorders

Initial screening for the noninsomnia disorders can be achieved in a clinical interview. For diagnostic confirmation of other sleep disorders, overnight PSG, a test in which a number of physiological variables are recorded during sleep, usually is required. Most clients presenting with the symptoms of primary insomnia do not need PSG to confirm the diagnosis. The recent Practice Parameters for the Evaluation of Chronic Insomnia from the American Academy of Sleep Medicine (Chesson et al., 2000) state that PSG is unnecessary for the routine evaluation of insomnia. The symptoms and characteristics of insomnia do not lend themselves to accurate assessment using PSG (Morin, 2000; Reite, Buysse, Reynolds, & Mendelson, 1995; Smith, Smith, et al., 2003). However, the American Academy of Sleep Medicine does recommend PSG for people with symptoms of insomnia when a sleep-related breathing disorder, narcolepsy, periodic limb movements, or a parasomnia is suspected; an underlying neurological disorder is suspected; and the client has shown to be refractory to all treatment for insomnia. As noted earlier, speaking to a bed partner can assist in the diagnosis of other sleep disorders.

Behavioral Assessment

Questionnaires. Several retrospective sleep questionnaires that inquire about sleep habits over a specified timeframe have been developed for clinical and research applications. The 19-item PSQI (Buysse, Reynolds, Monk, Berman, & Kupfer, 1989) is a brief, self-rated questionnaire that inquires about the client's sleep for the past month. The PSQI is sensitive to change after treatment (Currie et al., 2000, 2004; Mimeault & Morin, 1999) and has strong psychometric properties (Backhaus, Junghanns, Broocks, Riemann, & Hohagen, 2002; Carpenter & Andrykowski, 1998). A related scale, the Sleep Impairment Index (Morin, 1993) is a seven-item scale that covers similar dimensions of insomnia. This index is also psychometrically strong (Bastien, Vallieres, & Morin, 2001) and sensitive to change after treatment (Currie et al., 2004; Morin, Colecchi, Stone, Sood, & Brink, 1999).

The advantages of questionnaires for assessing sleep behaviors are that they are easy to administer in a variety of clinical settings, they are inexpensive, they provide sufficient detail on a client's sleep behavior for a preliminary evaluation of whether a sleep problem exists, the information correlates with prospective sleep diaries (Smith, Nowakowski, et al., 2003), and they are sensitive to treatment effects (Currie et al., 2004; Edinger, Wohlgemuth, Radtke, Marsh, & Quillian, 2001; Mimeault & Morin, 1999). On the negative side, retrospective questionnaires use a single sample method of data collection (Smith, Nowakowski, et al., 2003). Clients may selectively report their most recent night of sleep or the worst-case scenario (Gehrman et al., 2002). They also lack sufficient specificity concerning sleep disorders. For example, a high PSQI score can indicate the presence but not the type of sleep disorder.

Self-report instruments are available for measuring other facets of disturbed sleep. For example, the Stanford Sleepiness Scale (Hoddes, Zarcone, Smythe, Phillips, & Dement, 1973) and the Epworth Sleepiness Scale (Johns, 1991) assess subjective propensity to fall asleep. Although daytime sleepiness is a common symptom of insomnia, several studies have found no significant difference between sleepiness ratings in insomniacs and noninsomniacs (Sateia et al., 2000), obviously calling into question the discriminant validity of these scales. Reporting on a sample of more than 700 good and bad sleepers, Lichstein et al. (2004) found that Stanford Sleepiness Scale and Epworth Sleepiness Scale scores correlated higher with ratings of sleep quality than quantitative sleep measures such as SOL and TST. The Insomnia Impact Scale (Hoelscher, Ware, & Bond, 1993) assesses both daytime and nocturnal consequences of insomnia. Items cover problems such as mind racing at

night, memory problems from sleep loss, calling in sick after a bad night of sleep, and excessive worry about insomnia. Norms on the Insomnia Impact Scale were published recently (Lichstein et al., 2004).

Self-Monitoring. Prospective monitoring via a sleep diary is the preferred procedure for complementing interview data on insomnia (Lacks & Morin, 1992; Smith, Smith, et al., 2003). A standard sleep diary includes items for recording bedtime and rising time, parameters commonly used to quantify sleep (TST, SOL, awakenings, WASO, and SEF), and ratings of sleep quality. Clients can also record the time and duration of any naps, consumption of caffeinated beverages, the use of sleep aids, and the application of sleep hygiene principles (Bouchard et al., 2003; Morin, 1993). Latter items include the number of times the insomniac leaves the bed when unable to sleep and the use of relaxation exercises. In addition to aiding in diagnosis, regular completion of the sleep diary during treatment can augment therapeutic gains. Feedback on the diary values (e.g., weekly averages for sleep measures) can be a powerful incentive for clients when making changes in their sleep habits. Clients are more motivated to implement sleep improvement techniques when they can observe improvements in their sleep. Data derived from the sleep diary have proven to be both reliable and valid (Currie, 2006; Lacks, 1988; Smith, Nowakowski, et al., 2003), although diary estimates usually disagree with PSG assessment of the same sleep parameters (Carskadon et al., 1976; Edinger & Fins, 1995; Rosa & Bonnet, 2000). Normative data on the sleep diary are also provided in Lichstein et al. (2004).

Actigraphy. A popular and cost-effective alternative to PSG is emerging in actigraph technology. The principles and procedures involved in actigraphy are rooted in basic behavioral assessment. Actigraphy provides psychologists with the means to detect and quantify human movement with the aim of inferring states of wake or sleep from the specific pattern of movement (Smith, Smith, et al., 2003). Parameters such as the rate of sampling, timeframe (e.g., 1, 2, 7, to up to 30 days depending on battery duration), and detection threshold are set by the researcher. Internally reliable estimates of common indices of insomnia severity can be produced (Sadeh et al., 1995), which are sensitive to change after treatment

(Brooks, Friedman, Bliwise, & Yesavage, 1993; Currie et al., 2000). When compared with the gold standard of PSG, however, the movement-based sleep estimates from the actigraph are prone to large measurement errors. In cases of insomnia, disagreement between actigraph and PSG estimates of sleep duration can vary from only a few minutes to more than an hour (Sadeh et al., 1995). Nevertheless, actigraphs have an advantage over PSG in assessing insomnia because sleep can be studied over many nights in the patient's natural sleep environment with minimal inconvenience. Actigraph information can augment the data from an interview and self-report measures.

Selection of Treatment Targets and Referral

In the field of behavioral sleep medicine, interview information and data from other assessment measures are pooled to develop a cognitive-behavioral conceptualization of the case. Clinicians should focus their attention on sleep habits, cognitions, and misguided coping attempts that are maintaining the client's insomnia. Figure 26.1 displays the conceptualization of the case of Peter presented earlier. This client is typical of many insomniacs. He reported to be a "night owl" in his youth with chronic but mild sleep dysfunction. The client's sleep difficulties were exacerbated by two primary psychological events, work stress leading to major depression and the onset of alcohol dependence. Peter's attempts to cope with the insomnia (drinking more at night, napping during the day) eventually worsened his insomnia. Peter's irregular sleep pattern and maladaptive coping persisted despite abstinence from alcohol.

The clinical interview profile in this case identified several targets for cognitive-behavioral therapy. The clinician highlighted the impact of Peter's irregular sleep pattern on the maintenance of his insomnia and associated consequences.

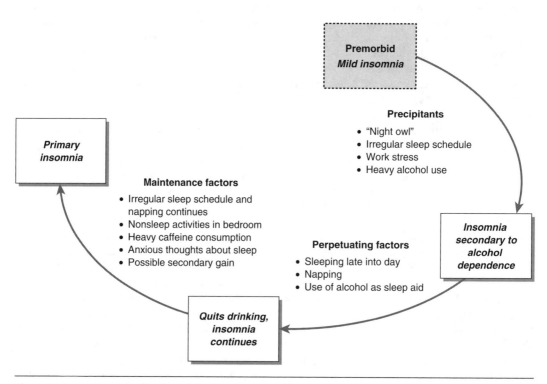

Figure 26.1   Conceptualization of the Development of Insomnia in Peter

SOURCE: Adapted from Currie, S. R., Wilson, K. G., Pontefract, A. J., & deLaplante, L. Cognitive-behavioral treatment of insomnia secondary to chronic pain, in *Journal of Consulting and Clinical Psychology, 68.* Copyright © 2000, American Psychological Association.

The interview also revealed several examples of poor sleep hygiene behaviors in the client (drinking excessive caffeine, watching TV in bed, reading stimulating material before sleep). The main interventions in cognitive-behavioral therapy, stimulus control and sleep restriction, are intended to correct these maladaptive habits. Importantly, the client self-identified his own goals for sleeping better, noting the expected benefits for himself and his family.

Individual and group cognitive-behavioral therapy are the treatments of choice for such a clear case of psychophysiological insomnia. A recent study found no difference between individual and group-based therapy for insomnia (Bastien, Morin, Ouellet, Blais, & Bouchard, 2004). Unfortunately, not all people have ready access to professionals trained in the behavioral treatment of insomnia. Other treatment options include medication and self-help therapy (see Currie, in press, for a review of self-help for sleep disorders). Medication remains the most commonly used intervention for insomnia, although concerns about the long-term efficacy and appropriateness in cases of chronic insomnia have been voiced (Morin, Hauri, et al., 1999). Table 26.1 provides a brief overview of the pros and cons of various treatment options for insomnia.

SUMMARY

Trouble sleeping is a common mental health concern, with approximately 15% of adults being affected. Although dozens of sleep disorders have been described in the literature, insomnia is the most prevalent in the general population. It is also one of the most challenging to assess and treat. Insomnia can encompass a wide range of symptoms and varying degrees of functional impairment and often co-occurs with numerous other mental and physical disorders. The most widely used diagnostic classification system for insomnia is the *DSM*, although the ISCD is comparable in terms of basic symptom specification. The ISCD system is preferred by sleep specialists because it also depicts insomnia as being maintained by learned cognitive and emotional arousal over the sleep experience. A primary goal of the clinical interview, which can be either structured or semistructured, is to identify these learned behaviors so they may be targeted for change during treatment. The interview documents the severity and history of insomnia, screens for other sleep disorders, explores the contribution of psychological factors in the onset and maintenance of insomnia, and identifies what additional assessment procedures

Table 26.1   Comparison of Treatment Options for Insomnia

	Individual	Group	Self-Help	Medication
Pros	• Flexible • Better adherence • Tailored interventions	• Cost-effective • Group support	• Wide dissemination • Cost-effective	• Minimal effort needed • Most accessible
Cons	• Expensive • Difficult to access	• Hard to tailor interventions • Adherence may be low	• Adherence is unknown • Misdiagnosis • Misapplication of skills	• Long-term efficacy not established • Daytime impairment
Efficacy				
Δ SOL	30 minute$\downarrow$ 50% improvement		20 minute$\downarrow$ 34% improvement	25 minute$\downarrow$ 30% improvement
Δ Quality	28% improved		11% improved	20% improved
Short-term cost	+++	++	+	++

SOURCES: Currie (in press); Smith, Smith, et al. (2003); Roehrs & Roth (2000).

NOTES: Δ = change in parameter from baseline to posttreatment; SOL = sleep onset latency; + = least expensive; ++ = moderately expensive; +++ = most expensive.

may be needed. The functional analysis, evaluating the precipitants, antecedents, possible secondary gains, and perpetuating factors, is considered the hallmark of behavioral interviewing. It is an ongoing process that begins at the initial assessment and continues throughout psychological treatment.

A number of interviewing obstacles may present during the assessment. There may be an objective-subjective discrepancy such that insomniacs overestimate time to fall asleep and underestimate sleep duration. The interviewer may also encounter externalization of causes of sleep dysfunction, different stages of readiness to change, and psychiatric comorbidity. Given that insomnia is often comorbid with another medical or psychiatric disorder, it is important to distinguish between primary and secondary insomnia, although the latter is still quite amenable to psychological treatment. Interview information and data from other assessment measures, such as questionnaires, self-monitoring, and actigraphy, are pooled to develop a cognitive-behavioral conceptualization of the case to guide selection of treatment targets. The interviewing style illustrated in this chapter would serve as the foundation for ongoing cognitive-behavioral management of insomnia.

REFERENCES

Aloia, M. S., Arnedt, J. T., Riggs, R. L., Hecht, J., & Borrelli, B. (2004). Clinical management of poor adherence to CPAP: Motivational enhancement. *Behavioral Sleep Medicine, 2*, 205–222.

American Psychiatric Association. (1987). *Diagnostic and statistical manual of mental disorders* (3rd ed., Rev.). Washington, DC: Author.

American Psychiatric Association. (1994). *Diagnostic and statistical manual of mental disorders* (4th ed.). Washington, DC: Author.

American Sleep Disorders Association. (1997). *International classification of sleep disorders: Diagnostic and coding manual.* Lawrence, KS: Allen Press.

Ancoli-Israel, S., & Roth, T. (1999). Characteristics of insomnia in the United States: Results of the 1991 National Sleep Foundation Survey I. *Sleep, 22* (Suppl. 2), S347–S353.

Backhaus, J., Junghanns, K., Broocks, A., Riemann, D., & Hohagen, F. (2002). Test-retest reliability and validity of the Pittsburgh Sleep Quality Index in primary insomnia. *Journal of Psychosomatic Research, 53*, 737–740.

Balter, M. B., & Uhlenhuth, E. (1992). New epidemiologic findings about insomnia and its treatment. *Journal of Clinical Psychiatry, 53*, 34–39.

Bastien, C. H., Morin, C. M., Ouellet, M., Blais, F. C., & Bouchard, S. (2004). Cognitive-behavioral therapy for insomnia: Comparison of individual therapy, group therapy, and telephone consultations. *Journal of Consulting & Clinical Psychology, 72*, 653–659.

Bastien, C., Vallieres, A., & Morin, C. M. (2001). Validation of the Insomnia Severity Index as an outcome measure for insomnia research. *Sleep Medicine, 2*, 297–307.

Beck, A. T., Epstein, N., Brown, G., & Steer, R. (1988). An inventory for measuring clinical anxiety: Psychometric properties. *Journal of Consulting and Clinical Psychology, 56*, 893–897.

Beck, A. T., Ward, C. H., Mendelson, M. M., Mock, J., & Erbaugh, J. (1961). An inventory for measuring depression. *Archives of General Psychiatry, 4*, 561–571.

Bouchard, S., Bastien, C. H., & Morin, C. M. (2003). Self-efficacy and adherence to cognitive-behavioral treatment of insomnia. *Behavioral Sleep Medicine, 1*, 187–199.

Breslau, N., Roth, T., & Rosenthal, L. (1996). Sleep disturbance and psychiatric disorders: A longitudinal epidemiological study of young adults. *Biological Psychiatry, 39*, 411–418.

Brooks, J. O., Friedman, L., Bliwise, D. L., & Yesavage, J. A. (1993). Use of wrist actigraphs to study insomnia in older adults. *Sleep, 16*, 151–155.

Brower, K. J. (2001). Alcohol's effects on sleep in alcoholics. *Alcohol Health & Research World, 25*, 110–125.

Buysse, D. J., Reynolds, C. F., Monk, T. H., Berman, S. R., & Kupfer, D. J. (1989). The Pittsburgh Sleep Quality Index: A new instrument for psychiatric practice and research. *Psychiatry Research, 28*, 193–213.

Carpenter, J. S., & Andrykowski, M. A. (1998). Psychometric evaluation of the Pittsburgh Sleep Quality Index. *Journal of Psychosomatic Research, 45*, 5–13.

Carskadon, M. A., Dement, W. C., Mitler, M. M., Guilleminault, C., Zarcone, V. P., & Spiegel, R. (1976). Self-reports versus sleep laboratory findings in 122 drug-free subjects with complaints of chronic insomnia. *American Journal of Psychiatry, 133*, 1382–1388.

Chang, P., Ford, D. E., & Mead, L. A. (1997). Insomnia in young men and subsequent depression: The Johns Hopkins Precursors Study. *American Journal of Epidemiology, 146*, 105–114.

Chesson, A., Hartse, K., Anderson, W. M., Davila, D., Johnson, S., Littner, M., et al. (2000). Practice parameters for the evaluation of chronic insomnia. *Sleep, 23*, 237–241.

Currie, S. R. (2006). Sleep dysfunction. In M. Hersen (Ed.), *Clinician's handbook of adult behavioral assessment* (pp. 401–430). New York: Elsevier.

Currie, S. R. (in press). Self-help treatment of insomnia. In P. L. Watkins & G. A. Clum (Eds.), *Handbook of self-administered therapies.* New York: Lawrence Erlbaum.

Currie, S. R., Clark, S., Hodgins, D. C., & el-Guebaly, N. (2004). Randomized controlled trial of brief cognitive-behavioral interventions for insomnia in recovering alcoholics. *Addiction, 99*, 1121–1132.

Currie, S. R., Clark, S., Rimac, S., & Malhotra, S. D. (2003). Comprehensive assessment of insomnia in recovering alcoholics using daily sleep diaries and ambulatory monitoring. *Alcoholism: Clinical and Experimental Research, 27,* 1262–1270.

Currie, S. R., Wilson, K. G., Pontefract, A. J., & deLaplante, L. (2000). Cognitive-behavioral treatment of insomnia secondary to chronic pain. *Journal of Consulting and Clinical Psychology, 68,* 407–416.

Edinger, J. D., & Fins, A. I. (1995). The distribution and clinical significance of sleep time misperceptions among insomniacs. *Sleep, 18,* 232–239.

Edinger, J. D., Wohlgemuth, W. K., Radtke, R. A., Marsh, G. R., & Quillian, R. E. (2001). Cognitive behavioral therapy for treatment of chronic primary insomnia: A randomized controlled trial. *JAMA, 285,* 1856–1864.

Espie, C. A. (1991). *The psychological management of insomnia.* Chichester, England: Wiley.

Espie, C. A., Inglis, S. J., Tessier, S., & Harvey, L. (2001). The clinical effectiveness of cognitive behavior therapy for chronic insomnia: Implementation and evaluation of a sleep clinic in general medical practice. *Behavior Research & Therapy, 39,* 45–60.

Fichten, C. S., Creti, L., Amsel, R., Brender, W., Weinstein, N., & Libman, E. (1995). Poor sleepers who do not complain of insomnia: Myths and realities about psychological and lifestyle characteristics of older good and poor sleepers. *Journal of Behavioral Medicine, 18,* 189–223.

Ford, D. E., & Kamerow, D. B. (1989). Epidemiological study of sleep disturbances and psychiatric disorders. *Journal of the American Medical Association, 262,* 1479–1484.

Gehrman, P., Matt, G., Turingan, M., Dinh, Q., & Ancoli-Israel, S. (2002). Towards an understanding of self-reports of sleep. *Journal of Sleep Research, 11,* 229–236.

Harvey, A. (2001). Insomnia: Symptom or diagnosis? *Clinical Psychology Review, 21,* 1037–1059.

Harvey, A. (2002). A cognitive model of insomnia. *Behavior Research & Therapy, 40,* 869–894.

Hoddes, E., Zarcone, V., Smythe, H., Phillips, R., & Dement, W. C. (1973). Quantification of sleepiness: A new approach. *Psychophysiology, 10,* 431–436.

Hoelscher, T. J., Ware, J. C., & Bond, T. (1993). Initial validation of the Insomnia Impact Scale. *Sleep Research, 22,* 149.

Johns, M. W. (1991). A new method for measuring daytime sleepiness: The Epworth Sleepiness Scale. *Sleep, 14,* 540–545.

Kaplan, H. I., & Sadock, B. J. (2002). *Synopsis of psychiatry* (9th ed.). Baltimore: Lippincott Williams & Wilkins.

Lacks, P. (1987). *Behavioral treatment for persistent insomnia.* Toronto, ON: Pergamon.

Lacks, P. (1988). Daily sleep diary. In M. Hersen & A. S. Bellack (Eds.), *Dictionary of behavioral assessment techniques* (pp. 162–164). New York: Pergamon.

Lacks, P., & Morin, C. M. (1992). Recent advances in the assessment and treatment of insomnia. *Journal of Consulting & Clinical Psychology, 60,* 586–594.

Lichstein, K. L., Durrence, H. H., Riedel, B. W., Taylor, D. J., & Bush, A. J. (2004). *Epidemiology of sleep.* Mahwah, NJ: Lawrence Erlbaum.

Lichstein, K. L., Durrence, H. H., Taylor, D. J., Bush, A. J., & Riedel, B. W. (2003). Quantitative criteria for insomnia. *Behavior Research and Therapy, 41,* 427–455.

Lichstein, K. L., McCrae, C. S., & Wilson, N. M. (2003). Secondary insomnia: Diagnostic issues, cognitive-behavioral treatment, and future directions. In M. L. Perlis & K. L. Lichstein (Eds.), *Treating sleep disorders: Principles and practice of behavioral sleep medicine* (pp. 286–304). Toronto: Wiley.

McCall, W. V., & Reynolds, D. (2000). Psychiatric disorders and insomnia. In M. H. Kryger, T. Roth, & W. C. Dement (Eds.), *Principles and practice of sleep medicine* (3rd ed., pp. 640–646). Toronto: W.B. Saunders.

Miller, W. R., & Rollnick, S. (2002). *Motivational interviewing: Preparing people to change* (2nd ed.). New York: Guilford.

Mimeault, V., & Morin, C. M. (1999). Self-help treatment for insomnia: Bibliotherapy with and without professional guidance. *Journal of Consulting & Clinical Psychology, 67,* 511–519.

Montplaisir, J., Nicolas, A., Godbout, R., & Walters, A. (2000). Restless legs syndrome and periodic limb movement disorders. In M. H. Kryger, T. Roth, & W. C. Dement (Eds.), *Principles and practice of sleep medicine* (3rd ed., pp. 742–752). Toronto: W. B. Saunders.

Morawetz, D. (2003). Insomnia and depression: Which came first. *Sleep Research Online, 5,* 77–81.

Morin, C. M. (1993). *Insomnia: Psychological assessment and management.* New York: Guilford.

Morin, C. M. (2000). The nature of insomnia and the need to refine our diagnostic criteria. *Psychosomatic Medicine, 62,* 483–485.

Morin, C. M., Colecchi, C., Stone, J., Sood, R., & Brink, D. (1999). Behavioral and pharmacological therapies for late-life insomnia: A randomized controlled trial. *Journal of the American Medical Association, 281,* 991–999.

Morin, C. M., Hauri, P. J., Espie, C. A., Spielman, A. J., Buysse, D., & Bootzin, R. R. (1999). Nonpharmacologic treatment of chronic insomnia. *Sleep, 22,* 1134–1156.

Ohayon, M. (1996). Epidemiological study on insomnia in the general population. *Sleep, 19,* S7–S15.

Ohayon, M. (2002). Epidemiology of insomnia: What we know and what we still need to learn. *Sleep Medicine Reviews, 6,* 97–111.

Ollendick, T. H., Alvarez, H. K., & Greene, R. W. (2004). Behavioral assessment: History of underlying concepts and methods. In M. Hersen (Ed.), *Comprehensive handbook of psychological assessment: Behavioral assessment* (pp. 19–34). Hoboken, NJ: Wiley.

Partinen, M., & Hublin, C. (2000). Epidemiology of sleep disorders. In M. H. Kryger, T. Roth, & W. C. Dement (Eds.), *Principles and practice of sleep medicine* (3rd ed., pp. 558–579). Toronto: W.B. Saunders.

Pilowsky, I., Crettenden, I., & Townley, M. (1985). Sleep disturbance in pain clinic patients. *Pain, 23,* 27–33.

Prochaska, J. O., DiClemente, C. C., & Norcross, J. C. (1992). In search of how people change: Applications to addictive behaviors. *American Psychologist,* *47,* 1102–1114.

Reite, M., Buysse, D., Reynolds, C., & Mendelson, W. (1995). The use of polysomnography in the evaluation of insomnia. *Sleep, 18,* 58–70.

Resnicow, K., Dilorio, C., Borrelli, B., Hecht, J., & Soet, J. E. (2002). Motivational interviewing in health promotion: It sounds like something is changing. *Health Psychology, 21,* 444–451.

Roehrs, T., & Roth, T. (2000). Hypnotics: Efficacy and adverse effects. In M. H. Kryger, T. Roth, & W. C. Dement (Eds.), *Principles and practice of sleep medicine* (3rd ed., pp. 414–418). Toronto: W.B. Saunders.

Rosa, R. R., & Bonnet, M. H. (2000). Reported insomnia is independent of poor sleep as measured by electroencephalography. *Psychosomatic Medicine, 62,* 474–482.

Roth, T. (2004). Measuring treatment efficacy in insomnia. *Journal of Clinical Psychology, 65*(Suppl. 8), 8–12.

Sadeh, A., Hauri, P. J., Kripke, D. F., & Lavie, P. (1995). The role of actigraphy in the evaluation of sleep disorders. *Sleep, 18,* 288–302.

Sateia, M. J., Doghramji, K., Hauri, P. J., & Morin, C. M. (2000). Evaluation of chronic insomnia. *Sleep, 23,* 243–308.

Schramm, E., Hohagen, F., Grasshoff, U., Riemann, D., Hajak, G., Hans-Gunther, W., et al. (1993). Test-retest reliability and validity of the structured interview for sleep disorders according to *DSM-III-R. American Journal of Psychiatry, 150,* 867–872.

Simon, A., & VonKorff, M. (1997). Prevalence, burden, and treatment of insomnia in primary care. *American Journal of Psychiatry, 154,* 1417–1423.

Smith, L. J., Nowakowski, S., Soeffing, J. P., Orff, H. J., & Perlis, M. L. (2003). The measurement of sleep. In M. L. Perlis & K. L. Lichstein (Eds.), *Treating sleep disorders: Principles and practice of behavioral sleep medicine* (pp. 29–73). Toronto, ON: Wiley.

Smith, L. J., Smith, L. J., Nowakowski, S., & Perlis, M. L. (2003). Primary insomnia: Diagnostic issues, treatment, and future directions. In M. L. Perlis & K. L. Lichstein (Eds.), *Treating sleep disorders: Principles and practice of behavioral sleep medicine* (pp. 214–261). Toronto, ON: Wiley.

Trinder, J. (1988). Subjective insomnia without objective findings: A pseudo diagnostic classification? *Psychological Bulletin, 103,* 87–94.

Üstün, T. B., Privett, M., Lecrubier, Y., Weiller, E., Simon, A., Korten, A., et al. (1996). Form, frequency, and burden of sleep problems in general health care: A report from the WHO Collaborative Study on Psychological Problems in General Health Care. *European Psychiatry* (Suppl. 1), 5S–10S.

Weissman, M. M., Greenwald, S., Nino-Murcia, G., & Dement, W. C. (1997). The morbidity of insomnia uncomplicated by psychiatric disorders. *General Hospital Psychiatry, 19,* 245–250.

Wong, M. M., Brower, K. J., Fitzgerald, H. E., & Zucker, R. A. (2004). Sleep problems in early childhood and early onset of alcohol and other drug use in adolescence. *Alcoholism: Clinical & Experimental Research, 28,* 578–587.

Zammit, G. K., Weiner, J., & Damato, N. (1999). Quality of life in people with insomnia. *Sleep, 22*(Suppl. 2), S379–S385.

27

PHYSICAL ABUSERS IN THE FAMILY

LOUISE S. ÉTHIER AND CARL LACHARITÉ

Society gives parents legal authority over their children and imposes a social and moral obligation on them to take care of their children and educate them. Children have a right to respect of their physical integrity and to development of their full potential (Prilleltensky, Nelson, & Peirson, 2001). In North American culture not all aggressive acts toward children are considered abusive (spanking as a disciplinary measure immediately comes to mind); only those that go beyond what is socially accepted are considered abusive.[1] In fact, the diverse ways in which parents exercise power over their children are subject to social and legal norms that evolve over time and reflect the community in which these people live (Chamberland, 2003).

In our cultural context, child physical abuse can be defined as the brutal, excessive, or irrational act of a parent who attacks the physical or psychological integrity of a child using physical means and causing injury (Strauss, 1979; Strauss, Hamby, Finkelhor, Moore, & Runyan, 1998).

In this chapter we examine physical abuse in the family, focusing on the parent-child relationship but not excluding spousal violence. Many families live with both spousal abuse and child maltreatment. Concomitance rates are between 6% and 14% in the general population (Appel & Holden, 1998; Margolin, Gordis, Medina, & Oliver, 2003) and between 20% and 100% in clinical populations, with a median rate of 40%

(Appel & Holden, 1998). Although most authors agree that concomitance refers to the concurrent presence of spousal abuse and child maltreatment in the same family, it is difficult to define the problem more precisely given the multiple combinations possible of the various forms of violence, both spousal and parental. Furthermore, the same person can be both the victim and the abuser, rendering the analysis of situations involving concomitant abuse even more complex. In a review of 20 studies, Appel and Holden (1998) identify five types of family dynamics in situations of concomitant abuse: the man/father is responsible for both spousal and parental abuse; the male partner abuses his spouse, and she maltreats the child; the man abuses the woman, but both parents are abusive toward the child; the spousal abuse is bidirectional, and both parents abuse their child; or each member of the family is both a victim and an abuser.

Our objective is to address the interview of parents who are physically abusive toward their children and often toward their partner. Although parental abuse is not confined to economically underprivileged families, most of studies on physical abuse have dealt with populations that are economically, socially, and psychologically disadvantaged.

In this chapter, we examine the conditions that are conducive to a successful interview and the specific content of an interview designed for diagnosis and counseling purposes. Our discussion is particularly aimed at future professionals and practitioners in health care and social services who work with abusive parents in the context of a counseling relationship. Although evaluation of parental behaviors, cognitions, and affects is a key aspect of such work, our objective here is not to propose a form of interview aimed at detecting and confirming situations of parental physical abuse. That being said, the information provided is not incompatible with that type of task.

Parents who physically abuse their children are in regular contact with health and social services professionals through services received by their children or their family. In that context, the main purpose of interviews between professionals and parents is to provide direct support to parents rather than investigate allegations of physical abuse. Even in cases where allegations have been officially confirmed, professionals working in youth protection and other services play an important role in helping these parents.

The intervention objectives presented in this chapter are not a substitute for a discussion of formal programs aimed at helping parents modify their abusive behaviors toward their children. Such programs usually are implemented in institutions whose mandate is to intervene in situations of confirmed child physical abuse. They are often part of a larger multi-intervention structure that includes individual interviews and strategies with these parents. Professionals who work in these programs usually have undergone specific training to develop their skills in analyzing the personal situations of abusive parents and maltreated children and in applying specialized intervention strategies. Although this chapter is based on such intervention models, its primary purpose is to provide information on the representations and characteristics of violent parents in order to target concrete ways of facilitating individual interviews and counseling with these parents.

The content of interviews and interventions is inevitably influenced by the practitioner's theoretical perspective or representation of the abuse phenomenon. Practitioners who perceive family violence as a result of the male-female power struggle will adopt an intervention approach influenced by feminist theory (Pence & Paymar, 1993), whereas those who perceive family violence as a reproduction of childhood abuse will be more influenced by attachment or social cognitive theory (Crittenden & Claussen, 2000). The main theories explaining family violence are summarized in this chapter. These approaches, based on a large body of empirical research, may guide the actions taken by health and social service professionals.

DESCRIPTION OF THE PROBLEM

Sociocultural Influences

Relationships between family members are not experienced exclusively on a private level; they are also an extension of the social world in which the people live (Doise, 1990; Levy, 1984; Moscovici & Duveen, 2000). Chamberland (2003) identified four social cognitive patterns that contribute to facilitating, trivializing, and justifying the use of physical violence in family relationships and particularly in parent-child relationships. The first pattern is based on a negative conception of childhood, what Miller (1986) calls "poisonous pedagogy." Children are seen as malicious beings that need to be trained. This conception usually is accompanied by a view of the world outside the family as a hostile environment in which human beings are in a perpetual state of confrontation. The second pattern is based on a limited conception of interpersonal violence. When social representations of abuse are built around the central notion that violence involves only physical assaults that leave marks, other acts of violence not meeting such a limited criterion tend to be excluded (Berger, Knutson, Mehm, & Perkins, 1988; Ney, 1987). The third pattern is based on a rigid conception of power in family relationships in which children are in a position of strict submission to adults, a notion often associated with the idea that women are in a position of submission to men (Bugental & Johnson, 2000). The fourth pattern is based on the premise that the care and upbringing of children is designed to fulfill parental goals rather than children's needs. Social representations of parenting form the foundation of this collective pattern. Work by Baumrind (1996) sheds light on a social conception of upbringing that is parent-centered as opposed to child-centered. (See Figure 27.1.)

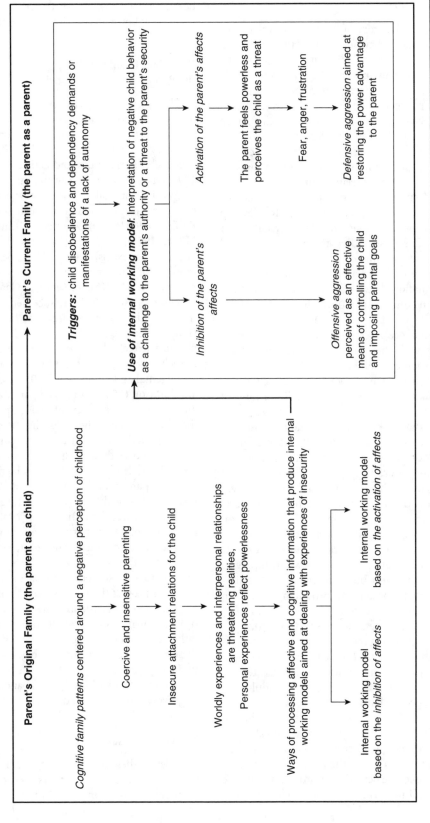

Figure 27.1   Conceptual Framework of Manifestations of Violence and Physical Abuse in the Parent-Child Relationship

Family History

The other category of factors that explain violent parental behaviors involve the childhood experiences of abusive adults and particularly the individual cognitive patterns they have constructed with their attachment figures. Attachment theory and in particular social cognition research by authors such as Bowlby (1980, 1982), Crittenden (1989), Crittenden and Claussen (2000), and Main (1991) have been a particularly important contribution to our understanding of the origins of abuse in parent-child relationships.

Children exposed to rejecting, hostile, or intrusive parental behaviors tend to develop cognitive patterns that exclude information or inhibit affects. According to the authors cited earlier, child victims of abuse develop internal working models based on a defensive exclusion of information. These children concentrate their attention on information that helps them predict the onset of negative parental behaviors (hypervigilance). For other children, the relationship with their attachment figures is built around their exposure to unpredictable parental conduct that fluctuates between relatively sensitive behaviors and parental manifestations of anger and frustration that can lead to verbal or physical abuse. These children tend to exclude or inhibit cognitive information that comes from the relationship with their parent (because that information does not enable them to properly predict when the parent will behave aggressively) and concentrate their attention on affects engendered by the relationship. The activation of affects (especially anger, fear, and the need for comforting) in children and the intense expression of those affects in the relationship with their parents contribute somewhat to "regulating" parental conduct by producing affects in the parent reciprocal to those of the child (e.g., guilt, pity, tenderness, depressive feelings).

Internal working models acquired in the original family tend to stabilize as the child grows up if the family conditions do not change (Crittenden & Claussen, 2000). By adolescence and adulthood battered people have developed, little by little, an insecure state of mind in their attachment and intimate relationships. When critical situations arise, such as interpersonal conflicts, their insecurity will dictate their behaviors toward other people, particularly toward their intimate partner and their children. These behaviors may be defensive (Bowlby, 1980; Crittenden, 2001; Main, 1991) or pattern driven (Bugental, 1992).

Episodes of Violence in the Parent-Infant Relationship

Physical assault is used by parents as a means of reaching specific objectives (e.g., to control or discipline their child); it is perceived by certain parents as being uncontrolled and impulsive (Dietrich, Berkowitz, Kadushin, & McGloin, 1990; Dix, Reinhold, & Zambarano, 1990).

Abusive parental behaviors appear to be triggered primarily by child disobedience (Hastings & Rubin, 1999; Holden, Coleman, & Schmidt, 1995; Milner, 1993), extreme behavior such as temper tantrums or excessive crying, and demands for more autonomy or a lack of autonomy on the part of the child (Malo, Moreau, Chamberland, Léveillée, & Roy, 2002). Disobedience acts as a trigger or detonator in parents at risk for abuse (Bugental & Clayton, 1998, 1999). Parents interpret negative child behavior as a direct challenge to their authority or a threat to their security.

Bugental and Happaney (2000) and Bugental and Johnson (2000) examined parental violence and the sequence of events triggered by child disobedience. First, the child's negative behavior is interpreted as a threat to the parent's internal security and leads to feelings of powerlessness. Second, the child is perceived as having power over the parent, and so the parent desperately seeks to restore the power advantage in his or her favor. Third, the entire behavioral sequence is accompanied by negative emotions (anger, frustration, discouragement, guilt, fear). When this occurs, the use of physical abuse is similar to the conduct of someone trying to react to an attack or protect themselves from danger.

Abusive parents usually make attempts to control their own emotions and behaviors and try to influence their child's negative behavior. However, these attempts translate into ambiguous and contradictory messages to which the child reacts by avoiding the relationship (fear) and increasing negative behaviors (child distress, anger).

The Gender Issue

Most studies on violence and child physical abuse are based on assaults perpetrated by mothers. Are the conceptual models explaining parental abuse developed in such studies valid for understanding the violent behaviors of fathers? It is difficult to answer that question given the current state of knowledge. In the 1990s, studies aimed at understanding the male role in families where child abuse was encountered were so few in number that for all practical purposes the field of study was nonexistent (Lansky, 1992; Sternberg, 1997). Haskett, Marziano, and Dover (1996) published a review of empirical studies on situations of physical child abuse, focusing on the type of samples used. They showed that of the 77 studies published between 1989 and 1994, the majority (52.3%) involved only mothers. And yet most studies with both mothers and fathers revealed gender differences. Men appear to resort more easily to physical violence in their intimate interpersonal relationships.

A study by McGloin and Widom (2001) suggests that men who have been abused as children or have lived in poor socioeconomic conditions are more vulnerable once they reach adulthood than women who have had similar experiences. Based on a population sample composed of 14,138 children born in 1991–1992 in the United Kingdom and followed until 1998, Sidebotham and Golding (2001) show that abusive fathers and mothers present the same risk factors (e.g., history of abuse and foster home placement, depression, drug addiction) but show differences in the magnitude of those risk factors. Fathers under the age of 20 years are 6.3 times more at risk of maltreating their children than other fathers, whereas mothers under the age of 20 years are only 3.2 times more likely to be abusive. Fathers with a history of depressive problems are 3.6 times more at risk of abusing their children, and mothers with a history of depression are only 1.8 times more likely to be abusive. Fathers who were placed in foster care as children are 6.0 times more at risk of abusing their children, compared to 1.5 times for mothers.

Prevalence of Abusive Behaviors in Mothers and Fathers

According to data gathered by the U.S. Department of Health and Human Services (2001), it is estimated that 1,100 children died in 1999 as a result of abuse and neglect. One third of child abuse cases involved primarily men. In Canada, according to the incidence study carried out by Trocmé, MacLaurin, and Fallon (2001), more than half of abuse cases investigated by child protection services involved mothers. However, these data appear to be distorted by the fact that mothers often declare that they are living on their own, without a stable spouse, possibly to prevent their social assistance payments from being reduced. According to the same study, when only two-parent families are counted, men are the perpetrators in 71% of cases of physical abuse and 69% of cases of emotional maltreatment. In fact, the percentage of mothers involved is greater only in cases of neglect, for all types of family composition, with or without a declared spouse (Trocmé et al., 2001).

Despite greater prevalence of male abusers, child maltreatment research has focused primarily on mothers, without taking into account the presence of a father or paternal figures (Lacharité, Éthier, & Nolin, 2006). Information available on male abusers comes almost exclusively from research on spousal abuse (Phares, 1996) and does not provide a proper comparison of the violence perpetrated by mothers and fathers. In addition to the fact that there is a significant lack of data on abusive fathers, rare are studies that explore counseling strategies to improve the parenting skills of these men. Smith and O'Leary (2001) note that we are currently facing the need to combine what has been learned in research on spousal abuse with knowledge we have gained from studies of family violence.

INTERVIEWING STRATEGIES

Interviews with physically abusive parents should ideally take place in a social service setting. Three elements must be emphasized here. First, practitioners must ensure that they are never the only source of support offered to physically abusive parents. The needs manifested by these parents and the complexity of the factors involved in the problem of physical abuse mean that the help needed often goes beyond the work that a single practitioner can perform. Second, multiple modes of intervention must be put into place to address the parents' needs and the complexity of the problem. Individual interviews with parents should be part of a much larger array of measures (e.g., legal, psychosocial, educational tools) that include group interventions and developmental guidance. Third, one-on-one interviews with abusive parents must also aid them in becoming involved in other support measures. Individual interviews therefore represent a form of guidance within a set of integrated services aimed at putting a stop to family violence.

Practitioners who work with abusive parents should be trained and supervised so they represent a reassuring figure for the parent (empathy and warmth but also the ability to motivate, to make the parents take responsibility for their acts and guide them in their efforts to change). Moreover, practitioners must be comfortable enough to define a framework for the interview (objectives and ways to reach the objectives), ask diagnosis-related questions, and create a counseling relationship while taking into account the safety of the parent and his or her family members. According to Kelly and Wolfe (2004), the ideal practitioner should have both the skills needed to motivate parents to change their violent conduct and the skills needed for working with families and maltreated children.

Abusive people tend to diminish the importance of their acts and may show signs of impatience and even anger when confronted with the reality of their behaviors. Men, in particular, may make the practitioner feel helpless and fearful.

The childhood abuse and family violence experienced by the majority of abusive parents predispose them to protecting themselves from others and interpreting offers to help as traps to be avoided. These parents place little value on attachment to other people and sensitivity toward them. At the beginning of the counseling process practitioners must display an attitude conducive to making a link with the abusive parent, an attitude that is cordial but direct. Most parents appreciate it when the practitioner clearly explains the situation facing the parent, what is expected of them, and the consequences if they do not live up to the agreement (e.g., "If you stop coming to our sessions, I will have to notify your social worker of your withdrawal from the program."). It can be very useful and even therapeutic to have parents sign a "contractual" agreement that states the framework of the counseling relationship. The agreement must allow parents to express their opinions and to propose modifications based on their needs and expectations. It requires the consent of the parent and represents a commitment on the part of both the counselor and the parent. At this point the practitioner explains the type of services provided, how the program works, and confidentiality rules (Table 27.1).

Initial interviews are designed to gain a better understanding of the parent's situation so that a preliminary diagnosis can be made. Gathering information is not always easy because of the complexity of situations of abuse and because of distrust on the part of the parents (Table 27.1). The collection of diagnostic information can entail more than one interview and sometimes the opinion of more than one professional (e.g., in cases of drug addiction and mental health problems). The third part of Table 27.1 deals with the principles of interviewing during the counseling process.

INTERVIEWING OBSTACLES AND SOLUTIONS

The main obstacle in interviews with fathers and mothers who physically abuse their children is the lack of collaboration; these parents are not inclined to spontaneously assume responsibility for their abusive conduct and may react to attempts to help them. Their reactions may be in the form of avoidance or fleeing behaviors or may translate into graver consequences, such as increased abuse of their child or violent behavior directed at the people who reported the abuse to authorities. Lack of parental collaboration therefore opens the door to two pitfalls: heightened isolation of the parents and an increased threat to people around them. Defensive reactions should not be seen as being independent of one another but rather as part of the same continuum: Parents who react to outside interventions with increased abuse often are those who are the most isolated or cut off from any source of parenting guidance.

Lack of collaboration of parents during interviews often is based on their perception that the interviewer is seeking to control their behavior and dispossess them of the power they are trying to establish in the relationship with their child. The interviewer is consequently perceived not as a source of support but as one of oppression that they need to eliminate or that requires them to defend themselves. Avenues for solutions in such situations lie in the practitioner's skill in building a counseling alliance with the parent. To accomplish this it is important to explore, with the

Table 27.1   Counseling Relationship Framework

1. Defining the Interview Framework

   • The practitioner must clearly explain his or her role and the objectives of the interviews.
   • The practitioner must explain the confidentiality rules and specify what type of information will be shared with the team of professionals (e.g., withdrawal from the sessions, the child's safety).
   • The practitioner must explain, in the most concrete way possible, the logistics of the interviews (time, place, schedule, number of sessions), the responsibilities of the parent (e.g., to attend all the meetings, be on time, pay a given amount), and the responsibilities of the professional (e.g., availability, breaks for holidays).
   • It is important that the parent have a good understanding of the objective of the interviews and consent to them before beginning the assessment or counseling process.

2. Beginning of the Interview

   • It may be difficult to gather information from abusive parents; they are distrustful, are afraid of losing custody of their child, or are in denial of their violent behavior. The parent often is reacting to or is even angry with child protection services or the other parent.
   • The practitioner must take the time to understand the parents' point of view, motivation, and expectations and must accept the fact that the parents are resistant and accept their representation of the facts without removing all sense of responsibility (abuse is unacceptable, it destroys the people who are most important to them).
   • The practitioner must support and encourage the parents' motivation in seeking help; the simple fact of attending the interview must be seen as the beginning of change.

3. Throughout the Interview

   • The trust that develops between the parent and the practitioner is the key to an effective counseling relationship and the collection of valid information needed for a differential diagnosis. This attitude must be combined with a clear position as to the parent's responsibility for his or her conduct.
   • Despite an appearance of collaboration, establishing the trust of the parents is a long and difficult process. Relationships they have had as children have made them distrustful.
   • The practitioner must watch for signs of demotivation (e.g., absence, arriving late, lack of involvement in the interview) and must discuss these problems with the parent.
   • The practitioner must not engage in a power struggle with the parent, who often sees interpersonal relationships as being based on power and conflict.
   • The practitioner must reframe the parent's conduct. For example, striking a child may be a means for the parent to teach the child respect for authority or help the child survive in a hostile world. Once the parent's intention is understood, the practitioner proposes a more appropriate way to educate the child.
   • The practitioner must ensure the security of the parent, who may be both a victim and abuser or may be a suicide risk.
   • Plan ahead, with the parent, for crisis situations, during summer or Christmas holidays, for example. Where should they go? Whom should they call? What should they do?

parent, the answers to the following questions: "How and under what conditions can I be considered a relevant source of help and support in the eyes of this parent?" "Who else but me has the possibility and capability of being considered relevant by this parent?"

When parents are forced by child protection authorities to participate in counseling or therapy, they often feel misunderstood and unjustly treated. In many cases they display a superficial commitment or passive resistance to change. As noted by Wolfe (1999), these attitudes must be addressed in the first stage of intervention aimed at modifying abusive behavior. It is crucial for the practitioner to acknowledge a parent's lack of motivation or denial of the problem in order to continue the intervention. Parents will feel more at ease with a practitioner who is able to bring up and discuss their lack of motivation than with a practitioner who ignores the problem throughout the interviews. However, decreased resistance to change must not be confused with actual change, namely putting an end to violence in the family (Miller & Rollnick, 2002).

During the first stage of intervention, it is important to get the parent to acknowledge that there is indeed a problem and then increase his or her awareness of the needs and feelings of children. Any attempts made too early in the counseling process aimed at, for example, implementing time-outs or better communication with children could be used by parents as another means of controlling or abusing their children and female partners (Adams, 1988; Gondolf & Russell, 1986; Dankwort, 1988, quoted in Scott & Crooks, 2004).

Because of their own history, parents who abuse their loved ones have never developed a proper awareness of violent behaviors or of the repercussions of such acts on the people around them. For example, confining a child to his bedroom all day with no food is not seen as harmful to the child but as a way of teaching him respect and obedience. The parent believes that such a punishment will change the child's behavior. The child's fearful reaction convinces the parent that the punishment is effective. The practitioner should reframe the abusive conduct by emphasizing the parent's intention to "educate the child" while proposing more positive methods.

Motivation of these parents is never completely achieved and is subject to fluctuations. Abusive parents have little inclination to continue their efforts throughout the intervention process. Attrition rates in intervention programs for abusive men range from 28% to 90% (De Hart, Kennerly, Burke, & Follingstad, 1999). According to Rooney and Hanson (2001), the main reasons for demotivation of abusive parents are the instability of this clientele and the characteristics of the programs offered.

Parents who display violent behaviors often lead a chaotic life that reflects their material and emotional instability. For example, a hasty move to another city is their way of avoiding child protection services for fear of losing custody of their child or avoiding their landlord or a money lender because they have financial problems. A change in the family dynamics, such as a breakup in the marriage or the placement of a child in foster care, often leads to intense emotional reactions (intense anxiety, fears, aggressiveness, sadness) that are expressed not verbally but through actions such as alcohol and drug use, increased abuse, or discontinuation of treatment. Over the course of the interviews, the practitioner must take into account any breakups and changes that occur in the parent's life and gain a proper

understanding of the meaning of such events in order to maintain the parent's motivation to continue getting help.

Among factors that contribute to the demotivation of parents, Leigh, Ogborne, and Cleland (1984) note a long waiting time (several weeks) before getting help and a poor evaluation of their needs and characteristics. For example, a parent with little education who displays cognitive problems will feel excluded in a group of parents with better verbal skills (Rooney & Hanson, 2001).

It is not easy to develop a trusting relationship between the counselor and parent. Despite appearances of collaboration, parents more or less consciously expect to be deceived, ridiculed, or attacked. By displaying a reassuring but not complacent attitude, the practitioner must promote a relationship in which the parent feels secure. Just as a battered child will reject a warm reception on the part of her parent, the practitioner must display patience in convincing the parent that he now has resources to help him change his behaviors, that he can indeed be helped, and that he is no longer in danger. Abusive parents often were abused as children, and they constantly feel threatened, hence their propensity for violent and impulsive reactions.

Case Illustration With Dialogue

Samples of a Filmed Interview With Mark, 26 Years of Age[2]

The following are two episodes of a clinical interview conducted with a physically abusive father. Although our example involves a father, the content of the interview could equally be applied to abusive mothers. As stated previously, our objective is not to propose a form of interview designed to detect, investigate, and confirm situations of parental physical abuse. In the case presented here, a child protection services investigation had already confirmed that the father was physically abusive.

This initial interview leads to a better understanding of the father's situation in view of arriving at a diagnosis and planning a counseling process with him. The interview is divided into two parts, the first part aimed at determining the type and severity of the abuse, the father's sensitivity toward his child, and his motivation to cease his violent behavior. The second part is aimed at gaining a better understanding of the father's history, the reproduction of abuse he suffered as a child, his attachment history, and the presence of trauma.

The interview is designed to be used in a counseling relationship where the father has voluntarily agreed to get help. His acceptance of help may be total or partial and does not mean that he will not show resistance to help offered by the practitioner. In many cases, especially when child protection services are involved, parents agree to counseling because they do not want to lose custody of their child.

History. Mark was raised by his aunt until he was 3 years old, after which he lived 1 year with his mother. From 4 to 7 years of age, he lived with his maternal grandmother. This grandmother appears to be Mark's only parental figure. From age 7 to 13 he was placed in a foster home because of his violent behavior. His relationship with his foster mother was perceived as positive. At age 14, he went back to living with his grandmother. At age 16 he lived in a couple relationship with a dancer who worked in a bar, and then he went to live with an uncle, who treated him abusively. Mark has had alcohol and drug addiction problems since childhood. He apparently started drinking at the age of 8.

Present Situation. Mark has no stable employment and little schooling. He has been living with his female partner since the age of 18 and has two children, a 6-year-old daughter and an 8-year-old son. Spousal abuse (unreported), child abuse (confirmed). According to the psychosocial report, Mark is impulsive and hits his son while under the influence of alcohol. The violence toward his daughter is mainly verbal, in addition to inappropriate punishments. In court, Mark obtained the right to supervised visits with his two children once a month. The judge ordered him to undergo individual therapy and to join a detoxification program.

First Part. Exploration of violent episodes; characteristics of these episodes, and description of the parent's motivation to modify his behavior.

Interviewer	Mark
The judge has ordered you to undergo individual therapy as a condition to returning to live with your children. . . . You are currently allowed to see your children once a month. . . . You have agreed to meet with me.	[5-second silence.] Yes [smiles].
[Framework and confidentiality: The practitioner states his framework, the number of meetings, and their duration and explains the confidentiality rules.]	[Agrees by nodding his head, fiddles nervously with his hands.]
What has brought you to the protection services?	[15 seconds, does not answer.]
Do you want to tell me about it?	In our system, the best guy always wins [smiles].
What do you mean? I would like to understand your point of view as to what brought you to the protection services?	Well, they said that I hit . . . that I was violent with my kids. [Does not take responsibility for the violence.]
And you, what do you think? Do you agree with what the protection services said?	[Smiles.] . . . Sometimes I dunno what I'm doing, that's for sure . . . when I go to (intelligible). . . . It's mostly . . . it's Dave who gets knocked around. . . . [Justification and limited conception of violence.]
Dave is your son?	Yes.
How old is he?	He's 8.
Could you give me an example of what is going on with your son?	Sometimes I'll grab him by the arm . . . when he doesn't listen to me. [Conception of authority in parent-child relationships.]

(Continued)

(Continued)

Interviewer	Mark
Do you have a recent example of something that happened?	[Smiles.] Well, the other day . . . when they called the DPJ . . . [the protection services]. I hit him because he wouldn't listen. . . . I told him to shut, pardon my French, "the fuckin' T.V." . . . He wouldn't listen, so I got mad. . . . The neighbor, she's the one who called the police . . . that's what my wife told me. . . . When there's something that bugs me, I don't say nothin', or I get pissed off. [The child's disobedience triggers the offensive assault.]
So you got "pissed off" at Dave. What exactly happened?	He pretended he didn't hear. . . . I smacked him behind the head and he started yelling at me . . . so I slammed him against the wall. [The child's behavior is interpreted as a challenge to authority.]
If you think back on this event, what really made you angry?	[8 seconds.] . . . When he was yellin' at me. [Violence detonator, threatening the father's security.]
When he was yelling, what was going through your head?	. . . I couldn't help it; it just happened. . . . I hit him. [Impulsiveness, feeling of loss of control.]
What condition was Dave in?	He was bleeding, my wife brought him to the hospital, . . . the doctor said it could've been bad.
How bad?	Yeah, it could've been worse. . . . I didn't kill him or nothin'. . . . [smiles]. [Trivialization of violence.]
What consequences do you think it could have for Dave?	I told the judge already. . . . I know I can hit pretty hard.
Can you tell me what happens when you lose control over yourself?	. . . I get mad too fast . . . especially when I've had a couple of drinks. [Justification for the violence.]
You find that you're violent toward your son especially when you've been drinking? [The practitioner knows that Mark will undergo an evaluation to assess the type and the severity of his alcohol and other substance abuse.]	. . . Yeah. . . . I yell. . . . I ain't patient [silence]. I used to smoke up all the time, and I was always hammered. It's a bit better now, I drink less than before, booze is not my thing. [Trivialization of and justification for the violence.]
You are violent when you have been drinking, but are you violent when you are sober?	It happens. . . . I ain't patient. [Trivialization of the violence.]
What happens when you aren't patient?	I yell mostly. . . .
When you are impatient, do you yell . . . and hit?	It happens . . . not that often [Father's resistance, even denial?]
Who gets hit in the family?	[4 seconds] . . . Dave [looks upset].
Only Dave? [The practitioner does not insist at this point, knowing that the physical and psychological abuse probably is not directed only toward Dave.]	Yes. [Father's denial.]
Why Dave?	He doesn't listen. . . . He's stubborn. . . . He's got no respect. [Trivialization of the abuse.]

Interviewer	Mark
Do you think it helps Dave become more obedient when you hit him?	Not all the time [chuckles]. . . . He listens when I get mad, then after, he starts all over again.
Do you think he might be afraid of you?	Maybe, yeah. . . . Everyone is scared [chuckle]. [Minimizes the effect, resistance.]
Does it affect you when you think of what is happening with Dave?	Yes . . . a bit. [Minimizes the effect.]
How does it affect you?	[8-second silence.] I don't like it, that's for sure. [Avoids emotional content.]
You don't like it. . . .	[Does not answer.]
Would you like to have other ways to help Dave become more obedient? [At this point in the process, the social worker does not mention more positive methods of upbringing.]	Well, yeah [sad look]. That's what I'm here for.
Are there things you like to do with your son, times when you enjoy being with Dave?	When we fight for fun [laughs].
What it is like during those times?	We fight for fun, we roughhouse, I show him how to fight [smiles]. [Mark teaches his son to fight so he can defend himself better?]
Do you enjoy doing other things with your son?	. . . I watch movies on TV with him.
Do you think he likes having fun with you?	Yeah, he likes it [smiles].
Who, currently in your life, could help you diminish your violent behavior? [Exploring his need for help, parent's ability to make up for what he has done.]	My wife. She screams at me when I hit him. . . . She don't like it. She said she'd leave with the kids if I don't change [smiles]. [Emotional distance.]
It helps you when she sets her limits?	I don't want her to leave with the kids [wrings his hands].
Does your wife find it hard, your abuse?	Yes, she finds it hard.
What are you willing to do so that she doesn't leave with the children?	I gotta stop drinking, I drink too much. [Acknowledgment of only one part of the problem.]
What are you going to do to stop drinking and stop your violent behavior?	Well, I'm comin' here and I'm goin' to see [names the drug counselor]. I see him tomorrow.

Second Part. Understanding the client's life story. The objective is to identify and evaluate the effects of certain elements from the past on present behavior, especially the reproduction of abuse suffered attachment relationships that the parent had as a child and trauma experienced.

What do you remember about the people who raised you? Your relationship with the person you consider most as a parent?	I didn't really have no parents. . . . My mother didn't take care of me. . . . It was my grandmother.
Do you consider your grandmother to be your parent?	Yes.
When you think about her, and the relationship you had with her, what word or memory comes to mind?	It was hell, we would always argue. We almost never had fun together. One day when I was 13, when I left the foster home, my mom was supposed to take me back, to try, but she ended up not taking me because this one time, she got on my nerves and she called

(Continued)

(Continued)

me a bad name so I grabbed her and struggled with her and I threw her against the wall. . . . It was always stuff like that [laughs].
[Confusion in his thoughts, dissociation between affect and content.]

As far back as you can remember, when you were a child, how were things with your mother?

[14-second silence.] . . . It wasn't her that took care of me, my aunts would give me a bath [laughs]. She was strict, if you'd ask her for a quarter she'd start yelling, she never wanted. . . .

Can you describe to me how she was strict?

She'd always have a fit. . . . She'd yell all the time.

You mentioned that the person you considered as a parent was your grandmother. Could you tell me about the relationship you had with her?

She was less strict, she'd always say no, but it'd really mean yes [19 seconds].

How would you describe the relationship with her?

[8 seconds.] . . . This one time she ran after me, with an axe. . . . I'd pissed her off big time [laughs].
[Laughter, sign of dissociation between affect and content.]

With an axe?

Yeah . . . 'cause I screamed some bad names at her; I called her a bitch, and other names. . . . Let's just say I'd had a couple too many.

What was different with your grandmother for you to consider her as your parent?

She was the only one to calm me down. . . . She came and saw me in my foster home. The rest of my family, I didn't give a damn.

When something bothered you when you were a child, you had trouble staying calm?

I punched holes in the walls; I'd break everything around me.

Do you remember anything in particular that bothered you to the point of reacting like that?

No, nothing.

You lived in a foster home from age 7 to 13. What type of relationship did you have with your foster family?

[27 seconds . . . Sign of trauma.]
Janine, . . . she was nice, whenever I decided she was nice [laughs]. I was impossible, but she never laid a hand on me, she'd never say bad things. When we'd go strawberry picking she'd let me keep the money, but she'd tell me to keep some for later, that it was important not to spend everything.

What would best describe your relationship with her?

[26 seconds.] . . . It wasn't like with my mom.
[Reaction time, sign of trauma.]

What was different?

I was treated better there. I even still visit them, once or twice a year. Once things turned bad, I slapped her across the face. She grabbed me by the arm and took me up to my room. She wasn't out of hand, I asked for it, 'cause she was nice.

You found her nice? Do you remember something about that?

Well, you didn't get slapped on the head and kicked in the ass; you didn't get called dirty names. My family, I don't talk to them no more.

When you think about the persons in your original family and your foster family, who do you feel closer to?

To my grandmother.
[The following interview will reveal that Mark reacted strongly to his grandmother's death when he was 19 years of age and married; he overdosed on pills and had to be hospitalized.]

Do you think that the reactions you had as a child have something to do with your fits of anger today?

[8 seconds.] . . . Maybe they do. . . . I dunno.

Differential Diagnosis and Behavioral Assessment

Parents' unresolved issues from their own childhood may be projected into the child, resulting in high levels of anger and reactivity that are quickly minimized, denied, or justified by the child's perceived badness (Bugental, Lewis, Lin, Lyon, & Kopeikin, 1999).

In the interview we gathered the information needed to arrive at a preliminary diagnosis of Mark's situation. The diagnosis will be completed with an assessment of the type of drug and alcohol addiction involved. The link between parental violence and drug and alcohol use has been clearly established (Chaffin, Kelleher, & Hollenberg, 1996; Walsh, MacMillan, & Jamieson, 2003) and must be factored into counseling programs for abusive parents.

A psychometric assessment often is crucial to arriving at a reliable diagnosis. The following are valid instruments for clinical work: the Childhood Trauma Questionnaire, developed by Bernstein and Fink (1998), composed of 28 questions dealing with childhood trauma (emotional abuse, physical abuse, sexual abuse, emotional neglect and physical neglect); the Revised Conflict Tactics Scales, a marital conflict resolution questionnaire by Strauss, Hamby, Boney-McCoy, and Sugarman (1996) made up of 10 subscales (negotiation used by the respondent, psychological aggression committed by the respondent, physical assault, sexual coercion and injuries inflicted by the respondent on his or her partner, and five subscales dealing with acts committed by the respondent's male or female partner); the Parent Child Conflict Tactics Scale, developed by Strauss and Hamby (1995), composed of 27 items designed to distinguish nonviolence, psychological abuse, and severe or very severe abuse in disciplinary measures; the Millon Clinical Multiaxial Inventory III (Millon & Davis, 1997), used to identify personality disorders in at-risk populations; and the Dissociative Experiences Scales, developed by Carlson and Putnam (1993), made up of 28 items and five scales (amnesia, depersonalization, derealization, absorption, and imaginative involvement).

Information we collected in the interview show that Mark's childhood was marked by physical abuse and ruptures with his attachment figure and that he shows signs of unresolved trauma (e.g., his long reaction times, loss of control evident in his behaviors, "doesn't know what he is doing").

His mode of communication is avoidant (he avoids or inhibits affects), and he shows a lack of empathy for his son, Dave. He minimizes the gravity of his violent acts. A breakup with his wife could lead to intense emotional reactions (e.g., violence, medication overdose). Nevertheless, Mark wants to get help, he values his relationship with his wife and children (he has positive experiences with son), and he is aware of his substance abuse problem (he has tried to stop using drugs and alcohol). He had two positive mother figures during his childhood (his grandmother and Janine, his foster mother). Many of his behaviors are reactions to childhood traumas.

As noted by Kelly and Wolfe (2004), practitioners must gain a better understanding of the effects of childhood traumas on adult abuse. When such intense emotional experiences remain unresolved, they can lead not only to depression (Naar-King, Silvern, Ryan, & Sebring, 2002) but to a series of psychic mechanisms, such as anxiety and symptoms of post-traumatic stress, sudden outbursts of anger, cognitive distortions, identity disorders, avoidance, and mental dissociation,[3] that are highly detrimental to parenting (Brière, 1996; Kluft, 1996; McClosey & Walker, 2000; Putman, 1997).

Parental violence is also associated with delinquency and crime. Child maltreatment, especially when it occurs before the age of 12 years, is significantly linked to delinquency in adolescence and adulthood. This link is greater for males than females (Stouthamer-Loeber, Loeber, Homish, & Wei, 2001; Widom, 1989).

Finally, studies have found that family violence is associated with personality disorders, including borderline personality disorder, in abusive men (Hamberger, Hastings, 1991). Violent women who physically abuse their husbands display depressive problems and various personality disorders (Henning, Jones, & Holdford, 2003).

Selection of Intervention Programs

Intervention Without Exclusion

In intervention programs, mothers are perceived as child protectors and fathers as child abusers. Although abusive mothers often are separated from their children when the latter are temporarily or permanently placed in foster care, efforts to improve the mother-child relationship clearly are more common than in the case of father-child relationships (Scott & Crooks, 2004).

Intervention with fathers is not only less common but often paradoxical in the sense that fathers must demonstrate the motivation to change without receiving all the help that is needed to fulfill that objective. As noted by Featherstone (2001), Martin (1984), and Sternberg (1997), practitioners probably consider fathers too difficult to reach or less important to the development of the child. Others propose that if the father has a harmful impact on the mother-child relationship, it is preferable that his visits be cut short, supervised, or simply stopped (Bancroft & Silverman, 2002).

The type of intervention currently used with abusive fathers consists of therapy sessions and supervised visits. The father usually meets with his child (frequency varies according to each case), generally outside the family home and under the supervision of a person designated by the child protection services. This type of limited intervention may be prove to be necessary, especially in cases of severe abuse or where the father is highly resistant to making changes in his behavior, but it cannot be considered a general formula to apply in all cases of family violence. This practice is now being challenged in favor of placing greater emphasis on intervention designed to support and improve the parenting skills of fathers (Harne & Radford, 1995; Scott & Crooks, 2004). Although the crisis brought on by an injunction requiring a father to undergo therapy or legal action preventing him coming into contact with his children may sometimes be a necessary evil, it may prove to be therapeutically counterproductive. All the clinical efforts must be then be focused on managing the effects of the restrictions rather than on the actual problem of violence (Kelly & Wolfe, 2003).

The exclusion of abusive fathers from the intervention process reinforces their lack of sense of responsibility for their behavior and in doing so places the emphasis for change on the women's shoulders. Moreover, the exclusion of fathers does not take into account the emotional ties that develop between a father and his children. Children stay emotionally connected to their father, even if he is violent (Boss, 1999; Wallerstein & Blakeslee, 1989). Some children seek to understand the loss or abandonment of their father, even after many years. Others are torn between their desire to see him and their relief of no longer having to deal with his abuse and anger (Peled, 1998). Furthermore, these same

men excluded from their family may ultimately become father figures for 6 to 10 children over the course of their life (Scott & Crooks, 2004). They go from family to family and are thus at high risk of abusing other children (Daly & Wilson, 2000). Women, on the other hand, reproduce the model of abuse by repeatedly choosing a violent partner.

Intervention Targets

For intervention to be successful, it is important to identify the attitudes and beliefs that characterize abusive parents. These parents believe that they have rights over their close ones and that they can legitimately exercise those rights through various forms of control, by using force and violence. For example, abusive fathers often demand strict obedience from their spouse and children and respect and dedication to their desires and needs. When their loved ones do not conform to such expectations, the fathers feel scorned or unjustly treated (Francis, Scott, Crooks, & Kelly, 2002). Abusive mothers often expect their children to fulfill their emotional needs and be available to them. These mothers perceive themselves as being powerless in the family and tend to attribute negative intentions to their spouse and children (Bugental, Brown, & Reiss, 1996; Bugental, Lewis, et al., 1999; Bugental et al., 2002).

Parents who exhibit violent behaviors are hypervigilant in recognizing the least sign of rejection, lack of respect, or disobedience on the part of their children. Such behavior creates extreme tension in the family as the members try to avoid any confrontation and violent outbursts. Controlling behaviors, hypersensitivity to rejection, and the feeling that they have the right to dominate significant others have also been found in men who abuse their spouses (Dutton, 1996, 1998; Hamberger & Hastings, 1991). Wife batterers expect their partner to be available to meet their personal physical, emotional, and psychological needs (Pence & Paymar, 1993). Such controlling and demanding attitudes toward the wife are easily transferred to the children (Bancroft & Silverman, 2002), which would explain the high rate of combined spousal and parental abuse (Edleson, 1999).

Abusive parents tend to focus on their own needs at the expense of the needs of their children. Bancroft and Silverman (2002) note that abusive fathers take an interest in their children when it is convenient for them, when their emotional state of mind permits it, or when they can receive public recognition. These fathers are rarely able to talk about the personal interests of their daughter or son, their circle of friends, or their favorite activities (Francis et al., 2002). The tendency for abusive parents to be focused on their own rights and needs at the expense of others must form the basis for any intervention program aimed at countering family violence.

Effectiveness of Intervention Programs

Wolfe and Wekerle (1993) maintain that intervention with abusive parents must fulfill eight key requirements: decrease the symptoms of psychological distress or personality disorders that make it difficult for these adults to adapt; reduce their impulsive, angry, and hostile reactions toward their children; increase the effectiveness of their parenting methods; make their beliefs and expectations regarding their children more realistic and decrease the rigidity of their parenting; make their lifestyle less chaotic and reduce their substance abuse or other practices that hinder parenting; take into account spousal abuse or a history of abusive male partners; take into account chronic financial problems and other stressors associated with poverty; and address social isolation of the family.

After an exhaustive 10-year review of intervention programs for abusive parents, Dufour and Chamberland (2003) concluded that the majority of intervention programs do not address the needs identified by Wolfe and Wekerle (1993) and that their efficacy has yet to be demonstrated. Nevertheless, although no one program for abusive parents stands out as more effective, most of the interventions reviewed were promising insofar as positive changes had been observed in mothers (e.g., decreased maternal depression and decreased abusive conduct). Our understanding of the efficacy of interventions with abusive fathers is sketchy because men often are excluded from child protection services. The little reliable data we have relates to wife batterers, who often also abuse their children.

A meta-analytic review by Babcock, Green, and Robie (2004) that examined the efficacy of 22 programs for abusive men shows that they have little impact, whether they take a psychoeducational approach aimed at eliminating authoritarian behaviors and male attitudes and values regarding power over close ones or a cognitive-behavioral approach designed to teach nonviolent assertive behaviors, communication skills, and social skills. Nevertheless, the programs with the highest rates of efficacy and the lowest rates of attrition are those developed by Taft, Murphy, Elliot, and Morrel (2001, cited in Babcock et al., 2004) and Waldo (1988). The first program is composed of behavioral techniques and group therapies, with particular attention paid to parental motivation (reminder phone calls and supportive handwritten notes). The second program, relationship enhancement, inspired by work done by Guerney (1977), is aimed at developing interpersonal skills and putting an end to the abuse. Interventions include role playing and exercises given as homework to increase interpersonal skills, empathy toward others, and partner communication. Finally, the program emphasizes identifying and controlling emotions (Waldo, 1988).

One of the reasons for the ineffectiveness of intervention programs for abusers is the lack of judgment in the target population (Babcock, Green, & Robie, 2004; Dufour & Chamberland, 2003; Scott & Wolfe, 2000). These programs deal with men and women who have varying degrees of motivation, different substance abuse problems, and a wide range of personal problems (e.g., personality disorders, unresolved trauma, criminal activities). Kinard (2002) notes that in many cases the services available to family members are not geared to their specific needs. Thus, numerous programs are aimed at enhancing the family's social support network without making the link between supporting the family and decreasing abusive behaviors. Other programs are aimed at improving parenting and communication skills without addressing the problem of parental or spousal abuse.

Continuity of Services

The majority of intervention programs for abusive parents last between 18 and 24 months (Éthier & Lacharité, 2000) and those for abusive men between 3 and 12 months (Austin & Dankwort, 1999). Although no studies have assessed the efficacy of interventions based on their duration, we are of the opinion that once the objective of an intensive program has been reached, certain services should continue to be offered on a less intensive basis to prevent second offenses and to reinforce the parents' newly acquired skills. We have seen that most families where abuse occurs have multiple psychological and social needs that cannot be met over a short period of time. At best, properly targeted intervention programs may decrease or put an end to abusive behaviors directed at children or the spouse, but these behaviors ca reemerge during times of stress or increases in child behavior problems, especially in the teenage years (Éthier, Lemelin, & Lacharité, 2004) and in the event of marital breakups, financial problems, or conflicts with family and friends.

Summary

In this chapter we have emphasized how important it is that interviews and individual counseling relationships with abusive parents be part of a logical integration of services for these parents and their families. The needs displayed by abusive parents and the complexity of the factors involved in physical abuse are such that the help needed goes beyond the work of a single practitioner. Consequently, multiple modes of intervention must be put into place to address the parents' needs and the many complex aspects of the problem.

An integrated approach means targeting professional practices based on the needs of parents and their families over an intensive period of treatment, followed by support services aimed at reinforcing the fathers' and mothers' parenting skills, maximizing the resources available to them, and preventing repeat incidents of abusive behavior. Integrated services for a family should not be confused with the superimposing of independent services; we need integrated professional practices designed for abusive parents, the type of relations and alliances that practitioners need to develop so that these parents feel supported and helped in a coherent and integrated manner. All contacts with professionals must project a common vision of their situation and involve complementary forms of help and support. The suggestions made in this chapter are aimed at standardizing interviewing practices, just one aspect in the process of helping abusive parents.

Notes

1. In 1994, 68% of American adults approved of spanking as a disciplinary measure (Strauss & Mathur, 1996). In 1999, 50% of Canadian parents approved of this form of discipline (Clément, Bouchard, Jetté, & Laferrière, 2000).

2. This interview was conducted as part of a Fonds Quebecois de la Recherche sur la Société et la Culture (FQRSC)–funded research project. The father voluntarily agreed to be filmed. The majority of parents, approximately two thirds, refuse to be videotaped.

3. Dissociation is a disruption in the usually integrated functions of consciousness, memory, identity, and perception (American Psychiatric Association, 2000, p. 519).

References

Adams, D. (1988). Treatment models for men who batter: A profeminist analysis. In K. Yllo & M. Bograd (Eds.), *Feminist perspective on wife abuse* (pp. 176–199). Newbury Park, CA: Sage.

American Psychiatric Association. (2000). *Diagnostic and statistical manual of mental disorders* (4th ed., Text rev.). Washington, DC: Author.

Appel, A. E., & Holden, G. W. (1998). The co-occurrence of spouse and physical child abuse: A review and appraisal. *Journal of Family Psychology, 12*(4), 578–599.

Austin, J. B., & Dankwort, J. (1999). The impact of a batterers' program on battered women. *Violence Against Women, 5*(1), 25–42.

Babcock, J. C., Green, C. E., & Robie, C. (2004). Does batterers' treatment work? A meta-analytic review of domestic violence treatment. *Clinical Psychology Review, 23*, 1023–1053.

Bancroft, L., & Silverman, J. C. (2002). *The batterer as parent: Addressing the impact of domestic violence on family dynamics.* Thousand Oaks, CA: Sage.

Baumrind, D. (1996). Parenting: The discipline controversy. *Family Relations, 45*, 405–414.

Berger, A. M., Knutson, J. F., Mehm, J., & Perkins, K. A. (1988). The self-report of punitive childhood experiences of young adults and adolescents. *Child Abuse & Neglect, 12*(2), 251–262.

Bernstein, D. P., & Fink, L. (1998). *Childhood trauma questionnaire: A retrospective self-report.* San Antonio: The Psychological Corporation.

Boss, P. (1999). *Ambiguous loss: Learning to live with unresolved grief.* Cambridge, MA: Harvard University Press.

Bowlby, J. (1980). *Attachment and loss: Vol. 3. Loss: Sadness and depression.* New York: Basic Books.

Bowlby, J. (1982). Attachment and loss. *American Journal of Orthopsychiatry, 52*, 664–678.

Brière, J. (1996). A self trauma model for treating adult survivors of severe child abuse. In J. Brière et al.

(Eds.), *The APSAC handbook on child maltreatment* (pp. 140–157). Thousand Oaks, CA: Sage.

Bugental, D. B. (1992). Affective and cognitive processes within threat-oriented family systems. In I. E. Sigel (Ed.), *Parental beliefs systems: The psychological consequences for children* (2nd ed., pp. 219–248). Hillsdale, NJ: Lawrence Erlbaum.

Bugental, D. B., Brown, M., & Reiss, C. (1996). Cognitive representations of power in caregiving relationships. Biasing effects on interpersonal interaction and information processing. *Journal of Family Psychology, 10,* 397–407.

Bugental, D. B., & Clayton, L. J. (1998). Interpersonal power repair in response to threats to control from dependent others. In K. Miroslaw, G. Weary, & G. Sedek (Eds.), *Personal control in action: Cognitive and motivational mechanisms* (pp. 341–362). New York: Plenum.

Bugental, D. B., & Clayton, L. J. (1999). The paradoxical misuse of power by those who see themselves as powerless: How does it happen? *Journal of Social Issues, 55*(1), 51–64.

Bugental, D. B., Ellerson, P. C., Lin, E. K., Rainey, B., Kokotovic, A., & O'Hara, N. (2002). A cognitive approach to child abuse prevention. *Journal of Family Psychology, 16*(3), 243–258.

Bugental, D. B., & Happaney, K. (2000). Parent-child interaction as a power contest. *Journal of Applied Developmental Psychology, 21*(3), 267–282.

Bugental, D. B., & Johnson, C. (2000). Parental and child cognitions in the context of the family. *Annual Review of Psychology, 51,* 315–344.

Bugental, D. B., Lewis, J. C., Lin, E. K., Lyon, J., & Kopeikin, H. (1999). In charge but not in control: The management of teaching relationship by adults with low perceived power. *Developmental Psychology, 35,* 1376–1378.

Bugental, D. B., Lyon, J. E., Lin, E. K., McGrawth, E. P., & Bimbela, A. (1999). Children "tune-out" in response to the ambiguous communication style of powerless adults. *Child Development, 70*(1), 214–230.

Carlson, C. B., & Putman, F. W. (1993). An update on the Dissociative Experiences Scale. *Dissociation, 6,* 16–27.

Chaffin, M., Kelleher, K., & Hollenberg, J. (1996). Onset of physical abuse and neglect: Psychiatric, substance abuse and social risk factors from prospective community data. *Child Abuse & Neglect, 20*(3), 191–203.

Chamberland, C. (2003). *Violence parentale et violence conjugale: Des réalités plurielles, multidimensionnelles et interreliées* [Parental and marital violence: Plural, multidimensional, and interdependent realities]. Quebec: Presses de l'Université du Québec.

Clément, M. E., Bouchard, C., Jetté, M., & Laferrière, S. (2000). *La violence familiale dans la vie des enfants du Québec, 1999* [Family violence in the lives of children in Quebec, 1999]. Quebec: Institut de la Statistique du Québec.

Crittenden, P. M. (1989). Internal representational models of attachment relationships. *Infant Mental Health Journal, 11,* 259–277.

Crittenden, P. M. (2001). Attachment. In E. Habimana, L. S. Éthier, D. Pétot, & M. Tousignant (Eds.), *Manuel de psychopathologie de l'enfant et de l'adolescent* [Textbook of child and adolescent psychopathology] (pp. 67–94). Chicoutimi, PQ: Gäétan Morin.

Crittenden, P. M., & Claussen, A. H. (2000). *The organization of attachment relationships: Maturation, culture, and context.* Cambridge, UK: Cambridge University Press.

Daly, M., & Wilson, M. (2000). Family violence: An evolutionary psychological perspective. *Virginia Journal of Social Policy & the Law, 8,* 77–121.

De Hart, D. D., Kennerly, R. J., Burke, L. K., & Follingstad, D. R. (1999). Predictors of attrition in a treatment program of battering men. *Journal of Family Violence, 14,* 19–34.

Dietrich, D. L., Berkowitz, L., Kadushin, A., & McGloin, J. (1990). Some factors influencing abusers' justification of their child abuse. *Child Abuse & Neglect, 14*(3), 337–345.

Dix, T., Reinhold, D. P., & Zambarano, R. J. (1990). Mothers' judgment in moments of anger. *Merrill-Palmer Quarterly, 36*(4), 465–486.

Doise, W. (1990). Les représentations sociales [Social representations]. In J. Beauvois, M. Bromberg, J. Deschamps et al. (Eds.), *Traité du psychologie cognitive. Tome 3. Cognitions, représentations, communication* [Handbook of cognitive psychology: Vol. 3. Cognitions, representations, communication] (pp. 113–172). Paris: Dunod.

Dufour, S., & Chamberland, C. (2003). *Quelle est l'efficacité des interventions en protection de l'enfance* [How effective are child protection interventions]? Unpublished document, Centre of Excellence for Child Welfare, University of Toronto.

Dutton, D. (1996). Jealousy, intimate abusiveness and intrusiveness. *Journal of Family Violence, 11,* 411–423.

Dutton, D. (1998). *The abusive personality: Violence and control in intimate relationships.* New York: Guilford.

Edleson, J. L. (1999). The overlap between child maltreatment and woman battering. *Violence Against Women, 5,* 134–154.

Éthier, L. S. & Lacharité, C. (2000). Comment prévenir l'abus et la négligence envers les enfants [How to prevent child abuse and neglect]. In F. Vitaro (Ed.), *La prévention des problèmes d'adaptation chez les jeunes* [Prevention of adaptation problems in youth] (pp. 284–301). Montreal: Les Presses de l'Université de Montréal.

Éthier, L. S., Lemelin, J. P., & Lacharité, C. (2004). A longitudinal study of the effects of chronic maltreatment on children's behavioral and emotional problems. *Child Abuse and Neglect, the International Journal, 28,* 1265–1278.

Featherstone, B. (2001). Putting fathers on the child welfare agenda. *Child and Family Social Work, 6,* 179–186.

Francis, K., Scott, K. L., Crooks, C., & Kelly, T. (2002). *Caring dads: Evaluation strategies and preliminary data.* Paper presentation at the Victimization of Children & Youth: An International Research Conference, Portsmouth, NH.

Gondolf, E., & Russell, D. (1986). The case against anger control treatment programs for batterers. *Response, 9*, 2–5.

Guerney, B. G. (1977). *Relationship enhancement: Skill training programs for therapy, problem prevention and enrichment.* San Francisco: Jossey-Bass.

Hamberger, K., & Hastings, J. (1991). Personality correlates of men who batter and nonviolent men: Some continuities and discontinuities. *Journal of Family Violence, 6,* 131–147.

Harne, L., & Radford, J. (1995). Reinstating patriarchy: The politics of the family and the new legislation. In R. Morely (Ed.), *Children living with domestic violence: Putting men's abuse of women on the child care agenda* (pp. 68–86). London: Whiting & Birch.

Haskett, M. E., Marziano, B., & Dover, E. R. (1996). Absence of males in maltreatment research: A survey of recent literature. *Child Abuse & Neglect, 20*(12), 1175–1182.

Hastings, P. D., & Rubin, K. H. (1999). Predicting mothers' beliefs about preschool-aged children's social behavior: Evidence for maternal attitudes moderating child effects. *Child Development, 70*(3), 722–741.

Henning, K., Jones, A., & Holdford, R. (2003). Treatment needs of women arrested for domestic violence. A comparison with male offenders. *Journal of Interpersonal Violence, 18*(8), 839–856.

Holden, G. W., Coleman, S. M., & Schmidt, K. L. (1995). Why 3-year old children get spanked: Parent and child determinants as reported by college-educated mothers. *Merrill-Palmer Quarterly, 41*(4), 431–452.

Kelly, T., & Wolfe, D. A. (2004). Advancing change with maltreating fathers. *Clinical Psychology: Science & Practice, 11*(1), 116–119.

Kinard, E. M. (2002). Services for maltreated children: Variations by maltreatment characteristics. *Child Welfare League of Canada, 81*(4), 617–645.

Kluft, R. P. (1996). Treating the traumatic memories of patients with dissociative identity disorder. *American Journal of Psychiatry, 153*(7), 103–110.

Lacharité, C., Ethier, L. S., & Nolin, P. (2006). Vers une théorie écosystémique de la négligence envers les enfants [Toward an ecosystemic theory of child neglect]. *Bulletin de Psychologie, 59*(4). 381–394.

Lansky, M. (1992). *Fathers who fail: Shame and psychopathology in the system.* Hillsdale, NJ: Analytic Press.

Leigh, I., Ogborne, A. C., & Cleland, P. (1984). Factors associated with patient dropout from an outpatient alcoholism treatment service. *Journal of Studies on Alcohol, 45,* 359–362.

Levy, R. I. (1984). Emotion, knowing, and culture. In R. A. Shweder & R. A. Levine (Eds.), *Culture theory: Essays on mind, self, and emotions* (pp. 214–237). Cambridge, UK: Cambridge University Press.

Main, M. (1991). Metacognitive knowledge, metacognitive monitoring, and singular (coherent) vs. multiple (incoherent) models of attachment: Findings and directions for future research. In C. M. Parkes, J. Stevenson-Hinde, & P. Marris (Eds.), *Attachment across the life cycle* (pp. 127–159). London: Routledge.

Malo, C., Moreau, J., Chamberland, C., Léveillée, S., & Roy, C. (2002). Émotions, cognitions et réactions des pères en situation disciplinaire: Semblables ou différentes de celles des mères [Emotions, cognitions, and reactions by fathers in disciplinary situations: Similar to or different from those of mothers]? *Revue Internationale de l'Éducation Familiale, 6*(1), 41–56.

Margolin, G., Gordis, E. B., Medina, A. M., & Oliver, P. (2003). The co-occurrence of husband-to-wife aggression, family-of-origin aggression, and child abuse potential in a community sample. *Journal of Interpersonal Violence, 18*(4), 413–440.

Martin, J. (1984). Neglected fathers: Limitations in diagnostic and treatment resources for violent men. *Child Abuse & Neglect, 8,* 387–392.

McClosey, L. A., & Walker, M. (2000). Posttraumatic stress in children exposed to family violence and single-event trauma. *Journal of American Child and Adolescent Psychiatry, 39,* 108–115.

McGloin, J. M., & Widom, C. S. (2001). Resilience among abused and neglected children grown up. *Development and Psychopathology, 13,* 1021–1038.

Miller, A. (1986). *L'enfant sous terreur* [The terrorized child]. Paris: Aubier.

Miller, W. R., & Rollnick, S. (2002). *Motivational interviewing* (2nd ed.). New York: Guilford.

Millon, T., & Davis, R. (1997). The MCMI-III. Present and future directions. *Journal of Personality Assessment, 68,* 69–85.

Milner, J. S. (1993). Social information processing and physical child abuse. *Clinical Psychology Review, 13*(3), 275–294.

Moscovici, S., & Duveen, G. (2000). *Social representations: Explorations in social psychology.* New York: Blackwell.

Naar-King, S., Silvern, L., Ryan, V., & Sebring, D. (2002). Type and severity of abuse as predictors of psychiatric symptoms in adolescence. *Journal of Family Violence, 17*(2), 133–149.

Ney, P. G. (1987). Does verbal abuse leave deeper scars? A study of children and parents. *Canadian Journal of Psychiatry, 35*(5), 371.

Peled, E. (1998). The experience of living with violence for preadolescent children of battered women. *Youth and Society, 29,* 395–430.

Pence, E., & Paymar, M. (1993). *Education groups for men who batter. The Duluth model.* New York: Springer.

Phares, V. (1996). Conducting non sexist research, prevention, and treatment with fathers and mothers. *Psychology of Women Quarterly, 20,* 55–77.

Prilleltensky, I., Nelson, G., & Peirson, L. (2001). *Promoting family wellness and preventing child maltreatment.* Toronto: University of Toronto Press.

Putman, F. W. (1997). *Dissociation in children and adolescents.* New York: Guilford.

Rooney, J., & Hanson, R. K. (2001). Predicting attrition from treatment programs for abusive men. *Journal of Family Violence, 16*(2), 131–149.

Scott, K. L., & Crooks, C. (2004). Effecting change in maltreating fathers: Critical principles for intervention planning. *Clinical Psychological Science Practice 11,* 95–111.

Scott, K. L., & Wolfe, D. A. (2000). Change among batterers: Examine men's success stories. *Journal of Interpersonal Violence, 15*(8), 827.

Sidebotham, P., & Golding, J. (2001). Child maltreatment in the "children of the nineties": A longitudinal study of parental risk factors. *Child Abuse & Neglect, 25*(9), 1177–1200.

Smith, A. M., & O'Leary, S. G. (2001). Examining partner and child abuse: Are we ready for a more integrated approach to family violence? *Clinical Child and Family Psychology Review, 4,* 87–107.

Sternberg, K. (1997). Fathers: The missing parents in family violence research. In M. Lamb (Ed.), *The role of the father in child development* (3rd ed., pp. 284–308). New York: Wiley.

Stouthamer-Loeber, M., Loeber, R., Homish, D. L., & Wei, E. (2001). Maltreatment of boys and the development of disruptive and delinquent behavior. *Development and Psychopathology, 13,* 941–955.

Strauss, M. A. (1979). Measuring intra-family conflict and violence: The Conflict Tactics Scale. *Journal of Marriage and the Family, 41,* 75–88.

Strauss, M. A., & Hamby, S. L. (1995). *Measuring physical and psychological maltreatment of children with the Conflict Tactics Scales.* Durham: University of New Hampshire.

Strauss, M. A., Hamby, S. L., Boney-McCoy, S., & Sugarman, D. B. (1996). The Revised Conflict Tactics Scales. *Journal of Family Issues, 17,* 283–316.

Strauss, M. A., Hamby, S. L., Finkelhor, D., Moore, D. W. & Runyan, D. (1998). Identification of child maltreatment with the Parent-Child Conflict Tactics Scale: Development and psychometric data for a national sample of American parents. *Child Abuse & Neglect, 22*(4), 249–270.

Strauss, M. A., & Mathur, A. K. (1996). Social change and trends in approval of corporal punishment by parents from 1968 to 1994. In D. Fresher, W. S. Horn, & K. D. Bussmann (Eds.), *Family violence against children. A challenge for society* (pp. 91–105). New York: Walter de Gruyter.

Trocmé, N. M., MacLaurin, B. J., & Fallon, B. (2001). Canadian incidence study of reported child abuse and neglect: Methodology. *Canadian Journal of Public Health, 92*(4), 259–263.

U.S. Department of Health and Human Services. (2001). *Child maltreatment 1999: Report from the states to the National Center on Child Abuse and Neglect.* Washington, DC: U.S. Government Printing Office.

Waldo, M. (1988). Relationship enhancement counselling groups for wife abusers. *Journal of Mental Health Counseling, 10,* 37–45.

Wallerstein, J., & Blakeslee, S. (1989). *Second chances: Men, women, and children a decade after divorce.* New York: Tickmor & Fields.

Walsh, C., MacMillan, H. L., & Jamieson, E. (2003). The relationship between parental substance abuse and child maltreatment: Findings from the Ontario Health Supplement. *Child Abuse & Neglect, 27,* 1409–1425.

Widom, C. S. (1989). Child abuse, neglect and adult behavior. Research design and findings on criminality. *American Journal of Orthopsychiatry, 50,* 355–367.

Wolfe, D. (1999). *Child abuse: Implication for child development and psychopathology* (2nd ed.). Thousand Oaks, CA: Sage.

Wolfe, D. A., & Wekerle, C. (1993). Prevention of child physical abuse and neglect: Promising new directions. *Clinical Psychology Review, 13,* 501–540.

28

BEHAVIORAL MEDICINE CONSULTATION

JOHN G. ARENA

This chapter focuses in on the consultative role of a mental health professional who specializes in behavioral medicine or health psychology. It is meant as a step-by-step primer on behavioral medicine consultation. It concentrates mainly on the clinical components of the typical behavioral medicine consultation for chronic pain rather than specific consultative research. The author assumes that the consultation was initiated by a primary care provider rather than a specialist. This chapter focuses on consultation in a general medical and surgical hospital and consultation by a private practitioner and includes many clinical hints for the mental health professional. Finally, it reviews selected literature in four areas that are deemed most promising for future research in behavioral medicine consultation.

Behavioral medicine consultation is a branch of psychology that began in the 1960s and grew out of the behavior therapy movement. Just as the field of behavior therapy involved the application of learning theory, which was based on laboratory and animal experimental models, to a traditional mental health population, behavioral medicine (and hence behavioral medicine consultation) was a natural offshoot of behavior therapy. Indeed, behavioral medicine and health psychology typically involve the application of well-established and empirically sound learning theory principles to a traditional medical domain, such as pain, insomnia, eating disorders, and obesity.

Behavioral medicine consultation also can trace its roots to the psychosomatic medicine and liaison psychiatry movements. The psychosomatic medicine movement in psychiatry, which began in the 1940s, involved application of psychodynamic psychotherapy to traditional medical problems, and the current liaison psychiatry field grew out of the psychosomatic medicine realm and entails a combination of psychosomatic medicine and psychopharmacological approaches.

Today, behavioral medicine consultation generally involves not only behavior therapy but also cognitive therapy approaches and components of system theory, developmental and social psychology, and neuropsychology. But the mortar that holds behavioral medicine and behavioral medicine consultation together is an empirical approach to the assessment and treatment of traditional medical problems.

This chapter is meant as a primer for psychologists working in a consultative role with medical professionals. It focuses on chronic pain for two reasons: That is where the expertise of the author lies, and dealing with people who suffer from chronic pain is the bread and butter of the typical psychologist in a general medical and surgical hospital.

Why Is There a Need for Behavioral Medicine Consultation?

One reason why behavioral medicine approaches are increasingly used in medicine is the changing nature of the treated illnesses. Modern, mechanistic-based medicine is very effective in dealing with acute illnesses caused by infections and accidents. However, modern medicine often fails with chronic illnesses, many of which are influenced by lifestyle choices and are strongly affected by psychological and behavioral factors. It is estimated that as many as 80% of primary care visits are for problems that involve lifestyle and psychological factors.

Another reason for the growth of behavioral medicine treatments is the emphasis on prevention and cost containment in modern health care. Psychological interventions in traditionally medical realms have increased at an exponential rate in the past quarter century and have proven effective with a variety of illnesses, such as chronic headache, arthritis, low back pain, irritable bowel syndrome, obesity, and hypertension. Today, research points to the targeted use of educational, behavioral, psychological, and psychophysiological interventions in a medical setting as simple, safe, and inexpensive treatments that can dramatically improve health outcomes and reduce the need for more expensive medical approaches. Therefore, there is a strong and growing need for behavioral medicine consultation.

Before the Consultation

The Basic Knowledge Set

Before a mental health professional begins the behavioral medicine consultation process, he or she should have a basic understanding of the area in which he or she is consulting. For a psychologist, that involves a doctoral degree, which includes a year of predoctoral internship and at least a year of postdoctoral fellowship. It is presumed that during this training, you will have obtained a significant amount of exposure to the area in which you will consult (e.g., if you

plan to do genetic counseling, you should have some experience in genetic counseling).

For someone who plans to consult on chronic pain, the basics include a good generalist education (too often, people with an extremely specialized education miss things that the average psychologist would not, such as how to distinguish between a pain patient and a schizophrenic suffering from somatic delusions) that covers treatment of depression, anger, anxiety, and stress, with specialized training in cognitive-behavioral therapy for pain, biofeedback, relaxation therapy, hypnosis, pain psychoeducation (e.g., pacing), and other stress reduction techniques (e.g., exercise, vacations, pet therapy). Although the author assumes that the reader is familiar with the assessment and treatment techniques of his or her specialty, because this chapter is using chronic pain to illustrate the points made, later in the chapter we will review the chronic pain interview (the chief assessment tool used for chronic pain), cognitive-behavioral therapy, biofeedback, and relaxation therapy (the primary nonpharmacological treatment modalities used for chronic pain).

It is very helpful for any psychologist who plans to perform consultation, especially consultation in a hospital setting, to have a basic understanding of system theory. System theory is a reaction against the reductionist movement in psychology and is an attempt to present a basic theory of all behavior, not just the behavior of individuals but of governments, institutions, groups, and so on. It is an attempt to address complexity and diversity in general laws and concepts. It is believed that no matter how complex or diverse a system is, if you can apply these general rules to it, break it down into its organizational parts, you can understand that system.

It is this author's belief that a basic understanding of system theory is necessary because the consultant psychologist often must understand how individuals function by themselves, how individuals function as groups, and how individuals function within organizations such as hospitals, governments, and professional organizations. Arredondo, Shealy, Neal, and Winfrey (2004) emphasize how important it is for psychologists who consult to understand how "(a) organizations work independently and as part of larger systems; (b) ecological and contextual systems act as forces to influence individuals, groups and other systems; and (c) sociocultural values and forces (race, religion, etc.) influence and affect behavior and change" (p. 796).

One other point must be made. A strong ethical background is essential for a behavioral medicine consultant. Often the questions mental health professionals are asked to deal with in medical settings involve such complex and difficult ethical and moral issues as genetic counseling, HIV prevention, assessment of risk for organ transplant rejection, and competency. The psychologist who is not keenly aware of the ethical guidelines of the profession is setting himself or herself up for potentially serious legal and professional problems. Any mental health professional consulting in the medical arena should have taken course work on ethics and should take continuing education classes on ethics at least once a year.

The Essential Texts

For anyone who plans to consult with medical providers, it is essential to understand basic medical terms. Every behavioral medicine consultant should have immediate access to a *Physician's Desk Reference,* which gives basic information about medications (now readily available on the Web); a medical dictionary, which explains medical terms; a *Merck Manual* or other medical text that describes and provides basic information on numerous medical disorders; and an anatomy textbook, such as *Gray's Anatomy,* which goes over the functions of the various muscles and bones in the body.

In addition to these general reference books, there are basic medical texts specific to the disorders you might be consulting on. For example, for pain there is the *Textbook of Pain,* by Wall and Melzack (1994), and *Bonica's Management of Pain* by Loeser, Turk, Chapman, and Butler (2002). For low back pain, there is no definitive text. However, there are very good reviews, such as those by Atlas and Deyo (2001). Although it is somewhat dated, the headache Bible for medical clinicians remains *Diamond and Dalessio's The Practicing Physician's Guide to Headache* (Diamond & Solomon, 1999), now in its sixth edition.

The Office

Although the location of your office is not as essential to behavioral medicine consultants who are in private practice, it is extremely important to mental health clinicians in general medical and surgical hospitals. For private practitioners, it is helpful, but not essential, to locate your office close to your primary referral sources. However, for clinicians in hospitals, the selection of an office is quite important. Although there is a perception among laypeople that hospitals are quiet places, nothing could be further from the truth. Having an office located in a busy and therefore loud section of the hospital is not conducive to interviewing and is especially counterproductive if one is using psychophysiological treatments such as relaxation therapy and biofeedback, which require a quiet environment.

In the author's experience, having an office close to but not in the primary care setting is optimal. Primary care settings are quite busy places, and the hectic atmosphere often is a hindrance to relaxation and to establishing a rapport with patients. If it is a large primary care practice, being located in the clinic but as far as possible from the examination room area is fine. Furthermore, it is the author's experience that the mental health professional located in the primary care setting often becomes the mental health clinician for all staff members. Staff members will come in and out of your office discussing their personal difficulties. Sometimes this interferes with time management, preventing the mental health clinician from completing progress notes and seeing patients in a timely manner. Although to some extent this facilitates rapport between the mental health and medical practitioners, it can detract significantly from the limited time the clinician has for patient care.

THE BEGINNING OF THE COLLABORATIVE CONSULTATION

Obtaining Appropriate Referral Sources

The initial approach to the medical provider depends on the setting. Although there is wide variability, generally clinicians in private practice have a more difficult time approaching medical providers than do clinicians who are hospital based.

Private practitioners who are new to a location commonly have a greater hurdle to overcome than those who have roots in the area, either through an internship, practicum, past residence, or graduate school. In this situation, the mental health provider is starting from scratch. Mass mailings to all the appropriate medical providers in the area generally are necessary, although in the author's experience the response rate on these often is quite low. One should join the local psychological association and become acquainted with the other psychologists in the area so as to avoid turf battles (e.g., if psychologist X gets all his referrals from physician Y, it is proper form to avoid soliciting referrals from physician Y, at least without the approval of psychologist X) and to avoid potential dead ends (e.g., if numerous colleagues have attempted to establish a relationship with a particular provider and all attempts have been rebuffed, you probably should not put a lot of energy into soliciting referrals from that provider).

One helpful strategy is to find out when the local medical association meets (this is especially very helpful for primary care physicians) and then ask for 5 minutes of their time to describe your services. It is good to have business cards and a one-page synopsis that outlines the types of patients you can best treat.

The private practice mental health provider who offers behavioral medicine consultation services should also go to meetings of other medical organizations that specialize in your area of behavioral medicine consultation. For example, if you specialize in chronic pain consultation, you should consider going to the local acupuncture, anesthesiology, chiropractic, neurology, neurosurgery, orthopedic, physiatry, and rheumatology meetings. If you specialize in diabetes, consider going to the area cardiology, endocrinology, nephrology, nutritionist, ophthalmology, and podiatry meetings. If you are not new to the area, you probably have past contacts with the medical providers or contacts in the area (not just colleagues or past teachers and supervisors; often friends and family are quite helpful) who can introduce you to appropriate providers.

If the mental health provider is located in a hospital, the job of initially approaching the appropriate medical providers who will become your referral sources is quite easy. Psychology colleagues who are already well established in the institution will introduce you to the appropriate referral sources. If you are the only mental health provider in your institution, the person who hired you or the chief of staff of the medical center will do the introduction. In a hospital, it is very simple to walk to the potential referring provider's area and introduce oneself. Again, it is quite useful to have a one-page sheet explaining your area of expertise to give to colleagues.

Regardless of whether you are in private practice or located in a hospital, your initial approach to the provider should be quite brief (5 minutes or so). Introduce yourself, explain what you do quickly and succinctly, and ask whether you can contact the provider to talk further with him or her.

The Initial Talk With the Potential Referral Source

Most medical practitioners are extremely busy. If they agree to see you again, you have already created a spark of interest in your services. The first one-on-one meeting allows you to explain what you can do to help the practitioner. It cannot be emphasized enough: Prepare for what you are going to say ahead of time and do not promise more than you can deliver.

What you should say should be jargon free and helpful to the clinician. For example, if you believe that you are going to be able to help treat a provider's chronic pain patients, focus on treatment outcome results and the types of patients you can and cannot help. Although you may be quite excited about the psychometric properties of a scale you have developed to examine modeling factors in pain patients, the average medical provider is not and probably will be annoyed that you are wasting his or her valuable time discussing it. Along the same line, although you may be an expert in psychiatric nomenclature, using jargon such as *bipolar I, euthymic, pathognomonic,* and *psychotomimetic* is not helpful. The goal here is to show not how smart you are but what you can do to help the provider.

Clearly and honestly outline the limitations of your services. For example, if there are types of patients that research has shown you cannot help, clearly state that. If you do not work well with certain types of patients, for whatever reason, then tell the medical provider that. It is essential to not promise more than you can deliver. The psychosomatic medicine and liaison psychiatry waves in medicine have passed because they offered much more than they delivered. The behavioral medicine movement could also fail for just this reason. Readers are referred to the seminal 1982 paper in this area by Stewart Agras, where he strongly cautions against this problem. One area where behavioral medicine may have overpromised is that of cognitive rehabilitation. In the late 1980s to mid-1990s many rehabilitation hospitals began offering cognitive rehabilitation. Many of those programs have closed because they could not demonstrate clinically significant outcomes (although increasing the vocabulary of a brain-injured person from 10 words to 14 may be statistically significant, it is not clinically significant).

The readers may benefit from the author's mistakes in this instance. When the author took his first position at a large Department of Veterans Affairs general medical and surgical hospital and a large medical college teaching hospital, he was filled with a lot of book knowledge and excitement about the field of behavioral medicine and of psychology's ability to treat patients with chronic pain. The author presented the rosiest scenario about psychological treatments and what psychology had to offer medical providers. It took the author 12–18 months to make up for this error, and he was lucky that the experienced clinicians he was talking to attributed his presentation to youthful enthusiasm and energy rather than unthinking zealotry. Remember, medical providers understand that these are difficult disorders. If they were easy to treat, they would not need to refer their patients to you. Therefore, it is essential to acknowledge that these are difficult cases, and you will not be "curing" all patients sent to you.

A few other points must be articulated. In preparing for the initial meeting with the potential referring provider, it is useful to practice what you are going to say with a spouse or friends. Listen to the feedback they give you. If they cannot understand something clearly, go over it until they can understand it. If they think you are going too fast, slow up your rate of speech. It is also a good idea to videotape yourself during at least one of these role modeling sessions. Often, seeing yourself on videotape will force you to confront certain habits or behaviors that may interfere with good communication skills (e.g., nodding too much, saying "ah" between words, poor eye contact, inappropriate smile). Although colleagues have found audiovisual presentations to be helpful, the author has never used them for initial introductions, finding them too formal. In addition, too much can go wrong with such presentations, and when you have only a few minutes to get your point across, even a 5-minute delay

caused by a technical glitch can be disastrous. Also, if you are visiting a private practitioner's office, the equipment is cumbersome. In your initial, 20-minute presentation, it is very useful to have written materials to give to the provider. These materials can be many pages in length and can include articles that you think would be useful. Often, a provider has time to meet with you only at lunchtime. This informal setting can actually quite productive, although there are some pitfalls. First, if you are meeting in a restaurant, do not order anything that is likely to spill on you (e.g., a hot dog with mustard and relish), and if you are brown-bagging it, make sure you prepare something similarly appropriate. Second, it is sometimes expected that you will pick up the bill for this lunch and, if you are just starting out, this is added expense that you may not be able to afford. Third, if you are going out to a restaurant, it is often better to meet the provider at the restaurant, which will reduce your demands on the provider's time and prevent the referring provider from seeing your car (which might not project the desired professional image). This initial introduction should be considered the essential meeting that will pave the way for subsequent meetings and prime the pump for a two-way learning process between the referring medical provider and the mental health professional.

THE COLLABORATIVE CONSULTATION

Subsequent Discussions With the Referral Source

Once you have established a referral source, the collaborative process does not end. Indeed, it is just beginning. This collaborative process can be quite punitive or rewarding, depending on a number of factors, including the consultant's and the provider's personality styles, the provider's practice style, the consultant's interpersonal skills (especially picking up subtle cues that the referring provider gives off), the consultant's relationships with the provider's staff, and the consultant's reputation in the community.

Some of these things can be ascertained by asking the provider directly, and we strongly suggest that you do so. However, some things can be discovered only through repeated interactions and experiences with the provider. It is important to develop a good working relationship not only with the provider but also with the provider's staff. In a large teaching hospital, this includes students, nurses, and receptionists. In private practice, this includes nurses, receptionists, and fiscal staff. In more than 25 years of experience conducting behavioral medicine consultation, the author has found that in every instance of a discrepancy between what the provider said and what the provider's staff said, the provider's staff was more accurate, particularly with regard to the provider's practice style.

The behavioral medicine consultant should attempt to ascertain two things from the provider before receiving any consults: the provider's preferences on specific information about the patient and the provider's preferences on how much information he or she wants regarding behavioral medicine research. In both instances, there is a wide range of variability among providers.

Some providers want weekly updates on their patient's progress faxed or e-mailed to them immediately. Others simply want to send their patient to you and have no wish to hear further from you about their progress, believing that you now "own" the patient (an unfortunate term that is still used too frequently in medical practice). Still others want a brief summary of treatment every month or at treatment's end. Other practitioners want you to phone them about the patient's status. Generally, providers want some feedback from the consultant after the initial consultation and after treatment is over. They usually want some global measure of treatment success and, if the treatment was not successful, any suggestions on whom they may refer the patient to for additional help. But you should not assume; ask about his or her preferences.

Failing to understand the provider's preferences concerning patient progress can lead to an irritated provider and a cessation of referrals. This is especially salient in a private practice setting because in the medical setting—especially now that most institutions have electronic record charting—it is easy for the provider to check on the status of a patient by simply bringing up his or her chart. However, in private practice no such easy access to your medical records is possible, and without your feedback, the provider is blind to patient progress.

Additionally, it is important to not take the word of the provider at face value but to verify his or her preference based your additional experiences with him or her. Often, people say

not what they really mean but what they believe others want to hear. So if a provider initially tells you that he or she wants information on patients only at the end of treatment but is constantly calling for updates on patients, you may infer that the provider wants more frequent feedback.

It is also important to ascertain how much information the provider actually wants about what you do and whether he or she is interested in current research in your area. This is best done by asking the provider what his or her preferences are and, as you build a relationship with the provider, using this feedback to hone the information you give to him or her. Do not assume that the provider is interested in getting a solid understanding of what you do. In the author's experience, many providers do not want to know what you do except whether it works and what it is called. It is a rare provider that wants detailed information, including articles about what mental health providers do. In the author's experience in the chronic pain field, it is best to give the provider who asks for general information a how-to chapter on chronic pain from a psychological treatment perspective. If the provider asks for more or comments on certain aspects of the chapter, further information is provided. However, it is a rare medical provider who has the time or inclination to become deeply informed about mental health techniques. When such a collaborative effort exists, it is often reciprocated, and it becomes a great learning experience for both medical and mental health providers. For example, in the area of chronic pain, the author has known providers who were interested in comparisons of pharmacological and nonpharmacological treatments, others who were interested in the pathophysiology of chronic pain disorders, and still others who were interested in epidemiology of chronic pain disorders, and we embarked together on a collaborative and mutually beneficial process. The important thing here is to not force the provider to learn what he or she doesn't want to. To do so will only bring frustration to both of you.

Subsequent Discussions With the Referral Source

Portions of this section appeared originally in a chapter on headache in the primary care setting (Arena & Blanchard, 2005).

A rather delicate issue is the personality, reasoning, and desires (conscious or unconscious) underlying the behavioral medicine referral from a provider. You will get an overall feeling about this after receiving a couple of referrals from the provider. If possible, try to find out what the provider really wants from the referral and why the provider is truly referring the patient to you. The documented referral question does not always contain the only reason for a referral. It is important to keep in mind that a primary care provider will not generally refer a patient to a mental health professional unless the patient has proved refractory to a number of pharmacological and medical interventions.

Does the primary care provider want the mental health provider to grant absolution, to say that it was not his or her fault that this patient did not improve, that no primary care provider could help this patient? If this is the case, it is important to include phrases such as "this very difficult pain management case" or "this complex pain problem" in your report. As you develop a relationship with that particular provider, you may want to do some brief psychotherapeutic interventions concerning this attitude. For example, in your conversations with the primary care provider, you can delicately discuss how difficult you find some of these patients to work with, how having patients who prove refractory to treatment can be frustrating, and how you and others have dealt with such types of patients.

Does the provider want you to identify whether the patient has significant psychological problems that interfere with medical treatment response rather than wanting you to treat the patient? Some primary care providers do not want a mental health professional to be involved in the pain treatment process but want to understand better the psychological makeup of their pain patients. In this instance, education and time are your best assets because as the provider gets more information about the psychological aspects of pain, the provider will quickly see the benefits of nonpharmacological treatment (and the fact that it takes specialized skills to help their patients).

Is the primary care provider referring the pain patient because this a very difficult patient that the provider wants to "dump" on the mental health professional? If this is the case—and the mental health professional will quickly realize this, generally after four or five completely inappropriate consults who have failed to respond to nonpharmacological treatment (if they make the mistake of treating them)—psychoeducation typically will fail. Generally the best approach is

to discourage that particular provider from sending referrals.

Is the provider at his or her wits' end and going on a fishing expedition in hopes of finding something that might work? This is the most common referral problem, and it is actually easy to deal with. Timely education about when to send a patient to a behavioral medicine professional usually also does the trick.

Finally, is the provider looking for an excuse not to treat this patient and hoping that a psychologist's report will give him or her the justification? Here, education of the provider about when to transfer a patient to another primary care provider and discussion of transference and countertransference is appropriate. One way to do this is to discuss difficult patients you have had and how you have had to transfer patients to other mental health providers because you just couldn't work with someone. Usually, this begins a dialogue that most medically oriented professionals have never had, and they are often grateful for the chance to discuss such a sensitive topic.

One way some behavioral medicine consultants try to help both themselves and the referring provider is to have either a separate checklist that providers can attach to consults or a list of usual reasons for referrals to the behavioral medicine specialist that providers can refer to when formulating referrals for difficult patients. The medical care provider fills out the referral slip (e.g., a checklist), which does not go in the patient's chart, to indicate reasons for referral (e.g., "The patient is refractory to numerous treatments," "I believe there may be mental health problems," "I think that this patient is depressed."). This is often a useful tool for the mental health professional in the primary care setting.

BEHAVIORAL MEDICINE CONSULTATION FOR THE CHRONIC PAIN PATIENT

As noted earlier, this chapter uses chronic pain to illustrate the various points made. The author assumes that the reader is familiar with the basics of chronic pain, such as characteristics of the various pain syndromes, and epidemiology issues, such as incidence and prevalence of pain disorders as a function of race, gender, cultural factors, and age. In this section we will review the chronic pain interview (the chief assessment tool used by behavioral medicine specialists to evaluate chronic pain) and cognitive-behavioral therapy, biofeedback, and relaxation therapy (the primary nonpharmacological treatment modalities used for chronic pain). Throughout, the author will give clinical hints.

The Clinical Interview

The importance of a clinical interview for a pain patient cannot be overstated. The clinical interview is the means by which most information is gathered to form a diagnosis and a treatment plan. Good clinical assessment is the keystone of good treatment and care. The essentials of a good interview for a purely psychiatric disorder and a good pain interview are quite similar, with one major exception: The clinician conducting a pain interview should not discuss any psychiatric or psychological factors until he or she has obtained all data about the pain problem. Too often, pain patients believe that the psychologist thinks, "The patient's pain is all in his or her head," and is really interested only in psychological problems. Some even bait the practitioner in an attempt to get him or her to prematurely focus on psychological factors in order to reinforce this false perception of behavioral medicine procedures and processes (e.g., "A couple of drinks really makes my pain better," "When my pain gets really bad, I want to kill myself," "Emotional stress really makes my pain much worse."). If you are pressed by a patient to discuss psychological issues prematurely, a suggested response is, "I really do want to discuss that, and I promise you that we'll get to that issue later on in the interview. But first, I need to understand your pain as well as I possibly can."

Even basic demographic questions in the behavioral medicine interview are important. For example, a practitioner's approach to a 65-year-old pain patient probably will be very different from the approach to a 25-year-old. In the latter instance, the primary focus may be on getting the patient back to work as quickly as possible, whereas with an older adult the major concern might well be on improving quality of life. This decision should be a collaborative one between the patient and the practitioner and should be communicated to the medical practitioner who requested the consult. (Surprisingly, age does not appear to have much effect on psychological pain treatment outcome.) Marital status often is an important clinical sign: If a patient is 40 years old

and has been married six times, the clinician may want to explore whether there is a basic inability to establish a long-term relationship with someone or whether the patient's poor decision-making skills have generalized to other aspects of his or her life and behavior. Educational level often is central in that it is generally easier to retrain a person with a high school education for a job, and there are more potential jobs available for a high school graduate than for a person with a fourth-grade education. Finally, socioeconomic status often is vitally important with pain patients, not only because of the added stress of financial difficulties but because of the limited choices that low–socioeconomic status people have for increasing pleasant life events (so essential for successful pain treatment) and pacing themselves (e.g., when you are the sole parent with three small children you cannot take breaks between tasks). So the mental health professional should not ignore basic demographic information when consulting with medical patients.

A behavioral medicine consultant uses the same format for questions about pain as one use for a psychological disorder such as panic: focus on a description, location, and first occurrence of the pain; any psychological or physical events occurring around pain onset; frequency, intensity, and duration; what makes the pain better or worse; associated symptoms; modeling factors; familial history (what family members do when the pain is severe); and previous pain treatments. Blanchard and Andrasik (1985) published a sample headache interview that might be used as an example of a pain interview protocol. Alternatively, the reader may contact the author and obtain a copy of interviews he uses for his patients with headache and lower back pain.

During the interview, the behavioral medicine consultant who specializes in pain should be looking for things that simply do not make sense, such as constant, unremitting pain that does not change in intensity throughout the day regardless of the activity one is involved in, pain that is not improved when a person is distracted or concentrating hard on something, or a patient who wants a fourth back surgery even though the previous three have failed and the surgeon does not believe he or she would benefit from another surgery. These usually are good prognostic indicators of poor treatment outcome.

Another thing a behavioral medicine consultant who specializes in pain should search for in any interview is a deviation from the golden mean. In other words, look for extremes and not automatically apply a psychological interpretation to a patient's behaviors, while also considering obvious psychological explanations for a patient's pain problems. To illustrate, when patients characterize their pain, look for those who floridly and dramatically describe their pain (in a classic hysteric response) and those who try to dismiss the importance of their pain or talk about it dispassionately, as if they were discussing the weather (classic "la belle indifference"). Patients who matter-of-factly state, "It's a bad pain," or who floridly state, "It's like a spiderweb of pain, a labyrinth. I feel like my brain is too big for my skull—like someone is taking a skinny pair of pliers and twisting and pulling my brain out through my eyeball," are both likely to be poor treatment responders. When asking about family members' responses when patients are in pain, the behavioral medicine specialist is interested in both those who dote excessively on the patient and those who actively try to punish the patient for his or her pain.

From an interpretive perspective, the author is reminded of two very dramatic and different examples. He once received a six-page report on a pain patient from a well-respected local psychologist. Three of the six report pages involved a psychodynamic interpretation of the patient's curious behavior during the interview: The patient was continually taking sips from a long straw attached to a 32-ounce water bottle. When the author asked the patient why he sipped water constantly, the patient explained, and medical records verified, that he had had radiation therapy for throat cancer, which destroyed his salivary glands, and so his mouth and throat were extremely parched and needed to be regularly lubricated. If the local psychologist who had seen the patient originally had asked him why he was sipping water, the psychologist would have arrived at a more accurate and certainly much shorter report.

This example also illustrates another extremely important point in behavioral medicine consultation. Consultation is a collaborative process and often entails back-and-forth discussion with the consultant and the referring provider. If the psychologist had consulted with the referring physician about the patient's behavior, this psychologist would have been informed about the patient's medical condition, and the

erroneous interpretation would have been prevented.

In a different vein, the author once failed to follow up on a temporal relationship with a patient's head pain, which began after the patient saw his brother murdered. When the author finally did follow up, he discovered that the patient's brother had been shot in the head in front of the patient and that the patient's headache location was exactly where his brother had been shot. The patient had even described the headache as a "shooting pain." Treating the patient's posttraumatic stress disorder and survivor guilt eliminated the headaches, whereas the techniques directed at his psychological pain problem did not have any effect. The point of this vignette is that it is especially important for the behavioral medicine consultant to look at the entire picture rather than focus solely on the patient's pain problem. (Of course, an alternative meaning would be to remember basic psychodiagnostic skills when interviewing pain patients.)

Some final notes regarding the clinical interview are warranted. Ask about depression, anxiety, and anger. These are the three emotions that have been implicated in causing or maintaining pain. Nearly all pain patients need to be treated for one or more of these conditions. Most patients with low back pain that the author treats have a major depression diagnosis, and a substantial proportion of headache patients have a major depression or dysthymia diagnosis. Many pain patients have additional psychiatric diagnoses, such as generalized anxiety disorder, agoraphobia, panic disorder, posttraumatic stress disorder, and substance abuse. Remember to include a brief mental status examination with each pain intake. Every clinician has stories of patients who seemed to be functioning within normal limits until the very end of the interview, when, asked questions such as "Do you have any special powers?" or "Have you ever heard or seen things that others couldn't see or hear?" reported that they "cause the sun to rise every morning and set every evening" or that voices were carrying on a conversation about their behavior and situations, telling them to do "bad, evil things." Finally, one peculiar phenomenon that occurs often with pain patients and seems to be a clinical predictor of poor response to treatment is the presence of an "everything would be perfect in my life if I just didn't have this darn pain" attitude during the interview. Such patients deny any problems in their lives, they have no marriage or children problems, they love their in-laws, and their boss and coworkers could not be more understanding. If a patient has had pain for more than 6 months, it *has* affected his or her marriage and family life. Such denial often covers up serious psychopathology.

The Written Consultation Report

There is no "typical behavioral medicine consultation report." Every consultant has his or her own style, tailored to his or her needs depending on a number of factors, including the complexity of the case presented, the referring provider's choices, and the amount of time the consultant has available at report-writing time. Clearly, a straightforward tension headache consult in a patient with few secondary psychiatric problems calls for a different type of response than a complex regional pain syndrome (also known as reflex sympathetic dystrophy) consult in a patient with many psychiatric problems and a clear potential for secondary gains. After getting to know a provider's preferences, an experienced behavioral medicine consultant will tailor the consultation report to the preferences of the referring provider. For example, this author has many referring providers who tell him they have time to read only the "Summary and Recommendations" section and usually do so only if it is two paragraphs long or less. In reports for these providers, the author places this section before all others, at the front of the consultation report, and meticulously keeps to the space requirement (making sure the paragraphs are not too long). Similarly, the amount of available time a consultant has often dictates what gets written: On hectic days, a one-page consultation report that gives just the essentials may have to suffice, whereas on other days, when you have unexpected cancellations and no-shows, you may have time to do a complete four- to six-page report.

This chapter does not cover what should go into the consultation report; it is assumed that behavioral medicine consultants have specialized knowledge in their field and know what they want to impart to the referring provider. Formats of the consultation reports are also very individualized (this author prefers to include sections called "Referral Question," "Interview Data," "Mental Status Examination," and "Summary and Recommendations"). However, one particular

consultation response warrants discussion here: If you find a patient to be inappropriate for your particular treatment, do not just say that in the report. This author has seen one-sentence consult reports ("Patient inappropriate for our services"), but such a response should never be given. The behavioral medicine consultant should explain why the patient is inappropriate for his or her treatment (e.g., "The patient has proved refractory to a course of my treatment already," "Secondary gains are of such magnitude and so inculcated into the patient's life that there is little likelihood of positive treatment response," or "The patient suffers from cluster headaches that have been shown to be nonresponsive to psychological interventions.") and state whether he or she believes that another type of provider may be able to help the patient. By doing so, the consultant will avoid irritating the referring provider and will be educating him or her about which types of patients are suitable candidates for treatment. Referring providers—especially primary care providers—respect a consultant who does not take on every treatment case, no matter how lost the cause. Similarly, if the behavioral medicine consultant believes that no one is going to be able to help a patient, it is important to tell the provider that and explain why. This will prevent unnecessary testing and save the patient and referring provider time and money.

Description of Treatment Choices

Although there are as many nonpharmacological treatments for chronic pain as there are grains of sand on the beach, three primary psychological treatments are available today: biofeedback, relaxation therapy, and cognitive-behavioral therapy. This section briefly describes these three modalities.

Biofeedback, as it is generally used today, is a procedure in which the therapist monitors the patient's bodily responses (e.g., muscle tension, surface skin temperature, or respiration rate) through a machine and then feeds this information back to the patient (Arena & Devineni, in press). Feedback usually is presented to the patient either through an auditory modality (e.g., a tone that goes higher or lower as muscle tension increases or decreases) or a visual modality (e.g., a computer screen where surface skin temperature is graphed on a second-by-second basis). Through this physiological feedback, it is expected that a patient will learn how to control his or her bodily responses. A more formal definition of biofeedback is "a process in which a person learns to reliably influence psychophysiological responses of two kinds: either responses which are not ordinarily under voluntary control or ordinarily are easily regulated but for which regulation has broken down due to trauma or disease" (Blanchard & Epstein, 1978, p. 2).

Two general theories underlie the use of biofeedback for most chronic pain disorders. The first is a direct psychophysiological theory, which attributes the origin or maintenance of the pain to specific physiological disorder, which biofeedback training modulates in a therapeutic direction. For example, it has traditionally been assumed that tension headache is caused by sustained contraction of skeletal muscles in the forehead, neck, and shoulder regions. Through the use of biofeedback, the patient learns to decrease muscle tension levels, leading to a decrease in headache pain. The second theory is predominantly psychological and postulates that there is a relationship between situational stress and the pain disorder in question. Through the use of biofeedback, the patient learns to regulate physiological responses such as muscle tension or sympathetic nervous system activity, leading to a decrease in overall stress levels, which brings about symptomatic relief of the pain. It is not necessary to view these theories as competing; they may be more appropriately viewed as complementary. Most clinicians subscribe to both theories, depending on the patient's presenting problem, clinical findings, and medical history.

Relaxation therapy is a systematic approach to teaching people to gain awareness of their physiological responses and achieve both a cognitive and a physiological sense of tranquility without the use of the machinery used in biofeedback (Arena & Blanchard, 1996). There are various forms of relaxation therapy (see Lichstein, 1988, or Smith, 1990, for excellent reviews of the various types of relaxation therapy). The major forms are progressive muscle relaxation therapy (Jacobson, 1929), meditation (Lichstein, 1988), autogenic training (Luthe, 1969–1973), and guided imagery (Bellack, 1973). By far, the most widely used relaxation procedures in pain are variants of Jacobsonian progressive muscle relaxation therapy and guided imagery.

Four theories underlie the use of relaxation therapy for chronic pain reduction. The first theory is a general stress reduction theory, which simply states that most patients who have chronic pain are under a great deal of stress. If they can learn how to deal with that stress and cope more effectively with stressors in life using relaxation procedures, there should be a corresponding decrease in pain. The second theory postulates that most types of pain are either caused or maintained by elevated levels of muscle tension, muscle sprain, strain, or spasm, and if the patient can learn how to reduce muscle tension levels through relaxation therapy, there will be a corresponding reduction in pain levels. The third theory involves the effect of relaxation on general sympathetic nervous system arousal. It is believed that people with chronic pain disorders often have sympathetic abnormalities (either a continuously overaroused sympathetic nervous system or a sympathetic nervous system that fails to modulate correctly). Relaxation therapy appears to decrease sympathetic nervous system arousal and modulate sympathetic outflow, thus decreasing pain levels. The fourth theory is a distraction theory and simply postulates that relaxation therapy acts as a distraction technique for people with chronic pain. As with biofeedback, these theories are more appropriately viewed as complementary theories.

Because relaxation therapy and biofeedback are believed to directly influence a person's physiology and psyche, they are commonly called psychophysiological interventions.

Cognitive-behavioral therapies for pain are based on the assumptions that a person's thoughts, emotions, and behaviors influence his or her physiology and that each of these four modalities can influence the others. Therefore, cognitive-behavioral treatments generally involve identifying thoughts, emotions, and behaviors that routinely precede or exacerbate pain, with the therapist subsequently teaching patients in a systematic manner to modify these thoughts, feelings, and behaviors. Cognitive-behavioral therapies for pain are generally combined with relaxation or biofeedback procedures. Stress reduction techniques (including exercise) and psychoeducation about pain and things such as pacing of one's activity levels are also incorporated under the rubric of cognitive-behavioral therapy. Cognitive-behavioral techniques often are used to deal with the emotional sequelae of the pain—the depression, anger, and anxiety that so often follow chronic pain problems.

Please see Arena and Blanchard (2005) for a review of the headache treatment outcome literature, and Arena and Blanchard (2002) for a somewhat dated review of the treatment outcome literature for other pain disorders.

Clinical and Consultative Aspects of Biofeedback, Relaxation, and Cognitive-Behavioral Therapy for Pain

Although this section concentrates on aspects of treatment that focus on the patient and the referring provider, it is important for the behavioral medicine consultant to understand that when one does so, he or she is effectuating change only on an individual, idiographic level. Often, behavioral medicine problems involve challenges that are much wider than individual patients and their providers. Many times, the problems are at a more macro level: societal and organizational. For example, behavioral medicine consultants who specialize in smoking cessation or eating disorders may find that they can effect more meaningful change by transforming societal attitudes about smoking or by passing laws requiring that nutrition information about complete portion sizes be made available at every restaurant. Genetic counselors may find that they can help more people by intervening with their organizations or employers to get them to pass policies that will not discriminate against people who prove positive for specific genetic markers. In chronic pain, professionals may want to work on changing public attitudes by making people aware that just because a patient looks healthy does not mean that he or she actually is healthy and is "just ripping off the system." They may want to educate medical professionals about the natural course of pain (e.g., just because a pain patient is walking perfectly one day does not mean that he or she is a malingerer; pain naturally waxes and wanes, and on rare good days patients display no overt pain behaviors). This is why an understanding of system theory and community psychology is so important for the behavioral medicine consultant. Change comes in many ways, not just in a one-to-one encounter. With that caveat in mind, let us now focus on problems that arise in biofeedback training, relaxation therapy, and cognitive-behavioral therapy with the chronic pain patient.

From a practical perspective, relaxation therapy is one of the most versatile and least troublesome procedures mental health professionals can conduct. Relaxation probably is the closest intervention to an aspirin that we in the behavioral sciences have; it is a general, as opposed to specific, treatment, and it is useful for a wide variety of clinical problems, including anxiety and general stress reduction, anger management, chronic pain, hypertension, and insomnia. Although there are some practical difficulties—common-sense problems that pop up that are generally the fault of the therapist being in a hurry or inexperienced (e.g., forgetting to ask whether a patient needs to go to the bathroom before you start or whether the patient is hard of hearing)—six potential problems are common in relaxation therapy. The first three problems are specific to relaxation therapy, and the latter three are shared by biofeedback or cognitive-behavioral therapy:

Patients Falling Asleep. It is important to caution patients to try hard not to fall asleep during relaxation because they will not learn much if they are sleeping. Despite your patients' best efforts, about 10% will fall asleep. Depending on where they are in the process (and whether you are making a tape or CD of the session), you can either awaken the patient and go on with the relaxation procedure or simply awaken the patient and end the procedure. The author strongly recommends making a tape or CD of each session for aid in practice, however. If you do this, just continue with the relaxation procedure and give the patient the tape or CD. He or she will usually be able to listen to the tape or CD to the end and get the benefit of the relaxation procedure. The author cautions against calling the patient's name. Rather, simply speaking in a louder and louder voice usually does the trick. Also, therapists should be aware of their own feelings when patients fall asleep during relaxation and try not to get irritated. After all, this generally means that the patient became very relaxed. Becoming irritated will be counterproductive and interfere with the therapist-patient relationship.

Intrusive Thoughts. One major problem that patients seem to have with relaxation therapy is intrusive ("busy") thoughts. Alert patients before the initial session that they may at first have problems with such thoughts entering their mind. Tell them to simply expect that those thoughts will happen. Some thoughts will be productive thoughts, such as "Oh, how relaxed I am feeling," whereas other thoughts will be unproductive, such as problems at work, tasks that need to be finished, or meals that have to be cooked. Tell the patient that they should not attempt to stop those unproductive thoughts because that will only exacerbate the problem. Inform them that as they get better at relaxation, the problem will lessen. Also tell them when they are practicing at home not to get frustrated when the thoughts occur; rather, let them play themselves out and return to the relaxation when they are over.

These suggestions usually work with most people. For those who are having severe intrusive thoughts after numerous sessions, suggest a mild form of thought stopping: "Imagine these thoughts are like a freight train, and at the first thought they become chained or linked together. In order to stop them, try to imagine a stop light that flashes, and in your mind say, 'STOP!' Immediately replace that unproductive thought with a more productive thought such as, 'I am learning to relax myself more quickly' or 'I am feeling the relaxation spreading throughout my muscles.'"

Erections. About 5% of male patients have a spontaneous erection during relaxation therapy, regardless of the gender of the therapist. This is normal and should be completely ignored by the therapist. The presence of an erection during relaxation means absolutely nothing and should be treated as such. If the patient makes a remark about his arousal (a rare occurrence in the author's experience), simply say that you did not notice it and go on with the session. Discretion is often the better part of valor.

Generalization. This is a problem for all psychological techniques, but much less so for relaxation therapy because it is something that most people like doing. For relaxation therapy, as well as biofeedback, patients should be told to periodically check their emotional and physiological arousal, and if it is elevated, they should practice the relaxation or biofeedback until the arousal is reduced or eliminated. The primary problem for relaxation appears to be one of remembering to conduct the response in the real world. We usually give patients strategies to remember, such as choosing something they do 5–10 times during the day to act as a reminder cue (e.g., every time they look at themselves in a mirror or answer

the phone), placing some colored or smiley face adhesive dots up in their home, workplace, and vehicle as a reminder cue (remember to tell the patient to wait 1 or 2 weeks before using them as a cue, so as to allow them to habituate to the dots), setting and resetting a wristwatch alarm, setting their cell phone alarms, or setting and resetting an electronic kitchen timer (especially useful with pain patients because kitchen timers do not require complex eye-hand coordination, as a wristwatch alarm does, and are quite loud and impossible to ignore).

For biofeedback, the response is more difficult to bring into the everyday world. There are many ways in addition to those just listed that clinicians use to deal with this problem. First, small, portable biofeedback devices can be given to the patient to assist in everyday practice. Second, training first on a recliner, then on a comfortable chair with arms, proceeding to an uncomfortable chair with arms, followed by an uncomfortable chair without arms, and, finally, standing often helps patients bring the biofeedback response into the real world. Other clinicians use stressful conditions during biofeedback (e.g., a mental arithmetic task or a negative imagery procedure) to make the biofeedback training similar to everyday living stressors and prepare the patient for its use in similar situations.

Generalization is an extremely difficult problem with cognitive-behavioral therapy. Every mental health professional has had the experience of patients who can successfully alter their maladaptive cognitions in the office but simply cannot do so in real-life situations, or patients who can be extremely assertive during role playing but cannot do so when their best friend inadvertently and unknowingly insults them. Often with chronic pain patients—who have fallen into the pain-depression cycle of isolation, decreased interactions with family and friends, and decreased frequency of pleasurable events in their life—seemingly very positive and self-reinforcing homework assignments become quite difficult to accomplish. For example, in an attempt to break this pain-depression cycle, nearly all pain patients are given homework assignments to increase the frequency of pleasurable events in their life. Patients are highly resistant to this idea and will come up with seemingly endless reasons why the must stay at home and watch TV. Here, problem-solving techniques and the treatment adherence techniques outlined later in this section are essential. Often, even though pain patients have a good time engaging in pleasurable activities, they do not want to do them again. Arena (2002) presents a case report of just how difficult it can be to get a patient to go fishing, a nearly always pleasant activity among nondepressed males. Such treatments take great perseverance and patience on the part of the therapist.

Panic Attacks and Relaxation-Induced Anxiety. Although they are not discussed often, a subset of patients experience increased tension and anxiety during relaxation therapy and, occasionally, biofeedback. In its extreme, this response may take the form of a panic attack. (For an excellent theoretical discussion of relaxation-induced anxiety, please see the seminal work by Heide and Borkovec, 1983.) People who suffer from generalized anxiety or panic disorders, or those who are very anxious during the preliminaries to the first session of relaxation therapy, are at greater risk for relaxation-induced anxiety and panic attack. Patients who increase significantly their muscle tension levels or who decrease significantly their hand temperature during a first session of biofeedback are also at greater risk. Because relaxation-induced anxiety can lead patients to drop out of treatment, it should be carefully assessed. Have high-risk patients focus more on the somatic aspects of the biofeedback or relaxation training rather than focus on cognitive factors (e.g., stress how the muscles feel rather than how quiet the patient's mind is). Also emphasize that patients are always in control during relaxation therapy and will always be aware of what is going on around them, what they are doing, and what the therapist is saying.

Despite all preparations, panic attacks may occur occasionally. These usually take the form of patients opening their eyes during the procedure, crying, stating that they feel very nervous, or attempting to leave the therapist's office. It is essential for the therapist to assume a calm demeanor. Novice therapists especially seem to have trouble with this and often pick up on the intense affect of the patient and contribute to it with their own fears and concerns. It is important to remember that, to the best of the author's knowledge, no one has ever died from a panic attack, although they are quite frightening. Therefore, stay calm, speak in a slow and low

voice with a relaxed tone, and act as if things are going to be fine. Even if you are extremely concerned and anxious, don't show it.

Next, before the patient can tell you what he or she is experiencing, tell the patient what he or she is feeling. This lets the patient know that you understand what he or she is experiencing, that you are competent, and that whatever else you say will be accurate as well (e.g., "Right now you're feeling really nervous, like something terrible is going to happen to you; you may even feel as if you are going to die. Your heart is pounding, your thoughts are racing, you are breathing very rapidly and shallowly, your mouth is dry, you're sweating a lot, you can't catch your breath, and you just want to get out of here. Don't worry; nothing that you feel now is permanent. It will all be over in a few minutes."). Get the patient a glass of water and a tissue and then wait for the patient to calm down. Another technique the author has used is to have patients breathe diaphragmatically along with you. If at all possible, prevent the patient from fleeing the office because this can lead to avoidance of relaxation and a pairing of relaxation or biofeedback with anxiety.

It is important to remember, especially if you are an insight-oriented psychotherapist, not to try to act as "super therapist" and give patients insight into why they are having these feelings. This is not to say that those questions and insights are not important, but during and immediately after a panic attack is not the time to gather such information or impart such interpretations. They are best left for subsequent sessions.

Usually, if you follow these suggestions, the patient will calm down and feel well enough to leave the office or continue discussion (it is strongly recommended not to continue with the procedure during that session). The next session, spend some time discussing with the patient how he or she felt and whether he or she wants to continue with the biofeedback or relaxation therapy. Most patients who do not drop out of therapy will continue with the regimen.

Treatment Adherence. The bane of all psychological and medical techniques is treatment adherence. Even adherence to medical regimens that could prevent death or serious physical consequences, such as HIV or diabetes treatment regimens, is quite low. Psychological treatment adherence is no different. Estimates are that less than 50% of patients adhere to a relaxation regimen, even though relaxation leads to an immediate positive payoff in the sense that it generally feels good, provides one with a subjective feeling of relaxation, and often leads to a reduction in pain, anger, and anxiety. Dropouts among pain patients for psychological treatments are quite high. To facilitate psychological pain treatment adherence, the author has found four things helpful:

First, make sure that you, the mental health clinician, explain clearly the rationale for the use of the particular treatments used. A handout is quite helpful here, as is repeating the rationales over multiple sessions and asking the patient to explain out loud what they are doing and why (if you have not done this before, prepare to be shocked at how little your patients remember and understand what you have told them). If patients understand the rationale for your intervention, they are more invested in the treatment.

Second, if at all possible, call patients the day before to remind them about their appointments. This will significantly reduce your no-show rate. It is axiomatic, but you cannot help someone if he or she does not appear for your therapy sessions.

Third, attempt to enlist the family members as cotherapists. At the very least, this will prevent deliberate or inadvertent sabotage of your treatment plan by them. Moreover, often family members can grasp the concepts you are trying to impart to the patient better than the patient can and may be able to explain them in words that the patient understands. Please do not forget children when you bring the family in. Pain patients especially get secondary gains from their children, so having the children give the parent attention and praise when he or she does the relaxation exercises is a strong reinforcer for treatment adherence.

Finally and most important, try to enlist the referring provider and his or her staff as cotherapists. This is essential when dealing with medical patients. Although we may not like it, mental health professionals are on the bottom rung of the prestige ladder in many patient's minds and we (psychiatrists included) are perceived as not being "real doctors." Many patients discount what we say. However, the referring physician and his or her nurses and physician's assistants are generally perceived as holding high status, so when they emphasize to the patient that it is paramount for

them to practice their relaxation exercises, this has a great impact. This impact cannot be overstated. The author—who works in two teaching hospitals and is the lead psychologist in one and a tenured professor in another—has had numerous instances in which he suggested things to patients and they refused to try them. But when he asked a junior medical student dressed in a white coat to suggest the same things to the patients, the patients both agreed to try them and thanked the student profusely for the great suggestions. (Teaching is a humbling experience.)

This is also why it is so important to have a collaborative relationship with the referring provider and a good relationship with his or her staff. In order for the referring provider to be able to reinforce the patient's treatment regimen, he or she must be aware of the treatment regimen and have a general understanding of what the components of the regimen are. The referring provider's staff also should know about the regimen; because of their busy schedules, most physicians are unable to directly talk to their patients when they phone in for questions or prescriptions, so the nurse or physician assistant acts as an intermediary. It is quite powerful when they remind the patient of the importance of practicing their relaxation exercises twice a day or of making sure they do at least one fun thing every day.

FUTURE DIRECTIONS IN BEHAVIORAL MEDICINE CONSULTATION

It is not the purpose of this chapter to provide an in-depth review of the behavioral medicine consultation literature. However, it is clear that new trends and areas for future directions are beginning to emerge. This section briefly focuses on four such trends: use of tele-health consultation as a treatment delivery method for behavioral medicine, use of behavioral medicine consultants in genetic counseling, the role of the behavioral medicine consultant in HIV and AIDS, and comparisons of various types of consultation models or styles.

Tele-Health Consultation. Probably the most interesting and exciting trend in behavioral medicine consultation today is the growing field of tele-health consultation. Mental health professionals and behavioral medicine specialists have many treatments that work. However, many patients cannot participate in such treatments because they live too far from the treating facility, preventing them from coming in for regular office visits. In addition, patients may face travel difficulties as a result of domestic, work, transport, or other constraints such as preexisting physical disability. Many behavior medicine consultants are not located in a treating facility but must travel to get to a facility for a consultation or treatment. Overcoming the challenges of time and distance is paramount to the development of services that promote equitable access to care, regardless of location. If behavioral medicine consultations and treatments could be offered in a home setting or a remote clinic site nearer to the patient's home or work, better continuity of care, more cost-effective treatment delivery, and improved outcomes may be realized.

Many studies have demonstrated the utility of tele-health for mental health consultation. Sorvaniemi, Ojanen, and Santamaki (2005) presented a follow-up of 60 patients who had used a videoconferencing system for an initial psychiatric consultation for entrance into a psychiatric hospital. Results indicated few technical problems and wide acceptance by both staff and patients. The ability to have a consultant always available, day and night, to evaluate the patient immediately, without the consultant having to travel to the facility, is a true advantage, especially in rural areas or for small facilities where psychiatric admissions are rare in off-hours (where it would be cost-prohibitive to keep a mental health professional available in-house 24 hours a day).

Arena, Dennis, Devineni, Maclean, and Meador (2005) evaluated the preliminary efficacy and feasibility of an analog telemedicine system for delivery of psychophysical treatment for vascular headache. Four subjects, ranging in age from 52 to 64, with at least 30 years of headache duration, were given an eight-session combined relaxation and thermal biofeedback regimen. Results indicated that three out of four subjects improved on measures of headache activity (overall headache severity, peak headache activity, and number of headache-free days), with one subject showing clinically significant improvement. It was tentatively concluded that telemedicine delivered treatment was feasible. Notably, they experienced few significant problems, either with equipment failure or with subjects objecting to the concept of remote treatment delivery. Indeed, subjects readily seemed to grasp and accept the telemedicine application. All were able to voice the obvious advantages of such a delivery system to the experimenter, although some expressed initial reluctance or discomfort because of the novelty of the delivery medium. It was concluded that these findings were encouraging for follow-up study of the clinical efficacy, cost-effectiveness, and broader viability of pain treatment via distance technology.

There were several of concerns and limitations regarding this pilot study, however. First, sample sizes of 10 or less per group do not allow definitive conclusions, either clinically or statistically. A larger-scale outcome study with at least 15 subjects per group seems warranted to test the reliability of these findings. Second, subjects in this study were provided only eight treatment sessions (five of relaxation therapy and three of thermal biofeedback), raising questions about the adequacy of treatment. It can be argued that a longer intervention (12–16 sessions), as is typical with clinic-based approaches, would have improved the efficacy of the treatment, especially for two of the subjects, who appeared to be showing some positive response to psychophysiological intervention but did not reach their criterion for clinical improvement of 50% or greater reduction in pain. Moreover, a novice therapist who had less than 10 hours of training in psychophysiological interventions conducted this study. It seems plausible that a more experienced therapist would have produced better treatment outcomes.

Arena, Hannah, and Meador (submitted) corrected for all these limitations. Preliminary results indicated that more than half of the subjects in each group were treatment successes (50% or greater reduction in pain), with no major difficulties with the equipment or patient acceptance of the procedure. Thus, it appears that behavioral medicine treatments such as relaxation and biofeedback are especially amenable to tele-health approaches.

Genetic Counseling. Probably the best-researched area of behavioral medicine consultation is that of predictive genetic counseling. This is one of the newest and fastest-growing areas of behavioral medicine consultation, with nearly half of the research being published since 2000. With completion of the mapping of the human genome, genetic counseling issues are going to increase at an exponential rate in the coming decades. The emotional sequelae of being told that you or your fetus has a genetic marker for a disease often are complex and overwhelming.

In addition to their primary job of dealing with the emotional aspects of genetic counseling, behavioral medicine consultants are dealing with other, equally important concerns. Although no one would dispute the right of patients to have knowledge about their own genetic heritage and the ability of a person to voluntarily obtain testing, many other issues of complex medical, psychological, ethical, sociological, religious, and moral concerns are at the forefront of such counseling. For example, are in utero testing and subsequent abortion acceptable for serious disease that probably will lead to an early death? Is it acceptable for diseases that probably will not be fatal but are serious enough to leave the baby with a significantly diminished quality of life or a shortened life span? What about genetic markers for diseases that probably likely manifest themselves in adulthood, such as diabetes, dementia, and cardiovascular disease? In adults, can potential employers insist on genetic testing before employment, and can the results used to deny people employment? Can insurance companies charge higher premiums for people who screen positive for certain diseases or deny coverage for such people? Do spouses or potential spouses have a legal or ethical right to know about potential genetic problems? These are questions that genetic counselors deal with every day.

The literature is replete with solid research grappling with these issues for a diverse number of disorders. Areas in which genetic counseling is currently available include Alzheimer's disease and other dementias (Hedera, 2001; Sadovnick, 2001), breast and ovarian cancer (Geirdal et al., 2005), chronic granulomatous disease (James, Holtzman, & Hadley, 2003), colorectal cancer (Codori et al., 2005), congenital heart disease (Coleman, 2002), hearing loss (Dagan, Hochner, Levi, Raas-Rothschild, & Sagi, 2002), Huntington disease (Decruyenaere et al., 2004), Machado-Joseph disease (Gonzalez et al., 2004), myotonic dystrophy type 1 (Prevost et al., 2005), and sickle cell disease (Opawoye, 1999).

In this young but well-researched field, a number of studies stand out that lead to further research directions. Halbert et al. (2005), using a survey method, examined cancer-specific distress among African American women being targeted for participation in counseling and testing for ovarian and breast cancer. Results indicated that African American women aged 50 and younger, those who were unemployed, and women with a personal history of breast or ovarian cancer may be the most vulnerable to elevated levels of distress during genetic counseling and testing. They concluded that greater attention to psychological issues, including concerns about cancer and cancer risks, may be needed during genetic counseling and testing for the specific genetic marker with these women. Clearly, this research must be expanded beyond survey methods and to other populations, such as Hispanic and Asian patients. Others have expanded this research to look at the psychological effects of genetic counseling in adolescent daughters of women with breast cancer (Cappelli et al., 2005).

Pieterse, van Dulmen, Ausems, Beemer, and Bensing (2005) examined how fulfilling patient's expectations in cancer genetic counseling affects the outcome of counseling. Results demonstrated a previsit to postvisit significant increase in correct knowledge and perceived self-control and a significant decrease in anxiety and risk perceptions. However, although risk perception decreased, marked overestimation of risks persisted. Decrease in anxiety and risk perceptions was significantly less pronounced in affected (i.e., those with the genetic marker) than in unaffected participants. The better participants perceived their needs to be fulfilled, the better their perceived self-control and the lower their anxiety scores were. Thus, it was concluded that genetic counselors should focus on meeting the emotional needs of their counselees and ensuring that their knowledge requirements are met. Further research looking at ways to accomplish both of these tasks (e.g., videotaped and written materials, repeated visits) is clearly needed.

In a very important article, Martin and Wilikofsky (2004) discuss the essential role of primary care clinicians in genetic counseling. They point out that the role of primary care clinicians is different from the usual role of genetic counselors. Primary care clinicians often are involved in the early stages of identifying who may benefit from genetic assessment, helping patients to decide when it is appropriate to pursue genetic information, and preparing them for consultation. Primary care practitioners are by nature much more directive in their approach than the usual nondirective approach advocated in genetic counseling. More important, primary care clinicians often have a working knowledge of the patient's family, the context in which genetic information has its impact. They are likely to care for family members in addition to the identified patient and probably are better situated to adopt a family-based approach to managing genetic risk. The authors note that primary care involves a longitudinal perspective, in which genetic information takes on new meaning and sometimes more urgency as diseases progress, family members are newly diagnosed, and patients enter new phases of the life cycle. Given the increasing emphasis by managed care on the use of primary care providers in medicine, more research into this area is sorely needed.

HIV and AIDS. The role of the behavioral medicine consultant in dealing with HIV and AIDS is of paramount importance, and the field has grown exponentially since the early 1980s, when the disease was first identified. HIV, which is believed to be the cause of AIDS, is a retrovirus. Retroviruses differ from a virus in that they are smaller and less complex, and their inner core consist of a single strand of RNA rather than DNA. Because a genome based on RNA has an outer cell envelope composed largely of material found in the human cell membrane, the immune system has a difficult time telling the difference between the HIV virus and normal human cells, which is why retroviruses defeat the body's immune defense system so easily. This leads to the very significant and pervasive symptoms of AIDS, such weight loss, fever, night sweats, marked fatigue, severe depression, memory loss, diarrhea, pneumonia, and swollen lymph glands. In addition to the physical and psychological consequences of the disease, people with HIV and AIDS also have to deal with the social stigma of the disease because it is transmitted through sexual contact with an infected person, by sharing needles or syringes (primarily for drug injection) with someone who is infected, or, less commonly in the United States and other developed countries, through transfusions of infected blood or blood clotting factors. People with HIV and AIDS also have to deal with their own fears about dying as a result of the disease and other people's often unrealistic fears regarding disease transmission.

There has been an explosion of all types of research in HIV and AIDS since their identification, and the behavioral aspects of the disease have been especially well investigated. In this section, we will use some recent studies to briefly illustrate how behavioral medicine consultation has contributed to the improved health of patients with HIV and AIDS. Blanch et al. (2002) examined the efficacy of a cognitive-behavioral group therapy program for a heterogeneous groups of patients with HIV and AIDS referred for mental health services. They examined depression and anxiety before, during, and after a 16-session group therapy program. Results indicated reductions in anxiety and depression after treatment and at follow-up. More such studies must be conducted, examining factors such as the patient's age, race, psychiatric diagnosis, preexisting level of depression, and anxiety.

Roberts (2002) has demonstrated that physician consultation style is highly correlated with treatment adherence for an HIV or AIDS pharmacological regimen. He found that when patients were dissatisfied with their care, it was often because there was a mismatch between the patient's expectations of care and the physician's consultation style. Results also showed that good-quality physician-patient relationships tended to promote adherence, whereas lesser-quality relationships impeded it. Roberts argued that strengthening and promoting the relationships between physicians and patients with HIV and AIDS should be an absolute priority, both at the interpersonal level of physician-patient interactions and at the organizational level. Research into provider-patient interactions and organizational relationships for HIV and AIDS and other behavioral medicine areas, such as chronic pain, obesity, and diabetes, is vitally needed.

Sargent, Sorensen, Greenberg, Evans, and Acampora (1999) examined the efficacy of residential detoxification for substance abusers with HIV and AIDS. They outline the program and explain the advantages of such a program over traditional detoxification for patients with HIV and AIDS. Further research examining innovative substance abuse treatment for HIV and AIDS as well as many other behavioral medicine areas is vitally needed.

Pain is also a very significant problem in patients with AIDS. In one survey of more than 200 patients with AIDS (Hope, Williams, Barton, & Asboe, 2001), 67% reported experiencing significant pain during the past 4 weeks. They noted that patients in poorer health, patients reporting more pain, and those developing severe pain used services more than other patients. They concluded that improved pain management would lead to substantial cost containment, better quality of life, and less use of outpatient services. Lefkowitz (1996) advocates developing separate pain treatment guidelines for patients with AIDS rather than simply using cancer pain treatment guidelines, as most clinicians do. Unfortunately, and surprisingly, there are still no clear-cut pain treatment guidelines specifically for AIDS that the author is aware of. This is clearly a future research direction that needs to be addressed.

Comparisons of Various Types of Consultation Models, Protocols, or Styles. In a field as established as behavioral medicine consultation, one might expect that research comparing various models or protocols of consultation would be vast and growing. Unfortunately, that is not the case. Although there is some literature, it is mostly in the genetic counseling and the HIV and AIDS area. This section selectively reviews this literature. However, it is obvious that additional research in this area is sorely needed.

Brain et al. (2005) assessed psychological harm, satisfaction, and preferences after two differing genetic counseling protocols (a short version and an extended version) in 28 patients at risk for colorectal cancer. Extended counseling involved two sessions before testing for the genetic marker, whereas the shortened testing involved a single session. No differences were found in psychological harm and patient satisfaction. Subject preferences for either treatment protocol were inconsistent. The authors suggest that preintervention information be given, as well as a tailored counseling approach based on this information.

In an elegant study, Hunter et al. (2005) compared three different types of intervention approaches to prenatal diagnosis counseling in women of advanced age. The study compared three randomly assigned counseling methods—individual, group, and use of a decision aid—for 352 women age 35 or older and 225 of their partners. All participants showed a significant increase in knowledge and a decrease in decisional conflict after the intervention. However, group intervention participants showed a significantly greater increase in knowledge than those in

the individual counseling intervention. Although all participants reported high levels of satisfaction, those in individual counseling were significantly more satisfied than those receiving group counseling or the decision aid.

Wang, Gonzalez, Milliron, Strecher, and Merajver (2005) compared the use of a CD-ROM information program for patients at risk for a genetic marker for breast cancer given before genetic counseling, a feedback checklist of counselees' misperceptions completed before the genetic counseling and given to the counselor, and genetic counseling only, with a standard genetic counseling condition. They found that women who viewed the CD-ROM spent less time with the genetic counselor and were less likely to undergo genetic testing than those who did not. The feedback checklist resulted in greater gains in terms of knowledge of genetics and breast cancer.

Helmes, Bowen, and Bengel (2002) looked at women's preferred physician involvement in the decision to obtain genetic testing for breast cancer risk (making up their own minds or leaving it up to the physician). Women in a primary care clinic were given both a telephone survey and a questionnaire to fill out. Results indicated that although the majority preferred to make up their own minds, less educated women, women with less knowledge about breast cancer, and women with higher external locus of control preferred to let the physician make the decision for them.

In the HIV and AIDS area, a number of studies that compare various types of consultation models, protocols, or styles stand out. Gomez, Klein, Sand, Marconi, and O'Dowd (1999) compared two models of how behavioral medicine consultants delivered mental health care to patients with HIV and AIDS: on site, in the infectious disease clinic, or in a specialized psychiatric HIV and AIDS clinic setting. The on-site model improved compliance with the treatment regimen and was preferred by staff to the specialized psychiatric HIV and AIDS clinic. However, compliance with the initial mental health evaluation remained below 50% in both settings. This area—behavioral medicine consultation setting—warrants additional research in many more behavioral medicine specialty areas (e.g., primary care provider setting vs. consultant's office for obesity, diabetes, or pain).

Stepleman, Hann, Santos, and House (2006) compared a specific behavioral medicine consultation model—patient-centered consultation—to a standard physician-centered consultation model for patients with HIV and AIDS who were traditionally underserved (African American, Hispanic, rural, and low socioeconomic classes). In the traditional physician-centered consultation model, the physician determines whether the patient needs to see a mental health profession and sends a consult; in the patient-centered consultation model, the patient makes that decision. Stepleman and colleagues had patients attending an infectious disease clinic at a medical center teaching hospital fill out a questionnaire outlining a number of psychological issues that are commonly found among patients with HIV and AIDS. They then gave the patients the opportunity to decide whether they wanted to see a mental health professional. Psychological consultations from a 2-year period before and after the model was implemented were compared, indicating that the model increased consultation use. There was an 83% increase in consultation requests and a 91.5% increase in consultation participants. This is a very important study, not only because of the real-world comparison of two specific consultation styles but because of the study participants: traditionally underserved people in the health care system. Additional research along these lines is vitally needed and sorely lacking.

There has been little research in this important area outside genetic counseling and HIV and AIDS. In dental research, Almog et al. (2004) compared four consultation methods in an attempt to determine which helped patients best understand a proposed treatment plan for maxillary anterior diastema closure. The authors presented 24 subjects with the four types of consultation in random order: before-and-after photographs of other patients; diagnostic models with wax setups; resin-based composite aesthetic preview mockups; and computer imaging simulations. After viewing each method, subjects were queried about treatment acceptability. At the end of the demonstrations of all four methods, subjects were asked which consultation method helped them best understand the proposed treatment plan. Subjects preferred computer imaging simulation to the other three consultation methods, and they indicated that computer imaging simulation provided a better understanding of the proposed treatment plan for diastema closure. None preferred the traditional diagnostic models with wax setups.

Finally, not all of the consultation comparison literature is positive. Kidd, Marteau, Robinson, Ukoumunne, and Tydeman (2004) compared three consultation models for diabetes and found that none brought about demonstrated increases in patient question asking in clinical consultations or led to increases in diabetic control at follow-up.

SUMMARY

The consultative role of a mental health professional who specializes in behavioral medicine or medical psychology is complex and expanding. With the advent of cost-containment in medicine and the understanding that most chronic medical diseases have a strong lifestyle component, the behavioral medicine consultant is more essential than ever. This chapter was meant to be a step-by-step primer of how to engage in behavioral medicine consultation.

ACKNOWLEDGMENT

This chapter was supported by a Department of Veterans Affairs Medical Research Merit Review awarded to John G. Arena.

REFERENCES

Agras, S. (1982). Behavioral medicine in the 1980s: Nonrandom connections. *Journal of Consulting and Clinical Psychology, 50,* 797–803.

Almog, D., Sanchez, M. C., Proskin, H. M., Cohen, M. J., Kyrkanides, S., & Malmstrom, H. (2004). The effect of esthetic consultation methods on acceptance of diastema-closure treatment plan: A pilot study. *Journal of the American Dental Association, 135,* 1516, 1518.

Arena, J. G. (2002). Chronic pain: Psychological approaches. *Journal of Clinical Psychology. In-Session: Psychotherapy in Practice, 58,* 1385–1396.

Arena, J. G., & Blanchard, E. B. (1996). Biofeedback and relaxation therapy for chronic pain disorders. In R. J. Gatchel & D. C. Turk (Eds.), *Chronic pain: Psychological perspectives on treatment* (pp. 179–230). New York: Guilford.

Arena, J. G., & Blanchard, E. B. (2002). Biofeedback therapy for chronic pain disorders. In J. D. Loeser, D. Turk, R. C. Chapman, & S. Butler (Eds.), *Bonica's management of pain* (3rd ed., pp. 1755–1763). Baltimore: Williams & Wilkins.

Arena, J. G., & Blanchard, E. B. (2005). Assessment and treatment of chronic benign headache in the primary care setting. In W. O'Donohue, N. Cummings, D. Henderson, & M. Byrd (Eds.), *Behavioral integrative care: Treatments that work in the primary care setting* (pp. 293–313). New York: Allyn & Bacon.

Arena, J., Dennis, N., Devineni, T., Maclean, R., & Meador, K. (2005). A pilot study of feasibility and efficacy of telemedicine-delivered psychophysiological treatment for vascular headache. *Telemedicine Journal and E-Health, 10,* 449–454.

Arena, J. G., & Devineni, T. (in press). Biofeedback. In J. G. Webster (Ed.), *Wiley encyclopedia of medical devices and instrumentation* (6 vols., 2nd ed.). Hoboken, NJ: Wiley.

Arena, J. G., Hannah, S. L., & Meador, K. J. (submitted). *A comparison of standard office-based versus telemedicine-delivered biofeedback and relaxation therapy for chronic vascular headache.*

Arredondo, P., Shealy, C., Neale, M., & Winfrey, L. L. (2004). Consultation and interprofessional collaboration: Modeling for the future. *Journal of Clinical Psychology, 60,* 787–800.

Atlas, S. J., & Deyo, R. A. (2001). Evaluating and managing acute low back pain in the primary care setting. *Journal of General Internal Medicine, 16,* 120–131.

Bellack, A. (1973). Reciprocal inhibition of a laboratory conditioned fear. *Behaviour Research and Therapy, 11,* 11–18.

Blanch, J., Rousaud, A., Hautzinger, M., Martinez, E., Peri, J. M., Andres, S., et al. (2002). Assessment of the efficacy of a cognitive-behavioural group psychotherapy programme for HIV-infected patients referred to a consultation-liaison psychiatry department. *Psychotherapy and Psychosomatics, 71,* 77–84.

Blanchard, E., & Andrasik, F. (1985). *Management of chronic headache: A psychological approach.* New York: Pergamon.

Blanchard, E. B., & Epstein, L. H. (1978). *A biofeedback primer.* New York: Addison-Wesley.

Brain, K., Sivell, S., Bennert, K., Howell, L., France, L., Jordan, S., et al. (2005). An exploratory comparison of genetic counselling protocols for HNPCC predictive testing. *Clinical Genetics, 68,* 255–261.

Cappelli, M., Verma, S., Korneluk, Y., Hunter, A., Tomiak, E., Allanson, J., et al. (2005). Psychological and genetic counseling implications for adolescent daughters of mothers with breast cancer. *Clinical Genetics, 67,* 481–491.

Codori, A. M., Waldeck, T., Petersen, G. M., Miglioretti, D., Trimbath, J. D., & Tillery, M. A. (2005). Genetic counseling outcomes: Perceived risk and distress after counseling for hereditary colorectal cancer. *Journal of Genetic Counseling, 14,* 119–132.

Coleman, K. B. (2002). Genetic counseling in congenital heart disease. *Critical Care Nursing Quarterly, 25,* 8–16.

Dagan, O., Hochner, H., Levi, H., Raas-Rothschild, A., & Sagi, M. (2002). Genetic testing for hearing loss: Different motivations for the same outcome. *American Journal of Medical Genetics, 113,* 137–143.

Decruyenaere, M., Evers-Kiebooms, G., Cloostermans, T., Boogaerts, A., Demyttenaere, K., Dom, R., et al. (2004). Predictive testing for Huntington's disease: Relationship with partners after testing. *Clinical Genetics, 65,* 24–31.

Diamond, M. L., & Solomon, G. D. (Eds.). (1999). *Diamond's and Dalessio's the practicing physician's approach to headache* (6th ed.). New York: W. B. Saunders.

Geirdal, A. O., Reichelt, J. G., Dahl, A. A., Heimdal, K., Maehle, L., Stormorken, A., et al. (2005). Psychological distress in women at risk of hereditary breast/ovarian or HNPCC cancers in the absence of demonstrated mutations. *Family Cancer, 4,* 121–126.

Gomez, M. F., Klein, D. A., Sand, S., Marconi, M., & O'Dowd, M. A. (1999). Delivering mental health care to HIV-positive individuals. A comparison of two models. *Psychosomatics, 40,* 321–324.

Gonzalez, C., Lima, M., Kay, T., Silva, C., Santos, C., & Santos, J. (2004). Short-term psychological impact of predictive testing for Machado-Joseph disease: Depression and anxiety levels in individuals at risk from the Azores (Portugal). *Community Genetics, 7,* 196–201.

Halbert, C., Kessler, L., Collier, A., Wileyto, E., Brewster, K., & Weathers, B. (2005). Psychological functioning in African American women at an increased risk of hereditary breast and ovarian cancer. *Clinical Genetics, 68,* 222–227.

Hedera, P. (2001). Ethical principles and pitfalls of genetic testing for dementia. *Journal of Geriatric Psychiatry and Neurology, 14,* 213–221.

Heide, F. J., & Borkovec, T. D. (1983). Relaxation-induced anxiety: Paradoxical anxiety enhancement due to relaxation training. *Journal of Consulting and Clinical Psychology, 51,* 171–182.

Helmes, A. W., Bowen, D. J., & Bengel, J. (2002). Patient preferences of decision-making in the context of genetic testing for breast cancer risk. *Genetic Medicine, 4,* 150–157.

Hope, S. C., Williams, A. E., Barton, S. E., & Asboe, D. (2001). What do patients attending HIV and GUM outpatient clinics want from service providers? Results from a large-scale consultation exercise in west London. *International Journal of STD and AIDS, 12,* 733–738.

Hunter, A. G., Cappelli, M., Humphreys, L., Allanson, J. E., Chiu, T. T., Peeters, C., et al. (2005). A randomized trial comparing alternative approaches to prenatal diagnosis counseling in advanced maternal age patients. *Clinical Genetics, 67,* 303–313.

Jacobson, E. (1929). *Progressive relaxation.* Chicago: University of Chicago Press.

James, C. A., Holtzman, N. A., & Hadley, W.(2003). Perceptions of reproductive risk and carrier testing among adolescent sisters of males with chronic granulomatous disease. *American Journal of Medicine and Genetics Comprehensive Seminars in Medical Genetics, 15,* 60–69.

Kidd, J., Marteau, T. M., Robinson, S., Ukoumunne, O. C., & Tydeman, C. (2004). Promoting patient participation in consultations: A randomised controlled trial to evaluate the effectiveness of three patient-focused interventions. *Patient Education and Counseling, 52,* 107–112.

Lefkowitz, M. (1996). Pain management for the AIDS patient. *Journal of the Florida Medical Association, 83,* 701–704.

Lichstein, K. L. (1988). *Clinical relaxation strategies.* New York: Wiley.

Loeser, J. D., Turk, D., Chapman, R. C., & Butler, S. (Eds.). (2002). *Bonica's management of pain* (3rd ed., pp. 1755–1763). Baltimore: Williams & Wilkins.

Luthe, W. (Ed.). (1969–1973). *Autogenic therapy* (6 vols.). New York: Grune & Stratton.

Martin, J. R., & Wilikofsky, A. S. (2004). Genetic counseling in primary care: Longitudinal, psychosocial issues in genetic diagnosis and counseling. *Primary Care, 31*, 509–524, viii–ix.

Opawoye, A. D. (1999). Communicating basic genetics to patients with sickle-cell disease. *Eastern Mediterranean Health Journal, 5*, 1178–1182.

Pieterse, A. H., van Dulmen, A. M., Ausems, M. G., Beemer, F. A., & Bensing, J. M. (2005). Communication in cancer genetic counselling: Does it reflect counselees' previsit needs and preferences? *British Journal of Cancer, 92*, 1671–1678.

Prevost, C., Veillette, S., Perron, M., Laberge, C., Tremblay, C., Auclair, J., et al. (2004). Psychosocial impact of predictive testing for myotonic dystrophy type 1. *American Journal of Medical Genetics, 126*, 68–77.

Roberts, K. J. (2002). Physician-patient relationships, patient satisfaction, and antiretroviral medication adherence among HIV-infected adults attending a public health clinic. *AIDS Patient Care STDS, 16*, 43–50.

Sadovnick, A. D. (2001). Genetic counselling and genetic screening for Alzheimer's disease and other dementias. *Canadian Journal of Neurological Science, 28*(Suppl. 1), S52–55.

Sargent, R., Sorensen, J. L., Greenberg, B., Evans, G., & Acampora, A. P. (1999). Residential detoxification for substance abusers with HIV/AIDS. Walden House Detoxification Program. *Journal of Substance Abuse Treatment, 6*, 87–95.

Smith, J. C. (1990). *Cognitive-behavioral relaxation training: A new system of strategies for treatment and assessment.* New York: Springer.

Sorvaniemi, M., Ojanen, E., & Santamaki, O. (2005). Telepsychiatry in emergency consultations: A follow-up study of sixty patients. *Telemedicine Journal and E-Health, 11*, 439–441.

Stepleman, L. M., Hann, G., Santos, M., & House, A. S. (2006). Reaching underserved HIV-positive individuals using patient-centered psychological consultation. *Professional Psychology: Research & Practice, 37*(1), 75–82.

Wall, P., & Melzack, R. (1994). *Textbook of pain* (3rd ed.). New York: Churchill Livingstone.

Wang, C., Gonzalez, R., Milliron, K. J., Strecher, V. J., & Merajver, S. D. (2005). Genetic counseling for BRCA1/2: A randomized controlled trial of two strategies to facilitate the education and counseling process. *American Journal of Medical Genetics, 134*, 66–73.

AUTHOR INDEX

SUBJECT INDEX

ABOUT THE EDITORS

Michel Hersen, PhD (SUNY–Buffalo, 1966), is Professor and Dean of the School of Professional Psychology at Pacific University and a Clinical Professor in the Department of Psychiatry at the Oregon Health Sciences University. His research interests include assessment and treatment of older adults, behavioral assessment and treatment of children, single-case research, and administration. He is a fellow of Division 12 (Clinical Psychology) of the American Psychological Association and the American Board of Medical Psychotherapists and Psychodiagnosticians, which awarded him their Lifetime Achievement Award, and is a past president of the Association for Advancement of Behavior Therapy. He has held editorships with nine journals, including *Clinical Case Studies, Behavior Modification, Clinical Psychology Review,* and the *Journal of Anxiety Disorders.* He has edited or authored 223 papers and 128 books, including many classic reference volumes.

Jay C. Thomas, PhD (University of Akron, 1981), American Board of Professional Psychology, is Professor and Program Director of Counseling Psychology in the School of Professional Psychology at Pacific University. His research interests include applied research methodology, psychometrics, career and life development, and behavioral change. He is a member of the American Psychological Association, American Psychological Society, and the American Statistical Association. He has authored numerous research papers and book chapters and has edited several books, including *Understanding Research in Clinical and Counseling Psychology* and the *Comprehensive Handbook of Personality and Psychopathology.*

ABOUT THE CONTRIBUTORS

Jennifer R. Antick, PhD, is an associate professor in the School of Professional Psychology, Pacific University, Forest Grove, Oregon. She is a clinical health psychologist and currently serving as the director of psychological services for the School of Professional Psychology. She has coauthored several book chapters and articles on topics related to strengths-based interviewing, assessment, and treatment methods. Her areas of interest include patient–provider communication, common factors in therapy, medical decision making, and other issues unique to working in medical settings.

John G. Arena (PhD, State University of New York at Albany, 1983) has worked as a licensed clinical psychologist for both the Augusta Department of Veterans Affairs Medical Center, where he is currently the lead psychologist, and the Medical College of Georgia, where he is a tenured professor in the Department of Psychiatry and Health Behavior. Dr. Arena is a fellow of Divisions 18 (Psychologists in Public Service) and 38 (Health Psychology) of the American Psychological Association and a fellow of the Georgia Psychological Association.

Thröstur Björgvinsson, PhD, is program director of the Menninger OCD Treatment Program at the Menninger Clinic and associate professor, Menninger Department of Psychiatry and Behavioral Sciences, Baylor College of Medicine, Houston, Texas. He received his BA from the University of Iceland and his PhD in clinical psychology from Queen's University, Kingston, Ontario, Canada. He completed his cognitive behavior therapy internship at McLean Hospital/Harvard Medical School and a behavior therapy fellowship at the OCD Institute, Massachusetts General Hospital/Harvard Medical School. At the Menninger Clinic

Dr. Björgvinsson developed and launched a comprehensive residential treatment program for adults and adolescents that provides empirically validated treatments to patients with severe obsessive-compulsive disorder and other anxiety disorders.

Susan L. Bland (MSW, University of Washington, 1999) has been a clinical assessor at the University of Washington's Behavioral Research and Therapy Clinics since 2000. She conducts screening, diagnostic, and outcome assessments for the multiple research studies conducted at the clinic and has helped develop many of the instruments used in these studies. Before her work at the Behavioral Research and Therapy Clinics she worked as an intake assessor, intensive case manager, and family therapist at Eastside Mental Health, a community-based mental health clinic, where she worked with suicidal and chronically mentally ill clients and families in crisis.

Julia D. Buckner (MS, Florida State University, 2005) is assistant director of the Anxiety and Behavioral Health Clinic, Florida State University, Tallahassee. She is finishing her doctoral studies in clinical psychology at Florida State University. She has coauthored numerous book chapters on the delivery of empirically supported mental health services and serves as lead editor on a book that delineates culturally competent mental health delivery for diverse populations. She has also coauthored numerous scientific journal articles on anxiety and substance use disorders in such peer-reviewed journals as *Journal of Anxiety Disorders, Behaviour Research and Therapy, Journal of Psychiatric Research,* and *Behavior Modification.*

Tracy Carothers (MS, Pacific University, 2005) is a graduate student at the School of Professional Psychology, Pacific University,

Hillsboro, Oregon. She has coauthored numerous abstracts on neuropsychological assessment. In her predoctoral work, she has researched neuropsychological functioning and how it affects one's life experience. Specifically, she has researched the ecological validity of neuropsychological measures for adults with brain dysfunction, the cognitive abilities and psychological functioning of adult male and female offenders, and the relationship between juvenile delinquency and gender on an adolescent's neuropsychological performance.

Yolanda M. Céspedes, MA, is a doctoral candidate in clinical psychology at the University of Southern California. Her clinical and research interests include the influence of family processes on youth mental health and culture-responsive treatments for ethnic minority populations. She is completing her dissertation project exploring the cultural mechanisms underlying depression and suicidality among Latino adolescents.

Shawn R. Currie, PhD, is an adjunct associate professor in psychology and psychiatry at the University of Calgary, a licensed clinical psychologist, and director of the Mental Health Information Management and Evaluation Unit in the Calgary Health Region, Alberta. He completed his doctoral degree at the University of Ottawa in 1998 and trained as a clinical psychologist in Ontario and Alberta. In 2002, he received the University of Calgary's Faculty of Medicine Research Award and the New Researcher Award from the Canadian Psychological Association. He has authored and coauthored numerous publications on the assessment and treatment of insomnia in medical and psychiatric populations, chronic pain, and gambling and other addictions.

Michael Daniel received his PhD from the University of Memphis, Tennessee, and did an internship at the Long Beach VA Medical Center, California. He is an associate professor in the School of Professional Psychology at Pacific University, where he is the director of the neuropsychology track. Dr. Daniel is actively involved in teaching, research, clinical training, and clinical practice in neuropsychology.

Jill Davidson (MA, Pacific University, 2006) graduated with a double track in behavioral and organizational therapy from the School of Professional Psychology, Pacific University, Portland, Oregon. She currently works as a child and family therapist at LifeWorks NW in Portland. She has coauthored peer-reviewed articles and chapters about trauma and issues in interviewing and has contributed to presentations at various psychology conferences. Additionally, she has taught classes in behavior modification theory and practice.

Elizabeth T. Dexter-Mazza, PsyD, is a clinical psychologist. She received her doctoral degree in 2003 from Pacific University's School of Professional Psychology in Forest Grove, Oregon. She completed a 2-year postdoctoral fellowship at the University of Washington–Seattle. Upon completion of her fellowship she became a research scientist in the university's psychology department and the clinical director of the Behavioral Research and Therapy Clinics. She manages three outpatient research clinics and was a research therapist on a National Institute of Mental Health grant—a randomized control clinical trial evaluating dialectical behavior therapy (DBT). She is in private practice providing DBT and is a DBT trainer for Behavioral Tech, a training company.

Keith S. Dobson completed his PhD in 1980 and has been a professor in the clinical psychology training program at the University of Calgary, Alberta, since 1989. His research has focused on both cognitive models and mechanisms in depression and the treatment of depression, particularly using cognitive-behavioral therapies. His applied research includes efficacy analyses of cognitive therapy, trials of prevention programs in depression, and a large study investigating the relative efficacy of cognitive therapy, behavioral, activation and selective serotonin reuptake inhibitors in the treatment of depression. Dr. Dobson's research has resulted in more than 120 published articles and chapters, 7 books, and numerous conference and workshop presentations.

Sarah Duman, MA, is a doctoral candidate in clinical psychology at the University of Southern California. Her clinical and research interests include the relationships between marital conflict, parental attunement, and child problem behavior. She has published on the influence of marital conflict and aggressive parental problem solving on youth problem solving.

Barry A. Edelstein (PhD, University of Memphis, Tennessee, 1975) is professor of psychology at West Virginia University. His research interests include factors that influence older adult medical decision making and the effects of decision aids on medical decision making. He has published chapters and journal articles on the assessment of older adults and edited three clinical geropsychology texts. He provides consultation and clinical services to older adults at Hopemont Hospital, a psychogeriatric facility in Terra Alta, West Virginia.

Tiffany A. Edwards, MS, is a child and family mental health therapist with Lifeworks NW in Portland, Oregon. She has worked in various settings advocating for and implementing responsive, culturally appropriate standards for care. She has presented and organized diversity-related material at conferences and is involved in the Cultural Action Team at Lifeworks NW.

Lori Eisner is a graduate student in adult clinical psychology at the University of Miami, Florida. She received her BA from the University of Pennsylvania in 2002 and her MS from the University of Miami in 2006. Lori has been a coauthor on four articles and three book chapters, and she has presented at several national and international conferences. Lori's research has focused on educating family members about bipolar disorder and promoting acceptance of the disorder.

Louise S. Éthier has been a full professor in the Department of Psychology at the University of Québec in Trois-Rivières since 1991. She is a member of the Child Development and the Family Research Group and associate to the Canada Research Chair on Children and their Living Environments. She has a doctorate in social psychology from the École des Hautes Études en Sciences Sociales in Paris and a master's degree in clinical psychology from the University of Montréal. She is a certified clinical psychologist in family therapy. She has received extensive clinical training in France, Italy, the United States, and Canada in attachment and systemic intervention.

Emily Fine, MA, is a doctoral candidate in clinical psychology at the University of Southern California. Her clinical and research interests involve the study of neuropsychological deficits in suicidal people. Her dissertation focuses on the process and content of working and autobiographical memory, respectively, in the prediction of suicidality. She also works at Children's Hospital Los Angeles, where she conducts neuropsychological and mental health assessments with homeless late-adolescent drug users.

Randy Fingerhut is an assistant professor of psychology at La Salle University, Philadelphia, Pennsylvania. He received his BA in psychology from Emory University, Atlanta, Georgia, and his PhD in clinical psychology from the University of Miami, Florida. Dr. Fingerhut served as a postdoctoral fellow at the University of Pennsylvania Health System's Center for Cognitive Therapy. Dr. Fingerhut's research interests include bipolar disorder, postpartum depression, and cognitive-behavioral therapy.

Charles J. Golden (PhD, University of Hawaii, 1975) is board certified in clinical psychology and clinical neuropsychology. He is a professor of psychology at Nova Southeastern University, Ft. Lauderdale, Florida, where he coordinates the neuropsychology concentration and runs clinics in psychological and neuropsychological assessment. He served as president of the National Academy of Neuropsychology and the Assessment Section of Division 12 of the American Psychological Association. Dr. Golden has authored numerous publications and has been active in the development of the Luria-Nebraska and the use of the Stroop as a neuropsychological test.

Zarabeth L. Golden attends the University of Florida in Gainesville, Florida, as a joint psychology and art major. Ms. Golden won first prize in the behavioral sciences at the International Science and Engineering Fair when she was a senior in high school. She has five publications in professional journals and has made multiple presentations at the National Academy of Neuropsychologists and the American Psychological Association. Her work has been primarily in neuropsychological evaluation, assessment, and the impact of hyperbaric oxygen treatment on chronic brain injury in children and adults.

Melissa L. González, MA, is a doctoral student in clinical psychology at Louisiana State University. Her research and clinical interests include assessment and treatment of adults and children with developmental disabilities, specifically challenging behavior in these populations. She has coauthored book chapters and several articles in peer-reviewed journals including *Behavior Modification, Journal of Intellectual Disability Research,* and *American Journal on Mental Retardation.*

Kimberly R. Goodale holds master's and doctoral degrees in clinical psychology from Pacific University, Forest Grove, Oregon. During her doctoral training, she completed practicum training at St. John's Medical Center, conducting assessments and consultations with chronic pain patients. She completed her predoctoral internship at the Veterans Administration Hudson Valley Healthcare System in New York, where she gained extensive experience working with patients with a wide range of medical and psychiatric issues. Dr. Goodale has also published and presented research on a variety of health-related psychological issues. She is a psychologist resident at Northwest Occupational Medicine Center in Portland, Oregon.

Jed Grodin, MA, is a doctoral candidate in clinical psychology at the University of Southern California. His clinical and research interests focus on the mechanisms of change for psychotherapy. He is currently on internship at the VA Hospital in Long Beach, California.

Berglind Gudmundsdottir (PhD, University at Buffalo, State University of New York, 2006) is a clinical psychologist at the Psychological Health Services, National Trauma Center, Landspitali–University Hospital in Iceland. She has coauthored several journal articles on etiology, assessment, and factors associated with the maintenance of posttraumatic stress disorder in such peer-reviewed journals as *Behavior Therapy, Journal of Traumatic Stress, Depression and Anxiety, Psychological Assessment,* and *Behaviour Research and Therapy.* In her postdoctoral work she continues to research trauma recovery, with a particular focus on risk and resilience factors that help explain the development of psychological problems after a traumatic event.

Elise Hodges (PhD, Wayne State University, 2002) is on the faculty in the departments of Psychiatry and Neurology at the University of Michigan. Dr. Hodges completed her MA and PhD at Wayne State University in Detroit, Michigan, and a postdoctoral fellowship in clinical neuropsychology at the University of Michigan. Her research

interests include the neuropsychological effects of sleep-disordered breathing in children, the influence of maternal depression on cognition in children, and cognitive functioning in adults with non–small cell lung carcinoma undergoing adjuvant chemotherapy.

Stefan G. Hofmann, PhD, is an associate professor of psychology at Boston University and director of the social anxiety program at the Center for Anxiety and Related Disorders. He received his doctorate from the Department of Psychology at the University of Marburg, Germany. His main research interests are treatment research, translational research, social anxiety, and the psychophysiology of emotions. He is editor of *Cognitive and Behavioral Practice,* associate editor of *Cognitive Behaviour Therapy,* and consulting editor of the *International Journal of Psychology.*

Julie N. Hook (PhD, clinical psychology, Northern Illinois University, DeKalb, 2002) is an assistant professor and staff neuropsychologist at Rush University Medical Center, Chicago. She completed her predoctoral internship at the Ann Arbor Veterans Administration Hospital in Michigan and her postdoctoral fellowship in neuropsychology at the University of Michigan Hospital. She has received a number of awards for accomplishments in research and clinical supervision. Dr. Hook has published in journals such as the *Journal of Anxiety Disorders, Journal of International Neuropsychological Society,* and *Clinical Psychology: Science and Practice.*

Jonathan D. Huppert (PhD, Boston University, 1999) is an associate professor of psychology at the Hebrew University of Jerusalem, Israel, and adjunct associate professor of psychology in psychiatry at the University of Pennsylvania. He has coauthored more than 50 articles and book chapters on the nature and treatment of anxiety disorders and comorbidity. He has authored articles on generalized anxiety disorder, panic, social anxiety, and obsessive-compulsive disorder in numerous psychology and psychiatric journals. He serves on the editorial boards of the *Journal of Anxiety Disorders, Behavior Therapy,* and *Cognitive Therapy and Research.*

Philinda S. Hutchings (PhD, University of Kansas, 1978) is the program director and a professor of clinical psychology at Midwestern University, Glendale, Arizona. She has been a professor and director of internship and postdoctoral training at Nova Southeastern University Center for Psychological Studies in Ft. Lauderdale, Florida, and a professor, department chair, and dean of the Arizona School of Professional Psychology at Argosy University, Phoenix. She is a diplomate in clinical psychology, American Board of Professional Psychology. Her areas of clinical interest are the treatment of sexual trauma, depression, and psychotic disorders. Research interests and publications include sexual trauma and professional training issues.

Thomas Irwin, PhD, is on the faculty at Harvard Medical School and is the program director at the McLean Center at Fernside, Princeton, Massachusetts, a residential substance abuse treatment program at McLean Hospital. Dr. Irwin received his training at the University of Houston in the area of clinical psychology, where he developed expertise in substance abuse treatment. Since completing his doctorate, Dr. Irwin has been on the faculty at Mount Sinai School of Medicine, New York, where he participated in federally funded research activities focused on behavioral and psychopharmacological treatment for substance use disorders.

Sandra Jenkins is an associate professor at the School of Professional Psychology at Pacific University, Forest Grove, Oregon, where she has taught since 1989 and is director of human diversity. She received her doctorate in clinical psychology at the University of Oregon in 1985. She teaches psychodynamic psychotherapy and basic clinical skills and supervises psychodynamic and human diversity treatment teams. Her research interests include ethnic minority clients and psychology of women. Dr. Jenkins maintains a small private practice where she offers long-term psychodynamic therapy and psychological evaluations of ethnic minority children, adolescents, adults, and families.

Sheri L. Johnson is a professor of psychology at the University of Miami, Florida. She received her BA from Salem College, North Carolina, in 1982 and her PhD from the University of Pittsburgh in 1992. Her research has been funded by the National Alliance for Research in Schizophrenia and Depression, the National Institute of Mental Health, and the National Cancer Institute. She has authored more than 80 articles and chapters. She is an associate editor for *Applied and Preventive Psychology* and *Cognition and Emotion,* and she serves on the editorial board for *Psychological Bulletin, Psychology and Psychotherapy,* and *Journal of Cognitive Psychotherapy.* Dr. Johnson's research focuses on processes that contribute to episodes of mania.

Kathryn E. Korslund, PhD, is a research scientist in the Department of Psychology at the University of Washington and associate director of the Behavioral Research and Therapy Clinics in Seattle. She received her doctoral degree from the Medical College of Pennsylvania at Hahnemann University, Philadelphia, and completed a 2-year postdoctoral fellowship at the University of Washington. Dr. Korslund is the dialectical behavior therapy adherence coordinator responsible for evaluating treatment fidelity across several randomized controlled trials at the University of Washington and other institutions.

Lesley P. Koven (PhD, West Virginia University, 2004) is an assistant professor and clinical psychologist in the Department of Clinical Health Psychology at the University of Manitoba. Her clinical work focuses on the assessment and treatment of older adults in community and long-term care settings. She also provides health psychology services to people with cardiovascular illnesses, including consultation to the Winnipeg Regional Health Authority's cardiac rehabilitation program. She has coauthored several chapters on the psychological assessment and treatment of older adults. Her current research examines psychological interventions to reduce depression and emotional distress in family caregivers of people with dementia. She is on the board of directors of the Alzheimer Society of Manitoba.

Carl Lacharité (PhD, Université du Québec à Montréal, 1989) is a certified clinical psychologist in child psychotherapy and systemic family therapy. He holds a full professorship at the Department of Psychology at Université du Québec à Trois-Rivières. He is director of a research unit on child neglect in Québec and an active member of the Canadian Center of Excellence on Child Welfare. He is closely involved with several child protection agencies and community resources in Québec. He has lectured in several countries on professional practices toward parents and children in situations of child abuse and neglect and on fathering and child maltreatment.

Rebecca Loh is a third-year doctoral graduate student of clinical psychology at Boston University.

Gayla Margolin (PhD, University of Oregon, 1976) is a professor of psychology at the University of Southern California, where she also served as director of clinical training. Her major interests span marital and family conflict and violence, with a particular focus on children's resilience. She coauthored *Marital Therapy: Strategies Based on Social Learning and Behavior Exchange Principles* and has more than 100 publications on topics related to assessment and treatment of couples and families, reciprocal influences between family processes and individual well-being, and ethical issues in couple and family therapy and research.

Johnny L. Matson (PhD, Indiana State University, 1977) is a professor and distinguished researcher at Louisiana State University, where he is clinical director in the Department of Psychology. His research and clinical interests focus on intellectual disabilities and autism spectrum disorders in children and adults. Using a behavioral-biological approach, his research ranges from teaching social skills to the evaluation of side effects of psychotropic medications. He has more than 400 publications, including 30 books on mental retardation, autism, and severe emotional disorders. He is editor-in-chief of *Research in Developmental Disabilities* and *Research in Autism Spectrum Disorders* and has served on the editorial boards of several other professional journals.

Daniel S. McKitrick (PhD, University of Maryland, 1978) is a professor in the School of Professional Psychology, Pacific University, Portland, Oregon. As a former board member of the Oregon Psychological Association and former Oregon representative to the American Psychological Association Council of Representatives, Dan put multicultural advocacy among his highest priorities. He is Pacific's acting director of diversity and supervises a diversity team at the training clinic. Dan also has been a clinical consultant for the Intercultural Communication Institute for many years.

Jessica M. McLachlan, MSc, is a doctoral student in clinical psychology at the University of Calgary. She completed her BA at the University of Winnipeg in 2000. Her graduate training and research have been supported by funding from the Social Sciences and Humanities Research Council of Canada.

Alicia E. Meuret (PhD, University of Hamburg, Germany, 2003) is an assistant professor in the Department of Psychology at Southern Methodist University in Dallas, where she codirects the Anxiety, Stress and Chronic Disease Research Program. She has coauthored multiple chapters and articles on anxiety disorder treatment. She has developed and applied psychophysiological methods in experimental clinical psychology and therapy settings in her work in the Laboratory of Clinical Psychopharmacology and Psychophysiology at Stanford University School of Medicine and the Affective Neuroscience Laboratory at the Department of Psychology at Harvard University.

Jon Morgenstern, PhD, is a professor of clinical psychology in psychiatry at Columbia University College of Physicians and Surgeons and director of substance abuse treatment at New York Presbyterian Hospital. He is also a vice president at the National Center on Addiction and Substance Abuse at Columbia University. Dr. Morgenstern is a nationally recognized expert on the treatment of substance abuse, specializing in cognitive-behavioral psychotherapy. He directs an active treatment research program that has been funded by the National Institutes of Health for the past 16 years. Dr. Morgenstern has published more than 50 peer articles and coedited 2 books.

Kim T. Mueser, PhD, is a licensed clinical psychologist and a professor in the departments of psychiatry and community and family medicine at the Dartmouth Medical School in Hanover, New Hampshire. Dr. Mueser received his PhD in clinical psychology from the University of Illinois at Chicago in 1984. Dr. Mueser's clinical and research interests include the psychosocial treatment of severe mental illnesses, dual diagnosis, and posttraumatic stress disorder. He has given numerous lectures and workshops on psychiatric rehabilitation and is the coauthor of several books.

Angela Murray (MA, MSW, Sage Graduate School, University of Washington) is the lead clinical psychological assessor for the Behavioral Research and Therapy Clinics at the University of Washington, Seattle. She worked in the Border Baby Crisis program for drug-addicted infants in New York hospitals in the 1980s and has worked for several years on the New York State Seroprevalence Study with women and infants at risk and infected with HIV. For the past decade she has worked on research projects for men and women with borderline personality disorder and comorbid disorders.

Darcy C. Norling received her master's degree in clinical psychology from Pacific University, Forest Grove, Oregon, and is working toward her doctorate degree. She is a psychology intern at a local community mental health agency specializing in children and families and works part time as a therapist at the Portland dialectical behavior therapy clinic. Her research interests include resiliency factors in youth who have experienced abuse, neglect, and other forms of childhood maltreatment and empirically supported treatments for an array of childhood and adult disorders.

Poorni Otilingam, MPH, MA, is a doctoral student in clinical aging psychology at the University of Southern California. Her current clinical and research interests include examining relationship issues in older adult couples and families facing neurodegenerative disorders, understanding culturally based perceptions of dementia, and assessing and increasing awareness of Alzheimer's disease in lay and health professional populations. She has coauthored publications on long-term remission of substance use disorders, internalized stigma of mental illness, and auditory hallucinations.

Tamara Penix (PhD, University of Nevada, Reno, 2002) is an assistant professor of clinical psychology at Eastern Michigan University in Ypsilanti. Her areas of expertise include research, assessment, and treatment for the full range of sexual self-control problems in adults and juveniles and investigation of the newer cognitive and behavioral therapies, including acceptance and commitment therapy, dialectical behavior therapy, and mindfulness-based stress reduction. She has written a number of articles and book chapters and a workbook that applies empirically supported techniques to compulsive sexual behavior.

J. Anthony Richey (MS, Florida State University, 2004) is a doctoral candidate in the Department of Psychology at Florida State University,

Tallahassee. He graduated from Pennsylvania State University in 1999 with a dual degree in psychology and sociology. After graduation, he worked for 2 years as a project director and research coordinator in the Pennsylvania State University Department of Psychology. He is completing his doctoral dissertation and expects to receive his PhD in the spring of 2007. His primary research interests are panic disorder, taxometrics, and etiological models of anxiety.

David Roe, PhD, is a clinical psychologist and chair of the Department of Community Mental Health in the Faculty of Social Welfare and Health Studies at the University of Haifa, Mount Carmel, Haifa, Israel. Dr. Roe previously was an associate professor in the Department of Psychiatric Rehabilitation and Behavioral Health Care at the University of Medicine and Dentistry, New Jersey. His primary research interests are factors related to recovery from serious mental illness and their clinical, policy, and legal implications.

Johan Rosqvist (PsyD, Pacific University, 2002) is an assistant professor in the School of Professional Psychology, Pacific University, Portland, Oregon. He is completing his postdoctoral training at the Lake Oswego Anxiety Disorders Clinic and at the Portland Psychological Service Center. He is director of Pacific University's CBT Solutions Anxiety Clinic. He has coauthored numerous book chapters on the topics of evidence-based assessment, diagnosis, and treatment of anxiety disorders. He is author of *Exposure Treatments for Anxiety Disorders: A Practitioner's Guide to Concepts, Methods, and Evidence-Based Practice,* an authoritative text on exposure therapy.

Abraham Rudnick (MD, Hebrew University, Jerusalem, 1990; PhD, Tel Aviv University, 1999) is associate professor in the departments of psychiatry and philosophy, University of Western Ontario, London, Ontario, Canada. He is physician-leader of the Schizophrenia Program at Regional Mental Health Care, London, Ontario, Canada, a tertiary center affiliated with the Faculty of Medicine and Dentistry at the University of Western Ontario. He is clinical director of the North-of-Superior Program, which provides fly-in psychiatric services to remote communities in northern Ontario through the Department of Psychiatry at the University of Western Ontario. He is a certified psychiatric rehabilitation practitioner and serves on the board of PSR (Psychosocial Rehabilitation) Ontario.

Martin C. Scherrer (MSc, University of Calgary, 2004) is a PhD candidate in the Clinical Psychology Program at the University of Calgary, Alberta. He works in the depression research laboratory under the supervision of Dr. Keith Dobson. He has been primary author and coauthor on several book chapters, invited articles, and conference presentations in his areas of primary interest, which include cognitive-behavioral theory and therapy, specifically as applied to depression. His current research interests are in cognitive-behavioral models of depression and the development of depressed mood states in people with clinical depression and other disorders.

Norman B. Schmidt (PhD, clinical psychology, University of Texas at Austin, 1991) completed his clinical internship at Brown University Medical Center and a National Institutes of Health postdoctoral fellowship at the University of Texas at Austin. Currently, he is a professor of psychology at Florida State University, where he directs the Anxiety and Behavioral Health Clinic. An active researcher, Dr. Schmidt has published more than 150 articles and book chapters and several books. Dr. Schmidt has received numerous awards for his research, including the American Psychological Association's Distinguished Scientific Award for Early Career Contribution to Psychology in the Area of Applied Research.

Stefan M. Schulz (Dipl-Psych, University of Würzburg, 2003) is a research scholar in the Department of Psychology at Boston University. He is completing his doctorate in a joint program of the Department of Psychology I, University of Würzburg, Germany, and the Center for Anxiety and Related Disorders, Boston University, on the psychophysiology of social anxiety. Mr. Schulz is an expert in psychophysiological measurement and analysis. He has worked with socially anxious patients in individual and group settings.

Daniel L. Segal is an associate professor in the Psychology Department at the University of Colorado at Colorado Springs (UCCS), where he teaches undergraduate and graduate courses in clinical psychology. He received his PhD in clinical psychology from the University of Miami in 1992 and completed a postdoctoral fellowship in clinical geropsychology at Nova Southeastern University. His research interests include diagnosis and assessment in clinical psychology and geropsychology, suicide prevention and aging, and personality disorders across the life span. Dr. Segal's research has resulted in the publication of more than 75 journal articles and book chapters.

Andrea Shreve-Neiger (PhD, West Virginia University, 2005) is a clinical staff psychologist at the Erie Veterans Affairs Medical Center in Erie, Pennsylvania. She provides education and direct clinical services to returning troops and their families. She has authored and coauthored several book chapters on psychological assessment and treatment of older adults, several scientific journal articles on malingering and posttraumatic stress disorder, and a review article on religiosity, spirituality, and anxiety in spousal caregivers of older adults with dementia in Clinical Psychology Review. She completed her postdoctoral fellowship and predoctoral internship training at the VA Pittsburgh Medical Center.

Ann B. Sola, MS, MPH, is a doctoral candidate at the School of Professional Psychology, Pacific University, Portland, Oregon. She is in her fourth year and combines academic work with clinical experience. She is doing fieldwork at a clinic that serves Spanish-speaking clients. Her thesis was on conducting intake interviews with Latinos, and her dissertation is on countertransference with Latinos. Before entering the doctoral program she obtained an MPH from Johns Hopkins School of Public Health. For 15 years she worked as a qualitative health researcher for a variety of community and government agencies, developing programs for underserved and disfranchised populations.

Tiffany M. Stewart earned her PhD from Louisiana State University. She completed residency at the Medical University of South Carolina and is now a faculty member at the Pennington Biomedical Research Center in Baton Rouge, Louisiana. She served as assistant director for the Eating Disorders Program at Our Lady of the Lake Regional Medical Center for 2 years. Her research has focused on eating disorders and obesity, with a special emphasis on body image. Dr. Stewart has published articles and chapters on eating disorders, obesity, dieting, behavior therapy, mindfulness, and the assessment and treatment of body image. She also serves on the editorial board of the journal Body Image.

Dahamsara R. Suraweera (BA, California State University, Dominguez Hills, 2003) is a third-year doctoral student in the clinical psychology program at Central Michigan University. His research interests include idiographic and functional classification systems, addictive behaviors, sexual deviance, forensics, and scale development. He is working on projects involving violent offender treatment and gender biases in the judicial system and on developing a functional classification for sexual offenders. In his 2 years of clinical work, he has developed a strong interest in sexual offender risk assessment and treatment of addictive behaviors.

Paula Truax (PhD, University of Washington, 1995) is on the faculty of Kaiser Permanente and is formerly an associate professor in the School of Professional Psychology, Pacific University, Forest Grove, Oregon. She completed her internship and postdoctoral training at Wilford Hall Medical Center in San Antonio, Texas. She has authored and coauthored a number of articles and book chapters on depression, effectiveness research, and behavioral case conceptualization. Her research interests include effectiveness outcome research, clinical significance testing, depression, and anxiety disorder treatments.

Laura L. Vernon (PhD, University of Illinois at Urbana-Champaign, 2000) completed a predoctoral clinical internship at the San Francisco Veterans Affairs Medical Center and a clinical and research postdoctoral fellowship in the Trauma and Anxiety Disorders Clinic at Central Michigan University. She was an assistant professor in the Department of Psychology at Auburn University before joining the faculty of the Wilkes Honors College of Florida Atlantic University. Dr. Vernon's research and clinical interests focus on the intersection of emotion and psychopathology, particularly anxiety disorders. She is a licensed psychologist specializing in the assessment and treatment of stress and anxiety disorders and in couple and family issues.

Michael R. Walther (BS, Pennsylvania State University, 2004) is a first-year clinical psychology doctoral student at the University of Wisconsin–Milwaukee. Previously he was a research assistant at the Center for the Treatment and Study of Anxiety at the University of Pennsylvania's School of Medicine, where he assisted in a study examining the effectiveness of prolonged exposure in community settings for people with posttraumatic stress disorder. He has coauthored peer-reviewed journal articles on obsessive-compulsive disorder and trichotillomania.

Kriscinda Whitney (PhD, clinical rehabilitation psychology, Indiana University–Purdue University Indianapolis, 2002) is a clinical neuropsychologist at the Richard L. Roudebush Veterans Affairs Medical Center in Indianapolis and a clinical assistant professor in the Department of Psychiatry at the Indiana University School of Medicine. She is interested in the study of neuropsychological function across a variety of medical and psychiatric disorders. She has coauthored numerous journal articles and book chapters on the assessment of anxiety symptoms and cognitive dysfunction among people with schizophrenia. She is studying the effects of chemotherapy treatment on cognitive and mood symptoms in people with non–small cell lung cancer.

Donald A. Williamson earned his PhD from the University of Memphis and completed his residency at the Western Psychiatric Institute and Clinic, University of Pittsburgh. He is chief of health psychology at the Pennington Biomedical Research Center and is John S. McIllhenny Endowed Professor. His research has focused on obesity and eating disorders. Dr. Williamson has published research journal articles, book chapters, and one book on obesity, eating disorders, behavior therapy, behavioral medicine, and health psychology. He served as program director for the Eating Disorders Program at Our Lady of the Lake Regional Medical Center for almost 13 years.

Sara Wright (MS, Pacific University, 2004) is a graduate student in the School of Professional Psychology, Pacific University, Portland, Oregon. She completed her master's thesis on the relationship between the reasons people give for why they are depressed and the effectiveness of cognitive-behavioral treatment for depression, and her dissertation focuses on cognitive predictive factors in the development of posttraumatic stress disorder. She has coauthored a chapter on behavioral conceptualization and has presented at conferences case studies of complex obsessive-compulsive disorder and panic disorder with atypical fears. She currently is completing her predoctoral internship at Wright-Patterson Air Force Base in Dayton, Ohio.